World's Bible Dictionary

World's Bible Dictionary

An A to Z of biblical information
for the people of today's world

Don Fleming

WORLD
PUBLISHING
Grand Rapids, Michigan 49418 U.S.A.

Published in the United States of America by
World Bible Publishers, Inc., with permission
from the copyright holder, Bridgeway Publications,
GPO Box 2547, Brisbane 4001, Australia

ISBN 0-529-07309-9

WBD-14-6961

Manufactured in the U.S.A.

To my wife,
Gae

AARON

From the time Moses set out to free Israel from Egypt, Aaron his brother played an important part in the young nation's development. He remained in a position of influence and responsibility until the day of his death, forty years later (Exod 7:7; Num 33:39).

Early developments

Although Aaron was three years older than Moses (Exod 7:7), he willingly accepted Moses' supreme leadership of the nation. He became Moses' chief spokesman and personal assistant (Exod 4:10-16; 4:29-30; 7:1-2,10,19; 8:5,17,25). As Moses grew in confidence, he became less dependent upon Aaron in his public activities (Exod 9:13,22,33). Aaron, however, continued to support Moses, especially in prayer (Exod 17:12).

Aaron was one of the privileged few who went with Moses up on to the mountain of God. He was also one of those to whom Moses entrusted the leadership of Israel during his absence (Exod 24:1-2,9,14). Aaron proved to be a weak leader, and was easily persuaded to build an idol as a visible symbol of the invisible God (Exod 32:1-6,21-25). When Moses challenged the faithful to fight against this idolatry, the men of the tribe of Levi responded. God rewarded them by promising that in the new religious order, the Levites would be his chosen religious servants (Exod 32:26-29).

Levi was the tribe to which Moses and Aaron belonged (Exod 6:16-20). God had already told Moses that in the new religious order, Aaron and his sons were to be the priests, with Aaron the high priest (Exod 28:1-4). In the generations to follow, although all Levites were to be religious officials, only those of the family of Aaron could be priests (Num 3:3-10; see LEVITES; PRIESTS).

Troubles along the way

In spite of his devoted service to God, Aaron had his disappointments and failures. His two older sons made an offering contrary to the way God had instructed them, and were punished with instant death (Lev 10:1-3). On another occasion, he and his sister Miriam showed some jealousy against Moses because of Moses' supreme position in Israel. When Miriam, who had led the criticism, was punished with leprosy, Aaron confessed his wrong and asked God to heal her (Num 12:1-2,9-12).

Just as Aaron had been jealous of Moses' position as supreme leader, so other Levites grew jealous of Aaron's position as high priest (Num 16:1-11). God destroyed the rebels (Num 16:31-35) and sent a plague on the people who had supported them; but Aaron prayed for them and the plague stopped (Num 16:47-48). By the miraculous budding of Aaron's rod, God emphasized afresh that only those of the family of Aaron were to be priests (Num 17:1-11).

Moses and Aaron were guilty of disobedience to God when, in anger at the people's constant complaining, they struck the rock at Meribah. God punished them by assuring them that they would never enter the promised land (Num 20:2,10-13). Soon after, when the journeying Israelites reached Mt Hor, Aaron died. Before he died, however, there was a public ceremony to appoint Eleazar, Aaron's eldest surviving son, as the replacement high priest (Num 20:22-29).

ABARIM

Bordering the Jordan River on its eastern side was a region that in the south was commonly known as the Plains of Moab. Within this region was a mountainous area known as Abarim, which contained the prominent peak, Mt Nebo. Israel camped on the Plains of Moab while making final

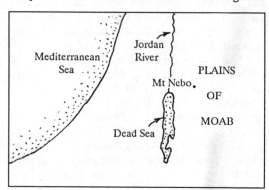

preparations to cross Jordan and conquer Canaan. From Mt Nebo Moses viewed the land on the other side of the river before he died (Num 33:47-48; Deut 32:49; 34:1,7).

ABBA

Abba was a common word in the Aramaic and Hebrew languages, and meant 'father'. It was a warm and informal term used in the everyday language of family life.

Jews of Old Testament times never used *abba* when addressing God, but Jesus used it when praying to his Father (Mark 14:36). The early Christians also addressed God as *Abba*; for, through Christ, God has adopted believers as his sons and made them joint heirs with Christ of his heavenly inheritance (Rom 8:15-17; Gal 4:5-6; cf. 3:26; see ADOPTION).

ABEL

The second son of Adam and Eve, Abel was a keeper of sheep. Like his elder brother Cain, he made an offering to God of things God had given him (Gen 4:1-4). Abel was a righteous man (Matt 23:35), and he offered his sacrifice in a thankful attitude of sincere faith (Gen 4:4; Heb 11:4). Cain was an unrighteous man (1 John 3:12) and offered his sacrifice in the wrong attitude. God therefore rejected his sacrifice (Gen 4:5; for further details see SACRIFICE).

In envy and anger, Cain killed Abel (Gen 4:8). But God gave to Adam and Eve another son, Seth, who helped maintain the sort of faith in God that Abel had shown (Gen 4:25-26).

ABIATHAR

When Saul ordered the slaughter of Ahimelech and the other priests at Nob, only one person escaped, and that was Ahimelech's son, Abiathar (1 Sam 22:18-20). He joined David and the others who were fleeing from Saul, and acted as priest for them (1 Sam 23:6,9; 30:7).

Later, when David became king, Abiathar and and another priest, Zadok, became part of David's royal court (2 Sam 8:17). At the time of Absalom's rebellion, when David was forced to flee Jerusalem, the two priests stayed behind to become spies on David's behalf (2 Sam 15:24-29,35; 19:11). At the time of Adonijah's rebellion, however, the two took different sides, Abiathar supporting Adonijah, and Zadok supporting Solomon. Upon becoming king, Solomon promoted Zadok to chief priest, but sent Abiathar into exile (1 Kings 1:5-8,43-45; 2:26,35).

ABIGAIL

Two women named Abigail are mentioned in the Bible (1 Sam 25:3; 2 Sam 17:25). The better known of the two is the wife of the foolish farmer, Nabal. Nabal almost brought disaster upon his household by his insulting refusal to supply David and his men with food in return for their service in protecting his farmlands against the raiding Philistines. Only quick thinking and wise words from Abigail saved the situation (1 Sam 25:2-35).

When Nabal unexpectedly died, David married Abigail (1 Sam 25:39-42). She became the mother of David's second son, Chileab (2 Sam 3:3).

ABIJAH (ABIJAM)

The Judean king Abijah (or Abijam) was one of several people of that name in the Bible. He was the second king of Judah after the division of the kingdom, and reigned from 913 to 910 BC (1 Kings 15:1-2).

Abijah was not wholly loyal to Yahweh, for he tolerated false religion in Judah (1 Kings 15:3). However, he was not as bad as his contemporary in Israel, Jeroboam, who had set up an official rival religion in the northern kingdom. When Abijah went to war with Jeroboam, he presumed God would give him victory because his kingdom was based on the Davidic dynasty and the Levitical priesthood (2 Chron 13:1-12). He did, in fact, defeat Jeroboam, not because God was in any way obliged to help him, but because his soldiers fought in an attitude of genuine reliance on God (2 Chron 13:13-22).

ABIMELECH

It seems that 'Abimelech' was used both as a royal title (among the Philistines) and as a personal name (among the Israelites). The meaning of the word was 'father-king'. The Bible mentions three Philistine rulers by this name and one notorious Israelite.

Among the Philistines

After the destruction of Sodom and Gomorrah, Abraham and Sarah moved through the south of Canaan and settled in the Philistine district of Gerar. Abraham, fearing that the Philistine king Abimelech might kill him in order to take Sarah for his own wife, preserved his life by saying that Sarah was his sister (Gen 20:1-2,13; cf. 12:11-13). Abimelech did indeed take Sarah, but before he had any sexual relation with her, God warned him that she was Abraham's wife (Gen 20:3-7). Abimelech avoided God's judgment by giving Sarah back to Abraham, along with compensation for the damage he had done to Sarah's honour (Gen 20:8-18).

Abraham remained in the region by Abimelech's permission (Gen 20:15), but his increasing prosperity made Abimelech wary. At Abimelech's suggestion, the two men made a treaty to ensure peaceful cooperation; but before entering the treaty, Abraham insisted that Abimelech's herdsmen return to him a well they had seized. The arrangement was sealed by Abimelech's acceptance of a gift from Abraham (Gen 21:22-32).

Eighty or so years later, when Abraham's son Isaac settled for a time in Gerar, he created tension with a later Abimelech through the same sort of deceit as Abraham's (Gen 26:1,7-11). In spite of opposition from Abimelech's men in repeatedly denying Isaac water, Isaac continued to prosper (Gen 26:17-22). This made Abimelech fear him, and on Abimelech's suggestion the two men renewed the treaty between the former Abimelech and Abraham (Gen 26:26 -32).

The other Philistine ruler whom the Bible calls Abimelech was Achish, ruler of the city of Gath (see Introduction to Psalm 34). David, in fleeing from Saul, had looked for safety in Gath, but when Achish was warned that David could be an Israelite spy, he decided to kill him. When David acted as a madman, Achish was easily deceived and drove him out of the city (1 Sam 21:10-15).

Among the Israelites

During the period of the judges, an ambitious Israelite named Abimelech was the cause of much unnecessary bloodshed. He was one of Gideon's seventy sons, and his mother was a Shechemite. Upon Gideon's death, Abimelech killed all his brothers (except one who escaped) and established himself 'king' in Shechem (Judg 9:1-6). When, after three years, the Shechemites plotted to assassinate him, Abimelech discovered the plot and slaughtered the plotters (Judg 9:22-41).

With his pride hurt, Abimelech was now driven on in senseless fury. He massacred the innocent citizens of Shechem, along with those of another town whom he thought might have been opposed to him. But his blind rage led to a lack of caution, and this in turn brought about his death (Judg 9:42-56).

ABISHAG

When David was old and sick, the nurse chosen to be with him constantly was Abishag. One of her duties was to lie with him in bed to give him warmth. Although she was not a concubine, some people apparently thought she was (1 Kings 1:1-4). After David's death, his son Adonijah asked the new king Solomon for Abishag as a wife. Since a new king inherited the concubines of the former king (cf. 2 Sam 3:7-10; 12:7-8; 16:22), Solomon considered Adonijah's request to be an attempt to gain David's throne. He therefore executed Adonijah for treason (1 Kings 2:13-25).

ABISHAI

With his brothers Joab and Asahel, Abishai joined David during David's flight from Saul. The brothers, though related to David and strong supporters of him, were a constant worry to David because of their hotheadedness. Abishai seems to have been the most violent of the three (1 Sam 26:6-9; 2 Sam 2:18-24; 3:30,39; 16:9-10; 19:21-22; 21:16-17). He became one of the highest ranked officers in David's army, being commander of that group of 'mighty men' known as The Thirty (2 Sam 23:18-19). In battle he commanded large divisions of the fighting forces (2 Sam 10:9-10; 18:2).

ABNER

When Saul, the first king of Israel, established his administration, he appointed his cousin Abner as commander-in-chief of his army (1 Sam 14:50-51). Abner first met David on the occasion of Goliath's defeat (1 Sam 17:55-57). David served under Abner as a loyal officer (1 Sam 18:5), but later Abner led Saul's troops in trying to capture the fleeing, yet innocent, David (1 Sam 26:5,14-15).

After Saul's death, Abner appointed Saul's son Ishbosheth as king in opposition to David (2 Sam 2:8). Although Abner was a strong leader, his troops were not as good as David's and they steadily lost ground over the next two years (2 Sam 3:1,6). Meanwhile Ishbosheth became increasingly jealous of Abner, who was the real power supporting him. When Ishbosheth accused Abner of wanting the throne for himself, Abner deserted Ishbosheth and joined David (2 Sam 3:7-11).

Abner then set to work to win allegiance to David from all the previous supporters of Ishbosheth (2 Sam 3:17-21). But he was treacherously murdered by David's commander Joab, in retaliation for Abner's earlier killing of Joab's brother in battle (2 Sam 3:24-30; cf. 2:12-23). Without the leadership of Abner, Ishbosheth's 'kingdom' quickly collapsed (2 Sam 4:1-5:1).

ABRAHAM

Originally called Abram, Abraham received his new name from God in confirmation of God's promise that he would be father of a multitude of people (Gen 17:5-7). In fulfilment of this promise, Abraham became the physical father of the Israelite nation (Matt 3:9; John 8:37). Because he accepted God's promise by faith, he is also the spiritual father of all who accept God's promises by faith, regardless of their nationality. As God in his grace declared Abraham righteous, so he declares righteous all who trust in him (Gen 15:6; Rom 4:11).

Response to God

Abraham was brought up in Mesopotamia, and the people among whom he lived were idol worshippers (Gen 11:28-31; Josh 24:2). Yet he worshipped the one true God (Gen 14:22; 18:25; 21:33). Abraham gave proof of his faith by obeying God when God told him to move out from his family group to a new land to which God would direct him (about 1925 BC; Gen 12:1,4; Neh 9:7; Acts 7:2-4; Heb 11:8-10).

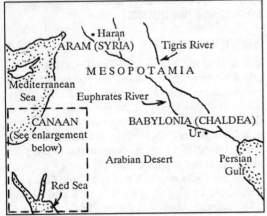

God's purpose in choosing Abraham was to produce through him a nation (Israel; 2 Cor 11:22), to give that nation a land to dwell in (Canaan; Gen 12:5-7), and to bring from that nation one man (Jesus Christ; Rom 9:4-5) who would be saviour of the world. Through Abraham, people of all nations would receive the life-giving blessing that God had prepared for mankind (Gen 12:1-3; Gal 3:14,29).

At the time of their migration to Canaan, Abraham and his wife Sarah (originally Sarai) had no children. Abraham was at that time seventy-five years of age. He and Sarah were accompanied by Abraham's nephew, Lot, and a large household of labourers whom Abraham needed to look after his flocks, herds and working animals (Gen 12:4,16; 14:14). A drought in Canaan convinced Abraham that he should look for better pastures in Egypt. But the Egyptian ruler found him deceitful, and Abraham was forced to leave Egypt in disgrace (Gen 12:10,20; 13:1).

Nevertheless, Abraham and Lot continued to prosper. In fact, they became so wealthy that when they returned to Canaan, they had to settle in different parts of the land to prevent trouble between their households (Gen 13:1-2,6). Lot settled in the fertile region east of the Dead Sea (Gen 13:10-11). Abraham settled in the centre of Canaan, and received God's reassuring promise that one day his descendants would possess Canaan as their national homeland (Gen 13:14-18). Later he rescued Lot from an invading army of Mesopotamians. He demonstrated his belief that God alone controlled

Canaan's affairs, when he made a sacrificial offering to God's priest (Melchizedek) and refused to accept any reward from the Canaanite rulers (Gen 14:1-24; cf. Heb 7:1-2,4,6).

God's covenant

God's promise to Abraham (namely, that he would be the father of a great nation) originated entirely in the sovereign will of God. God chose Abraham, Abraham believed God's promise, and in response God accepted Abraham as righteous (Gen 15:6). In confirmation of his promise, God told Abraham to prepare a covenant ceremony where normally the two parties to the covenant would pass between the parts of slaughtered animals. In this case, however, only God (symbolized by a smoking fire-pot and a flaming torch) passed between the animals, showing again that God alone took responsibility to fulfil the covenant promises. All that Abraham had to do was believe (Gen 15:7-10,17-21).

After ten years in Canaan, Sarah and Abraham had not been able to produce a son. Sarah therefore suggested that Abraham obtain his son through their slave-girl, Hagar (Gen 16:1-3). But the son born of this relationship was not the one God had promised. Abraham's promised heir would come through his wife Sarah. It was at this time that God gave the names 'Abraham' and 'Sarah'. The new names

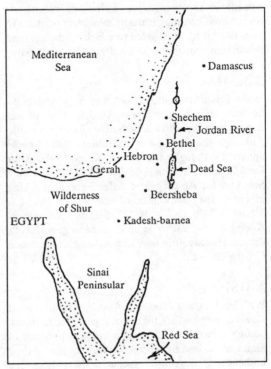

emphasized that they would yet be the parents of a multitude of people (Gen 17:1-7,15-19).

In further confirmation of his covenant with Abraham, God commanded Abraham and all future male descendants to make a permanent mark in their bodies. This mark, circumcision, was both a symbol of God's faithfulness to his covenant and a sign that Abraham believed God's promises and acted upon them. Circumcision sealed Abraham's faith and demonstrated his obedience (Gen 17:9-11; 17:23; Rom 4:9-12; Acts 7:8; see CIRCUMCISION; COVENANT).

Sarah found it difficult to believe that she would yet have a child. God had just reassured Abraham (Gen 17:17-19), and now he sent heavenly messengers to reassure Sarah (Gen 18:9-14). The same messengers told Abraham that judgment was about to fall on the wicked cities of the region where Lot lived (Gen 18:16-21). Abraham hoped that God might spare the cities, but he did not realize how bad they were. The cities were destroyed, though Lot escaped (Gen 18:32; 19:29).

Abraham's heir

Upon moving with his flocks and herds into the Philistine region, Abraham again brought disgrace upon himself when he deceived the ruler in whose territory he dwelt (Gen 20:1-3). This failure of Abraham, particularly at a time so close to the birth of the promised son, showed again that God's blessing upon Abraham depended entirely upon divine grace, not upon human good works (Rom 4:1-5).

The promised heir, Isaac, was born to Abraham and Sarah when Abraham was about one hundred years old. Abraham had accepted God's promise by faith, in spite of the apparent impossibility of such an old couple producing children. God was faithful to his promise (Gen 21:2-3; Rom 4:17-21).

An even greater test of faith came when God told Abraham to offer his son as a human sacrifice. If Isaac was killed, God could no longer fulfil his promise of a multitude of descendants for Abraham through Isaac. Yet Abraham obeyed, believing that God could bring Isaac back to life (Gen 22:1-2; Heb 11:17-19). Abraham's obedience proved the genuineness of his faith. Though he offered Isaac, he did not kill him. God provided a substitute, and Isaac's life was given back, as it were, from the dead (Gen 22:13; Heb 11:19; James 2:21-24).

When Sarah died, Abraham bought a piece of ground within Canaan as a burial place for her. In doing so he showed once more his faith in the ultimate fulfilment of God's promise concerning his descendants' permanent homeland. He now legally owned part of the territory which they would one day possess (Gen 23:1-4,16-20; cf. 49:29-33).

Since Isaac was to succeed Abraham as heir to Canaan and ancestor of the promised nation, Abraham required Isaac to remain in Canaan but not to marry one of the Canaanite women. He therefore sent his chief servant north to find a wife for Isaac among Abraham's relatives (Gen 24:3-6).

The Genesis account of Abraham concludes with the note that he had other descendants through minor wives, but these were not part of the promised nation (Gen 25:1-6). One hundred years after first moving to the promised land, Abraham died (Gen 25:7). He was buried in the burial ground with Sarah, as a final demonstration of his faith in God's promises (Gen 25:8-10).

Example of faith

Repeatedly, the New Testament refers to Abraham as an example of the truth that God accepts people and declares them righteous on the basis of faith. The Jews had to learn that physical descent from Abraham was no guarantee of salvation (Matt 3:9; John 8:39-44; Rom 9:7). The case of Abraham shows clearly that salvation has nothing to do with personal good works (Rom 4:1-5), religious rituals (Rom 4:9-12) or the law of Moses (Rom 4:13; Gal 3:16-18). It is entirely dependent upon God's grace and is received by faith (Rom 4:16).

The promises given to Abraham find their ultimate fulfilment in Jesus Christ, through whom people of all nations are saved (Luke 1:72-73; Gal 3:8,14,16). When believers become Christ's people, they become, through him, Abraham's descendants also, and so share in the blessings promised to Abraham (Rom 4:16-17; Gal 3:9,29; Eph 3:6).

Abraham's faith is a further example in that it is not only a faith that saves, but also a faith that the true believer lives by. Abraham's offering of Isaac showed that faith proves its genuineness by obedience (Heb 11:17-19; James 2:21-23). Always Abraham looked beyond his immediate circumstances, believing that God would give him a better and more lasting dwelling place (Acts 7:5; Heb 11:8-10,13-16).

ABSALOM

Absalom, the third son of David, first features in the Bible story when his sister Tamar was raped by Amnon, their older brother by a different mother (2 Sam 3:2-3; 13:1-22). Absalom was determined to have his revenge, no matter how long he had to wait.

After two full years he found a suitable opportunity, and had Amnon murdered. He then fled into exile (2 Sam 13:23-27).

After three years without a recognized heir to David in Jerusalem, David's army commander Joab was worried about the stability of David's dynasty. He therefore worked out a cunning plan to re-establish Absalom in Jerusalem, without the necessity for Absalom to face trial for murder (2 Sam 13:38; 14:1-24). Although Absalom returned from exile, David refused to receive him into the palace. But after two years Absalom forced his way in (2 Sam 14:28-33).

Over the next four years Absalom built up a following for himself among the country people, particularly those from the south (2 Sam 15:1-7). He then launched a surprise attack, seizing the throne and forcing David to flee for his life (2 Sam 15:8-18; 16:20-23). But one of David's chief advisers stayed behind as a spy in Absalom's court. By appealing to Absalom's vanity, he was able to persuade Absalom to ignore the wise words of Absalom's chief adviser (2 Sam 15:32-37; 17:1-14). As a result Absalom decided to glorify himself in a full-scale battle with David's army. His troops were no match for David's hardened soldiers, and he himself was killed (2 Sam 18:1-15).

ACHAIA

In the days of the Roman Empire, Achaia was the southern of two Greek provinces, the other being Macedonia (Acts 19:21; Rom 15:26; 2 Cor 9:2; 1 Thess 1:8). Formerly, in the days of the Greek Empire, Macedonia was the centre of Greek power, but under the Romans the political situation had changed and the name Achaia was usually identified with Greece (Acts 18:27; 20:2; see GREECE). The administrative centre of Achaia was Corinth, and the educational centre, Athens (Acts 17:21; 18:1,12; 2 Cor 1:1).

A church was founded in Corinth during Paul's second missionary journey, and another at the port of Cenchreae nearby (Acts 18:1-18; Rom 16:1; 1 Cor 16:15; see CORINTH). There were also Christians in Athens (Acts 17:34; see ATHENS). Paul revisited the area during his third missionary journey (Acts 19:21; 20:1-3), when he collected money that the churches of Achaia, like other churches, had put aside to help the poor Christians in Judea (Rom 15:26; 2 Cor 9:1-2). Some years later, Paul planned to spend a winter at Nicopolis, on Achaia's west coast, but the Bible does not record whether he was able to fulfil his plans (Titus 3:12).

ACTS, BOOK OF

Evidence from early Christian records, as well as from the book itself, indicates that Luke wrote the book of Acts. The book was the second of two volumes that Luke wrote, the first being Luke's Gospel.

Luke wrote for a person named Theophilus, with the purpose of giving Theophilus an account of Christianity from the birth of its founder to the arrival of its greatest apostle in Rome (Luke 1:1-4; Acts 1:1-2). Sections of Acts that are written in the first person show that Luke was with Paul on some of Paul's missionary travels (Acts 16:10-17; 20:5-37; 21:1-17; 27:1-28:31). (For further details concerning the author see LUKE.)

The value of Acts

Acts provides a good base for an intelligent understanding of much of the New Testament. Paul wrote his earlier letters during the period covered by Acts, and the present-day reader will have a better understanding of those letters, and other letters of the New Testament, once he is familiar with Acts. The book is also an important document for an understanding of significant developments in world history. Secular historians acknowledge Luke to be an accurate and reliable writer, and the findings of archaeology confirm the exactness of the technical expressions he uses in relation to places and officials (Acts 13:7; 16:12,35; 18:12,16; 19:31,35).

From the title of honour that Luke gives Theophilus, it seems that Theophilus was an official in the Roman government (Luke 1:3; cf. Acts 23:26; 26:25). Whether he was or not, there is no doubt that at the time Luke wrote his Gospel and Acts (in the early AD 60s), the Roman government was paying increasing attention to Christianity. Luke is therefore concerned to point out that Christianity was not in any way rebellious to Roman rule and was not a threat to law and order.

Christians were sometimes involved in civil disturbances, but Luke shows by one example after another that the Christians were not the cause of the trouble. Consistently the Roman authorities acknowledged the Christians to be innocent (Acts 16:37-39; 18:12-16; 19:31,37; 23:29; 25:18; 26:31-32; 28:30-31). In almost every case where there was trouble in connection with the Christians, the Jews were to blame (Acts 9:23,29; 13:50; 14:2,5,19; 17:5; 17:13; 18:12-17; 21:27). Christianity was not an illegal religion according to Roman law. On the contrary it was the legitimate continuation of the religion established by Abraham and developed through

Moses, David and the Israelite nation (Acts 2:31-33; 13:26-33; 15:15-18; 26:22-23; 28:23).

This progression from the old Jewish era to the new Christian era came about through Jesus Christ. He was the Messiah of whom the Jewish religion spoke and for whom it had prepared the way (Acts 2:36; 3:18; 9:22; 17:3; 18:5,28). Though he had now physically left the world and returned to his heavenly Father, he was in a sense still in the world. Through the Holy Spirit he indwelt his followers, and through them he continued to work (Acts 1:4-5; 2:33; 3:6,16; 4:30-31; 5:31-32). The spread of the gospel and the growth of the church was the ongoing work of Christ, acting by his Spirit through his followers (Acts 8:29,39; 9:17,31; 10:19,45; 13:2,4; 15:28; 16:6-7; see HOLY SPIRIT).

Summary of contents

Continuing the story from where Luke's Gospel ended, Acts begins by recording Jesus' promise of the Holy Spirit, his ascension, and the appointment of an apostle to replace Judas (1:1-26). On the Day of Pentecost, Jesus' promise was fulfilled when the Christians received the Holy Spirit (2:1-36). That same day three thousand people responded to

Peter's preaching of the gospel and were added to the church (2:37-47). Thousands more were added a few days later (3:1-4:4). This rapid growth brought opposition from the Jewish leaders (4:5-31).

The rejoicing among the Christians was interrupted by God's severe judgment on two people who deceived the church (4:32-5:11). Nevertheless, the church increased its numbers, though at the same time the Jewish leaders increased their opposition (5:12-42).

Until now the Christians had been popular with the common people, but this changed when one of the leading Christians, Stephen, made it clear that Christianity was not simply an improved form of Judaism. The Jews killed him (6:1-7:60) and began a violent program of widespread persecution against the Christians (8:1-3). As a result of the Christians' being driven from Jerusalem, the gospel spread to Samaria and Caesarea (8:4-40). Meanwhile Saul, the chief persecutor, repented and believed in Jesus (9:1-31).

Peter travelled from Jerusalem down to the Mediterranean coast (9:32-43) and preached the gospel to Gentiles in Caesarea with great success (10:1-48). Back in the Jerusalem church many were

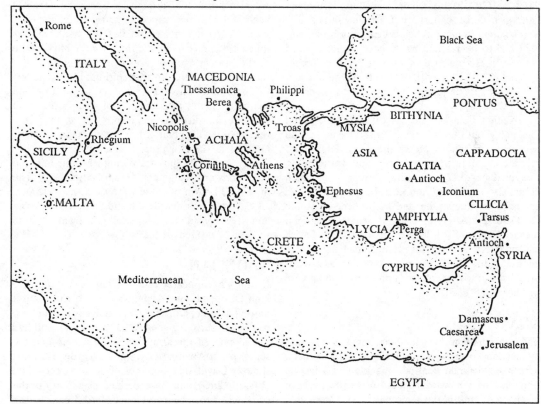

uneasy that Gentiles were being welcomed into the fellowship of Jewish Christians without first submitting to the Jewish law (11:1-18). In Antioch in Syria more Gentiles believed and the first Gentile church was formed (11:19-30). But in Jerusalem, Jewish opposition increased. In an effort to satisfy the Jews and avoid further unrest, Herod executed the apostle James and tried unsuccessfully to execute Peter (12:1-25).

Christianity spread further when Paul and Barnabas, with Mark as their assistant, set out from Antioch on a missionary journey to Cyprus and Asia Minor (13:1-14:28). When Jewish legalists tried to force Christians to keep the Jewish law, a meeting in Jerusalem upheld the gospel as Paul preached it (15:1-35). Paul then set out on his second missionary journey, this time taking Silas and Timothy as his partners. They travelled through Asia Minor to northern Greece (15:36-16:40) and then south to Athens (17:1-34). After eighteen months in Corinth they returned to Antioch (18:1-22).

Paul's third missionary journey took him to Ephesus in Asia Minor, where he stayed three years (18:23-19:41). He spent some months in Greece and, when he had finished his work there, returned to Palestine (20:1-21:14). Upon arrival in Jerusalem, Paul met fierce opposition from Jewish legalists who considered him a rebel. When a riot broke out, Paul had to be rescued by the local Roman guard (21:15-40). His defence of himself brought further violence (22:1-23:10), with the result that he was sent to Caesarea to be judged by the Roman governor, Felix (23:11-35).

Neither Felix nor his successor, Festus, found Paul guilty, but they left him in prison for more than two years, merely to please the Jews. Paul could tolerate the injustice no longer and appealed to Caesar (24:1-25:12). A visiting expert on Jewish affairs also found Paul innocent, but since Paul had appealed to Caesar, he had to be sent to Rome (25:13-26:32). After an eventful sea voyage, Paul reached Rome (27:1-28:16). As usual, the Jewish leaders rejected his message. The Roman authorities allowed him some freedom, so that he was able to preach the gospel openly and unhindered till his case was heard (28:17-31).

ADAM

The name 'Adam', which is the name of the first human, is also the common Hebrew word for man, both man the individual and mankind as a whole. The root of the word appears originally to have meant 'red', and is the same as that for 'red soil'.

The two words are used together in the sentence, 'The Lord God formed man (*adam*) of dust from the ground (*adamah*)' (Gen 2:7).

Adam represented the climax of God's creation. He shared his physical origin with other animals in being made of common earthly chemicals, yet he was uniquely different in that he was made in the image of God (Gen 1:27; 2:7; see CREATION; MAN). God gave Adam a wife, Eve, who shared his unique nature (Gen 2:21-23), and this nature has passed on to the human race which has descended from them (1 Cor 15:45-49).

Mankind's first parents lived in a beautiful parkland for their period of testing and training. There they had opportunity to develop in body, mind and spirit, through doing physical work, making choices, learning skills, relating to each other and living in fellowship with God (Gen 2:15-23). But instead of submitting to God, Adam attempted to live independently of God and so fell into sin (Gen 3:1-7). In so doing he brought judgment upon himself and upon the whole human race which, in effect, existed in him (Gen 3:14-19; Rom 5:12; see DEATH; SIN).

Only Jesus Christ can undo the damage that Adam has caused. Through his death, he becomes head of a new race of people, those saved by God's super-abundant grace (Rom 5:14-19). As Adam was the first of a race of people fitted for the physical life of the present age, so Jesus Christ is the first of a race of people fitted for the spiritual life of the age to come. As all who are in physical union with Adam share the deathly consequences of Adam's sin, so all who are in spiritual union with Christ share the resurrection life that Christ has made possible (1 Cor 15:21-22,45-49; see also IMAGE).

Adam lived 930 years, during which he fathered many sons and daughters (Gen 5:1-5; cf. 1:28). The most well known of these were Cain, his firstborn; Abel, whom Cain murdered; and Seth, whom Adam and Eve considered a special gift from God to replace Abel (Gen 4:1-8,25).

ADONIJAH

During what appeared to be the last days of the aged king David, his son Adonijah decided to establish himself as king before David died. He was the eldest of David's surviving sons (cf. 2 Sam 3:2-4), and had the support of the army commander Joab and the senior priest Abiathar (1 Kings 1:5-7). But God had showed David that Solomon was to succeed him (1 Chron 28:5), and Solomon had the support of the commander of the royal bodyguard Benaiah, the other leading priest Zadok, and the prophet Nathan (1 Kings 1:8). As a result of swift action by Nathan, David promptly declared Solomon to be king. The ambitious Adonijah could do nothing but cry to Solomon for mercy (1 Kings 1:6-53).

Soon after David's death, however, Solomon executed Adonijah for treason. He considered Adonijah's request for Abishag as wife was a claim to David's concubines, and therefore a claim to David's throne (1 Kings 2:13-25; see ABISHAG).

ADOPTION

A number of different words are used in the Bible to picture God's gracious act of saving the repentant sinner and giving him a new and living relationship with God. For example, it is an act of regeneration (new birth), for it gives spiritual life to one who is dead in sins (see REGENERATION). It is an act of justification, for it makes the sinner right with God on account of Christ's atoning death on his behalf (see JUSTIFICATION). It is also an act of adoption, for it makes the believer a son of God.

New status

The picture of adoption comes from a practice that was well known to people of Bible times. If a wealthy man had no descendants, he could carefully choose some trustworthy person to be his son. This adopted person then had the status of a responsible adult son, who would become the next head of the family, receive the family inheritance and carry on the family name (Gen 15:2-3).

When the Bible uses adoption as a picture of what God has done, the emphasis is on the status and dignity he places on those whom he brings into this close relationship with himself. Old Testament Israel is a good example of this gracious act of God; for he chose Israel from among all the peoples of the world and made the nation his son (Exod 4:22; Deut 14:1; Hosea 11:1; Rom 9:4).

Christians as God's sons

The New Testament develops the idea of sonship more fully, showing that God makes repentant sinners his sons. He brings them into such a close relationship with himself that they can speak to him as sons to a Father (Rom 8:15; Gal 4:6).

There is no conflict between the pictures of new birth and adoption. New birth shows that God gives life to those who are spiritually dead; adoption shows that God makes believers his special possession and gives them the full status of mature adult sons (Rom 8:15; Gal 3:23-26; 4:1-7; Eph 1:5; 1 John 3:1). This is possible only through the death of Jesus Christ, and it is true only of those who have faith in him (Gal 3:26; 4:4-5).

As sons of God, believers enjoy the spiritual privilege of access to God (Rom 8:15-16) and inherit here and now his spiritual blessings (Rom 8:17; Gal 4:7). They can look forward to the full and unhindered enjoyment of these blessings at the return of Jesus Christ (Rom 8:23; 1 John 3:2). (See also FATHER.)

ADULTERY

The teaching of the Bible is that sexual relations are lawful only between husband and wife. A sexual relation between two people who are not married is usually called fornication; a sexual relation between a married person and someone other than that person's marriage partner is usually called adultery (Exod 20:14; Rom 12:9,20; Gal 5:19; 1 Thess 4:3-4; see also FORNICATION).

Old Testament regulations

According to the law of Moses, the punishment for adultery was death by stoning (Lev 20:10; John 8:3-5). Where there was a suspicion of adultery but no clear evidence, Israelite law set out a special procedure by which a priest could determine the case (Num 5:11-31).

The engaged as well as the married were considered adulterers if they had sexual relations with third parties. Again the penalty was death. The one exception was the case of a woman who had been raped (Deut 22:22-27).

Adultery was a sin against one's own marriage partner (Mal 2:11,14; cf. Hosea 2:2), as well as against the marriage partner of the new lover (Exod 20:14,17; 2 Sam 12:9; Prov 6:32-35). Unfaithfulness was at the centre of all adultery. The Old Testament prophets repeatedly spoke of Israel's unfaithfulness to God as spiritual adultery, or spiritual prostitution (Jer 5:7; 23:10; Ezek 16:30-38; 23:4-5,11; Hosea 9:1; see PROSTITUTION).

New Testament teachings

Like the Old Testament, the New Testament looks upon marriage as a permanent union. Therefore, the person who divorced and remarried was considered guilty of adultery (Mark 10:2-12; Luke 16:18; Rom 7:2-4). The exception that Jesus allowed concerned the case where persistent adulterous behaviour by one partner had already virtually destroyed the marriage (Matt 5:32; 19:7-9; see also DIVORCE). Jesus said that even the desire to have unlawful sexual relations was a form of adultery. Therefore, the best way to avoid adulterous acts was to avoid adulterous thoughts (Matt 5:27-30; 15:19; cf. Exod 20:17; James 1:14-15).

Paul pointed out that Christians in particular should avoid all immoral sexual relations, since their bodies are indwelt by the Holy Spirit and they themselves belong to Christ. For the Christian, there is a sense in which sexual sin is spiritual prostitution (1 Cor 6:13-20).

Although the New Testament announces God's judgment on those who are immoral and adulterous (Heb 13:4; 2 Peter 2:14), it also shows that God is ready to forgive those who, in sorrow for their sin, turn to him for mercy (1 Cor 6:9-11). Jesus rebuked the self-righteous who condemned adulterers but who could not see their own sin. At the same time he gave sympathetic support to those who acknowledged their sin and repented of it (Matt 9:11-13; Luke 18:9-14; John 8:3-11; cf. Rom 2:22).

Christians may rightly condemn adultery, but, remembering their own weaknesses, they should also forgive those who repent of their adultery. More than that, they should give them understanding and support as they seek to re-establish their lives (2 Cor 2:7; Gal 6:1-2; Eph 1:7; 4:32).

ADVOCATE

The word sometimes translated in the Bible as 'advocate' denoted a person who came and stood beside someone to help in a time of need. People today usually think of an advocate as one who pleads on behalf of another in a court of law, but only occasionally does the Bible use the word in this legal sense (e.g. 1 John 2:1). In most cases it uses the word in the broader sense of a counsellor or helper (e.g. John 14:26).

Jesus had been a counsellor or helper to his followers while he was with them, and promised that when he left them and returned to his Father, he would send them another counsellor, the Holy Spirit. The Holy Spirit would dwell with Jesus' followers, giving them the sort of teaching, guidance and help that Jesus had given them (John 14:16-17; 14:26; 15:26; 16:7; cf. Matt 10:19-20; Rom 8:26). (For further details see HOLY SPIRIT.)

While the Holy Spirit is within believers on earth, Jesus Christ appears before the Father as their advocate in heaven. Christians need this advocate because of the difficulties they face in a sinful world. Inevitably they will sometimes sin and as a result need God's forgiveness. Their sin does not cause them to lose their salvation, but it spoils their fellowship with God. In Jesus they have a heavenly advocate who, when they confess their sin, brings their case before the merciful God and asks his forgiveness. Just as Jesus' death and resurrection was the basis on which God accepted them as his people in the first place, so it is the basis on which God continues to forgive their failures (Rom 8:34; 1 John 1:9; 2:1-2).

Another picture of the risen Christ's work on behalf of his people is that of high priesthood. In this picture Jesus' work is similar to that of an advocate. He is his people's great high priest, who understands their needs and appears in the presence of God to plead for them (Heb 7:25; 9:24). (For further details see PRIEST, sub-heading 'The high priesthood of Jesus'.)

AFRICA

By far the most frequent mention of Africa in the Bible has to do with Egypt (see EGYPT; GOSHEN; NILE). The land of Ethiopia is also mentioned frequently, sometimes under the name of Cush (see ETHIOPIA). Other African nations mentioned in the Bible are Libya (2 Chron 12:3; 16:8; Dan 11:43), Put (Jer 46:9; Ezek 30:5; 38:5; Nahum 3:9), and Lud (Jer 46:9; Ezek 30:5). (For additional New Testament references to Africa see ALEXANDRIA; CYRENE.)

AGRICULTURE

See FARMING.

AHAB

Ahab reigned over the kingdom of Israel (the northern part of the divided Israelite state) from about 874 to 852 BC. Before coming to Israel's throne, he had married Jezebel, daughter of the king-priest of Phoenicia, in a political alliance that had disastrous consequences for Israel.

Besides accepting the Baal worship that Jezebel brought with her from Phoenicia, Ahab gave it official status in Israel by building a Baal temple in his capital city (1 Kings 16:29-33). Israel's long-established practice of mixing the worship of God (Yahweh) with the worship of Baal was bad enough, but Jezebel's intention was far worse. She wanted to remove the worship of God from Israel entirely and replace it with the worship of Baal. The Baalism promoted by Ahab and Jezebel was a threat to Israel's existence as God's people, and for this reason God sent the prophets Elijah and Elisha to oppose it. (For details of this aspect of Ahab's reign see BAAL; ELIJAH.)

God used Elijah to tell Ahab of a drought that he was about to send as punishment on the ungodly kingdom (1 Kings 17:1). Three years later he used Elijah to announce the end of the drought, but that end came in such a way as should have convinced Ahab that he could not serve both God and Baal (1 Kings 18:1-2,17-18,21,41-46).

Ahab, however, continued to try to serve two gods. He allowed the queen to try to kill the prophet who opposed her Baalism (1 Kings 19:1-2), yet at the same time he looked to another of God's prophets for directions that would bring him military victory against Syria (1 Kings 20:13-14,22). Ahab won a decisive victory (1 Kings 20:20-21), and the next year won another victory, again at the direction of one of God's prophets (1 Kings 20:22).

The victories should have convinced Ahab that God's power was not, like Baal's, limited to only certain places (1 Kings 20:28). When Ahab agreed to spare the enemy kings because of trade advantages he could win for himself, another of God's prophets condemned his actions (1 Kings 20:34-43).

Not only were Ahab's religious, military and trade policies contrary to God's purposes, but his administration in general was full of injustice. This was clearly shown in the way he gained Naboth's vineyard for himself. People could be easily bribed, local officials were corrupt, and there was no one to uphold the law on behalf of ordinary citizens (1 Kings 21:1-16). The prophet Elijah announced a horrible judgment on Ahab, and particularly on his murderous wife Jezebel (1 Kings 21:17-26).

God's judgment fell on Ahab in another battle with Syria. Most of the court prophets were corrupt, and gave Ahab whatever advice they thought would please him. The prophet Micaiah, by contrast, had consistently told Ahab the truth. When he told Ahab that the coming war would bring defeat, Ahab threw him into prison (1 Kings 22:1-28). Ahab ignored the message from God, and as a result met the dreadful death that Elijah had earlier announced (1 Kings 22:29-38).

Ahab's sons continued the evil of their father's reign (1 Kings 22:51-53; 2 Kings 3:1-3). The dynasty came to a bloody end through a revolution led by the ruthless Jehu (2 Kings 9:7-10; 10:1-11,17).

AHASUERUS

Known also as Xerxes I, Ahasuerus ruled over the Persian Empire from 486 to 465 BC. At that time the Jews had returned from exile and the temple in Jerusalem had been rebuilt (completed in 516 BC). The completion of the city walls, however, awaited the governorship of Nehemiah (who arrived in Jerusalem in 445 BC). Ahasuerus is therefore not involved in the events narrated in the books of Ezra and Nehemiah, though he is referred to in Ezra 4:6. He is the king who features in the story of Esther. (For further details see ESTHER; PERSIA.)

AHAZ

Politically and religiously, Ahaz's reign over Judah was disastrous. He came to the throne about 735 BC, when Assyria was rapidly expanding its power and becoming a threat to all the countries of the region.

To resist the Assyrian threat, Israel and Syria asked Judah to join them in a three-part defence alliance. When Ahaz refused, Israel and Syria attacked Jerusalem, planning to put a king of their own choice on Judah's throne. Ahaz panicked and, against the advice of Isaiah the prophet, asked Assyria to help defend him. Isaiah promised that faith in God, and nothing else, would bring lasting victory. In the short term, Assyrian help might save Jerusalem, but in the long term it would bring Judah under the power of Assyria (2 Kings 16:5,7-9; Isa 7:1-9; 8:5-8). (Concerning God's sign of assurance given to Ahaz in Isaiah 7:10-25, see IMMANUEL; VIRGIN.)

Ahaz's policies during the war with Israel-Syria almost ruined Judah's national economy. His hiring of Assyria was costly (2 Kings 16:7-8,17-18; 2 Chron 28:20-21), and though it enabled him to repel the Israelite-Syrian army, he lost thousands of soldiers killed in the battle (2 Chron 28:5-7). He almost lost thousands more as prisoners, but a prophet told the Israelites to send all the prisoners, and all the loot, back to Judah (2 Chron 28:8-15). Ahaz suffered further losses at the hands of invading Edomites and Philistines, and lost control of the important Red Sea port of Elath (Ezion-geber) (2 Kings 16:6; 2 Chron 28:17-18).

In addition to damaging Judah's political and economic standing, Ahaz corrupted Judah's religion. He worshipped the gods of the foreigners who had shown such strength in battle, and introduced their religion into Judah. He built a copy of their altar of sacrifice to replace the existing altar of sacrifice in the Jerusalem temple (2 Kings 16:10-16; 2 Chron 28:22-24), and built shrines for the foreign religions throughout the towns of Judah (2 Chron 28:25). He even burnt his son as a human sacrifice (2 Kings 16:2-4).

Ahaz did such harm to Judah's national life, that the nation's leaders refused to give him a burial place among the royal tombs (2 Chron 28:27). His son and successor Hezekiah soon began a vigorous reformation of Judah (2 Kings 18:1-6).

AHAZIAH

Israel and Judah, the northern and southern parts of the divided Israelite kingdom, each had a king named Ahaziah. Ahaziah of Israel was the son of Ahab and Jezebel, and during his brief two-year reign (853-852 BC) he continued to promote his parents' Baal worship (1 Kings 22:51-53). When the godly King Jehoshaphat of Judah cooperated with the ungodly Ahaziah in establishing a shipping fleet, God wrecked the ships. It impressed upon Jehoshaphat that God did not want him to have any close association with Ahaziah (2 Chron 20:35-37). After an accident, Ahaziah sought help from Baal gods, but Elijah stopped him. Ahaziah then plotted to kill Elijah, but his plans ended in his own death (2 Kings 1:1-16).

After Ahaziah's death, his brother Jehoram (or Joram) became king of Israel (2 Kings 1:17). Their sister Athaliah had married the Judean king (Jehoshaphat's son), whose name also was Jehoram. Through the Judean Jehoram and his wife Athaliah, the Baalism of Ahab and Jezebel spread to Judah. When Jehoram of Judah died, his son Ahaziah came to the throne (840 BC; 2 Chron 21:1,5-6; 22:1-2). Being very much under the influence of his mother, Ahaziah promoted Baal worship in Judah (2 Chron 22:3-4). However, he was killed after reigning only one year (2 Chron 22:2). He had gone to visit his uncle, Jehoram of Israel, who had been wounded in battle, and got caught in Jehu's anti-Baal revolution (2 Chron 22:5-9; cf. 2 Kings 9:16-28).

AHIJAH

Ahijah the prophet is the most important of several people of that name in the Bible. He features in two incidents. The first was when he told Jeroboam that God was going to divide Solomon's kingdom and give ten of the twelve tribes to Jeroboam (1 Kings 11:28-38; see JEROBOAM). The promise was fulfilled with the division of the kingdom in 930 BC (1 Kings 12:15).

Jeroboam, however, ignored Ahijah's command to walk in the ways of God (1 Kings 11:38), and this resulted in the second incident involving Ahijah. Jeroboam wanted Ahijah's help, but, knowing that Ahijah was angry with him, he sent his wife disguised as someone else (1 Kings 14:1-5). Ahijah was aware of Jeroboam's trick, and announced that he would not escape God's judgment. He had rebelled against God, and therefore his dynasty would be destroyed (1 Kings 14:6-16). Again the words of the prophet came true (1 Kings 14:17-18; 15:29).

ALEXANDRIA

After his conquest in 333 BC, Alexander the Great of Greece built the city of Alexandria as a Mediterranean sea port for Egypt and named it after himself. It soon became the greatest Greek city of the time, and was famed for its architectural magnificence. It was the capital of Egypt during the Greek and Roman Empires, and was a busy centre of commercial and manufacturing activity. From here the famous grain ships of Alexandria carried Egypt's corn to Greece and Rome (Acts 27:6; 28:11).

The population of the city was a mixture of Greek, Egyptian, Jewish and Roman people (Acts 6:9; 18:24). The city became a centre of learning, famous for its Greek philosophers and its Jewish Bible scholars. Some non-canonical Jewish books of pre-Christian times were written in Alexandria (see CANON). More importantly, Alexandria was the place where seventy Jewish scholars prepared the first Greek translation of the Old Testament. This is known as the Septuagint (referred to in writing as LXX) and was widely used in New Testament times along with the Hebrew Old Testament (see SEPTUAGINT).

A feature of the Alexandrian school of Jewish Old Testament scholars was that their interpretations were detailed, earnest, philosophical and often extravagant. They developed the reputation of being learned and eloquent speakers. In the New Testament there is a record of one of them, Apollos, whose knowledge of Old Testament references to the Messiah was extraordinary. His knowledge of certain Christian teachings was lacking, but he was willing to learn. He soon developed into a powerful Christian preacher (Acts 18:24-28; see APOLLOS).

ALTAR

From the time of Noah there are biblical records of people who erected altars, usually to commemorate special religious experiences that people had with God. Some stories record the offering of sacrifices on these altars (Gen 8:20; 12:7; 13:18; 22:9; 26:25; 33:20; 35:3; Exod 17:15).

Even after the establishment of the tabernacle with its specially appointed bronze altar of sacrifice, Israelites at times erected altars to commemorate important events (Deut 27:5; Josh 8:30-31; 22:10; Judg 6:24-26; 2 Sam 24:18-25; 1 Kings 18:30). But these altars were not to be permanent or lavish. They were to consist simply of a mound of earth or a heap of loose stones, depending upon which

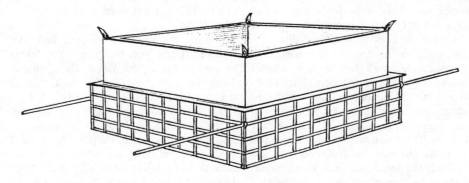

Altar of burnt offering

material was available in the region. The altars were not to be so high that they required steps, in order to avoid any immodesty which might occur if a person lifted up his robes while climbing the steps (Exod 20:22-26).

In the tabernacle, and later the temple, there were two altars, one in the open courtyard and the other inside the sanctuary. The one in the tabernacle courtyard was called the altar of burnt offering, for it was the altar on which all the animal sacrifices were offered. In appearance it was like a large wooden box overlaid with a metal variously described as bronze, copper or brass. It was five cubits square and three cubits high (a cubit being about forty-four centimetres or eighteen inches). This 'box' may have been filled with rocks and dirt to form a mound on which the sacrifices were burnt. Alternatively, the sacrifices may have been burnt on a grid inside the box. Extending halfway up the altar on the outside was a grating that supported a ledge. This may have had some use during the offering of the sacrifices (Exod 27:1-8).

The altar inside the sanctuary was positioned in the Holy Place against the veil, and was only for the offering of incense. It was much smaller than the altar of burnt offering, being only one cubit square and two cubits high. It too was made of wood, but its overlaying metal was gold, befitting the splendour of

the shrine in which it was placed (Exod 30:1-10; see also INCENSE; TABERNACLE).

Both the altar of burnt offering and the altar of incense had horn-shaped projections at their corners. The Bible does not explain the practical or symbolic significance of the horns, but blood was sprinkled on them in certain rituals (Exod 27:2; 29:10-12; 30:2; Lev 4:4-7; see HORN). The altars were also fitted with carrying poles, for they were taken with the people on the journey to Canaan (Exod 27:6-7; 30:4-5). (Concerning altars of false religion see BAAL.)

The Bible speaks of no literal altar for the Christian religion; only of the figurative 'altar' of Christ's atoning death. Sacrificial altars and their accompanying festivals belong to the old Jewish religion and have no place in Christianity. When certain Jews in the early church were tempted to combine Christian faith with sacrificial rituals, the writer to the Hebrews told them that such a combination is impossible. If people continue to join in eating sacrifices offered on the Jewish altar, they cannot join in receiving benefits from the sacrifice offered on the Christian 'altar', which is the death of Christ (Heb 13:10; cf. 1 Cor 9:13; 10:18).

AMALEKITES

Although the descendants of Esau were, on the whole, known as Edomites, there was one group of Esau's descendants who developed separately and were known as the Amalekites (Gen 36:1,9,12; Exod 17:8; Judg 3:13; 1 Sam 15:2,15). They were a race of wild desert nomads who were scattered in an area extending from the far south of Canaan across the Sinai peninsular.

When the Israelites were escaping from Egypt, the Amalekites raided the weak and defenceless who were lagging behind in the procession. Because of

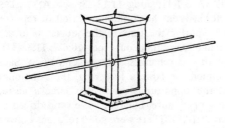

Altar of incense

this, God commanded that when the people of Israel were established in Canaan they were to wipe out the Amalekites (Exod 17:8-16; Deut 25:17-19).

In the meantime the Amalekites continued to attack the Israelites, both before they entered Canaan and after they had settled there (Num 14:45; Judg 3:13; 6:3,33; 10:12). Saul was commanded to destroy them completely, but although he won a notable victory, he failed to carry out the task fully (1 Sam 15:1-33). Those who survived continued their bandit-like raids, but with less frequency and less effect. Gradually the Amalekites were absorbed into other groups in the region and eventually the race died out (1 Sam 30:1-20; 1 Chron 4:41-43).

AMAZIAH

After the murder of his father Joash, Amaziah became king of Judah (796 BC; 2 Kings 12:20-21; 14:1-5). Determined to regain control of Edom (cf. 2 Kings 8:20), he planned to hire soldiers from Israel to help him. On advice from a prophet, he changed his mind and sent the hired soldiers home. He then fought the battle using Judean soldiers alone and won a great victory (2 Chron 25:5-13). Against the advice of a prophet, he took some of the idols he had captured from the Edomites and set them up as gods in his palace. In doing so he guaranteed his downfall (2 Chron 25:14-16). Swollen with arrogance and ambition, Amaziah then attacked Israel, in spite of being warned of the consequences. His country was defeated and Jerusalem plundered (2 Chron 25:17-24). Later he was assassinated by some of his own people (2 Chron 25:25-28).

Another Amaziah comes from the same general era. He was a priest who lived in Bethel during the reign of Jeroboam II of Israel. He opposed the preaching of the prophet Amos, and sent a message to the king accusing Amos of treason. When the king ignored the accusation, Amaziah tried to persuade Amos to return to Judah (Amos 7:10-13). Amos responded with an announcement of judgment on the false priest and his family (Amos 7:14-17).

AMEN

'Amen' is a transliteration from a Hebrew word meaning 'surely, truly, certainly, trustworthily'. It was used as a formula expressing agreement to a variety of statements or announcements; for example, an oath (Num 5:19-22), a blessing or curse from God (Deut 27:11-26; Jer 11:5), an announcement (1 Kings 1:36), a prophecy (Jer 28:6), an expression of praise (1 Chron 16:36; Ps 41:13; Jude 24-25), a prayer

(1 Cor 14:16), a statement (Rev 1:7) or a promise (Rev 22:20).

Since the promises of God find their true fulfilment (their 'yes', their 'amen') in Jesus Christ, he may be called 'the Amen'. He is what the Old Testament calls 'the God of truth', 'the God of the amen' (2 Cor 1:20; Rev 3:14; cf. Isa 65:16). Christians acknowledge this by adding their own 'amen' (2 Cor 1:20). Jesus, by introducing many of his statements with 'Amen' (i.e. 'Verily' or 'Truly'), guaranteed that those statements were true, certain, reliable and authoritative (Matt 8:10; 10:15,23,42; 11:11; 13:17; etc.). (See also TRUTH.)

AMMON

In the tableland region east of the Jordan River were the sister nations of Ammon and Moab. They were descended from the two daughters of Lot, and therefore were related to Israel (Gen 19:36-38). The chief city of Ammon was Rabbah, or Rabbath-Ammon (now known as Amman, capital of the present-day nation of Jordan) (Deut 3:11; 2 Sam 12:26). The national god of Ammon was Molech, or Milcom (1 Kings 11:5,7; see MOLECH).

National history

Ammon was a well watered region to the east of the Jordan River, with a number of streams that flowed through deep gorges into the Jordan. The most important of these streams was the Jabbok.

In the days before Israel's migration to Canaan, the Ammonites were pushed further east, away from the Jordan, by the Amorites. The Amorites overran all the land bordering the Jordan, from Bashan in the north to the Dead Sea in the south. Israel in turn conquered the Amorites, took the land for itself and divided it among the tribes of Reuben, Gad and half of Manasseh (Num 21:13,24-26,32-35; 32:1-5; Josh 13:8-12).

God approved of the Israelites' conquest of this territory, for they had taken it not from the Ammonites, who were related to them, but from the Amorites, who were under God's judgment (Deut 2:17-19,37; 3:1-11; Judg 11:12-23; see AMORITES). Therefore, when the Ammonites tried to repossess the area during the time of the judges, God used Jephthah to drive them out (Judg 10:6-9; 11:32-33).

With the changes that accompanied Saul's appointment as Israel's first king, the Ammonites seized the opportunity to invade Israel's eastern territory once more; but they were soon driven out (1 Sam 11:1-11). There were good relations between Ammon and Israel for much of David's reign, but when a new Ammonite king became aggressive, David's army drove the attackers back (2 Sam 10:1-14). When there was another attack the next year, David invaded Ammon, captured Rabbah, took control of the nation and forced the Ammonite people to work for Israel (2 Sam 11:1; 12:26-31).

David's successor, Solomon, took Ammonite women into his harem and worshipped the gods they brought with them (1 Kings 11:1,5,7,33). Solomon's son and successor, Rehoboam, was half-Ammonite, being the son of one of Solomon's Ammonite wives (1 Kings 14:21).

Ammon had repeated conflicts with Israel and Judah over the next two hundred years (2 Chron 20:10-11; 26:8; 27:5). When Assyria conquered Israel and took its people into captivity (722 BC), Ammon again took the opportunity to seize some of Israel's eastern territory. But the Ammonites' violence, cruelty and arrogance were inexcusable, and God's prophets assured them of a fitting punishment (Jer 49:1-6; Amos 1:13-15; Zeph 2:8-11). The Ammonites also joined the attackers to help with the final destruction of Judah, but their treachery only made their own destruction more certain (2 Kings 24:1,2; Jer 40:13-14; 41:1-3,10; Ezek 25:1-7).

As a result of conquests, first by Babylon and then by Persia, the nation of Ammon ceased to exist. Individual Ammonites continued to be a source of

trouble to the Jews (Neh 2:10; 4:7-9), but eventually the separate racial identity of the Ammonites disappeared.

AMORITES

There is some uncertainty concerning the identity of the Amorites mentioned in the Bible, for the name 'Amorite' had a variety of usages in early Bible times. Non-biblical records suggest that the word meant 'westerner' and referred to the early Semitic peoples who migrated to ancient Babylonia from Western Mesopotamia and Syria. They conquered the formerly powerful kingdom of Ur, and soon spread their rule throughout Lower, Upper and Western Mesopotamia.

Later these Amorites migrated down into Palestine, and were well established in certain areas by the time Abraham arrived (Gen 14:7,13). They intermarried so widely with the original Canaanites that it became common practice to use the words 'Canaanite' and 'Amorite' interchangeably as names for the whole mixed population of Canaan (Gen 15:16; Josh 24:15,18).

This intermarriage may explain why the biblical records indicate that the Amorites were descended from Ham, whereas non-biblical records suggest they were descended from Shem (Semites). Because most of the original Canaanites were descendants of Ham, the Amorites who later became Canaanites could regard both Ham and Shem as their ancestors (Gen 10:1,6,15-16). Nevertheless, there were some Amorite tribal groups in Canaan who maintained their distinct identity, as did other tribal groups (Exod 3:8; 13:5; 23:23; Josh 9:1; 12:8).

Israel and the Amorites

Prior to Israel's migration from Egypt to Canaan, the Amorite king Sihon had conquered all the Ammonite and Moabite territory east of the Jordan River as far south as the Arnon River. He made the former Moabite town Heshbon his capital (Num 21:26). When Sihon went to war against the journeying Israelites, the Israelites overthrew his army and seized his territory (Num 21:21-25). They also seized the adjoining northern territory of Bashan, which was ruled by another Amorite king (Num 21:33-35). This combined Amorite territory east of Jordan later became the homeland of the Israelite tribes of Reuben, Gad and the eastern half of Manasseh (Num 32:33).

Amorite kings west of Jordan (i.e. in Canaan) likewise lost their territory to the conquering Israelites (Josh 5:1; 10:5; 11:1-8). This area became the homeland of the remaining nine and a half Israelite tribes.

At various times throughout their history, the Israelites obtained cheap labour by forcing the Amorites and other conquered peoples to work as slaves on government projects (Judg 1:35; 1 Kings 9:20-21). In time the Amorites were absorbed into Israel and so disappeared as a distinct race. But their name survived as a general term for all the former inhabitants of Canaan (1 Kings 21:26; 2 Kings 21:11; cf. Gen 15:16).

AMOS

During the eighth century BC, there was widespread corruption in Israel and Judah. This stirred up opposition from men of God who condemned the people and announced God's judgment upon them. Of the four prophets of this time whose writings have been preserved in the Bible, the earliest was almost certainly Amos. The others were Hosea, Isaiah and Micah.

Characteristics of the age

Amos prophesied during the reigns of Jeroboam II in Israel and Azariah (or Uzziah) in Judah (Amos 1:1). These two kings between them expanded Israelite-Judean rule from Syria in the north to Egypt in the south, and from Philistia in the west to Ammon in the east (2 Kings 14:23-27; 2 Chron 26:1-15). With political stability and economic development, Israel and Judah entered an era of great prosperity. At the same time the religious and moral standards of society declined badly.

Previously, society had been built around the simple agricultural life. Now, with the rapid growth of commerce and trade, the merchants became

An Israelite market

the dominant people in society, and the farmers became the oppressed. City life developed, and with it came the social evils of corrupt government and commercial greed. Rapid prosperity for the few

meant increased poverty for most. As the upper classes grew in wealth and power, they exploited the lower classes. Bribery and corruption flourished, even in the law courts, leaving the poor with no way to obtain justice.

As a shepherd-farmer who had to deal with ruthless merchants and corrupt officials, Amos knew how bad the situation was and he spoke out against it (Amos 1:1; 7:14-15). He condemned the greed and luxury of the rich, for he knew that they had gained their wealth through cheating, oppression and injustice (Amos 2:6-7; 3:10,15; 5:10-12; 6:4-6; 8:4-6). Although they kept the religious festivals, all their religious activity was hateful to God so long as they persisted in social injustice (Amos 5:21-24; 8:3,10). Amos saw that the nation was heading for terrible judgment (Amos 6:14; 7:8-9).

Amos's message

By announcing God's judgment on some of Israel's neighbouring nations, Amos no doubt gained the enthusiastic attention of his hearers (1:1-2:3). He warned, however, that judgment was coming for Judah also (2:4-5), and particularly for Israel, the corrupt northern kingdom with whom Amos was mainly concerned (2:6-16).

As God's prophet, Amos had a responsibility to announce whatever God told him (3:1-8). He did this fearlessly, condemning the corruption of Israel's capital city Samaria (3:9-4:3) and the refusal of the people in general to heed God's warnings (4:4-13). God demanded repentance (5:1-27), and warned that the nation's corruption was leading it to certain destruction (6:1-14).

Three visions told Amos that God's patience with the rebellious nation could not last indefinitely (7:1-9). A local priest, tired of Amos's constant announcements of judgment, tried unsuccessfully to get rid of the troublesome preacher (7:10-17). Amos then revealed two further visions God had given him. The first emphasized that Israel was nearing its end (8:1-14), the second that there was no possibility of escape (9:1-10). Yet after the punishment of the captivity, God would restore the nation and bless its people again (9:11-15).

ANAK

Anak was a Canaanite whose descendants (called Anakim, plural of Anak) were giants. They lived in the south of Canaan in the hill country around Hebron. Because of the great size and fearsome appearance of the Anakim, the Israelites saw them as an obstacle to the conquest of Canaan. Only

Joshua and Caleb believed Israel could conquer them (Num 13:22-33; Deut 9:2).

Joshua and Caleb were, in fact, the ones who eventually led the attack on the Anakim. Most of the Anakim were slaughtered, the only ones who managed to escape being those who found refuge in the Philistine towns of Gaza, Gath and Ashdod (Josh 11:21-22; 14:6-15). Gath remained the home of giants for several centuries (1 Sam 17:4; 2 Sam 21:18-22).

ANATHEMA

See CURSE.

ANCESTORS

God has clearly taught his people to respect their parents (Exod 20:12; Eph 6:1-3; 1 Tim 5:8), and this naturally results in a respectful remembrance of those parents after they have died (Gen 35:20; 2 Tim 1:5). But no superstition is involved. The living are not able to call upon their dead ancestors for help, nor are they able to give their dead ancestors help, whether by praying to them, praying for them, or presenting offerings on their behalf. Those who die are, by their death, cut off from the world of the living. They join all their ancestors in the world of the dead (Gen 15:15; Judg 2:10; 1 Kings 1:21; 14:31; cf. 2 Sam 12:22-23).

If, generation after generation, people instruct their children in the knowledge of God, later generations will benefit from the faith and example of their ancestors. They will know the God of their fathers (Deut 6:3-7; 27:3; Ps 78:2-4; Joel 1:2-3; Luke 1:55; Acts 3:13). On the other hand, the forefathers might leave behind a bad example and a worthless manner of life for their descendants (Ezra 9:7; 1 Peter 1:18). Yet this should never be used as an excuse for wrongdoing. Each person is responsible for his actions, regardless of what his ancestors might have done (Ezek 2:3; 18:1-4,19-20).

Through their wrong behaviour, people of later generations can be a disgrace to the memory of their godly ancestors. Only through complete repentance can they be united with their believing forefathers as the true children of God (Mal 4:6; Luke 1:17; John 8:39-40,56).

God's faithfulness to believing ancestors should be an encouragement (Ps 22:4; Luke 1:72-73), his punishment on unbelievers a warning (Num 32:7-8; Zech 1:4-5). While it is true that the sinful ways of one generation can have lasting bad effects on later generations (Exod 20:5; Acts 7:51-52), it is also true

that the mercy of God is constantly available to those who submit to him (Exod 20:6). The clearest expression of this mercy is in Jesus Christ. Those of a former generation cannot help those of the present, but the living Christ can help all who call on him. To those who trust in him he gives the life that even physical death cannot destroy, eternal life (John 6:48-51,58).

ANDREW

Among those who responded to the preaching of John the Baptist was Andrew, a fisherman from Galilee. He was with John the Baptist in the region around the Jordan Valley when John introduced him to Jesus. Andrew quickly went and told his brother Peter that the Messiah of whom John had spoken had arrived, with the result that Peter soon met Jesus and believed (John 1:35-42). (For further details of Andrew's family see PETER.)

When Jesus later went to Galilee, the two brothers left their fishermen's work to join him in his work (Matt 4:18-20). Later again, Jesus included both brothers in his chosen group of twelve apostles (Matt 10:2; Mark 13:3; Acts 1:13). Two further references to Andrew record how he brought other people to Jesus (John 6:8-9; 12:21-22).

ANGELS

Angels are God's servants and messengers in the heavenly and spiritual realm, where they find true satisfaction in the unceasing worship and service of God. They were created before man, they belong to a higher order than man, and their number is countless (Ps 103:20; 148:2; Isa. 6:2-3; Dan 7:10; Luke 12:8-9; 15:10; Col 1:16; Heb 12:22; Rev 4:8; 5:11-12; 7:11).

Good and bad angels

At some time before the creation of man, some of the angels, under the leadership of one who became known as Satan, rebelled against God and so fell from their original sinless state (2 Peter 2:4; Jude 6). As a result there are good angels and evil angels. Christ has angels and so has Satan (Job 4:18; Matt 25:31,41; Jude 9; Rev 12:7-9).

Both good and bad angels are under God's sovereign rule, the difference between them being that the good angels are obedient and the evil angels rebellious. Even the chief of the evil angels, Satan, is no more than a created being under the authority of God. Satan and the evil angels who follow him can do their evil work only within the limits that God allows (Job 1:12; 2:6; see SATAN).

Because of the high position that angels have as God's heavenly servants, the Bible speaks of them as holy ones, as stars, and even as sons of God. Again these expressions may apply to good angels and bad angels (Job 1:6; 2:1; 5:1; 15:15; 38:7; Ps 89:5,7; Rev 9:1; 12:3-4,9). (The remainder of this article will be concerned only with good angels. For further discussion on evil angels see DEMONS.)

Dealings with mankind

Angels have many functions in relation to mankind, but above all they are God's messengers (Gen 19:1; 28:12; Exod 3:2; Num 22:22; Judg 2:1-4; 6:11; 2 Sam 24:16; 1 Kings 13:18; 19:5; Matt 1:20; 2:19; 13:41; 16:27; Luke 1:26-31; Acts 10:3-4; Gal 3:19; e.g. see GABRIEL). In many of the earlier Old Testament references, the angel (or messenger) of God appears to be almost the same as God himself. This is possibly because the angel is so closely identified with God as his messenger that when he speaks God speaks. The angel's temporary physical appearance is God's temporary physical appearance (cf. Gen 16:7-13; 21:17-18; 22:15-17; Exod 3:2-6).

To the godly, an angel may be a guide (Gen 24:7,40; Exod 14:19; Acts 8:26; 27:23), a protector (Ps 34:7; 91:11; Dan 6:22; 10:13,21; Matt 18:10), a deliverer (Isa 63:9; Dan 3:28; Matt 26:53; Acts 5:19), an interpreter of visions (Dan 8:16; Zech 1:8-14; Rev 1:1; 22:6) and, in fact, a sympathetic helper in all circumstances (Mark 1:13; Luke 22:43; Heb 1:13-14). Yet to the ungodly, angels may be God's messengers of judgment (Matt 13:39,41; 25:31-32; Acts 12:23; 2 Thess 1:7-8).

There are various categories of angels (Gen 3:24; Isa 6:2; Ezek 10:3; Col 1:16; 1 Thess 4:16; Jude 9; see MICHAEL). Angels themselves do not have a physical form and do not reproduce their kind as humans do (Matt 22:30). When God sends them as his messengers to humans, he may give them a form similar to that of humans, though they are usually sufficiently different to create a feeling of great awe (Judg 13:15-20; Matt 28:2-3; Luke 2:9; 24:4; John 20:12; Acts 1:10; 6:15).

Cherubim are spirit beings of one of the higher angelic orders. They usually feature as guardians of God's throne and protectors of his interests (Gen 3:24; Exod 25:17-22; Ps 80:1; Ezek 1:4-14; 10:1-22; cf. Rev 4:6-11; see CHERUBIM).

Great though angelic beings are, human beings should not worship them (Col 2:18; Rev 19:10; 22:8-9). Jesus Christ is the one whom people should worship; for he is God, and therefore far above angels (Heb 1:5-13; Eph 1:20-21; Col 2:10; Rev 5:11-14). Those who through faith are united with Christ will thereby share Christ's dominion in the age to come, and this will involve them in judgment of angels (Heb 2:5-9; 1 Cor 6:3).

ANGER

Sudden outbursts of temper are one of the fruits of man's sinful nature. The Bible therefore repeatedly pictures the evils of such behaviour and warns God's people to avoid it (Gen 49:6-7; Ps 37:8; Gal 5:19-20; Eph 4:31-32; Col 3:8). Uncontrolled anger can have far-reaching consequences, producing violence and even murder (Matt 5:21-22; Luke 4:28-29; Acts 7:54,57-58; 21:27-36). It is important that a person in a position of responsibility in the church not be quick tempered (Titus 1:7).

Yet there may be cases where it is right to be angry. Those who are faithful to God should be angry at all forms of sin, whether that sin be rebellion against God or wrongdoing against other people (Exod 16:20; 32:19; 2 Sam 12:5; Neh 5:6-7; Matt 18:32-34). But because the human nature of everyone is affected by sin, it is difficult for any person to be angry and at the same time not go beyond the limits that God allows (Ps 4:4; 106:32-33; Eph 4:26).

Certainly it is wrong for people to be so angry that they try to take personal revenge. God's people must be forgiving, and leave God to deal with those who do them wrong (Lev 19:18; Rom 12:19-21; see HATRED; REVENGE). If, in resisting wrongdoing, they are guilty of bad temper, they should not try to excuse their behaviour by claiming they are carrying out God's righteous purposes (James 1:19-20). God's anger is always pure, always just, always righteous (Exod 34:6-7; Rom 2:4-6; see WRATH).

ANIMALS

Since the Israelites were mainly an agricultural people, animals played a large part in their lives. Israelites raised cattle, sheep and goats extensively throughout their land, and these provided them with food products and materials for clothing (Num 32:1; 2 Chron 26:10; Prov 27:26-27). They used oxen to pull carts, plough fields and thresh grain (Num 7:6-8; 1 Kings 19:19; Amos 2:13; 1 Cor 9:9). They were to treat their working animals kindly and give them proper food and rest (Deut 5:14; 22:10; 25:4). (For further details see FARMING.)

Israelites did not keep pigs, considering them to be unclean animals whose meat was not fit to be eaten (Lev 11:7; Prov 11:22). However, there were pig farmers among non-Israelites who lived in the region (Luke 8:26,32; 15:15). Another animal that the Israelites loathed was the dog, for most dogs in those days were savage, disease-ridden animals that roamed the streets and fed on filth (2 Sam 16:9; 2 Kings 9:33-36; Ps 22:16; 59:6; Matt 7:6; Luke 16:21; 2 Peter 2:22).

For transport people in Bible times used asses (Josh 9:4; 1 Sam 9:3; 25:20; Matt 21:2-5), camels (Gen 24:10; 30:43; 31:17; 37:25; Isa 30:6) and horses

Camel transport

(Isa 28:28), though the latter were kept mainly for warfare (Josh 11:4; 1 Kings 10:28-29; Isa 30:16; 36:8). Mules, which combined the strength of the horse with the endurance of the ass, sometimes played an important part in Israel's communications (1 Kings 18:5; Ezra 2:66).

Many different animals lived in the forest and semi-desert regions of Palestine: lions (1 Sam 17:34; Ps 7:2; Isa 31:4; Jer 5:6; Nahum 2:11-12), bears (1 Sam 17:34; 2 Kings 2:24; Amos 5:19), foxes (Judg 15:4; Matt 8:20), wolves (Jer 5:6; John 10:12), hyenas (Isa 13:22), jackals (Isa 34:13; 43:20), wild asses (Job 39:5-8; Jer 14:6), wild oxen (Job 39:9; Ps 22:21), wild boars (Ps 80:13), and deadly snakes (Num 21:6; Isa 30:6; see SNAKE). The Israelites did not hunt for sport, but on occasions had to kill wild animals to defend themselves (Exod 23:29; Judg 16:5; 1 Sam 17:34-36; 2 Kings 17:26).

There were many other animals which, though wild, were not fierce, such as the hart, gazelle, roebuck, wild goat, ibex, antelope, rock badger, rabbit, hare and porcupine. The Israelites hunted some of these for food, but there were others that they were forbidden to eat (Lev 11:1-8; Deut 14:3-8; Isa 14:23; 34:11; see UNCLEANNESS). Hunters used bows and arrows, slingstones, and traps of various kinds such as nets and pits (Gen 21:20; 27:3; 1 Sam 17:40; Ps 57:6; 124:7; Ezek 19:8).

ANOINTING

In Old Testament times, it was a common practice to appoint priests, kings, and sometimes prophets to their positions by the ceremony of anointing. Holy oil was poured over the head of the person as a sign that he was set apart for the service of God. He now had the right, and the responsibility, to perform the duties that his position required (Exod 28:41; Num 3:2-3; 1 Kings 1:39; 19:16; 2 Kings 9:3; Ps 18:50; 28:8; 105:15). (Concerning the everyday eastern custom of anointing the heads of visitors and guests see HOSPITALITY.)

Things as well as people could be anointed. Moses anointed the tabernacle and its equipment to indicate that they were set apart for sacred use (Exod 30:22-30). The oil used to anoint the priests and the tabernacle was prepared according to a special formula that was not to be used for any other purpose (Exod 30:26-33). Official anointing carried with it the authority of God, and therefore no one could lawfully challenge the appointment (1 Sam 10:1; 24:6).

Anointing was also associated with the gift of God's special power, or the gift of his Spirit, for carrying out some specific task (1 Sam 16:13). Originally such anointing was a physical ceremony, but because of this spiritual significance, people began to use the word 'anoint' solely in a spiritual or

Anointing with oil

metaphorical sense. It symbolized the outpouring of God's Spirit in equipping a person for God's service (Isa 61:1; Acts 10:38).

This usage of the word was later extended even further, so that the Bible could speak of all who receive the Holy Spirit as being anointed (2 Cor

1:21-22; 1 John 2:20,27). Jesus was in a special sense God's Anointed (Luke 4:18; Acts 4:26-27; 10:38; see MESSIAH).

Concerning the practice of anointing in relation to such things as burial, massaging, healing and showing hospitality, see OIL; SPICES.

ANTICHRIST

Towards the end of the first century, there were certain false teachers who denied that Jesus Christ was fully God and fully man. In doing so they denied one of the basic facts of the Christian faith, and so showed themselves to be enemies of Christ. The name that the Bible gives to people who show such opposition to Christ is antichrist (1 John 2:22; 4:3; 2 John 7).

The spirit of antichrist is always in the world and has shown itself in many ways and in many people down the ages. It will have its last and most violent expression in the final great rebellion against God immediately before the return of Christ (1 John 2:18; cf. Ps 2:2-3; Dan 9:27; 11:36-39; Matt 24:15-21). More specifically, it seems that it will express itself in the leader of that rebellion, one who is variously known as *the* antichrist, the man of sin, the man of lawlessness and the wicked one.

Empowered by Satan, this last great antichrist will recognize no authority, Christian or otherwise, apart from his own, and will put himself in the place of God as the sole controller of mankind. He is probably the one whom the book of Revelation symbolizes by the beast with seven heads and ten horns (2 Thess 2:3-4,9-10; Rev 13:1-10). He is destined to perish in judgment at the return of Jesus Christ, and is therefore called also 'the son of perishing' (2 Thess 2:3,8; Rev 19:20).

ANTIOCH IN PISIDIA

Pisidia was the traditional name of a highland district in Asia Minor. When the Romans took control of Asia Minor, they replaced the many local districts with a smaller number of Roman provinces. Pisidia now fell within the Roman province of Galatia. Antioch lay within Galatia, on the border area between the two smaller districts of Pisidia and Phrygia (Acts 13:14; 16:6; for map see GALATIA). It is usually referred to as Pisidian Antioch to distinguish it from Syrian Antioch.

When Paul and Barnabas first came to Antioch, they preached in the Jewish synagogue on the Sabbath and there was a good response, both from Jews and from Gentiles (Acts 13:14,42-43). The next Sabbath almost the whole Gentile population of Antioch came to the synagogue to hear the missionaries preach. The Jewish leaders became jealous and angry, and drove Paul and Barnabas from the city (Acts 13:44-50; 2 Tim 3:11). The two missionaries, not lacking in courage, returned to the city soon after (Acts 14:21).

Antioch was one of the churches of Galatia that Paul addressed in his Letter to the Galatians (Gal 1:2; see GALATIANS, LETTER TO THE). Paul visited the churches of Galatia again on his second and third missionary journeys (Acts 16:6; 18:23).

ANTIOCH IN SYRIA

Soon after the sweeping conquests of Alexander the Great, the empire he established split into sectors under the control of his Greek generals. One of

Antioch in Syria

these sectors was centred on Syria, and in 300 BC the new rulers built the city of Antioch on the Orontes River as the administrative capital of the sector. They also built the town of Seleucia nearby, as a Mediterranean port for Antioch (Acts 13:1,4). With the conquest of the region by Rome in 64 BC, Antioch became the capital of the Roman province of Syria.

Christianity came to Antioch through the efforts of Greek-speaking Jewish Christians who had been driven from Jerusalem by violent Jewish persecution. The two people whose teaching most helped the church in its early stages were Paul and Barnabas. It was there in Antioch, during the stay of Paul and Barnabas, that people first gave the name 'Christian' to the followers of Jesus Christ (Acts 11:19-26; for the significance of the name see CHRISTIAN).

Upon hearing of the needs of poor Christians in Jerusalem, the Antioch church saw its responsibility to send gifts to help other Christians (Acts 11:27-30). Next it saw its responsibility to spread the gospel into more distant places where people had never heard it. The church therefore sent off Paul and Barnabas as its first missionaries (Acts 13:1-4). Antioch became the centre from which Christianity spread west into Asia Minor and Europe.

Paul and Barnabas returned to Antioch when they had completed their first missionary journey (Acts 14:26-28). Soon, however, they met trouble. Jews from the church in Jerusalem came to Antioch and tried to force the Gentile Christians to keep the Jewish law (Acts 15:1,5; Gal 2:11-13). As a result of the trouble that these Jewish teachers caused, the leaders of the Antioch church went to Jerusalem to discuss the matter with the leaders there. The Antioch leaders asserted that Christians were not bound by the Jewish law, and returned to Antioch with the reassuring knowledge that the Jerusalem leaders supported them (Acts 15:6-35).

Paul's second missionary journey also started and finished in Antioch (Acts 15:30-41; 18:22). He left from Antioch on his third journey (Acts 18:23), but finished the journey in jail in Caesarea (Acts 23:31-35). There is no record of any further visits Paul made to Antioch.

ANXIETY

In a world where people face daily troubles and future uncertainties, it is natural that often they become anxious (1 Cor 7:32-33). Those who trust in God, however, need not be burdened by anxiety. God understands their troubles and concerns, and he promises them his peace if they cast their cares upon him (Ps 55:22; Jer 17:8; Phil 4:6-7; 1 Peter 5:7; see PEACE; PRAYER).

Jesus reassures Christians with the promise that since God gives them life, he can also give them whatever is necessary to maintain life (Matt 6:25-30). God is a loving Father who knows how to care for his children. To refuse to trust him is to act like those who do not know him (Matt 6:31-32; cf. Luke 10:41-42; James 4:13-16).

In fact, people's anxiety concerning the affairs of life is often what prevents them from coming to know God. They refuse to give their serious attention to the one thing that can save them from anxiety, namely, the gospel of Jesus Christ (Matt 13:22). On the other hand, when people put God first by allowing him to reign in their lives, they find that he is able to relieve them of life's natural anxieties (Matt 6:33,34).

APOCALYPTIC LITERATURE

During the three centuries leading up to and including the New Testament era, the distinctive type of literature known as apocalyptic flourished among Jewish writers. The name 'apocalyptic' comes from the Greek apokalypto, meaning 'to reveal' (cf. Rev 1:1). The literature has been given this name because the authors presented their messages in the form of divinely sent visions that revealed heavenly secrets. The revelations were particularly concerned with coming great events.

The Old Testament books of Ezekiel, Daniel and Zechariah (also Isaiah Chapters 24-27) show some of the apocalyptic features that had begun to develop in the later prophetical writings. Likewise, some of the New Testament writings, such as the book of Revelation and Mark Chapter 13, contain apocalyptic features.

A message for difficult times

With Israel's release from captivity in 539 BC and its re-establishment in its homeland, many Jews expected that the messianic age was about to dawn. Their hopes, however, were disappointed, and one powerful nation after another continued to rule over Israel.

By this time, the ministry of Israelite prophets, which had never been as prominent after the captivity as before, had almost disappeared entirely. Apocalyptic writers replaced prophetic preachers as the interpreters of Israel's history. But whereas the prophets were largely concerned with denouncing Israel's unfaithfulness and assuring the people of their coming judgment, the apocalyptists were more concerned with condemning Israel's oppressors and announcing certain doom upon them.

A popular practice among apocalyptic writers was to write under the name of a respected Israelite of a previous era. Through prophecies and visions, this 'writer' from the former era then spoke of events from his time to the time of the actual writer, as a means of assuring the readers that God was always in control of events. He wanted to encourage God's people to endure their sufferings, in the assurance that God would soon overthrow evil and bring in the golden age.

Some features of the literature

Throughout the apocalyptic literature there is a sharp contrast between evil and good, between the present world and the age to come. In the present world God's people suffer because of the evil that hostile governments and ungodly people direct against them. In the age to come, by contrast, God's people will enjoy unending contentment, whereas those who are evil will be destroyed (cf. Isa 24:21-23; 25:6-12; Dan 7:9-14; Rev 19:1-5; 21:1-8).

Meantime, God's people must persevere. They have to realize that history must move along the path that God has determined for it, till the time comes for him to intervene decisively (cf. Ezek 39:1-6,21,25; Dan 12:6-13; Mark 13:24-27,32).

The visions reported by the apocalyptic writers were not usually in the form of scenes taken from real life. In most cases they contained features that were weird and abnormal, such as unnatural beasts and mysterious numbers (Dan 8:3-8; 9:24; 12:11-12; Rev 13:1-5,11-18). The visions had symbolic meaning and were often interpreted by angels (Ezek 40:2-4; Dan 8:15-19; Zech 1:9,19; 5:5-6; Rev 21:9,15). Such writings enabled the Jews to comment safely on the oppressors who ruled them; for they were able to use symbols (usually beasts) instead of the names of their overlords (Dan 7:1-8; Mark 13:14; Rev 13:1-4; 17:1-18).

In contrast to the prophets, who said, 'This is what God *said* to me', the apocalyptists said, 'This is what God *showed* me' (Jer 7:1-3; 23:18 with Zech 1:20; Rev 4:1). Yet in the biblical writings there is much overlap between the prophetic and the apocalyptic. The biblical apocalyptic writers, though they had similarities with other apocalyptic writers, also had the fervent evangelistic and pastoral spirit of the biblical prophets. Although they saw visions that carried symbolic meanings, they also had the prophet's awareness that they spoke words from God. And those words made spiritual demands upon people (Ezek 11:1-12; 33:30-33; Zech 1:1-6; 3:1; Rev 1:3; 2:1-7; 22:1-4,7,18).

APOCRYPHA
See CANON.

APOLLOS

Over the last two or three hundred years of the pre-Christian era, a strong community of Jewish biblical scholars had grown up in Alexandria in Egypt. Apollos came from this background. He had a detailed knowledge of Old Testament Scriptures concerning the Messiah and became a believer in Jesus.

When Apollos visited the newly established Christian community in Ephesus, it became clear that he lacked an understanding of some important Christian teachings. But he learnt from the fuller instruction that Priscilla and Aquila gave him, and was of considerable help in teaching the Ephesian church. When he decided to move across to Corinth, the Ephesian Christians wrote to the Christians in Corinth to recommend him to them as a worthy teacher (Acts 18:24-28).

Foolishly, the immature Corinthian Christians made favourites of different teachers who had helped them, and soon there was tension between various groups in the church. Among these groups was a pro-Apollos faction and a pro-Paul faction (1 Cor 1:11-12). Paul condemned this formation of factions. He pointed out that he and Apollos were not in competition, but worked in cooperation. They were fellow servants of God (1 Cor 3:4-9). No doubt Apollos likewise was opposed to the Corinthians' creation of factions. This was probably the reason why, after leaving Corinth, he thought it best not to return for a while, in spite of Paul's enthusiastic urging (1 Cor 16:12).

Apollos must have continued as a travelling Christian preacher for many years. Towards the end of Paul's life, when Apollos visited Titus in Crete, Paul urged Titus to welcome him and to give him all possible help in his service for God. Apollos may even have been the person who carried Paul's letter to Titus (Titus 3:13; cf. 1:5).

APOSTACY

One characteristic of the true Christian is that he perseveres to the end. He never gives up his faith in Christ. Those who profess faith in Christ and then wilfully give up that faith are guilty of apostacy (Matt 24:10-13; Col 1:21-23; 1 Tim 1:19-20; Heb 3:12-14; 2 Peter 2:20-22; 1 John 2:19; see PERSEVERANCE).

Apostacy is not backsliding in the sense of a temporary lapse in Christian practice. Nor is it a denial of Christ in a moment of weakness, such as Peter's failure at the time of Jesus' arrest (Luke 22:31-34,54-62; cf. John 21:15-19; see BACKSLIDING; DENIAL; TEMPTATION). Rather it is the deliberate rejection of the faith that a person once professed to have in Christ. It is a sin that the Bible severely warns against, for apart from Christ there can be no salvation. If a person has deliberately renounced Christ, there is no other way of salvation available to him. He has disowned and shamed Christ by an action similar to that of those who crucified him (Heb 6:4-6; 10:26-29).

There may be many damaging influences that lead a person away from God and cause him to commit apostacy. Two of the most common are false teaching and persecution (Matt 24:9-11; 1 Tim 4:1-3; 2 Peter 2:1-3; Jude 3-4,17-23).

APOSTLE

According to the word's original meaning, an apostle was 'a sent one'. Jesus gave the name to his chosen twelve because, after their time of preparation with him, he sent them out in the service of his kingdom (Mark 3:13-15; Luke 6:13). As twelve tribes had formed the basis of the old people of God, so twelve apostles would be the foundation on which God would build his new people, the Christian church (Matt 16:18; Eph 2:20; Rev 21:12,14).

Mission of the twelve

Jesus' purpose in sending out the twelve was to spread the message of his kingdom throughout Israel (Matt 10:5-7), as preparation for the world-wide mission to follow (Matt 28:19-20). He gave them a share in his messianic powers so that they could demonstrate the triumph of his kingdom through healing the sick and casting out demons (Matt 10:1,8; see KINGDOM OF GOD). They were to move through Palestine as quickly as possible, avoiding anything that would hinder progress or waste time, so that they might complete the first stage of their mission during Jesus' lifetime (Matt 10:9-14).

The apostles' early activity proved to them that the special powers Christ had given them worked (Mark 6:13,30). Even after Christ had returned to his Father, they continued to perform miraculous works, because the Spirit of the risen Christ now indwelt them. These miracles were evidence that they were truly Christ's apostles (Acts 3:12,16; 4:10; 5:12; cf. 2 Cor 12:12).

Part of Jesus' purpose in choosing the twelve to accompany him in his ministry was that, after his departure, they might be able to preach about him with the first-hand knowledge of eye witnesses (John 15:26-27; Acts 1:8; 5:32; 10:39-41; cf. Mark 3:14). Realizing that they had a specific ministry to the people of that generation, the apostles tried to maintain a unit of twelve personal associates of Jesus as the basis of the new community. They insisted, therefore, that the person to replace Judas in the apostolic group be one who, like the other apostles, had been a genuine eye witness of the ministry of Jesus from his baptism to his ascension (Acts 1:21-22; cf. Luke 24:46-48).

With the establishment and growth of the church, the apostles had fulfilled part of the mission for which Christ had chosen them. They provided the leadership for the early church in Jerusalem (Acts 2:42; 4:37; 5:1-5; 6:1-4), and were general overseers of the expansion of Christianity into the regions throughout Palestine and beyond (Acts 8:14-17; 10:46-48). Because of these developments, they were no longer constantly in Jerusalem and were no longer moving together as a group. When James was executed, they saw no need to replace him in order to maintain the unit of twelve, for it had now largely fulfilled its purpose (Acts 12:2; cf. Matt 28:19; Acts 1:8).

Apostles in the church

Initially apostles were concerned with announcing the good news that, through Christ, the new era had arrived (Matt 10:7; Acts 2:22-40). They then had the added responsibility of passing on the teachings of Jesus to those who believed (Matt 28:19-20). In this they had particular help and enlightenment from the Holy Spirit, as Christ had promised (John 14:26; 15:26; 16:12-15). Teaching therefore became one of the apostles' main duties in the church (Acts 2:42; 5:21,42; 6:4).

As the church grew, other people were acknowledged as having equal authority with the original apostles. They were not part of that unique group of twelve, but they were no less apostles. Among these were Paul, Barnabas, and James the brother of Jesus (Acts 14:14; Rom 16:7; 1 Cor 9:1; 15:8-11; Gal 1:19). Because people other than the original twelve might now be apostles, warnings were given against false apostles (2 Cor 11:13; Rev 2:2). Regardless of the assertions people made about themselves, a true apostle could be appointed only by God (Acts 1:24; 1 Cor 1:1; cf. Mark 3:13-14).

Although apostles increased in number beyond the original twelve, their position was still unique in the church. They were people to whom the Holy Spirit had given special gifts that enabled them to preserve, teach and develop the truths of the Christian gospel (1 Cor 1:1; 12:28; 14:37; 2 Tim 1:11). People accepted the apostles' teaching as having the authority of God's Word (Acts 2:42; Gal 1:8; 1 Thess 2:13; 2 Thess 2:15; 2 John 10), and added the apostles' writings to the collection of inspired Scriptures (2 Peter 3:15-16; cf. John 14:26; 16:13-14; see INSPIRATION).

Authority in teaching was only part of a wider authority that apostles exercised in the early church. Their authority extended over all areas of church life (Acts 5:1-11; 2 Cor 12:12; 13:1-3; 2 Thess 3:4,14; 1 Tim 1:20).

Yet on many occasions the apostles refused to use their authority to force Christians to submit to their rulings. They preferred that the Christians make decisions and take action themselves, and in so doing grow in spiritual maturity (Acts 11:2-4; 15:6; 2 Cor 1:24; 4:2,5; 10:8; 13:10; Philem 8-9). By helping such growth, they were again fulfilling their ministry (Eph 4:11-13).

The apostles did not pass their office on to the next generation. They were God's specific provision to link the ministry of Christ with the birth of the church, and to ensure that the church was built upon the right foundation (Eph 2:20). As the authoritative interpretation of Christ and the gospel became firmly established in written form (2 Thess 2:15; see GOSPEL; SCRIPTURES), and as the churches became firmly established through their local leaders (Acts 13:1-3; 14:23; 20:28; see ELDER), the necessity for apostles decreased. The apostolic office had served its purpose, and after the first century it died out.

AQUILA

Born of Jewish parents in Asia Minor, Aquila grew up to learn the trade of tentmaker. In due course he married a woman named Priscilla. In every place where the Bible refers to Aquila or Priscilla it speaks of them together, suggesting that they formed a useful and well respected partnership.

Aquila and Priscilla were living in Rome at the time of an outbreak of anti-Jewish feeling when the Emperor expelled all Jews from the city. They moved to Corinth in Achaia, the southern part of Greece, where they met Paul. It was possibly at this time that they became Christians (Acts 18:1-3). (For a map covering the area of their travels see ACHAIA.)

When Paul left Corinth for Ephesus eighteen months later, Aquila and Priscilla went with him,

and remained in Ephesus when Paul moved on (Acts 18:11,18-19). They probably helped to establish the church in Ephesus. In particular they were able to help Apollos, a newly converted Jewish teacher who had come to Ephesus from Egypt (Acts 18:24-26; see APOLLOS). They remained in Ephesus to help Paul when he returned to the city for a three-year stay (Acts 19:1; cf. 20:31), during which he wrote the letter known to us as 1 Corinthians. At this time the church in Ephesus used the house of Aquila and Priscilla as a meeting place (1 Cor 16:19).

Some time after this, when Jews were allowed back in Rome, Aquila and Priscilla returned to live there for a time. They continued to serve God wholeheartedly, and their house in Rome, like their house in Ephesus, became a church meeting place (Rom 16:3-5).

Many years later Aquila and Priscilla were living back in Ephesus, no doubt helping Timothy in the difficult work Paul had given him to do there. Paul's greeting to them just before his execution is the final reference to them in the New Testament (2 Tim 4:19; cf 1 Tim 1:3).

ARABAH

The Hebrews used the word *arabah* to denote semi-desert land. In particular they used the word as a name for that deep, hot and dry valley that ran north-south from the Sea of Galilee to the Gulf of Aqabah (the north-eastern arm of the Red Sea) (Deut 1:1; 2:8; 4:49; Josh 11:2; 18:18-19). The Dead Sea, which was the deepest part of this long valley, was known as the Sea of the Arabah (Deut 3:17). (For details see PALESTINE, sub-heading 'Arabah'.)

ARABIA

Only rarely does the Bible mention Arabia by name. It usually refers to the peoples of the region by the family or tribal groups to which they belonged. Often it refers to Arabia simply as 'the east' (Gen 10:30; 25:6; Judg 6:3; Isa 2:6; Ezek 25:4).

Many of the people descended from Noah (Gen 10:1-32), Abraham (through his concubine Keturah; Gen 25:1-6), and Esau (Gen 36:1-43) settled as tribal groups in Arabia. They were wandering shepherds rather than farmers, since most of the land was not suitable for cultivation and some of it was desert. Among the better known tribal groups were Joktam and Sheba in the south (Gen 10:25-29; 1 Kings 10:1-13; Ps 72:10,15; Isa 60:6) and Dedan and Kedar in the north (Isa 21:13-17; 42:11; Jer 25:23-24; 49:28; Ezek 25:13; 27:21).

These people camped at different places and lived in tents while looking after their flocks of sheep and goats (2 Chron 17:11; Ps 120:5; Isa 13:20; 60:7). Many of them were merchants who carried on profitable trading in gold, precious stones, cloth,

spices and other goods (Gen 37:25,28; 1 Kings 10:1-2,10-15; Job 6:19; Jer 6:20; Ezek 27:20-22; 38:13). They were also well known for their raiding and plundering of farms and villages (2 Chron 21:16-17; 22:1; Job 1:15; Ezek 25:4-5).

In New Testament times northern Arabia was occupied by an Arab tribe called the Nabateans, who at various times extended their power west to the Mediterranean and north to the Syrian capital, Damascus. They are mentioned once in the New Testament. After Paul's conversion, the Jews in Damascus opposed him violently. At the time of the unsuccessful attempt to capture him in Damascus, the city was under the control of the Nabateans (Acts 9:1-8,23-25; 2 Cor 11:32-33).

ARAM

The Arameans, or people of Aram, were one of the many groups of Semitic peoples who lived in the region of the Bible story. The ancestor from whom they took their name was Aram, the son of Shem, the son of Noah (Gen 10:22).

Arameans

By the time the Arameans first appear in the Bible story, they were living in the north-western part of Mesopotamia. This was the territory to which the father of Abraham came when he migrated with his family from Babylonia. They settled around the town of Haran (Gen 11:31).

Abraham later moved to Canaan, but the rest of his relatives remained in Aram (Gen 12:1,4-5). Consequently, they became known as Arameans, though actually they were descended not through Aram but through Arpachshad, another of Shem's sons (Gen 10:22-25; 11:10-32). When Abraham wanted to obtain a wife for his son Isaac from among his relatives, he had to send his servant back to Aram to fetch Rebekah (Gen 24:10; 25:20). (Some versions of the Bible call the Arameans Syrians, though the region was not known as Syria till centuries later.)

Jacob, son of Isaac and Rebekah, also went to Aram, where he obtained for himself two wives. Both of them were daughters of Laban, Rebekah's brother (Gen 28:2-5). Because Jacob had lived twenty years in Aram, and because his wives were from that region, he and his children became known as Arameans (Gen 31:20,38; Deut 26:5).

This explains how the practice developed of sometimes using the name 'Aramean' when referring to the forefathers of the nation Israel. The name was related to the place where the forefathers lived, not to their racial descent. The true Arameans do not become prominent in the Bible story till the time of the Israelite monarchy. By that time Aram was known as Syria (see SYRIA).

Aramaic

One of the greatest influences the Arameans had was through their language, Aramaic. The Aramaic language spread far and wide, and from the time of Israel's monarchy onwards was the language most commonly used throughout south-west Asia (2 Kings 18:26).

Written Aramaic used letters that were similar to Hebrew letters, and isolated sections of the Old Testament are written in Aramaic instead of the usual Hebrew (Ezra 4:8-6:18; 7:12-26; Jer 10:11; Dan 2:4-7:28). In the Persian Empire (539-333 BC) Aramaic was the official language (Ezra 4:7). With the conquests of Alexander the Great, the Greek language spread throughout his empire and became the official language. But in south-western Asia, Aramaic was still the most commonly used language, in spite of the increasing use of Greek. Aramaic was the language that Jesus and his disciples usually spoke (Mark 5:41; 7:34; 15:34), though they also spoke and wrote Greek, the language in which New Testament is written.

ARCHAEOLOGY

Throughout human history, each generation has left behind all sorts of objects that enable people of later generations to learn about life in former times. The science of archaeology, which is concerned with the study of ancient findings, is particularly useful in helping us understand the history, cultures, religions and languages of the biblical era. Although the truth of the Bible is not dependent upon such findings, archaeology has confirmed the reliability of the biblical record.

Methods

Many features of the ancient world can be readily investigated, because they are still standing and exposed to public view (e.g. the pyramids of Egypt). Others can hardly be investigated at all, because they lie beneath present-day settlements (e.g. the city of Damascus). The ruins that lie buried and can be excavated are some of the best sources of information on ancient civilizations .

As archaeologists dig into ruins, they are aware that human occupation of a site may have stretched over hundreds or thousands of years. When a town was destroyed, whether by conquest, earthquake, storm or flood, the usual practice for the new generation of builders was simply to level off the ruins and build on top of the flattened rubble and dirt. This rebuilding pattern may have been repeated a number of times over a long period. The result is that today the sites of many ancient towns are covered by mounds (Arabic: *tells*), which look like small tablelands. These mounds are a rich source of archaeological information.

Since archaeological investigation takes much time and money, archaeologists are usually able to investigate only a small area of a buried town. They try to choose those parts of the town that are likely to produce the most worthwhile results, such as palaces, government buildings, temples and selected houses. Beginning at the top level of the mound, they may dig down progressively through the layers,

gradually forming a trench that cuts through the mound. The layers reveal successively more ancient eras of the town's history. By carefully recording and investigating everything they find, archaeologists will in time be able to suggest the era and setting for different findings.

Many features help to indicate which period is being investigated. These include the nature of the soil, the type of pottery, building characteristics, metal articles, coins, jewellery and any inscriptions or other writings (see also WRITING). Scientists are often able to calculate the approximate date of animal and plant substances by using a technique known as Carbon-14. With knowledge continually increasing in all areas of science, archaeologists can call upon more and more expert help from research facilities all over the world. They are also aware that they must constantly review their earlier conclusions as more information becomes available.

Stone Age and Bronze Age

In biblical archaeology, the successive periods from prehistory to the fourth century BC are usually classified according to the successive technologies (Stone, Bronze, Iron). From the fourth century BC into the Christian era, the archaeological periods are usually classified according to successive empires (Greek, Roman).

The Stone Age, which covers an indefinite period extending back beyond 4000 BC, is divided into Palaeolithic, Mesolithic and Neolithic Ages, meaning respectively Old Stone, Middle Stone and New Stone Ages. The next eight hundred years, referred to as the Chalcolithic or Copper/Stone Age, leads to the Bronze Age, which lasted two thousand years from 3200 to 1200 BC. Much of the early part of the biblical record fits into the Bronze Age.

It is not the concern of the Bible to provide a detailed history of the world. The Bible's chief concern is to show how God, in a gracious response to man's rebellion, provided a way of salvation. God's plan of salvation began its major development

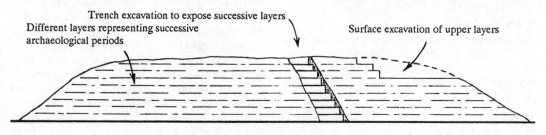

Trench excavation to expose successive layers
Different layers representing successive archaeological periods

Surface excavation of upper layers

Archaeological excavation mound (or *tell*)

with Abraham. God promised that from Abraham he would make a people, who would receive Canaan as their homeland and who would be God's channel of salvation to the world. Abraham enters the Bible story about the 20th century BC. The countless centuries before Abraham are passed over in only a few chapters (Genesis 1-11), whereas the seven centuries from Abraham to the end of the Bronze Age are spread across more than two hundred chapters (Genesis 12 to the opening chapters of Judges).

Out of the huge amount of archaeological evidence from the Bronze Age, certain discoveries have been particularly helpful in understanding some of the customs, laws, languages and other social features relevant to the Pentateuch. Important discoveries from the ancient Mesopotamian towns of Ebla (23rd century BC), Mari (18th century BC) and Nuzi (15th century BC) produce a picture of life in the region that is entirely consistent with the picture given in the biblical narratives of Abraham, Isaac, Jacob and their descendants.

Material from Egypt fits in harmoniously with the biblical accounts of Joseph's governorship and the Israelites' building of store-cities (see EGYPT). Ancient treaty documents between overlords and their subjects are in a similar form to the covenant between the God of Israel and his people (see COVENANT). Findings along the route of Israel's journey to, and conquest of, Canaan confirm and enlighten the biblical record.

Iron Age

The early days of Israel's settlement in Canaan correspond with the beginning of the Iron Age. In the biblical history, the Iron Age saw the establishment of Israel's monarchy, the division of the kingdom, the subsequent captivities, the destruction of Jerusalem and the subjection of the Jews, first to Babylon and then to Persia. The Iron Age, which began about 1200 BC, lasted almost nine hundred years to the stirring conquests of Alexander the Great about 330 BC.

Archaeological information from the Iron Age is enormous. The sites of many Israelite towns have been excavated, some with spectacular results. Outside Israel, discoveries at the ancient site of Ugarit (modern Ras Shamra) on Syria's Mediterranean coast have given us many enlightening details concerning the religions of Canaan that were such a stumbling block to Israel. Discoveries from the period of Ahab and Jezebel, for example, provide information about Baal worship that helps us to understand better the ministry of Elijah and Elisha (see BAAL).

For much of the period of the divided kingdom, Assyria was the dominant foreign influence in the affairs of Israel and Judah. Archaeological findings

Canaanite household idol discovered at Ugarit

reveal the extensive records that Assyrian kings kept of their reigns. Their many stone sculptures and inscriptions provide a good parallel to the biblical history of Israel and Judah, a number of whose kings are mentioned by name in the Assyrian records. These records also show the politically important achievements of some Israelite kings (e.g. Omri and Jeroboam II). Yet the prophet-writers of the Old Testament record give few details of these kings, considering them to be of only minor significance because of their religious unfaithfulness.

With the destruction of Jerusalem, the exile of the Jews in Babylon and their subsequent return to Palestine, Jewish national life entered a new phase. Babylonian findings confirm the biblical picture of the exile, and findings of the Persian Period confirm the biblical picture in the books of Ezra, Nehemiah and Esther. The era of Old Testament history was now over, and archaeology shows how the Persian Empire was increasingly feeling the effects of the spreading influence of Greece.

Greek and Roman Periods

Remains of buildings from the Greek Period are fewer than one might expect. The main reason for this is that builders of the Roman Period re-used large quantities of the Greeks' building materials in their own construction programmes. However, lengthy written records and thousands of documents from the period help compensate for this loss.

The widespread conquests of Alexander the Great introduced an era that brought dramatic change throughout the region of the Bible story. Greek culture and language became dominant everywhere. This had a great effect on Jewish history, bringing conflict between those Jews who gladly accepted the new ways and those who tried to resist them.

Out of this conflict arose religious parties such as the Sadducees and the Pharisees, along with other Jewish sects. One of these sects left behind a large library of Old Testament scrolls and other writings, which were discovered only in recent times. They were found in caves at Qumran near the Dead Sea, and are known as the Dead Sea Scrolls. They are one of the most spectacular finds from the period and have been of great help in the study of Old Testament manuscripts (see MANUSCRIPTS).

Rome took control of Palestine in 63 BC. This date provides a convenient starting point for a period that archaeologists see as one of transition between the Greek and Roman Periods. Most of the New Testament falls into this transition period. By AD 70, the date of the destruction of Jerusalem, the transition was over and the Roman Period well established. It lasted about three centuries.

Throughout Palestine there is much archaeological material that increases our knowledge of the region in New Testament times. This material is of great variety, from the impressive structures built by Herod the Great to everyday objects such as coins, pottery and glassware. Beyond Palestine, in Syria, Asia Minor, Greece and other areas of the New Testament story, archaeological discoveries confirm the accuracy of the New Testament in its references to matters of history, geography, culture, language and politics .

The scope of archaeology

No matter how much archaeology may help us to understand the world of the biblical period, we must bear in mind that it can neither prove nor disprove the truth of the Bible. The Bible's essential message concerns a relationship between God and man, and that is something that archaeology is not capable of investigating. It is beyond the scope of archaeology. Archaeology may, for example, shed light on the era in which Abraham lived, but it cannot evaluate the statement that Abraham believed God and God accepted him as righteous (Gen 15:6).

The main benefit of biblical archaeology is not in providing some sort of external assurance for Christian faith. Rather it is in providing a picture of life in Bible times that helps those who are separated by thousands of years from the people and events of which the Bible speaks.

AREOPAGUS

The Areopagus was an ancient and highly respected council of philosophers in Athens. The name came from the hill in Athens where the council originally met (commonly known as Mars Hill), though in New Testament times the council met in the commercial area of the town itself. The council consisted of philosophers from the two main schools of Greek philosophy, the Epicureans and the Stoics (see EPICUREANS; STOICS).

Athens was a famous centre of learning where people publicly discussed philosophy, religion and politics (Acts 17:21). The Areopagus was responsible for the orderly conduct of all public lecturing in Athens. When some of its members heard Paul preaching in the public places of the city, they invited him to give the Areopagus an account of his religion. From what they had heard, they thought he was announcing two new gods, whose names were 'Jesus' and 'Resurrection' (Acts 17:16-20).

Paul explained to the Areopagus the nature of the God they did not know. This God was the creator and controller of the universe, and the judge of all mankind. The death and resurrection of Jesus made forgiveness of sins available to all, but it also guaranteed judgment for those who refused to repent (Acts 17:22-31). Paul won the attention of the council with an explanation of the gospel that contained specific points relating to Epicurean and Stoic beliefs; but on the whole both groups rejected his teaching about the resurrection. There were a few, however, who believed (Acts 17:32-34).

ARISTARCHUS

Among the faithful helpers who travelled with Paul on his preaching tours was Aristarchus, a Christian from Thessalonica in the northern Greek province of Macedonia (Acts 19:29; 20:4). Though attacked during a riot in Ephesus (Acts 19:28-29), Aristarchus stuck firmly with Paul throughout the remaining journeys recorded in Acts. He accompanied Paul on his final visit to Palestine (Acts 20:1-6), probably stayed with him during his imprisonment there, and went with him on his journey to Rome (Acts 27:2). He remained with Paul during Paul's two-year imprisonment in Rome (Acts 28:16,30; Col 4:10; Philem 24).

ARK

An ark was a box-like container. In older English versions of the Bible, the word is used of Noah's floating animal-house (Gen 7:8-9), of the floating basket made for the baby Moses by his parents (Exod 2:3-5), and of the sacred box in the inner shrine of Israel's tabernacle (Exod 26:33).

Noah's ark

God's purpose in commanding Noah to build an ark was to provide a way of preserving people and animals through the judgment of the great flood (Gen 6:5-13; see FLOOD). The ark was not designed to sail the seas like a huge boat, but to float on the floodwaters like a huge box. It was about 133 metres long, 22 metres wide and 13 metres high, with a door in the side and a 44 centimetre light and ventilation opening running around the top of the wall, just below the roof overhang. It was divided horizontally into three decks, and vertically into a number of rooms. This helped to separate the animals and to brace the whole structure (Gen 6:14-20).

More important than the preservation of the animals was the preservation of the family of Noah. Noah's building of the ark demonstrated his faith and made possible the survival of a nucleus of believers through whom God could build a new people (Heb 11:7; 1 Peter 3:20; see NOAH).

Ark of the covenant

The gold covered wooden box known as the ark of the covenant, or covenant box, was Israel's most sacred religious article. It was approximately 110 centimetres long, 66 centimetres wide and 66 centimetres deep. Its ornamented lid, over which were mounted two golden cherubim, was the symbolic throne of God known as the mercy seat (Exod 25:10-22; see CHERUBIM). (For fuller details of the ark and for its significance in the tabernacle rituals see TABERNACLE.)

Ark of the covenant

When the Israelites moved from one camp to another, the ark was first covered with cloth, then carried by the Levites on shoulder poles. The ark usually went in front of the main procession (Num 4:5-6; 10:33). When the people crossed the Jordan River to enter Canaan, the Levitical priests carrying the ark again led the way. They stood in the middle of the dry river bed till all the people had crossed over (Josh 3:11-17). For the first battle in Canaan, God directed the priests to take the ark from the tabernacle and carry it around the city that had to be conquered (Josh 6:1-5).

Several generations later, Israelites again took the ark from the tabernacle and carried it into battle, this time against the Philistines. But they had not done so by God's directions, and the Philistines captured the ark (1 Sam 4:3-4,11).

After suffering terrible plagues during the time the ark was with them, the Philistines sent it back to Israel (1 Sam 5:1-12; 6:1-16). By striking dead some Israelites who looked into the ark, God impressed upon his people that the ark was sacred. They were not to treat it as an object of curiosity or superstition (1 Sam 6:19-20).

For the next twenty years the ark remained in a country house in Kiriath-jearim (1 Sam 6:21-7:2). When David conquered Jerusalem, he decided to take the ark there as part of his plan to make Jerusalem the religious centre of the nation. In putting the ark on a cart instead of using Levites to carry it, he was following the Philistines' practice instead of God's directions. The attempted move ended in tragedy (2 Sam 6:2-10). Three months later, after he had realized his mistake, David again tried to transport the ark, this time doing things properly (2 Sam 6:12-13; 1 Chron 15:13-15). With much rejoicing he brought the ark to Jerusalem and placed it in a tent specially prepared for it (2 Sam 6:14-19; 1 Chron 15:23-29).

When Solomon built the temple in Jerusalem, he placed the ark in the Most Holy Place (1 Kings 8:6-11). Apparently it was removed during the reign of the wicked Manasseh, but Josiah restored it to its rightful place (2 Chron 35:1-3). The Babylonians probably took the ark with them to Babylon after their destruction of Jerusalem in 587 BC (2 Kings 24:13). There is no record of what happened to it after that.

ARMOUR

The main pieces of armour worn by a soldier in ancient warfare were a coat of mail to protect the body, greaves to protect the legs, and a helmet to protect the head. These were usually made of bronze, though sometimes were made of leather (1 Sam 17:5-6; 1 Kings 22:34; Neh 4:16; Jer 46:4).

Soldiers who did the heavy fighting in the front ranks carried large shields, and the archers who came behind carried smaller shields (1 Sam 17:7; 2 Chron 14:8). Shields were sometimes made of

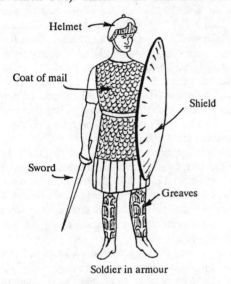

Soldier in armour

bronze (1 Kings 14:27), but less expensive types were made of rattan overlaid with leather. They could therefore be burnt (Ezek 39:9; see also WAR; WEAPONS).

The Christian is likened to a soldier who puts on the armour of God to fight against the evil forces of Satan. His defences against the enemy's attacks are truth, righteousness, faith and confidence in the Word of God and his own salvation (Rom 13:12; 2 Cor 6:7; Eph 6:10-18; 1 Thess 5:8).

ARNON

Originally the Arnon River belonged to the people of Ammon and Moab. But the Amorite king, Sihon, attacked from the north and overran much of their

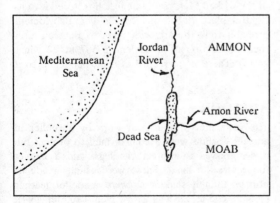

land. Eventually he was stopped at the Arnon River. The Arnon therefore became the boundary between the Amorites to the north and the Moabites to the south (Num 21:13).

When the Israelites under Moses were moving north towards Canaan, they conquered the Amorites and seized their territory (Num 21:24). Later, when Israel's territory east of Jordan was divided between its two and a half eastern tribes, the Arnon became the boundary between Israel's tribe of Reuben and the neighbouring Moabites (Deut 3:12,16).

ARTAXERXES

As Persian Emperor from 465 to 424 BC, Artaxerxes had control over Jerusalem during the time of the reforms of Ezra and Nehemiah. In the early part of his reign he responded to the complaints of local Palestinians by ordering that work on the rebuilding of Jerusalem cease (Ezra 4:7-23). But his decree made provision for him to reverse his decision at a later date if he so desired (Ezra 4:21).

In the seventh year of his reign, Artaxerxes did, in fact, reverse his decree, when he gave permission to Ezra to carry out reforms in Jerusalem (Ezra 7:7,11-26). His other significant decision in favour of the Jerusalem Jews came in the twentieth year of his reign, when he appointed Nehemiah governor and gave him full imperial support to rebuild and secure the city (Neh 2:1-8). For further details see EZRA; NEHEMIAH; PERSIA.

ASA

Judah was badly corrupted by Canaanite religions when Asa came to the throne (910 BC). He spent the early part of his reign trying to rid Judah of false religion, while at the same time he strengthened the nation's defences (2 Chron 14:1-8).

Strong faith and a strong army enabled Asa to defeat an enemy invader and won him encouraging words from God's prophet (2 Chron 14:9-15; 15:1-7). His religious reforms included the removal of the queen mother (one of the chief supporters of the Canaanite religions), the destruction of idols, and the banning of religious prostitutes (1 Kings 15:9-15; 2 Chron 15:8-15).

When Baasha, king of Israel, seized a border town and built a fort just north of Jerusalem, Asa paid money to Syria to break its treaty with Israel and attack her. When Israel turned to fight the attacking Syrians, Asa destroyed the offending fort and used the materials to build additional forts for himself (1 Kings 15:16-22). This policy of trusting in foreign nations showed a weakness in Asa's faith and brought him into conflict with God's prophet (2 Chron 16:7-10). Asa had another serious failure of faith late in his reign when, suffering from a disease in the feet, he looked for healing through pagan sorcerers instead of trusting in God (2 Chron 16:12-14).

ASCENSION

See JESUS CHRIST, sub-heading 'Resurrection and exaltation of Jesus'.

ASHDOD

Ashdod was one of the 'five cities of the Philistines', the other four being Ashkelon, Ekron, Gaza and Gath (Josh 13:3; 1 Sam 6:17-18; see PHILISTIA). The story most readily associated with Ashdod concerns the temple of Dagon that was in the town. When the Philistines captured Israel's ark of the covenant and placed it in the temple, the god Dagon fell down in front of the ark and broke in pieces (1 Sam 5:1-5).

As a result of enemy attacks that destroyed parts of the city (Isa 20:1; Jer 25:17-20), Ashdod was rebuilt several times during its long history. In New Testament times it was a prosperous town known as Azotus (Acts 8:40). Today it is a smaller town and is known by its original name, Ashdod.

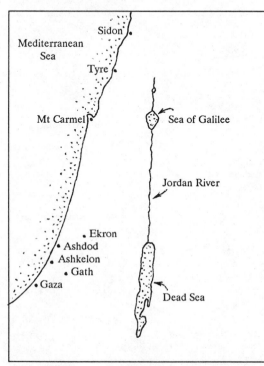

ASHER

The tribe of Asher was descended from Jacob through his maid Zilpah (Gen 30:12-13). In the division of Canaan under Joshua, this tribe received the coastal plain from Mt Carmel north to the Phoenician cities of Tyre and Sidon (Josh 19:24-31; Judg 5:17).

Like the other Israelite tribes, Asher did not drive out the local Canaanites, who still occupied a number of towns and districts. As a result Asher rarely controlled the Phoenician coast, and for most of its history had to be content with the coastal region around Mt Carmel and the neighbouring hill country (Judg 1:31-32). This was a fertile area whose olive orchards produced the best oil in Palestine (Gen 49:20; Deut 33:24).

ASHERAH, ASHERIM

Asherah was the name of a Canaanite Baal goddess of fertility (1 Kings 18:18-19; 2 Kings 23:4,7). (The plural form of the word in Hebrew was Asherim.) The names Asherah and Asherim were used of the goddess herself, of images of the goddess, and of the sacred poles and trees that represented the goddess. These idolatrous symbols often stood beside the Baal altars on the sacred hilltop sites known as high places, and were important in Baal rituals (Judg 6:25-26; 1 Kings 14:23; 15:13; Isa. 27:9). For details see BAAL.

ASHKELON

The ancient town of Ashkelon has passed on its name to successive settlements on the same site down to the present day. It is situated in the south of Palestine on the Mediterranean coast, and in Old Testament times was one of the 'five cities of the Philistines'. It was the Philistines' only port (Josh 13:3; Amos 1:8; Jer 47:7).

At the time of Joshua's invasion of Canaan, the Israelites captured Ashkelon (Judg 1:18), but the Philistines soon regained it. It remained one of their important towns during the time of their hostility to Israel prior to the reign of David (Judg 14:19; 1 Sam 6:17-18). After David broke their power, the Philistines lived alongside the Israelites without any major conflicts.

Though in many ways subservient to Israelite rulers, Ashkelon and neighbouring towns were still regarded as belonging to the Philistines. At times they suffered from the attacks of various invaders (Jer 47:5; Zeph 2:4). In spite of this interference, Ashkelon was still standing in New Testament times.

31

It was well known as the birthplace of Herod the Great, and benefited from his building projects. (See also PHILISTIA.)

ASHTORETH, ASHTAROTH

In the Hebrew language, Ashtaroth was the plural form of Ashtoreth. The Ashtaroth were among the Canaanite and Phoenician goddesses that proved to be such a temptation to the Israelites. Although a Baal was a male god and an Ashtoreth a female god, the two are often linked to represent the religion commonly known as Baalism (Judg 2:13; 1 Sam 12:10; 1 Kings 11:6). For details see BAAL.

ASIA

Over the centuries leading up to the New Testament era, the numerous independent states of Asia Minor had been brought under the control of firstly the Greeks, then the Romans. In the New Testament period a number of them were joined together to form what became known as the province of Asia. The local people, however, continued to use the names of the former states when referring to certain regions.

In the north-west of the newly formed province was the former region of Mysia, which included the towns of Troas, Assos, Adramyttium and Pergamum. In the south-east was part of the former region of Phrygia, the other part of which was in the neighbouring province of Galatia. The towns of Colossae, Laodicea and Hierapolis fell within the part of Phrygia that was in the province of Asia.

Phrygia was the region where Paul first entered the province of Asia (during his second missionary journey), but God did not allow him to preach there. Paul therefore headed north towards the province of Bithynia, but he was forbidden to preach there also. He then headed west across Mysia to Troas, from where he sailed for Europe (Acts 16:6-11).

When returning to Syria from Europe at the end of the journey, Paul called at Ephesus, chief city of the province of Asia, where he left Aquila and Priscilla. This marked the beginning of Christian work in the province. Only a few months later, Paul returned to Ephesus, and over the next three years carried on an extensive work of evangelism in and around the city (Acts 18:18-21; 19:1-20; 20:31; see EPHESUS).

It was no doubt during this time that churches were founded in neighbouring districts at Colossae, Laodicea and Hierapolis, possibly by disciples whom Paul had taught in Ephesus (Acts 19:8-10; Col 1:2,7; 2:1; 4:13). Churches were probably established also at Smyrna, Sardis, Philadelphia and Thyatira, which

were towns not far to the north of Ephesus (Rev. 2:8,12,18; 3:1,7).

The Jews of Asia were bitterly opposed to Paul and were a source of constant persecution (Acts 21:27; 24:18; 2 Cor 1:8-9; 2 Tim 1:15). The condition of the churches in Asia at the end of the first century is reflected in the letters that John wrote to seven churches there (Rev 2:1-3:22; see entries under the respective towns).

ASSURANCE

God wants believers to be assured of their salvation. He wants them to know without doubt that, having repented and trusted in Jesus, they have eternal life and will never perish (John 3:16; 6:47; 10:28; Heb 6:11,17-20; 7:25; 1 Peter 1:23; 1 John 5:12-13). God promises believers eternal security, and his promises are certain. God is faithful, and his promises can be trusted (John 6:37; Rom 10:13; 1 Thess 5:24; 2 Tim 2:19; Heb 10:22-23; 1 Peter 1:5).

What God has done

Believers have this assurance because their salvation depends not on anything they have done, but on what God has done for them in Christ. Through Christ's death, God has forgiven their sins and brought them into a new relationship with himself. God now accepts them as being 'in Christ' (Rom 3:24-25; 5:1; 8:1,33-34; Eph 1:7; Heb 10:14,17-18,22; Jude 24; see FORGIVENESS; JUSTIFICATION).

Further assurance comes from the fact of God's election. In his sovereign will and grace, God has elected, or chosen, believers to be his children, to have eternal life, to escape the wrath of God, and to share with Christ in the full blessings of the age to come (John 1:12-13; 6:37-39; Rom 8:29-30; Eph 1:4; 1 Thess 1:4; 5:9; 2 Tim 1:9; see ELECTION). Nothing can separate them from the love of God (Rom 8:35-39; Eph 2:4-5), and they receive from God the gift of the Holy Spirit as the guarantee of their eternal salvation. The Holy Spirit is God's mark of ownership upon them (2 Cor 1:22; Eph 1:13; 4:30; 1 John 4:13).

The response of believers

These great facts are all concerned with what *God* has done, and they are the basis of true assurance. In addition, however, there is an awareness within believers themselves that they are children of God (Rom 8:16).

This added assurance within believers comes from a variety of experiences relating to their new life. Such experiences include their desire to obey God (1 John 2:3-6), their sensitivity to sin (2 Tim 2:19; 1 John 3:4-10,19-21), their awareness of God's discipline in their lives (Heb 12:5-8), their love for others (1 John 3:14-15), their desire to know more of God and his Word (1 Peter 2:2-3), and their constant perseverance in the faith (Mark 4:18-20; 1 Peter 1:6-9; Heb 6:11-12). Without these evidences of a changed life, those who claim to have assurance of salvation are deceiving themselves (Titus 1:16; 1 John 2:4,9-11; 3:10; cf. Matt 7:22-23, 25:41-46). (See also BACKSLIDING; PERSEVERANCE.)

ASSYRIA

The land of Assyria was centred on the Tigris River in north-western Mesopotamia. Originally the land was known as Asshur, after the descendants of Asshur (son of Shem, son of Noah), who were among the early settlers in the region. Over many centuries they were joined by migrants from other regions in the neighbourhood, with the result that the race that developed was a mixture. The people were known by the name of the land, Asshur, and this name developed into Assyria. Among Assyria's chief cities was Nineveh, which later became the capital (Gen 10:11-12,22).

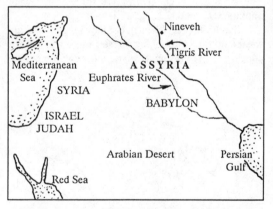

Assyria was one of the great nations of the ancient world, but it did not extend its power into Palestine till after the rise of a new dynasty about 900 BC. Assyria then set out to become the dominant power in the region, and after a series of conquests of other nations it turned its attention to Syria and Israel. On one occasion God sent his prophet Jonah to preach to the Assyrians so that they might repent and be saved from a threatened invasion (Jonah 3:1-10). God was preserving Assyria to be his means of punishing Israel (Isa 10:5).

The history of Assyria as it concerns the Bible story may be summarized according to its kings, many of whom are mentioned in the Bible. In the following summary, 'Israel' refers to the northern part of the divided Israelite kingdom, 'Judah' to the southern part.

Kings of Assyria

Tiglath-pileser III, also known as Pul (who reigned 745-727 BC), was the first Assyrian king to launch a major attack on Israel, but he withdrew after taking a bribe from the Israelite king, Menahem. Menahem's action was really a form of submission to Assyria, and it placed Israel under Assyrian influence (2 Kings 15:17-20). The prophets predicted that Assyria would soon conquer Israel completely (Hosea 10:5-8; Amos 7:17). The next king of Israel, Pekah, then combined with the king of Syria, Rezin, to attack Judah. Their aim was to take control of Judah and force it into a three-part alliance that might be able to withstand Assyria. But Judah's king, Ahaz, appealed to Assyria for help, and Assyria responded by conquering Syria and much of Israel (in 732 BC; 2 Kings 15:29,37; 16:1-9; Isa 7:1-9; 8:4; 17:1-3).

Shalmaneser V (727-722 BC), in response to a rebellion by another Israelite king, Hoshea, overran Israel and attacked the Israelite capital, Samaria. The siege had been in progress three years when Shalmaneser died (2 Kings 17:1-5).

Sargon II (722-705 BC), the new king of Assyria, wasted no time in bringing the siege to a triumphant conclusion. He crushed Samaria and took the people

Assyrian king

into captivity. This marked the end of the northern kingdom, Israel (in 722 BC; 2 Kings 17:6). In the meantime the southern kingdom, Judah, because of the disastrous policies of Ahaz, had fallen under the domination of Assyria and was forced to pay it heavy taxes (Isa 7:17; 8:5-8; 20:1-6).

Sennacherib (705-681 BC) met opposition from Judah when the new Judean king, Hezekiah, refused to pay further taxes (in 701 BC; 2 Kings 18:7). When Sennacherib besieged Jerusalem, Hezekiah repented of his rebellion and offered to pay whatever the

Assyrian soldier with bow and arrow

Assyrians demanded. Sennacherib took a large sum of money, but he deceived Hezekiah by refusing to lift the siege. Hezekiah appealed desperately to God for help, and God replied by miraculously destroying a large part of the Assyrian army. Sennacherib escaped home to Nineveh, but some time later he was assassinated (2 Kings 18:13-19:35).

Esarhaddon (681-669 BC), son of Sennacherib, succeeded his father as king (2 Kings 19:36-37). He was one the greatest kings to rule over Assyria. Soon after coming to the throne, he asserted his power over the weakened Judah (now ruled by the evil Manasseh) and over the more powerful Babylon (2 Chron 33:11).

Ashurbanipal (669-627 BC) continued the work that his father had begun in expanding Assyrian power. Under him the Assyrian Empire spread to an extent it had never known before.

After Ashurbanipal's death, Assyria's Empire began to crumble. Babylon was rising to power, and with the establishment of a new Babylonian dynasty in 626 BC, the Assyrians were soon driven out of Babylon. The Babylonians went from conquest to conquest, till in 612 BC they destroyed the Assyrian capital, Nineveh, as foretold by God's prophets. Nahum, in particular, rejoiced to see a fitting divine judgment fall on such a cruel and ruthless oppressor (Nahum 1:1; 3:1-7; cf. Isa 10:12; Zeph 2:13; see also NINEVEH). There was an attempt at some resistance in Assyria but it did not last, and within three years Assyria ceased to be a nation.

ATHALIAH

When Athaliah, daughter of Ahab and Jezebel, married Jehoram of Judah, the Baalism that Ahab and Jezebel had established in Israel spread to Judah. Athaliah was a strong influence on both her husband and their son, Ahaziah, who succeeded his father as king (2 Chron 21:4-6; 22:1-4). When Ahaziah was killed in Jehu's anti-Baal revolution (2 Chron 22:5-9; 841 BC), Athaliah seized the throne of Judah, killed all her grandchildren (except one who escaped) and established her mother's Baalism in Judah (2 Chron 22:10-12; 24:7).

Six years later, Athaliah was killed in a fresh anti-Baal revolution, this one centred on Jerusalem (2 Chron 22:12-23:15). The people then destroyed her Baal temple, Baal altars and Baal images, and restored the dynasty of David by placing her sole surviving grandson on the throne of Judah (2 Chron 23:16-21).

ATHENS

In the time of the New Testament, Athens was the world's great centre of learning. It was famous also for its magnificent architecture, seen in its many temples and public buildings. There is only one recorded occasion on which Paul visited the city, and on that occasion his evangelism was only moderately successful (Acts 17:15-34). Concerning Paul's debate with the philosophers of the city see AREOPAGUS; EPICUREANS; STOICS.

ATONEMENT

Atonement may be defined as that act of dealing with sin whereby sin's penalty is paid and the sinner is brought into a right relation with God. In the Old Testament the word is used mainly in connection with the offering of sacrifices for sin. The word does not occur in most versions of the New Testament, but it is used broadly in the language of theology in relation to the sacrificial death of Christ.

Man has sinned and is therefore under the judgment of God. He is guilty, the penalty is death, and there is no way he can, by his own efforts, escape this penalty. He is cut off from God and there is no way he can bring himself back to God (Ps 14:3; Isa 59:2; Rom 1:18; 3:20,23; 6:23; see SIN). God, however, gives man a way by which he may obtain forgiveness and be brought back to God. This is through the blood of a sacrifice, where blood is symbolic of the life of the innocent victim laid down as substitute for the guilty sinner (Lev 17:11; Heb 9:22; 1 John 4:10; see BLOOD).

Atonement is therefore not something that man can achieve by his own efforts, but something that God provides. Whether in Old or New Testament times, forgiveness is solely by God's grace and the sinner receives it by faith (Ps 32:5; 51:17; Micah 7:18; Eph 2:8). The Old Testament sacrifices were not a way of salvation. They were a means by which the repentant sinner could demonstrate his faith in God and at the same time see what his atonement involved. The sacrifices showed him how it was possible for God to act rightly in punishing sin while forgiving the repentant sinner. (See JUSTIFICATION; PROPITIATION; RECONCILIATION; REDEMPTION; SACRIFICE; SANCTIFICATION.)

The sacrifices of the Old Testament pointed to the one great sacrifice that is the only basis on which God can forgive a person's sins, the death of Christ. Through that death God is able justly to forgive the sins of all who turn to him in faith, no matter what era they might have lived in (Matt 26:28; Rom. 3:25-26; 4:25; Heb 9:15; 1 Peter 2:24). (See also DAY OF ATONEMENT.)

AUTHORITY

In some English versions of the Bible the two words 'power' and 'authority' are used to translate what is one word in the Greek. In such cases 'power' means 'the right to exercise power', and it is this aspect of power that is the subject of the present article. Concerning power in the sense of great strength or might, see POWER.

God is the one who has absolute authority (Ps 93:1-2; 115:3; Isa 40:20-23; Rom 9:20-24; 13:1; see GOD, sub-headings 'Eternal and independent', 'Majestic and sovereign'). Jesus Christ, being God, also had absolute authority, though he chose to exercise that authority in complete submission to his Father (John 5:19). He had the same authority on earth as he had in heaven, the same authority in time as he had in eternity (Matt 21:23-27; 28:18; John 5:27; 10:18).

By his authority Jesus Christ released sick and demonized people from the power of Satan (Matt 8:8-10; Mark 1:27) and instructed people in the truth of God (Matt 7:29). By that same authority he forgave people their sins (Matt 9:6), gave them eternal life (John 17:2), made them sons of God (John 1:12), and gave them the authority and the power to carry on the work of his kingdom (Matt 10:1; 28:18-20; 2 Cor 13:10; see KINGDOM OF GOD; APOSTLE).

As the words that the Son of God spoke carried with them God's authority, so did the words that the

Spirit of God inspired the authors of the Bible to write. The Scriptures, Old and New Testament alike, are God's authoritative Word to man (2 Tim 3:16; 2 Peter 1:21; see INSPIRATION).

God desires that every community of people be properly ordered for the well-being of all. Therefore, he has given authority to civil administrators to govern society (Jer 27:5; John 19:11; Rom 13:1-4; see GOVERNMENT), to parents to govern the family (Eph 6:4; 1 Tim 5:14; see PARENTS), and to elders to govern the church (Acts 20:28; 1 Peter 5:2; see ELDER).

AZARIAH

The Bible mentions almost thirty people who had the name Azariah. The only one who features prominently in the Bible story is the king of Judah who was more commonly known as Uzziah. For details see UZZIAH.

BAAL

Canaanite and Phoenician gods were known as Baals, or Baalim (the plural form of Baal in Hebrew; Judg 2:11; 10:10; 1 Kings 16:31). Goddesses were known as Ashtaroth (plural of Ashtoreth; Judg 2:13; 1 Sam 7:3-4; 12:10) or Asherim (plural of Asherah; 1 Kings 15:13; 18:19; 2 Kings 23:4).

The word *baal* was a common Hebrew word meaning 'master', 'husband' or 'owner'. When the Israelites entered Canaan and found that the local people believed every piece of land had a god as its 'owner', *baal* developed a particular use as a proper noun. It became the title or name of the god of the land, whether of the land as a whole or of a particular area of land. In some cases the local Baal took its name from the locality (Num 25:3; Deut 4:3), and in other cases a locality was named after the Baal (Josh 11:17; Judg 3:3; 2 Sam 5:20, 13:23). A locality may also have been named after the Ashtaroth (Josh 12:4).

Characteristics of Baal worship

Baal and his associate goddesses were gods of nature who, according to popular belief, controlled the weather and had power to increase the fertility of soil, animals and humans. Since Israelites knew Yahweh as creator of nature and God of all life, they readily fell to the temptation to combine the Canaanite ideas with their own and so worship Yahweh as another Baal (Hosea 2:5-10; 4:7-10). This identification of Yahweh with Baal was probably also influenced by the fact that Yahweh was Israel's husband and master (Heb: *baal*).

The Canaanites liked to carry out their Baal rituals at sacred hilltop sites known as 'high places'. This name was later applied to all places of Baal worship, not just those in the hills (2 Kings 14:4; 17:9,32; 23:13; Jer 17:2-3; 32:35). Among the features of these high places were the sacred wooden or

Baal as a weather god

stone pillars known as Asherim (plural of Asherah, the goddess they represented) (Deut 12:3; Judg 6:25-26; 1 Kings 14:23; 2 Kings 10:27; 17:10; 21:3,7; 23:6; Isa 27:9).

Israelites had often gone up into the hills to worship God (Gen 22:2; Exod 17:8-15; 24:12-18; cf. 1 Sam 9:12-14; 10:5,13) and in Canaan they easily fell to the temptation to use the local high places in their worship of Yahweh. These disorders would not have arisen if the Israelites had, from the beginning, obeyed God's command and destroyed all the high places in the land (Num. 33:52-53; Deut 12:2-3; 1 Kings 3:2; Jer 2:20; 3:6; Hosea 4:13).

Prostitutes, male and female, were available at the high places for fertility rites. These were religious-sexual ceremonies that people believed would persuade the gods to give increase in family, herds, flocks and crops (1 Kings 14:23-24; Jer 13:27; Hosea 4:10,14; 9:1-3,11-14; Amos 2:7-8). The people were also guilty of spiritual prostitution. Since the covenant bond between Israel and Yahweh was likened to the marriage bond, Israel's association with Baal and other gods was a form of spiritual adultery (Isa 1:21; Jer 13:27; Hosea 1:2; 2:5,13; 4:12; Micah 1:7).

God's judgment on Israel

Baal worship was a problem in Israel throughout most of the nation's Old Testament history. It began soon after the people entered Canaan (Judg 2:11-13; 3:7; 8:33; 10:6,10) and resisted repeated attempts at reform by various leaders. It remained firmly fixed in Israel's national life up till the captivity, when God' inevitable judgment fell (1 Sam 7:3-4; 1 Kings 15:9-14; 22:51-53; 2 Kings 17:7-18; 18:1-4; 21:1-3; 23:26-27).

Possibly the most dangerous period during this history was the reign of the Israelite king Ahab and his Phoenician wife Jezebel, who attempted to make Phoenician Baalism the official religion of Israel (1 Kings 16:31-33). This form of Baalism, under the lordship of the Phoenician Baal deity Melqart, was a greater threat to Israel than the local Canaanite Baalism. To meet the threat, God raised up the prophets Elijah and Elisha. Their ministry preserved the faithful through the crisis and led to the eventual removal of Phoenician Baalism. It was wiped out by Jehu's ruthless purge in the north, and by a similar, but less bloody, purge in the south (1 Kings 17-22; 2 Kings 1-11; see ELIJAH; ELISHA; JEHU).

Local Canaanite Baalism, however, was not removed. Israel's persistence in Baal worship was the chief reason for God's judgment in finally destroying the nation and sending the people into captivity (2 Kings 17:7-18 ; 21:10-15; Jer 9:12-16; 11:13-17; 19:4-9).

The time in captivity broke Israel's relationship with Baalism. When the nation was later rebuilt, Baalism was no longer a serious problem (Ezek 36:22-29; 37:23). People were so determined to avoid any link between Baal and Yahweh that they refused to use the word *baal* when referring to God as their husband or master. They used the alternative word *ish* (Hosea 2:16-19). By New Testament times Jews had developed a thorough hatred of idolatry in all its forms (see IDOLATRY).

BAASHA

Baasha came to Israel's throne (about 908 BC) by murdering the previous king and all those who were related to him. In so doing he brought the house of Jeroboam to an end as foretold by one of God's prophets. Another prophet, however, foretold that Baasha's house would suffer the same fate, and for the same reason, namely, religious corruption

(1 Kings 15:25-30; 16:1-4). There was constant war between Baasha and the Judean king Asa during the twenty-four years of Baasha's reign (1 Kings 15:16-22,33; for details see ASA).

BABEL

Babel was one of three important towns founded by the great warrior-hunter, Nimrod, in the land of Shinar. The other two towns were Erech and Accad. Shinar was the ancient name for the land of Babylon, or Babylonia. Babel was the ancient name for the city of Babylon, which later became the nation's capital (Gen 10:8-10).

The early settlers around Babel found that by combining their abilities and manpower they could achieve progress; but with their progress came an attitude of arrogant self-sufficiency. They considered themselves socially and technically more advanced than their neighbours, and as a symbol of their achievements they erected a towering structure in the town. The structure may have been a fortress,

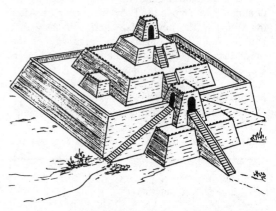

A ziggurat, or temple-tower

though more likely it was a temple built on a series of stepped platforms, similar to the Sumerian ziggurats. Whatever it was, God saw it as a symbol of the people's pride in trying to show themselves independent of him. Since they had used their united abilities to defy God, the divine response was to smash their ungodly unity decisively (Gen 11:1-9). See also BABYLON.

BABYLON

Although its boundaries varied from one era to the next, the land of Babylon was always centred on Mesopotamia, the region of the rivers Euphrates and Tigris. This was the region where the biblical story of early man takes place and where the Garden of Eden was located (Gen 2:10-14). In ancient times the northern part was often known as Akkad (or Accad; Gen 10:10), and the southern part as Sumer, then Shinar, and later Chaldea (Gen 10:10; 11:2,28; Ezek 12:13; 23:15). The land was named after its chief city, Babylon, which earlier was known as Babel (Gen 11:9; Jer 51:31; see BABEL).

Early history

The earliest known inhabitants of Babylon were the Sumerians, and the culture that developed through them provided the framework for the Babylonian civilization that followed. The Sumerians were later joined by Amorites and other Semites who migrated into the region. (The Semites were the descendants of Shem, one of the sons of Noah; Gen 10:1,21-31.) As a result of the intermingling of these peoples, the Sumerians eventually disappeared as a distinct race. Their culture, however, maintained its influence, lasting through the history of Babylon and surviving in part down to modern times.

By about 2000 BC the Amorites had become the dominant race among the Babylonian peoples. After overthrowing the powerful Sumerian dynasty that had reigned in Ur (chief Babylonian city of the time), they established their rule throughout Lower, Upper and Western Mesopotamia (see AMORITES). Abraham migrated from Ur to Canaan during this period (Gen 11:31).

With the defeat of the Sumerian Babylonians, the Amorite Babylonians set up a new kingdom, centred on the city of Babylon. This marked the

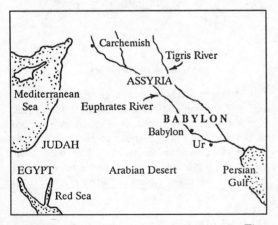

beginning of what has become known as the First Babylonian Dynasty. The greatest of its kings was Hummurabi, who reigned during the first half of the eighteenth century BC. He is chiefly remembered for writing a law-code that was far in advance of the

law-codes out of which it grew. It dealt with civil, criminal, social and commercial affairs, and provided a standard of justice better than anything the people of Babylon had previously known.

The chief god of the Babylonians, from this time to the end of the nation's history, was Marduk, or Merodach. The Sumerian god Bel was later

The Babylonian god, Marduk

identified with Marduk. Another god, Nebo, was considered to be Marduk's son (Isa 46:1; Jer 50:2; cf. Josh 24:2).

Involvement with Judah

The period of Babylon's involvement in Judah's affairs began more than a thousand years after the establishment of the First Babylonian Dynasty. During the intervening years Babylon had declined in power and had remained weak for centuries. New hope arose in Babylon about 740 BC when the nation began to grow in power again. During the reign of the Judean king Hezekiah (716-687 BC), Babylon tried to persuade Judah to join it in overthrowing Assyria, the dominating power of that era. God's prophet Isaiah opposed any such cooperation with an ungodly nation (2 Kings 20:12-19). Assyria at this stage was still too powerful for Babylon to conquer without help from other nations. For a time the Assyrian army even occupied the Babylonian capital (2 Chron 33:11).

Assyria's domination of Babylon lasted several decades, but with Assyria's gradual decline, Babylon began to reassert itself. In 626 BC Babylon began a new era when Nabopolassar established a new dynasty that spread its rule far and wide in what is now referred to as the Neo-Babylonian Empire. Nabopolassar gradually pushed back the Assyrians and finally overthrew them in 612 BC. This marked the end of the Assyrian Empire.

Babylonian power

Egypt, fearing the expanding power of Babylon, moved north to withstand it. After taking control of Judah and Syria, Egypt established a stronghold at Carchemish on the Euphrates River, in an effort to stop any further advances by Babylon. But in 605 BC the armies of Babylon under Nebuchadnezzar, son of Nabopolassar, conquered Egypt in the Battle of Carchemish (2 Kings 24:7; Jer 46:2-12). This meant

City gate, Babylon

that Judah now came under the control of Babylon. When the conquerors returned to Babylon they took with them captives from the conquered countries, including selected young men from the leading families of Jerusalem. Among these was the youth Daniel (Dan 1:1-6).

After three years the Judean king rebelled against Babylon, hoping that Nebuchadnezzar (who

had now become king of Babylon) would be too busy with wars elsewhere to deal with Judah. The Judean king depended on Egypt to support his rebellion, a policy that God's prophet Jeremiah opposed (Jer 2:18,36). When Nebuchadnezzar had dealt with rebellions elsewhere, he sent his armies to besiege Jerusalem. After a siege of three months, Jerusalem surrendered (597 BC). When the armies of Babylon returned home, they carried off most of Judah's wealth and took all its best people into captivity. Among these was the young man Ezekiel (2 Kings 24:1-17; Ezek 1:1-2).

Babylon appointed Zedekiah as the new Judean king, but after a while he too tried to rebel against Babylon, again by looking to Egypt for support. Jeremiah continued to oppose this policy, advising Judah to accept its fate as God's will and submit to Babylon (2 Kings 24:18-20; 2 Chron 36:11-14; Jer 21:1-10; 27:12-22; 37:6-10). But Zedekiah persisted in his rebellion and the armies of Nebuchadnezzar returned. This time the Babylonians plundered and burnt Jerusalem, killed the leaders of the rebellion, and took captive to Babylon all except those who were of no use to them (2 Kings 25:1-21; 2 Chron 36:11-21; Jer 39:1-10).

Before returning to Babylon, Nebuchadnezzar appointed a Jewish official, Gedaliah, as governor over those who remained in Judah. When Gedaliah was treacherously murdered, the remaining Judeans, fearing a revenge attack by Nebuchadnezzar, fled for their lives to Egypt (2 Kings 25:22-26; Jer 40:13-43:7). The attack on Judah came in 582 BC (Jer 52:30), but those who fled for safety to Egypt could not escape the Babylonians indefinitely (Jer 42:15-17; 43:8-13).

Babylon was now at the height of its power, and Nebuchadnezzar accepted homage from nations near and far (Dan 2:37-38; 4:20-22). His conquests, in the region covered by the biblical account alone, included Philistia, Sidon, Tyre, Moab, Ammon and Arabia (Jer 27:3-6; 47:4-5; 48:1-2; 49:2,17,28,30; Ezek 26:7; 28:2,21). Then, in 568 BC, he made the devastating attack on Egypt that the prophets had foretold (Jer 43:8-13; 46:13-19,25-26; Ezek 29:17-20; 30:10,24-26; 32:2,11).

Decline and fall

In many cases Babylon's victories over neighbouring nations were judgments on those nations by God. Babylon was merely the instrument of punishment God had used (Jer 27:3-6; Ezek 29:19; 30:10). In particular he had used Babylon to destroy Jerusalem and take the people of Judah into captivity (Jer 25:8-11; Hab 1:6). But the Babylonians had acted with such hostility against the Judeans and with such arrogance against God, that they had gone far beyond the limits God had set. Therefore, God would punish them as he had punished others (Jer 27:5-7; 50:23-25; 51:1-5,7-10,24; Hab 2:16-17), and would release the captive Judeans to return to their land and rebuild their nation (Isa 43:14; 48:14; Jer 25:12-14; 29:10).

A sign of hope that this expected release would occur came in 561 BC, when the new Babylonian king released the captive Judean king from prison and gave him a position of special honour (2 Kings 25:27-30; cf. 24:8-15). Meanwhile Persia was rising to power and, in 539 BC, under the leadership of Cyrus, it conquered Babylon and released the Jews (Ezra 1:1-4; Isa 21:2,9; 45:1-5; 48:14,20; Jer 50:1-5,8-10; 51:34-37; Dan 5:30-31). For further history of the Babylonian region after the Persian conquest see PERSIA.

The city of Babylon

One of Nebuchadnezzar's greatest achievements in the early days of his reign was to rebuild the city of Babylon, so that it became one of the showpieces of the ancient world (Dan 4:29-30). But in the eyes of God's prophets the city was a symbol of Babylon's pride, and that pride was embodied in the king. Both the king and the city were doomed to be destroyed (Isa 13:1-11,19; 14:4-25; 47:1-5; Jer 50:13-16; 51:64; see also NEBUCHADNEZZAR).

Even though Babylon was destroyed, in the minds of God's people it remained as a symbol of man who, in his pride and self-sufficiency, arrogantly defies God. In New Testament times Christians saw the Roman Empire, with its advanced civilization and organized opposition to God, as a first century expression of this spirit of Babylon (1 Peter 5:13; Rev 17:1-14,18). The book of Revelation pictures the overthrow of man in his worldwide opposition to God as the overthrow of the great and proud city of Babylon (Rev 16:19; 18:1-24). God again shows that his kingdom rules over all, and that he is the sovereign ruler over all the kingdoms that man may build (Rev 19:1-5; cf. Dan 2:44; 4:17).

BACKSLIDING

According to the word's common usage, a backslider is a Christian who has, through obvious sin or some other lapse, failed to persist in his Christian commitment. If such a person is a genuine believer, his failure will not be permanent, for God deals with his children by bringing them to repentance. Absence of such divine discipline is an indication

that the person was never really a child of God (Heb 12:6-8; 2 Peter 2:9).

A person may have failures, but if his faith is genuine any lapse will be only temporary. The true believer demonstrates the genuineness of his faith by continuing in it to the end (John 8:31; Col 1:21-23; James 5:19-20; 1 Peter 1:5). Perseverance is not a condition for salvation; but it is an evidence of salvation (Matt 24:13; see PERSEVERANCE).

In certain cases, what people call backsliding may be something far more serious. It may not be a temporary failure, but a settled attitude of rejection of what a person formerly believed. This is the sort of backsliding that Old Testament Israel was often guilty of, and is more correctly called apostasy (Jer 2:19; 5:6; 8:5; 15:6; Hosea 11:7; cf. Heb 10:26-31; 1 John 2:19). The difference between backsliding as a temporary failure and backsliding as apostasy is seen in the actions of the two disciples, Peter and Judas. Peter was restored, but Judas was lost (Luke 22:31-32,47-62; John 17:12; Acts 1:15-16; cf. 2 Cor 7:9-10; see APOSTASY).

BALAAM

At the time of Israel's migration to Canaan, the Moabite king Balak, fearing the Israelites, sent to Mesopotamia asking the soothsayer Balaam to come and put a curse on them. Balak hoped that Balaam's curse would ensure Israel's defeat (Num 22:1-6). (For the significance of a curse among Israelites and other ancient peoples see CURSE.)

God showed Balaam that he was not to go, because Israel was not to be cursed. Despite this, Balaam wanted to go, because he hoped to gain the reward Balak offered. God was angry with Balaam but in the end allowed him to go, in order to teach him some lessons (Num 22:7-20). Only God's mercy prevented Balaam from being killed along the way (Num 22:21-34).

Balak took Balaam to a place from where he could see the vastness of the Israelite camp. His purpose was to convince Balaam that the Israelites were a serious threat. But God had warned Balaam to speak only the words that God told him to speak. Balaam obeyed, and instead of announcing a curse on Israel he announced a blessing (Num 22:35,41; 23:1-12).

Disappointed at this result, Balak took Balaam to another place, where he could get a better view and so be persuaded to pronounce a destructive curse. But again Balaam announced a blessing on Israel (Num 23:13-26). A third attempt, from a third place, brought further blessing (Num 23:27; 24:1-9). Angrily Balak dismissed Balaam, but in response Balaam announced yet another lengthy blessing on Israel (Num 24:10-25).

However, Balaam too was angry. His failure to curse Israel meant that he did not receive the payment from Balak that he so much wanted. He therefore decided on a plan of his own. This plan had nothing to do with either blessing or cursing, but Balaam hoped it might bring destruction to Israel and so earn Balak's reward. He used foreign women to seduce Israelite men, and soon there was widespread immorality and idolatry in the Israelite camp. When God sent a plague that killed thousands, Balaam must have thought his plan was working, but swift action from the Israelite priest Phinehas saved Israel and brought death to Balaam (Num 25:1-9; 31:16; Josh 13:22).

The people of Old Testament Israel never forgot the evil of Balaam (Deut 23:5; Josh 24:9; Neh 13:2; Micah 6:5). Even in the New Testament, writers likened some of the false teachers of their time to Balaam. Like Balaam, such teachers were concerned solely with personal gain, even though their teaching was morally and religiously damaging to God's people (2 Peter 2:14-16; Jude 10-11). They encouraged God's people to join in idolatrous practices and to engage in immoral behaviour (Rev 2:14-15). God assured those who followed the way of Balaam that they were heading for destruction, but he promised those who resisted that they would enjoy his special reward (Rev 2:15-17; cf. Num 25:10-13).

BAPTISM

Christian baptism is a ceremony commanded by Jesus, by which Christians make a public confession that they have repented of their sins and committed themselves in faith to Jesus as their Saviour and Lord (Matt 28:19; Acts 2:38,41; 9:18; 10:47-48; 18:8; Rom 10:9). The Bible speaks of people going into the water to be baptized (Acts 8:38; cf. Matt 3:16), but it gives no detailed description of the act of baptism. The original meaning of 'baptize' was 'dip' or 'immerse', suggesting that believers were immersed in water.

Pre-Christian baptism

Although it had great significance in the birth and growth of the church as recorded in Acts, baptism was practised before this. Jews, it seems, baptized Gentile converts as part of their introduction into the Jewish religion. John the Baptist also practised baptism, demanding it of those who responded to his preaching and repented of their sins (Luke 3:1-8; John 3:22-23; Acts 13:24; 18:25).

John pointed out that the baptism he practised, though it may have pictured cleansing, could not in itself bring cleansing or give people the power to live pure lives. His baptism prepared the way for Jesus Christ, who would bring the blessings that John's baptism symbolized. Those who accepted Jesus as the Saviour-Messiah would enter the kingdom of God and, through Jesus' gift of the Holy Spirit, receive an inner power to live righteously (Matt 3:11; John 1:26-28,31,33; Acts 1:5; see BAPTISM WITH THE SPIRIT).

The baptism of Jesus

Even Jesus was baptized, though he had no sins to repent of. For this reason, John at first did not want to baptize him, but Jesus insisted. He wanted to show his oneness with the faithful in Israel who, by their baptism, declared themselves on the side of God and his righteousness (Matt 3:13-15).

Jesus' baptism was also his declaration, at the outset of his public ministry, that he knew what his work involved and he intended carrying it out fully. As the Messiah, he was the representative chosen by God for a people needing deliverance, which in this case meant man's deliverance from sin. Jesus' baptism in water prefigured a far greater 'baptism' that was yet to come; for he, as man's representative, would suffer God's judgment on man's sin through his death on the cross (Luke 12:50; Mark 10:38).

Having shown his intentions openly, Jesus then received openly the Father's gift of the Spirit's unlimited power to enable him to carry out his messianic work (Matt 3:16; John 3:34; Acts 10:37-38). The Father's expression of full satisfaction with his Son consisted of combined quotations from the Old Testament relating to God's messiah-king and God's submissive servant (Matt 3:17; cf. Ps 2:7; Isa 42:1). In both cases the God-appointed tasks could be carried out only in the power of the Spirit (Isa 11:1-2; 42:1-4).

Christian baptism

As Jesus preached the message of the kingdom, those who accepted his message and entered the kingdom showed the genuineness of their faith and repentance by being baptized. The disciples of Jesus, rather than Jesus himself, did the baptizing (John 3:22; 4:1-2). Just before he returned to his heavenly Father, the risen Christ told his disciples to spread the good news of his kingdom worldwide and to baptize those who believed (Matt 28:19). The book of Acts shows how the early Christians carried out his command (Acts 2:38,41; 8:12,35-39; 10:47-48; 16:13-15,31-33; 18:8).

Baptism was so readily acknowledged as the natural and immediate consequences of faith that the New Testament links the two inseparably. The object of saving faith is Jesus Christ and what he has done through his death and resurrection. Paul, the great interpreter of Christian belief and practice, saw baptism as more than just a declaration of faith; he saw it as having meaning that is tied up with the unique union that believers have with Jesus Christ (Rom 6:3; Gal 3:27).

According to Paul's teaching, baptism is an expression of union with Christ in dying to sin and being raised with Christ to new life. When Christ died and rose again, believers died and rose again, so to speak. They demonstrate this in their baptism, but they must also make it true in practice. They must live as those who are no longer under sin's power (Rom 6:1-11; Col 2:12). They are united with Christ in his baptism at Golgotha, as the Israelites were united with Moses in their redemption from Egypt (1 Cor 10:1-2).

Baptism is also a witness, or testimony. It declares that believers are cleansed from sin (Acts 22:16; cf. 1 Peter 3:21), given the Holy Spirit (Acts 10:47; cf. 1 Cor 12:13) and introduced into the body of Christ, the church (Gal 3:26-28; cf. 1 Cor 12:13).

Peter, like Paul, interprets Christian baptism in relation to the death and resurrection of Christ. He sees judgment and salvation pictured in baptism, as they were pictured in the flood of Noah's time. Christ died to bear God's judgment on sin, but he rose from death to new life. Through him believers are cleansed from sin and made sharers in a new and victorious life (1 Peter 3:20-4:1).

The community that believers enter through their conversion is not a man-made club, but the kingdom of God. They are therefore baptized not in the name of a human cult-figure, but in the name of God (Matt 28:19; 1 Cor 1:13). The early preachers constantly kept this in mind. Paul, for example, preferred someone else to baptize his converts, to avoid the appearance of building a personal following (1 Cor 1:14-16). Christians are disciples of Jesus Christ, and he alone is their Lord (Acts 2:38; 8:12; 10:48; 19:5; Rom 10:9).

Baptism of infants

The well known practice of baptizing infants, usually by sprinkling, is not specifically taught in the Bible. Nor does the Bible deal specifically with the related subject of the salvation of infants. Although the Bible shows that God has a special concern for children, its teaching about salvation is mainly concerned with those who are old enough to be responsible for their own decisions (Matt 18:1-6; 19:13-15; see CHILD).

Clearly, people are mistaken if they think that any sort of baptism, whether for adults or infants, guarantees a person's salvation regardless of his beliefs or actions as a morally responsible individual (Matt 3:7-10). Nevertheless, many Christians, while realizing that infant baptism does not guarantee salvation, see meaning in it, particularly for those in Christian families. They point out that in New Testament times whole households were baptized; though the narratives do not state whether those households included infants (Acts 16:15,33-34; 1 Cor 1:16).

The belief in the value of infant baptism among Christian families is related to the Old Testament idea of God's covenant with his people. God's covenant with Abraham, for example, included his household, and the males within that household were circumcised as the formal sign that they were part of that covenant (Gen 17:4,7,10-14; 21:4; see CIRCUMCISION; COVENANT).

Believers who practise infant baptism, while seeing it as a parallel to the Old Testament rite of circumcision, realize that, like circumcision, it is no assurance of salvation (Gen 17:23; Rom 2:25-29). Each person is born with a sinful nature and needs to exercise personal faith to be saved (Rom 3:22-23). Even the blessing of being brought up in a Christian family does not remove the need for the individual to repent and accept Christ if he is to become a child of God (John 1:12-13; 3:5-6).

BAPTISM WITH THE SPIRIT

The baptism with, in, or by the Holy Spirit was an event that John the Baptist foretold (Matt 3:11), that Jesus promised (Acts 1:4-5), and that Peter and Paul referred to (Acts 11:15-16; 1 Cor 12:13). Historically it took place on the Day of Pentecost, when the risen and glorified Christ gave the Holy Spirit to his disciples as he had promised and, in so doing, united them all into one body, the church (Acts 2:1-4,33; 1 Cor 12:13).

The early church

On the Day of Pentecost two separate groups of believers received the gift, or baptism, of the Spirit. The first group consisted of the one hundred and twenty mentioned in Acts 1:15, 2:1-4. The second consisted of the three thousand mentioned in Acts 2:37-42. There are several differences between the two groups.

The first group consisted of those who had been believers for some time and who had awaited Jesus' departure in order to receive the promised gift of the Holy Spirit. The second group consisted of those who became believers only after they heard Peter preach that day and who received the gift of the Holy Spirit immediately.

When those of the first group received the Holy Spirit, the experience was dramatic. But, because of the special circumstances in their case, such an experience should not be considered the normal experience of the Christian. Those disciples had lived with Jesus and could receive the Holy Spirit only after Jesus had returned to the Father (John 7:39; 16:7). The experience of those of the second group, who received the Holy Spirit when they believed, without any unusual happenings, was the normal experience of the Christian, then as well as now (Acts 2:38-41; see also TONGUES).

Only three exceptions to this normal experience are recorded in the New Testament, and all are related to the development of the early church. At first the church was entirely Jewish (Acts 2:5,22,41; 4:1-4), but when a number of Samaritans believed, a difficulty appeared. The Samaritans were a people of mixed blood and mixed religion who originated partly from Old Testament Israel, but they and the Jews hated each other. This division was not to be carried into the church. It seems, therefore, that before God gave the Holy Spirit to the Samaritans, he wanted the Jerusalem leaders to be assured that the Samaritans were true Christians, who were to be welcomed into the church on the same basis as the Jews (Acts 8:14-17).

Later, the apostles were even more amazed when a group of full-blooded Gentiles believed the gospel and received the Holy Spirit without the apostles doing anything at all. It was a repetition of what happened on the Day of Pentecost, but this time among Gentiles, not Jews (Acts 10:44-46; 11:15-17).

The third group who received the Holy Spirit in unusual circumstances consisted of some disciples of John the Baptist whom Paul met in an un-evangelized part of Asia Minor. At first they did not fully understand how the life and work of Jesus was the true fulfilment of John's ministry. When Paul explained this to them they believed, and showed themselves to be disciples of Jesus, not just of John, by being baptized as Christians. They then received the Holy Spirit, as the original disciples had on the Day of Pentecost (Acts 19:1-7).

The timeless, universal church

Paul pointed out, through a letter he wrote to a church of new converts in southern Greece, that there is a sense in which all Christians, regardless of era or nationality, have some part in the events of the Day of Pentecost. Through the baptism of the Spirit, all Christians, the moment they believe, are brought into the church and made sharers in the Holy Spirit (1 Cor 12:13). Jesus' promised gift of the Spirit, though initially received at Pentecost, extends through the ages to all who repent and believe the gospel (Acts 2:38-39; cf. 1:4-5; 2:33; see also HOLY SPIRIT).

BARNABAS

It is not known when Barnabas became a Christian, but he appears very early in the story of the Jerusalem church. He was a Jew from Cyprus (Acts 4:36) and was related to John Mark, whose family home was in Jerusalem (Col 4:10; Acts 12:12).

One who encourages others

In the early days of the Jerusalem church, Barnabas demonstrated his sacrificial spirit when he sold a field that he owned and gave the money to the apostles to help the poor Christians (Acts 4:36-37). Being a good man and full of the Holy Spirit (Acts 11:24), he was well known for the encouragement he gave people. For this reason he was given the name Barnabas (meaning 'son of encouragement'). His original name was Joseph (Acts 4:36).

Barnabas' gift of encouragement showed itself on a number of memorable occasions. When many of the Jewish Christians in Jerusalem were doubtful about Paul and his reported conversion, Barnabas gained acceptance for Paul with the leaders of the church (Acts 9:26-29). Being more open-minded than most of the Jewish Christians, he was later sent by the Jerusalem leaders to help at Antioch in Syria, where many non-Jewish people had become Christians. He, in turn, invited Paul to Antioch, and through the help they gave over the next year the church grew rapidly (Acts 11:19-26).

Missionary travels

A great partnership developed between Paul and Barnabas. Their first trip together was to Jerusalem, where they helped the church by taking an offering of goods and money from the Christians in Antioch (Acts 11:27-30; Gal 2:1). They then returned to Antioch, from where they set out on a missionary tour of Cyprus and parts of Asia Minor (Acts 12:25; 13:1-4,14; 14:12).

After returning to Antioch, the two missionaries met trouble when Jews from the Jerusalem church taught that Gentile Christians had to keep the Jewish law (Acts 15:1,5). The Jewish teachers argued so cleverly that they persuaded Barnabas to believe them (Gal 2:11-13). After Paul rebuked him, Barnabas saw his error. He then opposed the Jewish teachers and even went with Paul to Jerusalem to discuss the matter with the church leaders (Acts 15:2,12).

When Paul suggested that he and Barnabas revisit the churches of Asia Minor, a disagreement arose between them concerning whether to take Mark with them. As a result they parted. Barnabas took Mark to Cyprus, and Paul took Silas to Asia Minor (Acts 15:36-41; see MARK). Although this concludes the biblical record of Barnabas' travels, Paul continued to speak well of him. It is possible that Barnabas later became associated with Paul in Corinth (1 Cor 9:6).

BARTHOLEMEW

Nothing is recorded of Bartholemew except that he was one of the twelve apostles. In Matthew's list of the apostles, which groups the apostles in pairs, Bartholemew is linked with Philip (Matt 10:3). In the lists of Mark and Luke, Bartholemew comes after Philip (Mark 3:18; Luke 6:14). John does not mention Bartholemew, but he twice mentions Nathanael (who is not mentioned in Matthew, Mark or Luke). In John 1:45 Nathanael is linked with Philip, and in John 21:2 Nathanael is among the group of apostles, but there is no mention of Bartholemew. In view of all this, it is commonly believed that Bartholemew and Nathanael are the same person. If this is so, Bartholemew would have been his family name (Bar = son of), Nathanael his personal name. See also NATHANAEL.

BASHAN

Bashan was the region lying north of the Yarmuk River and east of the Sea of Galilee, though the name was occasionally used to cover a wider area. When Israel under Moses moved up from the south conquering all the territory between the Arnon and Jabbok Rivers, they continued on immediately to conquer the land of Bashan. This conquest must have included that part of the land of Gilead that lay between the Jabbok and Yarmuk Rivers (Num 21:24,31-35; for map and other details see GILEAD).

The battle in which the king of Bashan was defeated was fought at Edrei (Deut 3:1-3).

When all the conquered lands east of Jordan were divided between Israel's two and a half eastern tribes, Bashan fell within the tribal area of Manasseh (Josh 13:29-31). This Bashan region included within it sixty cities, the most important of which were Edrei, Ashtaroth and Golan (Deut 3:4; Josh 12:4-5; 21:27). The region was fertile and had good pastures. It was well known for its forests, sheep, and particularly the fine cattle it produced (Deut 32:14; Ps 22:12; Isa 2:13; Jer 50:19; Ezek 27:6; 39:18; Amos 4:1; Micah 7:14).

Israel maintained control of Bashan at least till the time of Solomon (1 Kings 4:13). Some time later it lost Bashan, but regained control in the reign of Jeroboam II (2 Kings 14:25). Israel lost Bashan again, this time without any hope of regaining it, when Assyria overran the northern and eastern sections of Israel and took the people into captivity (2 Kings 15:29). In New Testament times the regions of Iturea and Trachonitis fell within the territory of ancient Bashan (Luke 3:1).

BATHSHEBA

David took many wives for himself (2 Sam 3:2-5,14), but the circumstances surrounding his taking of Bathsheba brought him trouble for the rest of his life. While her husband Uriah was out fighting battles for David (he was one of David's leading soldiers; 2 Sam 11:3; 23:39), David made love to her and she became pregnant (2 Sam 11:2-5). He then thought of a murderous plan to have Uriah killed in battle, after which he took Bathsheba into his palace as a royal wife (2 Sam 11:6-27).

Nathan the prophet condemned David for murder and adultery, assuring David that his own family would be torn apart by murder and adultery (2 Sam 12:1-12). David repented of his sin (2 Sam 12:13; Ps 51), but God's forgiveness did not remove the evil example that David had already set before his family.

The child born to David and Bathsheba died (2 Sam 12:14-23), but later they had another son, Solomon (2 Sam 12:24). This son was the one chosen by God to succeed David as king (1 Chron 22:9-10). In David's closing years another son, Adonijah, tried to outdo Solomon in their claims for the throne, but Bathsheba's influence ensured that Solomon became king (1 Kings 1:11-31). When Adonijah then tried to use Bathsheba to advance himself in Solomon's court, Solomon executed him for treason (1 Kings 2:13-25).

BEELZEBUL

Jews of New Testament times used 'Beelzebul' as a name for Satan, the prince of demons (Matt 10:25; 12:24-27). It was a variation of the name Baal-zebub, a Baal god whose home (according to an ancient Canaanite belief) was in the Philistine town of Ekron (2 Kings 1:2). The name meant 'lord of flies', probably because the local people believed this god gave the citizens of Ekron protection against disease-carrying flies that plagued the area.

By contrast other people interpreted the name in a bad sense — lord of flies, and therefore lord of filth. This was the meaning the Jews had in mind when they used the name as a title for Satan. Satan was Beelzebul, for he was lord of all things unclean, in particular unclean spirits, or demons (Mark 3:21-22; Luke 11:14-15). (Concerning the Jews' accusation that Jesus cast out demons by Beelzebul, see BLASPHEMY.)

BEERSHEBA

Originally Beersheba was the name given to a well that Abraham dug in the dry southern region of Palestine known as the Negeb. Some years later, opponents of the Hebrews filled the well in, and Isaac had to dig it again (Gen 21:25-33; 26:18,32-33).

Well at Beersheba

The town that grew up around the well was also called Beersheba. Abraham, Hagar, Isaac, Jacob and the sons of Jacob all at some time either lived in or passed through Beersheba (Gen 21:14; 22:19; 26:23; 28:10; 46:1-5).

A number of important roads passed through Beersheba. Among these were the main north-south route from Canaan to Egypt, and the main west-east route from the Philistine coast to Edom (Gen 46:1-6; 2 Kings 3:8). (For a map of Palestine's main traffic routes see PALESTINE.)

After Israel's settlement in Canaan, the people of Israel commonly thought of Beersheba as the most southernly town of the occupied territory. The expression 'from Dan to Beersheba' meant 'from the northern boundary to the southern' (Judg 20:1; 2 Sam 3:10; 17:11; 24:2; 1 Kings 4:25). Centuries later, when the Jews reconstructed their nation after the captivity in Babylon, Beersheba again became an important settlement. The present-day town of Beersheba stands next to the ancient site and still marks the junction of well used traffic routes (Neh 11:25-30).

BEN-HADAD

Three Syrian kings in the Bible story had the name Ben-hadad. The first cooperated with Judah's king Asa in attacking Israel's king Baasha (1 Kings 15:16-22). The second fought with the Israelite kings Ahab and Joram (or Jehoram). (1 Kings 20:1-34; 2 Kings 6:24-7:20), but was later assassinated by Hazael, one of his generals (2 Kings 8:8-15). The third, who was Hazael's son and successor, began with some victories over Israel, but later lost to Israel repeatedly (2 Kings 13:3,24-25; Amos 1:4). For further details see SYRIA.

BENJAMIN

Of all Jacob's sons, the two born to Rachel were his favourites, Joseph and Benjamin. In giving his prophetic blessing on the future tribes of Israel, Jacob knew that the descendants of Joseph would be far more dominant than those of Benjamin (Gen 49:22-27).

Protected son

Since Rachel died while giving birth to Benjamin (Gen 35:16-19), Jacob had a special concern for Benjamin. To protect Benjamin from any possible harm, Jacob would not allow him to go to Egypt the first time his sons went to buy grain (Gen 42:4). He allowed Benjamin to go on the second journey only because he had no alternative (Gen 42:38; 43:13-15). Joseph, though delighted at seeing his younger brother again (Gen 43:16,29-34), used Benjamin to test the sincerity of his brothers before inviting the whole of Jacob's family to come and live in Egypt (Gen 44:2,12; 45:1-28).

Aggressive tribe

Little is recorded concerning Benjamin's character, but Jacob had sufficient insight to see that the tribe to be descended from him would be fiercely aggressive (Gen 49:27). Perhaps this characteristic developed in the tribe when, after the division of Canaan, it found itself squeezed into a narrow strip

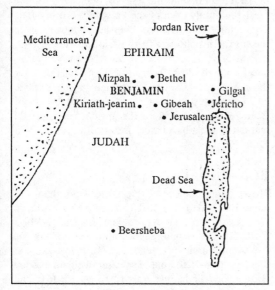

of land between Israel's two most powerful tribes, Ephraim to the north and Judah to the south (Josh 18:11-28). As a result Benjamin soon lost towns on its northern border to Ephraim (see BETHEL; GILGAL; JERICHO), and towns on its southern border to Judah (see JERUSALEM; KIRIATH-JEARIM). For other important Benjaminite towns see GIBEAH; GIBEON; MIZPAH.

The tribe of Benjamin soon became famous for its skilled fighters, many of whom were left-handed (Gen 49:27; Judg 3:15; 20:15-16; 1 Chron 8:40). On one occasion, when the men of Gibeah had committed a terrible crime that brought shame on all Israel, Benjamin chose to fight against the other tribes rather than punish its guilty citizens. As a result of the war that followed, Benjamin was almost wiped out (Judg 19-21).

Yet Benjamin, the smallest tribe in Israel, produced Israel's first king, Saul (1 Sam 9:21; 10:20-24). When Saul became jealous of David, the leading men of Benjamin encouraged Saul to kill him, no doubt because they saw David, and David's tribe Judah, as a threat to their own position (1 Sam 18:22-26; 22:7; 24:9; 26:19; Ps 7). When David later became king, some of the leading Benjaminites

maintained their hostility to him (2 Sam 16:5-8; 20:1-2).

Jerusalem, on the border between Benjamin and Judah, was still under enemy control when David became king. David's conquest of Jerusalem and his decision to make it his capital probably helped to win the allegiance of the Benjaminites (Judg 1:21; 2 Sam 5:6-7). The blessing that Moses promised the tribe of Benjamin was possibly fulfilled when Israel's temple was built in Jerusalem, which was officially in Benjamin's territory (Deut 33:12; Jer 20:2). When, after the death of Solomon, the northern tribes broke away from Judah, Benjamin was the only tribe in Israel to remain loyal to Judah and the Davidic throne (1 Kings 11:11-13,31-32; 12:21; 1 Chron 8:1,28).

Benjamin went into captivity in Babylon with Judah, and later returned from captivity with Judah (Ezra 4:1). Mordecai and Esther, who feature in a story of post-captivity Jews in a foreign land, were from the tribe of Benjamin (Esther 2:5-7). The apostle Paul also was from the tribe of Benjamin (Rom 11:1; Phil 3:5).

BEREA

Paul, accompanied by Silas, first visited Berea on his second missionary journey (Acts 17:10). The town was in the province of Macedonia in northern Greece, on the main road from Thessalonica in the north to Athens in the south. (For map of the region see ACTS, BOOK OF.)

The Jews of the local synagogue, unlike many of the Jews Paul met on his travels, were prepared to listen to Paul's teaching and test it against the Scriptures. As a result, many believed. However, Paul was forced to leave the young church when Jews from neighbouring Thessalonica forced him out of the town (Acts 17:11-14). Paul most likely revisited Berea on his third missionary journey (Acts 20:1-2). A representative from the Berean church joined his party to take an offering from the Greek churches to the poor Christians in Jerusalem (Acts 20:4; Rom 15:26; 2 Cor 8:1-4; 9:1-4).

BETHANY

There are two places called Bethany in the New Testament. The better known of the two was the village near Jerusalem, on the eastern slopes of the Mount of Olives. This was the village where Jesus' friends Mary, Martha and Lazarus lived, and where Jesus was anointed a few days before his crucifixion (Matt 26:6-13; Mark 11:1-11; John 11:1,18; 12:1-7).

The other Bethany ('Bethany beyond Jordan', sometimes called Bethabara) was in Perea, on the eastern side of the Jordan River. It was one of the places where John the Baptist preached and baptized (John 1:28).

BETHEL

When Abraham entered Canaan, one of his main camping places was near Bethel, in the hill country west of the lower Jordan. There he built an altar, and there he later returned after a time in Egypt (Gen 12:8; 13:3).

In those days the town was known by its Canaanite name, Luz. It was renamed Bethel (i.e. 'house of God') by Jacob, after he had a remarkable dream that made him feel he was in the dwelling place of God. From that time on, God was, to Jacob, 'the God of Bethel'. Many years later he returned to Bethel to fulfil vows he made on the night of his dream (Gen 28:11-22; 31:13; 35:6-7).

Bethel, along with other towns and villages of central Canaan, fell to Israel at the time of Joshua's conquest. When Canaan was divided among Israel's tribes, Bethel was on the border between Ephraim and Benjamin. It was allotted to Benjamin, but was occupied by Ephraim (Josh 8:9; 16:1; 18:11-13,21-22; Judg 1:23; 1 Chron 7:20,28; for map see BENJAMIN).

For a brief period after the conquest, the ark of the covenant was kept at Bethel (Judg 20:18,27-28). Bethel was an important religious and administrative centre in the time of Samuel and a school for prophets was established there. The school was still functioning in the time of Elijah and Elisha (1 Sam 7:16; 10:3; 2 Kings 2:3,23).

When the Israelite kingdom split into two, Jeroboam, king of the breakaway northern kingdom, set up golden idols at Dan and Bethel, the northern and southern border towns of his kingdom. The idolatry of Bethel, which God's prophets repeatedly denounced, was the reason why the altar and the town were eventually destroyed (1 Kings 12:28-33; 13:1-3; 2 Kings 23:15-20; Jer 48:13; Amos 3:14; 4:4; 5:5; 7:10-13).

With the rebuilding of Israel after the captivity, Bethel again became a settlement (Neh 11:31). It still existed in the time of Christ, though it is not mentioned in the New Testament.

BETHLEHEM

Known originally as Ephrath, Bethlehem was a small town a few kilometres south of Jerusalem. It was already an established settlement in the time of Jacob. Not far from the town was the place where Jacob buried his wife Rachel (Gen 35:19-20).

Bethlehem was situated in the tribal territory of Judah, in country that was hilly but suitable for growing grain and raising sheep (Ruth 1:1; 2:1-4; 1 Sam 17:15; Luke 2:8-15). It was the home of Israel's greatest king, David (1 Sam 17:12; 20:6; 2 Sam 23:14-16; cf. Ruth 4:11-17), and the birthplace of the great 'son of David', the promised Messiah, Jesus (Micah 5:2; Matt 2:1-6; Luke 2:4,11,15; John 7:42).

BETHSAIDA

Bethsaida was an important town on the northern shore of the Sea of Galilee (Mark 6:45). It was a base for fishermen who worked the rich fishing grounds of the lake. Among those fishermen were the brothers Andrew and Peter, who became two of Jesus' disciples. Another disciple, Philip, was also from Bethsaida (John 1:44).

On one occasion Jesus healed a blind man in Bethsaida (Mark 8:22), and on another occasion he miraculously fed five thousand people not far from Bethsaida (Luke 9:10-17). The people of Bethsaida, however, like the people of nearby Capernaum and Chorazin, stubbornly refused to accept the evidence that this Jesus was God's promised Messiah. Such a refusal only guaranteed for them a more severe judgment (Matt 11:21-24).

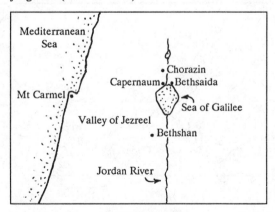

BETHSHAN (BETHSHEAN)

At the eastern end of the Valley of Jezreel, not far from the Jordan River, was the strategic town of Bethshan. (For the importance of the Valley of Jezreel see PALESTINE.) When the Israelites first settled in Canaan, they could not conquer Bethshan completely. Although the town was in the tribal allotment of Issachar, Manasseh soon took control of it in an unsuccessful attempt to drive out the local inhabitants (Josh 17:11-12; Judg 1:27). The town was still hostile to Israel in the time of Saul (1 Sam 31:10-12), but by the time of Solomon it was firmly under Israelite control (1 Kings 4:12).

BIBLE

This article is concerned solely with a summary of the Bible's contents, book by book. Concerning the Bible as the inspired and authoritative Word of God see INSPIRATION; REVELATION; WORD. Concerning the formation of the Bible and the organization of its contents see CANON; MANUSCRIPTS; SCRIBES; SCRIPTURES; SEPTUAGINT; WRITING. Concerning the present-day reader's understanding of the Bible see INTERPRETATION; QUOTATIONS.

Human sin and divine salvation

The first book of the Bible, Genesis (meaning 'origin' or 'beginning'), opens with a brief account of creation, chiefly as an introduction to the story of man. Although man failed repeatedly, God in his mercy preserved him and initiated a plan for his salvation. He chose Abraham, a man from Mesopotamia, promising to make of him a nation, to give that nation the land of Canaan as a homeland, and to use that nation as his channel of blessing to the world. Genesis traces the growth of Abraham's descendants over the next two or three centuries,

and closes with them settling down as a distinct and unified people in Egypt. These events mark the beginning of the nation Israel.

Over the next four centuries the Israelites so increased their numbers that the Egyptian rulers considered them a threat and made them slaves of the government. The book of Exodus (meaning 'a going out') records how Moses became the Israelites' leader, overthrew the oppressors and led his people out of Egypt (about 1280 BC). His intention was to lead them to a new homeland in Canaan, but first he took them to Mt Sinai, where they formally became God's people in a covenant ceremony. Then, over the next year, they organized themselves according to the laws God gave them for the new life that lay ahead. Many of these laws are recorded in the latter part of Exodus and in the next book, Leviticus (named after the Israelite tribe Levi, which had special responsibilities in religious affairs).

The book of Numbers takes its name from two census that Moses conducted in preparation for the move into Canaan. The book contains further laws, along with details of arrangements for the journey. But the people rebelled against God, and their entrance into Canaan was delayed forty years as a punishment. During this time most adults of the rebellious generation died and a new generation grew up. When the time drew near to enter Canaan,

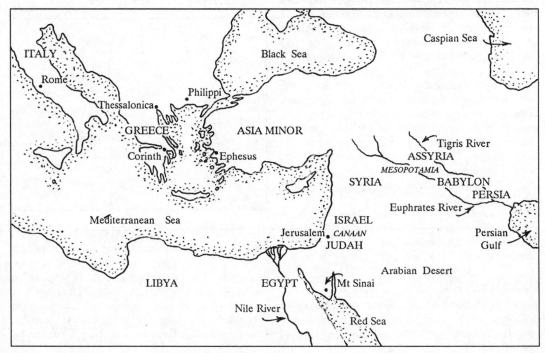

Moses repeated, and in some ways expanded and up-dated, the law for the new generation. The book that records this renewed instruction in the law is called Deuteronomy, meaning 'second law'.

Israel established in Canaan

Moses died before Israel entered Canaan, and his chief assistant, Joshua, became the nation's new leader. The book of Joshua records how Israel under Joshua conquered Canaan and divided the land among its twelve tribes.

During the following generations the people of Israel became increasingly rebellious against God. The book of Judges shows how they copied foreign religious practices and as a result brought God's judgment upon themselves, usually in the form of invasions from hostile neighbours. Israel had no central government, but when the people cried to God for help he provided specially gifted leaders from among them. These leaders were called judges, because they carried out God's judgment upon Israel's enemies and administered justice in local disputes. But among the ungodly people as a whole there were some who remained faithful, and the story of one such family is recorded in the book of Ruth.

In an effort to improve national stability, the people decided to establish a monarchy. Their spiritual leader at this time, Samuel, advised against this, for the cause of their troubles was not their system of government, but their ungodliness. The people, however, refused to listen to Samuel, with the result that Israel gained its first king, Saul (1050 BC). He was a failure, and the story of events leading to and including his reign is recorded in the book of 1 Samuel.

The book of 2 Samuel records the reign of the next king, David, who was a strong and godly king, in spite of some mistakes. He established a dynasty through which God promised to bring a messiah-king who would be the saviour of the world.

The nation divided

Solomon succeeded David, and the history of the Israelite kingdom from his time onwards is recorded in 1 and 2 Kings. Solomon spent much of his time developing the national capital Jerusalem, but in the process he treated his people harshly and created widespread unrest. When he died, the ten tribes to the north and east of Jerusalem broke away and formed their own monarchy. They still called themselves Israel and, after some early temporary arrangements, established their capital in Samaria. The two tribes to the south remained loyal to the

dynasty of David, whose kings continued to reign in Jerusalem. The southern kingdom became known as Judah, after its leading tribe.

Throughout the time of the divided kingdom, Israel and Judah had conflict with neighbouring countries, and sometimes with each other. Political, social and religious conditions steadily worsened, though a minority of people always remained true to God. Out of these, God chose some to be his messengers to his people. They condemned the people for their sin, warned them of judgment and instructed them in righteousness. They were known as prophets, and some of their writings have been collected and grouped together in a separate section of the Old Testament.

Captivity and return

As the prophets had warned, both parts of the divided kingdom were eventually destroyed. The northern kingdom was conquered by Assyria in 722 BC and its people taken captive into various parts of the Assyrian Empire. A little over a century later, Assyria was conquered by Babylon, who then advanced into the Palestine region. In a series of attacks starting in 605 BC, Babylon overpowered Judah and took its people into captivity, finally destroying Jerusalem in 587 BC.

The book of 1 Chronicles contains a shorter and parallel account of 1 and 2 Samuel, and the book of 2 Chronicles a shorter and parallel account of 1 and 2 Kings. But the books of Chronicles were written much later, after the kingdoms and Israel and Judah had been destroyed and the people were in captivity. A chronicle is an orderly record of events, and the books of Chronicles helped preserve national history and family records, in order to help those who were to re-establish the nation after the captivity.

When Persia conquered Babylon in 539 BC, the king of Persia quickly gave permission for captive peoples to return to their homelands. As a result captive Israelites returned to their land and set to work rebuilding Jerusalem. No longer was there a division between north and south. However, since most of those who returned were from the former southern kingdom Judah, the name Jew (short for Judean) soon became a name for Israelites in general.

The story of this reconstruction of Israel is told in the books of Ezra and Nehemiah, who were two of the more prominent leaders in post-captivity Israel. The book of Esther gives a glimpse of Jewish life in Persia during the same period. The three books cover a period of about one hundred years, and with them the historical section of the Old Testament comes to a close.

Wisdom teachers and song writers

In the arrangement of books in the English Bible, the historical books are followed by a group of five books that are largely poetical. The largest of these books is Psalms, which is a collection of 150 songs and poems that express the writers' feelings during their varied experiences. David wrote about half the psalms, but many of the authors are unknown.

Three of the books belong to a category of Hebrew literature known as wisdom literature. Wisdom teachers examined life's affairs with the aim of teaching people how to live rightly. The book of Job consists mainly of a debate between Job and his friends about the problem of human suffering. The book of Proverbs, as its name indicates, is a collection of wise sayings, the majority of which are from Solomon. Ecclesiastes (meaning 'the teacher' or 'the philosopher') is concerned with man's search for a meaning to life.

The remaining book in this group, the Song of Songs (or Song of Solomon), is neither a psalm nor a wisdom writing. It is a collection of love poems that recount the exchanges of love between a young man and a young woman.

Words of the prophets

The final section of the Old Testament consists of writings from the prophets. These were preachers who brought God's message to his people during the periods of the monarchy, the captivity and the later reconstruction of Israel. Each book, except for Lamentations, is named after the person who wrote it.

Isaiah and Jeremiah were probably the two most important prophets and their books are the longest. Isaiah belonged to the time of the divided kingdom and was concerned mainly with Judah. Jeremiah preached during the forty years leading up to and including the destruction of Jerusalem by the Babylonians. The book of Lamentations reflects the suffering of the Judeans at the hands of the Babylonians. Ezekiel and Daniel were among those Jerusalemites taken captive to Babylon, but whereas Ezekiel lived in one of the workers' camps, Daniel was taken into the palace and trained to be an administrator.

The twelve prophets who follow are usually called the Minor Prophets, not because they were less important than the previous four (usually called the Major Prophets), but because their books are

shorter. Hosea, Joel, Amos, Obadiah, Jonah, Micah, Nahum, Habakkuk and Zephaniah all belong to the period that began with the division of the kingdom and ended with the captivity in Babylon. The final three, Haggai, Zechariah and Malachi, belong to the period of Israel's reconstruction after the captivity, as recorded in Ezra and Nehemiah.

At the time the Old Testament story closes, Israel was back in its land but still under foreign rule, namely, the rule of Persia. When the Persians fell to the expanding power of the Greek Empire (334-331 BC), the Jews came under Greek rule. Several generations later, through persistent fighting during the years 165-143 BC, the Jews regained their independence. But in 63 BC they lost this independence to Rome, and were still under Roman rule when Jesus Christ was born.

Jesus and the early Christians

The books Matthew, Mark, Luke and John, known as the four Gospels, are concerned with the life and teaching of Jesus. They do not provide a detailed record of his life, but deal mainly with the three years or so leading up to and including his death and resurrection. At times the writers record the same events, but always in a way that is fitted to their separate purposes and the needs of those for whom they write.

After Jesus' resurrection and ascension, the apostles and other enthusiastic Christians spread the message of his salvation. This is recorded in the book of Acts, sometimes called the Acts of the Apostles. Much of the first half of the book is concerned with the work of Peter, John and others who worked in Jerusalem and surrounding areas. The second half of the book is concerned largely with the work of Paul, who made three main missionary journeys through Asia Minor and Greece and eventually reached Rome.

Letters from Christian leaders

Much of the rest of the New Testament consists of letters written by leading Christians of the first century. These have been arranged in sections. First are letters that Paul wrote to various churches in the course of his missionary activity. The letters are named after the churches to whom they were written and are arranged in order of length. The letters are Romans, 1 and 2 Corinthians, Galatians, Ephesians, Philippians, Colossians and 1 and 2 Thessalonians.

Following Paul's letters to churches are the letters he wrote to individuals. They are named after the people to whom they were written and likewise are arranged in order of length. The group consists of two letters to Timothy, one to Titus and one to Philemon.

The next group consists of eight letters that come from five writers. An unknown author wrote a letter (known as Hebrews) to Jewish Christians who were tempted to give up their belief in Jesus and go back to Judaism. The other seven letters are named after their authors. James the brother of Jesus wrote one, Peter the apostle wrote two, John the apostle wrote three, and Jude (probably another brother of Jesus) wrote one.

At the end of the New Testament is the book of Revelation. Although it contains letters written to churches, it is different in style from all the other books of the New Testament. Through a series of visions, God gave a revelation to the writer, who then passed it on to persecuted Christians. The message is that Jesus is still in control and the final victory of his people is certain.

BIRDS

Many of the birds mentioned in the Bible were large birds of prey, of which there were many species in Palestine. They fed on small animals that they killed themselves and on the carcasses of larger animals that had either died or been killed by wild beasts. They even fed on the bodies of dead soldiers that lay scattered over the battlefield after war. Among these birds were vultures, eagles, hawks, falcons, ravens, owls and kites. The law of Moses did not allow Israelites to use any of these birds as food (Lev 11:13-19; Job 9:26; 28:7; 39:26; Ps 79:2; Isa 34:15; Jer 49:16; Ezek 39:4; Matt 24:28). The ostrich, though not a bird of prey, was considered a wild and fearsome bird, living in desolate or deserted places (Isa 13:21; 34:13; Jer 50:39).

Quails

There were many migratory birds in Palestine, and almost every month some departed and others arrived. The most common among these birds were the cormorant, ibis, crane, pelican, stork, seagull and heron. Israelite law again prohibited the use of these

as food (Lev 11:13-19; Jer 8:7). It did not prohibit the eating of quails (Exod 16:13; Num 11:31-32; Ps 105:40).

Birds that were commonly seen around towns and villages were sparrows, swallows, doves and pigeons. Since these were allowable as food, people often caught them in traps, and then cooked and sold them (Lev 5:7; Ps 84:3; 91:3; Prov 26:2; Eccles 9:12; Amos 3:5; Matt 10:29). Israelites also kept chickens, both for their meat and for their eggs (1 Kings 4:23; Matt 23:37; 26:34).

BLASPHEMY

Bad or insulting language directed at a person or thing is usually referred to as a curse. When directed at God it becomes a blasphemy.

According to the law of Moses, blasphemy was an act not merely of disrespect to God but of rebellion against God. The penalty was death (Lev 24:10-23; 1 Kings 21:10; Acts 6:11; 7:58). Israelites by nature had a reverence for the name of God, and were not as likely to speak blasphemously of God as the Gentiles were (2 Kings 19:6,22; Ps 74:10,18). But they often *acted* blasphemously, as seen for example when they turned from God to serve idols (Ezek 20:27-28).

Jews of New Testament times accused Jesus of blasphemy because he claimed for himself powers that belonged to God only (Mark 2:7; 14:61-64). This was one reason why they persecuted Jesus and his followers. They even tried to make the followers of Jesus curse him — and that really would have been blasphemy (Acts 26:11). In fact, the Jews themselves were the ones guilty of blasphemy; for in speaking evil of Jesus they were speaking evil of God (1 Tim 1:13).

The blasphemy of the Holy Spirit was a sin that Jesus said could not be forgiven. This statement must be understood in its context. Jesus realized that many Jews did not clearly understand the nature of his messiahship, and did not know what he meant by referring to himself as 'the Son of man'. God could forgive people's doubts and misunderstandings about Jesus, but he would not forgive their deliberate rejection of the plain evidence that Jesus' works were good and they originated in God. When people called God's Spirit Satan and called good evil, they put themselves in a position where there was no way of acknowledging God's goodness. There was therefore no way of receiving his forgiveness (Matt 12:22-32; Mark 3:28-30).

If a person is distressed through thinking he cannot be forgiven because of some blasphemy he has spoken, he should realize that his distress is a sure sign that he has not committed the sin Jesus referred to. The sin Jesus condemned is not a rashly spoken curse, but a deliberate refusal of God; not a single act, but a persistent attitude. And so long as a person stubbornly persists in that attitude he cannot be forgiven.

BLESSING

Consistently the Bible refers to the gifts that God gives, whether material or spiritual, as blessings (Gen 9:1; Lev 25:21; Num 6:22-26; Ps 115:12-15; Prov 10:22; Eph 1:3; Heb 6:7). Often it contrasts God's blessings with his cursings or punishments (Deut 11:26-28; 27:12-13; 30:19).

Even in ordinary human relationships, to desire blessing or cursing for another person meant to desire benefits or calamities for that person (Gen 27:12; Num 22:6; Rom 12:14; Jas 3:10-11). A blessing in this sense was not a mere expression of good wishes, but an announcement that people believed carried with it the power to make the wishes come true (Gen 27:27-29,33; 49:1,28; Num 24:10; 2 Sam 7:29). (For a similar idea, but with opposite results, see CURSE.)

People gave blessings on important occasions, most notably at births, marriages and farewells (Gen 14:18-19; 24:60; Ruth 4:14-15; Mark 10:13-16; Luke 2:33-35; 24:50). Usually the person of higher status blessed the one of lower status (Heb 7:7; cf. Gen 14:18-20).

The blessing that people in Israelite families desired most was the prophetic announcement by which the head of the family passed on favours to his children (Gen 27:36-41; 48:8-22; 49:1-28; Deut 33:1-29; Heb 11:20-21; 12:17). Probably the most striking example of a blessing carrying with it the power of certain fulfilment was God's blessing to Abraham that promised him a people and a land (Gen 12:1-3; 26:24).

Since a blessing expressed the desire for a person's well-being, it was also used as a formal greeting, even from an inferior to a superior (Gen 47:7-10). A blessing could therefore become an expression of praise, and in this sense grateful people can bless God (Ps 28:6; 31:21; 41:13; Dan 2:19-20; Mark 11:9-10; Lk 1:68; Rom 1:25; Eph 1:3). A thanksgiving to God such as before eating a meal is sometimes called a blessing (Mark 6:41; 8:7; 14:22; 1 Cor 10:16).

There is another word sometimes translated 'blessed' that refers to the happiness or well-being of a person. It is usually used to denote the contented state of the person who lives uprightly according to God's principles and who, as a result, enjoys God's favour (Ps 1:1; 32:1; 41:1; Prov 3:13; Matt 11:6; 16:17; Luke 1:45; 12:37; Rom 4:6-9; James 1:12; Rev 16:15). When people enter God's kingdom and live under the kingly rule of Christ, they experience the sort of deep seated joy that Christ himself experienced. Such joy is a foretaste of the greater blessedness that will be theirs when they are with Christ in the day of his kingdom's final glory (Matt 5:2-11; 25:34; John 15:11; see JOY).

BLOOD

The special significance of blood in the Bible is that it commonly signifies death; not death through natural causes, but death through killing or violence. In the language of the Bible, anyone responsible for the death of another has upon him the blood of the dead person, and he who executes the guilty avenges the blood of the dead person (Num 35:19; 1 Kings 2:32-33,37; Matt 27:4,24-25; Acts 5:28; Rev 6:10; 17:6). Likewise the person who lays down his life for another is, so to speak, offering his own blood (2 Sam 23:15-17; Rom 5:6-9).

The life of the flesh

Blood has this special significance because 'the life of the flesh is in the blood' (Gen 9:4; Lev 17:11; Deut 12:23). However, the Bible's emphasis is not on blood circulating through the body, but on shed blood; not on blood's chemical properties, but on its symbolic significance. Since blood in the body represents life, shed blood represents life poured out; that is, death.

One of the principles on which Israelite law was based was that all physical life belonged to God and was therefore precious in his sight. This was particularly so in the case of man, because he was made in God's image (Gen 1:26). Any person who killed another without God's approval was considered no longer worthy to enjoy God's gift of life and had to be executed. In this case the executioner was not guilty of wrongdoing, because he was acting with God's approval. He was carrying out God's judgment (Gen 9:5-6). Therefore, until a murderer was punished, the blood of the murdered person cried out for justice (Gen 4:10; Num 35:33; Deut 19:11-13).

Animal life also belonged to God. God gave the flesh of animals to man as food, but the person who took the animal's life had to acknowledge God as the rightful owner of that life. He took the animal's life only by God's permission. He therefore poured out the animal's blood (representing the life that had been taken) either on the altar or on the ground. This was an expression of sacrificial thanks to God for benefits he received at the cost of the animal's life. Any drinking of the blood was strictly forbidden (Gen 9:4; Lev 17:3-7,10-14; 19:26; Deut 12:15-16,20-28).

The blood of atonement

Because of this connection between shed blood and life laid down, God gave the blood of sacrificial animals to man as a way of atonement. Man's sin made him guilty before God, and the penalty was death. But God in his mercy provided a way for the repentant sinner to come to him and have his sins forgiven, while at the same time the penalty for his sin was carried out. An animal was killed in place of the sinner. The person received forgiveness through the animal's blood; that is, through the animal's death on his behalf (Lev 17:11; see ATONEMENT; SACRIFICE).

This symbolic significance of blood was clearly illustrated at the time of the Passover in Egypt. The sprinkling of the blood around the door was a sign that an animal had died in the place of the person who was under judgment. The firstborn was saved through the death of an innocent substitute (Exod 12:13).

The blood of Christ

Man's flesh is kept alive by the blood that is in it, and when Jesus became man he took upon himself the nature of 'flesh and blood' (Heb 2:14; 5:7; cf. Matt 16:17; Gal 1:16; Eph 6:12). Man was under the penalty of death because of his sin; but when Christ, as man, died on the cross in the sinner's place, he made salvation possible. He broke the power of sin through his own blood (Acts 20:28; Eph 1:7; Titus 2:14; Rev 1:5; 5:9).

In the New Testament the expressions 'blood of the cross', 'blood of Christ' and 'death of Christ' are often used interchangeably (Rom 5:7-9; Eph 2:13,16; Col 1:20,22). To have life through Christ's blood means to have life through his death. There is no suggestion of using Christ's blood in any way that might be likened to the modern practice of a blood transfusion. Christ did not give his blood in the sense of a blood donor who helps overcome some lack in another person. He gave his blood through dying to bear the penalty of sin (Rom 3:24-25; Col 1:14; 1 Peter 2:24; 1 John 1:7). Those who 'share in Christ's blood' share in the benefits of his death through receiving forgiveness of sins and eternal life (John 6:54-58; 1 Cor 10:16).

The book of Revelation uses the symbolism of Christ's blood in relation to the presence in heaven of those killed for the sake of Christ. Yet their fitness to appear in God's presence is because of Christ's sacrifice, not theirs. They are cleansed through Christ's blood. This does not mean that they are washed in blood in the sense that clothes are washed in water, but that they are cleansed from sin through Christ's atoning death (Rev 7:14; cf. 1 Peter 1:2; 1 John 1:7).

Under the Old Testament system man's access to God was limited. Once a year, on the Day of Atonement, the high priest, and he alone, could enter the Most Holy Place, the symbol of God's presence. Even then, he could enter the divine presence only by taking with him the blood of a sacrificial animal and sprinkling it on and in front of the mercy seat. This blood was a sign of a life laid down in atonement for sin, so that the barrier to God's presence through sin might be removed (Lev 16:1-34; Heb 9:7,25; for details of the ritual see DAY OF ATONEMENT).

But Christ, the great high priest, entered the heavenly presence of God, not with his blood but through his blood. He entered by means of his death. Christ has no need to carry out blood rituals in heaven, for he has already put away sin by the sacrifice of himself (Heb 9:12,24-26). Just as he entered God's holy presence through his blood, so his people can have boldness to enter by the same blood. They claim for themselves the benefits of his death (Heb 10:19).

BOASTING

One result of pride and self-sufficiency is that people boast of their achievements instead of giving honour to God (Deut 8:11-14; Jer 9:23; Dan 4:30; 1 Cor 4:7; James 4:13-16). Such boasting is hateful to God and will bring from him a humiliating judgment (Isa 10:15-16; 37:23-29; Luke 18:10-14; cf. Matt 6:1-4; John 12:43).

Confidence in self is one of the things that prevent people from coming to God and receiving God's salvation. People cannot earn salvation as a reward for any good deeds they might do. They can only receive it as a gift that God gives freely to those who trust in his grace. There is therefore nothing of themselves that they can boast about (Rom 3:27-28; 4:1-5; 9:30-32; Eph 2:8-9). If they boast at all, they boast in what God has done, not in what they have done (Jer 9:24; 1 Cor 1:31; Gal 6:14; see also PRIDE).

The Bible records one occasion on which the apostle Paul boasted, even though he knew it was not the sort of thing a Christian should do. But his purpose was to answer certain people in Corinth who opposed him. These people too easily believed the boasting of men who set themselves up as super apostles (2 Cor 10:8,13; 11:1-5,16-21; 12:1-11). By contrast, most of the things that Paul boasted of were things that the normally boastful person would be ashamed to speak about, namely, his personal humiliations (2 Cor 11:23-30).

BOAZ

If the Rahab whom the Israelites saved at the time of Jericho's destruction is the same Rahab whose name appears in the genealogy of Jesus, then Boaz was descended from her (Josh 6:17; Ruth 4:18-22; Matt 1:1,5). He features in the book of Ruth as the man who helped the young Moabite widow Ruth and later married her (see RUTH).

Boaz was a godly man who was eager to reward Ruth when he learnt of her kindness to her widowed mother-in-law (Ruth 2:11-12). He protected her from the local youths (Ruth 2:8-9,22), supplied her with food and drink during her day's work (Ruth 2:9,14), rewarded her gleaning (Ruth 2:16-20) and gave her extra supplies of grain (Ruth 3:15). He showed no racial prejudice against her in spite of the traditional hostility between Israel and Moab (Ruth 2:6,10).

When Ruth asked Boaz to keep alive the name of her late husband by fulfilling the duties of a close relative, Boaz responded generously. He was open and honourable in all his dealings with her, whether concerning marriage or property (Ruth 3:11-13; 4:1-6). He married Ruth, and the child born to them was an ancestor of King David and of Jesus the Messiah (Ruth 4:18-22; Matt 1:1,5).

BODY

Although the Bible may speak of the body as being distinct from a person's spirit, soul, or mind (Micah 6:7; Matt 10:28; Rom 7:23-25), it also speaks of the body as representing the person himself (Neh 9:37; Rom 12:1; 1 Cor 13:3). This is because the Bible regards a human being as a unified whole, not as something that can be divided into separate independent parts.

Part of a unified whole

Man, as created in God's image, exists in a living body (Gen 1:27). For this reason the Christian's hope is not for the endless life of his spirit or soul in a bodiless existence, for a person without a body is not a complete person. Rather the Christian's hope is for the resurrection of his body to full and eternal life (2 Cor 5:1-5; see MAN). The Christian does not yet know the exact nature of this resurrection body, but he knows at least that it will be imperishable, beautiful, strong, suited to the life of the age to come, and patterned on Christ's glorious body (1 Cor 15:35-54; Phil 3:20-21; 1 John 3:2; see RESURRECTION).

Since the whole person is created in God's image and the whole person is destined for eternal glory, the Christian should not despise the body. He should not consider it something evil. He may be ashamed of the wrong things he does through his body, but this is all the more reason why he must exercise discipline over it (Matt 5:27-30; Rom 6:12-13; 8:13; 1 Cor 9:27; 1 Thess 5:23; James 3:3-5; see FLESH). Another reason to be careful of the way he uses his body is that it is God's temple, God's dwelling place within him (1 Cor 6:12-20). (Concerning the church as the body of Christ see CHURCH.)

Likewise in his dealings with unbelievers the Christian must remember that it is the whole person, not just the spirit or soul, that is made in the image of God. He should therefore do what he can to meet the bodily needs as well as the spiritual needs of his fellows (James 2:15-16; 1 John 3:17-18). In this he will be following the example of Jesus Christ (Matt 14:14-16; Mark 1:40-42); though like Jesus Christ he will realize that 'life is more than food and the body more than clothing' (Matt 6:25).

A wrong view

In the church of the first and second centuries a type of false teaching developed which asserted that the body, being material, was evil. This produced extremes of behaviour, from strict self-denial to unrestrained immorality. The false teachers claimed to have a special knowledge in relation to the world of matter and the world of spirit. Their 'knowledge', however, was false and its outcome was wrong behaviour (Col 2:23; 1 John 1:8; 3:10). (For further discussion see COLOSSIANS, LETTER TO THE; JOHN, LETTERS OF; KNOWLEDGE, sub-heading 'Knowledge and morality'.)

BOOK OF LIFE

It appears that different Bible writers used the expression 'book of life' in different ways. In Old Testament times it may have meant simply the register of all living people. It seems also to have had a special meaning as referring to the register of all who claimed to be God's people (Exod 32:32-33; Ps 69:28).

Among those known as God's people, from Old Testament times to the present, there are those who become apostates or who were not genuine believers in the first place. They demonstrate this by openly and deliberately rejecting God, and God removes their names from the book of life. True believers do not reject God, and God does not remove their names from the book of life. They are assured of eternal life in its fulness (Exod 32:32-33; Rev 3:5; 21:22-25; see APOSTACY; BACKSLIDING).

From this usage, 'book of life' has developed a more specific meaning. It becomes the register of all true believers — those whom God has chosen and who have received cleansing from sin through the blood of Jesus. Thus it becomes specifically the 'Lamb's book of life' (Luke 10:20; Phil 4:3; Rev 13:8; 21:27). In the coming judgment, all whose names are not written in the Lamb's book of life will suffer eternal punishment (Rev 17:8; 20:12-15).

BRANCH

One of the names that Israelites of Old Testament times gave to the expected Messiah was 'the Branch'. This arose from the Israelite expectation that the Messiah was to come from the 'tree' of David's dynasty (Jer 23:5; 33:15; cf. Isa 4:2; 11:1; see MESSIAH).

After the Jews' return from their Babylonian captivity, the name 'branch' was used in relation to Zerubbabel, the Jewish governor in Jerusalem. Zerubbabel was a descendant of David in the royal line that eventually produced Jesus the Messiah (Hag 2:21-23; Zech 3:8-10; 6:11-13; Matt 1:12-16; see ZERUBBABEL).

BREAD

To people in Bible times, bread was a basic part of the daily food. In everyday speech they often spoke of food in general as bread (Ps 37:25; Prov 31:27; Eccles 9:7; Isa 30:20; Matt 6:11; 2 Thess 3:8). (For details concerning the common bread of the people see FOOD. For the use of leaven in bread and for its symbolism in Israelite religion see LEAVEN; PASSOVER. For the meaning of the 'presence bread' in the tabernacle see TABERNACLE.)

Manna, that unusual food that God provided for the Israelites on their journey from Egypt to Canaan, was known as 'bread from heaven' (Exod 16:4; John 6:31; see MANNA). Jesus spoke of this

bread as a picture of himself, the true bread from heaven. He came from God as God's spiritual provision for man. He alone can bring salvation, and he alone can guarantee believers victory over death (John 6:32-40). This provision of salvation through Jesus is possible only because Jesus gave himself in sacrifice. By accepting the benefits of this sacrifice for themselves by faith, people can have eternal life (John 6:48-58).

Jesus also used literal bread as a symbol of his sacrifice. He told his disciples to eat bread and drink wine together, as a remembrance of him and as an expression of their unity with him and with one another (Matt 26:26-29; 1 Cor 10:16; 11:23-26; see FELLOWSHIP; LORD'S SUPPER).

BROTHER

Among the peoples of Bible times the word 'brother' had a wide meaning. Its obvious and most common meaning was to those who were children of the same parents (Gen 25:21-26; Matt 4:18-21). It was used also of a person who was more distantly related, such as a cousin or an uncle (Gen 14:12-14), a fellow member of the same community or nation (Gen 19:7; Lev 25:45-46; Acts 13:26; Rom 9:3), or one's fellow man in general (Lev 19:17; Matt 7:3). (See also NEIGHBOUR.)

Jesus used the expression 'brother' to indicate the closeness of the relationship between him and his followers (Matt 12:46-50; cf. Heb 2:11-12). Those who become Christ's people are therefore brothers to each other (Matt 18:15,21; Acts 9:17,30; 15:3,22; 1 Thess 5:25-27).

This shared brotherhood should help produce good relations between believers. They should be more tolerant of each other (Rom 14:10-15), more forgiving (1 Cor 6:5-8), more concerned (2 Thess 3:15), more self-sacrificing (1 John 3:17) and more loving (Rom 12:10; 1 John 2:9-11). They should realize that to sin against a brother is to sin against Christ (1 Cor 8:11-13), and therefore should make every effort to prevent, or correct, such sin (Matt 18:15-20; Rom 14:19-21).

BURIAL
See FUNERAL.

CAESAR

The name 'Caesar' was a Roman family name that became famous through Caesar Augustus, the man who in 27 BC introduced a new era in Roman affairs. Out of the disorder that characterized Rome and its colonies, Caesar Augustus founded what became known as the Roman Empire (Luke 2:1). People held him in such honour that later rulers took

A Roman Emperor

his name Caesar as their title (Luke 3:1). By New Testament times the common practice was to refer to the Emperor simply as Caesar (Mark 12:14; Luke 20:22; John 19:15; Acts 17:7; 25:11,25). For further details see ROME.

CAESAREA

A few years before the time of Christ, Herod the Great built a new city on the Mediterranean coast and named it Caesarea, in honour of the Roman Emperor. It was a magnificent city, but today only a few of its ruins remain.

The Palestine coast south of Mt Carmel had no good sites for harbours, because of the shallow waters and sandy shores. Herod therefore built an expensive artificial harbour for Caesarea, and the city soon became an important port. Being situated on the main north-south coastal road that linked Phoenicia and Egypt, the city developed into a prosperous centre for inland and overseas trade. It was also an important centre of administration from which the Herods, and later the Romans, governed the region (Acts 12:19; 23:33; 25:1-6).

When the Jews persecuted the early Christians and forced them to leave Jerusalem (Acts 8:1,4), Philip the evangelist went to live in Caesarea (Acts 8:40; 21:8). The apostle Peter helped the work, and soon a church was established there. One of the early converts was a Roman centurion, Cornelius (Acts 10:1,24,44-48). Later the apostle Paul also helped the church. He passed through Caesarea on a number of occasions and was for a time imprisoned there (Acts 9:30; 18:22; 21:8,16; 23:23-35; 24:24-27; 25:1-13).

This coastal city of Caesarea is not to be confused with the inland town of Caesarea Philippi. The latter was in the hill country of northern Galilee (Matt 16:13; see CAESAREA PHILIPPI).

CAESAREA PHILIPPI

According to the biblical record, Caesarea Philippi was the most northerly town of Palestine that Jesus visited. It was located in northern Galilee, near the source of the Jordan River (Matt 16:13; Mark 8:27). Like the much larger town of Caesarea on the Mediterranean coast, it was named in honour of the Roman Emperor. It was given the additional name Philippi in honour of Herod Philip, the provincial governor in whose territory it was located (cf. Luke 3:1).

CAIAPHAS

As Jewish high priest in Jerusalem during the time of Jesus, Caiaphas is chiefly remembered for his part in the crucifixion of Jesus. He was son-in-law of the former high priest Annas (John 18:13), he became high priest before Jesus began his ministry (Luke 3:2), and he was still high priest in the days of the early church (Acts 4:6).

During the time of Jesus, the members of the Sanhedrin (the Jewish Council) became increasingly hostile to him as they saw his fame growing. They feared that, if the Jews accepted Jesus as their Messiah and rebelled against Rome, the Romans would respond by crushing the Jews (John 11:47-48). Caiaphas, as leader of the Sanhedrin, suggested they get rid of Jesus. In his view, one man's death would save the nation. The words of Caiaphas had a prophetic meaning that he did not realize; for Jesus' death would indeed be a means of salvation, not just for Jewish people, but for people of all nations (John 11:49-52).

Acting upon the advice of Caiaphas, the Jews plotted to arrest Jesus (John 11:53; Matt 26:3-5). In the middle of the night, only a few hours before the dawn of Passover day, they captured him and took him to the house where Annas and Caiaphas lived. He was questioned first by Annas (John 18:12-14) and then by the Sanhedrin, whom Caiaphas had assembled in his house (Matt 26:57-58).

In reply to a question from Caiaphas, Jesus said that he truly was the Messiah from heaven and he was about to receive his eternal kingdom. Caiaphas promptly accused him of blasphemy. Although the meeting's conduct and verdict were illegal according to Jewish law, the Sanhedrin had no hesitation in condemning Jesus to death (Matt 26:59-66; Mark 14:61-64; see SANHEDRIN).

CAIN

Eldest of Adam and Eve's family, Cain was a crop farmer. Since man was to acknowledge God as the giver of all things, Cain brought some of his farm produce and presented it as an offering to God. Cain's brother Abel, being a shepherd, offered sheep. But whereas Abel presented his offering in sincerity and faith, Cain did not, with the result that God accepted Abel's offering but rejected Cain's (Gen 4:1-5; Heb 11:4).

Cain was envious and angry. He was told that if he wanted God to accept his sacrifice, he had to change his ways and overcome the sinful attitudes that were threatening to destroy him (Gen 4:5-7). Cain, however, refused to humble himself, and gave clear evidence of the evil within his heart by murdering his brother (Gen 4:8; 1 John 3:12). In punishment God drove him into a barren region. Cain still showed no sign of repentance, only fear of punishment. Yet God in his mercy promised to protect Cain from any possible revenge killing (Gen 4:8-16).

Free from the influence of those who still worshipped God, Cain set about establishing his own independent settlement. His descendants raised cattle and developed skills in arts and crafts, but morally they drifted further from God (Gen 4:17-24; cf. Rom 1:20-28).

CALEB

Although brought up a slave in Egypt, Caleb proved himself a responsible leader once the people of Israel began to organize themselves on the journey to Canaan. Within a short time he became one of the leaders of his tribe, Judah.

On the journey to Canaan

When Moses chose twelve representatives (one from each tribe) to go to Canaan and spy out the land, Caleb was the person chosen from the tribe of Judah (Num 13:2,6,17-20). At that time he was forty years of age (Josh 14:7).

The spies returned with a report that although Canaan was a fertile land, its inhabitants were fearsome, particularly the giant people of Anak who lived in the region of Hebron (Num 13:21-29; see ANAK). This report immediately discouraged the people from going ahead with the attack, but Caleb spoke up boldly, believing that in God's strength they could overcome the enemy (Num 13:30). The people, however, chose to accept the opinion of the unbelieving spies. They refused to trust God, and rebelled against the leadership of Moses (Num 13:31-14:4). Only Joshua, the spy who went as the representative of the tribe of Ephraim, supported Caleb (Num 14:6-9).

God responded to the people's rebellion by announcing that, since they did not want to enter Canaan, they would have their wish. During the next forty years all who were at that time twenty years of age or over (except Caleb and Joshua) would die in the wilderness (Num 14:28-35).

When, forty years later, a new generation had grown up and the people were about to enter Canaan, Moses appointed one leader from each of the twelve tribes to assist the new leader Joshua and the high priest Eleazar in the division of the land. Caleb was again chosen to represent Judah (Num 34:16-19).

Life in Canaan

After several years of battle, Canaan belonged to Israel and was divided between the twelve tribes. There were still groups of unconquered Canaanites scattered throughout the country, but each Israelite tribe was responsible for overcoming the enemies within its territory (Josh 13:1-7; cf. 15:63; 16:10; 17:12,18).

Caleb was now eighty-five years of age, but he was ready to show that his faith and courage were as strong as they had been forty-five years earlier. The people of Anak, whom the Israelites had once been afraid to fight, still occupied Hebron, the region that had been allotted to Caleb within the tribal territory of Judah. Caleb conquered them and took possession of their towns (Josh 14:6-15; 15:13-14).

The boldness of Caleb helped to develop the faith and courage of others. Having set an example by his conquest of Hebron, he offered his daughter as a wife to any man who could conquer the neighbouring town of Debir. The conqueror was Othniel, who later became a great leader in Israel (Josh 15:15-19; Judg 3:9-11).

CALENDAR

See MONTH.

CALL

In biblical usage, the word 'call' has a similarly wide range of meanings as it has in everyday usage. This wide range of meanings applies even when the Bible speaks of God's call to individual people, though certain usages stand out as being of greater theological significance.

God may call people in the sense simply of commanding them or inviting them; yet rebellious people often ignore his call (Isa 65:12; Jer 7:13; Matt 9:13; 22:3-6,14). More specifically, he may call people in the sense of choosing them or directing them according to specific purposes he has for them (Isa 43:1; 46:11; Hosea 11:1; Matt 4:21; Acts 16:10; Heb 11:8). In an even higher sense, he calls people by giving them his salvation and making them his own (Rom 1:6; 8:30; 1 Cor 1:24).

Christians are those who have responded to the call of God that they heard through the gospel. Their existence as God's people is the work of the sovereign God who, in his grace and mercy, has called them and saved them (1 Cor 1:2,26; Col 3:15; 2 Thess 2:14; 2 Tim 1:9). This aspect of the call of God is sometimes referred to as election (Rom 9:11; see ELECTION).

God's calling involves more than merely saving his people from the penalty of sin. He has called them to enjoy freedom (Gal 5:1,13), to practise holiness (1 Thess 4:7; 1 Peter 1:15), to be changed into Christ's likeness (Rom 8:29-30), to share in Christ's kingdom (1 Thess 2:12) and to proclaim Christ's message (1 Peter 2:9). He has also called them to share Christ's glory; though if they are to experience this fully, they must also share Christ's suffering (1 Peter 2:21; 5:10).

CALVARY

See GOLGOTHA.

CANAAN

The land of Canaan took its name from Canaan the son of Ham, who in turn was a son of Noah (Gen 10:1,6). The territory stretched along the Mediterranean coast from Phoenicia (Sidon) in the north to Philistia (Gaza) in the south, and extended inland to the hills of Syria and the valley of the Jordan River (Gen 10:15-19).

This was the land that God promised to give to Abraham and his descendants (Israel) as a national homeland (Gen 12:5-7; 13:12-17; cf. Exod 3:7-8; 6:1-4; Num 13:2,17). The land's boundaries were more clearly defined some centuries later when the

Israelites were about to take possession of it. The northern boundary went from the region of the Jordan's headwaters to the coast. The southern boundary went from the Dead Sea through Kadesh-barnea to the Brook of Egypt, which it then followed

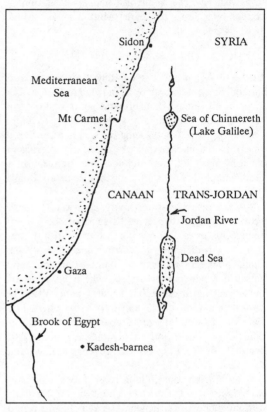

to the coast. The eastern boundary was the Jordan River and the western boundary the Mediterranean Sea (Num 34:1-12). (For details of the physical features of the land see PALESTINE.)

The Canaanite people

In the time of Abraham many tribal groups lived in Canaan along with the original Canaanites. Many of these tribal peoples feature in the history of Israel's origins and early development, but all were destined to lose their land to the Israelites (Gen 15:18-21; Exod 3:8; Num 23:29; see AMALEKITES; HITTITES; HIVITES; JEBUSITES; PERIZZITES; REPHAIM).

The most dominant of the peoples of Canaan were the Amorites. They had settled widely and intermarried extensively with the Canaanites, till the names 'Canaanite' and 'Amorite' became general terms that people used interchangeably to refer to the entire population of Canaan (Gen 12:5-7; 15:16; Josh 24:3,18; see AMORITES).

Conquest of Canaan

Though all the Canaanite peoples were religiously and morally corrupt, God gave them ample time to repent before he finally executed his judgment upon them. It was several hundred years from the time God warned of judgment to the time the judgment actually fell. Only when the Canaanites' wickedness had gone beyond the limits that God's tolerance allowed did God command the Israelites to destroy them and possess their land (Gen 15:16; Deut 7:1-5; 20:17-18).

When the Israelites conquered Canaan, they also conquered territory that bordered the Jordan River on the east and was occupied by the Amorites (Num 21:21-35). Two and a half of Israel's twelve tribes settled in this trans-Jordan territory. This means that Canaan itself (i.e. the area west of Jordan extending to the Mediterranean Sea) was occupied by only nine and a half tribes (Num 32:29-33; 34:13-15). (Concerning Israel's conquest of Canaan and subsequent history in the land see ISRAEL.)

CANDLESTICK

See LAMP.

CANON

According to the word's early usages, a canon was a rule, standard, measure or list. According to popular Christian usage, the 'canon' of Scripture is that collection of writings that the church acknowledges as the authoritative Word of God. In other words, it is the list of books that make up the Bible. It consists of the Old Testament canon, which had become established during the centuries before the time of Christ, and the New Testament canon, which became established during the early centuries of the Christian era.

Canonical books are those acknowledged as being written through the inspiration of the Holy Spirit (see INSPIRATION). Non-canonical books are religious books of the biblical era that are not acknowledged as being the inspired Word of God and have therefore not been collected in the Bible. They may be useful, and may even be referred to by the writers of the Bible (e.g. Num 21:14; Josh 10:13; 1 Chron 29:29; Jude 9,14), but they have no divine authority.

Israelite writers

From the beginning of their history as a nation, Israelites kept written accounts of their law and significant events in their history (Exod 24:4; Num 33:2; Josh 24:26; 1 Kings 11:41). Some of these writings were regarded as sacred and were kept at Israel's sanctuary (Deut 31:24-26; 2 Kings 22:8). Others were used as sources of information for the writing of books that later became part of the Bible (1 Kings 14:19; 15:7; 2 Chron 9:29; 12:15; 20:34).

While some people made written records of laws and events, others made collections of proverbs and psalms (1 Kings 4:32; Ps 72:20; Prov 25:1). In addition prophets often wrote down their messages (Isa 30:8; 34:16; Jer 36:2; 51:60) and people who recognized these messages as God's Word quoted them as authoritative (Jer 26:17-18; Dan 9:2).

The Old Testament collection

Under the guiding control of God, a recognized body of sacred writings was growing up in Israel. However, the formation of an official canon was not something that people planned. No person or group of persons decided to make an Old Testament canon. From the time of Moses people had clearly recognized certain writings as being the voice of God speaking to them, and as the years passed the collection of authoritative books grew. No one gave the books their authority. The books had authority within themselves, and people could do no more than acknowledge this.

No one knows for certain when the collection of sacred writings that we call the Old Testament was completed, but there are good reasons for thinking that Ezra and Nehemiah helped shape it towards its final form. They had come to Jerusalem in 458 and 445 BC respectively (Ezra 7:1-10; Neh 2:1-8), and played an important part in establishing the sacred writings as the basis of Israel's religious life in the post-captivity period (Neh 8:1-3,8; 9:1-3). Leaders of following generations probably completed what Ezra and Nehemiah had begun.

It seems clear that the Jewish canon (i.e. our Old Testament) was firmly established by the time of Christ (Matt 21:42; Luke 24:27; John 5:39). Towards the end of the first century AD a council of Jewish leaders confirmed that Jews recognized these books, and no others, as canonical. (For the composition of the Old Testament see SCRIPTURE. For the authority of the Old Testament canon that Jesus and New Testament writers acknowledged see INSPIRATION.)

Apocryphal writings

The third and second centuries BC produced many new Jewish writings. Some of these were vividly written and therefore were very popular, particularly in an age when great changes were occurring in the

Jewish world. But their popularity did not give them authority, and they were never accepted into the Jewish canon.

These non-canonical books are in two groups. One group is known as the Apocrypha (literally, 'hidden', but meaning 'disapproved' or 'outside'; i.e. outside the canon). The other group is known as the Pseudepigrapha (meaning 'written under a false name'). In popular usage, 'Apocrypha' often refers to the two groups together. Early Christians may have read the books (e.g. Jude 9,14), but they did not regard them as Scripture.

Early Christian writings

In the early days of the church, the 'Bible' that the Christians used was what we call the Old Testament (Luke 24:27,44; Acts 8:32; 17:2,11; Rom 1:2; 4:3; 9:17; 2 Tim 3:15-16). But with the coming of Jesus, Christians saw that God's revelation did not end with the Old Testament.

Jesus had promised the apostles that after he returned to his Father, the Holy Spirit would come to indwell them, enabling them to recall, interpret and apply his teachings (John 14:25-26; 16:13-15). The writings of the New Testament are part of the fulfilment of that promise. Apostles had God-given authority, and Christians recognized their teachings and writings as having the same authority as the Old Testament Scriptures (1 Cor 14:37; 1 Thess 5:27; 2 Thess 2:15; 3:14; 2 Peter 3:2; Rev 1:1-3).

A growing collection

As the writings of the apostles circulated, they gradually grew into a new collection in addition to, yet equal to, the Old Testament collection (2 Peter 3:15-16). It seems that when the early Christians evaluated the worth of the writings available to them, an important consideration was whether those writings came from the apostles or those who had the apostles' approval. The Gospels, the letters of Paul, the book of Acts, and the letters 1 Peter and 1 John were accepted everywhere as authoritative from the time they began to circulate.

During the latter part of the first century and the early part of the second, a number of other Christian writings were circulating widely. Some of these were useful, but they were not accepted by the churches as authoritative. In time Christians in general acknowledged that these writings were not inspired Scripture, with the result that they were excluded from the developing New Testament canon.

On the other hand there were some regions where it took longer for people to accept all the writings that are now part of the New Testament. Although a particular church or group of churches may have accepted an apostolic letter as having authority for them, churches elsewhere may not have immediately seen the relevance of the letter for all churches. No doubt there were many letters which, though having apostolic authority, were not preserved (1 Cor 5:9; cf. 1 Thess 3:17). Also, letters which were very short, or about which there were doubts concerning authorship, usually took longer to become widely known.

Completion of the canon

By the middle of the second century, churches in some places had a collection of books approximately equal to the present New Testament. But in other places there were still doubts about a small minority of books.

The damaging activity of false teachers was one factor that prompted church leaders to consider more closely which books were to be regarded as canonical and which were not. Church Councils met to discuss the matter at length, and by the end of the fourth century there was general agreement that the New Testament canon consists of the twenty-seven books that we recognize today.

Church Councils may have performed a useful service, but they could give no authority to the biblical books. The authority lay within the books themselves. They were the living Word of God (John 7:17; 1 Thess 2:13), and the Councils could do no more than acknowledge that authority. They did not create the canon, but merely acknowledged that Christians and churches everywhere recognized the books as being God's inspired and authoritative Word.

CAPERNAUM

The important town of Capernaum was on the north-west shore of the Sea of Galilee. Jesus seems to have made it the base for his ministry in Galilee, and it became known as his home town (Matt 4:13; 9:1; Mark 2:1; 9:33; John 6:24). Another lakeside town, Bethsaida, was close by (Mark 6:43-45; John 6:13,17; for map see BETHSAIDA).

Capernaum was large enough to have its own tax collectors. One of these was Matthew, who later became a disciple of Jesus (Mark 2:1,13-15; cf. Matt 17:24). Among the town's more important citizens were government officials and at least one Roman centurion (Matt 8:5; 17:24; John 4:46). There was a large Jewish population in Capernaum and the town had several synagogues. Jesus often taught in these synagogues, but the people's stubborn refusal to believe in him as the Messiah would one day bring God's judgment upon them (Matt 11:23; Luke 4:31; John 6:59).

CAPTIVITY

See EXILE; SLAVE.

CARMEL

Mount Carmel was the only major headland on the Palestine coast (Jer 46:18). It rose steeply from the sea, then extended inland in a mountain range about twenty kilometres long that divided between the Plain of Esdraelon to the north and the Plain of Sharon to the south. The mountains had good forests and pasture lands (Isa 33:9; 35:2; Jer 50:19; Amos 1:2; 9:3; Nahum 1:4). (For maps and other details of the region see PALESTINE.)

According to the beliefs of Baalism that Jezebel introduced into Israel from Phoenicia, Mt Carmel was a sacred Baal site. This gives added significance to the contest on Mt Carmel where Elijah defeated the prophets of Baal (1 Kings 18:17-46; see ELIJAH). (Mt Carmel had no connection with a town in Judah named Carmel; 1 Sam 15:12; 25:2-42.)

CENTURION

A centurion was an officer in the Roman army. The name came from the Latin *centurio*, indicating that originally it was the title for an officer in charge of a hundred soldiers. The favourable references to

Roman centurion

centurions in the New Testament suggest that they may have been carefully chosen because of their quality of character. Some even became believers in Jesus Christ (Matt 8:5-13; 27:54; Acts 10:1-2; 23:17-18; 27:43).

CHALDEA

Ancient Babylonia was occupied largely by people belonging to two racial groups, the Sumerians and the Amorites. In addition there were smaller tribal groups scattered throughout the region. The most important of the smaller groups were the Chaldeans, who lived in the south of Babylon around the lower reaches of the Euphrates and Tigris Rivers.

In the time before Abraham, the Babylonian rulers were mainly of Sumerian descent and their capital was the Chaldean city of Ur, from which Abraham originally came (Gen 11:28; Acts 7:4). About 2000 BC Babylonians of Amorite descent overthrew the dynasty in Ur and established a new capital at the city of Babylon. (For a map of the region and further details of Babylon's history see BABYLON.)

Many centuries later, during the period covered by the biblical books of Kings, a Babylonian of Chaldean descent seized the throne in Babylon (about 720 BC). Chaldeans continued to rule till Babylon was overthrown by Persia in 539 BC. As a result of this Chaldean domination, the practice arose of using 'Chaldea' as a name for the land of Babylon as a whole, and 'Chaldeans' as a name for Babylonians in general (Isa 13:19; 47:1; 48:14,20; Jer 25:12; Dan 5:30; 9:1).

The word 'Chaldeans' had also a more technical meaning, which had passed down from ancient times when certain Chaldeans became famous as astrologers, priests and wise men. This is the sense in which the Bible uses the name in the expression 'magicians, enchanters, Chaldeans and astrologers' (Dan 4:7; 5:7,11).

CHARIOT

When the Israelites entered Canaan under Joshua, they were successful in conquering the hill country, but had difficulty in conquering the plains. The reason for this was that the local Canaanites were well equipped with chariots (Josh 11:4; 17:16; Judg 1:19; 4:13; 1 Sam 13:5).

The use of chariots did not become common in Israel till the time of David, when Israel conquered many of the peoples of the plains and seized their chariots (2 Sam 8:3-4; 15:1). During the reign of

Solomon, Israel's chariot forces were expanded considerably, and from his time on they were an important part of Israel's army (1 Kings 4:26; 9:22;

An Assyrian chariot

10:26; 20:21; 22:35; 2 Kings 8:21; 9:21; 10:2; 13:7). The armies of other nations likewise relied heavily on chariots (1 Kings 22:31; 2 Kings 6:11-14; 18:24; 19:23; see also WAR).

CHASTISEMENT

Parents have a responsibility to discipline their children when they do wrong, but any punishment involved must arise out of love. The punishment is therefore better called chastisement. Parents who love their children will not ignore their children's wrongdoing, but will deal with it (Heb 12:6-9; cf. 2 Sam 7:14-15; Ps 89:26-33).

Chastisement should be both a penalty for wrongdoing and a form of training. It should teach the child to avoid what is wrong and do what is right, and so develop a life that is useful to himself and to others (Prov 13:24; 22:15; 23:14; 29:15). Parents, when chastising their children, therefore should act with proper understanding and without bad temper (Eph 6:4).

As parents correct and train their children, so God disciplines his children. Such discipline is proof to the believer that he is God's child and that God loves him (Deut 8:5; Prov 3:11; Heb 12:5-11; Rev 3:19). God's purpose in disciplining his children is to correct their faults, teach them obedience, and make them more into the types of people that he, in his superior wisdom, wants them to be (Ps 94:12; 1 Cor 11:32).

In carrying out this purpose, God may send his people various trials, such as suffering, defeat and loss. Sometimes these trials may be punishments for specific sins, but at other times they may not have any direct relation to wrongdoing (Ps 38:1-4; 118:18; John 9:1-3; 2 Cor 1:3-7; 12:7-10). They are simply the means God uses to remove imperfections from his

people and bring them closer to the fulness of growth he desires for them. Because he loves them, he will be satisfied with nothing less than their perfection (Eph 5:25-27; cf. Heb 5:8-9; see also SUFFERING; TESTING).

CHEMOSH

Bordering Israel in the region east of the Dead Sea was the nation Moab, whose national god was Chemosh. In times of religious corruption, Israel copied Moabite religious practices (Judg 10:6; 1 Kings 11:7,33), and in times of reformation got rid of them (2 Kings 23:13). The Moabites looked for help from Chemosh through offering child sacrifices (2 Kings 3:26-27; cf. Judg 10:6; 11:30-31,39), but Chemosh was powerless to save them from the judgment of God (Jer 48:7,13,46; see MOAB).

CHERETHITES

The Cherethites and Pelethites were people who lived among the Philistines and who, like the Philistines, probably came originally from Crete (1 Sam 30:14; Ezek 25:16; Zeph 2:5; see PHILISTIA). They were such good soldiers that David, upon conquering the Philistines, used them to form his personal bodyguard, under the command of the tough Benaiah (2 Sam 8:18; 20:23). They were fiercely loyal to David through the rebellions of Absalom and Sheba, and they supported David's chosen successor, Solomon, when there was an attempted coup against him (2 Sam 15:18; 20:7; 1 Kings 1:38). There is no mention of them after the death of David.

CHERUBIM

From the images that were made for the tabernacle and the temple, it seems that cherubim (plural of cherub) were winged creatures of some heavenly angelic order. They usually acted as guardians for the Almighty and his interests.

When man rebelled against God in the garden of Eden, God sent cherubim to guard the tree of life (Gen 3:24). In Israel's tabernacle, two cherubim images were attached to the lid of the ark of the covenant in the Most Holy Place. The lid of the ark, known as the mercy seat, was the symbolic throne of God, and the cherubim were symbolic guardians of that throne (Exod 25:18-22; 1 Sam 4:4; 2 Sam 6:2; 2 Kings 19:15; Ps 80:1; Heb 9:5). In Solomon's temple also, the Most Holy Place had images of guardian cherubim. They were so huge that side by side they stretched across the room from wall to wall (1 Kings 6:23-28). In Ezekiel's visions, cherubim supported the chariot-throne of God (Ezek 1:4-28; 10:1-22; cf. Ps 18:10).

Craftsmen who worked on the ornamentation of the tabernacle and the temple included cherubim in many of their designs. Cherubim were pictured on the coverings and curtains of the tabernacle (Exod 26:1,31), the walls of the temple (1 Kings 6:29; cf. Ezek 41:17-20,25), and the mobile lavers that belonged to the temple (1 Kings 7:29,36).

CHILD

One of God's purposes for human marriage is that a husband and wife produce children and build a secure and contented family. Godly people regard their children as a gift from God, and aim at bringing them up to know him and walk in his ways (Deut 6:6-9; Ps 127:3; Eph 6:4; 2 Tim 3:15). (Concerning the privileges and responsibilities of children in relation to their families and parents see FAMILY.)

However, in a world spoiled by sin, not all children grow up in a secure family environment. As a result they may be greatly disadvantaged and even exploited (Exod 22:22-24; Deut 26:12; 27:19; James 1:27; see ORPHAN).

Examples and illustrations

Jesus had a special concern for children and warned against ignoring or despising them. He pointed to their simple dependency on others as an illustration of the attitude that people must have if they are to enter the kingdom of God. People must realize that before God they are as helpless as children. They enter the kingdom of God not by their wisdom or achievements but solely by accepting God's grace (Matt 18:1-4; Mark 10:13-16).

When the Christian realizes that in God's eyes he has no more power or status than a child, he will be specially considerate of all other children, making sure he does nothing to cause them harm (Matt 18:5-10). The 'children' referred to here are both those who are children literally and those who are children in the sense of being new believers with childlike faith (cf. 1 John 2:12-13). Sometimes the young see truths that those of traditional views fail to see (Matt 21:14-16).

Another way in which the Bible speaks of believers as children is as children of God. In one picture they are born into God's family through the life-giving work of God himself (John 1:12-13; see REGENERATION); in another they are adopted into God's family and given the status of mature adult sons (Rom 8:15-17; Gal 4:5-7; see ADOPTION). As children of God, they are to develop the character of their Father (Matt 5:9,48; 1 Peter 1:14-16; 1 John 2:29; 3:10). In biblical language, 'to be a child of' sometimes means 'to have the character of' (1 Kings 21:13; Luke 7:35; Eph 2:2; 5:8; 1 Thess 5:5) or 'to be the subject of' (Eph 2:3; 2 Peter 2:14).

The Bible uses the picture of children in yet another way when it likens immature Christians to children who have not grown up. Like babies they still need the 'milk' of introductory teaching, when they should be feeding on the 'meat' of more advanced teaching (1 Cor 3:1-2; Heb 5:12-14). Love for the spectacular is another sign of immaturity. Christians should have the innocence of children in relation to evil, but in their minds they should be mature adults (1 Cor 13:8-11; 14:18-20).

CHINNERETH

Chinnereth was another name for Gennesaret. It applied both to the Lake of Gennesaret (the Sea of Galilee) and to the small Plain of Gennesaret on the lake's western shore (Num 34:11; Josh 19:35; Luke 5:1). For fuller details see PALESTINE, sub-heading 'Upper Jordan and Sea of Galilee'.

CHRISTIAN

The citizens of Antioch in Syria were the first people to give the name 'Christian' to believers in Jesus Christ (Acts 11:26). The language spoken in Antioch was Greek, and therefore the believers in that town spoke of Jesus not by the Hebrew word 'Messiah', but by the equivalent Greek word 'Christ'. (Both words meant 'the anointed one'; see MESSIAH.)

To people who were neither Jews nor believers, 'the anointed one' ('Christ') had no significance. To them the word seemed to be merely the name of a person, and the followers of that person they called 'Christ's people', or 'Christians'. Originally non-believers used the name 'Christian' as a nick-name, possibly in mockery (Acts 26:28). But it proved to be a suitable name, for it showed that the Christian religion was centred on Christ. Under some of the later Roman Emperors, believers in Jesus were persecuted merely for being Christians (1 Peter 4:16).

CHRONICLES, BOOK OF

In the Hebrew Bible the two books of Chronicles form one volume. The writer has not recorded his name, though he has mentioned some of the books and documents from which he gathered his information (1 Chron 9:1; 27:24; 29:29; 2 Chron 9:29; 16:11; 24:27; 33:19; 35:25). His account in some ways parallels the record found in the books of Samuel and Kings, but it is by no means a repetition. The Chronicler wrote for a particular group of people and with a particular purpose in mind.

Purpose of Chronicles

During the period covered by 1 and 2 Kings, the Israelite kingdom divided into two, the northern kingdom being known as Israel, the southern as Judah. When the people of the northern kingdom were taken into captivity by Assyria (732-722 BC), many became so widely scattered in the Assyrian Empire that they largely lost their national identity. When the people of the southern kingdom were taken into captivity by Babylon (605-582 BC), they remained together in Babylon and retained their national identity. It was people of this latter group who began returning to Palestine after Persia's conquest of Babylon in 539 BC.

Most of those who returned had never lived in Palestine and knew little of the operations of the Jerusalem temple in the days before its destruction. These were the people for whom the Chronicler wrote. He wanted to give them some background concerning their nation's history, and especially concerning its religion. He wanted them to realize that they were more than just a lot of migrants returning to the land of their forefathers. They were a continuation of that pre-captivity nation whose political life was based on the Davidic dynasty, and whose religious life was based on the Levitical priesthood.

Features of Chronicles

By carefully choosing and arranging his material, the Chronicler impressed upon the released captives the importance of rebuilding their nation according to God's design. They were not to be led astray by former bad examples. Though he traces the history of the nation from the time of its first king, Saul, to the time of the captivity in Babylon, he mentions Saul only briefly and says little about the northern kingdom. He is concerned almost entirely with the Davidic line of kings who reigned in Jerusalem.

The northern kingdom was a breakaway from the God-appointed kingdom of David. Its religion was a rebellion against the true worship of God that was centred on the temple in Jerusalem. The Chronicler's reason for scarcely mentioning the northern kingdom is that he does not want to interest his readers in its sinful ways. For him, David's is the only legitimate dynasty, Jerusalem the only legitimate capital, the temple the only legitimate sanctuary, and the Levitical priesthood the only legitimate religious order.

In concentrating on the history of the southern kingdom (i.e. the dynasty of David), the Chronicler wants to show what an important part the one and only God-given religion played in the national life of God's people. For this reason, features of Israel's religious organization that are omitted from Samuel and Kings are given in great detail in Chronicles. On the other hand, failures of individual Davidic rulers that are found in Samuel and Kings are omitted from Chronicles.

The Levites are of particular interest to the Chronicler. Whereas the writers of Samuel and Kings seldom mention them, the Chronicler speaks of them frequently, showing the important part they played in the nation's affairs. He wants his readers to see how God intended the Davidic type of civil administration and the Levitical type of religious order to function in harmony for the benefit of the nation.

Contents of 1 Chronicles

Genealogies were useful in showing the returning captives how they fitted into God's plan for the nation. After tracing the origins of Israel (1:1-54), the genealogies deal with the tribes of Judah and Simeon (2:1-4:43), the two and a half eastern tribes (5:1-26), the Levites (6:1-81), and the remaining tribes (7:1-8:40). The Chronicler then lists those who had recently gone to Jerusalem as the first group of returning captives (9:1-34).

After dealing very briefly with the reign of Saul (9:35-10:14), the Chronicler deals at length with the reign of David, beginning with David's rise to power (11:1-12:40). Having been made king, David brought the ark to Jerusalem and began organizing the singing and music that were to characterize public worship in Israel (13:1-16:36). When David said he wanted to build God a temple, God replied that he would build David a dynasty (16:37-17:27). The section closes with stories recalling David's greatness (18:1-22:1).

The final section of the book deals with David's preparations for the temple that his son Solomon would later build. Having encouraged Solomon for this task (22:2-19), David made detailed arrangements concerning the functioning of the priests and Levites (23:1-26:32). Arrangements for military and civilian leaders are much less detailed (27:1-34). Before his death, David presented the new king to the people (28:1-29:30).

Contents of 2 Chronicles

Solomon was a king of great wisdom and wealth (1:1-17). For the Chronicler, however, his chief importance had to do with his construction of the temple in Jerusalem (2:1-7:22). Building programs and clever trading activities contributed further to Solomon's greatness (8:1-9:31).

Although the northern tribes broke away from Jerusalem after Solomon's death, the Chronicler refused to recognize them as a separate legitimate kingdom. Solomon's son Rehoboam ruled well as long as he followed the teaching of the Levitical priests, but when he introduced foreign religious practices, God punished him (10:1-13:22).

Asa began a reform, but then he also departed from the ways of God (14:1-16:14). It was left to the next king, Jehoshaphat, to restore the nation to the ways of God. Priests and Levites played an important part in his reform (17:1-20:37). When Jezebel's Baalism spread from the north into Judah (21:1-23:21), priests and Levites were again leaders in the reform that got rid of it, the king on this occasion being Joash (24:1-27).

The prosperity of Judah under Uzziah and Jotham was followed by disaster and chaos under Ahaz (25:1-28:27), but Hezekiah then sought to correct matters with wide-sweeping reforms. The Chronicler deals with Hezekiah's religious reforms at length (29:1-31:21), but discusses his political reforms only briefly (32:1-33). After the evil reigns of Manasseh and Amon (33:1-25), there was a final reform under Josiah. The Chronicler's emphasis again is on the religious aspects of the reform (34:1-35:27).

Babylon's destruction of Jerusalem and the subsequent captivity are recorded, but with little detail. More important for the Chronicler's readers are the current realities of release from captivity and return to the homeland (36:1-23).

CHURCH

After the failure of mankind recorded in the early chapters of Genesis, God declared his purpose to choose for himself a people through whom he would work a plan of salvation for mankind. He began by choosing one man, Abraham, and promising to make from him a nation that would belong to God and be his channel of blessing to the world. The people of this nation, Israel, were therefore both the physical descendants of Abraham and the chosen people of God (Gen 12:1-3; Exod 6:7-8; 19:5-6; Ps 105:6; John 8:33,37; Acts 13:26).

This did not mean, however, that every person born into the Israelite race was, because of his nationality, forgiven his sins and blessed with God's eternal salvation. The history of Israel shows that from the beginning most of the people were ungodly and unrepentant. Certainly there were those who, like Abraham, trusted God and desired to follow him obediently, but they were always only a minority within the nation (Isa 1:4,11-20; Amos 5:14-15; Rom 11:2-7; 1 Cor 10:1-5; Heb 3:16). These were God's true people, the true Israel, the true children of Abraham (Rom 2:28-29; 4:9-12; 9:6-8).

From this faithful minority (or remnant) there came one person, Jesus the Messiah, who was the one particular descendant of Abraham to whom all God's promises to Abraham pointed. All God's ideals for Israel were embodied in him, and through him God fulfilled his promises of blessing for all mankind (Gal 3:14,16). Jesus then took the few remaining faithful Israelites of his day and made them the nucleus of the new people of God, the Christian church (Matt 16:18).

The church, then, was both old and new. It was old in that it was a continuation of that body of believers who in every age had remained faithful to God. It was new in that it would not formally come into existence till after Jesus' death, resurrection and ascension (Matt 16:18,21; Acts 1:4-5; Titus 2:14; 1 Peter 2:9). It was 'born' a few days after Jesus' ascension, on the day of Pentecost (Acts 2:1-4), and will reach its glorious destiny at Jesus' return (Phil 3:20-21; Heb 12:22-24; Rev 19:7-9).

God's new community

The word which Jesus used and which has been translated 'church' meant originally a collection of people — a meeting, gathering or community. It was the word used for the Old Testament community of Israel, and was particularly suitable for the new community, the Christian church, that came into being on the day of Pentecost (Exod 12:3,6; 35:1,4; Deut 9:10; 23:3; Matt 16:18; 18:17; Acts 5:11; 7:38; 8:1; 11:26).

On that day Jesus, having returned to his heavenly Father, sent the Holy Spirit to indwell his disciples as he had promised (Luke 24:49; John 7:39; 14:16-17,26; 16:7). This was the baptism with the Holy Spirit of which Jesus had spoken and through which all who were already believers were bound together to form one united body, the church (Acts 1:4-5; 2:33; see BAPTISM WITH THE SPIRIT).

From that time on, all who repent and believe the gospel are, through that same baptism with the

Spirit, immediately made part of that one body and receive the gift of the Holy Spirit (Acts 2:38,47; 1 Cor 12:13). This applies equally to all people, irrespective of sex, age, status or race, for all are one in Christ Jesus (Acts 2:17-18,39). The new people of God consists of Abraham's spiritual descendants, those who have been saved through faith in Christ, regardless of their nationality or social standing (Gal 3:14,28-29).

By his act of uniting in one body people who were once in conflict with each other, God has carried out part of a wider plan he has for his creation. That plan is for the ultimate removal of all conflict and all evil from the universe, and the establishment of perfect peace and unity through Jesus Christ (Eph 1:9-10; 2:13-16; 3:8-11).

The body of Christ

Christ and the church, being inseparably united, make up one complete whole, just as the head and the body together make up one complete person. Through his resurrection and ascension, Jesus Christ became head over the church and the source of its life and growth (Eph 1:20-23; 4:15-16; Col 1:18; 2:19; 3:1-4).

As the head has absolute control over the body, so Christ has supreme authority over the church (Eph 1:22-23). On the other hand, as the body shares in the life of the head, so the church shares in the life of the risen Christ. It is united with him in his victory over death and all the evil spiritual forces of the universe (Matt 16:18; Eph 1:21; 2:5-7; 3:10,21; Col 2:13-15).

If the picture of the body emphasizes the life, unity and growth that Christ gives to the church, the picture of marriage emphasizes the love that Christ has for the church. That love was so great that, to gain the church as his bride, Christ laid down his life in sacrifice (Eph 5:25; cf. Acts 20:28). Both pictures illustrate Christ's headship of the church (Eph 1:22-23; 5:23), and both make it clear that God can accept the church as holy and faultless only• because it shares the life and righteousness of Christ (Eph 5:26-27; Col 1:22).

This view of the church in all its perfection as the body of Christ is one that only God sees. Man sees the church in a world of sin and failure, where it is still troubled by imperfections (cf. 1 Cor 1:2 with 1 Cor 3:1-3; cf. Eph 1:1-4 with Eph 4:25-32). God sees the church as the total number of all believers in all nations in all eras — a vast, ongoing, international community commonly referred to as the church universal. Man sees it only in the form

of those believers who are living in a particular place at a particular time.

Within what man sees as the church there are genuine believers and those who have no true faith in Christ at all. Often it is difficult to tell the difference between the two, and the only certain division will take place at the final judgment. Only God knows which people are really his (Matt 13:47-50; 25:31-46; 1 Cor 4:3-5; 10:1-11; 2 Cor 13:5; 2 Tim 2:19).

The local church

While the Bible sometimes speaks of the church as a timeless and universal community, more commonly it speaks of it as a group of Christians meeting together in a particular locality. This community is the church in that locality. It is the local expression, a sort of miniature, of the timeless universal church (Acts 13:1; 15:41; 20:17; 1 Cor 1:2).

Each local church, though in fellowship with other local churches (Acts 11:27-30; 1 Cor 16:1-4; Col 4:15-16), is responsible directly to the head, Jesus Christ, in all things. The New Testament gives no guidelines for a central organization or head church to control all others. It lays down no set of laws either to hold the churches together in one body or to hold all the believers in one church together. Unity comes through a oneness of faith in the Spirit (Eph 4:4-6).

It is therefore better to think of the church not as an organization or institution, but as a family. Christ is the head, and all the believers are brothers and sisters (Gal 6:10; Eph 2:19; Rom 15:30; 16:1,23). The strength of the church comes not from some organizational system, but from the spiritual life that each believer has and that all believers share in common (Acts 14:23; Phil 1:7; 2:1-2; 1 John 1:3; see FELLOWSHIP).

According to Christ's command and the early church's example, those who repent and believe the gospel should be baptized (Matt 28:19-20; Acts 2:38,41; 10:48; see BAPTISM). By their faith they become members of Christ's body, the church, and they show the truth of this union by joining with the Christians in their locality. In other words, having become part of the timeless universal church, they now become part of the local church (Acts 2:41,47).

The Bible gives no instructions concerning where the church in any one locality should meet. (Churches in New Testament times seem to have met in private homes or any ready-made places they could find; see Acts 12:12; 19:9; 20:7-8; Rom 16:5,14-15; Col 4:15.) The meetings of the church are to be orderly and, what is more important, spiritually helpful (1 Cor 14:12,26,40). Christians must be built up through being taught the Scriptures and through having fellowship by worshipping, praying, singing praises and celebrating the Lord's Supper together (Acts 2:42; 20:7,27; 1 Cor 10:16-17; 11:23-33; 14:15; see LORD'S SUPPER; WORSHIP).

Christians must not look upon the church as a sort of private fellowship that exists solely for their own benefit. From the church they must go out to spread the gospel to others, baptizing those who believe, bringing them into the church, teaching them the Christian truths and making them true disciples of Jesus Christ (Matt 28:19-20; Acts 1:7-8; 8:4; Rom 10:14-17).

In addition, the church should be concerned with helping those who are the victims of sickness, hunger, conflict, injustice and other misfortunes (Matt 25:34-40; Rom 12:8,13; Gal 6:10; James 1:27). As with preaching the gospel, this ministry concerns both the church's own locality and distant regions (Matt 28:19-20; Acts 1:8; 2:45; 11:27-30; 13:2-4; Rom 15:25-26; see MISSION).

Leadership in the churches

Although the Bible gives clear guidelines concerning the responsibilities of the local church, it gives few organizational details. Christians grow in maturity as they exercise their judgment and carry out their responsibilities (Rom 12:6-8).

This does not mean that people may do as they like. The Spirit of the living Christ dwells within the church (1 Cor 3:16), and he has appointed leaders in the church to guide and feed it (Acts 20:28). Their task is to work out how to apply the Bible's timeless principles to the circumstances of their era and culture (1 Cor 14:26,40; 1 Thess 5:12-13; 1 Tim 3:15; 4:13-15; 2 Tim 2:7).

Those leaders who are chiefly responsible for the church's well-being are commonly called elders. Deacons are those who assist the elders by relieving them of some of the more routine affairs (Phil 1:1; 1 Tim 3:1,8; see ELDER; DEACON). People who fill these leadership positions may be gifted in various ways. God has given certain types of people to the church to help build it up — apostles, prophets, evangelists, pastors and teachers (Eph 4:11) — and such people can be expected to be in positions of leadership in the church.

Apostles and prophets appear to have been given to the church mainly to instruct and direct it during the period of its infancy (Eph 2:20; see APOSTLE; PROPHET). Evangelists are people with special ability in making known the gospel and establishing churches in places where previously there were none (Acts 14:1,21,23; 21:8; 2 Tim 4:5; see EVANGELIST). Pastors and teachers care for the church as a shepherd cares for his flock, feeding it with spiritual food and protecting it from spiritual dangers (John 21:15-17; Acts 20:28; 1 Tim 5:17; 1 Peter 5:2; see PASTOR; TEACHER).

The Bible does not divide people too sharply into one or other of these categories, as there is clearly some overlapping within the functions. Also some people may combine within them several of these gifts; e.g. Paul (Rom 15:20; 1 Tim 1:1; 2:7), James (Gal 1:19; 2:9-10), Timothy (1 Tim 4:13-16; 2 Tim 4:5), Barnabas (Acts 11:22-26; 14:14), Silas (Acts 15:32; 17:10-14) and others.

Responsibilities of church members

There is no suggestion in the Bible that people with these gifts are the only ones who do spiritual work in the church. On the contrary, the purpose of their work is to equip others to work. They build up the Christians and so prepare them for fuller Christian service (Eph 4:11-13). The gifted ones teach others who, in turn, pass on the teaching to others (2 Tim 2:2).

Every member of the church has some gift that the Holy Spirit has given him or her for the service of God (1 Cor 12:11,18). Just as the human body is made up of many parts, all with different functions, so is the church which is Christ's body. Yet with the variety there is equality. The church, unlike ancient Israel, has no exclusive class of religious officials who have spiritual privileges that ordinary people do not have (Rom 12:4-8; 1 Cor 12:12,27; Eph 2:18-20). There are many gifts, but Christians must use these gifts in dependence upon the Spirit's power and in accordance with the Spirit's teaching (1 Cor 12:4-11; 13:1-2; 14:37).

If a local church is to operate properly, each person in that church must find out which gifts the Holy Spirit has given him and then develop them (Rom 12:6-8; 1 Tim 4:14-16). When people act with such honesty and responsibility, there will be no pride on one hand or jealousy on the other. Instead, through the care of the members one for another, the church will be built up (1 Cor 12:14-30; see GIFTS OF THE SPIRIT).

Right attitudes and conduct

Another picture of the church is that of a building (1 Cor 3:9-10); specifically, a temple in which God dwells (1 Peter 2:5). Apostles and prophets form the foundation, other believers form the main building, and all is built around and built into Christ. This emphasizes again the cooperation and harmony that there should be among all within the church (Eph 2:20-22). It also emphasizes that the church must be holy, for it is God's dwelling place (1 Cor 3:16-17; 2 Cor 6:16-17).

Since God's church is holy, it must deal with those who are guilty of serious errors in wrong teaching or wrong behaviour (1 Cor 5:1,2; 6:1-5; Titus 1:10-13; 3:10). Wrongdoers must at least be warned or rebuked (2 Thess 3:14-15; 1 Tim 1:3-7; 5:19-20), both for their own benefit and for the benefit of others in the church who may be affected by their wrongdoing (1 Cor 5:6-7; 2 Tim 2:14-18; Heb 12:15; 3 John 9-10). Whatever action the church takes against wrongdoers should be with a view to restoring them to healthy spiritual life. It should not drive them further away from God and his people (2 Cor 2:5-11; Gal 6:1).

Some, however, may be so hardened in their sinful ways that they refuse to acknowledge their wrongdoing, and the church may have to expel them from its fellowship. Yet there is still the hope that because of such severe punishment, the wrong-doers may see the seriousness of their errors and turn from them (Matt 18:15-17; 1 Cor 5:1-5,11-13; 1 Tim 1:19-20).

The imperfections in the church can at times discourage people from full involvement in the church's life. Some may even be tempted to try to live as Christians while keeping themselves apart from the church. But a person cannot reject the church and still live the Christian life properly. The church is not a club that a few like-minded people have formed, but a community that God himself has formed (Matt 16:18; Eph 3:9-11; Col 3:15). It is the body of Christ, and all Christians are part of it. They must therefore learn to function as part of the body if they are to function properly as Christians. Participation in the life of the church is necessary for Christian growth and maturity (Eph 4:12-13).

CILICIA

In New Testament times, the Roman administration governed the province of Cilicia from the neighbouring province of Syria. People often spoke of Syria and Cilicia as one combined region (Acts 15:23,41; Gal 1:21). The main Roman road from Syria to Asia Minor passed through Cilicia, and Paul travelled this road when setting out on his second and third missionary journeys (Acts 15:41; 18:22-23; for map see PAUL).

Much of Cilicia was mountainous and a home for robbers. It was no doubt one of the places Paul had in mind when he spoke of the dangers he frequently faced from robbers (2 Cor 11:26). His home town of Tarsus was the chief city of Cilicia (Acts 21:39).

CIRCUMCISION

Circumcision was a minor surgical operation carried out on baby boys to remove the foreskin from the penis. It was practised among various ancient Near Eastern peoples and had certain health benefits, but for the Israelites it had, in addition, a special religious significance.

Meaning of circumcision

The first person God commanded to be circumcised was Abraham. God had made a covenant with Abraham to be his God, to give him a multitude of descendants who would be his special people, and to give those people Canaan as their homeland. Circumcision was the sign of that covenant (Gen 17:1-11; see COVENANT).

As a permanent mark in the body, circumcision symbolized the permanency of God's covenant with his people. Because of its significance for personal cleanliness, it symbolized also the purity that the covenant demanded of them. God required that Abraham, his household, and all his descendants throughout future generations be circumcised if they were to be his people according to the covenant (Gen 17:9-13; Acts 7:8).

Abraham believed God's promises and acted upon his commands. His circumcision sealed his faith and demonstrated his obedience (Rom 4:11). The covenant had originated in God's grace, but the Israelites had to respond with faithful obedience if they were to enjoy the covenant's blessing. If a man was not circumcised, he and his household were cut off from the covenant (Gen 17:14).

Circumcision was usually carried out when the child was eight days old (Gen 17:12; Lev 12:3; Luke 1:59; 2:21; Phil 3:5). But during Israel's years in the wilderness between Egypt and Canaan, the people failed to circumcise their new-born children. They neglected the first requirement of the covenant. Therefore, before they could take possession of the land promised to them in the covenant, they had to circumcise all who had been born during the previous forty years (Josh 5:2-9).

Jewish misunderstandings

If circumcision was a sign of cleanness, uncircumcision was a sign of uncleanness (Exod 6:12; Lev

26:41; Isa 52:1). Israelites prided themselves that, because they were circumcised, they were God's people. They called themselves 'the circumcised' (or 'the circumcision'; Gal 2:7-8; Eph 2:11; Col 4:11), and despised the Gentiles as 'the uncircumcised' (1 Sam 14:6; 17:26; 31:4; Eph 2:11).

In their self-satisfaction the Jews forgot that circumcision was also intended to be a sign of obedience (Gen 17:10). Therefore, the circumcised Jew who was disobedient to God was no better in God's sight than the uncircumcised Gentile. Though physically circumcised, spiritually he was uncircumcised, that is, unclean in God's sight (Jer 9:25-26; Acts 7:51; Rom 2:25; cf. Deut 10:16; 30:6). In fact, the uncircumcised person who obeyed God was more acceptable to God than the circumcised person who disobeyed him (Rom 2:26-27).

The Jews believed also that the only people who were God's people were those who kept the law of Moses. Since the law commanded circumcision, they believed that a person had to be circumcised to be saved (Lev 12:3; John 7:23; Acts 15:1,5; 21:21; see LAW).

But circumcision had never been a requirement for salvation. The law of Moses set out regulations for those who had already become God's people as a result of the covenant he had made with Abraham. The law was not a means of salvation, and neither was circumcision. Abraham was saved by faith, and that occurred before the law was given and at a time when he was still uncircumcised. He received circumcision later, as an outward sign of the inward faith that he already had (Rom 4:1-2,10-11; Gal 3:17-18).

Abraham may be the physical father of the Jews, but more importantly he is the spiritual father of all who are saved by faith, whether or not they are Jews and whether or not they are circumcised (Rom 4:11-12). The true Jews, the true people of God, are not those who have received circumcision, but those who have received inward cleansing from sin (Rom 2:28-29; Gal 6:15).

No longer necessary

Circumcision was a sign of God's covenant with Abraham, and that covenant reached its fulfilment in Jesus Christ. Through him, the one descendant of Abraham to whom all the promises pointed, people of all nations can receive the blessings of God's salvation (Gen 12:1-3; Luke 1:54-55,72-73; Rom 4:16-17; Gal 3:6-9,16,29). Now that Christ has come, the legal requirements of the former covenant no longer apply (Eph 2:15; Col 2:14-15). More than that, if a person tries to win God's favour by keeping those legal requirements, he cannot be saved (Gal 5:2-4). A person can be saved only through faith in Christ, and it makes no difference whether he is circumcised or uncircumcised (Rom 3:30; 1 Cor 7:19; Gal 5:6).

For the Christian, 'circumcision' is spiritual, not physical. It is the cleansing from sin and uncleanness that comes through Jesus Christ (Col 2:11-12). Those so cleansed are the true people of God, the true 'circumcision' (Phil 3:3; cf. Rom 2:28-29).

CITY

In the language of the Bible any organized human settlement may be called a city. This applies whether the settlement was large or small (Gen 4:17; 13:12; Deut 21:3; Jonah 1:2).

Larger cities were walled, with a central fortress to provide the citizens with defence against attack (Num 13:28; Josh 6:5; Judg 9:51; 2 Sam 5:7; 1 Kings 4:13; 2 Kings 14:13). During an attack, people living in the farming villages around the city took refuge inside the city walls (Num 35:2; Josh 17:11; 1 Sam 6:18). In some cases farmers had their fields outside

Gate of an Eastern city

the city and their homes inside. They worked in the fields during the day, but returned to the city before nightfall, when the gates were shut (Josh 2:5; Judg 9:43-44; see also WAR).

Immediately inside the main gate of the city was an open area where people sat, talked, sold goods and conducted business. It was also the place where the elders of the city sat to decide cases brought before them for legal judgment. This open area was popularly called the 'gate' of the city (Gen 19:1;

Deut 21:19; Ruth 4:1-2; 2 Kings 7:1). As commerce grew in Israel, city life became more and more characterized by greed and injustice, the chief offenders being ruthless merchants and corrupt officials. The gate of the city, instead of being a place to find justice and contentment, became a centre of bribery and oppression (Isa 29:20-21; Amos 5:10-15; 8:4-6).

Godly people saw the wickedness of city life as symbolic of the wickedness of man in general. To them the world was like one great evil city (Rev 11:8). They pictured human society, organized in arrogant defiance of God, as the great city Babylon, doomed to be destroyed (Rev 18:2-24; cf. Dan 4:30; see BABYLON).

By contrast, the eternal city where God will dwell with his people is called new Jerusalem, a city from which all forms of evil are excluded (Rev 21:2-4,22-27; see JERUSALEM). The Bible considers that Christians are already citizens of this heavenly city. In the present world they are considered to be temporary residents, whose real citizenship is in the 'Jerusalem which is above' (Gal 4:26; Phil 3:20; Heb 11:13-16; 12:22; 13:14; 1 Peter 2:11).

CITY OF REFUGE

Scattered throughout the tribes of Israel were forty-eight cities given to the Levites. Among these were six cities known as cities of refuge (Num 35:6-7).

A city of refuge was a place where a person who had killed another could flee for safety till the

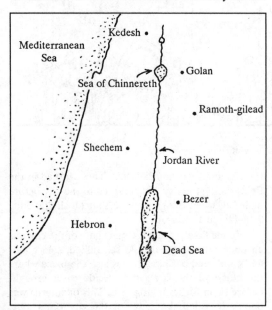

judges decided whether the death was intentional or accidental. If they found the person guilty of murder, he had to be executed. If they found he had caused the death accidentally, he could remain living in the city of refuge. This may have limited his freedom, but at least it gave him official protection. In the city of refuge he was safe from any revenge from the family of the dead person (Exod 21:12-14; Num 35:9-14; Josh 20:2-6).

There were three cities of refuge in Israel's territory west of Jordan (Kedesh, Shechem and Hebron), and three in its territory east of Jordan (Golan, Ramoth-gilead and Bezer). On each side of Jordan there was one city in the northern section, one in the central and one in the southern (Num 35:14-15; Josh 20:7-9). All six cities had clearly marked roads leading to them so that the refugee could reach safety quickly (Deut 19:2-6).

CLEANSING

See ATONEMENT; FORGIVENESS; UNCLEANNESS.

COINS

In the days before people used money in buying and selling, they usually paid for goods by exchanging other goods, such as farm produce, animals or jewellery. Later they found it more convenient to use precious metals, particularly silver, which they usually measured by weight.

Among the Israelites, the common unit of silver was the shekel, which was about sixteen grams (Gen 23:16; Lev 5:15; 1 Kings 10:29; Jer 32:9). Larger amounts were measured by the talent, which was about fifty kilograms (1 Kings 9:14; 16:24; 20:39). Merchants were sometimes dishonest and used extra heavy weights when weighing the buyer's money (Lev 19:36; Prov 11:1; Amos 8:5; Micah 6:11; see WEIGHTS).

When coin money came into use, the practice of weighing money gradually died out (Ezra 2:69; 8:27). Some of the old names for weights now became names for coins (e.g. see SHEKEL). Coins were of gold, silver or copper, depending on their value (Matt 10:9).

Money of various types was in use in Palestine during the New Testament era. There was official Roman money, local Jewish money, and old Greek money from the days of the former Greek Empire. The Jewish temple authorities accepted only certain types of money, which resulted in the practice of money-changers setting up business in the temple (Matt 21:12).

It is not possible to give accurate present-day equivalents of the values of ancient coins, but New Testament references give an indication of the values of some coins in the first century. For example, the coin mentioned in Jesus' story of the hired vineyard-workers, the Roman denarius,

Jewish shekel

Roman denarius

represented the wages of a labourer for one day (Matt 20:2). The denarius is mentioned also in Matt 22:19, Luke 10:35 and Rev 6:6. It was the approximate equivalent of the Greek drachma (mentioned in Luke 15:8). The smallest coin in use was the Jewish lepton (referred to in the story of the poor widow; Mark 12:41-44), and more than a hundred of these were needed to equal one denarius.

The Greek stater (referred to in Matt 17:27) was the approximate equal of the Jewish shekel, which paid the temple tax for two people (Exod 30:13; Matt 17:24-27). Originally the stater was a two-drachma coin, but when this coin went out of use, the name stater was given to the four-drachma coin.

One hundred drachmas (or a hundred denarii) was equal to one mina, the gold coin that the nobleman in Jesus' parable entrusted to each of his ten servants (Luke 19:13). Sixty minas equalled one talent. The talent was not a coin, but a unit used in counting large amounts of money. It is referred to in two other parables of Jesus (Matt 18:24; 25:15; see TALENT).

COLOSSAE

Although Colossae was on the main highway from Syria to Ephesus, Paul apparently did not visit the church there during his missionary travels recorded in Acts (Col 1:4; 2:1). Colossae was situated in a part of the province of Asia where Paul was forbidden to preach during his second missionary journey (Acts 16:6-8; for map see ASIA).

The church in Colossae was probably founded during Paul's stay in Ephesus on his third missionary journey, when the Ephesian converts took the gospel to the towns of the surrounding countryside (Acts 19:8-10). Epaphras appears to have been the person chiefly responsible for the establishment of the church in Colossae (Col 1:7). At the time Paul wrote his letter to the Colossian church, it met in the home of Philemon (Col 4:9; Philem 1-2,10-12; see COLOSSIANS, LETTER TO THE).

COLOSSIANS, LETTER TO THE

Paul was a prisoner at the time he wrote his letter to the Colossians (Col 4:3). Having appealed to the Emperor because of the injustice he met in Palestine, Paul came to Rome, accompanied by Luke and Aristarchus. He was held prisoner in Rome for two years, while he awaited the outcome of his appeal (Acts 25:10-12; 27:1-2; 28:16,30; Col 4:3,10,14).

While in Rome, Paul was visited by Epaphras, the man who had most likely founded the church in Colossae (Col 1:6-7; 4:12). (For details of Colossae and the origins of the church there see COLOSSAE.) Epaphras wanted Paul's help, as an unusual type of false teaching had appeared in Colossae. Paul wrote his letter to the Colossians mainly to deal with this false teaching.

The false teaching in Colossae

This teaching was an early form of Gnosticism, a type of religious philosophy that combined Christian belief with pagan mythology. In Colossae it had certain features taken from Judaism, mainly in relation to religious ceremonies. Gnostic religions had great interest in things mysterious or ritualistic (Col 2:16,20-21).

One of the chief concerns of the false teachers was with things they considered to be in conflict, such as good and evil, spirit and matter, God and man. Believing matter to be evil, they claimed that a God who is holy could not come in contact with man who is sinful. This meant, in their view, that Jesus Christ could not be both God and man.

The false teachers therefore taught that there were countless intermediate beings, part-spirit and part-matter, who bridged the gap between God and man. Those closer to God were more Godlike, those closer to man less Godlike, but together they controlled the material universe. A person had to worship them and win their favour if he wanted protection against the evil forces at work in the world (Col 2:8,18).

According to this teaching, Jesus Christ was one of these part-divine beings. Paul saw that if this was so, Christ's death was no longer able to cleanse man's sin and bring man to God; Christ was no longer the one mediator between God and man. Paul asserted that Christ is God, and he is over and above every being in the spirit world and the material world (Col 1:15-19; 2:9). Indeed, he is the creator of all things, the Saviour of mankind and the conqueror of the powers of evil (Col 1:20-22; 2:15). Through him, God has become man and is as inseparably united with his redeemed people as the head is with the body (Col 1:18; 2:19).

This union between Christ and his people has an important practical significance for the believer. It means that he too has victory over evil, and as a result is able to produce Christlike qualities in his life (Col 3:3-5,10).

Contents of the letter

Paul opens with a thanksgiving for the Colossians' faith and a prayer that their Christian growth may continue (1:1-14). He then announces the theme of his message, which is the greatness of Christ and his work. The foundational truths of Christianity centre on him and cannot be changed to suit human philosophies (1:15-23). These are truths that Paul teaches everywhere, and he wants all believers to stand firm in them (1:24-2:5).

Since false teaching leads people into bondage, Paul wants the Colossians to hold firmly to the truth of the gospel and so enjoy their freedom in Christ (2:6-15). They are not to submit to man-made religious systems, for their new life is bound up with Christ and with him alone (2:16-3:4). They should give expression to this new life by getting rid of old habits and developing qualities of character that are Christlike (3:5-17), whether in private life, in the home, or in society at large (3:18-4:6).

Paul keeps personal details till the end. He talks about various people, of whom some are with him, some about to visit Colossae, and some resident in and around Colossae (4:7-18).

COMFORT

See ENCOURAGEMENT.

COMMUNION

In simple terms, 'communion' means a sharing together in something that people hold in common. In present-day language, 'fellowship' is the word usually used to indicate communion (Acts 2:42; for further discussion see FELLOWSHIP).

The particular act of fellowship with Christ where Christians share together in a token or symbolic 'meal' of bread and wine is commonly called Holy Communion, or the Lord's Supper (1 Cor 10:16-17). (For further discussion see LORD'S SUPPER.)

COMPASSION

See MERCY.

CONCUBINE

Israelites of the Old Testament era lived in a world where it was common for a married man to take additional wives, known as concubines. The practice was contrary to God's plan for marriage (namely, one man and one woman united for life, to the exclusion of all others; see MARRIAGE), but human society had moved far away from God's plan (Rom 1:20-32).

Moses introduced laws to protect concubines for much the same reason as he introduced laws to protect slaves. Both slavery and concubinage were wrong, but the practices were so deeply rooted that they could not be removed immediately. However, laws could control them and so start a movement that would lead to their eventual removal (Exod 21:7-11; Deut 21:15-17; see also SLAVERY).

A man obtained his concubines sometimes by choosing them from among his slaves or war captives, and sometimes by receiving them as gifts. Through bearing him children, concubines helped strengthen his household and increase his social influence (Gen 16:1-2; 25:1; 29:24,29; 30:4-13; 36:12; Deut 21:10-11; 2 Sam 5:13-14; 2 Chron 11:21). Although Israelite law tolerated concubinage, it did not tolerate sexual relations with a person who was not one's marriage partner. To commit adultery with another man's wife was a far worse sin than to have several wives oneself (Lev 20:10; 2 Sam 11:2-5; 12:11-12).

God warned Israelite kings against glorifying themselves through building large harems, but most kings ignored his warnings (Deut 17:15-17; 2 Sam 15:16; 1 Kings 11:3; 2 Chron 11:21; cf. Esther 2:14). People considered the harem to be such a symbol of kingly power, that a new king established his claim to the throne by claiming the former king's harem (2 Sam 3:7-8; 12:7-8; 16:20-22; 1 Kings 2:21-22). Yet concubines proved to be a source of trouble to Israel's kings. The presence of so many wives and children in the palace created family conflicts (2 Sam 3:2-5; 13:20-22; cf. Gen 21:8-10; Judg 8:31; 9:2-5), and the idols that foreign concubines brought into the palace led believers away from God (1 Kings 11:4).

CONFESSION

In many languages, including the languages of the Bible, 'confession' is a word with a range of meanings. In the Bible's usage of the word, these meanings fall into two groups, those concerned with confession of sins, and those concerned with confession of faith.

Confession of sins

God is willing to forgive people's sins, but he requires on their part repentance and faith; that is, he requires that they see their sin as rebellion against God, that they confess it to God as deserving his punishment, that they turn from it decisively, and that they trust in God's mercy to forgive them (Ezra 10:10-11; Ps 32:5; 51:3-4; Matt 3:6; 6:12; Luke 18:13; 1 John 1:5-10).

There is no suggestion that sin causes the believer to lose his salvation and that confession is necessary to win it back. When a person turns to Christ for salvation, God declares him righteous and free from the penalty of sin, on the basis of what Christ has done. Failures will spoil a person's fellowship with God and he will need to confess them, but if his faith is truly in what Christ has done for him, his salvation is secure (1 John 1:6-9; 2:1-2). (For fuller details see JUSTIFICATION, sub-heading 'Justification and forgiveness'.)

If the person's sin has been against another person, he must also confess his sin to that person and put right any wrong he may have done (Num 5:6-8; Matt 5:23-24; James 5:16). Such confession is usually a private matter, but there may be cases where the person needs to make a public confession (Acts 19:18). Confession of sin is a necessary part of prayer, and a lack of confession could be one reason why prayers are not answered (1 Kings 8:33-36; Ezra 9:6-7; Neh 1:4-11; Ps 66:18; Dan 9:4-9; Matt 6:12; Luke 18:13). (See also FORGIVENESS.)

Confession of faith

If confession of sin is, in a sense, negative (admitting oneself to be a wrongdoer), confession of faith is, by contrast, positive (declaring oneself to be a believer in and follower of God). The confession of faith that Christians make is an open acknowledgment of their belief in Jesus Christ as the Son of God, the Messiah, the chosen one of God who died on the cross and rose victoriously to be crowned Lord of all (Matt 16:16; John 1:49; Rom 10:9; 1 Tim 6:12; 1 John 4:2,15).

Jesus made such a confession in relation to himself and suffered persecution as a result (Mark 14:60-62; John 18:33-37; 1 Tim 6:13). When his followers make a similar confession, they too may be persecuted (Matt 10:32-33; John 9:22; 12:42). Those who by their confession of faith identify themselves with Christ will be rewarded by God, but those who deny Christ will suffer God's judgment (Matt 10:32-33; 2 Tim 2:11-13; 1 John 2:22-23). One day all mankind will confess Jesus Christ as Lord, to the glory of God (Phil 2:11).

CONSCIENCE

There is within the human mind something that acts as a moral judge. It tells people what is right and wrong, urges them to do right, and gives them feelings of either innocence or guilt, depending on whether they obey or disobey it. This moral judge we call conscience (Rom 2:15-16; 1 John 3:19-21).

Although the Old Testament does not mention the word 'conscience', it certainly refers to the activity of conscience (Gen 3:7-8; 2 Sam 24:10; Job 27:6; Ps 32:3; 51:3-4). Conscience is not a perfect judge, because sin has affected the conscience as it has affected every other part of human nature (Luke 11:35; Eph 2:1-3). Therefore the conscience, like the rest of human nature, needs cleansing from the effects of sin, and this can come about only through the sacrificial death of Jesus Christ (Heb 9:14; 10:22).

The conscience also needs instruction, because it can only make judgments according to the knowledge it possesses (Rom 2:14-15; 1 Cor 8:7,10). The Christian must therefore train and discipline his conscience so that it is well instructed, pure, active and sensitive (Acts 24:16; Eph 4:17,23; 1 Tim 1:5,19; 2 Tim 1:3). A person may so ignore his conscience that it becomes defiled, hardened or dead (1 Tim 4:2; Titus 1:15).

A properly developed conscience will lead a person to do what is right, whether a written law demands it or not (Rom 13:5; 1 Peter 3:16). The Christian must be careful to have a clear conscience in all that he does (2 Cor 1:12; Heb 13:18). At the same time he must realize that a clear conscience does not necessarily mean that he is faultless (1 Cor 4:4-5). Sometimes his conscience may be clear in relation to something he would like to do, but he may decide not to do it because of the bad effect it could have on someone else (Rom 14:22-23; 1 Cor

10:28-29). His conscience must be clear before God, not just clear according to standards he sets for himself (Acts 23:1; Rom 9:1).

CONSECRATION

Consecration means setting apart people or things from the common affairs of life and dedicating them to God. In the religion of Old Testament Israel, these 'set apart' people or things were called 'holy', and the act of declaring, acknowledging or making them holy was called sanctification, consecration, or dedication (Exod 13:2; 29:1,27,36). (For details of this basic meaning of consecration see HOLINESS; SANCTIFICATION.)

The idea of consecration is common also in the New Testament. Though the word itself is not always used, the meaning is consistent with that of the Old Testament. Priests and the sacrifices they offered were consecrated to God (Exod 28:38,40-41), and Jesus seems to have been referring to priestly service when he spoke of himself as being consecrated to God (John 17:19). He set himself apart to do his Father's will, and this meant dying for sin (John 12:27; 17:4). Being the believer's great high priest, he offered himself as the perfect sacrifice (Heb 10:11-14; see PRIEST).

Jesus' priestly work not only brings forgiveness to believers, but it also sets them apart for God (John 17:19). This involves more than the salvation of believers; it involves the practical offering of themselves to God as living sacrifices (Acts 20:24; Rom 12:1).

Although selected people may be consecrated in the particular sense of being set apart for certain tasks (Jer 1:5; Gal 1:15-16), all Christians should be consecrated in the sense of being fully devoted to God. Christ has bought them at the price of his blood and they belong to him. They are disciples of their Lord and servants of their Master, and their commitment to him must be total (Matt 10:37-39; 1 Cor 7:23; 2 Cor 10:5; Col 3:23-24; see DISCIPLE; SERVANT).

CONVERSION

Although the the word 'conversion' may be rare in the Bible, the idea is common enough. A person is converted when he turns from darkness to light, from Satan to God, from dead idols to the living Christ (Acts 15:3; 26:18; 1 Thess 1:9-10; cf. Matt 13:15; 2 Cor 3:16). His changed life is the outward demonstration of that inward turning which the Bible more commonly calls repentance (Acts 3:19;

Acts 26:20; see REPENTANCE). Through repentance, the believing sinner receives the salvation of God. He is born anew; he is a new person (2 Cor 5:17; see REGENERATION; SALVATION).

CORBAN

See Vow.

CORINTH

The city of Corinth was a prosperous manufacturing and trading centre in Achaia, the southern province of Greece (see map page 7). An overland route went north from Corinth to Macedonia, and sea routes went east, west and south. The city was so well known for its immorality and vice that people of the time commonly referred to a person of loose morals as one who 'behaved like a Corinthian' (cf. 1 Cor 6:9-11,15-18).

Paul's first visit to Corinth was on his second missionary journey. He stayed eighteen months, and during that time he founded the Corinthian church (Acts 18:1-17). Another church was established at Cenchreae, the seaport a few kilometres east (Acts 18:18; Rom 16:1-2). Paul revisited the church at Corinth during his third missionary journey (Acts 20:2-3). He also wrote the church a number of letters, two of which have been preserved in the New Testament. (For the added information these letters give concerning life in Corinth see CORINTHIANS, LETTERS TO THE).

CORINTHIANS, LETTERS TO THE

Corinth was an important port in the Roman province of Achaia in the south of Greece. It was a lively commercial centre, and was well known for its colourful lifestyle and low moral standards (see CORINTH). Paul stayed in Corinth for eighteen months during his second missionary journey and established a church there (Acts 18:1-21). Since many of the people who made up the church came from a background of vice and immorality (cf. 1 Cor 1:26-27; 6:9-11), it is not surprising that problems arose in the church.

Background to 1 Corinthians

After leaving Corinth, Paul heard that some of the Christians had moral difficulties, so he wrote them a letter to pass on helpful advice. The letter has not been preserved (1 Cor 5:9). Paul saw problems arising in the Corinthian church and sent Timothy to Corinth in an effort to deal with them. Paul at this time was in Ephesus, and Timothy travelled to

Corinth by way of Macedonia (Acts 19:1,22; 1 Cor 4:17; 16:10).

Meanwhile some Corinthian believers visited Paul in Ephesus. They told him that factions had developed in the Corinthian church, because people had foolishly made favourites of different teachers (1 Cor 1:10-13). Paul heard also that there was immorality in the church (1 Cor 5:1) and that there

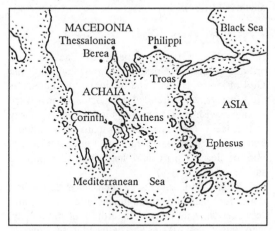

were disputes between Christians in the public law courts (1 Cor 6:1). Not long after this, a group of representatives from the Corinthian church arrived in Ephesus with questions about other problems (1 Cor 7:1; 16:17).

With all these matters before him, Paul decided to write at length to the Corinthian church. The letter is known to us as First Corinthians. Paul probably sent it to Corinth direct by boat, for he expected it to get there before Timothy (1 Cor 16:8-10).

Contents of 1 Corinthians

After his introduction (1:1-9), Paul deals with the immature and worldly attitudes that the Christians had shown through their quarrelling. The divisions were not because Paul had done anything wrong (1:10-17), but because the Corinthians had placed too much emphasis on human wisdom (1:18-31).

Paul then shows the difference between worldly wisdom and spiritual wisdom (2:1-16), and rebukes the Corinthians for their lack of spiritual growth (3:1-9). He warns that whether people help build up the church or help destroy it, they are accountable to God for their actions (3:10-23). Therefore, they should make sure that they have the right attitude towards God's servants (4:1-21).

Additional rebukes follow when Paul deals with the moral faults in the church: first a case of sexual immorality (5:1-13), then the matter of legal disputes

between members of the same church (6:1-11). He gives a specific warning against the temptations of prostitution in Corinth (6:12-20).

In answering the questions raised by the representatives from Corinth, Paul begins by dealing with difficulties in marriage relationships (7:1-16) and problems faced by the unmarried and widows (7:17-40). Concerning food offered to idols, Paul urges the Christians not to misuse their freedom (8:1-13). Whatever their rights, they should follow his example and deny themselves their rights for the sake of others (9:1-27). They should remember some of Israel's disastrous experiences with idolatry (10:1-13), and realize that idol feasts are a form of idol fellowship (10:14-22). Christians must consider what effect their behaviour will have on their fellow believers (10:23-11:1).

Concerning public worship, Paul talks about the orderliness that is required when people pray or prophesy (11:2-16) and when they eat the Lord's Supper together (11:17-34). He speaks of the variety of spiritual gifts in the church (12:1-31), emphasizing that Christians must exercise such gifts in love (13:1-13). In particular he deals with the gift of tongues, because some in Corinth were misusing it (14:1-40).

Another misunderstanding in the Corinthian church concerned the resurrection of believers at the return of Christ. Paul points to Christ's resurrection as the guarantee of the resurrection of all who are united with him (15:1-28). Whatever the nature of the resurrection body, it will be patterned on Christ's and suited to life in the eternal kingdom (15:29-58). Having reached this triumphant climax, Paul concludes his letter with a few final instructions and personal notes (16:1-24).

Background to 2 Corinthians

Paul planned to visit Corinth after finishing his work in Ephesus (Acts 19:21; 1 Cor 16:5-9). (Altogether Paul was in Ephesus three years; Acts 20:31.) When Timothy returned to Ephesus from Corinth, the news he brought was bad. Neither Paul's letter nor Timothy's visit had solved the problems. In fact, the situation had become worse, with the result that Paul made a quick trip to Corinth (as he had warned; 1 Cor 4:19-21) in an effort to deal with the rebels. There was a lot of opposition to Paul in Corinth, and the trip was very painful for him (2 Cor 2:1). This was only Paul's second visit to Corinth, and is the trip he refers to in 2 Cor 13:1-2 when he was about to visit the city a third time.

Upon returning to Ephesus, Paul heard that his visit, instead of helping to improve matters, had only made his opponents more rebellious. Rather than rush back in anger and perhaps later be sorry for his rashness, he wrote a letter. It was a very severe letter and was taken to Corinth by Titus. Though referred to in Paul's writings, the letter has not been preserved (2 Cor 2:3-4; 7:8; 12:18).

Having finished his work in Ephesus, Paul planned to go north to Troas and Macedonia, and then go on to Corinth. Titus was to return from Corinth via Macedonia and meet Paul in Troas, but Paul was so anxious to get news of the Corinthians' response to his severe letter, that he went across to Macedonia to meet Titus sooner (2 Cor 2:12-13; cf. Acts 20:1). The news Titus brought was good. The severe letter had brought the desired results and the Corinthians had at last submitted (2 Cor 7:5-6). With much relief, Paul wrote again to the church in Corinth, sending off with Titus the letter that we know as Second Corinthians (2 Cor 8:16-18).

Contents of 2 Corinthians

Paul begins the letter by encouraging the Christians in their various trials (1:1-11) and by explaining why he had made the painful visit and written the severe letter (1:12-2:4). Though the church had dealt with the person who had stirred up the rebellion, Paul wants them to be forgiving now that the man has repented (2:5-11).

As he praises God for the triumphant end to the recent troubles (2:12-17), Paul is reminded of the glorious liberty of the Christian gospel (3:1-18). He emphasizes the sincerity and confidence of the true servant of Christ (4:1-18), particularly in view of the glorious future Christians can look forward to in the afterlife (5:1-10). Yet Christians have an obligation in the present life to make the message of Christ known to others (5:11-21), no matter what opposition they meet (6:1-13).

Paul then speaks again of matters discussed in previous correspondence. He warns of some of the dangers in ungodly society (6:14-7:1), and expresses his joy at the Corinthians' response to his severe letter (7:2-16). He writes at some length about the collection of money to be sent to the poor in Jerusalem; for the Corinthians, in spite of making a good start the previous year, had now become lazy (8:1-15). He discusses arrangements for the collection (8:16-9:5) and speaks of the blessing of Christian giving (9:6-15).

The final section of the letter deals with Paul's status as an apostle; for the Corinthians were still troubled by travelling preachers who claimed that they were apostles but Paul was not. Paul contrasts

spiritual power with worldly boasting (10:1-18), and asserts that he is not inferior to others (11:1-15). He records his experiences as an apostle (11:16-33), especially one experience that was a genuine cause for boasting (12:1-10). In view of his plan to visit Corinth again soon (12:11-21), he urges all in the church to examine themselves so that he might not have to use his apostolic authority to discipline anyone (13:1-14).

CORNELIUS

In the Roman regiment based in Caesarea was an officer named Cornelius who worshipped the God of Israel. He was one of the people known as God-fearers, who attended synagogue services, kept certain Jewish laws, prayed to God and gave money to the needy. God saw that Cornelius was seeking a better understanding of him, so sent Peter to tell him of Jesus Christ and lead him to complete salvation (Acts 10:1-8).

Peter told Cornelius of what Jesus Christ had done for mankind through his life, death and resurrection. Any person, regardless of nationality, who repented of his sins and believed in Jesus would receive forgiveness (Acts 10:34-43). Not only did Cornelius and his friends believe, but they received the Holy Spirit as Jewish believers had previously (Acts 10:44-48; cf. 2:1-4). This was a significant event in the life of the early church, since it showed that God accepted Gentiles as he accepted Jews and gave his blessings to both without distinction (Acts 11:16-18).

CORNERSTONE

In ancient building practices, cornerstones were very important. The builders who laid the foundation had to shape and set the cornerstone of the foundation accurately, because the whole building was set out in relation to it. The building depended upon the cornerstone for its successful construction (Job 38:6; Isa 28:16; Jer 51:26).

As the builders moved on to the construction of the walls, they used additional cornerstones to tie the main walls together, thereby bringing stability to the whole structure. The placing of the chief cornerstone was always a satisfying achievement, because this was the stone that guaranteed the perfection of the whole building.

The cornerstone therefore provided a useful illustration of triumph and achievement. On one occasion when an Israelite king was on the edge of a humiliating defeat, he was likened to a useless stone that the builders had thrown away; but when he triumphed, he was likened to a stone that they had brought back and made the chief cornerstone (Ps 118:21-24).

In rejecting Jesus, the Jews were likened to builders who rejected the best stone of all. And just as a stone lying in the builders' path can be an obstacle to them, so Jesus was an obstacle to the Jews. As long as they would not believe in him, they could not be saved. They were like builders trying to complete the building without using the main stone. God then took the rejected stone (Jesus) and made him the chief cornerstone in the new house of God, the church. Christ is exalted to the highest place, and the whole church, which consists of 'living stones', is built around and built into him (Matt 21:42-43; Acts 4:11; Eph 2:19-20; 1 Peter 2:4-8). (See also STUMBLING BLOCK.)

COUNCIL

See SANHEDRIN.

COURAGE

One characteristic of the person who has a strong faith in God is courage in the midst of danger. There are, however, different kinds of dangers and different kinds of courage.

Courage may be obvious where a person is brave or heroic in circumstances of physical danger on every side, such as in war or natural disasters (1 Sam 14:6-15; 2 Sam 23:13-19; Acts 27:24-26; 2 Cor 12:25-26). It is obvious also in cases where, by speaking or acting in a certain way, a person knowingly faces consequences where there is a clear possibility of physical suffering (Num 13:30-32; Dan 3:16-18; Mark 6:17-18; John 2:13-17; Acts 4:13; 5:27-30). But greater courage may be necessary in cases where there is no immediate physical danger, but other pressures make it difficult to stand for what is right against a majority who want to do wrong (Prov 28:1; Luke 14:1-6; John 7:50-52; cf. Luke 22:54-62; Gal 2:11-14; see FEAR).

The believer's courage comes through his faith in God (Deut 3:22; 1 Sam 17:45-46; Ps 56:3-4; 1 Cor 16:13) and is maintained through prayer (Ps 27:14; Acts 4:29; Eph 6:18-19). But it still involves effort, since it requires a person to set out deliberately to do what he knows is going to be dangerous (Mark 15:43). Such courage is an example to others, urging them to greater confidence and increased boldness (Phil 1:12-14). Like the biblical expression 'Be of good courage', it is a way of giving encouragement to those who need it (Josh 1:6-7,9; 2 Sam 10:12; see ENCOURAGEMENT).

COVENANT

A covenant was an agreement between two parties that laid down conditions and guaranteed benefits, depending upon a person's keeping or breaking the covenant. It was sealed by some form of witness (Gen 21:22-32; 31:44-54; 1 Sam 18:3-4; Mal 2:14).

Covenants between God and man, however, differed from purely human covenants in that they were not agreements between equals. God was always the giver and man the receiver. Man could not negotiate an agreement with God or make demands upon him. God's promises originated in his sovereign grace alone, and man could do nothing but accept God's favours and directions.

Through one man to the world

From the time of the earliest recorded covenant (God's covenant with Noah, and with mankind through him), features of grace are prominent. The covenant originated in God's grace and depended upon God's grace for its fulfilment. The rainbow was the sign, or witness, that sealed the covenant (Gen 6:18; 9:8-17; see GRACE).

Having promised to preserve mankind (Gen 9:15-16), God revealed further that he had a plan of salvation for mankind. This plan again was based on a covenant that originated in God's grace. In his sovereign will God chose one man, Abraham, promising him a multitude of descendants who would become a nation, receive Canaan as their homeland, and be God's channel of blessing to the world (Gen 12:1-3; 15:18-21; 17:2-8; Acts 3:25).

God confirmed his promise to Abraham by a covenant ceremony. The ancient custom was for the two parties to kill an animal, cut it in halves, then pass between the two halves, calling down the fate of the slaughtered animals upon themselves should they break the covenant (Gen 15:9-11; Jer 34:18). But in Abraham's case, only God (symbolized by a smoking fire-pot and a flaming torch) passed between the halves of the animal. He alone made the covenant and guaranteed its fulfilment (Gen 15:17).

Yet Abraham had a responsibility to respond to God's grace, and his response would determine whether he would enjoy the covenant benefits. A truly spiritual relationship could exist only where man responded to God in faith and obedience. The rite of circumcision, which God gave as the sign and seal of the covenant, gave Abraham and his descendants the opportunity to demonstrate such faith and obedience. Those who responded to God's grace by being circumcised kept the covenant; those who did not were cut off from it. The covenant depended upon God, but only those who were obedient to God experienced the communion with God that was the covenant's central blessing (Gen 17:9-14; see CIRCUMCISION; OBEDIENCE.)

Developed through Israel

Once the nation promised to Abraham existed and was on the way to its promised homeland, God renewed the covenant made earlier with Abraham, this time applying it to the whole nation. Since Moses was the mediator through whom God worked in dealing with the people, the covenant is sometimes called the Mosaic covenant. It is also called the Sinaitic covenant, after Mt Sinai, where the ceremony took place.

God, in his sovereign grace, had saved the people of Israel from bondage in Egypt and taken them into a close relationship with himself. Grace was again the basis of God's covenant dealings (Exod 2:24; 3:16; 4:22; 6:6-8; 15:13; 19:4-6; 20:2). As in the covenant with Abraham, so in the covenant with his descendants, the central blessing was communion with God; for he was their God and they were his people (Gen 17:7; Exod 6:7; Lev 26:12). Again, the people would enjoy this blessing only as they were holy in life and obedient to God (Exod 19:5-6). The people understood this and agreed to be obedient to all God's commands. They were in no position to argue with God; they could do nothing but surrender completely to his will (Exod 24:7-8; see also LAW).

The two parties to the covenant were then bound together in a blood ritual. Half the blood was thrown against the altar (representing God) and half sprinkled on the people (Exod 24:3-8).

But this blood ritual was more than just a dramatic way of swearing loyalty to the covenant. The Passover had shown the people of Israel that blood symbolized life laid down to release those under condemnation of death (Exod 12:13). Blood was linked with release from the penalty of sin; therefore, the blood ritual at Sinai was an indication to Israel that it began its formal existence as God's covenant people in a condition of ceremonial purity (Heb 9:19-22; see BLOOD).

All this ceremonial procedure emphasized once more that the covenant with Israel, following the covenant with Abraham, was based on God's grace, not on man's effort (Gal 3:17-18). Nevertheless, the

people had to keep their part of the covenant if they were to enjoy its benefits (Exod 19:5; cf. Gen 17:9). God had no obligation to bless his people when they disobeyed his covenant commands, though in his mercy he was patient with them (Lev 26:27-33; Deut 4:25-31; 7:9-10; Neh 9:33; Heb 3:16-19).

Note on the form of the covenant

The covenant between God and Israel was of a kind that people of the time understood. It was similar in form to the common Near Eastern treaty by which a sovereign overlord made a covenant with his subject peoples.

Such a treaty was not a negotiated agreement. It was an authoritative document prepared by the overlord, declaring his sovereignty over his people and laying down the order of life he required of them. The features of these ancient documents are well illustrated in the book of Deuteronomy, which was written in the form of a covenant document. (For details see DEUTERONOMY. Concerning the illustration that likens the covenant between God and Israel to the marriage covenant see LOVE, sub-heading 'Steadfast love'.)

Towards a specific goal through David

After the promised nation had become established in the promised land, God revealed the next stage in directing his covenant purposes towards their ultimate goal. The promised offspring of Abraham through whom God would send his salvation to the world was Jesus the Messiah (Gen 12:3,7; Gal 3:16,29).

God prepared Israel to produce the Messiah by choosing from the nation one person, King David, and promising that his dynasty would be the channel through which the Messiah would come. God gave David this promise by means of a covenant that followed on from his earlier covenants, namely, those with Abraham and with the nation Israel (2 Sam 7:12-17; 23:5; Ps 89:3-4,28-37).

Jesus therefore was the true fulfilment of all God's covenant purposes. The Abrahamic covenant led to the Sinaitic covenant, which in turn led to the Davidic covenant, which led finally to Jesus Christ, the Saviour of the world (Luke 1:32-33,72-73; Acts 13:17-23).

The new covenant

Former covenants, then, were but a preparation for that saving work of God through Christ which the Bible calls the new covenant. Or, to put it another way, the new covenant fully develops the features consistently displayed in the former covenants.

Like the former covenants, the new covenant originates in the sovereign grace of God (Rom 3:24; 5:15-21; Eph 2:8-9; Titus 3:5). Through it God makes unworthy sinners his people and promises to be their God (Heb 8:8,10; 1 Peter 2:9-10). But if people are to enjoy that life-giving relationship with God which is the covenant's central blessing, they must respond to God's grace in faith and obedience (Gal 3:14; Heb 5:9; 1 Peter 1:2). Also, since faith involves perseverance, they must continue in the covenant (Col 1:23; cf. Heb 8:9; see PERSEVERANCE).

Yet there are great differences between the old and new covenants. All former covenants were imperfect — not in the sense of being wrong, but in the sense of being incomplete. They belonged to the era before Christ and therefore could not in themselves bring salvation. Only the atoning death of Christ can do that (see ATONEMENT). Therefore, until Christ came, there was always the need for a new covenant, one that carried with it better promises (Heb 8:6-9,13; 10:9-10).

The new covenant, in contrast to the old, is not concerned with a particular nation, nor is it concerned with any nation as a whole. Rather it is concerned with individuals, regardless of their nation. It does not demand obedience to a set of laws, but puts God's laws in people's hearts. It does not need priests to mediate between God and individuals, for all believers know God personally and have direct fellowship with him. There is no remembrance of sins through repetitive sacrifices, for all sins are at once removed and are gone for ever (Heb 8:10-12). (For further details of the contrast between the old and new covenants see HEBREWS, BOOK OF.)

Jesus Christ's atoning death is the basis of the new covenant. He is the mediator through whom God makes the covenant, and he is the sacrifice whose blood seals the covenant (1 Cor 11:25; Heb 9:15; 12:24). Through that same blood, sin is forgiven completely, so that God's people enter the covenant not with mere ceremonial cleansing, but with actual cleansing (Matt 26:28; cf. Heb 9:19-22). This is an eternal covenant, for there will never be another to follow it. Covenant grace is fully revealed, and the blessings that flow from it are eternal (Heb 10:16-18; 13:20).

COVET

The sin of covetousness covers a wide range of unlawful and self-centred desires. Selfish ambition, sexual lusts and common greed are all forms of covetousness (Deut 5:21; Ps 78:18; Prov 6:25; Matt 5:28; 1 Tim 6:9-10; James 4:2-3; 1 John 2:16). As the covetous person tries to get what he wants, his covetousness can produce all kinds of immoral and unlawful behaviour, such as stealing, oppression, deceit and violence (Exod 20:17; Josh 7:21; Micah 2:2; 1 Cor 5:9-11).

Among the Ten Commandments is one that forbids covetousness. This command differs from some of the others in that it deals with attitudes, whereas others deal with actions. Sins such as murder, adultery, stealing and lying are outward, but covetousness is inward. A person may not be guilty of sinful actions that are obvious to all, yet still be guilty of the hidden sin of covetousness (Matt 5:21-30).

Paul's realization of this in his own experience helped him see the incurable sinfulness of human nature (Rom 7:7-11; cf. Mark 7:22-23). He saw, in addition, that covetousness is a form of idolatry. A person's selfish desires may be so strong that the thing he covets takes the place of God in his life (Col 3:5; cf. Ps 10:3).

One reason why covetousness is so dangerous is that a good living, hard working, highly respected person can be guilty of it, yet not be aware of it. He may even mistake it for a virtue (Matt 19:16-22; Luke 12:15; see also WEALTH). God, however, puts it in the same group as some of the most horrible sins (Rom 1:29; 1 Cor 6:9-10; Eph 5:3).

The Christian can resist the temptation to covetousness through exercising sacrificial love. He will then be devoted to God rather than idolatrous, and generous to others rather than selfish (Matt 22:36-39; cf. 6:24,33; Eph 4:28; see also GIVING).

CRAFTSMAN

Among the craftsmen mentioned in the Bible are metal-workers (Exod 31:3-4; Isa 44:12; 54:16; Jer 10:9; 2 Tim 4:14), carpenters (2 Sam 5:11; Isa 44:13; Mark 6:3), wood-carvers (Exod 31:5; 1 Kings 6:32), stone-workers (2 Sam 5:11; 1 Kings 6:7), jewellers (Exod 28:11; 31:5), potters (Isa 41:25; Jer 18:1-4), spinners and weavers (Exod 35:25; Job 7:6; Isa 19:9), dyers (Exod 26:1; 2 Chron 2:7; Acts 16:14), tanners (Exod 26:14; Matt 3:4; Acts 9:43) and tent-makers (Gen 4:20; Acts 18:3). Tools that these craftsmen used are also mentioned occasionally (Gen 4:22; 1 Sam 13:20; 1 Kings 6:7; 7:9; 2 Kings 6:5; Isa 41:7; Jer 23:29).

People of the same craft, along with their families, usually lived in the same part of a town or village (1 Chron 4:21; Neh 11:35). Their common interests naturally produced a strong social bond. This was well demonstrated on one occasion in Ephesus. When Paul's preaching resulted in many

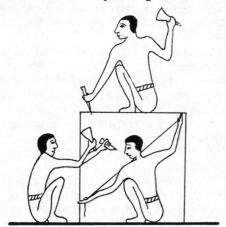

Stone-workers in ancient Egypt

idol worshippers being converted, the silversmiths saw him as a threat to their livelihood and used their collective power to oppose him vigorously (Acts 19:24-27). See also WORK.

CREATION

One of the basic Christian beliefs is that God created all things, and that all three persons of the godhead were involved in the acts of creation. God spoke and, by the power of his creative word, it happened (Gen 1:1-3; Job 33:4; Ps 33:6,9; 102:25; John 1:1-3; Heb 1:1-2).

The Creator and the universe

God alone is eternal; therefore, before his initial act of creation, nothing existed apart from him. He created all things, visible and invisible. Even spirit beings, though they may have existed before the physical universe, are creatures whom God has made (Gen 1:1-2; Job 38:4-11; Ps 33:6-9; 90:2; Isa 40:26-28; 42:5; John 1:1-3; Rom 11:36; Col 1:16; Heb 11:3; Rev 4:11). Once God had created matter, he used the materials of the universe to make and develop the features of the universe. He made animals and man, for example, out of materials he had made earlier (Gen 2:7,19).

Having created the universe, God did not then leave it to itself, as if it were like a huge clock that he wound up and left to run automatically. God is still active in the physical universe. He maintains what he creates. Though he is Lord of creation and distinct

from it, he works through it. He is over all things and in all things (Ps 147:8-9; Acts 17:24,28; Eph 4:6; Col 1:17; Heb 1:3; see also PROVIDENCE).

The universe exists, above all, for the praise and glory of God. He created it, not as an act of necessity, but as an act of free grace; not because he had to, but because he chose to (Isa 43:7; Acts 17:25; Rom 11:36; Eph 1:11; Col 1:16; Rev 4:11). It shows man something of God's love, power and wisdom (Ps 19:1-4; Jer 10:12; Rom 1:20).

God's 'rest' after creation indicated that he was completely satisfied with all his created works. In his grace he gave the created world to man and made him caretaker over it. God wanted man to enjoy his creation in fellowship with himself, and in so doing to share in his 'rest' (Gen 1:27-28; 2:1-3; Heb 4:3-10).

But man refused to submit to the Creator, and consequently ruined his relationship both with the Creator and with the creation. He brought disaster upon himself and upon the natural world (Gen 3:17-19; Rom 1:20-23; 8:20). Only when redeemed man enters his full salvation at the end of the age will the created world enter its full glory (Rom 8:21-23; Phil 3:21; see NATURE).

Story of creation

The chief purpose of the account of creation in Genesis is to provide an introduction to the story of man. It shows that God created everything out of nothing, and that he brought the universe through various stages of development till it was a fitting dwelling place for man (Gen 1:1,5,8,13,19,23,31; 2:4-7). Modern science may make man seem small, almost insignificant, in relation to the size and complexity of the universe, but the Bible takes a different view. It is concerned above all with man, and says little about how the physical universe operates (Ps 8:3-9).

If people want to find out more about the wonders of God's creation, they must do so by investigation and hard work, as God has appointed (Gen 3:19; Ps 111:2). God does not usually give such information by direct revelation. The Bible is not a textbook on science, nor is it concerned with the type of information that scientists are concerned with. Its purpose is not to teach scientific theories, but to give a short simple account of the beginning of things, and in language that people of any era or any background can understand.

The language of the creation story, like that of the rest of the Bible, is not the technical language of the scientist, but the everyday language of the common people (cf. Gen 1:16; 7:11-12; 40:22). The scientist may speak of the sun as the centre of the solar system, with the earth a minor satellite of the sun, and the moon a minor satellite of the earth. The Bible, by contrast, speaks of the heavens and the earth from the viewpoint of the ordinary person. To him the earth appears stationary, and the sun 'rises' and 'sets' as it moves around the earth (1 Chron 16:30; Eccles 1:5; Mal 1:11; Matt 5:45). The sun is the 'greater light' and the moon the 'lesser light' (Gen 1:16). The pictorial language of the Bible is different from the technical language of science, but the two are not necessarily in conflict.

Science may tell us much about God's creation, though it does so from a viewpoint that is different from the Bible's. Science can help us understand how nature works, whereas the Bible is concerned with showing that God is the one who makes nature work.

From science we may learn how the stars move, how the weather changes, or how plants grow, but from the Bible we learn that God is the one who makes these things happen (Ps 65:9-10; 78:20,26; 104:1-30; 147:8; Matt 5:45; 6:30). Although science may investigate how the creation developed, the Bible reveals that the development came about through the creative activity of the sovereign God. The 'laws of nature' are God's laws (Gen 1:1,7,11; 1:20,24; Heb 11:3).

CRETE

In Old Testament times the Mediterranean island of Crete was known as Caphtor. It was at one time the homeland of a people who, in the early days of the Old Testament story, sailed east and settled on Canaan's Mediterranean coast, where they became known as the Philistines (Deut 2:23; 1 Sam 30:14; Jer 47:4; Amos 9:7; see PHILISTIA; CHERETHITES).

The New Testament mentions Crete in the account of Paul's eventful voyage to Rome. While the ship was moving from one Cretan harbour to another, a fierce storm came up and blew the ship out to sea (Acts 27:7-21).

Possibly the first people to take the gospel to Crete were Jews who were converted on the day of Pentecost (Acts 2:11). Churches were established in Crete, but they later became troubled by various disorders. A national characteristic of the Cretans was that they readily accepted anything that made life easier and more enjoyable, and this created problems in their churches. The people accepted false teaching very readily (Titus 1:10-16).

When Paul visited Crete towards the end of his life, he had to deal with this problem. There were serious disorders in the churches, but Paul was not able to stay long. Therefore, when he moved on to other parts, he left Titus behind to continue the work of guiding and strengthening the churches (Titus 1:5; see TITUS, LETTER TO).

CROSS

Crucifixion was a form of torture and execution used by the Romans, not by the Jews. Yet Jesus knew that in the end this was the way the Jews would have him killed (John 3:14; 8:28; 12:32-33). Although the New Testament writers refer to the cruelty and injustice of Jesus' crucifixion (Acts 2:23; see CRUCIFIXION), their main concern is not with the physical horror of his death but with its theological meaning (1 Cor 1:18; 1 Peter 2:24).

The curse of the cross

Israelites of Old Testament times executed their criminals by stoning them. After an execution, they hung the body of the victim on a tree as a sign to all that he was under the curse and judgment of God (Deut 21:22-23). The Jews of Jesus' day, being under the rule of Rome, had no power to carry out executions themselves, but had to submit requests for execution to the Roman authorities. In the case of Jesus they did not even ask for him to be stoned when they saw it would be easier to have him crucified (Matt 27:22-23).

The Jews considered that Jesus' hanging on the cross had the same meaning as hanging on a tree. They considered, therefore, that he was under the curse of God. Actually, Jesus did bear the curse of God, but he did so on behalf of sinners, not because of any sin he had committed (Acts 5:30; 10:39; Gal 3:10-13; 1 Peter 2:24). Because the Jews had a wrong understanding of the curse Jesus bore in his death, his crucifixion was to them a stumbling block. They could not trust in Jesus' death on the cross as a way of salvation, and therefore they could not be saved (1 Cor 1:23; see CURSE; STUMBLING BLOCK).

God's way of salvation

To the writers of the New Testament, Jesus' death on the cross was the central point in the whole saving activity of God (1 Cor 1:23; 2:2; 15:3-4; see JUSTIFICATION; PROPITIATION). The cross therefore became a symbol for that salvation. The message of the gospel was the message of the cross (1 Cor 1:17-18; Gal 3:1; 6:12,14; Eph 2:16; Phil 3:18; see GOSPEL; RECONCILIATION). To the early Christians, the expression 'cross of Christ', like the expression 'blood of Christ', meant the same as 'death of Christ' (Rom 5:9-10; Col 1:20,22; see BLOOD).

The cross symbolized death not only for Christ, but also for the believer. Paul explained the meaning of the believer's baptism in relation to the cross of Christ. The believer's union with Christ means that he has, so to speak, died on the cross with Christ, been buried with Christ, and risen with Christ to new life (Rom 6:3-4; Gal 2:20; Col 2:12-14; see BAPTISM). The Christian demonstrates the truth of this practically by living a life of victory over the old sinful nature, the flesh (Gal 5:24; 6:14; see FLESH).

But death on a cross also meant humiliation. The believer must therefore be prepared for the sort of humiliation Christ suffered (Phil 2:8; Heb 12:2; 13:12-13; see PERSECUTION).

Christian self-denial

During his lifetime, Jesus warned people what to expect if they became his disciples. Jesus knew that his life would finish at the cross, and any person who followed him had to be prepared to take up his own cross and follow Jesus to a similar end (Matt 16:24-26; cf. John 19:17-18).

To bear one's cross is still a requirement for the person who wants to follow Christ. It means to sacrifice one's own interests for the sake of Christ. Christ does not require every disciple to suffer literal crucifixion, but he does require every disciple to be prepared for it, should it be God's will. If the disciple is prepared for that, he will be prepared for the lesser sacrifices and hardships that are involved in following Christ (Matt 10:37-38; Luke 14:27-33; see DISCIPLE).

CROWN

The Bible mentions two main types of crowns. One was the crown worn by a king, and as such was a sign of royalty and glory (Ps 21:1-3; Isa 28:5; 62:3; John 19:2-3; Rev 19:11-16). The other was the circle of leaves placed on the head of the winner of a sporting contest, and as such was a sign of victory (1 Cor 9:24-27; 1 Thess 2:19; 2 Tim 2:5). This latter type of crown is referred to frequently in reference to the final victory of Christians who faithfully persevere amid trials, sufferings and persecution (2 Tim 4:8; James 1:12; 1 Peter 5:4; Rev 2:10; 3:11; see also REWARD).

CRUCIFIXION

It is not certain where or when the practice of crucifixion originated, but it had been used as a method of execution long before the time of the Roman Empire. The Romans used it mainly against those accused of anti-government rebellion (Luke 23:18-19). When the Jews wanted to get rid of Jesus, they knew that if they accused him to the Roman governor of treason, they could call for his crucifixion (Luke 23:1-2,20-21).

Jesus' trial, before both the Jewish Council and the Roman governor, ignored many of the normal procedures, and was contrary to all accepted standards of justice (Matt 26:57-68; 27:11-31; see SANHEDRIN; PILATE). Once it was clear that Jesus was to be crucified, procedures followed a well established pattern.

The Bible gives no detailed description of the horrors that made crucifixion such a frightful sight, though it records the crucifixion story at length. This emphasizes the significance of the crucifixion as being central to the mission of Jesus and, indeed, to the entire history of mankind (1 Cor 2:1-5; Gal 6:14; 1 Peter 2:24). (For the theological meaning of the crucifixion see CROSS.)

Crucifixion was carried out in a public place outside the city (Matt 27:31,33,39; John 19:20; Heb 13:12), though the trial took place inside the city, usually at the governor's headquarters (Matt 27:27; see PRAETORIUM). The condemned person was first

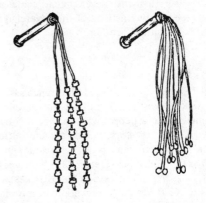

Scourges used by the Romans to flog prisoners

of all flogged (Matt 27:26), and then led off through the city to be crucified (Matt 27:31; Luke 23:27). He even had to carry the heavy piece of wood that formed the horizontal part of the cross on which he was to be crucified (John 19:17). If he was so weak from the flogging that he collapsed under the load, another person was forced to carry it for him (Matt 27:32).

At the place of crucifixion the usual procedure was to nail the victim's outstretched arms to the crosspiece, and then to lift this on to the vertical piece already fixed in the ground. The feet were then nailed (Luke 24:39; John 20:25). Though lifted up from the ground, the victim was close enough to the ground for people to read the accusation nailed to the cross above his head (John 19:19-20). People could also give him drugged wine to deaden the pain, though when it was offered to Jesus he refused it (Matt 27:34).

The soldiers who carried out the crucifixion received the victim's clothing (John 19:23-24). To prevent any attempted rescue, soldiers remained at the cross till the victim was dead (Matt 27:54). This may have taken several days, so to hasten the death they sometimes broke the victim's legs (John 19:31). This was not necessary in the case of Jesus. When, after about six hours on the cross, he knew that he had finished the work he had come to do, he triumphantly committed his spirit to God, bowed his head, and died (Mark 15:25,33-34,37; Luke 23:46; John 19:30).

CUBIT

Measurements of length recorded in the Bible were sometimes only approximate. People of Bible times, like people today, commonly estimated lengths and distances by measuring with fingers, arms or paces. The cubit was the distance from the elbow to the finger tip. It was equal to about half a pace, or a quarter of the distance between the finger tips when the arms were outstretched sideways.

The cubit became the basic unit for estimating length, depth and height (Gen 7:20; Deut 3:11; 1 Chron 11:23). Where exact measurements were required, such as in the construction of buildings, people used a standard cubit equal to approximately forty-four centimetres or eighteen inches (Exod 26:15-25; 1 Kings 6:2-6). (See also MEASUREMENT.)

CURSE

Cursing in the ancient Hebrew world was not a burst of bad language as it usually is in the world of today. It was a pronouncement of judgment believed to bring the release of powerful forces against the person cursed (Num 22:6; Judg 5:23; Job 31:30; Prov 30:10). For this reason it was as great a sin to curse a deaf person as it was to put a stumbling block in the path of a blind person. For the deaf person, not having heard the curse, could not defend himself with the more powerful 'blessing' of Yahweh (Lev 19:14; Ps 109:28).

God's curse on people or things was more than a pronouncement of devastating judgment; it was a punishment on sin (Gen 3:14; Prov 3:33; Dan 9:11; Matt 25:41; Mark 11:14,20-21; Heb 6:7-8). That is

why the judgments upon those who disobey God's commands are called curses, and the rewards to those who obey his commands are called blessings (Deut 27:11-26; 30:19; Josh 8:33-34; Zech 5:3; see BLESSING). Those who disobey the law fall under God's curse; but Jesus bore this curse when he himself became a curse in place of the sinner (Gal 3:10,13; see CROSS).

The Bible sometimes speaks of people or things that had to be destroyed as being 'put under the curse' or 'devoted'. That is, they were devoted to God for destruction (Deut 7:25-26; Josh 6:17-18; 7:1,11-12; 1 Kings 20:42; Mal 4:6) and could not under any circumstances be spared.

This was the sense in which Paul was willing to be cursed (Greek: *anathema*) in the place of his fellow Jews. He was willing to be cut off from Christ and totally condemned, so that his fellow Jews might be saved from judgment (Rom 9:3). He called for a similar judgment on any person who preached a false gospel (Gal 1:8) or who hated Christ (1 Cor 16:22).

On the other hand the saying 'Jesus be cursed' became a common saying among the opponents of Christianity during the time of Paul. It seems that in Corinth, some who spoke in strange tongues even used the expression in Christian meetings. Paul referred to this to demonstrate that speaking in tongues was not necessarily speaking by the Holy Spirit (1 Cor 12:3).

A 'woe' pronounced on people did not have the same sense of absoluteness as a curse. It was, nevertheless, to be taken seriously. It was either a stern warning or an announcement of catastrophe or judgment (Num 21:29; Isa 5:18-22; Ezek 24:9; Matt 11:21-22; Luke 6:24-26; Rev 8:13).

CUSH

Cush appears to have been the ancient name of the land of Ethiopia in Africa. The name Cushite, or person of Cush, was sometimes used as a general term for all the dark-skinned peoples of Africa. For details see ETHIOPIA.

CYPRUS

The island of Cyprus was located in the Mediterranean Sea. In former days it was called Kittim and its people were well known as sea traders (Num 24:24; Isa 23:1,12; Jer 2:10; Ezek 27:6; Dan 11:30).

Barnabas, one of the chief men in the early church, came from Cyprus (Acts 4:36). When the Jews killed Stephen and drove the Christians from

Jerusalem, some of those Christians took the gospel to Cyprus (Acts 11:19). Barnabas and Paul further helped the growth of the church in Cyprus by conducting a preaching tour that stretched from one end of the island to the other. A few years later Barnabas and Mark did further work there (Acts 13:2-6; 15:39). Paul sailed past the island on some of his later journeys, but there is no record that he visited the island again (Acts 21:3; 27:4).

Under the Roman administration, the capital of Cyprus was Paphos (Acts 13:6-7). There was a large Jewish population on the island and many synagogues (Acts 13:5-6). The Jews of Cyprus who became Christians had a much broader outlook than the Jews of Jerusalem, and were sympathetic to the expansion of the gospel among the Gentiles (Acts 11:20; 13:46; 21:16).

CYRENE

Cyrene was a Mediterranean port on the north coast of Africa. It was one of the many places in northern Africa where Jewish people settled during the centuries leading up to the New Testament era. As in other places, they built synagogues and carried on the religious traditions of their forefathers (see DISPERSION).

Many of the local people, attracted by the higher moral standards of the Jews, joined their synagogues, some as part members, others as full members (see PROSELYTE). The man named Simon who carried Jesus' cross on the way to Golgotha was either one of these Gentile God-fearers or a local Cyrenian Jew (Mark 15:21).

Jews, and possibly Gentiles, from Cyrene were in Jerusalem on the Day of Pentecost (Acts 2:10). Some of these apparently became Christians, for Cyrenian Christians were among those whom the Jews expelled from Jerusalem after they had killed Stephen. Cyrenian Christians were among the first to preach the gospel to the Gentiles, and played an important part in founding the church in Antioch in Syria (Acts 11:19-20). Among the prophets and teachers who led the Antioch church was a Cyrenian named Lucius (Acts 13:1).

CYRUS

As the king who led Persia to its conquest of Babylon in 539 BC, Cyrus was an important figure in helping to bring God's purposes for Israel to fulfilment (Isa 45:1). It was Cyrus who gave the captive Jews permission to return to their homeland and rebuild their national life and religion (Ezra 1:1-4). (For details see EZRA; PERSIA.)

DAGON

Dagon was one of the Canaanite Baal gods, and biblical references to it are all connected with the Philistines. There were temples for the worship of Dagon in the Philistine towns of Gaza and Ashdod (Judg 16:21-23; 1 Sam 5:1-5; see also 1 Chron 10:10). (For details see BAAL; PHILISTIA.)

DAMASCUS

One of the world's most ancient cities, Damascus has existed from at least the time of Abraham (Gen 14:15). It is important in the Bible story as capital of the nation Syria, which was very much involved in Israel's affairs from the time of the division of the Israelite kingdom in 930 BC to the conquest of Syria by Assyria in 732 BC. (For the history of Damascus during this period see SYRIA.)

The city of Damascus was on the major trade routes that crossed the region and was an important commercial centre (1 Kings 20:34; Ezek 27:18). It was also the religious centre of Syria. The ungodly Judean king Ahaz worshipped the Syrian gods there, and built a copy of the Syrian altar in Jerusalem (2 Kings 16:10-16; 2 Chron 28:22-24).

After Alexander the Great's conquest in 333 BC, Syria was made into an important province of the eastern part of the Greek Empire. But instead of making Damascus the provincial capital, the new rulers built a new capital at Antioch. With the Roman conquest of 64 BC, Damascus came under the administration of Rome, though for one brief period it was in the hands of an Arab king called Aretas (2 Cor 11:32-33).

The great persecutor of the early Christians, Paul, was converted to Christianity while on the way to Damascus (Acts 9:1-19). There were several

Market at Damascus

Jewish synagogues in the city, and the Jews opposed Paul so violently that he had to escape to save his life (Acts 9:20-25). After a period in Arabia, he returned to Damascus (Gal 1:17). It is not known how often Paul visited Damascus, though it is known that on several occasions he visited churches in Syria (Acts 15:41; Gal 1:21).

DAN

The tribe of Dan was descended from the elder of two sons whom Rachel's maid Bilhah bore to Jacob (Gen 30:1-6). In the original division of Canaan, Dan received its tribal portion on the Philistine coast between Judah and Ephraim (Josh 19:40-48; Judg 5:17; 13:1-2; 14:1; 16:23; for map see TRIBES).

Besides being squeezed between Israel's two most powerful tribes, the Danites were pushed back from the coast by the Philistines and the Amorites. The tribe therefore sent representatives north to look for a better place to live (Judg 1:34; 18:1-2). The place they decided upon was Laish, located in the fertile region of the Jordan headwaters in the far

north of Canaan. With the swiftness and ruthlessness that had characterized the tribe from the beginning, they slaughtered the people of Laish and seized the town for themselves, renaming it Dan (Judg 18:7-10; 18:27-29; cf. Gen 49:16-17; Deut 33:22).

From that time on, the towns of Dan and Beersheba marked respectively the northern and southern limits of the land of Israel (Judg 20:1; 1 Sam 3:20; 2 Sam 17:11; 24:2). When the nation was split in two after the death of Solomon, the southern tribes of Judah and Benjamin were separated from the northern tribes, who still called themselves Israel. The new limits of Israel were now Dan in the north and Bethel in the south. The breakaway king of Israel set up his own shrines in these two towns, in opposition to Judah's shrine in Jerusalem (1 Kings 12:28-30).

Dan's isolated location meant that it was open to enemy attack from the north (1 Kings 15:20). It was one of the first parts of Israel to fall when Assyria conquered the land and took the people into captivity (2 Kings 15:29).

DANCING

For the Israelites, dancing was a form of public rejoicing. Usually the women were the ones who danced, though men also danced on occasions (Exod 15:20; Judg 21:21; Jer 31:4,13). People danced to celebrate great national occasions such as victories over enemies (1 Sam 18:6-7), or private occasions such as the return of a long-separated member of the family (Luke 15:23-25). There were, however, indecent types of dancing, such as those associated with idolatry and certain forms of entertainment (Exod 32:19; Mark 6:21-22).

Children liked to dance in some of the games they played (Job 21:11; Matt 11:17), and people in general liked to dance at some of Israel's more joyous religious festivals (Judg 21:19-21). Dancing was part of Israel's public expression of praise to God after the crossing of the Red Sea (Exod 15:20-21) and during the bringing of the ark of the covenant to Jerusalem (2 Sam 6:14-15). In time, it became a regular part of Israel's public worship (Ps 149:3; 150:4). (See also MUSIC; SINGING.)

DANIEL

Through the example of his life and the visions recorded in his book, Daniel had a great influence upon people of later generations. The name that Jesus most commonly used of himself, the Son of man, was taken from Daniel's vision of the heavenly and universal king (Dan 7:13-14; Mark 2:28; 14:62); the writer to the Hebrews used Daniel as an example of the man of true faith (Heb 11:33); and John, in the book of Revelation, recorded visions that were based largely on those of Daniel (cf. Daniel Chapters 2,7 and 8 with Revelation Chapters 11, 12 and 13).

A man of faith

As a youth Daniel had been carried off captive to Babylon when Nebuchadnezzar first attacked Jerusalem (605 BC; Dan 1:1-6). Being handsome and intelligent, he was trained to be a courtier in Nebuchadnezzar's palace. He proved the genuineness of his faith in God by resisting the pressures upon him to conform to the ungodly ways of Babylon. God gave him success in his studies and the ability to interpret dreams (Dan 1:17,20).

This ability enabled Daniel to interpret a puzzling dream for Nebuchadnezzar. As a reward he was promoted to chief administrator in Babylon and head over Nebuchadnezzar's council of advisers (Dan 2:48). Daniel knew, however, that his success in interpreting Nebuchadnezzar's dream came only through his faith in God (Dan 2:16-19,24).

Daniel's trust in God showed itself also in the fearless way he told Nebuchadnezzar of the judgment that would fall upon him because of his pride (Dan 4:19,25). But Daniel had no joy in announcing the punishment, preferring rather that Nebuchadnezzar change his ways and so avoid the threatened judgment (Dan 4:27). In the time of a later ruler, Belshazzar, Daniel was even bolder in his denunciation of royal pride and arrogance (Dan 5:18-23).

Belshazzar was the last of Babylon's rulers, for it was during his reign that Persia, under Cyrus, conquered Babylon. By this time (539 BC) Daniel was at least eighty years of age, but he was given one of the highest positions in the new administration (Dan 6:1-2; cf. 1:21; 5:30). When jealous fellow administrators laid a trap that they thought would force Daniel either to deny his God or be put to death, Daniel refused to deny his God and God saved him from death (Dan 6:5,23).

One way Daniel maintained and demonstrated his faith was through prayer (Dan 2:17-23; 6:10). This applied not only to his involvement in great crises with heathen kings and governors, but also to his concern for the spiritual well-being of his own people, the Jews. On one occasion he humbly linked himself with the rebellious Israelite people as a whole in confessing their sin and asking God's mercy (Dan 9:1-19), and in reply received God's assurance of forgiveness (Dan 9:20-23). On another occasion his prayers were accompanied by three weeks of mourning and fasting (Dan 10:2-3), and once again his faith was rewarded by answered prayer (Dan 10:11).

The book of Daniel

Although the book of Daniel is commonly known as one of the Major Prophets, the Jews who arranged the books in their Bible included Daniel not among the prophets but among the miscellaneous writings. To them Daniel was a statesman who served God in a foreign palace, rather than a preacher who brought the message of God to his people. Nevertheless, the New Testament refers to Daniel as a prophet (Matt 24:15), for he was one through whom God revealed his purposes.

In broad outline, the purpose of the book of Daniel is to show to both Jews and foreigners that all nations and their rulers are under the control of God. The kingdoms of the world may fight against God, but in the end they must fall beneath the all-conquering power of his kingdom. The book of Daniel presents this message in two parts. The first deals with stories of selected people of God in a heathen country, the second with visions that God gave to his servant Daniel.

These revelations are concerned in the first place with the long period of confusion and conflict that followed the Persian period and reached its climax in the events of the New Testament era. Their meaning, however, is not limited to those events, for the New Testament writers apply features of them to the final triumph of God's kingdom, which is yet to take place.

Because of the many visions recorded in it, the book of Daniel has characteristics of that type of Hebrew literature known as apocalyptic (from the Greek *apokalupto*, meaning 'to reveal or uncover'). In apocalyptic literature the visions are always strange, with weird symbolism that often features fierce beasts. The overall purpose is to picture great conflicts out of which God and his people triumph (see APOCALYPTIC LITERATURE).

Contents of the book

After Daniel and his friends proved their faithfulness to God during their time of testing in the Babylonian palace (1:1-21), an occasion arose where Daniel showed his remarkable ability to interpret dreams. Nebuchadnezzar had a dream which, Daniel explained, showed that God is the ruler of the world and he sets up and destroys kingdoms according to his will (2:1-49).

Daniel's success at interpreting the king's dream brought promotion for him and his friends, but this in turn brought jealousy from some of the other officials. They accused Daniel's friends of treason for refusing to worship an idol that the king had set up, and had them thrown into a fiery furnace; but God saved them through their ordeal (3:1-30). When Nebuchadnezzar refused to heed Daniel's warning of the danger of pride, God humbled him. Nebuchadnezzar was then forced to acknowledge that Daniel's God was the one and only true God (4:1-37).

A succeeding king, Belshazzar, failing to learn from Nebuchadnezzar's experience, was responsible for his nation's destruction. In his reign Babylon fell to Persia (5:1-31). Daniel, now an old man but a leading official in the Persian administration, was the victim of a plot by jealous fellow officials. Though he was sentenced to death and thrown into a den of lions, God saved him (6:1-28).

The first of Daniel's visions was of four beasts that symbolized the successive empires of Babylon, Medo-Persia, Greece and Rome. In spite of their increasing opposition to God and his people, God's kingdom triumphed in the end (7:1-28). The next vision developed details of one of the four empires, namely, the Greek (8:1-27).

At the time of Daniel's visions, the Jews were still in captivity in Babylon, but expected to return to their homeland soon. In response to a prayer of Daniel on behalf of his people (9:1-19), God showed that he was now bringing his age-long purposes to completion. He would deal decisively with the whole problem of sin and bring in everlasting righteousness (9:20-27). Before that climax would arrive, however, the Jews would have intense suffering This would be so particularly during the Greek period, when they would suffer terrible persecution at the hands of Antiochus Epiphanes (10:1-12:13; for details see GREECE).

DARIUS

The first of three people named Darius mentioned in the Bible is Darius the Mede, who took control of Babylon when the city fell to the Medo-Persian armies in 539 BC (Dan 5:30-31). The name may be that of a Median leader whom the Persian Emperor Cyrus placed in charge of Babylon, or it may be another name for Cyrus himself (see also DANIEL; PERSIA).

Cyrus was succeeded in 530 BC by Cambyses, and Cambyses by Darius Hystaspes in 522 BC. During the reign of Darius Hystaspes the prophets Haggai and Zechariah aroused the Jews from their spiritual laziness, with the result that the temple in Jerusalem was rebuilt (Ezra 4:24; 5:6; 6:15; Hag 1:1; Zech 1:1; see EZRA; PERSIA). A later Darius, called Darius the Persian (Neh 12:22), ruled Persia from 423 to 408 BC.

DARKNESS

Apart from its literal meaning, darkness often has a figurative meaning in the Bible. Its most common figurative usage is as a symbol for evil. This symbolic usage is natural, for wrongdoers prefer darkness to light. It enables them to carry out their wrongdoing more easily (Neh 6:10; Ps 91:5-6; Isa 29:15; Jer 49:9; Luke 22:53; John 3:19-20; Rom 13:12-13; 1 Thess 5:2,7).

The world of mankind, because of sin, is a place of darkness and death. Believers need not fear this darkness, for God has become their light (Ps 23:4; 27:1; Micah 7:8; Eph 5:14). In fact, when people receive God's salvation they come, as it were, out of a kingdom of darkness into one of light (Isa 9:2; 42:6-7; Luke 1:76-79; Col 1:13). They must therefore no longer live as if they belonged to the darkness, but live as those who belong to the light (2 Cor 6:14; Eph 5:8-11; see LIGHT).

An intervention by God in human affairs may be accompanied by unnatural darkness (Deut 4:11; Matt 27:45-46). This is particularly the case if the intervention is one of judgment (Joel 2:2,31; cf. Rev 16:10-11). Therefore, the Bible may speak symbolically of a day of judgment as a day of darkness (Amos 5:20; Zeph 1:15). In keeping with this symbolism, the Bible depicts the final destiny of unrepentant sinners as a place of terrifying and everlasting darkness (Matt 8:12; 22:13; 2 Peter 2:17; Jude 13).

DAVID

From humble beginnings as the youngest son of a Bethlehem shepherd named Jesse, David rose to become Israel's greatest king. He established a dynasty out of which, according to God's plan, came the great Messiah, the son of David, who was Jesus Christ, Saviour of the world (1 Sam 16:1,11; 2 Sam 5:3-4,12; Isa 9:7; Luke 1:32-33; 2:11).

Early progress

After the failure of Saul as king, God directed Samuel to the young man David, whom Samuel marked out to be Israel's next king (1 Sam 13:14; 15:28; 16:11-14). It was many years before David became king, and during those years he steadily matured in mind and body. He became skilled in speech, writing and music, and developed into a brave fighter through having to defend his flocks against wild animals and raiding Philistines (1 Sam 16:18; 17:34-36; cf. Ps 23).

David's introduction to Saul's court was as one whose music relaxed the king's troubled nerves (1 Sam 16:16). After his victory over the Philistines' champion fighter, he became Saul's armour-bearer and full-time court musician (1 Sam 16:21; 17:50; 18:2). At this time a close friendship began to develop between David and Saul's son Jonathan. It lasted many years, and was ended only by Jonathan's tragic death in battle (1 Sam 18:1; see JONATHAN). David's successes in battle won him promotion, but further successes and growing popularity so stirred up Saul's jealousy against him that Saul tried to kill him (1 Sam 18:5-11).

By this time David had no doubt begun the psalm-writing activity for which he is well known. The biblical book of Psalms contains many of the songs and poems he wrote during his long and eventful career. In these writings David gives his personal views of many of the incidents that another writer records in the books of 1 and 2 Samuel (see PSALMS).

Flight from Saul

Unsuccessful in his direct attacks on David, Saul tried to have him killed in battle. He promised that if David could kill one hundred Philistines, he would give his daughter Michal to David for a wife. David again succeeded and, through marrying Michal, became part of the royal family (1 Sam 18:20-29). But Saul's jealousy resulted in further attempts to kill him (1 Sam 19:1,10-11; Ps 59).

After seeking temporary shelter with Samuel at Ramah (1 Sam 19:18), David returned in secret to find out from Jonathan whether it was safe for him to enter Saul's court. Upon discovering it was not, he obtained provisions from a priest at Nob and fled (1 Sam 20:1,12-14; 21:1-9).

When the Philistine city of Gath proved an insecure refuge (1 Sam 21:10-15; Ps 34; 56), David found a good hiding place in a cave at Adullam. Here he was joined by his family along with several hundred others, who for various reasons were dissatisfied with Saul's administration (1 Sam 22:1-2; Ps 57; 63; 142). From these people David built himself a strong fighting unit, which in later times became the central force of his royal army (1 Sam 22:2; 23:13; 1 Chron 11:10,15; 12:8-18). But as long as Saul was king, David never allowed his men to attack him (1 Sam 24:7; 26:9).

Saul's pursuit drove David increasingly into the semi-barren regions of Judah. David was pleased to use his fighting force to rescue the town of Keilah from the raiding Philistines (1 Sam 23:4), but he was

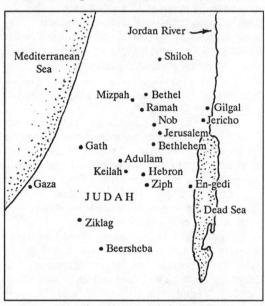

angry when the people of another Judean town, Ziph, betrayed him to Saul (1 Sam 23:19; Ps 54). On two occasions when he had an opportunity to kill Saul, he refused to (1 Sam 24:3-7; 26:5,9).

David supported his small army by protecting farmers against the raiding Philistines and then demanding food supplies as payment (1 Sam 25:7-8; 25:16,21). When one farmer refused to pay, David was saved from rash retaliation only by the quick thinking and wise words of the farmer's wife, Abigail. When the farmer died, David married Abigail (1 Sam 25:39).

Tired at the cruel pursuit by Saul and his Benjaminite supporters, David fell to the temptation to give up defending his righteousness. He decided to avoid further hardship by going and joining the enemy Philistines (1 Sam 26:19; 27:1-2; cf. Ps. 7; 11). From Philistia David enriched himself by carrying out brutal raids on neighbouring tribal people, though he repeatedly deceived the Philistine king concerning his activities. It was a disgraceful sixteen months David spent in Philistia, and, so far as we know, no psalm of his comes from this period (1 Sam 27:7-11). Only after his own camp was cruelly raided did David stop his ungodly behaviour and return to the Lord (1 Sam 30:1-7).

At this time the Philistines had gone to battle against Israel. David and his men had set out with the Philistines, but the Philistine leaders sent them back. They feared that David's men might betray them and fight for Israel (1 Sam 29:1-4). In the battle that followed, both Saul and Jonathan died (1 Sam 31:1-5), and David composed a song in memory of them (2 Sam 1:17-27).

Established as king

After Saul's death there was confusion in Israel. David was declared king in Hebron, which was in the area of his own tribe Judah in the south, but one of Saul's sons was declared king in the territory east of Jordan (2 Sam 2:3-4,8-9). After two years of conflict, the supporters of David overpowered their opponents. However, David executed the murderers of Saul's son, to make it clear that he had no desire to gain Saul's throne by murder (2 Sam 3:1; 4:9-12; cf. 1 :14-16).

For the next five years David ruled from Hebron (2 Sam 5:3-5). Being deep in the territory of Judah to the south, Hebron was not a suitable place from which to rule all Israel. Therefore, in an attempt to ensure the allegiance of the northern tribes, David decided to make Jerusalem his capital. Jerusalem was on a well fortified hill and belonged to no tribe, for it had remained under the control of the enemy since the time of Joshua. David conquered Jerusalem and soon united all the tribes under his rule (2 Sam 5:5-7,12).

David then set out to make Jerusalem the religious as well as the political centre of the nation. He brought the ark from the country house where it had sat neglected during Saul's reign, and placed it in a special tent he had erected for it (2 Sam 6:2,17; cf. 1 Sam 7:1-2; 1 Chron 13:6). The conquest of Jerusalem and the arrival of the ark there are celebrated in some of David's best known psalms (Ps 24; 68; 110). Further psalms show the ideals he aimed at in his government (2 Sam 23:1-7; Ps 101), and express his deep gratitude to God for all his gracious blessings (Ps 8; 103).

When David expressed his desire to build God a permanent house (meaning a temple), Nathan the prophet told him that God had a better purpose, and that was to build David a permanent house (meaning a dynasty). God had chosen David as the one through whose royal family he would bring the Messiah, the Saviour of the world (2 Sam 7:8-17; Ps 2:7-9; 89:19-37; Matt 22:42; Luke 1:68-70; Acts 13:22-23).

As David's military victories continued, Israel's power grew, showing that God was strengthening David's throne according to his promise. David's power spread beyond the borders of Israel, so that he dominated all the neighbouring peoples, from the Nile River and the Red Sea in the south to the Euphrates River in the north (2 Sam 8:1-18; cf. Ps 18). Unfortunately, pride in his expanding power prompted David to carry out a census. He knew he deserved God's punishment, but asked that it be mixed with mercy (2 Sam 24:10,14; cf. Ps 32).

David's military conquests had involved him in much bloodshed. Therefore, although God granted David's request for a temple, he considered that he was not a fit person to build it (1 Chron 28:3,6). That privilege was given to David's son, Solomon, though David helped him by preparing plans and setting aside money and materials for its completion (1 Chron 22:2-6; 28:11).

Family troubles

When he was at the height of his power, David committed a series of deliberate sins that affected the rest of his life. His sexual desire for Bathsheba led him to adultery and murder, as a result of which God assured him that his own family would be torn apart through adultery and murder (2 Sam 12:7-12). David confessed his sin and God in his mercy forgave him (2 Sam 12:13-14; Ps 51), but that did not remove the suffering and distress that David had brought upon himself and his family.

David's example of adultery and murder was followed in the family. One of the sons raped his sister, only to be murdered by another of the sons (2 Sam 13:11-14,28-29). The murderer, Absalom, fled into exile. Three years later he returned to Jerusalem, but it was a further two years before David allowed him back into the palace (2 Sam 13:38; 14:24,28,33).

Over the next four years Absalom strengthened his position, till he was able to launch a surprise rebellion. David was forced to flee Jerusalem, and Absalom seized the throne (2 Sam 15:1-7,14; Ps 3). In the battle that followed, Absalom was killed, in spite of David's instructions that no harm be done to him (2 Sam 18:5,14). Only after the people had shown they wanted David back as their king did he return to Jerusalem (2 Sam 19:9-15).

The peace of former times never returned to David's throne. Soon he had to deal with another rebellion, this one led by a man called Sheba, who tried unsuccessfully to lead the northern tribes to break away from David (2 Sam 20:1,22).

David's closing years were saddened by conflict in the palace concerning which son would succeed him as king. His choice was Solomon, but the ambitious Adonijah tried to seize the throne for himself before David died. Again the rebellion failed. These stirring events gave the weak and aged David renewed strength, and with great haste he had Solomon anointed as the new king (1 Kings 1:5-8,16-18,38-40). In due course he arranged a second anointing, this one public and with full regal ceremony, where he presented Solomon to the people as the divinely chosen successor (1 Chron 28:1-10; see ADONIJAH; SOLOMON).

Hope for the future

In spite of his failures, David was one of the greatest men that Israel produced. In the centuries that followed, when Israelites looked for the coming of the Messiah, the best example by which they could imagine an ideal king was that of David (Hosea 3:5). The Messiah was, as it were, a greater David (Ezek 34:23-24; 37:24-25). Being of David's family, he was known as David's son and he sat on David's throne (Isa 9:7; Jer 23:5; 33:15; Matt 12:23; 20:31; 21:15; Luke 1:32; John 7:42). Yet he was also David's Lord (Matt 22:42-45; cf. Ps 110:1). As to his humanity, the Messiah Jesus was descended from David, but as to his divinity he was the eternal Son of God (Rom 1:3-4; Rev 22:16; see MESSIAH).

Because many of David's psalms celebrate his victories and express the ideals that he looked for in his kingdom, the New Testament sometimes quotes them in relation to the Messiah Jesus (cf. Ps 2 with Acts 4:25; 13:33-34; 1 Cor 15:24-25; Heb 1:5; 5:5; Rev 12:5; 19:15; cf. Ps 110 with Matt 22:42-45; Heb 7:15-17,21-22). Other psalms speak of David's sufferings, and the New Testament quotes these also in relation to Jesus (cf. Ps 22 with Matt 27:39-43,46; John 19:24; Heb 2:12; cf. Ps 69 with Matt 27:34,38; John 2:17; 15:25; Rom 15:3).

Not all David's psalms, however, may be quoted as applying to Jesus, for many reflect David's wrong-doings. The reader's first consideration must be to consider the psalms in relation to the immediate circumstances about which David wrote (Ps 38:3; 41:4; 51:1-2). (For further details concerning the use of David's psalms in the New Testament see PSALMS, BOOK OF.)

According to the titles in the book of Psalms, David wrote 73 of the 150 in the collection. His poetry appears in 2 Samuel also (2 Sam 1:17-27; 3:33-34; 22:1-51; 23:1-7). His exceptional abilities as a musician and a poet were well known (1 Sam 16:17-18,23; 2 Sam 23:1). He used those abilities in organizing the services for the proposed temple and in setting up official groups of singers and musicians (1 Chron 6:31-32; 15:16-28; 16:7; Ezra 3:10; Neh 12:24,36,45-46). David served God faithfully in his own generation, and through his music and psalms has been of service to God's people throughout succeeding generations (Acts 13:36).

DAY

People in Bible times used the word 'day' with a wide range of meanings, as we do today. They may have used it for the normal 24-hour day (Num 10:11; Acts 20:7), for the hours of daylight in contrast to the hours of night (Luke 18:7; John 9:4), for a particular time or occasion (Jer 12:3; 16:19; Luke 6:23), or for a more lengthy period such as an age or era (John 8:56; 2 Cor 6:2).

In an age when there were no clocks as we know them today, people estimated the time of day according to the sun. Times were only approximate, for the number of hours of daylight varied throughout the year. Usually people counted the hours according to a 12-hour division from sunrise to sunset. Therefore, if the approximate time of sunrise was 6 a.m. (Gen 32:21,24,31; Mark 16:2), the third hour would be about 9 a.m. (Mark 15:25; Acts 2:15), the sixth hour would be about noon (Mark 15:33; Acts 10:9), the ninth hour would be about 3 p.m. (Mark 15:33; Acts 3:1), and the twelfth hour would be about 6 p.m., or sunset (Mark 1:32; John 11:9; cf. Matt 20:3,5-6,12; see also SABBATH).

During the time of the Roman administration, the twelve hours of night were divided into four periods, or watches (Matt 14:25; Luke 12:38). In former times, the Jews divided the night into three watches (Exod 14:24; Judg 7:19).

The contrast between day and night provided preachers with an obvious illustration to contrast good and evil. The present era is a night of moral darkness, in contrast to the day of light that will dawn at Christ's return (Rom 13:11-13; 1 Thess 5:4-8). The return of Christ is the great day that will bring the world's history to its climax (Phil 1:6,10; 2:16; Heb 10:25; see DAY OF THE LORD).

DAY OF ATONEMENT

Only one person, the Israelite high priest, could enter the Most Holy Place of the tabernacle, and he could do so only once a year, on the Day of Atonement (Lev 16:2; Heb 9:7). This was a day that the Israelites observed as a national day of cleansing from sin. It fell on the tenth day of the seventh month, a few days before the Feast of Tabernacles (Lev 16:29-34; 23:27-34; see FEASTS).

Rituals of the day

Throughout the Israelite year, regular sacrificial rituals dealt with sin in various ways. But even the best of these did not enable the offerer, nor even the priests, to come into the sacred presence of God in the Most Holy Place. Therefore, on this one day of the year, when entrance into God's presence was available, the high priest brought all the people's sins to God for his forgiveness.

Before offering a sacrifice on behalf of others, the high priest had to offer a sacrifice for himself and his fellow priests. He offered the priests' sin offering at the altar in the tabernacle courtyard, after which he took fire from the altar, along with blood from the sacrifice, into the tabernacle-tent. First he used the fire to burn incense in the Holy Place. Then, as he opened the curtain to enter the Most Holy Place, incense floated in and covered the mercy seat (lid of the ark, or covenant box), the symbolic throne of God. The high priest then sprinkled the blood of the slaughtered animal on and in front of the mercy seat (Lev 16:11-14).

On returning to the open courtyard, the high priest repeated the ritual, this time offering the people's sin offering (Lev 16:15-19). The sprinkling of the blood on the mercy seat reminded Israelites that even at the climax of their highest religious exercise, they could still not demand forgiveness. They could only cast themselves upon the mercy of God.

A second animal was then used in the people's cleansing ritual, but it was not killed. The high priest laid his hands on the animal's head, confessed over it the sins of the people, and sent it far away into the wilderness so that it could never return. This was a further picture to the people that their sins had been removed, though again at the expense of an innocent victim (Lev 16:8-10,20-22).

When the sin-cleansing ritual was finished, the high priest washed himself thoroughly with water. He then offered burnt offerings of consecration, first for the priests and then for the people. At the end of the day's activities, any others who had been in contact with the sin offering had also to wash themselves (Lev 16:23-28). (Concerning the different types of offerings in the Israelite sacrificial system see SACRIFICE.)

Atonement through Christ

The New Testament emphasizes that, although the Old Testament rituals were of benefit in showing people the seriousness of sin, they could not in themselves remove sin. They were only a temporary arrangement. Now that Christ has come, they are of no further use (Heb 9:6-10).

Jesus Christ, the great high priest, offered not an animal as a sacrifice; he offered himself. Through his sacrificial blood he has entered the presence of God, obtained eternal salvation, and cleansed the repentant sinner's conscience (Heb 9:11-14). His one sacrifice has done what all the Israelite sacrifices could not do (Heb 10:11-12). Entrance into the presence of God, which was restricted under the Old Testament system, is now available to all God's people through their high priest, Jesus Christ (Heb 10:19-22; cf. 9:8).

When the Israelite high priest had completed the sin-cleansing rituals in the tabernacle-tent, he reappeared to the people. Likewise Jesus Christ, having dealt with sin fully and having obtained eternal forgiveness for sins, will reappear to bring his people's salvation to its glorious climax (Heb 9:12,28; see also BLOOD).

DAY OF THE LORD

Israelites of Old Testament times looked for the day when God would intervene in the affairs of mankind, righting the wrongs and establishing his just rule on the earth. They called this divine intervention the day of the Lord (Isa 2:12-19; 13:6,9; Zeph 1:14-16; Zech 14:9).

Earlier 'days of the Lord'

Although the day of the Lord was usually considered to be something terrifying, Israelites often looked forward to it. The reason for this was that they believed that God was going to punish Israel's enemies and bring in Israel's golden age (Jer 46:10; Zeph 3:16-20). They failed to realize, however, that in that day God would punish *all* sinners, Israelites included, and save *all* the faithful, regardless of national or social status (Joel 2:30-32; Amos 5:18; Mal 3:1-4; 4:1-3).

Any catastrophic judgment, such as a flood, earthquake, locust plague, famine or war, could be called a day of the Lord (Joel 1:15-16; 2:1-2,11). But such a catastrophe was only a forerunner (and at the same time a guarantee) of the great and final day of the Lord (Joel 2:30-32; 3:14-18).

Jesus Christ's first coming was, in a sense, a day of the Lord, for through Christ God intervened in the affairs of mankind to conquer Satan, deal with sin and proclaim his kingdom (Matt 3:11-12; 4:14-17; Acts 2:16-21; see KINGDOM OF GOD). The 'last days' had begun (Acts 2:17; 1 Cor 10:11; 2 Tim 3:1; Heb 1:2; 1 Peter 1:20; 1 John 2:18). They will reach their climax when Christ returns at the end of the age to purge the world of sin and bring his kingdom to its victorious completion (Isa 2:2-4; Matt 24:29-31; 25:31-32; 2 Peter 3:3-4,10).

The final great 'day of the Lord'

Christ's people have always suffered persecution, but before the final great day of the Lord that persecution will become more severe (Matt 24:5-14; John 16:33; 2 Thess 1:5-12; see PERSECUTION). The spirit of antichrist, which has always been in the world, will express itself in a final great rebellion against God. There will be all sorts of pressures, both subtle and open, to force Christians to abandon their faith in Christ (Matt 24:15-24; 2 Thess 2:1-7; 1 John 2:18; see ANTICHRIST).

In a series of devastating judgments, God will pour out his wrath upon rebellious man (2 Thess 1:8; Rev 6:17; 14:9-11; 16:2). God will not pour out his wrath upon his own people; on the contrary he will protect them from it (Rev 7:1-3; 9:4; cf. Rom 5:9; 1 Thess 1:10; 5:9). Yet the rebels, instead of turning to God in repentance, will hate him and persecute his people even more (Rev 9:18,20-21; 11:7-10; 12:17; 16:9,21). The persecution will be so bitter that, for the sake of his people, God will shorten the day of his wrath. Although some believers will be killed for their faith in Christ, as far as God is concerned not one will be lost (Rev 6:9-11; 12:11-12; 20:4; cf. Matt 24:22; Luke 21:16-18).

Christ's return will be a day of judgment that will result in a separation between the wicked and the righteous. For one it will be a day of wrath, for the other a day of salvation (Matt 24:36-41; 25:32,46; Luke 21:27-28; Acts 24:15; Rom 2:5; Phil 1:6,10; 1 Thess 4:16-18; 2 Thess 1:5-8; Rev 22:12-15; see JUDGMENT; RESURRECTION).

In every era the circumstances of Christians vary from nation to nation. Christians in any place at any time could belong to the last generation of humanity as we know it. Therefore, the Bible urges Christians of all nations and eras to be alert and ready at all times for the onset of the final day of the Lord and the return of Christ (Matt 24:42-44; Mark 13:32-37; 1 Thess 5:2-6; 2 Peter 3:10-12).

However, no one knows when the end of the age will come, and Christians should not behave foolishly by thinking the world is about to come to an end (Matt 24:36; 2 Thess 2:1-2; 3:11-12). They must carry on with life normally, making long-term plans where necessary, yet remembering that God may intervene at any time (Luke 19:11-27; Acts 1:6-8; 1 Cor 15:5-7; Phil 1:9-10; 1 Thess 5:6,11,14).

DEACON

In the early days of the Jerusalem church, Christians shared their food and possessions so that all in the church had enough for their day-to-day needs. At first the apostles administered this daily welfare, but as the church numbers increased, new arrangements became necessary. To give the apostles more time for prayer and teaching, the church chose seven men whom the apostles appointed over the work. The words used to denote these men and their work were all related to *diakonos*, the common Greek word for servant or minister. It may be translated 'deacon' (Acts 6:1-6; cf. Rom 12:7; 2 Cor 11:8; Eph 6:21; Phil 1:1; Col 4:17; 1 Tim 3:8).

As the early churches grew in number and size, they saw an increasing need to organize their affairs properly. In time the common practice was for a church to have a group of people called deacons who had certain responsibilities in the church.

The word *diakonos* had such a broad meaning and usage that the Bible nowhere attempts to define the role and duties of deacons. The deacons were, however, distinct from the elders (GNB: leaders) (Phil 1:1; 1 Tim 3:1,8; see ELDER). Deacons had responsibility for a variety of ministries, but not the ministry of pastoral care and church leadership (cf. Acts 6:3-4; Rom 12:6-8).

Nevertheless, the story of the early Jerusalem church shows that a deacon's service is not limited to routine or welfare activities. Two of the seven administrators were also very useful preachers (Acts 6:5,8-10; 8:5). Other examples show that the church needs women deacons as well as men (Rom 16:1-2; 1 Tim 3:11; cf. Luke 8:1-3; 1 Tim 5:10).

Deacons must be spiritual people, for right attitudes are necessary even in organizing practical affairs (Acts 6:3). It is therefore important to check the character, behaviour and ability of people before appointing them deacons (1 Tim 3:10). Their lives must be blameless, whether in the sphere of family, church or society (1 Tim 3:8-13).

The case of the early Jerusalem church suggests a procedure for the appointment of deacons. The church elders invite the church members to select those they think suitable, then the elders, after due consideration, make the appointment (Acts 6:3). All must realize, however, that people can do the work of deacons properly only if the Holy Spirit has so gifted them, and only if he works through them (Rom 12:7; 1 Cor 12:4-7,11; 1 Peter 4:11).

DEAD SEA

One of Palestine's most unusual geological features is the Dead Sea. It is part of a deep north-south valley that extends along the Jordan River as far as the Gulf of Aqabah (north-eastern arm of the Red Sea) to the south. The Dead Sea, which is the lowest part of this valley, has a water level approximately 400 metres below sea level. It is about seventy-five kilometres long and fifteen kilometres wide. People in ancient times gave it the names Salt Sea and Dead Sea because it was extremely salty and, so far as they could see, nothing was able to live in it (Num 34:12; Josh 3:16; cf. Ezek 47:8-9). (See also PALESTINE, sub-heading 'Jordan Valley and Dead Sea'.)

DEATH

The Bible teaches that man dies as a result of sin (Gen 2:17; Rom 5:12). Yet it is not God's desire that man should die. Death is the enemy of man and God (1 Cor 15:26; Heb 2:15).

Results of Adam's sin

Physical and spiritual death are not completely separate. When sin entered the life of man through Adam, it changed everything. All man's life is now affected by the certainty of death (Rom 5:12-17). This involves physical death and spiritual death. The truth of this is demonstrated by the fact that the work of Christ, which reverses the effects of sin on man's behalf, brings the gift of spiritual life now (Rom 6:23) and in the end will bring victory even over physical death (1 Cor 15:21-22,44-45).

Some may think that since man is a creature of the natural world, physical death is inevitable. After all, death was apparently part of the world of nature before man sinned — leaves fell off trees, fruit was picked, and animals lived by eating other forms of life (Gen 2:15-16; 3:1). But it is not death in general that is the result of man's sin; it is the death of *man*. The truth that the Bible emphasizes is that man is not merely a creature of the natural world like the other animals. He is related to God in a way that makes him different from every other created thing. Man is unique, for he is made in God's image (Gen 1:27).

If physical death were merely the end of existence, man would have no need to fear it. The reason he fears it is his awareness that, when he dies, he does not escape the consequences of his sin, but goes to face them (Heb 9:27; see also SHEOL).

It has been suggested that, before man sinned, the spiritual life within him was so dominant that it prevented the natural physical deterioration that we today might expect. When sin entered man's life, his whole being was affected. His spirit no longer had control over his body, and physical deterioration resulted. Physical death was at the same time completely natural and completely the result of sin (Gen 3:19b). Physical effort and bodily functions

that should have brought pleasure brought pain and hardship instead (Gen 3:16-19).

There is no need to imagine the chaos of an over-populated world had man never sinned and no one ever died. It is death, not the termination of earthly existence, that is the enemy of God and man; and it is sin that makes death so hateful (1 Cor 15:26,55-56). There are examples to suggest that God could readily have brought a person's earthly existence to an end without the person having to pass through death (Gen 5:24; 2 Kings 2:11; 1 Cor 15:51; Heb 11:5; cf. Acts 1:9).

Present experience; future victory

The Bible uses the picture of an evil ruler to denote both death and the devil. Death is a sphere in which the devil rules (Heb 2:15). Man is a slave of sin and therefore under its power (Rom 5:14). He is not free to decide whether he will die or not. Physically he is condemned to death, and spiritually he is dead already (Eph 2:1,5; Col 2:13; 1 John 3:14). He is so under the dominion of death that his tendency towards sin is itself called death (Rom 7:24; 8:6,10). Sin cannot exist without death as its consequences (Rom 6:16,21; 7:5,13; James 1:15). To continue in sin is to continue in death; for sinners are in the sphere of death till they are saved out of it (Rom 8:23; 1 Cor 15:54).

While this connection between sin and death may seem natural and inevitable, it can be broken. Man is not the helpless victim of mechanical laws, but the subject of divine compassion. The same God who sends death as sin's penalty can give life as his gift (Rom 6:23).

Through the death of Jesus Christ, God has completely dealt with sin and death. Jesus died in man's place to take away man's sin and deliver him from the sphere of death (Rom 6:9-10; 2 Cor 5:21; Heb 2:9,14; 1 Peter 2:24). Satan uses death to bind man in fear, but God uses death to release man from Satan's power. Christ came to conquer death, and he did this by means of his own death. All who by faith belong to Christ share the benefits of that death (Rom 6:3-8; 2 Cor 5:14; Col 2:12-15). All who refuse Christ die in their sins, and so ensure for themselves an unalterable destiny that the Bible calls eternal destruction, outer darkness, the lake of fire and the second death (Matt 8:12; 25:46; John 8:24; Rev 20:14; see HELL).

Christ's saving work means that believers need no longer fear death. They know that one day it will be destroyed (Rom 6:9; 1 Cor 15:26,54-57; Rev 2:11; 20:6; 21:4). Although they still live in the sphere of death's influence, they have already passed out of death into life. They are free from the law of sin and death (John 5:24; Rom 8:2; 2 Tim 1:10; 1 John 3:14). Like other people, they may experience physical death, but they will never die in the sense that really matters (John 11:25-26; see HEAVEN).

DEBORAH

Two women named Deborah are mentioned in the Bible. The first of these was the maidservant of Rebekah who came with her from Paddan-aram when Rebekah married Isaac. She lived to a great age and died near Bethel (Gen 24:59; 35:8).

The better known Deborah was a respected civil administrator in Israel during the era of the judges. She lived near the town of Bethel, where she gave decisions in cases brought to her for judgment. Being a prophetess, she was well suited to discern God's will in difficult cases (Judg 4:4-5). She is chiefly remembered for directing Israel's victory over the forces of Sisera in northern Palestine. (For map see JUDGES, BOOK OF.)

With her army general Barak, Deborah led a force of Israelite soldiers up Mt Tabor, with the aim of drawing out Sisera's chariot forces into the plain of the Kishon River below (Judg 4:6-10). With prophetic insight, Deborah must have foreseen the outcome. There was a tremendous storm, the river flooded and, as Sisera's chariots became bogged, the Israelites rushed down upon them and won a great victory. Many details of the event are given in the song of victory that Deborah composed to celebrate the occasion (Judg 4:12-16; 5:1-22).

DEBT

Because debts place a person under obligation to his creditors, Paul sometimes used the word 'debt' to refer to a person's spiritual obligations. Paul considered that his obligation to preach the gospel was a debt he owed to people everywhere (Rom 1:14; 1 Cor 9:16). He believed also that Gentile Christians, having received the gospel by way of the Jews, owed a debt to their Jewish brothers. The Gentiles had an obligation to help the Jews in their poverty (Rom 15:27).

More frequently, however, the Bible uses the illustration of debt to refer to something bad, such as sin in general (Matt 6:12; 18:32-35) or bondage to the sinful human nature (Rom 8:12). Debt in this sense is a reminder of the difficulties of life in the everyday world, where debts can easily bring a person to ruin. The poor can easily be exploited, and

for this reason Israelite law aimed at protecting them from greedy money-lenders. (For details see LENDING.)

DECAPOLIS

The Romans gave the name Decapolis (meaning 'ten cities') to an extensive region situated largely south and east of the Sea of Galilee. Its inhabitants were mainly Gentiles. The New Testament mentions two of its localities, Gadara and Gerasa, and certain

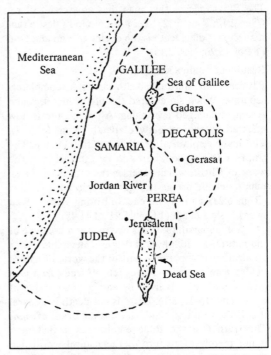

occasions on which Jesus visited the region. On one of these occasions Jesus healed a demon possessed man, though the incident brought him into conflict with local pig farmers (Matt 8:28; Mark 5:1,11-14; 7:31). Many of the people from the area joined the crowds that at one time followed Jesus (Matt 4:25).

DEDAN

Dedan was the name of a nomadic tribal group in northern Arabia. Their people were well known in Bible times as shrewd traders (Isa 21:13; Jer 49:8; Ezek 27:20; 38:13; see ARABIA).

DEDICATION

According to common usage, 'dedication' is another word for 'consecration'. The two words refer to the act of setting apart people or things from the ordinary affairs of life and presenting them to God for his service (Exod 13:2,12; 29:1,22; Num 7:10-11; 1 Sam 1:11,24-28; 1 Kings 8:63; 1 Chron 26:26; Ezra 6:16-17; for details see CONSECRATION).

The Jewish festival known as the Feast of Dedication celebrated the rededication of the Jewish temple after the defilement by Antiochus Epiphanes in the second century BC (John 10:22; for details see FEASTS).

DEFILEMENT

See UNCLEANNESS.

DEMONS

Both Old and New Testaments speak of the reality of the spirit world. Within this unseen world are spirit beings beyond number. They are commonly called angels, some of whom willingly serve God, though others have rebelled against him (Jude 6; see ANGELS). These rebellious, or fallen, angels are variously known as demons, evil spirits, spiritual hosts of wickedness, principalities, powers, rulers, authorities, evil spiritual forces, cosmic powers of evil, and angels of the devil. Their leader is Satan (Luke 10:17-18; Eph 6:12; Col 2:15; James 2:19; Rev 12:9; see SATAN). In relation to the ministry of Jesus, demons are usually called unclean spirits (Matt 10:1,8; Mark 6:7,13; see UNCLEAN SPIRITS).

Demons oppose God and are the spiritual force behind heathen religions and false gods (Deut 32:17; Ps 106:37; 1 Cor 10:19-20; Rev 9:20). Those who follow these religions usually fear demons, and often use magic and sorcery to resist demonic power. But God forbids magic and sorcery, for these things themselves involve cooperating with supernatural evil powers (Lev 19:26; 20:6; Gal 5:20; Rev 9:20-21; 21:8; see MAGIC). The only dealing Jesus would have with demons was one of total condemnation. He brought God's judgment upon them and freed demonized people from their power (Mark 1:27; Luke 8:2; 13:32; Acts 10:38).

Jesus' power over demons was a sign that the kingdom of God had come (Matt 12:28; see KINGDOM OF GOD). He gave his followers the power to cast out demons (Matt 10:1,8; Luke 10:17-18; Acts 16:16-18), and the ability to see whether prophets in the church were speaking through the influence of demons or the influence of God's Spirit (1 Cor 12:3,10; 1 Tim 4:1; 1 John 4:1-3).

Not all demonic activity is spectacular. Demons are busy in every sphere of human life and readily work through the normal activities of human nature

and human society (2 Cor 11:14-15; Eph 2:2-3; 6:12; James 3:15). The Christian should be aware of their evil purposes, but should not fear them. Christ has conquered them by his death and resurrection, and the Christian can claim that conquest for himself (Col 2:8-10,15; cf. Rom 8:38-39; Eph 1:18-21). The final demonstration of the conquest of demons will be at the last judgment, when God's punishment will remove them from human society for ever and send them to a place of fitting punishment (Matt 8:29; 25:41; Jude 6).

DENIAL

The New Testament speaks of two forms of denial, one bad, the other good. Denial in the bad sense has to do with openly disowning or rejecting God. A person denies God by declaring publicly that he does not belong to him (Matt 10:33; 26:70-72; Acts 3:13-14; 2 Peter 2:1; 1 John 2:22-23; Jude 4; cf. Rev 2:13; 3:8).

Wrong behaviour, even without words, can be a denial of the Christian faith (1 Tim 5:8; Titus 1:16). A person may deny Christ in a moment of weakness and, after genuine repentance, be forgiven (Luke 22:31-34; John 21:15-17). But the person who rejects God will be rejected by him (2 Tim 2:10-13; see APOSTACY).

Denial in the good sense has to do with the rejection of selfishness. A person 'denies himself' for the sake of Christ by allowing his life to be ruled by Christ instead of by himself. He is controlled by Christ's will, not by his own selfish desires. He promises to be obedient to Christ always, even if it should lead to death (Matt 16:24-26).

Jesus was the supreme example of self-denial, and in his case self-denial led eventually to death (Phil 2:5-8). Believers, being united with Christ, deny themselves by giving up worldly attitudes and desires, and living disciplined, godly lives (2 Cor 4:2; Gal 2:20; 5:24; Col 3:5; Titus 2:12; see OBEDIENCE; SELF-DISCIPLINE).

DERBE

Originally Derbe was part of the ancient kingdom of Lycaonia, but when Rome redivided Asia Minor, Derbe became part of the Roman province of Galatia (Acts 14:6; see GALATIA; LYCAONIA). Paul and Barnabas established a church in Derbe on their first missionary journey (Acts 14:20-21), and Paul visited the church on his second and third journeys (Acts 16:1; 18:23). It was one of the churches that Paul wrote to in his letter to the Galatians.

DEUTERONOMY

After receiving the law at Mt Sinai, Israel spent almost forty years in the wilderness region between Sinai and Canaan. During this time the adults died and a new generation grew up (cf. Num 14:28-35). Moses' repetition of the law for this new generation is recorded in the book called Deuteronomy (from two Greek words, *deuteros*, meaning 'second', and *nomos*, meaning 'law'). Concerning the authorship of the book and its relation to the previous four books see PENTATEUCH.

Characteristic style

Deuteronomy does more than simply repeat the law; it expounds the law, giving it a new emphasis. It shows that God wants more than legal correctness. He wants his people to obey him because they want to, not because they are forced to. He wants the relationship with his people to be one of warmth and love (Deut 6:3,5-7; 7:7-8,11; 8:5). The book's style is that of the preacher rather than the lawgiver; its audience is the people as a whole rather than the priests and judges (Deut 6:8-9; 8:6; 10:12-13).

The basis of Deuteronomy is the covenant between Yahweh and his people. In his sovereign grace, God chose Israel to be his people, and promised them Canaan for a national homeland (Deut 7:7; 8:1; 9:4-5). Israel could do nothing but accept God's grace and promise to serve him with loving obedience (Deut 5:6-7; 6:1-3; 10:12-13; see COVENANT).

In form Deuteronomy is similar to the normal covenant documents of the ancient Near East. When a sovereign overlord made a covenant with his subject peoples, he prepared a treaty document that declared his sovereignty over them and laid down the order of life he required of them. This is what God did with his people Israel, using Moses as his mediator.

Contents of the covenant document

Usually a treaty document began with an historical introduction in which the overlord, after announcing his name, recounted all he had done for his people. Deuteronomy opens with God's recounting all he had done for Israel (1:1-3:29) and urging the people to be loyal to him in return (4:1-43).

After the introduction came a statement of the covenant's basic requirements. For Israel the basic principles were in the form of ten commandments (4:44-5:33). Love would enable the people to do God's will. There was to be no treachery through forming alliances with foreign powers (foreign gods) (6:1-25). God was giving his people a good land, but they had to remember that life depends on more than the food people eat. It depends on spiritual forces found only in God (7:1-8:20). The people therefore were not to be stubborn (9:1-10:11), but were to have humble purity of heart towards God and towards their fellows (10:12-11:32).

Having established the basic principles, the treaty document then set out the detailed laws. Ancient custom allowed treaties to be updated from time to time to suit changing circumstances. In the case of the Israelites, they would no longer be together as a vast crowd moving through the wilderness, but would split up, spread out and settle down in an agriculturally fertile country. Moses' repetition of the law therefore included adjustments to fit in with the people's new way of life (e.g. 11:10-11; 12:20-22; 14:24-27; 18:6-8).

The updated covenant document dealt with a number of matters, including faithfulness in worship (12:1-13:18), honesty in religious and social matters (14:1-16:17), justice in government (16:18-19:21), respect for human life (20:1-21:23), sexual purity (22:1-23:25), protection for the disadvantaged in society (24:1-25:4), and integrity in family relations, business dealings and religious duties (25:5-26:15). The two parties then declared their loyalty to the covenant (26:16-19).

In keeping with the form of ancient treaties, the covenant also listed the rewards and punishments (blessings and cursings) that people could expect. If they were obedient, they would enjoy increased benefits from the overlord; if they were disobedient, they would suffer severe penalties (27:1-28:68). Having stated the conditions under which the covenant operated, Moses then formally renewed it (29:1-30:20). A further feature of the covenant was the twofold provision for its maintenance. First, the people had to assemble periodically to hear it read; second, the document had to be kept in the central shrine, where it served as an absolute standard of reference (31:1-29).

Moses summarized the covenant's contents in a song that the people were to memorize and sing (31:30-32:47). He brought the ceremony, and his leadership of Israel, to a fitting close by announcing prophetic blessings on each of Israel's twelve tribes (32:48-33:29). After viewing the promised land, he died peacefully (34:1-12).

DISCIPLE

During the lifetime of Jesus there were many who considered themselves to be his disciples. That is, they followed him and listened to his words, as pupils might listen to a teacher. Although these people may have thought Jesus to be the Messiah, many of them had a wrong understanding of the sort of person the Messiah would be. They expected him to be a political leader who would free the Jews from Roman domination and bring in the golden age (John 6:14-15,60-64). When they found that Jesus was not this type of leader, they withdrew from him (John 6:66-68).

Yet there were many, probably hundreds, who were true believers, true disciples (Luke 6:17,20). From these, Jesus chose twelve whom he appointed apostles (Luke 6:13; see APOSTLE). These twelve were Jesus' disciples in a special sense, and became known as 'the twelve disciples' or simply 'the disciples' (Matt 16:13; 20:17; 24:3; 26:17). After the resurrection and ascension of Jesus, all the followers of Jesus became known as disciples (Acts 1:15; 6:1; 9:1), and later as Christians (Acts 11:26; 1 Peter 4:16; see CHRISTIAN).

The cost of discipleship

Jesus pointed out that those who want to become his disciples (whether in his day or in ours) have to accept his lordship in their lives. He may require them to give up their occupations, friends, possessions or status for his sake. On the other hand, he may not. The fact is that every disciple must be *prepared* to give up such things, should Jesus so direct. Usually Jesus will require different people to make different sacrifices, depending on who they are and what work he wants them to do. But always there will be some sacrifice. Self-denial is the only way to discipleship of Jesus Christ (Mark 1:16-20; 8:34-38; 10:17-22,28-30; Luke 14:33; Phil 2:3-8; see DENIAL).

Just as Jesus carried his cross to the place of his crucifixion, so each of his followers has to take up his cross and be prepared to die for Jesus' sake (Matt 16:24-26; cf. John 19:17-18). Even if the Christian's discipleship does not lead to death, it will involve him in a certain amount of hardship, suffering and persecution (Matt 10:24-25; 24:9; John 15:20).

People therefore must consider beforehand what it will cost them to be Jesus' disciples. They must be prepared for a lifetime of commitment to him. There is no place for those who make a start and then give up (Luke 14:26-33;). Disciples must be ready to accept physical inconvenience (Luke 9:57-58), to put their responsibilities to Christ before all other responsibilities (Luke 9:59-60) and to be wholehearted in their devotion to Christ (Luke 9:61-62).

Characteristics of the true disciple

A disciple is a learner, and the disciples of Jesus learn from him (Matt 11:29; Eph 4:20). But merely to learn is not enough. They must put their learning into practice and maintain a consistent obedience if they are truly to be Jesus' disciples (John 8:31). They give visible proof that they are Jesus' disciples through practising genuine love towards each other and through bearing spiritual fruit in their lives (John 13:13-15,35; 15:8).

This practical love extends beyond the group of fellow disciples to all people everywhere (Matt 5:44-46). Jesus' disciples are therefore to take his message to others in order to make more disciples, no matter who the people are or where they live (Matt 28:19-20; see MISSION).

DISCIPLINE

See CHASTISEMENT; SELF-DISCIPLINE.

DISEASE

Sickness and disease are among the results of sin that entered the human race when Adam sinned (Gen 3:16-19). Jesus' healing of disease was one evidence that the kingdom of God had come and that Jesus had power over all the evil effects of sin (Matt 4:23; 8:17; 9:35; 12:28). The age to come will see the complete removal of all sickness and disease (Rev 21:4; 22:2).

At times God may use sickness to punish people for their sins (Num 12:1-10; 2 Kings 5:25-27; Ps 38:3-6; John 5:13-14; Acts 12:23). Other times he may use sickness to make them more reliant on his power and grace (2 Cor 12:7-10). In most cases, however, it is not possible to say why people suffer from sickness, disability or disease (John 9:1-3). The book of Job shows that no person should judge another with the accusation that his suffering is because of his sin (Job 42:7; see JOB, BOOK OF; SUFFERING).

Among the diseases and disabilities that the Bible mentions are leprosy (2 Kings 7:3,8; Luke 17:12; see LEPROSY), epilepsy (Matt 4:24), dysentery (Acts 28:8), nervous disorders (1 Sam 16:14-23; Dan 4:33), deafness (Lev 19:14; Mark 7:32), dumbness (Mark 7:37; 9:25), blindness (2 Sam 5:8; Mark 10:46; John 9:1), paralysis (John 5:4; Acts 9:33), bone deformities (Luke 5:18; 6:6; 13:11), boils (1 Sam 5:6; Isa 38:21), dropsy (Luke 14:2) and various fevers (Mark 1:30; John 4:52; Acts 28:8). (Concerning the connection between demon possession and certain diseases see UNCLEAN SPIRITS.)

The Israelite laws governing cleansing, foods and diseases provided a standard of hygiene that helped protect people from many harmful diseases (see UNCLEANNESS). Nevertheless, some sickness was inevitable. At a time when the knowledge and

Diseased beggar

facilities of modern medicine were not available, physicians and common people alike used whatever skills they had (Gen 50:2; Jer 8:22; Mark 5:26) and whatever treatments were available to them (2 Kings 20:7; Jer 46:11; Luke 10:34; 1 Tim 5:23). Many of the non-Israelite physicians were actually sorcerers (2 Chron 16:12; see MAGIC).

DISPERSION

During the centuries immediately before the New Testament era, Jews had become widely scattered across western Asia, eastern Europe and northern Africa. Some of these were descendants of people who had been taken captive to foreign lands by Assyria, Babylon and other invaders of Palestine. Some had fled as refugees in times of persecution; others had moved to different places in search of trade. All these people were known as 'Jews of the Dispersion' or 'the scattered Jews' (John 7:35; James 1:1; 1 Peter 1:1).

By New Testament times many of these Jews had lived in foreign countries so long that they had little or no knowledge of Palestinian languages such as Hebrew and Aramaic. Instead they spoke Greek, the common language of the Roman Empire, and so became known as Hellenists (from the word *hellas*, meaning 'Greece'). At the same time they maintained their Jewish identity through keeping the Jewish law. Wherever they lived they built

synagogues (Acts 13:5,14; 17:1,10; 18:1-4) and kept the traditions of their ancestors. Usually they went to Jerusalem for the more important ceremonies and festivals (Acts 2:1,5; 21:27-29).

DIVORCE

God's plan for marriage was that it be a permanent union between one man and one woman – a union broken only by death. Divorce was something God hated (Gen 2:24; Mal 2:16; Matt 19:3-6; Rom 7:2-4). From earliest times, however, mankind on the whole rejected God, and polygamy and divorce became common practices (Gen 6:1-8; Rom 1:20-27; see MARRIAGE).

Examples from Bible times

Among the Israelites of Moses' time, marriage disorders had become so widespread that Moses set out special laws designed to deal with the problem. In particular he wanted to stop easy divorce and protect women from unjust treatment.

For instance, if a man tried to find an excuse for divorcing his wife by accusing her (falsely) of sexual immorality before marriage, he was fined for his cruel accusation and prevented from divorcing her (Deut 22:13-19). He could divorce her only if there was a valid reason, and only if he gave her divorce documents that protected her rights should she want to marry someone else. He could not take her back if he later changed his mind, and she could not go back to him if her second marriage came to an end (Deut 24:1-4).

Moses' decision to permit divorce in certain circumstances was not because he approved of divorce. Rather he was trying to reduce divorce and restore some moral order to society. When Jews of later times quoted Moses' law as approval for divorce, Jesus referred them back to God's original standard. According to that standard, to divorce and remarry was adultery (Mark 10:2-12; Luke 16:18; 1 Cor 7:10-11). The only exception that Jesus allowed was the case where a person's adultery was already destroying the marriage (Matt 5:31-32; 19:3-9; see ADULTERY; FORNICATION).

A difficult situation arose in New Testament times when one partner in a non-Christian marriage later became a Christian. The Christian was not to divorce the non-Christian partner, but was to do everything possible to make the marriage work harmoniously. If the non-Christian partner was not willing to continue the marriage and departed, the Christian partner had to let it be so and consider the marriage at an end. The statement that in such cases the Christian partner was 'no longer bound' seems to mean that he or she was free to remarry (1 Cor 7:12-15).

A universal problem

In any society where there is a widespread breakdown of marriage, the result will be an increasing number of social and family problems. The Creator knows what is best for his creatures, and where people reject the plan he has laid down, they will have troubles (cf. Deut 10:13).

There is often no clear-cut solution to the complications that develop because of divorce and remarriage. In some cases, no matter what is done, some ideal will be broken. Moses accepted less than the best because of the people's 'hardness of heart', which suggests that the right course of action may sometimes mean choosing the lesser of two evils (Matt 19:8).

Repentant sinners can receive God's merciful forgiveness for divorce and adultery as they can for other sins (2 Sam 12:13; Ps 51:1-19; 145:14; Isa 43:25). Whatever people might have been guilty of previously, when God forgives them the church must also forgive them (1 Cor 6:9-11; cf. Matt 6:14-15). Although Christians must, like Jesus, uphold God's standards when others want to destroy them (Matt 19:3-9), they must also, like Jesus, give help to those who, having broken God's law, are later repentant (Luke 7:36-50; John 8:1-11; cf. Hosea 14:4).

DREAM

In everyday life, dreams are often related to matters that a person has been engaged in or been thinking about, and usually have no religious significance (Eccles 5:3). But the Bible records exceptional cases, where dreams did have religious significance. In circumstances where people had no written Word of God to guide them, or where God had an urgent message to pass on, he sometimes spoke to people directly through dreams (Gen 20:3; 31:24; 46:2-4; 1 Kings 3:5; Matt 1:20-24; 2:12). Dreams may have had meaning even when God did not speak directly, though these were rare (Gen 37:5-11).

Among people who did not know God, a dream with meaning usually required a person who knew God to interpret it (Gen 40:9-19; 41:1-32; Dan. 2:1-45; 4:4-27). Among God's people, a dream with meaning usually had a fairly obvious interpretation (Gen 37:5-10; 1 Kings 3:6-9; Acts 16:9-10).

Moses warned people to be careful in believing those who claimed that God had spoken to them through dreams. Such people were often false prophets, who led others astray (Deut 13:1-3; Jer 23:25,32). Moses was well aware that sometimes God may have spoken to the true prophets through dreams, but the Bible writers usually spoke of such experiences as visions rather than dreams (Num 12:6; see VISION).

DRESS

Styles of clothing varied among the different classes of people in Israel, and were often a means of showing a person's status (Gen 37:3; Josh 9:5; 2 Sam 13:18; Isa 3:18-23; Luke 16:19). Ceremonial clothing worn by people in high positions was often richly embroidered, sometimes with gold thread woven into the cloth (Exod 28:4,6,8,15; 39:3; Ps 45:13). There were special garments for special occasions

Israelite farming family

such as weddings and feasts (Isa 61:10; Matt 22:11; Luke 15:22; Rev 19:8; see ORNAMENTS). Practices that showed immoral tendencies, such as dressing in clothes of the opposite sex (transvestism), were forbidden (Deut 22:5).

From earliest times people used cosmetics and perfumes. Some of these developed from what were originally ointments. Most cosmetics were prepared from spices and vegetable oils, though some facial cosmetics were made from minerals (2 Kings 9:30; Jer 4:30; Ezek 23:40; see OIL; SPICES).

To express distress or mourning, people often tore their clothes, dressed in sackcloth, or put on cosmetics that made them look extra miserable (Gen 37:34; 2 Sam 3:31; 1 Kings 21:27; Job 1:20; Isa 58:3,5; Matt 5:16-18; 26:65; Acts 14:14; see SACKCLOTH). People taken captive were often humiliated by being made to walk barefoot or naked (Isa 20:4).

The Bible condemns the practice of making distinctions in the church through favouring those who are well dressed above those who are poorly dressed (James 2:2-5). It discourages God's people from dressing extravagantly, and emphasizes that good conduct is more desirable than lavish dress (Jer 4:30; Luke 20:46-47; 1 Tim 2:8-10; 1 Peter 3:3-5; cf. Col 3:9-10).

EARTHQUAKE

Earthquakes were well known events in the world of the Bible story (Exod 19:18; 1 Sam 14:15; 1 Kings 19:11; Amos 1:1; Zech 14:5; Matt 27:54; 28:2; Acts 16:26). The Bible writers often refer to earthquakes as evidence of God's mighty power (Judg 5:4; Ps 18:7; Isa 29:6; Joel 2:10; 3:16; Nahum 1:5; Hab 3:6; Matt 24:7; Rev 6:12; 8:5; 11:13; 16:18).

God may have used earthquakes, along with other forces of nature, to bring about his judgments, even in cases where the Bible does not specifically mention an earthquake. The destruction of Sodom and Gomorrah, the stopping of the Jordan River at the time of Israel's entrance into Canaan, and the collapse of the walls of Jericho may all have involved earthquake activity. These events occurred in the place and at the time God had earlier announced, showing that they had resulted from his direct intervention (Gen 19:12-14,24-28; Josh 3:7-8,13-17; 6:5,20).

EBAL

The mountains Ebal and Gerizim were in central Canaan and stood opposite each other on either side of the town of Shechem. The town and the mountains were closely linked in some important events in Israel's history (Josh 8:32-35; 24:1; for details see SHECHEM).

EBER

Eber was an early Semite (i.e. a descendant of Shem) whose two sons, Joktan and Peleg, began two notable lines of family descent (Gen 10:21,25). The line of descent through Joktan produced many of the Arab tribes (Gen 10:26-30), and the line through Peleg produced those tribes of Mesopotamia to which Abraham belonged (Gen 11:16-26). The name 'Hebrew', by which Abraham and his descendants were known, was taken from the name 'Eber' (Gen 10:21; 14:13; 39:17; Exod 1:22; see HEBREW). So too, it seems, was the name 'Habiru', by which semi-nomadic peoples in general were known. The word *eber* meant 'to pass over or through'.

ECCLESIASTES

The title 'Ecclesiastes' has been taken from the Septuagint, the first Greek translation of the Old Testament. The Hebrew word from which the translators took the title is *qohelet*. This is the name the writer of the book uses for himself, and it has been translated as preacher (RSV), teacher (NIV) and philosopher (GNB). The writer does not tell us his name, but he was no doubt a well known wisdom teacher of his time (Eccles 12:9).

Teaching style

In keeping with a common practice of the time, the author writes as if he were some well known person whose life would form a background for his own teaching. He takes as his starting point what was probably a saying of King Solomon, 'Vanity of vanities, all is vanity'. He then puts himself in Solomon's position and proceeds to show that all the wealth, pleasure, wisdom and power that a person may gain will, in the end, benefit him nothing if he has wrong attitudes to life and to God.

Ecclesiastes is not a story or argument that begins in the opening verse and moves through in an unbroken development to the last verse. Rather it is a collection of some of the writer's thoughts and ideas, probably written down later in life. Each section, however, is related to the central theme of the book. That theme is presented fairly clearly in the opening two chapters, then is restated and discussed, in part or in whole, in the following sections.

Being a wisdom teacher, the writer is concerned with some of the apparent contradictions of life (see WISDOM LITERATURE). He does not rely upon comfortable orthodox theories, but examines the frustrations and injustices that sometimes make life seem useless and without meaning. However, he is not a pessimist. He has a strong faith in God, and that faith gives him his interpretation of life.

Meaning of the book

The writer's interpretation of life is built around two main observations: first, that God is sovereign; second, that God is the Creator. His main ideas may be summarized as follows.

No matter what benefits people may gain for themselves in life, they lose them at death. Life seems useless (2:14,18; 6:1-6). Yet through it all God is in control, directing events according to his purposes (3:11a,14; 8:15b). The writer is frustrated that he cannot know God's purposes, but he never doubts that those purposes exist (3:11; 8:16-17; 9:1a). People should not therefore waste time searching after what God has kept for himself, but instead enjoy what God has given to them, namely, life (3:12-13; 5:18-19).

Not only does God control affairs in people's lives; he is the Creator who has given them his world. Therefore, they should accept whatever God determines for them and find enjoyment in God's world and in all their activities in that world (2:24; 9:7-10). That is not to say that they may be selfish and ill-disciplined. On the contrary, they will only enjoy life properly as they act with wisdom rather than folly, and as they do good rather than evil (7:5,7-9,19).

Summary of contents

Life seems at times to have no purpose (1:1-11). The search for a meaning to life through selfish ambition will lead to frustration. A person should accept what God gives and enjoy it (1:12-2:26). Having set out the central message of his book, the writer turns to consider some related matters: the control of God over life's affairs (3:1-15), the widespread injustice in the world (3:16-4:3), and the uselessness of self-centred achievement (4:4-16).

A collection of short messages encourages people to make the most of life's frustrations. The writer gives advice about religion, money and other matters (5:1-7:14), and suggests that the way to contentment is to practise moderation (7:15-8:17). Life presents people with great opportunities for true contentment (9:1-12), but they will have no contentment without wisdom (9:13-10:20). The final section therefore encourages people to have a positive attitude to life (11:1-8); for the Creator holds them accountable for the way they handle the gifts of creation (11:9-12:14).

EDOM

The name Edom meant 'red' and was given to Esau, his descendants, and the land they later occupied (Gen 36:1,8-9). Esau was red haired, he exchanged his birthright for red bean soup, and Edom was a land of red soil (Gen 25:25,30; 2 Kings 3:20,22).

Features of the land

Edom's territory stretched from the southern tip of the Dead Sea down to the northern tip of the Gulf of Aqabah (the north-eastern arm of the Red Sea). It was a mountainous region, divided down the centre by a semi-desert valley known as the Arabah. Chief among Edom's mountains was Mt Seir, after which the land was sometimes called (Gen 14:6; 32:3; 36:21; Deut 2:1,4,12; Josh 15:1; 1 Kings 9:26). (For details of the Arabah see PALESTINE.) The

Edomites' security depended largely on a strong defence system they had built throughout their mountains (2 Chron 25:11-12; Obad 1-4).

Chief of Edom's mountain towns were Sela, Bozrah and Teman (2 Kings 14:7; Isa 34:6; 63:1; Jer 49:20,22; Amos 1:11-12). Teman was famous for its wisdom teachers (Job 2:11; Jer 49:7; Obad 8-9). The other important population centres of Edom

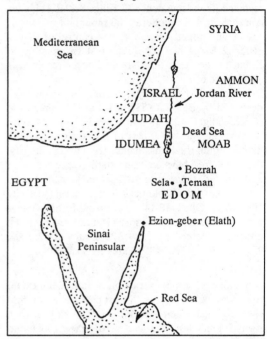

were the twin towns of Ezion-geber and Elath on the Gulf of Aqabah (Deut 2:8; 2 Chron 8:17). Since much of Edom's land was unsuitable for farming, and since Edom's Red Sea ports gave it control over important trade routes, many of the Edomites were traders rather than farmers (Amos 1:6,9).

Old Testament history of Edom

An important road known as the King's Highway ran through Edom. From Ezion-geber it went north over the mountainous plateau on the east of the Arabah to Moab, Ammon and Syria. The Israelites of Moses' time wanted to use this road on their journey to Canaan, but Edom and Moab refused permission, forcing the Israelites to detour around the borders (Num 20:14-21; 21:10-13,21-26; 33:35-37; Judg 11:15-24).

There was some conflict between Israel and Edom during the reign of Saul (1 Sam 14:47), but in the reign of David Israel conquered Edom and took political control of the country (2 Sam 8:13-14; 1 Kings 11:15-16). Solomon in turn established a fleet of ocean-going ships at Ezion-geber. These ships carried goods to and from India and other countries, thereby bringing him considerable profit (1 Kings 9:26-28; 10:22; 22:48).

The strategic and economic importance of Ezion-geber and Elath was one of the chief causes of later conflicts between Judah and Edom. When Judah weakened during the reign of Jehoram, Edom regained its independence (2 Kings 8:20-22). Under Amaziah, Judah conquered the mountain regions of Edom, and under Azariah it took control of Ezion-geber (2 Kings 14:7,22). Judah lost Ezion-geber to Edom in the reign of Ahaz and never regained it (2 Kings 16:6).

When Judah finally fell and Jerusalem was destroyed by Babylon (587 BC), the Edomites took wicked delight in joining with the Babylonians to try to wipe out the last traces of the ancient Israelite nation. When the Jerusalemites tried to flee the city, the Edomites blocked their path, captured them and handed them over to the Babylonians. They also joined the Babylonians in plundering the city (Ps 137:7; Obad 10-14). Because of this violent hatred of the Israelite people, God assured Edom of a fitting punishment (Jer 49:7-22; Lam 4:21-22; Ezek 25:12-14; 35:15; Joel 3:19; Amos 1:11-12).

Later history

Some time after the destruction of Jerusalem, Edom itself was destroyed, as the prophets had foretold (Mal 1:2-4). In their search for refuge and security, many Edomites moved west across the Arabah and settled in Judean territory around Hebron. Various Arab groups mingled with them, and the region later became known as Idumea (Mark 3:8).

Years later, after the Romans had conquered Palestine (63 BC), an Idumean named Herod was appointed 'king' of Palestine under the governing authority of Rome. This man, known as Herod the Great, was the person who tried to kill the infant Jesus (Matt 2:1-19; see HEROD). The modern nation of Israel includes this Idumean territory along with much of old Edom, and extends to the Red Sea port of Elath (or Elat).

EDUCATION

In early times there were no schools such as we know them today, and most children were educated at home. It was the responsibility of parents to teach their children the history and social customs of their nation, to instruct them in right living and to prepare them for adult life. This preparation involved teaching and training in reading, writing, crafts,

trades and household work (Exod 13:8,14; Deut 4:9-10; Prov 1:8; 4:1-9; 31:1). In the case of Israelites, parents had a particular responsibility to teach their children the religion given them by God (Deut 6:6-9). Christian parents have a similar responsibility (Eph 6:4; 2 Tim 1:5; 3:15; see FAMILY).

People of higher social status often received a more formal education through private instructors who were appointed as the children's guardians (2 Kings 10:1; Acts 7:22; Gal 3:24-25). Institutions known as wisdom schools were later established for the teaching and training of upper class people in philosophical thought (Eccles 12:9,11; Jer 18:18; see WISDOM LITERATURE). Prophets also had schools for the training of their disciples (2 Kings 2:3; 4:38; Isa 8:16; see PROPHET).

For the ordinary Israelite, the highest academic instruction he received was the teaching of the law of Moses. Originally the priests were the teachers, but by New Testament times the scribes had taken over most of the teaching activity (Deut 33:10; Ezra 7:6,10; Neh 8:1-4,8; Matt 23:2-3; see SCRIBES). The power of the scribes had developed along with the establishment of places known as synagogues, which became centres of instruction for Jewish people in general (Matt 4:23; Luke 4:16-21; see SYNAGOGUE).

Jewish men could, if they wished, receive a more thorough education in the Jewish law by becoming students of learned Jewish teachers (John 3:10; Acts 5:34; see RABBI). They usually sat at the feet of their teachers (Acts 22:3), and learnt by memorizing facts and having question-and-answer sessions with their teachers (Deut 31:19; Luke 2:46). These teachers often taught in the temple (Matt 26:55; Luke 2:46; cf. 19:47). (Concerning teachers in the church see TEACHER.)

In addition to education in this traditional religious setting, education in a Greek philosophical setting was also common in New Testament times. This created difficulties for Christians, because of the conflicts between values taught in this type of education and values taught in Christian homes and churches (1 Cor 1:20-25; Col 2:8).

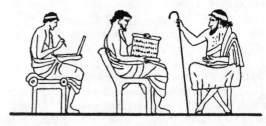

At school in Athens

Such conflicts will always exist. Christians may consider that when a government accepts responsibility for the education of its citizens, it is fulfilling part of its God-given task. It is helping provide for society's well-being (Rom 13:4). But this does not relieve Christian parents and church leaders of their responsibilities concerning the proper instruction, development and growth of those within their care (Eph 4:13-15; 6:4; 2 Tim 3:14-17; Heb 5:14; 13:17; see also ETHICS).

EGYPT

In spite of the ancient culture and civilization for which Egypt is famous, the feature highlighted in the Bible is that Egypt was a place of bondage out of which God redeemed his people (Exod 6:6-7; 15:1-12; 20:2; Deut 6:12; Josh 24:17). Throughout their history, the people of Israel celebrated their deliverance from Egypt, reminding themselves that God's grace and power alone had saved them (Lev 23:43; Deut 16:1-3; 1 Sam 10:17-18; Neh 9:16-17; Ps 106:7-12; Dan 9:15; Amos 2:10; Micah 7:15; Acts 7:17-19,36; see PASSOVER).

Egypt continued to be involved in the history of God's people, and is mentioned often throughout the period of the Old Testament period. Even the New Testament opens with a reference to Egypt,

for Mary and Joseph spent a time there with the baby Jesus (Matt 2:13-15).

The land and the people

Less than one twentieth of ancient Egypt was usable land, and almost the whole of Egypt's population lived in that area. Most of the remaining land was desert. Rain fell only rarely, and the country was dependent almost entirely on the Nile River for its water supply.

Egypt was divided into two main parts, Upper and Lower. Upper Egypt, to the south, was desert except for the Nile Valley, where soil left behind after the annual flooding of the Nile made the land usable for a few kilometres either side of the river. Lower Egypt, to the north, consisted mainly of the flat and often swampy Delta that stretched from Cairo (Memphis) to the Mediterranean Sea, 180 kilometres away (see NILE).

A stream called the Brook (or River) of Egypt, which formed part of the south-western boundary of the land promised to Israel, was not the Nile River but the Wadi El-Arish. It flowed out of the Sinai Peninsular into the Mediterranean Sea. This was a very practical boundary from Israel's point of view. It excluded the useless desert land of the Wilderness of Shur to the west, but included the usable farming and grazing land to the east (Num 34:1-5; Josh 15:4,47; 1 Kings 8:65; Isa 27:12).

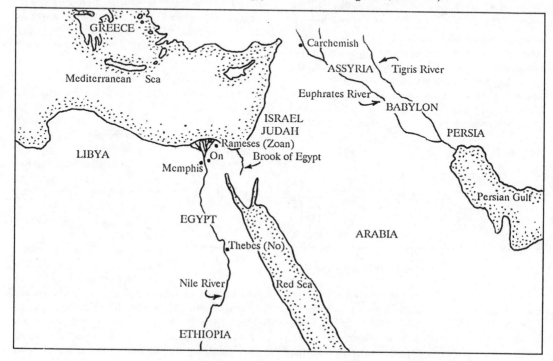

The people of Egypt appear to have been a mixture of Hamites and Semites. The descendants of Ham developed their own culture throughout lands of northern Africa, and were called Mizraim by the Hebrews (Gen 10:6; Ps 78:51; 105:23,27). From very early times, other peoples mingled with the Hamites, among them the Semites (descendants of Shem). The Semitic influence was mainly responsible for the advanced civilization that was well established in Egypt at the time Israel became prominent in the Bible story.

For most of this period the capital of Egypt was Memphis, on virtually the same site as present-day Cairo (Jer 44:1; Hosea 9:6; see MEMPHIS). Nearby was the city of sun worship, which the Egyptians called On and the Greeks called Heliopolis (Gen 41:45; Jer 43:13; cf. Isa 19:18).

Pharaoh was the title given to all Egyptian kings, and was used either by itself or attached to the king's personal name (Exod 5:1; 2 Kings 23:29; see PHARAOH). The people considered the king to be a god and did not question his laws.

Egyptians worshipped many gods, most of them gods of nature and therefore concerned with the Nile, on which the life of Egypt depended (Exod 12:12). Pharaoh was considered to be a god-king who embodied one of these gods. At his death he passed from the world of the humans to the world of the gods, which explains why the Pharaohs built for themselves elaborate tombs such as the pyramids.

Bible history up till the exodus

After about a thousand years of development and progress under successive Egyptian dynasties, the native Egyptian rulers gradually lost their power to aggressive chiefs among recent Semitic immigrants. These foreign chiefs (in Egyptian called Hyksos) eventually took over the country (about 1720 BC).

Migration of Semites to Egypt

The Hyksos continued the traditional Egyptian style of government, with the leader becoming the Pharaoh. Egyptian officials handled the day-to-day administration as previously. However, during the century and a half of the Hyksos dynasties, a number of Semites (such as Joseph) were appointed to high positions in the Egyptian government. At the same time official procedures and traditions remained thoroughly Egyptian (Gen 41:14,40-45; 43:32; 46:34; 47:22,26; 50:2-3,26).

Egyptian princes overthrew the Hyksos and established a new dynasty about 1570 BC. This was a turning point in Egyptian history, and the next five hundred years was the period of Egypt's greatest power and magnificence. For most of this time the capital was at Thebes in Upper Egypt. This was a magnificent city, a fact reflected in the Hebrew word no, by which the Israelites called the city (Jer 46:25; Ezek 30:16; Nahum 3:8; see THEBES).

Meanwhile the descendants of Jacob, who had migrated to Egypt during the time of the Hyksos, had multiplied greatly. The Egyptian rulers, fearing and despising these Semite migrants, introduced laws against them and eventually made them slaves. This provided the Pharaohs with a cheap work force for their extensive building programs. One of the cities that the Hebrew slaves built was Rameses (or Ra'amses) in the Nile Delta. (It was probably the former Hyksos capital, Avaris, rebuilt.) The building program included a palace, storehouses and defence installations (Exod 1:8-11; see RAMESES).

The Pharaohs lived in luxury and their large harems usually included many foreign women. It was therefore not unusual for non-Egyptian children to grow up in the palace (Exod 2:10). Pharaoh also had magicians and wise men, who were among his chief advisers (Exod 7:11; 8:19). (For Moses' conflict with Pharaoh see PHARAOH; PLAGUE.)

Bible history during the Israelite monarchy

Apart from the events that led up to and included the exodus (1280 BC), Egypt had little to do with Israel during the five hundred years of Egypt's greatest power. This time of Egyptian greatness came to an end about 1085 BC, and the story of the nation from then on is one of decline. The capital from 1085 to 660 BC was Rameses, renamed Zoan (Isa 19:11,13; 30:4).

About 970 BC Solomon, king of Israel, married the daughter of the Pharaoh of Egypt as part of a treaty designed to strengthen the security and commercial life of both kingdoms (1 Kings 3:1; 4:21; 10:28-29). But when that Pharaoh died, the new Pharaoh, fearful of Israel's increasing power, encouraged rebellions within Israel. He also supported guerilla attacks around its borders, and on one occasion he himself attacked and plundered Jerusalem (1 Kings 11:14-22,40; 14:25-27).

During the time of Israel's divided kingdom, both sections were at times tempted to rely on Egypt for help against Assyria. They were always disappointed (2 Kings 17:4-6; 18:21,24; Isa 30:1-3; 31:1). Also during this time Assyria destroyed the former Egyptian capital, Thebes (Nahum 3:8-10).

When Babylon conquered the Assyrian capital Nineveh in 612 BC, Pharaoh Necho of Egypt went to help what was left of Assyria to withstand Babylon. Josiah, king of Judah, opposed Necho, fearing that

An Egyptian god

this Egyptian-Assyrian alliance was a threat to his own independence. Judah was defeated and Josiah killed. Necho now considered himself controller of Judah and placed a heavy tax on it (2 Kings 23:28-35). But in 605 BC Babylon conquered Egypt in the Battle of Carchemish, and so became the new master of Judah (2 Kings 24:7; Jer 46:2).

After serving Babylon for a time, the Judean king rebelled, bringing a punishing invasion from Babylon. Babylon then appointed a new Judean king, Zedekiah, but after a while he too sought Egyptian aid in rebelling against Babylon, a policy that Jeremiah and Ezekiel strongly opposed (2 Kings 24:18-20; Jer 2:16-18,36-37; 21:1-10; 37:6-10; Ezek 17:12-16; 29:6-9). This brought a further attack by Babylon, resulting in the destruction of Jerusalem in 587 BC and the deportation of most of the Judeans to Babylon (2 Kings 25:1-21).

Gedaliah, a Judean official, was appointed by the Babylonians as governor of those who remained in Judah. He encouraged the people to submit to Babylon and not to look for support against Babylon from Egypt. But the pro-Egyptian group murdered Gedaliah. The remaining Judeans, fearing a revenge attack by Babylon, fled for their lives to Egypt (2 Kings 25:22-26; Jer 40:13-43:7).

Summary of later history

In another battle, in 568 BC, Babylon defeated Egypt again, this time not on foreign soil but in Egypt itself (Jer 46:13-24; Ezek 29:17-20, 30:20-26). Babylon then forced Egypt to join it in resisting the rising power of Persia, but the attempt was unsuccessful. Persia conquered Babylon in 539 BC, and conquered Egypt in 525 BC. Egypt rebelled against Persia whenever the opportunity arose, till in 341 BC the last native ruler of Egypt was removed (cf. Ezek 32:1-16).

With Alexander the Great's conquest in 332 BC, Egypt came under the rule of the Greeks. In New Testament times it was ruled by the Romans (Acts 21:38). In the third century AD it became a nominally Christian country, but in 641 AD it was conquered by the Moslems and has remained under Moslem control ever since.

EKRON

The town of Ekron was one of the 'five cities of the Philistines' (Josh 13:3; 1 Sam 6:17-18). It had a history of conflict with Israel from the time that Israel first entered Canaan. It changed hands between the Philistines and the Israelites frequently (see PHILISTIA). The Philistines considered Ekron to be the home of the god Baal-zebub (2 Kings 1:2-3; see BEELZEBUL).

ELAM

Elam was an ancient kingdom north of the Persian Gulf in the region of Mesopotamia. Later it became part of Persia, and its name was sometimes used as another name for Persia. For details see PERSIA.

ELATH

See EZION-GEBER.

ELDER

Within the community of God's people, God marks out certain people for responsibilities of care and leadership. The Bible refers to these people by a number of words, one of them 'elders'. This is the word that the Old Testament uses for those in Israel who exercised leadership in the community (Exod

24:1; Deut 21:1-6; Ruth 4:2-11; 1 Sam 8:4; see RULER), and that the New Testament uses for Jewish officials who administered Jewish affairs through the synagogue councils and the Sanhedrin (Mark 15:1; Luke 7:3; Acts 4:5; see SANHEDRIN; SYNAGOGUE). It is also the word that the New Testament uses for leaders in God's new community, the church (Acts 14:23; 15:4).

Developments in church leadership

The first Christian church was in Jerusalem, and in its early days its leadership came from the group of apostles whom Jesus had earlier appointed (Acts 4:37; 6:2; 11:1). God did not provide these apostles with a master plan of detailed procedures upon which they were to structure the church, whether in Jerusalem or elsewhere. Instead he left them to respond to the church's needs as his Spirit directed them. As the church grew, they introduced whatever organizational arrangements they considered necessary (e.g. Acts 6:1-6).

As the church expanded into neighbouring regions and countries, the apostles had increasing responsibilities outside Jerusalem. Soon the church in Jerusalem had its own group of governing elders, and these were distinct from the apostles (Acts 11:30; 15:6). The practice of appointing elders was later copied in other churches (Acts 14:23), though there is not enough information to indicate whether the form of church government was the same in all the churches.

The New Testament speaks consistently of leaders in the churches, though it does not always give them an official title (1 Cor 16:16; Gal 2:9; 1 Thess 5:12; Heb 13:7,17). Even where the Bible recognizes a title, the emphasis is usually more on the work the elders do than on the office they hold (Acts 20:17,28; 1 Thess 5:13; 1 Tim 3:1; 1 Peter 5:1-3).

English versions of the Bible use various words for church leaders – 'elders', 'overseers', 'guardians', 'bishops'. These names are translations of only two words in the Greek of the original New Testament, *presbuteroi* and *episkopoi*, and both words seem to apply to the same office and person. For example (quoting the RSV), in Acts 20:17 Paul sends for the elders (*presbuteroi*) of the Ephesian church, but when they arrive (v. 28) he calls them guardians (*episkopoi*). Likewise in Titus 1:5 he tells Titus to appoint elders (*presbuteroi*), and then in the same sentence (v. 7) he calls them bishops (*episkopoi*). In reference to any specific local church, the Bible always speaks of a plurality of elders (Acts 14:23; 20:17; Phil 1:1; 1 Thess 5:12).

Responsibilities of elders

Elders are likened to shepherds over a flock. They are the leaders of the church, whom God has placed over the church to guide it and care for it (Acts 20:28; 1 Tim 3:5; 5:17; Heb 13:17; 1 Peter 5:1-3; see PASTOR; SHEPHERD). Others in the church can help the elders by taking responsibility for many of the practical ministries of the church. In this way they give the elders more time for the important pastoral ministries God has entrusted to them (Acts 6:2-4; James 5:14; see DEACON).

All elders should have some ability at teaching (1 Tim 3:2), though some will be more gifted than others, and therefore more occupied than others, in public preaching (1 Tim 5:17). Through their own ministry and that of teachers from elsewhere, elders should provide the church with teaching that is upbuilding and protect it from what is harmful (Acts 20:28-30; Titus 1:9). Elders must therefore be people of discernment (1 Tim 1:3-7; 6:3-5; 2 Tim 2:14-16; 2 John 7-11).

In addition to having qualifications in relation to gift and ability, each elder must fulfil certain minimum requirements in relation to his character and behaviour. As a leader he is in a position of example to others, and therefore his family life and public reputation must be of the highest order (1 Tim 3:1-7; Titus 1:5-9). Any accusation of wrongdoing against an elder must be supported by witnesses. If the elder is proved guilty, he should be publicly rebuked, again because of the high standards required of those in positions of leadership (1 Tim 5:19-20).

Appointment of elders

The Bible gives no specific instructions concerning how elders are chosen or appointed. In the case of the churches that Paul and Barnabas established in Galatia, the first elders were appointed by those who planted the churches (Acts 14:23). Normally, a person should not be appointed an elder too soon after his conversion, as time is needed for Christian character and spiritual gift to develop (1 Tim 3:6; 5:22). If a church is left without elders, it is liable to lose direction (Titus 1:5,10-11).

Those who have the responsibility to appoint elders must realize that only the Holy Spirit can really make a person an elder (Acts 20:28; 1 Cor 12:11,28). They should also make sure, through prayer and consultation with the church as a whole, that those whom they appoint are those whom the church recognizes as elders. Church members must have confidence in their leaders if they are to respect them and heed their instruction (1 Thess 5:12-13;

Heb 13:17). They should also give the elders suitable payment for the work they do and the time they spend in the service of the church (1 Tim 5:17-18; cf. Gal 6:6).

With the passing of years and the growth of the church, additional elders will be needed. A person may recognize the direction in which his spiritual gift is developing and desire to be an elder (1 Tim 3:1; see GIFTS OF THE SPIRIT). People in the church will recognize his gift; in fact, elders have a responsibility to train those who appear to have leadership ability (2 Tim 2:2; cf. Acts 13:5; 16:1-3). The example of the apostles in the early church suggests that the existing elders are the ones who make the appointment (Acts 1:21-26; cf. 1 Tim 4:14; 5:22), but before doing so they find out the mind of the church (Acts 6:3; cf. 15:22).

Some may be tempted to avoid eldership because of the difficulties and tensions that come with it (1 Peter 5:2a). Others may be tempted in the opposite direction, and try to use the position of elder to further their personal ambitions (1 Peter 5:2b,3). Elders can learn how to be true shepherds of the flock by following the example of the Chief Shepherd, Jesus Christ, who gave himself for it (1 Peter 5:4; cf. John 10:11; Eph 5:25).

ELEAZAR

Of the many people named Eleazar whom the Old Testament mentions, the most important was Eleazar, the third of Aaron's four sons (Num 3:2). When Aaron became high priest, his four sons became his priest-assistants (Exod 28:1-4). After the death of the two older sons (Lev 10:1-2), Eleazar and his younger brother Ithamar were given greater responsibility. Eleazar was in overall charge of the Levites (Num 3:32). Within the division of the Levites according to their three family groups, Eleazar seems to have had responsibility for the Kohath group (which had the higher duties; Num 4:15-16), and Ithamar had responsibility for the other two groups (Num 4:28,33).

God had prepared Eleazar to succeed Aaron as high priest (cf. Num 16:37; 19:3-4), and directed that Aaron, before he died, publicly appoint Eleazar to office (Num 20:23-28). Eleazar then assisted Moses as Aaron had previously (Num 26:63; 27:2; 31:12; 32:2). God directed that when Moses died, the new leader Joshua would not speak to God face to face as Moses had, but would receive God's instructions through the high priest Eleazar (Num 27:18-23). God directed also that Joshua and Eleazar together were to be in charge of the work of dividing Canaan

between Israel's twelve tribes (Num 34:17; cf. Josh 17:4; 19:51; 21:1). (Concerning Eleazar's famous son see PHINEHAS.)

ELECTION

God is a loving and merciful God, and in his grace chooses people for purposes that he has planned. This exercise of God's sovereign will is called election.

In the Old Testament God's election applied particularly to his choice of Abraham and, through Abraham, to his choice of Israel to be his people (Gen 12:1-3; Neh 9:7-8; Isa 41:8-9). From this people he produced one man, Jesus the Messiah, chosen by him before the foundation of the world to be the Saviour of the world (Luke 9:35; Acts 2:23; 4:27-28; Eph 1:9-10; 1 Peter 1:20; 2:4,6). All who believe in Jesus, whether Jew or Gentile, are the true people of God, the true descendants of Abraham (Rom 9:6-9; Gal 3:14,26-29). God has chosen them to receive his salvation, and together they form God's people, the church (John 6:37,44; 15:19; 17:2,6; Eph 1:4-6; 2 Thess 2:13-14; 1 Peter 2:9). 'The elect' is therefore another name for the people of God (Matt 24:22; Luke 18:7; 2 Tim 2:10).

God's activity in determining beforehand what will happen, particularly in relation to people's destiny, is sometimes called predestination. This predestination originates in God himself, who acts according to his own will and purpose (Ps 139:16; Isa 14:24; 37:26; 46:9-10; Matt 25:34; Acts 2:23; 4:27-28; Eph 1:5; Rom 8:28-30; 1 Thess 5:9; see PREDESTINATION).

The gracious work of God

Election has its source in the sovereign love of God. No one deserves to be chosen by God, but in his immeasurable mercy he has chosen to save some (Rom 9:15; 11:5; Eph 1:5). God's choice of people does not depend on anything of merit in them. It depends entirely on his unmerited favour towards them (Deut 7:6-8; 9:6; Rom 11:6; 1 Cor 1:27-29; 2 Tim 1:9; James 2:5).

Neither does God choose people because he foresees their faith or their good intentions (Rom 9:11,16). Salvation is not a reward for faith. Faith is simply the means by which people receive the undeserved salvation that God, in his mercy, gives (Rom 9:16,30; Eph 2:8-9; see FAITH). Or, to put it another way, faith is the means by which God's eternal choice becomes a reality in their earthly experience (Acts 13:48; 1 Thess 1:4-9). By coming to believe in Jesus, they show that God has chosen them. Eternal life is not their achievement, but God's (John 6:37,40).

All the merit for a person's salvation is in Jesus Christ, whose work of atonement is the basis on which God can forgive repentant sinners (Rom 3:23-26; see JUSTIFICATION). They are chosen only because of their union with Christ, and they are to be changed into the likeness of Christ (Eph 1:4; 2 Tim 1:9; cf. Rom 8:29; 2 Thess 2:14).

No one can argue with God concerning his work of election, for all mankind is guilty before him and in no position to demand mercy from him. God is the sovereign Creator; human beings are but his rebellious creatures. The amazing thing is not that God shows mercy on only some, but that he shows mercy on any at all (Rom 9:14-23).

Election and calling

Sometimes the Bible speaks of God's choosing as his calling (Isa 41:8-9; 51:2; Rom 9:11), but other times it makes a distinction (Matt 22:14; see CALL). God chose his people from eternity (Eph 1:4; 2 Tim 1:9) and determined to save those whom he had chosen (Rom 8:28-29; Eph 1:5,11). The historical event when each chosen person repented, believed, and accepted God's salvation is sometimes spoken of as the call of God to that person (Rom 8:30; 9:23-24; 1 Thess 2:12; 2 Thess 2:13-14; 2 Tim 1:9).

Side by side with the truth of God's sovereign will is the truth of man's responsibility. The gospel is available to all, and those who refuse it have no one to blame but themselves (Rom 10:13; 1 Tim 2:3-4; 2 Peter 3:9).

The knowledge that God has chosen sinners to receive salvation is a great encouragement to those who preach the gospel. It urges them on in their preaching, so that people might hear the message of grace that is God's means of bringing his chosen to himself (John 10:14-16; 17:6-8; Acts 13:48; 18:10; Rom 10:13-14; 2 Tim 2:10). And the salvation of those who respond in faith is eternally secure; for it depends not upon their efforts, but upon the sovereign choice of God (John 6:37-40; 10:27-29; Rom 8:33-39; 11:29; see ASSURANCE).

Responsibilities of the elect

Although a person may feel secure because his salvation is centred in God, he is deceiving himself if he thinks that his behaviour is unimportant (2 Peter 1:9-11). There is nothing mechanical about election. Man is not a lifeless robot manipulated by some impersonal fate. He is a creature made in God's image, whose life depends upon a relationship with God. If a person has truly been chosen by God, he will show it by a life of perseverance in the faith he professes. The Bible often links statements about election with warnings and commands concerning the necessity for steadfastness, watchfulness and perseverance (Mark 13:13,22-23,27,33; Acts 13:48; 14:22; 1 Thess 5:23-24; 2 Thess 2:13-15; 1 Tim 6:11-12; see PERSEVERANCE).

Those whom God has chosen to be his people are, by that fact, chosen to be holy (Deut 7:6; Eph 1:4; 1 Peter 1:15). Since they belong to God, they are to be separate from sin and uncleanness, bringing praise to him (Isa 43:21; Eph 1:12; 2 Thess 2:13; see HOLINESS). They are to reflect the glory of Christ now, and will one day share in that glory fully (Rom 8:29-30; 9:23; 1 Cor 2:7; 2 Thess 2:14). Part of God's purpose in choosing them is that their lives might bear fruit for God, as they develop Christian character and do good for others (John 15:16; Eph 2:10). God has chosen them to be his channel of blessing to an ever-increasing number of people (1 Peter 2:9-10; cf. Gen 12:1-3).

Awareness of their election should not lead Christians to complacency. Rather the opposite, for God requires a higher standard of conduct in those who are his chosen people (Amos 3:2; Micah 3:9-12; 1 Peter 4:17). The way a person lives is the proof or disproof of his election (2 Peter 1:9-11; cf. Titus 1:1; 1 John 2:29; 3:10)).

ELI

At the time when Eli was chief priest and chief administrator in Israel, the tabernacle was at Shiloh, in central Israel. Eli sat outside the tabernacle to give advice and settle disputes, while his sons carried out the routine work connected with the sacrifices and ceremonies (1 Sam 1:3,9; 4:18).

Eli's sons were corrupt, but Eli did not remove them from office, even though he disagreed with their conduct. God announced to Eli, first through a prophet and then through the boy Samuel, that he would punish Eli's household with shame, poverty and early death. Only one would be left functioning as a priest, and eventually he too would be removed (1 Sam 2:12-36; 3:11-14). (For the fulfilment of these prophecies see 1 Sam 4:11; 14:3; 22:11-20; 1 Kings 2:26-27.)

ELIJAH

The chief purpose for which God raised up Elijah was to preserve in Israel the worship of Yahweh, Israel's covenant God. Israel had always been tempted to mix the worship of their God with the religious practices of local Baalism (see BAAL), but matters suddenly worsened after Jezebel became queen. Jezebel was daughter of the king-priest of Philistia and had married King Ahab of Israel. She brought with her a new and more dangerous form of Baalism, which she then tried to make the national religion of Israel. This was the Baalism of the god Melqart, whose influence had already spread south along the Mediterranean coast as far as Mt Carmel (1 Kings 16:30-33).

Early resistance to Baalism

Baal was supposed to control nature and fertility. Therefore, to show the powerlessness of Baal, Elijah announced a three-year drought throughout Israel and Phoenicia. God's miraculous provisions of food, both in Israel and in Phoenicia, showed that he, not Baal, was the God of nature (1 Kings 17:1-4,9,16; cf. Luke 4:25,26). Elijah's healing of the widow's son confirmed the woman's faith in the one true God (1 Kings 17:24).

After three years of drought, Elijah challenged Ahab to gather Baal's prophets to Mt Carmel for a public contest to show who was the true God, Yahweh or Baal (1 Kings 18:19-21). The Baal priests considered Mt Carmel to be one of their sacred sites, yet even there they were shamefully defeated (1 Kings 18:40). As a final proof that Israel's God, not Baal, controlled nature, Elijah announced that God would end the drought by sending a storm. That same day the drought ended (1 Kings 18:41-46; cf. James 5:17-18).

Elijah felt that he was fighting alone in his battle with Jezebel's Baalism (1 Kings 18:22; Rom 11:1-5). This feeling was strengthened when, in spite of his spectacular victory over Baal at Mt Carmel, nothing in Israel seemed to have changed. The people did not cease from their Baal worship, and Jezebel did not cease from her efforts to kill him. He therefore fled for his life (1 Kings 19:1-3).

God directed Elijah south to Mt Sinai, the place where, centuries earlier, he had established his covenant with Israel. There he showed Elijah the difference between spectacular public events and the quiet work of God within people's hearts. The former may have some use, but Israel would have truly lasting benefits only as people listened to the voice of God in their hearts and responded to it. God assured Elijah that a minority of people in Israel would make the quiet response of faithfulness to him (1 Kings 19:10-12,18).

For Israel's idolatrous majority, however, there would be further violent and spectacular events, but these would be in judgment against them rather than against Baal. God's instruments of judgment against Israel would be an enemy king Hazael, an Israelite king Jehu, and Elijah's successor Elisha (1 Kings 19:15-21).

Ministry fulfilled

In addition to opposing Ahab and Jezebel because of their Baalism, Elijah opposed them because of their greed and injustice. After their seizure of Naboth's vineyard, Elijah announced the judgment of God upon them (1 Kings 21:20-24). Ahab's son Ahaziah, who came to the throne after Ahab's death, continued the worship of Baal and likewise met opposition from Elijah. God preserved Elijah from Ahaziah's attempts to capture him, and then used Elijah to pronounce certain death upon the Baalist king (2 Kings 1:2-4,13-17).

The time had now come for Elijah to pass on to Elisha the responsibility for preserving the faithful and preparing judgment for the Baalists. Elijah tested his young successor to see whether he was prepared for the difficult and wide-ranging work ahead, or whether he would rather settle at one of the schools of the prophets (2 Kings 2:1-6). Elisha stayed with Elijah to the end, and in due course received Elijah's spiritual inheritance (2 Kings 2:9). Elijah's earthly life ended when he was taken up to heaven in a whirlwind (2 Kings 2:11).

Jews of a later era expected the return of Elijah immediately before the coming of the Messiah (Mal 4:5-6; Mark 6:15; 8:27-28). Jesus pointed out that this 'Elijah', this forerunner of the Messiah, was John the Baptist (Matt 11:10-14; 17:10-13; Luke 1:17).

On the occasion of Jesus' transfiguration, Elijah and Moses appeared together talking with Jesus about his coming death, and witnessing something of his coming glory. These two men, the great lawgiver and the great prophet, were representative figures from the former era. Their presence symbolized that the one to whom the law and the prophets pointed had now arrived. All the expectations of the former era were now fulfilled in Jesus Christ (Luke 9:28-31; cf. 24:27; see TRANSFIGURATION).

ELISHA

At the time of the ministry of Elijah and Elisha, Israel's ancient religion was threatened by the Baalism that Jezebel had brought with her from Phoenicia. Through her husband, King Ahab of Israel, Jezebel had tried to establish Phoenician Baalism as the official religion of Israel (1 Kings 16:30-33). The man who began the long and difficult job of removing this Baalism from Israel was the prophet Elijah (see ELIJAH). By God's direction Elijah passed on the unfinished task to Elisha (1 Kings 19:16,19), whose ministry lasted through the reigns of six Israelite kings. The extent of his ministry was about fifty years. The period was the latter half of the ninth century BC.

Successor to Elijah

From the beginning Elisha showed a willingness to succeed Elijah, in spite of the obvious difficulties ahead. Originally a farmer, he gave up his former way of life for the unpopular task of being God's messenger to the hardened and idolatrous people of Israel (1 Kings 19:19-21). Like Elijah, Elisha would have to move around the country, strengthening the believers and opposing the idolaters. Elijah tested him to see if he would try to avoid some of the difficulties by remaining at one of the schools for young prophets. But Elisha was determined to carry on Elijah's work. He was Elijah's spiritual heir, and he remained with Elijah to the end to receive the spiritual inheritance (2 Kings 2:1-12).

A miracle at the Jordan River quickly proved that God's power had now passed from Elijah to Elisha (2 Kings 2:13-14). Many more miracles would follow, showing what a serious threat Jezebel's Baalism was to Israel's national life.

Elisha's ministry was to be twofold. It was to be concerned on the one hand with preserving the faithful minority in Israel (the remnant), and on the other with preparing judgment for the unfaithful nation (1 Kings 19:15-18). His first two miracles symbolized these characteristics of blessing and cursing. To those who were in need he brought healing, but to those who rejected his message he brought judgment (2 Kings 2:19-25).

A combined Israelite-Judean attack on Moab gave Elisha the opportunity to demonstrate to the two kings his opposition to Baal. He refused to help the Baal-worshipping Israelite king, though he passed on advice to the godly Judean king (2 Kings 3:9-15).

Caring for the faithful minority

Faithful believers were rare in Israel, and Elisha had to help preserve them, lest the true worship of Yahweh vanish from the nation. He helped the poor widow of one of the godly prophets by giving her a miraculous supply of oil that saved her entire family (2 Kings 4:1-7). He also secured the future for a wealthy believer by giving her a son. When, years later, the son died, Elisha brought him back to life (2 Kings 4:8-37).

Many of the faithful were to be found in the schools where young men trained to be prophets. Like Elijah before him, Elisha moved around these schools, with the aim of strengthening those who could later help rebuild the religious life of the nation (2 Kings 2:1-7,15; 4:38; 6:1).

These communities were very poor. They had difficulty getting enough food to eat each day, and they lacked even the basic tools to rebuild their inadequate housing. In one place Elisha worked a miracle to save the day's food from being lost, and in another he miraculously recovered a borrowed tool that had fallen into the river (2 Kings 4:38-41; 6:1-7). On one occasion he miraculously multiplied a gift of food to feed a large group of his followers (2 Kings 4:42-44).

By the healing of Naaman, Elisha showed God's power to the commander of the army (Syria) that God was going to use to punish Israel (2 Kings 5:1-14; cf. 1 Kings 19:15-17). Naaman's knowledge of the one true God was still imperfect, but at least he had a more sincere faith in Yahweh than did many Israelites (2 Kings 5:15-19).

Preparing Israel for judgment

God's intention to use Syria to punish his people did not mean that Elisha had to desert Israel and join the Syrians. In fact, the Syrians saw him as an enemy and tried to capture him. Instead Elisha captured the Syrian soldiers and led them to the Israelite capital, Samaria. When the Israelite king wanted to kill them, Elisha directed him to feed them. The incident brought a temporary peace, and should have taught both nations that God controlled their destinies (2 Kings 6:8-23).

Neither king learnt much from the incident. The Syrian king attacked Jerusalem afresh, and the Israelite king blamed Elisha for the suffering that resulted (2 Kings 6:24-31). Elisha assured Israel's king that the siege would be broken and there would be plenty of food the next day. Yet when Elisha's prediction proved to be true, the king was slow to believe (2 Kings 7:1-15).

Syria's partly successful attacks on Israel were only the beginning. The attacks would become increasingly successful and violent. When Hazael of Syria murdered his king and seized the throne, a new era of terror began. Elisha wept when he saw the trouble that Hazael's cruelty would bring upon Israel (2 Kings 8:7-15; cf. 1 Kings 19:15). With Hazael now king of Syria, the time had arrived for Elisha to carry out his last major responsibility, the anointing of Jehu to be king of Israel. Jehu's job was to remove Jezebel's Baalism from Israel's leadership by destroying Ahab, Jezebel and all their Baal-worshipping family (2 Kings 9:1-10; cf. 1 Kings 19:16-17; see JEHU).

Elisha lived to see the divine judgment carried out, first on Ahab's family and then on Israel as a whole. After that, he saw the beginnings of Israel's recovery, and might have seen Israel overthrow Syrian power completely had not the Israelite king been lacking in faith (2 Kings 13:14-19). Even after Elisha's death, dramatic events at his burial place showed that the God he served was still alive and powerful (2 Kings 13:20-21).

ELIZABETH

Both Zechariah and Elizabeth, the parents of John the Baptist, belonged to the vast priestly family descended from Aaron (Luke 1:5). Elizabeth was also related to Mary the mother of Jesus (Luke 1:36). For some time Zechariah and Elizabeth were unable to have children, but in answer to their prayers (for they were godly people) God promised them a son. They were to name him John (Luke 1:6-7,13).

When Elizabeth was six months pregnant, Mary visited her, bringing news that she (Mary) was to be the mother of the promised Messiah (Luke 1:35-36,39-40). Elizabeth, far from being in any way jealous, was overjoyed, and interpreted the movement of the baby in her womb as a sign that it too was overjoyed (Luke 1:41-45). Elizabeth and Zechariah knew that their child was to become the forerunner of the Messiah (Luke 1:13-17). Some remarkable incidents at the child's birth caused even the local villagers to realize that this child was destined for greatness (Luke 1:57-66).

ENCOURAGEMENT

The subject of encouragement covers a wide range of issues and behaviour. This applies in relation to God's encouragement of his people and to his people's encouragement of one another.

One of the most common forms of encouragement is in giving comfort and help, whether to those who are sorrowful (2 Sam 10:2; Isa 61:2; Matt 5:4; Rom 12:15; see SORROW), those who fear (Exod 14:13; Ps 23:4; Matt 14:27; Rev 2:10; see FEAR), those who are persecuted (Ps 86:17; Isa 49:13; John 16:33; 1 Peter 4:12-14; see PERSECUTION), or those who are experiencing any other form of weakness, despair or suffering (Isa 40:1-2; Zeph 3:16; Matt 9:2,22; Acts 23:11; see SUFFERING). When God's people go through unpleasant experiences, one beneficial result is that they are able to comfort others who may have similar experiences (2 Cor 1:3-5).

But encouragement involves more than giving cheer to the disheartened. Positively, it involves giving support to people in such a way that they will have greater confidence, enthusiasm and strength in their lives and service for God (Deut 3:28; Zech 4:6-9; Acts 4:36; 9:26-27; 1 Cor 14:3-4; Phil 1:6; 4:19; see HOPE).

Encouragement may often include words of teaching, warning and perhaps rebuke, as mature leaders among God's people urge their fellows to greater effort in their devotion to God. This will require patience in those who give the advice and in those who receive it (Josh 1:6-7,9; 1 Cor 4:14; Col 1:28; 3:16; 1 Thess 2:11-12; 3:2; 5:14; Heb 13:22; see PATIENCE).

Through having right attitudes towards the giving and receiving of encouragement in all its forms, believers will develop Christian character. At the same time they will understand better the nature of God who, as Father, Son and Holy Spirit, is the God of all comfort (2 Cor 1:3; Phil 2:1; Acts 9:31). (Concerning references to the Holy Spirit as 'the Comforter' see HOLY SPIRIT.)

ENDURANCE

God has made it plain that his people will at times meet suffering, hardship, persecution and other trials. Through their endurance, however, they will prove God's faithfulness and develop true Christian character (Rom 5:3-4; 2 Cor 1:6; 2 Thess 1:3-4; 2 Tim 2:3-6,10-13; Heb 11:27; James 1:12; see PERSECUTION; SUFFERING; TESTING).

Endurance means that Christians will have to tolerate insults and injustice (1 Cor 6:7; 13:7; 2 Tim 3:10-11); but through persistence in prayer and the inward work of the Holy Spirit, they will be able to rejoice through it all (Rom 12:11-12; Gal 5:22). (For discussion on this aspect of endurance see PATIENCE.) Endurance means that Christians must always persevere, no matter what the difficulties and temptations. They must maintain their faith in Christ firm to the end (Matt 24:13; Eph 6:13; Heb 3:14; 6:15; Rev 13:10). (For discussion on this aspect of endurance see PERSEVERANCE.)

ENEMY

Although the Christian is to try to live peaceably with everyone (Rom 12:18), his identification with Jesus Christ means that some will oppose him.

Therefore, he will have enemies. The Christian's enemies become God's enemies, and God's enemies become the Christian's enemies (Exod 23:22; Ps 37:20; 55:2-3; Matt 10:22,36). In spite of this, the Christian is to love his enemies and do good to those who hate him (Matt 5:44; Luke 6:27; Rom 12:20; see HATRED).

The Bible speaks of enemies other than one's fellow human beings; for example, Satan, death and evil spiritual forces. But Christ has conquered all these through his death and resurrection, and in the day of his final victory he will destroy them for ever (Matt 13:39; Luke 10:18; 1 Cor 15:25-28; Col 2:15; Heb 10:12-13).

ENOCH

Death is one of the evil consequences of man's sin, and the genealogical record of the generations from Adam to Noah is characterized by repetition of the word 'death' (Gen 5:5,8,11,14,17,20). The case of Enoch, however, was different. He was a man who lived his life in such close fellowship with God that God took him to be with himself without Enoch's having to die first (Gen 5:22-24; Heb 11:5). In this way God gave hope to the righteous that death's apparent conquest is not permanent. God has power over it.

Thousands of years later, when Jews were becoming increasingly interested in heaven and the afterlife, there was much interest in Enoch. During the last centuries of the era before Christ, people wrote books in his name, and the New Testament quotes one of these as containing a prophecy from Enoch (Jude 14-15).

The only other person named Enoch in the Bible also belonged to the earliest period of biblical history. He was a son of Cain, but the Bible says little about him (Gen 4:17-18).

ENVY

See JEALOUSY.

EPHAH

An ephah was the basic measurement of capacity that the Israelites used when measuring volumes of grain. It was equal to about thirty-seven litres (Lev 6:20; Ruth 2:17; 1 Sam 17:17). Over the years the word 'ephah' became also the name of the container people used to measure the grain (Lev 19:36; Amos 8:5; Zech 5:6-9). (For fuller details of the system that Israelites used to measure capacity see MEASUREMENT.)

EPHESIANS, LETTER TO THE

Paul's letter to the Ephesians is more general than his other letters, in the sense that it deals with issues concerning the whole church rather than with those of a particular local church. In the letter Paul discusses the union that exists between Christ and the church, and the results that this union should produce in the lives of Christians. He says nothing specific about his relations with the Ephesian church or with individuals in the church, even though he spent more time with the Ephesian church than with any other (Acts 20:31).

At the time Paul wrote this letter, a particular type of false teaching had affected the churches in and around Ephesus. It seems that Paul's special messenger took a number of copies of the same letter and distributed them among the churches of the area. The name of the receiving church was probably written into the introduction of the letter as copies were distributed. If so, that would explain why some ancient manuscripts include the word 'Ephesus' in Paul's opening greeting, but others omit it. Paul's letter to the church in Laodicea may have been another copy of this letter (Col 4:16).

Background to the letter

Regardless of how many copies of the letter may have been distributed, there seems no doubt that one of those copies went to the church in Ephesus. Ephesus was a town on the west coast of Asia Minor and was famous for its heathen religions (Acts 19:35). This meant that the society from which the Christian converts came was one where superstition and false religious ideas were widespread (Acts 19:18-19,26-27). Paul saw that the church in Ephesus would be troubled by false teaching (Acts 20:29-30), and such teaching seems to have arisen by the time Paul was first imprisoned in Rome (Acts 28:16,30; cf. Eph 4:1).

The false teaching that affected the Ephesus area also affected neighbouring towns such as Laodicea and Colossae. From prison Paul wrote to these churches in an effort to correct the false teaching and the wrong conduct that had resulted from it. Tychicus was the messenger who took the letters to the churches and who passed on to them news of Paul's circumstances in Rome (Eph 6:21-22; Col 4:7,16).

It appears that the false teaching was an early form of Gnosticism. This was a type of religious philosophy that regarded Christ as neither fully human nor fully God, but as some sort of semi-angelic being. According to this teaching, Christ was far superior to the Christians who followed him, but both he and they needed help from unseen angelic powers if they were to reach the fulness of purity and perfection.

In reply Paul asserted that Christ is supreme over the universe, including all the angelic powers, good and bad. Angelic powers can add nothing to him (Eph 1:20-21). So far from anything in the universe filling up some lack in him, he fills the universe (Eph 1:23; 4:10; cf. Col 1:19). By his death and resurrection he has triumphed over the evil spiritual forces of the universe and, because of this, Christians likewise can have victory in their battles against evil (Eph 2:2-6; 6:12).

Paul considers not only individual Christians but also the church as a whole. The church is the body of Christ and shares with Christ in his triumph over all angelic powers (Eph 1:21-23; 2:6). The church is not humbled before angels. Rather angels are humbled before the church, for they see in it an overwhelming demonstration of the wisdom and power of God (Eph 3:10). All this is good reason for the Christians in and around Ephesus not to allow themselves to be persuaded by the clever, but false, teaching of the Gnostics (Eph 5:6).

Contents of the letter

In an opening expression of praise to God, Paul reminds his readers of the great blessings that they have because of their union with Christ. In fact, the whole universe will find its full meaning only in him (1:1-14). He prays that Christians might understand God's great purposes and experience his victorious power in their lives (1:15-23).

God saves helpless sinful people by his grace (2:1-10), and brings them into a united body, the church, where there is no distinction between Jew and Gentile. All are one in Christ (2:11-22). God unites Jews and Gentiles in one body, and this divine work displays God's wisdom. It also brings a response of love from those who have tasted his love (3:1-21).

Having been united in one body, God's people then grow spiritually through the gifts that the risen Christ has given them (4:1-16). They no longer follow former ungodly practices, because they now have new standards of behaviour (4:17-32). Their behaviour is patterned on the character of Christ (5:1-20), and as a result their relationships with everyone else change and become truly Christian (5:21-6:9). Because of the hostile powers of evil, the Christian life is a constant battle, but through the spiritual resources God has given them, Christians can have confidence and victory (6:10-24).

EPHESUS

Ephesus was the chief city of the Roman province of Asia (part of present-day Turkey). The church in Ephesus probably began through the work of Priscilla and Aquila, whom Paul left in Ephesus after visiting the city briefly at the end of his second missionary journey (Acts 18:18-21). (For map of the region see ASIA.)

Early developments

An important visitor during the early days of the Ephesian church was Apollos, a Jewish teacher from Alexandria in Egypt. Though eloquent, Apollos was lacking in the knowledge of certain Christian teachings, till Priscilla and Aquila taught him more accurately (Acts 18:24-28). The time of the church's greatest growth came when Paul returned at the beginning of his third missionary journey and spent three years in the city (Acts 20:31). During this time the zealous Ephesian converts evangelized most of the province of Asia (Acts 19:8-10).

The people of Ephesus were well known for their superstition and magic, and some dramatic events accompanied the people's response to Paul's preaching (Acts 19:11-20). The city was considered to be the home of the goddess Artemis (or Diana) and contained a magnificent temple built in her

Artemis (or Diana), goddess of Ephesus

honour (Acts 19:27-28,35). As the people of Ephesus turned in increasing numbers from the worship of Artemis to faith in Jesus, tensions developed in the city. The silversmiths who made small household shrines of the goddess found themselves going out of business and stirred up a riot. It was several hours before the city authorities were able to restore order (Acts 19:23-41).

Some time during his three years in Ephesus, Paul wrote the letter we know as First Corinthians (1 Cor 16:8-9,19). While in Ephesus Paul met violent opposition and suffered physical harm. On one occasion he almost lost his life (1 Cor 15:32; 16:8-9; cf. 2 Cor 1:8-9). Ephesus was no doubt the scene of some of the sufferings that Paul later records in 2 Cor 11:23-29, and it is possible that he suffered one of his imprisonments there.

Later difficulties

Before leaving Ephesus at the end of his third missionary journey, Paul warned that false teachers would trouble the church (Acts 20:17,28-31). This proved to be so, and Paul's letter to the Ephesians, which he wrote during his first imprisonment in Rome, deals with some of the wrong ideas that had become widespread in and around Ephesus (see EPHESIANS, LETTER TO THE).

After his release from Rome, Paul revisited the church in Ephesus to try to correct the wrong teaching. When he moved on, he left Timothy behind to continue corrective teaching. He also wrote Timothy two letters to help him in this task (1 Tim 1:3-7; 6:3-5; 2 Tim 1:18; 2:14-16). The false teaching that the apostle John condemned in his letters (written towards the end of the first century) was also centred in Ephesus (1 John 2:18-22; 4:1; 2 John 9-11).

Later the Ephesian church was troubled by another group of false teachers, the Nicolaitans. These people encouraged Christians to demonstrate their freedom by eating food that had been offered to idols and by engaging in sexual immorality (Rev 2:2,6; cf. 2:14-15).

Unfortunately, the Ephesian Christians had become so concerned with opposing false teaching year after year, that in the process their love for Christ had lost its original warmth. They had become harsh, critical and self-satisfied. God warned them that if they did not change and regain their original spirit of love, he would act against them in judgment and bring their church to an end. But those who triumphed over these attitudes would enjoy the fulness of eternal life (Rev 2:1-7).

EPHOD

An ephod was a short sleeveless linen garment, something like a long shirt or coat. It was a common piece of Hebrew clothing (1 Sam 2:18; 2 Sam 6:14), but in most cases where the Bible mentions an ephod the reference is to an article of the high priest's dress (Exod 28:4-30; 29:5).

The high priest's ephod was made of multi-coloured embroidered linen similar to the curtains of the tabernacle, but with gold thread woven into the cloth (Exod 39:2-3; cf. 26:31). It was held in place by two shoulder straps and bound at the waist by a sash (Exod 28:7-8). (For further details and an illustration of the high priest's dress see PRIEST.)

Since the ephod was the most distinctive article of the high priest's dress, people often referred to priests as those who 'wore the ephod' (1 Sam 2:28; 14:3; 22:18; Hosea 3:4). Sometimes a priest was asked to 'bring the ephod'. This was because within the flat pouch, or breastpiece, on the front of the ephod were two objects, the Urim and the Thummim, which the priest used to find out God's will (1 Sam 23:9-12; 30:7-8; Ezra 2:63; see URIM AND THUMMIM).

During the time of Israel's unfaithfulness in the period of the judges, Gideon made a golden ephod that soon became an object of idolatrous worship (Judg 8:26-27). On another occasion idolatrous priests, who were not even legally entitled to be priests, wore the traditional priestly ephod (Judg 17:5-6; 18:14-20).

EPHRAIM

Joseph and his Egyptian wife had two sons, Manasseh and Ephraim (Gen 41:50-52). When the aged Jacob gave his parting blessings to his family, he gave the firstborn's blessing to Joseph instead of to Reuben (because of Reuben's immorality with Jacob's concubine; Gen 35:22; 49:3-4; 1 Chron 5:1-2). This meant that Joseph would father two tribes in Israel instead of one. Jacob therefore raised Joseph's two sons to the same level as Jacob's other sons, so that Joseph's two sons would each have his own tribe (Gen 48:5-6). The tribe of the younger son Ephraim was destined to become stronger than that of the older son Manasseh (Gen 48:12-20).

Good territory

The tribe of Ephraim received as its inheritance possibly the best part of Canaan (cf. Gen 49:22-26). This was the central highland region between the Jordan River and the Mediterranean Sea (Josh 16:1-10). (For information about some of its more important towns see BETHEL; JERICHO; JOPPA; SHECHEM; SHILOH.)

Yet the Ephraimites were not satisfied. Since the fertile hills of the territory given to them were largely covered with forest, they complained that there was not enough land suitable for them to build villages to house all their people. Joshua told them to clear the forests and drive out the remaining

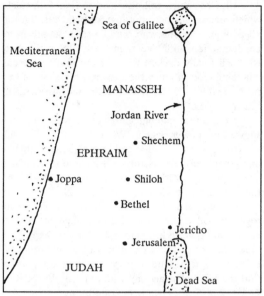

Canaanite people and they would find that they had plenty of land (Josh 17:14-18; see also Judg 17:1; 2 Sam 18:6).

Political ambition

Ephraim considered itself to be the leading tribe in Israel, and showed a spirit of jealousy when denied the status it believed it deserved. It complained to Gideon when he did not invite it to the battle against the Midianites (Judg 8:1), and to Jephthah when he did not ask it to join the battle against the Ammonites (Judg 12:1).

In particular, Ephraim was jealous of Judah, whom it saw as its competitor for leadership in Israel. When David (who was from the tribe of Judah) succeeded Saul as king of Israel, Ephraim supported Saul's son as a rival king, but after two years was forced to admit defeat (2 Sam 2:4,8-10; 5:1-3). Some years later Absalom rebelled against David, and once again Ephraim appears to have supported the anti-David forces (2 Sam 18:6-8).

When, after the death of Solomon, the northern tribes broke away from Judah, an Ephraimite led the revolt and became the first king of the breakaway kingdom (1 Kings 11:26-28; 12:20). This breakaway northern kingdom continued to call itself Israel, whereas the southern kingdom (which the dynasty of David continued to rule over in Jerusalem) became known as the kingdom of Judah. The northern kingdom Israel was so dominated by Ephraim that it

was often called Ephraim (Isa 7:2,9,17; 28:1; Hosea 4:17; 5:3; 9:3; see ISRAEL).

EPICUREANS

Greek philosophers of the New Testament period belonged mainly to two schools, the Epicureans and the Stoics. The Epicureans were named after their founder, Epicurus, a philosopher who taught in Athens about 300 BC. They believed that the world is neither permanent nor stable, and therefore people should not become too involved in its affairs. They should aim for maximum contentment through living calmly and avoiding all pain, desire, unpleasant feelings and superstitious fears. That was the way the gods lived, and that was why they took no interest in the life of man.

The Epicureans, with the Stoics, were members of the Areopagus, a council of philosophers that Paul addressed in Athens (Acts 17:18-19,22; see AREOPAGUS). The Epicureans would have agreed with Paul that God needs nothing from man (Acts 17:25), but they refused to accept his teaching on the resurrection (Acts 17:31-32). In later times their rejection of God and pursuit of pleasure led to carefree living, greed and immorality.

ESAU

As the firstborn of Isaac's twin sons, Esau was entitled to the family birthright. This meant that, upon his father's death, he would receive twice the inheritance of any other sons and become family head. Moreover, in the case of Isaac's firstborn, it included headship of God's chosen people and the right to possess the land of Canaan. But Esau was an unspiritual and irresponsible person, preferring temporary benefits to lasting blessings. Foolishly he sold his birthright to his ruthless twin, Jacob (Gen 25:29-34; Heb 12:16).

The custom was for the father to confirm the birthright by giving his special blessing before he died. Esau tried to gain this blessing ahead of Jacob, but again Jacob's cunning defeated him (Gen 27:1-29). Overcome with misery and anger, Esau tried to kill Jacob, but Jacob found out and escaped (Gen 27:30-38,41-45; Heb 12:17).

Although God's purpose was that his promises to Abraham and Isaac be fulfilled through Jacob and not Esau, that did not excuse either of them for their disgraceful behaviour (Gen 25:23; Rom 9:10-13). Nevertheless, God had a blessing for Esau. Esau would not father the nation that God would make his own, but he would father a nation that would establish a name for itself in the region. This was the nation Edom, which occupied the barren regions south and east of the Dead Sea (Gen 27:39-40; see EDOM).

Esau confirmed his position as being outside God's covenant blessings by marrying firstly two local Hittite women, and later a daughter of Ishmael (Gen 26:34-35; 28:8-9). When Jacob returned to Canaan after twenty years, Esau went to meet him. Fearful of what might happen, Jacob begged Esau's mercy, but Esau responded with such generous forgiveness that the dreaded meeting turned into a happy reunion (Gen 32:1-21; 33:1-16). The two brothers met again when together they buried their father Isaac (Gen 35:27-29).

ESCHATOLOGY

The word 'eschatology' comes from the Greek *eschatos*, meaning 'last', and commonly refers to the study of 'the last things'. This is a vast subject, and the following outline refers the reader to articles in this Directory that deal with its many topics.

In its broader aspects, eschatology is concerned with all matters relating to death and the afterlife (Ps 16:11; Dan 12:2; Luke 16:22-23; Heb 9:27-28; see DEATH; HADES; PARADISE; SHEOL). More specifically it is concerned with issues relating to the return of Jesus Christ and the new age that will follow (see JESUS CHRIST, sub-heading 'Christ's return and final triumph').

Human history is tied up with the mission of Jesus Christ. At his first coming Jesus brought God's plan of salvation to its fulfilment through his life and work, and particularly through his death and resurrection. God intervened in human history, and the 'last days' began (Heb 1:1-2; 1 Peter 1:20; see FULFILMENT). Those 'last days' have continued through the present age and will reach their climax at Christ's return. The coming 'day of the Lord' will be that final great intervention of God which brings human history to its destiny (Matt 24:29-31; 2 Peter 3:3-4,10; see ANTICHRIST; DAY OF THE LORD).

To have a proper understanding of matters concerning Christ's return, a person should consider them in relation to matters concerning Christ's earthly ministry as recorded in the Gospels. Christ's victory at his second coming will represent the triumphant climax of the kingdom that he brought to mankind at his first coming. The kingly Messiah and heavenly Son of man, having died for sin, will return to reign (Matt 25:31-34; see KINGDOM OF GOD; MESSIAH; MILLENNIUM; SON OF MAN). The return of Christ will bring about the victorious

resurrection of believers, but that resurrection is possible only because of the victorious resurrection of Christ (1 Cor 15:20-23; see RESURRECTION).

Christ's return will also lead to final judgment, which means judgment not just for believers, but for all people. The one who died to save people from condemnation and give them new life is the one who will finally declare whether they suffer eternal condemnation or enjoy the heavenly blessings of the new age (John 5:22; 2 Cor 5:10; see JUDGMENT; HEAVEN; HELL).

At his first coming Christ dealt with sin and showed his power over it. When he returns he will remove sin and all its evil consequences finally and completely. His victory will include the healing of the physical world, the destruction of death and the punishment of Satan (1 Cor 15:25-26; Rev 20:10; see NATURE; DEATH; SATAN). Christ and his people together will enter into the full enjoyment of the eternal life that he has made possible for them. The 'new heavens and new earth' will be a new order of existence where God is supreme and all people find their full satisfaction in him (1 Cor 15:28; Rev 21:1-4; 22:1-6; see ETERNITY; LIFE).

ESTHER

Esther was a Jewess who lived in Persia and became queen to the Persian king Ahasuerus, also known as Xerxes I. He reigned from 486 to 465 BC. The story of Esther is found in the book that is named after her. The book does not say who wrote it.

Features of the book

When an earlier Persian king gave the Jews permission to return to their homeland, many preferred not to go. Rather than face the hardships and risks involved in rebuilding Jerusalem and its temple, they made life more comfortable for themselves where they were. Their prosperity increased, but they showed little interest in re-establishing the Jewish religious order as a spiritual force among the Jewish people.

This attitude is reflected in the book of Esther, whose story is built around Jews in Persia. There is no mention of God in the book, apart perhaps from one reference to some unseen force that determines events (Esther 4:14). The closest indication of any spiritual awareness in the people is in one reference to fasting, though even then there is no reference to any type of prayer (Esther 4:16). Yet whether his people acknowledged him or not, God was still directing their affairs to ensure they were not destroyed.

Summary of the story

When the Persian king decided to replace his queen, the woman chosen was Esther, an orphan Jew who had been brought up by her cousin Mordecai. Mordecai worked around the palace where, on one occasion, he saved the king's life by reporting an assassination plot (1:1-2:23).

Some time later a proud and ambitious man named Haman became chief minister in the Persian government. Haman hated the Jews, and when Mordecai refused to bow to him, he determined to destroy all Jews throughout the Empire (3:1-15). While Haman cast lots (purim) to find the right day for the Jews' slaughter, Mordecai persuaded Esther to appeal to the king to have mercy on her people (4:1-5:14). Esther then revealed to the king that she was Jewish. When the king discovered that Haman wanted to wipe out a people that included his queen, and in particular that he wanted to kill the man who had saved the king's life, he executed Haman (6:1-7:10).

Mordecai then became chief minister instead of Haman. The day that had been chosen by the casting of lots (purim) for the slaughter of the Jews now became the day when the Jews took revenge on their enemies. The Jews' celebration of their victory was the origin of an annual Jewish festival known as the Feast of Purim (8:1-9:32). Through Mordecai the Jews enjoyed increased freedom and prosperity (10:1-3).

ETERNITY

Most people find it difficult to imagine eternity. This is largely because the only type of existence they have so far experienced is that of a world where everything happens within a framework of time and distance that can be measured. God alone understands eternity fully, because he alone is eternal (1 Tim 1:17). Man lives in a created order of which time is a part (Heb 1:2). Even the words he uses to speak of eternity come from a world governed by time.

The meanings of words

When the Bible writers referred to eternity, they usually used the word for 'age'. This was a word that denoted a long period of time, without specifying its beginning or end. The writers used the word in relation to things that were very old or that would last for a very long time (Ps 24:7; 125:1; Hab 3:6; Rom 16:25). Concerning the past, the word could mean 'a long time ago' (Josh 24:2; Luke 1:70); concerning the future, it could mean 'endlessness'

(Dan 2:44; 2 Peter 1:11). When they referred to immeasurable time, the writers may have used such expressions as 'to all ages' or 'from age to age', which have been translated as 'from everlasting to everlasting' and 'for ever and ever' (Neh 9:5; Ps 21:4; Rom 1:25; Eph 3:21; Jude 25).

The writers used similar expressions when they spoke of God as the eternal one (1 Chron 16:36; Ps 90:2; 106:48). Divine actions are called eternal, or everlasting, because of the character of the eternal God from whom they originate. This applies to both salvation and judgment (Isa 45:17; Jude 7), to life and destruction (John 17:2; 2 Thess 1:9).

From man's standpoint, eternity is the age to come, in contrast to the present age in which he lives (Mark 10:30; Eph 1:21). Eternal life, being the life of the age to come, is endless, because the age to come is endless. More importantly, it is life of a particular quality. It is a life that shares in some way the nature of God and that God gives to man through Jesus Christ (John 1:4; 5:21,24; 8:51; 17:2-3; see LIFE, sub-heading 'Eternal life'). Even in the present age, believers in Jesus Christ have the life of the age to come — eternal life, the life of the kingdom of God (Matt 19:16,24; John 3:3,5,15; Col 1:13; see KINGDOM OF GOD).

God's viewpoint and man's

Jesus' teaching concerning the nature of eternal life showed that it was more than merely life stretched out for ever. It was life of an entirely different order from the normal life of this world (John 4:14; 6:51,63; 17:3). Likewise eternity is not time stretched out for ever, but is something of an entirely different order. The realization of this helps to ease the difficulties that may arise in understanding God's foreknowledge. God is not limited by time, and therefore he sees time differently from the way man sees it (2 Peter 3:8).

An illustration that may help is that of a rod suspended horizontally in mid-air in a room. The rod has a beginning and an end, and represents time. The room represents eternity (assuming now that its floor, ceiling and walls are removed and it extends endlessly in all directions). From any point in the room (i.e. eternity), a person can see the whole rod (i.e. time). Man, who lives in time, might be likened to an ant moving along the rod. He has a record of what is past, he is conscious of what is present, but he does not know what lies ahead. God, from the viewpoint of eternity, sees the whole of time as eternally present before him. (See also TIME.)

It is therefore inadequate to think of God's eternity solely as everlasting existence. God is not limited in *any* way. His characteristics and qualities are immeasurable in every aspect of his being (Deut 33:27; Ps 103:17; 145:13; Isa 54:8; Rom 1:20; 1 Tim 1:17; see GOD).

ETHICS

Ethics is a broad subject whose particular concern is with right conduct in human behaviour. This includes every aspect of people's conduct, whether it involves others or not. People are answerable to God for *all* that they do (Heb 4:13; Rev 20:12).

God's standards

From the beginning man had within him some knowledge of right and wrong. God gave man a revelation of the standards of conduct he required in human relationships, and a person's conscience judged him according to those standards. This was so even when the person had rejected the knowledge of God (Rom 1:21-23; 2:14-15; cf. Matt 7:11; see CONSCIENCE; REVELATION).

When God took the people of Israel into a covenant relationship with himself, he gave them a law-code to regulate their national life. This written code was an application of the unwritten principles which God had placed in man from the beginning but which man had neglected. They were based on the truth that man's moral conduct should be a reflection of the moral character of God, in whose image he was made (Exod 19:6; Lev 11:44-45; 19:2; Matt 19:17; cf. Eph 4:24; see LAW).

The ethics of this Israelite law-code concerned a person's relationships with people and with God. In both cases the motive for right conduct was to be genuine love (Lev 19:17-18; Deut 6:3-7). Right conduct concerned all personal behaviour (e.g. Exod 20:12; 22:21-27; 23:1-8; Lev 18:6,19,22), yet it was more than merely a personal matter. People lived not in isolation but as part of a community, and God wanted the community as a whole to follow his standards (Exod 23:10-12,17; 32:7-10; Lev 19:9-10; Deut 20:10-20).

In giving his law to Israel at Mt Sinai, God's purpose was not that as Israelites kept it they could earn the right to become his people. Rather he gave the law to a nation that he had already made his people (Exod 4:22; 6:6-8; 24:3-4). Each person was a guilty sinner and received salvation only through coming in faith and repentance to God (Exod 32:33; 34:6-7; Ps 51:1-4; Isa 1:16-20). Salvation was a gift of God's grace, not a reward for keeping moral laws; though the person who received that salvation loved God's law all the more and had an increased desire to keep it (Ps 119:14-16,44-48; Rom 9:31-32; Gal 3:10,18).

Likewise in the new era introduced through Jesus Christ, no one is saved through keeping moral instructions, whether those instructions come from the law of Moses, the teachings of Jesus or the writings of the early Christian leaders. Salvation is by God's grace, and repentant sinners receive it by faith. But again, having received it they should be diligent to produce good works (Eph 2:8-10; Titus 2:11-12; James 2:18,26; 1 Peter 2:9-12; see GOOD WORKS).

Genuine love is once again the source of right behaviour. As new people indwelt by the Spirit of God, Christians can now produce the standard of righteousness that the law aimed at but could not itself produce (Rom 8:1-4; 13:8-10; 2 Cor 5:17; 1 John 2:3-6; see SANCTIFICATION).

Ethical teachings of Jesus

The foundation of Christian ethics is not what man himself might do, but what God through Christ has already done. Jesus was not primarily a teacher of ethics who showed people how to live a better life, but a Saviour who died and rose again to give repentant sinners an entirely new life (Rom 6:1-11; 2 Cor 5:15,17; 1 Peter 1:18-23; 4:1). God has made believers his sons, and they must now show this to be true in practice. Because God has acted in a certain way, Christians must act in a certain way (1 Cor 6:20; Eph 4:1; 5:1; 1 John 3:9-10; 4:7).

Jesus' teaching must therefore be understood in relation to his mission. He was not a social reformer, but the Saviour-Messiah who brought the kingdom of God to man. He did not draw up a code of ethics, but urged people to humble themselves and enter the kingdom of God. He knew that people would have worthwhile change in their behaviour only when they were truly changed within (Matt 4:23; 5:3,21-22; 12:28; 15:19-20; 18:4; 19:23; see KINGDOM OF GOD).

In dealing with standards of human behaviour, Jesus did not introduce any new set of values. He referred people back to the values which were already clearly set out in the Old Testament but which people had either ignored or distorted (Matt 5:17,43-44; 19:8-9; 22:37-40; see SERMON ON THE MOUNT).

Neither did Jesus present his teaching in the form of regulations applicable to all people in all circumstances, as if it were the law-code of a civil government. His requirement, for example, that people sell their houses or leave their families applied not in all cases, but only in those where people had put their interests before God's (Matt 19:16-22; Luke 9:57-62). But the principle on which that particular instruction was based (namely, that discipleship involves sacrifice) applies to everyone (Matt 10:34-39; 16:24-26).

If Jesus had set out a law-code, its regulations would have been suited to the way of life in first century Palestine, but unsuited to other cultures and eras. Instead, as each occasion arose, Jesus emphasized whatever aspect of God's truth was related to the circumstances (e.g. Matt 22:15-22; Mark 12:38-40; Luke 14:8-11). He also left behind with his followers the gift of the Holy Spirit who, generation after generation, helps Christians to interpret his words and apply their meaning. The teaching of Jesus never goes out of date (John 14:15-17; 16:13-15).

Motives and behaviour

Because God's work of redemption through Christ is the basis of Christian ethics, the relationship that believers have with Christ will largely determine their behaviour. Their understanding of Christian doctrine will enlighten them concerning Christian conduct. Their appreciation of what Christ has done will deepen their love for him and give them the desire to please him. They will want to obey his teachings (John 14:15; 15:4,10; 2 Cor 8:9; 1 Thess 2:4; 1 Tim 1:5; 6:3; Heb 13:21).

This obedience is not the fearful keeping of stern demands, but the joyful response to Christ's love (1 John 2:1-5; 4:10-12; 5:3; cf. Matt 11:29-30; see OBEDIENCE). It is not bondage to a new set of laws, but a freedom to produce the character that no set of laws can ever produce (Rom 8:2; Gal 5:1,13; Col 2:20-23; see FREEDOM).

The fact that Christian obedience is free from legalism is no excuse for moral laziness. Christians have a duty to be obedient (Rom 6:16; 1 Cor 9:21; 2 Cor 10:5; 1 Peter 1:14-16). They need to exercise constant self-discipline (1 Cor 9:24-27), and they will be able to do this through the work of Christ's Spirit within them (Gal 5:22-23; see SELF-DISCIPLINE). The work of the Holy Spirit helps believers produce that Christian character which is the goal of Christian ethics. The motivating force behind the conduct of Christians is their desire to be like Christ and so bring glory to God (Rom 13:14; 1 Cor 10:31; 2 Cor 3:18; Col 3:9-10,17; cf. Matt 5:48).

Being like Christ does not mean that Christians in different cultures and eras must try to copy the actions of the Messiah who lived in first century Palestine. It means rather that they have to produce the sort of character Jesus displayed and be as faithful in their callings as Jesus was in his (John 13:15; 15:12; Eph 4:24; 5:1-2; 1 Peter 2:21; 1 John 2:6). Christians know that in some bodily way they are to become like Christ at his return, and this should encourage them to become more like him in moral character now (Phil 3:17-21; 1 Thess 3:13; Titus 2:11-14; 1 John 3:2-3).

Christians live with the sure expectation that a better life awaits them in the heavenly kingdom. This, however, is no reason to try to escape the problems of the present life (1 Cor 15:54,58; Phil 1:23-24; 2 Tim 2:10-15). On the contrary, the affairs of the present life help develop personal character and communion with God, which give meaning to life now and will last through death into the age to come (1 Cor 13:8-13; 1 Peter 1:3-9).

The awareness of future judgment creates for Christians both expectancy and caution. This is not because they desire rewards or fear punishment, but because the day of judgment is the climax of the present life and the beginning of the new (Matt 25:14-30; 1 Cor 3:12-15; 2 Cor 5:10; 2 Tim 4:6-8; see JUDGMENT; PUNISHMENT; REWARD).

Applying Christian ethics to society

Christian ethical teaching is aimed, first of all, not at making society Christian, but at making Christians more Christlike. Their character and behaviour must reflect their new life in Christ (Rom 6:4; Eph 4:22-24; Col 2:6-7). But Christian ethics are not a purely private affair. Christians are part of a society where Christ has placed them as his representatives, and they must apply their Christian values to the affairs of that society (Matt 5:13-16; John 17:15-18; see WITNESS; WORLD).

The immediate community in which Christians must give expression to their standards is the family (Eph 5:22-6:4; see FAMILY; MARRIAGE). Beyond the family is the larger community where they live and work, and where they inevitably meet conduct that is contrary to their Christian understanding of righteousness, truth and justice (Eph 6:5-9; see JUSTICE; WORK). Over all is the civil government. Although Christian faith does not in itself make people experts on economics, politics or sociology, it does teach them moral values by which they can assess a government's actions (Rom 13:1-7; see GOVERNMENT).

Since the Creator knows what is best for his creatures, Christian ethics are the best for mankind. Christians should therefore do all they can to promote God's standards. A society will benefit if its laws are based on God's standards (Exod 20:13-17; Deut 5:29; Rom 13:8-10), though Christians should realize that it is not possible to enforce all those standards by law. Civil laws can deal with actions that have social consequences, but they cannot deal with the attitudes that cause those actions (cf. Matt 5:21-22; Eph 4:25-32).

In addition, the ethical standards of a society may be so poor that laws have to be less than ideal in order to control and regulate an unsatisfactory state of affairs (e.g. Exod 21:1-11; Deut 24:1-4; see DIVORCE; SLAVERY). This does not mean that Christians may lower their moral standards to the level of the civil law; for something that is legal according to government-made laws may still be morally wrong (cf. Matt 19:7-9). Nor does it mean (as the system known as Situation Ethics claims) that nothing is absolutely right or wrong, and that in certain situations Christians are free to disobey God's moral instructions, provided they feel they are acting out of love to others. The more knowledge Christians have of God's law, the more he holds them responsible to obey it (Luke 12:48; John 9:41; James 2:10-12; cf. Amos 3:2).

ETHIOPIA

Apart from Egypt, Ethiopia is the most frequently mentioned African country in the Bible. It was sometimes called Cush and its people were dark-skinned. It bordered Egypt to Egypt's south and, like Egypt, was centred on the Nile River. The region it occupied is today the northern part of Sudan (Isa 18:1-2; Jer 13:23; Ezek 29:10; for map of the region see EGYPT).

To most of the people of Palestine, Ethiopia was the most southern country they knew of. Writers frequently used its name poetically to symbolize the unlimited extent of God's sovereign rule (Ps 68:31; Isa 11:11; Ezek 30:4-5; Zeph 3:10).

Individuals from Ethiopia feature occasionally in the Old Testament story. During Israel's journey from Egypt to Canaan, Moses married an Ethiopian woman, probably after his first wife had died (Num 12:1). In later times an Ethiopian who worked in the palace of the Judean king saved the life of God's prophet Jeremiah (Jer 38:7-13; 39:15-18).

Ethiopia features in the biblical record mainly during the period of the divided Israelite kingdom, when it attacked Judah on at least two occasions (2 Chron 12:2-4; 14:9-15). Later it gained control over Upper Egypt, and for about half a century exercised a strong influence over Egypt. It even challenged Assyria, which was the leading power of the time (2 Kings 19:8-9; Nahum 3:8-9). The challenge brought little success and soon Ethiopia,

along with its ally Egypt, suffered a crushing defeat at the hands of Assyria (Isa 20:3-6). It subsequently fell under the control of Babylon, and then under the control of Persia (Esther 1:1).

In pre-New Testament times, Ethiopia was one of the many countries where Jews settled and established communities. Some Ethiopians attended the Jewish synagogues and became worshippers of the God of Israel (see DISPERSION; PROSELYTE). One of these worshippers of God, or 'God-fearers', was among the first non-Jewish people to become Christians in the time of the early church (Acts 8:27-38).

EUPHRATES

Among the rivers of west Asia, the Euphrates was the largest. It was often referred to as 'the great river' or simply 'the River' (Gen 15:18; Deut 1:7; Ezra 8:36; Neh 2:9; 3:7; Isa 7:20). The territory of the Euphrates and Tigris Rivers was known as Mesopotamia, and formed part of the ancient land of Babylon. This was the region where the garden of Eden was located (Gen 2:10-14). The ancient city of Ur was on the Euphrates (Gen 11:28; see UR).

The Euphrates formed the eastern boundary of the territory that God promised to Abraham and his descendants (Gen 15:18; Deut 11:24). Only at isolated times, however, did Israel extend its power that far (2 Sam 8:3).

During the time of the Assyrian Empire, the Euphrates formed a line of defence for Assyria against attacks from the west, and its name became

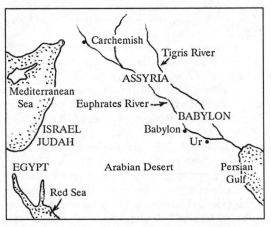

synonymous with Assyria (Isa 7:20; 8:7; Jer 2:18). When Babylon conquered Assyria in 612 BC, Egypt tried to prevent further Babylonian expansion by moving its army north through Judah to Carchemish on the western bank of the Euphrates (2 Kings

23:29; 2 Chron 35:20). But Babylon conquered Egypt at Carchemish and spread its rule west as far as the Mediterranean Sea and Egypt (2 Kings 24:7; Jer 46:2,6,10).

The city of Babylon, capital of the Babylonian Empire, was situated on the river Euphrates (Dan 4:29-30; see BABYLON). In the Persian Empire, which came after the Babylonian, the Euphrates formed the boundary between the Empire's eastern and western parts (Ezra 4:10; 5:3; Neh 2:9).

EVANGELIST

The English words 'evangelist' and 'gospel' come from the same word in the Greek. An evangelist is one who declares, preaches, brings, announces or proclaims the gospel (or good news). The noun 'evangelist' occurs only occasionally in the New Testament (Acts 21:8; Eph 4:11; 2 Tim 4:5), but the verb forms occur frequently (Matt 4:23; Luke 20:1; Acts 8:25; 14:7; Rom 10:15; 1 Cor 9:16; 15:1; Gal 4:13; cf. Isa 52:7; 61:1; see GOSPEL).

Although all Christians should make known the good news of Jesus Christ to others (Acts 4:20; 8:4; 11:20), evangelists are particularly gifted by God for this task. They are one of God's gifts to the church (Eph 4:11). In the early church they were mainly concerned with proclaiming the gospel to those who had not heard it, and establishing churches in places where previously there were none (Acts 8:5,40; 14:21; 16:10; Rom 10:14-15; 15:19-20; 2 Cor 10:16; see MISSION). Even established churches had need for someone to do the work of an evangelist among them (2 Tim 4:5), for there was a constant necessity to make known the facts of the gospel.

Men such as Peter, John, Philip, Barnabas, Paul, Silas and Timothy were evangelists. Some of them were at the same time apostles, prophets, pastors and teachers. This indicates, firstly, that there was considerable overlap between the gifts and, secondly, that one person could combine within him several gifts (cf. Acts 2:42; 14:14; 15:32; 1 Tim 2:7; 4:13-16; see APOSTLE; PASTOR; PREACHING; TEACHER).

No matter how the servant of the gospel may be classified or what era he may live in, the motivating force in his life and ministry is the love of God that he has experienced through Christ. He is thankful to God for the privilege of engaging in Christian service, and this makes him want to please his Master (2 Cor 5:14; Eph 3:7; 1 Tim 1:12-16; see SERVANT).

The evangelist knows that his work may involve risks, disappointments and hardships (Acts 15:26; 2 Cor 11:23-28; 2 Tim 2:10; 3:10-11). Yet he has an obligation to carry out the task God has entrusted to him, regardless of the personal cost (Matt 28:19; Rom 1:14; 1 Cor 9:16-17). He has a concern for those who have not yet heard or believed the gospel, and this drives him on to make it known; for only the gospel can save people from Satan's power and give them eternal life (Rom 10:14; 2 Cor 4:1-6; 5:11; Acts 20:19-26; cf. Ezek 3:17-21).

EVE

Originally the name 'Eve' was related to the word for 'life', and this was why Adam gave the name to his wife. She was 'the mother of all living' (Gen 3:20). God gave her to Adam as one equal with him in nature but opposite to him in sex, to be his companion and counterpart (Gen 1:27; 2:18-25). However, she too readily listened to the temptations of Satan and is blamed for leading Adam into sin (Gen 3:1-7; 2 Cor 11:3; 1 Tim 2:13-15; see ADAM).

EVERLASTING

See ETERNITY.

EVIL

If Christians believe in a God of love and power who created and controls the world, how can they explain the presence and power of evil in the world? This question commonly puzzles people, but the Bible gives no direct answer to it. As usual the Bible's response to the problem is practical rather than theoretical. It is more concerned with helping people develop character than with satisfying intellectual curiosity. And as people accept that help, they receive answers to some of the problems (cf. John 7:17). (Concerning the superior knowledge that Gnostics claimed to have regarding good and evil see KNOWLEDGE.)

The nature of man

God created the world good and he wanted man to enjoy it with him (Gen 1:31; 1 Tim 4:4; Heb 4:4,10). But since he created man as a morally responsible being with a freedom to make his own decisions, the possibility existed that man might misuse his freedom. He might choose to do what he knew he should not do (Gen 2:15-17). Maturity would come through making correct moral choices. The self-denial involved in rejecting tempting alternatives would strengthen character (cf. Heb 5:8,14).

God desired that man live in a relationship of love with him and with his fellow man; but man could not love if he was not free. If he were a robot, he could do what his maker programmed him to do, but he would not be able to love or enjoy anything. However, as freedom produced the possibility of devotion and goodness, so also it produced the possibility of rebellion and evil. Evil was not a product of the creative activity of God, but a product of the wrong use of freedom by morally responsible beings (Gen 3:1-7; James 1:12-13).

Life in a spoiled world

The Bible commonly speaks of evil in two different but related ways. Firstly, it speaks of evil in a moral sense similar to that considered above, where evil is the opposite of moral goodness (Prov 8:13; Jer 7:24; Micah 2:1; Matt 5:45; 15:19; Rom 7:19,21; 2 Thess 3:2; for details see SIN). Satan, through whom this evil entered the human race, is fittingly called 'the evil one' (Gen 3:1; Matt 13:19; 1 John 2:13; 5:19; see SATAN).

Secondly, the Bible speaks of evil in a more general sense, where it refers to calamities, conflicts, sufferings, misfortunes and even to things such as bad health and bad fruit. The word again means the opposite of good, but with a non-moral meaning (Deut 7:15; 2 Sam 15:14; Matt 7:17; Luke 16:25). Yet there is a connection between these two uses of 'evil'. Because the evil of sin has infected the world, calamities and misfortunes have become part of life in the world.

When the Old Testament says that God sends both good and evil, it is referring not to moral good and moral evil, but to life's blessings and troubles. Israelites in Old Testament times acknowledged God's overall control in all the affairs of life, both good and bad (Job 2:10; Isa 45:7). They saw that the evils of conflict, disaster and destruction were often God's means of punishing the wicked (1 Sam 16:14; Jer 35:17; Amos 3:6).

No cause for despair

Although the entrance of sin into man's world has spoiled God's purposes for mankind, it has not overthrown them. God can bring good out of evil (Gen 50:20; Rom 8:28). The troubles of life are not always God's judgments for specific wrongdoings. God usually does not explain why particular evils occur or why people suffer from them. Nevertheless, he consistently uses those evils to bring positive benefits (Hab 1:13; 3:17-19; Luke 13:1-5; John 9:2-3; 2 Cor 12:7-9; see SUFFERING). This, however, does not excuse the people who are responsible for the evils (Isa 10:5-11; Jer 51:5-10,34-36; Matt 26:24; Acts 2:23; Rom 3:8).

Probably the most feared of all evils is death, but God uses even death to fulfil his purposes for good. Through death he has conquered death and delivered people from the power of evil (Heb 2:14; see DEATH). Through Christ's death, believers can enjoy victory over evil while still living in the present evil world (Rom 6:7-11,14; Gal 1:4; see SALVATION). They will enjoy final victory when Christ returns to remove all evil, even to its last trace, and bring in God's new heaven and new earth (1 Cor 15:25-28; Rev 21:4,27; 22:1-3).

EXECUTION

Israelite law laid down the death penalty for certain offences, some of them religious, others civil (Lev 20:2,10,27; 24:16-17; Num 15:32-36; Deut 13:6-10; 22:20-24; 24:7). Even under the Roman system of law that operated in New Testament times, Paul accepted that the government had the right to carry out the death sentence in certain cases (Acts 25:11; cf. Rom 13:3-4).

Many of Israel's laws were specifically related to the particular relationship that existed between God and Israel under the covenant (e.g. Deut 13:6-10; cf. 5:2,6-7). However, the law that laid down the death penalty for murderers was based on a command that God gave long before the nation Israel existed. God's command was related to the fundamental sacredness of human life, for man exists in God's image. God therefore laid down that if any person wilfully killed another without divine permission, that person was no longer fit to enjoy God's gift of life (Gen 9:3-6; cf. Exod 21:23; Num 35:30-34).

The normal Israelite method of execution was stoning. There had to be at least two witnesses to the crime, and these had to participate publicly in the execution by throwing the first stones. This no doubt impressed upon people that they had to be absolutely certain in making an accusation against anyone (Lev 24:14; Deut 17:6-7; John 8:7; Acts 7:58). The dead body was then hung on a tree till evening as a sign that the executed person was under the curse of God (Deut 21:23).

Under the Roman administration of the New Testament era, prisoners were executed by either crucifixion or beheading (Matt 27:22; Mark 6:24-28; Acts 12:2; see CRUCIFIXION). Jews could pass the death sentence upon their own people for offences relating to Jewish law, but they could not carry it out. They had to hand over the prisoner to the Roman authorities, who alone had the power of execution (Matt 27:1-2). Yet when the Jews illegally stoned Stephen to death, the Roman authorities took no action against them. They probably thought it wise not to interfere when the Jews were so stirred up (Acts 7:58; cf. Matt 27:24; Acts 12:2-3).

EXILE

In the Old Testament 'the exile', or 'the captivity', refers to the period of approximately seventy years that followed Babylon's conquest of Jerusalem and deportation of the people into captivity in Babylon (2 Kings 24:1-25:21; Jer 25:11-12; 29:10; Dan 1:1-4; Ezek 1:1-3). (For details of the successive stages of this conquest and deportation see JUDAH, TRIBE AND KINGDOM. For details of life in captivity in Babylon see DANIEL; EZEKIEL.) The exile came to an end after Persia's conquest of Babylon in 539 BC, when the new ruler gave permission to the captive Jews to return to their homeland (2 Chron 36:22-23; Ezra 1:1-4; Isa 48:20; see CHRONICLES, BOOKS OF; EZRA).

In the New Testament 'the exile' refers to the Christian's life in the present world. Since the Christian is considered to be a citizen of heaven, his present life is like that of a foreigner or pilgrim in an alien country (Phil 3:20; Heb 13:14; 1 Peter 1:1,17; 2:11; see FOREIGNER).

EXODUS

Israel's escape from slavery in Egypt is commonly known as the exodus (meaning 'a going out'). The most likely date for the event is about 1280 BC, and the historical account of the event is given in the book of Exodus (see EXODUS, BOOK OF).

Significance of the exodus

The actual going out from Egypt was but one part of a series of events that gave the exodus its great significance in Israel's history. It was preceded by God's judgment on Egypt through a number of plagues (Exod 1-11; see PLAGUE); it came about through the decisive judgment on Passover night and the subsequent crossing of the Red Sea (Exod 12-15; see PASSOVER; RED SEA); and it was followed by the covenant ceremony at Mt Sinai, where God formally established Israel as his people (Exod 16-24; see COVENANT). After giving them his law, God directed them to the new homeland he had promised them in Canaan.

Throughout the years that followed, Israelites looked back to the exodus as the decisive event in their history. This was not just because the exodus led to the establishment of Israel's national independence, but more importantly because it

showed them what sort of person their God was. Yahweh revealed his character, showing that he was a God who redeems (Deut 15:15; 2 Sam 7:23; Neh 1:8-10; Micah 6:4; cf. Exod 6:6-8; 15:2,13; see REDEMPTION). The exodus was a sign to the people of this Redeemer-God's love (Deut 4:37; 7:8; Hosea 11:1), power (Deut 9:26; 2 Kings 17:36; Ps 81:10) and justice (Deut 6:21-22; Josh 24:5-7).

In demonstrating the character of God, the exodus gave assurance to God's people that they could trust in him. At the same time it reminded them that he required them to be loyal, obedient and holy (Lev 11:45; Deut 4:37-40; 5:6-7; 7:7-11; cf. Hosea 11:1-4).

The pattern repeated

Even with the destruction of Jerusalem in 587 BC and the subsequent captivity in Babylon, God's people never forgot his redeeming power. They looked for a 'second exodus' when he would again deliver them from bondage. They prayed that as he had first brought them out of Egypt and into the promised land, so he would now bring them out of Babylon and back to their homeland (Isa 43:1-7; 43:14-21; 48:20-21; 49:25-26; 51:9-11; 52:11-12; Jer 31:10-12; Micah 7:14-17).

The exodus theme is prominent also in the New Testament. The word 'exodus' (RSV: 'departure') is used of Jesus' death, by which he delivers people from the bondage of sin (Luke 9:31; cf. Col 1:13; Heb 2:14-15; see REDEMPTION). As the Passover lamb, he died in the place of those under judgment and so achieved redemption for them (1 Cor 5:7; 1 Peter 1:18-19; see PASSOVER). Those redeemed through Christ can therefore sing the song that the redeemed Israelites sang, but with new meaning (Rev 15:2-4; cf. Exod 15:1-21). They must also heed the lessons that the Israelites failed to learn in the wilderness years that followed their deliverance (1 Cor 10:1-11; Heb 3:7-19).

EXODUS, BOOK OF

The books that we today refer to as the five books of Moses (or the Pentateuch) were originally one continuous volume. The Hebrews made the division into five sections so that the extremely long book would fit conveniently on to five scrolls. Exodus, being only one part of a much longer book, is therefore best understood in connection with what precedes and what follows it. (For the authorship of Exodus see PENTATEUCH.) The name Exodus, meaning ' a going out', was given by those who made the first Greek translation of the Old Testament. It refers to the central event of the book, Israel's escape from Egypt.

Message of the book

God had promised that from the descendants of Abraham he would make a nation that would in a special sense be his people, and he would give them Canaan as their national homeland (Gen 12:1-3; 13:14-16; 17:6-8; 22:17-18). The chosen descendants of Abraham settled in Egypt in the fertile region of the Nile Delta. There, over the next four centuries, they multiplied and prospered (cf. Gen 15:13; Exod 12:41), till the time approached when they would be strong enough to move north and conquer Canaan. They were sadly disappointed when the Egyptian rulers, fearing the growing Israelite power, made them slaves. Among the cities built by the Israelite slaves was Rameses (Gen 15:14; Exod 1:8-12; see EGYPT; RAMESES).

But God had not forgotten the covenant he had made with Abraham. He therefore freed Israel from Egypt's power and set the people on their way to the promised land (Exod 2:24; 6:6-8). After three months journey they settled for a time at Mt Sinai. There God formally established his covenant with Israel as his chosen people, giving them a law-code and a religious order to govern their national life. The instructions concerning these matters begin in Exodus and carry on unbroken through Leviticus and into Numbers. The book of Numbers goes on to record how the people, after almost one year at Sinai, resumed their journey to Canaan (cf. Exod 19:1; Num 10:11).

The events of the exodus from Egypt and the establishment of the covenant at Sinai are therefore the main issues of the book of Exodus. Israel's experiences were part of the fulfilment of God's covenant promises. God was in control of events and was directing them towards the goals that he had set (Exod 14:31; 15:1-18; 19:4-6; 29:45-46; 33:14). Through all these experiences the Israelites began to understand the character of this God who had chosen them. Above all they came to know him as their Redeemer (Exod 3:13-17; 6:6-8; 20:2).

Summary of contents

God saw how the Israelites were oppressed in Egypt (1:1-22), and prepared Moses to be the deliverer to save them. Moses was brought up in the Egyptian palace, but after forty years in Egypt he renounced his Egyptian status and spent the next forty years in the barren regions of the Sinai Peninsular (2:1-25). There God revealed himself to Moses as Yahweh, the eternal and self-sufficient God who was going to use Moses to save his people from Egypt (3:1-4:17; see YAHWEH).

Moses then returned to Egypt. With his brother Aaron, who was his assistant, he tried to persuade Pharaoh to release the Israelites, but without success (4:18-6:27). This began a long conflict between Moses and Pharaoh, which resulted in repeated plagues upon Egypt (6:28-10:29; see PLAGUE). In the end God destroyed the eldest in each family in Egypt. He passed over the Israelite households,

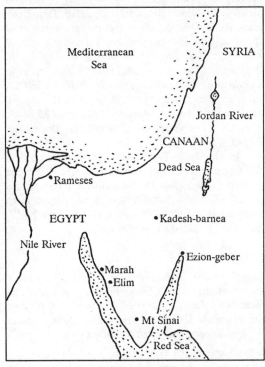

because they had already sacrificed a lamb in the place of the person under judgment. The Passover was God's great act of judgment for Egypt and redemption for Israel (11:1-13:16; see PASSOVER). The Israelites at last were free. When the Egyptians persisted in pursuing them, they were overthrown in the Red Sea (13:17-15:21).

In spite of the complaints of the journeying Israelites, God graciously preserved them through all their dangers and hardships, whether from thirst, disease, hunger or war (15:22-17:16). Because of the people's demands upon him, Moses appointed responsible men to help in the administration of Israel (18:1-27).

Once the people had established their camp at Mt Sinai, God prepared them for the formal establishment of his covenant with them (19:1-25;

see COVENANT). He gave the basic principles of the covenant in the form of the Ten Commandments (20:1-17), and added miscellaneous laws that were collected in a document known as the Book of the Covenant (20:18-23:33). The covenant was sealed in a blood ritual (24:1-18), after which God gave Moses instructions for the building of the tabernacle and the establishment of the priesthood (25:1-31:18; see PRIEST; TABERNACLE).

Before Moses had passed on these instructions to the people, they had already broken the covenant through their idolatry. God threatened to destroy the nation, but Moses pleaded with him for mercy. God heard Moses' prayer and, in response to further pleas, gave the assurance that he would not desert the people on their journey to Canaan (32:1-33:23). The covenant was then renewed (34:1-35) and the people got to work and built the tabernacle as God had instructed (35:1-40:38).

EZEKIEL

Among the people of Judah taken captive to Babylon in 597 BC was the young priest Ezekiel. (For an outline history of the era see JUDAH, TRIBE AND KINGDOM.) He was only twenty-five years of age at the time and, being a priest, no doubt hoped that soon he would be able to return to Jerusalem and begin his priestly duties in the temple. After he had been in Babylon five years, God made it plain to him that he would not return to Jerusalem. He would become a prophet, or messenger of God, to the Jews in Babylon (Ezek 1:1-3; 2:3,5,7; 3:4). His prophetic preaching lasted at least twenty-two years (Ezek 29:17), and much of it is recorded in the biblical book that he wrote.

Ezekiel's preaching

At the time Ezekiel began preaching in Babylon, Jerusalem had not been destroyed. He denounced the sins of its citizens, both those who had been taken to Babylon and those who were still in Jerusalem. He warned that when Babylon finally lost patience, it would destroy city and temple alike (Ezek 4:1-2; 5:12; 6:1-7; 7:5-9).

The exiles responded to Ezekiel's preaching by refusing to believe his prophecies of judgment, but when Jerusalem finally fell they accepted that he was a true prophet. People came to listen to him, but though they regarded him as an unusual and interesting person, they still took little notice of what he said (Ezek 33:21,30-33).

Certainly Ezekiel was unusual. He acted some of his messages with very unorthodox behaviour

(Ezek 4:1-17; 5:1-17; 12:1-16), gave the most striking and colourful illustrations (Ezek 16:1-63; 17:1-21; 23:1-49), and recounted the strangest visions (Ezek 1:4-28; 8:1-11:25; 37:1-28).

Ezekiel was not just a preacher of doom. He was concerned also with preparing God's people for the new age they could expect after their restoration to Palestine. In dramatic symbolic pictures he spoke of the ultimate destruction of evil and the triumph of God's people (Ezek 38:1-39:29). His picture of the golden age was one of an ideal national life, where God dwelt in the midst of his people and they worshipped him in a religious order that was perfect in every detail (Ezek 40:1-48:35).

Contents of the book of Ezekiel

After seeing a vision of the glorious chariot-throne of God (1:1-28), Ezekiel was called by God to take his message to a people who, God warned, would be very stubborn (2:1-3:27). Ezekiel then announced God's judgment on Jerusalem. Through a number of acted messages, he demonstrated the horrors of siege, slaughter and exile (4:1-5:17). The reason for the nation's judgment was its idolatry (6:1-14). Its judgment was certain, and all attempts to withstand Babylon's attacks were useless (7:1-27).

In a fresh series of visions Ezekiel was taken, as it were, to Jerusalem, where he saw people engaging in idolatry in the temple (8:1-18). As God sent his executioners through Jerusalem (9:1-11), his glorious chariot-throne began its sad departure from the city (10:1-22). The city's leaders were the ones chiefly responsible for its downfall (11:1-13), though God would preserve the faithful minority (11:14-25). By further acting and preaching, Ezekiel stressed the certainty of the coming siege and exile (12:1-28), and condemned the false prophets who were building up false hopes of security among the doomed people (13:1-23). Idolatry would now get its just punishment (14:1-15:8).

The nation as a whole had been unfaithful to God who had so lovingly cared for it (16:1-63), and Zedekiah the king had been treacherous in his political dealings (17:1-24). The people had no one but themselves to blame for the coming judgment (18:1-32), and no king would be able to save them (19:1-14). Exile in Babylon was certain (20:1-26), though after cleansing from the filth of idolatry there would be restoration (20:27-44). By further acted messages, Ezekiel indicated the ferocity of the Babylonians' attack on Jerusalem (20:45-21:32). The nation was corrupt beyond reform (22:1-23:49), and only by destruction could its filth be removed (24:1-27).

After recording a number of judgments against foreign nations — Ammon, Moab, Edom, Philistia (25:1-17), Tyre (26:1-28:19), Sidon (28:20-26), Egypt (29:1-32:32) — Ezekiel spoke of a new phase in his work, namely, the building up of the people in preparation for the return from exile (33:1-20). Jerusalem had now fallen (33:21-33) and Israel could look forward to better government in the future than there had been in the past (34:1-31). Enemies in the land would be removed (35:1-15); restoration was assured (36:1-38). The 'dead' nation would come to life again (37:1-28) and God's people could look forward to the day when all enemies would be destroyed (38:1-39:29).

Being a priest, Ezekiel pictured life in the new age as centring on an ideal temple, where God would dwell with his people and they would worship and serve him in true holiness. He described the temple (40:1-42:20), God's coming to dwell in it (43:1-12), and the service to be carried out there (43:13-44:31).

In Ezekiel's perfectly reconstructed national life, land for priests, Levites and king was justly allocated, and there was full provision for all the national religious festivals (45:1-46:24). Life was one of unending satisfaction, for it came from God himself (47:1-12). The tribes of Israel were given equal portions for their respective tribal territories (47:13-48:29), but the chief blessing was that God now dwelt in the midst of his people for ever (48:30-35).

EZION-GEBER

Ezion-geber (along with its twin town Elath, or Eloth) was situated on the northern tip of the Gulf of Aqabah, the north-eastern arm of the Red Sea. It was the port from which shipping routes went east and overland routes went north (Deut 2:8; 1 Kings 9:26). This meant that the nation that controlled Ezion-geber controlled much of the trade in the region (1 Kings 9:27-28; 10:22). (For fuller details of Ezion-geber's significance see EDOM.)

EZRA

In Old Testament times the books of Chronicles, Ezra and Nehemiah were apparently joined to form one continuous story. The book of Ezra begins at the point where Chronicles ends, the year 539 BC. In that year the Persian king Cyrus conquered Babylon and gave permission to the captive Jews to return to their homeland and rebuild their city and temple (2 Chron 36:22-23; Ezra 1:1-4).

Writer, priest and teacher

Ezra is traditionally believed to be the author of the book that bears his name. However, the events recorded in the first part of the book took place before Ezra was born.

After the decree of Cyrus in 539 BC, thousands of Jews returned to Jerusalem. Under the leadership of the governor Zerubbabel and the high priest Joshua, they began rebuilding the temple (Ezra 2:1-2; 3:1-2,8). But because of opposition from local people the work stopped, and nothing further was done till 520 BC, the second year of the Persian king Darius (Ezra 4:24). In that year the prophets Haggai and Zechariah began preaching, with the result that the people were stirred to action (Ezra 5:1-2; Hag 2:18), and within four and a half years completed the temple (Ezra 6:15).

In due course Zerubbabel, Joshua, Haggai and Zechariah all died, and without strong and godly leadership the nation drifted from God. During this time Ezra was born, and he grew up to be trained as a priest and a scribe. Scribes were people skilled in writing who made copies of the law of Moses. Ezra, however, did more than that. He studied the law diligently and became known for his learning and insight. In addition he was a godly person who practised what he knew. He also had the gift of being able to teach and explain the law clearly to others (Ezra 7:6,10-11; Neh 8:1-2,8-9).

Originally Ezra lived and worked in Babylon. Then, in the seventh year of the reign of Artaxerxes (458 BC), he obtained authority and finance from the king to return to Jerusalem and carry out reforms there (Ezra 7:1,6-7,13-15,21-24).

From the dates given in the book of Ezra, it can be seen that Ezra's move to Jerusalem was about eighty years after Zerubbabel's, and about sixty years after the completion of the temple. Because Ezra was preparing a book that recounted events before his time, he had to search through old documents and other historical records (cf. Ezra 4:7-8; 5:6-7; 6:1-2). Two sections of the book, which quote some of this material, are actually in the official language of the period, Aramaic (Ezra 4:8-6:18; 7:12-26). In one long section, Ezra has written in the first person (Ezra 7:27-9:15).

Contents of the book of Ezra

Upon hearing the decree of Cyrus in 539 BC, many of the Jews in Babylon returned to Jerusalem, though others chose to remain in Babylon (1:1-11). Those who returned were grouped according to their families and numbered about 50,000 (2:1-70). They quickly began the task of rebuilding the temple

(3:1-13), but opposition soon stopped the work (4:1-24). Sixteen years later the prophets Haggai and Zechariah stirred up the people to get working again and, in spite of further opposition, the work was completed – in 516 BC (5:1-6:22).

In 458 BC Ezra led another group of exiles back to Jerusalem. He carried with him authority from the Persian king to correct disorders and regulate the Jewish community according to the law of God (7:1-28). Through his strong faith in God, he and his company arrived safely in Jerusalem (8:1-36). Ezra was saddened to see that many Jews had married those who worshipped other gods. On behalf of the people he confessed their guilt to God (9:1-15). The people repented, then appointed officials who listed the offenders and ensured that they put away their heathen wives (10:1-44).

Later activity of Ezra

Ezra's reforms had been only partially successful, and it was not till Nehemiah came to Jerusalem as governor that the people showed any real willingness to leave their selfish ways. Nehemiah arrived in Jerusalem thirteen years after Ezra (cf. Ezra 7:7; Neh 2:1). Through Nehemiah's strong leadership, the wall of Jerusalem was rebuilt (Neh 6:15), after which Ezra read the law to the people and explained its meaning (Neh 8:1-2,8-9). Ezra was a notable man of prayer (Ezra 7:27-28; 8:21; 9:1-15; 10:1,6), and once again he led the people in confessing their sins and asking God's mercy (Neh 9:6-37).

At the dedication of Jerusalem's rebuilt wall, Ezra again played a leading part. The nation's chief citizens and religious officials were assembled and divided into two groups, led respectively by Ezra and Nehemiah. These two groups then marched around the wall of Jerusalem in opposite directions, meeting at the temple on the other side of the city. There they joined in a great service of praise to God (Neh 12:31-40). It was a fitting climax to the Bible's account of Ezra's ministry.

FAITH

In the original language of the New Testament, the noun 'faith' and the verb 'believe' are different parts of the same word. Although faith involves belief, by far the most important characteristic of faith (in the biblical sense) is reliance, or trust.

To have faith in a person or thing is to rely wholly on that person or thing, and not to rely on oneself. The Bible usually speaks of faith in relation to people's trust in, or dependence on, God and his works. This dependence may concern aspects of

physical life such as God's provision of food, health, protection from harm and victory over enemies (Ps 22:4-5; 37:3-4; 46:1-3; Matt 6:30-33; Heb 11:33-35), but above all it concerns aspects of spiritual life such as God's provision of salvation and eternal life (Ps 18:2; 40:4; 71:5; 73:26; Prov 3:5; Jer 17:7; John 3:16; Rom 1:16; 5:1).

Saved by faith

Whether in the era before Christ or after, people have been saved only through faith in the sovereign God who in his mercy and grace forgives sin; and the basis on which God forgives sin is the death of Jesus Christ (Rom 3:24-26; 4:16,22-25; 2 Cor 4:13; Gal 3:11; see JUSTIFICATION; SACRIFICE). People can never be saved from sin, never be accepted by God, on the basis of their good works or their law-keeping. They can do nothing to deserve or win God's favour (Rom 4:1-5; 9:30-32; 10:3-4). God saves people solely by his grace, and they receive this salvation by faith (Eph 2:8-9).

Faith in itself does not save. It is simply the means by which the sinner accepts the salvation that God offers. God's salvation is not a reward for a person's faith; it is a gift that no person in any way deserves, but he can receive it by faith (Rom 3:25; 5:15). For example, if someone out of the goodness of his heart decides to give a friend a gift, the friend must accept that gift if he wants to make it his own. But the gift is given freely; it is not a reward for the friend's act of acceptance.

Again, faith is not something a person can boast about. There is no merit in faith. All the merit lies in the object of faith, God, who through Jesus Christ has become the Saviour of mankind (John 3:16,18; 7:31; 17:20; Acts 20:21; 1 John 5:12-13). Consider another example. If a person in a sinking ship jumps into a lifeboat, that lifeboat will mean everything to him. His faith in jumping into it, far from being an act of merit, is an admission of helplessness. It is the lifeboat, the object of the person's faith, that takes him to safety.

Faith in God is not effort, but the ceasing of effort. It is not doing, but relying on what Christ has done. It is an attitude whereby a person gives up his own efforts to win salvation, no matter how good they be, and completely trusts in Christ, and in him alone, for his salvation (Acts 16:30-31; Gal 2:16). Without such an attitude, a person cannot receive God's salvation (Heb 11:6a).

The faith by which people receive salvation is not merely an acknowledgment of certain facts (though this is necessary, since the believer must know who and what he is trusting in; John 2:22; 3:12;

6:69; 8:24-25; Rom 10:9-10; Heb 11:6b; 1 John 5:20). Rather it is a belief by which a person commits himself wholly to Christ in complete dependence. It is not just accepting certain things as true (for even God's enemies may have that sort of belief; James 2:19), but trusting in a person, Jesus Christ. A person may say he has a general faith in God, but if he refuses to have specific faith in Jesus Christ, his 'faith' is a form of self-deception (John 5:24; 14:6; 1 John 2:23).

So basic is faith to Christianity, that the New Testament uses the name 'believer' as another name for the Christian (Acts 5:14; Rom 3:26; 1 Tim 4:12). Likewise it uses 'the faith' as another name for Christianity (1 Tim 5:8; 6:10,21).

Living by faith

Christians are not only saved by faith, they live by faith. They continue to rely on the promise and power of the unseen God rather than on what they see and experience in the visible world (1 Cor 2:5; 2 Cor 5:6-7; Col 1:23; 2:7; Heb 11:1). Their lives are lived in constant dependence on God. Christ has borne the penalty of sin on their behalf and now lives within them. Only as they trust in his power can they experience in practice the victory, peace and joy that their salvation has brought (Gal 2:20; 5:6; Eph 1:19). The strength of the faith by which they live depends largely on the strength of their personal relationship with Jesus Christ (Rom 14:1; 2 Thess 1:3; 2 Peter 1:5-8; 3:18).

A professed faith that does not produce a change for the better in a person's behaviour is not true faith; it is not a faith that leads to salvation. Those who have genuine faith will give clear proof of it by their good conduct (Gal 5:6; 1 Tim 5:8; James 2:18-26).

Sometimes the Bible speaks of faith in the special sense of trust in God to do something unusual or supernatural (Matt 9:22,28; 17:19-20; Mark 2:5; 9:23; Luke 7:9; 8:25; James 5:14-15; see DISEASE; MIRACLES; PRAYER). To some Christians God gives a gift of special faith that enables them to do what otherwise they could not do (Rom 12:3,6; 1 Cor 12:9; see GIFTS OF THE SPIRIT).

FALL OF MAN
See SIN.

FAMILY

According to God's plan for human life, people do not exist in isolation but as part of a vast society, and they are fitted for their part in that society by being brought up in families (Eph 3:14-15; 1 Tim 3:4). Stability, love and cooperation in the family will help produce similar qualities in society as a whole. (Concerning illustrations of the family in relation to Israel or the church see CHURCH; FATHER.)

Parents and children

With his ordering of human life, God has put it into the nature of man to exercise and accept authority. He has, for example, given parents authority over their children, and children naturally recognize that authority (Gen 22:7-8; Exod 20:12; Luke 2:51).

The Bible warns parents against misusing their authority or treating their children unjustly. It also teaches children that they must respect and obey their parents (Eph 6:1-4; Col 3:20-21). This does not mean that the family is intended to function in an atmosphere of harsh authority. On the contrary it will function best where there is an atmosphere of self-sacrificing love (Titus 2:4; cf. 2 Cor 6:11-13; Eph 5:25).

Parents who love their children will fulfil their duty to instruct and discipline them. They will not be able to do this, however, if they are ill-instructed or ill-disciplined themselves (Deut 11:18-19; 2 Sam 7:14-15; Prov 1:8; 13:1,24; 19:18; 29:17; Eph 6:4; 1 Tim 3:2-5; 5:14; Heb 12:7-11; see CHASTISEMENT). They must encourage open communication between themselves and their children (Deut 6:20-25; Josh 4:21-24). If parents act responsibly towards their children, they can expect to produce children who act responsibly (Prov 10:1,5; 22:6; 2 Tim 1:5). The training that produces this responsibility begins in the children's infancy, is carried out primarily in the home, and is based on the Word of God (Deut 6:6-9; 2 Tim 3:14-15).

The teaching that parents give their children must be supported by the example of right conduct in the parents' lives (Rom 2:21-24; 1 Thess 2:10-12). Parents must practise and teach self-sacrifice for the sake of others, so that the family is a place where people learn how to love others, forgive others, honour others and serve others (Eph 4:31-32; cf. Matt 20:25-27; John 13:12-15).

Wider responsibilities

Parents must be careful that concern for the family's well-being does not make them or their children self-centred. By practising hospitality and helping the needy, parents will encourage their children to have a generous attitude to those outside the family (Rom 12:13; 1 Tim 5:10; James 1:26-27; 1 John 3:17; see GOOD WORKS; HOSPITALITY). Such attitudes and conduct, besides benefiting others, will help those within the family develop godly character and produce a happy home (Ps 128:1-4).

Responsibilities within the family concern more than just the parents and children. They extend beyond the immediate family to those of the former generation who may no longer be able to support themselves. Regardless of the help that may come from the government, the church, or other sources, Christians have a responsibility for the well-being of their aged parents (Mark 7:9-13; 1 Tim 5:4,8; see also WIDOW).

FARMING

Since the majority of Israelites were farmers, a common practice in Israel was to indicate times of the year by features of the agricultural seasons, rather than by names of the months. Using the twelve months of our calendar for comparison, we can summarize the agricultural year in Palestine as follows:

Month	Weather		Agriculture
January	Cool	Rain	Sowing
February	Warmer	Rain	Almond blossom
March	Warmer	Rain	Citrus fruit harvest
April	Warmer	Dry	Barley harvest
May	Hot	Dry	Wheat harvest
June	Hot	Dry	First ripe figs
July	Hot	Dry	Grape harvest
August	Hot	Dry	Olive harvest
September	Hot	Dry	Dates, other fruits
October	Cooler	Rain	Ploughing time
November	Cooler	Rain	Winter figs
December	Cooler	Rain	Sowing

Israel's agricultural prosperity depended upon more than simply growing the right crops in the right seasons. The nation was in a special sense God's people, and its devotion to God was a basic factor that influenced seasonal conditions (Deut 11:8-17). Also, the annual religious festivals were related to the harvest seasons (Lev 23:10,14-15,39; see FEASTS; MONTH). In fact, the whole way of life in Israel was tied in with the annual agricultural cycle.

Ploughing and sowing

Like farmers elsewhere, Israelite farmers depended much upon the rain for the success of their crops. After the six months dry season, at the end of which all the harvesting for the year was over, the farmers awaited the coming of the rains. The ground was by now hard and dry, and had to be ploughed and broken up in preparation for the sowing of new crops (Exod 34:21; Jer 4:3).

Farmers normally ploughed with oxen, urging the animals on with a sharpened stick called a goad (Deut 22:10; Judg 3:31; 1 Kings 19:19; Luke 9:62; 14:19; see also YOKE). Ploughs originally were made

Ploughing

of wood, but later of iron (1 Sam 13:20). In hilly country where ploughing was difficult, farmers dug the ground by hand, using a hoe (Isa 7:25).

The rains that marked the arrival of the rainy season were known as the early, or autumn, rains (Deut 11:14; Jer 5:24; Joel 2:23) and were necessary for the sowing of the fields that followed (Gen 26:12; Matt 13:3). Rain fell irregularly throughout the cool season, helping the crops to grow. But the rains that farmers most eagerly looked for were the later, or spring, rains. These were necessary to bring the cereal crops to full growth before the dry season arrived (Deut 11:14; Prov 16:15; Jer 3:3; 5:24; Joel 2:23; Zech 10:1). Throughout the hot dry season that followed, farmers depended mainly on heavy dews to provide moisture for their crops (1 Kings 17:1; Isa 18:4; Zech 8:12; see WEATHER).

Cereal harvest

The first of the cereal crops to be harvested was the barley (Lev 23:10; Ruth 1:22; 2 Sam 21:9), and this was followed by the wheat (Lev 23:16-17; Judg 15:1). When harvesting, the farmer was not to reap to the borders of his field, and was not not to go back over the field to gather any grain he had missed when reaping. He was to leave this for the poor (Lev 19:9; Deut 24:19; Ruth 2:2-7,17).

Reapers cut the standing grain with a sickle (Deut 16:9; Mark 4:29), tied the stalks into sheaves (Gen 37:7; Deut 24:19), and then transported the sheaves either on animals or in carts to the threshing floor (Neh 13:15; Amos 2:13; Micah 4:12). The threshing floor was a hard flat piece of ground where oxen trampled the loosened sheaves so that

Harvesting

the grain fell from the stalks. The oxen were allowed to eat from the pile of straw as they trampled it (Num 18:27; Deut 25:4; 1 Sam 23:1; Hosea 10:11; 1 Cor 9:9). Another method of threshing was to drag large wooden or metal implements called threshing sledges over the pile of loosened sheaves (1 Chron 21:23; Amos 1:3).

The farmer then winnowed the grain, usually in the evenings when a soft breeze was blowing. Using a large fork, he threw the grain into the air so that the breeze blew away the chaff, while the grain itself fell to the earth (Ruth 3:2; Isa 30:24; Matt 3:12). He then sifted the grain in a sieve to remove impurities, before packing it into bags or baskets ready for household use (Amos 9:9; Luke 22:31). He burnt any dirty or useless straw, but stored the good straw away, to be used as food for animals (Judg 19:19; 1 Kings 4:28; Matt 3:12).

Fruit harvests

During the months that the farmers were reaping, threshing, winnowing and storing the cereal crops, the fruits were beginning to ripen. The first to ripen were the figs, which continued to bear fruit for about the next ten months (Num 13:20; see FIG). Next to be harvested were the grapes. Following the practice of the grain farmer, the vineyard keeper was not to go through his vineyard a second time to gather grapes he had missed when picking, but was to leave them for the poor (Lev 19:10). People ate grapes fresh or dried and used them to make a variety of wines (Num 6:3; 1 Sam 25:18; see GRAPES).

After the grapes were the olives, which workers harvested by shaking or beating the tree so that the fruit fell to the ground. It was then collected in baskets (Deut 24:20; Isa 17:6; Amos 8:2; see OLIVE). Finally came the harvest of dates and other summer fruits, which marked the end of the agricultural season (Amos 8:1).

The people were now well stocked with food for the winter months ahead. During these months the rains came and the farmers began preparing for the next annual cycle. (For details of other cereals, fruits and vegetables that the Israelites grew see FOOD.)

Flocks and herds

Only after the Israelites settled in Canaan did they became crop farmers and fruit growers. Before that, they and their forefathers had been mainly keepers of sheep and cattle. Abraham, Isaac and Jacob had moved around from place to place with their animals (Gen 13:1-7; 26:14-22; 33:13), the family of Jacob had kept flocks and herds in Egypt (Gen 47:1-6), and the people of Moses' time had brought animals with them when they left Egypt for Canaan (Exod 12:38; Deut 8:11-14).

Having settled in their new homeland, the Israelites continued to keep sheep and cattle. Some of the best regions for their animals were the grassy plains of Bashan and Gilead on the eastern side of the Jordan (Num 32:1,26,36; Deut 32:14; Ps 22:12; Micah 7:14).

Israelites were not great eaters of meat. In general they ate only the meat of cattle, sheep and goats, and usually only in connection with religious sacrifices or on special occasions (Gen 18:7; 27:9; Lev 7:15; 1 Sam 25:18; 28:24; Luke 15:23,29). They kept cattle mainly for their milk, which provided an important part of the Israelite diet (Gen 18:7-8; 2 Sam 17:29; Isa 7:22). They kept sheep mainly for their wool, which they used to make clothing (Lev 13:47; Prov 27:26; see SHEEP). Goats, which were able to live in harsher country than sheep, were kept for their hair, which people wove into cloth, and for their milk (Exod 26:7; 1 Sam 19:13; Prov 27:27).

Those who looked after animals usually became tough, hard people. Life for them was harsh and dangerous as they battled against the difficulties created by drought, heat, cold, wild animals and thieves (Gen 26:17-22; 31:39-40; Amos 3:12; John 10:12; see SHEPHERD).

Difficulties for farmers

There were no fences dividing one farmer's land from another's, the borders being marked by huge stones called landmarks. Farmers sometimes lost their land because of the dishonesty and violence of others (Deut 19:14). Much of Palestine's farming land was stony, and farmers had much hard work to do in digging up the stones before they could use the land for farming (Isa 5:2). They used most of the stones to make walls for sheep folds and vineyards, though in some cases they preferred to surround their vineyards with hedges (Num 22:24; Isa 5:5; Micah 2:12-13; Matt 21:33). But neither hedges nor stone walls could prevent thieving and violence (Matt 21:38-39; John 10:1).

In addition to these dangers, farmers were exploited and oppressed by wealthy merchants and government officials (Amos 5:11; 8:4-6). As a result many of them became poor and even lost their houses and lands to ruthless money lenders (Amos 2:7-8; Micah 2:1-2; James 2:6; 5:4).

Farmers had a constant battle also against natural enemies such as drought (1 Kings 17:7; Amos 4:7; Hag 1:11), locust plagues (Joel 1:4), hail storms (Hag 2:17), plant diseases (Amos 4:9) and hot winds from the desert that burnt up their crops (Isa 27:8; Jer 4:11; 13:24). Some of these difficulties may have come as judgments from God (Deut 28:1-24; see also SABBATICAL YEAR).

One of the qualities required in farmers, therefore, was patience amid the trials of life. Through hard work and perseverance they could expect in the end to enjoy the fruits of their work (2 Tim 2:6; James 5:7).

FASTING

Fasting was a common practice among Israelites in both Old and New Testament times. People went without food or drink for a period, usually for some religious purpose. It may have been to express sorrow (1 Sam 31:13; 1 Kings 21:27; Neh 1:4), repentance (1 Sam 7:6; Joel 2:12; Dan 9:3-4) or sincerity in prayer (2 Chron 20:3-4; Ezra 8:23).

The only official fast according to the Jewish law was the annual Day of Atonement (assuming that 'to afflict yourselves' means 'to fast'; Lev 23:27). The Jews later introduced a series of fasts to mourn the destruction of Jerusalem by Babylon in 587 BC (Zech 8:19). Because of the association of fasting with mourning, Jesus' disciples did not fast while he was with them. That was a time of joy. They fasted only when he was taken from them and killed; but their sorrow was turned into joy at his resurrection (Luke 5:33-35).

Both Old and New Testaments speak of those who fasted insincerely. Some people made a show of their fasting, thinking they were impressing others, and in particular impressing God; but they were only inviting God's condemnation (Isa 58:3-5; Matt 6:16-18; Luke 18:12). By contrast, God approved of true fasting, whether individual or collective, when it was combined with genuine prayer (Matt 4:1-4; Luke 2:37; Acts 13:2-3).

The Bible gives no explanation of the practical purpose of fasting. Examples of fasting in the New Testament show that it accompanied prayer when people faced unusually difficult tasks or decisions, or met unusually strong opposition from Satan. The purpose of the fast may have been to separate the person as much as possible from the common affairs of everyday life. This would enable him, without distraction, to concentrate all his spiritual powers on the important issues before him.

FATHER

A basic element in fatherhood is that it is related to origins, to bringing things into existence (Gen 17:5). Consequently, the Bible speaks about God as the Father of creation, for he is the source of all things (Num 16:22; Isa 64:8; Mal 2:10; Luke 3:38; Heb 12:9; James 1:17; see GOD). This is possibly one aspect of God's fatherhood that Paul refers to when he points out that all fatherhood comes ultimately from God. Earthly fathers exist only because there is a heavenly Father (Eph 3:14-15). (For the responsibilities of fathers in human society see FAMILY.)

People in Bible times used the word 'father' as a respectful way of referring to their ancestors (Ps 22:4; Heb 1:1; see ANCESTORS). They even used it to refer to their spiritual leaders, especially those who brought them to know God (2 Kings 6:21; 13:14; 1 Cor 4:14-15; 1 Tim 1:2,18; 1 Peter 5:13; cf. Matt 23:7-12). But the Bible's most important use of 'father' is in relation to God.

Father of his people

When the Bible speaks of God's fatherhood of his people, there is again a variety of meanings. In Old Testament times God was the Father of the nation Israel. He made Israel his people by covenant, and cared for them as a father cares for his children (Exod 4:22; Deut 1:31; 8:5; Hosea 11:1; Mal 1:6; John 8:41). In particular he was Father to the king of his chosen people, and more particularly still, of the Messiah, whom Israel's king foreshadowed (2 Sam

7:14; Ps 2:7; cf. Acts 13:33; Heb 1:5; see MESSIAH). In addition to all this, God was Father in a special sense to the true believers within the nation (Ps 103:13; Isa 63:16; Mal 3:17; John 8:42).

The New Testament shows that God is Father to *all* who believe in him — not just Israelites, but believers of all nations (Rom 1:7; 1 Cor 1:2-3). All people, regardless of nationality, are dead in sin, but those who repent of their sin and believe in Jesus are 'born again'. They receive new life from God and so become God's children (John 1:12-13; Eph 2:1; see REGENERATION). To use another picture, God adopts them into his family and gives them the status and privileges of full-grown sons (Gal 4:4-6; see ADOPTION). Believers therefore can speak to God confidently as their Father (Matt 6:9; Luke 11:9-13; Rom 8:15-16; see ABBA; PRAYER). Yet they must also reverence him, for he is their judge (Matt 6:14-15; 1 Peter 1:17).

God, on his part, cares for his children's needs and makes them heirs of his inheritance (Matt 6:32; Luke 12:32; Rom 8:17), though he also chastises them when they do wrong (2 Sam 7:14-15; Heb 12:7-11; see CHASTISEMENT). God's children are to develop lives whose character is like that of their Father (Matt 5:48).

Father of Jesus Christ

The highest sense in which God is Father is as the Father of Jesus Christ (John 1:18; 5:36; Rom 15:6; 2 Cor 1:3). But his fatherhood of Jesus is different from his fatherhood of believers (cf. John 20:17).

God did not make Jesus his Son as he makes believers his sons. Jesus always has been the Son of God. There is no suggestion that God the Father existed first and God the Son came into existence later. The Father and the Son, both being God, have existed eternally, but they have existed eternally in this relationship of Father and Son. Though distinct persons, they are inseparably united (John 10:30; 14:10; see SON OF GOD; TRINITY).

As the Son, Jesus alone has true knowledge of the Father. Therefore, only through the Son is the Father revealed to man, and only through the Son can man come to know the Father (Matt 11:27; John 1:18; 5:18; 10:15; 14:6-7).

FEAR

A person naturally fears those people, influences, objects and events that he sees as threatening, as being able to control, overpower or destroy him (Num 14:9; Ps 2:11; Luke 21:26; Heb 2:15; 10:27). In some cases this may be a cowardly fear (Prov

29:25; Gal 2:12), but in others a very healthy fear, amounting to respect or reverence (Gen 20:11; Lev 26:2; Rom 3:18; 1 Peter 2:18). In this latter sense people are to fear those who have authority over them (Lev 19:3; Prov 24:21; Rom 13:3,7; Eph 6:5), and particularly to fear God (Ps 34:11; Isa 8:13-15; Acts 9:31; 1 Peter 2:17).

The sinner has good reason to fear God; for God's punishment will one day fall upon him (Micah 7:16-17; Matt 10:28). By contrast the believer's fear of God is mixed with love for him (Deut 6:2,5; 1 Peter 1:8; 3:15). If the believer obeys God simply because he fears God's punishment, such obedience displays an immature love. The believer should obey God because he loves God (Deut 10:12; Rom 8:15; 1 John 4:17-18; 5:3).

Nevertheless, the believer's love for God is not a substitute for reverence, nor does it excuse him from judgment. God still requires obedience and holiness. He is the almighty judge as well as the loving Father. Therefore, the believer must have a healthy fear of him as well as a warm love for him (2 Cor 7:1; 1 Peter 1:16-17).

Such an attitude guarantees God's help in living a life that is pleasing to him and beneficial to the person himself (Ps 147:11; Prov 1:7; 8:13; 9:10; 10:27; 14:26; Phil 2:12-13). It also gives confidence not to fear the dangers and uncertainties of life (Ps 46:2; 112:1,7; Luke 12:4-5; 1 Peter 3:14-15).

FEASTS

Israelites were largely a farming people, and their religious festivals, or feasts, were built into the agricultural cycle (see FARMING). There were three main annual festivals: Passover-Unleavened Bread and Pentecost-Harvest at the beginning of the year, and Tabernacles-Ingatherings in the middle of the year. (For the Israelite calendar see MONTH.) On these three occasions all adult males had to go to the central place of worship, which was originally the tabernacle and later the temple (Exod 23:14-17).

The Israelite festivals recalled the nation's history, yet they were also relevant to the people's current experiences. Within the festivals there was a mixture of solemnity and joy, as the sinful people were humbled before their God yet thankful to him for his merciful salvation and constant provision (Lev 23:2,21; Deut 16:11-12).

Passover and Unleavened Bread

God decreed that the month during which the Israelites escaped from bondage in Egypt should be the first month of their religious year (Exod 12:2).

(This Jewish month fits somewhere into the period of March-April on our calendar.) In the middle of the month the people kept the Passover, followed by the week-long Feast of Unleavened Bread (Lev 23:5-8; Mark 14:1). The Passover recalled God's 'passing over' the houses of the Israelites when he killed the firstborn throughout Egypt (Exod 12:27). The accompanying Feast of Unleavened Bread recalled the people's hasty departure from Egypt when they had to make their bread without leaven (yeast), cooking as they travelled in order to save time (Exod 12:8,34,39). (For details of the Passover rituals see PASSOVER.)

Once the Israelites had settled in Canaan, the festival became an occasion to acknowledge God's care in giving them their grain harvest. At Passover time the barley was ready for harvest, but before the people could reap it and use it for themselves, they had to acknowledge God as the giver. Therefore, on the third day of the Feast of Unleavened Bread, they presented the first sheaf of reaped barley to God. They accompanied this with animal sacrifices that expressed confession, gratitude and dedication (Lev 23:10-14; Num 28:16-25).

Feast of Harvest (Pentecost)

After the Feast of Unleavened Bread, the people returned home and for the next six weeks were busy harvesting, first the barley and then the wheat. At the end of the wheat harvest they showed their thanks to God for their food by presenting to him two loaves of bread such as they would eat in their normal meals. Again there were additional sacrifices (Lev 23:15-21; Num 28:26-31).

Since this festival fell on the fiftieth day after Passover, it later became known as the Feast of Pentecost ('pentecost' meaning 'fifty') (Acts 2:1; see PENTECOST). It was also known as the Feast of Weeks, being a week of weeks after the offering of the first barley sheaf (Deut 16:9-10). More commonly it was called the Feast of Harvest or Feast of Firstfruits.

Between the two festival seasons

Following the cereal harvest there was much activity as the people threshed, winnowed and stored the grain. The hottest part of the year had now arrived, and over the next few months the figs, grapes, olives and dates ripened and were harvested. By the middle of the year, summer had almost gone, most farming activity was finished, and people began preparing for the mid-year festival season.

On the first day of the seventh month (within the period of September-October on our calendar) the ceremonial blowing of trumpets called the people together for a special day of rest and worship (Lev 23:24-25). This was to prepare them for the solemn cleansing from sin that followed ten days later on the Day of Atonement (Lev 23:26-32; for details see DAY OF ATONEMENT).

Feast of Tabernacles (or Shelters)

Five days after the Day of Atonement was the Feast of Tabernacles. The name 'tabernacle' in this case does not refer to the Israelite place of worship, but to small shelters, or booths, made of tree branches and palm leaves. During the festival people lived in these shelters in remembrance of Israel's years in the wilderness (Lev 23:34,39-43).

The festival was also known as the Feast of Ingatherings, because it marked the end of the agricultural year, when all the produce of the land had been gathered in and the people rejoiced in thanksgiving before God (Lev 23:39; Deut 16:13-15). The number of sacrifices at this feast was greater than at any other, though the number decreased a little each day (Lev 23:36; Num 29:12-38).

There are records of Israel's celebration of the Feast of Tabernacles after Solomon's completion of the temple and after the Jews' return from captivity in Babylon (2 Chron 8:12-13; Ezra 3:4). They still celebrated it in the time of Jesus (John 7:2), and had introduced into it a water-pouring ceremony. Jesus referred to this ceremony when he addressed the people on the final day of the feast, offering to satisfy the spiritual needs of all who came to him for help (John 7:37-39).

Feast of Purim

The Feast of Purim was not one of the feasts appointed by God through Moses. It was established in Persia in the fifth century BC by Mordecai, a leader of the large community of Jews that had grown up in Persia after the Babylonian captivity.

Haman, Persia's chief minister, had gained the king's approval for a plan to destroy the Jewish people. He determined the date to carry out his plan by casting lots, or purim (purim being the Hebrew plural of the Persian-Assyrian word pur, meaning 'lot') (Esther 3:7). In the end, however, Haman was executed and Mordecai made chief minister in his place. When Haman's 'lucky day' arrived, the Jews, instead of being slaughtered, took revenge on their enemies (Esther 9:1). Mordecai then ordered that Jews celebrate the great occasion with feasting, exchanging gifts and giving to the poor (Esther 9:20-28; see ESTHER). Jews have celebrated the festival to the present day.

Feast of Dedication

During the second century BC, the Greek ruler of the Syrian sector of the Empire, Antiochus IV Epiphanes, used his military power to try to destroy the Jewish religion. In a brutal attack he invaded Jerusalem and slaughtered the Jews. He then defiled the Jewish temple by setting up an altar in honour of the pagan gods and sacrificing animals that the Jews considered unclean.

A group of zealous Jews, the Maccabees, began a resistance movement against Antiochus, and after three years of untiring fighting won back their religious freedom (165 BC). They promptly cleansed and rededicated the temple, in celebration of which the Jews established the annual Feast of Dedication. It was the Jews' only winter festival (John 10:22-23).

FELIX

As Roman governor of Judea from AD 52 to 60, Felix had some influence on Jewish affairs in Palestine. Early non-biblical records show that he was corrupt and cruel, characteristics that are well illustrated in the story about him in the Bible.

After a riot by the Jews in Jerusalem, Paul was sent to Caesarea to be judged by Felix (Acts 23:26-35). Felix knew the Jews well, for his own wife was Jewish (Acts 24:24). He also knew sufficient of Christianity to realize that Paul was innocent of the charges the Jews laid against him (Acts 23:29; 24:22). Yet he kept Paul imprisoned for two years, simply to please the Jews and so prevent any further unrest (Acts 24:23,27). He was interested to hear of Paul's religious beliefs, and Paul could have gained his freedom had he paid the bribe Felix wanted (Acts 24:25-26). Paul refused to cooperate, so the heartless Felix left him in prison. In due course Felix returned to Rome, leaving the next governor to deal with the matter as best he could (Acts 24:27-25:5).

FELLOWSHIP

According to its basic biblical meaning, fellowship is concerned not with people enjoying each other's company, but with people participating together in something. Fellowship is communion — having a share in something.

Fellowship 'with' means sharing 'in'

An example of the biblical meaning of fellowship is the Lord's Supper, or Holy Communion. The believer's act of eating bread and drinking wine in the Lord's Supper is an act of fellowship with Christ, for it is a spiritual sharing in his body and blood. It is a participation in Christ and all that his sacrificial death means to the believer (1 Cor 10:16; see LORD'S SUPPER). By being united with Christ, the believer shares in him, has fellowship with him (1 Cor 1:9; Heb 3:14). Likewise the believer has fellowship with the Father (1 John 1:3) and with the Holy Spirit (2 Cor 13:14; Phil 1:21; Heb 6:4), for through faith in Christ he has become a sharer in the divine nature (2 Peter 1:4).

In all these cases the fellowship may involve only the individual believer and God. The believer may have fellowship with God, regardless of whether his fellow believers join with him. If others join with him, they may all have fellowship together with God. Therefore, when the Bible speaks of Christians having fellowship together, it means that together they have fellowship *with God*, not that they enjoy being with each other (1 John 1:3). But by having fellowship together with God, they will indeed be joined together in a true and happy union (John 17:21-22; 1 Cor 10:16-17).

Sin spoils the believer's fellowship with God. Those who think they can sin as they please and still have fellowship with God are deceiving themselves. By contrast those who live righteously will enjoy unbroken fellowship with God, because God in his grace cleanses the sins that they unknowingly commit (1 John 1:6-7).

Fellowship with Christ means not only sharing in the blessings that come through his sacrificial death, but also sharing in the sufferings that he endured (Phil 3:10; 1 Peter 4:12-14; Rev 1:9). But if people have fellowship with him in his sufferings, they will also have fellowship with him in his glory (2 Tim 2:11-12; 1 Peter 5:1).

Sharing in a common possession

As Christians jointly participate in Christ, so this fellowship binds them together (Acts 2:42). There is therefore a sense in which they have fellowship with one another, but again this fellowship is usually *in* someone or something that they have as a common possession (Phil 1:7; Heb 3:14; 2 Peter 1:4). Their fellowship is a joint sharing in a common faith (Titus 1:4), in a common salvation (Jude 3) and even in their common sufferings (2 Cor 1:7; Rev 1:9). They share in the gospel by helping those who preach it (Phil 1:5; 4:14-18), and share in the financial support of poor Christians by giving money to help them (Rom 15:27; 2 Cor 8:4; 9:11). From this latter example 'fellowship' developed the more specialized meaning of 'financial contribution' (cf. Rom 15:26; 2 Cor 8:4; 9:13).

There are certain things that the Christian is not to have fellowship with, not to share in, not to participate in. He is not to identify with another person in a way that shares in the wrongdoings of that person (1 Tim 5:22; 2 John 10-11). Neither is he to share in a marriage with a non-believer (2 Cor 6:14-15) or in a religious feast where food has been offered to idols (1 Cor 10:20-21). He is to have no part, no share, in anything that is sinful (Eph 5:11; Rev 18:4).

FESTIVALS

See FEASTS.

FESTUS

During his short governorship of Judea (AD 60-62), Festus had to judge the difficult case of Paul. The Jews knew that Festus was inexperienced in Jewish affairs and tried to take advantage of this to win their case against Paul. But Festus was aware of their cunning (Acts 25:1-5). He therefore arranged a proper trial and as a result was convinced of Paul's innocence. However, wanting to win the goodwill of the Jews, he refused to release Paul. Tired of this constant injustice, Paul appealed to the Emperor (Acts 25:6-12).

Festus now faced a difficulty. He had to send a person to the Emperor, without knowing the offence of which the person was supposedly guilty. He did not understand what made the Jews hate Paul. When Herod Agrippa, an expert on Jewish affairs, arrived at the governor's palace, Festus explained his problem. He was pleased to give his visitor the opportunity to hear Paul's case (Acts 25:23-27). Agrippa confirmed that Paul was innocent, but since Paul had appealed to the Emperor, Festus had no alternative but to send him to Rome (Acts 26:32).

FIG

Like olives and grapes, figs were plentiful in Israel and neighbouring countries (Deut 8:8; Judg 9:8-13; Jer 5:17). The saying 'to sit under one's own vine and fig tree' indicated the enjoyment of long-lasting peace, contentment and prosperity. On the other hand 'to lay waste one's vines and fig trees' indicated devastation and ruin (1 Kings 4:25; 2 Kings 18:31; Hosea 2:12; Joel 1:7,12; Micah 4:4). The cultivation of fig trees required years of patient labour, and the failure of a harvest was a major calamity (Prov 27:18; Luke 13:7; cf. Ps 105:33; Hab 3:17).

People ate figs either fresh or dried and often made them into cakes (1 Sam 25:18; 1 Chron 12:40; Nahum 3:12). They also believed that figs had some medicinal value (Isa 38:21).

Healthy fig trees bore fruit for about ten months of the year, though they lost their leaves and grew new ones according to the season (Matt 24:32). Jesus on one occasion was disappointed when he

Figs

found that a fig tree that should have had fruit on it (though it was not yet the season when the fruit could be picked) had no fruit at all. He saw the fruitless tree as symbolic of Israel, a nation that was useless to God. It produced no spiritual fruit and would fall under God's judgment (Mark 11:12-14; cf. Luke 13:6-9).

FIRSTBORN

In ancient Israelite society the firstborn son had special rights that were highly valued. He was the head of the family in the father's absence, and upon his father's death he received an inheritance double that of the other sons (Gen 49:3; Deut 21:17). The firstborn could, however, lose his birthright, either by selling it or through misconduct (Gen 25:31-34; 1 Chron 5:1-2).

At the time of Israel's escape from slavery in Egypt, God preserved the lives of the Israelites' firstborn, both people and animals. From that time on, the firstborn of all Israelite families, and the firstborn of their flocks and herds, became God's special possession (Exod 13:2).

In the case of the firstborn of animals, the owner dedicated a clean animal to God by sacrifice. He dedicated an unclean animal by the sacrifice of a clean animal in its place (since an unclean animal could not be offered in sacrifice) (Exod 13:11-15; Num 18:17-18). In the case of people, the parents ceremonially presented their firstborn to God, and then bought the child back by a payment of money (Num 18:15-16; Luke 2:7,23). For the service of the tabernacle, the Levites replaced the firstborn as God's special servants (Num 3:11-13,45; cf. Exod 32:29).

Because of the high status of the firstborn, the title developed a figurative usage. In Old Testament times, God considered the nation Israel to be his firstborn, his special people among all the nations of the world (Exod 4:22; cf. Deut 7:6; Hosea 11:1). In New Testament, times believers in Jesus Christ are God's firstborn, his chosen and privileged ones (Heb 12:23).

The Bible speaks of Jesus Christ as the first-born of his Father. This does not mean that he came into existence later than his Father, but that he is head of the Father's new people. He has authority over them, yet he graciously looks upon them as his brothers and sisters (Rom 8:29; Heb 1:6; 2:11-12). Jesus is also the firstborn of all creation. This means not that the Son of God was created, but that he existed before creation, has authority over it, and is its rightful heir (Col 1:15-17; Heb 1:2). Also, through his resurrection, he is the firstborn from the dead. He has authority over God's new creation, the church, and guarantees its final victory (Col 1:18; Rev 1:5).

FIRSTFRUITS

According to Israelite law, the people had to present to God the first portion of the harvest, whether of grain or fruit, as an expression of thanks to him for the entire harvest (Exod 22:29; 23:19). This offering may have been in the form of a cake made from the cereal, or in the form of a basket of cereal or fruit (Num 15:17-21; Deut 26:2).

In addition to the offerings of firstfruits by private individuals, there were offerings of firstfruits at Israel's national festivals. These included the Feast of Unleavened Bread (Lev 23:10-11), the Feast of Harvest, or Pentecost (Lev 23:15-17), and the Feast of Tabernacles, or Ingatherings (Exod 23:16; Lev 23:39). (For details see FEASTS.) The firstfruit offerings became the property of the priests and so formed one source of their food supply (Num 18:12-13).

Since people had to present their firstfruits before they could use the remainder of the harvest for themselves, firstfruits had a symbolic meaning. They were a sign of hope, a guarantee of greater things to come. This is the meaning of the New Testament illustrations of firstfruits. The risen Christ is called the firstfruits of believers who have died, because his resurrection guarantees the resurrection of all believers (1 Cor 15:20,23). The Holy Spirit, whom believers have already, is the firstfruits, or guarantee, of future glory (Rom 8:23).

Just as the firstfruits of the Israelites were the finest from their harvest, so God wants Christians to be the finest creatures in all his creation (James 1:18). Like the firstfruits, they belong especially to God (Rev 14:4). Paul sometimes spoke of the first people who became Christians in a locality as the firstfruits of the church in that place (Rom 16:5; 1 Cor 16:15).

FISH

Fish were plentiful in the Mediterranean Sea and in the Sea of Galilee, but there were none in the Dead Sea, as the water was too salty (Neh 13:16; Matt 4:18; Luke 5:1-7). According to the food laws set out by Moses, Israelites were allowed to eat fish (Deut 14:9-10; Luke 24:42-43; John 6:11; 21:9) and several of Jesus' apostles were fishermen (Matt 4:18,21; John 21:1-3). The Bible records one story of a fish so large that it was able to swallow a man whole (Jonah 1:17; 2:1; Matt 12:40).

People used various methods to catch fish. Some fished with a hook (Isa 19:8; Hab 1:15; Matt 17:27) but commercial fishermen usually used a drag-net. This was a net that they threw into the sea

Fishing on Lake Galilee

and dragged towards either the shore or the boat from which they were fishing (Hab 1:15; Matt 13:47-48; Luke 5:4-7; John 21:6-8). Most commercial fishing of this sort was done at night (Luke 5:5; John

21:3). Another type of net was the smaller cast-net, which the fishermen, standing on the shore or in shallow water, cast around him and then drew in (Isa 19:8; Matt 4:18-20).

After bringing their fish to land, the fishermen sorted them, putting the larger ones into baskets for sale and throwing the useless ones away (Matt 13:47-48). When the men were finished with their nets, they washed them (Luke 5:2), dried them (Ezek 26:5) and sometimes mended them (Matt 4:21). The Fish Gate was an entrance in Jerusalem's city wall that fishermen and traders used when bringing their fish into the city to sell (Neh 13:16; Zeph 1:10-11).

Jesus used illustrations from fishing in his preaching. As fishermen go looking for fish, so Jesus' disciples are to go looking for people to bring into his kingdom (Matt 4:19). As a fishing net contains both good and bad fish, so among those who claim to be in God's kingdom there are the true and the false. And as the good fish are separated from the bad, so the true and the false will be separated in the day of final judgment (Matt 13:47-50).

FLESH

Since flesh is one of the most obvious features of the human body, it is not surprising that the word 'flesh' developed a figurative usage in relation to human life. This usage was not limited to man's physical existence, for man's life within the physical world is inseparable from his moral imperfection. Inevitably, 'flesh' developed new meanings in relation to certain spiritual characteristics of man.

Physical life

Among the expressions that use 'flesh' in relation to man's physical nature are 'flesh and blood', 'flesh and bone' and 'flesh and heart'. These may mean no more than body, person, human life, mankind or something similar (Gen 6:12; Job 2:5; Ps 73:26; 78:39; Luke 3:6; John 1:14; 8:15; 2 Cor 5:16; 12:7; Gal 1:16; Phil 1:22-24; Heb 2:14; 1 Peter 1:24). A man and a woman united in marriage become one flesh, and people related to each other share the same flesh (Gen 2:24; 29:14; Rom 1:3; 4:1; 9:3; see also BODY).

On account of the usage of 'flesh' in reference to man's physical existence, the word is sometimes contrasted with 'spirit', that inner and higher aspect of man's life (Matt 26:41; 2 Cor 7:1; 1 Peter 3:18; see SPIRIT). Man's physical life, however, has been corrupted through sin, and this gives 'flesh' its

particular meaning in the writings of Paul. There it refers to sinful human nature (Rom 8:5; Eph 2:3).

Sinful human nature

The whole nature of man is infected by sin from birth. Adam, as the father and head of all mankind, rebelled against God and corrupted man's nature from the beginning. Each human being, because of his union with Adam, is born with this sinful nature (Ps 51:5; Rom 5:12; 7:18; see SIN).

Human nature (the flesh) is directed and controlled by sin, and rebels against God's law. It is incapable of being reformed and produces all the evil in man. Like a deadly disease it cannot be cured, and leads only to moral decay and death (Rom 7:5; 8:6-8; Gal 6:8; Col 2:23). The evil results of the flesh affect every part of the life and activity of man (Gal 5:19-21; cf. Matt 7:18).

Although Jesus was born with a human nature, his nature was not affected by sin. By living in complete obedience to God's law, dying for sin and rising victoriously from the dead, he condemned the flesh, so that mankind might no longer be enslaved by it (Rom 8:3-4; Heb 2:14-15; 4:15).

When a person trusts in the saving power of Christ, he receives new life and freedom through the Spirit of Christ who comes to dwell within him. But the flesh is not destroyed. The believer still lives in a world where everything, even his own nature, suffers from the effects of sin. The original sinful human nature remains with him till the end of his present earthly existence, but through Christ he is now free from its power (Rom 6:14,18; 8:1-2,10-12; see JUSTIFICATION).

Therefore, there is a continual conflict in the life of the believer, the flesh fighting against the Spirit (Rom 8:5; Gal 5:17). Before the believer had trusted in Christ and become indwelt by the Spirit, the flesh had ruled him as a cruel master. If, now that he is a believer, he readily gives in to the flesh, it will soon bring him under its power again. In view of this, the believer must ensure that his behaviour is controlled and directed by the Spirit (Rom 6:12-18; 8:4,13; 1 Cor 3:1-3; Gal 5:16). He has no obligation to the flesh; he owes it nothing. He must neither trust in it nor give it any opportunity to satisfy its evil desires (Rom 8:12; 13:14; Phil 3:3).

Christ has condemned the old nature by his crucifixion (Rom 6:6; 8:3). The person who belongs to Christ must accept this by faith and show it to be true by living according to his new nature (Rom 6:7-14; Gal 2:20; 5:24; Eph 4:22,24; Col 2:11; 3:5-10; see REGENERATION; SANCTIFICATION).

FLOOD

Early man's rebellion against God produced such widespread corruption that God announced he would destroy the rebels through a great flood (Gen 6:5-7,17). He would, however, preserve the godly man Noah and his family, and through them build a new people. God's means of preserving Noah's family, along with enough animals to repopulate the animal world, was through an ark that God told Noah to build (Gen 6:8-22; see Heb 11:7; 1 Peter 3:20; see ARK; NOAH).

The natural causes God used to bring about the flood were twofold – forty days heavy rain combined with what seems to have been earthquake activity that sent the waters of the sea pouring into the Mesopotamian valley (Gen 7:11-12). Even after the rain stopped and the earth settled, the flood waters took a long time to go down. Almost four months after the rain stopped, the ark came to rest in the Ararat range (Gen 8:3-4). Seven months later, grass and plants had grown sufficiently to allow Noah, his family and the animals to leave the ark and begin life afresh on the earth (Gen 8:14-19).

It appears that the area affected by the flood was the region of the Bible's story in the previous chapters. The information that Noah was able to obtain confirmed to him that the flood covered it all. (Expressions of universality such as 'all the earth', 'everywhere', 'all people', 'everyone', etc. are often used in the Bible with a purely local meaning, as they are today; cf. Gen 41:57; Deut 2:25; 1 Kings 4:34; 18:10; Dan 4:22; 5:19; John 1:4-5; Acts 2:5; 11:28; Col 1:23.)

The important point of the flood story is that the flood was a total judgment on that ungodly world (except for Noah and his family), as God had warned (Gen 6:17). It is a reminder that, at the return of Jesus Christ, sudden judgment will again fall on an ungodly world, though again God will preserve the righteous (Matt 24:36-39; 2 Peter 2:5,9; cf. Gen 9:13-15; 2 Peter 3:5-7).

FLOWERS

Very few flowers are named in the Bible. The most commonly mentioned are those of the lily family (Song of Songs 2:16; 6:2; Hosea 14:5; Matt 6:28). A type of wild rose is also mentioned (Song of Songs 2:1; Isa 35:1). The flower of the mandrake plant had a strong smell that people believed could excite sexual passion (Gen 30:14-16; Song of Songs 7:13).

People have always seen beauty in flowers, and flower patterns were prominent in the decorations of the tabernacle and the temple (Exod 25:31-34; 1 Kings 6:18,29-35; 7:26,49). Although they are beautiful, flowers do not last long. Because of this the Bible sometimes refers to them as symbols of the brevity and impermanence of life (Job 14:2; Nahum 1:4; James 1:10-11; 1 Peter 1:24).

FOOD

All food has been given by God, and people are to show their gratitude by thanking God for it and enjoying it (Gen 1:29; Eccles 9:7; Matt 6:11; Acts 14:17; 1 Cor 10:30-31; 2 Cor 9:10; 1 Tim 4:4). Although food is necessary for physical life, man's life is more than merely physical. Man needs more than food for the body. His life depends for its proper function upon spiritual forces that are found only in God (Deut 8:3; Ps 63:1; Matt 4:3-4; 6:25; John 6:27,35).

Just as a person needs to eat food if his physical life is to grow, so he needs to feed on God's Word if his spiritual life is to grow. As the newborn child feeds on milk, so the new Christian feeds his new life by learning the basics of Christian truth and practice. But a child must move on to solid food if it is to grow towards adulthood. Likewise the Christian must move on to a fuller understanding of God's Word if he is to grow towards maturity (1 Cor 3:1-2; Heb 5:12-14; 1 Peter 2:3).

Correct attitudes

The Christian's concern for spiritual food does not mean he can be indifferent to matters concerning food for the body. If a person speaks of having Christian faith but refuses to help the hungry, he is denying the Christian faith (Matt 25:42,44-45; Mark 6:33-44; James 2:14-17; 1 John 3:17). God taught Old Testament Israel that people were to make sacrifices in their business and domestic lives so that the poor would not go hungry (Lev 19:9-10; Deut 14:28-29; 15:7-11; Ps 132:15; Isa 14:30; 58:7). He teaches Christians similarly, emphasizing that they are to help all the hungry, even those who are their enemies (Luke 14:13; 16:19-25; Rom 12:20; cf. Luke 6:25,30).

Israelite law detailed which foods were or were not allowable. One of the forbidden foods was blood, because of blood's symbolic significance as representing life (Lev 17:14; see BLOOD). Other forbidden food was the meat of certain animals that Israelite law considered unclean (Lev 11:1-47; see UNCLEANNESS). Christians are not under these laws, and so are not restricted as the Israelites were (Mark 7:18-19; Acts 10:13-15; 1 Tim 4:3-4). At times, however, they should willingly forgo their freedom, so that they do not create unnecessary difficulties for those who still observe food laws like those given to Israel. Consideration for another person's well-being is more important than the food one eats (Rom 14:14,17,20; 1 Cor 10:31).

Apart from considering others, Christians must discipline their eating and drinking habits for their own sake. The Bible links gluttony and drunkenness as sins equally to be avoided (Prov 23:2,21; Luke 6:25; 1 Cor 11:20-22).

In ancient times, as in the present day, meals were an important part of social life. People ate meals together to show friendship and hospitality (Gen 18:6-9; 43:31-34; Mark 2:15; Luke 14:15-24), to confirm political and business agreements (Gen 26:28-31; 31:51-54), and to demonstrate fellowship with one another and with God (Lev 7:13-15; Deut 14:22-27; Luke 22:30; 1 Cor 10:17,21). This created difficulties for Christians when food at such meals had previously been offered to idols (1 Cor 8:1-8; 10:14-21; see IDOLS).

Fruit and vegetables

From earliest times plants and fruit trees were a ready source of food for mankind (Gen 1:29; 3:18). The Israelites, before they entered Canaan, received instruction in farming, so that they might gain the best results from their crops and orchards. They were warned also that when cutting down trees to construct siegeworks, they were to be careful not to destroy the fruit trees (Lev 19:23-25; Deut 20:19-20).

Among the vegetables found in the world of the Bible were beans, cucumbers, melons, leeks, onions, garlic, mallows and mustard (Gen 25:34; Num 11:4-5; 2 Sam 17:28; Job 30:4; Matt 13:31). Some of the better known fruits were figs, grapes, olives, pomegranates, apples, dates, sycamore, pistachio nuts and almonds (Gen 43:11; Deut 8:8; 34:3; Song of Songs 7:8; 8:5; Amos 7:14; Matt 7:16; see FIGS; GRAPES; OLIVES). People ate grapes fresh or dried (raisins) and crushed them to make various types of wine (Num 6:3; Deut 32:14; Ruth 2:14; 1 Sam 25:18; Joel 1:5; 3:18). Pomegranate juice made another type of popular drink (Song of Songs 8:2).

Olives were crushed to produce olive oil, which, because of its extensive use in cooking, was a basic necessity for the Hebrews. They mixed it with flour in preparing breads and cakes, and used it as a cooking fat for a variety of foods (Exod 29:2; Lev 2:4,14-16; 1 Kings 17:12-14; see OIL). The Hebrews also made a variety of sauces, usually by mixing the crushed flesh of certain fruits with other ingredients (Mark 14:20; see also SPICES).

Cereals

The Israelites' chief cereals were barley and wheat (Exod 9:31-32; 34:22; Deut 8:8). Cereal crops were important, mainly because the people obtained from them the flour to make the breads and cakes that were their staple diet (Gen 18:6; 21:14; 26:12; 37:7; 42:2; Exod 29:23; 2 Kings 4:42; Ezek 4:9; John 6:9). Cereals were so valuable that people at times used them instead of money when trading (Hosea 3:2). The price of grain, or the price of the bread made from it, was an indication of economic conditions in the land (2 Kings 7:1; Rev 6:6).

Flour was obtained by grinding the grain between two millstones (Exod 11:5; Isa 47:2; Matt 24:41; Rev 18:22). People made various sorts of cakes and breads. Sometimes they put honey in the mixture to sweeten it, and sometimes they added

Ingathering of food

leaven (yeast) to make the cake rise. This took time, and when people were in a hurry they may have omitted the leaven. Unleavened cakes were flat and heavy, leavened cakes round and light (Gen 19:3; Exod 12:33-34,39; Lev 23:17; 1 Sam 28:24; Matt 13:33; see LEAVEN). Cooking was done on an iron plate or in a clay oven (Lev 2:4-5; Isa 44:15; Hosea 7:4,6-7).

Food from animals

Animals that Israelites most commonly used for meat were those animals that were suitable for sacrifice, such as cattle, sheep and goats. But the Israelites were not great eaters of meat, and seem to have included it in their meals mainly on special occasions (Gen 18:7; Judg 6:19; 1 Sam 25:18; 28:24; Luke 15:23,29). Meat was either roasted or boiled (1 Sam 2:13-15; Ezek 24:3-5).

In addition to animals from the flocks and herds, certain wild animals also could be eaten. A meal made from the flesh of these animals was of special value (Gen 27:3-4; Deut 14:4-5). Fish also was allowed as food (Deut 14:9-10; Luke 24:42-43; John 6:11; 21:9).

The Israelites used milk, butter and cheese regularly in their meals (Gen 18:7-8; 1 Sam 17:18; 2 Sam 17:29; Prov 27:27; 30:33; Isa 7:22). They also ate the honey of wild bees, which was readily found in rocks and trees (Deut 32:13; Judg 14:8; 1 Sam 14:25). Poor people also ate locusts (Matt 3:4).

FOOL, FOLLY

In biblical usage, the word 'fool' has a wide range of meanings. Among these there is the usual variety of everyday meanings where the word applies to those who are careless, thoughtless, stupid, foolish, wicked or easily led (1 Sam 25:25; Prov 7:7; 9:13; 10:23; 17:7,18; 24:30; Matt 25:2; 2 Cor 11:16-20; 2 Tim 2:23). But the writers of the Bible also use the word with a particular meaning because of man's accountability to his Creator. They apply it to those who rely entirely on their own understanding and ability instead of relying on God. Foolishness in this sense is not so much denial of God's existence as rebellion against him (Ps 14:1; Prov 1:7; 12:15; Isa 32:6; Jer 4:22; Luke 12:20; Eph 5:17).

Therefore, the greatest fools may be those whom the world considers wise. They may think God's way of salvation through Christ's death to be foolish, but if they reject that salvation, they themselves are foolish (1 Cor 1:18-24). By calling God's work of salvation foolish, people display their ignorance. Such salvation is based on a wisdom that is beyond the capacity of man to understand fully (1 Cor 1:25; see WISDOM).

One of the most widely used terms of abuse in Jesus' time was a word that has also been translated 'fool'. Jesus referred to this abusive expression when illustrating that hate is the root cause of murder. Because God is concerned with people's attitudes as well as their actions, a person with uncontrolled hate is as liable to God's punishment as a murderer (Matt 5:21-22).

FOREIGNER

Almost every large community contains some people whom the community regards as foreigners. This often creates tensions (Num 12:1; Neh 13:23-25; Acts 18:2; 1 Thess 2:16), in spite of God's desire that there be tolerance and harmony (cf. Matt 5:9; Rom 12:18; Eph 2:14-16).

When the Israelites migrated from Egypt to Canaan, there were many foreigners among them (Exod 12:38). In Canaan there were more foreigners among them, because of the Israelites' failure to wipe out the local people (Josh 17:12; Judg 3:5). (Concerning the specific reasons for exterminating the Canaanites see CANAAN.) Israelites themselves brought in more foreigners by taking people captive in war and bringing them back to Israel to work as slaves and labourers (Num 31:9; Josh 9:22-24; 17:13; 1 Kings 9:21; see SLAVE).

God has a special concern for those who are resident foreigners or who belong to other minority groups that are liable to unfair treatment by the majority (Deut 10:17-19; Ps 146:9). He instructed Israelites to treat foreigners with tolerance and kindness, and to remember how they themselves felt when they were foreigners in Egypt (Exod 23:9; Deut 24:19-22; see HOSPITALITY).

Foreigners who worked for Israelites were to have one day rest in seven the same as Israelites (Exod 20:10). They were under the law of Israel (Exod 12:19; Lev 17:10; 18:26; 20:2; 24:16), but they also shared the national blessings of Israel (Deut 29:10-13; Josh 8:33; 20:9). They could join in some of Israel's ceremonies (Num 15:14; Deut 26:11), but they could not join in the Passover unless they had formally become members of the covenant people (Exod 12:48-50; see CIRCUMCISION; PROSELYTE). Under the new covenant, by contrast, there is no distinction between Israelites and foreigners. All believers are united in one body through faith, regardless of nationality (Gal 3:28; Eph 2:19; see GENTILE; RACE).

Among Old Testament Israelites there was a sense in which even they were foreigners. The land of Canaan belonged to God and the Israelites were like foreign visitors, or pilgrims – people whom God allowed to live for a time in his land. That was why, after Joshua divided the land among the families of Israel, no one was to sell any portion of land permanently (Lev 25:23; see JUBILEE).

In a sense all the inhabitants of the world are like foreign visitors, for the world is only their temporary dwelling place (1 Chron 29:15; Ps 39:12). This is particularly true of believers, whose real dwelling place is heaven (Heb 11:13-16; 13:14; 1 Peter 1:1,17; 2:11).

FOREKNOWLEDGE

Man's knowledge is governed by his awareness of a past, a present and a future, but God's knowledge is not. God is eternal, and his knowledge is not related to a sequence of events that he must experience in a world of time and space (Isa 57:15; Jer 23:24; see ETERNITY; TIME). Human language uses the word 'foreknowledge' in relation to God because it is the most convenient word available to indicate knowledge of events that man sees as future. From man's viewpoint, God's knowledge of the entire history of the universe is foreknowledge (Ps 139:4-6,16; Isa 46:9-10; Acts 2:23).

When the Bible speaks of God's foreknowledge it means more than merely that he knows what will happen. Usually God's foreknowledge is linked with God's purpose, which means that it is often the same as his pre-determined will. God's foreknowledge is according to his plan, and therefore may be another word for predestination (Acts 2:23; Rom 8:29; Heb 11:40; see PREDESTINATION).

God's sovereignty does not alter the fact that people are responsible for their actions. This may be a mystery beyond our understanding, but we do not solve the mystery by trying to weaken the truths of God's sovereign purposes and man's free will (Luke 22:22; Acts 2:23; see also ELECTION).

FORGIVENESS

Since wrongdoing spoils a relationship, forgiveness is necessary if the relationship is to be restored. Forgiveness does not mean pretending that some wrongdoing did not happen. It means recognizing the wrongdoing for what it is, and then in love forgiving it, forgetting it, and restoring the relationship with the forgiven person (Heb 10:17-18).

The basis of forgiveness

Man, being a sinner, has more than spoiled his relationship with God; he has also fallen under God's judgment. He is therefore in need of God's forgiveness if he is to escape that judgment (Exod 32:32; Rom 3:23-24). God alone can grant this forgiveness (Mark 2:7,10; Acts 5:31), but sinful man is in no position to demand it of him. No person has a *right* to forgiveness. Forgiveness is possible only because of the grace of God — the mercy that he exercises towards man even though man does not deserve it (Num 14:19; Ps 78:38; Rom 5:20; Titus 3:4-7).

God wants to forgive (Neh 9:17; Micah 7:18) but he requires repentance and faith in the sinner who seeks his forgiveness (Ps 32:5; 51:17; Luke 7:36-50; Acts 3:19; 10:43; 20:21; 1 John 1:9). There is no mechanical way of gaining forgiveness, such as by offering a sacrifice or reciting a formula. The sinner is dependent entirely upon God's mercy (Ps 51:1-4; Col 2:13).

This was so even in the sacrificial system of the Old Testament. There was no thought of bribing God by offering him sacrifices. On the contrary the sacrificial system was something God graciously gave to man as a means by which people might approach him and obtain forgiveness for their sins (Lev 17:11; cf. Ps 130:3).

In the sacrifices, God provided a way whereby a person could demonstrate his repentance, faith and obedience. Without such attitudes, a person benefited nothing from his sacrifices (Ps 50:9,13-14; 51:16-17; Isa 1:11,16-20).

The death of the animal in the place of the sinner also showed the sinner clearly that forgiveness of sin was possible only when the penalty of sin had justly been carried out. Forgiveness was costly. Without the shedding of blood there could be no forgiveness (Heb 9:22; cf. Lev 4:2-7; 16:15-19; see SACRIFICE). Christ's death is the basis on which God forgives all sins, past, present or future (Matt 26:28; Acts 13:38; Rom 3:24-26; Eph 1:7; Heb 9:11-14,26). And once God has forgiven sins, they are removed for ever (Ps 103:12; Isa 43:25; Col 2:13-14; Heb 8:12; 10:17-18).

Forgiveness in practice

Christ's followers have the responsibility to preach the forgiveness of sins, and because of this they become the means by which people either believe the gospel and are forgiven, or reject it and remain in their sins (John 20:22-23; Acts 13:38). Jesus on one occasion referred to the deliberate rejection of him as the blasphemy of the Holy Spirit, a sin for which there could be no forgiveness (Matt 12:31-32; for further discussion see BLASPHEMY).

Once people have been forgiven by God, they have the responsibility to forgive any who sin against them. This is more than a sign of their gratitude to God. It is a requirement laid upon them if they want to experience God's continued forgiveness of their own failures (Matt 6:12; 18:21-35; Mark 11:25; Luke 6:37; 7:47; 17:4; Eph 4:32). (Concerning the forgiven person's subsequent wrongdoings and their relationship to his salvation see JUSTIFICATION, sub-heading 'Justification and forgiveness'.)

FORNICATION

Fornication usually refers to sexual immorality by unmarried people, whereas adultery refers to sexual immorality by married people. Sometimes the Bible speaks of fornication to denote sexual immorality in general. It regards as immoral any sexual relations outside marriage or with any person other than one's marriage partner (Matt 5:32; 1 Cor 5:1; 6:13,18; 7:2; 1 Thess 4:3-4). The union of a man and a woman to become 'one' means, by definition, that it excludes all others (Gen 2:24; Matt 19:5-6).

Sexual relations without marriage

In ancient Israel it was of greatest importance to maintain one's virginity up till the time of marriage (Deut 22:13-21). Fornication by a person engaged to be married was treated as adultery (Deut 22:22-27; see ADULTERY). Unengaged people who had sexual relations were to marry, unless the girl's parents objected (Exod 22:16-17; Deut 22:28-29).

These laws impressed upon people that sexual intercourse is not merely a physical activity that people may engage in for their own pleasure, regardless of other considerations. It is part of a total commitment of a man and a woman to each other in a lifelong relationship (Rom 7:2). Those who treat sexual intercourse as no more than a physical function reduce themselves to the level of animals. They deny the dignity that God has given them as human beings designed for full inter-personal relations (Rom 1:24-27; 1 Cor 6:13,18; 2 Peter 2:12).

Wrong desires produce wrong behaviour

Often fornication occurs because people, instead of trying to avoid sexual temptation, encourage it. They do not control their thoughts and feelings, and soon they find that they cannot control their behaviour (Prov 6:23-27; 7:6-23; Matt 5:28; Col 3:5; 2 Tim 2:22; 1 Peter 2:11; cf. Gen 39:7-10; see TEMPTATION).

Human sexuality is one of God's gifts (Gen 2:18; 1 Tim 4:1-4) but, as with all God's gifts, people can properly enjoy it or shamefully abuse it. No matter how strong a person's sexual urges may be, the only satisfaction God allows for those urges is within the exclusive commitment of one person to another in lifelong marriage (1 Cor 7:2,9; 1 Thess 4:3-4; Heb 13:4; see MARRIAGE). As for prostitution, bestiality, incest and homosexual practices, God condemns them as perversions (Lev 18:6-18,22-23;

19:29; 20:10-21; Rom 1:26-27; 1 Cor 6:9-10,13-18; 1 Tim 1:9-10; Rev 21:8).

Some people may feel no shame concerning their sexual misbehaviour and may not even see it as sinful (Eph 4:19; 1 Peter 4:3-4; 2 Peter 2:12-14). This may be common among people who do not know God (Eph 4:17-19; 1 Thess 4:5), but should not be tolerated among those who call themselves Christians. The church should remove from its fellowship those who openly reject God's standards by persisting in shameful sexual misconduct (1 Cor 5:1-5,11).

There will always be people, both from outside the church and from within, who, being genuinely sorry for their sexual misconduct, turn from it and ask God's forgiveness. They can be assured that God will forgive, but they must also be assured that the church will forgive. Christians must be compassionate and understanding in giving support to those who have fallen into wrongdoing and need help (Matt 9:12-13; John 8:10-11; 1 Cor 6:9-11; 2 Cor 2:7; Gal 6:1-2; Heb 8:12).

FREEDOM

Sinful man is likened in the Bible to a slave, one who is in bondage to sin, Satan, the law and death. When by faith he receives God's salvation, he is freed from this slavery (Luke 13:16; John 8:31-34; Rom 6:17-18; Gal 4:5-7). This is an act of God's supreme grace that has as its basis the life, death and resurrection of Jesus Christ (Luke 4:17-19; John 8:36; Rom 7:4-6; 8:2; Heb 2:14-15).

Christian living

Although Christians are free from the law to which the ancient Israelites were bound, they are not free to do as they like. They have been saved by God's grace so that they might be free from sin, not so that they might fall under sin's power again (Rom 6:6-14; Gal 5:13; 1 Peter 2:16; 2 Peter 2:19). They must live as those who, through their union with Christ, have died to sin and received a new life where righteousness dominates (Rom 6:16-19; 1 Peter 2:24; 4:1-2).

Even when they are exercising their freedom correctly in relation to themselves, Christians must still consider whether they are exercising it correctly in relation to others. By controlling their freedom out of consideration for others, they demonstrate true Christian love (1 Cor 9:19-23; 10:23-24).

Personal sacrifice is necessary, but Christians must resist the pressure to submit to any set of moral or ceremonial laws that other Christians might try to impose upon them. Such laws may aim at controlling natural sinful tendencies, but in the end they will not be beneficial. They will lead only to frustration and renewed bondage (Gal 2:4; 5:1; Col 2:23). Laws might aim at righteousness, but Christians cannot achieve righteousness by keeping laws. They can achieve it only by exercising true freedom under the control of the indwelling Spirit (Gal 5:14-16; cf. 2 Cor 3:17).

Freedom in the Spirit does not mean that Christians need no self-discipline. On the contrary, self-discipline is an evidence of the Spirit's work in them (Gal 5:22-23; see SELF-DISCIPLINE). Though free from sin, Satan, death and the law, they are not free from God. They are slaves of God, because God is the one who has bought them. They belong to God (1 Cor 6:19-20; 7:22-23; see REDEMPTION). As God's slaves they have a responsibility to live righteously (Rom 6:17-22).

Besides being servants of God, believers are sons of God, and they enjoy the full liberty of sonship (John 8:35-36; Rom 8:12-17; Gal 4:1-7; see ADOPTION). They accept the authority of a loving Father, and respond with loving obedience. Their new 'law' of life is one that they obey because they want to, not because they are forced to. It is the law of Christ, which is a law of liberty and a law of love (1 Cor 9:21; Gal 5:13-14; 6:2; James 1:25; 2:12; see OBEDIENCE).

Wider responsibilities

Having experienced God's freedom, believers should then desire it for others. They should see that God desires man's freedom from sin and all its evil consequences: freedom from disease and suffering (Mark 5:1-6,18-19; Luke 13:16; Acts 10:38); freedom from hunger and poverty (Deut 15:1-11; 24:19-22; Matt 25:37-40; Acts 11:27-29); freedom from the domination of foreign nations and oppressive rulers (Exod 6:6; Nahum 3:18-19; Zeph 3:19; Rev 19:20); freedom from human slavery and social injustice (Exod 22:21-27; Deut 23:15-16; Luke 4:17-19; James 5:4-6); in fact, freedom from every type of bondage, even the bondage in the world of nature (Rom 8:21-24).

FULFILMENT

See PROPHECY; QUOTATIONS.

FUNERAL

The Israelites had elaborate customs for funerals, burials and mourning. The body of the dead person was washed (Acts 9:37), then anointed with oil or spices and wrapped in linen (John 11:44; 19:40; Acts 5:6). This was usually done by relatives or friends of the dead person (Mark 16:1). The burial followed with a minimum of delay (Acts 5:6,10).

As the funeral procession moved to the burial place, it was accompanied by mourning and wailing (Amos 5:16; Matt 9:23-24; Luke 7:12-14,32). The mourners tore their clothes and put on sackcloth as

Mourners at a funeral

a sign of their sorrow (2 Sam 3:31; see SACKCLOTH), but they were forbidden to follow superstitious heathen customs such as cutting themselves or making offerings for the dead (Lev 19:28; Deut 14:1; 26:14).

The body may have been buried in a specially prepared private tomb (Matt 27:60), a family tomb (Gen 23:19; 25:9; 49:31-32; Judg 8:32; 16:31), or a public burial ground (2 Kings 23:6; Matt 27:7). The Israelites did not usually burn the bodies of the dead, though there were exceptions. These included cases of execution of the wicked (Gen 38:24; Lev 20:14; 21:9; Josh 7;15,25) and cases where a body was badly damaged, decaying, or a danger to public health (1 Sam 31:12-13; Amos 6:10).

Funerals were usually conducted in a way that gave honour to the person who had died (2 Chron 16:14; Eccles 8:10). To leave a body unburied was therefore a mark of supreme disgrace (1 Sam 17:46; Eccles 6:3; Jer 16:6; 22:18-19; 36:30). A song may have been composed in praise of the one who had died (2 Sam 1:17-27; 3:32-34; 2 Chron 35:25), though in the case of an enemy a song may have been composed to disgrace him (Isa 14:4-21).

Another way in which Israelites showed their respect for those who had died was by adding decorations to their tombs (Matt 23:29). Often they whitewashed tombs so that people could see them at night; for anyone who touched a tomb, accidentally or otherwise, became ceremonially unclean (Matt 23:27; cf. Num 19:11,16).

This association of death with uncleanness reflects the truth that death leads to decay and corruption. The physical body eventually returns to the dust from which it was made (Gen 3:19; Eccles 3:20; John 11:39). But regardless of how the body returns to dust, whether through being buried, burnt or entombed, Christians are assured that Jesus will return to conquer death and raise them to new life. Their bodies will be changed into glorious spiritual bodies, suited to life in the age to come (1 Cor 15:42-51; Phil 3:20; 1 Thess 4:13-17; see DEATH; RESURRECTION).

GABRIEL

Angels, or messengers of God, feature frequently in the Bible record, but only rarely does the Bible give their names. One of those whom it names is Gabriel.

In the time of Judah's captivity, Gabriel made an appearance to Daniel as a man-like figure and explained the meaning of one of Daniel's visions (Dan 8:15-17). Later he appeared again, this time to bring God's answer to Daniel's prayer of confession on behalf of the nation. He assured Daniel that God would now restore the Jews to their land and bring his age-long purposes to fulfilment with the coming of the Messiah (Dan 9:20-27).

Centuries later, Gabriel was again used by God to reveal developments of these divine purposes. He announced to Zechariah the coming birth of the Messiah's forerunner (Luke 1:11-20), and then to Mary the coming birth of the Messiah himself (Luke 1:26-38). (See also ANGELS.)

GAD

Only nine and a half of Israel's twelve tribes settled in the area commonly known as Canaan (i.e. the land west of the Jordan River). The other two and a half tribes settled in the area east of Jordan. In this eastern area half of the tribe of Manasseh was in the north, the tribe of Gad in the centre and the tribe of Reuben in the south (Num 32:1-5,33; Josh 13:8-33). (For the settlement of the two and a half eastern tribes see REUBEN.)

Although the tribe was known as Gad (after the son of Jacob who fathered it; Gen 30:9-11), the area where it dwelt was commonly known as Gilead. Sometimes the names Gad and Gilead were used interchangeably (Josh 13:24-25; Judg 5:17; 11:5; 12:4; 1 Sam 13:7). (For the physical features of the region see GILEAD.)

Gad, like the other eastern tribes, was more open to attack than the western tribes, but the men of Gad were fierce fighters who drove back the invaders (Gen 49:19). They were not, however, able to withstand invasions for ever, and when Israel was later destroyed by Assyria, they were among the first Israelites to go into captivity (2 Kings 10:32-33; 15:29).

GADARA

The district of Gadara bordered the Lake of Galilee on its eastern side and extended south into the territory known as Decapolis. Gadara was not so thickly populated as other districts around the lake, and was inhabited mainly by Gentiles, some of them pig farmers. The Gadarenes were known also as Gerasenes after the chief town of the district (Matt 8:28; Mark 5:1,11-14). (For map and other details see DECAPOLIS.)

GAIUS

There are several people named Gaius in the New Testament, all except one of them connected with Paul. Paul baptized a man named Gaius in Corinth (1 Cor 1:14), and this was probably the person Paul stayed with on a later visit to Corinth (Rom 16:23). Another person named Gaius was from Macedonia (Acts 19:29) and another from Derbe (Acts 20:4). According to a variation in some texts of Acts 20:4, this latter Gaius may have been from Thessalonica, in which case he was possibly the same person referred to in Acts 19:29.

Later in the first century, the apostle John wrote a letter to a friend named Gaius. He was a person noted for his strong faith, exemplary life, generous hospitality and sincere love (3 John 1-6).

GALATIA

In the days before the Roman Empire, Asia Minor consisted of a collection of independent states. When it came under the control of the Romans, the whole area was redivided to form a number of Roman provinces. The large central province, which the Romans named Galatia, included parts of the ancient regions of Galatia in the north, Phrygia in the south-west, Pisidia in the south and Lycaonia in the south-east. (See map next page.)

Paul passed through south Galatia on a number of occasions and established churches in the towns of Antioch, Iconium, Lystra and Derbe. Sometimes the Bible writers refer to these towns as belonging to the Roman province of Galatia, but on other occasions they follow local practice and use the former names (Acts 13:14,51; 14:6,24; 16:6; 18:23; 1 Cor 16:1; Gal 1:2; 2 Tim 4:10). (Concerning the letter that Paul wrote to the churches of Galatia see GALATIANS, LETTER TO THE.)

GALATIANS, LETTER TO THE

Among the areas of Asia Minor evangelized by Paul was the southern part of the Roman province of Galatia. Paul established churches in the Galatian towns of Antioch, Iconium, Lystra and Derbe (Acts 13:13-14:23), then returned to his base in Antioch

in Syria (Acts 14:26-28). Most likely Paul wrote his letter to the Galatians while in Syrian Antioch at this time.

Purpose of the letter

Paul was disturbed when certain Jews from the church in Jerusalem came to Antioch teaching that Gentile converts had to be circumcised and keep the law of Moses (Acts 15:1,5). They argued so persuasively that even mature Christians such as Peter stopped eating with the Gentile Christians, fearing that they might break the Jewish food laws. Paul saw that such action was contrary to the gospel he preached, and he publicly rebuked Peter (Gal 2:11-13).

But worse was to follow; for the Jewish teachers had gone also to Galatia and spread their teaching among the newly planted churches there. When Paul heard this he was angry at the Jewish teachers and shocked that the Galatians had believed them (Gal 1:6; 3:1). He sent off to the Galatians a strongly worded letter, which in time became part of the New

Testament. In it Paul pointed out that there was only one gospel, the one he preached, and that the law of Moses has no authority over the believer in Jesus Christ. The believer, having been justified by faith in Christ, lives by the same faith. Though free from the Jewish law he is not lawless, but under the direction of the indwelling Spirit of Christ.

Contents of the letter

In the opening section of his letter, Paul emphasizes that the gospel he preaches is the only gospel. There is no other way to obtain salvation or live the Christian life. After rebuking the Galatians for so easily believing the Jewish teachers (1:1-10), he reminds them that the gospel he preached came direct from God (1:11-24), that it was supported by the apostles in Jerusalem (2:1-10) and that it offers salvation by faith alone (2:11-21).

The central portion of the letter shows how law-keeping has no place in Christianity. The Galatians should know this from their own experience of conversion (3:1-5), but the example of Abraham makes the point even clearer. Abraham was saved by believing the promise of God, not by keeping the law of Moses (3:6-14). The law was never intended to be a way of salvation, though in showing people their sin it helped prepare the way for the Saviour (3:15-4:7). Paul is concerned that the Galatians are being led into law-keeping (4:8-20), for this will lead only to bondage (4:21-31).

To conclude on a positive note, Paul instructs the Galatians in the enjoyment of the freedom they have in Christ. Law-keeping makes true Christianity impossible (5:1-12), but freedom under the direction of the Spirit produces Christian character (5:13-26). After some reminders of Christian responsibilities to others (6:1-10), Paul concludes by emphasizing again that the cross of Christ, not the law of Moses, is the basis of the gospel (6:11-18).

GALILEE

Galilee was the northern section of Palestine. It was a mountainous region that extended from the Lake of Galilee north to the Lebanon Ranges and west to the coastal plain. The Old Testament barely mentions it by name, since it was not in those days a distinct political territory. When the Old Testament refers to places in Galilee, it usually mentions them according to their location in the tribal areas of the region — Dan, Naphtali, Issachar, Zebulun and Asher (Josh 20:7; Isa 9:1; cf. Matt 4:12-15).

In New Testament times Galilee was a clearly defined region and a province of the Roman

Empire. It fell within the sub-kingdom of Herod Antipas (Mark 6:14-29; Luke 3:1; 23:6-12) and his successor Herod Agrippa I (Acts 12:20), but was under the overall rule of Rome. (For details see HEROD.)

The population of Galilee was a mixture of Jews and Gentiles, and this was one reason why the strict Jews of Judea despised the Galilean Jews (John 7:41,52). Added to this, Galilee was cut off from Judea by the territory of the Samaritans, a

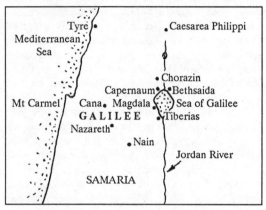

people of mixed blood and mixed religion who hated, and were hated by, the Jews (Luke 9:51-56; John 4:3-4,9).

Jesus grew up in Galilee (see NAZARETH) and spent most of the three and a half years of his public ministry there (Matt 2:22-23; 3:13; 4:12-16,23; 15:29; 17:22; 19:1; 21:11; 26:32,69; 27:55; 28:7,16). Some of the towns of Galilee that feature in the story of Jesus are Caesarea Philippi in the far north (Matt 16:13), Capernaum, Bethsaida, Chorazin, Magdala and Tiberias around the Lake of Galilee (Matt 4:13; 11:21-23; 27:56; Mark 6:45; John 6:17,23), and Nazareth, Cana and Nain in the hill country south of the lake (Luke 2:39; 4:16; 7:11; John 2:1-11; 4:46; 21:2). (For further details see separate entries under the names of these towns. For details of the physical features of Galilee see PALESTINE.)

GATH

One of the 'five cities of the Philistines', Gath was famous as the home of a number of giants, the most famous of whom was Goliath (Josh 13:3; 1 Sam 6:17-18; 17:4; 2 Sam 21:18-22; see also ANAK). It also became well known as the place where David took refuge from Saul (1 Sam 21:10-15; 27:1-12). Certain men of Gath became close friends of David. When David became king of Israel, he entrusted some of these men with important responsibilities (2 Sam

6:10-11; 15:19-21; 18:2). Others became full-time soldiers in David's army (2 Sam 15:18). (For a map of the region and other details see PHILISTIA.)

GAZA

The town of Gaza, on the Mediterranean coastal plain, was one of the 'five cities of the Philistines'. The other four were Gath, Ashdod, Ashkelon and Ekron (Josh 13:3; 1 Sam 6:17-18).

Gaza features in a number of Old Testament stories, among them those concerning Samson (Judg 16:1-3; 16:21-30). (For a map of the region and details of the Old Testament history of Gaza see PHILISTIA.) The sole New Testament reference to the town is in the story of Philip's meeting with an African official whom he led to faith in Christ (Acts 8:26-38). The present-day town of Gaza has been built on or beside the ruins of the old town.

GEDALIAH

In 587 BC the Babylonians destroyed Jerusalem, abolished Judah's monarchy, plundered the nation's treasures and took all its best people into captivity (2 Kings 25:1-21). They then appointed Gedaliah, son of a former Jerusalem official, governor over those Judeans who remained in the land (2 Kings 25:22; cf. Jer 26:24).

Gedaliah set up his headquarters at Mizpah, north of Jerusalem, and with Jeremiah's support followed a policy of submission to Babylon. He took no action against Judah's anti-Babylonian military leaders who had managed to escape the Babylonian army, but encouraged them, and other Judeans who had fled for safety, to return and settle around Mizpah (2 Kings 25:23-24; Jer 40:5-12).

One of Judah's former army commanders, Ishmael, opposed this policy of submission to Babylon and plotted to overthrow Gedaliah. When told of the plot, Gedaliah refused to believe it. That did not stop Ishmael from murdering him, along with all the Judean officials and Babylonian supervisors at Gedaliah's headquarters (2 Kings 25:25; Jer 40:13-41:3). That started a sequence of events that resulted in the rest of the Judeans fleeing to Egypt (2 Kings 25:26; Jer 41:4-43:13).

The Bible mentions four other men named Gedaliah. The first was a musician in the time of David (1 Chron 25:3,9), the second an ancestor of the prophet Zephaniah (Zeph 1:1), the third an official in Jerusalem who opposed Jeremiah (Jer 38:1-6), and the fourth a priest in the time of Ezra (Ezra 10:18).

GENESIS

Originally the first five books of the Bible were one. They were divided into their present form for convenience, and collectively are known as the Pentateuch (meaning 'five volumes'). The books are also commonly referred to as the books of Moses, because Moses has traditionally been regarded as the author (see PENTATEUCH).

Purpose of the book

The name Genesis means 'origin' or 'beginning', and comes from the title given to the book by those who first translated the Hebrew Old Testament into Greek. The book speaks of the origins of the universe, of man, of human sin and of God's way of salvation.

Although the Bible mentions matters relating to the beginnings of the universe and the early days of mankind, its main concern is not with the scientific aspect of these matters (see CREATION). The Bible is concerned rather with God and man and the relationship between them. It shows in the opening chapters of Genesis how man, though created sinless, rebelled against God and corrupted human nature. Man's sin brought with it God's judgment, but the judgment contained an element of mercy, as God repeatedly gave man the opportunity to start afresh. Still man rebelled, and still God did not destroy him.

This leads Genesis into its second and major section, which shows how God worked in human affairs to provide man with a way of salvation. God chose to work through Abraham, one of the few surviving believers. He promised to make from Abraham a nation, to make that nation his people, and to give them Canaan as a national homeland. From that nation God would bring a Saviour, through whom the blessings of God's salvation would go to all peoples of the world (Gen 12:1-3; 13:14-16). The book goes on to record the birth of this nation and the events that helped prepare it for its occupation of the promised land.

Outline of contents

Genesis begins with the story of creation (1:1-2:3) and the rebellion of man (2:4-4:26). As mankind spread, so did man's sin (5:1-6:4), till the rebellion became so widespread and so resistant to reform that God sent a flood that destroyed the entire generation, except for a few believers (6:5-8:19). From these believers, God made a new beginning and repopulated the devastated earth (8:20-10:32), but as man's security and independence increased, so did his rebellion against God (11:1-9). Judgment

inevitably followed, but in his grace God again preserved the faithful. One of these was a man from Mesopotamia named Abram, later renamed Abraham (11:10-26).

After God announced to Abraham his promise of blessing (11:27-12:3), Abraham and his household moved into Canaan. When a famine hit the land, they went to Egypt, but in due course they returned and settled at Hebron, west of the Dead Sea (12:4-14:24). (For a map and other details relevant to Abraham's varied experiences see ABRAHAM.)

God made a covenant with Abraham, in which he promised to give him a multitude of descendants (15:1-21); but the birth of Ishmael had no part in the fulfilment of that promise (16:1-16). God then confirmed the covenant with Abraham, giving the rite of circumcision as the sign and seal of the covenant (17:1-27). Some time later the promised son Isaac was born (18:1-21:34). God tested the faith and obedience of Abraham, but Abraham proved himself totally committed to God, no matter what the circumstances (22:1-23:20).

Isaac married and produced two sons, Esau and Jacob (24:1-25:26). In accordance with God's will, the blessing of Abraham passed to Jacob instead of to Esau. That, however, was no excuse for Jacob's ruthlessness and deceit in obtaining the blessing (25:27-28:9).

Jacob moved from Canaan to Mesopotamia to obtain a wife among his parents' relatives. He stayed in Mesopotamia for twenty years, during which he built up a large family. He then left to settle again in Canaan (28:10-31:55). But first he had to be reconciled to his brother Esau, who by this time had developed a prosperous settlement in neighbouring territory to the south-east (32:1-36:43).

Troubles arose among Jacob's twelve sons, with the result that one of them, Joseph, was sold as a slave and taken to Egypt. But God was controlling the affairs of his people, and through a series of remarkable events, Joseph eventually became governor over Egypt. When the entire region was devastated by a famine, his wise administration saved the nation (37:1-41:57). More than twenty years after Joseph's brothers had sold him as a slave, they met him in Egypt when they went there to buy food. The result was that the whole of Jacob's household migrated to Egypt and settled in the fertile Nile Delta (42:1-47:26).

In the specially marked-off area that Pharaoh had given them, Jacob's large family was able to live together and multiply without being corrupted by Egyptian ideas. Jacob saw that a prosperous future lay ahead for his descendants and announced his blessings on them before he died (47:27-49:33).

Years later Joseph died, but before his death he expressed his unwavering faith in God's promises. He knew that just as God's promise to Abraham of a nation had been largely fulfilled, so his promise of a homeland would also be fulfilled. The Israelites' increasing prosperity in Egypt was rapidly preparing them for the day when they would be strong enough to move north and take possession of the promised land (50:1-26).

GENTILE

The Hebrew word translated in English as 'Gentile' meant originally 'a nation'. When Israel became in a special sense God's people, Israelites used the expression 'the nations' ('the Gentiles') to refer to all non-Israelite people (Deut 7:6; Gal 2:15).

God's law prohibited Israelites from copying any Gentile customs that were likely to corrupt their religion (Deut 18:9). But they repeatedly ignored that law, with the result that eventually their nation was conquered and the people taken into captivity (2 Kings 17:7-8). The Gentiles, whose ways Israel had copied, then became the means God used to punish Israel (Judg 2:20-23; Isa 10:5-6).

Since God's purpose was that Israel take the message of his salvation to the Gentiles, Jesus announced the gospel to the Jews first. But he knew that on the whole they would not accept it and that as a result the gospel would go to the Gentiles (Isa 49:6; Matt 10:5-7; 12:18-21; 28:19; Luke 2:32; 4:25-28). Paul likewise preached the gospel to the Jews first, but when they refused it he turned to the Gentiles and there was a great response (Acts 13:46-48; 18:5-6; 22:21; 28:28; Rom 9:30-31; 11:11; 15:16).

Gentile people who did not know God had the reputation of being selfish, immoral, greedy, ungodly and idolatrous (Matt 5:47; 6:32; Rom 1:18-32; 1 Cor 12:2; Gal 2:15; Eph 4:17-19; 1 Thess 1:9; 4:5). Although they did not have the law of Moses as a guide, that was no excuse for their behaviour. Their own consciences told them that certain things were either right or wrong, and God would judge them accordingly (Rom 2:12-16).

In the eyes of the Jews, Gentiles had no hope of salvation, because they were excluded from the covenant promises that God gave to Israel (Eph 2:11-12). Only by becoming converts to the Jewish religion could they have hope of salvation (Matt 23:15; Acts 2:10; see PROSELYTE). It is therefore easy to see why, in the early days of the church, many Jewish Christians did not want to accept Gentiles into the church unless they kept the Jewish law (Acts 11:2-3; 15:1,5). It soon became clear, however, that the old Jewish regulations did not apply in the new community of God's people (Acts 15:8-11,19; Col 2:13-14). Gentiles and Jews were equals; more than that, they were united in one body (Rom 1:16; 3:29; 9:24; Gal 3:28; Eph 2:13-22; 3:4-6; Rev 5:9-10).

GENTLENESS

See HUMILITY; MEEKNESS.

GERASA

Gerasa was a town in Decapolis, south-east of the Sea of Galilee. It lay within the region of Gadara and gave its name to the surrounding district. As a result some of the Gadarenes were at times called Gerasenes, even though they may not have lived in the town itself (Mark 5:1-2; cf. Matt 8:28). (For map and other details see DECAPOLIS; GADARA.)

GERIZIM

Mount Gerizim stood beside the town of Shechem, opposite Mount Ebal. Both mountains were closely linked with Shechem in the history of Israel, and Mt Gerizim later became a sacred mountain to the Samaritans (Deut 27:11-14; John 4:20). (For details see SHECHEM.)

GETHSEMANE

Gethsemane was the name of a garden on the slopes of the Mount of Olives, just outside Jerusalem. Jesus went there frequently with his disciples (Luke 22:39; John 18:1-2) and prayed there in great agony the night before his crucifixion (Matt 26:30,36-45). The victory he won through that time of prayer enabled him to meet with confidence those who had come to the garden to arrest him (Matt 26:46-56; John 18:3-12). (Concerning the Mount of Olives see JERUSALEM, sub-heading 'Mountains and hills'.)

GIBEAH

The town of Gibeah was located in the tribal area of Benjamin (Josh 18:21,28; for map see BENJAMIN). It earned itself a bad reputation during the time of the judges when the men of Gibeah committed a serious crime and the leaders of Benjamin, instead of punishing them, defended them. The other tribes responded with an attack that almost wiped out Benjamin (Judg 19:1-21:24; Hosea 9:9; 10:9).

Gibeah was also the home town of Saul, Israel's first king. In spite of Benjamin's being the smallest tribe in Israel (1 Sam 9:21), Gibeah became the administrative centre of Saul's kingdom (1 Sam 10:26; 11:4; 14:16; 15:34; 22:6; 23:19; 26:1).

GIBEON

Being a Canaanite town of central Palestine, Gibeon should have been destroyed by Joshua's invading army. Instead the people of the town tricked the Israelites into promising to preserve them. The Israelites, though angry that the Gibeonites had deceived them, kept their promise and allowed the Gibeonites to live. The Gibeonites were forced to work for the Israelites as labourers, but the Israelites defended them against enemy attacks (Josh 9:3-27; 10:1-14). When Saul broke the treaty and murdered some of the Gibeonites, his sons were executed in 'blood for blood' justice (2 Sam 21:1-9).

Gibeon later became an important religious centre where the tabernacle was set up and the priesthood operated for many years. It was the last location of the tabernacle before Solomon replaced it with a permanent temple in Jerusalem (1 Chron 16:39; 21:29; 2 Chron 1:3,13).

GIDEON

Among the enemies that attacked Israel during the time of the judges were the Midianites. Their yearly raids devastated Israel (Judg 6:1-6), and when the people cried to God for help, he chose Gideon to save them. Gideon at first found it difficult to believe that God had chosen him for this task, but his faith was strengthened when an offering he prepared for God was miraculously burnt up (Judg 6:11-24).

Israel was in bondage to the worship of Baal. Therefore, if the people were to claim God's help, they had first of all to destroy the false religions. In Gideon's home town of Ophrah, Gideon's father was caretaker of the local Baal shrine, but when Gideon began his reformation, his father became the first convert. Others in the town were hostile (Judg 6:25-32).

This hostility did not last, for when Gideon called the people to battle, the people of his own clan (and therefore probably of his own town) were the first to respond. Others soon followed their example and Gideon was able to assemble a fighting force. Still uncertain of himself, Gideon twice asked God for miraculous signs to confirm that he was the one God had chosen (Judg 6:33-40).

God allowed Gideon only three hundred men to launch the attack, to impress upon him the need for total trust in God for success (Judg 7:1-8; Heb 11:32-33). Gideon's faith was greatly strengthened when he discovered, by secretly visiting the enemy's camp, that the Midianites were in the grip of an unnatural fear (Judg 7:9-15).

When the Midianites were awoken in the middle of the night by a terrifying noise and found themselves surrounded by Israelite soldiers, panic broke out. Some of the Midianites unknowingly attacked each other in the confusion, and others fled in fear. The larger Israelite force then swept in upon them (Judg 7:16-25).

Upon discovering that the Midianite kings had escaped across the Jordan, Gideon set out after them. He eventually captured them, but before executing them, he punished the leaders of one of the Israelite towns for earlier refusing to help him and his soldiers (Judg 8:1-21).

Gideon was now a national hero. To his credit he rejected the people's invitation to become their king (for God alone was their king), but he foolishly celebrated his victory over Midian by making a visible symbol of the invisible God. He may have had good intentions, but he opened the way for idolatry. Soon Gideon, his family and the people as a whole had returned to their former idolatrous ways (Judg 8:22-28).

GIFTS OF THE SPIRIT

According to common usage, the expressions 'gifts of the Spirit' and 'spiritual gifts' refer to those abilities that God gives to Christians for use in his service (Rom 12:6; 1 Cor 12:4). The Bible usually speaks of these gifts in relation to the local church, where, through the proper use of all the gifts, the members of the church are spiritually built up (1 Cor 12:7; Eph 4:11-12).

Variety of gifts

Different gifts and different forms of service do not indicate different levels of spirituality. All the abilities come from God, and he distributes them according to his will (1 Cor 12:4-7,11). The variety of gifts in the church is likened to the variety of functions in the human body. As the body functions best when each part carries out its function properly, so the church functions best when each person exercises his or her gifts properly, without pride, competition or jealousy (1 Cor 12:14-26). Although there is variety, there is unity (Rom 12:4-5; 1 Cor 12:12,27).

In several places the New Testament lists some of the gifts of the Spirit (Rom 12:6-8; 1 Cor 12:8-10; 12:27-31; Eph 4:11; 1 Peter 4:9-11). These lists, whether separately or combined, do not provide a complete catalogue of all the gifts, but give examples relevant to the writer's purpose. No list can be complete, because God's sovereign Spirit equips people according to the changing circumstances of different times and places (Acts 13:2; 1 Cor 12:7,11; Gal 2:9; 1 Tim 4:14). This work of the Spirit may begin with the God-given natural abilities that a person possesses even before he becomes a believer (Acts 9:15; Gal 1:15-16).

Sometimes the New Testament speaks of the gifted person as himself a gift whom God gives to the church. This is particularly so in the case of the teaching and leadership gifts (Eph 4:11; see APOSTLE; PROPHET; EVANGELIST; PASTOR; TEACHER). These gifts may not be as spectacular as some of the other gifts, but they are more important (1 Cor 12:28-31).

The more spectacular gifts include the power to heal sickness and disease (1 Cor 12:9,28; cf. Acts 3:6-8; 8:7; see HEALING), the ability to perform miracles (1 Cor 12:10; cf. Acts 9:36-41; 13:11; 2 Cor 12:12; see MIRACLES), special faith that achieves what normally seems unlikely (1 Cor 12:9; cf. Matt 17:19-20; Heb 11:33-40) and abilities relating to speaking in tongues, interpreting tongues and distinguishing between different types of spirits (1 Cor 12:10; cf. Acts 8:13-21; 1 Cor 14:13,27; 1 John 4:1; see TONGUES).

Other gifts may be less spectacular, but they are nevertheless important. These include the various capacities that people have for administering affairs, giving generously, helping others and showing mercy (Rom 12:8; 16:2; 1 Cor 11:28; cf. Acts 9:36; 2 Tim 1:16-18).

Using the gifts

While some people exercise their gifts mainly within their own locality (Acts 20:28-32; Col 4:12-13,17), others do so over a wider area, spending longer or shorter periods in various churches (Acts 11:25-26; 18:11; 20:31; 3 John 5-8). Church leaders should be constantly looking for those who show some ability and should help them develop it (1 Tim 4:14-16; 2 Tim 2:2; cf. Acts 13:5; 16:1-3).

At the same time individual Christians should desire spiritual gifts (1 Cor 14:1) and should pray for them (1 Cor 14:13), especially the more important gifts (1 Cor 12:31). Some, however, might seek gifts with the wrong motives; others, in spite of their good intentions, might wrongly assess their own abilities

(Rom 12:3-5; 1 Cor 12:1-3; 1 Tim 1:7; 2 Peter 2:1). Church leaders must therefore have the ability to distinguish between the true and the false (1 Thess 5:21; 1 John 4:1).

A person develops his spiritual gift by using it (Rom 12:6). He should work hard to achieve excellence in his performance (1 Tim 4:15) and must exercise his gift within the guidelines God has set out (1 Cor 14:27-31).

But good performance is not in itself enough. There must also be practical godliness in daily living (1 Tim 4:16). A person can carry out spiritual work properly only by the work of God's Spirit within him (1 Cor 2:12-13). If he exercises a spiritual gift in the wrong attitude, he may even cause harm (1 Cor 13:1-3). God gives gifts to build up the entire church, not to satisfy the pride or selfishness of the gifted individual. Each person must exercise his gift in a spirit of submission to others (1 Cor 12:7; 13:4-7; 14:5.26; 1 Peter 4:10; 5:5).

An indication of the Spirit's work in a person's life is not the spiritual gift he exercises, but the spiritual fruit he produces (Gal 5:22-23; cf. 2 Cor 3:17-18). Spiritual gift varies according to the ability that God gives, but spiritual fruit is the Christian character that God desires for all his people. Gifts are limited to service in the present world, but character will endure into the world to come. That is why the development of spiritual gift must be accompanied by a corresponding development in true Christian love (1 Cor 13:8-13).

GILEAD

The Bible uses the name Gilead in a number of ways, all of them in relation to the territory that Israel occupied east of the Jordan River. This area was a large tableland, broken by rivers that ran through deep gorges. (For details of trans-Jordan in general see PALESTINE, sub-heading 'Jordan Valley and Dead Sea'.)

Geographically, Gilead was the region between the Yarmuk River (southern boundary of the land once known as Bashan) and the northern tip of the Dead Sea (Deut 3:10). The Jabbok River divided this territory approximately in halves. The eastern part of the tribe of Manasseh lived in the northern half, and the tribe of Gad in the southern half (Deut 3:12-13). The Bible may refer to either half as Gilead. It calls the northern half (Manasseh) Gilead in Joshua 17:1,6 and half-Gilead in Joshua 13:29-31. It calls the southern half (Gad) Gilead in Joshua 13:24-25 and half-Gilead in Joshua 12:2. It mentions the two halves together in Deuteronomy 3:12-13.

There is yet another sense in which the Bible speaks of Gilead, and that is to refer to the whole of the former Amorite territory that Israel's two and a half eastern tribes occupied. This area included the land of Bashan in the far north and the tribal area of Reuben in the far south. Its southern border was the Arnon River, which divided Reuben from neighbouring Moab (Judg 10:8; 20:1; 2 Kings 15:29; see BASHAN; MOAB).

Gilead, like the rest of the area east of Jordan, had large open plains that were good for raising sheep and cattle. The region was also good for

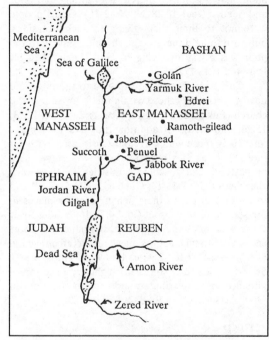

growing fruit and grain, and had some hilly areas of forest (Num 32:1,26,36; Jer 22:6; 50:19). It was famous for its balm, which people believed had healing properties and which they therefore used extensively in making medicines (Jer 8:22; 46:11; 51:8).

Chief towns of Gilead that feature in the Old Testament story are Jabesh-gilead (Judg 21:8-12; 1 Sam 11:1; 31:8-13), Mahanaim (Gen 32:1-2; Josh 21:38; 2 Sam 2:29; 17:24), Ramoth-gilead (Josh 21:38; 1 Kings 22:3-4; 2 Kings 8:28; 9:1-3), Succoth (Gen 33:17; Josh 13:27; Judg 8:4-16) and Penuel (Gen 32:31; Judg 8:4-17; 1 Kings 12:25).

In New Testament times the former land of Gilead fell partly within the Decapolis and partly within Perea. Towns of the region that feature in the New Testament story are Gadara, Gerasa and Bethany-beyond-Jordan (Matt 4:25; 8:28; Mark 5:1; 7:31; John 1:28; see DECAPOLIS; PEREA).

GILGAL

When Israel under Joshua crossed the Jordan to conquer Canaan, the first place they came to was Gilgal. There they set up a camp, which became the headquarters for the battles to follow (Josh 4:19; 6:11; 10:6).

Israel's entrance into Canaan was the beginning of a new way of life, and Joshua set up a memorial at Gilgal to mark the occasion (Josh 4:20). He also arranged for the circumcision of all those who had been born during the years in the wilderness but had not yet been circumcised. The significance of this mass ceremony was that circumcision was the sign of the covenant under which Israel inherited the land (Josh 5:2-9).

At Gilgal the Israelites kept their first Passover in Canaan. The forty years journey from Egypt was now formally over, and the daily supply of manna ceased (Josh 5:10-12). Gilgal was the administrative centre of Israel throughout the war and in the early days of the settlement program (Josh 10:6,9,15,43; 14:6). The headquarters was then transferred to Shiloh (Josh 18:1,8-10).

Later, Gilgal became an important religious town in Israel. It was one of the four towns in central Palestine that Samuel visited on his annual circuit. The school for prophets that he established there was still operating in the days of Elijah and Elisha (1 Sam 7:16-17; 2 Kings 2:1; 4:38).

Samuel also established in Gilgal a place of sacrifice for important national occasions (1 Sam 10:8; 13:8; 15:12). After Saul led Israel to victory in his first battle, the people arranged a public ceremony at Gilgal to confirm him king over a now united people (1 Sam 11:12-15). But Gilgal was also the place where Saul lost the kingdom through his wilfulness and disobedience (1 Sam 13:7-15; 15:12-33).

Gilgal remained popular with the people as a place of worship. Nevertheless, because of the self-righteousness and unspirituality of the worshippers, God's prophets repeatedly denounced Gilgal and the people who worshipped there (Hosea 4:15; 9:15; 12:11; Amos 4:4; 5:4-5).

GIVING

God is the giver of life and the ultimate provider of all that is necessary to maintain and enjoy life. This includes money and other possessions (Job

1:21; Eccles 5:19; 12:7; Matt 6:26-30; 1 Tim 6:17; James 1:17).

Since God is the ultimate owner of all things, his people should acknowledge that whatever they possess they hold on trust from him. They are answerable to him for the way they use these things, and by giving a portion back to him they express their thanks and worship. The offering, however, is also a sacrifice. It must be costly to the offerer personally if it is to be a genuine expression of devotion (Gen 4:3-4; 28:20-22; 2 Sam 24:24; Mal 1:8; Phil 4:18; see SACRIFICE).

Amounts and motives

This element of devotion does not mean that a person has to create feelings of heroic self-sacrifice or wait for the right mood before offering his gifts. Giving can be regulated and still be an act of devotion. The offering of tithes by Israelites was regulated, but it could still be an expression of the offerer's devotion. God was not pleased, however, when people offered tithes in a spirit of self-satisfaction (Deut 14:22-29; Luke 18:12). Israelites could further express their devotion by making voluntary contributions in addition to the compulsory tithes (Num 29:39; Neh 12:44; see TITHES).

Christians are not governed by the law-code of Israel, but the principles behind that law-code are written upon their hearts (Rom 7:6; Heb 10:16). The New Testament does not teach the Israelite tithing system for Christians, but it does teach that the amount Christians give should be in proportion to the income they receive (1 Cor 16:2; 2 Cor 8:3). It encourages Christians to give regularly, generously, and with thoughtful planning; though they should also give cheerfully, not grudgingly, and not under compulsion (1 Cor 16:2; 2 Cor 9:7).

God does not want to drive people into poverty (2 Cor 8:13), though he commends those who give more than they can reasonably afford (2 Cor 8:3). God views a person's gifts not in relation to their market value, but in relation to the offerer's total financial capacity (Mark 12:43-44; 2 Cor 8:2). He is not pleased with those who give in a way designed to deceive people or win people's praise (Matt 6:2; Acts 5:4). He promises his special care and a lasting reward for those who give generously because they love God and their fellow man (Matt 6:19-20; 2 Cor 9:6-12; Phil 4:17,19).

Generosity should be a characteristic of all those who know that they have salvation only because Jesus gave everything for them (2 Cor 8:9). Once they have responded to his grace by giving themselves to God, they will find that giving brings pleasure. They will even look for ways to increase it (2 Cor 8:4-5; 9:7; cf. Acts 20:35).

Distributing the contributions

In both Old and New Testaments, monetary and other gifts from God's people were used for two main purposes. These were the service of God and the help of the needy.

The tithes of the Israelites supported the Levites and priests, the servants of God in the Old Testament religious system (Num 18:21-28). On certain occasions the annual tithe (or perhaps an additional tithe) was shared also among the poor and needy (Deut 14:28-29; 26:12-15). God's people were not to limit their giving to such occasions, but were to help the poor at all times. Giving to the poor was a way of giving to God (Deut 15:10-11; Prov 14:31; 19:17).

Christians likewise are to give to the poor and needy, particularly those within the fellowship of the church (Luke 6:30,35; 12:33; Acts 11:29; Rom 12:13; 15:26; Gal 6:10). In addition they are to support financially those who carry out Christian service for them. This applies both to those who serve them in pastoral and teaching ministries in their own churches (1 Cor 9:13-14; Gal 6:6; 1 Tim 5:17-18) and to those who go on their behalf to other places in the service of the gospel (Phil 4:14-16; 3 John 8). If those who have the right to this financial support choose not to take it, gifts may be directed elsewhere (1 Cor 9:4-5,12,18; 2 Cor 11:8-9; 2 Thess 3:8-9). Sound wisdom and spiritual insight are necessary if gifts are to be distributed and used to the glory of God (Acts 6:3; 2 Cor 9:11,13; Phil 4:18,20).

GLORY

One of the common words that develops its own special meaning in the Bible is 'glory'. When used of people or things in relation to everyday life, it may indicate nothing more than honour, fame, power, wealth or splendour (Gen 45:13; 2 Kings 14:10; Isa 8:7; 17:4; Dan 2:37; Matt 4:8; 6:29; John 5:44; 7:18). But because it is used more frequently of the majestic all-powerful God, it develops a significance that makes it one of the characteristic words of both Old and New Testaments.

The glory of the unseen God

Revelations of God's majesty and power, such as through clouds, fire and lightning, were revelations of his glory (Exod 16:10; 24:16-17; Lev 9:23-24; Ps 29:3-4,7-9; Hab 3:3-4). Glory therefore became associated with brightness or shining. When God's glory, symbolizing his presence, filled the tabernacle and later the temple, its brightness was so intense that no human being could look upon it (Exod 40:34-35; 1 Kings 8:11; see SHEKINAH). Even when God allowed people a vision of his glory, it was usually so dazzling that it overpowered them (Exod 33:18-19; 34:8,29-30; Isa 6:1-5; Ezek 1:28; Luke 2:9; Rev 1:13-17).

Such visions were more than exhibitions of overpowering brightness; they were revelations of the nature of God. God's glory is an expression of his character — his goodness, love, justice, power and holiness (Exod 33:18-19; 34:6-7; Ps 29:3; Isa 6:3; John 12:41; Rom 3:23). Therefore, the Bible speaks of the revelation of God through nature and through history as the revelation of his glory (Ps 19:1; 96:3; see REVELATION).

The glory of Christ and his people

Jesus Christ is the greatest revelation of God's glory. The presence of God once dwelt among mankind in the glory that filled the tabernacle or temple, but now that glory dwelt among mankind in the form of a human being (John 1:14; James 2:1). The God whom no person could see, except in visions, now revealed himself in Jesus Christ (John 1:18; 2 Cor 4:6; Heb 1:3).

Yet, while believers saw in Jesus the glory of God, unbelievers did not (John 1:14; 2:11; 1 Cor 2:8). This was partly because Christ's glory during his earthly life was not a visible majestic splendour, such as he had as God before the world began. In becoming man he laid that glory aside; though the event known as the transfiguration was a foretaste of a greater glory that would yet be his (Matt 17:1-6; John 17:5; see TRANSFIGURATION). Following the triumph of his life, death and resurrection, God exalted him to heaven's highest place and gave him heaven's highest glory (Phil 2:6-11; Heb 2:9; 1 Peter 1:11,21).

One of the promises given to believers in Jesus Christ is that, as they share in Christ's sufferings in this life, so they will share in his glory in the life to come (Rom 8:17-18; 2 Cor 4:17; Phil 3:21; 2 Thess 2:14; Heb 2:10; 1 Peter 5:1,10). In a sense they share in Christ's glory now and increasingly become like Christ through their devotion to him (John 17:22; 2 Cor 3:18; 1 Peter 4:14). The great revelation of God's glory at the end of the age will bring salvation to believers and terror to the wicked (Isa 60:1-3; 66:18-19; Matt 16:27; 24:30; 25:31; Col 3:4; Titus 2:11-14).

Mere human beings cannot add to God's glory (in the sense of his majesty and power) but they can give him glory (in the sense of honour and praise).

They are to glorify him by their words and by their actions (1 Sam 6:5; Ps 96:8; Jer 13:16; Matt 5:16; Acts 12:23; Rom 4:20; 11:36; 1 Cor 10:31; 2 Cor 8:19; Eph 3:21; Rev 5:13; 14:7).

GNOSTIC

See KNOWLEDGE.

GOD

The Bible makes no attempt to prove the existence of God, but assumes it from the outset (Gen 1:1). This God is neither an impersonal 'force' nor an abstract 'principle' but a living person, and people find true meaning to existence by coming into a living relationship with him (John 17:3).

The personal God revealed

As people observe the physical world, they may conclude that there is an intelligent and powerful God who is the ultimate cause and controller of all things (Acts 17:23-27; Rom 1:19-20; Heb 3:4; see CREATION). As they reflect upon their awareness of right and wrong, they may conclude that there is a moral God to whom all rational creatures are answerable (Acts 17:23; Rom 2:15-16). However, God has not left mankind with only a vague or general knowledge of himself. He has revealed himself more fully through history, and he has recorded that revelation in the Bible (Jer 1:1-3; 2 Peter 1:21; see REVELATION). The central truth of that revelation is that there is only one God (Deut 6:4; Isa 44:6; Jer 10:10; Mark 12:29; 1 Thess 1:9; 1 Tim 2:5), though he exists in the form of a trinity (see TRINITY).

In any study of the character of God, we must bear in mind that God is a unified personality. He is not made up of different parts, nor can he be divided into different parts. Also, he is not simply a person who *has* certain qualities (e.g. goodness, truth, love, holiness, wisdom) but he is the full expression of these qualities. The Bible's way of putting this truth into words is to say that God *is* love, he *is* light, he *is* truth (John 14:6; 1 John 1:5; 4:16; see LOVE; LIGHT; TRUTH). (In the present article many of the qualities, or attributes, of God can be mentioned only briefly. For fuller details see the separate articles as indicated.)

Eternal and independent

Since it is impossible to give a complete definition or description of God, the Bible makes no attempt to do so. In addition, it forbids the use of anything in nature or anything made by man as a physical image of God, for such things can lead only to wrong ideas about God (Exod 20:4-5; Deut 4:15-19; see IDOLATRY).

When Moses asked for a name of God that would give the Israelites some idea of his character, the name that God revealed to him was 'I am who I am' (Exod 3:14). The name was given not to satisfy curiosity, but to tell God's people that their God was independent, eternal, unchangeable and able always to do what he, in his absolute wisdom, knew to be best. (Concerning this and other names of God see YAHWEH.)

God's existence cannot be measured according to time, for he is without beginning and without end. He is eternal (Ps 90:2; Isa 48:12; John 5:26; Rom 1:23; 16:26; 1 Tim 1:17; Rev 1:8; 4:8; see ETERNITY). He is answerable to no one. He does not need to give reasons for his decisions or explanations of his actions (Ps 115:3; Isa 40:13-14; Dan 4:35; Acts 4:28; Rom 9:20-24), though in his grace he may sometimes do so (Gen 18:17-19; Eph 1:9). His wisdom is infinite and therefore beyond the full understanding of man (Ps 147:5; Isa 40:28; Dan 2:20; Rom 11:33; 16:27; see WISDOM).

A God who is infinite has no needs. Nothing in the works of creation or in the activities of humans or angels can add anything to him or take anything from him (Ps 50:10-13; Acts 17:24-25; Rom 11:36). He is under obligation to no one, he needs no one, and he depends on no one. Whatever he does, he does because he chooses to, not because he is required to (Eph 1:11). But, again in his grace, he may choose people to have the honour of serving him (Ps 105:26-27; Acts 9:15).

Majestic and sovereign

As the creator and ruler of all things, God is pictured as enthroned in majesty in the heavens (Ps 47:7; 93:1-2; 95:3-5; Heb 1:3; see GLORY). Nothing can compare with his mighty power (Isa 40:12-15; 40:25-26; Jer 32:17; Rom 1:20; Eph 1:19-20; 3:20; see POWER).

God is the possessor of absolute authority and nothing can exist independently of it (Ps 2:1-6; Isa 2:10-12,20-22; 40:23; see AUTHORITY). He maintains the whole creation (Ps 147:8-9; Matt 5:45; Col 1:17), he controls all life (Deut 7:15; 28:60; Job 1:21; Ps 104:29-30; Matt 10:29) and he directs all events, small and great, towards the goals that he has determined (Gen 45:5-8; Ps 135:6: Prov 16:33; Isa 10:5-7; 44:24-28; 46:9-11; Amos 3:6; 4:6-11; John 11:49-53; Acts 2:23; 17:26; Rom 8:28; Eph 1:11; see PREDESTINATION; PROVIDENCE). Yet people have the freedom to make their own decisions, and they

are responsible for those decisions (Deut 30:15-20; Isa 1:16-20; Matt 27:21-26; Rom 9:30-32).

There are no limits to God's knowledge or presence. This is a cause for both fear and joy: fear, because it means that no sin can escape him; joy, because it means that no one who trusts in his mercy can ever be separated from him (Ps 139:1-12; Prov 15:3; Isa 40:27-28; 57:15; Jer 23:24; Heb 4:13). God is not only over all things, but is also in all things (Acts 17:24,27-28; Eph 4:6).

Since God is sovereign, people must submit to him and obey him. Refusing to do this, they rebel against him. They want to be independent, but instead they become slaves of sin (Gen 3:1-7; John 8:34; see SIN). They cannot escape God's judgment through anything they themselves might do. They can do nothing but repent of their rebellion and surrender before the sovereign God, trusting solely in his grace for forgiveness (Acts 17:30-31; Eph 2:8; see GRACE).

Man's rebellion, though in opposition to God, does not destroy God's sovereignty. God allows evil to happen, but he never allows it to go beyond the bounds that he has determined (Job 1:12; see EVIL; SATAN). God still works according to his purposes, for his own glory. He still causes to happen whatever does happen, even to the salvation of rebellious sinners (Isa 14:24; 37:26; Matt 25:34; Acts 2:23; Eph 1:5; 3:20; see ELECTION).

Invisible yet personal

From the above it is clear that God is not some impersonal 'force', but a personal being. He has knowledge, power, will and feelings. Human beings also have knowledge, power, will and feelings, but that does not mean that God is like man (Hosea 11:9). On the contrary, man has these attributes only because God has them; for man has been made in God's image (Gen 1:26; see IMAGE).

Being spirit, God is invisible (John 4:24; Rom 1:20; 1 Tim 1:17; Heb 11:27). Since human language cannot properly describe a person who has no physical form, the Bible has to use pictures and comparisons when speaking of God. It may speak of God as if he has human features, functions and emotions, but such expressions should not be understood literally (Gen 2:2; Num 12:8; Deut 29:20; 33:27; Ps 2:4; John 10:29; Heb 4:13).

Not only is God a person, but believers are so aware of a personal relationship with him that they can collectively call him 'our God' and individually 'my God' (Acts 2:39; Phil 4:19). They have an increased appreciation of God's character through their understanding of Jesus Christ; because, in the person of Jesus Christ, God became man and lived in man's world (John 1:14,18; 14:9; Col 1:15; see JESUS CHRIST). God is the Father of Jesus Christ (Mark 14:36; John 5:18; 8:54) and through Jesus Christ he becomes the Father of all who believe (Rom 8:15-17; see FATHER).

Unchangeable yet responsive

Although God is personal, he is unchangeable. Everything in creation changes, but the Creator never changes (Ps 33:11; Mal 3:6; Heb 1:10-12; 1 Peter 1:24). This does not mean that God is mechanical, that he has no emotions, or that he is the helpless prisoner of his own laws. What it means may be summarized from two aspects.

Firstly, the unchangeability of God means that, because he is infinite, there is no way in which any of his attributes can become greater or less. They cannot change for either better or worse. God can neither increase nor decrease in knowledge, love, righteousness, truth, wisdom or justice, because he possesses these attributes in perfection (Exod 34:6-7).

Secondly, God's unchangeability means that he is consistent in all his dealings. His standards do not change according to varying emotions or circumstances as do the standards of human beings. His love is always perfect love, his righteousness is always perfect righteousness (Heb 6:17-18; James 1:17). God's unchangeable nature guarantees that every action of his is righteous, wise and true.

We must not understand God's unchangeability to mean that he is unmoved by human suffering on the one hand or human rebellion on the other. In his mercy he may have compassion on the weak, and in his wrath he may punish the guilty (Exod 2:23-25; 32:9-10; James 5:4; 1 Peter 3:12). He may change his treatment of people from blessing to judgment when they rebel (Gen 6:6-7; 1 Sam 15:11,23) or from judgment to blessing when they repent (Joel 2:13-14; Jonah 3:10).

This does not mean that events take God by surprise and he has to revise his plans. He always knows the end from the beginning, and he always bases his plans on his perfect knowledge and wisdom (Num 23:19; 1 Sam 15:29; Isa 14:24; 46:9-10; Rom 11:29).

Righteous yet loving

When the Bible speaks of God as holy, the emphasis is not so much on his sinlessness and purity as on his 'separateness' from all other things. A thing that was holy, in the biblical sense, was a thing that was set apart from the common affairs of life and consecrated entirely to God. God is holy as the supreme and majestic one who exists apart from all else and rules over all (Exod 15:11; Isa 40:25; John 17:11; Rev 4:8-9; 15:4; see HOLINESS). Any vision of such a holy God overpowers the worshipper with feelings of awe, terror and unworthiness (Job 40:1-4; Isa 6:1-5; Hab 3:3,16; Rev 1:17).

Since holiness means separation from all that is common, it includes separation from sin. Therefore, God's holiness includes his moral perfection. He is separate from evil and opposed to it (Hab 1:12-13). The Bible usually speaks of this moral holiness of God as his righteousness (Ps 11:7; 36:6; Isa 5:16; Heb 1:9; 1 John 3:7; see RIGHTEOUSNESS). God's attitude to sin is one of wrath, or righteous anger. He cannot ignore sin but must deal with it (Ps 9:8; Isa 11:4-5; Jer 30:23-24; Rom 1:18; 2:8; see WRATH; JUDGMENT).

Yet God is also a God of love, grace, mercy and longsuffering, and he desires to forgive the repentant sinner (Ps 86:5; 145:8-9; Rom 2:4; Titus 3:4; 2 Peter 3:9; 1 John 4:16; see LOVE; PATIENCE). His love is not in conflict with his righteousness. The two exist in perfect harmony. Because he loves, he acts righteously, and because his righteous demands against sin are met, his love forgives. All this is possible only because of what Jesus Christ has done on man's behalf (Rom 3:24; see PROPITIATION). The God who is man's judge is also man's saviour (Ps 34:18; 50:1-4; 1 Tim 2:3; 2 Tim 4:18; Titus 3:4-7; see SALVATION).

GOLGOTHA

The name Golgotha, which is a transliteration of an Aramaic word meaning 'skull', was the name of the hill just outside Jerusalem where Jesus was crucified (Matt 27:33; Luke 23:33; John 19:17). (The name Calvary is not in the original New Testament, but has been taken from the Vulgate, a fourth century Latin translation. It comes from the Latin word for 'skull'.)

There is no certainty about which of several possible sites is Golgotha or how the hill got its name. But it was on a main road not far from one of Jerusalem's city gates, and a garden containing a tomb was nearby (Matt 27:39; John 19:20,41).

GOMORRAH

The city of Gomorrah was located near Sodom but, like Sodom, it was destroyed almost four thousand years ago. Its remains probably lie buried beneath the Dead Sea. (For details see SODOM.)

GOODNESS

People have always had difficult defining goodness. But whereas philosophers may struggle to define the abstract, the Bible talks about the concrete. It helps people understand goodness not by discussing the concept of goodness, but by pointing to people or things that are good.

When a young man questioned Jesus about moral goodness, Jesus replied by referring him not to a concept, but to a person — God. The way to understand goodness is through the person who is good and whose works are good (Matt 19:17). God's character reveals his goodness. It is a character that combines love, mercy, patience, faithfulness, justice, holiness and wrath in perfect balance (Exod 33:19; 34:5-7; Ps 86:5; Rom 11:22).

The biblical words translated 'good' contained a range of meanings, such as pleasant, beneficial, fitting, beautiful and honourable (Gen 1:4; Deut 6:18; Job 2:10; Eph 5:9). The added meaning that the words acquire in the Bible is largely because of their association with God. The goodness that the Bible teaches is the goodness that exists perfectly in God (Ps 100:5). This goodness was demonstrated in the life and ministry of Jesus (Acts 10:38), and the Holy Spirit desires to reproduce it in the lives of Christians (Gal 5:22).

All that God does is good (Ps 119:68; 136:1; Acts 14:17; 1 Tim 4:4). His people should recognize this, even when they meet hardships and difficulties (Job 2:10; Matt 7:11; Rom 8:28; Heb 12:10; James 1:17; see also CHASTISEMENT).

God desires the welfare of all mankind, and therefore he wants people to do good (Isa 1:17; 5:20; Gal 6:10). Though good works will not earn them salvation (for salvation is the gift of God and is received by faith), once they have received salvation they have an obligation to produce good works (Eph 2:8-10; Titus 2:14; see GOOD WORKS).

Likewise, although the law of God is good (Ps 119:39; Rom 7:12,16), obedience to the law will never produce a satisfactory standard of goodness (Rom 7:18-19). The reason for this is the sin that still infects human nature (Rom 7:13-14; see FLESH). But the believer can produce goodness through the power of the indwelling Spirit (Gal 5:22).

GOOD WORKS

Salvation from sin and condemnation comes not by human good works but by divine grace, and people receive this salvation through faith (Eph 2:8-9; Titus 3:5-7). No good deeds that people do can remove their sin, cancel its penalty, or make them acceptable to God (Isa 64:6; Rom 3:20; 8:7-8; 9:31-32). God forgives sin and declares people righteous solely on the basis of what Christ has done on their behalf (Rom 3:23-26; 2 Cor 5:21; see JUSTIFICATION). Once they have been saved, however, God's will is that they do good works. In fact, this is one purpose for which God saved them (Eph 2:10; Titus 2:14).

Christians will be equipped to carry out these good works as they learn more of the nature and purposes of God through the Scriptures (2 Tim 3:16-17; 2 Peter 3:18). Such good works will be of benefit to themselves as well as to others, and will be the means of bringing praise to God (Matt 5:16; Titus 2:7; 3:8; 1 Peter 2:12). They are one of the proofs of genuine faith (James 2:18), and arise from love and gratitude to God because of his free salvation (1 Thess 1:3; Heb 6:10).

Good works are no cause for pride. They are, after all, part of the Christian's duty (Luke 17:10). Nevertheless, Christians must carry out their good works not in a hard or legalistic spirit, but in an attitude of genuine love for others and with a clear conscience. They should be concerned with bringing praise to God, not to themselves (Rom 13:8-10; 1 Cor 10:31; Heb 13:18).

In the day of judgment God will test the works, good or otherwise, of all Christians. Those they have done out of selfishness or pride will bring no lasting benefit; those they have done for God's sake and according to his standards will bring an eternal reward (Matt 6:1; 1 Cor 3:11-15; 2 Cor 5:10; Rev 22:12; see JUDGMENT; REWARD).

GOSHEN

Goshen was the territory where the family of Jacob settled in Egypt. It was in the East Nile Delta and was suitable for raising flocks and herds (Gen 47:1-6). The descendants of Jacob lived there for about four hundred years, and during that time they multiplied enormously. The royal city of Rameses, which the Egyptians forced the Israelites to build by slave labour, was in Goshen (Gen 47:6,11,27; Exod 1:11; 12:37). Goshen was largely protected from the plagues that fell on other parts of Egypt during the time of Moses' conflict with Pharaoh (Exod 8:22; 9:26). (See also EGYPT.)

GOSPEL

In simple terms 'gospel' means 'good news'. When God's Old Testament people Israel were in captivity in Babylon and God announced to them that he was going to release them and bring them back to their homeland, that was good news (Isa 40:9; 52:7; 61:1-2). When Jesus came to release people from the bondage of Satan and give them new life, that too was good news (Luke 4:16-19).

Based on facts

The gospel that Jesus Christ proclaimed was that the promises God gave to Old Testament Israel were now fulfilled in him. The promised kingdom of God had come, and salvation was available to all who would repent of their sins and trust in him for forgiveness (Mark 1:14-15; see KINGDOM OF GOD).

Early Christian preachers, such as Peter, John, Stephen and Paul, preached the same message. But whereas Jesus' preaching of the gospel was during the period leading up to his death and resurrection, the early Christians' preaching followed his death and resurrection. They therefore laid great emphasis on Jesus' life, death and resurrection as historical facts that no one could deny. Those facts were the basis of the gospel they preached (Acts 2:22-42; 3:12-26; 7:1-53; 13:17-41; 1 Cor 15:1-7).

There is only one gospel (Gal 1:6-9). It is called the gospel of God, or the gospel of the grace of God, to emphasize that it originates in God and his grace (Acts 20:24; Rom 15:16; 1 Thess 2:2,8; 1 Tim 1:11). It is called the gospel of Christ, or the gospel of the glory of Christ, to emphasize that it comes to man only through Jesus Christ (Rom 15:19; 2 Cor 2:12; 4:4; 9:13). It is called the gospel of the kingdom, the gospel of salvation and the gospel of peace, to emphasize that those who believe it enter God's kingdom and receive eternal salvation and peace (Matt 9:35; Eph 1:13; 6:15).

A message of life

Because the gospel is inseparably linked with the great truths of God's saving work through Christ, 'gospel' has a meaning far wider than simply 'news'. It refers to the whole message of salvation, and even to salvation itself (Mark 8:35; 10:29; Rom 1:1-4; 1:16-17; Eph 3:7; 1 Peter 1:25; see JUSTIFICATION; SALVATION). Through it the power of God works, bringing life to those who accept it, and destruction to those who reject it (Rom 1:16; 2 Cor 4:3; Heb 4:2). Sometimes the single word 'gospel' is used for the body of Christian truth, or even for the whole new way of life that comes to man through Jesus Christ (Rom 16:25; Phil 1:7,27).

God entrusts the gospel to Christians so that they might preserve it and pass it on to others (Gal 2:7; 1 Thess 2:4; 1 Tim 1:11). Therefore, while it is God's gospel, it becomes in a sense their gospel

(Rom 2:16; 1 Thess 1:5; 2 Tim 2:8). Christians have a responsibility to spread this gospel worldwide, even though it may mean sacrificing personal desires and suffering personal hardships. They will carry out the task gladly when they appreciate what God's love has done for them through Christ (Matt 24:14; Mark 16:15; 1 Cor 9:16,23; 2 Cor 5:14; Eph 6:19-20; 1 Thess 2:2; see EVANGELIST; MISSION).

GOSPELS

Traditionally, the first four books of the New Testament have been called Gospels, probably because they record the gospel, or good news, of the coming of Jesus Christ, man's Saviour. Questions that naturally arise are why there should be four such books and why three of those books should contain so much material that is similar.

Preserving the message

After the resurrection and ascension of Jesus, his followers spread the good news of salvation through him, firstly in Jerusalem, and then throughout Palestine and neighbouring countries. They taught the stories and teachings of Jesus to their converts, who memorized them and passed them on to others (Matt 28:18-20; Acts 2:42; 2 Tim 2:2).

As the years passed, those who had seen and heard Jesus became fewer in number and more widely scattered. To preserve what these men taught concerning Jesus, various people began making written collections of things Jesus had said and done (Luke 1:1). There is no certainty concerning how or when the four Gospels were written. There is, however, enough evidence from within the books and from other first century sources to make the following explanation a possibility.

Three related accounts

Mark's Gospel appears to have been the first written. Mark had assisted the apostle Peter on missionary journeys that took them through the northern parts of Asia Minor and brought them eventually to Rome (cf. 1 Peter 1:1; 5:13). When Peter left Rome, Mark stayed behind, and was still there when Paul arrived as a prisoner, accompanied by Luke and Aristarchus (about AD 60; Acts 27:2; 28:16,30). (In letters Paul wrote from Rome, he mentions that Mark, Luke and Aristarchus were all with him; Col 4:10,14; Philem 24.) The Roman Christians asked Mark to preserve Peter's teaching for them, and this resulted in the writing of Mark's Gospel (see MARK, GOSPEL OF).

Meanwhile Luke also had been preparing an account of the life of Jesus. No doubt he had done much of his research during the two years he had just spent in Palestine with Paul (Acts 24:27). Others had already written accounts of the life of Jesus (Luke 1:1), and Luke was able to gather material from these and from people still living in the region who had seen and heard Jesus. Upon meeting Mark, Luke took some of Mark's material and added it to his own to fill out his record and so bring the book to completion.

Luke wrote his Gospel for a person of some importance (perhaps a government official) named Theophilus, to give him a trustworthy account of the origins of Christianity (Luke 1:1-4; see LUKE, GOSPEL OF). (Luke continued the story with a second volume, which recorded the spread of Christianity from Jerusalem to Rome; Acts 1:1; see ACTS, BOOK OF.)

Matthew's Gospel appears to have been written about ten years later. It was intended for Christians who were of Jewish background but who read Greek freely. The book shows a strong interest in the fulfilment of God's purposes concerning Israel's Messiah, and the responsibility of the Messiah's people to spread his message to the Gentiles. The place most commonly suggested for the writing of such a book is Antioch in Syria, which was closely connected with the Jewish churches of Palestine and with the mission to the Gentile nations (Acts 11:19-22,27-29; 13:1-4; 14:26-27; 15:1-3,22,30; see MATTHEW, GOSPEL OF).

By this time, Mark's Gospel had become widely known. Since it represented Peter's account of Jesus' ministry, it was well respected, and Matthew saved himself a lot of work by using material from it extensively in his own book. (About 90% of Mark is found in Matthew.) There is also a lot of material common to Matthew and Luke that is not found in Mark. This material is commonly referred to as Q and probably came from one or more of the many writings that had appeared over the years (Luke 1:1). It consists mainly of teachings and sayings from Jesus, in contrast to stories about him.

Because of the parallels between Matthew, Mark and Luke, the three books are often referred to as the Synoptic Gospels (meaning Gospels that 'see from the same viewpoint'). However, each contains material of its own that has no parallel in the other Gospels. In Mark this amount is very small, less than 5%. In Matthew the amount is about 28% and in Luke about 45%.

A different type of book

John's Gospel bears little similarity in form or style to the other three Gospels, though the general sequence of recorded events is the same. John wrote within the last decade or so of the first century, by which time the other three Gospels were widely known. His purpose was not to produce another narrative-type account of Jesus' ministry, but to use selected stories of Jesus, particularly his teachings, to instruct people in basic truths concerning Jesus' unique person and ministry.

Many people in the region where John lived (probably Ephesus) were troubled by false teachers. Some of these teachers denied that Jesus was fully God, others that he was fully man. John wanted people to be convinced that Jesus was the Messiah, the Son of God, and to find true life through him (John 20:30-31). John's Gospel therefore consists mainly of teaching, much of which comes from the recorded words of Jesus himself. In contrast to the Synoptic Gospels, action stories are comparatively few. Less than 10% of John's material is found in the Synoptics (see JOHN, GOSPEL OF).

GOSSIP

An ancient Israelite proverb expresses the truth that the more a person talks, the more he is liable to sin (Prov 10:19). This is one reason why the Bible constantly urges people to control their tongues (Ps 141:3; Prov 16:23; 17:27-28; James 1:19; 3:7-10). It is very easy to gossip. What starts as idle talk can easily lead to exaggerations, half-truths and false impressions, all of which can do great damage (James 3:2,5).

Gossip can become a habit; worse still, an enjoyable habit (Prov 11:13; 18:8). In spreading rumours, people may have the deliberate intention to slander others (Ps 31:13; 50:20; Prov 10:18; Rom 3:8) or they may just be foolish chatterers (Prov 26:20; Eccles 5:3; Matt 12:36), but either way they will probably cause trouble (Prov 26:18-20).

God links gossip with some of the most hateful sins (Rom 1:29-30), and constantly warns his people against it (Ps 101:5; Prov 10:19; 2 Cor 12:20; James 4:11; 1 Peter 2:1). All who are in positions of leadership or influence must be especially careful not to gossip (1 Tim 3:11; Titus 2:3). (See also TONGUE.)

GOVERNMENT

God is the supreme ruler of the world and he desires that all countries be governed orderly and justly. He is the source of all authority and he has given to governments, as his representatives on earth, the authority to administer society (Jer 27:5; Dan 4:17;

John 19:11). Citizens therefore have a responsibility to obey the laws of their country (Rom 13:1-2; cf. Jer 29:4-7). Christians share in this responsibility. Since they know that the authority of government comes from God, they should give their obedience willingly (Rom 13:5; 1 Peter 2:13-15).

The role of government

Two of the basic functions of civil government are to promote the well-being of society and to restrain wrongdoing in society. God has given to governments the right to reward good conduct and punish wrongdoing (Rom 13:4). Governments exist for the benefit of the people, and should desire to control affairs so that citizens can live peacefully and contentedly (1 Tim 2:1-2).

Christians are taught to cooperate with the government in pursuing these goals, and at the same time to maintain their loyalty to God (Mark 12:17; Rom 13:5-7; Titus 3:1; 1 Peter 2:17). They have a duty to pay taxes to the government for the benefits they receive from it, and a duty to be loyal to God because of all he has done for them (Luke 20:25; Rom 13:6-7).

Tensions will arise, however, when the ruling authorities pass laws that are unjust or anti-God. The only obligation to absolute obedience that God's people have is obedience to God. They may find that if they are to maintain their loyalty to him, they have to disobey the government. As a result they may suffer penalties (Dan 3:8-12; 6:13,16; Matt 10:18; Acts 5:29,40; 1 Peter 4:12-16). If that is the case, they must, like Christ, accept suffering without retaliation, praying for their persecutors and committing their cause to God (1 Peter 2:20-23; cf. Exod 3:7; Dan 3:16-18; Luke 6:28; 23:34; 1 Tim 2:1-2; see PERSECUTION).

At the same time God's people should be concerned about the government's behaviour. At times they may decide to speak and act in support of the principle of justice that the government is supposed to administer (Isa 3:14; 5:22-23; Micah 3:1-3; Acts 16:35-39; 22:25; 25:10-11).

The type of response that God's people make to unjust government action will depend to some extent on what rights citizens have in their country. In some countries Christians are in a similar position to Christians of New Testament times, having no rights in deciding who governs them or how they are governed. In other countries the citizens themselves decide who governs them, and they can openly try to influence government decisions. In such countries Christians can not only pray for God's will to be done on earth, but they can actively work for those values of justice, freedom, morality, honesty and compassion that God desires for human society (Matt 6:10).

One difficulty in all societies is that those in a position to bring about social change are the least likely to want it, for they are the ones who benefit most from the existing order (Isa 3:14-15; Ezek 34:4; Amos 5:11-12). Jesus refused to use violence, either to protect what was good or remove what was bad (Matt 26:52; John 18:36), but he did not keep silent when he saw disadvantaged and defenceless people ignored or exploited (Matt 21:13; 23:4,23; 25:42-45; Mark 12:20; Luke 6:24-25; 16:19-26; cf. Amos 2:6-7; Micah 2:1-2; Zeph 3:3; see JUSTICE).

This does not mean that the church should try to govern society. That is not the church's job. God has entrusted the government of society to civil authorities, not to the church (Rom 13:1,4). When governments misuse their God-given authority, God holds them responsible (John 19:10-12). In due course he will deal with them, in whatever way and with whatever means he chooses (1 Kings 11:29-37; Isa 1:23-26; Dan 5:24-28; Amos 6:4-7; Micah 3:1-4; Rev 18:1-2,24).

Limitations of government

Although governments can help society by their efforts to promote good and oppose evil, the basic problems of human sin cannot be overcome merely through government action.

The primary concern of Christianity is not to change society in the hope that people might improve, but to change people so that through them society might improve. The gospel is basic to God's work among mankind (Eph 4:17-24; Titus 2:14; see GOSPEL). But Christians cannot ignore problems in a society of which they are part (Amos 6:4-6). They have a joint responsibility to work positively for what is good (Matt 5:13) and openly condemn what is wrong (Matt 14:4; Eph 5:11).

As Christians understand more of God and his Word, they will understand more of the type of life God desires for mankind. The Creator knows what is best for his creatures, and his standards are best, not just for Christians but for everyone.

Yet if Christians, even with the help of God's indwelling Spirit, cannot live perfectly according to God's standards, non-Christians have much less chance. Because of the hardness of man's heart, God's ideal may be too high a standard to aim at in the laws that a government makes for society as a whole (Matt 19:8). While Christians may seek the highest standards for themselves and may try to persuade others to accept those standards, they cannot expect the government to enforce those standards by law (e.g. Matt 5:39-42).

Human society has been so spoiled by sin that when a government makes laws, it may be forced to choose the lesser of two evils. That does not mean that there is a change in God's standards. What was formerly evil is still evil. It does not become good simply because the government makes laws to regulate it (e.g. Matt 19:3-10).

Christians, therefore, should not be satisfied simply with doing what is legal (for something that is legal may still be morally wrong), but with doing what is right (Matt 5:21-24,46-48). The laws of the state may represent the minimum requirements for an ordered society; Christian morality goes beyond that, even to a person's thoughts and motives (Matt 5:27-29; see ETHICS).

GRACE

There is much in the Bible about grace, partly because there is much in the Bible about sin. Grace is the undeserved favour of God. People repeatedly sin and rebel against God, yet God in his grace is still ready to forgive them when they repent (Exod 34:6; Rom 5:20).

Saved by God's grace

The only way people have ever been forgiven their sin and saved from condemnation is by God's grace, and they receive this salvation through faith (Eph 2:8). People have never been saved through obeying the law or offering sacrifices (Rom 3:24-26; Gal 3:17-22). (Concerning the purpose of Old Testament regulations given to Israel see COVENANT; LAW; SACRIFICE.)

So much is grace a characteristic of God that the Bible calls him the God of grace (1 Peter 5:10; see also LOVE; MERCY). He chooses to save people because of his sovereign grace alone, not because of their good works (Rom 11:6; Eph 1:5-6; see ELECTION). Many of the stories that Jesus told illustrate God's grace (e.g. Matt 18:23-34; 20:1-16; Luke 7:36-50; 14:16-24; 15:11-32), but Jesus himself is the greatest demonstration of God's grace (John 1:14). He demonstrated that grace not only by the way he lived (John 1:17; 2 Cor 8:9), but particularly by his death on the cross (Rom 3:24-25; Gal 2:21; Heb 2:9).

Through Jesus' death, God is able to forgive freely all who repent of their sins and trust in him. More than that, God brings them into a right relationship with himself and declares them righteous (Rom 3:23-24; 4:5; 5:2; 1 Cor 1:4; Titus

2:11; 3:4-5). (For further discussion on God's work of grace through the death and resurrection of Jesus see FORGIVENESS; JUSTIFICATION; PROPITIATION; RECONCILIATION.)

God's grace in the lives of believers

Although salvation is a gift of God's grace and not a reward for good works, that is no reason for Christians to ignore good works. They are not free to live as they like or sin as they like. God's grace continues to work in their lives, giving them the inner power to discipline themselves, to do good, to endure suffering and to triumph over temptation (Rom 6:14-15; 2 Cor 12:9; 2 Tim 2:1; Titus 2:11-14; see FREEDOM; GOOD WORKS). They can carry out their Christian service properly only because God in his grace has given them the ability to do so (Rom 12:6).

God exercised his grace towards believers before they were born. That same grace operates continually towards them throughout life and will continue to be active towards them throughout the ages to come (Gal 1:15; Rom 5:2,21; Eph 2:7; 1 Tim 1:12-16).

Paul's practice was to begin and end his letters by speaking of the grace of God, or the grace of the Lord Jesus Christ. In this way he indicated that he was always conscious that the believer's whole life is lived in the atmosphere of God's grace (Rom 1:7; 16:20; 1 Cor 1:3; 16:23; Gal 1:3; 6:18).

GRAPES

From very early times grapes were widely grown throughout the Middle East (Gen 9:20; 14:18). Grape growing was well established in Canaan long before the Israelites arrived (Num 13:20,24; Deut 6:11). The Israelites in turn carried on grape growing as one of their main agricultural activities (Judg 9:27; 14:5; 21:20; Song of Songs 1:14; 7:12; Amos 4:9; 5:11,17).

Vineyards

A vineyard was usually a rectangular area planted with rows of grape vines and surrounded by a hedge to keep out animals and thieves. Often there was a tower where a person could keep watch over the workers in the vineyard (Song of Songs 2:15; Isa 5:1-2; Matt 20:1; 21:33). Workers usually pruned the vines in the spring, using specially made pruning hooks (Joel 3:10; John 15:2). They harvested the grapes in summer and, in keeping with Israelite harvesting practices, whatever they did not gather at the first picking they left for the poor (Lev 19:10; Deut 24:21; Obad 5).

Egyptians harvesting and trampling grapes

People ate grapes fresh and sometimes dried them to make raisins (Num 6:3; 1 Sam 25:18), but most of the grapes they crushed to make wine. They did this by trampling the grapes in a wine press, which was a pit hollowed out of solid rock (Isa 5:2; 16:10; 63:2; Matt 21:33; Rev 14:19-20).

Vines and vineyards provided prophets and teachers with useful illustrations. Old Testament writers likened Israel to God's vineyard. God took Israel from Egypt and planted it in a good land, doing everything possible for it so that it might bear fruit for him. But Israel failed to produce the fruit that God desired. God therefore ceased to look after it, with the result that enemies plundered and destroyed it (Ps 80:8-13; Isa 5:1-7).

Jesus on occasions used illustrations from the vineyard, mainly to contrast the Jews' rejection of him with the Gentiles' acceptance (Matt 20:1-15; 21:28-41). He also used the illustration of the grape vine, to show that if people truly are disciples, they will demonstrate it by the fruits that their union with him produces (John 15:1-11).

Wine

Processes of making wine were well known in the ancient world (Gen 9:20-21; Isa 25:6; Jer 48:11). People kept the fermented wine in earthenware pots or goatskin bags, though when goatskin bags became old and brittle they could not stand the pressure of new wine (Jer 13:12; 35:5; Mark 2:22).

Wine was a common drink of the Israelites, in both Old and New Testament times, and was one of the articles of daily food that they offered to God in sacrifice (Exod 29:40; Lev 23:13; Deut 11:14; 18:4; Judg 19:19; Jer 40:10; Matt 11:19). They considered a good supply of wine, along with other articles of daily food, to be one of God's blessings (Gen 14:18; 27:28; Deut 7:12-13; Prov 9:1-6; Isa 55:1).

People associated wine with merriment and joy (Ps 104:15; Eccles 9:7; Zech 10:7; John 2:1-10), though too much wine could lead to dullness of mind, unfitting behaviour and drunkenness (Prov 31:4-5; Isa 28:7; Hosea 4:11; Hab 2:15; 1 Peter 4:3; Rev 17:2). Israelite law therefore disallowed wine completely for certain people, such as priests and others who set themselves apart to God for special service (Lev 10:9; Num 6:3; Jer 35:8; Luke 1:15). The possibility of drunkenness brought strong warnings concerning the dangers of wine (Prov 20:1; 23:20; 23:29-35; Rom 13:13; 14:21; Eph 5:18). Drunkenness disqualified a person from a position of leadership among God's people (Isa 28:1-3; 56:9-12; 1 Tim 3:8; Titus 2:3).

Wine had some medicinal value and was used to help heal wounds and illnesses (Prov 31:6; Luke 10:34; 1 Tim 5:23). When mixed with spices it could help deaden pain. But when such a mixture was offered to Jesus on the cross, he refused it (Mark 15:23). The wine (vinegar) that he drank shortly after was the common wine of the people, not drugged wine. Jesus' purpose in asking for it was not to deaden his pain, but to moisten his mouth so that he could announce his final triumphant words loud enough for all to hear (Mark 15:36-37; John 19:28-30). (For the significance of wine in the Lord's Supper see LORD'S SUPPER.)

GREECE

Only occasionally does the Bible mention Greece by that name, though it frequently mentions parts of Greece. The ancient land of Javan, for instance, was possibly part of Greece (Gen 10:4; Isa 66:19; Ezek 27:13). In local language, Greece was *Hellas*, and Greeks were *Hellenes*.

Greece's influence on the world of the New Testament came through events resulting from the conquests of Alexander the Great in the fourth century BC. Yet, though there was a Greek Empire, there was no 'official' Greek nation. The country known today as Greece consisted in those times of various separate states. The most important of these was the northern state of Macedonia, which was the centre of the Greek Empire (Acts 16:12; 2 Cor 8:1; see MACEDONIA). In New Testament times the region referred to as Greece was the southern part of the Greek peninsular known as Achaia (Acts 19:21; 20:1-2; see ACHAIA).

The Greek Empire

The rise of Greek power in the pre-Christian era was rapid and spectacular. Alexander the Great, having come to power in Macedonia in 336 BC, rapidly overran what remained of the Persian Empire, and within a few years ruled a region that stretched from Greece to India (Dan 8:5-7,20-21; 11:2-3).

Wherever they went, the Greeks established their own rich culture. The Greek language became the most widely spoken language throughout the Empire, Greek architecture spread through the building of magnificent cities, and Greek philosophy changed the thinking of people everywhere (1 Cor 1:20-22). The Greeks brought progress to those they governed, and provided a standard of education, entertainment, sport and social welfare that their subjects had not known previously. Those who accepted this Greek culture were regarded as civilized; all others were regarded as barbarians (Rom 1:14).

Alexander, however, died while at the height of his power (323 BC), and within a short time his vast empire was divided among his generals (Dan 8:8,22; 11:4). By 301 BC the main divisions were a western

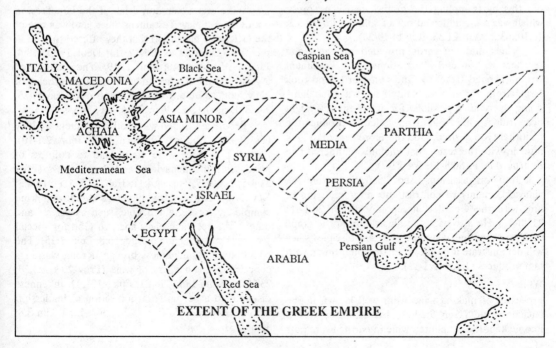

EXTENT OF THE GREEK EMPIRE

sector based on Greece, and two eastern sectors based respectively on Syria to the north and Egypt to the south.

At first Israel fell within the Egyptian sector and enjoyed a period of relative peace. During that time a group of seventy Jewish scholars translated the Hebrew Bible into Greek. This translation is known as the Septuagint (after the number of translators) and is usually referred to by the symbol LXX. In New Testament times both Jews and Christians used the Septuagint as well as the Hebrew Old Testament (see SEPTUAGINT).

Greek rulers in the Egyptian sector gave themselves the name Ptolemy. Some of the later Ptolemies became hostile to the Jews, but conditions

Greek coin showing Alexander the Great

worsened further when the Syrian sector conquered Egypt and brought Israel under its control (198 BC; Dan 11:14-16). Greek rulers in the Syrian sector were known as the Seleucids, after the name of the king who founded the dynasty. Most of the kings gave themselves the name Antiochus, after Antioch, the capital of the Seleucid kingdom that the founder of the dynasty built in 300 BC (Acts 11:20; 13:1; see ANTIOCH IN SYRIA).

Greek influence in Israel

After more than a century of Greek rule, Israel was feeling the heavy influence of Greek customs and ideas on the traditional Jewish way of life. Divisions began to appear among the Jewish people. Some Jews welcomed this Greek influence, even in their religion, because in this way they were able to win political favours from the Greek rulers and so gain important positions in the Jewish religious system. Other Jews firmly opposed all Greek influence, particularly Greek political influence in Jewish religious affairs.

When fighting broke out in Jerusalem between rival Jewish factions, the Seleucid king (Antiochus IV Epiphanes) welcomed the opportunity to deal with the Jews. He invaded Jerusalem, slaughtered all Jews who resisted, made others slaves, burnt the Jewish Scriptures, forced Jews to eat forbidden food and compelled them to work on the sabbath day.

Worse still, he set up a Greek altar in the Jewish temple, then took animals that the Jews considered unclean and sacrificed them to the Greek gods. To the Jews this was 'the awful horror' (GNB), 'the abomination that makes desolate' (RSV) (Dan 11:31). But Antiochus failed to realize that the Jews would not stand idly by and allow him to destroy their religion.

Resistance to Greek domination

The Jews' fight for religious freedom began through the zeal of an aged priest named Mattathias. He and his five sons (known as the Maccabees, after Judas Maccabeus, his son and the group's leader) escaped from Jerusalem, prepared a small army, and after about three years overthrew the pro-Greek party of priests. They then cleansed and rededicated the temple, restoring it to their people for traditional Jewish worship (165 BC). From that time on the Jews celebrated the great event in the annual Feast of Dedication (John 10:22).

Such an astonishing victory encouraged the Maccabees (also known as the Hasmoneans, after their old family name) to keep fighting till they had won political freedom as well. But the religiously strict Jews, who opposed Greek political interference in the Jewish religion, likewise opposed the Maccabees' drive for political power. Eventually these opposing viewpoints produced two parties that divided the Jewish people, the Sadducees and the Pharisees. The Sadducees wanted political power, but the Pharisees were content with religious freedom (see PHARISEES; SADDUCEES).

In spite of this opposition, the Maccabees carried on the war and after twenty years won political independence (143 BC). However, the Jews were now clearly divided. On one side were the pro-political priests and leaders, who were rich, powerful and favoured by the Hasmonean rulers. On the other side were the anti-political traditionalists, who were poor, powerless and favoured by the common people. The Jews were free of Greek rule, but they were weakened by internal divisions and within eighty years they fell to Rome (63 BC).

New Testament times

Though the Romans had succeeded the Greeks as rulers of the region, Greek was still the most widely spoken language. It was the common language of the Roman Empire as it had been of the Greek Empire (John 19:20; Acts 21:37; Rev 9:11; see HELLENIST). Because one language was spoken everywhere, Christianity was able to spread more quickly (Acts 14:1; 19:10).

Greek was also a rich language, able to express fine differences of thought and meaning. It was well suited to be the language of the New Testament, through which God revealed and preserved the teachings of the Christian gospel.

The New Testament records that many people of Greek origin became believers in Jesus and were active in Christian service. As early as the time of Jesus, certain Greeks had become interested in the new teaching that Jesus brought (John 12:20). In the period covered by the book of Acts, Greeks in different places responded to the preaching of the apostles (Acts 14:1; 17:4,12,34; 18:4) and churches were established throughout Greece itself, both in Macedonia and in Achaia (Acts 16:12; 17:1-4,10-12; 18:1-4; see ATHENS; BEREA; CORINTH; PHILIPPI; THESSALONICA). Sometimes the name 'Greek' was used as another name for Gentiles in general (Mark 7:26; Acts 19:17; Rom 1:16; 10:12; Gal 3:28).

GUIDANCE

Life involves the constant making of decisions, both major and minor, and believers naturally want to make decisions that are in accordance with God's will. They may believe that God is their guide (Ps 48:14) and they may pray for his guidance (Ps 31:3), but they can be assured of his guidance only on certain conditions. They must trust him fully, accept his authority in every part of their lives, and make every effort to live righteously (Prov 3:5-7).

A Christian mind

Many of life's decisions may be plainer than people think. Often what is required is not some special direction from God, but simply obedience to plain instructions that God has already given (e.g. Eph 4:25,28,32; see OBEDIENCE). However, people must know what is in the Bible if they are to obey it (2 Tim 3:15-17; cf. John 13:17).

As believers increase their understanding of the Bible, their thinking gradually changes. They learn to think christianly, even about issues where the Bible gives no direct instruction. Their minds are transformed by the Holy Spirit through the Word, and this helps them to know God's will and do what pleases him (Rom 12:2; Col 1:9-10; 3:10; cf. John 16:13; see KNOWLEDGE; MIND).

If people allow their lives to be directed by the Spirit through the Word, and if they do not self-confidently trust in their own wisdom, they can be assured that God will guide their decisions (Ps 25:8-10; Prov 3:5-7). He promises to give wisdom to those who in humility and faith ask for it (James 1:5-6; see PRAYER; WISDOM). He also encourages believers to discuss matters with those whose insight and experience can help them see issues more clearly (Prov 12:15; 1 Cor 7:1).

God does not want Christians to be uncertain or timid in the way they live. He wants them to think, pray, discuss and decide, and then to act confidently upon their decisions (Acts 6:3; 13:2-3; 15:25,28,36; 20:16; Rom 15:24-26; Titus 3:12). As they exercise their spiritual judgment in making decisions, they will grow towards maturity (Phil 1:9-11; Heb 5:14). On occasions, however, God may choose to direct people not so much through their minds as through compelling inner feelings, or even through dreams and visions (Acts 8:29; 10:9-16; 16:9; see DREAM; VISION).

Faith in practice

Christians believe that God controls all the affairs of life and works through those affairs for their good (Rom 8:28; Phil 1:12). They may believe that in certain circumstances God 'opens a door' and gives opportunities (1 Cor 16:8-9), and in others he 'closes a door' and denies opportunities (Acts 16:6-7). But circumstances in themselves are not always clear guidance. Favourable circumstances could be a temptation to take the path that is most naturally pleasing. Unfavourable circumstances could be a temptation to avoid the path that looks unpleasant (James 1:2-3,14; see TEMPTATION). Circumstances are not God's guidance for a certain action if that action is itself contrary to what the Bible clearly teaches (1 Sam 26:7-9).

God wants people to live their everyday lives positively, in a way that reflects the character of their salvation. He wants them to act in faith rather than ask for signs (2 Cor 5:7; cf. Matt 16:4); yet he may graciously give signs to those whose faith is not strong (Judg 6:16-18,36-40; Matt 12:20).

Christians should do what is right regardless of circumstances, rather than allow their circumstances to determine what they do (Phil 4:11-13). God does not want people controlled outwardly, as if they are no better than animals controlled by a harness. He wants people controlled inwardly, as the spirit of God renews their minds after the likeness of Jesus Christ (Ps 32:8-9; Eph 4:22-24).

HABAKKUK

Unlike most of the prophets, Habakkuk gives no specific statement to indicate the era during which he prophesied. Nevertheless, the contents of the book make it clear that he delivered his message during that period of the Judean kingdom, when Babylon had risen to power and was threatening to conquer Judah.

Background to the book

With its conquest of Assyria in 612 BC, Babylon had become the chief power in the region. It emphasized this by defeating Egypt in the battle of Carchemish in 605 BC (2 Kings 24:7; Jer 46:2). This victory gave it control over Judah, but it did not destroy Jerusalem until 587 BC, after it had lost patience because of Judah's repeated rebellions.

Babylon's conquest of Judah was part of God's will for his unfaithful and rebellious people. This raised a problem for Habakkuk, and his book shows how God dealt with his problem and answered his objections.

Summary of the book

Habakkuk begins by complaining to God that in spite of his preaching, Judah shows no signs of improving. He asks how long God will allow Judah to go unpunished (1:1-4). God replies that he is preparing the Babylonians (Chaldeans) to punish Judah (1:5-11). Habakkuk objects to this strongly. He asks: if God is holy, and if Judah is his people, how can he use Babylon to punish Judah when the Babylonians are worse sinners than the Judeans (1:12-17)? He awaits God's answer (2:1).

In due course God replies. His answer is that wickedness, whether of the Babylonians or the Judeans, will always bring defeat in the end, but the person who remains morally upright has nothing to fear. In the end God will give such a person victory (2:2-5).

The prophet has had his question answered, but he goes on to announce God's judgment on evil, particularly the evil of the Babylonians (2:6-20). The book concludes with a psalm that pictures, by a series of dramatic illustrations, the work of God in judgment upon evil (3:1-15). Its relevance to Habakkuk's question is seen in the final words, where Habakkuk learns to trust in the wisdom and justice of God. Habakkuk knows that the people of Judah deserve God's punishment. As for the Babylonians, the ones whom God uses to carry out that punishment, Habakkuk will leave God to deal with them according to his wisdom and justice (3:16-19).

HADES

The Greek word *hades* was used in Bible times as the equivalent of the Hebrew word *sheol*, the name used in the Old Testament for the world of the dead.

This world of the dead was the shadowy destiny that awaited all mankind, whether good or bad (Acts 2:27; cf. Ps 16:10; for details see SHEOL).

With Christ's conquest of death, there was no need to fear the world of the dead any longer. Hades was a fearful place only to those who would not trust in Christ. Hades spoke therefore of more than death in general; it spoke of the separation from God that followed death in the afterlife (Matt 11:23; 16:18; Rev 20:13-14).

In general, however, the word that the New Testament usually used for the place of eternal punishment was not *hades* but *gehenna*. This was a place of fiery torment (Matt 18:9; see HELL).

HAGAR

God promised Abraham and Sarah they would have a son through whom God would build a nation that would be his people. When Sarah was unable to bear children for Abraham, she suggested he try to produce a son through their Egyptian slave-girl, Hagar. Any child so born would legally belong to Abraham and Sarah (Gen 16:1-3).

Abraham followed Sarah's suggestion, with the result that Hagar bore him a son, Ishmael. God made it clear, however, that this was not the child he had promised (Gen 17:15-19). Ishmael would have a notable line of descendants, but God's covenant people would come through the child of Sarah yet to be born, Isaac (Gen 17:20-21).

Years later, after the birth of Isaac, trouble arose between Sarah and Hagar. This resulted in the expulsion of Hagar and Ishmael from Abraham's household (Gen 21:8-14).

In the New Testament Paul uses the story of Sarah and Hagar to illustrate the conflict that exists between those who are God's children through faith in his promises and those who are slaves to the law of Moses. The two cannot live together. Just as there was no place in Abraham's household for the slave Hagar, so there is no place in God's family for those who are slaves to the law (Gal 4:21-31).

HAGGAI

In 539 BC the Persian king Cyrus conquered Babylon and promptly issued a decree that allowed the Jewish captives to return to their homeland and rebuild Jerusalem. The outcome was that a good number of Jews moved out of Babylon and settled in Jerusalem. There they began to establish a new community under the leadership of the governor Zerubbabel and the high priest Joshua (Ezra 1:1-4;

2:1-2). They readily set up the altar and laid the foundation of the temple, but they just as readily lost their enthusiasm when local people began to oppose them. As the opposition increased, so did the Jews' discouragement, till eventually they stopped building (Ezra 4:1-5,24).

After sixteen years of inactivity, God raised up two prophets to arouse the people and get them working on the temple again. One of these prophets was Haggai, the other Zechariah (Ezra 5:1-2; Hag 1:1; Zech 1:1). The year was 520 BC.

People claimed that they had not been able to build because of opposition from enemies and hardship from famine. Haggai saw that these were not the reasons at all. The real reasons were the people's selfishness and laziness. The problem was spiritual, not political or material. Events soon proved Haggai to be correct; for when the people restarted building and opposition broke out afresh, the Persian king supported the Jews by giving them legal protection and financial assistance (Ezra 5:3; 6:6-12).

Contents of the book

Haggai's short book consists of four messages, all delivered within six months. His first message, which rebuked the people for their excuses in not building, brought quick results, and within a little over three weeks the people started building again (1:1-15). His second message encouraged them with the assurance that their work was part of the reconstruction of the Jewish nation, as a result of which the Messiah would come (2:1-9). His third message reminded them of the judgments that follow disobedience, and the blessings that follow obedience (2:10-19). His final message was a brief message of encouragement for Zerubbabel personally (2:20-23).

HALLELUJAH

Originally the word 'hallelujah' was a combination of parts of two Hebrew words, meaning 'praise' and 'Jehovah' ('Yahweh'). It has been transliterated into Greek and English as 'hallelujah' and means 'praise the Lord'. It was used mainly to open or close hymns of praise in public worship (Ps 106:1,48; 112:1; 113:1; 115:18; 146:1,10; 147:1,20; 150:1-6; Rev 19:1,3-4,6; see also PRAISE).

HAMATH

The city of Hamath was situated in the north of Lebanon, at the end of the Lebanon ranges and on the edge of the Syrian plain. In the time of David its leaders were friendly with Israel (2 Sam 8:9-10), and in the time of Solomon it was controlled by Israel (2 Chron 8:3-4). After Solomon's death it regained its independence, but it again came briefly under Israelite control during the reign of Jeroboam II (2 Kings 14:25).

At the northern end of the Lebanon ranges was a prominent gap known as 'the entrance of Hamath', where Lebanon opened on to the plains of Syria. This gap, or pass, marked Israel's ideal northern boundary (Josh 13:5; Amos 6:14), but only in times of unusual growth and prosperity was it the actual boundary (2 Kings 14:25). (For further details see LEBANON.)

HANNAH

As one of the two wives of Elkanah, Hannah lived in a household where there was unhappiness and tension. Elkanah's other wife, Peninnah, mocked Hannah because of Hannah's inability to have children (1 Sam 1:2-8). In her distress Hannah cried to God for a son, promising that if God answered her prayer she would give her son back to God to serve him for life. God gave her a son and she named him Samuel (1 Sam 1:9-20).

When Samuel was two or three years old, Hannah took him to the tabernacle and dedicated him to God for life. Features in her thanksgiving prayer reappear in the thanksgiving prayer of Mary the mother of Jesus (1 Sam 2:1-10; cf. Luke 1:46-55). When Hannah returned home, she left Samuel with the priest Eli, who was to bring him up as a dedicated servant of God. Hannah visited Samuel regularly and helped provide for his needs (1 Sam 2:11,18-20). After Samuel, Hannah had five more children (1 Sam 2:21).

HATRED

Hatred, in the sense of a deep-seated ill-feeling towards another person, is condemned as being one of the evil results of sinful human nature. It is the opposite of love and should not be found in the lives of God's people (Lev 19:17; Matt 5:44; Gal 5:20; Col 3:8; 1 Peter 2:1; 1 John 4:20). People whose lives are under the power of sin hate what is good, hate those who are righteous, and hate God (1 Kings 22:8; Ps 69:4; Micah 3:2; John 3:20; 15:18,23-25; 17:14).

God's people, by contrast, are not to hate those who hate them, but do them good (Luke 6:27). But they must hate wickedness, just as God hates it (Ps 97:10; 119:104; Prov 6:16-19; Isa 61:8; Heb 1:9; Jude 23; Rev 2:6).

Sometimes the Bible uses the word 'hate' in a special sense that has nothing to do with either the bitterness or the opposition outlined in the examples above. It is used in a situation where a choice has to be made between two things or two people. One is chosen, or 'loved', the other is rejected, or 'hated' (Gen 29:30-31; Mal 1:2-3; Luke 14:26-27; John 12:25; Rom 9:10-13).

HAZAEL

God told the prophet Elijah that Hazael of Syria would be God's instrument to punish Israel for its Baal worship during the reign of Ahab (1 Kings 19:15-17). Elijah's successor, Elisha, wept when he saw the suffering that the cruel Hazael would bring upon Israel (2 Kings 8:12-15).

Hazael began his brutal attacks on Israel during the reign of Ahab's son Joram (2 Kings 8:28-29). The attacks became more widespread during the reign of the next king, Jehu (2 Kings 10:31-33). They even spread into Judah, with attacks on coastal towns and on the capital, Jerusalem (2 Kings 12:17-18). Israel lost further territory to Hazael during the reign of Jehoahaz, and gained some relief only after Hazael's death (2 Kings 13:1-3,22-25). Israel looked longingly for the day when it would see a just punishment poured out on Syria because of Hazael's cruelty (Amos 1:3-5).

HAZOR

Before Israel's conquest of Canaan, Hazor was the chief city of the far northern region of Canaan. When the armies of Israel entered Canaan under Joshua, they conquered Hazor and burnt it (Josh 11:1,10-11). In the division of Canaan that followed, Hazor fell within the tribal area of Naphtali (Josh 19:32,36). Later the local people regained control of Hazor and rebuilt the city, though in due course the Israelites drove them out (Judg 4:2,23-24). In the reign of Solomon, Hazor became Israel's main defence outpost on its northern frontier (1 Kings 9:15).

HEAD

In most languages and cultures, a characteristic of everyday speech is to use the names of parts of the body (eyes, head, hands, feet, etc.) figuratively as well as literally. People in Bible times, for example, often referred to the head in a figurative sense. This was because they considered the head to be in some way representative of the person himself (1 Kings 2:32; Acts 18:6).

A person in Bible times might therefore show his shame or grief by covering his head, throwing dust on his head, or shaving his head (2 Sam 15:30; Isa 15:2; Jer 14:3; Rev 18:19). By contrast a person was honoured when someone anointed or crowned his head (Ps 23:5; Prov 4:9; Mark 14:3; Heb 2:9). Lifting up the head symbolized victory (Ps 3:3; 27:6; 110:7); hanging the head symbolized shame or grief (Lam 2:10; Luke 18:13).

When used figuratively of people or nations, 'head' could indicate leadership or authority (Deut 28:13; Judg 11:9; 1 Sam 15:17). The rulers of Israel were called the heads of Israel (Micah 3:1).

By New Testament times the figurative usage of 'head' was largely concerned with its being the source of life and the seat of authority. This is clearly seen in Christ's headship of the church. As the head is both the source and controller of the body's life, so Christ is the source of the church's life and has supreme authority over it (Eph 1:22; 4:15-16; Col 1:18; 2:10,19).

Another form of headship is found in the marriage relationship. The husband's headship of the wife results from the different responsibilities given to each as created by God. For the Christian husband and wife, this relationship should be patterned on Christ's self-sacrificing love for the church and the church's obedient love for Christ (Eph 5:23-25). While the husband's headship means that he has a certain authority, it does not mean that he is superior. There is an equality in status, though a difference in function. The husband is head of the wife in the same way as God the Father is head of God the Son. Yet the Son, though under the Father's authority, is equal with him (1 Cor 11:3; cf. John 5:19; 8:28-29; 10:30; 14:9-10; see HUSBAND; WIFE).

HEALING

Ultimately God is the only one who can heal, because he is the only one who can undo the effects of sin. Sickness and suffering are characteristics of a world that has been spoiled by sin (Gen 3:16-19), and healing is part of God's gracious work in caring for his wayward creatures (Exod 15:26; 2 Kings 1:3-4; Ps 103:3).

Jesus' miracles of healing showed his power over all the evil consequences of sin, and indicated that the kingdom of God had come (Matt 4:23; 8:17; 9:35; see MIRACLES). When that kingdom reaches its fulfilment in the new heavens and the new earth, all healing will be complete (Rev 22:1-4; cf. Rom 8:19-23).

Usually it is not possible to give a specific theological explanation of a particular suffering that a person experiences. However, in those cases where the suffering is a direct result of personal sin, God's healing is a sign also of his forgiveness (Ps 32:1-5; 41:3-5,11-12; John 5:13-14; James 5:15-16; see SUFFERING).

God may choose to heal people miraculously (Num 12:1-15; 2 Kings 5:8-14; Matt 8:2-3; John 4:46-54; 5:8-9), or by normal processes (2 Kings 20:1-7; Phil 2:27-30; 2 Tim 4:20), or not at all, depending on his sovereign will (2 Cor 12:7-10). He may protect people from diseases or he may not (Exod 15:26; 32:35; Job 1:12; 2:5-6; Jer 24:10). On some occasions God may heal out of his love and compassion, without a request from the afflicted (Matt 14:14; Luke 4:40); on other occasions he may

Healing the sick in Jerusalem

heal in response to the faith of the afflicted (Matt 9:27-30; Mark 5:34; 10:52; James 5:14-15). He heals those who have ordinary diseases and those who are demon possessed (Matt 8:16; Luke 4:41; see DISEASE; UNCLEAN SPIRITS).

Jesus gave his disciples a share in his healing powers, so that they could help him spread the message of the kingdom of God throughout Israel (Matt 10:5-8). These disciples continued this healing ministry in the early days of the church (Acts 3:1-11; 9:33-34). As the church spread, God gave similar gifts to other people (Acts 8:5-7; 14:9-10; 28:8-9). God's desire was that, as such people used their healing gifts in cooperation with other gifts he had given to other people, the church would enjoy well balanced growth (1 Cor 12:9,11,28-31).

HEART

Both Old and New Testaments speak repeatedly of the heart as the centre of a person's inner life. An examination of the hundreds of references to the heart in the Bible will show that the word is not limited in its meaning to one particular part of a person.

'Heart' may refer to a person's whole inner life – the person himself, what he really is (1 Sam 16:7; Ps 22:26; Prov 4:23; Matt 22:37; 1 Thess 2:4); or it may refer to attributes of his human personality such as his understanding (1 Kings 3:9; Prov 2:10; 1 Cor 2:9; Eph 1:18), desires (Deut 24:15; Prov 6:25; Matt 6:21; Rom 1:24), feelings (Judg 19:6; Prov 14:10; 15:30; John 14:27; James 3:14), determination (Exod 8:15; 1 Kings 8:58; Rom 6:17; Col 3:22), or character (1 Sam 13:14; Jer 5:23; Rom 2:29; 2 Thess 3:5; 1 Peter 3:4).

Sometimes 'heart' is used as another word for a person's spirit (Ps 51:10,17; Ezek 36:26), soul (Deut 4:29; Prov 2:10; Acts 4:32) or mind (1 Sam 2:35; Eph 1:18; Heb 8:10; cf. Matt 22:37). (See also MAN; MIND; SOUL; SPIRIT.)

The heart is what is sometimes called 'the inner man', and is the source of all the wrong that a person does (Prov 6:14,18; Jer 17:9; Mark 7:21-23; Rom 1:24-25; Eph 4:18; see SIN). Therefore, the heart must be cleansed to bring forgiveness; or, to use another picture, it must be re-created to bring new spiritual life. Only God can bring about this cleansing or re-creation (Ps 51:10; Ezek 36:26; Acts 8:21-22; Heb 10:22).

Since a person's heart determines his actions, he must be careful to have right attitudes of heart at all times (Lev 19:17; Ps 4:4; 1 Tim 1:5; James 3:14). God sees a person's inner condition and judges him accordingly (1 Sam 16:7; Ps 44:21; Matt 5:8; Rev 2:23; see also CONSCIENCE).

HEAVEN

People in ancient times did not understand the universe the way we understand it today. For them the universe consisted of 'the heavens and the earth'. The earth was where they lived and the heavens were the skies above, the place of the sun, moon, stars, clouds and birds (Gen 1:1,17,20; 15:5; Deut 4:19; 1 Kings 18:45; Matt 5:18; Heb 11:12).

A characteristic of human speech is that people often speak of realities and experiences beyond their understanding as being 'over', 'above' or 'higher than' them. Consequently, it was natural for people to speak of God as dwelling far, far above them in the highest place they could imagine, namely, heaven (Deut 26:15; 1 Kings 8:30,32; Ezra 1:2; Ps 2:4; Matt 5:45; 6:9; 7:21).

The Bible therefore speaks of heaven as being 'up'; not in the sense that it occupies a particular location in outer space, but in the sense that it represents a state of existence far beyond anything man can experience in the physical world. The Jews so identified heaven with God that they often used the word 'heaven' instead of 'God'. This was also a sign of respect for God, for it prevented them from using his name irreverently (Dan 4:26; Matt 19:23-24; Luke 15:18; John 3:27; see KINGDOM OF GOD).

Heaven is the dwelling place not only of God, but also of the angelic beings who worship him (Neh 9:6; Matt 18:10; 28:2; Mark 13:32; Luke 2:15). Jesus Christ came from heaven (John 3:31; 6:38), returned to heaven after his death and resurrection (Acts 1:11; Eph 1:20), at present appears in heaven on behalf of his people (Col 3:1; Heb 8:1; 9:24) and will one day return from heaven to save his people and judge his enemies (Acts 1:11; 1 Thess 4:16-17; 2 Thess 1:7-9).

Through the grace of God, heaven becomes also the eternal dwelling place of all those who through faith have become God's children (John 14:1-3; 2 Cor 5:1-2; Col 1:5; Heb 12:22-23; 1 Peter 1:3-5). For them, to be for ever in the presence of God is to be in paradise (Luke 23:43; 2 Cor 5:8; Phil 1:23; cf. 2 Cor 12:2-3).

From his present viewpoint on earth, man has no way of knowing what life in heaven will be like (1 John 3:2). No doubt people will be identifiable in heaven by their individual personalities just as they are on earth. The form of life, however, will be different from the form of life in the present world (cf. Matt 22:23-30; 1 Cor 15:35-44,50; see RESURRECTION).

When the Bible writers refer to some of the features of heaven, they are not giving literal descriptions of physical characteristics of heaven. They are merely using the only language available to them to try to illustrate and describe life as it will be in an entirely new order of existence (Matt 22:30; 26:29; John 14:2; Heb 12:22-23; 1 John 3:2).

This new order will find its fullest expression in what the Bible calls 'a new heaven and a new earth'. This again distinguishes it from the physical universe as we know it at present (Isa 66:22; 2 Peter 3:13; Rev 21:1-22:5). Although the Bible writers give few details of life in the new order, that life will not be one of laziness or idleness. It will be a life of joyful

activity in the worship and service of God (Rev 5:8-14; 14:2-3; 22:3).

HEBREW

The name 'Hebrew' comes from Eber, a descendant of Shem, the son of Noah. This means that the Hebrews were one of the Semitic peoples, Semites being those descended from Shem (Gen 10:21,25). Abraham was a Hebrew, being descended from Shem through Eber (Gen 11:10-26; 14:13). The descendants of Abraham, therefore, were also Hebrews (Gen 39:17; 40:15; 43:32).

In time the meaning of the name 'Hebrew' became more restricted in that it applied only to those who were descendants of Abraham through Isaac and Jacob. In other words, 'Hebrew' became simply another name for 'Israelite' (Exod 1:15; 2:6,11; 3:18; 5:3; 21:2; 1 Sam 4:6; 13:19; 14:11; 29:3; Jer 34:9; Jonah 1:9; Acts 6:1; 2 Cor 11:22; Phil 3:5). A third name, which came into use later, was 'Jew', and this has remained in common use till the present day (Jer 34:9; John 1:19; Acts 2:5; Rom 11:1; see JEW). (Concerning Hebrew as the language of the Old Testament see MANUSCRIPTS.)

HEBREWS, LETTER TO THE

Since the title 'To the Hebrews' is not part of the original writing, there is no clear statement in the Bible to indicate to whom the letter to the Hebrews was written. Nevertheless, the title reflects an early and widely held belief that it was written to a group of Hebrew Christians. The contents of the letter itself appear to support this belief.

Historical setting

With the increasing persecution of Christians during the reign of Nero (AD 54-68), tensions and fears arose in the church. This was particularly so among some of the Jewish Christians, who began to wonder if they had done right in giving up their Jewish religion and becoming Christians.

These people had believed, from the teaching of Jesus and his followers, that the Jewish religion no longer served God's purposes. They had been taught that the priesthood and sacrifices would come to an end and that the temple in Jerusalem would be destroyed. Yet, thirty years after Jesus' death, the temple was still standing and the Jewish religion was still functioning.

Because of the suffering that came through the persecution, some of the discouraged Jewish Christians were doubting Christianity's claim to be God's new and triumphant way to the eternal kingdom. It seemed to them that the Jewish religion was as firm as ever, whereas Christianity was heading for disaster. Some had stopped attending Christian meetings, and others had even given up their Christian faith and gone back to Judaism. The letter to the Hebrews was written to correct this backsliding.

The writer and his readers

Although the writer of this letter does not give his name, he must have been a well known Christian preacher of the time. Much of the letter is in the form of a sermon (Heb 13:22).

The content of the sermon makes it clear that the writer based his teachings on the same foundational beliefs as taught by other preachers such as Stephen, Peter, Paul and John. He was probably a Jew (Heb 1:1), though he wrote polished Greek and took his Old Testament quotations from the Greek version known as the Septuagint. Both he and his readers heard the gospel from the apostles or others who had personally heard Jesus preach (Heb 2:3).

Most likely the people who received the letter were a group of Jewish Christians who were part of a larger church. They may have lived in Italy (perhaps Rome), for a group of Italians who were away from home at the time join the writer in sending greetings to them (Heb 13:24). They knew Timothy and no doubt were pleased to hear that he had just been released from prison and would visit them soon (Heb 13:23). The writer also hoped to visit them soon (Heb 13:19).

The writer wanted to show these discouraged Jewish Christians that Christ was the true fulfilment of the Jewish religion. The Old Testament found its completion in him. Christ is far above prophets, angels, leaders and priests, and his sacrifice has done what all the Jewish sacrifices could never do. There is no need for any further developments in God's plan for man's salvation, because what Christ has done is final.

Contents of the letter

God may have used various types of people and various rituals to teach people about himself in Old Testament times, but with the coming of Jesus Christ such revelations are no longer needed. God now reveals himself through Christ (1:1-4). Christ is superior to all created things, including angels (1:5-14), and there is no salvation apart from him (2:1-4). In his great humility Christ became a man, willingly taking a temporarily lower position than angels in order to save man (2:5-18).

As the God-sent leader of God's people, Christ is greater than either Moses or Aaron (3:1-6). He leads his people to a better rest than the rest that Joshua led Israel to in Canaan. But, as in the time of Joshua, unbelief will prevent people from enjoying the rest that God provides (3:7-4:13). Christ is the great high priest of his people (4:14-5:10), but unstable Christians cannot appreciate this (5:11-14). They are in danger of forsaking Christ, the sole source of salvation, and going back to a system that is out of date and cannot save anyone (6:1-8). Believers must not lose heart, but persevere in the assurance of the salvation that Christ has obtained for them (6:9-20).

The priesthood of Melchizedek was not limited by time or nationality (7:1-10), and the priesthood of Christ is according to that timeless and universal order (7:11-28). He is a new priest and he officiates according to a new covenant (8:1-13). Priestly work under the old covenant was limited in that it could not take away the worshipper's sins (9:1-10), but the priestly work of Christ under the new covenant removes sins for ever (9:11-14). Likewise sacrifices under the old covenant were imperfect (9:15-22), but Christ's one sacrifice under the new covenant is perfect, complete and final (9:23-10:18).

In view of the perfection and finality of Christ's work, Christians must be confident. They must not lose heart (10:19-25). They must not turn back, but persevere in faith (10:26-39). Examples from Old Testament times show that if people had true faith they persevered. This was so even when they could not clearly see how God could fulfil his promises. Many suffered for their faith, but they stood firm regardless of the cost (11:1-40).

Christians must therefore face their difficulties with strength and endurance. They should not rebel or grow bitter when God uses their difficulties to test and train them (12:1-17). God is merciful, but he will also judge the rebellious (12:18-29). Christians must demonstrate the practical worth of their faith in the everyday matters of life (13:1-6), and offer the sacrifice of praise, obedience and good works, not the ritual sacrifice of animals (13:7-16). They should take notice of the teaching of their leaders and trust always in the saving power of God (13:17-25).

HEBRON

Hebron was a very old settlement in the south of Canaan. It was situated at the point where two main highways crossed, the north-south route from central Canaan to Egypt, and the east-west route from the Dead Sea to the Mediterranean coast (for map see

PALESTINE). Hebron was also known as Kiriath-arba and Mamre. Abraham, Isaac and Jacob all lived in the region at various times, and Abraham bought a piece of ground there for a family burial place (Gen 13:18; 18:1; 23:2,17-20; 25:9; 35:27; 37:14; 50:13).

At the time of Israel's conquest under Joshua, Hebron's local inhabitants were a tall powerfully built people whom many thought could never be conquered (Num 13:21-28,31-33). Caleb, however, believed otherwise (Num 13:30). Not only did he defeat them, but he received their territory as his family possession (Josh 14:12-15). Hebron, in the centre of this territory, became one of the three cities of refuge established west of Jordan (Josh 20:7-9; 21:9-13).

The town fell within the tribal allotment of Judah and soon became the chief town of the tribe. For seven years it was the capital of David's kingdom, till he conquered Jerusalem and made it his new capital (2 Sam 5:1-5). When Absalom tried to overthrow David, Hebron was the base from which he launched his rebellion (2 Sam 15:7-10). A later king, Rehoboam, recognized Hebron's strategic situation on the main highways, and fortified it as a key defence outpost (2 Chron 11:5-12).

HEIR

See INHERITANCE.

HELL

It is unfortunate that many of the older versions of the English Bible use the one word 'hell' to translate several words in the original languages. In the minds of most English-speaking people, hell is a place of terrible torment where the wicked dead are sent for final punishment. While this idea of hell may be true for the word *gehenna*, it is not true for other biblical words translated 'hell'. The Hebrew *sheol* and its Greek equivalent *hades* mean simply the place of the dead or the state of the dead.

Gehenna was the name Jesus used for the place of final punishment of the wicked. The word appears in the New Testament as a Greek transliteration of the Hebrew 'Valley of Hinnom'.

The Valley of Hinnom was a place just outside the wall of Jerusalem where, in times of apostasy, the people of Israel burnt their children in sacrifice to the god Molech (Jer 7:31). In the place where the people committed this wickedness, God punished them with terrible slaughter (Jer 7:32-34). Broken pottery was dumped in this valley, and the place became a public garbage dump where fires burnt

continually (Jer 19:1-13). Because of this association with judgment and burning, 'gehenna' became a fitting word to indicate the place or state of eternal punishment (Matt 10:28; 18:9; 23:33; Mark 9:43-48; cf. James 3:6).

According to the New Testament, the punishment of hell (gehenna) is one of eternal torment. It is likened to eternal burning (Matt 13:42; 18:8-9; Rev 20:10), eternal darkness (Matt 8:12; 22:13; 2 Peter 2:4,17), eternal destruction (Matt 7:13; Phil 1:28; 2 Peter 3:7,10) and eternal separation from God and his blessings (2 Thess 1:9).

Another symbolic picture of eternal punishment is that of a lake of fire prepared for the enemies of God (Rev 19:20; 20:10; cf. Matt 25:41). Into this lake God throws his great enemy, Death (Rev 20:14; cf. 1 Cor 15:26), along with all whose names are not written in the book of life (Rev 20:15). Just as heaven is something far better than the material symbols used to picture it, so hell is something far worse than the material symbols used to picture it. (See also JUDGMENT; PUNISHMENT.)

HELLENIST

During the last three centuries BC, Greek culture and language spread across the whole of the eastern Mediterranean region (see GREECE). Many Jews no longer spoke their native language, Hebrew, nor the related language, Aramaic, that had largely replaced it. The language they spoke was Greek, and because of this they were known as Hellenists (from the word *hellas*, meaning Greece).

Within Palestine, however, there were still many Aramaic-speaking Jews. Inevitably, tension developed between these and the Hellenists. In the early Jerusalem church the Greek-speaking Jews complained that their widows were being unfairly treated in the daily distribution of food. To solve the problem the church chose seven officials whom the apostles appointed to oversee the matter. It appears from the names of these officials that they were Hellenists (Acts 6:1-6).

When the Jerusalem Jews began to persecute the Christians, the Hellenist Christians were driven from Jerusalem. They preached the gospel wherever they went, to non-Jews as well as to Jews, and were the chief cause of the church's early expansion. Hellenists in many provinces became Christians, along with many God-fearing Greeks (Acts 8:1,4; 11:19-21; 13:43; 14:1; 17:1-4,10-12; 18:5-8; see also DISPERSION; PROSELYTE). Meanwhile the Aramaic-speaking Jews back in Jerusalem became a source of further trouble to the church (Acts 21:20-21,40).

HERESY

According to common usage today, heresy is false belief or false teaching. It is the misguided opinion of someone who denies the orthodox teaching of the Bible.

However, the word is used in this sense only once in the New Testament. Elsewhere it means sect or party. The Sadducees and Pharisees were sects within Judaism (Acts 5:17; 15:5). Orthodox Jews considered the Christians a Jewish sect who followed Jesus the Nazarene (Acts 24:5,14; 28:22).

When used by Christians, the word referred to factions created within a church through lack of love towards others (1 Cor 11:19). Those who created such factions showed that they were directed by the flesh, not by the Spirit (Gal 5:20). Such people were to be warned, then avoided, if they did not cease their divisive practices (Titus 3:10).

Because false teachers created factions, the word 'heresy' developed its more familiar meaning of 'false teaching'. The one biblical reference to heretics in this sense is to false prophets who deny Christ. By their belief they destroy themselves and by their teaching they destroy others (2 Peter 2:1; cf. 1 John 2:22,26; 4:1-3).

HERMON

Mount Hermon was in the far north of Palestine, at the southern end of the Lebanon Range. It was known to the Lebanese as Mt Sirion. The ancient Amorites called it Mt Senir (Deut 3:9; see also LEBANON). It was the highest mountain of the region, and water from its snow-covered heights was a major source of the Jordan River (Jer 18:14). It was included in the territory God promised to Israel, but Israel's control never extended beyond its southern foothills (Josh 11:16-17).

HEROD

Several rulers bearing the name 'Herod' feature in the New Testament record. Chief of these was Herod the Great, from whom the other Herods took their name. The prominence of the Herods had its origins in the confusion and corruption associated with Rome's rise to power just before the opening of the New Testament era.

Herod the Great

When Rome took control of Judea in 63 BC, it appointed as ruler a man who proved to be weak and easily used by others. He was very much under the influence of a part-Jewish Idumean friend,

Antipater, who was carefully and cunningly planning to gain control himself. (Idumea was a region in the south of Judea. It was inhabited by a mixture of Arabs, Jews and the remains of the nation once known as Edom.)

In the end Antipater won Rome's appointment as governor of Judea, with his two sons in the top positions beneath him. Throughout that period, the entire eastern Mediterranean region was troubled by power struggles and bitter conflicts, one of which resulted in Antipater being murdered and his two sons overthrown. One of these sons, who had developed even greater cunning than his father, escaped to Rome, where he persuaded the Romans to appoint him 'king' over the entire Palestine region. This was the person who became known as Herod the Great.

Through treachery and murder, Herod removed all possible rivals. Having made his position safe, he took firm control of Palestine and ruled it for the next thirty-three years (37-4 BC). He carried out

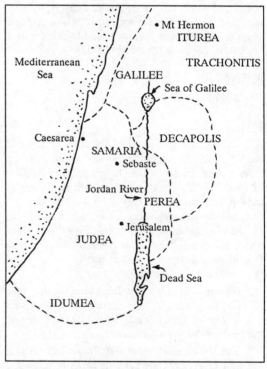

impressive building programs, two of his most notable achievements being the rebuilding of the city of Samaria (which he renamed Sebaste) and the construction of Caesarea as a Mediterranean port. In Jerusalem he built a military fortress, government buildings, a palace for himself and a magnificent

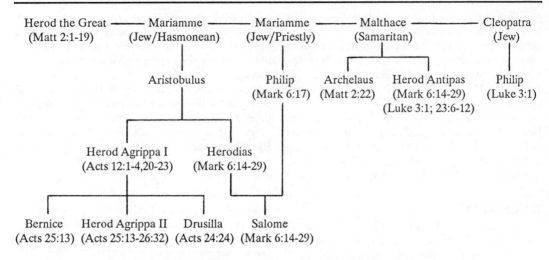

Herod the Great —— Mariamme —— Mariamme —— Malthace —— Cleopatra
(Matt 2:1-19) (Jew/Hasmonean) (Jew/Priestly) (Samaritan) (Jew)

Aristobulus Philip Archelaus Herod Antipas Philip
(Mark 6:17) (Matt 2:22) (Mark 6:14-29) (Luke 3:1)
(Luke 3:1; 23:6-12)

Herod Agrippa I Herodias
(Acts 12:1-4,20-23) (Mark 6:14-29)

Bernice Herod Agrippa II Drusilla Salome
(Acts 25:13) (Acts 25:13-26:32) (Acts 24:24) (Mark 6:14-29)

PART OF HEROD THE GREAT'S FAMILY

temple for the Jews (Matt 27:27; Mark 13:1; John 2:20; 19:13; Acts 23:10,35).

In spite of Herod's attempts to win Jewish support, the Jews hated him. This was partly because of his mixed-Jewish nationality (though he had adopted the Jewish religion) and partly because of his ruthlessness in murdering any that he thought were a threat to his position. His massacre of the Bethlehem babies was one example of his butchery (Matt 2:1-5,13,16-18).

Other members of Herod's family

Before he died (4 BC), Herod divided his kingdom among his three sons. Like their father, they could rule only within the authority Rome gave them.

The southern and central parts of Palestine (Judea and Samaria) were given to Archelaus, a man as cruel as his father but without his father's ability (Matt 2:22). The northern part of Palestine (Galilee) and part of the area east of Jordan (Perea) were given to Herod Antipas, the man who later killed John the Baptist and who agreed to the killing of Jesus (Mark 6:14-29; Luke 3:1; 23:6-12). The regions to the north and east of Lake Galilee (Iturea and Trachonitis) were given to Philip, a man of more moderate nature than the rest of his family (Luke 3:1). This man was half-brother to another Philip (mentioned in Mark 6:17).

Archelaus was so cruel and unjust that in AD 6 the people of Judea and Samaria asked Rome to remove him and rule them directly. From that time on, Judea and Samaria were governed by Roman governors (or procurators) until the destruction of Jerusalem in AD 70. The only exception to this was

the brief 'reign' of Herod Agrippa I, a grandson of Herod the Great. In AD 37 he took control of the former territory of Philip, and in AD 39 took control of the former territory of Herod Antipas. In AD 41 he gained Judea and Samaria, and for the next three years ruled virtually the whole area that Herod the Great once ruled (Acts 12:1-4,20-23). Upon his death in AD 41, Judea and Samaria returned to the rule of Roman governors.

Herod Agrippa II, son of Herod Agrippa I, received territories in the far north of Palestine, where he served Rome loyally from AD 48 to the destruction of the Jewish state in AD 70. He was an expert on Jewish affairs and bore the ceremonial title of king, but he had no authority over the Jews of Judea (Acts 25:13; 26:3,27,31). His sisters were Bernice and Drusilla (Acts 24:24; 25:13).

HERODIANS

The Herodians appear to have been a group of Jews who, unlike most of the Jews, were favourable to the rule of the Herods. Though the Pharisees would normally not be sympathetic to the Herodians, they were willing to cooperate with them in trying to find a way to have Jesus accused of law-breaking and, if possible, killed (Matt 22:15-17; Mark 3:6).

HESHBON

The city of Heshbon was situated on the tableland of Moab, about twenty kilometres east of the point where the Jordan River enters the Dead Sea. It was one of the chief cities of Moab, till lost to the

Amorites. The Amorites in turn lost it to the Israelites just before their attack on Canaan (Num 21:25-26; Deut 3:2). When the conquered territories were divided among Israel's tribes, Heshbon fell within the tribal area of Reuben (Num 32:2-5,37; Josh 13:15-21; Judg 11:26). (For map and other details see MOAB.)

Several centuries later, during the time of Israel's divided kingdom, Moab regained possession of Heshbon. But the city was doomed to destruction in the divine judgment that was to fall upon Moab (Isa 15:1,4; 16:8; Jer 48:1-2,45; 49:3).

HEZEKIAH

At the time of Hezekiah's accession to Judah's throne, his country was in a sad condition. The policies of Ahaz had left Judah economically weak, politically dominated by Assyria, and religiously corrupted through false religions (see AHAZ).

Upon becoming king, Hezekiah set out on the bold task of strengthening the nation's economy, overthrowing Assyrian domination, and reforming Judah's religion. This latter achievement won him praise as being Judah's greatest king to that time (2 Kings 18:1-8).

Religious reforms

The prophets of Hezekiah's time (he reigned from 716 to 687 BC) were Hosea, Isaiah and Micah. Hosea was by this time very old (cf. Hosea 1:1), Isaiah was very influential around the palace (Isa 1:1; 38:1) and Micah was preaching with such authority that the king was taking good notice of him (Micah 1:1; Jer 26:17-19). Yet none of the prophets records Hezekiah's reforms. Perhaps this was because the prophets were more concerned with the spiritual attitudes of people than with the revised procedures for temple worship.

Hezekiah began his reforms by assembling the priests and Levites and telling them plainly that neglect of the temple and its services was the reason for God's anger with Judah (2 Chron 29:1-11). He then sent them to cleanse and rededicate the temple. The common people responded to his reforms with such enthusiasm that the temple officials were unable to cope with all the sacrifices (2 Chron 29:12-36).

After this, Hezekiah arranged a great Feast of Passover and Unleavened Bread (2 Chron 30:1-12). He insisted, however, that before joining in the festival, people ceremonially cleanse themselves and remove all traces of false religion from Jerusalem (2 Chron 30:13-22).

Having cleansed Jerusalem of false religion, Hezekiah then cleansed the country areas (2 Chron 31:1). His desire was that the nation as a whole follow the religious order laid down by Moses and developed by David. He therefore organized the priests and Levites according to David's plan, and arranged for their proper financial support through the orderly payment and distribution of the people's tithes and offerings (2 Chron 31:2-19). Some of Hezekiah's leading officials made a collection of Solomon's proverbs to instruct the people further (Prov 25:1).

Political achievements

Assyrian influence in Palestine was at its peak during the time of Hezekiah. In the early part of his reign Assyria conquered the northern kingdom Israel and carried the people into captivity (722 BC; 2 Kings 17:6; 18:9-12). Meanwhile in the south, Hezekiah was busy strengthening Judah's independence. He improved its economy, increased its agricultural production, fortified its defences and improved Jerusalem's water supply (2 Chron 32:27-30). He then revolted against Assyria by refusing to pay further tribute (2 Kings 18:7).

As expected, Assyria sent its army to attack Judah, but Hezekiah had prepared Judah well and had equipped Jerusalem to withstand the siege (2 Kings 18:13; 2 Chron 32:1-6). He had also made a defence agreement with Egypt that he hoped would guarantee success. Isaiah opposed this dependence on Egypt. Judah's need was for quiet faith in God, not for military help from a foreign country (Isa 30:1-3,15; 31:1,3,5,8).

The Assyrian attack was far more damaging to Jerusalem than Hezekiah had expected. Even when the Assyrians had forced Hezekiah to pay them large amounts of money, they did not retreat. They were preparing to crush Jerusalem completely (2 Kings 18:14-37). On two occasions Hezekiah went in great distress to the temple to ask God's help, and on both occasions Isaiah brought God's reassuring answer (2 Kings 19:1-7,14-34). The outcome was that God intervened and dramatically overthrew the Assyrians (2 Kings 19:35-37).

Hezekiah had at one time become so sick that it appeared he would die. In answer to his prayers, God extended his life by fifteen years, enabling him to lead Judah through its period of conflict with Assyria (2 Kings 20:1-11). In gratitude to God, Hezekiah wrote a song of praise for his recovery (Isa 38:9-22).

Throughout this period Babylon was increasing in power and was looking for allies to help it conquer Assyria. An illness of Hezekiah gave the Babylonians the opportunity to visit him, in the hope of persuading him to join them against Assyria. Hezekiah was easily persuaded. He was very anti-Assyrian and very proud that his achievements for Judah had attracted Babylon's admiration (2 Kings 20:1-13; 2 Chron 32:24-25,31). Once again Isaiah condemned Hezekiah's willingness to enter into foreign alliances, for it would result in conquest by the allied nation (2 Kings 20:14-19). Hezekiah repented of his wrongdoing and completed his reign with Judah's independence still intact (2 Chron 32:26).

HIGH PLACES

See BAAL.

HIRAM

As king of Tyre in Lebanon, Hiram (or Huram) had always enjoyed good relations with the Israelite kings to the south. He helped David to build a palace (2 Sam 5:11) and later helped Solomon in his extensive building projects. He provided Solomon with huge amounts of materials and many skilled workmen in return for great quantities of farm produce (1 Kings 5:1-18). He lent Solomon money, in payment of which Solomon offered to give him a large section of Israel's northern territory (which bordered Lebanon) (1 Kings 9:10-14). The two kings also formed a trade alliance and became partners in a profitable shipping operation (1 Kings 9:26-28; 10:22). (For further details of Hiram's relations with Israel see SOLOMON.)

Another man named Hiram (or Huram) also features in the biblical record of this period. He was a highly skilled craftsman, also from Lebanon, whom Hiram the king sent to Jerusalem to do the bronze work and other decorations for Solomon's temple (1 Kings 7:13-14,40-46; 2 Chron 2:7,13-14).

HITTITES

The Middle Eastern political power known as the Hittite Empire lasted from about 1800 to 1200 BC. It extended from northern Palestine across Syria and into Asia Minor. Tidal, king of Goiim, was possibly a Hittite king of the era before the Empire was fully established (Gen 14:1).

Even after the Empire had collapsed, Syria was still sometimes referred to as the land of the Hittites. Likewise the people of various states and cities in Syria still called themselves Hittites (Josh 1:4; 2 Sam 24:6; 1 Kings 10:29; 11:1; 2 Kings 7:6).

However, the Hittites most often mentioned in the Bible are not those of the ancient Hittite Empire in the north, but those of smaller tribal groups in Canaan. They were probably the descendants of migrants from earlier Hittite kingdoms, and formed

Hittite king presenting his daughter to Pharaoh

one of the many tribal groups that occupied Canaan before the conquering Israelites drove them out (Gen 15:20; Exod 3:8; 23:28; Deut 7:1; Josh 3:10; Ezra 9:1).

The main area where the Hittites of Canaan lived was the central mountain region. This included the towns of Bethel, Jerusalem, Bethlehem, Hebron and Beersheba (Gen 23:2-16; 26:34; Judg 1:23,26; 2 Sam 23:39; Ezek 16:3). The Hittites were among the many Canaanite groups whom Solomon used as slaves in his building programs (1 Kings 9:20-21). Eventually they were absorbed into the Israelites and so ceased to be a distinct racial group.

HIVITES

Among the many tribal groups that occupied Canaan before the Israelites dispossessed them were the people known as Hivites (Gen 10:15-17; Exod 3:8; 23:28; Deut 7:1; Josh 3:10). They lived mainly in the mountain country of northern Palestine and Lebanon (Josh 11:3; Judg 3:3; 2 Sam 24:6-7), though some lived in Shechem and others as far south as Gibeon (Gen 34:2; Josh 9:3,7; 11:19). They were among the many Canaanite tribal peoples used as slaves in Solomon's building programs (1 Kings 9:20-21). Like other Canaanite groups they were eventually absorbed into Israel.

HOLINESS

The Hebrew word usually translated 'holy' had a much wider meaning than the English word 'holy'. To most English-speaking people 'holiness' usually indicates some ethical quality such as sinlessness or purity. To the Hebrews the word originally indicated the state or condition of a person or thing as being separated from the common affairs of life and consecrated wholly to God. (In Hebrew, also in Greek, the words 'holy' and 'sanctify' come from the same root.)

Ideas of separation for God

God was considered holy, because he was separate from man, and indeed from all created things (Exod 15:11-12; Ps 99:3; Isa 6:3; 8:13; Rev 3:7; 4:8). Israel was holy, because it belonged to God and was cut off from the religions and customs of the surrounding peoples (Exod 19:6; Deut 7:6). The Sabbath and other religious days were holy, because they were separated from the common days of the workaday world (Exod 31:15; Lev 23:4,21,24).

People who were removed from secular life and consecrated to the service of God were holy (Lev 21:6-8). Places and land withdrawn from common use and set apart for sacred use or given to God were holy (Lev 6:16; 27:21). Besides obviously holy things such as places of worship, less obvious things such as clothing, oils, food and produce were also holy if they were set apart for God (Exod 29:29-33; 30:25; 40:9; Lev 27:30; Matt 7:6; 23:17; Acts 6:13). The relation of a person or thing to God was what determined whether it was holy or common (see also DEFILEMENT).

Ideas of moral perfection

Because holiness signified separation from all that was common and everyday, the word naturally developed a wider meaning that included ideas of excellence and perfection. When applied to God this carried with it ideas of moral perfection. God's holiness meant that he was separate not only from the common everyday world but, above all, from sin (Hab 1:12-13).

As a result holiness developed the association with ethical qualities that we are familiar with in English. Because God was holy, his people were to be holy (Lev 11:44-45; Isa 57:15; 1 Peter 1:15-16). God's holiness meant also that one day he would judge sinners (see GOD; JUDGMENT).

The preaching of the Old Testament prophets was very much concerned with this ethical aspect of holiness. The prophets emphasized that it was useless for people to be ritually holy before God if they were not ethically holy in their daily lives (Isa 58:13-14; Amos 2:7). Likewise in the New Testament the writers emphasize this moral aspect of holiness. The holiness of God is to be reflected in his people in lives of purity, uprightness and moral goodness (Mark 6:20; Eph 1:4; 5:27; 1 Thess 4:7; Titus 1:8; Heb 12:10,14).

Holiness, however, is not something people can achieve by themselves. All mankind is defiled by sin (Rom 3:10,23), but Christ, the perfect man, died to take away man's sin. God can now accept repentant sinners as cleansed, because of what Christ has done (1 Peter 2:22-24). God declares believers in Jesus Christ holy; that is, he sanctifies them (1 Cor 6:11; 1 Peter 1:2). Having been declared holy, believers must make it true in practice. They must have lives of practical sanctification (Rom 6:8-11,19-22; see SANCTIFICATION).

HOLY SPIRIT

There is only one God, and this God has always existed in a trinity of Father, Son and Holy Spirit. Man's understanding of the Holy Spirit is therefore tied up with his understanding of the Trinity, and that in turn is tied up with the life and ministry of Jesus Christ. Yet, though the revelation reaches its climax in Christ, its origins are in the Old Testament.

The Old Testament period

When people of Old Testament times saw some remarkable demonstration of the power of God, they called that power by the Hebrew word *ruach*. This word was used in everyday speech without any particular reference to God and could have the meaning of wind (1 Kings 18:45), breath (Gen 7:15,22) or spirit (in the sense of a person's life or feelings) (Gen 41:8; 45:27).

In relation to God, *ruach* could apply to the wind that God used to direct the course of nature (Gen 8:1; Exod 10:19), to the breath of God's 'nostrils' or 'mouth', by which he did mighty deeds (Ps 18:15; 33:6), or to his spirit, through which he had power, actions and feelings as a living being (Gen 1:2; 6:3). The *ruach* of God indicated to the Hebrews something that was powerful and irresistible. It was not only full of life itself but was also life-giving (Judg 6:34; 2 Kings 2:16; Job 33:4; Ps 104:30; Ezek 37:14).

On certain occasions this Spirit of God, or power of God, came upon selected people for specific purposes. It may have resulted in victorious leadership (Judg 3:10; 6:34; Zech 4:6), superhuman strength (Judg 14:6,19; 15:14; 16:20) or artistic ability and knowhow (Exod 31:3-5). Frequently it produced unusual behaviour (Num 11:25-29; 1 Sam 10:6,10-11; 19:23-24). Always it was on the side of right and opposed to wrong (Ps 51:10-12; Isa 32:15-16; 63:10; Micah 3:8). Prophets who received God's messages and passed them on to his people did so through the activity of God's Spirit upon them (2 Sam 23:2; 2 Chron 24:20; Neh 9:30; Isa 61:1; Zech 7:12; see PROPHET).

God promised that a day was coming when not merely selected people, but all God's people, regardless of status, sex or age, would have God's Spirit poured out upon them (Joel 2:28-29; cf. Num 11:29; Ezek 36:27). And the one upon whom God's Spirit would rest in a special way was the Messiah (Isa 11:1-5; see MESSIAH).

In spite of all this, it is probably still true to say that when the Old Testament people spoke of the Spirit of God, they were thinking more of the living and active power of God than of a person within a trinity. They probably had no more understanding of the Spirit of God as a person within a triune Godhead than they had of the Son of God as a person within a triune Godhead.

These Old Testament believers, however, did not regard the Spirit as simply an impersonal force. They identified the Spirit with a personal God, yet at the same time they made some distinction between God the Almighty and his Spirit (Gen 1:1-2; 1 Sam 16:13; Ezek 37:26). It was all a preparation for the fuller revelation of the Trinity that came through the life and work of Jesus Christ.

The coming of Jesus

With the coming of Jesus, man received a much clearer revelation concerning the Spirit of God. People may not always have realized it, but every work ever done in people's hearts, whether in turning them initially to God or in creating new character within them, was the work of God's unseen Spirit. In more spectacular demonstrations of God's working, the Spirit of God had come upon selected people for certain tasks, but Jesus had the Spirit without limit. He lived his life and carried out his work through the unlimited power of God's Spirit working through him unceasingly (Isa 11:1-5; 42:1-4; Matt 1:18; 3:16-17; 12:28; Luke 4:1,14,18; John 3:34-35; Acts 10:38).

Through Jesus people now began to have a new understanding of the Spirit. As Jesus' baptism showed, God the Father was in heaven, God the Son was on earth, and God the Spirit had come from the Father to rest upon the Son (Matt 3:16-17). Through Jesus it was shown that the Spirit was more than merely the power of God. Certainly, the Spirit demonstrated the power of God, but people now began to see that the Spirit was a person – someone distinct from Father and Son, yet equal with them and inseparably united with them (Matt 28:19; John 14:15-17; 16:13-15; Acts 5:30-32; 1 Cor 12:4-6; see TRINITY).

Unlike the Son, the Spirit did not become flesh, but he was still a person, having knowledge, desires and feelings (Acts 16:6; Rom 8:27; 15:30; 1 Cor 2:11,13; Eph 4:30). Nor was the Spirit merely a 'part' of God. He was God himself (Acts 5:3-4; 1 Cor 3:16; 6:19-20).

The Spirit always had been fully God and fully personal, even in Old Testament times. The difference between Old and New Testament times was not that there was some change or development in the Holy Spirit (for since he is God, he is eternal and unchanging; Heb 9:14). There may have been a change in the way the Spirit worked, and there was a development in man's understanding of the Spirit, but the Spirit himself did not change.

With the coming of Jesus and the events that followed in the early church, people now had a better understanding of what God had been doing during the pre-Christian era. They now saw more in Old Testament references to the Spirit of God than the Old Testament believers themselves understood (cf. Joel 2:28-29 with Acts 2:16-18; cf. Zech 7:12 with Acts 7:51; 28:25; 1 Peter 1:11).

Once God had come into the world in the person of Jesus, Jesus became the means by which God gave his Spirit to others (John 1:33; 20:22). Jesus became the one mediator between God and man. No one could come to the Father except through Jesus, and no one could receive God's Spirit except through Jesus (John 14:6,16-17,26; 15:26; Acts 2:33).

Jesus' promise to his disciples

During his earthly life Jesus accepted the limitations of time and distance that apply to people in general. Consequently, the work that the Holy Spirit was doing in the world through him was limited to those times and places where Jesus worked. The Spirit was, so to speak, tied to Jesus.

Jesus, however, would not remain in the world indefinitely. After he had completed the work his Father had given him to do (a work that could be completed only through his death and resurrection), he would return to his Father, leaving his followers to carry on his work upon earth. To enable them to do this work satisfactorily, the Father would give them the same Spirit as had worked through Jesus (John 14:16-18; 15:26; 16:13-15).

This was why Jesus told his disciples that once he had returned triumphantly to his Father, they would do greater works than he had done. The power of the Spirit had previously been limited to the few years of one man's ministry in one place; but now that power would be poured out on *all* Jesus' disciples, and they would carry on his work in *all* countries, till the end of the age (John 14:12,16). In view of this, it was to the disciples' advantage that Jesus leave them and return to his Father; for then they too would be indwelt by God's Holy Spirit (John 14:17; 16:7).

The Holy Spirit is the Spirit of Christ

Although the Holy Spirit is a separate person from the Son, he is inseparably united with the Son, as the Son is with the Father (John 5:43; 14:26). The Holy Spirit is the Spirit of Jesus Christ. He bears the stamp of Jesus' character, as Jesus bore the stamp of his Father's character (Acts 16:6-7; Rom 8:9; Gal 4:6; Phil 1:19; 1 Peter 1:11; cf. Heb 1:3).

Through the Holy Spirit, Jesus continues to abide with his disciples, even though physically he is no longer in the world (John 14:18; Gal 2:20; Col 1:27). The Spirit is called the Counsellor or Helper, for he gives Jesus' followers the same counsel or help as Jesus gave them when he was physically with them. Through the Holy Spirit, the presence of Jesus, previously limited to first century Palestine, becomes timeless and worldwide (John 14:16,18,26; 15:26; 16:7).

It is impossible, therefore, to have the Spirit without having Christ. Equally it is impossible to have a relationship with God through the Spirit but not through Christ (Acts 2:38; Rom 8:9-11). The Spirit does not exalt himself above Christ, for the Spirit's task is to direct people to Christ (John 15:26; 1 Cor 12:3).

There is no competition between the Spirit and Christ, for the Spirit is the Spirit of Christ. Life 'in Christ' is life 'in the Spirit' and vice versa (Rom 8:1,9; 2 Cor 3:14-18). Just as Jesus received his authority from the Father, glorified the Father and taught people about the Father, so the Spirit receives his authority from Christ, glorifies Christ and teaches people about Christ (cf. John 8:28 with John 16:13; cf. John 17:4 with John 16:14; cf. John 17:8 with John 14:26, 16:15).

The Spirit and the early church

Because Jesus was to be the channel through whom God would give the Holy Spirit to believers in general, Jesus had to complete the work given him by his Father before believers could receive the Spirit. Moreover, the Father wanted to show his satisfaction with Christ's work by raising him from the dead and giving him glory. Only after such a triumphant conclusion to Christ's earthly ministry would the Father give the Spirit to others (John 7:39; 1 Peter 1:21).

Jesus therefore told his disciples to wait in Jerusalem after his ascension and they would receive the Holy Spirit as he had promised (Acts 1:4-5). The fulfilment of this promise came on the Day of Pentecost. Just as there were unusual happenings when God poured out the Spirit on Jesus, so there were when he poured out the Spirit on Jesus' disciples (Acts 2:1-4,33; cf. Matt 3:16-17; John 1:33; for details see BAPTISM WITH THE SPIRIT). The new age had dawned. God had promised to pour out his Spirit on all believers, regardless of status, sex or age, and that promise was now fulfilled (Joel 2:28-29; Acts 2:16-18,33,39).

Having received the Holy Spirit, the disciples then carried on the work of Jesus. Jesus had begun that work during the time of his earthly ministry (Acts 1:1-2), and he continued to do the work through his followers (Acts 3:6; 4:10,27-30; 5:12; cf. Luke 4:18).

Jesus was working through his disciples by the power of the Holy Spirit whom he had given them. Through that Spirit the disciples were bearing witness to Jesus, whose life, death and resurrection had changed the course of history. Jesus had made forgiveness available to the repentant, but judgment certain for the unrepentant. As the disciples made known this message, they presented their hearers with the alternatives of forgiveness and judgment (John 16:7-11; 20:22-23; Acts 1:8; 5:32).

All this may be summarized by saying that the Holy Spirit is the one who equips God's people for the task of spreading the gospel of Jesus, making disciples of Jesus and establishing the church of Jesus (Acts 1:8; 9:31; 13:2; 20:28). He gives different abilities to different people to enable the church to function harmoniously and fruitfully. These abilities are called gifts of the Spirit (1 Cor 12:4-7; see GIFTS OF THE SPIRIT).

Examples from the early church show that the Holy Spirit works in both spectacular and unspectacular ways. He gives Christians boldness in the face of opposition (Acts 4:8; 6:10; 13:9-10), yet also the quiet ability to organize church affairs smoothly (Acts 6:3). He guides Christians through inner promptings and visions (Acts 8:29,39; 10:19;

11:28), yet also through reasoned discussion (Acts 15:28). He directs Christian activity by opening new opportunities (Acts 13:4), yet also through closing others (Acts 16:6-7). (See also CHURCH; PROPHECY; TONGUES.)

Salvation through the Spirit

By nature man is dead in sin and under God's judgment, with no way of saving himself. Only by the work of the Holy Spirit can people be cleansed from sin and given spiritual life (John 3:5; 6:63; 16:7-11; 1 Cor 6:11; Eph 2:1-4; Titus 3:3-6; see REGENERATION). (Concerning the sin against the Holy Spirit see BLASPHEMY.) The Holy Spirit, having given believers new life, remains with them in an unbroken union. The Spirit dwells within them permanently (Rom 8:9-11; 1 Cor 6:19; 2 Tim 1:14; 1 John 3:24; 4:13).

Christians, then, may be described as those who are 'in the Spirit' (Rom 8:9), who 'have the Spirit' (Rom 8:9), who are 'led by the Spirit' (Rom 8:14) and who 'live by the Spirit' (Gal 5:25). The Spirit is God's seal, God's mark of ownership, upon them. He gives them the inner assurance that God has made them his sons, and he guarantees to them that they will inherit his eternal blessings (Rom 8:15-17; 2 Cor 1:22; Gal 4:6; Eph 1:13-14; 4:30; Heb 10:15-17).

Christian life and conduct

There is a constant conflict in the lives of believers, because the old sinful nature (the flesh) fights against the Spirit of God who has now come and dwelt in them (Rom 8:5-7; Gal 5:17; Eph 4:29-32). They triumph over the sinful desires of the flesh not by putting themselves under a set of laws, but by allowing God's Spirit to direct their lives (Gal 3:3; 5:16-25).

Because of their union with Christ, believers have died to the law. The Spirit has given them life and freedom − not a freedom to do as they like, but a freedom from the bondage that the law brings (Rom 7:6; Gal 5:1). Through the Spirit they now have the freedom, and the power, to develop the righteousness that the law aimed at but could never produce (Rom 8:1-4; 2 Cor 3:6,17; Gal 5:5; see FLESH; FREEDOM; LAW).

This change in the behaviour of believers does not happen automatically as a result of the Spirit's dwelling within them. It requires self-discipline and effort (Rom 12:9-13; 1 Cor 9:27; Gal 6:7-10; Eph 6:11-18; 2 Tim 2:1-6; see SELF-DISCIPLINE). But if the Spirit of Christ has control in their lives and is directing their self-discipline and effort, the result will be a quality of character that is like that of Christ himself (Rom 14:17; 2 Cor 3:18; Gal 5:22-23; see LOVE).

Such Christlike character is what the Bible calls the fruit of the Spirit (Gal 5:22). The production of spiritual fruit, not the exercise of spiritual gift, is the evidence of the Spirit's working in people's lives. Even those who are unspiritual can exercise abilities given them by the Spirit, but they cannot produce the character that only the Spirit of God can create (cf. 1 Cor 1:7; 3:1-4; 12:1-3).

A constant helper

Christians should not think that the Spirit-controlled life will be without disappointment, hardship or sorrow. If Jesus suffered, his followers can expect to suffer also (Matt 10:24-25; 2 Tim 3:12), but the Spirit of Jesus within them will help them maintain joy and peace through their sufferings (John 14:18,26; 16:33; Acts 13:52; 20:23; 1 Thess 1:5-6; 1 Peter 4:13-16; see JOY; PEACE).

When believers allow God's Spirit within them to have full control in their lives, they are said to be filled with the Spirit. This filling of the Spirit is not a once-for-all event, but the constant spiritual state of all who live in a right relationship with God and with others (Acts 6:3,5; 11:24; Eph 4:16; 5:18-21).

A person full of the Spirit is, in other words, a spiritual person (as a person full of wisdom is a wise person, or a person full of joy a joyful person; Acts 6:3,5,8; 9:36; 11:24; Rom 15:13-14). Yet this Spirit-filled person may receive additional 'fillings' in certain circumstances. That is, the person who truly lives by the Spirit can be assured of the Spirit's added help when special needs arise (cf. Acts 6:5 with 7:55; cf. Acts 9:17 with 13:9-11). Often the Spirit gives such special help to enable believers to have boldness when facing opposition because of their allegiance to Jesus Christ (Acts 2:4; 4:8-12,31; 7:55; 13:50-52).

Just as believers who allow God to control their lives are said to be filled with the Spirit, so those who allow the old sinful nature to control their lives are said to grieve the Spirit (Eph 4:29-32; cf. Acts 5:9; 1 Thess 5:15-19). Obedience and faith are as necessary for enjoying the Spirit's power as they are for receiving the Spirit in the first place (Acts 5:32; Gal 3:2).

Worship, prayer and the Word

The Holy Spirit creates unity and fellowship among Christians (1 Cor 12:12-13; 2 Cor 13:14; Eph 4:3-4; Phil 2:1-2; see FELLOWSHIP). When Christians join together in worship, the Holy Spirit is the one who unites them in a common purpose and directs their worship (Acts 13:2; 1 Cor 12:7-8). In fact, they can worship God acceptably only as the Spirit works in their thoughts and words (John 4:24; Phil 3:3; see WORSHIP).

True prayer, like true worship, is an activity that believers can carry out only through the activity of the Holy Spirit in them (Eph 6:18; Jude 20). Jesus Christ is their mediator in heaven (Rom 8:34; Heb 7:25), and the Spirit of Jesus Christ is within them on earth (Rom 8:9). As believers pray, the Spirit helps them and brings their real desires before God. This is particularly so when they themselves cannot find the right words to express those desires (Rom 8:26-27; Eph 2:18; see PRAYER).

Not only man's word to God, but also God's word to man involves the activity of the Spirit. Just as a person's own spirit, and no one else's, knows what is going on inside that person, so the Spirit of God, and no one else, knows what is going on within God. Therefore, only those who have the Spirit of God can properly understand the Word of God or teach it to others (1 Cor 2:10-13). Christian teachers or preachers, while they are careful to make sure that the hearers understand their message, must nevertheless rely upon the working of God's Spirit for that message to be effectual (Acts 4:8; 1 Cor 2:3-5; see PREACHING).

God's Spirit and God's Word are inseparable, because each works through the other. The Old Testament Scriptures were written by the inspiration of God's Spirit upon the writers (2 Tim 3:16; 2 Peter 1:20-21; see INSPIRATION). This same Spirit worked in his fulness through Jesus, and enlightened Jesus' followers by applying and developing his teachings (John 14:26; 16:12-15; 1 Peter 1:12). Through the work of the Holy Spirit in those men, the New Testament Scriptures came into being. As people read those Scriptures, the Spirit continues to bear witness to Jesus (John 15:26).

HOPE

Hope is a characteristic of genuine faith in God. Such hope is different from the hope that people in general might speak of. It is not a mere wish for something, but a strong confidence that is placed in God. It is the assured belief that God will do what he has promised (Ps 42:5; 71:5; Rom 4:18; Heb 11:1). Hope, according to its Christian meaning, is inseparable from faith (Rom 5:1-5; Gal 5:5; Heb 6:11-12; 1 Peter 1:21). Those without God have no

faith and therefore have no hope (Eph 2:12; 1 Thess 4:13; cf. Col 1:23).

The great hope for Christians is the return of Jesus Christ, when they will experience the fulness of their salvation and enter with Christ into the glory of the new age (1 Cor 15:19-23; Eph 1:18; Col 1:27; 1 Thess 5:8; 1 Peter 1:13). For Christians, then, to have the hope of Christ's return means to look forward to it eagerly; and the basis for such hope is Christ's atoning death and glorious resurrection. Christ's entrance into glory guarantees the entrance of believers into glory (Col 1:5; Heb 6:19; 1 Peter 1:18-21).

By its very nature, hope means that the thing hoped for has not yet arrived. Christ has not yet returned. Believers must therefore have patience as they wait for the day of their final salvation (Rom 8:23-25; Heb 11:1,39-40).

This patience contains no element of doubt, for Christian hope is the anticipation of something that is certain. God confirms the hope of salvation by giving believers the Holy Spirit. They have a living guarantee within them until the day their hope is fulfilled. The Spirit is God's mark of permanent ownership upon them (2 Cor 1:22; Eph 1:13-14; 4:30; see ASSURANCE).

Until Christ returns, the world will continue to be a place of imperfection and suffering. Christians must therefore persevere and be patient through all the difficulties they meet (Rom 5:3-5; 12:12). Their hope in Christ means that their endurance will be characterized not by grudging tolerance, but by positive enjoyment of all that life offers. Hope gives their lives purpose and stability (Rom 15:13; Col 3:1-4; 1 Thess 1:3; 2 Thess 2:16-17; Titus 2:11-14; see JOY; PATIENCE). At the same time they will work hard at keeping themselves free from sin; for their day of salvation is also their day of reckoning (1 John 3:2-3; cf. Matt 24:45-46; 2 Cor 5:10).

HOREB

Mount Horeb is another name for Mount Sinai. (For details see SINAI.)

HORITES

The Horites were the original inhabitants of the region around Mt Seir, south of the Dead Sea. When Esau and his descendants moved into the region, they overpowered the Horites and took possession of the land for themselves. It became part of the land of Edom, and the remaining

Horites were absorbed into the Edomites (Gen 14:6; 36:20-21; Deut 2:12,22; see EDOM).

HORN

Since wild animals used their horns to defend themselves or attack their enemies, Israelites often spoke of the horn as a symbol of power (Deut 33:17; 1 Kings 22:11; Ps 18:2; 22:21; 75:5,10; 92:10; Zech 1:21; Luke 1:69; Rev 5:6). Sometimes horns were symbolic of powerful rulers (Dan 7:7,24; 8:20; Rev 17:3,12).

People used certain types of horns as musical instruments, particularly on ceremonial occasions (2 Sam 6:15). In times of battle, the blowing of horns, like the blowing of trumpets or bugles, was

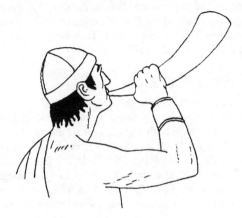

Blowing the horn for battle

a means of making declarations or sending signals (Josh 6:4,13; Judg 7:18; 1 Cor 14:8). Other horns were made into containers for the oil used in the ceremonial anointing of kings and priests (1 Sam 16:13; 1 Kings 1:39).

Ornamental horns projected from the four corners of the altars of the tabernacle. The priests applied the blood of certain sacrifices to these horns as part of the ritual for the cleansing of sin (Exod 27:2; 29:12; 30:1-2,10). Israelite law did not permit the widespread ancient practice of clinging to the horns of the altar to escape punishment for murder (Exod 21:14; 1 Kings 1:51; 2:29).

HOSANNA

Originally the word 'Hosanna' was a combination of parts of two Hebrew words that meant 'save' and 'pray'. When the word was joined to the name of God, Yahweh, the expression became both a prayer and an exclamation of praise: 'Save us, O Lord'.

The Hebrew form of the word occurs only once in the Old Testament, in Psalm 118. The scene is one of triumph, as Israel's king enters the temple for a public ceremony of praise to God for a recent victory in battle. His entrance is followed by a shout of 'Hosanna! Blessed is he who comes in the name of the Lord', accompanied by the waving of palm branches, as the people welcome their victorious king (Ps 118:25-27). 'Hosanna' later became an expression of praise in expectation of the great Saviour-Messiah.

In the New Testament the word is used in a setting similar to that of Psalm 118. When people in Jerusalem welcomed Jesus as their Saviour-Messiah, they shouted praises of 'Hosanna' and waved palm branches. By going direct to the temple, Jesus showed that his messiahship was concerned chiefly with spiritual issues, not political. In the temple also he was greeted with shouts of 'Hosanna', and again Jesus accepted the praise. He was indeed the promised Messiah (Matt 21:1-17; John 12:12-15; see MESSIAH).

HOSEA

At the time of the prophet Hosea's ministry (the eighth century BC) the ancient Israelite nation was divided into two kingdoms, Israel in the north and Judah in the south. Hosea began his ministry late in the reigns of Jeroboam II of Israel and Uzziah of Judah, and continued it through the reigns of succeeding kings (Hosea 1:1).

Unfaithful religion

Hosea's work was concerned with the north more than the south. Israel's religion had been corrupted through Baal worship, with the result that the nation was heading for judgment and would be taken captive to a foreign land.

Because the covenant between Israel and Yahweh was likened to a marriage covenant, Israel's association with other gods was really spiritual adultery (Hosea 4:17; 5:4; 6:10; 7:16; 8:5-6; see BAAL). Hosea saw a fitting illustration of this when his own wife Gomer left him for other lovers. She became a prostitute (Hosea 1:2; 2:2).

Gomer's pleasures did not last and she was sold as a slave. Hosea, who still loved his erring wife, had remained faithful to his marriage covenant, and when he found Gomer a slave, he bought her back (Hosea 3:1-3). Hosea's covenant love for Gomer pictured Yahweh's covenant love for his people. They too would go into captivity but, after being cleansed of their adulterous association with the

Canaanite gods, would be brought back to live in their land again (Hosea 2:17-20; 3:4-5; 14:4-7).

Corrupt society

During the reigns of Jeroboam II and Uzziah, Israel and Judah enjoyed political stability, economic prosperity and territorial expansion greater than at any time since the days of David and Solomon (2 Kings 14:23-27; 15:1-2; 2 Chron 26:1-15). This development, however, brought with it greed and corruption on a scale that neither Israel nor Judah had experienced previously. The two prophets who began to attack the social injustice and religious corruption of the age were Amos and Hosea. They came from different parts of the country, but both were concerned more with the northern kingdom than with the southern.

The particular social evils that the prophets attacked were connected with the exploitation of the poor by those of the upper classes. The people who benefited from the prosperity of the age were not the farmers (who made up the majority of the population) but the officials and merchants. They could cheat and oppress the poor as they wished, knowing that because of the corruption of the courts, the poor had no way of defending themselves (Hosea 4:1-2; 6:8-9; 12:7-8). Again, the judgment announced upon the nation was that of conquest and captivity (Hosea 5:14; 9:6; 10:3-8,13-15; see also Amos).

Outline of Hosea's prophecy

Hosea recounts his unhappy family experiences and shows how those experiences reflect the state of affairs in Israel (1:1-2:1). Like Gomer, Israel has been unfaithful to her husband God (Yahweh) (2:2-23), but as Hosea redeemed Gomer from slavery, so God will redeem Israel from the coming captivity (3:1-5).

The central section of the book is a collection of various short messages that Hosea preached over the years. The messages are not in chronological order, but all are connected with Israel's moral corruption. Corrupt religion produces a corrupt nation, whether in its everyday life (4:1-5:7), its foreign policy (5:8-14), its loyalty to God (5:15-6:6) or its concern for justice (6:7-7:7). The nation has rebelled against God by making alliances with foreign nations (7:8-16) and by giving itself to Baal worship (8:1-14).

Israel's punishment is therefore certain (9:1-17). The nation will reap what it has sown (10:1-15). The people have despised God's love (11:1-11) and exploited each other (11:12-12:14), and thereby have guaranteed captivity for their nation (13:1-16). But when the people repent, God will forgive them and bring them back to their land (14:1-9).

HOSHEA

The closing years of the northern kingdom of Israel were dominated by Assyria. When the Israelite king Pekah tried to oppose Assyria, the result was a disaster for Israel. Hoshea, a sympathizer with Assyria, assassinated Pekah and became king himself (2 Kings 15:29-30).

Hoshea survived as Israel's king only by buying protection from Assyria. When, with Egypt's help, he rebelled against Assyria by refusing to pay any further money, Assyria attacked Samaria (Israel's capital) and imprisoned Hoshea. After a three-year siege, Assyria crushed Samaria and took the people into captivity (2 Kings 17:1-6). This was the end of the northern kingdom (722 BC).

HOSPITALITY

Most people in Bible times recognized that they had a responsibility to practise hospitality. The custom was to welcome both friends and strangers and to give them food, water and other provisions to make them comfortable (Gen 18:1-8; 24:32; Exod 2:20; Deut 10:18-19; 23:4; Judg 13:15; 19:16-21; 2 Kings 4:8; Job 31:32; Luke 7:44-45; Acts 9:43; 16:15). A mark of special honour was to wash the guest's

A tent-dweller's hospitality

feet or to anoint his head with oil (Ps 23:5; Luke 7:37-38,44-46). The host was responsible to protect his guests as long as they were in his house (Gen 19:1-11; Judg 19:22-23).

God's people must be ready always to practise hospitality to those in need, whether close friends or people they have never seen before. And they must do so without expecting anything in return. Those who fail in this matter are in danger of God's chastisement (Isa 58:7; Matt 25:31-46; Luke 14:12-14; Rom 12:13; Gal 6:10; Heb 13:2; 1 Peter 4:9). Church leaders in particular should be an example to the rest of the church by their hospitality (1 Tim 3:2; 3 John 5-6). If Christians have not practised generous hospitality to others, they are in no position to call upon the church for financial support when they themselves are in need (1 Tim 5:9-10).

Christians have a special duty to give hospitality to travelling preachers and teachers of God's Word (Rom 16:23; 1 Cor 9:4-5; Titus 3:13-14; Philem 22; 3 John 5-8). They should give no hospitality at all to those who are false teachers (2 John 9-11).

HOSTS

God was, to the Israelites, the Lord of hosts. To them this signified a God of almighty power against whom no enemy could succeed. The armies of Israel were the armies of God, the hosts of Yahweh (1 Sam 17:45; cf. Josh 5:14-15). Yet as Lord of hosts, God is more than just God of the armies of Israel. He is God of the countless multitudes of angelic beings who live in constant readiness to carry out his commands (1 Kings 22:19; Ps 148:2; see ANGELS).

As a title indicating a God whose power is unlimited, 'Lord of hosts' is one of the most frequently used titles of God in the Bible. It occurs almost three hundred times (e.g. Ps 24:10; Isa 1:24; Jer 2:19; Zech 1:17; Mal 1:6,14; James 5:4).

HOUR

Like the word 'day', the word 'hour' is used in the Bible both specifically and generally. It may refer to a measured length of time or to an occasion or period (Matt 20:9,12; 24:44; 26:40,45; Luke 22:53; John 4:21; 5:28; 7:30; 12:27; for details see DAY; TIME).

HOUSE

Israel's conquest of Canaan under Joshua led to a new way of life for the Israelite people. One feature of this new way of life was a change in their type of domestic accommodation. Instead of being a wandering people who lived in tents and other temporary shelters, they were now a settled people who lived in houses (cf. Num 24:5; see TENT).

The Israelites built some of these houses themselves, but others they took over from the Canaanites. Often the houses were grouped together in villages or towns, where a surrounding wall protected them against attack. Farmers went out of the town and farmed their fields during the day, and returned to the safety of their homes at night (Judg 9:42-45; 1 Sam 6:18; 1 Chron 27:25).

The Israelite house

An ancient Israelite house was usually rectangular in plan, two storied, made of either stones or bricks, and covered on the inside walls with plaster (Lev 14:40-42; cf. Exod 5:7). The house had to be built on a solid foundation, and the whole structure was held together by being built into huge stones at the corners of the building (Isa 28:16; Matt 7:24-27; 21:42; see CORNERSTONE).

An Israelite house

Outside the house, steps led up to the roof, which was a flat area used as a place to relax, sleep, pray and worship (Jer 32:29; Mark 2:4; 13:15; Acts 10:9). A railing or low wall around the edge of the roof prevented people from accidentally falling off (Deut 22:8).

Inside the larger houses there was a central courtyard where women did much of the cooking, washing and other household work. Water pots, jars

183

and household utensils were usually kept in this courtyard (Isa 44:16; Jer 25:10; Ezek 24:3-5; Mark 7:4; Luke 22:55). A person stored his family's food and valuable possessions in the house, along with his farm tools and, at times, food for his animals (Judg 19:21). Windows were usually covered with lattice for security (Song of Songs 2:9).

The upper floor of a house may have consisted of one large room or may have been divided into several smaller rooms. This upper floor was used for sleeping, for accommodating guests, or for holding large gatherings (Luke 22:12; Acts 1:12; 20:8). In most houses furniture was simple, consisting only of those articles that were necessary (2 Kings 4:10). The houses of the rich, by contrast, were furnished lavishly (Amos 3:15; 6:4-6).

Making good use of the house

God's people are expected to use their houses, as they should use all things, for the glory of God (Col 3:17). The house should, above all, be a home, where children and adults can live together in a healthy and enjoyable family life (1 Tim 3:4,12; 5:14; see FAMILY).

But Christians must not use their houses solely for their own benefit. Their houses should be places where other Christians can enjoy fellowship (Acts 2:46; 16:15,34; 21:8) and perhaps have regular meetings (Rom 16:5; 1 Cor 16:19; Col 4:15). They should use their houses to practise hospitality at all times — not just in entertaining friends, but in providing generous help and friendship to the lonely, the poor and the needy (Isa 58:7; Matt 25:35; Heb 13:2; see HOSPITALITY).

HUMILITY

The words 'humility' and 'humble', which are from the same basic word, have a variety of meanings. In some cases they are associated with ideas of poverty or affliction (1 Sam 2:8; Ps 37:11,14; Isa 29:19; Phil 4:12; James 1:9), in others with ideas of embarrassment or shame (Isa 53:3,8; Acts 8:33; 2 Cor 9:4; 11:7; 12:21; Phil 3:21; James 1:10). Their most common usage, however, is in relation to attitudes of modesty, selflessness, gentleness, grace, meekness and forbearance. Humility in this sense is one of the virtues most pleasing to God. Its opposite, pride, is one of the evils most hateful to him (Num 12:3; Prov 6:16-17; Dan 5:22-23; Micah 6:8; James 4:6; 1 Peter 5:5; see PRIDE).

Jesus Christ is the great example of humility. In an act of total self-denial, the eternal Son of God humbled himself to the extent of taking human form and in the end dying to save sinful man (Phil 2:5-11). He was never boastful and never acted in a way that advanced his own interests. Always he submitted to his Father's will and served his fellow man (Matt 12:19-20; 20:28; John 5:30-32).

Just as Jesus humbled himself in living and dying for sinners, so sinners must humble themselves in repenting of their sins if they are to receive God's forgiveness. God gives the sinner no cause to boast in anything he might achieve. He can do nothing but acknowledge how helpless he is before God and humbly accept God's mercy (2 Chron 7:14; 12:6-7; 34:27; Luke 18:9-14; Rom 3:27; 10:3). Humility characterized Christ's kingship (Matt 21:5), and only through humility can anyone enter his kingdom (Matt 18:1-4).

Christians have a responsibility to develop humility in their lives. It is part of the life to which God has called them (Eph 4:1-2; Col 3:12), it is a characteristic of life in God's kingdom (Matt 20:20-27) and it is the product of the Spirit's work in the life of the individual (Gal 5:23). If they are to learn humility, they must be willing to take the lowest place and serve others (Luke 22:24-27; John 13:3-17). Such humility will help produce genuine fellowship in the church. It will prevent Christians from competing with each other to see who is the greatest among them (Mark 9:33-37; Rom 12:16; 2 Cor 10:12; Gal 6:3; Eph 4:2; Phil 2:3).

Those who look for status and praise may gain what they seek, but their reward will be short-lived (Matt 6:1-5,16). God exalts those who humble themselves, but humbles those who exalt themselves (Prov 3:34; 15:33; 18:12; Isa 2:11; 5:15; Matt 23:12; Luke 1:48-53: James 4:10; 1 Peter 5:6).

HUSBAND

God created man and woman as equal in status and worth, as joint bearers of the image of God (Gen 1:27). God also desired that man and woman live together in harmony, and with this in view he made them as the counterparts of each other. As husband and wife they were partners in a marriage relation where each was equipped to complement the other. Within this equality of status there was a difference of functions (Gen 2:21-25).

The need for regulations

Since the husband was given the role of originator of offspring, he bore the ultimate responsibility for the family (1 Cor 11:3,8-9; see also FAMILY; WIFE). But when sin entered the world, the husband was tempted to misuse his position and treat his wife as if she were his slave rather than his equal (Gen 3:16).

On account of this, the law of Moses introduced regulations that guaranteed the rights of the wife and protected her from exploitation by her husband. If a husband accused his wife of unfaithfulness, his accusation was not accepted without careful examination (Num 5:11-31). If an accusation was found to be false, the husband was punished (Deut 22:13-19). Husbands were in the habit of divorcing their wives for the most insignificant reasons, until Moses introduced a law to protect the wives (Deut 24:1-4; see DIVORCE).

If a man took one of his female slaves and made her a wife or concubine, he had to give her the full rights of a wife. He could not make her a slave again if he later grew tired of her (Exod 21:7-11; see CONCUBINE). When a man wished to marry a woman taken captive in war, he had to give her special consideration and care because of the new way of life she was being introduced to. If later she did not please him, he could not make her a slave again, but had to allow her to go free (Deut 21:10-14).

The Christian way

Teaching given to Christians in the New Testament has helped to restore the rights of the wife so that she might enjoy the equality with her husband that God intended from the beginning (Gal 3:28; 1 Peter 3:7). Both husband and wife have rights, but they also have obligations to each other. One cannot do without the other (1 Cor 7:3-4; 11:11-12; cf. Acts 18:2-3,26).

In their different roles, the wife must accept the husband's ultimate headship, and the husband must sacrifice himself for the sake of the wife. The husband has no authority to force his wife to follow some course of action merely because it pleases him. On the contrary he must treat her with special consideration and give her respect (Eph 5:23-25; Col 3:19; 1 Peter 3:7). The self-sacrificing love that the husband should exercise towards the wife is the same as that which Christ has exercised towards the church (Eph 5:25-31; see also MARRIAGE).

HYMN

See PRAISE; SINGING.

HYPOCRISY

Jesus repeatedly condemned the Jewish religious leaders of his time as hypocrites, because though they were outwardly religious, inwardly they were ungodly (Matt 22:18; 23:25; Mark 7:6-8; 12:15). They had no knowledge of God and his teaching, and could not see their own sin. They thought that their show of religion would impress people and please God, but it brought instead condemnation from Jesus (Matt 6:2-5; 23:13-36; Luke 12:56). While pretending to be sincere, they had evil motives (Luke 20:19-20; cf. 1 Tim 4:2). Their hypocrisy was, in fact, malice (cf. Mark 12:15 with Matt 22:18; see MALICE).

God's people must constantly beware of the dangers of hypocrisy. It shows itself in many ways, as, for example, when people accuse others of what they are guilty of themselves (Matt 7:5; Luke 13:15; Rom 2:1-3,19-24). It shows itself also when people flatter others, or when they change their stated opinions solely to please others (Ps 12:3-4; Gal 2:13). All insincerity, whether in speech or actions, is hypocrisy (1 Peter 2:1). Christians can learn to overcome it through practising genuine love and developing a sensitive conscience (Rom 12:9; 14:13; 1 Tim 1:5).

HYSSOP

It seems that hyssop was some sort of cereal plant that grew in Palestine. When several stalks were tied together it made a good brush, and as such was used

Hyssop plant

to apply blood in some of the Jewish rituals (Exod 12:22; Lev 14:4,6,49-52; Num 19:2-6; Ps 51:7; Heb 9:19). Its strong stalk enabled it to be used to pass a sponge of vinegar up to Jesus as he hung on the cross (John 19:29).

ICONIUM

The town of Iconium was situated in the south of the province of Galatia in Asia Minor. Paul established a church in Iconium on his first missionary journey and revisited the town on several occasions (Acts 14:1,21; 16:6; 18:23). Timothy, who accompanied Paul on some of his journeys, was well known in Iconium and was an eye-witness of some of the persecutions Paul suffered there (Acts 14:1-6; 16:1-2; 2 Tim 3:10-11). (For map and other details see GALATIA.)

IDOL

God's law-code given to Israel expresses in writing the timeless truth that Yahweh alone is God; there is no other. No image of any type should be an object of worship, whether used as a symbol of the true God or as the representative of some other (false) god (Exod 20:4-5; 34:17; Isa 42:8).

Since no man-made image can be a true representation of God, any such image cannot possibly increase a person's appreciation of God (Isa 40:18; 55:8-9). An image dishonours God through hiding his glory, and it misleads man through giving him a wrong idea of God (Deut 4:15-18; Rom 1:21-23).

Idolatry in Israel

Abraham, the father of Israel, came from a land of idol worshippers, but he renounced idols when he came to know the one true God (Josh 24:2,15). Some of Abraham's relatives, however, who did not share Abraham's faith, continued to have private household gods (Gen 31:19).

The penalty that Israelite law laid down for idol worship was death (Exod 22:20; Deut 13:2-5; 17:2-5). Yet the people of Israel repeatedly fell into idolatry through copying the practices of the people around them (Judg 2:12; 10:6; 17:3-6; Jer 44:15-19). Because they did not know what Yahweh looked like, they copied the forms of the gods of other religions (Exod 32:4; Deut 4:12; 1 Kings 12:28; Hosea 13:2). The form of idolatry that Israel most frequently fell into was Baalism (2 Kings 17:15-16; see BAAL). In addition the people sometimes took objects that had played an important part in God's dealings with Israel and wrongfully made them into objects of worship (Judg 8:27; 2 Kings 18:4).

At different times the kings of Judah carried out reforms in which they destroyed all the idols in the land (2 Chron 31:1; 34:4). But idolatrous tendencies were so deeply rooted in the lives of the people that they were never entirely removed. In the end they were the reason why God destroyed the nation and sent the people into captivity (2 Kings 17:7-18; 21:10-15). The period of captivity broke the people's association with the idols of Canaan, and when the Jews later returned from captivity, idolatry ceased to be a major problem (Ezek 36:22-29; 37:23; Hosea 2:16-19).

Idolatry in other nations

God's messengers condemned idolatry not only among Israelites, but also among Gentiles. As people observed the created world they should have recognized that there was a Creator, and responded by offering him thankful worship. Instead they

Assyrian idol

turned away from the Creator and made created things their idols (Rom 1:19-23). God's prophets mocked these lifeless idols and denounced both those who made them and those who worshipped them (Ps 115:4-8; Isa 2:8; 40:18-20; 41:6-7; 44:9-20; 46:1-2,5-7).

The reason for the prophets' condemnation of idols was not simply that idols were lifeless pieces of wood or stone, but that behind the idols there were demonic forces. Idols were enemies of God and were disgusting and hateful in his sight (Deut 7:25; 29:17; 32:16-17; Ezek 36:17-18; 1 Cor 8:4; 10:19-20).

Warnings to Christians

In turning to believe in the true and living God, a person automatically turns away from his idols (1 Thess 1:9). A refusal to turn from his idols shows that he has not really repented (Rev 9:20).

A common tendency among those who worship idols is a feeling that they are free to practise all kinds of sins, since a lifeless idol is unable to punish them (Rom 1:23-32; Eph 4:17-19). The self-satisfaction that comes from performing some act of idol worship produces a moral laziness and a relaxing of control over lustful desires. This is no doubt why the Bible often links idolatry with immorality (1 Cor 5:11; 10:7-8; Gal 5:19-20; Rev 9:20-21; 21:8; 22:15; cf. Num 25:1-2) and because immorality is a form of covetousness, idolatry is linked with covetousness (1 Cor 5:11; Eph 5:3,5). People may give so much attention to what they covet that the coveted thing takes the place of God and so becomes an idol (Col 3:5; see COVET).

Idolatry is linked also with wrong beliefs concerning Christ. Jesus Christ, the Son of God who died for sinful man, is the true God who gives believers eternal life. The substitutes invented by false teachers are false gods, and therefore believers must keep away from them (1 John 5:20-21).

Food offered to idols

In a society where the worship of idols is wide-spread, Christians sometimes face the problem of whether to eat food that others have previously offered to idols. This concerns food eaten in feasts at an idolatrous temple and food eaten in meals at home.

Some Christians may feel free to eat such food, for they know that the idol is only a piece of wood or stone and that it cannot in any way change the food. Others, having once worshipped idols as if they really had life, feel it would be wrong for them to eat such food. They could easily be led into sin through doing what they believe to be wrong. Christians who feel they have the right to eat idol food should therefore limit their personal freedom, so that they do not risk damaging another believer's life (1 Cor 8:1-13; 10:23-24,31-33; cf. Acts 15:20,29; Rom 14:13-23).

Another consideration is that eating together signifies fellowship. In the Lord's Supper, those who eat the bread and drink the wine are united together with Christ, spiritually sharing in him. Similarly, those who join in idol feasts are having fellowship with the idol or, worse still, with the evil spirit behind the idol (1 Cor 10:14-22; cf. Exod 32:4-6; Dan 5:1,4).

When Christians refuse to take part in idol feasts, it is because of this element of fellowship, not because the food itself is changed. When they buy food at the market or eat at the house of pagan friends, they have no need to ask whether the food has been offered to idols. If the food has no obvious idolatrous associations, they should eat it and be thankful to God for it (1 Cor 10:25-27). If, however, someone tells them the food has been offered to idols, they should not eat, because others might misunderstand and, thinking Christians may join in idol worship, fall into sin (1 Cor 10:28-30).

Towards the end of the first century AD, certain false teachers actually encouraged Christians to eat food that they knew had been offered to idols. They claimed this demonstrated the Christian's freedom from rules and regulations, but in practice it led to immorality (Rev 2:14,20). God promises a special reward to those who overcome such temptations (Rev 2:17,26-28).

IMAGE

This article is concerned solely with the subject of man's status as being made in the image of God. Concerning images in the sense of idols see IDOL. Also, the article uses the word 'man' as referring to mankind, not as referring to the male sex as distinct from the female. The image of God is expressed in all human beings alike, regardless of sex or race (Gen 1:27-28: 2:18; see MAN).

A unified being

Man is different from all other animals in that he alone is made in the image of God (Gen 1:26-27). This does not merely mean that certain 'parts' of man, such as his spiritual, moral or intellectual characteristics, reflect the nature of God. The whole man, the whole person, exists in God's image. The eternal God is in some way expressed in man, so that man is God's representative on earth. God has appointed man as the earthly ruler over the created world (Gen 1:27-28).

Certainly, one result of man's creation in God's image is that he has spiritual, moral and intellectual characteristics that make man different from all other creatures. If he were not in God's image, he would not, in the biblical sense, be man. Even if he had the same physical appearance as man, he would still be no more than an animal. An animal's 'animality' is within itself, but a man's humanity is not within himself. It depends for its existence on God.

Dignity and responsibility

In creating man in his image, God has given man a dignity and status that make his relation to God unique among God's creatures (Ps 8:3-8; Matt 10:31; 12:12). At the same time God limits man's independence. Man is not God; he only exists in the image of God. He cannot exist independently of God any more than the image of the moon on the water can exist independently of the moon. He may try to be independent of God, and will bring disaster upon himself as a result, but he cannot destroy the image of God. No matter how sinful he may be, he still exists in God's image (Gen 9:6; 1 Cor 11:7; James 3:9). It is the image of God within him that makes him man.

The story of Adam and Eve shows something of the dignity and responsibility that man has as being in God's image. As God's representative he has authority over the lower orders of creation (Gen 1:28-30; 2:15,19-20). God places him in a world where he can develop his mind and body through making rational choices and exercising creative skills. God wants him to enjoy fully his unique life, but he must do so in fellowship with God and submission to God. He does not have the unlimited right to do as he pleases, to be the sole judge of right and wrong (Gen 2:15-17).

Since God is unlimited and since man exists in God's image, there is a tendency within man to want to be unlimited. Yet the fact of his being in God's image means that he is not unlimited; he has no absolute independence. He falls into sin when he yields to the temptation to rebel against God and set himself up as the one who will decide what is right and what is wrong. He is not satisfied with his unique status as the representative of God; he wants to be God himself (Gen 3:1-7).

The perfect man

In contrast with Adam, Jesus shows what man in God's image should really be. Jesus accepted the limitations of humanity, yet found purpose and fulfilment in life, in spite of the temptations. As God's representative he submitted in complete obedience to his Father, and so demonstrated, as no other person could, what true humanity was (John 8:29; Phil 2:8; Heb 2:14; 4:15).

There was yet a higher sense in which Jesus reflected the image of God, a sense that could be true of no ordinary person. Jesus was not merely *in* the image of God; he *was* the image of God. As well as being human, he was divine. He was the perfect representation of God, because he was God. He had complete authority over creation, because he was the Creator (John 12:45; 14:9; 2 Cor 4:4; Col 1:15-16; Heb 1:3).

By his life, death and resurrection, Jesus undid the evil consequences of Adam's disobedience (Rom 5:12-20). But he has done far more than that. He has become head of a new community. Adam was made in the image of God and passes on that character to the human race that is descended from him. In like manner Christ shares his image with all who by faith are united with him (Rom 8:29). Although this image of Christ is something that

believers in Christ share now, it is also something that they must be continually working towards in their daily lives. It will reach its fullest expression at the return of Jesus Christ (1 Cor 15:49; 2 Cor 3:18; Col 3:10; 1 John 3:2).

While the world is still under the power of sin, man does not enjoy the authority over creation that his status as being in God's image entitles him to. Only at the final triumph of Jesus Christ will man, through Christ, enter his full glory (Heb 2:5-9; Rom 8:19-23). All mankind may exist in the image of God, but the only people who will bear God's image fully are those who by faith become united with Christ. Only Christians will be human as God intended man to be.

IMMANUEL

Meaning 'God with us', the name 'Immanuel' was given at first to a child born in the time of Ahaz, king of Judah (735-716 BC). The birth and naming of the child was a sign of assurance to the king and his people that God was with them to protect them during an enemy attack (Isa 7:10-16; see AHAZ).

The promise given to Ahaz was quoted in the New Testament by Matthew in relation to the birth of Jesus Christ. The virgin Mary also would conceive and give birth to a son named Immanuel, but in this case 'God with us' meant much more. In Jesus Christ, God actually came and lived as a man among the people of man's world (Matt 1:18-23; John 1:14). (For fuller discussion see VIRGIN.)

INCARNATION

The word 'incarnation' is commonly used to denote the truth that God became man in the person of Jesus Christ. The word itself is not found in the Bible, but comes from a Latin word meaning 'in flesh'. In relation to Jesus it means that, in him, God took a bodily form (John 1:14; 1 Tim 3:16). (For details see JESUS CHRIST, sub-heading 'God become man'.)

INCENSE

Incense was a substance produced by grinding and blending certain spices. When burnt it gave off thick white smoke and a strong smell, characteristics that gave incense its ceremonial usefulness.

Part of Israel's religious ritual was to burn incense on the altar inside the tabernacle in a symbolic offering of prayer to God (Exod 30:1; Ps 141:2; Rev 8:3; cf. Mal 1:11). In addition to burning incense at certain ceremonies (e.g. Lev 16:12-13), the priests burnt incense every morning and evening, to symbolize before God the unceasing devotion of his people (Exod 30:7-8; Luke 1:10).

Israel's law allowed only the priests to burn incense (Exod 30:7-9; Num 3:10). This restriction prompted Korah and other Levites to rebel against Moses and Aaron. Moses tested them by telling them to burn incense to see whether God approved. The outcome was that God destroyed them in a fiery judgment (Num 16:1-11,35).

The art of preparing incense was well known in Egypt and Arabia, and the Israelites had apparently learnt such skills from these people. But the formula God gave to Moses was to be used only for the incense of the tabernacle (Exod 30:34-38). One ingredient of the incense, frankincense, was also burnt with the cereal offering, and was placed on the sacred bread that was kept inside the tabernacle (Exod 30:34; Lev 6:15; 24:7). The wise men who visited the baby Jesus presented frankincense as an expression of their homage (Matt 2:11).

Spices used in the making of incense came from the gum of certain trees and from various plants and herbs (Song of Songs 4:14). Some of these were grown locally, but many were imported from the east and were an important source of income for ancient traders (Gen 37:25; Song of Songs 3:6; Isa 60:6; Jer 6:20). (For details of the ointments, medicines, cosmetics and perfumes that were made from spices and vegetable oils see OIL; SPICES.)

INHERITANCE

Israelites of Old Testament times considered an inheritance to be more than merely an amount of property received upon the death of one's parents. The inheritance was tied up with the family's portion of land originally allotted to it in Canaan (1 Kings 21:3-4; Micah 2:2). It was a gift that came from God (Gen 12:7; Deut 4:37-38; 12:10).

The New Testament shows that Christians also have an inheritance. This inheritance is tied up not with material possessions but with the kingdom of God. But like the Old Testament inheritance, it is a gift that comes from God himself (Matt 25:34; James 2:5).

Israel in the Old Testament

When Canaan was divided among Israel's twelve tribes, each tribal area was known as the inheritance of that tribe (Josh 15:20; 16:8; 18:2). Each tribal area was then divided among the families of that tribe, and each family portion was to remain with that family permanently. If a person later sold his portion

of the family land, it returned to the possession of the family in the Year of Jubilee (Lev 25:13-17; see JUBILEE).

The inheritance passed from one generation to the next through the male descendants, though if there were no sons, it could be shared among the daughters. If the daughters later married, they were to marry within their own tribe and so prevent the inheritance from passing to another tribe (Num 27:1-8; 36:1-13).

If there were no descendants at all, the land passed to the nearest living relative (Num 27:9-11). A childless widow could, however, ask the brother of her dead husband to act as a sort of temporary husband to her, so that she might produce a son who would inherit the dead husband's property and carry on his name (Deut 25:5-10; see WIDOW).

Whether concerning land or possessions in general, the eldest son received double the amount of the other sons. This special inheritance was known as the birthright (Gen 49:3; Deut 21:17). The firstborn could lose the birthright either by foolishly selling it or through misconduct (Gen 25:31-34; 1 Chron 5:1-2; see FIRSTBORN).

The Christian's inheritance

The New Testament uses the picture of an heir firstly of Christ, and then of the Christian. Christ is the heir of all things (Heb 1:2), and through him believers also become heirs. The blessings of salvation promised to Abraham were fulfilled in Christ, and believers inherit these blessings through him (Gal 3:14,16,29). Through the grace of God they become sons of God and receive eternal life (Rom 8:17; 1 Peter 3:7).

Although Christians enjoy this inheritance now, they will enjoy it more fully when Christ returns. Their salvation will then be complete. Because of the presence of the Holy Spirit within them, they can look forward to this inheritance with assurance (Eph 1:14,18; Titus 3:7; 1 Peter 1:4; see HOPE). Their expectation of this future inheritance gives them courage and perseverance amid present trials and difficulties (Heb 6:12; 11:13-16,39-40; Rev 21:7; see PERSEVERANCE).

INSPIRATION

According to long-standing Christian usage, the word 'inspiration' refers to that direct activity of God's Spirit upon the writers of the Bible that enabled them to write what God wanted them to write. In the following article the words 'inspiration' and 'inspire' are used only in this special sense. They do not refer to the sort of inspiration that an inspired musician, poet or painter may at times experience.

Although the Bible was written under the inspiration of God, there are many things recorded in the Bible of which God disapproves. The Bible sometimes records the words of people who were wrong in what they said (e.g. the false arguments of Job's friends or the misleading teachings of the Pharisees), for God reveals his truth by correcting what is false as well as by teaching what is right (Rom 15:4; 1 Cor 10:11; 2 Tim 3:16). It was not the speakers of those words who were inspired, but the writers who recorded them. God inspired the writers to record those things that would make his truth plain and expose man's errors.

From God, through man

The Greek word translated 'inspired' means literally 'God-breathed' (2 Tim 3:16). That is, God 'breathed out' his truth through human writers, so the words they wrote were the creation of God and bore his authority. The writers spoke from God. They were completely under the control of his Spirit and carried along by him to achieve his goals (2 Peter 1:19-20).

This does not mean that God used the writers without their personality or understanding playing any part. They were not impersonal instruments whom God used as a typist uses a typewriter. Rather they wrote intelligently out of circumstances that prompted them to write (e.g. Jer 29:1-9; Micah 2:1-3; John 20:30-31; Gal 1:6-9). They may have gathered their material from historical records, religious books, secular documents, conversations and other sources, but the whole work was under the direction of God. The final article was what God intended it to be (Luke 1:1-4).

The writers may not have been aware that their writing was inspired and would one day be part of the Bible. Yet what they wrote was God-directed. It was his message for man, written in man's language, but not corrupted by man's sin. The Bible is not partly divine and partly human; every part of it is divine, yet every part of it is also human. Each book says what God wanted to say, yet says also what its author wanted to say.

Jesus and his followers acknowledged the Old Testament writings as God's Word written by people who were inspired by God's Spirit. They considered the divine and human authorship inseparable (Matt 22:43; Acts 1:16; 4:25). Therefore, they could quote the spoken words of God as being the words of the Old Testament writer who recorded them (cf. Isa 29:13 with Matt 15:7-9; cf. Isa 65:1-2 with Rom 10:20), or they could quote the words of the Old Testament writer himself as being the words of God (cf. Ps 104:4 with Heb 1:7; cf. Ps 95:7-8 with Heb 3:7-8).

Though the Spirit guided the Bible writers in the words they used, the writers wrote according to their own styles and vocabularies. John's style is different from Peter's. Amos's vocabulary is different from Hosea's. With each book of the Bible, God chose the particular person whose nature, training, background and temperament were most suited to his purpose at the time. He used a wisdom teacher such as Solomon to write proverbs for Israel's guidance, and a university-trained person such as Paul to develop and apply Christ's teaching for the benefit of the early church.

There were also many literary forms among the writings of the Bible, but God spoke through them all. Sometimes he used very simple forms such as stories and word-pictures, other times more complex forms that involved strange visions and symbolic figures. Whatever the form, it accurately communicated God's message.

Choosing the right words

In spite of all the differences in the thinking and expression of the Bible writers, the actual words they wrote were those that God intended them to write. Words express thoughts, but they will express those thoughts correctly only if they are the right words. This is seen in some of the New Testament writers' quotations from the Old Testament. They give such close attention to the words used that they may even base an explanation or teaching on a particular word in an Old Testament portion (cf. John 10:34-35 with Ps 82:6; cf. Gal 3:16 with Gen 12:7).

At the same time it must be remembered that words are important only because of the truth they express. Therefore, the New Testament writers may at times quote Old Testament portions without a word-for-word exactness. They express the meaning without following the wording (cf. Rom 11:8 with Deut 29:4 and Isa 29:10; see also QUOTATIONS).

Authority of the Scriptures

Jesus acknowledged the Old Testament as the authoritative Word of God. It was a law that could not be lessened or cancelled (John 10:34-35). He referred to the Scriptures ('It is written . . .'; 'Have you not read . . .') as an absolute authority against which there could be no argument (Matt 4:4,7,10; 21:13,16; 22:29,31; Luke 16:17). He claimed the same absolute authority for his own words, for he was the living Word of God (Matt 24:35; Mark 8:38; John 1:14,18; 6:63; 7:16-17; 12:48-50).

The New Testament writers likewise upheld the absolute authority of the Scriptures (Acts 17:2-3,11; Rom 1:17; 12:19; Gal 3:10,13; 2 Tim 3:15-16; 1 Peter 1:16). To them the Scriptures were the 'oracles of God', the living, authoritative voice of God speaking to man (Rom 3:2; Heb 5:12). What the Scriptures said, God said (cf. Gen 12:3 with Gal 3:8; cf. Exod 9:16 with Rom 9:17). Just as the preaching of the biblical prophets were spoken revelations from God, so the books of the biblical writers were written revelations from God. Of both it was true to say, 'Thus says the Lord' (Amos 1:1-3; 3:8,13; Micah 1:1-2; 3:8; Isa 30:8-9; Acts 11:28; 13:1-2; 1 Cor 14:37; 2 Peter 1:19-21; Rev 1:1-3).

During his earthly life, Jesus promised his apostles that after his return to the Father, the Holy Spirit would come to them to remind them of Jesus' teaching and give them further teaching (John 14:25-26; 16:13-15). They were to pass this teaching on to those who became Christians (Matt 28:19-20). They did this not only through preaching but also through putting Jesus' teachings, and developments from them, into written form. And they claimed for their preaching and their writings the same authority as the Scriptures (1 Cor 2:13; Gal 1:8; 1 Thess 2:13; 4:2,15; 2 Thess 2:15; 3:14; 1 Peter 1:12; 2 Peter 3:2; Rev 22:18-19).

Paul and Peter were the two writers who spoke specifically of the Old Testament writings as being God-given (2 Tim 3:16; 2 Peter 1:21). Yet both of them speak of New Testament writings as having the same authority as the Old Testament.

In 1 Timothy 5:18 Paul quoted as 'Scripture' a statement whose first part came from Deuteronomy 25:4 and whose second part came from Luke 10:7, showing that he considered Luke's Gospel to have equal authority with the Old Testament. Likewise Peter, in 2 Peter 3:15-16, grouped the writings of Paul with 'the other Scriptures', showing that he considered Paul's writings to have equal authority with the Old Testament.

Living and active Word

The early church as a whole readily recognized many of the early Christian writings as Scripture, particularly those that came from the apostles or had the apostles' approval. But above all it was the truth within the books that impressed upon the readers that here indeed was God's Word speaking to them. As a result a new collection of writings began to take shape, known to us as the New Testament (see CANON).

Believers throughout the history of the church have likewise had an awareness that, as they read the Bible, God speaks to them through it (Heb 4:12). The same Spirit who inspired the writers enlightens believers as they read, and they receive the words of the Bible as God's final authority (1 Cor 2:12-15; 1 John 2:26-27; 5:7,10; see INTERPRETATION).

INTERPRETATION

The Bible is no ordinary book. It is the written Word of God, communicating God's purposes to man. But since those purposes are based on God's values, not man's, only those whose minds are instructed by God's Spirit can properly understand them. The Spirit of God is the true interpreter of the Word of God (1 Cor 2:10-12).

The work of the Holy Spirit

Just as the Spirit of God inspired the writing of the Scriptures in the first place (2 Tim 3:15-16; see INSPIRATION), so the Spirit helps Christians to interpret and apply those Scriptures (1 Cor 2:13). As they understand the circumstances in which the Holy Spirit inspired the original writings, the same Spirit can apply the meaning of those writings to them today. If Christians want the Scriptures to have a relevant message for them, their first duty is to find out what the Scriptures mean. God has given the Holy Spirit not to make Bible study unnecessary, but to make it meaningful.

To help Christians towards a clearer understanding of his Word, God has given to his church teachers, people specially equipped by the Spirit for this task (1 Cor 12:8,28; Eph 4:11-14; see TEACHER). Nevertheless, Christians have a duty to test what their teachers preach or write (1 Cor 14:29; 1 Thess 5:21), and if they are to do this satisfactorily they must know how to interpret the Scriptures.

Background and purpose

Because the world of the Bible was different from the world today, readers should learn whatever they can about the geographical and social features of the Bible lands. In particular they must understand the historical setting of the books of the Bible. They will understand the messages of the Old Testament prophets and the New Testament letter-writers only as they understand the circumstances in which the writers wrote. They will need to know who the writers were, when and where they wrote, and what purpose they had in writing (e.g. Micah 1:1; 2:1-3; Hag 1:1-6; 1 Cor 1:1-2,11; 5:1; 7:1; 1 Thess 3:1-6).

Some books clearly announce their subject and purpose (e.g. Nahum; Galatians), but others require readers to work through the material to find its central theme (e.g. Ecclesiastes; Ephesians). They may also have to consider what sources the writer has drawn upon and how he has used them in developing his message (e.g. Luke 1:1-4). As they understand a book's overall purpose, they will have a better understanding of the stories and teachings within the book (John 20:30-31).

Type of literature

Among the many forms within the Bible are prose narratives, poems, wisdom sayings, laws, visions, letters, genealogies and debates. Readers must interpret whatever they are reading according to the type of literature it is. People in Old Testament times recognized the differences between a teacher of the law, a prophet and a wisdom teacher (Jer 18:18) and interpreted their writings accordingly (see LAW; PROPHECY; WISDOM LITERATURE).

Unless people are reading the Bible in the original languages (Hebrew in the Old Testament, Greek in the New), whatever they are reading is a translation (see MANUSCRIPTS; SCRIPTURES). The words and expressions that the original writers used have to be understood in the context of their ancient cultures. Like other languages, the languages of the Bible contain idioms, word pictures and symbolism, and readers will misunderstand the writer if they interpret literally what he meant as a symbol or figure of speech.

In this respect it is particularly important to understand the features of apocalyptic writing (e.g. parts of Ezekiel, Daniel, Zechariah and Revelation) and the characteristics of Hebrew poetry (e.g. Psalms and many of the prophets). (For details see APOCALYPTIC LITERATURE; POETRY.)

Words and their meanings

Although readers must bear in mind such matters as background, purpose and literary form, their main concern is with the words themselves. This does not mean that readers must carry out a word by word study. In any language the unit of meaning will vary, depending on the style of the writer and the type of writing. In some places much may depend on one or two words (e.g. Gal 3:16), but in others one central idea may be built up over several lines (e.g. Ps 118:1-4).

A word's meaning is decided by the way the writer uses it in the sentence, paragraph or book, not by the way it developed out of other words in the long-distant past. A word may have variations of meanings in different contexts (e.g. 'sinner' in Eccles 2:26; Luke 7:39; Gal 2:15), and it is possible that

none of these is directly related to the word's linguistic origins (or etymology). Also, words change their meanings over the years. The meaning of a word in the Old Testament may be different from its meaning in the New, and different again from its meaning today (e.g. see HOLINESS; PROPHET).

Progressive revelation

The writing of the books of the Bible was spread over more than a thousand years, and throughout that time God was progressively revealing his purposes. He made known his purposes for mankind not in one moment at the beginning of history, but stage by stage as he prepared mankind for the fuller revelation that came through Jesus Christ (Heb 1:1-2; 1 Peter 1:10-12). There is therefore a basic unity to the Bible; it is one book. Although readers may understand each of the individual Bible books in its own context, they must also understand each book in the context of the Bible as a whole (see BIBLE).

It is therefore important to understand where each book of the Bible belongs in the developing purposes of God. This is especially so in the case of Old Testament books.

By interpreting a book in relation to its place in God's ongoing revelation, Christians will avoid two extremes. They will not treat the book as if it is merely an ancient document of historical interest, but neither will they try to 'christianize' the book by giving 'spiritual' meanings to its details. The Old Testament exists as Scripture in its own right (2 Tim 3:15-16) and Christians should recognize this. But because of their knowledge of the New Testament, they may see added significance in the Old (cf. Lev 16:1-28 with Heb 9:6-14). (For further details see QUOTATIONS; TYPOLOGY.)

However, the Christians' knowledge of the New Testament does not change the meaning of the Old. The Old Testament revelation might have been imperfect, but only in the sense of being incomplete, not in the sense of being incorrect. It was like the framework of a building still under construction. The fuller revelation in Christ does not correct the Old Testament revelation, but develops it and brings it to fulfilment (Heb 10:1; 1 Peter 1:10-12).

Accepting the Bible's authority

Even when readers allow for variations because of the progressive nature of biblical revelation, they will still meet cases where different statements or ideas appear hard to reconcile (cf. Matt 27:46 with Luke 23:46; cf. John 10:28 with Heb 6:4-6). It is dangerous to 'adjust' the meaning of one or the other to force it into some neatly ordered scheme of theological interpretation that people have worked out. In reading the Bible Christians need patience. In some cases answers to problems may come later, as their understanding of the Bible increases; in others they may not come at all.

Christians must also respect the authority of the Bible. They must allow the Bible to say what it wants to say, regardless of what they would like it to say. They come to the Bible as those who learn, not as those who are going to make it do things for them. Their first duty is not to bring isolated verses together to 'prove' their beliefs, but to accept the revelation in the form God gave it and to submit to its teachings. As they allow it to change their thinking and behaviour, they will have a better knowledge of the will of God and a greater likeness to the character of Christ (John 13:17; Rom 12:2; Col 3:10,16-17).

ISAAC

God promised Abraham and Sarah that, in spite of their old age, they would produce a child through whom God would carry on the process of fulfilling his covenant promises. That child was Isaac (Gen 17:19,21). The promises were that God would make Isaac's descendants into a people for himself, that he would give them Canaan as their homeland, and that through them he would bring blessing to the whole world (Gen 22:15-18).

Isaac and his father

It was entirely contrary to nature that a couple as old as Abraham and Sarah should produce a child, but this proved that it was the work of God (Gen 18:10-14; 21:5). God had made a promise, and Abraham and Sarah had acted on it in faith. Isaac was therefore a 'child of promise'. He was a living illustration that faith is the way to acceptance with God and enjoyment of his promises (Rom 4:17-22; 9:7-9; Gal 4:21-31). (For the contrast to the 'child of promise' see ISHMAEL.)

Abraham's faith was further tested when God told him to sacrifice Isaac (by that time a youth; Gen 22:6), the only person through whom God's promises to him could be fulfilled. Abraham obeyed, believing that God was able to bring Isaac back from death. In a sense Abraham did receive Isaac back from death, when God provided a lamb as a sacrificial substitute for him (Gen 22:1-2,12-13; Heb 11:17-19; James 2:21-23).

In seeking a wife for Isaac, Abraham insisted that she come not from the Canaanites (who were

under God's judgment) but from his own relatives in Paddan-aram. Since Isaac himself was not to leave the land promised to him (Canaan), Abraham sent his most senior servant to find the wife for him (Gen 24:2-6). The woman the servant found was Rebekah. Isaac was forty years old when he married her (Gen 24:58-67; 25:20).

Isaac and his sons

Isaac and Rebekah's faith in the promises of God was tested when they remained childless for twenty years. In answer to their prayers, God gave them twin sons, Esau and Jacob. God declared that his covenant people would come through Jacob, though Esau also would father a nation (Gen 25:21-26).

When a famine hit Canaan, Isaac proved his faith and his obedience by refusing to flee to Egypt (Gen 26:1-5). God rewarded him with increasing prosperity (Gen 26:12-14). Though on one occasion he lied to protect himself (Gen 26:7), he showed great self-control and tolerance when rival herdsmen were hostile to him (Gen 26:14-22).

Esau, the more outgoing of the two sons, was Isaac's favourite. Isaac determined to pass on the divine blessing to Esau, even though God had said it was to go to Jacob (Gen 27:4). But Rebekah and Jacob tricked Isaac into giving the blessing to Jacob (Gen 27:28-29). Later Isaac passed on the blessing of the Abrahamic covenant to Jacob knowingly and willingly (Gen 28:3-4).

Because of the deceit over Isaac's blessing, Esau tried to kill Jacob. Jacob escaped to Paddan-aram (Gen 27:41; 28:1-2,5). When Jacob returned more than twenty years later, there was a reunion between the two brothers (Gen 31:38; 33:4-5). Some time later Isaac died, and his two sons buried him in the family burial ground at Machpelah (Gen 35:27-29; 49:30-31).

ISAIAH

By the time of Isaiah, the Israelite nation had long been divided into two kingdoms — the northern kingdom Israel whose capital was Samaria, and the southern kingdom Judah whose capital was Jerusalem. Isaiah lived in Jerusalem, where he was an adviser to Judah's royal court (Isa 7:3; 37:2; 38:1; 39:3). He was married and had at least two sons (Isa 7:3; 8:3,18).

Isaiah began his work in the year of King Uzziah's death (740 BC) and continued through the reigns of three successive kings, Jotham, Ahaz and Hezekiah (Isa 1:1; 6:1). He was a man of moral uprightness who opposed the social evils of the time

(Isa 1:4,17; 3:9,14-15; 5:8-23). He was also a man of faith who consistently tried to persuade Judah's kings to trust in God rather than in foreign alliances (Isa 7:4-7; 30:15; 37:6-7). In addition he taught and trained a group of devoted disciples, whom he encouraged to maintain a firm faith in God in a time of widespread unbelief (Isa 8:16-17). According to doubtful Jewish tradition he was executed during the reign of the wicked Manasseh by being sawn in two (cf. Heb 11:37).

The book of Isaiah covers a lengthy period of about two hundred years. It deals not only with the reigns of the kings mentioned above, but also with Judah's captivity in Babylon and the restoration to Palestine that followed. Political, religious and social conditions varied greatly from one era to the next within this overall period. The following survey of the book includes background information on the different eras.

Isaiah's call to a sinful people (Chaps. 1-6)

During the long and prosperous reign of Uzziah (or Azariah), severe social and religious problems developed in Judah. Greed and injustice multiplied and, although the people maintained their religious exercises, they were thoroughly ungodly in their attitudes and behaviour. Isaiah's preaching was similar to that of Amos and Hosea, who had met similar problems in the northern kingdom. He defended the poor against exploitation by the rich, and tirelessly denounced Judah's social oppression and religious corruption.

Isaiah opened his book with an accusation by God that Judah had rebelled against him (1:1-9). The nation was religiously and morally corrupt (1:10-31), which was the opposite of what God had intended for it (2:1-22). Such a society was heading for a humiliating judgment (3:1-4:1), though after the judgment a new Israel would be born. The people of God would then consist of those whom God had saved and made holy (4:2-6).

In Isaiah's day, however, Judah had despised God's love, and the nation would surely be taken into captivity (5:1-30). Isaiah would have a difficult task in taking God's message to such a rebellious people, because most would reject the message. But God would preserve the few who remained faithful to him, and from these he would produce a new people for himself (6:1-13).

Judah in the reign of Ahaz (Chaps. 7-12)

At the time Ahaz came to the throne of Judah, the nearby nation of Assyria was growing in power (see AHAZ; ASSYRIA). Understandably, the countries in and around Palestine saw Assyria as a threat to their security.

To strengthen the defence against Assyria, the kings of Syria and Israel tried to persuade Ahaz to join them in a three-part alliance. When Ahaz refused, Syria and Israel joined forces to attack Jerusalem (735 BC), with the aim of setting a king of

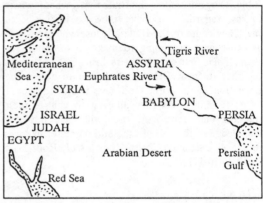

their choice on the Judean throne and so forcing Judah into the alliance. Ahaz was terrified, but Isaiah assured him that if he remained calm and trusted in God, Jerusalem would be delivered. Ahaz decided instead to ask Assyria to come and help him. Isaiah warned that this would lead to disaster, for Judah would then fall under Assyria's power. But Ahaz ignored him (7:1-25; cf. 2 Kings 16:7-8).

The common people likewise rejected the way of faith. God's judgment on Judah, by means of the Assyrians, was therefore certain (8:1-22). Yet out of the darkness to fall upon the nation would come a new leader, the great Messiah-Deliverer, to bring in a new era of light, joy and peace (9:1-7).

Isaiah then described the condition of the neighbouring kingdom Israel, which had become progressively weaker and was finally conquered by Assyria (in 722 BC; 9:8-10:4). But Assyria made the mistake of thinking it could treat God's people as it liked. Therefore, it too would be punished (10:5-34).

Judah meanwhile suffered and eventually would be destroyed, but God would preserve a remnant, the minority who remained faithful to him. From the people taken captive to foreign lands, a remnant would return to their homeland and the Messiah's kingdom would be set up (11:1-12:6).

Messages for various nations (Chaps. 13-23)

Not only Judah and Israel, but all nations were under the rule of God. He controlled their rise to power and their final destruction. Babylon, the first on a list of nations to be addressed by the prophet, had not yet risen to power, but when its day of glory came, it would bring about its own downfall. Its arrogant defiance of God guaranteed its destruction (13:1-14:23).

Assyria, the main threat in Isaiah's day, was also doomed (14:24-32). Moab would fall (15:1-16:14), and so too would Syria and Israel who had combined to attack Judah (17:1-14).

Judah was to make no foreign alliances for the purpose of withstanding Assyria (18:1-7). To rely on Egypt would be useless, because Egypt would be conquered (19:1-25). Alliances would lead only to eventual captivity (20:1-6). Babylonians, Edomites and Arabs would all suffer destruction (21:1-17), but when Jerusalem was besieged, the people had to keep trusting in God (22:1-25). Phoenicia, the great commercial power of the day, would also be judged (23:1-18).

Final judgment and salvation (Chaps. 24-27)

From the judgment of the nations of his time, Isaiah went on to consider God's final judgment of the world. God would make no distinction on the basis of class or status. The faithful alone would be saved, and they would praise him for his gracious salvation (24:1-25:12). The godly, who had suffered because of their loyalty to God, would finally have victory (26:1-21). After a shameful exile there would be a glorious return (27:1-13).

Judah in the reign of Hezekiah (Chaps. 28-39)

When Hezekiah succeeded Ahaz as king of Judah, he immediately set about changing Judah's foreign policy and reforming its religion. He then revolted against Assyria by refusing to pay further taxes (2 Kings 18:7; see HEZEKIAH). In doing so he sought military support from Egypt, an action that Isaiah opposed, just as he had opposed Ahaz's dependence on Assyria. Judah's need was not for foreign military aid but for quiet faith in God.

Bad leadership, both civil and religious, was one reason for Judah's decline and subsequent punishment (28:1-29). By allowing Jerusalem to be besieged and then miraculously saving it (701 BC), God showed that Judah did not need political alliances to guarantee its security (29:1-24). To rely on Egypt was particularly foolish (30:1-31:9).

Beyond the deliverance from the Assyrians, the prophet saw a kingdom of righteousness where Judah would be governed by a king according to the ways of God (32:1-20). The current crisis, out of which God would defeat Assyria and bless Judah (33:1-24), was a foreshadowing of the final great judgment of the world, when God would destroy all enemies (34:1-17) and bless his faithful people (35:1-10).

A historical appendix outlines the events that formed the background to the previous messages. The Assyrians attacked (36:1-22), but God brought about their defeat (37:1-38). Earlier God had preserved Hezekiah's life to enable him to lead Judah through the conflict with Assyria (38:1-22). Hezekiah, however, could not resist the temptation of yet another anti-Assyrian alliance, this time with Babylon. Isaiah saw that it would lead to eventual conquest and captivity in Babylon (39:1-8).

Captivity and return (Chaps. 40-48)

Between the events of Chapter 39 and those of Chapter 40 there is a gap of about 150 years. (Some suggest that Chapters 40-66 were not written by Isaiah, but come from some person or persons of a later generation.) The scene changes from Jerusalem of Hezekiah's day to Babylon in the time of the Jews' captivity.

During the 150 years that are omitted, Babylon had risen to power, conquered Assyria in 612 BC, then from 605 to 587 BC attacked Judah repeatedly, finally destroying Jerusalem and taking the people into captivity (see BABYLON). The events foreseen in Chapters 40-48 began to take place during this time of captivity. Cyrus of Persia was overpowering one nation after another in the region, and in 539 BC he would conquer Babylon and give permission to the Jews to return to their land.

God reassured his people that he was the all-powerful one. Though he had punished them in captivity, he would now lead them back to their land in triumph (40:1-31). He was raising up a deliverer, Cyrus, who would conquer Babylon and release the Jews (41:1-29; see CYRUS). There would be a new Israel, a true servant of God, through whom God would save the repentant of all nations (42:1-25).

All this would be a demonstration of God's power (43:1-28); for, while man-made idols were lifeless, Israel's God was the living, sovereign Lord (44:1-28). It was he who had raised up Cyrus to free the captive Jews (45:1-19). Babylon's gods would be powerless to save when the day of Babylon's destruction came (45:20-46:13). The once proud nation would die in shame (47:1-15). The Jews were to learn from their past mistakes and not fall into idolatry again (48:1-22).

The salvation of God's people (Chaps. 49-55)

Although God had chosen Israel to be his servant, Israel as a whole was a failure. But there were always some who remained faithful, and for their sakes God would restore the nation (49:1-50:3). God's true servant learnt obedience and perseverance through the things he suffered (50:4-11). It might have seemed impossible that mighty Babylon could be overthrown and the nation Israel rebuilt, but God had done the seemingly impossible in the past and he would do so again (51:1-23). The exiles were to prepare to return (52:1-12).

Just as people were startled at the sight of the servant's great suffering, so would they be startled at the sight of his great glory. The sufferer would become a conqueror (52:13-53:12; see SERVANT OF THE LORD). Judah's exile in Babylon was like the divorce of a wife from her husband, but God would now forgive her and take her back (54:1-17). The exiles would find full satisfaction, not by trying to make life comfortable for themselves in Babylon, but by returning to Jerusalem (55:1-13).

Present shame and future glory (Chaps. 56-66)

Looking ahead to the time of the Jews' resettlement around Jerusalem, the prophet saw that the golden age had still not come. With social and religious sins again characterizing Israel's national life, the prophet looked for a new Jerusalem yet to be.

Israel's new national life should have been based on God's law (56:1-8), but religious and civil leaders were as corrupt as those of former days (56:9-57:21). God rejected the worship of those who tried to impress him with their religion while at the same time they oppressed others (58:1-14). If they did not change their ways, God would act in judgment (59:1-21).

Returning to the scene in Babylon and the expectation of return, the prophet pointed out that foreigners would come to join the Jews in rebuilding Jerusalem and worshipping God there (60:1-22). The returned exiles would mourn when they saw the ruined city, but God would compensate them for former plunderings (61:1-62:12) and punish the plunderers (63:1-6).

On behalf of the nation, the prophet confessed its sin and asked God's forgiveness (63:7-64:12). Amid all the corruption there had always been a faithful remnant, and these were God's true people, the people of the Messiah's kingdom (65:1-25). God had always required right attitudes and behaviour (66:1-6), and only a genuinely spiritual life would fit people for the new age (66:7-24).

ISHMAEL

Of several men named Ishmael in the Bible, the best known is the son born to Abraham through his Egyptian slave-girl, Hagar. He was born as a result of Abraham and Sarah's failure of faith, when, feeling that Sarah could not produce the son God had promised them, they arranged for Abraham to produce the son through Hagar (Gen 16:1-3).

In New Testament times, Paul saw this as a picture of those who try to achieve salvation through law-keeping instead of through faith in Jesus Christ. As Ishmael was the child of a slave-girl, so they are the children of slavery. They are in bondage to the law instead of being free people in Christ (Gal 4:21-26).

Concerning Ishmael, God promised that he would grow into a fiery independent desert-dweller, and would produce a notable line of descendants (Gen 16:11-12; 17:20). But he was not the son that God had promised to Abraham as the one through whom he would build his covenant people. God's promises would be fulfilled through Isaac, the son who was later born to Abraham and Sarah (Gen 17:15-19).

When conflict arose between Sarah and Hagar, Hagar and Ishmael were forced to leave Abraham's household and establish their own independent existence (Gen 21:8-21). In New Testament times, Paul saw the expulsion of Hagar and Ishmael as an illustration that slaves of the law have no place in a family (the church) where people have the freedom of sons and through faith inherit God's promises (Gal 4:28-31).

Ishmael grew up to be a tough desert-dweller, as God had foretold (Gen 21:20; cf. 16:12). He married an Egyptian (Gen 21:21), and one of his daughters married Isaac's son, Esau (Gen 28:9). There was a temporary reunion between Isaac and Ishmael at the funeral of their father (Gen 25:7-10).

Many of the tribal peoples who grew up in the region around Canaan were descended from Ishmael (Gen 25:12-18). Even today many of the Arab peoples claim descent from him.

ISRAEL

God promised Abraham that he would make from him a great nation, that he would give that nation the land of Canaan as a homeland, and that through it blessing would come to people worldwide (Gen 12:1-3; 13:14-17; 15:18-21; 22:17-18). The nation became known as Israel, after Abraham's grandson (originally named Jacob) whose twelve sons were the fathers of the twelve tribes of Israel (Gen 32:28; 35:22-26; 49:1,28; 1 Chron 1:34; 2:1-2; see JACOB).

Beginnings of Israel's national life

When circumstances in Egypt were more favourable than in Canaan, Jacob and his family (about seventy people) moved to Egypt to live (18th century BC; Gen 46:26-27). When, after more than four hundred years in Egypt, they had multiplied till they could truly be called a nation, God used Moses to lead them out of Egypt, with the aim of bringing them into Canaan (about 1280 BC; Exod 12:40-41). Three months after leaving Egypt they arrived at Mt Sinai, where they remained for the next year. During that time Moses organized them as a national community, taught them the ways of God and officiated in a covenant ceremony that bound them to God as his people (Exod 19:1-6; 24:3-8; Num 10:11-12; see COVENANT; LAW).

In spite of promising to obey God, the people rebelled against him, with the result that he kept them from entering Canaan for forty years. During those years most of the adult population died, and a new generation eventually entered Canaan under the leadership of Joshua (about 1240 BC; Num 14:32-34; Josh 1:1-5; Heb 3:16-17).

Establishing the nation in Canaan

Israel conquered not only Canaan (i.e. the land between the Jordan River and the Mediterranean Sea) but also the land east of Jordan. This combined area was then divided between the twelve tribes, nine and a half tribes settling in Canaan, the other

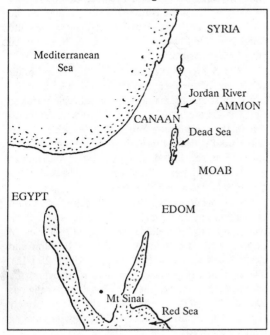

two and a half tribes in the area east of Jordan (Josh 13:7-8). (For the tribal divisions of the land see TRIBES.)

God instructed the Israelites to wipe out the Canaanites and remove all trace of their religion, but they failed to do so. As a result the Canaanite people left in the land were a source of trouble to Israel, and the Canaanite gods were the cause of Israel's falling into idolatry (Judg 2:1-3; see BAAL). When the people of Israel turned away from God, God used enemies to punish them; when they turned back to God and cried to him for mercy, he raised up deliverers (called judges) from among them to overthrow the enemy and lead the people back to himself (Judg 2:11-19).

There was little unity in Israel during this period. Each tribe looked after its own affairs without much concern for the others (Judg 21:25). The one leader who brought some measure of unity to Israel was the godly man Samuel. The people asked that Samuel appoint a king to succeed him, believing this would help give the nation stability. Samuel opposed this, pointing out that devotion to God was the source of national stability. When it became clear that the people would not listen to him, he allowed them to have their king (1050 BC; 1 Sam 8:4-9).

The early Israelite kingdom

Israel's first king, Saul, though a good soldier, was a failure as a national and spiritual leader. He was followed by David, who became probably Israel's greatest king.

David conquered Jerusalem (which till then had been held by the Canaanites), and set about making it the political and religious centre of the nation (1003 BC; 2 Sam 5:1-10). (For the significance of Jerusalem in Israel's history see JERUSALEM.) David expanded Israelite rule to the Euphrates River in the north, over Ammonite and Moabite territory to the east, over Philistine territory to the west, and to the Red Sea and Egypt in the south (2 Sam 8:1-4,11-14).

Solomon, who succeeded his father David as king, devoted himself to developing and beautifying Jerusalem, so that his national capital might be a place of incomparable splendour. But he was a hard ruler. The people hated his forced labour programs and heavy taxation schemes, and as soon as he died they took the opportunity to revolt. Only the king's tribe, Judah, along with neighbouring Benjamin, supported the Davidic king. The remaining tribes broke away, appointing as their king Jeroboam, a leader from the tribe of Ephraim (930 BC; 1 Kings 11:11-13,29-32; 12:20).

From that time on, the nation was divided into two, a northern kingdom and a southern kingdom. The northern kingdom, which consisted of ten tribes, still called itself Israel (though it was sometimes called Ephraim, after its leading tribe). The southern kingdom, which consisted of two tribes, was called Judah. (For details of the southern kingdom and its history see JUDAH, TRIBE AND KINGDOM.)

Northern part of a divided kingdom

Jeroboam made Shechem the capital of the northern kingdom (1 Kings 12:25). (The capital was later moved to Tirzah, and later still to Samaria, where it remained till the end of the kingdom; 1 Kings 15:21,33; 16:23-24.) Jerusalem remained the capital

of the southern kingdom, and kings of the Davidic dynasty continued to rule there (1 Kings 12:17,21; 22:41-42).

Jerusalem was also the location of the temple. Therefore, to prevent northerners from defecting to the south, Jeroboam built shrines at Dan on his northern border and Bethel on his southern border, complete with his own order of priests, sacrifices and festivals. Jeroboam's religious system combined Canaanite and Israelite practices, and led to a moral

and religious decay that would result in God's destruction of the kingdom (1 Kings 12:26-33; 16:19,26; 2 Kings 17:7-18).

Soon Israel was troubled by a type of false religion that was even more serious than that which Jeroboam had introduced. This was the Baalism of Phoenicia that the Israelite king Ahab and his Phoenician wife Jezebel tried to establish as Israel's official religion (1 Kings 16:29-34).

To resist Jezebel's Baalism, God raised up the prophets Elijah and Elisha. They helped to preserve the faithful minority of believers in Israel and so prevent Israel's ancient religion from being lost for ever. Part of Israel's punishment for its acceptance of Jezebel's Baalism was a series of destructive invasions by Syria that lasted many years (1 Kings 19:13-18; 2 Kings 8:12-13; 10:32-33; 13:3-8). (For a map showing Israel's position in relation to the major nations that became involved in its history see BIBLE.)

When the Syrian oppression of Israel was finally removed, Israel enjoyed a time of renewed growth and prosperity, particularly during the reign of Jeroboam II (793-752 BC; 2 Kings 14:23-25). The prosperity, however, resulted in much corruption, injustice, immorality and religious decay, and soon the prophets Amos and Hosea were announcing God's judgment on the sinful nation (Amos 7:8-11). The judgment came when Assyria conquered the northern kingdom and took the people into captivity in Assyria (722 BC; 2 Kings 17:5-6). This marked the end of the northern kingdom. Nineteen Israelite kings had ruled over it, and these had been spread over nine dynasties.

The Assyrians then resettled people from other territories of their empire into parts of the former northern kingdom, mainly the central region around Samaria. These people intermarried with Israelites left in the land, and combined their own religions with Israel's. From these people there developed a race, of mixed blood and mixed religion, known as the Samaritans. True Israelites despised them (2 Kings 17:24-33; see SAMARIA).

Meanwhile the kingdom of Judah to the south struggled to maintain its independence. Eventually it was conquered by Babylon, who, in a series of attacks, took the Judeans captive to Babylon and destroyed Jerusalem (587 BC; 2 Kings 25:1-12). Throughout the years of captivity in Babylon, the southerners retained their national and religious identity. Not so the northerners, who became widely scattered and were absorbed into the peoples among whom they lived.

The rebuilt nation

In 539 BC Persia conquered Babylon and allowed all captive peoples to return to their homelands. Many of the Judeans returned to Palestine and, under the leadership of the governor Zerubbabel and the high priest Joshua, began to rebuild the nation. The reconstructed temple was completed in 516 BC (Ezra 1:1-4; 5:1-2; 6:14-15).

Although back in their land, the people were still under the rule of Persia. They were at least united, for there was no longer a distinction between northerners and southerners. The restored nation could be called either Israel or Judah, because it was the true continuation of the ancient Israel, even though it consisted mainly of Judeans. Israelites therefore became known as Jews, the name 'Jew' being short for 'Judean' (see JEW).

After the early enthusiasm, spiritual life in the new nation soon declined. In an attempt to improve matters, the priest and teacher Ezra came to Jerusalem in 458 BC, with authority from the Persian government to reform the people (Ezra 7:1-10). But his efforts brought little success, and only when Nehemiah joined him thirteen years later was there any great change in Jerusalem. The Persian rulers had appointed Nehemiah governor of Jerusalem, and he and Ezra worked together to bring about wide-sweeping reforms (Neh 2:1-8; 8:1-4,8; 9:1-3).

Over the years that followed, a number of developments arose out of these reforms. They included the construction of buildings for worship and teaching called synagogues, the growth of a class of teachers of the law called scribes, and the establishment of a council to judge Jewish affairs called the Sanhedrin (see SYNAGOGUE; SCRIBES; SANHEDRIN).

The Greek and Roman periods

When the Greek conqueror Alexander the Great spread his power throughout the region (334-331 BC), Israel fell under Greek rule. Alexander's empire soon split into several sectors, Israel at first falling within the Egyptian sector, but later within the Syrian sector (198 BC).

By this time Greek customs and ideas were having some influence on the Jewish way of life, and this created divisions among the Jews. Some opposed this Greek influence and others encouraged it. Here we see the beginnings of the parties of the Pharisees and the Sadducees (see PHARISEES; SADDUCEES).

When fighting broke out in Jerusalem between these two Jewish factions, the Greek ruler in Syria showed his hatred of the Jews by trying to destroy them and their religion. The Jews fought back fiercely, regaining control of their temple in 165 BC, and eventually regaining full political independence in 143 BC. After 460 years under Babylon, Persia, and then Greece, the Jews were free again. (For further details of the events outlined above see GREECE.)

Though free from foreign domination, the Jews continued to fight among themselves. This so weakened the nation that it was unable to withstand the spreading power of Rome (who had succeeded Greece as the leading power of the region). In 63 BC Jewish independence came to an end. The politics of the region continued in confusion till 37 BC, when Herod, a part-Jew, was appointed 'king' over the Jews, though still under the overall control of Rome. Some time after Herod's death, Judea came under direct Roman rule, with Roman governors in charge (AD 6). (For details see HEROD.)

Among the Jews were anti-Roman extremists called Zealots, who were constantly looking for opportunities to fight against Rome. Finally, about AD 66, open rebellion broke out. The result was conquest by Rome and the destruction of Jerusalem in AD 70, thereby bringing Israel's national life to an end. (For details see ROME; ZEALOT.) Not until recent times (AD 1948) did Israel become a nation again.

Spiritual Israel

Although all the physical descendants of Jacob were God's chosen people Israel in the physical and national sense, not all were God's people in the inward and spiritual sense. Only those who turned from their sins and trusted in the saving mercy of God could be called the true Israel, the true people of God. This was so in Old Testament as well as New Testament times (Isa 1:4-20; Rom 2:28-29; 9:6-8; Gal 6:16).

Yet even these, the true people of God, did not experience the full blessings that God intended for his people. God's purposes for Israel found their perfect fulfilment in the Messiah, Jesus (see MESSIAH). The nation Israel was Abraham's natural offspring (John 8:37); the few faithful believers in Israel (often called the remnant) were his spiritual offspring (Rom 9:6-7; Gal 3:29); but the Messiah himself was the perfect offspring, the one in whom all God's purposes for Israel were fulfilled and through whom people of all nations are blessed (Gal 3:16; cf. Gen 12:1-3).

When people through faith are 'in Christ', they become Abraham's offspring through Christ and inherit God's promises through Christ. This is so regardless of their nationality (Gal 3:14,29; Eph 3:6). The true people of God includes all who have faith in him, not just those who belong to Israel. Like Abraham they are saved by faith, and therefore are spiritually his true descendants (Rom 4:11-12,16; Gal 3:26-29; 4:26-28; 6:16; 1 Peter 1:1; 2:9).

ISSACHAR

Nothing is known of the man Issachar apart from the fact that he was the fifth son that Leah bore to Jacob (Gen 30:17-18). The tribe descended from him inherited land that covered the important Plain of Esdraelon and Valley of Jezreel in northern Israel (see PALESTINE; JEZREEL). This territory lay between Mt Tabor to the north and Mt Gilboa to the south (Josh 19:17-23).

Important trade routes ran through Issachar's territory, connecting inland and coastal towns. The commercial activity that resulted, along with the good farming country of the area, brought much prosperity to Issachar. But its desire for prosperity meant that, except for one notable victory, it had to submit to the Canaanite people. Being equipped with an army of chariots, the Canaanites were well able to control the relatively flat country (Gen 49:14-15; Deut 33:18-19; Judg 4:12-15; 5:15). At least two national leaders of Israel came from Issachar (Judg 10:1; 1 Kings 15:27).

ITHAMAR

When Aaron and his four sons established Israel's priestly order, Aaron became the high priest and his sons were the priests who assisted him. Ithamar was the youngest of the four sons (Exod 28:1-4).

After the death of the two older sons, Eleazar and Ithamar received additional responsibilities. Eleazar, the senior of the two, had overall control of the Levites (Num 3:32), but Ithamar had specific responsibility for two of the three family divisions within the Levites (Num 4:28,33). He had earlier supervised the building of the tabernacle (Exod 38:21), and now he was the chief overseer of its maintenance (Num 4:24-33).

ITUREA

The region of Iturea lay between the Sea of Galilee and Damascus, and in early New Testament times was governed by Herod Philip, a son of Herod the Great (Luke 3:1; see HEROD). It was on the edge of the tableland region formerly called Bashan (Num 21:33; Ps 22:12; see BASHAN).

JABBOK

To the east of the Jordan River was a high tableland region divided into two by the Jabbok River. Before Joshua's conquest of Canaan, the area north of the Jabbok was controlled by the Amorite king Og. The area south of the Jabbok was controlled by another Amorite king, Sihon, who had taken the territory from the nations of Ammon and Moab. Israel conquered both kings, and the territory became the homeland of the two and a half tribes of Israel that settled east of Jordan (Num 21:21-26,31-35; 32:33). The town of Penuel, on the Jabbok River close to its junction with the Jordan, became a strategically important defence outpost (Judg 8:9,17; 1 Kings 12:25; see PENUEL).

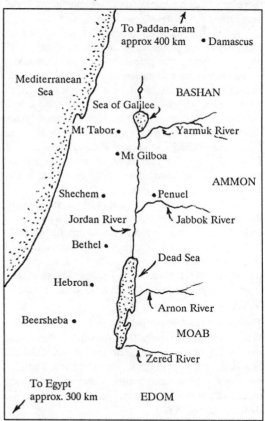

JACOB

Events relating to a child's birth often influenced parents in their choice of a name for the child. Isaac and Rebekah gave the second of their twin sons the name Jacob (meaning 'to hold the heel') because at the birth the baby Jacob's hand took hold of the heel of the first twin, Esau (Gen 25:24-26). When the two boys grew to adulthood, Jacob proved to be true to his name when he again took hold of what belonged to his brother, by cunningly taking from him the family birthright and the father's blessing (Gen 27:36).

From the beginning God made it clear that he had chosen Jacob, not Esau, as the one through whom he would fulfil his promises to Abraham. But that was no excuse for Jacob's trickery (Gen 25:23; Mal 1:2; Rom 9:10-13).

The line of descent from Abraham through Isaac and Jacob was the line God used to produce the nation that became his channel of blessing to the whole world (Gen 28:13-14). To the generations that followed, God was known as the God of Abraham, Isaac and Jacob (Gen 50:24; Exod 3:6; Deut 1:8; Matt 22:32; Acts 3:13). The nation descended from Jacob was commonly called Israel (after Jacob's alternative name; Gen 32:28), though in poetical writings it was sometimes called Jacob (Num 23:21; Isa 2:5; 43:28; Mal 3:6; Rom 11:26).

Building for the future

Jacob was a selfishly ambitious young man who was determined to become powerful and prosperous. By ruthless bargaining he took from Esau the right of the firstborn to become family head and receive a double portion of the inheritance (Gen 25:27-34; see FIRSTBORN). Later, by lies and deceit, he gained his father's blessing This confirmed the benefits of the birthright, in relation to both the family and the nation that was to grow out of it (Gen 27:1-29; see BLESSING). (Concerning the lesser blessings given to the elder brother see ESAU.)

To escape his brother's anger, Jacob fled north. His excuse was that he was going to Paddan-aram to look for a wife among his parent's relatives (Gen 27:41-28:5). Before Jacob left Canaan, God graciously confirmed the promise given to Abraham, and assured Jacob that one day he would return to Canaan (Gen 28:10-22).

It was twenty years before Jacob returned. In Paddan-aram he fell in love with Rachel, younger daughter of his uncle Laban, and agreed to work seven years for Laban as the bride-price for Rachel. Laban tricked Jacob by giving him Leah, the elder daughter, instead. He then agreed to give Rachel as well, but only after Jacob agreed to work another seven years as the extra bride-price (Gen 29:1-30).

Upon completion of the second seven years, Jacob decided to work an additional six years. His purpose was to build up his personal flocks of sheep and goats, which he considered to be compensation for Laban's repeated trickery. There was a constant battle, as two cunning dealers tried to outdo each other (Gen 30:25-43; 31:41).

During these twenty years Jacob also built a large family. Leah produced several sons, but Rachel remained childless. Rachel therefore gave her maid to Jacob, so that through the maid he might produce sons whom Rachel could adopt as her own. Not to be outdone, Leah did the same. Finally Rachel produced a son, Joseph, and he became Jacob's favourite (Gen 29:31-30:24). When at last Jacob and his family fled from Laban, Laban pursued them. In the end Jacob and Laban marked out a boundary between them and made a formal agreement not to attack each other again (Gen 31:1-55).

A changed man

As he headed for Canaan, Jacob knew that if he was to live in safety he would have to put things right with Esau. Esau by this time had established a powerful clan (Edom) in neighbouring regions to the south-east. Jacob was beginning to learn humility such as he had not known before and cried to God for help (Gen 32:1-12).

God taught Jacob, through a conflict he had one night with a special messenger from God, that his proud self-confidence had to be broken if he was really to receive God's blessing. The crisis in Jacob's life was marked by God's gift to him of a new name, Israel, 'an overcomer with God' (Gen 32:13-32). Jacob began to change. He humbled himself before Esau and begged his forgiveness, with the result that instead of further tension and conflict between the two brothers there was friendship and co-operation (Gen 33:1-17).

Jacob then crossed the Jordan into Canaan, where he demonstrated his faith in God's promises by buying a piece of land. He at least now had permanent possession of part of the land God had promised to him and his descendants (Gen 33:18-20). At Bethel God renewed his promises (Gen 35:1-15; cf. 28:13-22). As if to emphasize that this occupancy of Canaan was by God's grace alone, the writer of Genesis includes two shameful stories that show the unworthiness of Jacob's family to receive God's blessings (Gen 34:1-31; 38:1-30). The only son of Jacob to be born in Canaan was the youngest, Benjamin (Gen 35:16-26).

The family moved south to Hebron to be with the aged Isaac in his last few years (Gen 35:27-28). It seems that Jacob remained there while his sons took his flocks from place to place looking for pastures (Gen 37:14-17). Out of these circumstances came the dramatic sequence of events recorded in the long story of Joseph (see JOSEPH). The outcome of that story was that Jacob and all his family moved south through Beersheba and settled in Egypt (Gen 46:1-7,26).

Jacob lived in Egypt seventeen years (Gen 47:28). Before he died, he raised Joseph's two sons, Ephraim and Manasseh, to the same status as his own sons (Gen 48:1-6). This was because he had given Joseph the birthright that the eldest son had lost (1 Chron 5:1-2; cf. Gen 35:22). Now Joseph, through his two sons, would receive twice the inheritance of the other sons (Gen 48:14-16; 49:26). Jacob then announced his blessing on all his sons in turn (Gen 49:1-27; Heb 11:21). By insisting that his sons bury him in Canaan, he expressed his faith that Canaan would become the land of his descendants (Gen 47:29-31; 49:28-33; cf. 46:4). His sons carried out his wish (Gen 50:12-13).

JAMES THE APOSTLE

Two of the apostles had the name James. The lesser known was James the son of Alphaeus (Matt 10:3). It is possible that he is the same person elsewhere called 'James the less' or 'James the younger', names no doubt given to distinguish him from the better known James. If this is so, his father must have had two names, Alphaeus and Clopas (Matt 27:56; Mark 15:40; John 19:25).

The other apostle named James was the elder brother of the apostle John (Matt 10:2). In the Gospels, he is never mentioned by himself, but always together with his more famous brother. (Concerning the family background and personal experiences shared by the two brothers see JOHN THE APOSTLE.) Jesus had warned James and John that, as his followers, they could expect the sort of persecution he suffered. For James this came true a few years later when Herod Agrippa beheaded him (Matt 20:20-23; Acts 12:1-2).

JAMES THE BROTHER OF JESUS

Since the brothers and sisters of Jesus are usually mentioned in association with Mary the mother of Jesus, it is natural to assume that she was their mother (Matt 12:46; 13:55-56; John 2:12). If that is the case, it means that after the birth of Jesus, Joseph and Mary began to have normal sexual relations (Matt 1:25). The mention of James' name first in the list of Jesus' brothers and sisters indicates that he was next oldest in the family after Jesus.

From unbelief to church leadership

During Jesus' earthly life his brothers did not believe that he was the Messiah. They were religiously conservative, and they regarded Jesus' unorthodox teaching and lifestyle as an indication that he was suffering from some sort of religious madness (Mark 3:20-21,31; John 7:3-5). But by the time of Jesus' ascension they had become believers (Acts 1:14). This suggests that whatever happened at Jesus' special appearance to James after the resurrection, it helped turn James, and the other brothers, from unbelief to faith (1 Cor 15:7).

James soon became one of the chief men in the Jerusalem church. When Paul went to Jerusalem for the first time after his conversion, the two leaders he met were James and Peter (Acts 9:26-27; Gal 1:18-19).

Some years later, when Paul, Barnabas and Titus visited Jerusalem to deliver a gift from the Antioch church, the leaders they met were James, Peter and John (Acts 11:30; Gal 2:1,9). On that occasion James and his fellow leaders expressed their support for Paul's mission to the Gentiles (Gal 2:7-9). James again appears as a prominent leader of the Jerusalem church in the story of Peter's escape from prison (Acts 12:17).

Following Paul's first missionary journey, a group of Jews from the Jerusalem church came to Antioch teaching that Gentile converts had to be circumcised and keep the law of Moses (Acts 15:1,5). They claimed that James had sent them (Gal 2:12), but when church leaders later discussed the matter at a special meeting in Jerusalem, James denied this (Acts 15:24).

James, in fact, took the leading part on behalf of the Jerusalem church in confirming that Gentiles were saved by faith alone. In this he confirmed the truth of the message Paul preached. He asserted, moreover, that Gentile converts were not to be forced to obey Moses' law. But it would be helpful, he suggested, if Gentile Christians respected their Jewish brothers by not engaging in practices that Jews considered repulsive (Acts 15:13,19-21).

The people of Jerusalem in general developed a great respect for James, and he became popularly known as James the Just. The character of his life and teaching can be seen in the New Testament letter that bears his name (James 1:1; see JAMES, LETTER OF).

Opposition from fellow Jews

In spite of James' efforts, many in the Jerusalem church still refused to accept Gentile Christians as equals unless the Gentiles kept the law of Moses. When, many years later, Paul came to Jerusalem with an offering from the Gentile churches, he first met with James and the other elders (Acts 21:17-18).

He soon learnt from them that many in Jerusalem were hostile to him because of his refusal to force the law of Moses upon his converts. They therefore suggested that Paul demonstrate his respect for the Jewish law by joining in a temple ceremony. Although their suggestion was intended to help Paul, it resulted in his imprisonment (Acts 21:20-24).

The anti-Christian feeling in Jerusalem, far from diminishing, increased. History records that a few years later, in the early AD 60s, James himself was murdered by the Jews.

JAMES, LETTER OF

The author of the letter of James was most likely James the brother of Jesus. He was a leading man in the Jerusalem church and was highly respected by the Jews. (For further details of the author see JAMES THE BROTHER OF JESUS.)

Background to the letter

It seems that the letter of James was one of the earliest New Testament letters. It was written to Jewish Christians who had long been accustomed to the public worship of God in the synagogue, and who took their moral standards from the law of Moses.

These things were in some ways a help to Jewish Christians, but in other ways they were a hindrance. Some of the Christians held firmly to the law they had always followed, but they became so coldly legalistic that their Christianity lacked life and enthusiasm. Others erred in the opposite direction. They reacted against the restrictions they had once experienced under the law, and joined so freely in the common practices of the society around them that their behaviour became unchristian.

James dealt with these problems by giving instruction on the nature of Christian faith. Faith is more than intellectual belief, and more than obedience to a set of rules. It is something that is living and active, and it expresses itself in right behaviour. It does not give a person freedom to do as he likes, but leads a person to have a greater love for God and a greater love for his fellows. It enables the Christian, whether he be Jew or Gentile, to live positively and joyfully for God in an ungodly society, without accepting the ungodly standards of that society.

Contents of the letter

James realizes that Christians face many trials and testings in life, so he begins his letter by encouraging them to meet their trials and testings in the right attitude. If they do, they will grow in their Christian lives (1:1-18). This growth depends upon their being obedient to God's Word (1:19-27).

Low standards of behaviour may be acceptable in society at large, but Christians must not allow such standards to influence their behaviour. They must not, for example, favour the wealthy or ignore the poor, but love all people regardless of class, as God does (2:1-13). If they say they have faith, they must give proof of it by the way they live (2:14-26). They are to control their tongues (3:1-12) and are not to be guilty of unspiritual or selfish behaviour (3:13-18).

The attitude that produces such unchristian behaviour is what James calls worldliness (4:1-12). It causes Christians to live like the ordinary people of the world, whose chief concern is for their own advancement regardless of God's will and God's values (4:13-5:6). Christians should learn to be patient. They should put other people's interests before their own and prayerfully trust in God at all times (5:7-20).

JEALOUSY

There are two aspects of jealousy in the Bible, one bad, the other good. Jealousy in the bad sense is envy — the feeling of resentment or hate that a person has towards one who has more influence, power, ability, status, fame or possessions than he (Gen 30:1; 37:11; 1 Sam 18:8-9; Job 5:2; Ps 106:16; Matt 27:18; Acts 5:17; 1 John 3:12). Such jealousy is a characteristic of sinful human nature, but the Spirit of Christ and the power of love in a person's life can overcome it (Prov 27:4; Rom 13:13-14; 1 Cor 13:4; Gal 5:21; James 3:14-16).

Jealousy in the good sense is the desire a person has for the well-being of someone he or she loves. It is a desire so strong that it demands faithfulness and opposes all that would tempt to unfaithfulness (Num 5:12-15; Prov 6:32-35). This is what the Bible means when it speaks of God being jealous for his people. He desires their faithfulness and has a deep concern for their well-being (Exod 20:4-5; Deut 6:15; Josh 24:19; Ps 78:58; Zech 1:14; 1 Cor 10:21-22; James 4:5).

Likewise the godly leader who is concerned for the spiritual progress of God's people may speak of himself as being jealous for them (2 Cor 11:2). In the same way the person who is concerned to uphold the honour of God's name is jealous for God (1 Kings 19:10; Ezek 39:25). Jealousy may therefore include the idea of zeal for all that is right and opposition to all that is wrong (Num 25:11-13; Deut 4:24; Nahum 1:2; John 2:17; 2 Cor 7:11).

JEBUSITES

The Jebusites were descended from Canaan, the grandson of Noah, and were one of the native peoples of the land of Canaan. They lived in the central highlands, where their chief centre was Jerusalem, earlier known as Jebus (Gen 10:15-16; 15:18-21; Exod 3:8; Num 13:29; Josh 11:3; 15:63; 18:28). Jerusalem's position on a well fortified hill made the city extremely difficult to conquer (see JERUSALEM). Although Jerusalem fell at first to Joshua's conquering Israelites, the Jebusites soon retook it, and they kept control of it till the time of David (Judg 1:8,21; 19:10-11).

Jerusalem was so difficult to capture that the Jebusites confidently claimed that even the blind and crippled could beat off an attack. But David's men gained entrance through a tunnel used to carry water from a spring outside the city walls. They then launched a surprise attack and took the city (2 Sam 5:6-10).

In the years that followed, the Jebusites became absorbed into the Israelite population of Jerusalem. Eventually they disappeared as a distinct race.

JEHOAHAZ

Three kings in Israel and Judah had the name Jehoahaz. The first was the Judean king Ahaziah, for whom Jehoahaz was an alternative name. He reigned for only one year (842 BC; 2 Chron 21:16-17; 22:1; see AHAZIAH). The second was the son of Jehu who succeeded his father as king of Israel. He came to the throne in 814 BC and reigned for seventeen years. He was a worthless ruler, during whose reign attacks from Syria brought Israel almost to total collapse. If God had not mercifully intervened, the people would have been left homeless and the entire army destroyed (2 Kings 13:1-9).

The third king named Jehoahaz was a son of Josiah. He had a brief three-month reign over Judah (609 BC) in the kingdom's closing years. Pharaoh Necho, having just defeated and killed Josiah, considered himself the overlord of Judah and would not accept Jehoahaz as king. Necho threw Jehoahaz into prison and later took him to Egypt, where he eventually died (2 Kings 23:29-34). He was also known as Shallum (Jer 22:11-12).

JEHOASH

Many people in Bible times had the name Jehoash, or Joash in its shorter form (e.g. Judg 6:29-31; 1 Chron 4:22; 7:8; 12:3; 27:28; 2 Chron 18:25). The most important of them all were the two kings who

ruled during the time of the divided kingdom, one over Judah and the other over Israel.

To avoid confusion, Jehoash of Judah is often referred to as Joash. When his father Ahaziah was killed, the mother of Ahaziah killed Ahaziah's children and seized the throne of Judah. This woman, Athaliah, the daughter of Ahab and Jezebel, then established her parents' Baalism in Judah. The only child to escape her massacre was the year-old Joash, who was rescued by his aunt (wife of the high priest) and brought up secretly in the temple. After six years the high priest led a successful revolution that saw Athaliah killed, Baalism removed, and the child Joash placed on the Davidic throne (835 BC; 2 Kings 11:1-21).

The most influential person in Judah at that time was Jehoiada the high priest, who trained and instructed Joash. Because of Jehoiada's influence, Joash matured into a good king (2 Kings 12:2; 2 Chron 24:2-3). When he found inefficiency, and possibly dishonesty, among those responsible for repairing the temple, Joash acted decisively to have the work completed promptly (2 Kings 12:4-16; 2 Chron 24:4-14).

After Jehoiada's death, Joash and his people drifted into idolatry and even killed a priest who rebuked them (2 Chron 24:15-22). God's judgment fell upon Judah in the form of a costly invasion by Syria. Joash was assassinated by his own soldiers and was not even given a royal funeral (2 Kings 12:17-21; 2 Chron 24:23-27).

Jehoash of Israel came to the throne at a time when Syria was crushing his country (798 BC; 2 Kings 13:7-9). Though unfaithful to God, he respected God's prophet Elisha (2 Kings 13:11,14). In three battles against Syria he regained much of Israel's lost territory, and only lack of faith stopped him from regaining a lot more (2 Kings 13:15-19,25). He was chiefly remembered for a battle with Judah that he tried to avoid. In a stunning victory he plundered Jerusalem and taught the arrogant Judean king a timely lesson (2 Kings 13:12; 14:8-14).

JEHOIACHIN

At the time of Babylon's attack on Jerusalem in 597 BC, the Judean king Jehoiakim died and was succeeded by his eighteen year old son Jehoiachin (also known as Jeconiah, or Coniah). After three months resistance, Jehoiachin surrendered (2 Kings 24:6,8,12). The Babylonians then plundered Judah's treasures and took Jehoiachin captive to Babylon, along with the royal family, palace officials and most of Judah's best people (2 Kings 24:8-16; Esther 2:6;

Jer 22:24-30; 24:1; 27:20; 29:2). One of the captives was Ezekiel (Ezek 1:1-2).

In 561 BC a new Babylonian king released Jehoiachin from prison and treated him with special favour. To the captive Jews this was a sign of hope that one day they would all be released (2 Kings 25:27-30). When, after Persia's conquest of Babylon in 539 BC, the Jews were released and returned to Jerusalem, a grandson of Jehoiachin, Zerubbabel, became their governor (1 Chron 3:17; Ezra 3:2; Hag 1:1; Matt 1:12).

JEHOIADA

The Bible mentions a number of people named Jehoiada. The only one concerning whom it speaks in any detail is the chief priest in Jerusalem who was the main influence for good in the life of the Judean king Jehoash (or Joash) (2 Chron 22:10-24:25; for details see JEHOASH).

JEHOIAKIM

Undoubtedly Jehoiakim was one of Judah's worst kings. When his father Josiah was killed in battle with Pharaoh Necho (609 BC), the people of Judah made one of Josiah's younger sons king rather than the older Jehoiakim (2 Chron 35:20-25; 36:1-2). Pharaoh Necho, considering himself the master of Judah, replaced the people's choice with his own. His choice was Jehoiakim (also known as Eliakim) (2 Chron 36:3-5).

In order to raise the large amount of money that Pharaoh Necho demanded each year from Judah, Jehoiakim taxed his people heavily (2 Kings 23:35). At the same time he built himself luxurious royal buildings, forcing people to work in his selfish projects without payment (Jer 22:13-19).

Conflict with Jeremiah

The chief opponent of Jehoiakim was the prophet Jeremiah, who had begun his preaching earlier, in the reign of Josiah (Jer 1:1-3). At the beginning of Jehoiakim's reign, Jeremiah announced God's judgment on the sinful kingdom (Jer 26:1-6). This brought opposition from the palace (Jer 26:10-11), but Jeremiah escaped unharmed. Another prophet, however, did not. Jehoiakim was angry at his preaching and executed him (Jer 26:20-24).

Jeremiah warned that because of the idolatry of the king and his people, God would send the Babylonians against Jerusalem in judgment (Jer 25:1-9). This judgment began in 605 BC, the year in which Babylon conquered Egypt at Carchemish and so replaced it as Judah's overlord. In returning to Babylon, the conquerors took with them selected captives from the leading families of Jerusalem (2 Kings 24:7; Jer 46:2; Dan 1:1-4).

At God's direction, Jeremiah wrote down all the prophecies of the previous twenty-three years. After his secretary Baruch read them in the temple, the city leaders became so disturbed that they read them to Jehoiakim. The king defiantly burnt the scroll, and tried unsuccessfully to arrest Jeremiah and Baruch (Jer 36:1-26). Jeremiah then rewrote the scroll, with additions, and gave some encouragement to the frightened Baruch (Jer 36:27-32; 45:1-5).

Conflict with Babylon

After submitting to Babylon's overlordship for three years, Jehoiakim rebelled by refusing to pay further tribute (2 Kings 24:1). In depending upon foreign nations to support his rebellion, he met further opposition from Jeremiah (Jer 2:18,36). Babylon did not attack Jerusalem immediately, but encouraged other countries within its empire to raid Judah and so gradually weaken it (2 Kings 24:2-4).

In due course Babylon attacked Jerusalem (597 BC). Jehoiakim was taken captive and chained ready to be sent to Babylon, but he died before the journey began. No one mourned his death, and his body was thrown on the garbage dump outside Jerusalem, as if it were the carcass of an unclean animal (2 Chron 36:6; Jer 22:18-19; 36:30).

JEHORAM

Judah and Israel each had a king named Jehoram (often shortened to Joram). Judah's Jehoram was the son of the good king Jehoshaphat (1 Kings 22:50). However, he himself was wicked. He married Athaliah, daughter of the Israelite king Ahab and his Baalist wife Jezebel, and introduced the Baalism of Jezebel into Judah (2 Kings 8:16-18; 2 Chron 21:4-6). To make sure no one stopped him doing as he pleased, he killed all likely rivals. Because of his wickedness, Elijah assured him of a horrible death (2 Chron 21:11-15). During his reign Edom and Philistia broke free from Judah's rule (2 Chron 21:8), and Arab raiders plundered Judah with great success (2 Chron 21:16-17). In one attack they killed most of the royal family (2 Chron 22:1). Jehoram died a horrible death as predicted, and no one regretted his departure (2 Chron 21:18-20).

Israel's Jehoram (often called Joram, to avoid confusion) was brother-in-law to Judah's Jehoram. He was the second son of Ahab and Jezebel, and became king when his older brother Ahaziah died as a result of an accident (1 Kings 22:51; 2 Kings

1:2,17; 3:1). Though not as devoted to Baal as his parents, he remained in conflict with Elisha, the prophet who led God's opposition to Baal (2 Kings 3:1-3,13; 6:30-31). When wounded in battle with Syria, Joram returned to his summer palace in Jezreel to recover. There he was assassinated by his army commander Jehu, who then seized the throne and began a violent anti-Baal purge (2 Kings 8:28-29; 9:14-26).

JEHOSHAPHAT

Five people named Jehoshaphat are mentioned in the Bible (2 Sam 8:16; 1 Kings 4:17; 15:24; 2 Kings 9:2; 1 Chron 15:24). Of these the most important was the king of Judah who reigned in Jerusalem from 870 to 845 BC (1 Kings 22:42). He is noted for his reformation of Judah after the political and religious disorders that had developed towards the end of the previous king's reign.

Jehoshaphat began his reforms by destroying the Baal shrines and removing the cult prostitutes (1 Kings 22:46; 2 Chron 17:6). He then taught the people God's law by sending a teaching team of priests, Levites and civil administrators on a circuit of Judah's towns and villages (2 Chron 17:7-9). He was able to give his full attention to these programs because he had first of all strengthened Judah against any interference from hostile neighbours (2 Chron 17:2).

In an effort to remove injustice, Jehoshaphat reorganized Judah's judicial system. His desire was that all citizens receive fair treatment, regardless of their status. He set up courts and appointed judges in all the chief cities of Judah, with the chief court in Jerusalem. Some courts dealt specifically with religious matters, and these were under the control of the high priest. Others dealt solely with civil matters, and these were under the control of the chief governor (2 Chron 19:4-11).

Under Jehoshaphat, Judah's defences were greatly strengthened (2 Chron 17:2,10-13). King Ahab of Israel was so impressed that he persuaded Jehoshaphat to join him in a battle against Syria (1 Kings 22:1-4). Jehoshaphat, however, did not trust Ahab's court prophets, who seemed more concerned with pleasing Ahab than with telling him God's will. Only the prophet Micaiah told the truth (namely, that Israel would be defeated), but Ahab ignored his advice, went to war and was killed (1 Kings 22:5-36). A prophet rebuked Jehoshaphat for cooperating with the Israelite king, who was morally corrupt, a worshipper of Baal and an enemy of God (2 Chron 19:1-3).

Later, Jehoshaphat joined with Ahab's equally corrupt son in a commercial partnership involving a fleet of ships. By wrecking the ships, God showed Jehoshaphat once more that he was not to cooperate with the Baal-worshipping kings of Israel (2 Chron 20:35-37). Jehoshaphat had now learnt his lesson (1 Kings 22:49).

Jehoshaphat proved that faith in God, not cooperation with Israel, was the way to success when he won a great victory over a huge enemy invasion force. He called the people to the temple to pray (2 Chron 20:1-6,13) and in reply received God's assurance of victory (2 Chron 20:14-17). God then intervened to overthrow the enemy. Jehoshaphat's people plundered the defeated army and returned in triumph to Jerusalem to praise God for hearing their prayers (2 Chron 20:18-30).

JEHOVAH

See YAHWEH.

JEHU

After Jezebel of Phoenicia had married King Ahab of Israel, she set about establishing her Phoenician Baalism as Israel's official religion. God foretold through the prophet Elijah that Jehu would be his instrument to wipe out their dynasty and their Baalism (1 Kings 19:15-18; see BAAL).

Some years later, when Ahab's son had become king and Jehu had risen in rank to become Israel's army commander, a prophet anointed Jehu and declared him the new king (2 Kings 9:1-10). At that time Syria was attacking Israel, and Jehu was commanding Israel's army on its eastern border at Ramoth-gilead. However, he did not hesitate to leave the battle and head west for Jezreel, where the Israelite king Jehoram (or Joram) was recovering from wounds received in battle (2 Kings 8:28-29; 9:1-2,14,16).

Joram's mother Jezebel was with him at Jezreel; so was Judah's king Ahaziah, who was a grandson of Ahab and Jezebel and a nephew of Joram. Swiftly and mercilessly Jehu killed them all (2 Kings 9:17-37). He ordered the execution of seventy other descendants of Ahab, and displayed their heads as a warning that the wrath of God would fall on any who opposed him (2 Kings 10:1-11). He also killed some relatives of Ahaziah whom he happened to meet (2 Kings 19:12-14). The climax of his anti-Baal activity was the cold-blooded massacre of any others he suspected of being Baal worshippers (2 Kings 10:15-27).

In wiping out the dynasty of Ahab, Jehu was driven more by his desire for power than by his devotion to God; for he himself still worshipped at the idol shrines that Jeroboam had earlier set up (2 Kings 10:29,31). In spite of this he received God's reward for ridding Israel of Jezebel's Baalism. In fulfilment of God's promise, his dynasty lasted longer than any other in Israel. But people never forgot his butchery, and his dynasty was doomed to end, as it had begun, with violence (2 Kings 10:30; Hosea 1:4).

Jehu's massacre of all the chief administrators left Israel's government weak and unstable (2 Kings 10:11). His withdrawal from the eastern border left Israel open to attack from the Syrians (2 Kings 9:4-5,14-16). Hazael of Syria quickly overran most of Israel's eastern territory, and continued to trouble Israel throughout Jehu's reign (2 Kings 10:32-35; cf. 8:12; 1 Kings 19:17).

Another man named Jehu was a prophet who announced God's judgment upon an earlier Israelite king, Baasha (1 Kings 16:1,7,12). Later this same prophet brought God's message to the Judean king Jehoshaphat. He also wrote the court record of Jehoshaphat's reign (2 Chron 19:2; 20:34).

JEPHTHAH

Born of a prostitute and cast out by his family, Jephthah grew up in a tough and bitter world (Judg 11:13). When the people of his tribe decided to overthrow the Ammonites (who had oppressed them for eighteen years; Judg 10:7-8,17-18), Jephthah was the man they asked to be their leader. Jephthah accepted only after the tribal elders had agreed to his conditions, which were that after he had defeated the enemy, he would remain their leader and rule them as a civil governor (Judg 11:4-10).

Jephthah had sufficient faith to believe that God would give Israel victory (Heb 11:32-34). He was, however, only a recently reformed bandit, and he had little knowledge of the character of God or the law of God. By vowing, and then offering, his daughter as a human sacrifice in return for God's help towards victory, he was following the religion of the false gods whom Israel worshipped (Judg 11:29-40; cf. 2 Kings 3:27). He was certainly not following the teachings of Yahweh (cf. Lev 18:21; Deut 12:31).

When Jephthah attacked the enemy, he did not invite soldiers from the tribe of Ephraim to join in the main battle. The Ephraimites were offended and threatened him with violence. Jephthah responded in typically uncompromising fashion. He launched a furious attack and slaughtered the Ephraimites in thousands (Judg 12:1-6). He then settled down to the civilian rule that he had wanted, but after only six years rule he died (Judg 12:7).

JEREMIAH

Among the Old Testament prophets, Jeremiah is the one who reveals more personal details than anyone else. Like all the prophets he declared his opposition to false religious practices, wrong social behaviour and foolish government policies, but above all his writings display the unhappiness that was a feature of much of his life. This unhappiness resulted partly from his unpopularity with the community in general, but his greatest distress came from a feeling that God had been unfair to him.

We can understand Jeremiah's problems only as we see them against the background of conditions in Judah as set out in his book. Since the messages and events detailed in the book are not in chronological order, the following outline of events may help towards an understanding of the man and his work.

Forty years of preaching

Jeremiah began his prophetic work in 627 BC, the thirteenth year of the reign of Josiah, king of Judah (Jer 1:1-2). Josiah had carried out sweeping reforms, firstly to remove all the idolatrous and immoral practices that had become deeply rooted in Judah over the previous generations, then to re-establish the true worship of Yahweh (2 Kings 22:1-23:25). Jeremiah saw that in spite of the king's good work, there was little change in the hearts of the people. Judah was heading for terrible judgment. (Jeremiah Chapters 1-6, and possible parts of Chapters 7-20, seem to belong to the early period of Jeremiah's preaching.)

Meanwhile to the north, Babylon was growing in power, and with its conquest of Assyria in 612 BC, it established itself as the leading nation in the region. When Egypt, the leading nation to Judah's south, decided to challenge Babylon, Josiah tried to stop the Egyptians from passing through Palestine and was killed in battle (609 BC; 2 Kings 23:28-30). Considering itself now the master of Judah, Egypt removed Jehoahaz, the new Judean king, and made his older brother Jehoiakim king instead (2 Kings 23:31-37).

Jehoiakim was a cruel and ungodly ruler. He opposed Jeremiah because of his condemnation of Judah's sins and his forecasts of its destruction (Jer 22:13-19; 26:1-6,20-24; 36:1-32). (Much of Jeremiah

Chapters 7-20, along with Chapters 22, 23, 25, 26, 35, 36 and 45, belong to the time of Jehoiakim.)

When Babylon conquered Egypt at the Battle of Carchemish in 605 BC (Jer 46:2), it thereby gained control of Judah and took selected Jerusalemites captive to Babylon (Dan 1:1-6). When Jehoiakim later tried to become independent of Babylon, the Babylonian army, under Nebuchadnezzar, besieged Jerusalem. Jehoiakim died during the siege, and

Nebuchadnezzar, king of Babylon

three months later his son and successor Jehoiachin surrendered. Jehoiachin and most of the useful people were then taken captive to Babylon. The Babylonians appointed Zedekiah, another brother of Jehoiakim, as the new king (597 BC; 2 Kings 24:8-17).

Jeremiah and Zedekiah were constantly in conflict. Jeremiah assured Zedekiah that Babylon's overlordship was God's judgment on Judah for its sin. Judah should therefore accept its punishment and submit to Babylon. To resist would only bring invasion, siege, starvation, bloodshed and captivity (2 Kings 24:18-20; Jer 21:1-10; 24:1-10; 27:12-22; 28:12-14).

The opponents of Jeremiah assured Zedekiah that with the help of Egypt he could overthrow Babylonian rule. Foolishly, Zedekiah followed their advice rather than Jeremiah's, and brought upon Judah a long and devastating siege. In the end Babylon destroyed the city and its temple, and took the king, along with all remaining useful citizens, into foreign captivity (587 BC; 2 Kings 25:1-21; Jer 32:1-5,28-29; 33:1-5; 37:16-17; 38:17-18; 39:1-10). (The parts of Jeremiah that deal largely with the reign of Zedekiah are Chapters 21, 24, 27-34, 37-39 and 52.)

On more than one occasion during this long crisis Jeremiah was imprisoned (Jer 32:2; 37:15; 37:20-21; 38:1-6,13,28). Upon conquering the city, the victorious Babylonians released him and gave him full freedom to decide where he would like to

live, Babylon or Judah. Jeremiah decided to stay in Judah. The Babylonians placed him under the protection of Gedaliah, the Jewish governor whom they had appointed over the Judeans left in the land (2 Kings 25:22; Jer 39:13-14; 40:4-6).

Sadly, Gedaliah was murdered by some Judeans who were still opposed to Babylon (2 Kings 25:25; Jer 40:13-41:18). The remaining Judeans then fled for safety to Egypt, taking an unwilling Jeremiah with them (2 Kings 25:26; Jer 42:1-43:7). Jeremiah warned that they would not escape God's punishment by fleeing to Egypt, but, as always, the people refused to heed the message (Jer 43:8-44:30). The Bible records nothing further of Jeremiah's life, though there is one tradition which says that the Judeans in Egypt later stoned him to death. (The period of Gedaliah's governorship and the Judeans' flight to Egypt is dealt with in Jeremiah Chapters 40-44.)

Jeremiah's personal life

From the book of Jeremiah we learn much about the prophet's personal life. It appears that he was only about twenty years of age when he began his prophetic preaching (1:6). Apparently he never married (16:2) and for much of his life he had few friends (20:7). His own family opposed him (12:6) and the people of his home town plotted to kill him (11:19,21). The common people of Jerusalem cursed him (15:10), false prophets ridiculed him (28:10-11; 29:24-28), priests stopped him from entering the temple (36:5) and the civil authorities plotted evil against him (36:26; 38:4-6).

In addition to being imprisoned, Jeremiah was at times flogged (20:2; 37:15) and often threatened with death (11:21; 26:7-9; 38:15). Some people in positions of influence, however, were on occasions able to gain some protection for him against his persecutors (26:24; 38:7-13; 40:5-6).

There can be no doubt that Jeremiah loved his people and his country (8:18-22; 9:1-2; 14:19-22). It almost broke his heart to have to announce his country's overthrow and urge his countrymen to submit to the enemy (4:19-22; 10:17-21; 14:17-18; 17:16-17). He was deeply hurt when people accused him of being a traitor (37:13; 38:1-6), for his great desire was that the people heed his warnings and so avoid the threatened destruction (7:5-7; 13:15-17; 26:16-19; 36:1-3).

Jeremiah wished for peace, but he knew there could be no peace as long as the people continued in their sin. The false prophets, on the other hand, assured the people of peace, knowing that messages that pleased the hearers brought good financial rewards (6:13; 8:11). Jeremiah knew that the people's hopes would be disappointed, but this gave him no satisfaction, only greater distress (7:1-15; 14:13-18; 23:9).

Although it hurt Jeremiah to have to announce judgments on his own people, he did it faithfully as God's messenger (20:8-10). When the people responded with hatred and violence (11:19; 18:18), Jeremiah complained to God bitterly. He accused God of being unfair in giving him a cruel reward for his devoted loyalty (12:1-4; 15:10-12,17-18; 20:14-18). God rebuked Jeremiah for his self-pity, though he also strengthened him to meet further troubles. As long as Judah remained faithless, Jeremiah could expect opposition (12:5-6).

These experiences emphasized to Jeremiah the importance of an individual's personal relationship with God. Those who sincerely sought God found him; those who had no personal fellowship with God did not know him, no matter how outwardly religious they might have been (23:21-22). Jeremiah looked beyond the captivity to a day when there would be a new covenant between God and his people. This would be a covenant characterized not by a community's conformity to religious laws, but by an individual's personal relationship with God (31:31-34).

Outline of the book

The first six chapters of the book deal with the main features of Jeremiah's early ministry: his call to be a prophet (1:1-19); his denunciation of Judah for its unfaithfulness, idolatry and immorality (2:1-3:5); his demand for true, inward repentance (3:6-4:4); and his warning of the coming destruction of Jerusalem (4:5-6:30).

Chapters 7-20 record incidents and messages which, in general, demonstrate the sinful condition of Judah and, in particular, Jerusalem. Three topics are prominent in this section. The first concerns Judah's widespread sin and its certain punishment (7:1-8:17; 11:1-23; 16:1-17:13). The second concerns the approaching judgment on the capital city, Jerusalem (8:18-10:25; 13:1-15:9; 18:1-20:6). The third concerns Jeremiah's inner conflicts and his complaints to God (12:1-17; 15:10-21; 17:14-27; 20:7-18).

After this come five chapters of warnings. There are warnings to rulers, such as Zedekiah (21:1-10; 24:1-10), kings in general (21:11-22:9), Jehoahaz (Shallum), Jehoiakim and Jehoiachin (Coniah) (22:10-30). There are additional warnings to lying prophets (23:9-40), and messages concerning

God's control over the destinies of nations (23:1-8; 25:1-38).

Prophecies of captivity and return (Chapters 26-36) include a warning to the Jerusalemites to submit to Babylon or be destroyed (26:1-28:17); an assurance to those already in exile that there is no hope for an immediate return to Jerusalem (29:1-32); the promise of a new age after the nation's restoration (30:1-33:26); and guarantees that though treachery and rebellion will be punished, fidelity will be rewarded (34:1-36:32).

A unit of eight chapters then traces events in chronological sequence from the final siege of Jerusalem to the settlement of the Jews in Egypt: Jeremiah's imprisonment and rescue (37:1-38:28); the fall of Jerusalem (39:1-18); the appointment of Gedaliah and his brutal assassination (40:1-41:18); the migration to Egypt (42:1-43:7); and Jeremiah's message to the Jews in Egypt (43:8-44:30). An earlier message for Jeremiah's secretary, Baruch, is also recorded (45:1-5).

Finally there is a collection of messages for foreign nations: Egypt (46:1-28), Philistia (47:1-7), Moab and Ammon (48:1-49:6), Edom (49:7-22), Damascus, Kedar, Hazor and Elam (49:23-39), and Babylon (50:1-51:64). An historical appendix details matters relating to the fall of Jerusalem (52:1-34).

JERICHO

The ancient town of Jericho was destroyed and rebuilt many times, though sometimes the rebuilt town was beside, rather than on top of, the ruins of the former town. The present town of Jericho, the Old Testament town destroyed by Joshua, and the New Testament town visited by Jesus all occupied different sites, though these sites are within a kilometre or so of each other.

One reason for this constant settlement of Jericho was the presence there of a good spring of water. This ensured a constant supply of fresh water and made the place such an oasis that people called Jericho the city of palm trees (Deut 34:3). The town was located in a flat area of the Jordan Valley. To the east a small plain dropped away into the Jordan River, and to the west barren hills rose up to the central highlands.

Archaeological evidence indicates that Jericho was in existence in 8000 BC. Its first mention in the Bible concerns events about 1240 BC, when the Israelites under Joshua approached Canaan from the plains of Moab, crossed the Jordan River and conquered Jericho in their first battle in Canaan (Num 22:1; Josh 2:1-6:27).

Joshua announced a curse over Jericho, and for the next few hundred years no one dared rebuild the town properly, though some sort of settlement still existed there (Josh 6:26; Judg 3:13; 2 Sam 10:5). When a man named Hiel later rebuilt the city, he suffered the punishment announced by Joshua (1 Kings 16:34; cf. Josh 6:26). A school for young prophets was located at Jericho in the time of Elijah and Elisha (2 Kings 2:4-5,15-22).

There were further destructions and rebuildings of Jericho over the following centuries. The town was still in existence in New Testament times, having been rebuilt by Herod the Great. The narrow road that descended from Jerusalem through wild and rocky country to Jericho was dangerous because of bandits (Luke 10:30).

Jesus visited Jericho on his final journey to Jerusalem, and may have passed through the town on other occasions. Among those who benefited from Jesus' visit were some blind beggars and a well known tax collector (Matt 20:29-34; Luke 18:35-43; 19:1-11).

JEROBOAM

Two kings of Israel had the name Jeroboam. Both of them ruled over the northern part of the divided kingdom, but they were separated in time by more than a hundred years and they belonged to different dynasties.

Jeroboam the son of Nebat

The books of Kings consistently condemn Jeroboam the son of Nebat, the man who led the northern tribes to break away from the Davidic rule. But the chief reason they condemn him is religious rather than political; for Jeroboam established his own religion in the north in opposition to the Levitical system that was based on the Jerusalem temple (1 Kings 15:34; 16:19; 22:52; 2 Kings 10:31; 14:24; 23:15). This false religion, set up by Jeroboam and followed by other kings, was the reason God destroyed the northern kingdom and sent the people into captivity (2 Kings 17:21-23).

From his youth Jeroboam was capable and hard-working. Solomon was so impressed with the young man that he put him in charge of the Ephraim-Manasseh workforce (1 Kings 11:28). The ambitious Jeroboam cleverly used his position to gain a following among his fellow northerners, in opposition to the southerner Solomon, whose policies he found oppressive. From the prophet Ahijah, Jeroboam learnt that God would punish Solomon by splitting his kingdom and giving ten tribes to Jeroboam. When Solomon tried to kill Jeroboam, Jeroboam escaped to Egypt, where he remained till the end of Solomon's reign (1 Kings 11:29-40).

As soon as Solomon was dead, Jeroboam returned from Egypt and led a rebellion (930 BC). The northern tribes readily crowned Jeroboam their king, in opposition to Solomon's son, Rehoboam. Rehoboam still reigned in Jerusalem, but only over Judah and its neighbouring tribe, Benjamin (1 Kings 12:1-20).

Jeroboam made his capital in Shechem, but later shifted it a few kilometres north to Tirzah (1 Kings 12:25; 14:17; cf. 15:21,33). He was wary of the attraction that Jerusalem still held, fearing that if his people went there for religious ceremonies they might transfer their allegiance to Rehoboam. He therefore decided to set up his own independent religion. He built shrines at the towns of Bethel (near his southern border) and Dan (near his northern border), complete with his own order of priests, sacrifices and feasts. His religion attempted to combine the worship of Yahweh with Canaanite religion (1 Kings 12:26-33). A bold announcement of judgment by a prophet from Judah showed plainly that God would not accept this new religion (1 Kings 13:1-10). Ahijah repeated the announcement of judgment (1 Kings 14:1-18).

During his twenty-two years reign Jeroboam fought against the Judean kings, Rehoboam and Abijam (1 Kings 15:6-7). His costly loss to Abijam was a final demonstration to him that God would not help one who had broken away from the Davidic dynasty and the Levitical priesthood (2 Chron 13:2-20).

Jeroboam the son of Joash

This Jeroboam is usually referred to as Jeroboam II, to distinguish him from the person who established the breakaway northern kingdom. Jeroboam II was one of Israel's most powerful and prosperous kings, but religiously he was no better than the first Jeroboam. He ruled from 793 to 752 BC (2 Kings 13:13; 14:23-24).

At that time Syria had declined in power and Assyria was concerned with struggles far removed from Palestine. Jeroboam II was therefore able to strengthen his kingdom without interference from hostile neighbours. He brought territorial expansion and economic growth on a scale not seen in Israel since the days of David and Solomon (2 Kings 14:25-28). The prosperity, however, brought with it greed, injustice and exploitation that the prophets Amos and Hosea condemned fearlessly (Amos 1:1;

2:6-8; 3:15; 4:1; 5:10-12; 6:4-6; Hosea 1:1; 4:1-2,17-18; 6:8-9; 12:7-8; see AMOS; HOSEA).

Just as one prophet earlier had forecast the expansion of Israel's territory, so another now forecast God's judgment throughout that territory (2 Kings 14:25; Amos 6:14). Jeroboam would be killed and eventually Israel would go into captivity (Amos 7:9-11).

JERUSALEM

Jerusalem has existed for thousands of years and during that time the shape of the city has changed repeatedly — valleys filled in, hills taken away, other hills added by the accumulation of rubbish, and city boundaries altered from era to era. But the overall picture of an elevated city built on an uneven plateau remains as in Bible times.

Valleys and streams

The only convenient access to the city in ancient times was from the north, access on the other sides being hindered by cliffs that fell away into deep valleys. On the south-west side was the Valley of Hinnom, where at times idolaters set up altars on which they offered their children as burnt sacrifices to the god Molech (Josh 15:8; 2 Chron 28:3; 33:6). Jeremiah foretold God's judgment on these people by announcing that in the place where they killed their children, they themselves would be killed and their corpses left to rot in the sun (Jer 7:31-34; 32:35).

People also used the Valley of Hinnom as a place to dump broken pottery (Jer 19:1-13). Other rubbish accumulated, with the result that in later years the place became a public garbage dump where fires burnt continually. The Hebrew name 'Valley of Hinnom' translit-erated via the Greek is *gehenna*, which was the word Jesus used to indicate the place of final judgment on the wicked (Matt 5:29-30; 10:28; 18:9; 23:33; Mark 9:43-48; cf. Rev 20:10,15; see HELL).

Immediately to the east of the city another valley ran south, separating the city from the Mount of Olives. This was known as the Valley of Kidron or the Valley of Jehoshaphat. In the rainy season a swiftly flowing stream ran from the hills north of Jerusalem through this valley, ending in the Dead Sea (2 Sam 15:23; 1 Kings 2:37; 15:13; 2 Chron 30:14; Joel 3:2,12; John 18:1).

Between the city and the Kidron stream was the Spring of Gihon, whose waters King Hezekiah redirected into Jerusalem to improve the city's water supply (2 Kings 20:20; 2 Chron 32:30; 33:14). The water flowed into pools, or reservoirs, some of which were damaged when the Babylonians destroyed Jerusalem. They were later repaired in the time of Nehemiah (Neh 2:14; 3:15; cf. Isa 22:9-11). One of these reservoirs, the Pool of Siloam, was still in use hundreds of years later (John 9:7). Nearby was the Tower of Siloam which, somewhere about the time of Jesus, collapsed, killing eighteen people (Luke 13:4).

In addition to the Spring of Gihon, there was a spring at En-rogel, just outside Jerusalem to the south (Josh 15:7; 2 Sam 17:17). The Jerusalem leaders had a means of sealing up these springs so

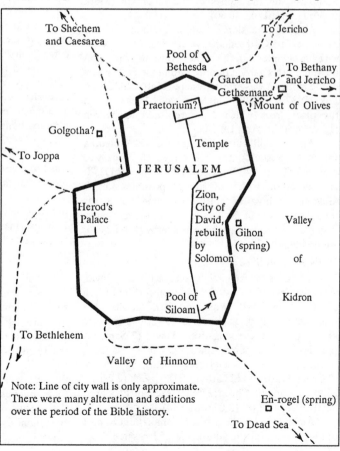

To Shechem and Caesarea

To Jericho

Pool of Bethesda

To Bethany and Jericho

Garden of Gethsemane

Praetorium?

Mount of Olives

Golgotha?

Temple

To Joppa

JERUSALEM

Zion, City of David, rebuilt by Solomon

Herod's Palace

Gihon (spring)

Valley

Pool of Siloam

of

Kidron

To Bethlehem

Valley of Hinnom

Note: Line of city wall is only approximate. There were many alteration and additions over the period of the Bible history.

En-rogel (spring)

To Dead Sea

that any besieging army would be without water (2 Chron 32:4). Apart from these two springs, Jerusalem had to depend for its water supply on rain water that was directed into stone reservoirs (2 Kings 18:31; Jer 38:6; John 5:2).

Mountains and hills

The commanding hill in Jerusalem was Zion, where for centuries a strong fortress enabled the city's previous inhabitants, the Jebusites, to withstand Israel's attacks. Finally, David defeated them (2 Sam 5:7; see JEBUSITES). The hill was also known as Moriah and was the place where David decided to build Israel's temple (2 Chron 3:1; cf. Gen 22:2). Both the city and the temple were figuratively called Zion (1 Kings 8:1; 2 Kings 19:31; Ps 2:6; 9:11; 48:12; 74:2; Isa 8:18; see ZION).

To the east of the Kidron stream was the Mount of Olives, so named because of its many olive orchards (2 Sam 15:30; 2 Kings 23:12-13; Ezek 11:23; Zech 14:4). The main road from Jerusalem to Jericho passed through the villages of Bethany and Bethphage on the slopes of the mountain (Mark 10:46; 11;1,11; Luke 10:30).

Also on the slopes of this mountain was a garden called Gethsemane, where Jesus often went with his disciples. On the night before his crucifixion he went to this garden to pray, and in the early hours of the morning was arrested there (Matt 26:30,36,47; Luke 21:37; 22:39,48). The Mount of Olives was also the place from which Jesus returned to heaven (Luke 24:50-51; Acts 1:9-12).

Another hill outside Jerusalem was Golgotha (meaning 'a skull'), the hill on which Jesus was crucified (Matt 27:33; Luke 23:33; John 19:17). It is not certain which of several possible sites is Golgotha or how the hill got its name, but it was on a main road not far outside one of the city gates. A garden containing a tomb was nearby (Matt 27:39; John 19:20,41).

Walls and buildings

From the days before Israel's conquest under David, Jerusalem was a walled city and well fortified (Josh 15:63; 2 Sam 5:6-7). Walls and fortifications were repaired, enlarged, or added to by various Israelite kings. Among these kings were David (2 Sam 5:9; the Millo was some tower or other defence fortification), Solomon (1 Kings 9:15), Rehoboam (2 Chron 11:5), Asa (2 Chron 14:7), Uzziah (2 Chron 26:9), Jotham (2 Chron 27:3), Hezekiah (2 Chron 32:5) and Manasseh (2 Chron 33:14).

Among the buildings that Solomon built as part of his program for the adornment of Jerusalem were an expensive temple, a magnificent palace, a military headquarters called the House of the Forest of Lebanon, an auditorium called the Hall of Pillars, a judgment court called the Hall of the Throne and a separate palace for the queen. All these buildings were contained within a large enclosure called the Great Court (1 Kings 7:1-12).

Several hundred years later, the armies of Babylon destroyed Jerusalem (587 BC). They broke down large sections of the city wall, burnt most of the houses and destroyed all the important buildings, including the temple and the palace (2 Kings 25:1-4,9).

When Persia conquered Babylon in 539 BC and allowed the exiled Jews to return to Jerusalem, the people first of all rebuilt the temple, completing it in 516 BC (Ezra 6:14-15). But during the next seventy years they did no major reconstruction work. The city was still in a state of disrepair and the wall surrounding the city had not been rebuilt. The Persians' appointment of Nehemiah as governor was specifically for this project of reconstruction (Neh 2:1-8). The book of Nehemiah shows how Nehemiah carried out the work, and gives details concerning different sections of the wall and the various city gates (Neh 2:13-3:32).

Herod the Great, with help from the Roman authorities, carried out major reconstruction work in Jerusalem during the period just before the New Testament era. The program included civil and military buildings (Matt 27:27; Mark 15:16; John 19:13; Acts 23:10,35).

To the Jews the greatest of Herod's works was the construction of a new temple (the previous temple having been destroyed by the Romans). It was built on the same site as the previous temples but was much larger and far more magnificent. It took many decades to build and was not completed till long after Herod's death (Mark 13:1; John 2:20; Acts 3:2; see HEROD; TEMPLE).

Old Testament history of Jerusalem

It seems that Jerusalem was originally known by its shorter name Salem, and was the city of which Melchizedek was priest-king (Gen 14:18). When the Israelites entered Canaan, the city was occupied by the Jebusites and was known as Jebus. Although the city at first fell to the conquering Israelites, the local people soon retook it. When the Israelites, after their conquest of Canaan, divided the land between their tribes, Jerusalem fell within the tribal area of Benjamin. By that time the Jebusites were firmly in control of Jerusalem again, and they remained in control till the time of David (Josh 15:8,63; 18:28; Judg 1:8,21; 19:10-11).

No doubt there were several reasons why David wanted to conquer Jerusalem and make it the capital of his kingdom. Firstly, a city that was so hard to conquer would make an excellent site for a capital. Secondly, the conquest of such a long-held enemy fortress was certain to win nationwide support for David. Thirdly, since Jerusalem was not in the possession of any Israelite tribe, there could be no cause for inter-tribal jealousy if he made it his capital.

Although the Jebusites thought their city was unconquerable (2 Sam 5:6), David's men took it in a surprise attack. They entered the city secretly through a water tunnel, which the Jebusites used for bringing water into the city from a spring outside the city walls (2 Sam 5:7-10).

David's plans were to make Jerusalem the religious as well as the administrative centre of his kingdom. He placed the ark of the covenant in a special tent erected for it in the city, and made arrangements for his son and successor, Solomon, to build a permanent temple on Mt Zion (2 Sam 6:17; 7:12-13; 1 Chron 15:29; 22:1-5; 28:11).

Solomon's plans, however, were for more than a temple. He wanted to make Jerusalem a national showpiece, and his building program included a luxurious palace and many other magnificent buildings. But his oppressive policies of forced labour and heavy taxes created a feeling of rebellion among the people. The outcome was that most of Israel broke away from Jerusalem after Solomon's death (1 Kings 12:1-19).

Only two tribes remained loyal to the throne of David, and together they became known as the kingdom of Judah, with their capital at Jerusalem as previously. The remaining ten tribes still called themselves Israel and formed a separate kingdom in the north, with their own capital and their own religious system (1 Kings 12:20-33).

From this point on the history of Jerusalem is to a large extent the history of Judah (2 Chron Chaps. 12-36; see JUDAH, TRIBE AND KINGDOM). Jerusalem fell under the domination of Babylon in 605 BC, and after repeated attempts at rebellion was finally destroyed by Babylon in 587 BC (2 Kings 24:1; 25:1-12).

After Persia conquered Babylon in 539 BC and released the captive people, the Jews returned to their land and reoccupied Jerusalem (Ezra 1:1-4; 6:15; Neh 2:17-20). Over the next century they rebuilt the temple, the city and the city walls, as outlined above. With the completion of Nehemiah's program, the Old Testament history of Jerusalem comes to an end.

Into the New Testament era

During the four hundred years between the close of the book of Nehemiah and the opening of the New Testament, Jerusalem continued to have a colourful history. In 333 BC the Greek conqueror Alexander the Great won a decisive victory over Persia and the next year became the new controller of Jerusalem. Soon, however, the Greek Empire split. In the east there were two main sectors, Egyptian and Syrian, with Palestine being controlled by Egypt till 198 BC, and then by Syria.

When, about 168 BC, fighting broke out among rival groups of Jews in Jerusalem, the Greek ruler in Syria, Antiochus IV Epiphanes, took the opportunity to invade Jerusalem, slaughter the Jews, and if possible destroy the Jewish religion. After setting up a Greek altar in the Jewish temple, he took animals that the Jews considered unclean and offered them as sacrifices to the Greek gods.

The Jews, led by a zealous group called the Maccabees, assembled a fighting force to resist Antiochus. After three years of fighting they won back their religious freedom and rededicated their temple (165 BC). The Maccabees decided to keep fighting till they had gained political freedom as well, and after twenty years were successful.

For the next eighty years Jerusalem remained independent, but the Jews' internal conflicts finally brought in the Romans who, in 63 BC, seized control of Jerusalem. After some initial confusion, Rome appointed as ruler of Palestine the man who became known as Herod the Great and whose extensive improvements to Jerusalem have been referred to above.

Jerusalem was the centre of opposition to Jesus and the place where he was eventually condemned and crucified (Matt 16:21; 23:37; Mark 11:15-18; John 11:55-57; 12:12,19). After Jesus' resurrection, his disciples remained in Jerusalem till they received the promised Holy Spirit. The early church became established in Jerusalem, from where it spread to nations near and far (Acts 1:4; 8:1-4,14; 11:22; Rom 15:26-27).

The Jerusalem church itself, however, had an unsettled early history. This was mainly because of its constant battle with narrow-minded Jewish legalists (Acts 11:2-3; 15:1-5). Paul tried to develop a sense of fellowship between the Jewish church in Jerusalem and the Gentile churches elsewhere (Acts 11:29-30; 21:20-26; Rom 15:25-27; Gal 2:9-10), but the city as a whole turned against him violently, as it had against Jesus (Acts 21:11-13,30-36; 22:22; 23:10-15,31-35).

Brief history to the present day

In AD 66 there was a revolt against Rome by a group of Jewish extremists, with the result that Rome attacked Jerusalem with its full force. In AD 70 most of the city, including the temple, was destroyed, as Jesus had foretold (Matt 24:1-2; Luke 19:41-44; 21:20-24).

The Romans rebuilt Jerusalem in AD 132, declaring it a pagan city from which all Jews were excluded. When Constantine became Emperor in AD 313, he declared Jerusalem a Christian city. In AD 637 the Muslims conquered Jerusalem, and in 691 erected their own mosque on the site where the Jewish temple previously stood. In 1542 the Muslim ruler rebuilt the city walls, and they still stand today. Except for brief and isolated periods, Jerusalem remained under Muslim control till 1967, when it was retaken by the Jews. The mosque on the temple hill, however, still stands.

JESUS CHRIST

'Jesus' was a common Jewish name and appears in the Greek language of the New Testament as the equivalent of the Hebrew 'Joshua' in the Old Testament. The name meant 'Yahweh (Jehovah) is our Saviour', and therefore was a fitting name to give to the one who would save his people, Yahweh's people, from their sins (Matt 1:21). 'Christ' was a Greek word equivalent to the Hebrew 'Messiah' (Matt 22:42). (For the significance of this name see MESSIAH.)

Life of Jesus

The writers of the four Gospels provide most of the information concerning Jesus' life and teaching, but they make no attempt to give a detailed biography of Jesus. They wrote at different times, for different people, in different places, for different purposes, and they selected their material accordingly (Luke 1:1-4; John 20:30-31). Yet there is no disagreement in the picture of Jesus they present: he is God and man, the Lord and Saviour of the world. (See also GOSPELS.)

For convenience we can divide the Gospels' record of Jesus' life into three main sections. The first has to do with his birth and early childhood, the second concerns his public ministry (i.e. his teachings, healings, miracles and other recorded activities) and the third centres on the events of his death and resurrection.

Stories that describe events surrounding Jesus' birth are recorded at some length. Nothing more is recorded of Jesus' childhood till he was twelve years old. Even at that early age Jesus knew that he existed in a special relation with God; for he was God's Son (Luke 2:42,49).

There is no record of the next eighteen years or so of Jesus' life. Then, when about thirty years of age (Luke 3:23), he was baptized and began his public ministry. His baptism showed on the one hand his complete willingness to carry out all God's purposes, and on the other his complete identification with the people whose sins he would bear. God then showed, through the descent of the Spirit in the form of a dove upon Jesus, that he had equipped him for this task (Matt 3:13-17; Acts 10:38; see BAPTISM; HOLY SPIRIT). Jesus had the Spirit's power in unlimited measure (John 3:34), but he had to exercise it in keeping with his position of willing submission to the Father.

Almost immediately after Jesus received this special power from the Father, Satan tempted him to use it according to his own will, independently of the Father; but Jesus overcame the temptation (Matt 4:1-11; see TEMPTATION). He then began to move about doing the work that his Father had entrusted to him.

This public ministry of Jesus seems to have lasted about three and a half years. He did much of his work in the northern part of Palestine known as Galilee (Matt 4:12,23), though he met his fiercest opposition in Judea in the south, particularly in Jerusalem, which was the centre of Jewish religious power.

The Jewish leaders considered that Jesus' claim to be the Son of God was blasphemy (Mark 2:7; 3:22; 14:61-64; John 7:25,40-44; 8:56-59; 11:55-57). Jesus knew that he eventually would be killed by the Jews in Jerusalem (Matt 16:21; 20:18-19; Luke 9:51), but he knew also that first he had to complete the work his Father had sent him to do (John 4:34; 9:4). Only when he had finished that work and the time appointed by his Father had come would he allow the Jews to take him and crucify him (John 7:30; 10:18; 13:1; 17:4-11).

Jesus' final week in Jerusalem was full of tension and activity and is recorded in greater detail than any other part of his life. He entered Jerusalem as Israel's Messiah-King, cleansed the temple, debated with the Jews and gave teaching to his disciples on many subjects. He then allowed his enemies to arrest him, treat him cruelly, condemn him falsely and finally crucify him. Three days later he rose from the dead and during the next six weeks appeared to his disciples and others on a number of occasions in various places (Acts 1:3). His final appearance concluded with his ascension to heaven, though heavenly messengers reassured his disciples that one day he would come again (Acts 1:9-11; cf. John 14:3).

God become man (the Incarnation)

In Jesus Christ, God became incarnate; that is, he took upon himself human form. Jesus Christ was the embodiment of God and, by coming into the world as man, made God known to man. This shows that Jesus must have existed as God before he was born into this world; for only one who was previously with God could make God known (John 1:1,18; 3:13; 12:41; 17:5; 1 Cor 10:4). When he became man, Jesus added humanity to the deity that he always had (John 1:14; Heb 1:3).

As the eternally existent Son of God, Jesus had no beginning (John 8:58; Col 1:17; Rev 1:8), but as a human being he had a beginning when he was born as a baby in Bethlehem. God became flesh (John 1:14; Gal 4:4; 1 Tim 3:16; 1 John 1:1-4; see SON OF GOD; WORD). This came about through the miraculous work of God's Holy Spirit in the womb of the virgin Mary, so that the child who was born, though having no human father, was nevertheless fully human. He was not an ordinary person whom God adopted as his Son, but a unique person who was actually God's Son (Luke 1:27,31,35).

In becoming man, Jesus did not cease to be God. His deity was not lessened in any way. When Philippians 2:7 says that Jesus, in being born a man, 'emptied himself', it does not mean that he lost, voluntarily or otherwise, any of his divine attributes or qualities. Its meaning is well explained in the verses before and after, where it is clear that to empty oneself means to deny oneself totally, to sacrifice all self-interest.

Jesus from all eternity had existed as God, yet he willingly sacrificed the supreme glory of heaven and took instead the place of a servant. What he sacrificed was not his deity, but the heavenly glories that were his by right. The limitation that he accepted in becoming man was not a lessening of his divine powers or being, but the limitation of living like other human beings in a world of imperfection and suffering (Phil 2:5-8; cf. John 17:5; 2 Cor 8:9; Heb 2:9).

Not only Jesus' physical form but also his human nature was like that of human beings in general; except that, whereas the human nature common to all other people is infected by sin from birth, Jesus' human nature was not. Because his oneness with mankind was complete, he was able to die for his fellow human beings and so free them from the evil results of sin (Rom 8:3; 2 Cor 5:21; Heb 2:14-15).

Fully God yet fully man

Though a man, Jesus retained his divine being and powers (Col 1:19; 2:9; Titus 2:13). His human and divine natures existed together — complete, united and inseparable — without either one lessening the other.

Jesus was still the creator and controller of the universe (Col 1:16-17; Heb 1:2-3), the Lord of life (Luke 7:22; John 5:21,26; 8:51; 10:10,28), the forgiver of sins (Mark 2:5,7,10; 2 Cor 5:19), and the judge of mankind (Matt 13:41-43; 25:31-32; John 5:26-27; 2 Cor 5:10). He was still the originator of divine truth (Matt 5:22,28,32,34,39,44; 12:5-8; Mark 13:31; John 14:6,10), the possessor of superhuman knowledge (John 6:64; 11:14; 18:4), the satisfier of man's deepest needs (Matt 11:28-30; John 4:14; 6:35; 11:25) and the object of man's worship (Matt 2:11; John 5:23; 9:38).

Being the Son of God, Jesus was equal in deity with the Father (John 10:30). So completely were they united that Jesus could say that whoever saw him saw the Father (John 14:9; cf. Matt 1:23; 2 Cor 4:4; Col 1:15; Heb 1:3). Therefore, whoever received him received the Father and whoever rejected him rejected the Father (Matt 10:40; Luke 10:16; John 12:44; 15:23; 1 John 2:23). Because he was God, Jesus demanded that total allegiance which only God could demand (Matt 10:37-39; Mark 8:34-35; John 3:36).

Yet at the same time Jesus was fully man (1 Tim 2:5; 1 John 1:1). He knew how it felt to be hungry, thirsty and tired (Matt 21:18; John 4:6; 19:28). He experienced poverty and sorrow as well as joy (Luke 9:58; 10:21; John 11:33-36; 15:11; Heb 5:7). He showed some of the emotional reactions common to human nature such as astonishment, disappointment, pity and anger (Mark 3:5; 6:6; 8:2; 10:14; Luke 7:9). He was inwardly troubled as he saw his crucifixion drawing near, and he desired the sympathetic company of his closest friends during his time of spiritual conflict in Gethsemane the night before his death (Mark 14:32-41; Luke 12:50; John 12:27).

A man who can help man

Jesus exercised self-control in all aspects of his life and behaviour, and had the same sorts of temptations that other people have (Matt 4:1-11;

Heb 2:17-18; 4:15; 1 Peter 2:23). Yet through it all he never sinned (Heb 4:15). Those who lived closest to him, and who saw more of him than anyone else, asserted that he never sinned (1 Peter 1:19; 2:22; 1 John 3:5). Even his enemies, when challenged to accuse him of sin, were unable to do so (John 8:46; cf. Matt 27:3-4).

On account of Jesus' endurance and obedience through all his temptations and sufferings, his life was one of continuous yet perfect development and maturing. The perfect boy grew into the perfect man, who thus became mankind's perfect Saviour (Luke 2:40,52; Heb 2:10; 5:8). He can sympathize with the normal human weaknesses that people experience, but more than that he can help people triumph over them (Heb 2:18; 4:15). Man's Saviour is God, but that God is one who has lived as man in man's world.

To deny that Jesus was either fully God or fully man is to deny that which is basic to Christian faith (1 John 2:22-25; 4:2-3; 5:6-12). It is only because of the divine oneness between Father and Son that Jesus could bring God to man, and only because of the human oneness between Jesus and his fellow man that he could bring man back to God (John 14:6-10; 1 Tim 2:4-6).

The obedient servant

In becoming man Jesus accepted the limitations that his humanity required. If, for example, he wanted to go from one place to another, he travelled the same as others and put up with the weariness of the journey. He did not use his divine powers to avoid the trials of human existence (John 4:3-6). He had taken upon himself the nature of a servant and he lived in obedience to and dependence on his Father. That was one reason why he prayed constantly (Mark 1:35; 6:46; Luke 6:12).

Jesus' acceptance of the limitations of human life meant also that if he wanted information he asked questions (Luke 2:46; Mark 5:30; 6:38; 9:21). Being God, he must have had all knowledge, but his human consciousness of that knowledge and the way he used it were always in submission to his Father's will.

Certain areas of Jesus' knowledge, therefore, may have been deliberately kept below the level of his human consciousness so that he could have no unnatural advantage over his fellows. But if his Father directed, Jesus could draw upon that knowledge (John 12:49; 14:10,24). As the obedient Son who took the humble place of a servant, he knew, and desired to know, only what his Father wanted him to know (Mark 13:32; John 8:55).

This may help to explain why on some occasions Jesus' knowledge was limited but on other occasions it was not. The Father allowed him certain knowledge that was in keeping with the mission for which the Father had sent him into the world. In these cases Jesus' superhuman knowledge was not to give him a type of magical solution to a problem, but to enable him to carry out the specific work that his Father required him to carry out at that particular time (Luke 6:8; John 1:47-49; 2:25; 4:18,29; 11:11-14; 12:49).

The superhuman knowledge that Jesus showed on such occasions was fully in keeping with the divine knowledge he repeatedly displayed in relation to the work his Father had sent him to do. That is why none of the events surrounding his death took him by surprise. He knew in advance that those events were part of his Father's will for him (Matt 12:40; 16:21; 20:18; John 3:14; 6:64; 12:7; 13:38; 14:29; 16:32).

In summary, then, Jesus exercised his divine knowledge in the same way as he exercised his divine power — always in complete dependence upon and obedience to his Father. He never exercised it for his personal benefit (John 5:19,30; 7:16; 12:49; cf. Matt 26:53-54).

If Satan tempted Jesus to use his divine powers for his own benefit, Jesus must have possessed those powers (Matt 4:3-4; 26:53-54). Any limitation on Jesus' physical capacity or knowledge was an indication not of a lessening of his divinity but of his submission to his Father's will (John 8:28-29). Although Jesus lived a genuinely human life, he did so in the perfection that his deity demanded.

Mission and teaching

All that Jesus did and said was in some way a revelation of who he was. He was not simply a doer of good works or a teacher of religious truths, but the Son of God who came into the world to save man. His works and words are inseparably tied up with the nature of his person and mission (John 5:19,24,30,36; 14:7,10; see SON OF GOD).

A central theme in all the works and teaching of Jesus was that in him the kingdom of God had come visibly into the world of mankind. The kingdom of God is the kingly rule of God, and Jesus proclaimed and exercised that rule as he released sick and demonized people from the power of Satan (Matt 4:23-24; 12:28). Even among people who were not diseased, Jesus preached the kingdom, urging them to enter the kingdom voluntarily in humble faith and so receive eternal life (Mark 1:15; Matt 6:33; 18:3; 19:16,19-23; see KINGDOM OF GOD). He assured the repentant and the unrepentant that they would stand before him, for better or for worse, when he returns at the end of the age to bring the kingdom to its triumphant climax (Matt 13:47-50; 19:28; 25:34,41; cf. 2 Cor 5:10).

In relation to the kingdom of God, Jesus often referred to himself as the Son of man. This title was taken from the heavenly figure of Daniel 7:13-14, to whom the Almighty gave a kingdom that was worldwide and everlasting (Matt 24:30-31; 25:31; Mark 8:38; 14:62; see SON OF MAN). Jesus rarely referred to himself as the Messiah, probably because of the widespread misunderstanding among Jews concerning the type of Messiah they wanted.

Jesus preferred the title 'Son of man' because it made people think about who he was. He wanted people to see for themselves that he, the Son of man, was both a heavenly figure and the Davidic Messiah (Matt 16:13-16; Mark 2:10,28; John 6:62; 9:35-36; 12:23,34; see MESSIAH). He wanted people to see also that he was the Lord's suffering servant. The Messiah had to die before he could reign in the full glory of his kingdom (Matt 16:21; 20:28; see SERVANT OF THE LORD).

Likewise Jesus' miracles were directed towards revealing who he was, though in a way designed to lead people to saving faith (Mark 2:9-12; Luke 4:18; John 9:16-17; 20:30-31; see MIRACLES). His parables had a similar purpose. They made people think, and those who understood and accepted their message entered the kingdom of their Saviour-Messiah (Matt 13:10-16; see PARABLES).

Having entered that kingdom, people had to live by its standards. Jesus' moral teaching, however, was not a code of legal regulations like the law of Moses; nor was it like the burdensome system of the rabbis. He wanted to change people inwardly and so produce a quality of life and character that no law-code could ever produce (Matt 5:21-22,27-28; 7:29; see ETHICS; SERMON ON THE MOUNT).

Jesus' teaching had authority because he came from God, made known the character of God to man, brought people into a relationship with the living God, and enabled them to reproduce within themselves something of the character of God (Matt 5:48; 11:25-27; John 7:16-18).

Jesus as Lord

The Greek word *kurios* (i.e. Lord) in the New Testament is the same word that was used in the Greek translation of the Old Testament for the Hebrew word *yahweh* (i.e. Jehovah) (cf. Ps 32:2 with Rom 4:8; cf. Isa 40:13 with Rom 11:34). In the original Hebrew, Yahweh, the name of God, was a mysterious name that Jews of later times considered so sacred that they refused to speak it. The name was linguistically connected with the words 'I am' and referred to the eternal, unchangeable, ever-present God (Exod 3:13-16; see YAHWEH). Jesus identified himself with Yahweh by calling himself 'I am' (John 8:58; see also John 4:26; 6:35; 8:12; 10:7,11; 11:25; 14:6; 18:5; Mark 14:62).

The New Testament writers also emphasized this identification of Jesus with the God of the Old Testament. Repeatedly they quoted Old Testament references to Yahweh as applying to Jesus (cf. Ps 16:8 with Acts 2:24-25; cf. Isa 40:3 with Mark 1:1-3; cf. Jer 9:23-24 with 1 Cor 1:30-31; cf. Isa 8:13 with 1 Peter 3:15; cf. Ps 110:1 with Matt 22:41-45).

Both the words of Jesus and the quotations of the New Testament writers reflect the Hebrew background of the New Testament. According to that background, to call Jesus 'Lord' is to call him God.

Most of the early Christians, however, did not come from a Hebrew background. They were Gentiles, not Jews, and they had no history of the usage of the name Yahweh to influence their thinking. Yet to them also, to call Jesus 'Lord' (*kurios*) was to call him God. Their understanding of *kurios* came from its usage in the Greek-speaking Gentile world in which they lived.

In common speech, *kurios* may sometimes have meant no more than 'sir' or 'master' (Matt 21:30; Luke 12:45; John 12:21; Acts 25:26), but it was also the usual word people used when referring to the Greek and Roman gods (1 Cor 8:5). The Greek-speaking Christians' use of this word for Jesus showed that they considered him to be God; not just one of many gods, but the one true God who was the creator and ruler of the universe, the controller of life and death (Acts 1:24; 13:10-12; 17:24; Rom 14:9,11; 1 Tim 6:15-16).

Through the resurrection and exaltation of Jesus Christ, God declared dramatically the absolute lordship of Christ (Acts 2:36; Rom 1:4; Phil 2:9-11). Believers in Christ gladly acknowledge him as Lord. They submit to him as to one who has complete authority over their lives, yet they love him as one who has saved them and given them new joy, peace and hope (John 20:28; Acts 10:36; Rom 10:9; 1 Cor 1:2-3; Eph 1:22-23; 2 Thess 3:16; Rev 22:20).

One day Jesus Christ will return in power and glory. In that great day there will be universal acknowledgment that he is indeed Lord (1 Cor 15:24-26; Phil 2:11; 2 Thess 1:7; Rev 19:16; see DAY OF THE LORD).

The death of Jesus

Great though the incarnation and unique life of Jesus may be, they are not in themselves sufficient to meet man's needs. The incarnate Son of God had also to die. Salvation is not through the birth of Christ, nor through his life, but through his death (Matt 20:28; Rom 3:25; 1 Cor 15:2-3; Heb 9:12-14; Rev 5:9-10).

Jesus knew that the chief purpose for which he had been given a human life was that he might offer that life back to God as a sacrifice for people's sins. Yet the offering of that life could be an acceptable sacrifice only because Jesus lived it in full obedience to his Father, without sin (John 4:34; 6:38,51; 8:29; 12:27; Rom 5:19; Heb 10:5-10).

This devotion to his Father's will drove Jesus on, even though he knew it was leading to crucifixion (Mark 8:31; 9:31; 14:36; Luke 9:51; 12:50; John 12:23-24; see CRUCIFIXION). He saw the whole of his life, including his suffering and crucifixion, as a fulfilment of the Old Testament Scriptures (Matt 26:53-54; Mark 14:21,27; Luke 4:18-21; 18:31-34; 22:37; 24:25-27; 24:44-46). This did not mean that he felt no distress or temptation in the face of death. More likely it increased his suffering, but he resisted all attempts to turn him away from the cross. He gave his life willingly (Matt 16:21-23; 26:53; John 10:18; 12:27).

Jesus' death, then, was not an unfortunate accident, nor was it the heroic deed of a martyr. It was the great act, the only act, by which God could deal with sin and release the guilty from sin's punishment. Jesus gave his life as a ransom. He paid the price to deliver guilty sinners from the power of sin and death (Matt 20:28; 26:26-28; 1 Tim 1:15; Heb 9:12-14; 1 Peter 1:18-20; see FORGIVENESS; REDEMPTION).

Although Jesus was crucified by wicked men, his death was according to God's plan (Acts 2:23). He was under the curse of God as he hung on the cross, but it was the curse he bore on behalf of sinners (Gal 3:13). He who was sinless bore the sins of those who were sinful (2 Cor 5:21; 1 Peter 2:24; see JUSTIFICATION). He who was not under God's judgment bore that judgment in place of those who were. He bore the wrath of God so that he might bring guilty sinners back to God (Rom 3:23-25; Col 1:20; 1 John 2:2; 4:10; see BLOOD; PROPITIATION; RECONCILIATION).

Christ's one sacrifice is sufficient to bring complete salvation. It needs nothing to be added to it. It does not need to be repeated. It is a finished work — complete, final, perfect (Heb 9:12,25-26; 10:12-14; cf. John 17:4; 19:30; Rom 8:31-39; Col 2:13-15)).

Resurrection and exaltation

Jesus' death was not for his own sins (for he had none) but for the sins of others. Therefore, death could have no power over him. He rose from death as proof to all that the Father was pleased with the Son's entire work. Jesus had made full atonement for sin and was the triumphant Lord, Messiah and Saviour (Acts 2:24,36; 3:13; Rom 1:4; 4:25; 1 Cor 15:3-4; Phil 2:8-11; Heb 2:14-15).

The resurrection body of Jesus, however, was not simply a corpse brought back to life. It was a glorified 'spiritual' body, belonging to an entirely new order of existence that he brought into being and that all believers will one day share in (1 Cor 15:20-23,42-49). God raised him up and gave him glory, exalting him to heaven's highest place (Acts 2:32-33; 5:30-31; Eph 1:20-22; 2:6; Heb 1:3; 2:9; 1 Peter 1:21).

Although he now existed in a glorified and exalted state, Jesus graciously made a number of appearances to his disciples over a period of forty days following his resurrection (Acts 1:3). Besides giving them further teaching, he proved to them that although his resurrection was a literal bodily resurrection, his resurrection state was uniquely different from his previous state. He could make himself visible to human eyes, or invisible, as he wished (Luke 24:31,39,43; John 20:19,26-27; see RESURRECTION).

When he disappeared from his disciples for the last time, Jesus showed by the means of his departure that he would appear to them no more. He would, however, send the Holy Spirit to be with them, as he himself had been with them. Jesus meanwhile would remain in the heavenly world, exalted in his Father's presence, till the time came for him to return (Luke 24:50-51; John 16:7; Acts 1:9-11; 2:33; 1 Peter 3:22; see HOLY SPIRIT).

Even in his exalted place in heaven, Jesus continues his work on behalf of his people. He claims the blessings of God for them, defends them against the accusations of Satan, and guarantees the continued forgiveness of their sins, all on the basis of his sacrificial death (Rom 8:34; Heb 7:25; 9:24; 1 John 1:7-9; 2:1; see ADVOCATE; PRIEST, sub-heading 'The high priesthood of Jesus').

Christ's return and final triumph

In considering the second coming of Jesus, we should not think of it independently of his first coming. His return and the events connected with it form the climax of what he did through his life, death and resurrection. All that he achieved at his first coming will find its full and final expression in the events of his second coming: the conquest of sin, death and Satan (1 Cor 15:54-57; Rev 20:10; cf. Heb 2:14); the salvation of man (Heb 9:28; cf. Eph 2:8); the gift of eternal life (Matt 25:46; 2 Cor 5:4; cf. John 5:24); the healing of the physical world (Rom 8:18-23; cf. Mark 1:31,42; 4:39); and the establishment of God's kingdom (Matt 25:34; 1 Cor 15:24-28; cf. Luke 17:21).

Jesus' second coming is that great and final 'day of the Lord' that people of both Old and New Testament eras saw as the climax of the world's history. God will intervene in human affairs and bring his purposes to fulfilment (Zech 14:9; 1 Cor 1:7-8; 2 Peter 3:11-13; see DAY OF THE LORD).

Preceding and accompanying this day of the Lord there will be great wonders in the heavens and great distress upon earth. In an event as sudden, as open and as startling as a flash of lightning, Jesus will return in power and glory to save his people and judge his enemies (Matt 24:27-31; 2 Thess 1:7-10; 2:8; Rev 19:11-16). Believers of former generations will be raised from death and, along with believers still alive, will enter a new order of existence in imperishable, spiritual bodies. They will then be with Christ for ever (1 Cor 15:20-23,42-57; Phil 3:21; 1 Thess 4:13-18; see RESURRECTION).

The above characteristics of Christ's return are expressed in the three Greek words that the New Testament most commonly uses of it. Christ's return is an *apokalupsis*, indicating a revealing of himself in majesty and power (1 Cor 1:7; 2 Thess 1:7; 1 Peter 1:7,13; 4:13). It is an *epiphaneia*, indicating his appearing visibly before people's eyes (2 Thess 2:8; 1 Tim 6:14; 2 Tim 1:10; 4:1,8; Titus 2:13). It is a *parousia*, indicating his coming, arrival and presence (Matt 24:3,27,37; 1 Thess 2:19; 3:13; 4:15; 2 Thess 2:1,8; 1 John 2:28).

Judgment is one of the inevitable consequences of Christ's return (Matt 24:30-31,40-42; 25:31-32,46). While unbelievers will have no way of escaping condemnation and punishment, believers can face the coming judgment with confidence. They know that Christ has already delivered them from the wrath of God (Rom 5:9; 1 Thess 1:10; 5:9).

Yet, though saved from eternal condemnation, believers are not saved from all judgment. They are answerable to God for the way they have lived on earth, and on that day they will face God and their lives will be examined (Rom 14:10; 2 Cor 5:10; 1 Thess 2:19; see JUDGMENT).

The second coming of Jesus, therefore, while it is something Christians look forward to (Titus 2:13; see HOPE), is also something that urges them to be holy, diligent and sincere in the way they live now (Phil 1:10; 1 Thess 3:13; 5:23; 2 Tim 4:8; 2 Peter 3:11-13; Rev 22:12). In addition it makes them more earnest in spreading the gospel of Jesus Christ throughout the world (Matt 24:14; 2 Peter 3:9-10; Rev 22:12-14). Since Jesus will return when least expected, Christians must be ready always (Matt 24:42-44; 1 Thess 5:2-6).

Not only believers, but the physical creation also will be redeemed at Christ's return. The world of nature, which has suffered because of man's sin, will receive its full glory. The triumph of Christ's kingdom is seen in a triumphant Christ reigning with his redeemed people over a redeemed earth (Rom 8:19-23; 2 Tim 2:12; Rev 5:9-10; 20:4).

Finally, having destroyed all enemies and removed all wickedness, Jesus Christ will have the satisfaction of seeing that the victory he achieved at the cross is effectual throughout the universe (Phil 2:10-11; Rev 11:15; 20:10). The Father had entrusted to him the work of overcoming all rebellion and bringing all things into perfect submission to the sovereign God. That work will now have reached its triumphant climax (1 Cor 15:24-28).

JEW

The name 'Jew' was not used in Old Testament times before the division of the Israelite kingdom. After the death of King Solomon, the kingdom was split into two parts, the northern part being known as Israel and the southern part as Judah. People of the southern kingdom, though Israelites by blood (since they were descended from Jacob, or Israel) were called Judeans, to distinguish them from those of the northern kingdom. The name 'Judean' was later shortened to 'Jew' (Jer 34:9).

Both northern and southern kingdoms were eventually destroyed and the people taken captive to foreign lands. When the descendants of these captives were later allowed to return to the land of Israel, most of those who returned belonged to the former southern kingdom (the Judeans, or Jews).

By this time the name 'Jew' was in common use. It was freely applied to all those now living back in the ancient homeland, without having any specific reference to the tribe they originally came from. In other words, it was used in general as a name for all Israelites (Ezra 6:7; Neh 6:6; Esther 3:6,10; Jer 44:1; Dan 3:8). By the time of the New Testament, the names 'Hebrew', 'Israelite' and 'Jew' were used interchangeably (Matt 2:2; John 1:19; Acts 2:5; Rom 1:16; 2:28-29; 11:1; 1 Cor 9:20; 2 Cor 11:22; Gal 2:14; Phil 3:5; see also HEBREW; ISRAEL; JUDAH).

JEZEBEL

By her marriage to King Ahab of Israel, Jezebel helped to join Phoenicia and Israel together in a political and religious alliance. She was daughter of the king-priest of the Phoenician cities Tyre and Sidon, and set out to make Phoenician Baalism the official religion of Israel. Ahab cooperated in the plan and built a royal Baal temple in Israel's capital, Samaria (1 Kings 16:29-33).

Soon, however, Ahab ran into opposition, his opponent being God's prophet Elijah (1 Kings 18:17-18). The ministry of the prophets Elijah and Elisha was aimed specifically at preserving the true worship of Yahweh in Israel when Jezebel's Baalism threatened to wipe it out (see ELIJAH; ELISHA).

Within a short time, Jezebel had killed a large number of God's prophets and replaced them with several hundred of her own (1 Kings 18:4,19). When,

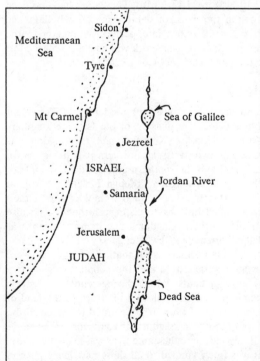

after a contest on Mt Carmel, Elijah defeated and killed the Baal prophets, Jezebel tried to kill him, but he escaped (1 Kings 18:40; 19:1-3).

Jezebel demonstrated her total lack of moral uprightness in the way she arranged for Ahab to seize the vineyard of Naboth. She set up people to make false accusations against the innocent Naboth, then, after having him executed, she seized his vineyard (1 Kings 21:1-16). Elijah announced a horrible judgment upon the dynasty of Ahab, and particularly upon the murderous Jezebel (1 Kings 21:20-25).

Even after Ahab's death, Jezebel still exercised much influence in Israel. For the next fourteen years two of her sons, Ahaziah and Jehoram, ruled as successive kings and promoted her religious policies (1 Kings 22:51-53; 2 Kings 1:17; 3:1-3). She and Jehoram were killed at Jezreel in Jehu's bloody revolution. Strong-willed to the end, Jezebel was determined to meet her executioner with royal dignity (2 Kings 9:22-37).

In New Testament times the church at Thyatira in Asia Minor was troubled by a woman nicknamed Jezebel. She was a false prophetess whose religion, like that of the original Jezebel, was characterized by idolatry and immorality (Rev 2:18-23).

JEZREEL

Among the important centres of northern Israel was the town of Jezreel in the tribal territory of Issachar (Josh 19:17-18). (This town is to be distinguished from the lesser known Jezreel in the tribal territory of Judah to the south; cf. Josh 15:56; 1 Sam 25:43.) Jezreel of the north was situated on the edge of the Plain of Esdraelon, where the plain began to slope down into the Valley of Jezreel. This region was often a battleground in Old Testament times, and Jezreel sometimes became involved in the fighting (e.g. 1 Sam 29:11; see PALESTINE).

When, during the time of the divided kingdom, the king of Israel established his capital in Samaria, he also built a summer palace at Jezreel. Ahab later expanded this palace by unjustly seizing the adjoining property belonging to Naboth (1 Kings 21:1-2,16). Ahab's wife Jezebel, their son Joram and others of the royal household were killed at Jezreel in Jehu's bloody revolution (2 Kings 8:29; 9:16-37; 10:11; Hosea 1:4-5).

JOAB

It seems that Joab and his brothers were among the several hundred people who joined David during his flight from Saul. The private army that David formed from these people later became the central fighting force in his royal army (1 Sam 22:1-2; 26:6; 30:9; 2 Sam 2:13). (For map covering the region of David's activities see DAVID.)

In the two-year civil war that followed Saul's death, Joab quickly established himself as David's military leader (2 Sam 2:28). He was also a close relative of David (1 Chron 2:13-16). When Saul's former commander, Abner, defected to David, Joab saw him as a threat and murdered him. Joab used the excuse that he was retaliating because Abner had killed his brother in battle. But David saw it as murder and never forgave Joab (2 Sam 2:12-23; 3:23-39; 1 Kings 2:5-6).

Not long after these events, David became undisputed king of Israel. In response to David's declaration that he wanted to take Jerusalem from its Canaanite inhabitants, Joab led a victorious assault on the city and was rewarded by being appointed commander-in-chief of the Israelite army (1 Chron 11:6; 18:15). He was a clever, brave and loyal soldier (2 Sam 10:6-19; 11:1; 12:26) who usually had David's interests at heart (1 Sam 12:27-28; 24:2-4). Nevertheless, there was no excuse for his cooperating with David in the killing of Uriah (2 Sam 11:6-25).

When, as a consequence of David's wrongdoing, his family started to break up, Joab tried to preserve the dynasty by ensuring that there was a recognized heir to the throne. He considered that the most suitable of David's sons for the position was Absalom, but Absalom had committed murder and fled to a neighbouring country. Joab therefore worked out a clever plan that enabled Absalom to return from exile without having to stand trial (2 Sam 14:1-24).

Once back in Jerusalem, Absalom heartlessly used Joab to pursue his own ambitions (2 Sam 14:28-33). When Absalom rebelled against David and seized the throne, Joab again upheld David. He brought the rebellion to a swift end by killing Absalom, even though it was against David's wishes (2 Sam 18:2,5,9-16). He then rebuked David for his lack of gratitude to those who had saved him (2 Sam 19:1-8).

Upon resuming his rule in Jerusalem, David appointed Absalom's general, Amasa, chief of the army in place of Joab. This was clearly unfair to Joab, who had been loyal to David and won him the victory (2 Sam 19:13). Soon there was another uprising against David. When Amasa proved himself to be a poor leader, Joab murdered him and took control of the army as of old (2 Sam 20:4-10,23).

In the palace conflict to decide which son would succeed the ageing David as king, Joab supported Adonijah in opposition to Solomon, who was David's choice (1 Kings 1:5-8,13,19; 1 Chron 28:5). On becoming king, Solomon executed Joab. A violent death seemed a fitting end for one whose life had been marked by so many acts of violence (1 Kings 2:28-35).

JOASH

See Jehoash.

JOB

The Old Testament book of Job is among the group of writings known as the wisdom books. In ancient Israel people recognized wisdom writings as being different from other writings. Wisdom teachers were a category distinct from other religious guides and leaders.

Wisdom teachers did not teach the law as did the priests, nor bring revelations from God as did the prophets. Rather they looked at the practical affairs of life and, as those who feared God and knew his law, gave advice for living. Sometimes they gave common sense instruction based on their observations of the experiences of life in general. Other times they investigated the puzzles of life when the facts of experience seemed to contradict the generally accepted beliefs. The book of Proverbs gives an example of the former type of teaching, the book of Job an example of the latter. (See also Wisdom Literature.)

Understanding the book

There is no certainty concerning who wrote the book of Job or when it was written. The book takes its name from the chief person in the story.

Job was a wealthy, intelligent, God-fearing man who lived in Uz, somewhere in the region east of Palestine. When a series of disasters ruined his prosperity, destroyed his family and struck him down with a terrible disease, his friends argued that his troubles must have resulted from his secret sins. Job denied this, even though it was the commonly held traditional belief. Job knew he was not perfect, but he also knew that the traditional belief did not explain everything. The long and bitter argument that followed takes up most of the book.

The reader of the book, however, knows what neither Job nor his friends knew. Satan had made the accusation that people serve God only because of the benefits they can get from him. If, instead, they receive only hardship and suffering, they will curse him (Job 1:9-11; 2:4-5). God allowed disasters to fall upon Job to prove the genuineness of Job's faith and at the same time enrich Job's experience of God. Job's sufferings were not a sign of God's judgment on him, but proof of God's confidence in him (Job 1:8; 2:3).

As the friends persisted with their unjust and cruel accusations, Job increasingly lost patience with them. Job's frustration drove him to protest to God, whom he saw as his only hope. In making his protests, Job may have been guilty of rash language, but at least he took his protests to the right person (Job 7:11-21; 13:13-28; 14:13-17; 17:3-4). He was finally satisfied, not through having all his questions answered, but through meeting the God to whom he had cried. God is not answerable to man, and he gave Job no explanation of his sufferings. Yet Job was content. He realized now that the unseen God was in control of all events and his wisdom was perfect (Job 42:1-6).

God then declared that the friends, in accusing Job of great sin, were wrong (Job 42:7). He also showed the error of the commonly held belief that suffering was always the result of personal sin. In addition he proved Satan to be wrong in his accusation that people worship God because of what they can get from him. Job had remained true to God even though he had lost everything. God now blessed Job with greater blessings than he had ever had before (Job 42:10).

Outline of contents

The book opens with a narrative section that recounts Satan's challenge to God and his attack on Job (1:1-2:13). The remainder of the book, except for the closing narrative, is in poetry. It starts with a complaint from Job (3:1-26) and this begins a long debate between Job and his three friends.

Eliphaz, the first of the friends to speak, states that Job's suffering must be because of his sin. Therefore, if Job repents he will have good health and prosperity again (4:1-5:27). Job rejects Eliphaz's accusations and complains to God about his unjust suffering (6:1-7:21). Bildad heartlessly reminds Job of his misfortunes, pointing out that they are a fitting punishment. He emphasizes that the traditional teaching is all-important (8:1-22). In his response, Job again complains to God about the injustice he suffers (9:1-10:22). Zophar, the shallowest thinker and most hot tempered of the three friends, then attacks Job (11:1-20), to which Job gives a lengthy and at times sarcastic reply (12:1-14:22).

The second round of argument follows the same sequence as the first. Eliphaz speaks and Job replies (15:1-17:16), Bildad speaks and Job replies (18:1-19:29), then Zophar speaks and Job replies (20:1-21:34). The third round begins in the same fashion, with Eliphaz speaking, followed by Job

(22:1-24:25). Bildad speaks only briefly, followed by Job (25:1-26:14), but Zophar does not speak at all. Job therefore proceeds to give a summary of his position (27:1-31:40).

A young man named Elihu, having listened to the debate in silence, now decides to speak. Angry that the friends have not convinced Job of his wrongdoing, Elihu claims he will answer Job with different arguments. But he adds little to what the other three have said (32:1-37:24).

As a fierce storm breaks, God himself now speaks to Job. He reminds Job, through chapter after chapter, of his divine wisdom in controlling all things, and he challenges Job to take the place of the Almighty and govern the moral order of the universe (38:1-41:34). Job cannot accept God challenge; he realizes he has been conquered. At last he submits, and in doing so he finds peace (42:1-6). God then rebukes the friends and expresses his approval of Job (42:7-17).

JOEL

Unlike most of the other prophets, Joel does not state the period during which he preached. This is no great hindrance to the reader, for the book is largely concerned with just one incident, a severe locust plague. The setting appears to be Jerusalem and the surrounding countryside.

Background and meaning

One possible date for the book is about 835-830 BC, during the reign of the boy-king Joash. This would explain why there is no mention of oppressive enemy nations such as Syria, Assyria and Babylon, which are constantly mentioned in the other prophets, for at that time those nations had not begun to interfere in Judean affairs. It would also explain why Joel makes no mention of the reigning Judean king, for the government was largely in the hands of the priest Jehoiada (2 Kings 11:1-21; 12:1). The prominence of Jehoiada could be partly responsible for Joel's interest in the temple and its services (Joel 1:9,13; 2:12,15-17).

An alternative suggestion is that the book belongs to the period following Judah's return from captivity. On this theory the most likely time of writing is either 520-510 BC, after the ministry of Haggai and Zechariah and the rebuilding of the Jerusalem temple (Ezra 5:1-2,15), or about 400 BC, a generation or so after the reforms of Ezra and Nehemiah (Neh 8:1-3,9; 13:30).

Joel interpreted the locust plague as God's judgment on Judah for its sin. He urged the people to repent, confident that God would renew his blessing upon them. God would not only renew their crops but also give them a greater knowledge of himself (Joel 2:12-14,23-27).

According to Joel's view, these events were symbolic of God's future blessing upon all his people and his judgment upon all his enemies. In New Testament times Peter saw a fulfilment of Joel's prophecy in the events that resulted from Jesus' death and resurrection. A new age had dawned, the Spirit had come upon all God's people, and judgment had become certain for all God's enemies (Joel 2:28-32; Acts 2:14-21).

Summary of contents

In very lively fashion, Joel describes the devastating effects of the locust plague, firstly upon the farmers and other country people (1:1-20), then upon the citizens of Jerusalem (2:1-11). He calls the people to

Locusts

gather at the temple and repent (2:12-17), and offers hope for renewed productivity in their fields and vineyards (2:18-27).

A far greater blessing, however, will be the gift of God's Spirit, enabling the people to know and obey him better (2:28-32). The locust plague and its removal picture the greater judgment and greater blessing yet to come (3:1-21).

JOHN THE APOSTLE

Various names have been used of John the apostle. Many of the people of his time referred to him as 'the disciple whom Jesus loved', perhaps because of his special relationship with Jesus (John 13:23; 19:26-27). Yet Jesus himself often referred to John and his older brother James as 'sons of thunder', perhaps because they were sometimes impatient and over-zealous (Mark 3:17; 10:35-40; Luke 9:49-56). John was one of the most highly respected leaders in the early church, and later generations knew him as 'the elder' (2 John 1; 3 John 1). (For his writings see JOHN, GOSPEL OF; JOHN, LETTERS OF.) He has traditionally been regarded as the writer of the book of Revelation (Rev 1:1,9; 22:8; see REVELATION, BOOK OF).

In the time of Jesus

John's father was a fisherman named Zebedee (Matt 4:21). His mother, Salome, appears to have been the sister of Mary the mother of Jesus (Matt 27:56; Mark 15:40; John 19:25-27). The family lived in a town on the shores of Lake Galilee, where James and John worked as fishermen in partnership with another pair of brothers, Peter and Andrew (Matt 4:18-21; Luke 5:10).

Most likely all four men had responded to John the Baptist's preaching. They became disciples of the Baptist and were part of that minority of true believers who looked expectantly for the promised Saviour. John was probably one of the two disciples (the other was Andrew) whom the Baptist first directed to Jesus Christ (John 1:35-40). Soon both pairs of brothers had become followers of Jesus (Matt 4:22), and later all four were included in Jesus' group of twelve apostles (Matt 10:2). Peter, James and John developed into an inner circle of disciples who were particularly close to Jesus (Mark 5:37; 9:2; 14:33).

As the ministry of Jesus progressed, Peter became increasingly more prominent. James and John, with their mother, tried to outdo Peter by going to Jesus and asking him to give the top two positions in his kingdom to them. They received no such guarantee from Jesus; only a rebuke for their selfish ambition and a promise of persecution ahead (Matt 20:20-28). By the time Jesus' ministry had come to an end, Peter and John were clearly the two leading apostles (Luke 22:8; John 19:26-27; 20:2-9; 21:20).

In the early church

After Jesus' return to his Father, Peter and John provided the main leadership for the Jerusalem Christians. Their boldness amid persecution was an example to all (Acts 1:13; 3:1-4,11; 4:13-20; 5:40). They were the first Christian leaders to show publicly that God accepted non-Jewish converts into the church equally with Jewish converts (Acts 8:14-17). John's willingness to preach in Samaritan villages was in marked contrast to his hostility to Samaritans a few years earlier (Acts 8:25; cf. Luke

9:52-56). With James the Lord's brother they formed a representative group who expressed the Jerusalem church's fellowship in the mission of Paul and Barnabas to the Gentiles (Gal 2:9).

The Bible contains little information about John's later activities, though there are early records outside the Bible that refer to him. According to these, John lived to a very old age (as Jesus had foretold; John 21:20-23) and spent most of his later years in Ephesus. From there he wrote his Gospel and the three letters that bear his name. It seems also that he was imprisoned on Patmos, an island off the coast from Ephesus, from where the book of Revelation was written (Rev 1:9).

JOHN THE BAPTIST

God's purpose for John the Baptist was that he be the forerunner of the Messiah. Even before John was born, God revealed to his parents that he had been specially marked out for this task. Like prophets of a former era, John was to live a life of hardship and self-denial, at the same time preaching a message of repentance to the people of Israel. Those who responded to his message in obedience and faith would thereby show themselves to be the true people of God. They would be ready to welcome the Messiah and so enter his kingdom (Luke 1:13-17,57-66,76-79; Matt 3:2).

Forerunner of the Messiah

People in Israel had long expected that Elijah the prophet would return before the coming of the Messiah (Mal 4:5). Jesus pointed out that this 'Elijah' was in fact John the Baptist (Matt 11:10-14; 17:10-13). John preached in the spirit and power of Elijah (Luke 1:17) and shared the harsh existence of Elijah, living in semi-barren regions where he wore rough clothing and ate wild food (Matt 3:4; Luke 1:80; 3:2; cf. 1 Kings 17:5-7; 19:4-9; 2 Kings 1:8; 2:8).

John began his preaching in that region of Palestine where the Jordan River approached the Dead Sea (Mark 1:4-5; Luke 3:2-3; John 1:28). God had called him to be a prophet (Luke 1:76; 7:26; 16:16; 20:6) and he preached after the manner of the Old Testament prophets. He condemned those who thought that their Israelite nationality guaranteed their salvation (Matt 3:7-10; cf. Amos 9:7-8), and denounced the greed, corruption and injustice of Israelite society (Luke 3:10-14; cf. Isa 5:8-23). The only ones who were truly God's people were those who repented of their sins and demonstrated their sincerity in baptism (Matt 3:1-2; cf. Isa 1:16-20).

The baptism that John proclaimed, though important, was not able to empower people for a new life. That power could come only through a greater baptism, the gift of the Holy Spirit; and that was a gift that only the Messiah could give. John was not the Messiah, but he was clearly preparing the way for the Messiah (Luke 3:3-6,15-17; John 1:6-7,19-28). He announced the kingdom of God (Matt 3:2).

Introducing the Messiah

John and Jesus were about the same age and were related (Luke 1:36), but their backgrounds and upbringing were different. John was the son of a priest and grew up in Judea in the south of Palestine (Luke 1:5-13,39-41,65,80), whereas Jesus was the son of a carpenter and grew up in Galilee in the north (Luke 1:26; 2:51).

There is no record of what association John and Jesus had during their childhood and youth. However, by the time they were about thirty years of age (Luke 3:23) they were at least familiar with each other's activities.

John knew enough about Jesus to know that Jesus was the better man and had no need for a baptism for repentance. But Jesus insisted that John baptize him. As a result of that baptism, John knew for certain (through the visible descent of the Spirit upon Jesus) that this one was the promised Messiah (Matt 3:13-17; John 1:33-34). By his baptism Jesus showed that he was on the side of those who, by responding to John's baptism, had shown themselves to be God's true people (see BAPTISM).

The followers of John developed into a clearly recognizable group, characterized by devotion and self-denial (Luke 5:33; John 3:23-25). They spread into regions so far from Jerusalem that it was a long time before some of them heard the full message concerning the Messiah of whom John had spoken (Acts 18:24-26; 19:1-5). Yet John was not interested in building a personal following, and he felt well satisfied when his disciples left him to follow Jesus (John 1:35; 3:26-30).

From the old era into the new

In moving widely around the Jordan region, John would have spent some time in areas west of Jordan controlled by Pilate and some time in areas east of Jordan controlled by Herod Antipas (Luke 3:1; John 1:28; 3:23). This brought John into conflict with Herod Antipas, whom he rebuked for marrying the wife of his brother, Herod Philip. Antipas replied by throwing John into prison (Mark 6:17-20; Luke 3:19-20).

Shut up in prison, John received only irregular, and possibly inaccurate, reports of Jesus' ministry. This made him wonder whether Jesus really was the Messiah he had foretold, so he sent messengers to ask Jesus directly (Luke 7:18-20). Jesus reassured John by pointing out that his works were those that the Old Testament prophets had spoken of when they foretold the messianic age (Luke 7:21-23; cf. Isa 35:5-6; 61:1-3).

Jesus reassured the people also, for he did not want them to lose their respect for John. There was nothing weak or uncertain about John. He did not look for comfort or prestige, but like a true prophet he endured a life of hardship for the sake of God (Luke 7:24-27). John was the last and greatest prophet of the era before Christ. But he did not live to see the fulness of the new era (for he was executed by Herod; Mark 6:21-29). The blessings of the Messiah's kingdom are such that the humblest believer of this new era is more blessed than the greatest believer of the old (Luke 7:28).

JOHN, GOSPEL OF

Both early tradition and evidence from the Bible itself indicate that 'the disciple whom Jesus loved' was John the son of Zebedee, and that this John was the author of John's Gospel (John 21:20,24).

The other Gospels mention John by name frequently, as he was one of the three apostles who featured prominently in much of the activity of Jesus. But his name never appears in John's Gospel. The writer, preferring to follow a common practice of not mentioning his own name, used instead the descriptive name by which he was well known (John 13:23; 19:26; 21:7; see JOHN THE APOSTLE). Perhaps John's use of this title showed his unending gratitude for all that Jesus had done for him.

The apostle at Ephesus

John was very old at the time he wrote his Gospel, and was probably the last survivor of the original apostolic group. There was even a belief that he would never die (John 21:23). Records from the period immediately after the New Testament era indicate that he lived his later years in Ephesus in Asia Minor, where he fought against false teachers. He probably wrote his Gospel within the last decade or so of the first century.

Wrong teaching about Jesus had developed over the years (Col 2:4,8,18-19; 1 Tim 6:3-5), and was to become very destructive with the Gnostic heresies of the second century. John was already dealing with early stages of these errors at Ephesus.

Certain teachers had come into the church and denied that God and man were perfectly united in Jesus. Some denied that Jesus was fully God, others that he was fully man. John opposed both errors. His book, however, was not intended merely as an attack on false teaching. He had a positive purpose, and that was to lead people to faith in Christ, so that they might experience the full and eternal life that Christ had made possible (John 20:31; cf. 1:4; 3:15; 4:14; 5:24; 6:27; 8:12; 10:10; 11:25; 14:6; 17:3).

From the opening words of the book, John asserted that Jesus was fully God (John 1:1) and fully man (John 1:14). As to his divinity, he was the eternal one who created all things (John 1:2-3) and who came from the heavenly world to reveal God to man (John 1:18; 3:13; 5:18-19; 6:62; 14:9,11) As to his humanity, he had a material body that possessed the normal physical characteristics (John 4:6-7; 9:6; 19:28,34) and that experienced the normal human emotions (John 11:35; 12:27).

Characteristics of John's Gospel

By the time John wrote his Gospel, the other three Gospels were widely known. Since John and his readers were no doubt familiar with them, there was no point in John's producing a similar narrative-type account of Jesus' life. John was concerned more with showing the meaning of incidents in Jesus' life. The stories he knew were beyond number (John 20:30; 21:25), but from them he made a selection, around which he built his book. He used this material to teach spiritual truth by showing what the chosen incidents signified. For this reason he called the incidents 'signs' (e.g. John 2:1-11; 4:46-54; 6:1-14; 11:1-44; see SIGNS).

Because the signs were designed to show that Jesus was the messianic Son of God (John 20:30-31), they were often followed by long debates with the Jews (e.g. John 5:1-15 followed by 5:16-47; John 9:1-12 followed by 9:13-10:39). These and other debates that Jesus had with the Jews provided John with his teaching material. He used the words of Jesus to teach the Christian truths he wanted to express (e.g. John 7:1-52; 8:12-59).

The contrast between John and the other Gospel writers is seen when one of John's 'signs' is recorded also in the other Gospels. The other writers did little more than tell the story, whereas John followed the story with lengthy teaching that arose out of it (e.g. cf. Matt 14:13-21 with John 6:1-14 and the teaching that follows in v. 26-65).

John's concern with the interpretation of events showed itself also in the way he recorded some of

Jesus' lengthy conversations with people (e.g. with Nicodemus in John 3:1-15 and with the Samaritan woman in John 4:1-26). Likewise he used his account of the Last Supper, reported briefly in the other Gospels, to provide five chapters of teaching on important Christian doctrines (John 13:1-17:26).

In John's Gospel, more than in the others, there is an emphasis on the reason for the Jews' hatred of Jesus. They considered that his claim to be God in human form was blasphemy, and they were determined to get rid of him (John 6:42; 7:28-30; 8:57-59; 10:33,39; 11:25,53). The strongest opposition to him was in Jerusalem, and John's Gospel shows that Jesus spent more time in Jerusalem than is recorded in Matthew, Mark and Luke (John 2:13; 5:1; 7:14,25; 8:20; 10:22-23; 11:1).

Summary of contents

In the introduction Jesus is presented as the eternal Word who became man (1:1-18). John the Baptist prepared the way for Jesus (1:19-28) and then baptized him (1:29-34), after which Jesus called his first disciples (1:35-51), presented his first 'sign' to them (2:1-11), then went to Jerusalem and cleansed the temple (2:12-25). Jesus spoke to Nicodemus about new birth (3:1-21), and John the Baptist spoke to the Jews about Jesus (3:22-36).

Upon leaving Judea, Jesus met and taught various people in Samaria (4:1-42) and performed a healing miracle in Galilee (4:43-54). Back in Jerusalem a further healing miracle resulted in a dispute with the Jews about Jesus' divine sonship (5:1-47). After a miracle in Galilee that provided food for a multitude, people wanted to make Jesus king (6:1-21). Jesus taught that the true 'food' for man's life was himself (6:22-71). Jesus' unbelieving brothers urged him to go to Jerusalem and perform his wonders at a festival that was about to take place (7:1-13), but when Jesus went he taught the people and aroused much opposition (7:14-8:11). He met more opposition when he taught that he was the light of the world (8:12-30) and the one who could set people free (8:31-59).

Jesus' healing of a blind man in Jerusalem brought him into further conflict with the Jewish leaders (9:1-41). This resulted in Jesus' contrasting himself as the good shepherd with them as worthless shepherds (10:1-30). After being further attacked, he went to the regions around the Jordan River, where many believed (10:31-42). At Bethany, just outside Jerusalem, he raised Lazarus from death, declaring himself to be the resurrection and the life (11:1-44). This was the event that finally stirred the Jews to plot his death (11:45-57).

After an anointing at Bethany (12:1-8), Jesus entered Jerusalem triumphantly (12:9-19) and gave his final public teaching (12:20-50). At the Passover meal with his disciples he demonstrated the nature of true service by washing their feet (13:1-20) and warned of the betrayer among them (13:21-38).

In the teaching that followed, Jesus told the disciples that as he had come from the Father, so he would return to the Father, after which he would send his Spirit to indwell them (14:1-31). They had to abide in him (15:1-17) and bear persecution for his sake (15:18-27). Jesus spoke further of the Holy Spirit's work (16:1-15), but in their confusion of mind the disciples scarcely understood him (16:16-33). He then prayed at length to his Father, not only for himself and his disciples, but also for those who would yet believe (17:1-26).

Upon going to Gethsemane to pray again, Jesus was arrested and taken to the high priest (18:1-27). From there he was taken to the Roman governor (18:28-40), humiliated before the people (19:1-16), crucified (19:17-30) and buried (19:31-42). On the third day he rose from the dead, appearing first to Mary and then to his disciples (20:1-25). The next week he appeared to the disciples again (20:26-31). Some time later he appeared to seven of the disciples at the Sea of Galilee (21:1-14), where he delivered a final challenging message to Peter (21:15-25).

JOHN, LETTERS OF

Towards the end of the first century, the churches in and around Ephesus suffered much tension and conflict because of false teaching (e.g. Rev 2:2-6; cf. Acts 20:17,29-30). Early records indicate that the apostle John lived in Ephesus at this time, and that he wrote his Gospel and three letters partly to counter some of the false views.

Background to 1 John

The chief trouble-maker in Ephesus was a man named Cerinthus. He had been influenced by Gnostic ideas concerning the relation between spirit and matter, and as a result developed wrong beliefs concerning Jesus Christ. Believing God to be pure and matter to be evil, he denied that Jesus Christ could be God and man at the same time. This led to a variety of wrong teachings. Some of these denied the full deity of Jesus, and others denied his true humanity (1 John 2:22; 4:2-3).

Many Christians became uncertain of their salvation; for if the Jesus who lived and died in this world was not at all times fully God and fully man, how could his death benefit man or satisfy God? To reassure Christians in their understanding of Jesus and the salvation he brought them, John wrote firstly his Gospel (John 20:31), and then the letter known as 1 John (1 John 5:13).

Gnostic ideas concerning spirit and matter, besides leading to wrong teaching about Jesus, led to wrong behaviour among believers. Cerinthus taught that the behaviour of the body could not affect the purity of the soul, and therefore believers could sin as they wished. John condemned such teaching (1 John 3:6). He emphasized that Christians must be obedient to God, must love others and must be disciplined within themselves.

Contents of 1 John

From the beginning of his letter, John emphasizes the two areas of Christian truth that were under attack — the eternal godhead yet full manhood of Jesus Christ (1:1-4) and the obligation on Christians to live pure, disciplined, obedient lives (1:5-2:6). All Christians are to follow Christ's commandment to be loving, and are to resist the pressures upon them from an evil world (2:7-17).

God's people must recognize that those with wrong teaching about Jesus Christ are of the devil (2:18-29), and so too are those who encourage Christians to sin (3:1-10). Behaviour is the test of the genuineness of a person's Christianity (3:11-24). Though steadfastly resisting error (4:1-6), Christians must consistently develop love, and in so doing they will become more assured in their salvation (4:7-21). Right belief is also necessary for assurance (5:1-5), and this belief centres on the uniqueness of Jesus Christ and his work (5:6-12). The practical results of assurance will be effectual prayer and victory over sin (5:13-21).

Background and contents of 2 John

The false teaching that John fought against in his first letter was being spread around the churches by travelling preachers. The letter that we know as 2 John was written to counter such teaching.

No names are mentioned in the letter, but it seems that 'the elder' who wrote it was John the aged apostle, and 'the elect lady' who received it was a church whose 'children' (members) had so far kept the true Christian teaching (v. 1-4). John wanted them to maintain right belief and right behaviour, and warned that false teaching, if allowed into the church, would ruin it (v. 5-13).

Background and contents of 3 John

In spite of his warnings about travelling preachers who had wrong teaching (2 John 10-11), John knew that many other travelling preachers were genuine Christians whose teaching was true and wholesome. But there was a problem in one church because a dictatorial person named Diotrephes refused to accept the travelling preachers into the church. He considered them representatives of John, whom he opposed.

John therefore wrote a letter (3 John) to one of the better leaders in the church, a friend named Gaius, to encourage and help him. In the letter John encouraged Gaius to keep helping the true preachers of the gospel (v. 1-8). He assured Gaius that if Diotrephes persisted in his present attitudes, then he himself would deal with him when he visited the church in the near future (v. 9-15).

JONAH

In contrast to the other prophetical books, the book of Jonah does not say who wrote it or why it was written. The book takes its name from the chief person in the story, a prophet who had become known for his accurate forecast of the growth of Israel (the northern part of the divided kingdom) under Jeroboam II (2 Kings 14:23,25).

Additional contrasts to other prophetical books are the small amount of the prophet's preaching recorded in the book, and the small amount that is written in poetry. The book is mostly narrative and is directed towards teaching one major lesson.

Purpose of the book

During a time of national prosperity such as Israel enjoyed under Jeroboam II, it was easy for people to become selfishly nationalistic. The only threat to Israel's continued prosperity was the rising power of Assyria to the north. When a hostile neighbour was planning to attack Assyria's capital Nineveh, God told Jonah to go and warn the Ninevites of the attack. He was to urge the people to repent of their wickedness, so that they might avoid destruction (Jonah 3:4-5,10).

Jonah preferred to see Nineveh destroyed. In his view, that would have been a fitting judgment on Assyria and a welcome relief to Israel. God had to show Jonah that he was the controller of all nations, and he would have mercy on whomever he wished (cf. Rom 9:15). God was not the God of Israelites only, but the God of all people and all nations (cf. Rom 3:29).

God was pleased when the Ninevites repented. In fact, their repentance was in sharp contrast to the stubbornness that usually characterized the people of Israel (Luke 11:32).

Since God's people had so often experienced the love and mercy of God, they were to show similar love and mercy to others. The lesson of the book reaches its climax in the final few verses. God took no pleasure in the destruction of men and women, and neither should his people. Rather they should, like God, desire their repentance and forgiveness (Jonah 4:10-11).

Contents of the book

When told to go and preach repentance to the Ninevites, Jonah disobeyed God and fled by ship in the opposite direction. When he was thrown overboard, God saved him by sending a great fish to swallow him alive (1:1-17). From inside the fish, Jonah thanked God for saving him, whereupon the fish vomited him out, still alive (2:1-10).

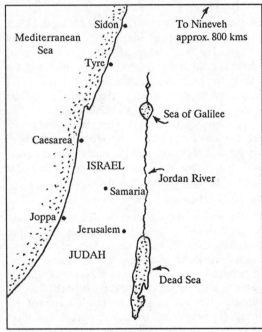

Jonah then went and preached to the Ninevites and they repented (3:1-10). This displeased Jonah, because they had now escaped the judgment he had hoped would fall on them. God then taught Jonah a lesson by destroying a big leafy plant that had been sheltering him from the burning sun. Jonah did not want the plant to die, and neither did God want the Ninevites to die (4:1-11).

JONATHAN

In the early days of Saul's kingship, the Israelite army consisted of two main divisions, one under the command of Saul, the other under the command of his eldest son, Jonathan (1 Sam 13:2; 14:49). Early in his career, Jonathan showed his sharp thinking and his courage when he took his armour-bearer and carried out a daring raid that threw the enemy Philistines into confusion. Though it was a risky adventure, it resulted in a notable victory for Israel (1 Sam 14:1-48).

When David became a member of Saul's court and then of his army, he and Jonathan became close friends (1 Sam 18:1-4). David's victories stirred up Saul's jealousy and hatred, but Jonathan defended him and intervened on his behalf. He successfully pleaded with his father to stop trying to kill David (1 Sam 19:1-7).

Unknown to Jonathan, Saul renewed his attacks on David (1 Sam 19:8-11). When Jonathan heard about this, he determined to find out Saul's real intentions towards David (1 Sam 20:1-23). Unlike his father, Jonathan showed no jealousy of David, even when his father reminded him that David was a threat to his own chances of becoming king (1 Sam 20:30-34).

Jonathan helped David escape, but neither he nor David plotted against the king. Their sole purpose was to save David's life. While remaining loyal to the king, Jonathan reassured David that nothing could change the relationship between them. He knew that David would be the next king, and he would be happy to serve under him as chief minister (1 Sam 23:16-18).

Some years later Jonathan was tragically killed in a battle with the Philistines. David's love for him is seen in the song of remembrance he wrote after his friend's premature death (1 Sam 31:2; 2 Sam 1:17-27).

JOPPA

In Old Testament days Joppa was Israel's only port on the Mediterranean coast. It lay between the plain of Sharon to the north and the land of the Philistines to the south.

When timber was brought from Lebanon to be used in the construction of Solomon's temple, it was floated down from Tyre and Sidon in rafts, received at Joppa, and then taken to Jerusalem (2 Chron 2:16). A similar arrangement was apparently used four hundred years later when Zerubbabel rebuilt the temple (Ezra 3:7). Joppa was the port where Jonah boarded a ship when he tried to flee from God (Jonah 1:3).

Joppa was one of the first places outside Jerusalem that the apostles visited in the early days of the church. There Dorcas was raised to life (Acts

9:36-43) and there Peter had a remarkable vision that changed his ideas about the evangelization of the Gentiles (Acts 10:1-48). The town still exists today, as part of Tel Aviv, and is known as Jaffa (or Yafo).

JORAM

See Jehoram.

JORDAN

The Jordan River, which formed the boundary along the eastern side of the land of Canaan, rose in the region of Mt Hermon in the north and finished in the Dead Sea in the south. It was an important feature of Palestine's geography and was of much significance in the history of Israel. For details see PALESTINE, sub-headings 'Upper Jordan and Sea of Galilee' and 'Jordan Valley and Dead Sea'.

JOSEPH OF ARIMATHEA

Among the members of the Jewish Council that condemned Jesus to death were at least two who disagreed with the decision. One was Nicodemus (cf. John 7:50-51), the other a man named Joseph who came from the Judean village of Arimathea (Luke 23:50-51; John 19:38-39).

Joseph was a just and righteous man, well respected, wealthy, and a follower of Jesus (Matt 27:57; Mark 15:43; Luke 23:50). Though he feared the Jews, he was bold enough to ask Pilate for the body of Jesus so that he might give Jesus an honourable burial. With Nicodemus he took the body down from the cross, anointed it with spices, wrapped it in linen and placed it in the tomb that he had prepared for himself (Matt 27:58-60; John 19:38-42).

JOSEPH THE HUSBAND OF MARY

Two lines of descent from David came together in Jesus. The royal line through Solomon and the kings of Judah came through Joseph, the legal father of Jesus, giving grounds for Jesus' right to the throne of David (Matt 1:1-16). The other line, through another of David's sons, also led to Joseph (Luke 3:23-31).

It is possible, however, that the genealogy in Luke is that of Mary rather than Joseph. Since the genealogy preserves only the names of the males, Joseph (according to this theory) would be 'son' of Heli only because he was married to Heli's daughter; that is, he would be Heli's son-in-law.

Both Matthew 1:16 and Luke 3:23 emphasize that Joseph was not the natural father of Jesus. Jesus was conceived in the womb of the virgin Mary by the direct activity of God's Spirit, without the help of any man. It is understandable that Joseph was called the father of Jesus (John 1:45; 6:42), because legally he was, but Joseph knew that he was not responsible for Mary's pregnancy. When he thought of breaking the engagement with Mary secretly (for he did not want to embarrass her), God told him that Mary was morally blameless and her pregnancy was miraculous (Matt 1:18-25; cf. Luke 1:26-35).

After the birth, Joseph showed a loving concern for both Mary and Jesus, and a readiness to act promptly when God directed him (Matt 2:13-15; 2:19-23). With Mary he took the baby to Jerusalem for the ceremonies required by the Jewish law (Luke 2:22). Later they settled in Nazareth in the north (Matt 2:23), but they went each year to Jerusalem for the Passover (Luke 2:41).

Joseph was a well known carpenter in Nazareth (Matt 13:55) and he taught his carpentry skills to Jesus (Mark 6:3). Apparently he was no longer alive when Jesus engaged in his public ministry, as the Gospel writers do not mention him in references to current members of Jesus' family (Matt 13:55-56; Mark 6:3; John 19:26-27). The brothers and sisters of Jesus were probably children of Mary and Joseph, born to them once they began sexual relations after the birth of Jesus (Matt 1:25).

JOSEPH THE SON OF JACOB

The story of Joseph is among the best known in the Bible. It spreads over more than a dozen chapters of Genesis and shows how God was fulfilling his promises to Abraham.

God had promised Canaan to Abraham and his descendants, but those descendants would be able to take possession of it only when they had sufficient numbers to do so. First of all, therefore, they had to develop as a nation, and the story of Joseph shows how this became possible. It recounts the events that led to their migration to Egypt and their subsequent growth and development. Although, after Joseph's death, they suffered a period of slavery, in due course they left Egypt and took possession of Canaan (cf. Gen 15:13-16).

From Canaan to Egypt

Joseph was Jacob's eleventh son but, being Rachel's firstborn, he soon became Jacob's favourite (Gen 30:22-24; 33:1-7). By the time Joseph was seventeen, his brothers so hated him that they decided to get rid of him. They sold him to traders who took him to Egypt, though they told their father that a wild animal had killed him (Gen 37:1-36).

In spite of his blameless behaviour, Joseph ended up in prison. Because of his good conduct, he was given a position of responsibility that proved to be of benefit to the other prisoners, but he waited in vain for anyone to help him (Gen 39:1-40:23). When at last someone told the king of Joseph's wisdom, Joseph was able to warn the king of a coming famine and advise him how to deal with it. The king was so impressed that he made Joseph the administrator of the famine relief program, and then governor of all Egypt (Gen 41:1-45; Acts 7:9-10).

Governor of Egypt

At the time of his appointment as governor, Joseph was thirty years of age (Gen 41:46). He married an Egyptian and they produced two sons, Manasseh and Ephraim (Gen 41:47-52).

Egypt alone had made preparations for the famine, with the result that people came from everywhere to buy food. Among these were Joseph's brothers. Although Joseph recognized them, they did not recognize him (Gen 41:53-42:8).

To see if his brothers had changed for the better over the years, Joseph cleverly arranged a striking sequence of events. He worked them into a trap from which they could have easily escaped by sacrificing their brother Benjamin, who was their father's new favourite. But they refused to forsake Benjamin (Gen 42:9-44:34). Joseph, satisfied that his brothers had experienced a genuine change of heart, told them who he was. He then sent wagons to Canaan to bring Jacob and all his family to Egypt (Gen 45:1-46:34; Acts 7:11-14).

Joseph arranged for all Jacob's family to settle in Goshen in the Nile Delta. There, separated from the Egyptians, they could multiply and develop without their culture or religion being corrupted by the Egyptians (Gen 47:1-12). Meanwhile Joseph continued as governor, and his economic policies saved Egypt from disaster (Gen 47:13-26).

Later events

Before Jacob died, he raised the two sons of Joseph, Manasseh and Ephraim, to equal status with the brothers of Joseph. Manasseh and Ephraim would therefore become heads of tribes in Israel. Joseph, by receiving two tribes instead of one, received the inheritance of the firstborn (Gen 48:1-22; 49:22-26; 1 Chron 5:1-2).

When Jacob died, Joseph's brothers feared he might now have revenge against them. Joseph was saddened by such mistrust and reassured his brothers that he would continue to look after them (Gen 50:1-21).

Joseph lived over ninety years in Egypt, but he still believed that Canaan was the land his people would one day possess. Before he died he showed his faith in God's promises by leaving instructions that when the people of Israel eventually moved to Canaan, they take his remains with them (Gen 50:22-26; Exod 13:19; Heb 11:22). His descendants buried his bones at Shechem, in the tribal area of Ephraim (Josh 24:32).

JOSHUA, BOOK OF

The subject of the book of Joshua is the conquest and division of the land of Canaan. Moses, who had led the people for the previous forty years, died before the people entered Canaan (his death having been recorded in the final chapter of the previous book, Deuteronomy). He was succeeded by the man from whom the book of Joshua takes its name.

Authorship, style and purpose

There is no statement in the book of Joshua telling us who wrote it, though some of the material may have been based on what Joshua himself wrote (e.g. Josh 24:25-26). The writer probably also used other historical books of that era (Josh 10:13), along with national and tribal records (Josh 18:8-9).

Although it outlines the conquest of Canaan, the book of Joshua does not give a detailed record of events. The battle for Canaan lasted a long time (Josh 11:18), at least five years (Josh 14:7,10), yet some of the more extensive battle campaigns are passed over in a few verses. By contrast, events of apparently little military importance are sometimes given in considerable detail.

The reason for this unevenness of treatment is that the book was intended to be not a chronological record of facts, but a prophetical interpretation of an important era of Israel's history. The writer's main concern was to show how God was revealing himself and his purposes through the experiences of his people Israel. (For the prophetical significance of the group of books to which Joshua belongs, the Former Prophets, see PROPHECY.)

Summary of contents

Chapters 1 to 5 deal with Israel's entry into Canaan. From the outset the emphasis is on the fact that God is giving the land to Israel. Nevertheless, the people, and particularly Joshua, must be courageous, trusting and obedient to God if their invasion is to be successful (1:1-18).

After spying out the land in order to plan the invasion intelligently (2:1-24), the Israelites crossed the Jordan River and set up camp at Gilgal. To impress upon people the religious significance of the invasion, the narrative emphasizes such matters as the ritual cleansing of the people, the leadership of the priests, the prominence of the ark of the covenant, the miraculous crossing of the Jordan, and the obedience to the covenant commands by those who were till then uncircumcised. The appearance of the angel of the Lord further demonstrated that the entire operation was divinely directed (3:1-5:15; see also JOSHUA THE SON OF NUN).

The overthrow of Jericho gave more examples of the religious significance of Israel's conquest: the role of the priests and the ark, the repeated use of the symbolic number 'seven' in the proceedings, and the judgment that followed disobedience to God's commands (6:1-7:26). Only after the leaders dealt with the sin, did Israel make further advances into central Canaan (8:1-29). The people then reaffirmed their obedience to the covenant by which God had given Canaan to them (8:30-35).

Having split Canaan by their drive through the central region, the Israelites then conquered the south (9:1-10:43) and the north (11:1-15). The summary that follows emphasizes again that Israel's occupation of Canaan was in fulfilment of God's promises (11:16-12:24). (For a map showing towns that the Israelites conquered and regions that the Israelite tribes subsequently occupied see JUDGES, BOOK OF.)

With Canaan now the possession of Israel, Joshua, together with the high priest and the tribal leaders, began the task of dividing the land between the twelve tribes. The area west of Jordan (Canaan itself) was divided between nine and a half tribes; the other two and a half tribes (Reuben, Gad and half of Manasseh) received their inheritance in the land east of Jordan that Israel had conquered in the time of Moses (13:1-14:5). Of the area west of Jordan, the largest and best portions went also to two and a half tribes — Judah (14:6-15:63) and the remainder of the Joseph tribes, Ephraim and the other half of Manasseh (16:1-17:18). The seven smaller tribes then received their tribal allotments (18:1-19:51). The Levites, who had no tribal area of their own, were given towns in all the other tribes (20:1-21:45).

Apart from the story of an early misunderstanding between the eastern and western tribes (22:1-34), nothing more is recorded of the era till the time of Joshua's final address to the nation many years later (23:1-16). Before he died, Joshua called Israel's leaders to assemble for another covenant renewal ceremony. Through them he reminded the people that if they wanted to enjoy the blessings of the covenant, they had to be obedient to its requirements (24:1-33).

JOSHUA THE SON OF JEHOZADAK

In 539 BC Cyrus of Persia conquered Babylon and immediately gave permission to the captive Jews to return to their homeland and rebuild Jerusalem and the temple. Chief among those who returned were the governor Zerubbabel and the high priest Joshua (or Jeshua) the son of Jehozadak (or Jozadak) (Ezra 2:1-2).

Joint leadership

Under the leadership of Zerubbabel and Joshua, the returned exiles set up the altar soon after they arrived in Jerusalem (Ezra 3:1-2). They laid the foundation of the temple the next year (Ezra 3:8-11), but when opposition discouraged the builders, the work stopped (Ezra 4:1-5).

Sixteen years later God raised up the prophets Haggai and Zechariah to stir up Zerubbabel, Joshua and the people to get to work once more on the temple (Ezra 4:24; 5:1-2; Hag 1:1-11). When work restarted, the prophets brought further messages of encouragement to the people through Zerubbabel and Joshua (Hag 1:12-15; 2:1-9).

The rebuilding of the temple was a preparation for the coming of the Messiah. When, in anticipation of this Messiah, the Jews conducted a coronation ceremony, the person they should have crowned was Zerubbabel, for he was not only governor but also a Davidic prince in the line of the Messiah (Matt 1:6,12,16). Instead they crowned the priest Joshua, to avoid any action that may have appeared to the Persians as treason. The ceremony emphasized that the joint rule of Joshua and Zerubbabel, the priest and the prince, foreshadowed the rule of the priest-king Messiah (Zech 6:9-14).

Dealing with sin

In a vision that the prophet Zechariah saw, Joshua the high priest was standing before God in dirty garments. Standing beside Joshua was Satan, ready to make the accusation that the people were unclean because of their long exile in idolatrous Babylon. They were therefore no longer fit to serve God or build him a temple. By clothing Joshua in clean garments, God showed that he had forgiven and cleansed his people (Zech 3:1-10).

Sadly, the people's renewed devotion was short-lived. Joshua's sons did not truly follow God and, like many of their countrymen, married unbelieving non-Jewish women. When rebuked by Ezra, they put away their foreign wives and offered sacrifices for their wrongdoing (Ezra 10:18-19).

JOSHUA THE SON OF NUN

Like Moses, Joshua was born and brought up in Egypt. He became Moses' chief assistant on the journey from Egypt to Canaan and, when Moses died, became Israel's new leader and led the people into Canaan. The name Joshua means 'Yahweh (Jehovah) saves'. Translated via the Aramaic into Greek, the name becomes 'Jesus'.

Assistant to Moses

Joshua's leadership qualities became evident soon after the Israelites left Egypt. When some raiding Amalekites attacked the Israelite procession, Moses hurriedly appointed Joshua to form and command a fighting force. Through courage and prayer, Israel won its first battle (Exod 17:8-14).

As Moses' chief assistant, Joshua kept watch when Moses entered God's presence on Mt Sinai (Exod 24:13) and when Moses spoke face to face with God in his tent (Exod 33:11). Joshua was so loyal to Moses that he wanted Moses to silence two men who prophesied, lest people listen to them and ignore Moses (Num 11:26-29).

When Moses sent representatives from the twelve tribes to spy out Canaan, Joshua was the representative from the tribe of Ephraim. Only he and Caleb, the representative from the tribe of Judah, believed that God could give Israel victory over the Canaanites. The people chose to accept the report of the ten unbelieving spies and tried to kill Joshua and Caleb. God announced that Israel would therefore remain in the wilderness for the next forty years, till all those currently over twenty years of age (except Joshua and Caleb) had died, and a new generation had grown up (Num 13:1-16; 14:6-10; 14:26-30).

Conqueror of Canaan

Forty years later, when the new generation was ready to enter Canaan, Moses appointed Joshua as his divinely chosen successor (Num 27:18-22; Deut 31:14; 34:9). Joshua would direct the conquest of Canaan and, with Eleazar the high priest, oversee the division of the land among Israel's tribes (Num 34:17; Deut 1:38; 3:28; 31:23). After Moses' death, God gave Joshua special encouragement for the tasks ahead (Josh 1:5-9).

Joshua's proven faith, combined with his long experience as an administrator and army general, enabled him to carry out the work entrusted to him. He organized the people and sought out information for the advance into Canaan (Josh 1:10-11; 2:1); he ensured that people and priests carried out the rituals God required of them (Josh 3:7-13; 5:2-3); and he submitted totally to God's directions (Josh 5:13-15). The book of Joshua records how Israel crossed the Jordan River, conquered Canaan and divided the land among its tribes (see JOSHUA, BOOK OF).

The entire operation for the conquest and division of Canaan showed Joshua's courage, faith, obedience and honesty (Josh 6:15-16; Heb 11:30). When he found wilful disobedience among the people, he dealt promptly with the guilty person (Josh 7:10-12,16,25). Victory followed, whereupon Joshua led the Israelites to Shechem, where they renewed their promise of obedience to God and his covenant demands (Josh 8:30-35).

Joshua then attacked to the south, but the people of Gibeon saved themselves by tricking the Israelites into making a peace treaty with them. The reason for the Israelites' mistake was their failure to ask God's direction; but, having made an agreement, they kept it (Josh 9:14-19). The outcome was that soon they had to defend the Gibeonites against an attack by hostile neighbours, but in doing so they experienced miraculous exhibitions of God's power (Josh 10:1-14). From this victory Joshua went on to conquer all southern Canaan (Josh 10:28-43), and then northern Canaan (Josh 11:1-15).

A godly administrator

After the conquest of Canaan, the Israelite tribes settled in their respective areas (Josh 14:1). But Joshua had constantly to remind the individual tribes to drive out the Canaanites from the scattered areas they still occupied (Josh 13:1; 17:16-18; 18:3). Joshua himself settled in a district that he had chosen, by God's permission, within the territory of his own tribe, Ephraim (Josh 19:49-50).

Nothing is recorded of Joshua's life till the occasion of his address to the nation just before his death (Josh 23:1). The people followed God throughout Joshua's time and the time of those he had trained, showing that he was as strong and godly a leader in civilian affairs as he had been in military affairs (Josh 24:31). In his final address he warned of the dangers of idolatry and challenged the people to maintain their faithfulness to God (Josh 24:14-15). He died at 110 years of age and was buried on his home property (Josh 24:29-30).

JOSIAH

After fifty-five years rule of the wicked Manasseh, plus two years rule of his equally wicked son Amon, Judah's spiritual condition was the worst it had ever been (see MANASSEH, KING OF JUDAH). Josiah became king when his father Amon was assassinated (640 BC) but, being only eight years old at the time, he was for some years under the direction of government officials (2 Chron 33:25; 34:1). At the age of sixteen he became a believer in the one true God, and at the age of twenty he began religious reforms that lasted many years (2 Chron 34:2-5).

Religious affairs

Possibly one of the influences that led Josiah to begin his reforms was the preaching of the prophet Zephaniah (Zeph 1:1). Another prophet, Jeremiah, began his ministry in the early years of Josiah's reforms (Jer 1:1-2; 3:6).

During the evil days of Manasseh, the temple in Jerusalem had been damaged and the law of God forgotten. In the sixth year of Josiah's reforms, workmen repairing the temple found scrolls of this long-forgotten law. Josiah was shocked to find how far Judah had departed from God. He soon learnt that the nation was heading for judgment, but God encouraged him to continue his reforms, so that the people might turn to God and avoid the threatened judgment (2 Kings 22:3-20).

With this encouragement from God, Josiah gathered Jerusalem's leading citizens together at the temple, where the law was read to them. He gained

Public reading of the law

their support in renewing the nation's covenant with God and in helping his ongoing reforms (2 Kings 23:1-3). An increasingly confident Josiah then destroyed all false shrines and other idolatrous objects throughout the country, and centralized the nation's public worship in Jerusalem, where it was

under his supervision (2 Kings 23:4-14,24; 2 Chron 34:6-7). He burnt the bones of the false prophets on their altar, after which he destroyed it (2 Kings 23:15-20; cf. 1 Kings 13:1-3,29-32).

Having removed idolatry, Josiah re-established the worship of Yahweh by keeping the Passover. This gave him the opportunity to organize the priests and Levites according to the order set out by David. He wanted to make sure that the entire worship procedure was conducted properly. The nation's leading officials joined Josiah in providing large numbers of sacrificial animals for the festival. It was the most spectacular Passover ever seen in Jerusalem (2 Chron 35:1-19).

Political affairs

One factor that assisted Josiah in carrying out such wide-sweeping reforms was the decline of Assyria. He was even able to extend his control into areas of the former northern kingdom that Assyria had conquered (2 Kings 23:15,19; 2 Chron 34:6-7).

Assyria eventually fell to Babylon in 612 BC. Pharaoh Necho of Egypt, fearing this expansion of Babylonian power, set out to attack Babylon. In doing so he had to pass through areas of Palestine that Josiah controlled. Foolishly, Josiah tried to resist him. The result was that Josiah was killed in battle (609 BC) and Judah fell temporarily under the overlordship of Egypt (2 Kings 23:29-30; 2 Chron 35:20-27).

Josiah was only thirty-nine years old when he died (2 Kings 22:1). Those of his people who later suffered under the cruel hand of his son Jehoiakim looked back with gratitude on his compassion and justice (2 Chron 35:25; Jer 22:15-19). Josiah won unqualified praise for his reforms (2 Kings 23:25), but few people were genuinely converted. Idolatrous ideas were so deeply rooted in the people's hearts that judgment on the nation was inevitable (2 Kings 23:26-27).

JOTHAM

The book of Judges records the story of Jotham the son of Gideon. After Gideon's death, another son, Abimelech, killed his brothers and, with the help of some worthless men from Shechem, established himself 'king'. Jotham, who was the only one of Gideon's sons to escape the massacre, told a parable to warn the Shechemites of the trouble they had brought upon themselves (Judg 9:1-21). His forecast of doom came true when Abimelech's ambition brought about his own death and the destruction of his supporters (Judg 9:57).

About five hundred years later another man named Jotham appears in the Bible story. He was the son of King Uzziah, and helped his father rule Judah when Uzziah became a leper in his later years (2 Chron 26:21). After his father's death (739 BC), Jotham maintained the policies of national development his father had introduced. Judah continued to enjoy prosperity (2 Chron 27:1-6; see also UZZIAH). Nevertheless, the greed and corruption of Uzziah's reign continued through the reign of Jotham. The prophets Hosea, Isaiah and Micah denounced the social and religious evils of the self-satisfied people (Isa 1:1; Hosea 1:1; Micah 1:1). (For details of social conditions in Judah during the reign of Jotham see ISAIAH; MICAH.)

JOY

Both Old and New Testaments use a variety of words to express the many aspects of joy, gladness, contentment and rejoicing. Joy is a characteristic of God, and he wants it to be a characteristic that is evident throughout all creation, particularly among his people (Job 38:7; Ps 16:11; 104:31; Luke 2:10,14; John 15:11; Phil 4:4).

Gladness and rejoicing are part of the everyday life that God desires for mankind. God wants people to enjoy him and all that he has given them for life in this world (Deut 14:26; Eccles 5:18-19; 9:7-9; Luke 1:14; 15:22-24; 1 Tim 6:17). However, all such enjoyment must be linked with right behaviour and self-discipline (Prov 23:16-21; Amos 6:4-7; Rom 13:13; 14:17; 1 Thess 5:7-8; 1 Peter 4:3).

Expressions of gladness and joy were a feature of public worship in ancient Israel (Deut 12:5-7; Ps 81:1-3; 100:1-2; 150:3-6). They were also a feature of the life of the early church (Acts 2:46-47; 5:41; 8:39; 13:52; Col 3:16).

Joy in a special sense becomes the possession of believers when by faith they come into union with Jesus Christ (John 15:4,11). This joy is more than simply a feeling of happiness when all is going well. That type of joy will be only temporary (Eccles 2:1-11). The joy that Christ gives is something that no circumstances can take away (John 16:22,33; 17:13; Rom 15:13). It is a quality of peace and strength that enables believers to rejoice even amid trouble and sorrow (Hab 3:17-18; Matt 5:10-12; 2 Cor 6:10; Col 1:24; James 1:2; see PEACE).

Sin in the lives of believers can spoil their experience of the joy God has given them. For this reason they must resist sin, along with its accompanying tendency to despondency. They must make a constant and wholehearted effort to be positive and joyful at all times (Phil 4:4; 1 Thess 5:16-18).

The more believers grow in their new life in Christ, the more the indwelling Spirit of Christ develops the quality of joy within them (Gal 5:22). This joy is inseparable from faith, love, peace and hope (Rom 5:1-5; 15:13; 1 Thess 1:3,6; Heb 10:34). The fulfilment of their joy will be to meet Christ at his return and enter with him into the full joy of the age to come (Isa 65:17-19; Matt 25:21; Jude 24; Rev 19:7-9). This glorious hope is a further cause for their rejoicing amid present sufferings (Rom 5:2; 8:18,24; 1 Peter 1:6-8; 4:13; see HOPE).

JUBILEE

Israelites counted their years in groups of seven. Every seventh year was called the sabbatical year (or rest year), because in that year all farmland was rested from normal agricultural activity (see SABBATICAL YEAR). After seven lots of seven years there was an additional sabbath year called the Jubilee, or Year of Restoration (GNB). In that year all land that had changed ownership during the previous forty-nine years returned to its original owner. This ensured the preservation of the just and fair distribution of land that had been made following Joshua's conquest. People who became poor could not lose their property for ever, and the rich could not gain control of the country through buying most of the land (Lev 25:8-12).

Since all land returned to the original owner in the fiftieth year, the sale price of land had to be reduced from its original value so that it was proportionate to the number of years that remained to the fiftieth year (Lev 25:13-17). If a person needed money he could sell his land, but as soon as possible either he or a close relative had to buy it back (Lev 25:25-28).

Laws for the return of land in the year of Jubilee applied only to farming and pastoral land, not to land in walled cities. This was because city land was not used for cultivation and therefore had nothing to do with the agricultural 'rest' years (Lev 25:29-34).

JUDAH, SON OF JACOB

Fourth son of Jacob, Judah soon established himself in the family as one who had genuine leadership qualities (Gen 29:31-35; 37:25-27; 43:1-10; 44:14-34; 46:28). Concerning his own sons he wanted to establish a strong family to carry on his name and inheritance (Gen 38:1-10). He himself, however, proved to be morally weak and an easy victim of sexual temptation (Gen 38:11-30).

Jacob saw clearly that Judah's tribe would become the leading tribe in the Israelite nation. It would conquer foreign enemies and rule over its brother tribes (Gen 49:8-12). Out of it came the great king David and finally the Messiah Jesus (Matt 1:3,6,16). (See also JUDAH, TRIBE AND KINGDOM.)

JUDAH, TRIBE AND KINGDOM

Even before Judah existed as a tribe, God had marked it out for a position of leadership in Israel (Gen 49:9-10). Both on the journey through the wilderness under Moses and in the conquest of Canaan under Joshua (1240 BC), Judah took the lead (Num 2:9; Judg 1:2). Once Israel settled in Canaan, Judah soon established its prominence among the twelve tribes.

A large and powerful tribe

In the division of Canaan among the Israelite tribes, Judah received the whole of southern Palestine between the Dead Sea and the Mediterranean Sea, as far south as the Wilderness of Zin and the Brook of Egypt (Josh 15:1-12). This was the largest of all the tribal areas. It was, in fact, too large to be occupied entirely by the Judeans, so the tribe of Simeon was invited to occupy part of it. Simeon, as a result, had no separate tribal area of its own and was soon absorbed by Judah (Josh 19:1,9).

The land occupied by Judah rose west of the Dead Sea into a high central mountain area (Josh 15:48; Luke 1:39), and then fell away through low hill country known as the Shephelah to the Philistine plain on the Mediterranean coast (Josh 10:40-41; 15:20-21,33,47). The southern portion of Judah was the dry region known as the Negeb (Josh 10:40; 15:19). (For further details of the physical features of Judah see PALESTINE. For some of its important towns see BEERSHEBA; BETHLEHEM; HEBRON; KADESH-BARNEA; KIRIATH-JEARIM; LACHISH. For towns on the coastal plain see ASHDOD; ASHKELON; EKRON; GATH; GAZA. For Judah's conflict with the Philistines, who occupied the coastal plain, see PHILISTIA.)

A natural division of hills and valleys separated Judah from the tribes to the north; the Jordan River and the Dead Sea separated it from the two and a half tribes to the east. Added to this, there was always some jealousy between Judah and the other tribes. During the reign of Israel's first king, Saul (who was from the tribe of Benjamin), the difference between Judah and the other tribes became so

noticeable that people often referred to Judah as distinct from the rest of Israel (1 Sam 11:8; 18:16).

Era of David and Solomon

After Saul's death (1010 BC), there was a much clearer division between Judah and the other tribes. The people of Judah appointed one of their own men, David, as king, but the other tribes appointed Saul's son, Ishbosheth, as king. For two years there was fighting between the two groups, but in the

end David's group won (2 Sam 2:4,8-10; 3:1). For the next five and a half years David reigned in Hebron over the whole of Israel. He then conquered Jerusalem and made it his capital, reigning over all Israel for a further thirty-three years (2 Sam 5:1-5). (For details of David's plans and purposes in making Jerusalem his capital see JERUSALEM.)

Solomon followed David as king of Israel, and further developed David's plans to make Jerusalem the religious as well as the political centre of the kingdom. In a building program that lasted more than twenty years, he built a magnificent temple, a luxurious palace and other impressive buildings in the national capital. But his policy of forced labour and heavy taxes made him unpopular, particularly with the northerners, whose farm produce and land he gave to foreign creditors to pay for his showpiece city (1 Kings 5:11; 9:1).

Division of the kingdom

When Solomon died (930 BC), his son Rehoboam, apparently aware of the anti-Jerusalem feeling throughout the northern tribes, tried to regain the northerners' allegiance. His first step was to have his coronation in the northern city of Shechem instead of in Jerusalem (1 Kings 12:1). But it was too late. Rebellion in the north, led by the Ephraimite Jeroboam, had been building up for years, and now the northerners decided to break away from Judah completely. They did so, making Jeroboam their king (1 Kings 11:26,28; 12:16,20).

From that time on the ancient nation Israel was split in two — a northern kingdom of ten tribes that continued to be known as Israel, and a southern kingdom of two tribes (Judah and Benjamin) that was known as Judah (1 Kings 11:11-13,29-32).

Judah was the smaller of the two kingdoms, both in area and in population, and it had the poorer country agriculturally. But it had greater political stability. It had an established dynasty, the dynasty of David, and a well fortified capital, Jerusalem. Its people, being mostly from one tribe, were fairly well unified. By contrast there was rarely any strong unity in the northern kingdom. Reasons for this were the greater number of tribes in the north, the large population of local Canaanites still living in the area, and the natural divisions created by mountains and rivers. Judah was more isolated, but Israel more open to foreign interference.

The kingdom of Judah

For the first sixty years of the divided kingdom there was constant fighting between Israel and Judah (1 Kings 14:30; 15:7,16), but the main difficulties for both nations came from the false religious practices that grew up among them. Baal worship was always a problem, particularly in the north. (For further history of the northern kingdom see ISRAEL.)

The kings Asa and Jehoshaphat carried out reforms in Judah (2 Chron 14:1-5; 17:3-6), but a greater threat to Judah's religion followed when a particularly evil form of Baalism from the north spread into the south. It was eventually removed, largely through the work of the priest Jehoiada (835 BC; 2 Kings 11:4-20).

In the years that followed, Judah developed agriculturally and commercially to an extent never before experienced. But with rapid growth in wealth came increased greed, corruption, injustice, violence and immorality. The prophets Isaiah and Micah condemned the sinful nation and announced the coming judgment of God (Isa 1:1-4; 5:13-25; Micah 1:1; 2:1-5; 3:9-12; see ISAIAH; MICAH).

Judah began to feel the divinely sent judgment when, through the disastrous policies of the Judean king Ahaz, Assyria began to interfere in Judean affairs. But Assyria's interference in Israel's affairs to the north was even more serious. Several of Israel's kings, and now Ahaz of Judah, had fallen under Assyria's domination, and maintained their rule only by paying heavy tribute to Assyria (2 Kings 15:17-20; 16:1-9; 17:1-3). Because of treachery and instability in Israel through a number of rebellions,

Defeated king forced to pay tribute to the king of Assyria

assassinations and changes of foreign policy, Assyria finally lost patience. In 722 BC it destroyed the northern kingdom and took most of the people into captivity (722 BC; 2 Kings 17:5-6).

Isaiah was probably the most important man in Judah during this era. He announced untiringly, to king and people alike, that Judah's only hope was to trust in God. The good king Hezekiah, who had introduced sweeping religious and political reforms (2 Kings 18:1-8), proved this to be true when God miraculously saved Jerusalem from what seemed certain conquest by the Assyrians (701 BC; 2 Kings 19:34-36; see HEZEKIAH; ISAIAH).

The next king, Manasseh, undid the good that his father had done. Under his rule Judah's spiritual condition became so corrupt that not even the reforms of Josiah and the preaching of Zephaniah were able to prevent the nation's collapse (2 Kings 21:1-15; 23:24-27; see JOSIAH; ZEPHANIAH).

Captivity and return

For the final forty years of Judah's history, the man who most clearly saw where Judah was heading was the prophet Jeremiah. He had a constant battle with kings, priests, government officials and the common people, as he tried to prepare the nation to accept the judgment that must now certainly fall upon it (Jer 21:3-10; see JEREMIAH).

Babylon, who had conquered Assyria in 612 BC, took control of Judah in 605 BC. The Judean king,

Jehoiakim, at first submitted but later rebelled. The outcome was that Babylon attacked Jerusalem and took most of the nation's wealth and best people into captivity in Babylon (597 BC; 2 Kings 24:1-17). Zedekiah was made king, but when he too rebelled, Babylon attacked Jerusalem again. This time it destroyed the city and took most of the remaining people into captivity (587 BC; 2 Kings 25:1-12).

The Babylonians appointed a Judean named Gedaliah as governor over the small community of Judeans left in the land. When Gedaliah was killed by some anti-Babylonian rebels, Babylon's army returned to deal with any possible uprising. Some of the Judeans escaped to Egypt, and most of the rest were captured and taken off to Babylon (582 BC; 2 Kings 25:22-26; Jer 52:30).

Persia conquered Babylon in 539 BC and gave the captive Jews permission to return to Jerusalem and rebuild their nation. Those who returned were mostly from the tribe of Judah, but since the old distinction between the northern and southern kingdoms no longer existed, the restored nation could be referred to as either Israel or Judah. As a result Israelites in general became known as Jews, the word 'Jew' being a shortened form of 'Judean' (see JEW). (For the history of this post-captivity period see ISRAEL.)

JUDAS

It seems that, after the treachery of Judas Iscariot in betraying Jesus, the name Judas became unpopular among Christians. Those who already had the name Judas often preferred some other name.

For example, in Jesus' group of twelve apostles there was a second man named Judas, but when writers mention him they point out that he was the son of a man named James, and not Judas Iscariot. To avoid confusion, this apostle apparently took another name, Thaddaeus (or Lebbaeus) (Matt 10:3; Luke 6:16; John 14:22; see THADDAEUS). One of Jesus' brothers was named Judas, but on becoming a believer he was known by the shorter name, Jude (Matt 13:55; see JUDE). A prophet named Judas in the Jerusalem church took another name, Barsabbas (Acts 15:22,27). (Concerning Judas the Galilean mentioned in Acts 5:37 see ZEALOT.)

Judas Iscariot

Judas the betrayer was commonly known as Iscariot (meaning 'man of Kerioth'), after the home town of his father, Simon (Matt 10:4; John 6:71). As treasurer for the group of twelve apostles, Judas had responsibility for funds donated for the poor. It later

became evident that he had been stealing some of the money for himself (John 12:5-6; 13:29).

Jesus had seen the evil in Judas' heart long before those final acts of treachery that resulted in Jesus' crucifixion (John 6:70-71; 17:12). Judas' criticism of Mary's anointing of Jesus showed his lack of spiritual insight (John 12:3-8). The other disciples still did not suspect him of disloyalty, even when Jesus told them there was a betrayer in their midst (Matt 26:20-25; John 13:2,21-30).

The Jewish leaders had been wondering how to arrest Jesus without creating a riot (Luke 22:1-2), but the defection of one of Jesus' apostles made their task easier. Judas demanded payment for his part in the plot, and the Jewish leaders agreed (Matt 26:14-16; Luke 22:3-6). The vital information that Judas gave the Jews concerned the secret place where Jesus prayed with his disciples. In the middle of the night, when the people of Jerusalem were asleep, Judas led an armed group of temple guards and Roman soldiers to the place. His final act of treachery was to identify the one to be arrested by kissing him (Matt 26:47-56; John 18:2-12).

Judas gained no satisfaction from his evil work. He knew he had done wrong in helping to crucify an innocent man, but he made no effort to correct the wrong. Instead he committed suicide; though first he tried to ease his conscience by returning the money that the priests had given him (Matt 27:3-5).

It seems that Judas went into a field and tried to hang himself, but in doing so he injured himself internally and his stomach burst. When his body was found, the priests took the betrayal money Judas had returned and with it bought the field in his name. Originally known as Potter's Field, the place was renamed Field of Blood and used as a cemetery for Gentiles (Matt 27:6-10; Acts 1:18-19).

JUDE

It is generally believed that the author of the letter of Jude was the younger brother of Jesus, whose original name Judas was later shortened to Jude (Mark 6:3). Jesus' brothers at first did not accept him as the Son of God and the Davidic Messiah (John 7:5), but the resurrection must have caused them to change their minds. They were among the foundation members of the Jerusalem church (Acts 1:14; cf. 1 Cor 15:7).

Purpose and content of Jude's letter

Jude's purpose in writing his letter was to oppose a type of false teaching which denied that practical self-control was necessary for those who had become

Christians. They claimed that when a person passed into a higher experience of spiritual life, the deeds of the body could no longer affect the purity of the soul. In fact, immoral behaviour could be a sign of spiritual maturity.

Jude's response to this was to warn his readers that those who taught and practised such immorality were perverting the gospel and bringing judgment upon themselves (v. 1-16). True Christians, besides learning more of Christian truth, kept themselves pure and developed practical godliness in their daily lives (v. 17-25).

The content of Jude is similar to that of 2 Peter. Perhaps one writer borrowed from the other; or, more likely, both used a type of argument that was common in opposing the false teaching. Such false teaching was widespread during the latter half of the first century, and seems to have been yet another early form of Gnosticism.

JUDEA

In 63 BC Rome took control of Palestine and made it a province of the Roman Empire. In those days Palestine was known as Judea, meaning 'land of the Jews'. The name was used sometimes for Palestine as a whole, as for example when Herod the Great

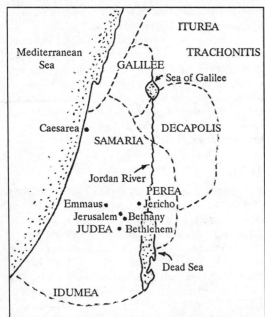

governed the region (Luke 1:5). But in general people thought of Palestine as consisting of three sections, the northern known as Galilee, the central as Samaria and the southern as Judea (John 4:3-4).

When Herod died in 4 BC, his former territory was divided among his sons, the central and southern parts going to Archelaus (Matt 2:22).

Archelaus was so cruel and unjust that in AD 6 the Jews in Judea asked Rome to remove him and rule over them directly. From that time on, the combined Judea-Samaria section was governed by Roman governors and was officially known as the Roman province of Judea. The administrative centre was Caesarea.

Judea had a brief period without Roman governors from AD 41 to 44, when Herod Agrippa I was allowed to rule (Acts 12:1-4,18-23). Apart from that, Roman governors controlled Judea till the destruction of the Jewish state in AD 70. Roman governors of Judea mentioned in the Bible are Pontius Pilate (Luke 3:1; 23:1), Felix (Acts 23:24,33) and Porcius Festus (Acts 25:1-5).

The people of Judea were, on the whole, true Jews. They were fiercely proud of their national and religious purity and were devoted to the traditions of their forefathers. They despised the Galilean Jews, who lived in a region of mixed Jewish-Gentile population (Matt 26:69,73; John 7:41,52), and they despised the Samaritans, who were people of mixed blood and mixed religion (John 4:9; 8:48). Above all they despised Jesus. They never accepted him as many in Galilee did, and finally they crucified him (Matt 23:37).

Some of the towns of Judea that feature in the story of Jesus are Bethlehem, Bethany, Bethphage, Emmaus, Jericho and Jerusalem (Matt 2:1; Mark 11:1; Luke 10:30; 24:13). (For further details see separate entries under the names of these towns. For details of the physical features of Judea see PALESTINE.)

JUDGE

When disputes arise between people, it is necessary to have an independent person, a judge, who is competent to decide the matter. In the early days of Israel's national life, Moses judged all legal disputes, but when this work became too much for one person, he appointed officials to help him (Exod 18:17-26). These were men chosen from the elders of the people, and as the administration of Israel developed they became a clearly recognized official body in the nation (Num 11:14-17; Deut 16:18; 21:2; Josh 8:33). (Concerning the national deliverers whom the book of Judges refers to as judges see JUDGES, BOOK OF.)

In their administration of justice, judges were to be strictly impartial, favouring neither the poor nor the rich (Exod 23:2-3,6; Deut 1:16-17; see JUSTICE). Under no circumstances were they to accept bribes (Deut 16:19-20). When cases were too difficult for them, they were to take them to the priests to decide (Deut 17:8-9; 2 Chron 19:8-11). Despite these laws, in later times Israel's administration became so corrupt that judges and priests favoured anyone who paid them well (Amos 2:6-7; 5:12; Micah 3:11; Zeph 3:3). They became so biased that they refused a fair hearing to anyone whom they did not like (Mark 14:55-56; John 7:51).

Disputes may sometimes arise in the church, but a Christian should not take a fellow believer before a civil judge to settle a disagreement between them. Such matters should be settled by spiritual people within the fellowship. A Christian should be prepared to suffer wrong rather than force his rights to the extent of creating a lawsuit with another believer (1 Cor 6:1-7).

Christians must be prepared to forgive, and this forgiveness must extend to opponents who are openly anti-Christian (Matt 5:10-11,38-42). There may, however, be cases where Christians feel they should demand their legal rights in order to clear Christianity of false accusations (Acts 16:36-39; 22:25; 25:10-11). (See also JUDGMENT.)

JUDGES, BOOK OF

Between Israel's conquest of Canaan and the setting up of the monarchy, there was a period of about two hundred years known as the period of the judges. With no formal or centralized administration, Israel relied largely on specially gifted men or women whom God raised up to provide leadership. They were called judges because they carried out God's judgment, either by driving out enemies who forced their rule upon the Israelites, or by settling disputes among the Israelites themselves. The activities of the judges are described in the book of Judges and in the opening chapters of the first book of Samuel (Judg 3:10; 4:4; 10:2-3; 12:7-14; 15:20; 1 Sam 4:18; 7:15-17).

Features of the era

The basic cause of the Israelites' troubles during the period of the judges was their disobedience. They had failed to carry out God's instructions to destroy the Canaanite people left in the land after Joshua's conquest (Deut 7:2-4; 9:5; Judg 1:21,27-36). The result was that the Israelites followed the false religious practices of the Canaanites.

In judgment God used the Canaanites, along with people from neighbouring lands, to oppress

Israel (Josh 23:4-5,12-13; Judg 2:11-15,20-23). When, after years of oppression, the Israelites cried to God for help, he raised up deliverers (judges) from among them to overthrow the enemy (Judg 3:9,15; 4:3; 10:10-16). But once they were enjoying peace and prosperity again, the people slipped back into idolatry (Judg 2:16-20; 8:33; see BAAL).

Israel's territory was at the time divided into tribal areas. Of the twelve tribes, nine and a half occupied the region between the Jordan River and

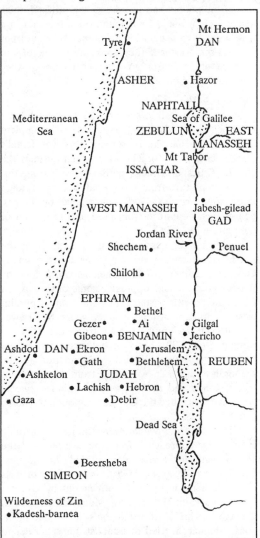

the Mediterranean Sea (i.e. Canaan itself). The other two and a half tribes occupied the plateau region east of Jordan. The enemy conquests usually involved only part of Israel, and there were cases where different enemies controlled different parts of the country during the same period (e.g. Judg 10:7-8; 11:5; 13:1).

There was little unity between tne Israelite tribes during the period of the judges. They were separated from each other by settlements of the unconquered Canaanite peoples (Judg 1:19,27-36; 4:2-3) and were usually slow to help each other in times of crisis (Judg 5:16-17; 12:2). Most people were concerned only for their own interests (Judg 15:9-13; 20:12-14).

If the people had loved and served God, their loyalty to him would have bound them together in a true unity. The demand for a monarchy would not have arisen. Instead, they took advantage of the absence of a central government to do as they pleased (Judg 17:6; 21:25).

Contents of the book

A summary of Joshua's conquests that introduces the book shows that the conquest was incomplete (1:1-36) and that the reason for this was Israel's disobedience (2:1-10). The writer then outlines the characteristics of Israel's national life during this time — departure from God, Baal worship, foreign domination, cry to God, deliverance by judges, peace, then departure from God and repetition of the pattern (2:11-3:6).

The first oppression of Israel came from the north, lasted eight years, and was overthrown by Othniel of Judah (3:7-11). Then Moab, helped by Ammon and Amalek, oppressed some of the eastern tribes along with parts of Benjamin and Ephraim west of Jordan. After eighteen years Moab was overthrown by Ehud, a man from the tribe of Benjamin (3:12-30). Shamgar delivered part of the coastal region from Philistine domination (3:31). Deborah and Barak, with help from a number of tribes, conquered the oppressors who for twenty years had controlled the Galilean region in the north (4:1-5:31).

Invaders from Midian were the next to trouble Israel. They approached from the east, crossed the Jordan, and for seven years raided the helpless Israelites as far west as Gaza and as far north as Naphtali. They were finally driven out by Gideon, who came from the tribe of Manasseh in central Canaan (6:1-8:35). After Gideon's death, one of his sons, Abimelech, tried to establish himself ruler in central Canaan. After a short but violent reign he was killed (9:1-57).

Little is known of the activities of the judges Tola and Jair (10:1-5). Then for eighteen years the Ammonites imposed a cruel rule over the area east of Jordan (and over parts of some western tribes as

well). They were conquered by Jephthah, one of the eastern tribes' greatest heroes (10:6-12:7). After Jephthah came the judges Ibzan, Elon and Abdon (12:8-15). For forty years the Philistines dominated the territory inland from the coast, spreading across the tribal territories of Dan and Judah. With his spectacular one-man victories against them, Samson began the movement that eventually broke their dominance (13:1-16:31).

A separate section at the end of the book highlights the lack of a central government to administer justice in inter-tribal affairs. As a result people did as they pleased, something that was well illustrated by the actions of the tribes Dan and Benjamin.

Dan was originally located on the central coast, but it found itself being squeezed out of its territory by oppression from the Philistines and expansion from the stronger tribes that bordered it (Judah and Ephraim). Determined to maintain its tribal identity and its independence, Dan went looking for a new location. With a ruthless disregard for the rights of others, it gained its new territory in the far north (17:1-18:31).

The tribe of Benjamin became involved in an inter-tribal dispute when some of its people were guilty of violence against members of another tribe. When it ignored a nationwide demand for justice and refused to punish the offenders, the other tribes attacked it and almost wiped it out (19:1-21:25).

JUDGMENT

Judgment has many aspects. It may concern legal procedures and announcements, or it may concern private acts of examining, discerning or criticizing. It is something that people do and something that God does. It takes place in the lives of people now and will take place in their encounter with God at the end of the age.

God the judge

As creator of man and ruler of the universe, God is the supreme judge (Gen 18:25; Ps 67:4; 94:2; 96:13; John 8:50; Heb 12:23). His judgment is always just because it is according to his own perfect standards, but it is also mixed with mercy (Ps 9:8; 36:5-6; 89:14; Rom 2:12-16; 2 Tim 4:8; James 2:13; Rev 16:5; see MERCY).

God's judgment is not merely another word for his condemnation and punishment. True judgment involves both discernment and action, and the two are inseparable. First the judge makes a distinction between what is right and what is wrong, then on the basis of his findings he takes action. The purpose of that action is to condemn the person who is wrong and vindicate the person who is right (Deut 1:16-17; 16:18-20; 1 Kings 3:9,28; Jer 5:28; Ezek 7:27).

For this reason persecuted believers in Old Testament days often looked forward to God's judgment. Though downtrodden, they knew they were in the right, but because of the corruption of the courts they had no way of gaining a hearing and therefore no chance of getting justice. They longed for the day when God would act in true judgment, righting the wrongs, declaring them to be right, and sentencing their opponents to punishment (Ps 7:6-8; 9:8,12; 10:2,12,17-18; 82:1-4; see JUSTICE).

Persecuted believers in the New Testament era could likewise long for the day when God would intervene in judgment, bringing relief to them and punishment to their persecutors (2 Thess 1:4-8; Rev 6:10; 11:18). Christ's death makes the judgment and condemnation of evildoers certain, because by that death Satan himself was judged and condemned (John 12:31-33; 16:8-11).

Everyday judgments

Making judgments between right and wrong is part of the process of living (Luke 7:43; 12:57). This is particularly so in the case of Christians who, having an understanding of the mind of God, are better able to judge between the good and the evil (John 7:24; 1 Cor 2:15-16; Heb 5:14). In the church they must make judgments concerning what is said (1 Cor 10:15; 14:29; 1 Thess 5:20-21) and what is done (Acts 15:19; 1 Cor 5:3,12; 6:1-3).

When exercising this judgment, Christians must first of all judge themselves, to make sure they are not guilty of the things concerning which they accuse others. God will judge them according to the standard they use to judge others (Matt 7:1-5; Rom 2:1-3). It is important, therefore, that they exercise strict self-examination and self-correction, otherwise they may experience God's judgment upon them in the form of various sufferings (1 Cor 11:28-32; Heb 12:6; see CHASTISEMENT).

There are some things, particularly in the lives of others, concerning which Christians should not make judgments at all. In such cases God is the only one capable of making right judgments (1 Cor 4:3-5; James 4:11-12). They should not be harshly critical of those of weaker faith, but should concentrate on strengthening them (Rom 14:3-4,13).

Jesus Christ the judge

The purpose of Jesus' first coming was not to be a judge but to be a saviour; not to condemn sinners but to save sinners (John 3:17; 12:47). It is at his second coming that Jesus will carry out God's work of judgment (Matt 25:36-41; John 5:22,26-30; 2 Cor 5:10; 2 Thess 1:7-8; 2 Tim 4:1).

Although Jesus' first coming was not for the purpose of judgment, it did, in a sense, result in judgment. When people faced him they had to make a decision either to accept him or reject him; and the decision they made was their own judgment on themselves. It determined whether they would be saved or condemned (John 3:19; 9:39; cf. Rom 1:24,26,28).

People who considered themselves good, who heard Jesus' teachings and saw his mighty works yet deliberately rejected him, condemned themselves. They would suffer greater punishment than those whom they considered wicked but who had never heard of Jesus (Matt 11:20-24; Mark 12:40; Luke 12:47-48; John 9:39-41).

Final judgment

All people will one day stand before Christ, the supreme judge. This includes those who are living at Christ's return and those who have died throughout the thousands of years of the world's history (Matt 10:15; 25:31-32; Acts 10:42; 17:31; Rom 14:10; Heb 9:27; 1 Peter 4:5). Because no one knows when that judgment will be, people should live in a state of constant readiness for it (Matt 24:36,42-44). At that judgment each person's behaviour will be judged, even hidden actions and secret thoughts, because such works are evidence of what a person really is (Matt 12:33-37; 16:27; Rom 2:6,16; 1 Cor 4:5; 2 Cor 5:10; Rev 22:12).

Being perfect in holiness, God cannot treat evil as if it does not matter. His love for all that is right is so strong that he reacts against all that is wrong in righteous anger and holy wrath (Rom 1:18; 2:5; Eph 5:6; Rev 6:17; see HELL; PUNISHMENT).

As far as believers are concerned, this wrath has fallen on Jesus Christ. Through him believers have the forgiveness of their sins and so escape the wrath that is to fall on sinners at the final judgment (Rom 3:24-26; 5:9; 2 Cor 5:21; Eph 1:7; 1 Thess 1:10; 5:9; see FORGIVENESS; JUSTIFICATION; PROPITIATION).

Since Christ has borne their sin and brought them into a right relationship with God, believers can face God's judgment with confidence (Rom 8:33; 1 John 4:17). They do not fear condemnation, because once they are 'in Christ' there can be no condemnation (John 3:18; 5:24; Rom 8:11). Since their names are in the book of life, they have no fear of the judgment of death (Rev 20:11-15; cf. Luke 10:20; Phil 4:3; Rev 21:27).

This confidence does not mean that believers are going to escape all judgment. There will be an examination of their lives and works that will reveal whether they have lived for God or for themselves; whether they have followed God's standards or the standards of the world. That examination will determine the reward or rebuke they will receive (Rom 14:10; 1 Cor 3:8-15; 2 Cor 5:10; see HEAVEN; REWARD).

JUSTICE

Throughout the Bible, justice is closely connected with righteousness. Both words have a breadth of meaning in relation to character and conduct, and both are commonly concerned with doing right or being in the right (see RIGHTEOUSNESS).

God, the sovereign ruler of the universe, is perfect in justice (Gen 18:25; Deut 32:4; Rev 15:3). At the same time he is merciful. Sinful man can have hope only because of the perfect harmony of justice and mercy within the divine nature (Exod 34:6-7; Zeph 3:5; cf. Job 4:17; Mal 3:6-7). There is no way that sinful man can bring himself into a right relationship with a just and holy God, yet God is merciful to him. Through Jesus Christ, God has provided a way of salvation by which he can bring the repentant sinner into a right relationship with himself, yet be just in doing so (Rom 3:26; see JUSTIFICATION).

In addition to the justice that is evident in God's way of salvation, justice should be evident in the common affairs of human society. This is the aspect of justice that the present article is chiefly concerned with. The perfect expression of justice in governing human society is seen in the authority exercised by Jesus the King-Messiah (Isa 9:7; John 5:30; Acts 22:14; see KING). But God desires justice in the operations of all earthly governments, and likewise in private dealings between individuals (Deut 16:18-20; 25:13-16).

Basic concerns

Since man exists in God's image (Gen 1:27), there is within him an awareness of things being right or wrong, good or bad, just or unjust. The law of God is, as it were, written on man's heart (Rom 2:14-15). Though sin has hindered man's understanding and dulled his conscience, the law of God remains within him. It is this unwritten law that makes it possible for man to know what justice is and to draw up law-codes to administer justice in society.

The ancient Hebrew law-code demonstrates how the universal and timeless principles of justice can be applied to the cultural and social habits of a particular people and era. Moses' law, given by God himself, sets out the type of justice that God requires (Deut 16:18; 32:44-47).

Justice must be the same for all, rich and poor alike (Exod 23:3,6-7; Deut 1:15-17). Laws must not be designed to suit the people of power and influence, but must protect the rights of those who can be easily exploited, such as foreigners, widows, orphans, debtors, labourers and the poor in general (Exod 21:1-11; 22:21-27; 23:6-12; Deut 14:28-29; 15:11). Also penalties must fit the crime, being neither too heavy nor too light (Exod 21:23-25; see PUNISHMENT).

Although the history of Israel mentions many kings, judges and other administrators who upheld such principles of justice (2 Sam 8:15; 23:3-4; Ps 101:1-8; Isa 33:15-16; Jer 22:15), it also mentions many who ignored them (1 Sam 8:3; 2 Kings 21:16; Eccles 5:8; Isa 5:23; Jer 22:17; see RULER). In both Old and New Testament times godly people were fearless in condemning injustice, whether committed by civil authorities or religious leaders. Civil power gives no one the right to do as he likes, and religious exercises are no substitute for common justice (Isa 1:14-17,23; 59:14-15; Amos 5:11-12,21-23; Micah 7:3; Mark 11:15-17; 12:40; Luke 6:25; 16:19-25; James 5:1-6).

Influence for good

God's way of dealing with the sinfulness of human society begins not with changing the social order, but with changing individuals. Those individuals, however, are part of society, and they will help change society as they promote the values of life they have learnt through coming to know God (Matt 5:13,16; 1 Cor 7:21-24; Eph 4:17-24; 5:8-11). Genuine moral goodness includes within it a concern to correct social injustice. This involves not merely condemning evil, but positively doing good (Isa 1:17; Amos 5:15,24; Micah 6:8; Matt 23:23; Luke 3:10-14; Col 4:1; James 1:27).

Political conditions vary from one country to another, and these will largely determine the extent to which God's people can actively try to persuade the government to improve social justice. Much depends on what rights citizens have to choose their government and influence its decisions (see GOVERNMENT). But no matter what type of government they live under, God's people should always work to promote values of human dignity (cf. Ps 8:5-8). In so doing they may undermine unjust practices and eventually see them removed (Eph 2:13-16; 5:25; 6:5-9; Philem 16; see RACE; SLAVE;

WOMEN; WORK). No government, however, can relieve them of their personal responsibility to help the disadvantaged in society (Lev 25:35-40; Isa 58:6-7; Matt 5:9; 25:34-36; Luke 10:30-36).

Bearing with injustice

Christians may suffer injustice in the form of discrimination and even persecution, both from governments and from citizens. Like Jesus they must accept any such opposition bravely and not try to retaliate (Rom 12:19-21; 1 Peter 2:15,21-23; 3:13; 4:16; see PERSECUTION). There may be cases where they claim their rights in support of those principles of justice that government officials are supposed to administer (Acts 16:35-39; 22:25; 25:10-11), but they should not use their rights for selfish purposes.

When Jesus told his followers that they were not to demand 'an eye for an eye', he was not undermining the basis of civil justice (which does demand 'an eye for an eye' and positively 'returns evil for evil' by imposing a penalty to fit the offence). Rather Jesus was telling his followers that the spirit ruling in their hearts must not be the same as that which operates in a code of legal justice. God's people must always be prepared to sacrifice their rights and even do good to those who harm them (Matt 5:38-42; 1 Cor 6:7-8; Phil 2:4; cf. 1 Cor 9:15).

JUSTIFICATION

The English words 'justification' and 'righteousness' are different parts of the same word in the original languages of the Bible. This applies to the Hebrew of the Old Testament and the Greek of the New (see also RIGHTEOUSNESS).

Meaning of 'justify' in the Bible

Most commonly the Bible uses the word 'justify' in what might be called a legal sense. The picture is that of a courtroom where the righteous person is the one whom the judge declares to be right. The person is justified. In other words, to justify means to declare righteous, to declare to be in the right, to vindicate. It is the opposite of to condemn, which means to declare guilty, to declare to be in the wrong (Deut 25:1; Job 13:18; Isa 50:7-8; Matt 12:37; Luke 18:14; Rom 8:33).

A person who tries to show that he is in the right is said to be trying to justify himself. He is trying to declare himself righteous (Job 32:2; Luke 10:28-29; 16:14-15). He may even go to the extent of condemning God in order to justify himself, declaring God to be wrong and himself to be right (Job 40:8). It is in this sense of declaring a person to be right or wrong that the Bible may speak of God

as being justified. People acknowledge that he is in the right and that his judgments are correct (Ps 51:4; Luke 7:29; Rom 3:4; cf. Rev 16:5).

Some may argue that to justify means to *make* righteous (cf. Rom 5:19 RSV), but if such is the case it is important to understand what is meant by being 'made' righteous. A person is not made righteous in the sense that a piece of metal placed in a fire is 'made hot'. He is made righteous only in the sense of being declared righteous. He is put in a right relationship with God (Rom 5:19 GNB). The word has to do with a legal pronouncement, not with changing a person from one thing to another by placing some new moral power within him (Rom 4:1-3; 5:17-19; Phil 3:9).

Just as condemn does not mean 'make wicked', so justify does not mean 'make good'. Nevertheless, one result of the believer's justification is that his life is changed so that righteousness (in the sense of right behaviour), not sin, becomes its chief characteristic (Phil 3:9-10; James 2:17-23; 1 Peter 2:24; 1 John 3:7; see SANCTIFICATION).

Justification by faith

The fullest explanation of justification is in the writings of Paul. There the teaching centres on God's great act of salvation by which he declares the repentant sinner righteous before him. Instead of having the status of one who is guilty and condemned, the sinner now has the status of one who is right with God. God brings him into a right relationship with himself, giving him a right standing before him (Rom 5:1-2; 8:33).

This is entirely an act of God's grace, for it is impossible for a person to have any right standing before God on the basis of his own deeds. Even his best efforts to keep the law will not help. Since man is a sinner and under God's condemnation, there is nothing he can do to gain acceptance with God (Ps 143:2; Rom 3:28; 9:31-32; Gal 2:16). God accepts man not because of anything man has done, but solely because of his own mercy (Isa 55:7; Micah 7:18; Rom 3:24; Eph 2:8).

However, this gracious work of justification takes place only in those who trust in God. It is through faith that people are justified; more specifically, through faith in Jesus Christ. Christ has done the work and they accept the benefits of that work by faith (Rom 1:17; 3:22,28; 4:2-5; 5:1; Gal 2:16; 3:11; see FAITH; GRACE).

The basis of God's merciful act of justification is the death and resurrection of Jesus Christ (Rom 3:24-25; 4:23-25; 5:9,17-19; Gal 2:21). God now sees the believer as 'in Christ' and therefore he declares the believer righteous. And the person whom God declares righteous *is* righteous — not in the sense that he is a perfect person who cannot sin any more, but in the sense that God gives him a righteousness that is not his own, the righteousness of Christ. God accepts the believing sinner because of what Christ has done. Jesus Christ becomes, as it were, his righteousness (1 Cor 1:30; 2 Peter 1:1).

Justification and substitution

Although the word 'justification' tells us that God declares the sinner righteous, it does not tell us the hidden mysteries of divine activity that make it possible for God to do this. The mysteries of God's will and the wonders of his salvation are beyond the ability of man to understand fully. But since justification is concerned with the processes of law, a further illustration from the law court may suggest the way God has worked.

In this courtroom scene, God is the judge and sinful man is on trial (Rom 2:2,5-6; 3:23). God loves man and wants to forgive him (1 John 4:16; 2 Peter 3:9), but God's love requires that he act justly (i.e. righteously). Any judge who acquitted a guilty person simply because he liked that person would be called unjust. He might claim to be loving, but his love would be no more than an irrational emotion divorced from moral justice and righteousness. True love, by contrast, is so zealous for the other person's well-being that it reacts in anger against all that is wrong (cf. Heb 12:6).

God is love and wants to forgive the sinner, but because he is a God of love he cannot ignore sin or treat it as if it does not matter. His act of forgiveness, if it is based on love, will involve his dealing with sin.

Being a God of love, God must punish sin, but at the same time (being a God of love) he provides a way whereby sinners need not suffer the punishment themselves. He has done this by becoming a man himself, living in man's world, and then taking the punishment of man's sin through Jesus Christ's death on the cross (Rom 3:24; 5:9; 2 Cor 5:18). God is both the judge and the one against whom man has sinned, yet at the same time he is the one who bears the penalty of man's sin. He forgives the sinner only at great cost to himself (John 3:16; 2 Cor 8:9; see SACRIFICE).

Jesus died in the place of, or as the substitute for, guilty sinners (1 Peter 2:24). Whereas Adam's sin brought death, Christ's death brings life (Rom 5:15,18). Being fully man, Jesus could be a substitute for his fellow man, but only because he was sinless and completely obedient. He fulfilled all God's

righteous requirements under the law (Matt 3:15; Phil 2:8; 1 Peter 2:22; 1 John 3:5). One who broke God's law would be under condemnation himself and could not take the place of another (Gal 3:10). Jesus, however, kept God's law perfectly. He was absolutely righteous in the fullest moral sense of the word, and so was able to bear the law's punishment on behalf of those who had broken it (Gal 3:11-13; 4:4-5).

When he died, the sinless Jesus suffered the punishment that man's sin deserved. 'He bore our sins' (1 Peter 2:24). Because of the death of Christ, God is now able to forgive the repentant sinner and accept him as righteous before him. The believer is now in a right relationship with God, because Christ is in a right relationship with God (2 Cor 5:21). God's justice and God's mercy operate in harmony, because both are outworkings of his love. His justice is satisfied in seeing sin punished, and his mercy flows out in seeing sin forgiven. In his love God justifies the guilty but repentant sinner, yet he does so justly and righteously (Rom 3:26; 4:5; see also PROPITIATION).

Justification and forgiveness

God's forgiveness is more than what the ordinary person usually means when he talks of forgiveness. It is more than merely the removal of hostility or the ignoring of wrongdoing. When God forgives the sinner, he also justifies him, bringing him into a right relation with himself (Rom 5:6-11). God not only removes condemnation, he also gives righteousness (Rom 4:6-8,22; 5:17,19; 2 Cor 5:19,21; Phil 3:9). Forgiveness is something the believer continues to be in need of because he is still likely to sin (Matt 6:12); justification is a once-for-all act, a declaration by God that he accepts the believer in his Son (Rom 5:1-2).

The forgiveness that the believer needs day by day is concerned not with the basic work of justification, but with the believer's daily enjoyment of fellowship with God. Although the penalty of sin has been paid, the evil effects of sin are still in the world and the believer cannot escape them. His failures may disappoint himself and God, but as he confesses them he is assured of God's forgiveness (1 John 1:7,9; see CONFESSION; FORGIVENESS). His justification, however, is never in question.

Christ's death deals with sin's penalty for all believers, whether they belong to generations past, present or future. In like manner it deals with the penalty for all the sins of each individual believer, whether those sins be in the past, present or future (Rom 3:22-26; Heb 9:15).

KADESH-BARNEA

The town of Kadesh-barnea (or Kadesh) was the main settlement in the far south of Palestine. It was an oasis town between the Wilderness of Zin to the north, the Wilderness of Paran to the south, the Wilderness of Shur to the west, and the Arabah to the east (Gen 16:7,14; 20:1; Num 13:26; 20:1; see PALESTINE).

Kadesh appears to have been the Israelites' main base during their forty years in the wilderness. It was the place where the twelve spies reported to the people after their fact-finding mission to Canaan, and where Moses planned the final journey

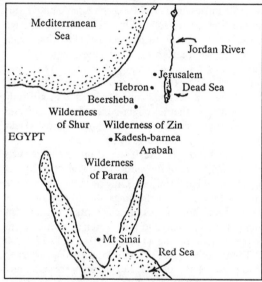

to Canaan about forty years later (Num 13:25-26; 14:32-34; 20:14-21). Little is known of events at Kadesh during the intervening years. Two recorded incidents were Miriam's death and Moses' striking of the rock in search of water (Num 20:1-14; 27:14).

Moses intended that after the conquest of Canaan, Israel's southern border would run from the Dead Sea through Kadesh-barnea to the Brook of Egypt, which it would follow to the Mediterranean Sea (Num 34:1-5). Though Israel's conquest reached Kadesh, the town that later generations usually recognized as marking Israel's southern border was Beersheba, almost fifty kilometres to the north. The wilderness of Zin lay between the two towns (Josh 10:40-41; 15:1-3; 2 Sam 17:11; 24:2).

KEDAR

Kedar was the name of one of the nomadic tribal groups of northern Arabia. The people of Kedar lived in tents, kept flocks of sheep and goats, and dealt shrewdly in various trading activities (Ps 120:5; Isa 60:7; Jer 49:28-29; Ezek 27:21; see ARABIA).

KENITES

The name Kenites usually refers to that tribal group within the Midianite people to which Moses' in-laws belonged. This group had apparently mingled with the ancient Kenite people (who were among the early inhabitants of Canaan) and so were referred to as both Kenites and Midianites (Gen 15:19; Exod 2:15-21; Judg 1:16; 4:11). The Israelites allowed the Kenite in-laws of Moses, and their descendants, to live among them in Canaan, and at times showed a special concern for them (Judg 1:16; 1 Sam 15:6; 30:26-29; 1 Chron 2:55; Neh 3:14).

KILL

See DEATH; EXECUTION; SACRIFICE.

KINDNESS

Like many words that indicate qualities of character and behaviour, 'kindness' has a very broad meaning. It may be well understood through the study of a number of words closely associated with it.

In older versions of the English Bible, kindness is one of the words used to denote God's covenant love for Israel (Micah 6:8; see LOVE, sub-heading 'Steadfast love'). It is also used in connection with God's goodness, patience and forbearance (Rom 2:4; Gal 5:22-23; Titus 3:4; see GOODNESS; MERCY). Christians likewise are to be kind, particularly in being patient with people and circumstances that test or annoy them (2 Cor 6:6; Eph 4:32; Col 3:12-13; see PATIENCE). The meekness of Christ is a demonstration of his kindness (Matt 11:28-30; see MEEKNESS).

KING

As the sovereign ruler of the universe, God is the all-powerful and glorious king who reigns for ever and rules over all (Ps 10:16; 24:8,10; 95:3; 103:19; Jer 51:57; Dan 4:17; 1 Tim 1:17; Rev 15:3). In particular he is king to his people, who live under his absolute lordship (Ps 98:6; Mal 1:14). This was well illustrated in the covenant that God made with Israel at Mt Sinai. In response to God's sovereign act of graciously taking Israel to be his people, the Israelites promised to live in obedience to all his commands (Exod 19:5-6; 24:3).

During the period of the Old Testament, Israel's national life functioned under various types of government — the absolute leadership of Moses (Num 12:6-8), a federation of self-governing tribes (Josh 24:1), a united monarchy (1 Sam 11:15), a divided monarchy (1 Kings 12:17-20; 15:1) and a governorship controlled by a foreign overlord (Neh 5:14). However, the people were to regard God as their king, regardless of the type of government they lived under. The New Testament teaches that the same principle applies to Christians, who in different countries and eras may live under different types of governments (Luke 20:25; 1 Peter 2:13-17; see GOVERNMENT).

Establishment of Israel's monarchy

In the early days of Israel's settlement in Canaan, there was no monarchy and no central government. The various tribes looked after their own affairs (Judg 21:25). During this period, the people of Israel were repeatedly unfaithful and disobedient to God, and this brought God's judgment upon them in the form of repeated invasions from hostile neighbours (Judg 2:13-19). In their search for greater national stability, the people decided to follow the pattern of neighbouring nations and appoint a king who would rule over the whole nation through a central government (1 Sam 8:4).

This desire for a king was really a rejection of God — not in the sense that an Israelite monarch replaced God as the leader of the government, but in the sense that the people tried to solve their problems without submitting to God. Their troubles arose from their sins, not from their system of government. Therefore, the way to overcome those troubles was to turn from their sins to God. Instead they chose to ignore God and to try to solve their problems by changing the political system. They did not want a way of life where their well-being depended on their spiritual relationship with God (1 Sam 8:7-8).

Samuel warned that having a king would not improve matters if the people remained disobedient. In the days before they had a king they had been punished for disobedience, and under a king they would be punished just the same (1 Sam 12:9-15).

Characteristics of the kings

During the period before the setting up of the monarchy, God had rescued Israel from foreign oppression by raising up deliverers (called judges) in response to the people's repentance. Through the power of God's Spirit, these leaders carried out God's judgment on the oppressors and restored Israel's independence (Judg 2:16-19; 3:10; 6:34; 11:29; 13:25). This type of activity continued into the

reign of Israel's first king, Saul (1 Sam 10:6,10; 11:6), but the next king, David, was the last of the Spirit-gifted leaders (1 Sam 16:13-14). David established the sort of dynasty that the people had looked for. They wanted a system where the throne would pass on automatically from the king to his son, generation after generation. In such a system there was no need for God's provision of specially gifted people.

From what they had seen in the nations round about, the Israelites knew that kings could be oppressive because of their desire for personal power and wealth. But when Samuel warned them of this, they ignored him (1 Sam 8:9-20).

Centuries earlier, Moses had anticipated this desire for an Israelite king. He therefore gave specific instructions to prevent Israelite kings from following the pattern of other kings, who built for themselves military glory, large harems and excessive wealth (Deut 17:14-17). Above all, the Israelite king was to have a personal copy of God's law and study it carefully, so that he might govern Israel justly and righteously according to God's standards (Deut 17:18-20; cf. 2 Sam 23:3-7; Ps 101:1-8).

The history of the Israelite monarchy records the development of the sorts of problems that Moses and Samuel had expected. Only by taxing the people heavily were many of the kings able to support their large royal households, finance their extravagant building programs and pay foreign overlords to support their throne (1 Kings 4:1-7; 5:13-17; 12:4; 2 Kings 15:20; 23:35). Some kings brought justice and peace to the people, but others were cruel and corrupt (1 Kings 21:1-14; 2 Kings 18:1-6; 21:16; 2 Chron 17:3-4,9; Jer 22:13-17). The entire period of the monarchy was marked by a striking mixture of obedience and disobedience to the instructions set out in the law of Moses (Deut 17:14-20; cf. 1 Kings 3:9,28; 10:14-22,26; 11:1-7; 2 Kings 11:12; 22:11-13; 2 Chron 19:4-11).

Repeated disobedience among the kings was one reason for the nation's decline and fall. In the end the nation was conquered, the people taken into captivity, and the monarchy brought to an end (2 Kings 17:21-23; 21:10-15; 23:26-27).

The ideal king

With the increasing disorder that characterized Israelite life during the period of the monarchy, people looked back to the time of David as the nearest Israel had ever been to having an ideal king (Ps 89:20-21; Acts 13:22). Each king of the dynasty of David was, in a sense, God's son, because through him God exercised his rule. The coronation ceremony was the occasion when God formally adopted the king and anointed him for the task of ruling his people (2 Sam 7:14-16; Ps 2:7; 20:6; 45:7; 89:3-4,26-29).

In spite of the failure of their kings and the termination of the monarchy, the Israelite people still hoped for the day when the dynasty of David would be restored to power. They looked for one who would be the ideal king, the great descendant of David whom they called the Lord's 'anointed one', or, in the Hebrew language, 'the Messiah' (Isa 11:1; Jer 23:5; Ezek 34:23-24; 37:24; see MESSIAH). In contrast to the kings of a former era, this king would rule with perfect wisdom, power, love and justice (Isa 9:6-7; 11:2-5; Jer 33:15).

Jesus Christ was this promised king (Matt 2:2; 21:5,9). However, he was not the sort of king many of the Jews expected; for his chief concern was not with bringing in a political golden age, but with bringing sinful people to submit to the rule of God in their lives. His kingdom was not concerned with national glory; it was a kingdom of a different type from the political kingdoms of the world (John 6:15; 12:13-16; 18:33-37; see KINGDOM OF GOD). Unrepentant sinners did not want a king whose concern was for such a kingdom, and in the end they had him crucified (Matt 27:29,37,42; John 19:15,19; cf. Luke 19:14).

Through the resurrection and exaltation of Jesus, God showed that Jesus Christ was indeed his chosen king, and the early preachers enthusiastically proclaimed his kingship and his kingdom (Acts 2:36; 4:26-27; 5:31; 8:12; 17:7; 19:8; 28:23,31; Phil 2:9-11). This kingship will be displayed openly on the day when Jesus Christ returns in glory as King of kings and Lord of lords (Rev 17:14; 19:15-16; cf. Matt 25:31,34,40).

KINGDOM OF GOD

Most of the biblical references to the kingdom of God are found in the teachings of Jesus recorded in the four Gospels. The subject of the kingdom of God was central in Jesus' teaching. Yet nowhere did Jesus say exactly what the kingdom was, and neither did the writers of the New Testament who followed him, even though they too spoke of the kingdom.

Perhaps the reason for this was that people who knew the Old Testament should already have been familiar with the idea of God's kingdom. Jesus' teaching on the kingdom was a development of the Old Testament teaching, showing that through him the kingdom found its fullest meaning.

What the kingdom of God is

Throughout the Bible the kingdom of God is the rule of God. It is not a territory over which he reigns, but the rule which he exercises. It is defined not by a geographic location, an era of existence, or the nationality of a people, but by the sovereign rule and authority of God (Exod 15:18; Ps 103:19; 145:10-13).

Jesus likewise understood God's kingdom as God's rule rather than as a territory or a people. The person who seeks God's kingdom seeks God's rule in his life (Matt 6:33); the person who receives God's kingdom receives God's rule in his life (Mark 10:15). The prayer for God's kingdom to come is a prayer that his rule be accepted, so that his will is done on earth as it is in heaven (Matt 6:10). The kingdom is a realm in the spiritual, rather than the physical, sense. The person who enters the kingdom of God enters the realm where he accepts God's rule (Matt 21:31).

The world at present is in a state of rebellion against God's rule, because it is under the power of Satan (2 Cor 4:4; 1 John 5:19; see WORLD). Therefore, when the kingdom of God came among mankind in the person of Jesus Christ, the rule of God was demonstrated in the defeat of Satan. As Jesus proclaimed the kingdom, he healed those who were diseased and oppressed by evil spirits, and in so doing he gave evidence of his power over Satan (Matt 4:23-24). His deliverance of people from the bondage of Satan was proof that God's kingdom (his authority, power, rule) had come among them (Matt 12:28; Mark 1:27; Luke 10:9,17-18).

There is a sense, therefore, in which all people experience the kingdom; for all people experience (or one day will experience) the sovereign authority of God, either in blessing or in judgment (Matt 12:28; Rev 11:15,18; 19:15-16). But the important aspect of the kingdom that the Gospels emphasize is that it came among mankind through Jesus. Because John the Baptist announced the coming of the kingdom of Jesus, he brought to a close the pre-kingdom era (Matt 3:2; Luke 16:16). Even the most insignificant person in the new era enjoys blessings that the greatest person of the former era never knew (Matt 11:11).

Note: The kingdom of God and the kingdom of heaven are different names for the same thing. The Bible uses the expressions interchangeably (Matt 19:23-24). Jews had developed the practice of showing great respect for the name of God, and because they feared that they might use that name irreverently, they often used the word 'heaven' instead of 'God' (Dan 4:25-26; Luke 15:18; John 3:27). Matthew, who wrote his Gospel for the Jews, usually (but not always) speaks of God's kingdom as the kingdom of heaven, whereas the other Gospel writers call it the kingdom of God (Matt 19:14; Mark 10:14; Luke 18:16).

Both present and future

In contrast to the popular Jewish belief that God's kingdom was a future national and political kingdom to be centred on Israel, Jesus pointed out that God's kingdom was already present among them. It was present in him (Luke 10:9; 17:20-21).

When people willingly humbled themselves and submitted to the rule of Christ, they immediately entered Christ's kingdom. And by entering the kingdom they received forgiveness of sins and eternal life (Matt 21:31; Mark 10:14-15; John 3:3). Not only those of Jesus' time, but people of any era, when they believe in him, immediately enter his kingdom and receive the kingdom's blessings (Rom 14:17; Col 1:13).

Yet Jesus spoke also of the kingdom as something belonging to the future (Mark 14:25), whose establishment could take place only after he had suffered and died (Luke 18:31-33; 22:15-16; 24:26; Rev 5:6-12; 11:15). Even for those who were already believers, Jesus spoke of his kingdom as something yet future, which they would enter at his return (Matt 7:21-23; 13:41-43; 25:31-34). For this reason Christians, who are already in the kingdom, also look forward to the day when they will inherit the kingdom (1 Cor 15:50; 2 Peter 1:11).

A person may well ask how the kingdom of God can be something that is present here and now, yet be something that awaits the future. The answer lies in our understanding of the kingdom of God as the sovereign rule of God. Believers enter the kingdom as soon as they believe, but they will experience the full blessings of the kingdom only when Christ returns to punish evil and reign in righteousness (1 Cor 15:24-26; see DAY OF THE LORD; RESURRECTION).

To 'enter the kingdom of God' is to 'have eternal life' or to 'be saved'. The Bible uses these expressions interchangeably (Matt 19:16,23-25). Just as the believer experiences the kingdom of God now and will do so more fully in the future, so he has eternal life now but will experience it in its fulness when Christ returns (John 5:24,29). Likewise he has salvation now, but he will experience the fulness of his salvation at the return of Christ (Eph 2:8; Heb 9:28). Eternal life is the life of the kingdom of God, the life of the age to come; but

because the kingdom of God has come among mankind now, people have eternal life now (Matt 25:34,46; John 3:3,5,15; 5:24).

The mystery of the kingdom

The truth that the teaching of Jesus makes clear is not simply that God's kingdom is present in the world now, but that people can enter that kingdom now, even though the world is still under the power of Satan. This is a truth that people did not understand till Jesus explained it. He referred to this present aspect of the kingdom as a mystery, or secret (Mark 4:11). By using the word 'mystery', Jesus did not mean that he was telling people something to confuse them. He meant rather that he was telling them something that previously God had kept secret but was now making known. (Similar uses of 'mystery' occur elsewhere in the New Testament; cf. Rom 16:25-26; Eph 1:9-10; Col 1:26; see MYSTERY.)

In Old Testament times people expected God's kingdom to come in one mighty act, when God would destroy all earthly kingdoms and establish his rule throughout the world (Dan 2:44-45; Zech 14:9; see SON OF MAN). It seems that, to some extent, John the Baptist also had this idea of the kingdom of God. That may have been why he became worried when Jesus did not immediately set up a world-conquering kingdom (Matt 3:11-12; 11:2-3; cf. Luke 24:21; Acts 1:6).

To reassure John, Jesus pointed out that the miracles of healing he performed were in keeping with the Old Testament prophecies concerning the Messiah's mission. His kingdom had begun (Matt 11:4-6; see MESSIAH; MIRACLES). That kingdom was not yet established in the world-conquering sense that John and others expected, but it had begun to do its work by delivering people from the power of Satan and offering them new life in Jesus Christ (Luke 17:20-21).

God's kingdom is present now, though not in the form it will have after the great events at the climax of the world's history. It is hidden rather than open. It is entered voluntarily, not forced upon mankind with irresistible power. This is the mystery of the kingdom, the previously unknown purpose of God that Jesus revealed.

Parables of the kingdom

Jesus emphasized this mystery of the kingdom in the parables recorded in Matthew 13 (Matt 13:11; see PARABLE). The parable of the seed and the soils shows that because people are free to accept or reject the message of the kingdom, most reject it.

But those who accept it experience great spiritual growth in their lives (Matt 13:18-23; cf. 23:13). The parable of the wheat and the weeds teaches that in the present world those who are in God's kingdom live alongside those who are not; but in the day of judgment, when God's kingdom will be established openly, believers will be saved and the rest punished (Matt 13:24-30,34-43).

The parables of the mustard seed and the yeast illustrate that although the kingdom may appear to have insignificant beginnings, it will one day have worldwide power and authority (Matt 13:31-33). The parables of the hidden treasure and the valuable pearl illustrate that when a person is convinced of the priceless and lasting value of the kingdom of God, he will make any sacrifice to enter it (Matt 13:44-46). Nevertheless, there are both the true and the false among those who claim to be in God's kingdom. The parable of the fishing net shows that these will be separated in God's decisive judgment at the close of the age (Matt 13:47-50).

Practical demands of the kingdom

Although a person may desire the kingdom of God above all else (Matt 6:33; 13:44-46), no person can buy his way into it. The right of entry into that kingdom is the gift of God and, as with God's other gifts, people must accept it humbly by faith (Mark 10:15; Luke 12:32). The work of God produces eternal life within a person and introduces him into the kingdom of God. It is a work that no person can do, no matter how hard he tries; yet God does it for any person who trusts in him (Mark 4:26-29; 10:17,23-27; John 3:3,15).

Neither a person's good deeds nor his status in life can gain him entrance into the kingdom of God. What God demands is repentance — a total change that gives up all self-sufficiency for the sake of following Christ as king (Matt 4:17; 5:20; 19:23; Luke 9:62). It is a decision that requires the full force of a person's will (Luke 16:16).

All who enter God's kingdom come under his rule, where he teaches them the qualities of life that he requires of them. Yet they look upon his commands not as laws that they are forced to obey, but as expressions of his will that they find true happiness in doing (Matt 5:3,10; 1 John 5:3-4). They learn that the principles that operate in the kingdom of God are different from those that operate in the kingdoms of the world (Matt 20:20-28; John 18:36). Having come into the enjoyment of the rule of Christ themselves, they then spread the good news of his kingdom throughout the world (Matt 10:7; 24:14; Acts 8:12; 19:8; 28:23,31).

Those who serve the kingdom of God may bring persecution and suffering upon themselves (Matt 10:7,16-22; Acts 14:22; 2 Thess 1:5). God, however, will preserve them through their troubles and bring them into the full enjoyment of his kingdom in the day of its final triumph (Luke 18:29-30; 2 Tim 4:18; 2 Peter 1:11).

The kingdom and the church

God's purpose was that when the Messiah came, the people of Israel would be the first to hear the good news of the kingdom. Upon accepting the Messiah, they would enter God's kingdom and then spread the good news to all nations (Isa 49:5-6; Matt 10:6-7; 15:24). But when Israel on the whole rejected the Messiah, God sent the message to the nations direct. Gentiles who believed entered the kingdom, but Jews for whom the kingdom had been prepared were excluded (Matt 8:10-12; 20:1-16; 21:33-43; Acts 13:46-47; 28:23-31).

The reason many of the Jews rejected Jesus was that he did not bring them the type of kingdom they were looking for. They wanted a Messiah who would be a political deliverer, and they wanted a kingdom that would bring material prosperity. Jesus was opposed to both ideas (John 6:15; 18:36). Even the apostles did not fully understand the nature of the Messiah and the kingdom, but they did not, as others, reject Jesus. They knew that he was indeed the Messiah of God who brought to mankind the kingdom of God and eternal life (Matt 16:13-16; John 6:66-69).

The believing minority among the Jews (the old people of God, the nation Israel) became the nucleus of the new people of God, the Christian church. To build the old people of God, God chose twelve tribes; to build the new people of God, he chose twelve apostles. As they preached the good news of Jesus Christ, the apostles opened the kingdom to all who wished to enter. They carried God's authority with them, so that when they acted in obedience to his word, their work on earth was confirmed in heaven (Matt 16:18-19; Acts 8:12; 20:24-25; 28:31).

As a result of the apostles' preaching of the kingdom of God, people believed. The faithful of old Israel became God's true Israel; believers of other nations became Abraham's spiritual offspring (Rom 2:28-29; Gal 3:28-29; 6:16). The church came into being and grew. In the great acts of God seen on the Day of Pentecost and during the months that followed, the apostles saw the power of the kingdom of God at work in a way they had never imagined (Mark 9:1).

However, the church is not the kingdom, just as Israel was not the kingdom. The church and the kingdom are things of a different kind. The kingdom is the rule of God; the church is a community of people. It is the new community of God's people, just as Israel was the old community. The kingdom works through the church, but it is something far wider than the church. It worked in the days before the church was born, and it will continue to work till the day of God's final triumph (1 Cor 15:24-28; Rev 11:15). In the meantime the church is the means by which God's rule should most clearly be seen in the world (John 17:23; Rom 14:16-18; Eph 3:10; see CHURCH).

KINGS, BOOKS OF

The two books of Kings (which were originally one book) trace the history of Israel over approximately four centuries from the end of David's reign to the beginning of the captivity in Babylon. The books record the division of the Israelite kingdom into two parts, and the history, decline and fall of the separate kingdoms (see ISRAEL; JUDAH, TRIBE AND KINGDOM).

Characteristics of the books

Although they are based on history, the books of Kings were not written merely as historical records. The ancient Hebrews grouped the books among the prophetical writings. Prophecy is God's revelation of himself and his purposes, and in these books he reveals himself in the history of Israel and Judah, showing how all affairs are under his control. The story deals with surrounding nations only as those nations are of significance in the divine purposes (see PROPHECY).

The presentation of Israel's history as prophetic history is partly because many of the historians in Israel were prophets (e.g. 1 Chron 29:29; 2 Chron 9:29; 33:19). The author of Kings (who is not named) most likely used some of the records of the prophets, along with the official records of various kings, in preparing his book (1 Kings 11:41; 14:19,29). Large portions of the books of Isaiah and Jeremiah are found also in Kings.

Because the writer of Kings is showing the purpose and meaning of Israel's history, he does not try to record all the events of any one era. Nor does he always place events in chronological order. Rather he selects and arranges his material according to his prophetic purpose. He deals with kings more in relation to their religious significance than their political achievements. He may record the reign or achievements of a politically important king only briefly (e.g. Omri; 1 Kings 16:21-28), but deal with politically unimportant events in great detail (e.g. the ministry of certain prophets; 1 Kings 17-22; 2 Kings 1-9). His purpose is to help his readers understand God better as they see him at work in the history of Israel.

Contents of 1 Kings

The opening section of 1 Kings deals with the reign of Solomon. It shows how he became king (1:1-53) and made his throne secure, firstly by removing all possible opponents (2:1-46), then by equipping himself with wisdom (3:1-28) and reorganizing the administration (4:1-34).

Solomon then prepared workers and materials for an extensive national building program (5:1-18). In Jerusalem, the capital, he built a magnificent temple for God (6:1-38), along with many impressive government buildings (7:1-12). Upon completing the temple (7:13-51), he placed in it the ark of the covenant (8:1-21) and dedicated the temple to God (8:22-9:9). He carried out building projects in country regions (9:10-25) and increased his wealth through clever trading activity (9:26-10:29). At the same time he fell into idolatry and brought God's judgment upon his kingdom (11:1-43).

Rehoboam, Solomon's son, saw the judgment of God fall when the kingdom split into two. Only the southern tribes remained loyal to the Davidic dynasty in Jerusalem. Together they became known as the kingdom of Judah. The ten tribes to the north broke away and formed their own kingdom (still called Israel) under the rebel leader, Jeroboam (12:1-33).

False religion in the north soon brought an announcement of divine punishment (13:1-14:20). The false religion spread to the south (14:21-15:8), though there was a reformation under the king Asa (15:9-24). Meanwhile the northern kingdom suffered from wars and assassinations, till Omri established a new dynasty (15:25-16:28).

When Omri's son and successor Ahab married Jezebel of Phoenicia, the Baalism of Phoenicia threatened to become Israel's national religion. The prophet Elijah was God's servant to help preserve Israel and punish the Baalists (16:29-17:24). Elijah won a great victory over the prophets of Baal on Mt Carmel (18:1-46), but when the people of Israel still did not give up their Baalism, God strengthened and reassured the discouraged Elijah (19:1-21). Through Elijah's help, Ahab saved Israel from a Syrian attack (20:1-43), but he was doomed to suffer God's judgment (21:1-29). He was killed in a later battle (22:1-40). Meanwhile in Judah to the south, King Jehoshaphat carried out extensive religious and political reforms (22:41-53).

Contents of 2 Kings

Elijah was succeeded as prophet by Elisha (1:1-2:14), who soon proved that the miraculous power of God worked through him as it had through Elijah (2:15-3:27). He performed a number of miracles to help preserve the faithful minority in Israel who still trusted in God (4:1-6:7). He performed other miracles to warn the unfaithful in Israel of God's judgment (6:8-8:15). Jezebel's Baalism, however, continued to flourish, and even spread to Judah (8:16-9:10).

An army commander named Jehu led a revolt against the ruling house of Ahab and Jezebel, which resulted in the removal of Jezebel's Baalism from Israel (9:11-10:36). Then a priest named Jehoiada led a revolt that wiped out Jezebel's Baalism from Judah (11:1-21). The true worship of Yahweh was restored in Judah (12:1-21), but there was no such reformation in Israel (13:1-14:22).

With the decline of Syrian power, Israel (under Jeroboam II) and Judah (under Azariah) enjoyed security and prosperity (14:23-15:7). After Azariah's death there was chaos in Judah, which resulted in the disastrous reign of Ahaz (15:8-16:20). The northern kingdom likewise declined after the death of Jeroboam II. Eventually it was conquered by Assyria and its people taken captive into different

Assyrians taking Israelites into captivity

parts of the Assyrian Empire (17:1-41). Only Judah remained in the national homeland, and with new policies under the godly Hezekiah the nation freed itself from Assyrian domination (18:1-20:21). But the fifty-five year reign of the evil Manasseh reduced the nation to a condition that made judgment certain (21:1-26).

Josiah repaired the temple and reformed the nation (22:1-23:27), but he was not able to save Judah from destruction. After his death, Judah lost its independence, first to Egypt and then to Babylon (23:28-37). Babylon conquered Jerusalem, took the best people into captivity, and appointed Zedekiah as king in Jerusalem (24:1-17). After Zedekiah proved treacherous, the Babylonians returned and destroyed Jerusalem. More people were taken into captivity and the nation Judah soon came to an end (24:18-25:30).

KIRIATH-JEARIM

Prior to Israel's conquest of Canaan, the inhabitants of Kiriath-jearim were known as Gibeonites, after the name of a more important town in the region (Josh 9:3,17; see GIBEON). Kiriath-jearim was on the border between Benjamin and Judah, and was known also as Kiriath-baal, Baalah, Baale-judah and Kiriath-arim (Josh 15:9,60; 18:14,21-28; 2 Sam 6:2; Ezra 2:25). It is chiefly remembered because during the time of Saul and David the ark of the covenant rested there for twenty years (1 Sam 7:1-2; 2 Sam 6:2; for maps see BENJAMIN; JUDAH).

KISS

Kissing was a very ancient custom among Israelites and other peoples of the region. It was a sign of affection between relatives, between friends and between lovers (Gen 29:11; Song of Songs 1:2; 8:1; Matt 26:48; Luke 15:20). It was also a sign of homage to a king (1 Sam 10:1; Ps 2:12; cf. Matt 26:49) or devotion to an idol (1 Kings 19:18; Hosea 13:2). In New Testament times kissing became the customary form of greeting between Christians (Rom 16:16; 1 Peter 5:14).

KNOWLEDGE

Among man's many abilities is the ability to think, know and reason. His knowledge may range from knowing people to knowing things. It may be both practical and theoretical, and it may cover the concrete and the abstract, the seen and the unseen. Above all, man has the capacity to know God. That knowledge is to be valued above all others and will affect all others (Jer 9:23-24; John 17:3).

A relationship

God desires that the people of his creation know him. This does not mean merely that they should know about him, but that they should know him personally through coming into a relationship with him (Jer 24:7; 31:34; Hosea 6:6; John 17:3; 1 John 4:6,8; 5:20). Similarly God knows those who are his – those whom he has chosen, those whom he has taken into a spiritual union with himself (Deut 34:10; Amos 3:2; Matt 7:23; John 10:27; 2 Tim 2:19). In fact, people can know God only because God has first known them; that is, loved them, chosen them and made them his own (Exod 33:17; Jer 1:5; John 10:14; Gal 4:9).

Because knowledge, in biblical language, can mean 'to be brought into a close relationship with', a man and a woman were said to 'know' each other when they had sexual relations (Gen 4:25; 19:8; Matt 1:25). Knowledge could also mean 'to have dealings with', 'to be concerned with', or 'to regard' (Deut 33:9; Rom 7:7; 2 Cor 5:16,21).

The Bible also speaks of knowledge according to the word's more common meaning in relation to understanding and learning. Yet even in such cases the knowledge usually has a very practical purpose. When people come to a knowledge of the truth, they grow in that truth through learning more of God and his ways (Ps 119:125; 1 Tim 2:4; 2 Peter 1:5; 3:18; see TRUTH). If people profess to be God's people but do not know or obey his law, they only bring God's judgment upon themselves (Isa 5:13; Jer 4:22; Hosea 4:6; John 9:39-41; Heb 5:12-13). The person who exercises a reverent submission to God has already taken the first step towards true knowledge. To refuse to go further is to act like a fool (Prov 1:7,22; 2:1-5; 8:10; see WISDOM).

Christian experience

People need at least some knowledge before they can have true faith in Jesus Christ as Saviour. Therefore, Christians must make known the facts about Jesus Christ (Rom 10:14). Those who believe must increase their knowledge of God and all that he has done for them through Jesus Christ. As a result they will know more of the power that Christ has made available to them, and will be able to worship him better (Eph 1:17-23).

If Christians are to make correct decisions in life and develop character of true quality, they must increase their knowledge of God and his Word. They cannot expect to do God's will unless first they know it (Ps 32:8-9; Phil 1:9-11; Col 1:9-10; see GUIDANCE).

The knowledge that Christians are to seek can be obtained only as their minds are renewed and developed according to their new life in Christ (Rom 12:2; Col 3:2,10; see MIND). They must remember, however, to put into practice what they learn (Ps 119:34; John 13:17; James 1:22; 1 John 2:4). They must remember also that in using their knowledge, they should act with humility before God and with

love and consideration for their fellow man (Dan 10:12; 1 Cor 8:1-2; 13:2).

Knowledge and morality

There is therefore no suggestion in the Bible that a person's knowledge excuses him from self-discipline. This was one of the errors of Gnosticism, a heresy that did much damage to the church during the second century. (The word 'Gnostic' comes from the Greek word *gnosis*, meaning 'knowledge'.)

Forerunners of the Gnostics appeared in the church in New Testament times. These 'knowing ones' claimed to have a knowledge not shared by ordinary Christians, a claim that Paul strongly denied. The treasures of God's wisdom are found in Christ, not in Gnosticism, and are available to all God's people, not just to those who are specially enlightened (Col 2:2-4,8-10,18-19; 3:1-3; cf. 1:9,28; see COLOSSIANS, LETTER TO THE).

The Gnostics' belief that all matter was evil led to opposite extremes of behaviour. Some of the Gnostics followed strict laws in an effort to avoid contact with the material world. Others, realizing that withdrawal from the material world was not possible, made no such effort. They even claimed that behaviour was irrelevant, because by their superior knowledge they had risen above the evil material world into a realm where deeds were of no importance. They could sin as they liked and still be Christians. The apostle John met this claim with a flat contradiction (1 John 3:9; see JOHN, LETTERS OF).

John pointed out that knowledge, far from being a substitute for morality, leads to morality. If a person knows God, he will keep God's moral commandments (1 John 2:3-4). If he knows Christ, he knows that Christ died to save people from sin and turn them to the way that is right (1 John 2:29; 3:5-6,24; see ASSURANCE).

KORAH

During Israel's journey through the wilderness, two groups combined to rebel against the leadership of Moses and Aaron. One was a group of 250 prominent Levites under the leadership of Korah who were envious that only Aaron and his family were allowed to be priests. The other group was headed by two from the tribe of Reuben who were envious of Moses' position as national leader (Num 16:1-3).

In a public demonstration of whom he had chosen to be his priests, God put Korah to the test. He challenged Korah and his fellow Levite rebels to burn incense, something that normally only Aaron and his sons were allowed to do (Num 16:5-19). Korah and the two Reubenites were separated from the 250 Levites for the test. The outcome was that the three leaders were swallowed up by the earth, and the 250 Levites were burnt to death by fire from God (Num 16:32,35; Jude 11).

Centuries later, descendants of Korah restored some respectability to the family name when they became gatekeepers, singers and musicians in the temple (1 Chron 6:31-38; 15:17,19; 16:41-42; 26:19). They collected or wrote a number of psalms that have been preserved in the Bible (Ps 42; 44-49; 84-85; 87-88).

LABAN

After the father of Abraham migrated to the region of Paddan-aram in northern Mesopotamia, some of the family settled there. Others, such as Abraham and Lot, moved south into Canaan (Gen 11:31-12:5). Laban became a prominent member of one of the families that remained in Paddan-aram. He shared with his father in giving permission for his sister, Rebekah, to marry Abraham's son, Isaac (Gen 24:15,29,50-51). Later he gave his own daughters, Leah and Rachel, to be wives of Isaac's son, Jacob (Gen 28:2; 29:15-30). Laban's deceit of Jacob in the marriage arrangements began a long contest of trickery between the two, as each tried to outdo the other. (For details see JACOB.)

LACHISH

The important town of Lachish was located in the mountain pass that led from Hebron down to the Mediterranean coast. It was conquered by Israel in the time of Joshua (Josh 10:3-5,32) and later became an important military outpost for the defence of Jerusalem and other highland towns (2 Kings 18:13-17; 2 Chron 11:5,9; Jer 34:7; Micah 1:13; see PALESTINE). It was resettled after the Jews' return from captivity, but never regained its previous importance (Neh 11:25,30).

LAKE OF FIRE

See HELL.

LAMB

Most of the Old Testament references to lambs are related to sacrificial rituals. (For references to matters other than sacrifice see SHEEP.) Abel's offering was probably a lamb (Gen 4:4), Abraham considered a lamb to be the natural animal for a burnt offering (Gen 22:7-8), and the Israelites in Egypt offered sacrificial lambs at the time of the original Passover (Exod 12:3-8; see PASSOVER). In the religious system that God gave Israel, lambs were one of the animals most commonly used for sacrifice (Lev 3:1,7; 4:32; 9:3; 12:6; 14:10; 23:12; Num 28:4,11; 29:13; Ezra 6:17; 7:17; Ezek 46:4-15; see BLOOD; SACRIFICE).

A lamb offered in sacrifice had to be without defects, symbolizing its fitness to be the guiltless substitute for the guilty offerer (Exod 12:5-6; Lev 4:32; 9:3). Although it was necessary to shed the blood of a sacrificial animal, no animal sacrifice in itself could take away a person's sin (Heb 9:22; 10:4). Jesus Christ, the Lamb of God, achieves what all the animal sacrifices could not achieve. He willingly gave his life as a sacrifice for guilty sinners, and through his sacrifice takes away their sin (John 1:29; Acts 8:32; 1 Peter 1:18-19).

In the visions of the book of Revelation, the Lamb again symbolizes Jesus Christ. Having died for sin, he has now overcome death and is the Lord of life and salvation (Rev 5:6,9,12; 7:14; 12:11). He is the conqueror of Satan, the Saviour of his people, the judge of mankind, the King of kings, and the object of heaven's worship (Rev 7:17; 14:1,10; 17:14; 19:7; 21:23; 22:1,3).

LAMENTATIONS

The five chapters of the book of Lamentations are five poems that lament Babylon's destruction of Jerusalem in 587 BC. The poems deal with the people's suffering during the siege and in the days immediately after, when the Babylonians ruled over the few Judeans who remained in the country round about (2 Kings 25:1-26; Jer 40:1-41:18).

Although it is often assumed that Jeremiah was the writer of Lamentations, the book does not say who wrote it. Whoever the author was, he must have lived in the time of Jeremiah, for he was in Jerusalem during the siege that led to the collapse of the city. The poems give a vivid picture of the horrors of those days. (For events surrounding the fall of Jerusalem see JEREMIAH.)

In three of the five poems, the twenty-two verses that make up the poem begin in turn with the twenty-two successive letters of the Hebrew alphabet. One poem has sixty-six verses grouped in twenty-two sets of three. In this poem, which is the central poem in the collection, all three verses in each set begin with the same letter, and these sets of initial letters likewise follow the order of the

Hebrew alphabet. The remaining poem (the last in the collection) again has twenty-two verses, but does not follow the usual alphabetical arrangement.

Contents of the book

The first poem pictures the plundered city now ruined and deserted. It was a pitiful sight, yet a fitting punishment for the city's sins. The second poem pictures the widespread starvation in the city at the height of the siege, and shows how misleading were the false prophets' assurances of deliverance. In the lengthy third poem the writer admits that Jerusalem's sufferings are God's righteous judgment, and urges the people to accept God's discipline and seek his forgiveness. In the fourth poem there is a contrast between Jerusalem's former glory and its present ruin, and in particular a contrast between the former luxury of the leaders and their present humiliation. The final poem, written a little later, shows the hardship and dangers faced by the people left behind in Judah.

LAMP

Various types of lamps are mentioned in the Bible, some for indoor use (2 Kings 4:10; Dan 5:5; Matt 5:15; Acts 20:8), others for outdoor use (Ps 119:105; Matt 25:1; John 18:3). They were made of a variety of materials (clay, metal or wood) and were of

Ancient lamps

different shapes and designs, but they all functioned in much the same way. Basically, a lamp consisted of a bowl to hold the fuel (oil) and a cloth wick that soaked up the oil for the flame (Exod 27:20; Matt 25:3-4).

A lamp was so important for everyday living in the ancient world that it was almost a symbol of life itself (2 Sam 21:17; Job 29:2-3; Prov 13:9; Rev 18:23). The Word of God and the servants of God are at times likened to lamps, since they provide light from God in a world of darkness (Ps 119:105; Matt 5:16). The lamp was therefore a fitting symbol of the witness that the people of God bear to him (Luke 12:35; John 5:33,35; cf. 1:7).

Lampstands

In the tabernacle built by Moses, seven lamps were fitted to a single lampstand to provide light for the

Holy Place. God gave Moses no dimensions for the lampstand, but it weighed about thirty-five kilograms, was made of one piece of gold and was richly ornamented. The common people provided the oil for the lamps, and the priests checked the lamps each morning and evening to ensure they

Tabernacle lampstand

were kept burning (Exod 25:31-40; 27:20-21). In Solomon's temple there were ten lampstands, five against each of the two side walls (1 Kings 7:49).

Many years later, when the Jews had returned from captivity in Babylon and were rebuilding their temple, the prophet Zechariah had a vision of a seven-branched temple lampstand. Two olive trees, one each side of the lampstand, fed the lamps miraculously with a continuous supply of oil. This symbolized the continuous supply of God's supernatural power, which would ensure the satisfactory completion of the temple (Zech 4:1-14). It probably also symbolized the witness of God's people (Rev 11:3-4).

In the book of Revelation, lampstands feature in one of the visions that John saw. In this vision, seven lampstands represented seven churches, to which God directed John to write seven letters (Rev 1:11-13,20). Each church was to be a witness to Jesus Christ, but if it failed in its task and ignored God's warnings, God could 'remove the lampstand' by bringing the church to an end (Rev 2:5).

LAODICEA

Like Colossae and Hierapolis, Laodicea was situated in a fertile valley east of Ephesus in the Roman province of Asia. It was an important educational, commercial and administrative centre.

Although Paul was the first to take the gospel to Asia, there is no indication that he visited the town during his missionary travels recorded in Acts (Col 2:1). The church was probably founded at the time of Paul's lengthy stay in Ephesus during his third missionary journey, when the zealous Ephesian converts took the gospel throughout the surrounding countryside (Acts 19:8-10; Col 4:12-13). (For map and other details see ASIA.)

When Paul wrote to the church in Colossae, he wrote also to the church in Laodicea. He wanted the two churches to exchange their letters, so that both churches could read both letters (Col 4:16). This letter to the Laodiceans was never collected as part of the sacred writings.

Another letter to the Laodicean church has been preserved, this one written towards the end of the first century (Rev 3:14). The letter is Christ's message to the church and is largely one of criticism. The citizens of Laodicea in general were prosperous and self-satisfied, and this spirit of self-satisfaction carried over into the church.

The Laodiceans prided themselves that they had all they needed, and even believed that their material prosperity had resulted from their spiritual goodness. Because of their reliance on material things they could not exercise true faith in God, and their lives could not demonstrate that Christ brings complete satisfaction. Jesus condemned their comfortable spiritual pride and tried to make them see themselves as he saw them — poor, blind and naked. They had to realize that Christ alone could produce truly spiritual qualities in their lives, and he could do this only when they turned from their sin and humbly sought his help (Rev 3:15-22).

LAST DAYS

See ESCHATOLOGY.

LAW

The word 'law' is used in many ways in the Bible. It may be used of commandments or instructions in general, whether given by God, civil administrators, teachers or parents (Gen 26:5; Exod 18:20; Prov 3:1; 6:20; see also GOVERNMENT). Frequently it is used of the written Word of God (Ps 119:18-20,57-61), sometimes applying to the Old Testament as a whole and sometimes to part of the Old Testament, such as the five books of Moses (Matt 5:17; Luke 24:44; John 1:45; 15:25; see PENTATEUCH). Occasionally it means a principle of operation (Rom 7:21,23; 8:2). The most common usage of the term, however, concerns the law of God given to Israel through Moses at Mt Sinai (Exod 24:12; Deut 4:44; Ezra 7:6; John 1:17; Gal 3:17,19). It is this meaning of 'law' that is the chief concern of the present article.

God's covenant with Israel

In his grace God made a covenant with Abraham to make his descendants into a great nation and to give them Canaan as their national homeland (Gen 17:1-8). Over the next four hundred years God directed the affairs of Abraham's descendants so that their numbers increased and they became a distinct people. They were then ready to be formally established as a nation and to receive the land God had promised them. At Mt Sinai God confirmed the covenant made previously with Abraham, this time making it with Abraham's descendants, the nation Israel (Exod 24:7-8; see COVENANT).

God had chosen Israel to be his people, saved them from slavery in Egypt, and taken them into a close relationship with himself, all in fulfilment of his covenant promise made to Abraham. Everything arose out of the sovereign grace of God (Exod 2:24; 3:16; 6:6-8). But if the people were to enjoy the blessings of that covenant, they had to respond to God's grace in faithful obedience. The people understood this and promised to be obedient to all God's commands (Exod 24:7-8).

The law that God gave to the people of Israel at Sinai laid down his requirements for them. Through obedience to that law the people would enjoy the life God intended for them in the covenant relationship (Lev 18:5; cf. Rom 7:10; 10:5; Gal 3:12). The ten commandments were the principles by which the nation was to live, and formed the basis on which all Israel's other laws were built (Exod 20:1-17).

Characteristics of Israelite law

No part of the lives of the Israelites was outside the demands of the covenant. The law applied to the whole of their lives and made no distinction between moral, religious and civil laws. Laws may have been in the form of absolute demands that allowed no exceptions (e.g. 'You shall not steal'; Exod 20:15), or in the form of guidelines concerning what to do when various situations arose (e.g. 'If a man borrows anything and it is hurt or dies . . .'; Exod 22:14), but the two types were equally binding.

Israel's law-code was suited to the customs of the time and was designed to administer justice within the established culture. Unlike some ancient law-codes, it did not favour the upper classes, but guaranteed a fair hearing for all. It protected the rights of people who were disadvantaged or defenceless, such as orphans, widows, foreigners, slaves and the poor (Exod 22:22; 23:6,9,12). The penalties it laid down were not brutal or excessive, as in some nations, but were always in proportion to the crime committed (Exod 21:23-24).

Jesus' attitude to the law

The covenant made with Israel at Sinai and the law that belonged to that covenant were not intended to be permanent. They were part of the preparation for the coming of Jesus Christ, through whom God would make a new and eternal covenant (Gal 3:19,24; Heb 9:15).

Jesus was born under the law (Gal 4:4) and was brought up according to the law (Luke 2:21-24,42). He obeyed the law (Matt 17:27; John 2:13) and he commanded others to obey the law (Matt 8:4; 23:1-3,23). Jesus did not oppose the law, though he certainly did oppose the false interpretations of the law that the Jewish leaders of his time taught. He upheld and fulfilled the law by demonstrating its true meaning (Matt 5:17-19,21,27,31,33,38,43).

Frequently Jesus pointed out that the law was good and holy and that God gave it for man's benefit (Matt 22:36-40; Luke 10:25-28; cf. Rom 7:12,14). By contrast the Jewish leaders used the law to oppress people, adding their own traditions and forcing people to obey them. In so doing they forgot, or even opposed, the purpose for which God gave the law (Matt 23:4; Mark 7:1-9; see TRADITION). Jesus knew that the law, as a set of regulations, was part of a system that was about to pass away (Matt 9:16-17; cf. Heb 8:13). His death and resurrection would mark the end of the old covenant and the beginning of the new (Heb 9:15).

Under the new covenant people still have to respond to God's covenant grace with obedience, but the expression of that obedience has changed. Instead of being bound by a set of rules, they have inner spiritual power to do God's will. Instead of having to offer sacrifices repeatedly, they have their sins taken away once and for all. Instead of having to approach God through priests, they have direct fellowship with God (Jer 31:31-34; Heb 8:8-13; 10:1-4,16-18).

Salvation apart from the law

People have never received the forgiveness of sins through keeping the law. Under the old covenant, as under the new, they were saved only through faith in the sovereign God who, in his grace, forgave them and accepted them. Abraham, David and Paul lived respectively before, during and after the period when the old covenant and its law-code operated in Israel, but all three alike were saved by faith (Gen 15:6; Rom 3:28; 4:1-16,22; Gal 3:17-18; Eph 2:8; 1 Tim 1:14-16). Salvation depended upon God's promise, not upon man's effort. It was a gracious gift received by faith, not a reward for keeping the law (Gal 3:18,21-22; see PROMISE).

Contrary to popular Jewish opinion, the law was not given as a means of salvation (Rom 9:31-32). It was given to show the standard of behaviour God required from his covenant people. As a set of official regulations, it was given solely to the nation Israel and was in force for the period from Moses to Christ. But as an expression of the character and will of God, it operated on principles that are relevant to people of all nations and all eras. It expressed in a legal code for one nation the principles that are applicable to mankind in general (Rom 2:12-16; 13:8-10). Through the law given to Israel, God showed to mankind the righteous standards that his holiness demanded.

At the same time the law showed the extent of man's sinfulness, for his behaviour repeatedly fell short of the law's standards. The law therefore showed up man's sin; but when a person acknowledged his sin and turned in faith to God, God in his grace forgave him (Rom 3:19-20,31; 5:20; 7:7; Gal 3:11,19). (Concerning the rituals of the law for the cleansing of sin see SACRIFICE.)

Those who broke the law were under the curse and condemnation of the law (Deut 27:26; Gal 3:10). Jesus Christ, however, lived a perfect life according to the law, and then died to bear the law's curse. By his death he broke its power to condemn those who take refuge in him. Believers in Jesus are freed from the law's curse. They have their sins forgiven and are put right with God (Rom 7:6; 8:1-3; 10:4; Gal 3:13; Eph 2:15; Col 2:14).

Jesus Christ is the true fulfilment of the law. The law prepared the way for him and pointed to him. Before his coming, the people of Israel, being under the law, were like children under the control of a guardian. With his coming, the law had fulfilled its purpose; the guardian was no longer necessary. Believers in Jesus are not children under a guardian, but full-grown mature sons of God (Gal 3:23-26; 4:4-5; cf. Rom 10:4; see ADOPTION).

Christian life apart from the law

It was some time before Jewish Christians in the early church understood clearly that the law was no longer binding upon them. They still went to the temple at the set hours of prayer and possibly kept the Jewish festivals (Acts 2:1,46; 3:1). Stephen seems to have been the first Christian to see clearly that Christianity was not part of the Jewish system and was not bound by the Jewish law (Acts 6:13-14). Then Peter had a vision through which he learnt that Jewish food laws no longer applied. He was harshly criticized by certain Jews in the Jerusalem church when they found he had been eating freely with the Gentiles (Acts 10:15; 11:2-3).

These Jews later tried to force Gentile converts to keep the law of Moses (Acts 15:1), and argued so cleverly that Peter tended to follow them, until Paul corrected him (Gal 2:11-16). When some of the leading Christians met at Jerusalem to discuss the matter, they agreed that Gentiles were not to be put under the law of Moses (Acts 15:19). It was now becoming clear, and Paul's teaching soon made it very clear, that there was no difference between Jews and Gentiles concerning requirements for salvation and Christian living. People were saved by faith alone, not by the law, and they lived their Christian lives by faith alone, not by the law (Rom 3:21-31; Gal 3:28).

When he met opposition to his teaching, Paul pointed out how it was impossible for a person to be saved through keeping the law (Rom 9:30-32; Gal 2:16; 5:4; Phil 3:9). Equally it was impossible for a person to grow in maturity and holiness through keeping the law, or even selected parts of it (Gal 3:2-5; 5:1-3; James 2:10-11).

The actions of Paul in occasionally observing Jewish laws were not for the purpose of pursuing personal holiness. They were for the purpose of gaining him acceptance among Jewish opponents whom he wanted to win for Christ. Such actions were purely voluntary on Paul's part (1 Cor 9:19-23; cf. Acts 15:19-21; 16:3; 21:20-26). If people tried to force Paul to keep the law, he would not yield to them under any circumstances (Gal 2:3-5).

Paul explained the uselessness of trying to grow in holiness through placing oneself under the law. He pointed out that the more the law forbids a thing, the more the sinful human heart wants to do it (Rom 7:7-11). This does not mean that there is anything wrong with the law. On the contrary, the law is holy, just and good. The fault lies rather with man's sinful nature (Rom 7:12-14; see FLESH).

Free but not lawless

Although the law aims at righteous behaviour, a person cannot produce righteous behaviour by keeping the law. He can produce it only by claiming true Christian liberty and living by the inner spiritual power of the Holy Spirit (Rom 6:14; 8:3-4; Gal 5:13-23; see FREEDOM; HOLY SPIRIT). But the same Holy Spirit who empowers inwardly has given clear guidelines for behaviour in the written Word. It is not surprising, then, to find that those guidelines contain quotations from the law of Moses to indicate the type of character and conduct that a holy God requires (Matt 22:36-40; Rom 7:12; 13:8-10; Eph 6:2; Heb 8:10; James 2:8-12).

Christians are not under law but under grace. Yet they are not lawless (Rom 6:15). They have been freed from the bondage of the law and are now bound to Christ (Rom 7:1-4). The law of Christ is a law of liberty, one that Christians obey not because they are forced to but because they want to. The controlling force in their lives is not a written code but a living person (1 Cor 9:21; Gal 6:2; James 1:25; 2:12).

As Jesus demonstrated his love for the Father by keeping the Father's commandments, so those who truly love Jesus will keep his commandments (John 14:15,21; 15:10; 1 John 2:3-4,7; 5:3). And in so doing they will practise love, which itself is the fulfilment of the law (John 13:34; Rom 13:8-10; Gal 5:14; 1 John 5:2-3).

LAYING ON OF HANDS

One of the symbolic actions we meet a number of times in the Bible is the laying on of hands. It contained within it a wide range of meanings.

In Israel's sacrificial system, before a person offered his animal in sacrifice, he laid his hands on the animal's head, indicating that the animal was his representative in bearing his sins (Lev 1:4; 4:1-4). When Israel's tribal leaders, acting on behalf of the whole nation, laid their hands on the heads of the Levites, they symbolized that the Levites were their representatives in the service of God (Num 8:10-11). When the church in Antioch sent out Paul and Barnabas as missionaries, the elders of the church laid their hands on them, symbolizing the church's identification with the two men as their missionary representatives (Acts 13:3).

From these examples it seems that important elements in the laying on of hands were those of identification and fellowship. This again appears to be so in those cases where the apostles laid their hands on people who received the Holy Spirit in unusual circumstances (Acts 8:17; 19:6; see BAPTISM WITH THE SPIRIT).

Sometimes laying on hands symbolized more than representation or identification. It symbolized appointment to office. Moses appointed Joshua as his successor by the laying on of hands (Num

27:22-23). Church leaders appointed missionaries, teachers, elders and deacons to their positions by the ceremonial laying on of hands (Acts 6:6; 13:3; 1 Tim 4:14; 5:22; 2 Tim 1:6).

The laying on of hands seems in some cases to have indicated transferal. It may have been a transferal of sin, such as happened when the high priest confessed the sins of Israel over the head of a goat on the Day of Atonement (Lev 16:21-22); or it may have been a transferal of good, such as happened when a father passed on his blessing to his children (Gen 48:14-16; cf. Mark 10:16).

Jesus and the apostles sometimes laid their hands on those whom they healed, possibly to symbolize the passing on of God's power and blessing (Mark 6:5; Luke 4:40; 13:13; Acts 9:17). In some cases the laying on of hands may have been a type of acted prayer (Acts 28:8; cf. James 5:14-15).

LAZARUS

Jesus once told a story of a beggar named Lazarus who lay full of sores at the gate of a rich man. When both men died, Lazarus entered into the joy of God's heavenly kingdom, but the rich man entered into torment in the place of punishment (Luke 16:19-23).

The rich man called for Lazarus to come and bring relief to his suffering, but he learnt to his disappointment that no person could pass from Lazarus' world to his (Luke 16:24-26). He then asked to send Lazarus back from the world of the dead into the world of the living, to warn the rich man's brothers of the horrors that lay ahead. Again he was disappointed. If people are so self-centred that they ignore the plain message of the Bible, even the miracle of someone rising from the dead will not make them change their ways (Luke 16:27-31).

Some time later, another man named Lazarus did in fact rise from the dead. This was Lazarus of Bethany, the brother of Mary and Martha (John 11:1-44). But, as Jesus had pointed out, such an event had little effect on those who had consistently resisted God through rejecting the message of the Bible. They still resisted, even when they witnessed the miracle of someone coming from death back to life (John 11:46-50; cf. 5:38-40,45-47). Rather than accept the evidence and humbly submit to God, they tried to destroy the evidence. They planned to kill Lazarus (John 12:9-11).

Jesus' raising of Lazarus started that final burst of hostility which, within one week, brought about

Jesus' death (John 11:53; 12:1,17-19). (For details of Lazarus' family see MARTHA.)

LEAH

Being the mother of six of Jacob's twelve sons, Leah had an important role as one of the mothers of the Israelite nation (Gen 30:1-19; 35:23). She was not the wife Jacob chose for himself, and the ill-feeling between her and Jacob's chosen wife Rachel created many difficulties in Jacob's household. (For details see JACOB; RACHEL.)

LEAVEN

Among the Hebrews, leaven (or yeast) was very important. It had a practical use in making bread and a symbolic significance in religious rituals.

People made leaven by mixing the flour of certain cereals with water, and allowing the mixture to stand till it fermented. When making leavened bread, they mixed this fermented portion with dough, so that when the dough was baked in the oven the bread would rise (Matt 13:33; 1 Cor 5:6). Leavened bread was light and rounded, unleavened bread heavy and flat. An easier way of making leaven for future batches of bread was to remove a small piece of leavened dough before baking and leaving it stand till it too fermented.

The first mention of any ritual significance of leaven was at the time of the Passover when Israel escaped from Egypt. During the week that followed the Passover escape, the people had no time to bake their bread leavened. They had to carry their dough and baking pans with them, baking as they went (Exod 12:11,18,34,39). Each year from that time on, the people were to hold a symbolic re-enactment of the Passover along with a week-long Feast of Unleavened Bread. This was to remind them of Israel's hurried and unceremonious departure from Egypt. They were to leave no leaven in their houses during the week of the feast (Exod 12:14-20; 23:15; Mark 14:1; see PASSOVER).

Nothing containing leaven was to be offered on the altar of sacrifice. This was probably because leaven spoiled easily, and there was to be no trace of corruption in the sacrifices (Exod 23:18; 34:25; Lev 2:11; 7:12; 10:12). However, leavened bread, representing the ordinary food of the people, was presented to God at the Feast of Harvest, as an expression of gratitude to him for their daily food (Lev 23:15-20). Leavened bread offered with the peace offering was not burnt on the altar, but eaten in the meal that followed (Lev 7:11-14).

Because it tended to corrupt and because it affected everything it touched, leaven developed a deeper symbolic meaning. Jesus saw the Pharisees, the Sadducees and Herod as evil influences that spread through Israel as leaven spreads through a lump of dough. He warned his disciples to beware of the leaven-like effect of such people. Their hypocrisy, teaching and ungodliness could quickly have a corrupting effect on others (Matt 16:5-12; Mark 8:15; Luke 12:1-3).

Just as Israelites cleaned all leaven out of their houses at the time of the Passover, so Christians should clean the leaven of sin and wrong teaching out of their church. If left unchecked, sin will spread yeast-like through the church (1 Cor 5:6-8; Gal 5:7-9).

In one of Jesus' parables, by contrast, leaven is used figuratively in a good sense. Just as leaven spreads through the dough into which it is put, so will Christ's kingdom spread throughout the world (Matt 13:33).

LEBANON

Lebanon was the name of a mountain range north of Israel between Phoenicia and Syria. It ran parallel to the coast, leaving only a narrow coastal plain for the Phoenician cities, most important of which were Tyre and Sidon (see PHOENICIA). The range gave its name to much of the surrounding territory, and even today the nation that occupies this region is called Lebanon.

The Lebanon Range actually consisted of twin parallel ranges. The western half was referred to simply as Lebanon, and the other half as East Lebanon or Antilebanon (Josh 13:5). The range extended from Mt Hermon, in the border regions of Israel, north to a mountain pass known as 'the entrance of Hamath'. This was the gap between the twin ranges where Lebanon opened on to the Syrian plain (see HAMATH; HERMON).

Lebanon was considered to be the northern boundary of the land promised to Israel (Deut 11:24), but Israel's conquest under Joshua extended no further than Mt Hermon (Josh 11:16-17). The rest of the Lebanon Range remained unconquered (Judg 3:1-3). Only for two brief periods, first during the reign of Solomon and later during the reign of Jeroboam II, did Israel's territory reach as far as the entrance of Hamath. This was considered the ideal northern border of Israel (2 Chron 8:3-4; 2 Kings 14:25; Amos 6:14).

The lower slopes of Lebanon towards the Phoenician plain were very fertile (Ps 72:16; Hosea 14:5-7). Further up the mountains were the great forests of cedar trees for which Lebanon became famous (Ps 104:16; Song of Songs 5:15). These mighty cedars were symbols of majesty and strength (2 Kings 14:9; Ps 92:12-13; Isa 35:2; 60:13), but they could also be symbols of pride and arrogance (Isa 2:12-13; 10:33-34; Ezek 31:3-14). Cedar from Lebanon was beautiful, enduring and expensive, and people considered that anything made from it was the finest and best (Song of Songs 3:9; Ezek 27:5). Solomon used it extravagantly in the building of his temple, palace and government buildings (1 Kings 5:1-11; 7:1-8).

LENDING

God expected all Israelites to realize that because they existed in a special relation to him, they were not to take advantage of their fellow Israelites. A person was not to exploit someone in need, but to show mercy. He was to help with the necessities of life and treat the needy person as an equal. He could lend money or goods to the poor, but he was not to charge interest (Exod 22:25; Lev 25:35-38; Ps 15:5; Ezek 18:10-13).

Repayment of loans

Though not allowed to take interest from the poor, a creditor could, if he wished, ask for temporary possession of some article belonging to the debtor, as a guarantee that the debtor would repay the loan. But he was not to take items essential to a person's everyday living. For example, he could not take a millstone, as it would leave a person with no way of grinding flour to make food for his family. If he took clothing as a guarantee, he had to return it by evening, so that the person would not have to sleep in the cold (Exod 22:26-27; Deut 24:6,10-13). A creditor could give employment to a debtor who wished to repay a debt by working for him, but he could not make the man a permanent slave (Lev 25:39-40).

Disorders arose when creditors took advantage of debtors, and debtors took advantage of friends whom they had asked to guarantee them. A person could get himself into trouble by agreeing to be a financial guarantor for a friend (or a stranger) if he did not have enough money to honour his promise. Also, the debtor could get himself so far into debt that the guarantor could be ruined. Wise advisers therefore warned guarantors against making rash promises, and even suggested they withdraw their guarantees from dishonest debtors before it was too late (Prov 6:1-5; 11:15; 17:18; 22:26).

Although dishonest debtors were a problem, dishonest creditors were a much greater problem. The Bible records cases of ruthless creditors who ignored the laws that Moses had laid down. They seized debtors' food and clothing (Amos 2:6-8; 5:11; 8:6), farm animals (Job 24:3), and houses and land (Micah 2:2,9). Some even took members of the debtors' families and made them slaves (2 Kings 4:1; Neh 5:1-5).

Release from debt

These disorders existed in spite of the law which laid down that, at the end of every seven years, Israelites were to forgive debts owed them by fellow Israelites. They were to consider themselves one big family, where no one would be driven into poverty or refused a loan in a time of need, even if the year for releasing debtors was approaching. God promised to reward those who were generous to their fellows (Deut 15:1-11). (Concerning the year for releasing debtors see SABBATICAL YEAR.)

As with the law concerning interest on loans, the law concerning release from debt did not apply to cases involving foreign debtors. In those cases normal business procedures applied (Deut 15:3; cf. 23:20).

Lessons for Christians

In all these laws the emphasis was on helping fellow Israelites in need. The background to the laws was the simple farming society of ancient Israel. What the laws condemned was the exploitation of the disadvantaged, not the investment of money to set up or expand business, such as one might find in a more commercially developed society.

Jesus too condemned the exploitation of the needy through taking interest on a private loan (Luke 6:34), but he apparently approved of wise investment to earn income (Luke 19:23). He did not, however, approve of investment and trading where a person was so concerned with making money that he neglected the needy (Matt 25:42-45; Luke 6:24-25; 16:19-25; cf. James 4:13; 5:1-6). The New Testament encourages Christians to give to those in need (Luke 6:30-31; Rom 12:13), and discourages them from getting into debt (Rom 13:8).

The generosity of creditors in helping the needy and forgiving debtors is frequently used in the New Testament to picture truly godly attitudes. It is an illustration of that mercy and grace by which God forgives people their sins and by which they should forgive each other (Matt 6:12; 18:21-35; Luke 7:41-48). By contrast, the bondage that binds the debtor to his creditor is an illustration of that bondage to the old nature from which Christians have been freed by Christ (Rom 8:12-13).

LEPROSY

Among the health laws God gave to Israel through Moses were laws concerning leprosy. However, both biblical scholars and medical scientists have clearly shown that what the Old Testament calls leprosy is not always the disease that we today call leprosy. The word used of leprosy in the Old Testament had a broad meaning and denoted a number of infectious skin diseases, some of which could be cured. It applied even to germ-carrying fungus or mildew on clothes and buildings (Lev 13:1-17,47-59; 14:33-53).

The laws given through Moses were concerned not with treating the disease, but with isolating the infected person so that others in the community did not become infected. If a person saw any abnormality in his skin, even if only a rash, boil or falling out of the hair, he had to report it to the priests. The priests then isolated him till they were certain whether or not it was a dangerous disease. If it was not, the person carried out a cleansing ceremony and returned to normal life in the community. But if it was real leprosy the person was excluded from the community entirely (Lev 13:18-46).

This exclusion of lepers from normal society resulted in many of them becoming beggars (Lev

13:45-46; Num 5:2; 2 Kings 7:3,8; Luke 4:27; 17:12). Important people may not have become beggars, but they still had to be isolated from the community (2 Chron 26:21).

Any leprous-type disease made an Israelite ceremonially unclean and therefore unable to join in the normal religious life of the nation. If he was healed, he had to go to the priest and carry out a cleansing ceremony before he could join in religious activities again (Matt 8:1-4).

The cleansing ceremony lasted eight days. The healed person, previously 'dead' through his disease, symbolized his death by the ritual killing of a bird, symbolized his cleansing by draining the bird's blood into a bowl of pure water, and symbolized his new life of freedom by releasing a second bird that had been stained with the blood of the first. The priest then sprinkled the person with the blood of the bird seven times, after which the person washed and shaved. He then returned to the community, but not yet to his own dwelling place (Lev 14:1-9). After waiting a further seven days, he offered sacrifices, then resumed normal religious, social and family life (Lev 14:10-32).

LEVI

Levi, the third son of Jacob, had a ruthless zeal in fighting against what he thought was wrong, and this characteristic passed on to his descendants (Gen 29:31-34; 34:25-26; Exod 32:26-28). Jacob announced that because of his son's violence, the descendants of Levi would be scattered in Israel (Gen 49:5-7); but because of their zeal against idolatry in the time of Moses, God made their scattering honourable. The people of Levi's tribe became God's special servants throughout the nation. Although they had no tribal territory of their own, they were given cities in all the tribal territories (Exod 32:28-29; Num 35:2,8; Deut 33:8-10; see LEVITE).

One of Jesus' chosen twelve apostles had the name Levi, though he had an alternative name, Matthew (Matt 9:9; 10:3; Mark 2:14; Luke 6:15; see MATTHEW).

LEVITE

The Levites were the servants, or ministers, in the Israelite religious system. They were descended from the third son of Jacob and formed one of the tribes of Israel (Gen 29:31-34; see LEVI). The Levites were divided into three sections that corresponded to the three families descended from Levi's three sons, Gershon, Kohath and Merari (Exod 6:16; Num

3:14-20). God appointed them to their privileged religious service as a reward for their zeal against idolatry (Exod 32:26-29; Deut 33:8-10).

Although the Levites had general duties in the tabernacle and temple ceremonies, only those of one family within the tribe, the family of Aaron, were priests (Exod 6:16-25; 29:9). Priests alone carried out the blood rituals of the sacrifices, and priests alone entered the inner shrine of the tabernacle (or later the temple) (Num 3:5-10; see PRIEST).

Duties concerning the tabernacle

After helping to construct the tabernacle (Exod 38:21), the Levites had the duty of setting up, taking down, maintaining and transporting the tabernacle on the journey to Canaan (Num 1:50-51). The Gershon group looked after the curtains and other hangings, and had two wagons to carry their load (Num 3:21-26; 7:7). The Merari group had care of all the timber and metal parts, and had four wagons to carry their load (Num 3:33-37; 7:8). The Kohath group looked after the sacred furniture, most of which they carried on shoulder poles (Num 3:27-32; 7:9; 1 Chron 15:14-15).

On the journey the Levites travelled in the centre of the procession (Num 2:17). When a camp was set up, they camped immediately around the tabernacle (Num 1:52-53; 3:23,29,35,38).

Representatives of the people

Since God had saved the Israelites' firstborn through the Passover judgment, all their firstborn belonged in a special sense to God. For the service of the tabernacle, however, God used the Levites instead of the firstborn (Num 3:11-13,40-51).

In a dedication ceremony involving cleansing rituals and sacrificial offerings, Moses and Aaron presented the Levites to God for his service (Num 8:5-13). God then gave the Levites back to Aaron to help him and the other priests in their work (Num 8:14-19). Leaders of the people also took part in the ceremony, to indicate symbolically that the Levites were the people's representatives (Num 8:9-10).

Levites began their service at the age of thirty, though this was apparently preceded by a training period of five years. They ceased their main duties at the age of fifty, but were still able to help in various ways (Num 4:3; 8:23-26). Having no time to earn a living as others, the Levites received their income in the form of tithes offered by the people (Num 18:21-28; see TITHES).

Although Levi had no tribal area of its own, Joshua gave the Levites cities in each of the other tribes. The number of cities in each tribe was in proportion to the size of the tribe (Num 35:1-8; Josh 21:1-3). There were forty-eight Levitical cities and these were divided among four groups – the priestly Kohathites (Aaron was a Kohathite; Exod 6:16-20), the non-priestly Kohathites, the Gershonites, and the Merarites. The cities for the priestly group were all within easy reach of Jerusalem, where the temple was later built (Josh 21:4-8). Among the forty-eight cities were six cities of refuge (Josh 20:1-9; see CITY OF REFUGE).

Temple service

In arranging the functions for priests and Levites in Israel's temple services, David divided the Levitical singers and musicians into the usual three family groups. The respective leaders were Heman, Asaph and Ethan (Jeduthan), all of whom are mentioned as writers of psalms (1 Chron 6:1,31-48; 15:16-22; 2 Chron 5:12; Ps 73-83; 88; 89).

Other duties of Levites included cleaning the temple (1 Chron 23:28), helping the priests in the temple rituals (1 Chron 23:28-32), serving as temple guards (1 Chron 9:17-27) and looking after the furniture, food and spices used in the ceremonies (1 Chron 9:28-32). Some of the Levites served as judges and officials of various kinds (1 Chron 23:4; 26:20).

When David found that there were too many Levites for the amount of work available, he divided them into twenty-four groups according to their family descent. The groups served in rotation one week every six months, though all groups were on duty for the annual festivals (thereby making up the remaining four weeks of the year) (1 Chron 23:1-24; 24:18-19; 25:9-31; 26:1,12).

Errors, reforms and developments

Over the following centuries, the nation and many of its kings frequently fell into idolatry. Priests and Levites usually played an important part in the reforms that godly kings carried out (2 Chron 17:7-9; 19:8-11; 29:1-16; 30:21-22; 34:8-13), though at times they were slow to respond to the king's directions (2 Chron 24:4-13). A feature of some of the reforms was the organization of temple duties for priests and Levites according to David's original plan (2 Chron 29:25-30; 31:2-19; 35:1-15).

When, after seventy years captivity in Babylon, the Jews were released, many Levites were among those who returned to Jerusalem (Ezra 2:40-42). They supervised the reconstruction of the temple and participated in ceremonies connected with the building's beginning and completion (Ezra 3:8-11; 6:16). At first they were properly organized for religious service (Ezra 6:18), but later they were neglected by those who should have supported them with their tithes. Nehemiah corrected this problem by organizing an orderly system of tithing (Neh 10:37; 11:3; 12:27,47).

Another result of Nehemiah's reforms was increased activity in teaching the law. The Levites helped the priests and scribes in this work (Neh 8:7-9), but the good work of these early leaders was not maintained by those of later generations. The result was the development of that form of Jewish religion known in New Testament times as Judaism (see SCRIBE; SYNAGOGUE). Nevertheless, people of New Testament times still saw Levites as a class of people distinct from both the priests and the scribes (Luke 10:25,31-32; John 1:19; Acts 4:36).

LEVITICUS

Israel's priesthood was commonly known as the Levitical priesthood (Heb 7:11), and the book that deals more than any other with that priesthood is known as the Levitical book, or Leviticus. The priests, however, were only one family in the tribe of Levi. Matters relating to the non-priestly Levites are dealt with in the next book, Numbers. There is no break between these books, because what we call the five books of Moses (or the Pentateuch) were originally one book (see PENTATEUCH).

Features of the book

God had brought the people of Israel out of Egypt and set them on their way to Canaan, all according to the covenant promises he had given to Abraham. After three months they arrived at Mt Sinai, and there God established his covenant with them. He declared Israel to be his people, and they responded by promising to do whatever he required of them (Gen 12:2; 15:18-21; 17:6-8; Exod 2:24; 6:6-8; 19:4-6; 24:7-8). The regulations that God laid down under the covenant begin in Exodus and carry on through Leviticus into Numbers.

First of all God announced the covenant's basic principles and some of its practical requirements (Exod 20-23). He then gave his plans for a central (but portable) place of worship, the tabernacle, and for a priesthood to oversee religious affairs (Exod 25-40). He gave the people a sacrificial system by which they could express their relationship with him (Lev 1-10); he set out laws to regulate cleanliness and holiness (Lev 11-22); he gave details concerning festivals and other special occasions (Lev 23-27); and he outlined certain duties, particularly in relation to the Levites (Num 1-10).

A central theme of Leviticus is that priests and common people alike were to be pure in their relations with God and with one another. Because God was holy, they were to be holy (Lev 11:44-45; 20:26). This holiness extended to every part of the people's lives, including personal cleanliness and public health. The laws of cleanliness, besides having practical usefulness, were an object lesson in a more basic problem, the problem of sin.

In his grace God helped his people deal with sin by giving them the sacrificial system. It taught them the seriousness of sin and gave them a way of approach to him to seek his forgiveness. People did not have to try to squeeze forgiveness from an unwilling God; God himself took the initiative by giving them the blood of animals to make atonement for their sin (Lev 17:11; see BLOOD; SACRIFICE). Whether repentant sinners knew it or not, their sacrifices could not in themselves take away sin. The basis on which God accepted the blood sacrifices of the ancient Israelites was the perfect blood sacrifice yet to be offered, the sacrifice of Jesus Christ (Heb 9:22; 10:1-4,11-14).

Contents of the book

With the tabernacle now completed, God gave the Israelite people his regulations for the sacrifices. There were five basic sacrifices – the burnt offering, the cereal offering, the fellowship offering, the sin offering and the guilt offering (1:1-6:7). God gave additional details of these offerings for the priests who officiated (6:8-7:38). Moses ordained Aaron and his four sons as priests, after which they began their duties (8:1-9:24). Two of the sons were struck dead when they tried to act independently of God (10:1-20).

God then set out his requirements in relation to cleanliness. He laid down laws concerning food, disease and bodily health (11:1-15:33), and followed with regulations concerning the Day of Atonement and the sacredness of blood (16:1-17:16). Further instructions on practical holiness concerned sexual relationships and a range of miscellaneous matters (18:1-20:27). There were additional rules specifically concerned with priests (21:1-22:33).

Israel was to have a regulated timetable of festivals to acknowledge the overruling care of God throughout the year (23:1-24:23). Sabbatical and jubilee years were designed to prevent the rich from gaining control over the poor (25:1-55). God promised blessing for obedience, but warned of judgment for disobedience (26:1-46). Honesty was essential at all times, and people had to treat their vows seriously (27:1-34).

LIE

Deceitful actions as well as deceitful words are wrong and are condemned by God. People can act lies as well as speak them (Gen 27:8-23; Jer 23:32; Acts 5:1-4; Eph 4:25; 1 John 2:4; 4:20). A person is considered guilty even when he tells only half the truth, if his purpose is to hide the full truth (Gen 20:1-3,9-13). Likewise a person is guilty when he twists the truth to make it acceptable to others (Jer 8:8-9; 14:13-15). If a person makes false accusations against the innocent, he is guilty of lying and is assured of God's severe punishment (Deut 19:15-19; 1 Kings 21:8-19).

People tell lies to deceive others, yet at the same time they lead themselves astray (Amos 2:4). They reject the way of truth and therefore open the way for falsehood to control their thoughts and actions (John 8:44-47; Rom 1:25-32; 2 Thess 2:9-12; see TRUTH). They seek safety through their lies, but the safety proves to be deceptive (Isa 28:15,17; Ezek 13:8; cf. Heb 6:18).

Although lying is one of the natural results of sinful human nature (Col 3:9), there is no excuse for it in the lives of God's people. The Spirit within them is the Spirit of truth, and he can enable them to overcome the sinful tendencies of the old nature (John 14:17; Gal 5:16,24-25; 1 John 2:21). God consistently tells his people that they are not to lie (Exod 20:16; Lev 19:11; Eph 4:25). A hatred of lying is one of the marks that they are God's people (Zeph 3:13; Rev 14:5). The person who habitually lies is giving an indication that he has never known God's salvation and the new life that comes with it. He will not escape God's punishment (Prov 19:5; Rev 21:8,27).

A further reason for the Christian's avoidance of lying is that he is a child of God. God does not lie (Num 23:19; Titus 1:2; Heb 6:18) and his children are to grow to be like him (Col 3:9-10). By contrast, Satan is the father of lies, and his children naturally reflect his nature (John 8:44).

LIFE

God is the source and controller of all life. He brings it into existence, sustains it, and brings it to an end, all according to his purposes (Gen 2:7; Num 16:22; Deut 32:39; Job 34:14-15; Ps 36:9; Eccles 12:7; Matt 10:28; Luke 12:20; 1 Tim 6:13).

Human life is especially sacred, for man exists in God's image. Israelite law therefore considered that any person who murdered another was no longer worthy to enjoy God's gift of life and had to be executed (Gen 9:5-6; Num 35:33; see IMAGE). The law required that even when people killed animals for food, they had to carry out the killing with fitting acknowledgment that the life belonged to God (Gen 9:4; Lev 17:2-4,10-14; Deut 12:15-16; see BLOOD).

The life of man

Though it is common to make a contrast between man's physical life and his spiritual life, God's intention is that all aspects of man's life be united harmoniously. God wants man to enjoy his physical life fully, but to do so in a right relationship with himself (Deut 8:1,3; 30:15-20; Ps 16:9-11; Eccles 5:18-20; 9:9-10). The life that is proper to man is one in which physical and spiritual aspects find their fulfilment as a unity (see MAN).

Sin, however, has so changed the character of man's life that it is no longer as it should be. Because of sin, the whole of man's life has become affected by the power of death. The result is that physically man is doomed to death and spiritually he is dead already (Rom 5:12; 6:23; Eph 2:1; 4:18; see DEATH). He is cut off from God and therefore is cut off from true spiritual life, the life that is life indeed, eternal life (1 Tim 6:19).

The Bible may speak of man's life from two aspects, physical and spiritual (Gen 25:7; 27:46; John 5:40; 6:33), but these two aspects are not opposed to each other. Nor are they completely separate from each other. The life that a person lives in his physical earthly existence finds new meaning when he is 'born again'. He then receives spiritual life as the free gift of God (John 1:13; 3:5-6; Eph 2:5; see REGENERATION). He finds life in its truest sense; he begins a new existence (Mark 8:35; John 12:25).

Even though physical death is the common experience of mankind, the believer will never be separated from God (John 8:51; Rom 8:38-39). His physical death is viewed as a temporary 'sleep'. At Christ's return, God will raise him to resurrection life, where sin and death will have no more power (John 11:11,25-26; 1 Cor 15:20-26,51-57).

Eternal life

Life in its highest sense is what the Bible calls eternal life (1 Tim 6:13,15-16,19). In referring to this life as eternal, the Bible is emphasizing its quality rather than its length. The word 'eternal' comes from the Greek word for 'age' or 'era'. Eternal life is the life of the age to come. It is the life that belongs to the eternal and spiritual world in contrast to the life of the temporal and physical world (John 4:10,13-14; 6:27,35,40). Certainly, that age will be unending (John 6:51; 8:51), but more importantly it will be an age when man enjoys the close personal relationship with God for which he has been made. He will enjoy the life that God desires him to live (John 6:63; 10:10; 17:3; Eph 2:1,5-6; Phil 1:21; see ETERNITY).

This eternal life has its source in God. In fact, it is a characteristic of the nature of God himself. It has been revealed to man through Christ, became a possibility for man through Christ, and is available to man only through Christ (John 1:4; 5:26; 14:6; Col 3:4; 1 John 5:20).

Man cannot achieve eternal life by his own efforts. It comes solely as the gift of God (John 10:28; Rom 6:23; 1 John 5:11). But God gives this gift only to those who repent of their sins and commit themselves in faith to Jesus (John 3:16; 11:25; 17:3; 20:31; Acts 11:18; 1 John 5:12). God wants people to have confidence and assurance in the eternal life that he gives them. Those who have eternal life have salvation; those without it are under condemnation (John 3:18,36; 5:24; 1 John 5:13; see ASSURANCE; SALVATION).

Being part of a world affected by sin and death, the believer may have to pass through physical death, but he will never die in the sense that really matters (John 11:25-26). He has eternal life now (John 5:24; Eph 2:1; 1 John 3:14), and can look forward to the experience of that life in its fulness in the age to come. When Jesus Christ returns, the believer will be raised from death to enjoy the resurrection life of glory, perfection, power and immortality (Matt 25:46; John 5:28-29; 6:40; Rom 2:7; 6:22; 1 Cor 15:42-44; 2 Cor 5:4; 2 Tim 1:10; see RESURRECTION).

LIGHT

By common usage, in Bible times as well as today, light is figuratively associated with things that are good. In like manner darkness is usually associated with things that are bad (Job 30:26; Ps 112:4; John 3:19-20; see DARKNESS).

In particular, light is associated with God. He is clothed in light, he dwells in light, he is light. Because God is separate from all creation, and especially from all things sinful, light is symbolic of God's holiness (Ps 104:2; Dan 2:22; 1 Tim 6:16; 1 John 1:5). It is also symbolic of the holiness that should characterize God's people. As light can have no partnership with darkness, so God's people should have no partnership with sin (Prov 4:18-19; Isa 2:5; Rom 13:12-13; 2 Cor 6:14; Eph 5:8-11; 1 John 1:6-7; 2:9-10; see HOLINESS).

Just as the uniqueness of God is symbolized by light, so is the uniqueness of Jesus Christ, who is God-become-man (Matt 17:2; Acts 9:3-5; Rev 1:16). Jesus likened his coming into the world to the coming of light into darkness. He is the light of the world, who brings the life and salvation of God into a world that is dark and dead because of sin (Matt 4:16; John 1:4-5; 3:19; 8:12; 12:35-36,46; 2 Cor 4:6; cf. Ps 27:1).

Those who turn to Christ for salvation are, by God's grace, transferred from a kingdom of darkness into a kingdom of light (Col 1:12-13; 1 Peter 2:9). They become lights in the world, as they take the good news of Jesus Christ to those who are still in darkness (Matt 5:14-16; Acts 13:47; Phil 2:15; Rev 11:4; see WITNESS). God's Word is also a light, as it guides them along the path of life (Ps 119:105; Prov 6:23; see LAMP).

LOAN

See LENDING.

LONGSUFFERING

See PATIENCE.

LORD

For the use of 'Lord' among the Israelites of Old Testament times see YAHWEH. For the use of 'Lord' among the followers of Jesus in New Testament times see JESUS CHRIST, sub-heading 'Jesus as Lord'.

LORD'S DAY

Christians in the early churches met together often (Acts 2:46; Heb 10:25). Although the frequency of meetings varied from place to place, the common practice seems to have been that all the Christians in a church met together at least on the first day of each week (Acts 20:7; 1 Cor 11:20; 16:2). By the end of the first century, Christians commonly referred to the first day of the week as the Lord's day, probably because it was the day on which Jesus rose from the dead as the triumphant Lord (John 20:1,19; cf. Acts 2:36; Rom 1:4; Phil 2:9-11). (Concerning the difference between the Lord's day and the Jewish Sabbath see SABBATH.)

LORD'S SUPPER

In both the New Testament and the present day church, the Lord's Supper is known by a number of names. Paul calls it, literally, the supper of the Lord, because Christians keep it on the Lord's authority and in his honour (1 Cor 11:20). Paul speaks of it also as a communion, meaning an act of fellowship, or sharing together, in Christ (1 Cor 10:16; see COMMUNION). Luke calls it the breaking of bread, referring to part of the meal as a shortened title for the whole (Acts 2:46; 20:7). Another name, the Eucharist (from the Greek word for 'thanksgiving'), refers to Jesus' act of giving thanks for the bread and wine (Mark 14:23; 1 Cor 11:24).

The last supper

Jesus instituted the Lord's Supper while eating a Passover meal with his disciples the night before his crucifixion (Luke 22:8,12,15). (For details of a Passover meal see PASSOVER.) During the meal Jesus took some of the bread and wine from the table and passed each in turn among his disciples, inviting them to eat and drink. The bread and wine were symbols of his body and blood, which he was to offer on the cross as a sacrifice for the forgiveness of sins (Matt 26:26-28; cf. Isa 53:4-6,10).

God had once made a covenant with Israel and sealed it with blood (Exod 24:6-8; see COVENANT). Through Jeremiah he promised a new covenant, one that would bring forgiveness of sins and give new life through the indwelling Spirit (Jer 31:31-34; cf. Ezek 36:26-27). Jesus established this covenant, his blood sealed it, and the supper he instituted is a reminder of its meaning to those who believe in him. The Old Testament system, having reached its fulfilment, is replaced by the new covenant with its unlimited blessings (Matt 26:28; 1 Cor 11:25).

When Israelites observed the Passover, they reminded themselves that their lives had been saved only through the death of the Passover lamb. When Christians observe the Lord's Supper, they remind themselves that they have eternal life only through the death of Christ (1 Cor 11:23-24; cf. 5:7).

Christians keep the Lord's Supper not only in remembrance of Christ's death, but also in anticipation of his return. When that day comes, bread and wine will no longer be necessary. Christ and his people will be together for ever in the triumphant kingdom of the Messiah. In that day there will be far more blessed fellowship between Christ and his people, likened to a heavenly feast with new wine (Matt 26:29; Luke 22:16,18; 1 Cor 11:26).

The practice of the church

From the earliest days of the church, Christians joined regularly to eat the Lord's Supper. It seems that at first they ate it as part of their ordinary meals, and may even have done so daily (Acts 2:42,46). Later they ate it less frequently, perhaps weekly (Acts 20:7), but the practice of combining it with a common meal continued for some time.

These common meals were called love feasts, and were occasions when the rich could show love and fellowship by sharing food generously with the poor. At Corinth, however, many of the rich greedily ate their own food, without waiting for others to arrive and without sharing it with others. Instead of being a love feast, it was a selfish feast. Instead of being a supper in honour of the Lord, it was very much a supper for themselves (1 Cor 11:20-22; cf. Jude 12).

Paul reminded the Corinthian church that if Christians make a mockery of the Lord's Supper through wrong behaviour, they may bring judgment upon themselves. They must therefore examine themselves and correct any wrong attitudes they may have towards the Lord's Supper (1 Cor 11:27-34).

Far from being a cause of division among Christians, the Lord's Supper should be something that binds them together. Christians demonstrate their unity in Christ as they share in the same bread and the same wine. They show that they are united with each other and with Christ in one body (1 Cor 10:17; cf. 11:18-21).

Eating bread and drinking wine together in the Lord's Supper is more than just a remembrance of Christ's suffering and death. It is a spiritual sharing together in the body and blood of Christ, a fresh enjoyment of and proclamation of the benefits of his death. It is not a time of mourning, but a time of joyful fellowship with the risen Lord (1 Cor 10:16; 11:26; cf. John 6:48-51; Acts 2:46-47).

The Lord's Supper is therefore an important part of worship in the church. It is enriched when fittingly combined with prayers, singing, preaching, the reading of the Scriptures and instruction in Christian teaching (cf. Acts 2:42; 1 Cor 14:26; Col 3:16; see WORSHIP).

LOT

When Abraham and his household moved from Mesopotamia into Canaan, his nephew Lot went with him. He also went with Abraham into Egypt, and then back into Canaan (Gen 11:26-31; 12:1-5,10; 13:1).

Like Abraham, Lot was a wealthy owner of sheep and cattle. When trouble developed between Abraham's and Lot's workers, the two households separated. Lot chose for himself the fertile pasture lands around Sodom and Gomorrah, east of the Dead Sea (Gen 13:5-11). Lot's choice was selfish and it soon brought him trouble. Mesopotamian invaders raided his territory, plundered his goods and took Lot himself captive. Only swift action by Abraham rescued him (Gen 14:1-3,12-16).

Lot established himself in the city of Sodom and continued to increase in prosperity. But Sodom and the neighbouring city of Gomorrah were so morally corrupt that God decided to destroy them (Gen 13:12-13; 18:20-21). Lot did not agree with the immoral practices of Sodom (2 Peter 2:7-8), though he apparently did nothing to oppose them. He was even prepared to allow the sexual perverts of the city to rape his daughters, in order to save two guests from homosexual assault (Gen 19:1-11). Lot was so much at home in Sodom that even when God's judgment was about to fall on the city, he did not want to leave (Gen 19:15-20).

The two daughters of Lot, still affected by the evil influences of Sodom, forced their father into immoral sexual relations with them. The two children born as a result marked the beginnings of two nations, Ammon and Moab (Gen 19:30-38).

LOVE

In the language of the Bible, as in most other languages, the word 'love' has a very broad meaning. It may apply to God's love for man (Deut 7:12-13; John 3:16), to man's devotion to God (Ps 91:14; 1 Cor 8:3), to pure sexual love between a man and a woman (Prov 5:18-19; Song of Songs 2:4-5), to impure sexual activity such as in prostitution (Jer 4:30; Hosea 2:12-13), to love between members of a family where sexual feelings are not involved (Gen 22:2; Ruth 4:15), to an attitude of kindness towards others, whether friends or enemies (Lev 19:17-18; 1 Sam 18:1,16; Matt 5:43-46; John 11:3), or to the desire for things that brings pleasure or satisfaction (Prov 20:13; 1 Tim 6:10).

Where the Bible gives teaching about love, the centre of love is usually the will, not the emotions. Such love is a deliberate attitude, not an uncontrollable feeling (Matt 5:44-46). This characteristic of love is seen in both God's love and man's. The Bible commands people to love; it commands them to act in a certain way, regardless of how they feel (Deut 11:13; 22:37-39; John 13:34; 15:17; Eph 5:25; Titus 2:4; 1 John 4:20-21).

Christian love does not mean that a person tries to create feelings within himself towards another, but that he acts towards the other in a way he knows he should (Luke 10:27,29,37). The reason why he so acts is that God's love rules his life, making him want to do God's will (Rom 5:5; 2 Cor 5:14; 1 John 4:19). The more he acts towards another in love, the more favourable his feelings will become towards that person.

God's love

The love that God has for man originates solely in God's sovereign will. He loves people because he chooses to love them, not because they in any way deserve his love (Deut 7:7-8; Jer 31:3; Rom 5:8; Eph 1:4; 2:4-5; 1 John 3:1; 4:10).

This was seen clearly in Jesus Christ, who throughout his life helped those in need and by his death saved helpless sinners. Man's salvation originates in the love of God, and that love found its fullest expression in the cross of Jesus Christ (Matt 14:14; Mark 10:21; Luke 7:13; John 3:16; 15:13; Gal 2:20; Eph 2:4-7; 5:25; 1 John 4:9; see also MERCY). Jesus Christ could perfectly express God's love, because he and the Father are bound together in a perfect unity in which each loves the other (John 3:35; 10:30; 14:31; 15:9; 17:24).

So much is love the dominating characteristic of the divine nature that the Bible declares that God *is* love. Everything that God says or does is in some way an expression of his love (1 John 4:8,16).

If we find this statement hard to understand when we think of God's wrath and judgment, the reason is probably that we misunderstand the nature of love. God's love is not an irrational emotion divorced from justice and righteousness, but a firm and steadfast attitude that earnestly desires the well-being of his creatures. God has such a love for what is right that he reacts in righteous anger against all that is wrong. God's wrath is the outcome of his love (Hab 1:13; 1 John 1:5; see WRATH).

God wants to forgive the sinner, but because he is a God of love he cannot treat sin as if it does not matter. He cannot ignore it. His act of forgiveness, being based on love, involves dealing with sin. At the same time, because he is a God of love, he provides a way of salvation so that sinners need not suffer the punishment themselves. He has done this by becoming man in the person of Jesus Christ and taking the punishment himself on the cross (John 1:14-18; 3:16; Rom 5:8; Gal 2:20; 1 John 4:10; see ATONEMENT).

This same love causes God to discipline, correct and train his children, so that they might develop into the types of people that he, in his superior wisdom, wants them to be. God's love towards man is an authoritative love; man's love in response is an obedient love (John 14:15,21; 16:27; 1 John 2:4-5; 4:19; 5:2-3). God's chastisement may seem painful rather than pleasant, but to ask God to cease his chastisement is to ask him to love us less, not

more (Heb 12:5-11; see CHASTISEMENT). Love desires perfection in the one who is loved, and will not be satisfied with anything less (Eph 5:25-27; James 4:5).

Christians should accept whatever happens to them as being in some way an expression of God's love and as being in accordance with God's purposes for them (Rom 8:28; see PROVIDENCE). God's gift of his Son is the guarantee that all his other gifts will also be an expression of his love (Rom 8:32). His love is everlasting and measureless. Nothing in life or death can separate believers from it (Jer 31:3; Rom 8:35-39; Eph 3:18-19).

Man's love

It is the duty of man to love God with his whole being. He is to be devoted to God and obedient to him (Deut 6:5; 10:12; Ps 18:1-3; Matt 22:37). As a result of such devoted obedience he will learn more of the meaning of God's love and so will increasingly experience joyful fellowship with God (Ps 116:1-4; John 14:21-23; 1 Cor 2:9; 8:3; 1 Peter 1:8; 1 John 4:7,12,19).

Love for God will at times create difficulties. Conflicts will arise as people put loyalty to God before all other loyalties, desires and ambitions (Matt 6:24; 10:37-39; John 3:19; 1 John 2:15-17). Genuine love involves self-sacrifice (Eph 5:25; cf. Rom 14:15; 1 Cor 13:4-7).

Faith and obedience are just as basic to a relationship with God as is love. If people claim to love God but do not trust in him or obey him, they are deceiving themselves (John 14:15,24; Gal 5:6; James 2:5). Likewise they are deceiving themselves if they claim to love God but do not love their fellow human beings (Rom 13:10; 1 John 3:10,17; 4:8,20). Christians must have the same loving concern for others as they have for themselves (Matt 22:39; Phil 2:4). Love is a characteristic of those in whom the Spirit of Christ dwells; for when they receive God's salvation in Christ, the Holy Spirit fills them with God's love (John 15:9-10; Rom 5:5; Gal 5:22; Eph 3:17-19; 5:1-2).

Christians should exercise this love towards everyone, and in particular towards fellow Christians (John 13:34; 15:12-17; Gal 6:10; 1 Peter 3:8; 1 John 3:16-17). Such an exercise of love provides evidence that they really are Christians (John 13:35; 1 John 3:14) and helps them grow towards spiritual maturity (1 John 4:12,17). The church of God is founded upon love and builds itself up through love (Eph 3:17; 4:16). A unity of love between Christians will be clear evidence to the world that the claims of Christianity are true (John 17:20-23).

Although love for each other is something God demands, people should not practise that love solely as a legal requirement. They must act sincerely and display right attitudes, even when they feel no natural affection for the person concerned (Exod 23:4-5; Lev 19:17-18; Rom 12:9; 1 Cor 13:4-7; 1 Tim 1:5). Good deeds may be worthless in God's sight if they do not arise out of sincere love (1 Cor 13:1-3; Rev 2:2-4).

Steadfast love

In the Old Testament the special love that God had for Israel was signified by the Hebrew word *chesed*. It is difficult to find an exact equivalent of this word in English. The RSV translates it mainly as 'steadfast love', the GNB as 'constant love', and the older English versions as 'mercy', 'kindness' and 'loving kindness' (cf. Gen 32:10; 39:21; Ps 100:5; 118:1-3; Isa 54:10; Hosea 2:19; Micah 7:18).

The distinctive feature of *chesed* is covenant loyalty or faithfulness. A covenant is an agreement between two parties that carries with it obligations and blessings, and in the case of God and Israel this covenant was likened to the marriage bond. The two parties were bound to be loyal to each other (Deut 7:9,12; Neh 1:5; see COVENANT). God exercised loyal love and covenant faithfulness to his people, and this was to be the basis of their trust in him (1 Kings 8:23; Ps 13:5; 25:7; 103:17; 136:25; Hosea 2:19; Micah 7:20). Yet so often the people were not faithful to God in return. Their covenant love vanished (Hosea 6:4; 11:1-4).

This *chesed* — this faithful devotion, this loyal love — is what God most desires from his people (Hosea 6:6). It also shows the quality of love that God requires his people to exercise towards others (Prov 3:3-4; Hosea 12:6; Micah 6:8).

LUKE

According to evidence from early records, Luke was a Gentile who was born in Antioch in Syria. By profession he was a doctor (Col 4:14), but he also became a skilled historian. His most memorable writing was a lengthy account of the development of Christianity from the birth of its founder to the arrival of its greatest missionary in Rome. The first part of this record is called Luke's Gospel, the second part the Acts of the Apostles (Luke 1:1-4; Acts 1:1-2).

Luke first appears in the biblical record when he joined Paul and his party in Troas during Paul's second missionary journey. This is shown by Luke's inclusion of himself in the narrative — 'we sought to go into Macedonia . . . we made a direct voyage' (Acts 16:10-11). Luke went with Paul to Philippi (Acts 16:12,16) and remained there when Paul and his party moved on (indicated by the use of 'they', not 'we', in Acts 17:1). It seems that Luke lived in Philippi for some time. When Paul passed through Philippi on his way to Jerusalem at the end of his third missionary journey, Luke rejoined Paul's party. This is indicated by the renewed use of 'us' and 'we' in the narrative (Acts 20:5-6). (For a map of the area of Luke's movements see ACTS, BOOK OF.)

From this time on, Luke kept close to Paul. This explains why the sea journey to Palestine and the events that followed in Jerusalem and Caesarea are recorded in some detail (Acts Chapters 20-26). Paul and his party were in Palestine for at least two years (Acts 24:27), and Luke no doubt used this time to gather information from eye-witnesses of the life of Jesus to include in his Gospel. He was a very thorough and discerning person, who was careful to see that his story of Jesus was meaningful and accurate (Luke 1:1-4).

Luke travelled with Paul on the eventful sea voyage to Rome (Acts 27:1; 28:16) and remained with him during his two years imprisonment there (Acts 28:30; Col 4:14; Philem 24). Although he was close to Paul throughout those years, Luke says almost nothing about himself in his record. He seems to have been a humble person, never self-assertive, but always dependable. When the aged Paul, after being released and later recaptured, sat cold and lonely in prison awaiting his execution, Luke alone stayed with him (2 Tim 4:11).

LUKE, GOSPEL OF

Of the four Gospels, Luke is the longest and most orderly. It gives a greater overall coverage of the life of Jesus than the other Gospels, though like them it does not attempt to provide a biography of Jesus. The author has gathered and arranged his material with a certain purpose in mind, and with much skill has produced a book that contains more well known stories of Jesus than any other.

Writing the book

In his opening statement, Luke mentions briefly how he prepared his Gospel. Since he himself had never seen or heard Jesus, he obtained the material for his book from careful research of existing records and from the accounts of eye-witnesses (Luke 1:1-4). He followed his Gospel with a second volume, known to us as the Acts of the Apostles (Acts 1:1-3; see ACTS, BOOK OF).

Though a doctor by profession (Col 4:14), Luke was also an accurate historian, and he liked to date biblical events according to secular history (Luke 1:5; 2:1-2; 3:1-2). In addition he was a reliable Christian worker who spent many years of Christian service with Paul. (For further details see LUKE.) Luke probably assembled much of the material for his book while he was helping Paul during the two years of Paul's imprisonment in Palestine (cf. Acts 21:17; 23:31-33; 24:27).

Later, Luke travelled with Paul from Palestine to Rome (Acts 27:2; 28:16). There he met Mark (Col 4:10,14; Philem 24). Mark also had been preparing a Gospel, and Luke was able to take some of Mark's material, combine it with his own, and so bring his book to completion. (For further details see GOSPELS.)

Purpose and characteristics

Luke prepared his Gospel for a person of some importance (probably a government official) named Theophilus, to give him a trustworthy account of the life of Jesus (Luke 1:1-4). In his second volume, written for the same person, Luke traced the spread of Christianity (Acts 1:1).

However, Luke was concerned with more than just recording history. He wrote with a distinctly Christian purpose. He wanted to show that God in his love had a plan for man's salvation, that Jesus came to be man's Saviour, and that Jesus' followers then spread the message of that salvation worldwide (Luke 1:17; 2:11; 3:4-6; 4:18,21; 19:10; 24:44-48; cf. Acts 1:8). This salvation was not for Jews only, but for people everywhere, regardless of nationality or race (Luke 2:32; 3:6-8; 4:25-27; 7:9; 10:29-37; 17:11-18).

In a society where many were disadvantaged, Luke showed that God's salvation was available equally to all. Many of the socially despised would receive it, but many of the socially respectable would miss out (Luke 7:29-30; 10:30-37; 16:19-31; 18:9-14; 19:1-9). Among the disadvantaged people that Luke wrote about as being blessed by God were slaves (Luke 7:2-7; 12:37), aliens (Luke 10:30-37; 17:16), lepers (Luke 4:27; 17:11-18), the poor (Luke 1:53; 2:7; 6:20; 7:22) and women (Luke 2:36-38; 7:37-48; 8:2; 13:11-13), in particular, widows (Luke 4:25; 7:12-15; 18:1-7; 21:1-4).

Summary of contents

The Gospel of Luke falls naturally into major sections, the first of which covers the birth and childhood of Jesus. After an introduction (1:1-4), Luke records the prophecy of John's birth (1:5-25),

the prophecy of Jesus' birth (1:26-38), Mary's visit to Elizabeth (1:39-56), John's birth (1:57-80), Jesus' birth (2:1-20), temple ceremonies following his birth (2:21-40) and a visit to Jerusalem when Jesus was twelve years old (2:41-52).

A short section deals with the beginning of Jesus' public ministry. It includes the preparatory preaching of John the Baptist (3:1-20), the baptism of Jesus (3:21-22), Jesus' genealogy (3:23-38) and the devil's temptation of Jesus in the wilderness (4:1-13).

Luke then gathers together, in one section, material relating to the work Jesus did over a period of about three years, mainly in Galilee. This material includes Jesus' sermon in the synagogue at Nazareth (4:14-30), various healings (4:31-44), the call of his first disciples (5:1-11), further healings (5:12-26), the call of Matthew (5:27-32) and explanations of the nature of true religion (5:33-6:11). After the appointment of twelve apostles (6:12-19), there are further teachings (6:20-49), miracles of compassion (7:1-17), explanations to John's disciples (7:18-35) and demonstrations of forgiveness and devotion (7:36-50). Jesus' teaching in parables (8:1-21) is followed by demonstrations of his power over storms, demons and sickness (8:22-56). The section concludes by recounting the work of the twelve (9:1-27), the transfiguration of Jesus (9:28-36) and some failures by the apostles (9:37-50).

Much of the next, very long, section is found only in Luke. The section deals mainly with Jesus' ministry in Samaria and around the Jordan Valley, and leads to his triumphal entry into Jerusalem. It begins with Jesus' reminder of the cost of discipleship (9:51-62) and his sending out of an additional seventy disciples to hasten the spread of the gospel into all regions of Palestine (10:1-24). Then follow teachings and stories about love (10:25-42), prayer (11:1-13), inward cleansing (11:14-36), hypocrisy (11:37-12:3), anxiety (12:4-34), readiness for the crises ahead (12:35-13:9), the nature of Christ's kingdom (13:10-14:24), true discipleship (14:25-35), repentance (15:1-32), wealth (16:1-31), forgiveness, faith and gratitude (17:1-19), the coming of the son of Man (17:20-18:8), self-sufficiency (18:9-30), the Messiah's ministry (18:31-43) and the responsibilities of the Messiah's servants (19:1-27).

At last Jesus reached Jerusalem, and a short section deals with his few days there before his crucifixion. After his triumphal entry into the city and his cleansing of the temple (19:28-48), he came into conflict with the Jewish leaders (20:1-21:4) and spoke of coming judgment (21:5-38).

Finally, Luke deals with events relating to the death and resurrection of Jesus. Jesus prepared for his last Passover with his disciples (22:1-13), then spent some time with them in the upper room (22:14-38) before going to Gethsemane, where he was arrested (22:39-53). He was brought before the Jewish leaders (22:54-71), then before the Roman governor (23:1-25), and afterwards taken outside the city and crucified (23:26-56). On the third day he rose from the dead (24:1-12) and appeared to his disciples in various places (24:13-43). Six weeks later, after giving further teaching and a final blessing, he departed from them (24:44-53).

LYCAONIA

Originally, Lycaonia was a small kingdom in Asia Minor. When the Romans incorporated Asia Minor into their Empire, they drew new boundaries and Lycaonia was split between the provinces of Galatia, Cappadocia and Cilicia. It is the Galatian part of Lycaonia that is referred to in the New Testament

account of Paul's first missionary journey. Paul established churches in the Lycaonian towns of Lystra and Derbe, and these were among the churches that he addressed in his letter to the Galatians (Acts 14:6). Although the local people spoke Greek, the chief language of the Roman Empire, they continued to use their own Lycaonian language (Acts 14:11).

LYCIA

The small province of Lycia in south-west Asia Minor was important mainly for its two ports, Myra and Patara. From these ports ships sailed east to Phoenicia, south to Egypt and west to Greece and Italy. The Bible records two occasions when ships on which Paul travelled called at the ports of Lycia (Acts 21:1-2; 27:5-6).

LYSTRA

Lystra was a town in the ancient kingdom of Lycaonia in Asia Minor (Acts 14:6). When the Romans took control of Asia Minor, they redivided it to form a number of provinces. Lycaonia was split between the provinces of Galatia, Cappadocia and Cilicia, with Lystra falling within Galatia.

When Paul and Barnabas first visited Lystra, they healed a crippled man. The local people were impressed and, thinking Paul and Barnabas were two of the Greek gods, they prepared to offer sacrifices to them. Because Paul and Barnabas did not understand the local language, they were not aware at first what was happening. When they found out, they quickly stopped the people and proclaimed publicly the nature of the one and only true God (Acts 14:8-18).

Jews from neighbouring Antioch stirred up the people of Lystra against the missionaries, and Paul was nearly killed (Acts 14:19-20). The wounds Paul received at this time may have been those he referred to when he later wrote to these Christians (Gal 6:17). Timothy, who came from Lystra and who accompanied Paul on some of his missionary travels, may have witnessed the incident (Acts 16:1-2; 2 Tim 3:10-11).

MACEDONIA

Macedonia was the northern part of the land known today as Greece, and the centre of power during the time of the Greek Empire. It later became an important province of the Roman Empire. Ships from the port of Troas in Asia Minor connected with the port of Neapolis in Macedonia, from where the main highway led through the Macedonian town of Philippi, Amphipolis, Apollonia and Thessalonica towards Rome (Acts 16:11-12; 17:1). Another route went south from Thessalonica through Berea to Athens (Acts 17:10-15). The administrative centre of the province was Thessalonica.

Paul passed through Macedonia on his second missionary journey and established churches in a number of towns (Acts 16:9-40; 17:1-14; see BEREA; THESSALONICA; PHILIPPI). He revisited the area during his third missionary journey (Acts 19:21; 20:1-6; 1 Cor 16:5; 2 Cor 2:13; 7:5). At this time Paul was organizing a collection of money for the poor Christians in Jerusalem, and the Macedonian

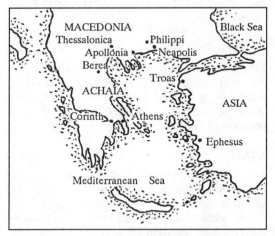

churches cooperated generously (Rom 15:26; 2 Cor 8:1-4; 9:1-4). After being released from his first imprisonment in Rome, Paul visited Macedonia again (1 Tim 1:3).

MAGIC

People have from earliest times had the desire to use supernatural (occult) forces to help them know the future. The foretelling of events in this way is sometimes called divination (Acts 16:16-18). Magic, witchcraft and sorcery go beyond divination in that they seek to use occult powers not merely to foretell future events but also to influence those events.

Such magic often has an evil intent, being directed at enemies by means of curses, spells and ritualistic actions. Sometimes it may have a partly good intent in trying to reverse evil spells and curses (Num 24:1,10; 1 Sam 6:2; 2 Kings 17:17; 21:6; Dan 2:2; Rev 9:21). But divination and sorcery derive their power from the demons of the spirit world, and for this reason the Bible condemns them (Lev 19:26,31; 20:6,27; Deut 18:10-11; 2 Kings 21:6; 23:24; Gal 5:19-20; Rev 9:21; 21:8; 22:15). Sorcerers often used their powers in deliberate opposition to God (Acts 13:8; 19:19; 2 Tim 3:8).

Among the methods of divination and sorcery mentioned in the Bible are throwing arrows into the air and observing the pattern formed when they fall

(Ezek 21:21), consulting idolatrous figures or images (Ezek 21:21), looking into the liver of a sacrificed animal (Ezek 21:21), consulting the spirits of the dead (1 Sam 28:8-9), studying the movements of the stars (Isa 47:13), gazing into a bowl or large cup of water (Gen 44:5,15) and using wristbands and veils in weird rituals to cast deadly spells over people (Ezek 13:17-19). Magicians were among the chief advisers to kings in many ancient countries (Exod 7:11; Dan 2:2).

Divination, witchcraft and all these associated practices are contrary to the ways of God, not only because they depend on evil spiritual powers for their operation, but also because they are a denial of faith. True believers walk humbly with their God, accepting that, no matter what the circumstances, God is still in control of their affairs. Having been saved by faith, they now live by faith (Gal 2:20; Eph 4:17-24; Col 1:11-13; Heb 11:6).

Jesus Christ has triumphed over all the unseen powers of evil, and through him believers too can triumph (Eph 1:19-21; 2:6; Col 2:8-10; 3:1-3). They believe in the power of the living Christ, but they do not treat that power as if it is magical (Acts 19:13-16).

MALACHI

A prophet was a messenger from God, and the meaning of the Hebrew word 'Malachi' is 'my messenger'. Some regard the word 'Malachi' in the opening verse not as a person's name but as a statement that the writer is a genuine messenger from God. (The same word is used in Malachi 3:1, where it is not the name of a person.) The usual understanding, however, is that the writer, in calling himself Malachi, is introducing himself by his name, as do the other writing prophets.

Background to the book

As a result of the Persian king's decree that released captive peoples (539 BC), many Jews returned to Jerusalem. In spite of some initial selfishness among themselves and opposition from local people, the Jews completed the rebuilding of their temple in 516 BC. However, with no one to replace the original strong leaders, people of later generations drifted from God.

In 458 BC a Jewish priest named Ezra came from Persia to Jerusalem to carry out much-needed reforms among the Jewish people (Ezra 7:7,11-26). He was joined in 445 BC by another Jew from Persia, Nehemiah, who became Judea's new governor (Neh 2:1-8). Jerusalem was full of social and religious disorders, and these two men worked together in an effort to lead the people back to God (Neh 8:1,8,9; 12:26,31,36,38). It seems that Malachi brought his message to the people some time during this period of reform by Ezra and Nehemiah. He does not give the date of his prophecy, but the sins he rebukes are similar to those that Ezra and Nehemiah had to deal with (cf. Mal 2:7-9 with Ezra 10:18-19; Neh 13:28-29; cf. Mal 2:10-11,14-16 with Ezra 9:1-10:44; Neh 10:30; 13:23-27; cf. Mal 3:5 with Neh 5:1-13; cf. Mal 3:8-12 with Neh 10:35-38; 13:10-14).

The Jews of Jerusalem thought that because they were back in their land and the temple was in operation again, they would now enjoy the unlimited blessings of God. This did not prove to be so, and as a result they began to doubt whether God really cared for them.

Malachi responded to the people's complaints by pointing out that the fault was on their side, not God's. They had, by their sins, created barriers that hindered the flow and enjoyment of God's love. The people, refusing to admit their faults, rejected Malachi's message and argued bitterly against the accusations that God brought to them through his messenger (Mal 1:2,6-7; 2:17; 3:7,13). There were some, however, who loved and respected God, and for these Malachi had a special message of encouragement (Mal 3:16-17; 4:2).

Summary of contents

In answering the people's complaint that God no longer loves them, Malachi gives them undeniable evidence that God's love has never forsaken them (1:1-5). He then shows how their sins are the reason for their present unhappy spiritual condition. They have demonstrated their wrong attitude to God in many ways: their offering of disgraceful sacrifices (1:6-14); the worthless behaviour of the priests (2:1-9); the sexual immorality that has produced divorce from Israelite partners and marriage to idol-worshippers (2:10-16); their irreverent complaining against God; and their cheating him of the offerings due to him (2:17-3:18).

The day of the Lord is approaching, when God will intervene in the affairs of mankind and deal decisively with the wicked. At the same time he will rescue his own and lead them into lives of new joy and freedom (4:1-6).

MALICE

One of the most destructive fruits of sinful human nature is malice — the desire to harm someone or the feeling of pleasure at someone's misfortune (Ps 41:5; Ezek 25:6; Titus 3:3; 1 Peter 2:1). Malice is often the cause of false accusations (Exod 23:1; Ps 35:11; Matt 22:18; see HATRED).

Unless people deal with their malice, it will bring God's punishment upon them (Rom 1:29; 2:2). It is an attitude that should have no place among God's people (1 Cor 5:8; Eph 4:31; Col 3:8; 1 Peter 2:1). The way to overcome malice is through the proper exercise of Christian love (1 Cor 13:6; see LOVE).

MAMRE

Mamre was a locality in Hebron named after the man who owned it. Its prominent oak trees, which possibly were considered sacred, were a well known landmark (Gen 13:18; 14:13,24; 18:1; 23:19). (For details see HEBRON.)

MAN

In dealing with the subject of man, this article is concerned not with men as distinct from women, but with humanity as a whole — mankind. Concerning the distinctiveness of men and women as being of different sexes see MEN; WOMEN.

Made in God's image

Basic to any study of the nature of man is the fact that God created man in his own image (Gen 1:27; 9:6; James 3:9). Man is therefore unique among all God's earthly creatures. He has a God-given authority over the material world in which he lives (Gen 1:26; Ps 8:3-8) and a God-given capacity for fellowship with the unseen, sovereign, eternal God (Acts 17:26-27).

The Bible does not attempt to divide man too sharply into separate 'parts' such as physical, spiritual, moral, mental, emotional and the like, for man is a unified whole. It is the whole person that is in God's image (see IMAGE). The Bible uses words such as 'body', 'mind', 'soul', etc. not to indicate the number of parts that make up the human being, but to emphasize different aspects of man's life as it appears in different contexts.

For example, we must not think that, because Jesus told people to love God with all their heart and soul and mind and strength, a person is made up of four parts (Mark 12:30); or that, because Paul prayed for the Thessalonians to be kept blameless in spirit, soul and body, a person is made up of three parts (1 Thess 5:23); or that, because Jesus spoke of the destruction of soul and body, a person is made up of two parts (Matt 10:28). Some of these words are used in different ways by different people at different times. Sometimes two words may have virtually the same meaning; other times they may have quite different meanings.

Aspects of man's nature

Both 'soul' and 'spirit' have a range of meanings in the Bible. The basic meaning of 'soul' (Hebrew: *nephesh*; Greek: *psyche*) has to do with a person's (or animal's) existence as a living being. It is often translated 'life' or 'person' (Gen 1:21,24; 2:7; Exod 1:5; Ezek 18:4,27; Matt 16:26; Acts 2:41,43; Phil 2:30; see SOUL). The basic meaning of 'spirit' (Hebrew: *ruach*; Greek: *pneuma*) has to do with that unseen, life-giving force that comes from God — the 'breath of life' that he gives to all persons (and animals), that belongs to him, and that he takes back at death (Gen 7:22; Num 16:22; Eccles 12:7; Heb 12:9; James 2:26; see SPIRIT). With regard to these meanings, we might say that a person is *nephesh* (a living being) because he has *ruach* (the life-force that comes from God).

However, the Bible uses both *nephesh* and *ruach* (and their Greek equivalents in the New Testament) to refer to certain aspects of human life where man is different from other animals. Human emotions, will-power and understanding may in some cases be linked with the soul (Gen 42:21; Deut 6:5; John 12:27; Acts 4:32), in others with the spirit (Exod 35:21; Ps 77:6; Mark 2:8; 8:12; 1 Cor 14:14-15).

More importantly, the higher and spiritual aspect of human life that other animals do not share may be called the soul (Heb 13:17; 1 Peter 2:11) or the spirit (Rom 8:10; 2 Tim 4:22). The physical and non-physical aspects of man may be referred to as body and soul (Matt 10:28) or body and spirit (1 Cor 7:34; 2 Cor 7:1). That aspect of man that continues in a bodiless existence after death may be referred to as a soul (Acts 2:27; Rev 6:9; 20:4) or a spirit (Heb 12:23; 1 Peter 3:18).

Such bodiless existence is only temporary. God's purpose is not that a person should live endlessly merely as a soul or a spirit. His purpose for man is that he find his full salvation as a whole person in a resurrected and glorified body (1 Cor 15:35-54; see BODY).

Soul and spirit are not the same. Yet it is not easy to distinguish between them (Heb 4:12). We should not think of them as two 'parts' of man which, put together in a certain proportion, make up man's inner life (as hydrogen and oxygen, put together in a certain proportion, make up water). It is probably better to think of them as the inner life of man viewed from different aspects. The Bible most frequently refers to this inner life as the heart. Depending on which aspect of the inner life is emphasized, the heart may refer to the soul (Deut 4:29; Acts 4:32), the spirit (Ps 51:10,17; 1 Cor 2:9,11) or the mind (1 Sam 2:35; Heb 10:16; see HEART; MIND).

Failure and triumph

The story of the Bible is the story of man's failure and God's gracious salvation. God intended man to live in harmony with his Creator, his fellow man, his physical environment and his inner self. But through his sin, man fell into a state of conflict in every aspect of his being (Gen 3:8-24; see SIN). Man has become, so to speak, infected by the disease of sin, and this infection affects every part of his nature. The tendency to do wrong is within the nature a person is born with. This 'diseased' human nature is commonly called 'the flesh' (Ps 51:5; Rom 5:12; 8:7; 13:14; see FLESH).

Through his sin, man has brought himself under God's judgment. He is guilty before a holy and just God, and there is nothing he can do to escape condemnation (Num 32:23; Rom 3:23; 5:12; Eph 2:3; Heb 10:31). God, however, has provided a way of salvation.

God became man in the person of Jesus Christ, who lived the human life perfectly and finally died to bear sin's punishment on behalf of his sinful fellow man (Rom 8:3; Heb 4:15). Through the man Jesus Christ, man can regain what he lost through the man Adam. Man can enjoy the harmony with his Creator, with his fellow man, with his physical environment and with his inner self that God intended for him from the beginning. The image of God in man, which was spoiled by sin, can be restored through Christ (1 Cor 15:22; Eph 4:24; Col 3:10; see IMAGE, sub-heading 'The perfect man').

The evil consequences of man's sin may be summarized under the word 'death' (Gen 2:17; Rom 6:23; Eph 2:1). Christ reverses all those evil consequences. The salvation that he has achieved includes even the conquest of physical death (Acts 2:24; Heb 2:14-15; see DEATH; LIFE). Those who trust in Christ for their salvation can look forward to the fulfilment of that salvation when Christ returns and raises the dead (Rom 8:18-25; 1 Cor 15:49-57).

Man's glory will be experienced by those who are united with Christ. Their whole person will experience this glory, and therefore they must, in their whole person, remain devoted to God and blameless in behaviour till Christ returns (Mark 12:30; 1 Thess 5:23; see RESURRECTION). For those who refuse Christ's salvation, there is nothing to look forward to but fearful judgment (Heb 9:27; 10:27; see JUDGMENT).

MANASSEH, KING OF JUDAH

Of all Judah's kings, Manasseh was by far the worst. No sooner had he established his power than he began a program of demolishing all the reforms that his father Hezekiah had introduced. With fanatical anti-God zeal, he reintroduced foreign religious practices of every kind (2 Kings 21:1-9). Fifty-five years of his rule corrupted Judah to the extent that its destruction was inevitable (2 Kings 21:10-16).

Towards the end of Manasseh's reign, Assyria attacked Judah and took Manasseh captive. Fearful of God's punishment, he repented of his wrong and decided to reform. But his limited reforms were not able to undo the damage he had done over the previous half-century, and they produced no lasting results (2 Chron 33:10-20). He died in 642 BC (2 Kings 21:17-18). Even the sweeping reforms of Josiah a few years later were not able to rid Judah of Manasseh's evil (2 Kings 23:24-27).

MANASSEH, TRIBE OF

Among the tribes of Israel there were two, Ephraim and Manasseh, that took their names not from Jacob's sons but from his grandsons. Ephraim and Manasseh were the sons of Joseph.

When Jacob determined to give the firstborn's blessing to Joseph instead of to Reuben (for Reuben had disqualified himself by raping one of his father's concubines; Gen 35:22; 49:3-4; 1 Chron 5:1-2), he raised Joseph's two sons to the same status as Joseph's brothers (Gen 48:5-6). As a result Joseph, through his two sons, received two tribes, but each of his brothers received only one. Though Manasseh was born before Ephraim, Ephraim's tribe was senior to Manasseh's (Gen 48:12-20).

Manasseh differed from all other tribes in Israel in that it was divided into two portions. Half the tribe lived in Canaan (the area between the Jordan River and the Mediterranean Sea) and the other half lived in the area east of Jordan (Josh 22:7). In all there were nine and a half tribes in Canaan and two and a half east of Jordan.

The two tribes that settled east of Jordan with half of Manasseh were Reuben and Gad (Num 32:1-5,33; Josh 13:8-33). (For an outline of the settlement and history of the eastern tribes see REUBEN.) The land occupied by the eastern half of Manasseh was the most northern of these three

tribal areas. Its northern part was commonly known as Bashan, and included the towns Golan and Edrei (Josh 13:29-31; 22:7; see BASHAN). Its southern part was sometimes known as Gilead, a name commonly applied to the neighbouring tribe Gad, and even to the entire region east of Jordan. Ramoth-gilead was an important frontier town where Gilead bordered Gentile territory to the east (1 Kings 22:3; see GILEAD; RAMOTH-GILEAD).

West of Jordan the other half of Manasseh occupied good land to the north of the tribe of Ephraim (Josh 17:1-12). Although Ephraim and Manasseh between them received one of the largest and best portions of Canaan, they still complained

that they had not enough land. Joshua gave them no more, but told them to make better use of the land they already had. They could do this by clearing the forest and driving out the remaining Canaanites (Josh 17:14-18). Within the northern part of this territory was part of the Plain of Esdraelon, site of many of Israel's battles (see PALESTINE). (For the important towns of West Manasseh see BETHSHAN; JEZREEL; MEGIDDO.)

MANNA

Manna was a type of food that God first gave to the Israelites soon after they left Egypt. It remained their daily food for the next forty years (Exod 16:4; Num 11:6; Ps 78:23-24). It was not, however, their only food (Exod 18:12; Lev 7:14-15; 11:2-3,9; Num 11:31-34). God's provision of the manna ceased once the people arrived in Canaan (Josh 5:12).

The people of Israel gave the food the name 'manna' (meaning 'What is it?') because they did not know what else to call it (Exod 16:15,31). We today do not know exactly what the manna was or how it was made. Possibly it was a substance prepared by insects that sucked the gum from trees. It formed during the night and was ready to be collected in the morning. It was fine, flaky, tasted like wafers mixed with honey, and could be cooked in various ways (Exod 16:14,23,31; Num 11:7-9).

God supplied the manna every morning, and the people had to eat it the same day. The only exceptions concerned the Sabbath rest day. There was no manna on Saturday mornings, but God gave two days' supply each Friday, half of which the people kept for use on Saturday. Because the manna spoiled quickly, the people preserved the supply for Saturday by baking or boiling it beforehand. Moses controlled the collection and distribution of the manna so that no one had too much or too little (Exod 16:4-5,15-18,23).

The command that prohibited keeping the manna overnight tested the people's obedience. The promise that ensured complete Sabbath rest through the double supply each Friday tested their faith. But in both matters they failed (Exod 16:19-30).

In accordance with God's instructions, Moses put part of the manna in a jar, to keep as a memorial of how God fed his people in the wilderness. This jar was later placed in the ark of the covenant together with Aaron's rod and the stone tablets inscribed with the law (Exod 16:31-35; Heb 9:4).

God also used the manna to teach the Israelites that their lives depended not merely on the food they ate, but on their spiritual relationship with God (Deut 8:3; cf. Matt 4:4). Jesus compared the gift of manna to satisfy man's physical hunger with the gift of himself to satisfy man's spiritual hunger. He did not need to make food fall from heaven, for he himself was the true bread from heaven (John 6:31-35). He gave himself as a sacrifice for sin, so that those who trust in him may have eternal life (John 6:48-51; cf. Rev 2:17).

MANUSCRIPTS

It appears that the books of the Bible were written originally on scrolls of papyrus, a material made from dried and flattened strips of papyrus reed (see WRITING). Papyrus did not last well, and the original writings all perished long ago. But from the beginning people had made copies of the original writings, and others continued to make copies down through the centuries. These copies are known as manuscripts (abbreviated MS in the singular, MSS in the plural).

Although the original writings were written by ordinary people in ordinary human language, they were at the same time written under the special direction of the Spirit of God. They expressed the truth as God wanted it expressed (see INSPIRATION). The copies that have survived, however, have suffered some damage from people who have copied or used them.

Because methods of mechanical printing were unknown in ancient times, people who made copies of the Scriptures had to write them out by hand. Writing skills varied and copyists at times made errors. Some of the common errors were to misread the master copy, misspell words, or misplace, omit, or repeat words or lines. There were also cases where copyists deliberately changed the wording to make a sentence mean what they thought it should mean. Yet, in spite of human failings, God has preserved his Word. There are so many good manuscripts in existence that people with the necessary skills are able to determine the original wording fairly accurately.

Old Testament manuscripts

The language of the Old Testament, Hebrew, reads from right to left and was written originally with consonants only. The absence of vowels caused no problem to the readers, as they could mentally

וַיְהִי אַחֲרֵי מֹות מֹשֶׁה עֶבֶד יְהוָה וַיֹּאמֶר יְהוָה אֶל־יְהֹושֻׁעַ בִּן־נוּן מְשָׁרֵת מֹשֶׁה לֵאמֹר׃ מֹשֶׁה עַבְדִּי מֵת וְעַתָּה קוּם עֲבֹר אֶת־הַיַּרְדֵּן הַזֶּה אַתָּה וְכָל־הָעָם הַזֶּה אֶל־הָאָרֶץ אֲשֶׁר

Hebrew writing, showing 'points', or vowel signs

put in the vowels as they read. But with the spread of the Aramaic language and then Greek during the latter centuries BC (see ARAM; GREECE), Hebrew had become less widely known in Palestine in New Testament times. After the destruction of the Jewish state in AD 70, the use of Hebrew declined even further. This decline continued, till Hebrew ceased to be a commonly spoken language.

Over an extended period from the sixth to the eleventh centuries AD, Hebrew scholars called

Massoretes introduced a system of vowel signs, or 'points', to ensure that the meaning of the original writing was not lost. These vowel points were dots and other symbols placed below or above the consonants to show what the word was and how it should be pronounced. The version of the Old Testament that the Massoretes established is commonly called the Massoretic Text (MT).

Until the discovery of the Dead Sea Scrolls in 1948, the oldest known manuscripts of the Old Testament were from the ninth to the eleventh centuries AD. The reason why no earlier manuscripts survived was that when manuscripts became too old or worn to use, the Hebrew scholars buried them, rather than let them fall into dishonourable use. In making fresh manuscripts, the Hebrew copyists were almost fanatical at preserving every letter exactly as it was in the former manuscripts. As a result they made few errors.

Versions and translations from the ancient past confirm the general reliability of the Hebrew manuscripts. Among the most important of these are the Dead Sea Scrolls, a collection of Old Testament and other writings belonging to a Jewish community that lived in the region of the Dead Sea about 130 BC to AD 70.

There is added confirmation of this reliability in the copies of early translations that were based on Old Testament manuscripts older than any available today. These include translations into Greek in the second century BC, into Syriac in the

first century AD, and into Latin in the fifth century AD. Further confirmation comes from the Samaritan version of the Pentateuch and from quotations from the Old Testament found in Jewish writings of the first five centuries AD. (See also SEPTUAGINT.)

New Testament manuscripts

In New Testament times Greek was the language commonly spoken throughout the lands of the Bible story. The books of the New Testament were written in Greek — not classical Greek, but the everyday language spoken by ordinary people. From the

Καὶ ὄντος αὐτοῦ ἐν Βηθανίᾳ ἐν τῇ οἰκίᾳ Σί-
μωνος τοῦ λεπροῦ, κατακειμένου αὐτοῦ ἦλθεν
γυνὴ ἔχουσα ἀλάβαστρον μύρου νάρδου πιστικῆς
πολυτελοῦς· συντρίψασα τὴν ἀλάβαστρον κατέχεεν
αὐτοῦ τῆς κεφαλῆς. ἦσαν δέ τινες ἀγανακτοῦντες
πρὸς ἑαυτούς, Εἰς τί ἡ ἀπώλεια αὕτη τοῦ μύρου

Greek writing in miniscule, or lower case, letters

beginning, people made copies of letters that Paul and others had written, as well as copies of the Gospel records, and sent them to churches far and near. All this took time, and many years passed before all the writings were gathered together to form the complete New Testament as we know it today (see CANON).

Greek manuscripts were of two types, those written entirely in uncial (or capital) letters, and those written in miniscule (or lower case) letters. Writing in uncials was more common in the earlier centuries, but it was gradually replaced by the more convenient miniscule script.

Copyists' errors are more common in the Greek manuscripts of the New Testament than in the Hebrew manuscripts of the Old Testament. But the variations in the Greek manuscripts do not seriously affect our understanding of what the New Testament writers wrote. There are in existence over five thousand manuscripts of the Greek New Testament (in part or in whole), and although these increase the number of variations, they also increase the possibility of eliminating the errors.

The most valuable manuscripts come from the period of the fourth to the sixth centuries AD, though there are earlier ones. As a rule, the earlier the manuscript, the more likely it is to be correct. On the other hand a more recent manuscript could be more accurate if it was copied from a much

```
ΝΑΒΟΥΧΟΔΟΝΟ
ϹΟΡΒΑϹΙΛΕΥϹΒΑ
ΒΥΛШΝΟϹΚΑΙΗΝ
ΤΟΥΤШΠΛΙϹΘΡΕ
ΠΤΗΘΥΓΑΤΗΡΑΜΙ
ΝΑΔΑΒΑΔΕΛΦΟΥ
ΠΑΤΡΟϹΑΥΤΟΥΚΑΙ
ΤΟΟΝΟΜΑΑΥΤΗ
ΕϹΘΗΡΕΝΔΕΤШ
ΜΕΤΑΛΛΑΞΑΙΑΥ
ΤΗϹΤΟΥϹΓΟΝΕΙϹ
ΕΠΕΔΕΥϹΕΝΑΥΤΗΝ
ΕΑΥΤШΕΙϹΓΥΝΑΙ
ΚΑΚΑΙΗΝΤΟΚΟΡΑ
ϹΙΟΝΚΑΛΗΤШΕΙΔ
```

Greek writing in uncial, or capital, letters

earlier and more reliable manuscript. One way of checking the accuracy of manuscripts is to compare them with early translations of the New Testament, or with quotations from the New Testament in the writings of early authors.

As they study all this evidence, experts are able to assess the value of manuscripts and arrange them in groups according to their common features. It has become apparent that different groups of manuscripts belonged originally to different regions (e.g. Rome, Alexandria, Byzantium). This gives scholars an indication of the types of manuscripts that were in use at various stages of the early church's history, and so helps towards determining the exact wording of the original writing.

A reliable text

Using all the material available to them, those skilled in the processes outlined above are able to prepare accurate editions of the Hebrew Old Testament and the Greek New Testament. These books are called texts. Modern translations of the Bible are made from these texts, not from the ancient manuscripts. Most of the manuscripts are carefully preserved in museums or places of learning around the world.

No doubt as there are further discoveries and further insights into ancient languages and practices, there will be further revisions of the Hebrew and Greek texts. Any changes will probably be only minor, as history has shown that changes made to the text through fresh discoveries have been comparatively few and unimportant. In spite of damage to the ancient manuscripts through wear and tear, misuse, copyists' errors and government opposition, the Scriptures have remained intact, essentially as they were when first written. God has preserved his Word in such a way that no important teaching is anywhere affected.

MARK

It was not unusual for Jews in the Roman Empire to have both Jewish and Roman names. In the case of John Mark, his two names reflect respectively this Jewish and Roman background.

In Jerusalem

Mark was a Jew brought up in Jerusalem. His parents were reasonably wealthy, as they owned a large house and had servants (Acts 12:12-13). (Also, at least one of Mark's close relatives was wealthy enough to own land; Acts 4:36-37; Col 4:10.) Mark's house must have been a regular meeting place for the apostles and other Christians in Jerusalem, as

Peter, on escaping from prison, knew that he would find the Christians there (Acts 12:12). If this was the house usually used by the apostles as a meeting place, it was the house of 'the upper room' where Jesus had earlier gathered with his disciples (Luke 22:11-13; Acts 1:13; cf. also John 20:19,26).

There is a further point in favour of the suggestion that Mark's house was the house of the upper room. This is the reference Mark himself makes to a certain young man who had followed Jesus and the disciples from the house to the Garden of Gethsemane, clothed only in his nightwear (Mark 14:51-52). It was a common practice for an author to include a brief personal detail or story but not to mention his own name directly (cf. John 13:23; 2 Cor 12:2).

With Paul and Barnabas

Whether the house of the upper room was Mark's home or not, Mark certainly would have known Peter and the other leading Christians who often visited his home (Acts 12:12-14). When Paul and Barnabas visited Jerusalem with an offering from the church at Antioch, they met Mark. They were so impressed with him that they took him back to Antioch, and later took him with them on what has become known as Paul's first missionary journey (Acts 12:25; 13:5).

After only a short time, Mark left Paul and Barnabas and returned to Jerusalem (Acts 13:13). To Paul this showed that Mark was not reliable, and he refused to allow Mark to go with him and Barnabas on their next missionary journey. Paul and Barnabas quarrelled over the matter and parted. Paul went ahead with his planned journey, but with a new partner, while Mark went with Barnabas to Cyprus (Acts 15:36-41).

In Rome and Asia Minor

There is no record in the Bible of Mark's activities over the next ten years or so. There is, however, evidence in other early records that he spent some time with Peter, helping Peter to evangelize the provinces of northern Asia Minor where God had not allowed Paul to preach (1 Peter 1:1; cf. Acts 16:6-8).

Peter and Mark then visited Rome and taught the Christians there. When Peter left Rome, the Roman Christians asked Mark (who had stayed behind) to preserve the story of Jesus as they had heard it from Peter. In due course Mark produced the book known as Mark's Gospel, a book that strongly carries the flavour of Peter (see MARK, GOSPEL OF).

Mark was still in Rome when Paul arrived as a prisoner the first time (Philem 23-24). Mark had matured over the years, and Paul readily acknowledged this. He bore no grudges, and recommended Mark to the Colossian church as one who could be of great help to it (Col 4:10).

On leaving Rome, Mark most likely went to Colossae as planned. He was probably still there when Paul later wrote to Timothy (who was in Ephesus, not far away), asking him to get Mark and bring him to Rome. Paul was back in prison after a brief time of freedom and travel, and he wanted to see Timothy and Mark before he was executed (2 Tim 4:11).

Whether the two reached Rome before Paul's execution is uncertain, but Mark was certainly in Rome at the time of Peter's visit soon after. Over their years of working together, Mark and Peter had become so close that Peter called Mark his son. Mark may even have been converted through Peter, back in the days when Peter frequented Mark's house in Jerusalem. Now, as Peter neared the end of his life, he linked Mark's name with his own in writing a letter to the churches of Asia Minor that together they had helped to establish (1 Peter 1:1; 5:13).

MARK, GOSPEL OF

John Mark, the writer of Mark's Gospel, was the young man who set out with Paul and Barnabas on their first missionary journey (Acts 12:25; 13:5). Later he worked closely with Peter, so closely in fact that Peter called Mark his son (1 Peter 5:13; see MARK). There is good evidence that Peter and Mark visited Rome about AD 60 (just before Paul arrived in Rome as a prisoner; Acts 28:16) and taught the church there for a time. Over the next few years Mark spent some time in Rome, while Peter revisited churches elsewhere. The Roman Christians asked Mark to preserve Peter's teaching for them, and the result was Mark's Gospel.

Mark, Peter and the Romans

Many features of Mark's Gospel reflect the interests and character of Peter. Apart from the events in Jerusalem at the time of Jesus' death and resurrection, most of Jesus' ministry recorded in Mark took place in Galilee in the north. Peter's home town of Capernaum seems to have been Jesus' base (Mark 1:21,29; 2:1; 9:33).

The account in Mark shows the characteristic haste of Peter in the way it rushes on from one story to the next. On the whole the language is more clearcut than in the parallels of the other Gospels, and reported statements are more direct. There is vivid detail, particularly in the record of Jesus' actions and emotions (Mark 1:41; 3:5; 4:38; 6:6; 10:14,16,21,32). Peter's genuineness is seen in that his mistakes are recorded (Mark 9:5-6; 14:66-72), whereas incidents that might be to his credit are omitted (cf. Matt 14:29; 16:17).

During the decade of the sixties, the Roman persecution of Christians increased, particularly after Nero blamed Christians for the great fire of Rome in AD 64. Just before this, Peter had written from Rome (code-named Babylon; 1 Peter 5:13) to encourage Christians who were being persecuted (1 Peter 1:6; 2:20-23; 3:14-17; 4:12-16). Not long after this he himself was executed (2 Peter 1:14; cf. John 21:18-19). Mark's Gospel reminded the Roman Christians (by quoting from Peter's experience of the life and teaching of Jesus) that they would need strength and patience to endure misunderstandings, persecution, false accusations and even betrayal (Mark 3:21,30; 4:17; 8:34-38; 10:30; 13:9,13; 14:41,72; 15:19,32).

Since the story of Jesus was set in Palestine, the Gentiles in Rome needed explanations of some matters. Mark therefore helped them by translating Hebrew or Aramaic expressions (Mark 3:17; 5:41; 7:11,34; 15:22,34) and explaining Jewish beliefs and practices (Mark 7:3-4; 12:18,42; 14:12; 15:42).

Mark's view of Jesus

Mark's Gospel records more action than the other Gospels, but less of Jesus' teaching. Nevertheless, the book has a basic teaching purpose. Though Mark wrote in different circumstances from John and for different people, his basic purpose was the same, namely, to show that Jesus was the Son of God (cf. John 20:31). Mark makes this clear in his opening statement (Mark 1:1).

According to Mark, the ministry of Jesus from beginning to end showed that he was a divine person in human form, the God-sent Messiah. At Jesus' baptism, the starting point for his public ministry, a statement from God showed what this unique ministry would involve. The statement, combining Old Testament quotations concerning the Davidic Messiah and the Servant of Yahweh, showed that Jesus' way to kingly glory was to be that of the suffering servant (Mark 1:11; cf. Ps 2:7; Isa 42:1; see MESSIAH). The heavenly Son of man, to whom God promised a worldwide and everlasting kingdom (Dan 7:13-14), would receive that kingdom only by way of crucifixion (Mark 8:29-31,38; 9:31; 10:45; see SON OF MAN).

The death of Jesus is therefore the climax of Mark's Gospel. That death came about through Jesus' open confession to Caiaphas that he was both messianic Son of God and heavenly Son of man, and he was on the way to his kingly and heavenly glory (Mark 14:61-64). Demons knew Jesus to be the Son of God (Mark 3:11; 5:7), his disciples recognized it (Mark 8:29), his Father confirmed it on the Mount of Transfiguration (Mark 9:7), Jesus declared it to disciples and enemies (Mark 13:32; 14:61-62) and even a Roman centurion at the cross was forced to admit it (Mark 15:39).

Summary of contents

An introductory section deals with Jesus' baptism and his subsequent temptation by Satan (1:1-13). The story then quickly moves on to deal with Jesus' ministry in Galilee and other northern regions.

After gathering together his first few disciples (1:14-20), Jesus carried out a variety of healings (1:21-2:12) and added Matthew (Levi) to his group of disciples (2:13-17). Through several incidents he showed that the true religion he proclaimed was not concerned simply with the legal requirements of the Jewish law (2:18-3:6).

From Galilee Jesus appointed twelve apostles whom he could send out to spread the message of his kingdom (3:7-19). He illustrated the nature of that kingdom by dealing with critics (3:20-35), telling parables (4:1-34), overcoming storms, evil spirits, sickness, hunger and death (4:35-6:56), demanding moral rather than ceremonial cleanliness (7:1-23), and demonstrating by teachings and miracles the importance of faith (7:24-8:26).

The record of this part of Jesus' ministry concludes with Peter's acknowledgment of his messiahship (8:27-33), Jesus' reminder of the cost of discipleship (8:34-9:1), the Father's declaration at Jesus' transfiguration (9:2-8), the disciples' inability to heal a demon-possessed boy (9:9-29), and Jesus' teaching on the necessity for humble submission in his kingdom (9:30-50).

Jesus' ministry from his departure from Galilee to his arrival in Jerusalem dealt with such matters as divorce (10:1-12), children (10:13-16), wealth (10:17-31) and ambition (10:32-45). Near Jericho he healed a blind man (10:46-52).

On the Sunday before his crucifixion, Jesus entered Jerusalem as Israel's God-sent Messiah (11:1-11). In the days that followed, he cleansed the temple and warned of the terrible judgment that was to fall on the Jewish nation because of its rejection of the Messiah (11:12-12:12). On many occasions the Jews disputed with him publicly (12:13-44), but privately he told his disciples of coming judgments and warned them to keep alert (13:1-37).

After his anointing at Bethany (14:1-11), Jesus prepared for the Passover, instituted the Lord's Supper, then went and prayed in the Garden of Gethsemane (14:12-42). He was arrested (14:43-52), taken to the high priest's house (14:53-72), brought before Pilate (15:1-20), taken away and crucified (15:21-47). On the third day he rose from the dead (16:1-8), after which he appeared a number of times to his disciples and gave them final teaching (16:9-20). (These last twelve verses are not in the oldest and best manuscripts.)

MARRIAGE

From the beginning God's ideal for marriage has been that one man and one woman live together, independent of parents, in lifelong union (Gen 2:18-24; Matt 19:4-6). This ideal union is broken only by death, in which case the surviving partner is free to remarry (Rom 7:2-3; 1 Cor 7:39; 1 Tim 5:14).

Polygamy in the Old Testament

The early history of mankind is one of almost total departure from God, so that only a very small minority of mankind retained any real understanding of God (Gen 6:1-8; Rom 1:20-27). Polygamy, the practice of having several wives at the same time, became so widespread that even God's people did not always regard it as wrong (Gen 25:6; 2 Sam 5:13; 1 Kings 11:1-3). Inevitably, jealousy and conflict resulted, leading them eventually to recognize that God's ideal of monogamy was best (Gen 21:8-10; 29:21-30:24; Deut 21:15-17; Judg 8:30-9:6; 1 Sam 1:4-8; 2 Sam 3:2-5; 1 Kings 11:1-8).

In ancient Israel it was considered a matter of social shame if a wife did not have children (Gen 16:1; 30:1; 1 Sam 1:10-11; Luke 1:7). According to one custom, if a wife was not able to have children, she may have allowed her husband to produce a child by her maidservant. All legal rights over the child belonged to the wife, not the maid (Gen 16:2; 30:1-8). (Concerning the case where a married man died without leaving children see WIDOW.)

Marriage customs

Among the ancient Israelites, engagement to marry was almost as binding as marriage. Unfaithfulness within an engagement was considered as bad as adultery (Deut 22:23-27; Matt 1:18-20). Parents usually chose the marriage partners for their sons and daughters (Gen 21:21; 24:1-4; 38:6; Ruth 3:1-5), though they may have taken into consideration any preference that a son or daughter indicated (Gen 24:58-61; 34:4,8; Judg 14:2; 1 Sam 18:20-21).

The custom was for the bridegroom to give some payment or service to the parents of the bride as the price for the daughter he had taken from them (Gen 29:18,30; 34:12; 1 Sam 18:25). The bride's parents usually gave a gift to the married couple which, in wealthy families, often consisted of servants or land (Gen 29:24,29; Judg 1:15; 1 Kings 9:16).

Both the bridegroom and the bride wore special clothes for the wedding ceremony and the associated festivities (Isa 61:10; Jer 2:32; Rev 19:7-8; 21:2). The bridegroom had his best man, and the bride her bridesmaids (Ps 45:14; John 3:29). The bridegroom and his friends went and brought the bride from her father's house to his own house, where the feast was held (Ps 45:14-15; Matt 25:1-13). The wedding feast was a time of great celebration, and all who were invited as guests were given special clothes for the occasion (Matt 22:1-4,11-12; John 2:1-11). Festivities sometimes went on for a week (Gen 29:27; Matt 9:14-15).

Total union

Whatever the traditions or procedures, marriage is more than a social custom or a legal arrangement. It is also more than a sexual relationship. It is an unselfish giving of each partner to the other in a union that excludes all others. God intends people to have and to enjoy sexual relations, but only as part of a total relationship where a man and a woman commit themselves to each other for life (Matt 19:5-6; Heb 13:4). Divorce is not part of God's plan for mankind (Mal 2:16; Matt 5:32; 19:8-9; see DIVORCE).

Human sexuality is one of the gifts of God to mankind and, like all God's gifts, it can be properly enjoyed or shamefully abused (1 Thess 4:4-5; 1 Tim. 4:3-4). The Bible encourages a healthy enjoyment of sex within marriage (Prov 5:18-19; Eccles 9:9; Song of Songs 1:12-13; 7:6-13; 8:1-3), but it forbids sexual relations before marriage or with any person other than one's marriage partner (Lev 18:6-18; 20:10; Deut 22:20-22; Mal 2:14; Mark 6:18; Rom 7:2; cf. Matt 5:27-28; see ADULTERY; FORNICATION). It condemns prostitution, incest, bestiality and homosexual practices as perversions. They are sins against one's own body (Lev 18:22-23; 19:29; 20:14-17; Rom 1:26-27; 1 Cor 6:9-10,13-18; Rev 22:15).

In marriage as God intended it, there is an equality between the man and the woman (Gen 2:23-24). Though there may be physical, emotional and psychological differences between the male and the female, the two complement each other so that each is equipped to do what the other cannot. Together they form a unit, with each dependent on the other (1 Cor 7:3-4; 11:11-12).

God holds the man ultimately responsible for the household that comes into being through the marriage (Gen 3:9-12; 1 Cor 11:3; cf. Rom 5:12). Husbands have at times thought this responsibility gives them special privileges that allow them to treat their wives as inferiors instead of as equals (Gen 3:16), but such a state of affairs was not God's original intention. Sin has spoiled the marriage relationship as it has spoiled everything else in human society. However, because of the exercise of Christian love, Christian marriage ought to achieve marital harmony, even in circumstances where other marriages do not.

Christian love is the sort of self-sacrificing love that Christ exercised — serving others rather than pleasing self. Husband and wife must exercise such love towards each other (Eph 5:1-2), though the husband in particular is required to make sacrifices (Eph 5:25-29).

Likewise husband and wife must exercise submission to each other (Eph 5:21), though the wife in particular is required to recognize the husband's headship of the family (Eph 5:22-24). Where each is prepared to sacrifice self-interest for the sake of the other, the marriage will be enriched (Eph 5:33; see HUSBAND; WIFE). It will also be a fitting picture of the relationship between Christ and his church (Eph 5:29-32).

Special considerations

Since their relationship with Christ governs all their other relationships, Christians should not marry those who do not share their faith in Jesus Christ (2 Cor 6:14-16; cf. 1 Cor 7:39). However, where one partner of a non-Christian marriage later becomes a Christian, the marriage should be maintained. God understands the circumstances, and the Christian should do everything possible to make the marriage work harmoniously (1 Cor 7:12-16).

In certain circumstances it may be God's will for a person not to marry, and this may at times require much self-discipline (Jer 16:2; Matt 19:12; 1 Cor 1:7-8,17,32-35). Even among those who intend to marry, self-discipline is necessary. They must take into consideration the added responsibilities that marriage brings (1 Cor 7:32-34), and must not marry hastily, particularly when there is the possibility of increased social and economic hardship (1 Cor 7:25-31). But if an unmarried person is constantly aflame with sexual passion, it may be better to marry, lest the temptations prove to be too great (1 Cor 7:9,36-38; cf. 7:5).

While the Christian teaching on marriage is based on principles that the Creator set out for his creatures, it also acknowledges the weaknesses of human nature and the need to deal with them sensibly. Christian morality requires God's people to uphold his standards when others want to destroy them. At the same time Christian love requires them to give support to those who, having ignored God's law, are sorry for their sin and need help in rebuilding their lives (John 8:1-11; 1 Cor 6:9-11; Gal 6:1-2).

MAR'S HILL

See AREOPAGUS.

MARTHA

Martha, Mary and their brother Lazarus lived in the village of Bethany, just outside Jerusalem (John 11:1,18). Jesus knew the family well (John 11:5), for he had probably been there often to get away from the crowds and enjoy some rest and fellowship. That was probably why he rebuked Martha on one occasion. She busied herself with much preparation for a special meal, whereas Jesus was looking only for some quiet and relaxing conversation with his friends. Mary, realizing this, talked with Jesus, and in so doing she benefited from the words he spoke (Luke 10:38-42).

Some time after this, Lazarus fell ill. The sisters sent for Jesus, but by the time Jesus arrived, Lazarus was dead (John 11:1-6,17). Martha and Mary were convinced that if Jesus had been there, he could have done something to stop Lazarus from dying (John 11:19-21,28-32).

Martha still believed that Jesus had the power to do anything (John 11:22) and, in response to Jesus' question, she reaffirmed her faith in him as the Messiah, the Son of God (John 11:25-27). Jesus' resurrection of Lazarus demonstrated not only the power that Jesus had over death, but also the unity that Jesus had with his Father in all his works (John 11:41-44).

A few days later, when Jesus and his disciples were having a meal with Lazarus and his two sisters, Mary anointed his feet with costly ointment. Jesus saw this as a symbolic anointing in preparation for his burial, which would soon take place (John 12:1-8). When, during the last few days before the crucifixion, Jesus and his disciples went out to Bethany at night to sleep, this house was probably the place where they slept (Mark 11:11-12,19; Matt 21:17). (If the anointing by Mary referred to above was the same as that recorded in Matthew 26:6-13, the person called Simon the leper was possibly Martha's father or husband.)

MARTYR

A martyr is a person who stands firm in the midst of persecution and willingly suffers death rather than deny his faith (Acts 7:54-60; 12:1-2; 22:20; Rev 2:13). The word 'martyr' comes from the Greek word that is used in the New Testament for 'witness' and 'testimony'. The martyrs were those who died because of their witness, or testimony, to their Lord (Rev 6:9-11; 12:11; 17:6; 20:4).

In the end the victors will be the martyrs, not their opponents. The basis of this assured victory is the death and resurrection of Christ, who is himself the faithful and true witness (2 Tim 4:6-8,18; Rev 12:10-11; 20:4; cf. 1:5, 3:14). (See also PERSECUTION; WITNESS.)

MARY

Six women in the New Testament had the name Mary. The lesser known of these were the mother of John Mark (Acts 12:12; for details see MARK), a member of the church in Rome (Rom 16:6), and a woman who was wife of Clopas and mother of two sons, James and Joseph (Matt 27:56; Mark 15:40,47; 16:1; John 19:25).

This last-named Mary was one of several women from Galilee who helped look after the needs of Jesus and his disciples. They travelled with Jesus around Palestine and were present at his crucifixion. Another in that group was also named Mary. She came from the town of Magdala in Galilee and was known as Mary Magdalene, to distinguish her from the other Marys (Matt 27:55-56; Luke 8:1-3).

Mary Magdalene had become a follower of Jesus early in his ministry, when he had healed her of evil spirits (Luke 8:2). On the morning of Jesus' resurrection, she and some others, including Mary the mother of James and Joseph, went to anoint the body of Jesus, but found the tomb empty (Matt 28:1-5; John 20:1). She brought Peter and John to the tomb, then, after they had left, met the risen Jesus (John 20:2-18).

Another Mary was the sister of Martha and Lazarus. The three lived at Bethany, just outside Jerusalem, and were close friends of Jesus (John 11:1,5). In the biblical record, Mary and Martha are usually mentioned together. (For further details see MARTHA.)

The mother of Jesus

By far the most important Mary in New Testament times was the mother of Jesus. She was blessed above all women, for God chose her to be the mother of the Messiah (Luke 1:28,32,42-43).

At the time God revealed this to Mary, she lived in the town of Nazareth in Galilee, where she was engaged to be married to a local carpenter named Joseph. (Concerning the families from which Mary and Joseph came see JOSEPH, HUSBAND OF MARY.) God revealed to Mary that, while still a virgin, she would become pregnant. This would come about through the direct creative power of God's Spirit, so that her son would be unique. Though fully human, he would also be the Son of God (Luke 1:30-35).

Mary accepted the will of God for her without question (Luke 1:38). She praised God that he chose her, just an ordinary person from a humble family, to be the means by which he would bring his blessing to the world. Through her baby, God was going to fulfil the great promises given to Abraham and David (Luke 1:46-56).

For the next three months Mary stayed with her friend and relative, Elizabeth, in Judea. When she returned to Nazareth pregnant, Joseph was deeply troubled, but he too submitted to God's will after he received a revelation of the divine purposes (Luke 1:56; Matt 1:18-25).

Some months later, Joseph and Mary moved to Bethlehem in Judea for a census, and there the baby was born (Luke 2:1-7,19). When Joseph and Mary later took the baby to Jerusalem for certain Jewish ceremonies, Mary learnt a little of what lay ahead. Although her son would be a Saviour, he would also attract bitter opposition, which would in turn cause Mary pain and sorrow (Luke 2:22-23,34-35).

Because of the threat of violence from Herod, Joseph sought safety for Mary and the baby Jesus by taking them to Egypt. After Herod's death the family returned to Palestine and settled in Nazareth (Matt 2:13-14,19-23).

Joseph and Mary brought Jesus up to be obedient to his parents and to be instructed in the teachings of the Old Testament (Luke 2:42-46,51). They did not, however, have a clear understanding of the unique relationship that Jesus had with his heavenly Father (Luke 2:49). Even when he began his public ministry, Jesus found it necessary to remind his mother that he was to use his divine power solely in accordance with his Father's will. He

would not use it simply to please friends and family (John 2:3-4).

The children born to Mary and Joseph after Jesus were James, Joseph, Simon, Judas and at least two daughters (Matt 13:55-56; Mark 6:3). When Jesus set out on his public ministry, his brothers did not believe him to be the Messiah. They thought that he was suffering from some sort of religious madness. On one occasion when they expressed their annoyance with him, Mary was with them (Mark 3:21,31-35; John 7:3-5).

Yet Mary was convinced of her son's messiahship and remained devoted to him even to the cross (John 19:25-27). Jesus' resurrection seems to have changed his brothers, for in the days immediately after his ascension, they along with Mary were among the group of Jerusalem believers who met for fellowship and prayer (Acts 1:14; cf. 1 Cor 15:7).

MASTER

Throughout the countries of the region of the Bible story, many households were very large and included slaves and hired workers. The head of the household was commonly referred to as the master, and he exercised considerable authority (Gen 14:14; 24:2,9; 1 Sam 25:14,17).

In recognition of the dangers that accompanied such authority, Israelite law laid down that a master did not have the right to treat his servants as he wished. He had to recognize their rights, and be fair and honest in all his dealings with them (Exod 21:8-11,20,26-27; see SLAVE).

The New Testament further emphasizes the responsibility of masters towards their servants. Christian masters in particular are to be careful the way they treat their servants, because they themselves are answerable to a master, Jesus the Lord (Eph 6:9; Col 4:1; see WORK).

All Christians are servants of this divine Master and must give him their total allegiance (Matt 6:24; see JESUS CHRIST, sub-heading 'Jesus as Lord'). One day their Master will assess their faithfulness in service and reward them accordingly (Matt 25:14-30; Mark 13:33-37; Rom 14:4; 1 Cor 4:1-5; see also STEWARD).

MATTHEW

When the Gospel writers Mark and Luke give the list of the twelve apostles, they name Matthew but do not record his occupation (Mark 3:18; Luke 6:15). When they mention the tax collector who responded to Jesus' call and invited his fellow tax collectors to a feast to meet Jesus, they call him not Matthew, but Levi, which was his other name (Mark 2:14-17; Luke 5:27-32). It is almost as if, to be kind to Matthew, they deliberately avoid mentioning that he was once a tax collector. Jews in general despised those of their own people who collected taxes on behalf of Rome. They regarded them as dishonest and unpatriotic people who had lost their self-respect (see TAX COLLECTOR).

Matthew's response to the call of Jesus changed his attitude to life completely. This is seen in the Gospel traditionally associated with Matthew. The book itself does not state whether Matthew was the person who actually wrote it, but there is good evidence to suggest that, no matter who wrote it, it came from material that Matthew had prepared. And far from hiding the fact that he was once a tax collector, Matthew states it clearly. He uses the name Matthew, not Levi, in his account of Jesus' call (Matt 9:9-13), and in his list of the twelve apostles he states his previous occupation (Matt 10:3). The book reflects a tax collector's gratitude to Jesus for calling such a person to be an apostle. (See also MATTHEW, GOSPEL OF.)

At the time he first met Jesus, Matthew lived and worked in Capernaum on the shore of the Sea of Galilee (Mark 2:1,13-14). He had a good income (Matt 9:9) and owned a house large enough to accommodate a good number of people (Luke 5:29). But he left all this to join Jesus in the urgent and risky business of spreading the good news of the kingdom of God (Matt 10:5-23). Though the Bible gives no details of Matthew's later activities, he was involved in the establishment of the church after Jesus' resurrection (Acts 1:13).

MATTHEW, GOSPEL OF

Nowhere does this Gospel say who wrote it, though the title given to it in the second century reflects the traditional belief that Matthew was the author. Whether or not Matthew actually produced the finished product, it seems clear that his writings (referred to in second century documents) must have at least provided a major source of material for the book.

Origin of Matthew's Gospel

It appears that Mark's Gospel, written during the first half of the decade of the sixties, was the first of the Gospels. Its purpose was to preserve Peter's account of Jesus' ministry for the Christians in Rome. Other people had also prepared written accounts of the life and teachings of Jesus, and from

these Luke began to write an account of Jesus' life to present to a high ranking government official (Luke 1:1-4). A few years later, probably in the decade of the seventies, Matthew's Gospel appeared. It was written mainly for Greek-speaking Jewish Christians, probably those of the churches of Syria and neighbouring regions to the north of Palestine (see GOSPELS).

Matthew had a clear purpose in writing. He therefore chose and arranged his material carefully, to fit in with his overall plan. He saved himself the work of writing fresh narratives of the ministry of Jesus by using most of the material from Mark's Gospel, along with material from some of the same sources as Luke had used. But Matthew used this material differently from Mark and Luke, by making it serve his central purpose. He added a lot of material not contained in the other Gospels, and the characteristic flavour of his Gospel comes from this additional material.

A teaching purpose

Included in the material found solely in Matthew are many quotations from the Old Testament. He introduces most of these by a statement showing how the Old Testament was fulfilled in Jesus (Matt 1:22; 2:15,17,23; 4:14; 8:17; 12:17; 13:35; 21:4; 27:9).

Matthew was particularly concerned to show that Jesus was the promised Messiah, the son of David, the fulfilment of God's purposes in choosing Israel (Matt 1:1,17; 2:6; 9:27; 11:2-6; 15:22; 16:16; 21:9; 26:63-64). In Jesus the kingdom of God had come among mankind (Matt 4:17,23; 5:3; 12:28; 18:1-4; 24:14; see KINGDOM OF GOD), though Jesus the king was not the sort of king most people had expected (Matt 2:6; 4:8-10; 21:5; 25:31,34; 26:52-53; 27:11).

Unbelieving Jews often attacked those of their fellow Jews who were Christians. Matthew's Gospel gave reassurance to these Christians that they were not people who had wandered away from the teaching of the Jewish religion, but people who had found the true fulfilment of it. Jesus did not contradict the Jewish law; rather he brought out its full meaning (Matt 5:17).

The Gospel of Matthew therefore showed the Jewish Christians the nature of the kingdom into which they had come, and the requirements it laid upon them. They were to have high standards of behaviour (Matt 5:3-12; 5:22,28,42,44; 20:21-27) and were to be energetic in spreading the good news of the kingdom to others (Matt 5:13-16; 10:5-8; 24:14; 28:19-20). The unbelieving Jewish traditionalists, on the other hand, were consistently condemned (Matt

3:9; 23:1-36). They missed out on the kingdom, with the result that the gospel was sent to the Gentiles, and many believed (Matt 8:11-12; 11:21-24; 12:21; 12:38-42; 21:43). Jesus had laid the foundation of his church, and no opposition could overpower it (Matt 16:18).

Because of its basic purpose of instruction, Matthew's account of the life of Jesus records more teaching and less action than the accounts of Mark and Luke. His material is not in chronological order. It is arranged according to subject matter around five main teaching sections, each of which concludes with a statement such as 'When Jesus had finished these sayings . . .' (Matt 7:28; 11:1; 13:53; 19:1; 26:1). The first of these sections concerns behaviour (Chapters 5-7), the second deals with spreading the message of the kingdom (Chapter 10), the third consists of parables of the kingdom (Chapter 13), the fourth concerns attitudes to others (Chapter 18), and the fifth discusses the coming of the end (Chapters 24-25).

Summary of contents

The opening section of Matthew begins with a genealogy of Jesus (1:1-17), the story of his birth (1:18-25), the escape from Herod (2:1-18) and the subsequent move to Nazareth (2:19-23). Many years later, Jesus was baptized by John (3:1-17), after which he suffered temptations by Satan (4:1-11). He then returned to Galilee, where he began his public ministry and gathered together his first disciples (4:12-25). The section concludes with the Sermon on the Mount (5:1-7:29).

As Jesus continued to cast out demons, heal the sick, calm storms and welcome sinners, people saw that he was different from other Jewish teachers (8:1-9:17). Some saw that he was the Messiah (9:18-34). Jesus then appointed twelve apostles and sent them out as his assistants in spreading the news of his kingdom. First, however, he reminded them of the cost of being his disciples (9:35-10:42).

After commending John who had prepared the way for his kingdom (11:1-19), and urging others to enter the kingdom (11:20-30), Jesus showed that his kingdom was concerned with more than legal correctness (12:1-21). This stirred up the Jewish traditionalists against him, causing Jesus to warn them that they were only preparing a more severe judgment for themselves (12:22-50). A number of parables emphasized that Christ's kingdom was the only way to life. To reject it meant eternal destruction (13:1-52).

Though rejected by some and feared by others (13:53-14:12), Jesus continued to bring help and healing to many (14:13-36). He emphasized the need for inner cleansing (15:1-20) and showed that faith is the way to blessing (15:21-16:12). The disciples knew that Jesus was the Messiah (16:13-20), but Jesus warned that death lay ahead for him and perhaps for them (16:21-28). After his transfiguration (17:1-8), he repeated that the Messiah would be cruelly treated and killed (17:9-27). Those in the Messiah's kingdom therefore needed to be characterized by a humble and forgiving spirit (18:1-35).

After dealing with questions concerning family responsibilities (19:1-15), Jesus showed how wealth hindered entrance into God's kingdom (19:16-30). The blessings of that kingdom came by God's grace (20:1-16), and therefore there was no room for selfish ambition (20:17-34).

Jesus then entered Jerusalem as the messianic king (21:1-11), cleansed the temple (21:12-17), and in a series of disputes with the Jews showed how their rejection of the Messiah was leading them to national catastrophe (21:18-22:46). In particular he condemned the religious leaders (23:1-39), and privately he told his disciples to be prepared both for the coming destruction of Jerusalem and for the climax of history when he returns (24:1-51). Three stories illustrated the need for constant readiness (25:1-46).

While the Jews plotted to capture him, Jesus prepared for the crucifixion that he knew awaited him (26:1-19). After the Last Supper in Jerusalem and a time of prayer in the Garden of Gethsemane (26:20-46), he was arrested, condemned by the Jewish Council, handed over to the Roman governor and crucified (26:47-27:66). But he rose from death (28:1-15) and, before finally leaving his disciples a few weeks later, entrusted to them the task of spreading his gospel worldwide (28:16-20).

MEASUREMENT

There is no certainty about present-day equivalents of many of the measurements given in the Bible. These measurements probably varied considerably even in Bible times. (Concerning measurements of weight and the cheating that was common where there were few official standards, see WEIGHTS.)

Measures of capacity for grain and for liquids sometimes had different names. The largest measure of capacity was the homer, or cor, equal to about 370 litres (Lev 27:16; 1 Kings 4:22). The homer, or cor, was divided into ten smaller measures. In the case of grain this measure was called an ephah (Judg 6:19; Ezek 45:11) and in the case of liquids a bath (Ezra 7:22; Ezek 45:11). The grain measure, the ephah, was divided into ten omers (Exod 16:36). The liquid measure, the bath, was divided into six hins (Lev 23:13). A hin was divided into twelve logs (Lev 14:10).

People in ancient times, as in the present day, often measured length by calculating according to the span of their fingers, the length of their arms, the distance they could walk in a set time, and so on. The basic measurement of length, the cubit, was the approximate distance from the elbow to the tip of the finger. More exactly, the cubit was about forty-four centimetres or eighteen inches (Exod 25:23; Deut 3:11; Rev 21:17; see CUBIT). Half a cubit was a span, the distance from the tip of the thumb to the tip of the little finger on an outstretched hand (Exod 28:16; 1 Sam 17:4). A handbreadth, or four

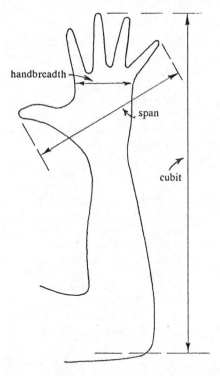

fingers, was the distance across the hand at the base of the four fingers. It was equal to about a third of a span (Exod 25:25; Jer 52:21).

Longer distances may have been calculated in cubits (Num 35:4), but more often they were estimated approximately; for example, the distance a fired arrow might travel (Gen 21:16), the length of a ploughed furrow (1 Sam 14:14), or the distance a person could walk in a day (Num 11:31; Gen 30:36). A Sabbath day's journey was the distance that the Jewish leaders laid down as the maximum a person was allowed to travel on the Sabbath day. It was about one kilometre (Exod 16:29; Acts 1:12).

MEDIA

Media was an ancient kingdom to the north of Persia. It appears in the Bible story mainly as a partner of Persia, who had conquered it in the reign of the Persian king Cyrus. The combined army of Media and Persia conquered Babylon in 539 BC, after which Persia became the supreme power in the

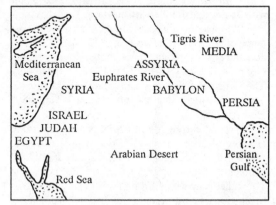

region. Medes shared as equals with Persians in the military and civil administration of the Persian Empire, and sometimes the names Medes and Persians were used interchangeably (Ezra 6:1-3; Esther 1:3,14,19; Isa 13:17; 21:2; Jer 51:11,28; Dan 5:30-31; 6:8,28; 8:20; 9:1; 11:1). (For further details see PERSIA.)

MEDIATOR

Man, because of sin, is cut off from God and unable to bring himself back to God (Gen 3:22-24; Isa 59:2; Eph 2:3; Col 1:21; see SIN). Therefore, there needs to be a mediator who can stand between sinful man and a holy God, and somehow bring man back to God. The only person who can really do this is Jesus Christ. He alone was truly man and truly God, and, being sinless, he bore the penalty of sin on man's behalf. Through him repentant sinners can be brought back to God and enjoy the fellowship with God that he desires for them (2 Tim 2:5-6; 1 Peter 3:18; see RECONCILIATION; REDEMPTION).

The work of Jesus through his life, death and resurrection is therefore the basis on which God deals with man's sin and brings repentant sinners back to himself. This applies even to believers who lived in Old Testament times. Such people may not have known about Jesus' death, but the eternal God did (Rev 13:8).

Through the nation Israel God taught man the principles of his salvation. He chose Israel to be his people and gave them an order of priests and sacrifices as a means of approaching him (Exod 19:5-6; Lev 5:27-30; Num 3:10; see COVENANT; PRIEST; SACRIFICE). In making the covenant with Israel, God used Moses as the mediator (Exod 24:3-8; Acts 7:38; Gal 3:19-20). The people, in their approach to God, used the priests as mediators (Lev 5:17-18; 16:15-17; Heb 5:1).

With the coming of Jesus Christ, the covenant with Israel had fulfilled its purpose. God has now established a new and eternal covenant, Jesus Christ being the mediator (Heb 8:6; 9:15; 12:24). He is also the priest through whom people approach God (John 14:7; Heb 4:14-16; 9:24; 13:15; 1 Peter 2:5). The basis on which this new covenant operates is Christ's sacrificial death (Col 1:21-22; 1 Tim 2:5-6; Heb 9:11-15).

Yet the earthly life of Christ is also important. Because of his experiences as one who has lived in the world of ordinary people, he understands the problems of believers. As a result he can plead sympathetically with God on their behalf, as well as bring God's help to them (Heb 2:17-18; 4:15; 7:25). (For further details see PRIEST, sub-heading 'The high priesthood of Jesus'.)

MEEKNESS

In the Bible, meekness is so closely linked with humility, gentleness and kindness that the reader may have difficulty distinguishing between them. Together they represent a quality of human nature that was found perfectly in Jesus Christ (2 Cor 10:1), and that is desirable in all those who follow him (Eph 4:1-2).

There is nothing weak or colourless about meekness. It is the very opposite of all that is self-centred, and therefore is a quality of strength. It enables a person not merely to be patient when suffering unjust criticism or persecution, but to be positively forgiving (Col 3:12-13; Titus 3:2; see PATIENCE). The meek person does not demand revenge, but leaves the matter in God's hands (Num 12:1-3; 16:4-5; 1 Peter 2:20-23). He does not insist upon his rights, but when circumstances arise where he is forced either to defend himself or correct an opponent, he does so with gentleness (2 Tim 2:25; 1 Peter 3:15).

Jesus is the perfect example of meekness. He never made a show to attract praise for himself, and never damaged the faith of even the weakest believer (Matt 12:19-20; 18:5-6; 21:5). Yet he never hesitated to denounce cruelty, pride, injustice and hypocrisy, even when it made him unpopular (Matt 15:7-14; 21:12-13; 23:13,33). He submitted to his Father and served his fellow man (Matt 20:28; John 5:30), and he expected others to do likewise. As the meek and gentle one, he accepted the burden of sin on behalf of repentant sinners. At the same time he demanded that they accept his lordship in their daily lives (Matt 11:28-30; cf. Ps 25:8-10).

Meekness is a characteristic of life in Christ's kingdom (Matt 5:5); therefore, those who enter that kingdom must exercise meekness (Matt 20:25-26). They will learn to do this as the indwelling Spirit of God changes them into the likeness of Christ and produces the quality of meekness in them (Gal 5:22-23; Phil 2:3-5). (See also HUMILITY.)

MEGIDDO

The town of Megiddo in northern Canaan fell to Israel at the time of Joshua's conquest, though the local inhabitants were not totally destroyed. In the division of Canaan among Israel's tribes, Megiddo came within the tribal allotment of Issachar. The neighbouring tribe of Manasseh was more powerful and took over the town, claiming it could drive out the remaining Canaanites, but it was not able to (Josh 12:7,21; 17:11; Judg 1:27).

In the days of Solomon, Megiddo was an important administrative centre in the north. It was also a strategic defence city (1 Kings 4:12; 9:15-19). Being situated at the western end of the Plain of Esdraelon, at the point where the main north-south and east-west highways crossed, it was involved in a number of important battles (Judg 5:19; 2 Kings 9:27; 23:29). (For map and other details of the region see PALESTINE.) In the symbolism of the book of Revelation, Megiddo is the scene of the last great battle, when God destroys all enemies (Rev 16:16. 'Armageddon' means 'hill of Megiddo').

MELCHIZEDEK

When Abraham was returning from victory over a group of invaders, he was met by Melchizedek, the ruler of the Canaanite city-state of Salem. (This appears to be the place later known as Jerusalem.) Like Abraham, Melchizedek was a worshipper of the Most High God. In fact, he was God's priest, and he reminded Abraham that God was the one who had given Abraham victory. Abraham acknowledged this by offering to God a costly sacrifice, which he presented through God's priest (Gen 14:17-20; Heb 7:1-4).

Several centuries later, when the nation Israel had settled in Canaan, David conquered Jerusalem and made it his national capital. To celebrate his victory he wrote a psalm to be sung by the Levitical singers. It was as if David had become a successor to Melchizedek and heir to all Melchizedek's titles. As ruler of Salem, he was like a king-priest who represented God to his people and whose authority seemed unlimited (Ps 110:1-7).

When the psalm was applied literally to David, it was extravagant, but in later times Jews applied it to the expected Messiah. Jesus agreed that this was a correct application (Matt 22:42-45). A song of lavish praise, extravagant when applied to David, was fitting when applied to Jesus Christ.

Jesus Christ is a high priest after the order of Melchizedek, and his priesthood is complete and eternal. Like Melchizedek, Christ is a king and a priest, a combination not allowed in the traditional Israelite system. The Levitical priests of Israel kept family records of people's ancestry, birth and death, to confirm a person's right to the priesthood. But there were no such records for Melchizedek, as his type of priesthood was not limited by time or Levitical laws. In this way he foreshadowed Christ, whose priesthood is for all people of all eras and all nations (Heb 7:3,15-17; see PRIEST, sub-heading 'The high priesthood of Jesus').

MEMPHIS

The ancient Egyptian city of Memphis, though not in existence today, was situated on almost the same site as the present-day city of Cairo; that is, on the Nile River, about 180 kilometres from its mouth. It was the administrative centre of the first king to unite Upper and Lower Egypt (about 3000 BC), and was capital of Egypt for much of the period before Abraham. It continued to be an important city up till the time of its conquest by Alexander the Great in 332 BC (Isa 19:13; Jer 44:1; 46:14,19; Ezek 30:13; Hosea 9:6). (For map and other details see EGYPT.)

MEN

In the social and family order that God has set out for human society, men and women have complementary roles. Though equal in status before God (Gen 1:27; Gal 3:28; 1 Peter 3:7), they are different in body and personality, so that each is suited in different ways to deal with different needs and responsibilities.

The basic unit of human society is the family, and the ultimate responsibility for the family's well-being rests with the man. As husband he must care for his wife, and as father he must care for his children. In relation to his wife he must treat her as an equal (Eph 5:25,28; 1 Peter 3:7; see HUSBAND), and in relation to his children he must bring them up with love, firmness and understanding (Eph 6:4; Col 3:21; see FAMILY).

Sexual passion is usually stronger in men than in women, and for this reason the Bible gives special warnings to men concerning sexual temptations (Prov 7:6-23; Hosea 4:14; Matt 5:28; 1 Thess 4:4-5; 2 Tim 2:22; Titus 2:6; see ADULTERY; FORNICATION; PROSTITUTION). Older men are to be an example to younger men in demonstrating the worth of a life of self-control (Titus 2:2).

In the church both men and women have their special responsibilities (1 Tim 2:12-15; see WOMEN). Again men are warned not to misuse their position, and in particular not to talk and act in a way that is boastful or arrogant (1 Tim 2:8). No matter what their position, whether in the church, the family or society, they are accountable to God. And the greater the responsibility, the stricter will be the judgment (1 Cor 11:3; Eph 6:9; James 3:1).

MENAHEM

Few Israelite kings were as ruthless in achieving their ambitions as Menahem. In 752 BC he seized the throne by murdering the previous king, then smashed any opposition to his rule with the most brutal cruelty (2 Kings 15:14,16). He survived for ten years, but only by buying the protection of Assyria. This policy was not only economically costly to Israel, but it also opened the way for eventual conquest by Assyria (2 Kings 15:17,19-20).

MERCY

A characteristic of God is that he is merciful and compassionate (Exod 34:6; Neh 9:17; Ps 103:13; 2 Cor 1:3; Eph 2:4). This characteristic showed itself very clearly in Jesus Christ who, being God, became man and demonstrated the mercy that God has towards man (Matt 9:36; 14:14; Luke 7:13).

The most striking demonstration of divine mercy is God's great act of salvation in saving sinners from the just consequences of their sins and giving them forgiveness and eternal life (Num 14:18-19; Ps 86:5; Isa 63:9; Rom 2:4; 11:32; Titus 3:4-5; 1 Peter 2:3). Even in the rituals of the Old Testament, the sinners were dependent entirely on God's mercy for their acceptance with God. It was God's mercy, not their own religious acts, that saved them. For this reason God's throne was called the mercy seat. It was the place where God symbolically sat and where he mercifully accepted repentant sinners into his presence (Exod 25:21-22; cf. Heb 4:16; see TABERNACLE).

Those who claim to be God's people must also be merciful and compassionate (Luke 6:36; 10:36-37; Col 3:12; 1 Peter 2:10). This means more than that they should have pity and concern for others. They must actually *do* something (James 2:15-16; 1 John 3:17-19). In particular they should give help to those in society who are liable to be disadvantaged, such as orphans, widows, aliens, the persecuted, the afflicted and the poor (Deut 14:28-29; 24:19; Prov 19:17; Micah 6:8; Zech 7:9-10; Luke 10:29-37; Rom 12:8; James 1:27). They should show mercy even to those who annoy or oppose them (2 Kings 6:21-22; Luke 6:35; Rom 12:20; Eph 4:32).

Jesus' parables and other teachings are a constant reminder that God takes notice of the way people treat others. God promises that he will have mercy upon those who practise mercy to others (Matt 5:7; 25:34-40). Those who show no mercy to others will receive no mercy from God in the day of judgment (Matt 18:21-35; Luke 16:24-26; James 2:13). (See also GRACE; LOVE.)

MESOPOTAMIA

Originally the name 'Mesopotamia' was given to the fertile land around the upper reaches of the Euphrates and Tigris Rivers (Gen 24:10; Deut 23:4; Judg 3:8-10; 1 Chron 19:6). By New Testament times it applied to the whole of the Euphrates-Tigris

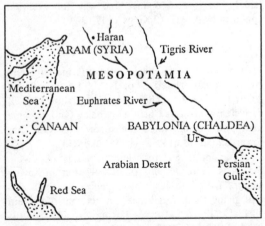

valley, so that even the city of Ur, which was near the mouth of the Euphrates, was considered to be in Mesopotamia (Acts 2:9; 7:2). (For details see ARAM; ASSYRIA; BABYLON; EUPHRATES; SYRIA; TIGRIS.)

MESSIAH

The word 'messiah' is a Hebrew word meaning 'the anointed one'. Israelites of Old Testament times anointed kings, priests, and sometimes prophets to their positions by the ceremony of anointing. In this ceremony a special anointing oil was poured over the head of the person as a sign that he now had the right, and the responsibility, to perform the duties that his position required (Exod 28:41; 1 Kings 1:39; 19:16; see ANOINTING). In the Greek speaking world of New Testament times the word 'christ', also meaning anointed, was used as a Greek translation of the Hebrew 'messiah'.

Old Testament expectations

The most common Old Testament usage of the title 'anointed' was in relation to the Israelite king, who was frequently called 'the Lord's anointed' (1 Sam 24:10; Ps 18:50; 20:6). In the early days of Israel's existence, when it was little more than a large family, God signified that the leadership of the future Israelite nation would belong to the tribe of Judah. From this tribe would come a great leader who would rule the nations in a reign of peace, prosperity and enjoyment (Gen 49:9-12).

Centuries later, God developed this plan by promising King David (who belonged to the tribe of Judah) a dynasty that would last for ever (2 Sam 7:16). The people of Israel therefore lived in the expectation of a time when all enemies would be destroyed and the ideal king would reign in a world-wide kingdom of peace and righteousness. This coming saviour-king they called the Messiah.

In promising David a dynasty, God promised that he would treat David's son and successor as if he were his own son (2 Sam 7:14). From that time on, Israelites regarded every king in the royal line of David as, in a sense, God's son; for he was the one through whom God exercised his rule. The Messiah, David's greatest son, was in a special sense God's son (Ps 2:6-7; Mark 10:47; 12:35; 14:61).

Because of their expectation of a golden age, the Israelite people saw victories over enemies as foreshadowings of the victory of the Messiah and the establishment of his kingdom. They praised their kings in language that was too extravagant to be literally true of those kings. The language expressed the ideals that Israel looked for in its kings, but it could apply fully only to the perfect king, the Messiah (e.g. Psalms 2, 45, 72, 110).

Messianic interpretations

The idealism of the prophets was not fulfilled in any of the Davidic kings of the Old Testament, but this did not cause the people of Israel to lose hope. They constantly looked for the one who would be the great 'David' of the future, the great descendant of David the son of Jesse (Ps 89:3-4; Isa 9:2-7; 11:1-10; Jer 23:5; Ezek 34:23-24; Micah 5:2). This king, this Messiah, was Jesus Christ (Matt 1:1; 9:27; 12:22-23; 21:9; Luke 1:32-33,69-71; Rev 5:5).

One of David's best known psalms, Psalm 110, was interpreted by Jews of Jesus' time as applying to the Messiah, though they consistently refused to acknowledge the messiahship of Jesus. Jesus agreed that they were correct in applying this psalm to the Messiah, but he went a step further by applying it to himself (Ps 110:1; Matt 22:41-45).

Since the king of Psalm 110 was also a priest, Jesus was not only the messianic king but also the messianic priest (Ps 110:4; Heb 5:6; 7:1-28; see PRIEST, sub-heading 'The high priesthood of Jesus'). This joint rule of the priest-king Messiah had been foreshadowed in the book of the prophet Zechariah (Zech 6:12-13).

The Messiah was, in addition, to be a prophet, announcing God's will to his people. As the Davidic kings in some way foreshadowed the king-messiah, so Israel's prophets in some way foreshadowed the prophet-messiah. Again the ideal was fulfilled only in Jesus (Deut 18:15; Luke 24:19; John 6:14; 7:40; Acts 3:22-23; 7:37; Heb 1:1-2).

Jesus and the Jews

Although Jesus was the Messiah, he did not at the beginning of his ministry announce his messiahship openly. This was no doubt because the Jews of his time had a wrong understanding of the Messiah and his kingdom.

The Jews had little interest in the spiritual work of the Messiah. They were not looking for a spiritual leader who would deliver people from the enemy Satan and bring them under the rule and authority of God. They looked rather for a political leader who would deliver them from the power of Rome and bring in a new and independent Israelite kingdom, where there would be peace, contentment and prosperity. If Jesus had announced himself publicly as the Messiah before showing what his messiahship involved, he would have attracted a following of the wrong type (see KINGDOM OF GOD; MIRACLES).

While not refusing the title 'Messiah', Jesus preferred to avoid it when speaking of himself. Instead he called himself the Son of man. This was a title that had little meaning to most people (they probably thought Jesus used it simply to mean 'I' or 'me'), but it had a special meaning to those who understood the true nature of Jesus' messiahship (see SON OF MAN).

Just as Jesus opposed Satan who tempted him with the prospect of an earthly kingdom, so he opposed those who wanted him to be king because they thought he could bring them political and material benefits (John 6:15,26; cf. Matt 4:8-10). When other Jews, by contrast, recognized Jesus as the Messiah in the true sense of the word, Jesus told them not to broadcast the fact. He was familiar with the popular messianic ideas, and he did not want people to misunderstand the nature of his mission (Matt 9:27-30; 16:13-20). He did not place the same restrictions on non-Jews, for there was little danger that non-Jews would use his messiahship for political purposes (Mark 5:19; John 4:25-26).

Later in his ministry, when he knew that his work was nearing completion and the time for his crucifixion was approaching, Jesus allowed people to speak openly of him as the Messiah (Matt 21:14-16). He even entered Jerusalem as Israel's Messiah-king and accepted people's homage (Matt 21:1-11). But when he admitted before the high priest Caiaphas that he was the Messiah, adding a statement that placed him on equality with God, he was accused of blasphemy and condemned to death (Mark 14:61-64). When asked by the governor Pilate if he was a king, Jesus agreed that he was, though not the sort of king Pilate had in mind (Matt 27:11; John 18:33-37; cf. Acts 17:7).

The Messiah's death and resurrection

Even true believers of Jesus' time still thought of the Messiah solely in relation to the establishment of God's kingdom throughout the world at the end of the age. Because of this, many believers were puzzled when Jesus did not immediately set up a world-conquering kingdom (Matt 11:2-3; Luke 24:21; Acts 1:6). Jesus pointed out that with his coming, God's kingdom had come; the messianic age had begun. He was the Messiah, and his miracles of healing were proof of this (Isa 35:5-6; 61:1; Matt 11:4-5; Luke 4:18; 18:35-43).

What the disciples could not understand was that the Messiah should die. Like most Jews they knew of the Old Testament prophecies concerning God's suffering servant (Isa 49:7; 50:6; 52:13-53:12; see SERVANT OF THE LORD), just as they knew of the prophecies concerning God's Messiah, but they did not connect the two. Jesus showed that he was both the suffering servant and the Messiah. In fact, it was in response to his disciples' confession of him as the Messiah that he told them he must die (Matt 16:13-23; 17:12; Mark 10:45; Acts 4:27).

Immediately after this, at the transfiguration, the Father confirmed that Jesus was both Davidic Messiah and suffering servant. He did this by an announcement that combined a statement from a messianic psalm with a statement from one of the servant songs of Isaiah (Matt 17:5; Ps 2:7; Isa 42:1; cf. also Matt 3:17).

The idea of a crucified Messiah was contrary to common Jewish beliefs. The Jews considered the Messiah as blessed by God above all others, whereas a crucified person was cursed by God (Gal 3:13). That is why the Christians' belief in a crucified Jesus as the Saviour-Messiah was a stumbling block to the Jews (see STUMBLING BLOCK).

Jesus' resurrection provided the solution to this apparent difficulty. Even the disciples did not understand when Jesus foretold his resurrection (Mark 8:29-33; 9:31-32), but afterwards they looked back on the resurrection as God's final great confirmation that Jesus was the Messiah (Luke 24:45-46; Acts 2:31-32,36). He was God's anointed one (Acts 10:38; cf. Isa 61:1; Luke 4:18).

Title and name

So firmly was the Messiah identified with Jesus after his resurrection, that the Greek word for Messiah (Christ) became a personal name for Jesus. The two names were often joined as Jesus Christ or Christ Jesus, and frequently the name 'Christ' was used without any direct reference to messiahship at all (Phil 1:15-16,18,21). In general the Gospels and the early part of Acts use 'Christ' mainly as a title ('Messiah'), and Paul's letters use it mainly as a name.

In the eyes of unbelieving Jews, Jesus was not the Messiah, and therefore they would not call him Jesus Christ. They called him Jesus of Nazareth, and his followers they called Nazarenes (Matt 26:71; John 18:4-7; Acts 24:5). To unbelieving non-Jews, however, the Jewish notion of messiahship meant nothing. To them 'Christ' was merely the name of a person, and the followers of this person they called Christians (Acts 11:26). (See also JESUS CHRIST.)

MICAH

The best known of several Micahs in the Bible story is the prophet whose book is part of the Old Testament (Micah 1:1; Jer 26:18). (For details of this Micah see MICAH, BOOK OF).

Another prophet had a variation of the same name, Micaiah. He lived in the time of King Ahab of Israel, and Ahab hated him. Whereas the other court prophets said only those things that pleased Ahab, Micaiah spoke the truth, whether Ahab liked it or not (1 Kings 22:5-9). When he told Ahab that a coming battle would bring defeat, Ahab threw him into prison. The outcome proved (as Micaiah had asserted) that he spoke the truth and that the other prophets were liars (1 Kings 22:13-36).

An earlier Micah lived in the time covered by the book of Judges. He was a thief and an idol worshipper whom his mother made priest of her household shrine. But Micah did not come from the priestly tribe, so when a Levite happened to visit his house, Micah made him priest instead (Judg 17:1-13). After some time, representatives of the tribe of Dan stopped at Micah's house while on a journey north in search of a new tribal homeland (Judg 18:1-6). When the Danites later moved north to settle, they again visited Micah. On this occasion they raided his shrine, robbed him of his images, and threatened him with death when he resisted (Judg 18:11-26). They then continued their journey and established Micah's idolatrous religion in their new homeland (Judg 18:27,31).

MICAH, BOOK OF

Of the four eighth century prophets whose writings have been preserved in the Old Testament, Micah was the last. Amos and Hosea had brought God's message mainly to the northern kingdom Israel, whereas Isaiah and Micah were more concerned with the southern kingdom Judah. The two men prophesied during the same period (Isa 1:1; Micah 1:1) and both were especially concerned with the sins of Jerusalem. The two books contain many similarities, and it has been suggested that Micah might have been one of Isaiah's disciples (cf. Isa 8:16).

Social conditions

With the prosperity of the eighth century came the social evils of greed, corruption, injustice and immorality. Those who profited most from the economic development were the merchants, officials and other upper class city dwellers. Corruption in the law courts made it easy for these people to do as they wished, while poorer class people found it impossible to gain even the most basic justice (Micah 3:9-11; 7:3).

Micah was particularly concerned with the injustice done to the poor farmers. He was from a farming village himself (Micah 1:1), and he saw that the corruption of Israel and Judah was centred in the capital cities, Samaria and Jerusalem (Micah 1:5; 6:9).

Because of the injustice of the officials and merchants with whom they had to deal, the farmers were forced to borrow from the wealthy to keep themselves in business (Micah 3:1-3; 6:10-12). The wealthy lent them money at interest rates so high that the farmers found it impossible to pay their debts. The wealthy then seized the farmers' possessions as payment. First they seized their clothing and household items (Micah 2:8), then, when these were not sufficient, their houses and land (Micah 2:1-3,9). The farmers then had to rent back their land from their new masters, thereby increasing the farmers' burden even more.

These practices showed no knowledge of the character of God or the nature of true religion. The people still followed the sacrifices and ceremonies of the Israelite religion, but Micah warned that formal religion was hateful to God if justice and love were absent (Micah 6:6-8). Unless they repented, God would send the people into captivity and leave their homeland desolate (Micah 3:12; 6:16).

Religious leaders also were corrupt. Preachers had comforting words for the upper class people from whom they received their income, but they condemned the prophet Micah for his forthright speaking (Micah 2:6,11; 3:5). Hezekiah the king, however, heeded Micah's warnings. He managed to achieve some reformation in Judah, and as a result God postponed the day of judgment (Jer 26:18-19; cf. Micah 3:12).

Eventually, in the reign of a later king, the judgment fell. Yet Micah saw that beyond the judgment lay the hope of a restored nation, a glorious kingdom and an ideal king (Micah 2:12-13; 4:1-4; 5:2,4).

Summary of the book

From his prophetic viewpoint, Micah gives a picture of the judgment about to fall on Israel and Judah (1:1-16). He goes on to point out that the reason for the judgment is the oppression of the poor by the corrupt leaders (2:1-3:12). But, looking further ahead, he sees that after captivity in a foreign land, Israel's shame will be replaced by glory (4:1-5:1), and God's chosen king will reign over his people in an ideal kingdom (5:2-15). Returning to the present, Micah announces God's accusations against his people (6:1-16), then confesses their sin to God and pleads for God's mercy (7:1-20).

MICHAEL

In all the biblical references to him, Michael the archangel is in conflict with the enemies of God's people. When, in the time of Daniel, the Jews suffered a number of setbacks because of opposition from the ruling Persian authorities, Michael came to the Jews' rescue. An evil spirit was behind the rulers of Persia and had prevented a messenger of God from reaching Daniel, but the good spirit Michael overpowered the evil spirit and freed the heavenly messenger (Dan 10:12-14).

The messenger knew that later he would be opposed by an evil spirit working on behalf of Greece (the nation that would succeed Persia as the Jews' ruler), but he was confident that Michael's help would again bring him victory (Dan 10:20-21). Opposition to the Jews would increase, but God's people could always depend on Michael to fight for them (Dan 12:1).

Among Jewish writings of the period between the Old and New Testaments, there are a number that mention Michael. One of the New Testament writers, Jude, refers to an incident from one of these books to illustrate a point in his message. Satan had claimed that Moses' body belonged to him, but Michael again fought on behalf of the man of God (Jude 9).

Michael is mentioned also in the visions of the book of Revelation. The context concerns conflict in the spirit world, with Michael and his angels fighting on behalf of God's people against the devil and his angels. The vision reassures the persecuted people of God that the final victory will be theirs (Rev 12:7-9). (See also ANGELS.)

MICHAL

When Michal, the younger daughter of King Saul, fell in love with David, Saul promised her to David as wife, provided David could kill one hundred Philistines as the bride-price. Saul, being jealous of David, hoped David would be killed in the attempt, but David was spectacularly successful (1 Sam 18:20-27).

Not long after the marriage, Saul laid a plot to kill David in David's house, but Michal's quick thinking saved him (1 Sam 19:11-17). When David was forced to flee from Saul, Saul took Michal and gave her as wife to another man, Paltiel (1 Sam 25:44).

After Saul died, David came out of hiding and was proclaimed king, though some of Saul's former followers disputed his right to the throne. David then forced Michal's return to him as his wife. This strengthened his claim to Saul's throne, but it left Paltiel broken-hearted (2 Sam 3:13-16). There seems to have been no revival of Michal's original love for

David. She was actually hostile to him when he danced for joy at bringing the ark to Jerusalem. She bore him no children (2 Sam 6:16,20-23).

MIDIAN

The Midianites were a nomad people descended from Abraham and his concubine Keturah (Gen 25:1-2). They inhabited the dry barren lands on the western edge of the Arabian desert, extending around the Gulf of Aqabah and into the Sinai Peninsular. They lived in tents, kept sheep and

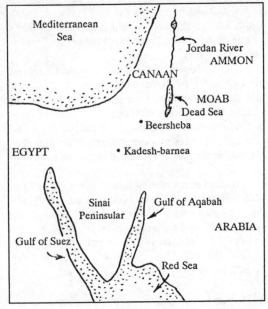

travelled on camels (Judg 6:1,5-6; Isa 60:6; Hab 3:7). From early days they seem to have mingled with the Ishmaelites, who were descended from Abraham through another woman, the slave-girl Hagar (Gen 25:12; 37:28,36; Judg 8:24-26).

Moses lived with a Midianite family after he fled from Egypt. The head of the family, Reuel (or Jethro), was a prominent tribal chief, and Moses married one of his daughters (Exod 2:15-21). Some years later, Hobab, Moses' Midianite brother-in-law, helped guide the travelling Israelites through some of the semi-desert country where he had grown up (Num 10:29-32). Moses' in-laws are also called Kenites, indicating that the section of Midian to which they belonged had intermarried with the Kenites, one of the ancient peoples of Canaan (Gen 15:19; Judg 1:16; 4:11).

When the Israelites were approaching Canaan, the Midianites, fearful of Israel's power, combined firstly with the Moabites and then with the Amorites in opposing Israel's progress. They were beaten by the Israelites twice (Num 22:4,7; 25:6-18; 31:1-12; Josh 13:21). They raided Israel repeatedly during the time of the Judges but were eventually overthrown by Gideon (Judg 6:1-6; 7:24-25; Isa 9:4; 10:26; see GIDEON).

MILCOM

See MOLECH.

MILETUS

On the west coast of southern Asia Minor were the important towns of Miletus and Ephesus. They were about fifty kilometres apart and fell within the Roman province of Asia. (For map and other details see ASIA.)

When Paul visited Miletus towards the end of his third missionary journey, he invited the elders of the church at Ephesus to come and meet him at Miletus. He gave them some important instructions and warnings and then left for Jerusalem (Acts 20:15-17). He visited the town on at least one other occasion, not long before his final imprisonment and execution (2 Tim 4:20).

MILLENNIUM

The word 'millennium' means 'a thousand years'. Though not found in the Bible, the word refers to the thousand years mentioned in one of the visions of the book of Revelation (Rev 20:4-6).

Symbolism in Revelation

Revelation belongs to a type of literature known as apocalyptic, where teaching is given in the form of strange visions with symbolic meanings (see APOCALYPTIC LITERATURE). Readers of the first century, being familiar with that type of literature, probably understood the visions without too much difficulty. Readers of later generations have had much greater difficulty, and this has resulted in a variety of interpretations of the details of the book (see REVELATION, BOOK OF).

Among the interpretations of Revelation 20:4-6 there have been three main viewpoints, popularly called amillennial, premillennial and postmillennial. Because of the book's apocalyptic characteristics, which involve angelic beings, strange beasts and mysterious numbers, many interpreters hesitate to measure off an exact period of one thousand years calculated to the year, month and day. There is considerable agreement, however, that the thousand years represent a long period, whether precisely measured or not.

The different viewpoints are largely concerned with determining what the thousand years reign of Christ refers to (v. 4), and this in turn is tied up with the meaning of the words 'came to life' (v. 4-5). Also, the different viewpoints usually consider these matters in relation to the return of Christ, even though Revelation 20 does not mention the return of Christ.

Thousand years reign with Christ

Those who believe that the thousand years reign of Christ refers to his present exaltation in glory are called amillennialists (a meaning 'without'), because they do not believe that the vision refers to a literal reign of Christ on earth. They consider that the martyrs who 'come to life' and reign with Christ are believers of the present Christian era. Through their union with Christ in his death and resurrection, they have already been made alive and made to sit with him in the heavenly places (Eph 2:1,6). According to this view, the other 'coming to life', which takes place at the end of the thousand years, refers to a resurrection of all mankind that takes place at the return of Christ. This resurrection leads to final judgment (Acts 24:15). God's people then enter with him into the full enjoyment of the eternal age (Rev 21:1-4).

By contrast, other interpreters consider that the thousand years reign of Christ refers to a literal reign on earth. Since Christ must return to earth before (pre) this reign can begin, they are called premillennialists. They consider that the martyrs who 'come to life' and reign with Christ are believers who are raised to life at Christ's return (1 Cor 15:51-52; 1 Thess 4:16). According to this view, the other 'coming to life', which takes place at the end of the thousand years, refers to a second resurrection. This occurs at the end of the earthly millennium, when the wicked are raised to face final judgment (John 5:28-29). After this comes the eternal age, where God and his redeemed people dwell together in unending joy (Rev 21:1-4).

The postmillennial view is that Christ will return after (post) the millennium. This view is not as widely held as the two previous views. It has similarities with the amillennial view in its interpretation of the two groups who 'come to life' and in its understanding that the thousand years reign of Christ does not refer to a literal reign on earth. However, it has a rather more optimistic view of life in the world prior to Christ's return. Whereas the amillennial and premillennial views expect greater opposition from the forces of antichrist (2 Thess 2:1-12), the postmillennial view expects an era of peace and contentment, brought about through the evangelization of the world. According to this view, the thousand years reign of Christ refers to the rule of the kingdom of God in the world (Matt 24:14; Rom 11:11-15).

Thousand years binding of Satan

In the visions of Revelation Chapter 20 the thousand years reign of Christ seems to correspond with the thousand years of Satan's imprisonment (Rev 20:1-3). At the end of this time Satan is released, then, after a brief but violent rebellion, destroyed (Rev 20:7-10).

The amillennial and postmillennial view understands the binding of Satan to refer to his conquest by Christ at the cross, so that man might no longer be enslaved by him (Heb 2:14-15; cf. Luke 10:17-18; 11:20-22). On this view, the rebellion of Satan refers to the great outbreak of evil by the forces of Satan at the end of the present age. The destruction of Satan comes, therefore, at the return of Christ (2 Thess 2:3-8; Rev 16:12-21).

The premillennial view understands the binding of Satan to refer to his inability to interfere during the coming earthly reign of Christ (Matt 25:31). On this view, the rebellion of Satan refers to a final attempt by Satan to overthrow Christ's kingly rule. The destruction of Satan comes, therefore, at the end of Christ's earthly reign (1 Cor 15:25-28).

The central truth

In spite of the different viewpoints concerning the thousand years reign of Christ, all are agreed that it speaks of the triumph of Christ that he shares with his people (Matt 19:28; Rom 5:17; Col 2:13-15; 2 Tim 2:12). All are agreed also that the return of Christ is the hope of the church, and that it encourages Christians to greater devotion, increased holiness and more enthusiastic evangelism (Matt 24:42; Luke 19:11-26; Acts 1:7-11; Titus 2:11-14; 1 John 3:2-3; 2 Peter 3:11-13). See also ANTICHRIST; DAY OF THE LORD; ESCHATOLOGY; HEAVEN; HELL; JUDGMENT; KINGDOM OF GOD; RESURRECTION; SECOND COMING.

MIND

Man, being made in the image of God, is different from all other animals (Gen 1:27; see IMAGE). One of the differences is that indefinable characteristic of man called the mind. Man's mind does not result solely from the fact that he has a brain, for other animals also have brains. There is something within man enabling him to commune with God, to think, to reason and to understand in a way that animals do not. The Bible sometimes calls this the mind, though frequently it calls it the heart (Prov 2:2-3; Heb 10:16; see HEART). The point that the Bible emphasizes is that because man has a mind he must think and behave differently from the other animals (Ps 32:8-9; Prov 1:2-6; 18:15; Matt 22:37; Phil 1:9-10; 1 Peter 1:13-15; 2 Peter 2:12-16; see KNOWLEDGE; WISDOM).

Like the rest of man's nature, the mind of man has become corrupted through sin (Rom 1:21; 8:7; 2 Cor 3:14; 4:4; Col 1:21; Eph 4:17-18). Therefore, when a person repents and believes the gospel, his mind is renewed because of his union with Jesus Christ (Rom 8:5-6; Eph 4:22-24). The believer must then show that this is so. He must develop a new attitude of mind, which will result in a new pattern of behaviour (Rom 12:2; 2 Cor 10:5; Phil 2:5; 4:8; Col 3:2,10; 1 Peter 4:1).

This use of the mind is to be seen not only in the way believers behave, but also in the way they worship and serve God. They must use their minds to pray and sing intelligently (1 Cor 14:15; Col 3:16; see PRAYER; SINGING), to understand Christian teaching (Prov 2:1-5; 1 Cor 2:11-13; 2 Tim 2:7; see INTERPRETATION), to find out God's will (Rom 12:2; Eph 5:17; Col 1:9; see GUIDANCE), to preach the gospel effectively (Acts 17:2-4; 19:8-10; see PREACHING), and to teach the Scriptures in a way that will build up the hearers (Col 1:28; Titus 1:9; see TEACHER).

MINISTER

Christian ministry is a very broad subject and may be conveniently studied through looking at topics that deal with its various aspects. According to its most common biblical usage, 'ministry' simply means 'service'. A person who ministers to others is one who serves others; a minister of God is a servant of God (Deut 10:8; Ps 103:21; Joel 2:17; Matt 8:15; 25:44; 27:55; 2 Cor 3:6; 6:4; 11:15,23; for details see SERVANT).

Different forms of the biblical word translated 'minister' denote a variety of people and the work they do in the church (Rom 12:7; Eph 6:21; Col 4:17; Heb 6:10; see GIFTS OF THE SPIRIT). The same word, transliterated 'deacon', refers to a recognized class of church helpers (Phil 1:1; 1 Tim 3:8; see DEACON). The pastoral leaders of the church, who are distinct from the deacons, are also ministers (Eph 4:11-12; Col 1:7; 1 Tim 1:12; 2 Tim 4:5; see APOSTLE; ELDER; TEACHER; PREACHING). The perfect minister, who is an example to all others, is Jesus Christ (Matt 20:28; John 13:14-16; Rom 15:8).

MIRACLES

God is shown in the Bible to be a God of miracles. But miracles do not feature consistently throughout the biblical record. Rather they are grouped largely around three main periods.

The first of these periods was the time of the Israelites' bondage in Egypt, which challenged God's purposes to establish his people as an independent nation. By mighty acts God saved his people and brought them into the land he had promised them (Deut 4:34-35; Josh 4:23-24). The second period was that of Elijah and Elisha, when Israel's religion was threatened with destruction. By some unusual miracles God preserved the minority who remained faithful to him, and acted in judgment against those who tried to wipe out the worship of Yahweh from Israel (1 Kings 19:15-18). The third period was that of the coming of the kingdom of God through Jesus Christ and the establishment of his church through those to whom he had given his special power (Acts 2:22; 3:6; 4:10; 1 Cor 12:10,28-29; 2 Cor 12:12).

Of all the miracles, the greatest are those that concern the birth and resurrection of Jesus. God's act in becoming man is itself a miracle so great that it overshadows the means by which it happened, namely, the miraculous conception in the womb of a virgin (Matt 1:18-23; John 1:14; see VIRGIN). The resurrection is a miracle so basic to the Christian faith that without it there can be no Christian faith (1 Cor 15:12-14; see RESURRECTION).

Miracles and nature

If we believe in a personal God who created and controls the world (Gen 1:1; Col 1:16-17), we should have no trouble in believing the biblical record of the miracles he performed. The physical creation is not something self-sufficient or mechanical, as if it were like a huge clock that, once wound up, runs on automatically till finally God stops it. The God of creation is a living God who is active in his creation (John 5:17).

God deals with people as responsible beings whom he has placed in a world where everything is in a state of constant change. Being sensitive to the needs of his creatures, he may work in his creation in an extraordinary, even miraculous, way for their benefit (Exod 17:6; Josh 10:11-14; 2 Kings 4:42-44; Mark 6:47-51).

On the other hand, God does not work miracles every time someone wants him to. If he did there would be chaos. God's control of the universe is designed to produce order (Job 38:4-41; 39:1-30; Ps 147:8-9,16-18; Matt 5:45).

Since God is the controller of nature, he may have performed many of his miraculous works not by doing something 'contrary to nature', but by using the normal workings of nature in a special way. The miracle was in the timing, extent or intensity of the event.

Such divine activity may help to explain events such as the plagues of Egypt, the crossing of the Red Sea, the crossing of the Jordan River, the collapse of Jericho's walls and some of the healings performed by Jesus. But even if these can be explained as having natural causes, they were still miracles to those who saw them. They happened as predicted, even though the chances of their so happening appeared to be almost nil (Exod 7:17; 8:2; Josh 3:8-13).

This still leaves unexplained the large number of miracles for which there seem to be no natural causes. Such supernatural interventions by God are not attacks on the so-called laws of nature. What we call the laws of nature are not forces that make things happen, but statements of what man has discovered concerning how nature works. It is God who makes things happens; the 'laws of nature' merely summarize the processes by which such things happen. When God acts supernaturally, his actions may be contrary to the way man has usually seen nature work, but his actions do not break any laws of nature. They merely provide new circumstances through which nature works.

God is always the creator of life, the healer of diseases, the calmer of storms and the provider of food, whether he does so through the normal processes of nature or through some miraculous intervention. Through the ages God has sent the rain to water the grapes to produce the wine, but he may choose to hasten the process by turning water into wine immediately (John 2:1-11). God has also at times withheld the rain and so caused trees gradually to dry up, but again he may choose to intervene and hasten the process (Matt 21:18-19).

The purpose of miracles

Miracles were usually 'signs', that is, works of God that revealed his power and purposes (Exod 7:3; Deut 4:34; Isa 7:11; Matt 16:1; John 2:11; 6:14; 20:30; Acts 2:43; see SIGNS). However, men of God never used miracles just to impress people or to persuade people to believe them (Matt 12:38-39; Luke 23:8). It was the false prophet who used apparent miracles to gain a following (Deut 13:1-3; Matt 24:24; 2 Thess 2:9-11; Rev 13:13-14). God's miracles were usually linked with faith (2 Kings 3:1-7; Dan 3:16-18; 6:22; Heb 11:29-30).

This was clearly seen in the miracles of Jesus Christ. Jesus used miracles not to try to force people to believe in him, but to help those who already believed. He performed miracles in response to faith, not to try to create faith (Matt 9:27-29; Mark 2:3-5; 5:34,36; 6:5-6). Frequently, Jesus told those whom he had healed not to spread the news of his miraculous work. He did not want to be bothered by people who wanted to see a wonder-worker but who felt no spiritual need themselves (Matt 9:30; Mark 5:43; 8:26).

Nevertheless, it is clear that many of those who saw Jesus' miracles were filled with awe and glorified God (Matt 9:8; Luke 5:26; 7:16; 9:43). To those who believed in Jesus as the Son of God and the Messiah, the miracles confirmed the truth of their beliefs and revealed to them something of God's glory (John 2:11; 11:40; Acts 14:3; Heb 2:3-4; see MESSIAH). There was a connection between the miracles of Jesus and the era of the Messiah. This may explain why miracles were common in the early church but almost died out once the original order of apostles died out (Matt 10:5-8; Luke 9:1; 10:9; Acts 4:16,29-30; 5:12; Rom 15:19; 1 Cor 12:9-10; 2 Cor 12:12).

In the record of some of Jesus' miracles there is no mention of faith. It seems that on those occasions Jesus acted purely out of compassion (Matt 8:14-15; 14:13-14; 15:32; Luke 4:40; 7:11-17; John 6:1-13); though, as always, he refused to satisfy people who wanted him to perform miracles for their own selfish purposes (John 6:14-15).

Jesus' miracles demonstrated clearly that he was the Messiah, the Son of God (John 20:30-31), and that the power of the Spirit of God worked through him in a special way (Matt 12:28; Luke 4:18). Being both God and man, he had on the one hand authority and power to work miracles, but on the other he always acted in dependence upon his Father (John 5:19; 14:10-11). His miracles were always in keeping with his mission as the Saviour of the world. They were never of the senseless or unbelievable type such as we find in fairy stories. Jesus did not perform miracles as if they were acts of magic, and he never performed them for his own benefit (cf. Matt 4:2-10).

Jesus' miracles and the kingdom of God

In Jesus the kingdom of God had come among mankind. The rule of God was seen in the miracles by which Jesus the Messiah delivered from the power of Satan people who were diseased and oppressed by evil spirits (Matt 4:23-24; 11:2-6; 12:28; see KINGDOM OF GOD). This victory over Satan was a guarantee of the final conquest of Satan when the kingdom of God will reach its triumphant climax at the end of the world's history (Rev 20:10).

To Christians, Jesus' miracles foreshadow the age to come. His raising of the dead prefigures the final conquest of death (Matt 11:5; John 11:24-27,44; 1 Cor 15:24-26; Rev 21:4). His healing miracles give hope for a day when there will be no more suffering (Matt 9:27-29; Mark 1:40-42; Rev 21:4). His calming of the storm foreshadows the final perfection of the natural creation (Matt 8:24-27; Rom 8:19-21). His provisions of food and wine give a foretaste of the great banquet of God in the day of the kingdom's triumph (John 2:1-11; Matt 14:15-21; 15:32-38; 26:29; Rev 19:9).

MIRIAM

Most likely the unnamed sister who looked after the baby Moses was Miriam (Exod 2:1-8). She was the eldest of three children who grew up to play a leading part in the establishment of Israel as a new and independent nation (1 Chron 6:3; Micah 6:4). She was a prophetess, and led the celebration that followed Israel's victory over Egypt at the Red Sea (Exod 15:19-21).

Later, Miriam and Aaron became jealous of Moses because of the supreme power he exercised in Israel (Num 12:1-2). Miriam was chiefly to blame, and God punished her with a sudden outbreak of leprosy; but when Moses prayed for her, she was healed. However, just as a daughter who had been publicly rebuked by her father had to spend seven days in shame, so did Miriam. Seven days was also the normal period of isolation for the cleansed leper (Num 12:9-15; cf. Lev 14:8).

Miriam died in the wilderness between Egypt and Canaan. She was buried at Kadesh-barnea (Num 20:1).

MISSION

God has entrusted to his people the task, or mission, of spreading the message of his salvation to the world. The people who carry out this mission are therefore called missionaries. The present article uses the words 'mission' and 'missionary' in this broad sense, and not as technical names for specific organizations or people who work full time in church-sponsored activities in foreign countries.

Mission is necessary because man's sin has cut him off from the life of God and left him in the power of Satan (Gen 3:24; Rom 1:21-25; John 3:19; Gal 5:19-21; 1 John 5:19). God, however, has made a

way of salvation (and it is the only way; John 3:16; 14:6; Acts 4:12; Rom 5:17), but if the people of the world are to receive this salvation, God's people must first of all tell them about it (Rom 10:13-15; 2 Cor 5:18-19).

The Bible records the development of God's plan for the salvation of man worldwide. God chose one man (Abraham) to father one particular nation (Israel) through whom God's blessing would go to all nations. Israel was to be God's representative in bringing the nations of the world to know him (Gen 12:2-3; 22:18; Exod 19:5-6; Isa 49:6; Zech 8:22-23). Although Israel as a whole failed to carry out its task, out of it came one person, Jesus Christ, who was the Saviour of the world (Luke 2:10-11; Gal 3:16). He built a new people of God, the Christian church, to whom he entrusted the mission of taking the message of his salvation to people everywhere (Matt 28:19-20; Acts 1:8; 13:47).

Jesus and world mission

Israel failed to be God's light to the nations, partly because the people were so self-satisfied in their status as God's chosen people that they had no concern for others. They considered themselves assured of God's blessing, and the Gentile nations assured of his judgment; but in this they deceived themselves (Jonah 4:2,11; Matt 3:9; Rom 2:25-29; 3:29; 9:6-7,15).

Despite Israel's failure, it was still the nation God chose and prepared to produce the world's Saviour. Jesus therefore announced his salvation to Israel before spreading the message farther afield among the Gentiles (Matt 15:24; cf. 4:23; 13:54). He instructed the twelve apostles to do likewise (Matt 10:5-6). (For the mission of the twelve during the lifetime of Jesus see APOSTLE.) Even Paul, who was not one of the original twelve, believed he had an obligation to preach to the Jews first (Acts 13:46; 18:6; Rom 1:16).

Jesus had always anticipated a wider mission to the Gentiles (Matt 8:11-12; 21:43; 28:19; John 10:16; 20:21). He told his disciples, and through them the church, to look upon the initial work in Palestine as the foundation for a wider reaching work into the Gentile world (Luke 24:46-47; Acts 1:8). He encouraged a sense of urgency in this mission by saying that he would return and bring in the new age only after his followers had preached the gospel worldwide (Matt 24:14).

Planting churches in new areas

The New Testament record of the expansion of the early church shows the sort of work the church must be prepared for if it is to fulfil its mission. Of first importance is the personal life and testimony of the Christians themselves. Through their witness the gospel spreads (Acts 8:4-6; 11:19-21; Col 1:7). But God wants more than to save people. He wants to see them baptized, made disciples of Jesus, instructed in Christian teaching and built into local churches (Matt 28:19-20; John 17:20-21; Acts 1:8; 2:41-47; 11:26; Col 1:25,28; see BAPTISM; DISCIPLE; TEACHER).

While all Christians should bear witness to Jesus, God chooses and equips certain people for the specific task of breaking into unevangelized areas with the gospel (Acts 9:15; Rom 10:14-15; 15:20; 2 Cor 10:16; Gal 1:16; see EVANGELIST). As a church recognizes such gifted people, it may send them out to devote their whole time to preaching the gospel, making disciples and planting churches. In doing so, the home church becomes a partner with its missionaries in the gospel (Acts 13:1-4; 14:27; 16:1-2; 18:22-23; cf. Phil 1:5).

Paul was a missionary sent by a church into unevangelized areas, and his example shows that the missionary must have plans and goals. Like Paul, the missionary may make no attempt to preach in every town and village, but concentrate on planting churches in the main population centres (Acts 13:14; 14:1,8,20; 16:12; 18:1; 19:1). These churches then have the responsibility to spread the gospel into the surrounding regions, though they will be able to do so only if they themselves are spiritually healthy (Acts 13:49; 19:8-10; 1 Thess 1:8).

Whatever his strategy, the missionary must also be flexible. He must be sensitive to God's will in changing situations, and be prepared to alter his plans if God so directs (Acts 16:6-10; 18:21; 1 Cor 16:7-9,12).

Adapting to different situations

There is only one gospel, but its presentation may be adapted to the background and needs of different audiences. Paul's preaching in the Jewish synagogues differed from his preaching to non-Jewish idolaters (Acts 13:14-41; 14:11-17; 17:22-31). Nevertheless, it is often the case that those who appear ready-made to accept the gospel refuse it (e.g. Jews who already knew the Bible; Acts 13:45; 14:1-2; 17:1-5,13), and the most unlikely people accept it (e.g. idolaters, robbers, adulterers and perverts; Acts 19:18-20,26; 1 Cor 6:9-11).

Christianity must not be identified with one level of society or one race. There should not therefore be an emphasis on one class of people to the neglect of the rest (Acts 16:14; 17:4,12; 18:3,7-8;

1 Cor 1:26; 2 Cor 8:1-2; Eph 2:14-15; 1 Tim 6:1-2,17). Nor should there be an emphasis on one type of proclamation to the neglect of the rest (1 Cor 9:22). The missionary may make the gospel known through preaching, discussion, debating or teaching; he may use religious buildings, public places or private homes; he may deal with mass audiences, small groups or individual enquirers (Acts 2:40-41; 5:25; 6:9-10; 8:27-29; 11:12; 14:1; 16:13,32; 17:19; 20:22; 21:39-40; 28:17).

The time that the missionary spends in one centre may vary from a few weeks to a few years (Acts 17:2; 18:11; 20:31). Patience is necessary, but that does not mean that the person must remain indefinitely in one place preaching the gospel to unresponsive people, when people in other places have not yet heard (Matt 10:11-14; Acts 13:51; 17:13-14; 19:8-9).

Independence of new churches

To avoid making a church dependent on him, the person who plants the church should be careful about starting programs that can only operate if he is there permanently (Acts 18:20; 20:38; 1 Cor 2:5). He should concentrate on making the Christians true disciples who can carry on the work of Christ, both in helping the church and in reaching out to the lost (Matt 28:19; Eph 4:11-13). In particular he should train those who show signs of being gifted for the more important ministries of the church (2 Tim 2:2; see GIFTS OF THE SPIRIT).

Having taught the Christians to trust in the Lord, the missionary must show that he also trusts in the Lord, by leaving them to learn by experience how to live as Christ's people (Acts 14:23; 20:32). If he has built up the new Christians in the knowledge of God and his Word (Acts 11:26; 20:27), they will be able to maintain their Christian commitment after he has gone. They should even be able to spread the gospel into the surrounding regions (Acts 13:49,52; 19:10; 1 Thess 1:8-10).

Though the founder of the church may leave it, he does not abandon it. Through letters, visits and periods of temporary residence he can help it to grow (Acts 15:36; 20:2-3; 1 Cor 5:9; 7:1; 16:5,12).

Each church, if it is to stand by itself, must also be able to govern itself. God has provided for the leadership of local churches through giving certain people the necessary abilities to be elders. The founder of the church has the responsibility to appoint such leaders in the church (Acts 14:23; 20:17; Titus 1:5; see ELDER). (Concerning Paul's exercise of authority in the churches he established, see APOSTLE.)

People in different churches will pray, sing, teach and worship in a variety of ways, depending on their background and culture. When the missionary plants a church in a culture different from his own, he must not impose his culture upon the new Christians, but encourage them to find suitable ways of expressing their newfound faith (cf. 1 Cor 16:20; Col 3:16-17).

Christianity can function in any age and in any culture. The New Testament is not a book of rules giving instructions on the practical details of church procedures, but a collection of stories and letters providing guidance for a Spirit-directed people (Acts 20:28; 1 Cor 2:12-13; 6:5; 7:6,40; Phil 1:9). Flexibility will enable the missionary to change patterns of activity to meet the needs of different types of people (Acts 15:10; 1 Cor 9:20-23; Gal 2:12-14). (For the principles of church life that should guide those who establish new churches see CHURCH.)

When establishing a church in a new area, the missionary may choose not to accept financial support from the local people, to avoid being a burden or creating misunderstanding (1 Cor 9:12; 2 Cor 12:14-18). He might choose to do part-time secular work to help support himself, or receive gifts of money from churches elsewhere (Acts 18:3; 20:33-34; 2 Cor 11:7-9; Phil 4:15-18; 1 Thess 2:5,9; 2 Thess 3:7-8).

Evangelism and social concern

Jesus demonstrated true Christian love by helping the poor, the sick, the despised and the victims of injustice. He taught his disciples to do likewise (Matt 8:2-3,6-7; 9:11; 25:34-35; Mark 8:1-2; 12:40; Luke 10:36-37; James 5:1-6; 1 John 3:17).

Following Jesus, the early missionaries saw people not merely as souls to be saved, but as people whose bodies and minds were also in need. They were concerned for the whole person, not just part of the person. They therefore accompanied their preaching with acts of compassion, and taught the newly founded churches the social responsibilities that the gospel placed upon them (Acts 5:12; 9:34; 16:16-18; Rom 13:8-10; Gal 2:10; 6:10; 1 Tim 5:3-5; 6:18; James 1:27).

Like Jesus, however, the early missionaries did not carry out their practical ministries or use their miraculous powers as a method of evangelism. They did not do good deeds for people simply to try to convert them. They did good deeds because it was their Christian duty to do so, whether or not the people were Christians or even likely to become Christians (Acts 3:6; 5:15-16; 19:11-12; 28:8-9; James 2:15-16; see GOOD WORKS; MIRACLES).

As Christians carry on the mission that Jesus started, they show people the type of world that God wants. They work towards the goal that God has for the removal of all the effects of sin, not only in individuals and human society but also in the world of nature (Rom 8:19-23; Rev 21:4; 22:1-2; see JUSTICE; NATURE).

But the root of the world's problems is man's sin, and the basic task of the church's mission is to make known the gospel of Jesus Christ. The gospel is God's provision to deal with man's sin. As people respond to that gospel, they come into a right relationship with God, and then set about producing character and behaviour that is in keeping with their Christian faith (Matt 28:19-20; Luke 24:47; Acts 1:8; Rom 1:16; 15:20; Titus 3:8).

MIZPAH

The name Mizpah came from a common Hebrew word meaning 'watchtower' or 'watchpost', and was given to a number of places referred to in the Bible. The earliest mention is to a place that features in the story of Jacob where he and Laban made an agreement not to be treacherous to each other in future. They called the place Mizpah, since God was witness to their agreement, the one who 'watched' between them (Gen 31:44-50).

In relation to the history of the nation Israel, the most important town that had the name Mizpah was in the central hill country of Palestine. It was one of four administrative and religious centres that Samuel visited on his annual circuit (1 Sam 7:5-12,16). The town was located in the tribal area of Benjamin and had previously featured in one of the most disastrous events in Benjamin's early history (Judg 20:1-7; 21:1-8). Israel's first king, Saul, who was from the tribe of Benjamin, was publicly declared king in Mizpah (1 Sam 10:17-24; for map see BENJAMIN).

During the period of the divided kingdom, Mizpah became an important defence outpost on Judah's northern border with Israel (1 Kings 15:22). After the destruction of Jerusalem it became the centre from which Gedaliah, the governor appointed by Babylon, administered the scattered remains of the former kingdom (2 Kings 25:23,25; Jer 40:6-16; 41:1-18).

Other places in Palestine named Mizpah were near Mount Hermon in the far north (Josh 11:3), in Gilead east of Jordan (Judg 10:17; 11:11,29,34), and in the low foothills west of the central highlands (Josh 15:38). There was also a Mizpah in Moab south-east of the Dead Sea (1 Sam 22:3).

MOAB

Among the peoples of the Palestine region who were related to the Israelites were the Moabites. They, along with the Ammonites, were descended from Lot through the children that resulted from Lot's immorality with his two daughters (Gen 19:36-38; see also AMMON). The Moabites lived in the tableland region east of the Jordan River and the Dead Sea, an area of good pastures suitable for raising

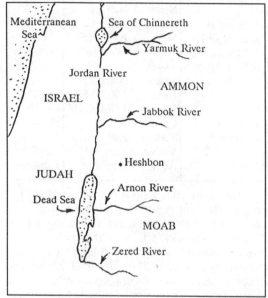

sheep (Num 22:1; 2 Kings 3:4; Isa 16:1-2). The Moabites' chief city was Heshbon (Isa 16:4; Jer 48:2) and their national god was Chemosh (Jer 48:7,46; see CHEMOSH).

Early history

Conflicts with other peoples of the region meant that Moab's boundaries changed from time to time. At the time Israel invaded Canaan, Moab controlled only the southern portion of the territory east of the Dead Sea — from the Arnon River south to the Zered River. All Moab's former territory north of the Arnon had been taken by the Amorite king Sihon, who then made Heshbon his capital (Num 21:13,26).

In leading the Israelites north towards Canaan, Moses reached the Arnon River without having any conflict with Moab (Num 21:10-13). Now that he was entering territory controlled by the Amorites, Moses asked their permission to travel along the well used road known as the King's Highway that passed through their territory (Num 21:21-22; Deut 2:26-29). When the Amorites responded with attack,

the Israelites crushed their army and seized their territory (Num 21:23-25; Deut 2:30-37; 29:7-8; see AMORITES).

The Moabites feared this Israelite advance. Previously they had refused to supply the Israelites with food and water, but now they increased their opposition. They hired a soothsayer named Balaam to put a curse on them, believing this would ensure their destruction (Num 22:1-6). Balaam was unable to put a curse on Israel, but God put a curse on Moab (Num 23:20-21; 24:17; Deut 23:3-6; see BALAAM).

Israel continued to advance, and eventually conquered Canaan. When all the conquered lands (on both sides of the Jordan) were divided among Israel's twelve tribes, the tribe of Reuben received the former Moabite territory that Israel had taken from the Amorites. The Arnon now became Israel's border with Moab (Deut 3:12,16).

Moab and Israel

During the time of the judges, Moab, with help from Ammon, exercised control over parts of Israel for eighteen years (Judg 3:12-14). The joint oppressors were finally overthrown by the Israelite hero, Ehud (Judg 3:15-30).

Moab had further conflict with Israel during the reign of Saul (1 Sam 14:47), and became subject to Israel's overlordship during the reign of David (2 Sam 8:2). After the decline of Israelite power through the division of the kingdom, Moab regained its independence (2 Kings 3:6-27), and gathered allies in an attempt to conquer Judah; but God saved his people (2 Chron 20:1-12,20-23).

In its arrogance, Moab repeatedly boasted of its glory and mocked God's people. As a result it brought upon itself the assurance of divine judgment (Isa 16:6-7,13; Jer 48:29-39; Zeph 2:8-11). Moab was among those whose raids helped to weaken Judah in the days of Babylon's final assault on Jerusalem (2 Kings 24:1-2), and so made its own destruction inevitable (Ezek 25:8-11).

God's prophet warned that when that day of judgment came, all Moab's desperate pleas for help would be useless (Isa 15:1-9; 16:1-7,12). The conquests by Babylon and Persia saw the prophecies of judgment fulfilled, and Moab's national existence came to an end (Jer 48:42).

Despite Moab's overall hostility to Israel, there were occasions when individual Moabites showed kindness to Israelites (e.g. 1 Sam 22:3-4). The most notable example was that of the young widow Ruth, who sacrificed her own interests to help her Israelite mother-in-law (Ruth 1:2-5,16-18; 2:1). Ruth later married an Israelite. She became an ancestress of Israel's King David, and therefore an ancestress of the Messiah Jesus (Ruth 4:13,17; Matt 1:1,5).

MOLECH

Molech (or Milcom) was the national god of the Ammonites, whose land bordered Israel's territory east of Jordan. A well known feature of the worship of Molech was the sacrifice of children by fire, a practice that in Israel carried the death penalty (Lev 18:21; 20:2-5; 2 Kings 23:10; Jer 32:35).

When Solomon married an Ammonite wife, he built a shrine for Molech, though there is no record of his using it to offer child sacrifices. The shrine was not destroyed till the reign of Josiah, three hundred years later (1 Kings 11:5,7; 2 Kings 23:10,13).

In spite of the penalties and warnings, there were many occasions throughout Israel's history when people were guilty of offering child sacrifices (Judg 10:6; 11:30-31,39; 2 Kings 17:17; 21:6; 2 Chron 28:1-3; Ps 106:38; Jer 7:31; Ezek 16:21; 20:31; 23:39). There is no record of child sacrifices by the Israelites after the Babylonian captivity.

MONEY

The Bible recognizes the possession and use of money as a legitimate part of life in human society. (Concerning the types of money in use in Bible times see COINS.) But the benefits that money brings are temporary, and those who become over-concerned with increasing their wealth eventually bring trouble upon themselves (Matt 6:19-23; 1 Tim 6:9-10; see WEALTH).

Poverty is not desirable either, and people should use their money to help those who are in need (Deut 15:7-10; James 2:15-16; see POOR). Christians have a responsibility to give their money generously, both as an offering to God and as a service to his work in the world (2 Cor 9:6-13; see GIVING).

MONTH

Records from the time of Solomon show that the Israelites followed a calendar of twelve months to the year (1 Kings 4:7). The successive months, however, do not correspond to the twelve successive months of the calendar used throughout most of the world today.

The Israelite year began with the new moon of mid-spring, which was some time during the second half of March on our calendar. Some of the names that the Israelites originally gave to the various

months were changed in later times. The list below contains both old and new names, depending on which is mentioned in the Bible. A common practice was to refer to a month by its number rather than by its name; for example, 'the fourth month' rather than 'Tammuz' (2 Kings 25:3).

Number	Name		Modern
1 Exod 12:2	Abib	Exod 23:15	Mar-Apr
	Nisan	Neh 2:1	
2 Gen 7:11	Ziv	1 Kings 6:1	Apr-May
3 Exod 19:1	Sivan	Esther 8:9	May-June
4 2 Kings 25:3	Tammuz		June-July
5 Num 33:38	Ab		July-Aug
6 1 Chron 27:9	Elul	Neh 6:15	Aug-Sep
7 Gen 8:4	Ethanim	1 Kings 8:2	Sep-Oct
8 Zech 1:1	Bul	1 Kings 6:38	Oct-Nov
9 Ezra 10:9	Chislev	Neh 1:1	Nov-Dec
10 Gen 8:5	Tebeth	Esther 2:16	Dec-Jan
11 Deut 1:3	Shebat	Zech 1:7	Jan-Feb
12 Esther 3:7	Adar	Ezra 6:15	Feb-Mar

The above table follows the calendar used for religious festivals, most of which were regulated according to the new moon and the full moon (Lev 23:6,24,39; Num 28:11). It seems that there was also a secular calendar, which differed from the religious calendar by six months. This meant that the first day of the seventh month of the religious calendar was New Year's Day on the secular calendar. In everyday speech people often referred to the time of the year not according to the number or name of the month, but according to the festival season (John 2:13; 5:1; 6:4; 7:2; Acts 2:1; 12:3; 20:6,16; see FESTIVALS).

MOON

From early times people recognized the importance of the moon, as well as the sun, in helping to produce a variety of weather and a cycle of regular seasons (Gen 1:14-18; Ps 104:19). Early calendars were based on the phases of the moon (see MONTH), and so were Israel's annual religious festivals (see FEASTS). The new moon marked the beginning of the month, and the full moon the middle of the month (Lev 23:24,39).

The day of each new moon was a holy day on which the Israelite people offered sacrifices and held a feast. Like other holy days, it was announced by the blowing of trumpets (Num 10:10; 28:11; 1 Sam 20:5; Ezra 3:5; Ps 81:3; Ezek 46:1). The Israelites were guilty of the same wrong attitudes towards the ceremonies of the new moon as towards other religious ceremonies, and as a result God's prophets condemned them (Isa 1:13-14; Hosea 2:11; Amos 8:5; cf. Col 2:16; see also SABBATH).

God strictly prohibited any worshipping of the moon. Again there were times when the Israelites broke his commandment (Deut 4:19; 2 Kings 23:4-5; Jer 8:1-2).

MORDECAI

Mordecai was a Jew who lived in the Persian capital and whose cousin Esther became queen to the Persian Emperor (Esther 2:5-7,17). Between them, Mordecai and Esther saved the Jewish people from threatened destruction, and Mordecai later became the Emperor's chief minister (Esther 10:3). (For details see ESTHER.)

MOSES

The life of Moses divides conveniently into three periods of forty years each. The first period ended with his flight from Egypt to Midian (Acts 7:23-29), the second with his return from Midian to liberate his people from Egyptian power (Acts 7:30-36; Exod 7:7), and the third with his death just before Israel entered Canaan (Deut 34:7).

As the leader God chose to establish Israel as a nation, Moses had absolute rule over Israel. God spoke to the people through him (Exod 3:10-12; 24:12; 25:22). Moses' position was unique. No other person of his time, and no leader after him, had the face-to-face relationship with God that Moses had (Exod 24:1-2; 33:11; Num 12:6-8; Deut 34:10).

Relations with Egypt

Moses was the third child of Amram and Jochabed, and belonged to the tribe of Levi. His older sister was Miriam and his older brother Aaron (Exod 6:20; 1 Chron 6:1-3). Through a series of remarkable events, the young child Moses was adopted into the Egyptian royal family but grew up under the influence of his godly Israelite mother (Exod 2:8-10; Heb 11:23). From his mother he learnt about the true and living God who had chosen Israel as his people, and from the Egyptians he received the best secular education available (Acts 7:22).

By the time he was forty, Moses was convinced God had chosen him to rescue Israel from Egypt. But his rash killing of an Egyptian slave-driver showed he was not yet ready for the job. To save his life he fled from Egypt to live among the Midianites, a nomadic people who inhabited a barren region that spread from the Sinai Peninsular around the Gulf of Aqabah into the western part of the Arabian Desert. By such a decisive act, Moses demonstrated his total rejection of his Egyptian status (Exod 2:11-15; Acts 7:23-29; Heb 11:24-25).

In Midian Moses lived with a local chief named Jethro (or Reuel), from whom he probably learnt much about desert life and tribal administration. He married one of Jethro's daughters, and from her had two sons (Exod 2:16-22; 18:1-3).

During Moses' forty years in Midian, Israel's sufferings in Egypt increased. God's time to deliver Israel from bondage had now come, and the person he would use as the deliverer was Moses (Exod 2:23-25; 3:1-12). Because the Israelites had only a vague understanding of God, Moses had to explain to them the character of this one who would be their redeemer. He, the Eternal One, would prove himself able to meet every need of his people, but they had to learn to trust in him (Exod 3:13-15; 6:2-8; see YAHWEH).

In response to Moses' complaint that the Israelites would not believe him, God gave him three signs (Exod 4:1-9,30). In response to his excuse that he was not a good speaker, God gave him Aaron as a spokesman (Exod 4:10-16; 7:1-2). Moses then returned to Egypt, where the elders of Israel welcomed him (Exod 4:20,29,31).

God warned Moses that his job would be difficult and that Pharaoh would not listen to his pleas for freedom for the Israelites (Exod 4:21-23). Pharaoh's response to Moses' initial meeting was to increase the Israelites' suffering, with the result that they turned bitterly against Moses (Exod 5:1-21). God gave Moses further assurance that Pharaoh would be defeated, but when Moses told the people, they were too disheartened to listen (Exod 6:1,9).

Moses again put his request to Pharaoh, and again Pharaoh refused (Exod 7:1-13). God therefore worked through Moses and Aaron to send a series of plagues upon Egypt, resulting in the overthrow of Egypt and the release of Israel (Exod 7:14-15:21; see PHARAOH; PLAGUE).

Israel's lawgiver

Having crossed the Red Sea, the Israelites headed through the semi-barren countryside for Mt Sinai. They complained constantly, sometimes because they had no water (Exod 15:23-25; 17:2-3), other times because they had no food (Exod 16:2-3). In each case God enabled Moses to satisfy their needs. He also answered Moses' prayer in giving victory over some raiding Amalekites (Exod 17:8-13).

When Jethro met Moses on the journey, he quickly saw that the heavy burden of leading the people was wearing Moses out. People brought even their minor personal disputes to Moses for his judgment (Exod 18:13-18). Jethro suggested that Moses share the load by appointing others to judge lesser cases, leaving Moses to judge only the more difficult ones. Moses heeded Jethro's advice, and so took the first steps in organizing the administration of Israel (Exod 18:19-27).

Jethro returned home, and the Israelites moved on to Mt Sinai. They remained there for the next year (Exod 19:1; Num 10:11), during which God prepared them for the life that lay ahead for them as an independent nation under his lordship.

There now had to be some recognized standard for the recently appointed officials to administer. God therefore gave the basic principles of the law in the form of ten simple commandments (Exod 20:1-17), which were probably the principles Moses had been using as his standard all the time. The

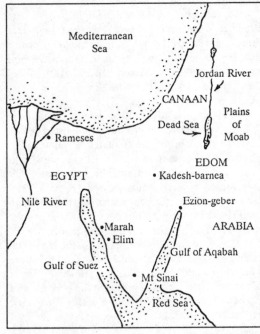

miscellaneous laws collected in the remainder of Exodus, and in the books of Leviticus, Numbers and Deuteronomy, were based on these principles. As Moses judged the cases brought before him, the people accepted his decisions as having the authority of God. Many of these decisions became the basis of laws for the future (Exod 18:16; Num 15:32-40; 27:5-11; see LAW).

Mediator of the covenant

God then formally established his covenant with Israel in a ceremony at Mt Sinai. Moses, who acted as the mediator or go-between, announced God's covenant commands to the people, and the people declared their willingness to obey. Moses sealed the covenant by blood, sprinkling half of it on the people and half of it against the altar (representing God) (Exod 24:3-8; see COVENANT). He took the leaders of the people with him up into the mountain, where they saw the glory of God, but Moses alone entered God's presence. He remained there about six weeks and received God's directions for the construction of the tabernacle and the institution of the priesthood (Exod 24:9-18; 25:40).

While Moses was absent on the mountain, the Israelites built an idol. God told Moses he would destroy the nation and build it afresh, using Moses as the new 'father'. Moses, thinking more of God's glory than his own fame, successfully pleaded with God not to destroy the people (Exod 32:11-14). Nevertheless, God could not ignore Israel's sin. When he allowed a limited judgment to fall upon the people, Moses again pleaded for them, even offering to die on their behalf (Exod 32:30-34).

In response to God's statement that he would not go to Canaan with such a rebellious people, Moses again pleaded for them. Once more God answered Moses' prayer, this time promising Moses his presence (Exod 33:1-3,12-16). This encouraged Moses to ask even more. He asked for a greater understanding of the nature of God, and God replied by revealing to him more of his character and glory (Exod 33:17-23). This revelation took place when Moses returned to the mountain to receive fresh copies of the law (Exod 34:1-9). His face became so dazzling because of his meeting with God that on certain occasions he had to cover it with a cloth (Exod 34:28-35; 2 Cor 3:7-18).

A patient leader

Moses' gracious response to Israel's disgraceful behaviour, both on the journey from Egypt and at Mt Sinai, showed that although he was a strong and decisive leader, he was not hot-headed or self-assertive. He was a humble man (Num 12:3), whose patience was demonstrated constantly.

After the fatal judgment on Aaron's rebellious sons Nadab and Abihu (Num 10:1-2), the other two sons thought it better to burn their portion of the sacrifice in sorrow rather than eat it. Their action was wrong, but it came from good motives. Moses, with understanding and sympathy, saw this and so said no more (Lev 10:16-20). In a later case of wilful blasphemy, and in another of deliberate disobedience to God's law, Moses refused to act hastily. In both cases he waited for God to show him how to deal with the offenders (Lev 24:12; Num 15:34).

When Moses married a Cushite woman (his first wife had apparently died), Miriam and Aaron criticized him. The real reason for their attack, however, was their jealousy of Moses' leadership. Though Moses made no effort to defend himself, God rebuked Miriam and Aaron. Again Moses showed his forgiving spirit by asking God's mercy on his critics (Num 12:1-13). His generous nature was shown also on a previous occasion, when Joshua had wanted to protect Moses' status as a prophet by stopping others from prophesying. Moses replied that he wished all God's people were prophets (Num 11:27-29).

Following the people's refusal to accept Joshua and Caleb's report and move ahead into Canaan, God again threatened to destroy the nation and rebuild it through Moses. Once more Moses prayed earnestly that God would forgive the people (Num 14:11-19). Although God did not destroy the people, he refused to allow the unbelieving adult generation to enter Canaan. Israel would therefore remain in the wilderness forty years, till the former generation had passed away and a new had grown up to replace it. Only then would Israel enter the promised land (Num 14:26-35).

Some time later later there was a widespread rebellion against Moses and Aaron, headed by Korah, Dathan and Abiram. As usual Moses left the matter with God rather than take action to defend himself (Num 16:4-5). In righteous anger God threatened the rebellious nation with destruction, but again Moses prayed for them (Num 16:20-24,44-48).

The one occasion on which Moses lost his temper with the people was at Meribah. By his rash words and disobedient actions he misrepresented God before the people and brought God's judgment upon himself. Because of his position of leadership, the cost of his failure was high. God punished him by not allowing him to enter Canaan (Num 20:10-13; Ps 106:32-33).

Later events

About forty years after Israel left Egypt, the new generation prepared to enter Canaan. During a long detour that Israel was forced to make around Edom, Aaron died (Num 20:21-29). As the people of Israel moved north, they conquered large areas of good land east of Jordan, with the result that two and a half tribes asked to settle there instead of in Canaan. This at first worried Moses, because it seemed they were repeating the unbelief of their forefathers. He showed that he was fair and reasonable by agreeing to the two and a half tribes' proposal to help conquer Canaan first and then return to settle east (Num 32:6-8,20-23).

When sexual immorality and foreign religious practices threatened Israel at this time, Moses took decisive action (Num 31:1-54). He also conducted a census, for the double purpose of determining Israel's military strength for the attack on Canaan and making arrangements for the division of the land (Num 26:1-2,54-56).

Moses showed no bitterness at being refused entry into the land, but was concerned only that Israel have a godly leader (Num 27:12-17; cf. Deut 3:23-28). That leader was to be Joshua, though Joshua would not have the absolute authority that Moses had. Civil and religious leadership were to be separated. Joshua would not, like Moses, speak with God face to face, but would receive God's instructions through the high priest (Num 27:18-21; cf. Deut 31:7-8,14,23; 34:9-12).

During the remaining weeks before he died, Moses repeated the law for the sake of the new generation that had grown up since the first giving of the law at Sinai. This teaching, recorded in the book of Deuteronomy, was in the style of the preacher rather than the lawgiver. It was an exposition of the law rather than a straight repetition (Deut 10:12-22; see DEUTERONOMY).

Moses was a prophet, one who brought God's message to the people of his time, and this was well demonstrated in his final messages to his people (Deut 18:18; cf. 6:1-9). He wanted the people to remind themselves constantly of the law's requirements by memorizing a song he had written for them (Deut 31:30; 32:44-46) and by conducting periodic readings of the law (Deut 31:10-12).

Shortly before he died, Moses announced his prophetic blessings on the various tribes of Israel (Deut 33:1-29). According to the permission God had given him earlier, Moses then climbed the peak (Pisgah) of Mt Nebo in the Abarim Range to view the magnificent land his people were to possess. He died at the age of 120 and was buried in the territory east of Jordan (Deut 34:1-8).

Moses' writings

Throughout his time as Israel's leader, Moses was busy as a writer. When Israel escaped from Egypt, he wrote a song celebrating the overthrow of the enemy at the Red Sea (Exod 15:1), and he recorded Israel's subsequent conflict with Amalek (Exod 17:14). In the initial covenant ceremony at Sinai, he wrote God's commandments in a book (Exod 24:4), and added further writings when the covenant was renewed a few weeks later (Exod 34:27). He kept a full record of the stages of Israel's journey from Egypt to Canaan (Num 33:1-2).

When he repeated and expounded the law for the new generation that was about to enter Canaan, Moses recorded his teaching in a book, which was then kept safely inside the tabernacle (Deut 31:9,24-25). At this time he also wrote a song (Deut 31:22,30). Another song credited to him has been collected in the book of Psalms (Ps 90).

From the time of Israel's settlement in Canaan, people regarded Moses as the writer of the law (Josh 8:31; 2 Chron 34:14; Neh 8:1; Mark 12:19,26). Over the years it became common practice to use the name 'Moses' as a title for Israel's law in general (Luke 5:14; Acts 6:11,13; 15:1), and as an overall title for the first five books of the Bible (Luke 16:31; 24:27; John 5:46-47; Acts 15:21; 26:22; 28:23; see PENTATEUCH). In fact, Moses symbolized all that the old covenant represented in the purposes of God. His greatness in Israel was unchallenged.

Great though Moses was, he was but a servant in God's vast household. He fulfilled his duty by helping to prepare the way for one who was God's Son and man's Saviour (Mark 9:4-8; Heb 3:2-6).

MUSIC

Music was one of the earliest expressions of man's artistic and cultural development (Gen 4:21). It was widely used, along with singing and dancing, to celebrate great occasions, whether private or public, domestic or national, secular or sacred (Gen 31:27; Exod 15:20-21; 2 Sam 6:14-15; 2 Chron 20:28-29;

Harp, lyre, horn and drum

Ps 92:1-3; 144:9; Isa 5:12; Amos 6:5; Dan 3:4-5; see also DANCING; SINGING). At other times people played or listened to music purely for relaxation or enjoyment (1 Sam 16:16-17,23; 18:10; Job 21:11-12; Ezek 26:13; 33:31-32; Lam 5:14; Rev 18:22). Music also accompanied mourning and singing at funerals (Matt 9:23; Luke 7:32; see FUNERAL).

Hebrew musical instruments were of three kinds — stringed, wind and percussion. Chief among the stringed instruments were the harp (1 Sam 10:5; 2 Sam 6:5; 1 Kings 10:12; Isa 5:12) and the lyre (Gen 4:21; 31:27; 1 Sam 10:5; 16:23; 2 Sam 6:5). The main wind instruments were the flute (Isa 5:12; Jer 48:36; Matt 9:23), the pipe (Gen 4:21; 1 Kings 1:40; Job 21:12; Matt 11:17), the horn (2 Sam 6:15) and the trumpet (Num 10:2; 31:6; Amos 3:6; Matt 24:31). Percussion instruments included cymbals (2 Sam 6:5; Ps 150:4; 1 Cor 13:1), tamborines (Gen 31:27; 1 Sam 10:5; 2 Sam 6:5; Job 21:12) and timbrels (Exod 15:20; Judg 11:34; Ps 150:4). In the music that David organized for Israel's temple worship, the main instruments were harps, lyres and cymbals (1 Chron 15:16,19-21; 16:5).

MYSIA

The region known as Mysia was originally occupied by one of the independent states of Asia Minor. It was taken over by the Greeks and later by the Romans, and incorporated into the Roman province of Asia. Politically Mysia no longer existed in New Testament times, but people still used the old name to refer to the north-west region of Asia Minor. Towns of this region that are mentioned in the New Testament are Troas, Assos and Adramyttium (Acts 16:6-11; 20:6,13-14; 27:2; for map see ASIA).

MYSTERY

In New Testament usage, a mystery is not a puzzle or a secret that leaves a person in ignorance, but a truth that God reveals to man. It usually refers to something that man normally would not know, but that God in his grace makes known to him (Eph 3:4-5; Col 1:26; Rev 17:7). The truths concerning salvation through Jesus Christ are mysteries in this sense. Man could not work them out by himself, but God who planned salvation from eternity reveals them to him (Rom 16:25-26; 1 Tim 3:9,16).

Jesus taught his disciples that there was a mystery concerning the kingdom of God (Matt 13:11). He revealed that God has already established his kingdom in the world, even though the world is still under the power of Satan. God does not yet force people to submit to the kingdom's authority. Consequently, those who are not in the kingdom live in the world alongside those who are. The decisive separation will take place on the day of judgment (Matt 13:24-30,36-43; see KINGDOM OF GOD).

Paul's preaching was a revelation of the mystery of the gospel and the mystery of Christ (Eph 6:19; Col 2:2; 4:3). He showed that God's plan of salvation through the gospel was to unite Jewish and Gentile believers in one body through Jesus Christ. All share equally in the full blessings of God, without any distinction on the basis of nationality (Eph 3:3-6; Col 1:26-27; cf. Rom 3:21-24). This unified body is a picture, a foretaste and a guarantee of the unity that there will be throughout the universe when God, through Christ, finally removes all rebellion and disharmony (Eph 1:9-10; 3:9-10; cf. 1 Cor 15:25; see GOSPEL).

A further mystery reveals how believers can participate in the blessings of this coming glorious age. God will remove all the effects of sin and death from his people for ever, through the resurrection of the dead and the transformation of all believers to a new state of existence in spiritual, imperishable bodies (1 Cor 15:51-53; see RESURRECTION).

NAHUM

At the time of Nahum's prophecy, Assyria had passed the peak of its power and was heading for inevitable conquest by the rising power of Babylon. Nahum, as God's spokesman, announced a fitting judgment on Assyria, enlivening his message with graphic descriptions of the destruction of Assyria's capital, Nineveh.

Background to the book

About one hundred years previously, Assyria had conquered the northern kingdom Israel and taken its people into captivity (722 BC; 2 Kings 17:6). It then applied pressure to the southern kingdom Judah. Through the reign of one Judean king after another, there was tension and conflict between Judah and Assyria (2 Kings 16:7-20; 18:7-37; 19:1-37; 2 Chron 28:20-21; 30:6; 33:11).

By the time Josiah became king of Judah (640 BC), Assyria had weakened sufficiently for Josiah to carry out extensive political and religious reforms in Judah. Nahum was most likely one of those prophets who began to preach in Judah during the revival of prophetic activity that occurred during Josiah's reign.

Most nations of the region had at some time suffered from the brutality of Assyria (Nahum 3:19). Nahum, who had been deeply stirred over Assyria's injustice and cruelty, had a feeling of satisfaction that at last a fitting divine judgment was to fall upon the ruthless oppressor (Nahum 2:10,13; 3:5-7,19). Nineveh was conquered by the armies of Babylon in 612 BC.

Summary of the book

Nahum opens his book with striking word-pictures showing that God takes vengeance on those who fight against him, though he protects those who trust in him (1:1-15). The prophet then describes the coming attack on Nineveh (2:1-9), which is to be punished because of the fierce cruelty with which it destroyed its victims (2:10-13). A third poem gives a further description of Nineveh's overthrow. The reason given this time is the nation's unrestrained greed for wealth and power (3:1-19).

NAME

To the Israelites of Bible times, the name of a person had much more significance than it does in most countries today. This applies to the giving of names and the usage of names.

Names given for a purpose

Many factors influenced Israelite parents in their choice of names for their children. In some cases the name was connected with happenings at the child's birth (Gen 10:25; 25:24-26). In other cases parents gave names that expressed their joys or sorrows at the time of the birth (Gen 29:32-35; 35:16-18), or expressed their hopes for their own or the child's future (Gen 30:24). God at times directed parents to give names that were a prophecy of coming events (Isa 8:3-4,18; Hosea 1:4,6,9).

A person in a position of power could give a new name to someone within his authority as an indication of blessing or appointment to a place of honour (Gen 17:5,15; cf. Phil 2:9). In some cases a new name may have been given to indicate a new character (Gen 32:28).

Where there was such a connection between name and character, the request to know a person's name was a request to know the character indicated by the name (Gen 32:29; Exod 3:13; Judg 13:17). Sometimes people remembered a new revelation of God's character by calling him by a special name that summarized the revelation in a few words (Gen 22:14; Exod 3:14; 17:15; Judg 6:24). To know a person's name (in this sense) was to know the person himself (Exod 33:12; Ps 9:10; 79:6).

The name meant the person

Since the name represented the person, Israelites considered it important that a man have descendants to carry on his name (Num 27:4; Deut 25:5-6; see INHERITANCE). It was a matter of great shame for a person to have his name blotted out (Josh 7:9; 2 Sam 14:7; Prov 10:7). Those who honoured a person's name honoured the person; those who dishonoured a person's name dishonoured the person (Exod 20:7; Lev 18:21; 1 Kings 1:47; Isa 29:23; Matt 6:9; Rom 2:24; 1 Tim 6:1).

When an Israelite was called by the name of another person, it meant that he was united with that person so closely as to belong to him (Deut 28:9-10; Isa 4:1; Jer 14:9; 15:16; 25:29; Matt 28:19; 1 Cor 1:13-15). In the same way, when a person spoke or acted in the name of another person, it meant that he spoke or acted as if he were that person (Deut 18:20; 1 Sam 25:5; Matt 18:20; John 16:23-24; Acts 3:6,16; 9:27-29; Col 3:17).

According to this common biblical usage, to make known a person's name meant to make known the character and activity of the person (Ps 22:22; 99:3; John 17:6; Acts 9:15). To do something for the sake of a person's name was to do something for the sake of the person's good character or for the sake of the person himself (Ps 109:21; Acts 9:16). To call upon a person's name was to call upon the person himself (1 Kings 18:24; Ps 99:6; Acts 2:21). Therefore, those who called upon the name of the Lord could be assured that the Lord himself would save them (Ps 54:1; Acts 4:12; Rom 10:13).

NAPHTALI

Naphtali was the younger of two sons whom Rachel's maid Bilhah bore to Jacob (Gen 30:7-8). The tribe descended from him settled in the north of Canaan, and together with the neighbouring tribe of Zebulun occupied much of the region later known

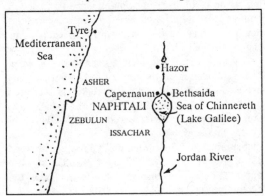

as Galilee. This was the region to the north and west of the Sea of Chinnereth (Lake Galilee) where Jesus grew up and where he spent most of the time recorded of him in the New Testament. The country was mainly hilly, with good pastures and fertile soil

(Gen 49:21; Deut 33:23; Josh 19:32-39; 20:7; Isa 9:1; Matt 4:12-16). (For other features of the region see BETHSAIDA; CAPERNAUM; CHINNERETH; GALILEE; HAZOR.)

In Old Testament times the men of Naphtali proved to be good fighters when called upon to help the other tribes in battle (Judg 4:6,10; 5:18; 6:35; 7:23; 1 Chron 12:34). The tribe itself, however, was open to attack from the north (1 Kings 15:20). It was among the first tribes to go into captivity when Assyria invaded and finally destroyed Israel (2 Kings 15:29). Yet out of this land of darkness and defeat came light and salvation in the person of Jesus Christ (Isa 9:1; Matt 4:12-16).

NATHAN

Several men named Nathan are mentioned in the Bible, one of them being a son of David in the line of descent that produced the Messiah (2 Sam 5:14; Zech 12:12; Luke 3:31). But the best known Nathan is the prophet who belonged to David's court. It was he who revealed that the permanent temple David desired to build was not necessary, and that God was more concerned with building a permanent dynasty for David (2 Sam 7:1-17). God allowed the temple to be built, though by David's son, not by David himself (2 Sam 7:12-13; 1 Chron 28:3,6).

Nathan was again God's spokesman when he announced God's judgment on David because of his sin with Bathsheba (2 Sam 12:1-15). Nathan seems also to have been the person through whom God revealed that Solomon would be David's successor as king (2 Sam 12:24-25; 1 Chron 28:5-6; 1 Kings 1:17). Significantly, Nathan came to the defence of Solomon when Adonijah challenged him (1 Kings 1:11-14,22-24,32-34). Like many prophets, Nathan was a court historian (1 Chron 29:29; 2 Chron 9:29; 29:25).

NATHANAEL

Only John's Gospel mentions Nathanael, though he is probably the same person whom Matthew, Mark and Luke call Bartholemew. (For the identification of the two names see BARTHOLEMEW.) He lived in Galilee and was introduced to Jesus by Philip (John 1:43-45; 21:2).

Nathanael was an honest person, free of deceit (John 1:47). At first he had difficulty believing that the Messiah should come from the small Galilean town of Nazareth, but he was quickly convinced when he learnt first-hand of Jesus' supernatural knowledge (John 1:48-49). Jesus assured Nathanael that the Messiah was more than just a person with superhuman knowledge. He was the divinely given mediator, God's unique 'ladder' that connected earth and heaven. Jesus' mission was to bring God to man and to make it possible for man to come to God (John 1:50-51).

NATION

Within God's overall government of human society, he has allowed a great variety of nations. Most of these have arisen out of commonly held interests or characteristics such as race, language, homeland culture, religion and law-code (Gen 10:32; Deut 32:8; Acts 17:26).

In Old Testament times God chose one nation, Israel, to belong to him (Exod 19:5-6). This was not because Israel was better than other nations (Deut 7:6-7; 9:9), but because God wanted a channel of communication through which he could send his blessings to all the people of the world (Gen 12:3; 22:17-18; see ELECTION). God loves all nations and desires their good (Isa 19:24-25; Amos 9:7; Matt 28:19; Acts 1:8; 13:47).

Nevertheless, nations may fall under God's judgment, and God may use other nations to punish them. This does not mean that those whom God uses as his instruments of judgment are free to do as they like. If they do wrong, they too may fall under God's judgment (Isa 10:5-19; 37:23-26; Hab 1:6-7; 2:15-17). God may also use nations as his instruments to bring deliverance and blessing (Isa 45:1-5), for he controls the destinies of all nations (Jer 18:7-10; Dan 4:17).

Sometimes people become nationalistic to the extent of putting pride in their nation ahead of moral values. God may have to remind them that national power and glory can be very shortlived. The only lasting kingdom is the kingdom of God (Dan 2:44; 4:30,34). God's people may well love the nation to which they belong (Jer 8:18-22; Matt 23:37; Rom 9:3) and be loyal citizens (Rom 13:1-7; 1 Peter 2:13-14; cf. Jer 29:4-7), but their first allegiance must always be to God (Exod 20:3; Mark 12:17; Acts 5:29; see GOVERNMENT).

Israelites of Old Testament times made such a clear distinction between themselves and others that their usual word for 'nations' developed the special sense of 'other nations' (often translated 'Gentiles' or 'heathen') (Deut 18:9; Ps 2:1; Isa 11:10; 30:28; 36:18; 49:22; Jer 10:1-5,10; see GENTILE). Israelites of New Testament times made the same mistake as many of their ancestors in thinking that their nationality guaranteed their salvation (Matt 3:9; Rom 9:6). God accepts people into his family on the basis of their faith, not their nationality (Luke 4:25-27; Rom 2:28-29; 4:1-3,16-17).

This truth is clearly demonstrated in that vast international community known as the Christian church. The concern of this community is to win people of all nations for Christ and promote a true fellowship in which there are no national or racial barriers (John 17:20-23; Gal 3:28; Eph 2:13-16; Rev 5:9; 7:9; see RACE).

NATURE

By God's appointment, man is the earthly ruler of the created world. God's intention was that as man brought the physical world under his control, nature would enter into fuller glory and man would enter into greater blessing (Gen 1:28). Nature's destiny was tied up with man's. Therefore, when man sinned and brought suffering upon himself, nature also suffered (Gen 3:17-18; Rom 8:20,22). Only when redeemed man enters his full glory will nature enter its full glory (Rom 8:19-23).

Different attitudes to nature

People who do not believe in God may not agree with the Christian that man has authority over nature. They may consider that man has no more rights than animals, plants, or even lifeless things such as minerals. As a result they may worship rocks or trees, and sometimes may treat animals better than they treat people. The outcome of their belief is not that they raise nature to the level of man, but that they lower man to the level of the animals (Rom 1:20-25).

God's people, while not giving animals, plants and minerals a higher place than God intended for them, should nevertheless realize that these things have a place and purpose in God's order. This was demonstrated in the law God gave to ancient Israel. He allowed his people to plant trees for fruit or to clear forests to establish settlements (Lev 19:23-25; Josh 17:18), but he did not allow them to chop down trees unnecessarily. People could not destroy forests and orchards simply to use the trees for building siegeworks. They were to use only those trees that were not useful for anything else (Deut 20:19-20).

Likewise God taught his people to be kind to animals. They were to give proper food and rest to the animals that worked for them, and were not to use their animals in any way that could be considered cruel (Deut 5:14; 22:10; 25:4). In killing animals they were not to be heartless or thoughtless. They had to consider the animal's instincts and feelings, and remember the need to maintain the balance of nature (Exod 23:19b; Lev 22:28; Deut 22:6-7). In particular they had to acknowledge that God was the owner of all life, and that they could take the life of an animal only by his permission (Lev 17:13-14; Deut 12:15-16,23-24; Ps 50:10-11; see BLOOD).

Man's responsibility to God

Although given authority over nature, man is not to treat nature according to his own selfish desires. He does not have unlimited right over nature, for he is merely the representative of God in administering what God has entrusted to him. God is the owner of nature (Ps 24:1-2; see CREATION), and man is answerable to God for the way he treats it (Gen 2:15; Ps 8:6-8).

According to the gracious permission given him by God, man may use nature for his own benefit. God allows man to take minerals from the earth, to enjoy the fruits of plant life, to cut down trees to build houses, to eat the meat of animals, and to kill insects and animals that threaten his life (Deut 8:7-10; 12:15; Josh 6:21). But God does not give to man the right to desolate the land solely for monetary gain, or to destroy life solely for his own pleasure. Man's attitude to nature should be a reflection of the care over nature that the Creator himself exercises (Ps 104:10-30; Matt 6:25-30; 10:29).

God gave specific laws to the people of Israel concerning their attitude to nature in the matter of farming. He told them to rest their land one year in seven. If they failed to, he would force them to rest it by driving them from it (Lev 25:3-7; 26:34-35,43; see SABBATICAL YEAR). God assured the Israelites that he would use nature as a means of blessing them when they obeyed him, but of punishing them when they disobeyed him (Deut 11:13-17; 28:1-24; 2 Chron 7:14).

It seems that God so created the natural world that, when man acts towards it without restraint, he helps bring ruin to it and to himself (Isa 24:5-6). Christians know that man's sin affected nature from the time man rebelled in Eden (Gen 3:17-19), but they know also that when they are finally delivered

from the effects of sin, nature also will be delivered (Rom 8:19-23).

In their personal lives Christians work towards the goal of their deliverance from the consequences of sin. They should work towards similar deliverance in all things affected by sin. Not only should they purify themselves because of the likeness they will one day bear to Christ, but they should also help towards the healing of nature in view of the full glory God has planned for it (Phil 3:20-21; Titus 2:11-14; 1 John 3:2-3).

NAZARETH

The chief importance of Nazareth is that it was the place where Jesus lived most of his life. It is not mentioned in the Old Testament, and is mentioned in the New Testament only in connection with the story of Jesus.

Nazareth was situated in the hilly country of the northern part of Palestine known as Galilee. It had no great political importance, though it was close to several trade routes that passed through Palestine. Citizens of rival towns did not have a high opinion

Nazareth

of it (John 1:43-46). The town today is within the borders of modern Israel, and is larger and more important than it was in Jesus' day.

Jesus' parents were originally from Nazareth, but before his birth they moved south to Bethlehem in Judea (Luke 2:4). After Jesus' birth the family went to Egypt to escape the murderous Herod, and it was probably about two years later that they returned to Palestine and settled again in Nazareth (Matt 2:19-23; Luke 2:39). Jesus spent his childhood in Nazareth (Luke 2:40,51; 4:16), and seems to have continued living there till he was about thirty years of age, at which time he began his public ministry (Mark 1:9; Luke 3:23).

A common Jewish practice was to identify a person by the name of the town he came from. Jesus was often referred to — by friends, enemies, angels, demons, common people, government officials, and even by himself — as Jesus of Nazareth (Matt 26:71; Mark 1:23-24; 16:5-6; Luke 24:19; John 18:5; 19:19; Acts 2:22; 22:8).

The people of Nazareth, who had seen Jesus grow up in their town, were surprised that he could preach so well, especially since he had not studied at any of the schools of the rabbis. They were also angry that he would not perform miracles to please them. On one occasion they tried to throw him over one of the cliffs in the hills around Nazareth (Matt 13:53-58; Luke 4:16-30; Mark 6:1-6).

In New Testament times the unbelieving Jews refused to call Jesus by his messianic name 'Christ', and refused to call his followers 'Christians'. They called him simply Jesus of Nazareth or Jesus the Nazarene, and called his followers Nazarenes (Acts 24:5). Even today, in Hebrew and Arabic speech, Christians may be called Nazarenes.

NAZIRITE

The word 'Nazirite' is used to indicate both a type of vow and the person who made such a vow. It is not to be confused with Nazarene (the name given to a person from the town of Nazareth), but comes from the Hebrew word *nazir*, whose meaning indicates that a Nazirite vow was one of separation (Num 6:2). A person could make a Nazirite vow if he (or she) wanted to show openly that he had set himself apart to God for some special purpose over a certain period.

During the period covered by his vow, the Nazirite kept three special laws. First, he refused wine and anything that was likely to produce it, to demonstrate his refusal of life's enjoyments and to avoid any possibility of drunkenness. Second, he let his hair grow long, as an open sign to all that he was living under the conditions of a Nazirite vow. Third, he avoided anything dead, to emphasize to himself and to others the holiness that his service for God demanded (Num 6:3-8).

If a person broke his Nazirite vow deliberately, there was no remedy. If he broke it accidentally, he could ask forgiveness through offering sacrifices. But the time he had kept his vow was lost and he had to begin again (Num 6:9-12; cf. Amos 2:11-12). At the end of the period of his vow, he offered sacrifices, shaved his head and was released from the three Nazirite restrictions (Num 6:13-21).

Probably the best known Nazirite in the Bible was Samson, whose parents dedicated him to God at birth to be a Nazirite for life. Samson had little regard for the Nazirite laws concerning the drinking of wine and contact with dead bodies, though he did allow his hair to remain uncut. When he finally broke that law too, he broke the last remaining link in his declared devotion to God (Judg 13:3-7; 14:9-10,19; 16:19-20).

Samuel and John the Baptist were possibly Nazirites for life (1 Sam 1:11; Luke 1:15). It appears that on one occasion Paul took a short-term Nazirite vow upon himself (Acts 18:18; cf. 21:23-26).

NEBO

Mount Nebo was a prominent peak in the hilly region of Abarim on the Moabite tableland, east of the Jordan River (Num 33:47). It was the place where the aged Moses went to view the promised land and where, a short time later, he died (Deut 32:49-50; 34:1,5-6; see ABARIM).

NEBUCHADNEZZAR

Towards the end of the seventh century BC, the ancient nation Babylon rose again to international prominence, largely through the new dynasty that had been established by Nabopolassar. The greatest king of this dynasty was Nabopolassar's son and successor, Nebuchadnezzar (or Nebuchadrezzar).

Nebuchadnezzar became king soon after he led Babylonian forces to victory over Egypt at the Battle of Carchemish in 605 BC (2 Kings 24:7; Jer 46:2). One outcome of this was that Judah fell under Babylonian power. After a series of Babylonian attacks over several years, Jerusalem was finally destroyed and its people taken captive to Babylon (587 BC). Nebuchadnezzar was the Babylonian king throughout this time, and the books of 2 Kings, Jeremiah, Ezekiel and Daniel mention him by name repeatedly. (For details of his dealings with Judah and his military successes among the nations of the region see BABYLON.)

Through his contact with Jews at his court in Babylon, Nebuchadnezzar learnt about the Jews' God, Yahweh. Upon seeing how this God revealed mysteries and miraculously saved people from death, he concluded that Yahweh must have been the greatest of all the gods (Dan 2:47; 3:29). However, he was a proud man, whose great empire-building achievements led him to believe that he could ignore God and take no notice of the warnings given him by God's messenger Daniel. The result was that

God punished Nebuchadnezzar with a disease of temporary madness, till he learnt that God was the sovereign ruler over the kingdoms of the world (Dan 4:27-33).

The Bible gives no clear indication whether Nebuchadnezzar's acknowledgment of the sovereign rule of God had any lasting effect on his behaviour. Babylon proved to be an arrogant nation, and God's prophet saw all its pride and evil embodied in its king (Isa 14:4-11). There is no certainty that the prophet had Nebuchadnezzar or any other king specifically in mind, but his warning has a timeless relevance. Those who ambitiously desire the highest place, the greatest honour and supreme power are in danger of being brought down to the lowest place, the greatest shame and complete weakness (Isa 14:12-20).

Nebuchadnezzar was undoubtedly the greatest king of this period of Babylonian supremacy. He reigned more than forty years and died in 562 BC. He was succeeded by his son Evil-merodach (Jer 52:31).

NEGEB

Much of southern Palestine between the Dead Sea and the Sinai desert was dry semi-barren country to which the Hebrews gave the name *negeb* (meaning 'dry'). The region features prominently in the Old Testament story from the time of Abraham onwards (Gen 13:1; Num 13:25-29; 1 Sam 30:14). (For details see PALESTINE, sub-heading 'Negeb'.)

NEHEMIAH

As governor of Jerusalem and author of a book, Nehemiah is an important character in the biblical record of Israel's reconstruction after the captivity in Babylon. All that we know of Nehemiah comes from the book that he wrote (Neh 1:1).

Circumstances of the time

When Persia conquered Babylon and released the captive peoples (539 BC), many Jews returned to Palestine. One of their first achievements, in spite of some early setbacks, was the reconstruction of the temple in Jerusalem. But the city wall remained in ruins, and only when Nehemiah came to Jerusalem as governor in 445 BC was it rebuilt. This was more than ninety years after the first group of people had returned from captivity (Neh 2:1; cf. Ezra 1:1-4). (For events leading up to the time of Nehemiah see EZRA.)

Nehemiah was a man of very forceful character who had the ability to motivate people. He was a great organizer and leader, but more importantly he was a man of prayer who trusted God, feared God and obeyed his commandments (Neh 1:4; 2:4; 4:20; 5:15; 6:11; 7:2; 13:17,25,30). He was fearless in dealing with opponents (Neh 4:14,20; 6:8,11; 13:8), yet sympathetic and self-sacrificing in helping the needy (Neh 5:11,14-18).

Most of the book of Nehemiah seems to have come from the personal records that Nehemiah kept during his governorship of Jerusalem. The book is therefore largely in the first person. Nehemiah had two periods as governor of Jerusalem, an earlier period lasting twelve years and a later period of unknown length (Neh 5:14; 13:6-7).

Summary of Nehemiah's book

Nehemiah first became governor as a result of a visit to Persia by some Jews from Jerusalem. At that time Nehemiah held a trusted position in the Persian palace, and the Jews no doubt hoped he could persuade the king to support them against the attacks of their opponents (1:1-3). Being a man of prayer, Nehemiah prayed about the matter for four months before asking the king for help. The king responded by giving him authority, materials and finance to go to Jerusalem to repair the city and rebuild its walls (1:4-2:10). It was probably at this time that Nehemiah was appointed governor.

After surveying the damage, Nehemiah outlined his plans to the people, gained their support, and organized a building program in which people of all types participated (2:11-3:32). When opponents tried to stop the work, Nehemiah presented the matter to God, but at the same time made arrangements to strengthen the defence of the city (4:1-23). He also acted decisively to stop the rich in Jerusalem from taking advantage of the poor, who were suffering added hardship because of the current difficulties (5:1-19). Outside enemies tried by various means to stop the work, but without success. In the end the wall was finished (6:1-7:73).

Before the wall was dedicated, Ezra read and explained parts of the law of Moses, first to the people and then to the leaders. After that the people celebrated the Feast of Tabernacles (8:1-18).

Following further confession, the people swore to God an oath of obedience, which their leaders put in writing and signed on their behalf (9:1-10:39). An added arrangement before the dedication ceremony was to increase Jerusalem's security by increasing its population. Many people from country areas came to live in the city (11:1-12:26). Ezra and Nehemiah then led the people in an impressive dedication ceremony (12:27-13:3).

At the end of twelve years service, Nehemiah returned to Persia for a time. Without his strong leadership the people weakened and old enemies gained influence in the city. Upon arriving back in Jerusalem, Nehemiah dealt fearlessly with the enemies (13:4-9) and corrected Jerusalem's social and religious disorders with his usual decisiveness (13:10-31).

NEIGHBOUR

Moses' law laid down the principle that a person was to love his neighbour as himself (Lev 19:17-18; see also Exod 20:13-17; 22:10-14; Deut 15:2; 27:24). In trying to avoid the responsibility this placed upon them, people sometimes asked who exactly was their neighbour. On one occasion Jesus answered the question with the story of a Samaritan who helped a man who had been attacked by robbers. The point of the story was that any person in need was one's neighbour (Luke 10:29-37). Neighbours in this sense include even enemies (Matt 5:43-47).

Love of God and love of one's neighbour combine to form the basic requirements God has placed upon mankind (Matt 22:36-40; Rom 13:8-10; Gal 5:14; James 2:8). The person who claims to love God but does not love his neighbour is deceiving himself (1 John 4:20; cf. Prov 3:28; 14:21; see also BROTHER).

NEW BIRTH

See REGENERATION.

NICODEMUS

Most of the Jewish leaders arrogantly rejected Jesus' teaching, but Nicodemus had a sincere desire to know the truth. He was a respected Pharisee and a member of the Jewish Council, or Sanhedrin (John 3:1; 7:50), but he was also willing to admit that Jesus' miracles showed that God was with him (John 3:2; cf. 2:23-25).

At first Nicodemus had difficulty understanding Jesus' figurative teaching concerning the new birth (John 3:3-10), but he did not dismiss the teaching. He showed courage in opposing the prejudice of his fellow councillors against Jesus, and suggested that at least they ought to give Jesus a fair hearing (John 7:48-52).

When the Sanhedrin finally condemned Jesus to crucifixion, Nicodemus and at least one other member disagreed with the decision. That man was Joseph of Arimathea. He and Nicodemus showed publicly that they were followers of Jesus by taking

his body down from the cross and giving him an honourable burial (Luke 23:50-53; John 19:38-42).

NILE

Although the Bible mentions the Nile River mainly in relation to Egypt (Gen 41:17-19; Ezek 29:3), the river passes through many countries, among them Ethiopia (GNB: Sudan) (Isa 18:1-2). The length of the Nile is about 5,600 kilometres.

Very little rain fell in Egypt, with the result that the country depended almost entirely upon the Nile for its water supply. The fertility of its land also depended upon the Nile. Because of the silt left behind after the river's annual flooding, otherwise barren land became usable (Isa 23:3,10; Amos 8:8; 9:5).

Apart from the land that extended out a few kilometres on either side of the river, plus the land of the well watered delta region (together totalling less than one twentieth of Egypt's entire land area), Egypt was a desert. In Egypt the failure of the Nile to flood was the equivalent of a drought in other

Fishing in the Nile

countries. It ruined the farming, fishing and cotton industries, and created widespread unemployment (Gen 41:1-3; Isa 19:5-10). Prophetic announcements of judgment on Egypt therefore often included graphic pictures of the drying up of the Nile (Ezek 29:1-10; 30:12; Zech 10:11). It seems that God used some of the physical characteristics of the Nile Valley in bringing the plagues on Egypt during the time of Moses (Exod 7:14-10:29; see PLAGUE).

NINEVEH

Situated on the Tigris River in northern Mesopotamia, Nineveh was one of the great cities of the ancient world, and became capital of the powerful

Assyrian Empire (Gen 10:11-12; 2 Kings 19:36). (For map of Assyria and details of Nineveh's history see ASSYRIA.) On one occasion the city was saved from a threatened invasion when the people responded to the preaching of God's prophet Jonah (Jonah 1:1; 3:1-10; 4:11; Matt 12:41; see JONAH).

Though the Assyrians were used by God to punish his people Israel, they were one of the most brutal oppressors in recorded history. The prophets of God assured them of a fitting divine punishment (Isa 10:5,12-16; Nahum 1:1; 3:1-7; Zeph 2:13; see NAHUM). This judgment fell in 612 BC, when the besieging Babylonians overcame Nineveh's defences by bursting open the water gates, breaking through the wall and flooding the city (Nahum 2:6-8). The Babylonians then plundered and smashed the city, leaving it a heap of ruins. It was never rebuilt (Nahum 2:9-10; 3:1,7; Zeph 2:13-15).

NOAH

The early history of mankind is one of rebellion against God and rejection of the revelation that God had given to man (Gen 6:5-6; cf. Rom 1:20-25). Conditions became so morally corrupt that God decided to destroy the rebellious people and to make a new beginning. The new 'father' for mankind would be the one man who had remained faithful to God, Noah. When all the people around him were ungodly, Noah remained blameless. He was a righteous man who lived in unbroken fellowship with God (Gen 6:8-11).

Saved through the flood

Noah preached righteousness to those around him, but they would not listen to him (2 Peter 2:5). God's way of dealing with the corrupt and unrepentant people was to send a great flood to destroy them (Gen 6:17; see FLOOD).

God told Noah to build a huge ark in which he, his family, and at least one pair of all the animals of the region could find safety and so be preserved through the disaster (Gen 6:12-14,19; 7:1-2; see ARK). Noah demonstrated his faith in God by doing all that God commanded him (Gen 7:5; Heb 11:7). As a result, all in his household were saved (Gen 7:7; 8:16-19; 1 Peter 3:20), so that they, with the preserved animals, could begin life on earth afresh (Gen 8:17).

After Noah offered sacrifices of dedication and thanksgiving, God warned him not to expect a golden age, because man would always be sinful. Yet God in his grace would allow sinful man to continue to live on his earth, and would not destroy him with a flood again (Gen 8:20-22). God confirmed this promise by making a covenant with Noah and with mankind through him (Gen 9:8-13).

Repopulating the region

With this new beginning, God gave Noah similar responsibilities to those he had originally given to Adam — responsibilities to populate the earth and look after it (Gen 9:1-3; cf. 1:28-30). The following chapters of Genesis record how the descendants of Noah's three sons, Japheth, Ham and Shem, spread throughout the region, and as a result different ethnic groups, languages and cultures developed (Gen 9:18-19; 10:5,20,31).

Of the peoples who developed from Japheth, Ham and Shem, those descended from Ham's son Canaan were doomed to have their land taken from them by the descendants of Shem. This was partly because Canaan had particularly disgraced Noah when he and Ham found him lying drunk and naked in his tent (Gen 9:20-27).

Noah lived to a great age. During the centuries after the flood, he had the satisfaction of seeing the growth of his descendants and the re-establishment of a healthy human society (Gen 9:28-29; 10:32).

NUMBER

A characteristic of languages in general is that they often use numbers in their idioms and figures of speech (cf. English: 'two or three', 'by the dozen', 'a thousand times'). So it is with the languages of the Bible (Gen 31:7; Lev 26:8; Amos 1:3; 1 Cor 14:19; Rev 5:11). Other numbers seem to have been used as round figures, particularly the number forty (Judg 3:11; 5:31; 8:28; 1 Sam 4:18; 17:16; Jonah 3:4; Acts 1:3; 7:23,30,36).

Modern research has still not discovered the full meaning of words that the ancient Hebrews used in counting and classifying large numbers of people. When more is known, it may help to explain some of the puzzling statistics recorded in the Old Testament (e.g. 1 Kings 20:29-30; 2 Kings 19:35).

In some cases numbers were used symbolically, especially where teaching was given through visions, as in the books of Ezekiel, Daniel, Zechariah and Revelation. The number seven was a significant number in Hebrew symbolism. Much of the Hebrew social, cultural and religious system was from the beginning based on a unit of seven (Exod 20:8-11; see SEVEN). The number ten was common. It was a natural unit for counting and helped produce a simple decimal system (Exod 18:21; 26:1,16; 27:12; 34:28; Lev 5:11; 6:20; 27:32). The number twelve most likely gained its biblical significance from the fact that Israel was built upon twelve tribes (Exod 28:21; Num 1:44; 7:84-87; Josh 4:8; Matt 10:1-2; Rev 21:12,14).

NUMBERS, BOOK OF

A person reading Numbers must bear in mind that he is reading only part of a larger book. The 'five books of Moses' (or Pentateuch) originally were one book, the division into five volumes being purely for convenience. Numbers has greater significance once the reader sees it as part of this larger work. (Concerning the authorship and purpose of this larger work see PENTATEUCH.)

Significance of Numbers

In fulfilment of his promises to Abraham, God had made Abraham's descendants into a nation, saved them from Egypt and was now taking them to their new homeland, Canaan. The person he had given them as their leader was Moses (Gen 12:2; 15:18-21; Exod 3:10-12; 6:4-8; for map and other details see MOSES).

After three months' journey, God settled the people temporarily at Mt Sinai. There he established his covenant with them and gave them laws to govern their lives as his people. At the point where Numbers begins, Israel had been at Sinai almost one year (Exod 19:1; Num 1:1).

During their time at Sinai, the people had received much instruction in religious, moral and social matters (Exod 20-24). They had also built the tabernacle (Exod 25-40), established a priesthood and a sacrificial system (Lev 1-10), and begun to regulate their national life according to the laws God had laid down (Lev 11-27). The people were now preparing themselves to depart from Sinai and head for Canaan (Num 1-10).

The book of Numbers opens with Moses about to conduct a census so that he could prepare an army for the conquest of Canaan. The journey to Canaan should have taken only a few weeks, but instead it took almost forty years. The reason for the delay was the people's rebellion against God. Out of fear and distrust they refused to enter Canaan, with the result that God left them in the wilderness till all that adult generation had died and a new generation had grown up. At the end of Numbers, almost forty years after its beginning, Moses took another census, this time to organize the new generation for the conquest of Canaan. The book of Numbers takes its name (in the Greek, Latin and English versions) from these two census.

Since the two census represent only a small part of the book, the Hebrew title 'In the Wilderness' gives a better indication of the book's contents. Most of the book is concerned with the journey from Sinai to the borders of Canaan, and much of this journey was through wilderness country. There are very few details of the wasted years of 'wanderings' in the wilderness (Num 32:13).

Contents of the book

To begin with, Moses conducted a military census (1:1-54). He also set out arrangements for camping and marching (2:1-34), paying particular attention to the Levites, whose duty it was to transport, erect and look after the tabernacle (3:1-4:49). After giving additional religious and civil laws (5:1-6:27), Moses accepted offerings from Israel's leaders for the use of the Levites, and then dedicated the Levites to God's service (7:1-8:26). Israel kept the Passover and awaited God's sign for them to break camp and set off (9:1-10:10).

The procession moved off (10:11-36), but soon the people became complaining and they criticized Moses (11:1-12:16). Worse still, they refused to go into Canaan when they heard of the opposition that lay ahead. In so doing, they rebelled against God and consequently condemned themselves to die in the wilderness (13:1-14:45).

God impressed upon the people the necessity for obedience in all circumstances (15:1-41). Soon, however, there was another rebellion when a group of leaders challenged the authority of Moses and Aaron. They were destroyed in a dramatic divine punishment (16:1-17:13). In view of these rebellions, God gave further laws and regulations (18:1-19:22). Moses and Aaron lost patience with the complaining people, but their rash behaviour brought judgment upon themselves (20:1-13).

After being forced to detour around the land of Edom (20:14-21:20), the Israelites conquered all the Amorite territory east of Jordan and set up camp on the Plains of Moab in preparation for the attack on Canaan (21:21-22:1). Attempts by the king of Moab to destroy the Israelites were unsuccessful, though the Israelites almost destroyed themselves through their immoral behaviour with neighbouring peoples (22:2-25:18).

Moses conducted a new census (26:1-27:23) and gave further laws and regulations (28:1-30:16). In a military victory over the troublesome Midianites, the Israelites gained some welcome profits (31:1-54). As the time approached for the Israelites' attack on Canaan, Moses set out plans for the division of the land that they were to occupy. This included the land already conquered east of Jordan and the land yet to be conquered in Canaan itself (32:1-36:13).

OATH

According to Hebrew thought, when a person took an oath he called down a curse upon himself if he was not telling the truth (Mark 14:71) or if, after making a promise, he did not keep his word (2 Sam 3:8-10). In swearing by the name of God, a person was inviting God to take decisive action against him should he be false to his oath (1 Sam 19:6; 2 Kings 2:2; Jer 42:5; Ezek 17:18-19; see CURSE).

There were various rituals that people followed in swearing oaths. Where two parties bound themselves to a contract by oath, they sometimes carried out a ritual where they passed between portions of slaughtered animals, calling down the fate of the animals on themselves should they break their oath (Jer 34:18; cf. Gen 15:9-20). A person might, as he swore an oath, raise his hand above his head or, if swearing to another, place his hand under the other man's thigh (Gen 24:2-3; Deut 32:40).

People could swear oaths before local judges or at the sanctuary altar (Exod 22:10-11; 1 Kings 8:31). A special ritual was available when a woman was suspected of adultery and she wanted to swear her innocence (Num 5:11-31).

When Israelites swore by the name of God, they were to be careful not to swear falsely (Lev 19:12). Under no conditions were they to swear by the name of a false god (Amos 8:14). If a person swore a rash oath and later regretted it, he could ask forgiveness through presenting a guilt offering and making any compensation that may have been necessary (Lev 5:4-6; 6:5; cf. 1 Sam 14:24-29).

Even God sometimes bound himself by an oath; for example, in his covenant promises to Abraham (Gen 15:5-20; 22:16-17; Luke 1:68-73; Heb 6:13-14), to David (Ps 89:34-36; Acts 2:30), to the messianic king (Ps 110:4; Heb 7:15-22,28), and to his redeemed people (Heb 6:16-17). Although he had no need to take an oath (since his word is always sure), in his grace he confirmed his promise by an oath, so that believers might be doubly certain of their ultimate salvation (Heb 6:17-20).

Wrong practices developed among the Jews concerning the taking of oaths. Some considered that if, in swearing an oath, they did not actually use the name of God, they were not bound by that oath. They felt no guilt if they swore 'by heaven', 'by earth', 'by Jerusalem' or 'by the head' and then broke their promise, for such oaths did not use God's name. Jesus told them that if they were truthful and honest in all their day-to-day behaviour, they would not feel the need to swear oaths at all. *Everything* a person says should be true and straight-forward (Matt 5:33-37; 23:16; James 5:12).

OBADIAH

The Bible mentions at least twelve people named Obadiah. The most important is the prophet who wrote about the Edomites (see OBADIAH, BOOK OF). Of the remainder, the best known is the manager of Ahab's royal household. When all around him were worshipping Baal, this man remained faithful to God. He protected God's prophets from Jezebel's violence, and on one occasion carried a message from Elijah to Ahab (1 Kings 18:1-16).

OBADIAH, BOOK OF

The book of Obadiah is largely an announcement of judgment upon Edom for its part in helping Babylon in the destruction of Jerusalem in 587 BC (Obad 10-14; cf. Ps 137:7; Ezek 35:5,12,15). Edom, being descended from Esau, was a brother nation to Israel-Judah, and therefore should have helped Jerusalem in its final hour (cf. Gen 25:23-26; 32:28; 36:1,8-9). Instead the Edomites took the opportunity to plunder the helpless city (Obad 11,13). They even captured the fleeing Jerusalemites and sold them to the Babylonian conquerors (Obad 14; for map and other details see EDOM).

Contents of the book

Edom prided itself in the strength of its mountain defences and the cleverness of its political dealings. Neither, however, would save it from the divine judgment that would fall upon it because of its active cooperation in the destruction of Jerusalem (Obad 1-16).

But whereas God would destroy Edom totally, he would bring Judah out of captivity and back to its land, where it would rebuild its national life. It would even spread its power into former Edomite territory (Obad 17-21).

OBEDIENCE

Since God is the Creator and Lord of the universe, people should obey him (Deut 4:35-40). To those who obey him, he promises blessing; to those who disobey him, cursing (Deut 11:27-28; 27:10; Josh 5:6). Obedience means to hear God's voice, to accept his authority and to do what he commands (Exod 15:26). Disobedience means to refuse to hear God's voice, to reject his authority and not to do what he commands (Jer 7:24). Adam's disobedience brought ruin to mankind, but Christ's obedience (an obedience throughout life even to death) brings salvation (Rom 5:19; Phil 2:8; see also SIN).

God commands all people everywhere to repent and believe the gospel (Mark 1:15; Acts 17:30; 1 John 3:23). Therefore, faith in Christ is obedience; unbelief is disobedience (Acts 6:7; 2 Thess 1:8; Heb 5:9; 1 Peter 4:17). Having exercised faith in Christ, the true believer will give clear evidence of this by a life of constant obedience to God (1 Peter 1:14-16; 1 John 5:1-3).

Religious exercises are never a substitute for obedience to the commands of God. The person who says he loves God but deliberately disobeys God's Word is only deceiving himself. Love for God leads to obedience, not disobedience (1 Sam 15:22; Luke 22:42; John 14:15; 15:10,14-15). If a person develops the habit of obeying God, he will become a true servant of righteousness and therefore a true servant of God. By contrast, if a person develops the habit of obeying the sinful human nature, he will become a servant of sin and therefore useless to God (Rom 6:12-18).

Christians have a responsibility to submit to the various types of authority that God has established in human society. In the family, children are to obey their parents (Eph 6:1; Col 3:20). In the sphere of work, employees are to obey their employers (Eph 6:5; Col 3:22). In any community or nation, people are to obey the laws of that community or nation (Rom 13:1; Titus 3:1; 1 Peter 2:13). In the church, Christians are to obey their leaders (Phil 2:12; 1 Thess 5:12; Heb 13:7).

In any sphere of life, people with authority may at times command Christians to do something that is contrary to what God has taught in his Word. In such cases, Christians must be prepared to obey God rather than man, even though their actions may bring unwelcome consequences upon themselves (Acts 5:29,40).

OFFERING

See GIVING; SACRIFICE.

OIL

In most cases the oil that the Bible mentions is olive oil. Olive trees were grown extensively in Palestine, and Israel exported oil to other countries (1 Kings 5:11; Ezek 27:17; Hosea 12:1). Other fruits and plants were also a source of oil. Workers obtained the oil by crushing the fruit, flowers or leaves. This was sometimes done through grinding the substance, using either a thick stick in a bowl or a stone roller in a hollowed out rock. Sometimes the oil was trodden out in a press, other times squeezed out from a sack by twisting it with sticks (Exod 27:20; Deut 33:24; Micah 6:15).

People used oils in the preparation of food (Exod 29:2; Lev 2:4; 1 Kings 17:12-14), as fuels for lamps (Exod 27:20; Zech 4:2-3,12; Matt 25:3-4), as

Squeezing oil from flowers

medicines and ointments (Isa 1:6; Luke 10:34), as cosmetics (2 Sam 14:2; Esther 2:12; Ps 104:15; Song of Songs 1:12; 5:5) and for rubbing on the body to bring soothing and refreshment (Ruth 3:3; 2 Sam 12:20; Amos 6:6; Luke 7:37-38; John 12:3). The use of oil in anointing the sick may have had some medicinal purpose, but its chief significance may have been symbolic, demonstrating faith (Mark 6:13; James 5:14).

It was a custom to show honour to a person by anointing his head with oil (Mark 14:3). This was particularly so when a host welcomed a special guest (Ps 23:5). On festive occasions anointing contributed to the joy and merriment of the occasion. As a result oil, like wine, became a symbol of rejoicing (Ps 45:7; 104:15; Isa 61:3; Joel 1:10).

Besides being widely used in Israel's everyday life, oil was frequently used in its religious rituals. It was part of some sacrifices (Exod 29:2,40; Lev 8:26; Num 6:15; 7:19), was offered as both firstfruits and tithes (Exod 22:29; Deut 12:17), was used as fuel for the tabernacle lamp (Exod 27:20) and was put on people in certain ceremonies (Lev 14:10-18).

Oil was used to anoint priests, kings and at times prophets, to symbolize their setting apart for God's service and their appointment to office (Exod 28:41; 1 Sam 10:1; Ps 89:20-21; 1 Kings 1:39; 19:16; Zech 4:11-14). It was used also to anoint things that were set apart for sacred use, such as the tabernacle and its equipment (Exod 40:9-11). The oil used to anoint the priests and the tabernacle was prepared according to a special formula, which was not to be used for any other purpose (Exod 30:23-33; cf. Ps 133:2). (See also ANOINTING; SPICES.)

OLIVE

Olive trees, both wild and cultivated, were among the most common trees of Palestine (Deut 8:8; Judg 15:5; 1 Chron 27:28; Luke 22:39). They grew also in Mesopotamia and other places in the region (Gen 8:11). The trees grew to about six metres in height, and although their timber was of no use in building construction, it could be used to make furniture and ornamental articles (1 Kings 6:23,31). The Israelites used branches of olive trees to help make shelters for the Feast of Tabernacles (Neh 8:15).

Mostly, however, people grew olive trees for their fruit, which could be crushed to produce oil (Exod 27:20; Lev 2:4; 2 Kings 18:32; Micah 6:15; see OIL). Farmers harvested the olives by shaking or

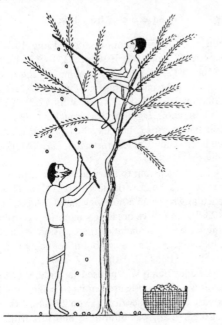

Harvesting olives

beating the tree so that the fruit fell to the ground. They then collected the fruit in baskets (Deut 24:20; Isa 17:6; 24:13; Amos 8:2). To obtain higher quality fruit and larger harvests, they sometimes grafted branches from good quality trees on to wild trees. To graft branches from wild trees on to good trees was 'contrary to nature' (Rom 11:17-24).

In the symbols and pictures of the Bible, the olive tree had a variety of meanings. It was a symbol of peace (Gen 8:10-12), fruitfulness (Ps 128:3-4), freshness (Ps 52:8), pleasantness (Jer 11:16), beauty (Hosea 14:5-7), God's Spirit (Zech 4:1-6), God's family (Rom 11:17-24) and God's witnesses (Zech 4:11-14; Rev 11:3-4).

ONESIMUS

In New Testament times, households often included slaves, and many of these slaves became Christians. One slave who became a Christian was Onesimus.

Onesimus had worked in Colossae for a man named Philemon, but he ran away and came to Rome. There he met Paul and was converted. Paul knew Philemon, so when Onesimus decided to return to his master, Paul wrote a letter to Philemon, urging him to forgive Onesimus and receive him back (Philem 10-19; for details see PHILEMON).

ORDAIN

Though a common word in the traditional language of the church, 'ordain' is not common in the Bible. It is not present at all in most modern versions. The word usually means 'appoint', as for example when Jesus appointed apostles (Mark 3:13-14; John 15:16; see APOSTLE), and the apostles appointed church leaders (Acts 6:3,6; 14:23; see DEACON; ELDER).

People were not to make such appointments hastily. They had to have confidence that those appointed possessed the God-given gifts for the tasks, and they expressed that confidence through the ceremony of laying on hands (Acts 6:6; 1 Tim 4:14; 5:22; see LAYING ON OF HANDS).

ORNAMENTS

Just as it is natural for people to want to make themselves attractive by the clothes they wear, so it is natural that they should want to add to their appearance by wearing ornaments (Ezek 16:10-13). In ancient times valuable ornaments were also used for making payments or investing wealth (Gen 24:22,53; Exod 11:2; 35:22; 2 Sam 1:24).

People wore ornaments especially on important or joyous occasions (Isa 61:10; Jer 2:32). At times certain people received ornaments to indicate their honoured status in a household or society (Gen 41:42-43; Esther 3:10; Luke 15:22). But excessive adornment was condemned. Such extravagance was usually the characteristic of prostitutes (Jer 4:30) or the haughty and corrupt women of the upper classes (Isa 3:18-23). Good conduct, not lavish adornment, is what makes people truly attractive (1 Tim 2:8-10; 1 Peter 3:3-5; see also DRESS)..

ORPHAN

God has a special concern for orphans (Deut 10:18; Ps 68:5), and he wants his people to have similar concern (Deut 26:12; James 1:27). In circumstances where orphans are left poor or defenceless, people who are cruel or greedy can easily take unfair advantage of them (Exod 22:22; Job 24:3,9; Isa 10:2; Jer 5:28). Although God will punish the oppressors (Deut 27:19; Ps 10:12-15; Mal 3:5), he expects his people to defend the oppressed against injustice (Deut 24:17; Job 29:12). He also expects them to help provide the needy with the necessities for everyday living (Deut 16:14; Job 31:16-17).

PALESTINE

Palestine is the name commonly used for the land that in ancient times was known as Canaan. When the Israelites first occupied Canaan, they met some of their strongest opposition from the Philistines, the people from whom Palestine takes its name (see CANAAN; PHILISTIA). The natural boundaries of the land were the Mediterranean Sea in the west, the Jordan River in the east, the Lebanon Range in the north and the Sinai Desert in the south.

The main physical features of Palestine ran approximately north-south in more or less parallel lines. Bordering the Mediterranean Sea was a coastal plain rising into an area of low foothills called the Shephelah, which rose further into the broad central mountains. These mountains then fell away into a deep valley called the Arabah, through the northern section of which flowed the Jordan River. East of Jordan the land rose sharply, then opened on to an uneven tableland. (For Palestine's vegetation, animal life, climate and agriculture see ANIMALS; BIRDS; FARMING; FLOWERS; FOOD; TREES; WEATHER.)

Coastal plain

Palestine's coastal plain, from the Phoenician town of Tyre in the north to the Israelite town of Gaza in the south, was about 220 kilometres in length. In Phoenicia, where the Lebanon Range was close to the coast, the plain was very narrow (see LEBANON;

PHOENICIA), but south from Lebanon it gradually widened till interrupted by the Mt Carmel Range.

Extending inland from the Mt Carmel Range to Jezreel was the Plain of Esdraelon, through which flowed the Kishon River (Judg 5:21; Hosea 1:5). From Jezreel the plain led into the Valley of Jezreel,

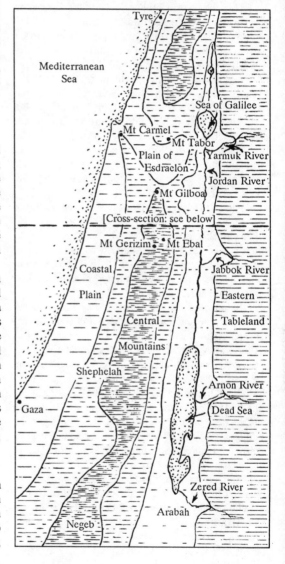

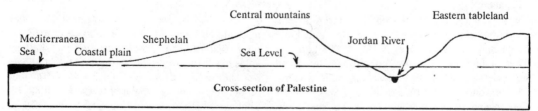

Cross-section of Palestine

which extended east as far as the town of Bethshan near the Jordan River. Other towns of the region were Jokneam, Megiddo, Ibleam and Shunem (Josh 17:11; 1 Sam 28:4; 1 Kings 4:12). (For details of towns mentioned in this article see entries under the names of the towns.)

This whole area (i.e. the Plain of Esdraelon and the Valley of Jezreel) was sometimes referred to as the Valley of Jezreel and played an important part in Israel's history. To the north of the valley was Mt Tabor, and to the south Mt Gilboa. Many of Israel's battles were fought in this area, partly because the main north-south (Syria to Philistia) and east-west (Bethshan to Mt Carmel) roads passed through the valley. Megiddo, where the two roads crossed, also commanded the western entrance to the Plain of Esdraelon and consequently was of strategic importance to Israel (Judg 4:6; 5:19-21; 6:33; 1 Sam 29:1; 31:1,8,12; 2 Kings 9:16,27,30; 23:29; Zech 12:11).

Along the coast immediately to the south of Mt Carmel was the small Plain of Dor (Josh 17:11; 1 Chron 7:29) and farther south the larger Plain of Sharon. Though much of Sharon was marshy, it had some pastoral and forestry lands. In Old Testament times it was fairly thinly populated (1 Chron 27:29; Song of Songs 2:1; Isa 35:2).

Because of sandy shores and shallow waters, there were no good sites for harbours south of Mt Carmel. A low headland enabled a small harbour to be built at Joppa, and in Old Testament times this was Israel's only Mediterranean port. Other towns in the area were Ono and Lod (or Lydda) (2 Chron 2:16; Ezra 3:7; Neh 11:35; Jonah 1:3; Acts 9:35-36,38; 10:5-8). In New Testament times the magnificent city of Caesarea, built by Herod the Great and equipped with an artificial harbour, became the administrative centre and chief port of the Roman province of Judea (Acts 18:22; 25:1-6).

From Joppa south to Gaza was the Plain of the Philistines, whose five main towns were Ekron, Ashdod, Ashkelon, Gaza and Gath. The plain and its lowland hills were good for farming, but became drier and less fertile towards the south. (For further details of this region see PHILISTIA.)

Shephelah

The low hill country between the narrow coastal plain and the high central range was called the Shephelah (Deut 1:7; Josh 9:1-2; 10:40; 12:8; Jer 17:26; Obad 19). It consisted of many hills and valleys, down which flowed swift mountain streams. This produced a fertile region that was suitable for growing sycamore trees and raising sheep and cattle (1 Kings 10:27; 1 Chron 27:28; 2 Chron 9:27; 26:10).

Certain valleys in the Shephelah provided the only convenient routes from the coastal plain up to the central highlands, and consequently were the scene of many battles. The most important of these valleys was the Valley of Aijalon, where the main route from the coastal plain climbed up through Gezer and Beth-horon to the chief highland towns (Josh 10:11-12; 16:3; 1 Kings 9:16-17; see 'Central mountains' below).

To the south of the Valley of Aijalon was the Valley of Elah leading up through Libnah (Josh 10:29-31; 1 Sam 17:2; 2 Kings 19:8), and slightly farther south another valley leading up through Lachish (2 Kings 18:13-17). Of lesser importance were the valleys of Sorek and Zephathah (Judg 16:4; 2 Chron 14:10).

Central mountains

Rising from the coastal plain/Shephelah on the west and the Jordan Valley/Arabah on the east were the central mountains of Palestine. For convenience they may be considered a single mountain range broken into two unequal sections.

The smaller northern section consisted mainly of the mountains of Galilee and was separated from the remaining section by the Plain of Esdraelon and its associated Valley of Jezreel. These hills and the adjacent plain and valley covered much of the tribal areas of Dan, Naphtali, Issachar, Zebulun and Asher (Josh 20:7; Isa 9:1).

In the north of Galilee the mountains were higher than those in the south, more thickly forested and more thinly populated. In Old Testament times the chief city of the northern part was Hazor, originally a Canaanite stronghold but later one of Israel's northern defence outposts (Judg 4:2; 1 Kings 9:15). Towards the south the mountains were more suited to farming. This south Galilean hill country was the region where Jesus grew up and where he spent most of the three and a half years of his public ministry. Some of the towns of the region were Nazareth, Cana and Nain (Matt 21:11; Luke 2:39; 4:16; 7:11; John 2:1-11; 4:46; 21:2). (For other towns in Galilee see 'Upper Jordan and Sea of Galilee' below.)

Hills to the south of the Plain of Esdraelon marked the beginning of the long section of the range that stretched through central and southern Palestine. First were the hills of Samaria. These were not as high as those of north Galilee, the only prominent mountains being Mt Gerizim and Mt Ebal, which stood on opposite sides of the town of

Shechem (Deut 27:12-13; Judg 9:7). Other important towns were Tirzah and Samaria. In the early days of the divided Israelite kingdom, Tirzah was the northern capital (1 Kings 14:17; 15:33; 16:6-8,15-19). Samaria was made the capital after Tirzah and remained so till the end of the northern kingdom. The city's position on a hill overlooking the surrounding territory made it an excellent site for a capital (1 Kings 16:23-24; 20:1; 2 Kings 6:24; 17:5). North of Samaria was the small Plain of Dothan, which provided an alternative route from Jezreel to the coast (Gen 37:17,28; 2 Kings 6:13).

Further south was the hill country of Ephraim, Benjamin and part of neighbouring Judah. This was a fertile forest region broken by steep valleys. These valleys proved to be good defences against attackers, particularly in the days following Joshua's conquest when the Israelites were struggling to keep hold of their newly won territory (Josh 17:17-18; Judg 5:14; 7:24; 12:15).

To the west the Valley of Aijalon led down from the towns of Beth-horon and Gezer through the Shephelah to the Philistine coastal plain (Josh 10:9-12; 16:3,5; 18:13-14). Since this valley provided a main route from the coastal plain to Israel's highlands, it was a frequent battlefield and became well fortified with Israelite defence outposts (1 Sam 13:17-18; 1 Kings 9:16-17; 2 Chron 8:5; 11:10; 25:13; 28:18).

On the other side of the highlands another valley provided the way down to the east. The route went from Bethel through Ai and Michmash to Jericho on the broad plain of the Jordan Valley (Josh 16:1-2; 18:11-13; 1 Sam 13:2-5,23; 14:1-5; Luke 10:30; 19:1).

This part of the central highlands was one of the most thickly populated regions of Canaan. Some of its other well known towns were Shiloh, Mizpah, Ramah, Gibeon, Gibeah, Kiriath-jearim, Beth-shemesh, Emmaus, Jerusalem, Bethlehem and Bethany (Josh 9:3,17; 18:25-28; 1 Sam 6:12; 7:15-17; 14:1-3; 17:12; Matt 2:1; Mark 11:1; Luke 24:13).

To the south of this collection of towns the hills gradually flattened, the rainfall decreased, the land became less fertile and the population was more thinly spread. The chief town in this region was Hebron (Gen 23:17-19; 2 Sam 2:11; 3:20; 15:10). It was situated about half way between Jerusalem and Beersheba and was on the main route from Jerusalem to Egypt (Num 13:21-22).

Another route led west from Hebron through Lachish down to Ashkelon and Gaza on the main coastal route to Egypt. Because of their strategic positions, Hebron and Lachish were heavily fortified (2 Chron 11:5-12).

This barren region of southern Judah was the place to which David fled in escaping from Saul. Some of the places mentioned in the story are Adullam, Keilah, Ziph, En-gedi, Maon, Horesh and

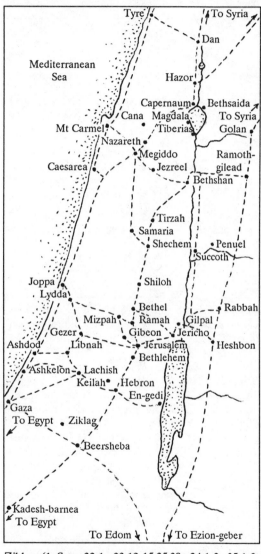

Ziklag (1 Sam 22:1; 23:13-15,25,29; 24:1-2; 25:1-2; 27:6-10; for map see DAVID). The central mountains had by now flattened into a broad tableland that stretched south into the Negeb.

Negeb

The Negeb is literally 'the dry', and was the name given to the dry southern part of Palestine between the Dead Sea and the Sinai Desert. Its approximate northern boundary ran from Gaza on the coast east to the Dead Sea. Its approximate southern boundary ran from Ezion-geber at the north-eastern tip of the Red Sea to the Brook of Egypt (Wadi El-Arish), which it followed to the coast. The chief towns of the Negeb were Beersheba in the north and Kadesh-barnea in the south. The Wilderness of Zin fell

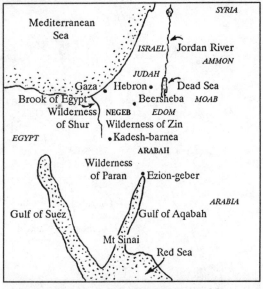

within the Negeb, and the Wildernesses of Shur and Paran bordered it to the west and south respectively (Gen 20:1; Exod 15:22; Num 10:12; 13:26; 20:1; 32:8; 33:35-37; 34:4).

In Old Testament times much of the Negeb was occupied by the tribe of Judah. The northern part attracted more people than the southern, because it was more suitable for grazing and farming. The Philistines continued to occupy much of the coastal plain, and other tribal groups occupied various areas at different times (Gen 20:1; 26:1; Num 13:29; 1 Sam 27:10; 30:14). Water was always a problem in this dry region (Gen 16:7; 26:17-23; Josh 15:19).

There were two main roads linking Egypt and Palestine. The 'Way of the land of the Philistines' went along the coast (Exod 13:17), the 'Way of the Wilderness of Shur' went through the centre of the Negeb (Gen 16:7). This latter route passed through the towns of Kadesh-barnea, Beersheba, Hebron, Jerusalem, Shiloh and Shechem, and was a well used route even as early as the time of Abraham (Gen 20:1; 21:32; 37:14; 46:1). It may have been used by some of the twelve spies when they went north to spy out Canaan (Num 13:21-23), and was probably used by Joseph and Mary when they fled to Egypt to escape from Herod (Matt 2:13-15).

This north-south road was crossed at Beersheba by a west-east road connecting Gaza on the coast with Edom inland. The section of the road that went east from Beersheba through the Valley of Salt and the Wilderness of Zin to Edom was known as the 'Way of the Wilderness of Edom' (2 Sam 8:13; 2 Kings 3:8; 14:7).

Upper Jordan and Sea of Galilee

The Jordan River rose in the region of Mt Hermon in the Lebanon Range. From there it flowed south through a region that was quiet and isolated, till the tribe of Dan conquered the people and seized the territory for itself. In Old Testament times the town of Laish, which the Danites renamed Dan, became the northernmost town of Israel (Judg 18:27-29; 1 Sam 3:20; 1 Kings 12:29). In the New Testament record the town of Caesarea Philippi, which was in the same locality, was the northernmost point that Jesus visited (Matt 16:13).

South of Dan the Jordan flowed through a small lake, then into a second and larger lake known in the Old Testament as the Sea of Chinnereth and in the New Testament as the Sea (or Lake) of Galilee, the Lake of Gennesaret, and the Sea of Tiberias (Num 34:11; Matt 15:29; Luke 5:1; John 6:1). The hills around the Sea of Galilee, particularly those to the north-west, provided Jesus with some quiet spots where he went to pray and teach his disciples (Matt 5:1; 14:23; 15:29; 28:16).

The lake itself was 200 metres below sea level and contained plenty of fish (Matt 4:18; Luke 5:1-9; John 21:1-8). The area around the lake was well populated and was the scene of much of Jesus' public ministry. On the northern shore of the lake were two towns, each with a large Jewish population, Capernaum and Bethsaida. Capernaum seems to have been Jesus' base for his northern ministry (Matt 4:13; Mark 2:1; 6:45; 9:33; John 6:17). In the hills behind Capernaum was another town that Jesus visited, Chorazin (Matt 11:21-23).

On the western shore of Lake Galilee were the largely Gentile towns of Magdala and Tiberias. Also bordering the lake to the west was the small Plain of Gennesaret (or Chinnereth) (Matt 15:39; Mark 6:53; John 6:23).

To the east of the lake was the less populous district of Gadara, where the land rose steeply from the water's edge and opened on to good farming country. The people of the district were mainly Gentiles, some of them pig farmers, and were known as Gadarenes (after the local district) or Gerasenes (after the larger district where Gadara was located) (Matt 8:28,30-32; Mark 5:1,11-13). Spreading out farther to the north and east was the rich pastoral land of Bashan. Two of its main towns were Golan and Edrei (Deut 32:14; Josh 12:1-5; 21:27; Jer 50:19; see BASHAN).

Jordan Valley and Dead Sea

From the Sea of Galilee the Jordan flowed south through a deep valley till it entered the Dead Sea, 400 metres below sea level. The valley immediately south of the Sea of Galilee was fertile and good for farming, but further south it began to become desolate, till it was little better than a desert where it entered the Dead Sea (Mark 1:4-5,9-13).

For much of its length the river was difficult to cross, and so formed a good barrier against invasion from the east. There was thick jungle along the water's edge on either side of the river, from where steep banks rose up to the floor of the main valley (Jer 12:5; 49:19; Zech 11:3). These banks collapsed at times and dammed the stream, which was probably what happened at the time of Israel's crossing under Joshua (Josh 3:14-17). Normally, people could cross the river only at certain places where there were natural fords (Josh 2:7; Judg 3:28; 7:24; 12:5; 2 Sam 19:15,18).

Between the Sea of Galilee and the Dead Sea a number of streams fed the Jordan from the east, the most important of them being the Yarmuk and the Jabbok. Another, of lesser importance, was the Cherith (Deut 3:16; 1 Kings 17:3). Two towns of the region, Succoth and Penuel, were strategically located close to the Jordan and Jabbok Rivers. There was a ford across the Jordan nearby, and defence fortifications were built at Penuel (Gen 32:22,31; 33:17; Judg 8:8,16-17; 1 Kings 12:25).

The region east of Jordan, particularly the central part, was commonly known as Gilead. In the time of Moses, Israel had taken the land from the Amorites, but the earlier occupants were the Ammonites (in the central region) and the Moabites (in the southern region). Their respective capitals were Rabbah and Heshbon (Num 21:24-26; Deut 3:11; 4:46). The Israelites' chief defence outpost on the eastern frontier was at Ramoth-gilead (2 Kings 8:28; 9:14). (For maps and other details see AMMON; GILEAD; MOAB.)

In the Jordan Valley and to the west of the river were the towns of Gilgal and Jericho (Josh 4:19). Because of a natural spring of freshwater at Jericho, the town had the appearance of an oasis and was called the city of palm trees (Deut 34:3). Another natural product of the Jordan Valley was a special type of clay that was used in making articles of bronze (1 Kings 7:46).

The Dead Sea was known also as the Salt Sea, because of the large amounts of salt and other chemicals in the water (Josh 15:5; 18:19). No fish could live in it and no vegetation grew around its shores, except at places where fresh water entered from streams on the eastern side. There were no streams on the western side, but cultivation was possible at isolated points where there were fresh-water springs, such as at En-gedi (Song of Songs 1:14).

It is believed that Sodom and Gomorrah were located near the southern end of the Dead Sea. Through earthquake activity the sea apparently spread further south, covering whatever may have remained of the ancient cities (Gen 19:24-28).

Arabah

From the eastern side of the central highlands, the land fell away sharply into a deep valley that ran from the Sea of Chinnereth (Sea of Galilee) along the Jordan River to the Dead Sea, from where it continued south to Ezion-geber on the Gulf of Aqabah (the north-eastern arm of the Red Sea). The section north of the Dead Sea was commonly known as the Jordan Valley, and the section south as the Arabah.

Originally, *arabah* was a common Hebrew word meaning 'burnt' or 'dried up', and was used of dry or semi-desert wasteland. It was a fitting word to give as a name to the barren valley south of the Dead Sea (Deut 1:1; 2:8).

The name Arabah was not restricted to this one region. On occasions the whole valley, both north and south of the Dead Sea, was called the Arabah. The Dead Sea was known as the Sea of the Arabah, and a small stream that entered the Jordan near its entrance to the Dead Sea was known as the Brook of the Arabah (Deut 3:17; 4:48-49; Josh 3:16; 11:2; 12:1-3; Amos 6:14). In the days of Israel's expansion under Jeroboam II, the Sea of the Arabah marked Israel's southern boundary (2 Kings 14:25).

An important road called the King's Highway ran from Ezion-geber along the plateau on the eastern side of the Arabah through Edom, Moab and Ammon into Syria. The Israelites under Moses wanted to use this road on their journey to Canaan, but Edom and Moab refused permission, forcing the Israelites to make a lengthy and tiring detour around the borders (Num 20:14-21; 21:10-13,21-26; Judg 11:15-24).

The Arabah contained good quantities of iron and copper (Deut 8:9). Workers mined and smelted the minerals at various places along the valley, then transported them down the King's Highway (the

Arabah road; Deut 2:8) to a refinery at Ezion-geber, from where large ocean-going ships carried them east (cf. 1 Kings 9:26-28; 10:22).

Political divisions

For details of the history of Palestine and its political divisions in Old Testament times see AMORITES; CANAAN; ISRAEL; JUDAH; and articles under the names of the various Israelite tribes and towns. In New Testament times there were three commonly recognized regions in Palestine itself (northern, central and southern; see GALILEE; SAMARIA; JUDEA), and two in the former Israelite territory to the east of Jordan (northern and southern; see DECAPOLIS; PEREA).

PAMPHYLIA

The province of Pamphylia was in southern Asia Minor, bordering the Mediterranean Sea (Acts 27:5). Paul visited the province twice on his first missionary journey. There is no mention of his preaching there when he passed through it the first time (Acts 13:13-14), but on his return he preached in the main town of Perga. He then went to the nearby port of Attalia, from where he sailed back to his home church in Syria (Acts 14:24-26). (For map see ACTS, BOOK OF.)

PARABLES

From ancient times people have used pictures and stories from nature, history and everyday life to teach moral and spiritual truth. Broadly speaking, these pictures and stories are called parables. The Old Testament contains a number of stories that may be considered parables (Judg 9:8-15; 2 Sam 12:1-4; 2 Kings 14:9), but by far the majority of parables in the Bible were spoken by Jesus.

Purpose of Jesus' parables

Jesus' parables were more than mere illustrations. They were stories designed to make people think, and often the hearers had to work out the meaning for themselves. The crowds that followed Jesus were often a hindrance, as many of the people were more interested in seeing him perform miracles than in making a spiritual response to his ministry. Jesus' parables helped separate those who were genuinely interested from those who were merely curious (Mark 4:1-2,11-12).

This separation occurred as people exercised their minds to work out the meaning of the parables. Those who desired to know more of Jesus and his teaching found the parables full of meaning. As a result their ability to understand the teaching increased. Those who had no real interest in Jesus' teaching saw no meaning in the parables at all and so turned away from him. As a result their spiritual darkness became darker, and their hardened hearts harder. Because their wills were opposed to Jesus, their minds could not appreciate his teaching. Their sins therefore remained unforgiven (Matt 13:10-17; Mark 4:10-12).

Although the teaching of parables may have caused the idly curious to lose interest in Jesus, the basic purpose of a parable was to enlighten, not to darken. A parable was like a lamp, and a lamp was put on a stand to give people light, not hidden under a bowl or a bed to keep people in darkness. The more thought people gave to Jesus' teaching, the more enlightenment and blessing they received in return. On the other hand the less thought they gave to it, the less chance they had of understanding any spiritual truth at all (Mark 4:21-25).

Parables of the kingdom

Because Jesus' parables separated between the true and the false, many of them were concerned with the subject of the kingdom of God. God's kingdom had, in a sense, come in the person of Jesus Christ. He announced the kingdom, and people's response to his message determined whether they entered the kingdom (Matt 13:18-23; 21:28-33,42-43; 22:1-14; see KINGDOM OF GOD).

This was seen clearly in the parable of the sower, where the different types of soil illustrated the different responses that people made to the teaching of Jesus. Only those who wholeheartedly accepted it were God's people (Matt 13:1-9,18-23). This parable was the key to understanding the others (Mark 4:13). When the Jews, for whom the kingdom was prepared, rejected Jesus, Gentiles were invited and there was a great response (Matt 22:1-10). Thus Gentiles, who in Old Testament times had not received the preparation for God's kingdom that the Jews had received, entered into its full blessings along with believing Jews (Matt 20:1-16).

Jesus pointed out that in the present world there will always be a mixture of those who belong to God's kingdom and those who do not. When the final judgment comes, however, only the genuine believers will share in the triumphs of the kingdom (Matt 13:24-30,34-43,47-50; 25:1-46).

God's kingdom, then, is assured of final victory. From its insignificant beginnings among the ordinary people of Palestine it spreads throughout the world (Matt 13:31-33). It is of such value that to enter it is worth any sacrifice (Matt 13:44-46). It is something that reaches its fulfilment through the work of God himself (Mark 4:26-29).

Further characteristics of the parables

Whether or not Jesus' parables are directly related to the subject of the kingdom in the manner just outlined, Jesus usually intended them to teach only one or two points. In some cases he mentioned these points (Matt 21:43; Luke 12:21; 15:7,10), but in others he left the hearers to find out for themselves (Mark 12:12-13; Luke 7:40-43; 19:11-27). Likewise

Sowing the seed

instead of giving a direct answer to a question or criticism, Jesus sometimes told a parable by which the hearer himself could work out the answer (Luke 10:29-30; 15:2-3).

It is therefore important, in reading a parable, to find the chief purpose for which Jesus told it, and interpret the parable according to this purpose (Luke 18:1,9). There is no need to find meanings for all the details within the parable, as these are often nothing more than parts of the framework of the story. Indeed, it can be misleading to interpret some of these details, because in doing so we may miss, or distort, the meaning that Jesus intended.

For example, in the parable of Matthew 20:1-15 Jesus was not teaching that an employer should give his workers equal pay for unequal work. Rather he was showing that even the most unlikely people enter God's kingdom and, by God's grace, they receive its full blessings (Matt 20:16). Similarly in the parable of Luke 16:1-17 he was not advising people to use cunning or dishonesty in their business dealings. Rather he was teaching that if believers use

their material possessions wisely, they are guaranteed heavenly riches of permanent value (Luke 16:9-11).

Whatever the main point of each of Jesus' parables may have been, Jesus was inevitably forcing his hearers to a decision. He wanted people to listen and think (Matt 18:12; 21:28; 22:17), but more than that he wanted them to decide and act (Matt 18:35; 21:45; Luke 10:37). And the challenge that Jesus brought through his parables is still relevant today (Matt 13:9,43).

PARADISE

Originally the word translated 'paradise' in English versions of the Bible meant 'a garden'. The word was used of the Garden of Eden (Gen 2:8-10; Ezek 28:13). This association with a place of beauty and perfection was probably the reason why the word in later times was used of heaven (Luke 23:43; 2 Cor 12:3; Rev 2:7; cf. Rev 22:1-5; see HEAVEN).

PARAN

Paran was a barren region in the Sinai Peninsular. It was located south of Kadesh-barnea and west of Ezion-geber. (For map and other details see KADESH-BARNEA.) Refugees at times escaped to Paran, and the people of Israel camped there on their way from Egypt to Canaan (Gen 21:21; Num 10:12; 13:25-26; 1 Kings 11:17-18).

PARENTS

Probably the most basic of all human relationships is that between a man and a woman. Only through it can human life be perpetuated (Gen 1:27-28). Yet this relationship involves more than sexual relations for the sake of producing children. Sex is only one part of a total relationship in which a man and a woman marry and commit themselves to each other for life (Matt 19:5-6).

It is within this total marriage relationship, not outside it, that God intends children to be born and grow up. God's design is for children to be brought up in families where both parents live together and accept their responsibilities. Those responsibilities include providing for their children's physical and social needs, and teaching them the true values of life (Ps 128:1-3; Prov 1:8; 31:21,27; Col 3:20-21; cf. 1 Kings 1:5-6).

In the case of Christian parents, the training of their children will aim to bring them to know God and walk in his ways (Deut 6:5-9; Eph 6:1-4; 2 Tim 1:5; 3:15). Christians will learn how to deal properly with their children as they understand more about the way their heavenly Father deals with them (Heb 12:5-11; James 1:16-17; see FATHER). (For fuller details of parental responsibilities see FAMILY.)

PASSOVER

The Feast of Passover was God's appointed way for the people of Israel to celebrate their miraculous escape from Egypt (Exod 12:14,24). The name of the feast recalled God's act of 'passing over' the houses of the Israelites while killing the firstborn of the Egyptians (Exod 12:27). However, God withheld judgment from the Israelite households only when he saw the blood of the sacrificial animal around the front door. The blood was a sign that an innocent life had been taken in place of the one under judgment (Exod 12:5,7,12-13,21-23; cf. Lev 17:11; see BLOOD).

Regulations and practices

The month of the Passover became the first month of the Jewish religious year (Exod 12:2). (This was the season of spring in Israel and corresponds with March-April on our calendar.) Late in the afternoon of the fourteenth day, each household killed a lamb, which the people ate in a sacrificial meal that night. This was now the beginning of the fifteenth day according to Israelite reckoning, for they considered sunset to mark the end of one day and the beginning of the next (Exod 12:6,8).

Each Passover meal was a re-enactment of the first Passover meal, when people prepared and ate it in haste, dressed ready for their departure in the morning (Exod 12:11,25-27). They did not cut up the animal and boil it, but roasted it whole over an open fire. They made their bread without yeast (leaven), to save time waiting for the dough to rise. The entire meal was deliberately kept simple, to keep the people from any feeling of self-glory. They were to burn the leftovers, and so prevent any defilement of the solemn occasion through the meat's spoiling or the people's keeping portions as sacred charms (Exod 12:8-10).

Following the Passover, and joined to it, was the seven-day Feast of Unleavened Bread. The two were considered one festival (Deut 16:1-8; Mark 14:1). Having removed leaven from their houses before preparing the Passover, the people kept their houses free of leaven for the week after the Passover (Exod 12:14-20). This reminded them that, having been saved through the Passover, they had fled from Egypt hastily, cooking unleavened bread as they travelled (Exod 12:33-34,39). (Concerning the offerings made at the Feast of Unleavened Bread see FEASTS.)

Once the Israelites arrived in Canaan, they were to celebrate the Passover only at the central place of worship. At first this was the tabernacle, and later the temple (Deut 16:5-6; Josh 5:10-11; 2 Chron 8:12-13; 30:1; 35:1; Luke 2:41; John 2:13; 11:55).

All adult male Israelites had to attend the Passover celebration (Exod 23:14,17), and so could foreigners, provided they had accepted circumcision and so become part of the covenant people (Exod 12:43-49). There were special provisions for those Israelites who were unable to attend because of unavoidable circumstances (Num 9:6-13; cf. 2 Chron 30:17-20). The reforms that became necessary at various times in Israel's later history show that people had frequently neglected or misused the Passover (2 Chron 30:5; 35:16-18).

Jesus' last Passover

By the time of Jesus, the Passover had developed into a set form with a number of added rituals. Although people killed the lamb at the temple, they ate the meal privately with friends and relatives (Luke 22:8-13). Among the additions to the meal was a cup of wine, for which the head of the household offered a prayer of thanks (or blessing; 1 Cor 10:16), and which he passed around among the participants, both before and after the eating of unleavened bread (Mark 14:22-24; Luke 22:15-20).

Singing also became part of the celebration, the participants singing a collection of psalms known as the Hallel (Psalms 113-118). They usually sang the first two psalms before eating the lamb, the other psalms after (Mark 14:26).

It appears that on the occasion of Jesus' last Passover, he and his disciples ate the meal a day earlier than the official time, and probably without a lamb (Luke 22:15; John 13:1). If this was so, the reason was probably that Jesus knew that he himself was now the Passover lamb. On the next day he would lay down his life at the same time as the animals were being killed in preparation for the meal that was to follow that night (John 18:28; 19:14,31,42).

Jesus' death on the cross was the great act of redemption of which the Israelite Passover was but a picture (cf. Exod 12:5 with 1 Peter 1:18-19; cf. Exod 12:46 with John 19:36; cf. Exod 12:21,27 with 1 Cor 5:7). Once Jesus had died, the Passover was of no further use. It was replaced by a new remembrance ceremony, the Lord's Supper (Matt 26:17-30; 1 Cor 10:16; 11:23-26; see LORD'S SUPPER).

Nevertheless, the New Testament refers to the requirements of the Passover to provide a lesson for Christians. Just as the Passover festival meant that Israelites removed leaven from their houses, so the sacrifice of Jesus Christ means that Christians should remove sin from their lives (1 Cor 5:7-8; see LEAVEN).

PASTOR

Ephesians 4:8-11 states that pastors and teachers were among the risen Christ's gifts to the church. The grammatical link between the two words in the original language indicates that they refer to the same people, pastor-teachers.

Another point that is clearer in the original language than in English is the connection between the words 'pastor', 'shepherd' and 'flock'. All come from the same Greek root. A pastor, or shepherd, is one who leads and cares for God's flock, the church (John 21:15-17; Acts 20:28-29; 1 Peter 5:1-4). In referring to leaders of God's people as shepherds, the New Testament writers were following a well established Old Testament usage of the word (Num 27:17; Isa 63:11; Jer 50:6; see SHEPHERD). But whereas the shepherd-leaders of Israel were often concerned only for themselves (Ezek 34:2-6), the Christian's example of a shepherd-leader, Jesus Christ, gave himself for the flock (Matt 9:36; 10:6; John 10:1-15; 1 Peter 5:1-4).

One reason why pastors must also be teachers is that their means of feeding the flock is the teaching of the Word (Acts 20:28; see TEACHER). Some may move from place to place, spending periods of varying lengths in different churches (Acts 11:25-26; 20:31). Others may be settled residents of particular localities, and most likely be elders in their local churches (Acts 20:28-32; Col 4:12-13). Elders must have pastoring abilities (1 Peter 5:1-4) and teaching abilities (1 Tim 3:2). Their leadership and care of the church involves feeding it on teaching that is wholesome and protecting it from teaching that is harmful (Acts 20:29; 1 Tim 1:3-7; 6:3-21; Titus 1:9; see ELDER).

It is not the duty of the pastor-teachers to carry out all the service of God in the church. They must not encourage the Christians to be totally dependent on them. On the contrary they should use their God-given gifts in such a way that all the Christians are better equipped to carry out God's service and better able to understand Christian teaching. In this way individual Christians will grow to spiritual maturity and the church as a whole will be built up (Eph 4:11-16; cf. Ezek 34:2-6).

PATIENCE

Among the many qualities that the Spirit of God develops in the life of believers is that of patience (Gal 5:22). Some older English versions called it longsuffering, and at times forbearance. Patience is that quality of character that develops within believers as they learn to put up with people and things that test, try or annoy them (Rom 5:3-4; Eph 4:1-2; James 1:3-4). The specific feature of Christian patience is that believers exercise it in a spirit of love, joy, humility and forgiveness (1 Cor 13:4,7; Col 1:11; 3:12-13; cf. Matt 18:23-35).

Patience is a characteristic of God himself. He is patient with sinners, withholding his judgment and providing instead a way of salvation (Ps 103:8-9; Jonah 4:2; Rom 3:25-26; 1 Peter 3:20). Those who respond to his patience in faith and repentance receive his forgiveness; those who despise or ignore it fall under his punishment (Exod 34:6-7; Rom 2:3-4; 9:22; 1 Tim 1:16; 2 Peter 3:9).

Jesus was the perfect example of forbearance and longsuffering (Matt 26:50-53; Luke 9:51-56; 1 Tim 1:16; 1 Peter 2:21-23). His example assures Christians that patience is more than tolerance; it is endurance and steadfastness (2 Thess 3:5; Heb 12:3). God's people must be prepared to endure insults, hardship, injustice, persecution, suffering and trials of every kind (1 Cor 4:12; 6:7; 2 Cor 1:6; 2 Thess 1:3-4; Heb 11:25-27; James 1:12; 5:10-11). This sort of patience is especially necessary for those who serve God in the work of evangelism and church care (1 Thess 5:14; 2 Tim 2:10,24; 3:10-11; 4:2).

Patience also means perseverance, whether in particular matters such as prayer (Rom 12:12; Col 4:2) or in the overall matter of steadfast commitment to the end (Matt 24:13; Col 2:23; Heb 10:36). What Christians look for is the return of Christ. Although, in the meantime, they must bear patiently with the trials of life, their expectancy of Christ's return gives purpose to their perseverance. It is their Christian hope (Heb 6:11-12; James 5:7-8; see HOPE; PERSEVERANCE).

PAUL

Through his evangelistic activity, church leadership, theological insights and extensive writings, Paul had an immeasurable influence on the development of Christianity. He spread the gospel and planted churches regardless of national or racial barriers, and in so doing he changed the traditional views of God-fearing people. He interpreted Christ's life and developed Christ's teachings in a way that provided a firm theological framework for Christian faith and practice.

Background and conversion

Paul's original name was Saul. He was a full-blooded Jew, born in Tarsus in south-east Asia Minor (Acts 9:11; 22:3; Phil 3:5). He inherited from birth the privilege of Roman citizenship (Acts 16:37; 22:26-28; see ROME), and he grew up to speak, read and write Greek and Hebrew fluently (Acts 21:37,40). The Greek influence in his education gave him the ability to think clearly and systematically, and the Hebrew influence helped to create in him a character of moral uprightness (Phil 3:6).

As a religiously zealous young man, Paul moved to Jerusalem, where he received instruction in the Jewish law according to the strict traditions of the Pharisees. His teacher was the prominent rabbi, Gamaliel (Acts 22:3; 23:6; 26:5). Like all Jewish young men he learnt a trade, in his case, tent-making (Acts 18:3).

Zeal for the Jewish law stirred up Paul against the Christians. He considered that Stephen was a rebel against the law and that therefore he deserved execution (Acts 6:13; 7:58; 8:1; Phil 3:6). With the support of the Jewish Council (the Sanhedrin), Paul then led the persecution against the Christians, imprisoning men and women alike (Acts 8:3; 9:1-2; 26:10-11; Gal 1:13; 1 Tim 1:13).

Paul considered the Christians to be guilty of blasphemy in believing in a Messiah who died on a cross; for a person who died on a cross was under God's curse (Acts 26:11; Gal 3:13). But while on the way to Damascus to capture Christians, Paul had a dramatic experience that changed him completely. Jesus' personal revelation to Paul convinced him that Jesus was alive (Acts 9:3-5; 22:14; 26:8,15; 1 Cor 9:1). This meant that Jesus was no longer under God's curse. He had died, not because he was a lawbreaker, but because he willingly bore the curse on behalf of those who were. Jesus' resurrection was now the unmistakable evidence of God's approval of him (Rom 1:4; Gal 3:13; 6:14).

Linked with Paul's conversion was the Lord's revelation that he was going to use Paul as his messenger to the Gentiles (Acts 9:15; 26:15-18; Gal 1:11-16). From that time on, Paul never ceased to wonder at the work of God in saving the opponent of Christianity and turning him into an ambassador for Christianity. It gave Paul an appreciation of the grace of God that affected every aspect of his life (1 Cor 15:8-10; Eph 3:8; 1 Tim 1:12-17). (The date of Paul's conversion was about AD 32.)

Preparation for future ministry

After his conversion, Paul remained for a while in Damascus, trying to convince the Jews that Jesus was Lord and Messiah. Part of the next three years

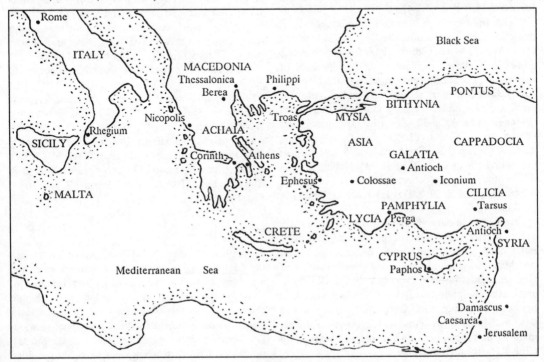

326

Paul spent in Arabia, after which he returned to Damascus. When violent opposition from the Jews threatened his life, he escaped to Jerusalem (Acts 9:22-26; Gal 1:17-18). Most of the Christians in Jerusalem doubted whether Paul's conversion was genuine. Not so Barnabas. After he introduced Paul to Peter and James the Lord's brother, the tension eased (Acts 9:26-28; Gal 1:19-20). But attempts by the Jews on his life again forced him to flee. He sailed from Caesarea to northern Syria, from where he went overland through Cilicia to Tarsus (Acts 9:29-30; 22:17-21; Gal 1:21).

Paul's next visit to Jerusalem was eleven years later (cf. Gal 1:18; 2:1). Little is known of those eleven years, though they must have been important years of preparation for Paul's future work. Paul spent the final year of this preparation period at Antioch in Syria. In response to an invitation from Barnabas, he had come from Tarsus to help the newly formed Antioch church (Acts 11:25-26). At the end of the year, Paul and Barnabas took a gift of money from Antioch to Jerusalem to help the poor Christians there (Acts 11:29-30; Gal 2:1).

Peter, John and James the Lord's brother, as representatives of the Jerusalem church, received the gift from the Antioch church and expressed their complete fellowship with the mission of Paul and Barnabas to the Gentiles (Gal 2:9-10). Paul and Barnabas then returned to Antioch, taking with them the young man John Mark (Acts 12:25).

Breaking into new territory

Having a desire to spread the gospel into the unevangelized areas to the west, the Antioch church sent off Paul and Barnabas as its missionaries (Acts 13:1-2; about AD 64). Accompanied by John Mark (who had gone with them as their assistant), Paul and Barnabas went first to Cyprus, where they proclaimed the message from one end of the island to the other (Acts 13:4-6).

From there the group went to Perga in Asia Minor. At this point John Mark left the other two and returned to Jerusalem (Acts 13:13). Paul and Barnabas then moved inland, planting churches in the Galatian towns of Antioch, Iconium, Lystra and Derbe (Acts 13:14; 14:1,8,20). To strengthen the new churches, they returned to Perga by the same route as they had come, and then sailed back to their home church in Syria (Acts 14:21-28).

This trip, commonly referred to as Paul's first missionary journey, showed how Paul thought carefully about his missionary work. He established some basic patterns, which he followed on later trips as his field of missionary activity expanded.

For example, Paul set himself certain guidelines concerning how and where he preached. He felt an obligation to preach to the Jews first, since their entire national history had prepared them to receive the Christian gospel (Acts 13:14,46; Rom 1:16).

On entering a town, Paul usually preached first in the synagogue, where God-fearing Gentiles, as well as Jews, provided him with a well prepared audience (Acts 13:14,43-44,48; 14:1; 17:1-4,10). His preaching in the synagogue was usually based on the Old Testament (Acts 13:15-41). His preaching in other places, where people knew nothing of the Old Testament, was usually based on the more general revelation of God in the natural creation and the human conscience (Acts 14:12-18; 17:17-31; Rom 1:19-20; 2:14-16).

Paul's aim was not merely to preach the gospel or make converts, but to bring people into a relationship with Jesus Christ that would change their lives. The life of Christ was to be reproduced in the lives of Christ's people (2 Cor 5:17; Eph 4:17-24; Col 2:6-7; 3:1-4). However, Paul did not leave these people to live in isolation. In each locality he built them into a church, or body, where the lives of all would be enriched as they contributed to, and shared in, the life of the body (1 Cor 12:12-14; see CHURCH). From the Christians within each church, Paul appointed suitable people as elders, in order to give leadership to the church (Acts 14:23; 20:28; see ELDER).

As independent units, each of them answerable to Christ as head (Eph 1:22-23; 4:15-16), churches then had the responsibility to evangelize the areas round about. For this reason Paul usually chose important towns along the main highways and trade routes as centres in which to plant churches. Once strong churches were established in these centres, the gospel would spread quickly to the surrounding regions (Acts 13:49; 16:11-12; 19:10; Rom 15:19-20; 1 Thess 1:8).

Trouble from Judaisers

There had always been some Jews in the Jerusalem church who believed that Christians had to follow the regulations of the Jewish law. Some of these people, known as Judaisers, came to Antioch in Syria and taught so persuasively that even Peter and Barnabas were influenced by them (Acts 15:1; Gal 2:11-14). Paul quickly dealt with the problem in Antioch, but soon he heard news that the Judaisers had spread their teaching to the new churches of Galatia. Without delay he wrote and sent off the letter that we know as Galatians (Gal 1:6-8; 3:1-3; see GALATIANS, LETTER TO THE).

For the rest of his life Paul opposed unceasingly any attempt to place Christians under the law of Moses. One of the great themes of his teaching was that Christ's death and resurrection has freed Christians from all forms of bondage, and given them a power to produce a quality of character that no law-code could ever produce (Rom 6:15-18; 7:4; 8:1-4; Gal 5:1,14; Col 2:13-14; 1 Tim 4:1-4). He was uncompromising in insisting that, through the grace of God, people are justified and sanctified by faith, regardless of lawkeeping (Rom 3:28; 6:19).

Paul's careful exposition of the meaning of Christ's death and resurrection (namely, that it is the basis of man's entire salvation) was one of his most influential contributions to the development of Christian doctrine (Rom 3:24-25; 5:1-2,6-11; 6:3-11; 1 Cor 1:21-24; 2 Cor 5:19-21; Gal 2:20-21; Eph 1:7; Phil 3:8-9; Col 1:20; 1 Tim 2:5-6; see JUSTIFICATION; SANCTIFICATION).

With these truths clear in mind Paul went to Jerusalem, along with others from Antioch, to deal with the problem that the Judaisers had created (Acts 15:1-5). The Jerusalem leaders supported Paul and expressed their disapproval of the Judaisers (Acts 15:11,19,24). They also sent a letter to the troubled churches to reassure them in what they had believed (Acts 15:23-33; 16:4).

Into Europe

In view of the recent troubles, Paul decided to revisit the churches of Galatia. When he and Barnabas split because of a quarrel concerning whether to take Mark with them, Paul chose Silas as his partner. Soon he added Timothy as a young assistant (Acts 15:36-41; 16:1-3; about AD 49). This marked the beginning of what is commonly referred to as Paul's second missionary journey.

Although Paul planned his movements, he was also responsive when God redirected him. As a result he moved from the churches of Galatia up to Troas, from where he sailed to Macedonia in northern Greece (Acts 16:6-11). He established churches in Philippi (Acts 16:12-40), Thessalonica (Acts 17:1-9) and Berea (Acts 17:10-14), after which he moved to the southern part of Greece known as Achaia. He preached with only moderate success in Athens (Acts 17:15-34), and then moved across to Corinth, where he stayed eighteen months (Acts 18:1-11).

During this time in Corinth, Paul wrote the two letters that we know as 1 and 2 Thessalonians (cf. Acts 18:5; 1 Thess 3:1-6; 5:1; 2 Thess 1:1; 2:14; see THESSALONIANS, LETTERS TO THE). Some of the matters Paul dealt with in these letters concerned the return of Jesus Christ. Throughout his writings Paul showed Christ's return to be the great hope, the assured expectation, the joyous climax towards which the Christian moves (Rom 8:18,23-24; 1 Cor 15:20,51-57; Phil 3:20-21; 1 Thess 1:10; 3:12-13; 4:13-18; see HOPE). It is also a sober reminder to Christians that, in view of their future meeting with Christ, they should be careful how they live now (1 Cor 4:5; 2 Cor 5:10; 1 Thess 5:1-11; see SECOND COMING).

From Corinth Paul sailed for Ephesus. After a short stay there, he sailed for Palestine, where he visited the church in Jerusalem before returning to Antioch in Syria (Acts 18:18-22).

Developing churches

After a time with the church in Antioch, Paul set out on what is known as his third missionary journey (about AD 53). Once more he visited the churches of Galatia, after which he moved to Ephesus on the west coast of Asia Minor (Acts 18:23; 19:1). He stayed there three years (Acts 20:31), during which time his disciples evangelized much of Asia Minor (Acts 19:9-10). His work in Ephesus brought extraordinary results among a wide variety of people (Acts 19:9,18-20,24-26).

The entire record of Paul in Acts is only an outline of his travels and experiences. He suffered many beatings, imprisonments and other hardships not mentioned in Acts (2 Cor 11:23-28), and met particularly violent opposition in Ephesus (1 Cor 15:32). During his three years in Ephesus he also had to deal with many problems that had arisen in the Corinthian church. He wrote the church a number of letters, and on one occasion made an urgent trip to Corinth to deal with the more serious matters. (For details of these travels and writings, not mentioned in Acts, see CORINTHIANS, LETTERS TO THE.)

Although Paul based his missionary plan on the establishment of churches in the key cities of a region, the plan would work only if those churches were strong and healthy. For this reason Paul gave repeated instruction to congregations and leaders on the quality of life required within the church. He emphasized the transforming work of the Holy Spirit in people's lives (2 Cor 3:17-18; Gal 5:18-24; Eph 5:15-20), the loving consideration that Christians should have for each other (Rom 14:13,19; 1 Cor 10:24; Gal 6:1-2; Phil 2:4), the importance of right teaching in the church (2 Cor 4:1-2; 1 Tim 1:3-5; 3:15; 2 Tim 2:15,24), and the need for the public life of the church to be orderly, God-honouring, and spiritually helpful to all (1 Cor 11:17-22; 14:12,26,40;

1 Tim 5:16-17; Titus 1:5; see CHURCH; GIFTS OF THE SPIRIT; HOLY SPIRIT).

Ephesus and Corinth were the two churches that gave Paul the most concern on these matters. They were also the two places where he stayed longest. After his three years in Ephesus he moved north to Macedonia (Acts 20:1), from where he travelled further through the region, possibly as far as Illyricum (Acts 20:2; Rom 15:19). He then travelled south to Corinth, where he spent a further three months (Acts 20:3).

For some time Paul had been collecting money from Gentile churches to help the poor Christians in the Jerusalem church. He hoped that when he and representatives from the Gentile churches took this money to Jerusalem, it would help towards healing the ill-feeling that many Jerusalemites had towards their Gentile brothers (Rom 15:25-27; 1 Cor 16:1-4; 2 Cor 8:1-9:15). Upon completing this mission in Jerusalem, Paul hoped to visit Rome (Acts 19:21; Rom 15:28-29).

In preparation for this visit to Rome, Paul wrote (from Corinth) a lengthy letter to the Roman church, setting out in systematic fashion the basics of the Christian faith. If Rome, the centre of the Empire, was to be a centre from which the gospel could spread, the church there had to have a clear understanding of the gospel (Rom 1:10-13; 15:14-16; see ROMANS, LETTER TO THE). Just as Paul had wanted to make sure that the church in Corinth was strong before he moved west to Rome (2 Cor 10:15-16), so he wanted to be sure that the church in Rome was strong before he moved farther west to Spain (Rom 15:23-24).

With these plans in mind, Paul and his party moved from Corinth back to Macedonia, across to Troas and down to Miletus (Acts 20:4-6,15). There he met the leaders of the Ephesian church, warning them of troubles that lay ahead for their church (Acts 20:17,28-30). After visiting Christians in a number of other ports, Paul reached Jerusalem (Acts 21:15; about AD 57).

Final break with Jerusalem

The Jerusalem Jews, some Christians among them, had always been suspicious of Paul, mainly because of his refusal to acknowledge the Jewish law as either a way of salvation or a rule of life. Yet Paul was always prepared to adjust to Jewish practices voluntarily, if he thought such action would gain him acceptance with the Jews and give him the opportunity to win them to Christ (1 Cor 9:19-23). He tried such an approach when he arrived in Jerusalem, but the Jews misunderstood. A riot

resulted and Paul ended up in prison (Acts 21:17-40; 22:1-30). The Roman commander then sent Paul to stand trial before the Jewish Council, but that also finished in a riot (Acts 23:1-10). He therefore sent Paul to the provincial governor, Felix, in Caesarea (Acts 22:31-33).

Paul's accusers were unable to convince Felix that Paul was guilty, but Felix left Paul in prison to prevent any further trouble with the Jews (Acts 24:22-27). When, after two years, Festus replaced Felix as governor, he continued the injustice. As a result Paul claimed his right as a Roman citizen and appealed to the Emperor for justice (Acts 25:10-12). Before Paul left for Rome, a visiting expert on Jewish affairs, Herod Agrippa II, confirmed that Paul was innocent (Acts 26:32).

Through one crisis after another, Paul had shown himself to be a person of great physical courage and mental alertness. Earlier, when saved at the last moment from being beaten to death by the rioting Jews in Jerusalem, he had insisted on speaking to those who wanted to murder him, and he even brought them to silence (Acts 21:35-40). More than once he surprised the Roman military commander by his quick thinking (Acts 21:37-40; 22:25-29). Before the Jewish Council his speedy assessment of the situation enabled him to change proceedings to suit himself (Acts 23:6). With calm reasoning he convinced Felix of his innocence (Acts 24:10-23), and his alertness before Festus enabled him to seize the opportunity to get to Rome at last (Acts 25:9-12). He was now sent off to Rome by sea, under a Roman guard (Acts 27:1-2).

Although a prisoner, Paul did not hesitate to give advice to the ship's officers, warning them against sailing further in dangerous weather. They ignored his advice and the ship was soon in trouble (Acts 27:10-11,14,20). When, after two weeks of terror, the ship was about to sink, Paul's leadership prevented panic and ensured that all on board got to land safely (Acts 27:29-38,42-44).

The place they landed was the island Malta (Acts 28:1). Some months later they arrived in Rome, where Paul was kept under guard while awaiting the hearing of his case (Acts 28:11,16; about AD 60). He was allowed visitors and could speak openly in making known the Christian gospel (Acts 28:17,30-31).

Two years in Rome

Among those who came to Rome to see Paul was a Christian from Colossae named Epaphras (Col 1:7-8; 4:12). There had been false teaching in the Colossian church, and Epaphras sought advice from

Paul concerning how to deal with it (Col 2:16-23). Although Paul had not personally founded the church in Colossae (Col 2:1), he gladly sent off a letter to help the church through its difficulties (see COLOSSIANS, LETTER TO THE).

Another arrival from Colossae was a runaway slave named Onesimus, whose master Philemon owned the house in which the Colossian church met (Philem 1-2). Onesimus had heard the gospel from Paul, become a Christian, and now thought he should return to his master. Paul therefore wrote to Philemon, urging him to welcome Onesimus back (Philem 10-13,16; cf. Col 4:9; see PHILEMON).

Since Paul's friend Tychicus was to take these letters to Colossae (Col 4:7-9), Paul decided to send additional letters with Tychicus to other churches in the area, such as those at Ephesus and Laodicea (Eph 6:21-22; Col 4:16). False teaching similar to that in Colossae had created difficulties in churches of neighbouring towns. (For details see EPHESIANS, LETTER TO THE.)

Paul possibly wrote his letter to the church in Philippi during this imprisonment in Rome (though he may have written the letter elsewhere, during a previous imprisonment). Paul still had freedom to welcome visitors and speak openly of the kingdom of God (Phil 1:12-13; 2:19,25). He had just received a gift that the Philippian church had sent to him with Epaphroditus, and he wrote to thank them for it (Phil 4:18; see PHILIPPIANS, LETTER TO THE).

In these letters from prison, Paul gave some of his richest teaching concerning the person of Jesus Christ. False ideas about Christ had forced Paul to set out clearly some of the important truths that people were forgetting or distorting (Eph 1:17-23; 3:4,14-19; Phil 2:5-11; 3:8-10; Col 1:15-20; 2:8; 3:1-4; see JESUS CHRIST).

False ideas had also grown up concerning Christian behaviour and the nature of the church. Paul therefore wrote of the eternal purposes that God was bringing to fulfilment through the church collectively (Eph 1:11-14; 2:11-22; 3:3-12; 4:1-16; 5:27; Phil 2:12-16; Col 1:24-28) and through the lives of his people individually (Eph 1:3-10; 5:1-2,21; 6:10-18; Phil 1:9-11; 2:5,12-13; 3:12-16; 4:8-9; Col 1:9-14; 3:12-17).

The final triumph

Throughout his imprisonment Paul had remained hopeful that he would be released and so be able to visit various churches again (Phil 1:25,27; 2:24; Philem 22). It seems certain that he was released and that with Timothy, Titus and others he visited a number of places. One of those places was Crete, where Titus remained for a while to help correct difficulties in the churches (Titus 1:5). Paul also visited Ephesus, where he left Timothy, again to help strengthen the churches after a period of instability (1 Tim 1:3,19-20; 3:12-16; 5:20-22; cf. Acts 20:29-30).

Paul then moved north to Macedonia (1 Tim 1:3; cf. Phil 2:24). Possibly it was about this time that he received news of affairs in Crete and Ephesus that prompted him to write letters to his two fellow workers (see TITUS, LETTER TO; TIMOTHY, LETTERS TO). Among other places he visited were Corinth, Miletus and Troas (2 Tim 4:13,20). About this time Paul must have been arrested again, for the next mention of him is as a prisoner in Rome once more. This time he expected not release, but execution (2 Tim 2:9; 4:6-8).

From prison Paul wrote his last letter, known to us as Second Timothy (see TIMOTHY, LETTERS TO). It seems that Timothy was still in Ephesus and that Mark was in nearby Colossae (cf. Col 4:10). These two men, who had started out with Paul many years earlier as his young assistants, were the two he most wanted with him in his final days (2 Tim 4:9,11).

With Christianity facing increasing dangers, many of the Christians had deserted Paul, leaving only Luke to support him in his imprisonment (2 Tim 1:15; 4:10-11,16). Paul wanted Timothy and Mark to come as quickly as possible and to bring with them Paul's books, parchments and warm clothing; for winter was approaching (2 Tim 4:13,21). It is not known whether they reached Rome in time. According to tradition Paul was executed in Rome about AD 65.

PEACE

In the original languages of the Bible, the word 'peace' had a meaning far wider and richer than that which people commonly associate with the word today. In the Old Testament, peace (Heb. *shalom*) included a range of ideas, such as completeness, wholeness and well-being. The New Testament, though using the Greek word for 'peace', retained the breadth of ideas found in the Old Testament and so gave the word a richer meaning.

Wide-ranging blessings

According to the Hebrews' understanding, peace was a state of well-being that included good health, prosperity, contentment, security and harmonious relationships (Ps 29:11; 37:37; 85:8-9; Isa 26:1-4; 32:17-18; 60:17; Lam 3:17; Zech 6:13; 8:12; Luke 11:21; 1 Cor 14:33; Eph 4:3). A prayer for God's peace upon a person, nation or church was a prayer for the wide-ranging blessing of God (Num 6:26; Ps 122:6; Luke 2:14; Rom 15:33). The greeting of 'Peace!' with which people greeted each other was both an enquiry after and a wish for a person's well-being (Judg 6:23; 18:6; 19:20; 1 Sam 25:6,35; Matt 10:13; John 20:21; 1 Cor 1:3; Eph 1:2; 6:23; 1 Peter 1:2; 5:14).

Since peace was often linked with the blessing of God, it became linked also with God's salvation (Isa 26:11-13; Luke 1:79; 19:42; Acts 10:36; Rom 5:1; 16:20). When God's prophets warned the Old Testament Israelites of certain judgment if they continued in their sin, false prophets comforted the rebellious people with false assurances of salvation (Jer 8:10-11,15; 14:19; Ezek 13:10). But there could be no salvation, no peace, for the wicked (Isa 48:22). After the years of exile in Babylon, however, the good news of peace would prepare a repentant people for salvation from captivity and return to their homeland (Isa 52:7-10; cf. Eph 6:15).

Peace with God through Jesus Christ

No matter what expressions of salvation people of Old Testament times experienced, the fulness of salvation awaited the coming of Jesus Christ, the Prince of Peace (Isa 9:6; Luke 1:79). The peace he brought is an everlasting peace (Luke 2:14; John 14:27 16:33; 20:21-22). It is available to all people now and will reach its fullest expression in a restored universe at the end of the age (Isa 9:7; 65:17-25; Rev 21:1-5,22-24).

This complete restoration to peace, fulness, wholeness and well-being is possible only because Jesus, by his death, dealt with the cause of the world's trouble, sin. He bore God's judgment on sin, so that the divine hostility against sin might be removed and repentant sinners might have peace with God (Isa 53:5-6; Rom 5:1-2; Col 1:20-22; see PROPITIATION).

When people, through God's grace, have peace with God, they also have peace with one another. They become members of the kingdom of God, where all disharmony and injustice are removed, whether in matters of race, age, sex or status (Rom 14:17,19; Eph 2:14-17; 4:3; see RECONCILIATION).

Christians preach this gospel of peace to others (Matt 10:13; John 20:21; Acts 10:36; Eph 6:15), though they realize that at times it may cause division; for while some will gladly accept it, others will violently oppose it (Matt 10:34-36). In spite of this, Christians must do all they can to help people in general to live together peacefully (Matt 5:9; Rom 12:18; Heb 12:14).

Not only do Christians have peace *with* God through Christ, they also have the peace *of* God through Christ. That peace does not mean that they will have a trouble-free life. Rather it means that they now enjoy a state of spiritual wholeness and well-being that gives them strength and calmness even in the midst of suffering and trials (John 14:27; 16:33; Gal 5:22; Col 3:15; Phil 4:7).

PEKAH

The closing years of the kingdom of Israel (the northern part of the divided kingdom) were marked by the domination of Assyria. The Israelite kings Menahem and Pekahiah had survived only by buying protection from Assyria. The commander of the Israelite army, Pekah, tired of this pro-Assyrian policy, assassinated Pekahiah, seized the throne and tried to make Israel independent of Assyria (2 Kings 15:19,23-25,27).

Pekah formed an alliance with Rezin, king of Syria, with the aim of withstanding Assyria. In an attempt to force Ahaz of Judah to join their alliance, Pekah and Rezin attacked Jerusalem. Ahaz, against the advice of the prophet Isaiah, went to Assyria for help. Assyria replied by conquering Syria (732 BC), then overrunning much of northern and eastern Israel and taking the people into captivity (2 Kings 15:29; 16:5-9; for details see AHAZ). Pekah's policy had proved disastrous, and he was assassinated by Hoshea, a sympathizer with Assyria, who then became king (2 Kings 15:30).

PENTATEUCH

From early Christian times, and possibly before, the first five books of the Old Testament have collectively been known as the Pentateuch. The name comes from two Greek words, *penta* meaning 'five', and *teuchos* meaning 'a volume'. The Hebrews usually referred to the whole Pentateuch as 'the law' (2 Chron 17:9; Neh 8:14,18; Matt 5:17; 11:13; 12:5; Luke 24:44). It was originally one continuous book, but was divided into five sections for convenience. The English titles of the five separate books are taken from the early Greek translation known as the Septuagint.

Authorship

Age-old Hebrew and Christian tradition recognizes Moses as the author of the Pentateuch, though the Pentateuch itself nowhere names its author (2 Chron 35:12; Neh 13:1; Mark 12:26; John 5:46). The Bible speaks frequently of Moses' literary activity. He wrote down the law that Israel received from God

(Exod 24:4; 34:27; Deut 31:9,24), he kept records of Israel's history (Exod 17:14; Num 33:2) and he wrote songs and poems (Exod 15:1; Deut 31:22,30).

Moses would certainly have been familiar with the family records, ancient songs and traditional stories that people had preserved and handed down from one generation to the next (cf. Gen 5:1; 6:9; 10:1; 11:10,27). Like all writers he would have used material from a variety of sources, particularly if writing about times and places other than his own (cf. Gen 26:32-33; 35:19-20; 47:26; Num 21:14). In addition he received direct revelations from God and spoke with God face to face (Exod 32:7-8; 33:11; Num 12:6-8).

In different eras, critics who reject Moses' authorship of the Pentateuch have suggested various theories for a much later composition. Most of these theories are based on the different names used for God, the similar or contrasting features in narrative accounts, the varying features of Israel's religious system, and the usage of certain words and phrases. Broadly speaking, these critics have suggested four independent documents that date no earlier than the period of Israel's monarchy, and that a later editor (or editors) combined into one. The four documents are referred to respectively as J (because it speaks of God as Jehovah, or Yahweh), E (because it speaks of God as Elohim), D (because it bases its content on Deuteronomy) and P (because it deals mainly with matters of priestly interest).

These theories have been argued, answered, revised and contradicted many times over. Debating the mechanics of composition, however, may not always be profitable. The important consideration is not how the Pentateuch was written, but what it means. It stands in both the Hebrew and Christian Bibles as a book whose unity is clear and whose message is the living Word of God (John 5:39,45-47; 7:19; Luke 16:31; Acts 15:21).

Message

Genesis introduces the basic issues concerning God, man and the world. It shows that God made man good and desired man to live in harmony with him. Instead of doing so, man rebelled; yet God in his grace did not destroy him. Even when God gave man the opportunity to start afresh, man went the same way as before. God still extended his favour, promising to work through one of the few remaining believers (Abraham) to bring blessing to the whole world.

God promised that Abraham would produce a notable line of descendants, that those descendants would enjoy a special relationship with himself, and

that he would give them a national homeland. In due course Abraham started the family and his descendants began to multiply, but through a variety of circumstances they eventually found themselves slaves in Egypt. The book of Exodus shows that God, faithful to his promise, gave them a leader (Moses) through whom he brought them out of Egypt, gave them his law, and established them in a special covenant relationship with himself. He was their God and they were his people.

Leviticus and the beginning of Numbers give details of how the people were to maintain and enjoy their covenant relationship with God. The remainder of Numbers shows how the people moved on towards the promised land, and Deuteronomy shows the life God required of them once they settled in that land.

The grace of God and the sovereign choice of God are prominent themes in the Pentateuch. The deliverance from Egypt was the great turning point in the people's history, the covenant was the basis of their existence, and the law was the framework for their behaviour. The purposes of God were on their way to fulfilment (cf. Gen 12:1-3; Gal 3:16; cf. Deut 18:18-19; Acts 3:18-23).

PENTECOST

The word 'pentecost' means 'fifty', and comes from the Greek translation of the Old Testament. It refers to the Israelite harvest festival that was held fifty days after Passover. In the Old Testament this festival is called the Feast of Harvest, the Feast of Firstfruits and the Feast of Weeks. In the New Testament it is called the Feast of Pentecost (Lev 23:5-6,15-16; Acts 2:1; 20:16; 1 Cor 16:8; for details see FEASTS).

Pentecost is significant in the New Testament story because on that day the church was born. Christ the Passover lamb had been sacrificed; then, fifty days later, God poured out his Spirit on that small group of disciples who were the firstfruits of his new people, the church of Jesus Christ (Acts 2:1-4; cf. 1 Cor 5:7). (Concerning the extraordinary happenings that day see BAPTISM WITH THE SPIRIT; TONGUES.)

PENUEL

One of the more important towns in Israel's territory east of Jordan was Penuel. It was in the centre of the region popularly called Gilead, situated on the Jabbok River, close to the point where the Jabbok joins the Jordan (Gen 32:22,31). Various Israelite leaders, recognizing the strategic importance of the Jordan and the Jabbok as defence barriers, built special fortifications at Penuel (Judg 8:9,17; 1 Kings 12:25). (For map and other details see GILEAD.)

PEREA

Running down the eastern side of the Jordan River and the Dead Sea was a narrow strip of territory that in New Testament times was known as Perea. It was part of the tableland area that originally belonged to Ammon and Moab, but after Israel's conquest was occupied by the tribes of East Manasseh, Gad and Reuben. The region in general was popularly called Gilead (see AMMON; GILEAD; MOAB).

In New Testament times Perea was occupied mainly by Jews. For this reason Jews travelling between Judea and Galilee often detoured across Jordan and through Perea, rather than go through the territory of the Samaritans. Jews commonly referred to the area as 'beyond Jordan' (Matt 4:25; John 3:26).

Jesus at times visited Perea (Matt 19:1; John 1:28; 10:40). He also visited neighbouring Decapolis, the other region that bordered Jordan's east bank (Matt 4:25). (For a map showing the two regions see DECAPOLIS.)

PERGAMUM

The town of Pergamum was in the province of Asia, on the west coast of Asia Minor (Rev 1:4,11; for map see ASIA). The Bible does not record how or when the church there was founded, but it does mention difficulties that the church experienced towards the end of the first century. The difficulties were mainly connected with the religious system known as Emperor worship, which in the province of Asia had its headquarters in Pergamum (cf. Rev 2:13). (Concerning Emperor worship see ROME.)

On the whole the Christians in Pergamum stood firm and refused to join in the Emperor worship. At least one of their number was martyred (Rev 2:12-13). There were some, however, who taught and practised Nicolaitan teaching, which encouraged Christians to join in idolatrous feasts and to practise immorality. Jesus declared he would judge those who denied him in this way, and reward those who refused to compromise with the State religion (Rev 2:14-17).

PERIZZITES

The Perizzites were one of the many Canaanite groups that occupied Canaan before the Israelites drove them out (Gen 13:7; 15:20; Exod 3:8; Deut 7:1; Josh 3:10). They lived mainly in the hills of central Palestine and are found in Bible narratives concerning Bethel, Shechem and the tribal territory of Ephraim (Gen 13:2-7; 34:26-30; Josh 17:15). They were used as slaves in Solomon's building programs and were eventually absorbed into Israel (1 Kings 9:20-21).

PERSECUTION

Those who love evil rather than good will inevitably want to persecute those who desire to live godly lives (John 3:19-20; 2 Tim 3:12). Christians should not be surprised when they suffer persecution. If they show themselves to be Christ's people, they can expect the sort of opposition that Christ suffered. They should consider it a privilege to suffer for Christ's sake (Matt 5:10-11; John 15:20; Acts 5:41; 2 Cor 12:10; 1 Peter 4:12-13).

Both Jesus and the New Testament writers taught Christians that they should pray for their persecutors. Certainly they should not try to return evil upon those who attack them. God's people should have confidence in him that, when they are persecuted, they will know how to act and what to say (Matt 5:44; 10:17-20; Rom 12:14; 1 Peter 2:21-24; 4:14-16).

Persecution tests the genuineness of a person's faith, but true believers will endure it, knowing that God will not forsake them (Matt 13:21; Rom 5:3-5; 8:35; 2 Cor 4:9; 2 Thess 1:4). The early Christians proved the reality of God's presence with them when they suffered persecution, much of which was at the hands of the Jews (Acts 4:29-31; 5:17-21; 7:54-56; 18:9-10; 2 Tim 4:17).

This persecution came first from the Sadducees (Acts 4:1-3; 5:17,27-28), then from the Pharisees, whose fiery leader was the young Saul of Tarsus (Acts 7:58-8:3; 9:4; Gal 1:13; Phil 3:6). When Saul the persecutor was converted to Paul the Christian preacher, he himself was persecuted by the Jews, violently and unceasingly (Acts 9:15-16; 14:19-20; 16:22-24; 21:35-36; 2 Cor 11:23-25). In his preaching Paul warned of the persecution that believers could expect; yet people continued to turn to God. And as Paul warned, they met opposition from their fellow citizens (Acts 14:22; 1 Thess 1:6; 2:13-16).

During the reign of Nero the persecution of Christians became government policy throughout the Empire. Government officials and common people alike hated the Christians for their refusal to follow the practices of a society that they considered idolatrous and immoral (1 Peter 2;12; 4:12-16). So severe was the persecution that some Christians were tempted to give up their faith in the hope of avoiding trouble (Heb 10:32-36).

Although official persecution later died down, it increased again towards the end of the century during the reign of the Emperor Domitian. But no matter how great the persecution, God's people are repeatedly assured that in the end they will triumph (Rev 2:13; 6:9-11; 12:11; 19:1-2).

PERSEVERANCE

God requires of Christians not only that they believe the gospel, but also that they persevere in living according to the gospel, regardless of the difficulties they meet. Perseverance is proof of the genuineness of faith and leads to spiritual maturity (John 8:31; Acts 14:22; Rom 5:3-4; Col 1:21-23; Heb 3:12-14; 4:1-11; 6:11-12).

When Jesus called people to believe in him, he made it clear that he was calling them into a continuous relationship with himself. Belief involved more than just a momentary decision; it involved a life of following him as a true disciple to the end (Mark 8:34-38; 13:13; Luke 9:57-62; John 15:4-6; cf. 6:60,66-68). In one of his parables Jesus showed that some people profess to be believers, but later, by their lack of perseverance, prove not to be (Mark 4:15-20).

Christians are able to persevere because of the power of God working within them (Phil 1:6; Col 1:11; 1 Peter 1:5; Jude 24; Rev 3:10). In addition to giving his people the promise of his power, God demands that they exercise self-discipline and effort. Christians must be on their guard and persistent in prayer if they are to endure firmly to the end (Luke 21:36; Col 4:2).

If people have true faith in God, they will prove it by their steadfast trust in his power and promises. Their perseverance is not something God rewards by giving them salvation, but something that gives proof of their salvation. It shows that their faith is genuine (Mark 13:13,22-23; Luke 21:36; Phil 3:13-14; 2 Tim 4:7-8).

At times people may be tempted to give up their Christian commitment. The source of their troubles may be the trials of life, persecution, desire for personal prosperity, worry, laziness or false teaching (Mark 4:17-18; 13:13; 1 Tim 4:1; 6:10; Heb 2:1; 10:32-39). Christians can fight against these temptations by training themselves in godliness, resisting the pressures of the world, continuing steadfastly in the truth they have believed, learning more of God through the Scriptures, and giving

themselves wholeheartedly to whatever work God has entrusted to them (2 Thess 2:14-15; 1 Tim 4:7,15; 6:11-12; 2 Tim 2:10; 3:14-17; Heb 4:14; 6:1-3; 10:23; Jude 20-21).

The outcome of Christian endurance will be the experience of salvation in its fullest expression at the return of Jesus Christ (Rom 8:24-25; 2 Tim 4:7-8; 1 Peter 1:6-9; Rev 2:26-28). The expectation of Christ's return is therefore a constant incentive to perseverance (Matt 24:45-51; 1 Thess 5:23; 2 Tim 2:11-12; James 5:8; 2 Peter 3:14,17; 1 John 2:28).

PERSIA

The boundaries of Persia varied from era to era, but the name Persia is usually associated with the territory on the northern side of the Persian Gulf. In ancient times the north-western part of this territory (the area that bordered the Mesopotamian Plain) was known as Elam (Gen 14:1). At times the Bible

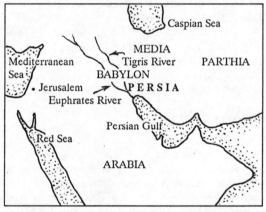

makes a distinction between Elamites and Persians (Ezra 4:9), but usually Elam is simply another name for Persia (Isa 11:11; 21:2; Jer 25:25; 49:35-39). Regions to the north of Elam that were later closely allied with Persia were Media and Parthia (Esther 1:18; Acts 2:9).

Persia's period of greatest power was during the reign of the Emperor Cyrus. Having come to the Persian throne about 558 BC, Cyrus proceeded to enlarge his territory, as one by one he conquered kingdoms large and small. One of his greatest triumphs was the conquest of Media. Media then became Persia's strongest ally, and its leaders shared in the civil and military leadership of the expanding Persian Empire. So closely were the Medes and the Persians associated that people sometimes used their names interchangeably. The greatest victory for the Medo-Persian army came in 539 BC, when it conquered Babylon and Cyrus became undisputed ruler of the region (Isa 13:17; 21:1-10; 44:28; 45:1; Jer 51:11,28; Dan 5:30-31; 8:20; 9:1; 10:1).

Upon becoming ruler of Babylon, Cyrus quickly gave permission for all the people held captive by Babylon in foreign lands to return to their homelands. As a result many of the Jews returned to Jerusalem, where they soon began rebuilding the temple and the city (Ezra 1:1-4). They completed the temple in 516 BC, in the reign of a later Emperor, Darius (Ezra 6:14-15). (This Darius is a different person from Darius the Mede, the man who led the Medo-Persian attack on Babylon over twenty years previously; cf. Dan 5:30-31.)

When at times non-Jewish people of the region opposed and persecuted the Jews in Jerusalem, the Persian rulers protected the Jews (Ezra 5:3-6:12; Neh 2:9-10; Esther 8:9-14). The Persian government

Persian Emperor

even gave the Jews funds to help carry out their program for the reconstruction of their nation and religion (Ezra 6:8-10; 7:14-16,21-24; Neh 2:7-8). At times the Emperor gave his personal support to Jewish leaders who went from Persia to Jerusalem to teach and reform the Jewish people (Ezra 7:11-20; Neh 2:5-8).

The capital of Persia was Susa, or Shushan (Esther 1:1-3; 2:3; 9:11; Dan 8:2). The Empire was divided into provinces ruled by Persian or Median nobles (satraps), with local people under them as governors and other officials (Ezra 4:8-10; 5:3,14; 6:2; 7:21; Neh 2:9; 5:14; 7:2; Esther 3:1; 8:9; 10:3).

Persian rule lasted about two hundred years, but the biblical narratives cover little more than the first half of this period. Several Emperors feature in the record.

Emperor	Reign BC	Events and references
Cyrus	558-530	Babylon conquered (539); Jews released; temple begun (538) (Ezra 1:1-4; 3:7; 5:13-15; Isa 44:28; 45:1; Dan 6:28; 10:1).
Cambyses	530-522	–
Darius	522-486	Temple finished (516) (Ezra 4:24; 5:3-6:15; Hag 1:1; Zech 1:1)
Ahasuerus	486-465	Jews given increased liberty (Esther 1:1-10:3)
Artaxerxes	465-424	Special powers given to Ezra (458) and Nehemiah (445) (Ezra 7:1-13,21; Neh 2:1-8; 5:14; 13:6)

PETER

Simon Peter was one of the earliest believers in Jesus. Like his brother Andrew, he was probably a disciple of John the Baptist, till John directed them to Jesus (John 1:40-41; cf. Acts 1:15,21-22). Jesus immediately saw the man's leadership qualities and gave him a new name, Peter (or Cephas), meaning 'a rock' (John 1:42). (The two names are from the words for 'rock' in Greek and Aramaic respectively.)

This initial meeting with Jesus took place in the Jordan Valley (John 1:28-29,35). Not long after, there was another meeting, this time in Galilee, when Peter became one of the first believers to leave their normal occupations and become active followers of Jesus (Matt 4:18-22). When Jesus later selected twelve men from among his followers and appointed them as his special apostles, Peter was at the head of the list (Matt 10:2).

Peter and Jesus

The son of a man named John (or Jonah) (Matt 16:17; John 1:42; 21:15), Peter came from Bethsaida on the shore of Lake Galilee (John 1:44). Either he or his wife's parents also had a house in the neighbouring lakeside town of Capernaum, which became a base for Jesus' work in the area (Mark 1:21,29-30; 2:1). Peter and Andrew worked as fishermen on the lake, in partnership with another pair of brothers, James and John (Matt 4:18; Luke 5:10). These men all became apostles of Jesus. Although they had never studied in the Jewish religious colleges, they developed skills in teaching and debate through their association with Jesus (Acts 4:13).

From the beginning Peter showed himself to be energetic, self-confident and decisive. Sometimes he spoke or acted with too much haste and had to be rebuked (Matt 14:28-31; 16:22-23; 19:27-28; Mark 9:5-7; Luke 5:4-5; John 13:6-11; 18:10-11; 21:7), but he never lost heart. He went through some bitter experiences before he learnt of the weakness that lay behind his over-confidence. Jesus knew that Peter had sufficient quality of character to respond to the lessons and so become a stronger person in the end (Mark 14:29,66-72; Luke 22:31-34).

As Jesus' ministry progressed, Peter, James and John became recognized as a small group to whom Jesus gave special responsibilities and privileges (Mark 5:37; 9:2; 14:33). Peter was the natural leader of the twelve and was often their spokesman (Mark 1:36-37; 10:27-28; Luke 12:41; John 6:67-68; 13:24; 21:2-3; Acts 1:15-16). On the occasion when Jesus questioned his disciples to see if they were convinced he was the Messiah, Jesus seems to have accepted Peter's reply as being on behalf of the group. In responding to Peter, Jesus was telling the apostles that they would form the foundation on which he would build his unconquerable church (Matt 16:13-18; cf. Eph 2:20).

When Peter's great testing time came, however, he denied Jesus three times (Luke 22:61-62). Jesus therefore paid special attention to Peter in the days following the resurrection. He appeared to Peter before he appeared to the rest of the apostles (Luke 24:34; 1 Cor 15:5; cf. Mark 16:7), and later gained from Peter a public statement of his devotion to his Lord (John 21:15).

In accepting Peter's statement and entrusting to him the care of God's people, Jesus showed the other disciples that he had forgiven and restored Peter. At the same time he told Peter why he needed such strong devotion. As a prominent leader in the difficult days of the church's beginning, Peter could expect to receive the full force of the opposition (John 21:17-19; cf. Luke 22:32).

Peter and the early church

The change in Peter was evident in the early days of the church. He took the lead when there were important issues to deal with (Acts 1:15; 5:3,9), and he was the chief preacher (Acts 2:14; 3:12; 8:20). But no longer did he fail when his devotion to Jesus was tested. He was confident in the living power of the risen Christ (Acts 2:33; 3:6,16; 4:10,29-30). Even when dragged before the Jewish authorities, he

boldly denounced them and unashamedly declared his total commitment to Jesus (Acts 4:8-13,19-20; 5:18-21,29-32,40-42). On one occasion the provincial governor tried to kill him, but through the prayers of the church he escaped unharmed (Acts 12:1-17; cf. 1 Peter 2:21-23; 4:19).

Peter had been brought up an orthodox Jew and did not immediately break his association with traditional Jewish practices (Acts 3:1; 5:12-17). Yet he saw that the church was something greater than the temple, and he readily accepted Samaritans into the church on the same bases as the Jews (Acts 8:14-17). He showed his increasing generosity of spirit by preaching in Samaritan villages and in the towns of Lydda and Joppa on the coastal plain (Acts 8:25; 9:32,36).

In spite of all this, a special vision from God was necessary to convince Peter that uncircumcised Gentiles were to be accepted into the church freely, without their first having to submit to the Jewish law (Acts 10:9-16). As a result of the vision he went to Caesarea, where a God-fearing Roman centurion, along with his household, believed the gospel and received the Holy Spirit the same as Jewish believers (Acts 10:17-48). More traditionally minded Jews in the Jerusalem church criticized Peter for his broadmindedness. Peter silenced them by describing his vision and telling them what happened at Caesarea (Acts 11:1-18).

Another factor in Peter's changing attitudes towards Gentiles was the influence of Paul. The two men had met when Paul visited Jerusalem three years after his conversion (Gal 1:18). They met again eleven years later, when Peter and other Jerusalem leaders expressed fellowship with Paul and Barnabas in their mission to the Gentiles (Gal 2:1,9).

Although Peter understood his mission as being primarily to the Jews (Gal 2:7), he visited the mainly Gentile church in Syrian Antioch and ate freely with the Gentile Christians. When Jewish traditionalists criticized him for ignoring Jewish food laws, he withdrew from the Gentiles. Paul rebuked him publicly and Peter readily acknowledged his error (Gal 2:11-14). When church leaders later met in Jerusalem to discuss the matter of Gentiles in the church, Peter openly and forthrightly supported Paul (Acts 15:7-11).

A wider ministry

Little is recorded of Peter's later movements. He travelled over a wide area (accompanied by his wife) and preached in many churches, including, it seems, Corinth (1 Cor 1:12; 9:5). Early records indicate that he did much to evangelize the northern parts of Asia

Minor. The churches he helped establish there were the churches to which he sent the letters known as 1 and 2 Peter (1 Peter 1:1; 2 Peter 3:1).

During this time Mark worked closely with Peter. In fact, Peter regarded Mark as his 'son' (1 Peter 5:13). There is good evidence that at one stage they visited Rome and helped the church there. When Peter left for other regions, Mark remained in Rome, where he helped the Christians by recording for them the story of Jesus as they had heard it from Peter. (For the influence of Peter in Mark's account see MARK, GOSPEL OF.)

Later, Peter revisited Rome. Mark was again with him, and so was Silas, who acted as Peter's secretary in writing a letter to the churches of northern Asia Minor. In this letter Peter followed the early Christian practice of referring to Rome as Babylon (1 Peter 1:1; 5:12-13). The letter shows how incidents and teachings that Peter witnessed during Jesus' life continued to have a strong influence on his preaching (cf. 1 Peter 1:22 with John 15:12; cf. 1 Peter 2:7 with Matt 21:42; cf. 1 Peter 2:12 with Matt 5:16; cf. 1 Peter 3:9 with Matt 5:39; cf. 1 Peter 4:15-16 with Mark 14:66-72; cf. 1 Peter 4:7 with Luke 22:45-46; cf. 1 Peter 4:19 with Luke 23:46; cf. 1 Peter 5:1 with Mark 9:2-8; cf. 1 Peter 5:2 with John 21:16; cf. 1 Peter 5:5 with John 13:4,14; cf. 1 Peter 5:7 with Matt 6:25).

At this time Nero was Emperor and his great persecution was about to break upon the Christians. Peter wrote his First Letter to prepare Christians for what lay ahead. He wrote his Second Letter to give various reminders and warn against false teaching. (For details see PETER, LETTERS OF.) By the time he wrote his Second Letter he was in prison, awaiting the execution that Jesus had spoken of about thirty years earlier (2 Peter 1:13-15; cf. John 21:18-19). According to tradition, Peter was crucified in Rome some time during the period AD 65-69.

PETER, LETTERS OF

The Christians addressed in 1 Peter lived mainly in the northern provinces of Asia Minor bordering the Black Sea (1 Peter 1:1). These were places that Paul had not been allowed to enter (Acts 16:7-8), but that Peter had helped to evangelize, most likely with John Mark as his assistant (1 Peter 5:13).

Purpose in writing 1 Peter

It was the era of the Roman Emperor Nero (who ruled from AD 54 to 68) and persecution against Christians was increasing everywhere. At the time of writing, Peter was apparently in Rome. This was the heart of the Empire and the place that Christians referred to as Babylon, the symbol of man's arrogant opposition to God and his people (1 Peter 5:13). Paul had recently been executed (2 Tim 4:6), and Peter felt that a more violent persecution was about to break out.

Peter therefore wrote to warn Christians not to be surprised or ashamed when they met persecution (1 Peter 4:12,16). They were to bear their sufferings with patience, even if it meant death, and they were to bear intelligent witness to their faith in Christ (1 Peter 2:20-23; 3:14-15; 4:19). Always, however, they had the assurance of a living hope and a glorious future (1 Peter 1:3-8).

Contents of 1 Peter

At the outset Peter reminds his readers that while God wants his people to have assurance of their salvation, he also tests their faith to prove its genuineness (1:1-12). True faith produces qualities of holiness and love in the lives of Christ's followers (1:13-2:3) and builds them into a community whose life and vigour should bring blessing to people everywhere (2:4-10).

This leads Peter to consider the responsibility Christians have to maintain good conduct in society (2:11-17), even when people in general are against them (2:18-25). Likewise in the home and in the church they must work towards peace and harmony (3:1-12).

Suffering is inevitable if Christians live rightly, and in this matter Christ is the perfect example (3:13-22). But just as Christ's suffering was not without purpose, so neither is the suffering of his followers. It should lead them to more disciplined and fruitful lives for God (4:1-11) and help them to experience that deep-seated joy that Christ himself experienced (4:12-19).

Because church leaders have such a vital work to do among believers in times of difficulty, Peter gives some special instruction for them (5:1-5). He concludes his letter by urging all his readers to be humble and to keep alert at all times (5:6-14).

Purpose in writing 2 Peter

It seems that Peter wrote the letter known as Second Peter only a year or so after he wrote First Peter, and that he sent it to the same people (cf. 2 Peter 3:1 with 1 Peter 1:1). It seems also that Peter was in prison, most likely in Rome, and expected to be executed soon (2 Peter 1:14-15). When he heard that false teachers were moving around the churches causing trouble, he promptly sent off this short but uncompromising letter.

The main error that Peter opposed was the claim by the false teachers that, since faith alone was necessary for salvation, Christians could live as they pleased. Immoral practices were not wrong for those who had gained a higher knowledge of spiritual things, and in fact were evidence that they had gained true freedom (2 Peter 2:1-3). (Concerning the similarities between 2 Peter and Jude see JUDE.) The other error of the false teachers was their mockery of the return of Jesus Christ.

Contents of 2 Peter

Peter counters the false teaching about Christian behaviour by showing that when a person is saved by faith, his whole life is changed in the direction of virtue, morality, self-control, godliness and love (1:1-15). God's power to change lives is a fact to which Old Testament writers and New Testament apostles bear witness (1:16-21). Then, in a strong denunciation of the false teachers, Peter describes their immoral character and announces their certain punishment (2:1-22).

As for Christ's return, it also is certain, and the scoffers are only deceiving themselves (3:1-7). Any apparent delay in his return is for the purpose of giving sinners the opportunity to repent and escape the coming judgment. Christians likewise must be ready for his return, for they too are accountable to God (3:8-18).

PHARAOH

Egyptian kings were known by the title Pharaoh. To the Egyptian people Pharaoh was a god-king, one who embodied a god during his life and went to the world of the gods at his death (see EGYPT). The Bible, however, treats the various Pharaohs as it treats the kings of other nations. They were mere human beings under the sovereign control of God (Rom 9:17; cf. Isa 44:28).

Some Pharaohs are mentioned favourably in the Bible. The Pharaoh whom Abraham visited was more honest in his behaviour than Abraham (Gen 12:10-20), and the Pharaoh of Joseph's time was sensible and generous (Gen 41:37-45,55; 45:16-20; 47:20-22; 50:4-6). Later, other Pharaohs oppressed the Israelites and made them slaves. One even tried to kill all their babies (Exod 1:8-16,22).

The most infamous of the Pharaohs was the man who opposed Moses and hardened his heart against God. From Moses' first meeting with him, he showed that he despised God and had no intention of releasing the captive Israelites (Exod 5:1-2). He was determined to resist God at all costs, in spite of the repeated opportunities God gave him to repent and in spite of the warnings God gave him through a series of plagues (Exod 7:11-13; 8:8,15,28-32). By confirming Pharaoh in his hardness of heart, God showed the greatness of Pharaoh's evil and the justice with which he punished it (Exod 9:12; Rom 9:14-18; see PLAGUE).

In the final plague on Egypt, the firstborn in all Egyptian families, including Pharaoh's, died. This prompted Pharaoh at last to release the Israelites (Exod 11:1-9; 12:29-32). When Pharaoh changed his

Egyptian Pharaoh

mind and tried to recapture the Israelites, he and his soldiers were killed in a mighty judgment at the Red Sea (Exod 14:5-9,28).

Most of the remaining Pharaohs of the Bible story are mentioned in relation to Egypt's political and military involvement with Judah during the time of the Israelite monarchy (e.g. 1 Kings 3:1; 11:40; 2 Kings 18:21; 23:29; see JUDAH). Some of them feature in prophetic announcements of judgment upon Egypt (e.g. Ezek 29:1-32:32; see EGYPT).

PHARISEES

The Pharisees were one of the two main parties within Judaism in New Testament times, the other being the Sadducees. The origins of the two parties go back to the second century BC, when Greek influence in Jewish affairs created divisions among the Jewish people.

Most of the Pharisees came from the working classes and tried to preserve traditional Jewish practices from the corruption of foreign ideas and political ambition. The Sadducees came mainly from the wealthy upper classes. Their chief concern was not with following tradition, but with using the religious and social structures of Jewish society to gain controlling power for themselves. (For fuller details concerning the origins of the two parties see SADDUCEES.)

Lawkeeping

Once the Sadducees had gained priestly power, they furthered their own interests by emphasizing the need to keep the temple rituals. The Pharisees, by contrast, emphasized the responsibility to keep the law in all aspects of life, not just in temple rituals. In this the Pharisees supported the traditions that the teachers of the law (the scribes) had developed and taught. The scribes had expanded the law of Moses into a system that consisted of countless laws dealing with such matters as sabbath-keeping (Matt 12:1-2; Mark 3:1-6; Luke 13:10-14), ritual cleanliness (Matt 23:25; Mark 7:1-9), fasting (Luke 18:11-12), tithing (Matt 23:23) and the taking of oaths (Matt 23:16-22; see also SCRIBES).

Being members of such a strict party, many of the Pharisees regarded themselves alone as being the true people of God, and kept apart from those who did not follow their beliefs and practices. The name 'Pharisees' meant 'the separated ones' (Acts 15:5; 26:5; cf. Gal 2:12).

The Pharisees criticized Jesus for not keeping their laws (Matt 12:10-14; 15:1-2; John 9:16), but Jesus condemned the Pharisees for not keeping God's law. They were more concerned with maintaining their traditions than with producing the type of character and behaviour that God's law aimed at (Matt 5:20; 15:1-10; 23:23-26). They were concerned with outward show rather than with correct attitudes of heart. They wanted to impress people rather than please God (Matt 23:2,5,27-28).

Jesus' criticism of the Pharisees caused them to hate him. They even cooperated with the Sadducees (the priests) to get rid of him (John 11:47-53; 18:3). Although the Sadducees had the chief positions in the Sanhedrin (the Jewish Council that condemned Jesus), many Pharisees were Sanhedrin members. At least one of the Pharisees, Nicodemus, became a believer in Jesus (John 3:1; 7:45-52; 19:38-40; see SANHEDRIN).

Other beliefs and practices

While lawkeeping was the Pharisees' main concern, other distinctive beliefs added to the tension in their relationship with the Sadducees. The Pharisees, for example, believed in the continued existence of the soul after death, the resurrection of the body and the existence of angelic beings, whereas the Sadducees did not (Matt 22:23; Acts 23:8).

The Pharisees' belief in the resurrection was probably one reason for their favourable attitude to Christians in the early days of the church. They did not object to multitudes of people believing in the resurrection of Jesus. While the Sadducees angrily opposed the Christians, the Pharisees seem to have regarded the Christians as sincerely religious Jews with orthodox beliefs and practices (Acts 2:46-47; 4:1-2; 5:12,17,25-28).

Another belief of the Pharisees, also in contrast to the beliefs of the Sadducees, was that all events were under the control of God, and man did not have independent right to interfere with what God had decreed. They therefore thought it wise not to oppose the Christians, lest they oppose a movement that had God's approval (Acts 5:34-39).

This attitude of tolerance towards Christians changed suddenly when the Pharisees understood Stephen to have spoken against the law of Moses. They turned violently against the Christians, and in fact it was a Pharisee, Saul of Tarsus, who led the persecution (Acts 6:13-14; 7:57-58; 8:3; 23:6).

After the destruction of Jerusalem by Rome in AD 70, the Sadducees and the smaller Jewish parties died out. This left the Pharisees in full control of the Jewish religion. A separate Pharisee party was no longer necessary, for Judaism as a whole now followed the Pharisee tradition.

PHILADELPHIA

Situated on the edge of a fertile region of the Roman province of Asia, Philadelphia was the outlet for the produce of the region. There is no record of how the church there was established, but it was only small and it suffered much from the persecutions of the Jews (Rev 3:7-9). God assured the Christians that they, not the persecutors from the synagogue, were his true people. He would protect his church and reward those in it who remained faithful to him (Rev 3:9-13). (For map see ASIA.)

PHILEMON

Among the letters Paul wrote while imprisoned in Rome (see Acts 28:16,30) were two that went to the town of Colossae in Asia Minor. One was for the church in Colossae, the other for Philemon, the Christian in whose house the Colossian church met (Philem 2). In both letters Paul mentions that Epaphras, Mark, Luke, Aristarchus and Demas are with him in his imprisonment (Col 1:7-8; 4:10,12,14; Philem 23-24). In both letters he sends a message to Archippus, who was engaged in God's work in

Colossae (Col 4:17; Philem 2). In particular, Paul talks about Onesimus, a slave who had worked in the house of Philemon (Col 4:9; Philem 10).

Onesimus had fled from his master and, in search of a new life of freedom, had found his way to Rome. There he met Paul, repented of his wrongdoing and became a Christian. He knew that, being a Christian, he should return to his master to correct the wrong he had done. Paul knew Philemon well, and was in fact the person through whom Philemon had first believed the gospel (Philem 19). Paul therefore wrote to Philemon, and though his letter was only a brief personal note, it has been preserved as part of the sacred writings.

Contents of the letter

Paul greets Philemon with a note of thanks that Philemon's faith has been such an encouragement to the Colossian church (1-7). He then asks Philemon to forgive Onesimus (8-14) and to welcome him back as a brother in Christ, as if he were welcoming Paul himself (15-20). He closes with a few personal notes and greetings from his friends (21-25).

PHILIP

There were two men named Philip among the early disciples of Jesus. These are commonly referred to as Philip the apostle and Philip the evangelist. (Concerning two other men named Philip, who were members of Herod's family, see HEROD.)

Philip the apostle came from the fishing town of Bethsaida on the shore of Lake Galilee. When Jesus first went to Galilee at the beginning of his ministry, Philip was among the first to respond to his call. Immediately, he brought Nathanael to Jesus (John 1:43-46). Later, Jesus appointed Philip one of his twelve apostles (Matt 10:3). Philip features in the story of Jesus' feeding of the five thousand (John 6:5-7), but he was slow to understand how Jesus' miraculous works demonstrated the unique relationship between Jesus and his Father (John 14:8-11). Just before the last Passover, Philip helped a group of visiting Greek worshippers to meet Jesus (John 12:20-22). A few weeks later he witnessed Jesus' return to his Father (Acts 1:9-13).

Philip the evangelist was one of the seven men whom the Jerusalem church chose to administer its welfare program (Acts 6:1-6). Following the killing of Stephen and the expulsion of Christians from Jerusalem, Philip went to Samaria, where many responded to his preaching (Acts 8:4-13). He then travelled south towards Gaza and led a God-fearing Ethiopian official to faith in Jesus Christ (Acts

8:26-39). From there he moved north along the Mediterranean coast, preaching in all the towns as far as Caesarea (Acts 8:40). The next mention of Philip is about twenty-five years later, when Paul's party stayed with him in Caesarea for a few days. He had four daughters who had the gift of prophecy (Acts 21:8-9).

PHILIPPI

The city of Philippi was an important administrative centre in Macedonia, the northern part of Greece. (For map see MACEDONIA.) It was named after Philip of Macedon (the father of Alexander the Great), who conquered it about 356 BC and made it into one of his strategic cities. During the Roman civil war, Philippi was the scene of a vital battle in 31 BC, after which the victor gave the city the status of a Roman colony (Acts 16:12). (For the privileges that citizens of a Roman colony enjoyed see ROME, sub-heading 'Roman citizenship'.)

Philippi was on the main route from Rome to Asia Minor. Its port was Neapolis (Acts 16:11-12). Paul and Silas visited Philippi on Paul's second missionary journey, and found their first converts among a group of God-fearing Gentiles who met for prayer at the river bank (Acts 16:13-15). When the missionaries healed a demonized girl, their opponents stirred up trouble and had them thrown into prison (Acts 16:16-24). But this resulted in more people turning to Christ (Acts 16:31-34). Though released the next day, Paul and Silas had to leave the city, but they left behind the beginnings of the church in Philippi (Acts 16:39-40).

Paul appears to have visited Philippi twice on his third missionary journey — once when travelling through Macedonia south to Achaia (Acts 20:1-2), and once when returning through Macedonia to Troas (Acts 20:6). He probably visited Philippi again after release from his first Roman imprisonment (1 Tim 1:3).

The Philippian church saw itself as a partner with Paul in his missionary work and helped support him financially (Phil 1:7-8; 4:14-18). The church brought Paul much joy and drew from him warm expressions of true friendship (Phil 1:4; 4:1; see PHILIPPIANS, LETTER TO THE).

PHILIPPIANS, LETTER TO THE

At the time of writing this letter, Paul was being held prisoner (Phil 1:13). Over the course of his ministry Paul was held prisoner many times (2 Cor 11:23), though the only places of imprisonment mentioned in the biblical record are Philippi (Acts 16:23), Jerusalem (Acts 22:23-30), Caesarea (Acts 24:23-27) and Rome (Acts 28:16,30). Of these four places, Rome is the most likely as the place from which Paul wrote his letter to the Philippian church. Ephesus has also been suggested as a possibility. There is no doubt that Paul met severe opposition in Ephesus (1 Cor 15:32), but there is no certainty that he was imprisoned there.

Purpose of the letter

If the letter was written from Rome, the occasion was probably Paul's two-year imprisonment when he was awaiting the outcome of his appeal to Caesar (Acts 25:12; 27:1; 28:16,30). The church in Philippi sent one of its members, Epaphroditus, to Rome to help Paul and to give him a gift from the church. Paul wrote this letter to the Philippians to thank them for the gift (Phil 1:5; 4:18) and to correct wrong attitudes that had developed among some in the church (Phil 2:1-4,14; 4:2-3).

The Philippian church was the first church Paul established in Europe (Acts 16:11-40; see PHILIPPI) and he seems to have had a special affection for it (Phil 4:1). His letter to it was warm and optimistic, expressing the hope of a quick release and an early visit to Philippi (Phil 1:25,27; 2:24).

Contents of the letter

After thanking the Philippians for their partnership in the gospel, Paul prays for their further spiritual growth (1:1-11). Far from being discouraged because of his imprisonment, he rejoiced over the good that has come from it (1:12-26).

Paul encourages the Philippian believers to be united (1:27-30) and to develop the same humility and concern for others as Christ had (2:1-11). They must demonstrate in practice the nature of their salvation (2:12-18). For two examples of practical Christianity, he refers them to Epaphroditus and Timothy (2:19-30).

Developing the idea of Christian completeness, Paul shows that it comes not from lawkeeping, but from the power of the living Christ within (3:1-16). The certainty of Christ's return should encourage Christians to be more holy (3:17-21), as they submit to each other and trust steadfastly in God (4:1-7). In a final note of thanks, Paul assures them that God will reward their sacrificial giving (4:8-23).

PHILISTIA, PHILISTINES

The territory of Philistia consisted largely of the plainlands that stretched along the Mediterranean coast of Palestine. The region was known in ancient times as 'the land of the Philistines', from which we get the modern name 'Palestine'. The coast road from Egypt to Palestine was known as 'the way of the land of the Philistines', and the Mediterranean Sea was sometimes called 'the Sea of the Philistines' (Exod 13:17; 23:31).

Establishment in Palestine

It is believed that the Philistines came originally from Crete, known in ancient times as Caphtor. They were well established in Palestine by the time they begin to feature in the Bible story (Gen 10:14; Deut 2:23; Jer 47:4; Amos 9:7). They followed the Canaanite religions, and the Bible treats them as native Canaanites. They worshipped the common

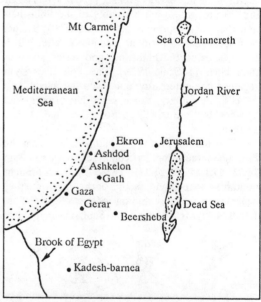

gods and goddesses of Canaan (the Baals and the Ashtaroth), as well as their own local Baal gods such as Dagon and Baal-zebub (Judg 16:23; 1 Sam 5:1-5; 31:8-13; 2 Kings 1:2; 1 Chron 10:8-12; see BAAL; BEELZEBUL; DAGON).

There were five main population centres in the Philistine territory, and these became known as 'the five cities of the Philistines' — Gaza, Ashdod, Ashkelon, Gath and Ekron. The leaders of these cities were known as 'the five lords of the Philistines' (Josh 13:2-3; Judg 3:3; 16:5,8,27,30; 1 Sam 5:11; 6:4,12,16-18; 7:7; 29:6-7).

Involvement with Israel

Abraham, and later Isaac, settled for a time in Philistine territory in the south of Canaan. Although they had reasonably good relations with the Philistine leader, their herdsmen and the Philistine herdsmen were frequently in conflict (Gen 20:1-18; 21:25-34; 26:1-33; see ABIMELECH).

When the Israelites under Joshua conquered Canaan, they took control of most of the hill country but were not able to gain similar control over the plain country occupied by the Philistines. As a result the Philistines reasserted their independence and became a source of trouble during Israel's early days in Canaan (Josh 10:41; 11:21-22; 13:3; Judg 3:1-3,31; 10:6-7; 13:1; 14:1-15:20).

The Philistines suffered a major setback when Samson brought about the death of all their leading civilian and military rulers (Judg 16:1-31). After they had recovered, the Philistines attacked Israel and captured the ark of the covenant (1 Sam 4:1-11). But the ark brought so much trouble to the Philistines that they soon returned it (1 Sam 5:1-7:2). Samuel then led Israel to national repentance, after which Israel defeated the Philistines and seized some of their cities (1 Sam 7:5-14). The Philistines soon regained their territory and even advanced into Israel's hill country. Some years later, after Saul became king, the Israelites drove them out (1 Sam 13:19-14:47).

This did not mean that Saul was free from the Philistine threat. Conflicts continued to arise (1 Sam 14:52; 17:1-54; 23:27-28). These conflicts brought military fame to David, though at the same time they brought him jealousy and hatred from Saul (1 Sam 18:6-9,14,30). In fleeing from Saul, David on two

Philistine soldiers

occasions found refuge in the Philistine city of Gath, and even used Gath as a base from which to operate his private army (1 Sam 21:10-15; 27:1-12). David pleased the Philistine ruler with his raids on various tribal peoples (1 Sam 27:8-12), but he was prevented from fighting for the Philistines against Israel (1 Sam 29:1-4,11). When Saul died in battle against the

Philistines, David became Israel's new king (1 Sam 31:1-7; 2 Sam 2:4; 5:1).

David wasted no time in driving the Philistines from the Israelite hill country that they had seized. He smashed their power decisively, so that they were never again a serious threat to Israel (2 Sam 3:18; 5:17-25; 8:1).

After the death of David, Israel's control over the Philistines relaxed and the two peoples lived independently side by side with only occasional conflicts. Any conflicts usually were concerned with border towns that changed hands from time to time (1 Kings 15:27; 2 Kings 8:22; 2 Chron 17:11; 26:6).

Among other nations that invaded Philistia at different times were Syria (2 Kings 12:17), Assyria (Isa 20:1), Egypt (Jer 47:1) and Greece. As foretold by the prophets, the nation was eventually destroyed (Jer 47:4-7; Ezek 25:15-17; Amos 1:6-8; Zeph 2:4-7; Zech 9:5-8).

PHINEHAS

Of the biblical characters named Phinehas, the most important was the zealous priest who was Aaron's grandson (Exod 6:25). Phinehas' father, Eleazar, had succeeded Aaron as high priest (Num 20:25-26), and Phinehas proved himself to be a loyal supporter. When Israelite men brought God's judgment upon themselves through their immorality with foreign women, Phinehas dealt with the rebels. His swift action saved Israel from destruction (Num 25:1-8; see also 31:1-7). God rewarded Phinehas' zeal by promising that his descendants would become the chief priestly family in Israel (Num 25:10-13; cf. Judg 20:27-28). Though zealous for God's standards, Phinehas proved to be fair and reasonable when he had to listen to complaints and settle disputes (Josh 22:13-16,30-34).

A later priest named Phinehas had no concern at all for God's standards. He and his brother, who were sons of the priest Eli, corrupted the priesthood so badly that God removed them in a dramatic judgment. The two were killed the same day (1 Sam 1:3; 2:12-17,34; 4:4,11).

PHOENICIA

To the north of Palestine, along the narrow coastal strip between the Mediterranean Sea and the Lebanon Range, was the land known in Bible times as Phoenicia. Today the land falls largely within the country known as Lebanon, though the Bible most commonly refers to it by the names of its chief towns, Tyre and Sidon (Ezra 3:7). Other important towns were Zarephath and Byblos (1 Kings 17:9). The wealth of the Phoenicians came partly from their fleets of merchant ships and partly from the large forests of cedar trees in the Lebanon Range (see LEBANON).

Commercial power

Tyre and Sidon appear to have been founded in the period 3000-2500 BC (Gen 10:19). When Israel conquered Canaan about 1240 BC, Tyre and Sidon withstood the invasion and remained independent

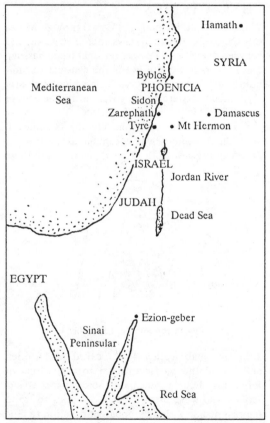

of Israel throughout most of their history. They were Israel's closest northern neighbours (Tyre was almost on the border; Josh 19:29) and, apart from the occasional conflict, lived alongside Israel fairly peaceably (Judg 18:7; cf. 10:12).

One of the greatest Phoenician kings, Hiram (who reigned from 979 to 945 BC), had very close trade relations with the Israelite kings, David and Solomon (2 Sam 5:11; 1 Kings 5:1,12). He supplied timber, stone and craftsmen for Solomon's extensive building programs (1 Kings 5:8-12; 7:13-14; 9:11) and joined with Solomon in developing a profitable trade transport. Goods from Mediterranean countries

were received at Tyre, taken overland to Israel's Red Sea port of Ezion-geber, then shipped east in the kings' jointly owned fleet. Goods that the ships brought back from the east brought further profits to the two kings (1 Kings 9:26-28; 10:11,22; cf. 22:48).

Phoenicia's ships were beautifully made (Ezek 27:3-7) and were sailed by skilful seamen (1 Kings 9:27; Ezek 27:8-9). They carried a huge variety of goods (Ezek 27:12-25), which so enriched Phoenicia that other nations often tried to break through its defences and capture its wealth (Ezek 26:3-4,7-14; 27:10-11).

Religious influence

In the century after Hiram, another Phoenician king, Ethbaal, became involved in Israel's affairs when he gave his daughter Jezebel to be the wife of the Israelite king Ahab (about 874 BC). Ethbaal was also high priest of the Baal religion in Phoenicia, and Jezebel soon set about making Phoenician Baalism the official religion of Israel (1 Kings 16:31-33).

This Phoenician Baalism, centred as it was on the Baal god Melqart, was far more dangerous to Israel than the local Baalism practised by the country people in Canaan (see BAAL). The ministry of Elijah and Elisha was specifically concerned with

Melqart

opposing the Phoenician Baalism, by preserving the faithful minority in Israel and initiating judgment on the unfaithful majority (1 Kings 19:13-18; see ELIJAH; ELISHA). Phoenician Baalism was later wiped out from Israel by the ruthless Jehu (2 Kings 9:11-10:36).

However, through the marriage of Jezebel's daughter to the king of Judah, Phoenician Baalism had spread to Judah (2 Kings 8:16-18). Again it was dramatically removed, though with less bloodshed (2 Kings 11:1-21).

Judgment and blessing

With the wealth it had obtained through clever trading, Phoenicia saw itself as all-powerful, a god among the nations. Because of its arrogance, God assured it of a fitting punishment (Isa 23:1-18; Ezek 28:1-9,16-18,21-23; Zech 9:2-4). Phoenicia's chief oppression of Israel was not through military might but through commercial power. It heartlessly seized Jerusalem's wealth and even traded Israelite war prisoners solely for monetary profit (Joel 3:4-6; Amos 1:9).

In fulfilment of the judgments God announced on Phoenicia, the nation suffered repeatedly over the following centuries. In 587 BC the Babylonians besieged the main cities (Jer 27:3-6; 47:4). They captured Sidon that year, but found Tyre more difficult to capture. This was mainly because the city was in two parts, one on the mainland coast, the other on an island a short distance from the shore. The Babylonians finally took the city in 574 BC, but they received very little reward, for the people of Tyre had apparently managed to ship out much of their wealth during the years of siege (Ezek 29:18).

After the fall of Babylon to Persia (539 BC), the Phoenician cities recovered and enjoyed a lengthy period of prosperity. Eventually they fell to Alexander the Great, Sidon in 333 BC, Tyre the year after. In taking Tyre, Alexander first destroyed the mainland city, then emptied the rubble into the sea to form a road by which he attacked the island city. The inhabitants who previously thought they were safe were then slaughtered in a terrible bloodbath (cf. Ezek 26:3-6,12-14).

Once more the cities of Phoenicia recovered. In spite of further conflicts, they were well populated in New Testament times, though under the overlordship of Rome (Luke 6:17; Acts 12:20). Jesus visited the region on at least one occasion (Mark 7:24,26), and people from the region visited Galilee to hear Jesus teach (Mark 3:8).

In the early days of the church, when fierce persecution drove the Christians from Jerusalem, many of them fled to the cities of Phoenicia. There they preached the gospel and established churches (Acts 11:19). Paul enjoyed a close fellowship with the Phoenician churches and visited them whenever possible (Acts 15:3; 21:2-6; 27:3).

PHRYGIA

Originally a small kingdom in Asia Minor, Phrygia was divided in two when the Romans redrew the provincial boundaries in Asia Minor. Under the Roman administration the western part of Phrygia, which included the towns of Colossae, Laodicea and Hierapolis, fell within the province of Asia. The eastern part fell within the province of Galatia (Acts 2:10; 16:6; 18:23). (For maps see ASIA; GALATIA.)

PHYLACTERIES

When God told the people of Israel through Moses that they were to bind his laws upon their hands and between their eyes, he was no doubt emphasizing that his people were to live in the constant remembrance of his law. Not only their actions but also their thoughts were to be governed by the law of God (Exod 13:9,16; Deut 6:8; 11:18).

Taking God's instructions literally, Israelites of later times wrote selected commands of the law on small strips of cloth or parchment, placed these

Phylactery worn on the forehead

strips in small leather boxes called phylacteries, and bound the phylacteries on to their arms or foreheads. Jesus condemned those Pharisees and scribes who wore extra large phylacteries to try to impress people with their apparent devotion to God (Matt 23:5).

PILATE

In the Roman government of Palestine, the regions of Judea and Samaria were governed by procurators, or governors, sent out from Rome. (Galilee and other parts to the north and east were governed by Rome through the sons of Herod the Great.) Pilate governed Judea and Samaria from AD 26 to 37 (Luke 3:1). His headquarters were at Caesarea, though during the Jewish festivals he moved to Jerusalem to keep order in the city (Matt 27:27; see PRAETORIUM).

Early records indicate that Pilate hated the Jews, and on occasions deliberately provoked them to riot by displaying images of Roman gods in Jerusalem. In one incident he massacred some of the Galilean Jews who had created a disturbance while in Jerusalem for one of the festivals (Luke 13:1-2). This may have contributed to the hatred that existed between Pilate and Herod Antipas, the governor of Galilee (Luke 23:6-12).

Besides being cruel, Pilate was a coward. This is seen clearly in the event for which he is chiefly remembered, the crucifixion of Jesus.

The Jewish Council, the Sanhedrin, had earlier condemned Jesus to death for blasphemy, but it had no power to carry out the death sentence. Only the Roman governor could authorize execution. The Jews therefore worded their accusation to try to convince Pilate that Jesus was a traitor to Rome and should be executed (Luke 22:66-23:5).

Pilate knew that Jesus was not a political rebel and that the Jews had handed him over because they were jealous of his religious following (Luke 23:4-5,14-15; Matt 27:18). His knowledge of Jesus' innocence only increased his crime in condemning Jesus. He had tried to calm the Jews with offers that he hoped would please them while enabling him to release Jesus, but the Jews refused his offers (Luke 23:16; Matt 27:15-23). Pilate's concern was only for himself. His great fear was that he could be in trouble with the Emperor if a riot broke out. Therefore, to satisfy the Jews and protect his own interests, he crucified the man he knew to be innocent, and released the man he knew to be a murderer (John 19:12,16; Luke 23:24-25).

A few years later Pilate was involved in another religious conflict when he slaughtered a number of Samaritans on their sacred mountain. He was ordered back to Rome to answer for his actions, and never returned to Judea. According to tradition he died by committing suicide.

PILGRIM

See FOREIGNER.

PISGAH

It seems that Pisgah is not the name of a particular locality, but an ordinary Hebrew word used for the peak of a hill or mountain. Usually it is a peak that gives a good view over the surrounding countryside (Num 21:20; 23:13-14). The most commonly known Pisgah is the peak of Mt Nebo in the Abarim Range east of Jordan. This was the peak from which Moses viewed the land of Canaan before he died (Deut 3:27; 32:49; 34:1; see ABARIM).

PISIDIA

Pisidia was a mountainous region in the south of the Roman province of Galatia. Its most important town was Antioch, where Paul established a church that spread the gospel throughout the region (Acts 13:14,49; 14:24). (For map and other details see ANTIOCH IN PISIDIA; GALATIA.)

PLAGUE

Different versions of the Bible use a variety of words to describe the many disasters, plagues, diseases and sicknesses that afflict mankind (e.g. Exod 8:2; 9:3; 1 Kings 8:37; Ps 91:6,10; Jer 14:12; Luke 7:21; 21:11; see also DISEASE).

The ten plagues of Egypt were judgments of God on the stubborn nation and its king. Both people and king were bitterly opposed to Yahweh, the God of Israel, and were devoted followers of Yahweh's real enemies, the Egyptian gods (Exod 9:27; 12:12). These were gods of nature and were therefore connected with the Nile River, upon which Egypt depended entirely for its agricultural life. God may have used the physical characteristics of the Nile Valley to produce the plagues, but the timing, intensity and extent of the plagues showed clearly that they were judgments sent directly by God (Exod 8:21-23,31; 9:1-6,22,33).

God in his mercy gave advance notice of the plagues and consistently gave Pharaoh the chance to repent; but the longer Pharaoh delayed, the more he increased the judgment that was to fall on him (Exod 9:15-19). The tenth plague was God's final great judgment on Egypt and at the same time his act of redemption for his people. Previously the Israelites escaped the plagues without having to do anything, but this time their safety depended upon carrying out God's commands. Their redemption involved faith and obedience (Exod 12:1-13; see PASSOVER).

POETRY

Much of the Old Testament is written in poetry. This applies especially to the Psalms, the wisdom books and the prophetical books, though poems and songs are scattered throughout the prose narratives of other book (see SINGING).

Unlike English poetry, Hebrew poetry has no rhyme or metre. It relies for its expression and style upon a rhythm of sound and thought produced by a careful arrangement of words and sentences. The form that is most common in the Bible is called parallelism. This form can be varied and developed in many ways, but basically it consists of sentences arranged so as to balance each other.

If the first part of a verse contains the main thought, the following part (or parts) may add weight to this thought by repeating it in a slightly different form (Ps 27:1; 104:7; Isa 2:7; 5:20-22). In some cases the two parts of a verse may be arranged to contrast with each other by stating two opposite truths (Ps 37:9; Prov 19:4,12). Alternatively, the second part may add to the first for the purpose of giving an application or leading to a climax (Ps 56:4; 68:18; Jer 31:20).

Poetry was sometimes written in the form of an acrostic based on the 22-letter Hebrew alphabet. In the simple acrostic, the first word of each verse began with a different letter, the sequence following the order of the Hebrew alphabet from the first letter to the last (e.g. Psalms 25, 34; Lamentations Chapters 1, 2 and 4). Other acrostics were divided into twenty-two sections of a number of verses each, with all the verses in each section beginning with the same letter. Psalm 119 has twenty-two sections of eight verses each; Lamentations Chapter 3 has twenty-two sections of three verses each.

The New Testament, though written in Greek and mainly in prose, contains quotations from Old Testament poems. It also records poems from its own era that the writers composed in the Hebrew style discussed above (Luke 1:46-55,68-79; 2:29-32). In addition there are quotations from what appear to be early Christian hymns (Eph 5:14; 1 Tim 3:16) and occasional quotations from Greek poetry (Acts 17:28; Titus 1:12).

POOR

One of the realities of life is that society will always contain people who are poor and disadvantaged (Deut 15:11; Matt 26:11). This is not what God intended for the world, but when man introduced sin into the world, human society suffered.

This does not necessarily mean that those who are poor are suffering the direct consequences of their own sin. Although there are cases where this may be so (Prov 6:9-11; 10:4; Hag 1:9; Luke 19:24), there are other cases where poverty has no direct connection with personal wrongdoing (Job 1:8-22; Rev 2:9). As with all human suffering, there may be physical, moral, social, religious, political, historical and geographical factors that help produce the problem (see SUFFERING). Christians may be poor

through no fault of their own (Acts 11:27-30; 2 Cor 8:1-5), but they should not behave as if there is no God in whom they can trust (Matt 6:25-33).

The inevitability of poverty is no reason for anyone to be indifferent to the poor. Israelite law required people to restrict their own income-earning activities, in order to provide opportunities for the poor to try to support themselves (Exod 23:11; Lev 19:9-10,13). In addition, people were to give money, food and goods to help the poor (Exod 22:25; Lev 25:35-38; Deut 15:7-8; 16:9-12; 26:12; Esther 9:22; Job 29:16). (Concerning regulations designed to prevent money-lenders from exploiting the poor see LENDING.)

New Testament teaching also requires those with money and possessions to help those who lack them. Generous giving to those in need is a specific duty of Christians (Matt 25:34-40; Luke 14:13; Rom 15:26; Gal 2:10; James 2:15-17; 1 John 3:17; see GIVING). God has a special concern for the poor. He guarantees his blessing upon those who help them and his judgment upon those who take unfair advantage of them (Ps 41:1; Prov 17:5; 19:17; 21:13; 29:14; Isa 10:1-2; Amos 2:7-8).

God gave special laws to Israel to ensure that in legal disputes judges did not favour the rich against the poor, and were not prejudiced against the rich in favour of the poor (Exod 23:3,6). The poor, as well as the rich, could be guilty of wrongdoing (Prov 30:8-9). However, as corruption and oppression increased, the poor were easily exploited. Often they had no way of gaining justice and cried out helplessly to God to defend them (Ps 69:33; 82:3-4; cf. Ps 109:31; 140:12; Isa 11:4; 32:7).

Those who trusted in God amid widespread unfaithfulness and opposition sometimes likened themselves to the helpless poor. They were poor in the sense that they had nothing in themselves to rely upon, but trusted entirely upon God for their salvation. Such people, in any era, are the true citizens of God's kingdom (Ps 86:1-2; Matt 5:3). Even when they are materially poor, they are often happier than those who are rich, because, being more dependent upon God, they know him better (Luke 4:18; 6:20; 21:1-4; 2 Cor 6:10; cf. Rev 2:9; 3:17). This is a further reason why Christians should not favour the wealthy or despise the poor (James 2:1-6; see WEALTH).

POWER

Some English versions of the Bible use the word 'power' to translate different Greek words. In some cases the meaning has to do with great strength or

346

the ability to exercise that strength (1 Cor 1:18; Eph 1:19; Rev 5:13). In other cases it has to do with authority, or the right to exercise authority (Matt 21:23; 28:18; John 1:12; Rom 13:1). The present article is concerned with the first of these meanings. For the second meaning see AUTHORITY.

Evidences of God's power

The Old Testament repeatedly speaks of God's immeasurable power. This power was demonstrated through his creation of the universe (Ps 33:6-9; Isa 40:21-23; Jer 10:12-13), his activity in nature (Ps 29:3-10; 66:5-7), his control of history (Exod 9:16; Ps 33:10; Isa 40:15-17) and his saving acts on behalf of his people (Exod 15:4-12; 32:11; Ps 106:8; 111:6; Isa 40:10-11).

These evidences of God's power are referred to also in the New Testament (Luke 1:49; Rom 1:16,20; 15:19; Heb 1:10-12; Rev 7:12; 15:8). The life and ministry of Jesus Christ provide particularly clear evidence of God's power (Luke 4:14,36; 5:17; 9:1; see MIRACLES; KINGDOM OF GOD). The supreme demonstration of God's power is the resurrection of Jesus (Rom 1:4; Eph 1:19-20).

Saving power at work

God's promise to believers is that the same power as raised Jesus from death is available to them. Just as Jesus conquered sin and death, so can those who trust in him. They have victory over sin now and are assured of victory over death at Jesus' return (Rom 6:5-11; 8:9-11; Phil 3:9-11; 1 Cor 6:14; 15:42-44,54-56).

The entire salvation God has made available to mankind operates by God's power. This salvation includes saving sinners from eternal condemnation and giving them victory over sin in their lives as believers (Rom 1:16; 6:14; 1 Cor 1:18,24; 2:5; Eph 1:18-20; 3:20; 1 Peter 1:3-5). This power becomes theirs through the Spirit of God within them (Acts 1:8; Rom 15:13; Eph 3:16; cf. Micah 3:8; Zech 4:6; see HOLY SPIRIT).

Although they have this power of God within them, believers are not to seek exhibitions of it that will draw attention to themselves (2 Cor 12:9; 13:4). They should be humble and dependent on God, so that he alone may be the one in whom people trust and to whom they give praise (Acts 3:12-16; 1 Cor 2:4-5; 2 Cor 4:7; Phil 4:13; 1 Thess 1:5; 2 Peter 1:3).

PRAETORIUM

Originally the praetorium was the headquarters of a Roman army commander, whether the supreme commander in Rome or a lesser commander in one of the provinces. Later it became also the official residence and administration centre of the provincial

Reading an edict from the praetorium

governor (Matt 27:27; Mark 15:16; Acts 23:10,35; 25:6,13-14). On one occasion when Paul was held prisoner, he mentioned that he was guarded by soldiers from the praetorium (Phil 1:13).

PRAISE

One characteristic of the life of God's people is that they constantly praise him. Praise is an expression of homage, adoration and thanksgiving to God either in prayer or in song, and may be accompanied by various expressions of joy (Exod 15:1-2,20-21; Ps 35:18; 63:5; 71:8; 150:1-6; Isa 12:2-6; Luke 2:13-14; Acts 2:47; 3:8; Col 3:16; Rev 5:9-14; see DANCING; MUSIC; SINGING).

Believers offer praise to God because of who he is and what he has done. Their praise is part of their worship of God, and it will reach its fullest expression in the age to come (Ps 7:17; 66:1-4; 104:1; 138:1-2; Luke 24:53; Rev 19:4-5). All living things, and especially God's people, have a duty to praise God. They offer this praise both individually and collectively (Ezra 3:10-11; Ps 34:1-3; 35:18; 117:1-2; 135:1-2; 150:6; Joel 2:26; Acts 16:25; Heb 13:15; 1 Peter 2:9). (For fuller discussion on the subject see WORSHIP.)

God's people should desire that their lives and actions bring praise to God. They should not seek praise for themselves (Prov 27:2; Matt 6:2; John 12:43; 2 Cor 9:1; Eph 1:12; Phil 1:11; Col 1:3-4; 1 Thess 2:6). Yet it is true that, if they live uprightly and behave properly, others will naturally want to give them praise (Prov 31:28,31; Acts 16:2; 1 Cor 11:2,17; 1 Peter 2:14).

PRAYER

Prayer is that activity of believers whereby they communicate with God, worshipping him, praising him, thanking him, confessing to him and making requests of him. This article will be concerned mainly with those aspects of prayer connected with requests, whether personal or for others. Concerning other aspects of prayer see CONFESSION; FASTING; PRAISE; WORSHIP.

God's power and man's helplessness

Believers pray because they know that God is the source of all good, the controller of all events and the possessor of supreme power (Neh 1:4-5; 9:6; Matt 6:9). By praying they acknowledge that they have no power to bring about the things they pray for, but God has. Believers are in the position of inferiors to a superior. They have no right to try to force God to do what they want, but by their prayers they are admitting their own helplessness and their complete dependence on God (Mark 9:17-24; Rom 9:20; 11:33-34). They are, in effect, inviting God to work his solution to the matter concerning which they are praying.

The answer to a prayer depends not upon the will-power, zeal or emotions of the person praying, but upon the wisdom and power of God. God looks not for an effort to work up feelings, but for a humble and helpless spirit that trusts entirely in him (Ps 51:17; Prov 3:5-6; Luke 18:10-14). The merit is not in the prayer, but in God who answers the prayer. Only when believers recognize their helplessness can they really pray in the right spirit; for then they acknowledge that God can do what they cannot (John 15:5). Their helplessness causes them to trust in God, which means, in other words, that they exercise faith.

Man's faith and God's will

Faith, therefore, is a basic requirement of all true prayer (Matt 8:13; Mark 9:23; 11:24; Heb 11:6; James 1:6-8). People do not need large amounts of faith. All they need is enough faith to turn in their helplessness to God (Matt 21:21-22). Faith has no merit in itself, as if God needs people's faith to help him do things. God has complete power in himself. Faith is simply the means by which believers come to God and ask him to exercise that power (Mark 11:22; Acts 3:16; 4:24-31).

Since faith is part of the very nature of prayer, it is impossible for people to use prayer to get their own way. Those who try to use prayer in such a way iare not really praying at all. They are arrogantly commanding God instead of humbly depending on him; they are wanting their will to be done instead of God's (Matt 20:20-23; James 4:3).

Long and impressive prayers will not persuade God; neither will an outward show of zeal and earnestness (Matt 6:5-8; Mark 12:38-40). If believers expect to have their prayers answered, they must pray in the name of Jesus, not in their own name. That is, they must pray for what Jesus wants, not what they want. They must desire that certain things will happen for Jesus' sake, not for their own sake. They must desire that glory be brought to God, not to themselves (John 14:13; 16:23-24).

Answers to prayer

God promises to answer the prayers of his people, but only if they offer those prayers out of pure motives, according to his will, and with a genuine desire to glorify God (Num 14:13-20; Matt 6:10; 18:19; John 14:13; 1 John 5:14-15). Believers should bear in mind that they have no right of their own to come into God's presence with their requests. They come only because Christ has made entrance into God's presence possible and because God in his grace accepts them. They come before God humbly and reverently, but they also come confidently (Heb 4:14-16; 10:19-22).

While God's people can pray with assurance, there is no guarantee that God will immediately give the things they pray for. In fact, he may not give them at all. The reason for this may be that he has something else in mind that will, in the end, be better for themselves, better for others and more glorifying to God. If people pray in the right spirit and with the sincere desire that God's will be done, they are assured God will answer their prayers. In so doing he may give something different from what was requested. He gives what people would have asked for if they had the full knowledge that he has (Matt 7:7-11; 26:38-46; John 11:32,37,40-45; 2 Cor 12:8-10; Eph 3:20).

If believers live righteous and godly lives, they can have confidence that God hears and answers their prayers. But disobedience, unconfessed sin and an unforgiving spirit are hindrances to prayer (Ps 66:18-19; Isa 1:15-17; Mark 11:25; Heb 5:7; James 5:16; 1 Peter 3:12; 1 John 3:22).

Believers are to pray with the mind as well as with the spirit (1 Cor 14:15; cf. Rom 12:2; Col 1:9). However, they may not always know how exactly to express their prayers or what exactly to pray for. In such cases the Spirit of Christ, who operates through them in all true prayer, presents the prayers to God on their behalf (Rom 8:26-27,34; Eph 6:18; Heb 7:25; 1 John 2:1; Jude 20).

Matters for prayer

Prayer is an exercise for Christians collectively as well as individually. It is one of the functions of the church, particularly of the leaders of the church (Matt 18:19; Acts 1:14; 2:42; 6:4; 12:12; 13:3; 20:36).

The Bible gives many examples of the matters believers are to pray about. In their concern for the world, they are to pray that the kingly rule of God will have its rightful place in people's lives (Matt 6:10; Rom 10:1; 1 Tim 2:1-4). They are to pray that God will send his servants into the world to bring people to know God (Matt 9:37-38), and that God will protect and guide those servants to make their work fruitful (Acts 12:5; Rom 15:30-31; 2 Cor 1:11; Eph 6:19; Phil 1:19).

Concerning the church, Christians should pray that they and their fellow believers might know God and his purposes better, be strengthened by God's power, have unity among themselves, grow in love, develop wisdom, exercise right judgment, endure hardship with joy, and bring glory to God by lives of fruitfulness and uprightness (John 17:20-23; Eph 1:16-23; 3:14-19; 6:18; Phil 1:9-11; Col 1:9-11; 4:12). They should pray also for the physical well-being of each other (James 5:16).

Believers are to pray for those who treat them unkindly (Job 42:10; Matt 5:44), and ask for mercy on those who have sinned and brought disgrace on themselves and on God (Exod 32:11-13; 34:9; 1 Sam 12:23). They are to pray for civil rulers, so that God's will might be done on earth and people might live in peace (Matt 6:10; 1 Tim 2:1-2).

In relation to themselves, believers should pray in times of temptation and when they have spiritual battles (Matt 6:13; 26:36-46). They are to pray for God's guidance (Luke 6:12-13; Acts 1:24-25), for wisdom (James 1:5-8), for protection (Neh 4:8-9; Ps 57:1-3), and for the necessities of life (Deut 26:15; Matt 6:11). By prayer they can overcome anxiety (Phil 4:6; 1 Peter 5:6-7).

Praying always

People can engage in prayer anywhere and at any time (Gen 24:12-13; Neh 2:4; Luke 5:16; 6:12; 18:10; Acts 10:9; 1 Tim 5:5). In addition to developing the habit of speaking to God freely regardless of time or place, believers should set aside certain times when they can be alone with God and pray. Even Jesus recognized the need for set times of prayer (Dan 6:10; Matt 14:23; Mark 1:35). A person may pray in any position, such as standing or kneeling, with hands stretched out or hands lifted up, with head bowed or head uplifted (1 Sam 1:26; 1 Kings 8:54; 18:42; Ezra 9:5; Luke 18:11,13; John 11:41; Eph 3:14; 1 Tim 2:8).

Praying in faith does not mean that there is no need for persistence in prayer. On the contrary faith involves perseverance. Believers do not have to beg from a God who is unwilling to give; nevertheless they pray constantly, since their prayers are an expression of their unwavering faith. They know that their heavenly Father will supply his children's needs (Mark 14:38; Luke 11:5-13; 18:1-8; Eph 6:18; Col 4:2; 1 Thess 1:2; 5:17).

PREACHING

The Bible often mentions preaching and teaching together, for the two are closely related. It seems at times that there is little difference between them. The same person was usually both a preacher and a teacher (Matt 4:23; 11:1; Acts 5:42; 15:35; Col 1:28; 1 Tim 2:7; 2 Tim 4:2; see TEACHER).

Sometimes preaching is proclamation, such as in announcing the good news of the gospel to those who need it (Luke 4:18; 9:6; Acts 8:4,12,40; 17:18; Gal 1:11,16; 1 Thess 2:9), while teaching is more concerned with the instruction of those who already believe the gospel (John 14:26; Acts 18:11; 20:20; 1 Cor 4:17; Col 2:7; 3:16; 1 Tim 4:11). Teaching is necessary also for those who do not believe (Luke 4:31; 5:3; 21:37; Acts 4:2; 5:21,25; 18:11; 2 Tim 2:24-26), while preaching the great facts of the gospel of Jesus Christ is still necessary to challenge the believer (Rom 1:15; 16:25; 2 Cor 4:5; Col 1:28; 2 Tim 4:2).

It is therefore probably better not to make too sharp a distinction between preaching and teaching. To preach the gospel is to preach Christ. God's message for believers and non-believers centres in him. The gospel is more than just the message of salvation; it is the whole new life in Jesus Christ (1 Cor 1:23-25; 15:1-2,11-12; 2 Cor 1:19-22; 4:5-6; see GOSPEL).

Authority in preaching

God wants mankind to learn about him, to know him personally and to be instructed in what he desires for them. He has therefore revealed himself to man; he has spoken to man. He has done this dramatically through his Son Jesus Christ, but he has also given a written revelation through the Scriptures (John 1:1,14; 2 Tim 3:16-17; Heb 1:1-2; 2 Peter 1:20-21).

Since God has given these Scriptures to his people, those who preach and teach them have a special responsibility to God. God has entrusted his revelation to them, and therefore they must be careful how they use it. They must make it known in a manner that is faithful to its meaning and at the same time beneficial to the hearers (1 Cor 4:1-2; 2 Tim 2:15).

Preachers and teachers, though they reveal and announce a message that is not their own, should treat that message as if it were their own. It must become, as it were, part of them before they give it out to others (Jer 20:8-9; Ezek 2:8-10; 3:1-3; Rev 10:8-11). They are doing more than merely passing on someone else's message; they are instructing their hearers (Acts 20:20). But the only authority in their instruction is that of the Word they preach (Acts 20:27). The spiritual authority of the message comes from God, not from the preacher (1 Cor 1:17; 2:1-5; 4:1-2; 2 Cor 4:7).

Honesty in preaching

If a person is dependent on God for the benefits his preaching brings to others, he will express his dependence through constant prayer. He will also live righteously, so that his life is consistent with his message (1 Thess 1:5; 1 Tim 4:16). Yet he must put thought and effort into his ministry (Col 1:28-29) and must work constantly at improving the quality of his performance (1 Tim 4:13-15).

Among the dangers that the preacher faces is the temptation to adjust his message to win approval from the audience. This is the fault for which false prophets were consistently condemned in the Old Testament (Isa 30:8-11; Jer 5:31; 23:16-17,21-22). By contrast the true messenger of God says what needs to be said, whether or not it is what people want to hear (Jer 1:17; Micah 3:8; Mark 12:14; 2 Tim 4:2). Whatever Scripture he is expounding, he interprets and applies it honestly. He does not twist it to make it mean something different from what the biblical author intended (2 Cor 4:2). At all times his concern is to gain God's approval, not to win people's praise (2 Tim 2:15; cf. John 12:43).

PREDESTINATION

God is the sovereign ruler of the universe, one who is perfect in wisdom and power and who determines all things according to his will (Isa 46:10; Dan 4:35; Acts 4:28; Eph 1:11). Predestination means that he 'pre-destines' what will happen — he sees, knows, plans, prepares, appoints and decides what will happen (Ps 33:10-11; Prov 16:33; Isa 14:26-27; 22:11;

37:26-27; Acts 17:26-27; Rom 8:29-30; Eph 1:5-6; 1 Peter 1:20).

Divine will and human response

God's predestination does not mean that people are the helpless victims of unalterable fate. They have the freedom to make their own decisions, and they are fully responsible for what they do (Luke 22:22; Acts 2:23; 4:27-28; Rom 14:10,12; see also PROVIDENCE).

Predestination is concerned with the controlling will of God in all things, whether matters concerning the universe as a whole (Ps 135:6-7; Heb 1:10-12), the nations of the world (Deut 7:6-8; Dan 4:32) or individual people (Jer 1:5; Acts 9:15). The entire life and work of Jesus Christ was according to the pre-determined purpose of God (Matt 8:17; 12:17; Luke 24:44-47; Acts 4:25-27; 1 Peter 1:20). The particular aspect of predestination that is concerned with God's salvation of sinners through Christ is commonly referred to as election (Rom 8:29-30,33; Eph 1:4; 1 Peter 1:2; see ELECTION).

People receive eternal life, not because of their efforts to earn it, but because God in his grace gives it to them freely. God makes the offer to all, but most refuse it; and God holds them responsible for their choice (John 3:16-19; 8:24). Those who accept it, however, realize that only God's grace has drawn them to the Saviour and given them the eternal life that God has prepared for them (John 6:37,40,44; 10:27-29; 17:2; Acts 13:48; 1 Thess 5:9).

A purpose to life

God saves believers because of his eternal purpose, not because of their good works or their efforts at holiness (2 Tim 1:9; cf. Eph 2:8-9). But once they are saved, they must produce good works and make every effort to be holy. Assurance of predestination, far from making them self-satisfied, gives them purpose in life (Eph 1:4; 2:10; 2 Thess 2:13). God's will is not only to make them his sons (Eph 1:5), but to change them to become like his only Son (Rom 8:29). And one day they will share the Son's glory (Rom 8:30; 2 Thess 2:13-14).

Although believers see the purposes of God at work in their present lives, beyond that they see his purposes for the future. According to his perfect will, he has built his chosen ones into one body, the church (Eph 1:11-13; 2:13-16; Col 3:15). This united body is a visible part of a far greater work that God is doing according to his eternal plan. That plan is designed to bring an end to all the conflict in the universe and restore all things to perfect unity through Jesus Christ (Eph 1:10; 3:9-11).

PRIDE

Pride is possibly the most common sin of all. It is the root sin, the means that Satan used in successfully tempting man to rebel against his maker (Gen 3:1-6; 1 John 2:16). It remains a characteristic feature of fallen human nature and one of the hardest evils to overcome (Prov 16:18; Dan 5:20; Obad 3; Mark 7:21-22; Rom 1:28-30).

The essence of pride is self-centredness. The pleasure of the proud person is not simply to have something, but to have more of it than anyone else; not simply to be something, but to be better than anyone else (Prov 14:21; Matt 23:5-7,12; 1 John 2:16). Pride causes a person to rebel against God because God is above him, and to despise his fellow human beings because he considers them below him (Exod 5:2; Isa 14:12-15; Luke 18:9-11).

To feel pleasure at being praised is not pride, provided the pleasure comes from having pleased someone else (Matt 25:21). But if the pleasure is that of delighting in oneself or holding a high opinion of oneself, that is pride (Matt 6:2,5; John 12:43). In like manner, to feel pleasure in some other person or thing (to feel proud of it) is not pride in the sinful sense, providing it is only unselfish admiration (Hag 1:8; Gal 6:14). But if the pleasure is a feeling of conceit, the pride is sinful (Isa 25:11; Dan 4:30).

Pride is a sin that is particularly hateful to God (Prov 8:13; 16:5). Those who practise it bring against themselves God's opposition, and guarantee for themselves a humiliating punishment (Lev 26:19; Prov 29:23; Isa 13:11; 16:6; Dan 4:37; Luke 1:51; 18:14; James 4:6). (See also BOASTING; HUMILITY; HYPOCRISY.)

PRIEST

In ancient religions, priests were mediators between the people and their gods. They were religious officials whose duty was to pass on the instructions of the gods to the people and offer the people's sacrifices to the gods (Gen 41:45; 47:22; Exod 2:16; 18:1; 2 Kings 11:18; Acts 14:13).

The earliest priest of the one true God that the Bible mentions is Melchizedek. He was God's representative to whom Abraham offered gifts, and man's representative through whom Abraham drew near to God (Gen 14:17-24). Such priests were rare, as God had not yet given mankind an organized religious system. Among the ancestors of Israel, the head of the family usually acted as the family priest (Gen 8:20; 22:13; 31:54; 46:1). Before Israel was formally established as God's people by covenant, Moses served as the nation's priest (Exod 3:13-15,18; 24:2,6,8,12).

Aaronic (or Levitical) priesthood

At the establishment of Israel's religious system, Aaron and his sons were the priests, Aaron being set apart as the high priest. In the generations that followed, only male descendants of Aaron could be priests. Those who belonged to the same tribe as Aaron (the tribe of Levi), but who were not of Aaron's family, were responsible for many of the practical aspects of Israel's religious affairs, but they were not priests (Exod 6:16-25; 32:25-29; Num 3:2-3; 3:9-10; see LEVITES).

Priests mediated between the people and God. They presented the people's sacrifices to God (Heb 8:3; see SACRIFICE), and passed on God's instruction to the people (Mal 2:7). They were to be the teachers and moral guides of the nation (Deut 27:9-10; 31:9-13; 33:10). They also carried out daily functions in relation to the altar in the tabernacle courtyard (Lev 6:12,14) and the altar and lamp inside the Holy Place (Exod 27:20-21; 30:7-8). Only priests could enter the Holy Place, and only the high priest could enter the Most Holy Place. Even then he could do so only once a year, on the Day of Atonement (Lev 16:2-3; Heb 9:6-7; see DAY OF ATONEMENT).

Representative functions

As religious officials representing the people, priests wore clothing that set them apart from others. An ordinary priest's clothing was fairly plain, consisting of a full-length long-sleeved white coat and a white cap (Exod 28:40-43). The high priest's clothing, by contrast, was both distinctive and colourful.

Although the high priest wore a white coat similar to that of the ordinary priests (Exod 28:39), it was largely hidden from view because of a blue robe that he wore over it (Exod 28:31-35). Over the blue robe was a multi-coloured garment called an ephod, which was the most prominent garment of the high priest's dress (Exod 28:5-14; see EPHOD). Tied to the ephod was a flat pouch called the breastpiece, inside which were the Urim and Thummim (Exod 28:15-30; see URIM AND THUMMIM). On his head the high priest wore a turban with a gold plate declaring 'holiness to the Lord' (Exod 28:36-39).

The high priest's dress was intended to display dignity and splendour (Exod 28:2). It also showed symbolically that the high priest acted not as an individual but as the representative of the whole nation. He had the names of the tribes of Israel engraved on stones on the breastpiece and on stones on his shoulder pieces, so that when he went into the presence of God he symbolically took the people with him (Exod 28:9-12,21,29).

Turban

Gold plate

Breastpiece

Ephod

Blue robe

Linen coat

High Priest

Before the priests could begin their service, they were appointed to their position in an elaborate dedication ceremony. Since they themselves were not free from sin, they had to offer sacrifices for themselves before they could act on behalf of others (Exod 29:1-37; cf. Heb 7:27). Because they were aware of their own need for forgiveness, the priests should have had a sympathetic understanding of the weaknesses of the people on whose behalf they ministered (Heb. 5:1-3).

Priests were to maintain disciplined behaviour, moral uprightness and ceremonial cleanliness (Lev 10:8-11; 21:1-8,13-14; 22:1-9). Any priests who had physical defects could not carry out representative functions for the people, though they could share in less public priestly activity (Lev 21:16-24).

The people provided the income of those who did religious work on their behalf. They gave a tithe (i.e. a tenth) of their own income to the Levites, and the Levites in turn gave a tenth to the priests (Num 18:25-28; see TITHES). The priests received further income from portions of sacrifices, animal firstlings and harvest firstfruits that were allotted to them. This income helped compensate for the priests' lack of tribal or family land (Num 5:9-10; 18:8-20; Deut 18:1-5; 26:1-4).

Other responsibilities

One of the priests' duties was to ensure that people maintained a high level of cleanliness, whether in matters of ceremonial holiness, physical health or personal hygiene (Lev 13:3,10,20,30; 14:2-3,36,48; 15:13-15,28-30; Matt 8:4; see UNCLEANNESS). Priests also supervised the keeping of vows (Lev 27:1-25; Num 6:6-12; see VOWS) and assisted civil officials in giving judgments in certain moral issues (Num 5:11-31; Deut 17:8-13; 19:15-21; 21:1-9). They had ceremonial and practical functions in national affairs such as mobilization for war, land allocation and public celebrations (Num 10:1-10; Josh 3:14-17; 14:1; 19:51; 1 Chron 15:24; 2 Chron 13:12).

By the time of David there were too many priests for the amount of work to be done. David therefore divided the priests (and the Levites) into twenty-four sections, each of whom served for one week every six months (1 Chron 24:1-6; Luke 1:8). The remaining four weeks of the year were taken up with the annual festivals, which all males were to attend and which therefore required all priests to be on duty (Exod 23:14-17).

Changing role of the priests

Throughout Israel's history there were both good and bad priests. Many were zealous for righteousness and had a good influence on national leaders and the people as a whole (Num 25:1-13; 2 Sam 15:27; 1 Kings 1:8; 2 Kings 12:2; 2 Chron 11:13-17; Ezra 5:1-2; Neh 8:1-9; see EZRA; JEHOIADA; JOSHUA THE SON OF JEHOZADAK; PHINEHAS; ZADOK).

Some of the nation's better kings gave priests important leadership responsibilities in an effort to reform the nation and administer it according to God's law (2 Chron 17:7-9; 19:8-11; 29:3-4,11; 31:2-5; 34:8-9,20-21; 35:1-6; see CHRONICLES, BOOK OF). Other priests, however, were rebellious, corrupt, immoral and idolatrous. They were among the chief causes of the nation's ultimate destruction (Lev 10:1-2; 1 Sam 2:12-17; 3:10-14; 2 Kings 16:11-16; Isa 28:7; Jer 2:8; 6:13-15; Ezek 22:26; Hosea 6:9; Micah 3:11; Zeph 3:3-4; Mal 2:7-8).

After the captivity in Babylon, the Jews moved back to their homeland and rebuilt the nation. By this time a new emphasis had developed on teaching the law of Moses, and a new group of teachers had become prominent in Israel. These were known as scribes, or teachers of the law (see SCRIBES). As the years passed, the priests became more concerned with exercising political power, though they still carried out ceremonial functions (Luke 1:8; 5:14).

By New Testament times two major religious parties dominated Jewish affairs. The scribes were the main influence in the more traditionally religious party, the Pharisees, but the chief priests controlled the politically dominant party, the Sadducees (Acts 5:17; see SADDUCEES). All these people, whether priests or scribes, Sadducees or Pharisees, readily cooperated to get rid of Jesus (Matt 21:15,45-46; 22:15,23; 26:57; 27:41; Mark 11:18; John 11:57).

High priesthood of Jesus

The writer of the book of Hebrews pictures the life, death and present ministry of Jesus as that of a great high priest. Jesus' high priesthood, however, belongs not to the order of Aaron (for Jesus was not a descendant of Aaron) but to the order of Melchizedek. This was a higher priesthood than Aaron's, for it was not limited to one era, one nation, one family or one class of people. Christ's priesthood is therefore timeless and is available to all mankind (Heb 7:1-3,11-17,23-25).

Although Christ did not belong to the Aaronic priesthood, his priestly work followed the pattern of the Aaronic priesthood. Yet it was far superior, for it achieved perfectly what the Aaronic priesthood merely pictured. Like the Aaronic priests, Christ was appointed to his position by God. He also had a sympathetic understanding of the problems of those whom he represented before God. But, unlike the Aaronic priests, he was without sin and so had no need to offer sacrifices for his own sins before acting on behalf of others (Heb 2:17-18; 4:15-16; 5:1-6; 7:26-28).

Aaronic priests offered sacrifices repeatedly, but the sacrifices could never make people perfect, because they could never take away sins. Christ offered *himself* as a sacrifice. By that one act he completed his sacrificial work and brought perfect cleansing to all believers (Heb 10:1-4,11-14). The Aaronic high priest could enter the Most Holy Place (God's symbolic dwelling place) only once a year, and then only by taking with him the blood of a sacrificial animal. Christ, through his own blood, entered the actual presence of God and secured an eternal salvation (Heb 8:1-2; 9:6-14,24-26).

Because Christ is in God's presence as their heavenly representative, Christians can now enter God's presence. They need no earthly priest to mediate on their behalf. Through Christ they can come to God directly and confidently, knowing that they can depend on Christ's help in pleading for their needs before God (Heb 4:14-16; 7:25; 9:24; 10:19-22; Rom 8:34; 1 John 2:1; see ADVOCATE).

Christians have added confidence in Christ's concern for them when they see the prayer that he prayed for his disciples shortly before his crucifixion (John 17:9-26). Furthermore, they know that Christ's personal entrance into the presence of God is the guarantee that one day they too will personally enter the presence of God, and find there an eternal dwelling place (Heb 6:19-20).

All God's people are priests

Although Israel's religious system had an appointed order of priests, there was a sense (not specifically connected with the religious system) in which all the people were priests. Israel, as the chosen people of God, was a kingdom of priests, a holy nation. The people of Israel were to serve God, both by bringing him worship and by being his representatives in making him known to other nations (Exod. 19:5-6; Isa 61:6).

The words recorded in Exodus 19:5-6 applied to the Old Testament people of God, but in the New Testament the same words are applied to the new people of God, the Christian church. Christ's people are now God's chosen race, a kingdom of priests and a holy nation (1 Peter 2:9-10; cf. Rev 1:6; 5:9-10). They serve God by bringing him the sacrifice of worship and praise (1 Peter 2:5; cf. Heb 13:15) and by making him known to the nations of the world (1 Peter 2:9; cf. Rom 15:16).

PRISCILLA

When the Bible mentions the husband and wife team of Aquila and Priscilla (or Prisca), it usually mentions Priscilla first (Acts 18:26; Rom 16:3; 1 Tim 4:19). This is unusual, but the Bible gives no reason for such usage. Perhaps Priscilla was more active or more prominent than Aquila in the Christian work in which they were constantly and wholeheartedly engaged. (For details see AQUILA.)

PRISON

God has given governments the right to send law-breakers to prison (Rom 13:4), but he forbids brutal or excessive punishments. The punishment must be in proportion to the crime (Exod 21:23-25).

In Bible times all sorts of places were used as prisons. In some cases there were official state prisons (Gen 39:20; 2 Kings 17:4; Mark 6:17; Acts 12:4; 16:24), though in other cases a prisoner may have been locked in the soldiers' barracks at the palace (Jer 32:2), dropped into an old disused well (Jer 38:6), or kept under guard in a private house (Acts 28:16,30). Often the prison conditions were bad (Jer 37:18-20), the food poor (2 Chron 18:26) and the treatment cruel (Judg 16:21,25; Jer 52:11; Ezek 19:9).

Such conditions were not as common in Israel as in neighbouring countries, because the law of Moses encouraged respect for justice and human life. The guilty were to be punished, but they were not to be degraded (Deut 25:3; cf. Num 15:34). (For further details see PUNISHMENT.)

PROMISE

Israelites of the Old Testament era made their promises usually in the forms of covenants, oaths and vows. They therefore understood the promises of God in relation to such forms (Exod 6:8; Deut 9:5; Eph 2:12; Heb 6:13; see COVENANT; OATHS; VOWS). In the New Testament, although the idea of the covenant is present, there is little concerning oaths and vows. Usually the emphasis is on the promise, and most of the promises are made by God (2 Cor 1:20; Titus 1:2).

Some of these promises are in the nature of fulfilled prophecies, where God's promises of Old Testament times find their fulfilment in the events of Christ and the gospel (Luke 1:32-33,72-73; Acts 13:23,32; Rom 1:2; 15:8; Gal 3:14; Heb 9:15; cf. Gen 12:1-3; 2 Sam 7:16; Jer 31:31-34). Others concern the gift of the Holy Spirit to the church (Luke 24:49; Acts 1:4; 2:33,39), and the blessings of the believer in the age to come (Heb 10:36; James 1:12; 2:5; 2 Peter 3:4,13; 1 John 2:25).

The New Testament therefore refers to the entire gospel and its blessings as being based on promise. That is, salvation is God's gift, dependent on God's faithfulness and in no way a reward for human effort or merit (Gal 3:18; 4:23-28; 2 Tim 1:1; Heb 4:1; 10:36). God's promises are contrasted with the law given to Israel; for whereas the law demanded obedience, the promises require only faith to accept them (Rom 4:13-16; Gal 3:17-18; 3:21-22; Eph 3:6; Heb 8:6; 11:13).

God is always faithful to his promises. He has given added assurance of this by giving the Holy Spirit to the believer as a guarantee that he will do what he has promised (Eph 1:13-14; Heb 6:13;

10:23; 2 Peter 3:9). God's people likewise should be faithful to their promises, even when it involves them in personal inconvenience (Deut 23:23; Ps 15:4; 2 Cor 1:17-20).

PROPHECY, PROPHET

In present-day language the words 'prophecy' and 'prophet' are usually used in relation to foretelling events; a prophet is one who predicts (for example, a weather prophet). This was not the basic idea associated with the work of a prophet in Old Testament times. In those times prophecy meant making known the will of God; a prophet was God's spokesman.

This definition of a prophet was well illustrated in the case of Aaron, who was Moses' prophet, or spokesman (Exod 4:10-16; 7:1-2). Moses was the leader of Israel, but Aaron was the person who announced Moses' instructions to the people. In the same way the prophet announced God's will to the people of his time (1 Kings 22:8; 2 Kings 22:14-20; Jer 1:7,9; Ezek 3:4,27; Amos 3:7).

A true prophet could be appointed only by God (Jer 1:5; Ezek 2:3-7; Amos 7:15). He was therefore known as a man of God (1 Sam 2:27; 9:6; 1 Kings 13:1-2), a messenger of God (Hag 1:13), or a servant of God (2 Kings 17:23; 21:10; Jer 7:25). Sometimes he was called a seer (meaning 'one who sees') because he may have seen God's message in a vision (1 Sam 9:9,18-19; Zech 1:7-8).

Prophetical books

The arrangement of books within the Hebrew Bible gives a further indication of the Israelites' understanding of prophecy. They divided their Bible (our Old Testament) into three sections, which they called the Law, the Prophets and the Writings. The Law consisted of the five books of Moses. The Prophets consisted of the Former Prophets (Joshua, Judges, Samuel and Kings) and the Latter Prophets (Isaiah, Jeremiah, Ezekiel and the twelve so-called Minor Prophets). The Writings consisted of the miscellaneous other books.

It becomes clear, as we look at the composition of the Former Prophets group, that the books that we call historical the Israelites called prophetical. This is because these books were written from the prophetic point of view, showing how God was working out his purposes in the lives of his people. Most of Israel's historians were in fact prophets (1 Chron 29:29; 2 Chron 9:29; 12:15). In summary we might say that in the Former Prophets God revealed himself in the history of Israel, and in the Latter

Prophets he revealed himself through the words of his spokesmen.

Because they understood prophecy in this way, the Israelites excluded Chronicles from the Former Prophets and Daniel from the Latter Prophets. Chronicles was written from the priestly point of view rather than the prophetic. Daniel was written in the apocalyptic style rather than the prophetic. (See APOCALYPTIC LITERATURE.)

Professional and writing prophets

The prophets whose writings have become part of the Old Testament are commonly referred to as the writing prophets. Their writings date from the eighth century BC, but prophets had been active in Israel long before the eighth century. Even before the establishment of Israel's monarchy, prophets had been preachers and spiritual guides in Israel (Judg 4:4; 1 Sam 3:20; 2 Sam 7:2).

In the days of Samuel there were many young prophets in Israel. These young men had plenty of enthusiasm, but their emotional and sometimes uncontrolled behaviour helped to give prophets a poor reputation (1 Sam 10:5,9-12; 19:20-24; 2 Kings 9:11; cf. Amos 7:14). In an effort to redirect this religious enthusiasm for the spiritual benefit of the nation, Samuel established a school of prophets at Ramah. This was followed by the establishment of additional schools in other centres (1 Sam 19:18-20; 2 Kings 2:3,5; 4:38).

The setting up of these schools did not bring an immediate solution to the problem of emotionalism. Nevertheless, when Israel's religion was under threat from the Baal worship introduced by Jezebel, the prophets Elijah and Elisha found many faithful followers of God in these schools. These young men (the 'sons of the prophets') helped maintain the worship of the true God in a nation that had become unfaithful (2 Kings 2:1-7,15; 4:38; 6:1).

A person did not have to be a member of one of these schools to be a prophet. By the time of the writing prophets two hundred years later, many from these schools were more concerned with being religious professionals than with spiritually feeding God's people. Very few of the writing prophets appear to have been professionals. Their emphasis was that the true prophet had been called by God, not that he had received specialist training (Jer 1:4-8; Amos 7:14-15).

True and false prophets

Religion was an important part of Israelite life, and people often consulted prophets about their affairs. Consequently, many of the prophets operated near Israel's public places of worship (1 Sam 9:11-12; 10:5; 1 Kings 13:1-2; 18:30; Jer 35:4; Amos 7:12-13). Some of them were advisers to kings and officials, so that leaders could ask God's directions when they faced important decisions (2 Sam 7:1-3; 24:11-12; 1 Kings 22:6-8; 2 Kings 19:1-7; Jer 38:14-17).

Prophets received their income from those to whom they ministered, and this tempted them to say the sorts of things they knew their hearers wanted to hear. This assured them of good payment, but it brought condemnation from genuine believers. Because of their dishonesty and greed they were known as false prophets (1 Kings 22:5-8,13-18; Jer 6:13-14; 23:16-17; Micah 2:11; 3:5-7,11).

True prophets denounced the false prophets as being appointed by themselves, not by God. They were not God's messengers, but spoke according to their own selfish desires (Jer 14:14; 23:21-22; Ezek 13:1-3,17). Instead of rebuking the people for their sin and so running the risk of becoming unpopular, the false prophets assured the people that God was pleased with them. The truth was that the people were heading for judgment, and the corruption of the prophets was only adding to that judgment (Jer 23:11-17; Ezek 13:8-16,22).

The test of a prophet, whether he was true or false, was not whether his predictions came true, for even the predictions of false prophets could come true. The test was rather whether he led people in the ways of God (Deut 13:1-5; Jer 23:21-22,29-32). Nevertheless, if a prophet made a bold assertion that his prediction would come true and it did not, he was clearly a false prophet (Deut 18:22).

If prophets were truly God's messengers, their chief concern was not with foretelling events, but with leading people to repentance and obedience (Micah 3:8; 7:18; Zeph 2:1-3). They often opposed false religious practices, not because the practices themselves were wrong, but because the people carried them out in the wrong attitude. Religious exercises were no substitute for morality. They were of value only when the people were doing God's will in their daily lives. God would accept his people's worship only if they conducted themselves with righteousness before him and justice to others (Isa 1:12-17; Amos 5:21-24; Micah 6:6-8).

Current events and future hopes

Since the prophet's chief purpose was to bring God's message to the people of his time, prediction was not an essential part of the message. However, it often played a part, because the God who is concerned about the present also controls the future. As the prophet urged the people to turn from their sins and obey God, he may therefore have spoken of events that would follow the people's obedience or disobedience. His predictions were not merely to satisfy curiosity about the future, but had an important moral purpose. They showed people what God required of them now (Isa 1:18-20; Hosea 11:1-11; 14:1-7).

Predictions of this sort were usually conditional, even though the prophet may not have mentioned the conditions in his prophecy. For example, a prediction of blessing may not have been fulfilled, because the people were disobedient. A prediction of punishment may not have been fulfilled, because the people repented (Jer 18:7-10; 26:17-19; Jonah 3:4,10).

The prophets, like all the godly in Israel, looked forward to the day when God would punish all enemies, cleanse the earth of sin and establish his righteous rule in the world (Isa 24:17-23; 32:1-4). The one who would rule in this golden age they called the Messiah (cf. Ps 2:1-7; see MESSIAH).

But while the prophets pictured the Messiah as a king, a conqueror and a saviour, they also spoke of a prophetic figure whom they pictured as a servant, a sufferer and a victim. What they did not see was that both pictures applied to the same person. The Messiah was a king and a servant, a conqueror and a sufferer, a saviour and a victim (Deut. 18:15; Isa 9:6-7; 11:1-5; 52:13-14; 53:4-7; Zech 6:12-13; 12:10).

Another point that the prophets did not see was that this person would fulfill God's purposes not all at once, but through two separate entrances into the world. The New Testament makes it clear that this promised person was Jesus Christ (Matt 11:2-6; 22:41-45; Luke 1:32-33; 24:19,25-26; 1 Peter 1:10-12; Rev 5:5). The Messiah's first coming began with Jesus' birth and ended with his death, resurrection and ascension. At his second coming he will judge mankind and lead his people into the era of the new heavens and the new earth (Heb 1:5-9; 9:27-28; Rev 19:11-16; 21:1-4).

Problems concerning time

This apparent disregard for time is a common feature of Old Testament prophecy. A prediction may contain some parts fulfilled within the prophet's lifetime, other parts fulfilled within a generation or two, and other parts still unfulfilled (e.g. Joel 2:24-32; Hag 2:20-23).

It seems that the reason for this is that the prophet sees things from God's point of view; and God does not live in the sort of time system that operates in the world of mankind. The prophet sees

and knows in a way that is different from that of ordinary people. It is as if he steps out of the present world into the world of eternity, where time as we know it does not exist (2 Peter 3:8; Rev 1:8; see ETERNITY; TIME).

The prophet may therefore speak of events in language of future, present or even past tense (Isa 9:6-7; 53:1-9; Jer 51:52-57). Events may be separated by thousands of years as the ordinary person sees them, but they may not be separated at all in the message spoken by the prophet. He may group events together almost as if they happened about the same time (Isa 53:1-12; 61:1-9; Ezek 34:20-24; cf. 1 Peter 1:10-12).

The language of prophecy

Early prophets such as Deborah, Samuel, Nathan, Ahijah, Elijah and Elisha have left little or no record of their prophecies. It is clear, however, that they sometimes passed on their messages by means of stories and symbolic actions (2 Sam 12:1-7; 1 Kings 11:29-31). Over the following centuries, prophets increasingly wrote down their messages as well as, or sometimes instead of, speaking them (Isa 30:8; Jer 29:1,25; 36:1-4). Some also acted them (Isa 20:1-6; Jer 19:1-3; Ezek 5:1-12).

Most of the prophecies that have been written down are in the form of poetry. One reason for this is that poetry is often more effective than prose in expressing a person's deepest thoughts and feelings. Poetry is also easier to memorize, and this helped people to remember and pass on the message. (For further details see POETRY.)

New Testament prophets

John the Baptist, the forerunner of Jesus, continued the line of Old Testament prophets into the New Testament era (Matt 11:10,13; cf. Luke 2:36). He proclaimed God's will to the people and called them to repentance. At the same time he announced the blessings that would follow if they obeyed his message, and the judgments that would follow if they rejected it (Matt 3:7-12; Luke 3:3-7,16-18). He was the last prophet before Jesus Christ, in whose life, death, resurrection and final triumph all the Old Testament prophecies of salvation and judgment found their complete fulfilment (Matt 26:56; Luke 24:25-27).

In a sense Jesus too was a prophet. He was the one through whom God spoke (Heb 1:1-2), the great prophet that the people of Israel had always looked for as part of their messianic hope (Deut 18:15; John 6:14; 7:40; Acts 3:19-23; see MESSIAH). As a prophet he brought a message that people recognized as an authoritative word from God (Matt 7:28-29; 11:21; Luke 7:16; 24:19).

Jesus, in turn, established the new community of God's people, the Christian church, and in this community he appointed prophets to have a part. They were one of his gifts to the church (1 Cor 12:28; Eph 4:11). Jesus had promised that his Spirit would enable the leaders of the early church to recall, interpret and apply his teachings, and so build up the church (John 14:26; 15:26; 16:13; cf. Acts 2:24; 4:13; 6:4).

Apostles and prophets were Christ's special provision for the early church, to ensure that it was built on a proper foundation and in accordance with God's plan (Eph 2:20; 3:4-6; see APOSTLE). As the authoritative Christian teaching became increasingly available in written form, the need for apostles and prophets diminished. It seems that they were no longer needed after the first century.

Like Old Testament prophets, New Testament prophets were concerned with more than simply foretelling future events. Certainly they revealed God's will concerning people and events, and often they gave special instruction in particular situations (Acts 11:27-30; 13:1-2; 21:9-11; Rev 1:3; 10:7; see REVELATION). But above all the prophets built up God's people through bringing them the message of God in the power of the Spirit (Acts 15:32; 1 Cor 14:3-5,31). Even people who were not Christians could see the relevance of prophetic messages and, through repentance and faith, find salvation (1 Cor 14:24-25).

Prophets were closely linked with teachers and, like teachers, encouraged and strengthened their hearers through expounding the Scriptures (Acts 13:1; 14:22; 15:32; see TEACHER). It seems that they also received messages direct from God (1 Cor 14:6,26; Rev 1:1-3) and sometimes spoke with little or no preparation (1 Cor 14:29-31).

This did not mean that the prophets had no control over the urges they might have felt (1 Cor 14:32). Nor were people to accept their words without question simply because they were known as prophets. The hearers had to test everything according to the apostolic teaching, to see whether or not the prophets were building people up in the truth of God (1 Cor 14:29; 1 Thess 5:20-21; 1 John 4:1; cf. 1 Cor 14:37-38; Gal 1:8; 2 John 10).

Some people who were not regular prophets in the church may have prophesied in exceptional circumstances (Acts 19:6; cf. 2:17). This increased the possibility that false prophets might appear. God therefore gave to certain people the special gift of being able to discern more readily the difference between the true and the false (Matt 7:15; 24:24; 1 Cor 12:10; Rev 2:20).

PROPITIATION

Very rarely does the word 'propitiation' appear in modern English. This is largely the reason why present-day versions of the English Bible prefer to use alternative expressions. In simple terms, to propitiate means to turn away a person's anger by giving him an offering.

The wrath of God

God is holy, and therefore he is always opposed to evil. The Bible describes this opposition to evil as the wrath or anger of God (Deut 11:16-17; John 3:36; Eph 5:6). It is not an anger such as the bad temper that sinful people often display, but an anger that contains no trace of sin. It is the attitude of one who loves goodness and hates evil to such an extent that he cannot overlook wrongdoing. He cannot treat sin as if it does not matter (2 Kings 23:26; Jer 21:12; Hab 1:13; Rom 1:18; 2:5; Heb 1:9; Rev 14:8-11; 19:1-2).

Man through sin has cut himself off from God and placed himself under the wrath of God. He is unable to have fellowship with God, unable to please God and unable to bring himself back to God (Isa 59:2; Rom 8:7-8; Eph 2:3; Col 1:21).

God always has an attitude of wrath against sin, and there is nothing man can to do to propitiate God (i.e. to pacify, appease, calm the anger of or win the favour of God). Pagans used to try to escape the wrath of their gods by offering sacrifices; that is, they tried to propitiate their gods. But sinful man cannot act towards God like this. None of his efforts can quiet God's wrath against sin or win his favour. (For similar ideas of making offerings to turn away wrath see Exod 32:30-32; Prov 6:34-35; 16:14; Isa 16:1-7; 47:11.)

The love and mercy of God

God's opposition to man's sin is connected with his concern for man's good. God is a God of love, and he reacts in holy and just anger against all that is wrong in his rebellious creatures. Sinful people justly deserve the punishment that God's holy wrath requires, but God is patient with them and has no pleasure in punishing them (Ps 78:38; Rom 2:2-4; 2 Peter 3:9). In fact, he provides a way whereby they need not suffer the punishment themselves.

This was demonstrated in the sacrificial system that God gave to Israel. The sinner was in a hopeless position where there was nothing he could do to escape God's wrath. Yet God in his love provided a way of dealing with sin, so that the punishment on sin could be carried out, while at the same time the sinner could be forgiven.

God allowed the repentant sinner to kill an animal as a substitute for himself, so that the animal suffered the penalty that the offerer, because of his sin, should have suffered. Pardon was not something that the sinner had to squeeze from an unwilling God, but was the merciful gift of a God who wanted to forgive. God's anger was turned away (i.e. God was propitiated) not by the efforts of man but by his own gracious gift. God provided the propitiation (Lev 17:11; see BLOOD; SACRIFICE).

The sacrifice was not man's gift (in the sense of a bribe) to win God's favour, but God's provision to bear the divine judgment on sin. God's act of forgiveness, being based on love, involved his dealing with sin. God's wrath and God's love, far from being in conflict with each other, operated in harmony (Isa 53:4-5,10-11; 54:8; Micah 7:18; John 3:16-21,36; Rom 6:23).

The sacrifice of Christ

Sacrifices belonging to the Old Testament system had real meaning for the genuinely repentant sinner. They enabled him to see that God was acting justly in dealing with his sins, and gave him a way of expressing his faith in God's forgiving love (Heb 9:22). But the blood of animals could not take away sins (Heb 10:4). Only the blood of Jesus Christ – his death on the cross – can do that. In view of Christ's death, God was able to 'pass over', temporarily, the sins of Old Testament believers. God forgave them on credit, so to speak, for their sin was not actually removed till Christ died (Rom 3:25-26).

It becomes clear, now that the climax of God's plan of salvation has been reached through Christ, that the only thing that propitiates God is the death of Christ. Again, God provides the way. He himself becomes the sacrifice that secures the propitiation. A loving God willingly pays the penalty on behalf of those under his judgment (2 Cor 5:19; 1 John 4:10). God's holy wrath against sin has been satisfied by Christ's death, and therefore he can show mercy on the believing sinner. He can forgive the sinner, yet still be just in doing so (Rom 3:25-26; Heb 2:17; 1 John 2:2).

PROSELYTE

Throughout the cities of the Roman Empire there were communities of Jews who kept the traditions of their ancestors and attended synagogues regularly.

These were known as Jews of the Dispersion, or the scattered Jews (see DISPERSION).

Many Gentiles in these cities, being attracted to the Jewish religion by the morally upright lives of the Jews, attended the synagogue services and kept some of the Jewish sabbath and food laws. These people became known as God-fearers, or worshippers of God (Acts 10:1-2; 16:14). Some went even further and were circumcised and baptized as Jews. They were known as proselytes, or converts to Judaism (Acts 2:10; 6:5). Many of these Gentile proselytes and God-fearers, having already come to know and worship the God of Israel, readily became Christians when they first heard the gospel of Jesus Christ (Acts 13:43; 14:1; 17:4).

PROSTITUTION

In the ancient world, as in the modern, prostitution was widespread (Gen 38:15; Josh 2:1; Judg 11:1; 16:1; 1 Kings 3:16; Prov 2:16; 6:26; Luke 15:30). In Israelite law the penalty for prostitution was death, usually by stoning (Lev 19:29; 21:7,9; Deut 22:21; John 8:5).

Prostitutes bring lasting damage to themselves and their lovers. The Bible gives strong warnings against them (Prov 2:16-19; 5:1-14; 6:23-27; 7:1-27). A Christian in particular should have no union with a prostitute, since he already is spiritually united with Jesus Christ (1 Cor 6:15-20).

Although the Bible condemns prostitution, it does not reject prostitutes as being without hope of salvation. In the time of Jesus, prostitutes and other socially despised people were usually more willing to listen to the message of Jesus than were religiously respectable people. Some believed in him and found forgiveness (Matt 9:11-13; 21:31-32; Luke 7:37-50; 15:1). (See also ADULTERY.)

In Old Testament times Israel was unfaithful to God in leaving him and going after false gods. This unfaithfulness was likened to the behaviour of an unfaithful wife who leaves her husband to become a prostitute (Isa 1:21; Jer 13:27; Ezek 16:1-63; Hosea 1:2; 2:13; Micah 1:7). Israel's idolatry, besides being spiritual prostitution, involved physical prostitution. In many of the idolatrous religions, prostitutes were available for sexual rites that people believed gave increase in family, crops, flocks and herds (1 Kings 14:23-24; Jer 3:6-10; 13:22-27; Hosea 4:7-14; Amos 2:7-8; see BAAL).

God's prophets sometimes likened political and commercial agreements between Israel and pagan nations to acts of prostitution. Such agreements were often unions of shame designed solely for personal advantage. They ignored God's standards and defied his authority (Isa 23:17; Nahum 3:4). This anti-God spirit, symbolized by the prostitute, found its expression in New Testament times in the Roman Empire. It will find its fullest expression in the days of man's final great rebellion prior to the return of Jesus Christ (Rev 17:1-18).

PROVERBS

In ancient times as in the present, people gain wisdom from experience and condense that wisdom into short sayings called proverbs. The biblical book of Proverbs is largely a collection of miscellaneous Hebrew proverbs, most of them from Solomon (Prov 1:1; 10:1; 25:1). It also contains lectures for youth (Chapters 1-9) and wisdom teaching borrowed from neighbouring countries (Prov 30:1; 31:1). (See also WISDOM LITERATURE.)

Characteristics of the book

Living is a very practical matter, and sound common sense is necessary if a person is to handle life's everyday affairs satisfactorily. The wisdom teachers of Israel and neighbouring countries visited each other and exchanged such wisdom (1 Kings 4:30-34; 10:1; cf. Acts 7:22). But the Israelites were careful not to take from their neighbours any teaching that was coloured by foreign ideas of idolatry, immorality or self-seeking. The basis of the Israelite wisdom was the fear of God (Prov 1:7).

Because of this, the wisdom taught in the biblical book of Proverbs is not worldly wisdom, but godly wisdom. Worldly wisdom can encourage selfish ambition regardless of the needs of others; godly wisdom will encourage a life of practical righteousness based on the law of God.

Israelite proverbs are therefore useful for all God's people, even though they may live in different countries and eras. The proverbs are concerned with all sorts of subjects, small and great. Some deal with apparently minor matters such as talking too much or having bad table manners. Others deal with wider social issues such as contributing to the good of society or making far-reaching political decisions. Among the topics that most frequently occur in Proverbs are wisdom, folly, laziness, family life, speech, friendship, life and death.

Most of the book of Proverbs is written in simple two-line units of poetry. The characteristic parallelism of Hebrew poetry makes the two-line units easy to remember (see POETRY). Usually the second line either repeats the truth of the first line (Prov 16:16) or expresses its opposite (Prov 11:5).

Sometimes the second line develops or applies the first (Prov 3:6). This easily remembered poetic form encourages people to memorize the teaching, so that it will readily come to mind when needed. In reading Proverbs, it is better to stop and think about each unit of instruction than to read the book straight through as if it were a letter or narrative.

Outline of contents

The opening section of Proverbs is a lengthy talk from a 'father' to a 'son' (meaning, most likely, from a teacher to a pupil) on the importance of choosing wisdom and avoiding folly. The teacher gives the basis of his instruction (1:1-7), emphasizing that wisdom is of use to people only if they heed it (1:8-33). Wisdom brings its own reward (2:1-22) and enables a person's life to be useful for God and beneficial to himself (3:1-4:27). In particular, it helps a person overcome temptation to sexual immorality and other evils (5:1-7:27). Wisdom is eternal and is available to all people (8:1-9:18).

This basic instruction in the value of wisdom prepares the reader for the first major collection of proverbs. Of about 3,000 proverbs that Solomon wrote or collected (1 Kings 4:32), 375 are collected here. In places proverbs concerned with the same subject have been grouped together, but in general, teaching on any one subject is scattered throughout the section (10:1-22:16).

Two shorter sections collect together sayings from various other wise men. The sayings here are longer than those of Solomon and often cover several verses (22:17-24:22 and 24:23-34). Following this is a further collection of Solomon's proverbs. This collection was added more than two hundred years after the time of Solomon, at the time of Hezekiah's reforms (25:1; cf. 2 Chron 29:1-31:21). It consists of 128 proverbs (25:1-29:27).

The book concludes with three shorter sections. The first of these comes from the wisdom of Agur, a non-Israelite (30:1-33). The second comes from the wisdom of King Lemuel, another non-Israelite (31:1-9). The final section is an anonymous poem in praise of the perfect wife (31:10-31).

PROVIDENCE

The word 'providence', though not found in the Bible, is commonly used to describe God's control and government of all things. He maintains the universe and cares for his creatures according to his perfect love, wisdom and power. He directs all affairs, small and great, according to his purposes and brings them to their appointed goal (Ps 147:8-9;

Eccles 3:11; Isa 10:5-7; Matt 10:29; Eph 1:11; Phil 2:13; 1 Tim 6:15).

God's providence is evident everywhere — in the physical creation (Ps 29:3-6; 78:13-16; 104:27-28; Matt 6:26,28; Acts 14:17), in the events of world history (Prov 21:1; Amos 9:7; Luke 1:52; Acts 17:26; Rom 9:17) and in the lives of individuals (Gen 30:1-2; Job 1:21; Prov 16:33; Matt 6:25,30; 10:30; Luke 1:53). God's people are particularly aware of these truths, because they see God at work in everything (Eph 4:6).

Christians see not only God's love in his preservation of nature, but also his purpose in directing it towards its final glory (Matt 5:44-45; Rom 8:19-23; Col 1:17). They see that his direction of history has produced Jesus the Saviour and will lead to victory over all evil at the final triumph of Christ's kingdom (Gal 4:4; Col 1:20; 2 Thess 2:3-8). They see God at work in their own lives, lovingly controlling all their affairs in order to lead them to greater spiritual maturity (Rom 8:28; Phil 4:12-13; James 1:2-4; see also PREDESTINATION; SUFFERING).

Providence is not fate. There is no suggestion that because of God's controlling power everything happens mechanically. Neither nature nor man is the helpless victim of unalterable impersonal laws that determine the course of events. All things and all people are in the hands of the living God who is responsive to their needs (Gen 50:20; Jer 17:7-10; Jonah 4:11; Matt 8:26; 15:32; James 5:17-18; see MIRACLES; PRAYER). Also, people cannot excuse their mistakes by trying to put the blame on God's providence. People are moral beings and God holds them responsible for all their actions (Deut 30:15-18; Rom 2:15; cf. Luke 22:22; Acts 4:27-28).

PSALMS, BOOK OF

A psalm is a hymn of praise to God designed to be sung to the accompaniment of music. The book of Psalms is a collection of 150 such hymns.

One hymn book for all

The collection of the various psalms into one volume seems to have taken place gradually over a long time. Although each psalm is a unit in itself, not necessarily connected with those before or after it, certain psalms have been grouped together. They may have come from smaller collections already in existence (e.g. those of the 'sons of Korah'; see Ps 44-49), and may have been arranged in a certain order (e.g. Ps 120-134). Five groups (or books) make up the collection. The five books are Psalms 1-41, 42-72, 73-89, 90-106 and 107-150.

At the end of each of the first four books, an expression of praise has been added to mark the close of the book. The very last psalm, the 150th, has been placed where it is to form a climax to the entire collection.

Within the hymn book there are psalms for all occasions. Some were written specifically for use in public worship and temple festivals (e.g. Ps 38); others were adapted from personal psalms (e.g. Ps 54). Some were written for use on great national occasions such as coronations, victory celebrations and royal weddings (e.g. Ps 2, 18, 45); others arose from circumstances in the lives of private individuals (e.g. Ps 3, 75). The psalms may have expressed joy and confidence on the one hand, or terror and uncertainty on the other.

Writers of the psalms

Many of the psalms have titles that give the name of the writer or the name of the person(s) from whose collection they were taken (e.g. Ps 41, 42). David is named as the author of 73 psalms, which is almost half the collection. He was a gifted musician and

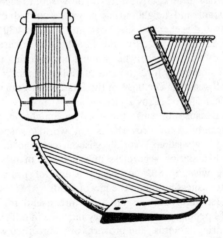

Stringed instruments

writer (1 Sam 16:23; 2 Sam 23:1), and was the person who established the various groups of singers and musicians for the temple services (1 Chron 15:16-28; 16:7,37-42).

David arranged the singers and musicians into three groups under the leadership of three men taken from the three family groups that made up the tribe of Levi. The three men were Asaph, Heman and Ethan (or Jeduthun) (1 Chron 6:31-48; 15:17-19; 16:5,42), and between them they wrote a number of psalms that have been included in the book of Psalms (e.g. Ps 50, 73-78, 88-89). The book also contains two psalms credited to Solomon (Ps 72, 127) and one to Moses (Ps 90).

Language of the psalms

Hebrew poetry has certain characteristics that the reader needs to know if he is to interpret the psalms correctly. The rhythm in Hebrew poetry comes not from metre and rhyme as in English poetry, but from the balanced arrangement of words and sentences. For this reason, Hebrew poetry can retain some of its style even when translated.

The balanced arrangement of Hebrew poetry is well demonstrated in the book of Psalms. Often the writer expresses one central idea by making parallel statements that have virtually the same meaning (Ps 7:16). Sometimes only one or two words are changed (Ps 118:8-9). The writer may make further emphasis by giving an application of his central idea (Ps 37:7), by contrasting two truths (Ps 68:6), or by otherwise developing his theme through a careful arrangement of related statements (Ps 4:3-5).

In some psalms the writer may repeat a verse to provide a refrain (Ps 42:5,11; 46:7,11). In others he may begin successive verses with successive letters of the Hebrew alphabet ('from A to Z', so to speak). This produces a type of verse known as an acrostic (e.g. Ps 25, 34, 119). (See also POETRY.)

The titles of the psalms, though not necessarily written by those who wrote the psalms, often include directions for those in charge of the music. The directions may indicate the type of instruments to be used (Ps 4, 5) and the tune to which the song is to be sung (Ps 53, 56, 58). Words such as Shiggaion (Ps 7), Miktam (Ps 16) and Maskil (Ps 55) are Hebrew words of uncertain meaning. They may indicate the type of hymn or the occasion on which it should be sung. 'Selah' is probably a musical term used to indicate a variation in the music, such as a pause, the repetition of a line, or a change in the volume or speed of the music (Ps 89:37,45,48).

Interpreting the psalms

Like all writings of the Old Testament, the psalms must be interpreted in their historical context. The present-day reader's first responsibility is to understand each psalm as its author intended it to be understood.

However, the New Testament writers often saw meanings in the psalms that the original writers were not aware of. Jesus Christ was the fulfilment of all that God intended the nation Israel to be. The Davidic kings of Israel foreshadowed the greatest of all Davidic kings, Jesus the Messiah. When writing about the Davidic kings, the psalmists freely spoke of Israel's ideals of triumph and glory, but those ideals found their perfect expression only in Jesus Christ (cf. Ps 2 with Acts 4:25-31; 13:33-34; Heb 1:5; 5:5; cf. Ps 45 with Heb 1:8-9; cf. Ps 110 with Matt 22:41-46; Heb 7:15-17; see MESSIAH).

The failures of the Davidic kings, however, indicate how far they fell short of God's perfect requirements. In a psalm that speaks of the ideal qualities of the Davidic king there may also be references to the king's sins. The New Testament writers may therefore quote from one part of a psalm and apply it to Christ (cf. Ps 69:4,9,21 with John 2:17; 15:25; Matt 27:34,38), though other parts of the same psalm may refer to the Davidic king's sins and therefore could never apply to Christ (cf. Ps 69:5 with 1 Peter 2:22; 1 John 3:5).

Just as the reader must interpret each psalm according to the psalmist's purpose, so must he interpret a New Testament application of a psalm according to the New Testament writer's purpose. As the psalmists were concerned with suffering and victory, so are the New Testament writers as they consider the work of Christ

When the godly of the Old Testament era suffered for righteousness' sake, they anticipated Christ's sufferings (cf. Ps 22:1-18; Matt 27:39-46). (This may be likened to the experience of Christians who, when they suffer for righteousness' sake, share in Christ's sufferings; 2 Cor 1:5; Phil 3:10.) Similarly, when godly kings of Israel won great victories, they anticipated the triumphs of Christ (cf. Ps 68:17-18; Eph 1:18-23; 4:8-10).

Christ, the true embodiment of Israel, so shared his people's sufferings that in the end he bore the full force of God's wrath against sin. But he came out victorious, so that people can enter a kingdom greater than Israel ever imagined (cf. Ps 22:19-31 with Phil 2:7-11; Rev 5:9-14).

PUNISHMENT

As the supreme Lord and the perfect judge, God is the source of all justice. He loves what is good and is the giver of all the blessings that man receives (Zeph 3:5; Matt 19:17; James 1:17). He also hates what is evil and requires just punishment on the sin that man commits (Ps 94:1-2; Rom 12:19; Heb 10:30).

Order in society

God desires that human society function justly and orderly. Therefore, he has given to man the responsibility to administer justice in society and to carry out fitting punishments on wrongdoers (Rom 13:1-4; 1 Peter 2:13-14; see GOVERNMENT).

Such punishments must always be just. They must not be relaxed to favour people of power and influence such as the rich; nor must they be imposed rashly to take advantage of defenceless people such as the poor (Exod 23:3,6; cf. Rom 2:11; James 2:6). Always the punishment must be in proportion to the crime (Exod 21:22-25; Deut 25:1-13; Gal 6:7). Where the wrongdoing involves loss or damage, the wrong-doer should compensate the person who suffers the loss or damage (Exod 22:1-6; Luke 19:8).

Punishment of the wrongdoer should be carried out primarily because the person deserves it, not because the ruling authorities want to use him to teach others a lesson (Deut 13:10; 19:19; 25:2; Luke 23:41; Heb 2:2). If, however, the punishment serves to warn others or reform the wrongdoer, so much the better (Deut 13:11; 19:20).

Eternal punishment

Being a holy and righteous judge, God must punish sin (John 5:26-29; Rom 2:1-6). But God's holiness and righteousness are not separate from his love. He has therefore provided a way of salvation so that when people repent of their sins and trust in his mercy, they can receive forgiveness. Christ bears the punishment of their sins for them (Heb 9:28; 1 Peter 2:24; see JUDGMENT; PROPITIATION). Those who repent are forgiven and receive eternal life. Those who refuse to repent remain unforgiven and suffer eternal punishment (Matt 25:46; 2 Thess 1:9).

The word 'eternal' indicates the nature, rather than the length of time, of the life or punishment. They belong to the eternal and spiritual world in contrast to the temporal and material world. Nevertheless, there is a terrible endlessness about the punishment, as Jesus clearly pointed out (Mark 9:43-48; see HELL).

There is no indication in the Bible that God's judgment of condemnation on the wicked will be reversed. The judgment is final, and therefore the punishment is eternal (Matt 8:12; 13:41-42; John 3:36; Rom 2:5-11). The punishment is not for the purpose of correction. It is for the purpose of carrying out the penalty that the person, because of his sin, deserves (1 Peter 1:17; Rev 16:6).

PURIFICATION

See UNCLEANNESS.

QUOTATIONS

New Testament writers frequently quote the Old Testament, and in doing so show their acceptance of the Old Testament as God's authoritative Word (see INSPIRATION). But in some cases the New Testament quotations differ from the Old Testament originals. In others the meanings given to the quotations in the New Testament differ from those of the Old Testament originals.

Different wording in Old and New Testaments

Since the Old Testament was written in Hebrew and the New Testament in Greek, any quotation of the Old Testament in the New requires translation. This naturally brings a change in wording. Sometimes the New Testament writers made their own translations. Usually, however, they used the existing translation of the Old Testament known as the Septuagint (abbreviated LXX), which Jewish scholars had made in the third and second centuries of the era before Christ (see SEPTUAGINT).

Just as a preacher today may use an alternative translation to give the desired emphasis, so did the New Testament writers. They used the translation that suited their purposes (cf. Isa 28:16 with Rom 10:11).

In many cases, again like preachers today, the New Testament writers made their quotations from memory. As a result their quotations do not follow the Old Testament originals word for word. They were concerned with the meaning rather than the wording of the passages they quoted (cf. Rom 11:8 with Deut 29:4; Isa 29:10). In other cases, however, they were concerned with the wording rather than the meaning. They may even have based a teaching on the meaning of a particular word (cf. Gal 3:16 with Gen 12:7).

Writers and preachers, ancient and modern, often quote passages from well known writings merely to give liveliness or colour to their writings. The New Testament writers at times did likewise. They were so familiar with the Old Testament that they quoted its words naturally. They may not have intended any connection between the Old and New Testament contexts (cf. 2 Cor 6:16-17 with Exod 29:45; Isa 52:11; 2 Sam 7:14).

The nature of fulfilment

Certain passages of the Old Testament are quoted repeatedly in the New Testament. This suggests that there was in New Testament times a collection, either oral or written, of selected Old Testament passages in common use among the churches. For example, Psalm 118:22-23, Isaiah 8:14 and Isaiah 28:16 are used in such passages as Matthew 21:42, Acts 4:10-12, 1 Peter 2:1-10, Romans 9:33 and Romans 10:11. Similarly Zechariah 12:10-14 is found in Matthew 24:30, John 19:37 and Revelation 1:7.

Psalm 69 is quoted in Matthew 27:34, John 2:17, John 15:25, Acts 1:20, Romans 11:9-10 and Romans 15:3.

These selections of Scripture are all used in relation to Jesus Christ, for the New Testament writers understood them as having their fulfilment in him. The primary meaning of that fulfilment was not simply that Old Testament predictions had now come true, but that the Old Testament work had now been completed. The Old Testament was written not merely to predict New Testament events, but to record what God was doing in working out his purposes for mankind. The New Testament writers saw that in Christ God had brought that work to completion, to fulfilment, to finality.

God was the controller of history. His repetitive activity in judgment and salvation, bondage and deliverance, reached its climax in one great act of judgment and salvation at Golgotha. There God gave absolute deliverance to those who were in hopeless bondage. He completed the pattern that he had been working among mankind through the history of Israel. In Christ he brought his plans to fulfilment (Exod 6:6-8; Isa 11:15-16; Hosea 2:14-15; 1 Cor 5:7; 10:1-13; Rev 5:9; 15:3).

Israel's Old Testament history was the record of the ongoing revelation of God. It was not just a record of events, but a record of what God was doing. What the Old Testament writers saw, though having meaning in its own day, developed greater significance through the New Testament events. Christians now saw Jesus as the goal towards which all God's Old Testament activity had been moving. They saw Jesus as the centre of all history. The old era prepared the way for him; the new results from him.

Jesus and the Old Testament

Now that God's purposes had been fulfilled in Jesus Christ, the New Testament writers discovered in the Old Testament writings greater truths than the original writers were aware of (1 Peter 1:10-12). While accepting the original meaning of the writings, the New Testament writers expanded that meaning because of the fuller revelation that had come through Jesus Christ.

Promises may have already been fulfilled in the Old Testament, but now they had a greater fulfilment in the New (Deut 12:9; 25:19; Josh 21:45; Heb 4:1-10). Psalms, prophecies and songs may have been written at first concerning some Old Testament person or event, but now they had new meaning because people saw them as foreshadowings of Christ (cf. quotations from Psalm 2 in Acts 4:25-26;

13:33; cf. quotations from Psalm 45 in Heb 1:8-9; cf. quotations from Psalm 69 in John 2:17; 15:25; 19:28-30; Acts 1:20; cf. quotation of Isa 7:14 in Matt 1:23).

The New Testament writers saw Jesus the Messiah as the fulfilment of all God's purposes for Israel. He was the great descendant of Abraham through whom Israel received its supreme glory and through whom people of all nations are blessed (Gen 12:1-3; Gal 3:16).

Since Jesus was the one to whom the entire Old Testament pointed, he fulfilled the Old Testament (Matt 4:14-16; 8:17; 12:17-21). The New Testament writers were so convinced of this that they spoke of a 'fulfilment' even when they saw only a striking similarity between Old and New Testament events. For example, as Israel came out of Egypt, so did Jesus (Hosea 11:1; Matt 2:15). As there was loud weeping when the Babylonians took the Israelites captive, so was there when Herod slaughtered Jewish babies (Jer 31:15; Matt 2:17-18).

Although Israel repeatedly failed and suffered God's punishment, the people still hoped for a glorious future. Jesus Christ, the true fulfilment of Israel, not only suffered for his people's sins, but he completed perfectly what Israel had failed to do (cf. Isa 53:4 with Matt 8:17; cf. Isa 42:1-4 with Matt 12:18-21). The New Testament fulfils the Old in that Jesus Christ became all that Israel should have been but never was (cf. Isa 53:5-6 with 1 Peter 2:24-25; cf. Zech 9:9-11 with Matt 21:5; 26:28-29; see SERVANT OF THE LORD).

Like Israel in general, David's kingdom in particular failed to fulfil God's purposes. David's psalms reflect both his sorrow over Israel's failures and his expectation of better things to come. He looked for the day when God's people would enjoy his blessings in a kingdom of righteousness. The ideals that David longed for found their fulfilment in David's great descendant, Jesus the Messiah (cf. Ps. 40:6-8 with Heb 10:5-9; cf. Ps 110:1 with Matt 22:44). (For discussion on the use of David's psalms in the New Testament see PSALMS, BOOK OF, sub-heading 'Interpreting the Psalms'.)

RABBAH

To the east of the Jordan River was the land of the Ammonites, whose capital city was Rabbah, or Rabbah-ammon. Though at times conquered, the city was repeatedly rebuilt. It is known today as Amman, capital of the present-day nation of Jordan (Deut 3:11; Jer 49:1-2; Ezek 21:20; Amos 1:13-14). Most references to Rabbah in the Bible are related to conflicts between Ammon and Israel-Judah (e.g. 2 Sam 11:1; 12:26-31). (For map and other details see AMMON.)

RABBI

'Rabbi' was a Hebrew word meaning 'my teacher' or 'my master'. Pupils used the word when addressing their teachers (Matt 23:7; Mark 9:5; John 1:38; 3:25-26), and it was a common title that Jesus' disciples used in addressing him (Matt 26:25; John 6:25; 9:2; 13:13-14; 20:16). People in general used the word as a title of respect for prominent teachers in the community (Luke 3:12; 10:25; John 1:49; 3:2). The word also had a more specialized meaning as a formal title for the Jewish teachers of the law known as scribes (cf. Luke 2:46; Matt 23:7; Acts 5:34; 22:3; see SCRIBES).

RACE

In spite of the many ethnic groups in the world, there is one race that includes them all, the human race. There is a basic unity to the human race, for all people share a common origin (Acts 17:26; Rom 5:12; 1 Cor 15:47-48). There is also a basic equality, for all people exist in the image of God (Gen 1:27; see IMAGE).

No person is favoured with God's salvation on account of his race. All have sinned and are under the judgment of God, but all can be saved through accepting the salvation that God in his grace offers (Rom 2:9-10; 3:19,23-24).

From the time of man's earliest rebellion, God worked in human history to produce one who would be a saviour for all mankind. The fact that this saviour was one of mankind meant that he had to come from one of the many races and nations of mankind. God's choice of Israel as his people was specifically for the purpose of producing this saviour (Luke 2:10-11,32; Rom 9:4-5; cf. Gen 12:1-3; see ELECTION; COVENANT).

Through being God's channel of blessing to the world, Israelites enjoyed certain blessings, but that did not mean that they automatically received salvation from the penalty of sin. Israelites, whether in Old or New Testament times, had to repent and believe, the same as people of other races, if they were to be saved. Salvation is solely by God's grace, and people accept it by faith (Isa 1:16-20; Luke 3:6-8; 11:32; John 8:39,44; Rom 9:30-32; Eph 2:8; see REMNANT).

Since all are saved on the same basis, there can be no inequality in the church. Believers of all races

are united in one body (Gal 3:28; Eph 2:13-16; see FOREIGNER; GENTILE). God intends his church to be a showpiece to the world. Through the union of people of different races in one body, the church demonstrates the unity that God has planned for the whole universe (Eph 1:9-10; 3:6-10).

RACHEL

When Jacob went to Paddan-aram to find a wife, he met and fell in love with Rachel, the younger daughter of his uncle, Laban. Jacob worked seven years for Laban as payment for Rachel, but when the wedding day came, Laban deceived Jacob by giving him the older daughter, Leah, instead. After the wedding festivities he gave Rachel also to Jacob, but made Jacob work for him an extra seven years as payment for her. Laban also gave each of the two daughters a slave-girl as a wedding gift (Gen 29:1-30).

While Leah produced several sons for Jacob, Rachel remained childless. She then gave her maid to Jacob, so that the maid might bear sons whom Rachel could adopt as her own. Leah did likewise with her maid, after which she produced more sons of her own. Jacob already had ten sons and a daughter by the time Rachel gave birth to her first son, Joseph (Gen 29:31-30:24).

Although Laban had enriched himself through his daughters' bride price (Jacob's years of hard work), he now planned to exclude them from the inheritance, in favour of his sons. This made Rachel so angry that when Jacob and his family left Paddan-aram for Canaan, she took her father's idols with her. According to local custom, these gave her some claim to his inheritance (Gen 31:1-21). Laban never regained his idols, but Jacob made sure that Rachel did not keep them once the family entered Canaan (Gen 31:34-35; 35:1-4).

Rachel died when giving birth to Benjamin, the only son of Jacob born in Canaan. She was buried near Ramah, on the road from Bethel to Bethlehem (Gen 35:16-20; 1 Sam 10:2; Jer 31:15). Centuries later, Jeremiah imagined the dead Rachel mourning from her tomb as her descendants were led past on their way to captivity in a foreign land (Jer 31:15). She might likewise have mourned over the slaughter of the Jewish babies by Herod (Matt 2:16-18).

RAHAB

The name Rahab appears in English versions of the Bible as belonging to a woman who features in the book of Joshua, and to a mythical sea monster that features in the poetical books. But in the Hebrew Bible the two do not share the same name. There is a difference in spelling.

A woman in Jericho

Before Joshua opened his attack on Canaan, he sent two men to spy out the first city they would meet, Jericho. In Jericho the men met Rahab, a prostitute whose house was attached to the city wall. Rahab had heard sufficient of Israel's God to fear his power, but she believed in his mercy to save her. She protected the spies from the local authorities, and in return asked protection for herself and her family when the Israelites attacked Jericho (Josh 2:1-14; Heb 11:31).

Rahab further demonstrated her faith by being obedient to the instructions that the spies gave her. She protected the spies as requested, and did as they had told her in preparation for Israel's attack. As a result the Israelites preserved her and her family when Jericho fell, and accepted them into Israel as part of the nation (Josh 2:15-24; 6:17,22-25; James 2:25). If this Rahab is the person of that name who married Salmon, she was mother of Boaz and an ancestor of Jesus the Messiah (Matt 1:1,5-6).

A mythical sea monster

Rahab the mythical sea monster was considered by people of the Middle East to symbolize the forces of chaos over which God had victory in creating an orderly world (Job 9:13; 26:12; 38:8-11). Poets at times wrote about God's overthrow of Egypt in the Red Sea as if it were the overthrow of the sea monster Rahab (Ps 89:9-10; Isa 51:9-10). From this there developed the poetical usage of 'Rahab' as another name for Egypt (Ps 87:4; Isa 30:7).

RAMESES (RA'AMSES)

One reason why the Israelites of Moses' time were slaves in Egypt was that the Pharaoh wanted a cheap work-force to carry out his spectacular building programs. Among the cities that the Israelites built was Rameses (or Ra'amses), where the buildings included a magnificent palace, large storehouses and defence fortifications (Exod 1:8-11). Rameses was probably the former Hyksos capital, Avaris, rebuilt. (For map and other details see EGYPT.)

Rameses was located in that part of the Nile Delta where the family of Jacob had originally settled (Gen 47:11). This was the region from which Jacob's multitude of descendants set out on their flight from Egypt over four hundred years later (in 1280 BC; Exod 12:37). Rameses was also apparently known as Zoan (Ps 78:12,43), which from 1085 to 660 BC was the capital of Egypt (Isa 19:11,13; 30:4; Ezek 30:14).

RAMOTH-GILEAD

As its name indicates, Ramoth-gilead was in the territory of Gilead, east of the Jordan River. It was in the region of the ill-defined border between the tribes of East Manasseh and Gad, and was one of the three cities of refuge in Israel's trans-Jordan territory (Josh 20:8-9). (For maps and other details see CITY OF REFUGE; GILEAD.)

Ramoth-gilead's chief importance was as a defence outpost on the nation's eastern frontier. Many battles were fought there, and the town often fell to invading armies (1 Kings 22:1-40; 2 Kings 8:28-9:16). It was among the first places to fall when Assyria conquered Israel and carried the people into captivity (2 Kings 15:29).

RANSOM

See REDEMPTION.

REBEKAH

As the wife of Isaac, Rebekah had an important part in God's development of a people for himself according to the promise he gave to Abraham (Gen 22:15-18; 24:3-4,67). Isaac and Rebekah were without children for twenty years, but then Rebekah gave birth to twin sons, Esau and Jacob (Gen 25:20-26). Though God had told her that the covenant would be fulfilled through the younger son rather than the older (Gen 25:23; Rom 9:10-13), she had no right to work out a scheme to

Israelite slaves building cities in Egypt

deceive Isaac. She was determined that nothing would prevent Jacob from receiving the blessing (Gen 27:6-29).

When Esau plotted to kill Jacob, Rebekah thought out another scheme, this time to protect Jacob. She decided to send him north to her brother in Paddan-aram. Again she deceived Isaac, this time by persuading him that the reason Jacob should go north was to find a wife among her people (Gen 27:41-28:5).

There is no record that Rebekah ever saw her favourite son again. Upon her death, she was buried in the burial ground that Abraham had bought for his family (Gen 49:31).

RECONCILIATION

Through his sin man has made himself the enemy of God. He is separated from God, under the wrath of God and unable to have fellowship with God (Rom 1:18; 8:7-8; Eph 2:3; Col 1:21). Man needs to be reconciled to God; that is, he needs to be brought back from a state of hostility to a state of peace; from being an enemy to being a friend.

The only way that reconciliation can occur is through the removal of the cause of hostility. Christ did this when he died on the cross; he bore man's sin. God's holy wrath against sin was satisfied, but only at great cost to himself. God was in Christ, reconciling sinners to himself. Because of what he has done through Christ's death, God can in his love accept the repentant sinner back to himself (Rom 5:6-9; 2 Cor 5:18-19,21; see PROPITIATION).

Once God has dealt with sin according to his standards of justice and holiness, he can reconcile guilty sinners. Reconciliation is God's work, not man's. The fault is on man's side, but the removal of hostility is entirely the work of God (2 Cor 5:18-19). Man is brought into a right relationship with God only through the outworking of God's grace in the death of Jesus Christ (Rom 5:10-11; Eph 2:12-16; Col 1:20,22). Sinners receive the benefits of this reconciliation when they respond to God in faith and repentance (Rom 5:1; 2 Cor 5:20).

Peace now replaces hostility (Eph 2:3,14-17). This peace is more than the absence of hostility; it is a state of spiritual well-being brought about through a right relationship with God. It is a peace that comes from God through Christ's conquest of sin, and it enables believers to be confident and calm in a world still hostile to God (John 14:27; Rom 5:1; 8:6; 16:20; Phil 4:7,9; see PEACE).

Having experienced the gracious work of God's reconciliation, believers should preach it to others,

so that others might be reconciled to God (2 Cor 5:18). In addition they should desire that people be reconciled to each other. Christ's work destroys traditional hostilities in human relations and brings peace (Eph 2:14-16).

Whether within the community of believers or outside it, Christians should try to live peaceably with others (Matt 5:23-26; Rom 12:18-21; 2 Cor 6:11-13), and should encourage the same attitude in others (Matt 5:9). They should also work towards the reconciliation of man to the world of nature in which he lives. Such a reconciliation is part of the purpose for which Christ died (Rom 8:19-23; Col 1:16,20; see NATURE).

RED SEA

When the Bible speaks of the Red Sea, it refers only to the northern part where the sea divides into two arms, between which lies the Sinai Peninsular. The western arm is the Gulf of Suez (Num 33:10) and the eastern arm the Gulf of Aqabah (Num 14:25; 21:4; 1 Kings 9:26; see also EZION-GEBER).

The Red Sea through which the people of Israel passed during their miraculous escape from Egypt was literally the 'Sea of Reeds'. This was a large

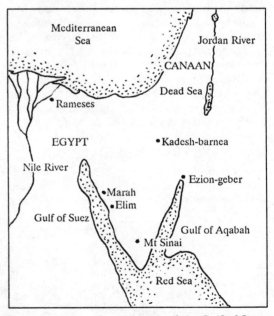

shallow expanse of water north of the Gulf of Suez, somewhere near the line of the present-day Suez Canal (Exod 13:18). God saved the Israelites by sending gale force winds that blew all night and dried up enough of the water to form a passage for his people to cross to the other side (Exod 14:21-22).

Just before daybreak, when all the Israelites had crossed over, the Egyptians attempted to follow. By then the wind had dropped and the sea waters began to return to normal, bringing first confusion, then panic, and finally destruction to the Egyptian chariot force (Exod 14:24-28; 15:4).

REDEMPTION

In Bible days a slave could be set free from bondage by the payment of a price, often called the ransom. The whole affair was known as the redemption of the slave (Lev 25:47-48). (The words 'redeem' and 'ransom' are related to the same root in the original languages.) The Bible speaks of redemption both literally (concerning everyday affairs) and pictorially (concerning what God has done for his people) (Ps 77:15; Titus 2:14).

In the Old Testament

Under Israelite law, both people and things could be redeemed. In family matters, all Israelites had to redeem their firstborn. Since God had preserved Israel's firstborn during the Passover judgment, they rightly belonged to him. Therefore, the parents had to redeem their firstborn by a payment of money to the sanctuary (Exod 13:2,13; Num. 18:15-16; see FIRSTBORN). In matters of property, if a person became poor and sold land he had inherited from his ancestors, either he or a relative had to buy the land back (redeem it) as soon as possible (Lev 25:25; Ruth 4:3-6; see SABBATICAL YEAR).

If Israelites vowed to give God their children, animals, houses or land, they could redeem those things, again by a payment of money to the sanctuary (Lev 27:1-25; see VOWS). If a person was under the death sentence because his ox had killed someone, his relatives could redeem him (since the death was accidental) by a payment of money to the dead man's relatives (Exod 21:28-30). In all these cases there was the idea of release by the payment of a price.

Often God is said to have redeemed Israel; that is, to have delivered Israel from the power of its enemies (Jer 31:11; Micah 4:10). The greatest of these acts of redemption was at the time of the exodus, when God delivered Israel from captivity in Egypt (Exod 6:6; 15:13; Ps 106:9-10; see EXODUS). Centuries later, after Israel (Judah) had been taken captive to Babylon, there was a 'second exodus', when God again redeemed his people from bondage (Isa 44:22-23; 48:20).

In these acts of redemption of Israel there is no suggestion that God paid anything to the enemy nations, as if he was under some obligation to them. Nevertheless, there is the suggestion that redemption cost God something; for he had to use his mighty power in acts of judgment to save his people (Exod 32:11; Deut 4:37-38; 9:26,29; Isa 45:13; 52:3; 63:9).

In the New Testament

Besides being an everyday practice, redemption was a fitting picture of God's activity in saving sinners. Those who sin are slaves of sin and under the sentence of death, and have no way of releasing themselves from bondage (John 8:34; Rom 6:17,23; 1 John 5:19; cf. Ps 130:8). Jesus Christ came to give his life as a ransom for those under this sentence of death. His death brought forgiveness of sins and so released them from sin's bondage (Matt 20:28; Rom 3:24-25; Gal 3:13; Eph 1:7; Col 1:14; 1 Tim 2:6; Rev 1:5).

Sinners are therefore redeemed by the blood of Christ. The ransom price he paid for them was his life laid down in sacrifice (Heb 9:12; 1 Peter 1:18-19; Rev 5:9). They are freed from the power of sin in their lives now (Heb 2:14-15), and will experience the fulness of their redemption when their bodies also are freed from the power of sin at Christ's return. That event will bring about not only man's final redemption but also the release of the world of nature from sin's corrupting power (Luke 21:28; Rom 8:21-23; Eph 4:30).

Paul at times makes a slightly different use of the illustration of slavery and redemption to remind Christians of their present responsibilities. When people are redeemed from the bondage of sin and the curse of the law, they come into a new life of liberty as the sons of God. Sin no longer has power over them, and they must show this to be true by the way they live (Rom 8:2; Gal 3:13-14; 4:4-7; cf. Titus 2:14).

Yet, though free from sin, Christians are not free to do as they like. Because they have been bought with a price, they are now, in a sense, slaves of God. They must therefore be obedient to him, their new master (Rom 6:16-18; 1 Cor 6:19-20; 7:22-23; see SERVANT; SLAVE).

REFINE

Metal-workers were common in the ancient world, and used their skills in a variety of ways (Gen 4:22; Exod 31:4; Judg 17:4; Isa 41:7; 44:12; 54:16). If they wanted to obtain pure metals from the raw materials they worked with, they first of all had to refine the metals. This was particularly so in the case of precious metals such as silver and gold (1 Chron 28:18; Mal 3:2-3).

The metal was placed in a fire of intense heat so that, as the metal melted, impurities could be removed. The refining process tested and purified

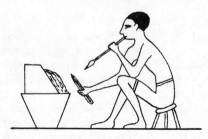

Egyptian refiner

the metal. It was a vivid picture of the way God tests and purifies his people through the sufferings and hardships they experience (Ps 66:10; Prov 17:3; Isa 1:25; 48:10; 1 Peter 1:7; see TESTING).

REGENERATION

Man, being a sinner, is spiritually dead, and unable to give himself spiritual life. He is cut off from God, with no hope of salvation through anything he might plan or do. God, however, can save man from this hopeless condition by forgiving his sins, giving him new life and restoring him to a right relationship with himself. This experience is called the new birth, or regeneration, and is entirely the work of the Spirit of God within a person. It takes place when the person humbly submits himself to Jesus Christ and trusts him for forgiveness, salvation and life (John 1:12-13; 3:3-6; Eph 2:1,5; Titus 3:5).

To be regenerated means, in other words, to be born anew, to be spiritually re-created. This is not something man can do. It is entirely the work of the merciful and sovereign God (John 1:13; 3:5; Titus 3:3-7; James 1:18; 1 Peter 1:23; cf. Ps 51:10; Ezek 11:19). Without it the sinner remains in his hopeless state and is incapable of experiencing spiritual life (John 3:5-6). Through it a person becomes a child of God and enters the kingdom of God (John 1:12-13; 3:3,5; see also ADOPTION).

The regenerated person is a new person (2 Cor 5:17; 1 Peter 2:2; cf. Gal 6:15). He has a new life inwardly, characterized by a renewed mind that governs all his thinking and attitudes (Rom 12:2; Eph 4:23-24; cf. Ezek 36:26-27; Jer 31:33). He also has a new life outwardly, characterized by loving behaviour towards others, hatred of sin and victory over the world's temptations (Col 3:10,12-13; 1 John 2:29; 4:7; 5:4,18; cf. 1 Cor 5:7-8).

REHOBOAM

Upon the death of Solomon, Rehoboam his son became king of Israel (930 BC). He inherited the judgment that God had previously prepared for the throne of Solomon (1 Kings 11:11-13).

Aware that the northern tribes were dissatisfied with the Jerusalem government, Rehoboam tried to hold their allegiance by going north to Shechem for his coronation ceremony (1 Kings 12:1). He also decided to take a firm stand against any tendency to weaken Jerusalem's control of the north. But his efforts were in vain, with the result that the ten northern tribes broke away from David's dynasty and formed their own kingdom under Jeroboam (1 Kings 12:2-20). The Davidic kingdom, though still centred on Jerusalem, was reduced to the tribe of Judah and one neighbouring tribe.

Though Rehoboam thought of sending his army to force his rule upon the north, he changed his mind when a prophet told him that the division was a judgment sent by God (1 Kings 12:21-24). For three years Rehoboam followed the way of God faithfully. This was partly because of the good influence of a large number of priests and Levites who had fled from the north to Jerusalem rather than cooperate with Jeroboam's idolatry (2 Chron 11:13-17). During this time he ruled well, improving the nation's defences and training his sons to be administrators (2 Chron 11:5-12,23).

As Rehoboam's strength increased, so did his pride. Soon he tried to show himself independent of God by copying the Canaanite religions (1 Kings 14:21-24; 2 Chron 12:1,14). God punished him by allowing Egypt to invade and plunder the land. Only a last minute confession of sin from Rehoboam and his governors saved Judah from destruction (2 Chron 12:2-13).

REMNANT

Although the nation Israel as a whole was God's people, only a minority of the people ever truly believed. While the majority carried out their rituals without any attitude of genuine repentance or faith, there were always the few who were truly devoted to God. This faithful minority is consistently referred to as the remnant. Israel may have been God's people in the national sense, but the remnant were God's people in the spiritual sense. They were the true Israel (Rom 9:6-7,27).

When God's people of Old Testament times rebelled against him, the prophets announced God's judgment upon them. Time and again the prophets declared that God had rejected his unfaithful people but would preserve the faithful remnant. One task of the prophets was to build up and encourage the remnant (1 Kings 19:18; Isa 1:9; 8:16-19; 10:20-23; 28:5; Jer 15:19-21).

The prophets saw that events were heading towards a judgment far greater than anything the people had met previously. The nation would be conquered, Jerusalem destroyed and the people taken into captivity. But God would still preserve a remnant, so that after a time in captivity, some would return to Jerusalem to rebuild the temple, the city and the nation (Ezra 9:13-15; Isa 11:11-12,16; Micah 2:12).

After the return, the people as a whole again became unfaithful to God, but there was always a remnant of faithful believers. From this remnant the Messiah eventually came (Micah 5:2-3,7-8; Zech 8:11-12; Mal 3:16-18; Matt 1:18-21; Luke 1:5-7; 2:25-38).

Still the majority of Israel rebelled against God, this time rejecting the Messiah. But there was a remnant who received him. This faithful minority of old Israel became the nucleus of the new people of God, the Christian church (Luke 24:44-49; John 20:20-22; Acts 1:13-15; 2:1-4).

Within a few years the church consisted largely of non-Jews. Within it, however, were the believing Jews, the faithful remnant, the spiritual Israelites who believed in Jesus the Messiah and became part of his church (Acts 13:43; 16:1; 17:2-4; 18:8; Rom 2:28-29; 9:6-8; 11:1-5).

REPENTANCE

Repentance is a turning from sin to God (Deut 30:1-2; 2 Chron 6:26-27; 7:14; Neh 1:9; Ps 78:34; Isa 55:7; Jer 8:6; 31:18-19; Ezek 18:21; Mal 3:7; Matt 11:20-21; Luke 15:7; 16:30; Acts 3:19; 8:22; 14:15; 26:19-20; Rev 9:20-21). The open demonstration of this turning to God is sometimes called conversion (Acts 15:3; cf. 26:17-18; 1 Thess 1:9-10). Jesus and the New Testament preachers commanded people to repent, because without repentance there can be no salvation (Matt 3:2; 4:17; Mark 6:12; Luke 5:32; 13:3; 24:47; Acts 2:38; 11:18; 17:30).

It is true that faith is the means by which people receive salvation (Rom 3:22-25; Eph 2:8), but faith that does not involve repentance is not true faith. It is not a faith that leads to salvation. Faith means complete trust in Jesus Christ and his atoning death. It means that a person has total dependence on Christ for his entire salvation (see FAITH). But such trust is impossible so long as a person still clings to anything of himself. He cannot rely upon the work of Christ for the forgiveness of sin unless he turns from that sin (Mark 1:15; Acts 11:21; 20:21; 26:18; 1 Thess 1:9).

Because faith involves repentance and repentance involves faith, the Bible in some places speaks of forgiveness as depending on faith (Acts 10:43; 13:38-39), in others as depending on repentance (Luke 24:47; Acts 3:19,26). But the preaching of repentance, like the preaching of faith, must be related to the death and resurrection of Jesus Christ (Luke 24:46-47).

While it is true that people must exercise faith and repentance if they are to be saved, it is also true that neither faith nor repentance would be possible in the heart of self-centred man apart from the gracious work of God. God is the one who brings conviction of sin within people and gives them the readiness to repent and believe (Acts 5:31; 11:18; cf. John 6:65; 16:7-11).

Repentance involves a complete change in the mind and will of the believer. It is more than mere sorrow for sin; it is surrender to God. A person may be sorry for his sin because of its consequences, but still have no thought for God. True repentance recognizes the character of sin as deserving God's judgment, and turns from that sin to ask God's forgiveness. Sorrow for sin that ignores God leads only to self-pity and despair. Godly sorrow leads to repentance and new life (2 Cor 7:9-10; cf. Job 42:5-6; Ps 51:1-17; Luke 18:13). It proves its genuineness in a complete change of behaviour (Luke 3:8-14; 19:8; 2 Cor 5:17; 1 John 2:4-6).

A different usage of the word 'repent' is found in the Old Testament, where writers sometimes use it in relation to God. The word simply has to do with a change in God's dealings with people. It has nothing to do with any divine sin or failure (Gen 6:6; 1 Sam 15:11; Jer 18:7-10; Jonah 3:8-9; cf. Ps 110:4; Jer 4:28).

REPHAIM

Prior to Israel's conquest of Canaan, the Rephaim were scattered over a wide area on both sides of the Jordan. They were one of many groups who were to be destroyed when Israel took possession of Canaan (Gen 14:5; 15:20; Deut 2:9-11,19-21). They were of large stature (comparable in size to the Anakim; see

ANAK), and were feared by other peoples of the region (Deut 2:10-11,20-21; Josh 12:4). There was a valley west of Jerusalem known as the Valley of Rephaim (Josh 15:8; 2 Sam 5:18).

RESURRECTION

Both Old and New Testaments record examples of ordinary people who died and were brought back to life. In all these cases the kind of life to which they returned was the same kind of life as they had known previously. They experienced a normal human existence again, and in due course died a normal human death (1 Kings 17:22; 2 Kings 4:32-35; Luke 7:12-15; 8:49-55; John 11:39-44; Acts 9:37-41). The present article, however, is concerned with a type of resurrection that is an entirely new order of existence, where death has no more power (Rom 6:9; 1 Cor 15:54; 2 Cor 5:4).

Death and the afterlife

Old Testament believers did not have a clear understanding of eternal life, though they did at times express the hope of a resurrection through which they would have deliverance from the power of death. Likewise they expected a resurrection of the wicked that would be followed by punishment (Ps 49:14-15; Dan 12:2). The reason their understanding was so limited was that Jesus Christ had not yet come. By Christ's death God broke the power of death and revealed the nature of resurrection life (2 Tim 1:10; Heb 2:14-15). A minority of Jews, the Sadducees, refused to believe in a resurrection of any sort (Matt 22:23).

Death is a consequence of sin, and therefore salvation from sin must include victory over death if that salvation is to be complete. It must involve the resurrection of the body to a new and victorious life. Because Jesus' death and resurrection conquered sin and death, the believer in Jesus can look forward to salvation from sin and death (Rom 4:24-25; 6:8-10; 8:11; 1 Cor 15:26,54-57).

God created man as a unified whole, and therefore he deals with man in the totality of his being. God does not divide man into physical and spiritual 'parts'. Man's final destiny, whether for salvation or damnation, is connected not with death but with the resurrection of the body, after which the person faces final judgment (Dan 12:2; John 5:29; Acts 24:15; see DEATH).

Assurance of Jesus' resurrection

Man's only basis of hope for a victorious resurrection is the resurrection of Jesus (John 11:25; 1 Cor 15:20-21,45-49). Throughout his ministry Jesus pointed out that he was not only to die but was also to rise from death (Mark 8:31; 9:9,31; John 2:19-21). In spite of Jesus' clear statements, his disciples often displayed a lack of understanding concerning his coming crucifixion and resurrection. Therefore, when Jesus met with them after his resurrection, he made sure that they knew it was a true bodily resurrection (Luke 24:39-43; John 20:20,27; 1 Cor 15:4-7).

Nevertheless, there was something uniquely different about Jesus' body after his resurrection. On some occasions his physical appearance seems to have changed, for his friends did not at first know who he was (Luke 24:30-31,36-37; John 20:14-15; 21:4,12). On other occasions they recognized him immediately (Matt 28:9; John 20:26-28).

In his resurrection body Jesus was capable of normal physical functions (Luke 24:41-43), but he was also able to appear and disappear as he wished. Although always with his disciples invisibly, he could make himself visible to them if he so desired (Luke 24:31; John 20:19,26; cf. Matt 18:20). The last time he appeared to them, he disappeared in a way that showed that he would appear to them no more, until he returned in power and glory at the end of the age (Acts 1:3,9-11).

Jesus' resurrection changed the apostles from people who were confused and cowardly into people who were assured and courageous (Acts 2:14,36; 4:13,18-20,29-31; 5:27-29). By his resurrection he had conquered death and made salvation sure, and they were witnesses of these things (Luke 24:46-48; Acts 2:24,32; 5:30-32; 10:39-43).

The resurrection was therefore a central theme in the apostles' preaching. It had a significance that people could not ignore (Acts 2:22-24; 4:2,33). Jesus was alive and, through his disciples, was continuing the work he had begun during the time of his earthly ministry (Acts 3:15-16; 4:10; cf John 14:12-18; see HOLY SPIRIT).

Not just the original disciples but all disciples are changed because of Jesus' resurrection (Eph 2:5-6; Rev1:17-18). Paul, who had not known Jesus during the time of Jesus' earthly ministry, claimed that the resurrection gave him assurance of eternal life and confidence in his Christian service (Acts 23:6; 25:19; Rom 1:4-5; 1 Cor 9:1; 15:8,14-15; 2 Tim 2:8). The resurrection of Jesus is essential for a person's entire salvation (1 Cor 15:14,17,19; Rom 4:24-25; 8:10-11). This is one of the truths that believers express when they are baptized (Rom 6:3-4; 10:9; Col 2:12; see BAPTISM).

Having become united with Christ through faith, believers share in the resurrection life of Christ. God's power worked in Christ in raising him to new life, and that same power can work in those who have come into union with Christ. Christians have a new life. They share in Christ's conquest of sin, and so can claim victory over sin in their everyday lives (Rom 6:6-11,13; 7:4; 8:10; Eph 1:19-20; Phil 3:10).

Future resurrection

Only through Jesus' resurrection can believers have the assurance of a future resurrection. Through their union with him, they can look forward to an entirely new order of existence where sin and death have no more power (1 Cor 15:20-26,54-57; 1 Peter 1:3-4). This new order of existence will begin at the return of Jesus Christ, when the resurrection of believers will take place (John 6:40,54; 1 Cor 15:52; 1 Thess 4:16-17).

Believers have no way of knowing exactly what the resurrection body will be like. But they know at least that it will be imperishable, glorious and strong, suited to the life of the age to come just as the present body is suited to present earthly life. The link between the future resurrection body and the present physical body may be compared to the link between a plant and the seed from which it grows. The plant is different from the seed, but in a sense it is the same thing. Similarly, the believer's resurrection body will be different from his present body, but he will still be the same person (John 6:40; 1 Cor 15:35-38,42-44).

As Adam's body was the pattern for the bodies of people in the present life, so Christ's resurrection body is the pattern for the bodies of believers in the life to come (1 Cor 15:45-49; Phil 3:20-21). The Christian's expectation at the resurrection is not for the giving of life to a corpse, but for the changing of his whole person into the likeness of Christ (1 John 3:2; cf. Rom 8:29; 2 Cor 3:18).

The resurrection of the ungodly is a different matter. Whatever form their resurrection will take, they will not be given spiritual and imperishable bodies. Their resurrection will result not in life, but in judgment, condemnation and eternal destruction (Dan 12:2; Matt 10:28; John 5:29; 1 Cor 15:50; Rev 20:6,12-14; see HELL).

REUBEN

As the eldest of Jacob's twelve sons, Reuben had the right to the blessing of the firstborn (Gen 35:23; 46:8). At times he showed qualities of character and leadership (Gen 37:21-30; 42:22,37), but he lost the firstborn's rights because of his immorality with one of his father's concubines. As a result the civil leadership of Israel went to the tribe of Judah, the religious leadership to Levi, and the double portion of the inheritance to Joseph. This meant that Joseph received the right to have two tribes (which were descended from his sons, Ephraim and Manasseh) (Gen 35:22; 49:3-4; 1 Chron 5:1-2).

In the time of Moses, certain Reubenites were jealous that a man from the tribe of Levi (Moses), rather than one from the tribe of Reuben, was overall leader in Israel (Num 16:1-3,12-14). God punished their rebellion in a dramatic judgment (Num 16:25-33).

When the Israelites conquered and divided Canaan in the time of Joshua, the tribes of Reuben, Gad and half of Manasseh settled east of the Jordan River in territory taken from the Amorites (Num 21:11-35; Josh 13:8-12). This entire eastern territory was often called Gilead, though strictly speaking Gilead was only one part of it (Judg 10:8; 20:1). (For map and other details see GILEAD.) Reuben was the most southern of the eastern tribes, occupying land that originally belonged to Moab (that is, before Moab lost it to the Amorites) (Num 21:26; Josh 13:15-23). (For the physical features of the region see MOAB.)

The reason the two and a half tribes asked for this area was that it had good pasture lands and they had large flocks and herds (Num 32:1-5,33). But their situation east of Jordan separated them from the other tribes, and at times led to tension and misunderstanding (Josh 22:1-34; Judg. 5:16-17).

Further difficulties arose for the eastern tribes because their position left them more open to attack than the western tribes (1 Kings 10:32-33). At the time of Israel's collapse several hundred years later, the eastern tribes were among the first to be taken into captivity (2 Kings 15:29).

REVELATION

Since God is supreme and sovereign, answerable to no one, he has no need to make himself known to man. Yet in his grace he has chosen to do so, and man is responsible to God concerning what he learns from him (Deut 29:29). The activity of God in making himself and his truth known to man is called revelation.

Revelation through nature and conscience

God has given man a general revelation of himself through nature. The created world tells people everywhere something of the sovereign power, glory and love of God (Ps 19:1-4; 104:1-32; Acts 14:17; 17:26-27; Rom 1:19-20). Many, however, though recognizing the natural world to be full of wonder and beauty, refuse to accept it as evidence of the presence and power of God (Rom 1:21). When people humbly submit to God in faith, they see him revealing himself to them through nature (Gen 9:13-16; Ps 29:3-10; Hab 3:1-19; Matt 6:26,30; see also CREATION; NATURE).

In addition to providing a general revelation through nature, God has revealed something of himself through the basic knowledge of right and wrong that he has put within the hearts of all people. This unwritten standard, which makes possible the operation of the human conscience, is sometimes called 'natural law' (Rom 2:15; see CONSCIENCE).

The revelation through conscience, like the revelation through nature, gives man some understanding of God, but it does not give him the detailed knowledge that is necessary for salvation. Such knowledge comes through the more specific revelation God has made through his spoken and written Word (1 Cor 1:21).

Revelation through Christ and the Word

Earlier revelations of God to individuals prepared the way for the fuller revelation that God gave mankind through the nation Israel (Gen 12:1-3; 17:1-8,16; Exod 3:2-6). The entire Old Testament history of Israel was itself a revelation of God. Through his prophets and other special messengers, God taught his people and interpreted the events of their history to make himself and his purposes known to them (Num 12:6-8; Amos 3:7; Heb 1:1; see PROPHECY). The Old Testament Scriptures are a revelation of God.

However, something even greater than this was necessary to save man fully from the consequences of his sin and bring him into a right relation with God. God himself became man and made himself known perfectly through Jesus Christ (John 1:14,18; 14:8-9; Heb 1:2). The gospel of Jesus Christ reveals how God, through Christ, is able to forgive guilty sinners, declare them righteous and build them into a unified body, the church (Rom 1:17; 16:25-26; Eph 3:5-6; see GOSPEL; MYSTERY).

When people come to Christ in repentance and faith, they receive a fuller revelation and a personal understanding of God (Matt 11:27; 16:17; Gal 1:16). Because revelation is solely an activity of God and is exercised according to his sovereign will, God may choose to give additional special revelations to certain people (Acts 9:10-16; 1 Cor 14:30; 2 Cor

12:1,7; Gal 1:11-12; 2:2; Eph 3:3; see APOCALYPTIC LITERATURE; PROPHECY; VISION).

Just as God had given revelations during the time leading up to Christ's coming, so he gave them during the time immediately after Christ's coming. Previously he had given revelations through the history of Israel; now he gave them through the events of the early church. And just as God used prophets and others to record and interpret his pre-Christ revelation, so he used apostles and others to record and interpret his post-Christ revelation (1 Cor 2:10,13; 2 Peter 3:15-16). The New Testament joins with the Old Testament to form the complete written revelation that God has given to man (see INSPIRATION; SCRIPTURE).

From all this it becomes evident that God's revelation is progressive. This does not mean that later revelations contradict those that were earlier; it means rather that later revelations develop the earlier, as God works towards the completion of his purposes through Jesus Christ (Eph 1:9-12; 3:3-11; 1 Peter 1:10-12; see INTERPRETATION, sub-heading 'Progressive Revelation').

REVELATION, BOOK OF

As its title suggests, the book of Revelation reveals things that might otherwise remain unknown. The revelation came from God and the risen Christ by way of the book's writer to first century Christians, and it concerned things that were soon to take place (Rev 1:1). The traditional view is that the person named John who wrote the book was the apostle John, though there is no statement in the book to make this identification certain.

Background to the book

The church of the first century was persecuted almost from the beginning. Persecution at first came mainly from the Jews, but as the century progressed, civil authorities also turned against the Christians. The two main periods of persecution from the Roman Emperors came in the sixties under Nero and in the nineties under Domitian. It was during this latter period that John, having been imprisoned for his Christian testimony, received the revelation recorded in this book (Rev 1:9-10).

Patmos, the place of John's imprisonment, was an island off the coast from Ephesus in the west of Asia Minor. Upon receiving the revelation, John wrote it in a book, then sent it with a messenger to the mainland to deliver to a group of seven churches in Asia Minor. The order in which the churches are listed probably represents the order in which they were visited by the messenger who delivered the letters. From these centres the message would no doubt spread to other churches of the region (Rev 1:11; for map see ASIA).

By this time the government was enforcing Emperor worship as a settled policy, with the result that Christians were being imprisoned, tortured and even killed (Rev 2:10,13; 6:9-11). People in general were becoming anti-Christian. To make matters worse, false teachers were troubling the churches by encouraging Christians to participate in pagan religious practices (Rev 2:14,20-21). Some Christians were renouncing their faith, others losing heart. Many were confused, for it seemed that Jesus Christ, the almighty king whom they expected to return in triumph, was either unable or unwilling to save them from the power of Rome.

Through John, Jesus reassured the suffering Christians that he was still in control, though he did not want them to build up any false hopes. He gave no guarantee of quick relief. Rather he prepared them for greater endurance, by revealing the extent of the troubles yet to come and the eternal reward for those who stood firm for him. In God's time he would return to punish all enemies, save his people, and bring in a new and eternal era.

Interpretation of the book

The book of Revelation belongs to a category of literature known as apocalyptic. (The name comes from the Greek *apokalypsis*, the word translated 'revelation' in Rev 1:1.) In apocalyptic literature God gives revelations to people by means of strange visions explained by angels. The visions often feature fearsome beasts and mysterious numbers, and are usually concerned with great conflicts out of which God and his people triumph (see APOCALYPTIC LITERATURE).

Because Christians of the first century were familiar with apocalyptic literature, they would have readily understood Revelation, but Christians of a different era and culture usually find the book difficult to interpret. Some interpret it as applying wholly to the time of John; others interpret it as applying wholly to the future, when God will bring the world's history to an end. Some see the book as a continuous history of the world from John's time to the end; others see it not as a record of historical events but as a presentation of the victory of the gospel in symbolic pictures. There are countless variations in the interpretation of the book, both as a whole and in its details.

In an attempt to solve the difficulties of the book of Revelation, some people simply choose the scheme of interpretation that suits them and reject the rest. But this is not the best way to understand the book's message. The book is not a collection of puzzles designed to amuse Christians in their spare time by giving them mysteries to solve. It is a book given to strengthen and guide Christians in a time of persecution. The pictures are taken from life under Roman rule as the Christians of John's time knew it, but the principles are applicable in any era.

Anti-Christian persecutions and divine judgments have been repeated throughout the church's history, from John's time to the present. But in every era Christians have triumphed through their troubles because of Christ's victory on the cross (Rev 12:11). Opposition will continue till the world's last great crisis comes and Jesus Christ returns. In that day the triumphant Saviour will banish evil, save his people, and bring in a new age of peace and joy (Rev 19:13-16; 22:1-5).

Contents of the book

After greeting the seven churches to whom the book is sent (1:1-8), John describes his vision of the risen and exalted Christ, who is Lord of all the churches (1:9-20). Then follow the seven letters. Each of the letters consists of a greeting from the risen Christ, a statement concerning the state of the church, a warning, an instruction and a promise (2:1-3:22). John then has two visions. In the first the Almighty is seated upon his throne and is worshipped as the Creator (4:1-11). In the second the Lamb is victorious out of death and is worshipped as the Redeemer (5:1-14).

Following this are three series of judgments, each based on the symbolic number seven. In the first series a seven-section scroll is unrolled section by section by breaking one seal for each section. As the scroll is unrolled, each section reveals a vision relating to some aspect of suffering and judgment. There is an interval before the breaking of the final seal, when further visions reassure the faithful. No matter what they suffer, God will preserve them for his heavenly kingdom (6:1-8:5).

In the second series of judgments, each of the seven visions is announced by the blowing of a trumpet. Again there is an interval before the final vision, when further visions reassure the faithful of victory. They may suffer persecution, and perhaps martyrdom, but because of Christ's victory they are triumphant (8:6-11:19).

Before the third series of judgments, John receives a number of visions to show the conflict and ultimate triumph that God's people can expect. One vision is of a dragon that tries to destroy a woman and her child (12:1-17); another is of a beast that rises out of the sea to fight against God and his people (13:1-10); and a third is of a beast that rises out of the earth in support of the previous beast (13:11-18). However, the redeemed, not the beasts, are the victors (14:1-5), while the wicked suffer destruction (14:6-20).

The third series of judgments then follows, with seven angels pouring out seven bowls of God's anger upon a rebellious world (15:1-16:21). The overthrow of rebellious mankind is pictured in the destruction of a prostitute (17:1-18) and the burning of Babylon (18:1-19:5). The triumph of God and his people is pictured in a wedding feast, the victorious reign of Jesus Christ, the defeat of Satan and the last great judgment (19:6-20:15).

Finally, John has a vision of a new heaven and a new earth, where God dwells with his people in a new order of existence (21:1-22:5). In view of the salvation and judgments that lie ahead, the book urges Christians to be faithful to God, and urges others to accept God's offered mercy (22:6-21).

REVENGE

Whether in Old or New Testaments, the Bible teaches that people are not to take personal revenge for what they consider to be wrong done to them. They should forgive the offender and allow God to deal with the person as he sees fit (Lev 19:18; Deut 32:35; Rom 12:19; Rev 5:9-11; see WRATH). In the law of Moses, as in the teachings of Jesus, God's people are taught not even to bear a grudge against their enemies. Far from returning evil for evil, they must positively do good to those who do evil to them (Exod 23:4-5; Lev 19:17-18; Matt 5:44-48; 18:35; see FORGIVENESS).

Although individuals have no God-given right to pay back wrongdoers, civil governments have. They are to execute judgments fairly, and not give a light punishment for a serious offence or a heavy punishment for a minor offence. The punishment must be in proportion to the crime — 'an eye for an eye, a tooth for a tooth, a bruise for a bruise, a scratch for a scratch' (Exod 21:22-24; Rom 13:4; see GOVERNMENT; CITY OF REFUGE; JUDGE).

When Jesus rebuked people for living according to this rule, he was not criticizing the law of Moses. Jesus supported the law of Moses (Matt 5:17), but he opposed people who used the principle of civil justice ('an eye for an eye', etc.) as an excuse for personal revenge. The spirit that rules in the hearts of God's people is not the same as that which rules in the code of legal justice (Matt 5:38-42).

REWARD

The Bible speaks of rewards in both good and bad senses; that is, rewards may result from either the good or the evil that a person does. This article is concerned only with rewards in the good sense, namely, the gifts God gives to his people for their faithfulness and service. (Concerning rewards for wrongdoing see PUNISHMENT.)

Rewards are not the same as salvation or eternal life. God saves sinners solely by his grace and gives eternal life as a free gift, not as a reward for personal effort (Rom 6:23; Eph 2:8-9; see FAITH). Nevertheless, Christians are answerable to God for the way they live. One day they will stand before God to give an account of themselves and receive what they deserve, whether good or bad, according to the way they have lived (2 Cor 5:10; James 2:12; see JUDGMENT).

It is possible for Christians to be saved eternally but to receive no reward when God makes an assessment of their lives at the final judgment. This can happen if they live for themselves instead of for God. They build their lives according to the world's values instead of according to God's. When God tests what they have built, the test will show it to be worthless. They will lose all, though they themselves will be saved (1 Cor 3:11-15).

If Christians look for their reward in the form of praise from fellow believers, they will miss out on the eternal reward from God (Matt 6:1,5; 1 Cor 4:5). God rewards those who are diligent in their Christian service, who persevere amid trials, who endure sufferings patiently and who make sacrifices for the sake of others (Matt 5:12; 6:4; 10:40-42; Gal 6:9-10; 1 Thess 2:19-20; 1 Peter 5:1-4; 2 John 8). Yet when they have faithfully done all this, they still do not deserve God's rewards. They have merely done their duty (Luke 17:10).

God's rewards are therefore evidences of his immeasurable grace. They are out of all proportion to the good that people do (Matt 24:45-47; 25:21). They should not be likened to material prizes such as people receive after a competition. Rather they represent the greater capacity that people have to enjoy those lasting realities of the kingdom of God around which true Christians have built their lives (Matt 5:3; 25:21; 2 Tim 4:8).

RIGHTEOUSNESS

The words 'righteous' and 'righteousness' are found much more in biblical language than in everyday language. Both words, however, are concerned with everyday matters, and for this reason some modern versions of the Bible prefer to use such words as 'right', 'fair', 'just' and 'honest'. A righteous person is one who, among other things, does right or is in the right.

The source of righteousness

Perfect righteousness is found in God alone. He is perfect in goodness and has a perfect knowledge of what is right and what is wrong (Deut 32:4; Ps 145:17; Isa 45:21; Rom 9:14; Heb 6:18). Since God made man in his image, man also has a sense of righteousness. If people are characterized by proper behaviour and moral uprightness, the Bible may speak of them as righteous (Gen 7:1; Ps 15:2; Prov 12:3-10; Luke 1:6; 2 Cor 9:9-10).

This righteousness is not a moral perfection that people achieve by their own efforts, but a right relationship with God that people enter into through faith and obedience (Isa 50:9; Hab 2:4; Rom 3:4-5; 9:31-32; 10:3-4; Gal 3:11-12). It is a righteousness that pleases God and guarantees his help (Ps 45:7-8; Isa 56:1; 1 Peter 3:12).

The legal setting

Righteousness is not simply a private affair; it is a matter also for social concern. God's righteousness demands social justice (Isa 5:7-9; Amos 5:6-7,24). Justice, in fact, is a prominent characteristic of righteousness in the Bible (see JUSTICE).

The Bible commonly uses 'righteousness' and related words in a legal setting, where a judge must administer justice righteously. The judge in some cases is God (Gen 18:25; Ps 96:13; Eccles 3:17; Acts 17:31; 2 Tim 4:8; Rev 19:11), in other cases a civil official (Lev 19:15; Deut 4:8; Ezek 23:45; cf. John 7:24). The innocent and the guilty are respectively the righteous and the wicked. In acquitting the innocent, the judge declares him to be in the right, or righteous; in condemning the guilty, the judge declares him to be in the wrong, or wicked (Deut 25:1; 1 Kings 8:32; Job 32:1; Mal 3:18; Matt 13:41-43; 27:19; Rom 2:5-8).

This legal sense of righteousness gives meaning to the biblical teaching of justification by faith. (In both Hebrew and Greek the words 'righteous' and 'justify' come from the same root.) To justify means to declare righteous. Justification is God's act of declaring righteous those who put their faith in Christ and his saving work. God does not *make* believers righteous in the sense of improving them to a standard of behaviour that satisfies him, but rather he *declares* them righteous. Christ has met God's righteous demands by paying sin's penalty on

behalf of sinners. God is therefore able to declare repentant sinners righteous, yet himself remain righteous in doing so (Rom 1:16-17; 3:21-26; 4:1-3; 5:1-2; Gal 2:15-16; 3:21-22; Phil 3:9). (For details of this aspect of the believer's righteousness see JUSTIFICATION.)

Though righteous deeds, or good works, cannot save anyone, once people are saved their lives should be full of righteous deeds (Eph 2:8-10; Phil 1:11). Once God has declared them righteous, they must make it true in practice by living righteously (Rom 6:13,18-19; Eph 4:24; 5:9; Phil 3:8-10; 1 Tim 6:11; 1 Peter 2:24; 3:14).

ROCK

The Old Testament often speaks of God as being like a rock to his people. The reference is to the security and safety that God gives to those who trust in him. Just as a high rocky cliff can be a refuge or fortress, so God is a refuge and fortress to his believing people (Gen 49:24; Ps 18:2; 28:1; 62:2; 78:35; Isa 32:1-2).

A rock is also a solid foundation (Matt 7:24). This is probably the central idea in Jesus' statement to the apostles, through their representative Peter, that they were the rock on which he would build his unconquerable church (Matt 16:18; Eph 2:20). (See also CORNERSTONE; STUMBLING BLOCK.)

ROMANS, LETTER TO THE

In his letter to the Romans, Paul gives his most carefully developed exposition of the gospel. He sets out to teach in a progressive and orderly manner the basis of the salvation in Christ that he preached. While Paul intends this presentation of the gospel to be a means of teaching Christian truth in general, he gives it in the form of a letter that he had specific reasons for writing.

Background to the letter

The church in Rome was already well established when Paul wrote this letter to it. (For the origins of the church there see ROME.) At the time of writing, Paul was in Corinth in the south of Greece (Rom 16:23; cf. 1 Cor 1:14), and he sent the letter with a lady from the Corinth region who was travelling to Rome (Rom 16:1-2).

Paul had not yet been to Rome (Rom 1:13; 15:22-23), but he had definite plans to pay a visit in the near future. First, however, he was going in the opposite direction, to Jerusalem. He wanted to deliver to the poor Christians in Jerusalem a gift of money that he had been collecting among the

Gentile churches of Greece and Asia Minor (Acts 19:21; Rom 15:23-27).

Rome was the centre of the Empire. In Paul's plan the church there had to be firmly established in an understanding of the Christian gospel, so that it could be a centre from which the gospel could spread west. In sending this letter, Paul hoped to strengthen the church and prepare it for further teaching that he would give when he arrived (Rom 1:11-12,15; 15:14-16,29). From Rome he planned to move into unevangelized areas farther west, till eventually he reached Spain (Rom 15:20,24,28).

In former years there had been a strong anti-Jewish feeling in Rome, and on at least one occasion Jews had been expelled from the city (Acts 18:2). But they had now returned, and there were many Jews in the Roman church alongside their Gentile fellow citizens.

Paul considered it necessary to speak at times specifically to the Jews (Rom 2:17-19; 3:9; 4:1), at other times specifically to the Gentiles (Rom 11:13-16,28; 15:14-16). He warned against any anti-Jewish feeling among the Gentiles (Rom 11:17-24; 15:27) and encouraged Jews and Gentiles to be tolerant of each other (Rom 14:1-15:5). The gospel is for all people equally, because all are sinners under God's judgment and they can be saved only by God's grace (Rom 1:16; 2:9-11; 3:9,23-24; 10:12; 11:32; 15:8-9).

The chief emphasis in Paul's exposition is that people are put right with God — justified, declared righteous — solely through God's grace, and they receive this divine blessing by faith (see FAITH; GRACE; JUSTIFICATION). All people are under the power of sin and are unable to save themselves from its penalty, whether through religious ritual, the keeping of the law or personal good works (see GOOD WORKS; LAW; SIN). Even when saved by grace through faith, believers are still dependent on God for victory over sin. Only the Spirit of God within believers can deliver them from the evil power of the sinful human nature, the flesh (see FLESH; HOLY SPIRIT; SANCTIFICATION).

Contents of Romans

Paul introduces himself by speaking of his longing to visit the Roman Christians (1:1-15). He wants to write about the gospel, and the heart of the gospel is God's act of declaring righteous those who have faith in Jesus Christ (1:16-17).

Salvation is entirely the work of God. It cannot be the work of man, because man is a helpless sinner. Pagans, who have rejected the light of God, are sinners (1:18-32), but so are Jews, who claim to know God (2:1-29). All people are sinners (3:1-20), and therefore if God is to declare anyone righteous, it must be entirely by his grace. The basis of God's gracious salvation is the sacrificial death of Jesus Christ on the sinner's behalf (3:21-31).

Abraham was justified by faith; his salvation had nothing to do with good works, law-keeping or rituals. Abraham might therefore be called the spiritual father of all who believe (4:1-25). Believers have confidence because of what God has done for them through Christ (5:1-11); they no longer fear the power of sin, because God's grace is always sufficient to overcome it (5:12-21).

This does not mean that believers may be careless about sin. On the contrary they should live as those who share Christ's conquest of sin and whose behaviour is characterized by righteousness. They have new life in Christ (6:1-23).

Christians are free from the law. They realize that if they try to put themselves back under the law in order to triumph over the sinful human nature, the result will be frustration and despair (7:1-25). Victory comes rather through the indwelling Spirit of the living Christ. The Spirit enables believers to practise the righteousness that the law aimed at but could never produce (8:1-11). The same Spirit gives believers confidence in every aspect of salvation, whether in the present life or in the glorious triumph of the age to come (8:12-39).

Paul's great disappointment is that Israel, the people whom God prepared for this salvation, have on the whole rejected it (9:1-5). As always God has preserved the faithful minority, but the majority have missed out, because they have tried to achieve salvation by keeping the law. Gentiles, by contrast, have accepted it by faith and so are saved (9:6-10:4).

Israelites have no excuse, for the gospel has been plainly preached to them (10:5-21). Although there will always be a minority of Israelites who believe, Paul hopes that the widespread Gentile response to the gospel will stir the unbelieving majority of Israelites to respond likewise. Then all mankind will enjoy the salvation of God as never before (11:1-36).

In gratitude to God for his mercy, believers should live lives of devotion to God. They should contribute to the healthy life of the church and be forgiving to those outside the church who oppose them (12:1-21). Christians should cooperate with the government and show love to everybody (13:1-14). One expression of love is to be considerate of fellow believers who have differing opinions on matters of lesser importance (14:1-15:13).

Part of Paul's reason in writing to the Roman Christians on these matters is that, as God's apostle to the Gentiles, he has a special responsibility to them. At the same time he stresses that he wants the Gentile Christians to show fellowship towards Jewish Christians (15:14-33). He concludes his letter by sending greetings to many Christians whom he has met in other places over the years and who now live in Rome (16:1-27).

ROME

Within a hundred years of the rise of Greek power under Alexander the Great (334-331 BC), Rome had begun to overrun colonies of the Greek Empire and form them into outlying provinces of Rome. Rome first came into prominence in the affairs of Palestine when the Roman general Pompey seized control of Jerusalem and brought Judea under Roman control (63 BC).

The Roman Empire

After the assassination of Julius Caesar (44 BC), Rome went through a disastrous time of civil war, political confusion and social turmoil. Thousands of people were poor and unable to find work. There was little law and order, corruption was widespread, and ambitious army commanders were constantly plotting for more power.

Out of this instability and tension there arose a leader who was able firstly to control and then to correct the disorders. In 27 BC he took the name Caesar Augustus and became the first ruler of what became known as the Roman Empire (Luke 2:1). The people held him in such honour that rulers of the Roman Empire after him took his name Caesar as the title of the Emperor (Luke 3:1; 20:22; Acts 17:7; 25:11,25).

There was a widespread feeling of gratitude to Augustus for the peace and order that he brought, and people began praising him as if he were a god. This marked the beginning of Emperor worship, which developed into the official religion of the Empire. The Romans tolerated other religions, provided they had first been registered with the government. But the law still required all people to carry out acts of worship to the Emperor's image, even though they may have belonged to some other (registered) religion.

The Romans did not force Jews to obey this law, as they knew that Jews would not bow to any idol. Christians also refused to worship before the Emperor's image, but as long as the Roman officials thought that Christianity was merely a sect within the Jewish religion, they took no action against the Christians. However, once they knew that Christianity was a new religion, different from Judaism and therefore outside Roman law, they persecuted the Christians cruelly.

One of the severest outbreaks of persecution occurred after the great fire of Rome (AD 64), which the Emperor Nero blamed on the Christians. At the same time the Romans were becoming increasingly impatient with the Jews, particularly the Jerusalem Jews, who were angry at Rome's mismanagement of their affairs. A Jewish political group known as the Zealots (or Patriots) were so opposed to Roman

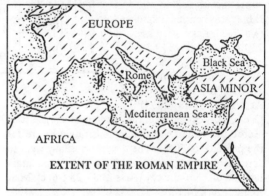

EXTENT OF THE ROMAN EMPIRE

rule that they were prepared to fight against it (see ZEALOT). The outcome was that the Romans came and, after overcoming stubborn Jewish resistance, destroyed Jerusalem without mercy (AD 70). The fall of Jerusalem marked not only the downfall of the Jewish nation, but also the end of Judaism's dominance as a religious force.

By this time the Roman Empire extended over much of Europe, northern Africa and western Asia. It lasted for at least another three hundred years, but then began to fall apart. Finally, in AD 476, Rome itself was overthrown by the Germans.

Provinces of the Empire

From the days of the Empire's beginnings, Rome's plan was to place a Roman governor in charge of each province of the territory it seized. A series of events in AD 37 resulted in a different arrangement for the province of Judea (which included the region commonly known as Samaria). The ruler over Judea was not a Roman but a Palestinian (Herod the Great) who had persuaded Rome to appoint him 'king' of Judea. He was not a sovereign king, for he was under the overall control of Rome (see HEROD).

In BC 4, Herod the Great died and his son Archelaus succeeded him. Archelaus was so cruel and unjust that in AD 6 the Jews of Judea asked Rome to remove him and rule them directly through their own officials. From that time on, Judea was ruled by Roman governors (or procurators). The only exception to this was a period of about three years from AD 41 to 44, when Herod Agrippa I was governor over almost the entire region once ruled by his grandfather, Herod the Great (Acts 12:1-4,20-23).

Roman governors of Judea mentioned in the Bible are Pontius Pilate (AD 26-36; Luke 3:1; 13:1; 23:1,6,24; John 18:29-38; 19:38), Felix (AD 52-59; Acts 23:26,33; 24:25) and Porcius Festus (AD 59-62; Acts 25:1-5,13-14; 26:24).

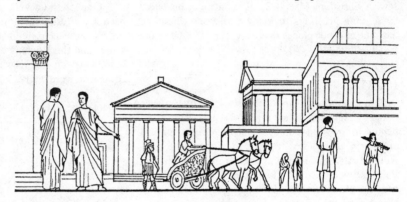

Rome in New Testament times

Caesarea, a city built on the Mediterranean coast by Herod the Great, was the administrative centre for the province of Judea. The governor usually went to Jerusalem during Jewish festivals to help maintain law and order in the city (Acts 23:33; 25:1-6; cf. Matt 27:1-2; Mark 14:1-2).

Since there was always a possibility of riots breaking out in the provinces, governors were ready to act as soon as there was any sign of rebellion (John 11:48-50; Acts 17:6-9; 19:40; 21:31-36). They were also responsible for the administration of justice and the collection of taxes (Luke 2:1; Acts 19:38; 25:9-10; Rom 13:1-7). Administrators in some of the provinces were called proconsuls (Acts 13:7; 18:12; 19:38).

There was widespread travel throughout the Roman Empire. Government officials, businessmen and soldiers moved to all parts of the Empire, often settling in places that the Romans called colonies. These were towns established as centres of Roman life in the non-Roman world of the provinces, and their citizens had the privileges of Roman citizenship and self-government. Pisidian Antioch, Lystra, Troas, Corinth and Philippi were all Roman colonies (Acts 16:12). The Romans built an extensive system of roads to link these and other major towns to Rome and to each other.

Paul appreciated the stability that Roman rule produced and the advantages that the government's development programs provided for the spread of Christianity (Rom 13:1-7; cf. 1 Peter 2:13-17). Like the Romans he had a spirit of enterprise, a mind for planning and a vision for the world (Rom 15:19-20; 2 Cor 10:16; Col 1:6). He moved from province to province along the Roman roads, aiming to establish churches in the major towns. Once there were strong churches in these towns, the gospel would spread quickly into the regions round about (Acts 13:14,49; 14:1,6-7,20-21,24; see MISSION). In particular, Paul saw the importance of having a strong church at the centre of the Empire (Acts 19:21; Rom 1:9-13; 15:14-15,23-24).

Roman citizenship

Originally a Roman citizen was a person who lived in Rome, where citizens enjoyed special privileges given them by the Emperor. Later, the Roman government extended this citizenship to people of other cities and provinces. They extended it also to people who had given outstanding service to the Empire, and even to those who could afford to buy it (Acts 22:28a). This citizenship passed on to the person's children (Acts 22:28b). People did not have to be of Roman blood to be Roman citizens (Acts 16:37; Phil 3:5).

A person who was a Roman citizen had rights not enjoyed by other citizens. He could not be beaten by local officials (Acts 16:36-39; 22:25-29) and could not be executed without a verdict from a general meeting of the people. If he was not satisfied with the standard of justice he received, he could appeal direct to the Emperor (Acts 25:10-12,25-27; 26:32; 27:1-2; 28:16).

The city of Rome

Built on the famous 'seven hills' in 753 BC, Rome was one of the world's great cities. In the era of the New Testament it had a population of more than one million. Included in this population were people of many nationalities, some of whom the Romans expelled if they thought they were going to become troublemakers (Acts 18:2).

The Bible does not say how the church in Rome began. The church may have been formed partly by Romans who were converted in Jerusalem on the Day of Pentecost and who took their new-found faith back to Rome (cf. Acts 2:10,14,41). In addition, Christians from other parts of the Empire no doubt travelled to and from Rome or went there to live, and these might have had some part in founding the church there (Rom 16:1-16). Paul's letter to the church in Rome makes it clear that at the time of writing he had not yet visited Rome (Rom 1:10-15; 15:20-22; see ROMANS, LETTER TO THE).

Paul was at one time held prisoner in Rome for two years (Acts 28:16,20,30). It was probably during this time that he wrote the letters known to us as Colossians, Philemon, Ephesians and Philippians (Eph 6:20; Phil 1:13; Col 4:10; Philem 23). At the end of his two years imprisonment Paul almost certainly was released, though it is impossible to be sure of the details of his later movements.

After further travels Paul was arrested and taken to Rome as a prisoner once again, but this time he knew he had little chance of being released (2 Tim 1:17; 2:9; 4:6-8). From Rome he wrote his last letter, a personal note to Timothy known to us as 2 Timothy. It seems that soon after writing the letter he was beheaded (about AD 62).

Possibly about this time Peter arrived in Rome, along with Silas (or Silvanus), his fellow worker. Using Silas as his secretary, Peter wrote a letter to the churches of the northern part of Asia Minor that he had helped to evangelize. In this letter (known to us as 1 Peter) he referred to Rome symbolically as Babylon (1 Peter 5:12-13).

The reason for this use of Babylon as a name for Rome was that Rome, like Babylon of Old Testament times, was the clear expression of man's rebellion against God. It was the embodiment of the arrogant spirit of man who, in the pride of his power and achievements, defies God and persecutes his people (Rev 17:1-18). The downfall of Babylon pictures more than the downfall of Rome. It pictures the final overthrow of the entire world system that man has built and organized in opposition to God and his people (Rev 18:1-24).

RULER

Any society must have some sort of leadership if it is to function effectively. In primitive societies the heads of families provided that leadership (Gen 14:14; 32:3-6). As societies developed, the leadership

came from recognized officials who administered the affairs of the community (Ruth 4:2). There is great variety in the types of rulers who feature in the Bible, but the Bible consistently encourages God's people to do what they can to cooperate with their rulers for the good of society as a whole (Jer 29:7; Titus 3:1; 1 Peter 2:13-14).

Leadership in Old Testament Israel

Even when the Israelites were slaves in Egypt and had no government of their own, senior men in the community were recognized as leaders (Exod 3:16; 4:29; 12:21). After the establishment of the Israelite nation under Moses, seventy elders were appointed to share the civil leadership with Moses. In the early days of Israel's national life, these elders served as judges in matters of civil law (Exod 18:17-26; Num 11:16-17,24-25).

As Israel's administration developed, elders and judges became two separate groups of officials (Deut 21:2; 22:15; 25:7-8; Josh 8:33; 20:4; Judg 11:5; Micah 7:3; Zeph 3:3-4; see JUDGE). Religious affairs, however, were under the control of priests (see PRIEST).

God wanted Israel to recognize him as their supreme ruler and to obey his laws. The priests and elders were merely the administrators of those laws. But the people failed to follow God's laws, and the first few centuries of their national life in Canaan were marked by repeated judgments from God in the form of invasions from neighbouring nations. In response to the people's repentance, God raised up deliverers from among them to overthrow the enemy and re-establish his rule among them. But the peace was often followed by periods of disobedience, which brought renewed suffering (Judg 2:13-19; see JUDGES, BOOK OF).

In search of stability, the people asked to have a king to rule over the whole nation, as neighbouring nations had. This was a rejection of God, for it was an attempt by the people to correct their problems by changing from one political system to another, rather than by changing from rebellion against God to obedience (1 Sam 8:4-7; see KING). The people got the monarchy they wanted, though even under the new system of government the elders retained considerable influence in the nation (1 Kings 8:1; 20:7; 21:8; 2 Kings 23:1).

After the Jews' captivity in Babylon and return to their homeland, the Persian overlords appointed prominent Jews to positions of leadership in the nation (Ezra 7:25-26; Neh 5:14; 7:2). During this period religious leaders became more and more involved in civil affairs. Their authority grew rapidly through the function of synagogues that began to appear throughout the country, and through the establishment of a national Jewish council called the Sanhedrin (Matt 23:2-4; 26:59; John 7:32; 9:22; see SANHEDRIN; SCRIBES; SYNAGOGUE).

Conditions in New Testament times

In spite of being under the rule of firstly Greece and then Rome, the Jewish leaders were able to maintain firm control over their people in many of the everyday affairs of life. In New Testament times they had considerable influence with the Roman authorities. In fact, the Jewish leaders were the ones really responsible for the crucifixion of Jesus (Matt 27:1-2,20; Acts 4:8-10).

Jesus recognized the authority of civil rulers, though he pointed out that they were responsible to God for the way they used their authority (Luke 20:25; John 19:11). Although he refused to use force against unjust treatment (Matt 26:52; John 18:36), Jesus showed, by being outspoken on one occasion and defiantly silent on another, his contempt for the misuse of power (Luke 13:32; 23:9). When the rulers put him on trial, his conduct before them showed them clearly that he saw no justice in their actions. Yet he tried neither to escape nor to retaliate. In the end he was executed (Matt 27:11-14; John 19:9-11; 1 Peter 2:23).

Christians likewise must recognize the authority of the civil rulers (Rom 13:1-7; 1 Peter 2:13-14,17), though they too will at times see the need to speak out against injustice (Acts 16:37-39; 25:8-11). Like Jesus they may suffer at the hands of unjust rulers (Matt 10:18; Acts 12:2-3), but they must not return evil for evil (Rom 12:17-19; 1 Peter 2:20-21; 3:14; see GOVERNMENT; JUSTICE).

Because of their loyalty to God, Christians may at times have to disobey laws that are anti-Christian. As a result they may suffer imprisonment and even death (Acts 5:29,40-41; 1 Peter 4:16; Rev 13:6-7; 18:24). Through it all, however, God will be faithful to them, and in the end they will be the victors (1 Peter 4:19; Rev 2:10-11; 20:4; see MARTYR).

RUTH

Ruth is the chief character of the book of the same name. The story is set in the period of the judges (see JUDGES, BOOK OF) and shows that at a time when the people of Israel as a whole turned away from God, some remained faithful to him. When the majority easily slipped into the worship of false gods, individuals here and there still exercised simple trust in God. In spite of the widespread moral failure,

purity and honesty had not entirely disappeared. In an era of selfishness, there was still loving concern for others. And God, on his part, was still directing affairs in the everyday lives of his people for their good.

Contents of the book

The story begins when Elimelech, Naomi and their two sons went to the country of Moab to escape famine in Israel. Both sons married Moabite girls (one of them being Ruth), but when Elimelech, and later the two sons, died, Naomi and Ruth returned to Israel. They settled in Naomi's home town of Bethlehem (1:1-22).

Being poor, Ruth went gleaning to get food for Naomi and herself. Unknown to her, the man in whose field she gleaned was Boaz, a close relative of the late Elimelech. When Boaz learnt of Ruth's kindness to Naomi, he showed particular kindness to her in return (2:1-23; see BOAZ).

Naomi believed that Boaz was Elimelech's closest living relative. She therefore suggested that Ruth ask Boaz to produce through her a child who, according to custom, would be recognized as child of the dead man. This child would grow up to carry on the dead man's name and inheritance. Boaz was willing to do as Ruth requested, but in all honesty he told her that there was a closer living relative than he (3:1-18).

This close relative had another responsibility besides producing a child to carry on the name of Elimelech and his son. The man had also to buy the family property, which Naomi had been forced to sell because of her poverty. In this way he would preserve the inheritance of Elimelech and his son. But since the child to be born would eventually inherit this family property, the close relative asked that Boaz, rather than he, fulfil the duties of the close relative. Boaz was delighted, because he had wanted to marry Ruth and he was happy to produce a son and heir through her. The son became the grandfather of King David and an ancestor of Jesus the Messiah (4:1-22; cf. Matt 1:1,5-6).

SABBATH

The word 'sabbath' comes from the Hebrew word meaning 'to cease'. In the Genesis story of creation, God ceased from his work of creation after six days, then rested on the seventh (Gen 2:1-3). It seems that from early times people in general recognized a week of seven days (Gen 8:10,12; 29:27), and God's people in particular ceased their work one day in seven. This was for two purposes: firstly, to set the day apart for God instead of using it for themselves; secondly, to rest from their daily work and so gain refreshment (Exod 16:22-30).

God's appointment for Israel

When God formally established Israel as his people and gave them his laws, one of the laws was that they had to rest from their work every seventh day. The day was set apart especially for God and was, in fact, a sign that the people were bound to God by covenant. Anyone who did his work on that day was to be put to death (Exod 20:8-11; 31:13-17; Num 15:32-36; Deut 5:15). Among the religious exercises of the Sabbath were the offering of sacrifices and the renewing of the 'presence bread' in the tabernacle (Lev 24:5-9; Num 28:9-10).

Working animals, such as oxen and donkeys, also had rest one day in seven (Deut 5:14; cf. Neh 13:15-21), and the land had rest one year in seven (Lev 25:3-4; see SABBATICAL YEAR). A festival day on which people were to do no work was also called a Sabbath, though it may not have coincided with the usual weekly Sabbath (Lev 16:29-31; 23:30-32; John 19:31).

Much of the Jewish Sabbath-keeping was not pleasing to God, because of the wrong attitudes of many of the people. Some were annoyed because it interrupted their money-making activities (Amos 8:5), and others used the day for their own pleasure, without concern for God (Isa 58:13-14; Jer 17:21-23). Through despising God's covenant requirements, the people in the end brought destruction upon the nation (Ezek 20:23-24; 23:38).

After the return from captivity in Babylon, Nehemiah introduced special laws to prevent people from working and trading on the Sabbath (Neh 13:15-22). Over the next few centuries the teachers of the law (the scribes) built up a system of countless Sabbath regulations to add to the simple require-ments of the law of Moses (cf. Mark 2:23-24; Luke 14:3-4; John 5:10; Acts 1:12). Through schools and synagogues, the teachers of the law spread and enforced their regulations. In doing so they often disregarded the Word of God, and as a result came into conflict with Jesus (Luke 13:10-17; see SCRIBES; SYNAGOGUE; TRADITION).

The new era

Jesus pointed out that although God gave rules to guide people concerning what they may or may not do on the Sabbath, it was always right to do good on the Sabbath (Matt 12:9-13). Just as God's daily work in caring for his creation does not break the Sabbath law, neither did Jesus' work in healing the sick on the Sabbath (John 5:16-18). Life is more important than ritual. God gave the Sabbath to man for his benefit, not for his discomfort. The Sabbath was intended to ease man's burden, not increase it (Matt 12:1-8; 23:4).

As Lord of the Sabbath, Jesus knew best how to use it. While he kept the law of God (Matt 5:17; Luke 4:16), he opposed the traditions of the scribes and Pharisees (Mark 7:6-9). At the same time he knew that the law-code that Moses had given to Israel had fulfilled its purpose and was about to pass away. A new age was about to dawn (Matt 9:16-17). Jesus' death and resurrection marked the end of the law as a binding force upon God's people (Rom 7:6; 8:1-3; 10:4; Col 2:14).

Christians are free from the bondage of the Israelite law and must not become its slaves. This applies to all the requirements of the law, whether concerning the Sabbath or any other matter (Gal 4:8-11; Col 2:16).

On the other hand Christians can learn from the law. Although that law was given to a particular people (Israel) for a particular period (from Moses to Christ), the idea of a weekly day of rest existed before the time of Moses and continued after the time of Christ. It was taken from the symbolic rest of God, which expressed his satisfaction in bringing his creative work to its goal with the creation of man (Gen 2:1-3; Exod 20:11).

From the beginning of human existence, God has wanted people to find true rest through coming into a living relationship with their Creator. God desires also that within that relationship, they enjoy the created world and all their activity in it (Eccles 5:18-20; 12:1; Heb 4:1-4). The one-day-in-seven rest is a reminder to them that when work so dominates them that they have no time to cease from it, then it has become a god. Restful contemplation is as essential as energetic activity in the worship and service of God (cf. Ps 46:10).

Even when the early Christians no longer kept the Jewish Sabbath, they still set aside time each week for fellowship with God and with one another. This was usually the first day of the week, a day that they called the Lord's Day, because it was the day of Jesus' resurrection (John 20:19; Acts 20:7; 1 Cor 16:2; Rev 1:10).

Sunday did not replace Saturday, as if it were a Christian Sabbath to replace the Jewish Sabbath. Nevertheless, it provided the opportunity to give practical expression to those values of cessation from work and devotion to God that God desired of mankind from the beginning.

There were some people in the early church who wanted to recognize certain days as having some kind of legal sacredness; there were others who refused such recognition, since the church was not regulated by law. Paul taught that each person be tolerant of the other's view, and that Christians treat every day in a way that acknowledges and honours God (Rom 14:5-6).

SABBATICAL YEAR

A sabbatical year was a year when all farming land was given rest from agricultural activity. It was supposed to occur every seventh year throughout Israel's history. There was also to be release for debtors and a public reading of the Mosaic law every seventh year. Although these latter two functions were not specifically connected with the year of rest for the land, they were probably arranged to coincide with it.

Rest for the land

Just as people and their working animals rested one day in seven, so the land was to be rested one year in seven. By ceasing agricultural activity during this year, the Israelites had the opportunity to recognize in a special way that God was the rightful owner of the land. They were merely tenants, and could not treat God's land as they wished. Also, the rest from farming gave the land the opportunity to clear itself of pests and restore its natural powers of production (Exod 23:10-11; Lev 25:1-7,23).

The people had no reason to fear a shortage of food during the sabbatical year. God would bless every sixth year with double the normal produce, so that people could store up food for use the following year. In addition there would be enough natural growth during the sabbatical year for people such as the poor who could not store up in advance. There would also be enough for the flocks and herds (Lev 25:6-7,12,18-22). If the people disobeyed God's laws and did not rest the land one year in seven, God would force them to rest it by driving them from it (Lev 26:34-43; cf. 2 Chron 36:20-21; Jer 34:13-22).

Release for debtors

At the end of every seven years, Israelites were to forgive any debts owed them by fellow Israelites. They were to consider themselves one big family, where those who had money helped those who were in need. They were not to refuse anyone a loan, even if the year of release was approaching. However, in the case of foreigners who owed Israelites debts, normal business procedures applied (Deut 15:1-11).

Israelites who were slaves of their fellow Israelites were also released in the seventh year. Foreigners who were slaves of Israelites apparently did not enjoy this privilege (Deut 15:12-18; Lev 25:44-46; see SLAVE).

Reading of the law

One of the priests' duties in the year of release was to gather the people together for a public reading of the law, to remind them of their responsibilities as God's people. This reading was to take place at the central place of worship when the people assembled to celebrate the Feast of Tabernacles (Deut 31:9-13).

SACKCLOTH

People put on sackcloth as a sign of mourning, whether for those who had just died (Gen 37:34; 2 Sam 3:31), for some personal distress (Job 16:15), or for a national disaster (Esther 4:1; Lam 2:10). They also put on sackcloth as a sign of sorrow for personal sins (1 Kings 21:27-29; Neh 9:1-2) or urgency in prayer (Dan 9:3). The sackcloth was worn either over the top of, or instead of, their normal clothing (2 Kings 6:30; Job 16:15; Jonah 3:6; see DRESS).

SACRAMENT

According to common usage, the word 'sacrament' refers to some formal religious act that is an outward sign of an inward spiritual truth. The two sacraments commanded by Jesus are baptism and the Lord's Supper (Matt 28:19; 1 Cor 11:23-24). They are also called 'ordinances', meaning rites or ceremonies established by divine command.

Baptism is an outward expression of faith in Christ and what he has done for believers through his death and resurrection (Acts 2:38; Rom 6:3-4; see BAPTISM). The Lord's Supper is an outward expression of fellowship with the risen Christ and his people, through recalling his sacrificial death and proclaiming its eternal blessings (Matt 26:26-29; 1 Cor 10:16-17; 11:26; see LORD'S SUPPER).

SACRIFICE

From earliest times people expressed their devotion to God through presenting to him offerings and sacrifices. Some sacrifices expressed thanks, as the person presented to God the best of his crops or animals (Gen 4:4; 8:20). Others emphasized fellowship, both with God and with man, as the offerer ate part of the sacrifice in a meal with relatives and friends (Gen 31:54). Other sacrifices were for forgiveness of sins, a slaughtered animal bearing the penalty that the offerer, because of his sins, should have suffered (Job 42:8). These basic elements of the sacrifices were later developed in the ceremonial law of Israel.

The offerer and his offering

Whether before or after the institution of Israel's ceremonial law, the heart attitude of the worshipper was always more important than his gifts. Abel offered his sacrifice in humble faith and God accepted it. Cain offered his sacrifice in a spirit of arrogance and God refused it. Even if Cain's sacrifice, like Abel's, had involved the shedding of blood, it would still have been unacceptable to God, because Cain himself was ungodly and unrepentant (Gen 4:2-5,7; Heb 11:4; 1 John 3:12).

The Bible's first specific statement concerning the particular significance of blood did not come till the time of Noah. The first clear revelation of the value of blood for atonement had to wait till the time of Moses (Gen 9:3-6; Lev 17:11).

God revealed his purposes progressively as people were able to understand them, but always his acceptance of the offering depended on the spiritual condition of the offerer. The sacrificial system of Israel did not ignore this principle; rather, it had this principle as its basis. Therefore, when people carried out the rituals mechanically, without corresponding faith and uprightness, the prophets condemned their sacrifices as worthless (Isa 1:13-20; Amos 5:21-24; Micah 6:6-8).

God's gift of the blood of atonement

The Passover in Egypt marked an important stage in God's revelation of the special significance of blood. Blood was a symbol of life; shed blood was therefore a symbol of death; in particular, death through killing (Gen 9:4-6; Num 35:19,33; see BLOOD). In the original Passover, the blood of the lamb was important, not because of any chemical property in the blood itself, but because it represented the animal's death. The blood around the door showed that an animal had been killed instead of the person under judgment (Exod 12:13).

In Israel's sacrificial system God provided a way of atonement through the shed blood of animals. Through sin man was separated from God and under the penalty of death, and there was nothing he could do to save himself. There could be no forgiveness of his sin, no releasing him from its consequences, apart from death. God, however, provided a way of salvation through the blood (that

is, the death) of a guiltless substitute. The blood of atonement was not an offering from man in the hope of squeezing pardon from an unwilling God. On the contrary it was the merciful gift of a God who was eager to forgive (Lev 17:11). The escaping of divine punishment was not something man brought about, but was due to God himself (see PROPITIATION).

Although an animal substitute had to bear the death penalty so that the sinner could be forgiven (Heb 9:22), the blood of an animal could not itself take away sins (Heb 10:4). Nevertheless, it enabled the sinner to see that God, in forgiving sins, was not ignoring those sins but dealing with them. The only blood able to forgive sins is the blood of Jesus – his death on the cross. God knew of Jesus' atoning death even though it had not yet occurred (1 Peter 1:18-20), and because of that he was able to 'pass over', temporarily, the sins of believers of former generations. He forgave them, one might say, on credit, for their sins could not be actually removed till Christ died (Rom 3:25-26; Heb 9:15).

The sacrificial system helped people see what salvation involved, but it was not in itself a means of salvation. Under the old covenant, as under the new, people were saved not through their works, but through the grace of a merciful God. The repentant sinner could do nothing but accept God's salvation by faith (Rom 4:13,16,22; Gal 3:17-19; Eph 2:8-9). The benefit of the sacrificial system was that it gave people a means of communication with God, by which they could demonstrate their faith and seek God's forgiveness (1 Sam 1:3; Isa 56:7).

Ritual requirements

God set out the legal requirements for the various sacrifices in great detail, and these details should have helped the Israelites understand the meaning of what they were doing. The sacrificial animal, for instance, had to be without defects, to symbolize that it was free from condemnation and therefore fit to be the guiltless substitute for the guilty sinner (Lev 1:3,10; see LAMB).

No matter what a person offered, it had to be the property of the offerer, so that it had meaning as 'part' of himself. As an offering, it was a personal possession that he gave. As a sacrifice, it cost him something. It impressed upon him that he could not treat the removal of sin lightly. Devotion to God was not to be treated cheaply.

At the same time God did not want to drive people into poverty. In many cases he therefore allowed grades of offerings, so that each person could make an offering that was suited to his financial capacity (Lev 1:3,10,14; 5:7-13).

By laying his hands on the animal's head, the offerer indicated that it was bearing his guilt and that he desired God to accept it on his behalf (Lev 1:4; 16:21). The unpleasant task of killing the animal (which was carried out beside the altar, not on it) reminded the offerer of the horror of sin (Lev 1:11). The priest collected the blood in a basin to apply to various places as a visible sign that a life had been taken to bear the curse and penalty of sin. Unused blood was poured out on the ground beside the altar (Lev 1:5; 4:7; 16:14).

Some burning occurred with all the sacrifices, though the amount that was burnt varied. The parts to be burnt were usually burnt on the altar of sacrifice, though in some cases they were burnt in an isolated place away from the central camp (Lev 1:9; 2:2; 3:3-5; 4:10-12,35; 7:5). The portions not burnt were eaten, sometimes by the worshippers and the priests (including the priests' families) and sometimes by the priests alone (Lev 2:3,10; 6:26; 7:15-17,32; 22:11).

Five main offerings

Israel's sacrificial system had five main categories of sacrifice, though there were variations of these on certain occasions. The major categories were the burnt offering (Lev 1:1-17; 6:8-13), the cereal (or grain) offering (Lev 2:1-16; 6:14-23), the peace (or fellowship) offering (Lev 3:1-17; 7:11-38), the sin offering (Lev 4:1-5,13; 6:24-30) and the guilt (or repayment) offering (Lev 5:14-6:7; 7:1-10). Although the different types of sacrifices were for different purposes, there were elements of atonement and devotion associated with them all (Lev 1:5; 2:2; 3:2,5; 4:5-7; 5:18).

The burnt offering, so called because the whole animal was burnt upon the altar, indicated the complete consecration, or self-dedication, of the offerer to God (Lev 1:9; cf. Gen 8:20; 22:2; Exod 10:25; Rom 12:1). A burnt offering, offered on behalf of the entire nation, was kept burning on the altar constantly, as a symbol of the nation's unbroken dedication to God (Exod 29:38-42).

The cereal (or grain) offering and its associated wine (or drink) offering demonstrated thanks to God for his daily provision of food. Cereal and wine offerings were not offered alone, but always with burnt offerings or peace offerings. The wine was poured over the animal sacrifice on the altar, and a handful of cereal was burnt with it (Lev 2:4-10; 23:13,18; Num 15:1-10).

The peace offering expressed fellowship, a truth demonstrated in the meal that accompanied it. After initial blood ritual, burning ritual and presentation of a portion to the priest, the worshipper joined with his family, friends, the poor and the needy in eating the remainder of the animal in a joyous feast (Lev 7:11-18; Deut 12:7,12; 1 Sam 9:12-13).

The sin offering was compulsory for the person who became aware that he had broken one of God's laws. In cases of sin by priests or the nation as a whole, the priests sprinkled the animal's blood inside the Holy Place, burnt parts of the animal on the altar of sacrifice, and burnt the remainder outside the camp (Lev 4:7,10,12). In the case of sin by private citizens, the priests sprinkled the blood at the altar of sacrifice, burnt parts of the animal on the altar, and ate what remained (Lev 4:27-30; 6:26,30).

The guilt offering was offered in those cases where the person's wrongdoing could be given a monetary value. Such wrongdoing would include forgetting to pay tithes, causing damage to property, or failing to pay for goods (Lev 5:15; 6:1-5). The person presented an offering (similar to the sin offering for a private citizen) and repaid the loss, along with a fine of one fifth of its value (Lev 5:16; 6:5).

Limitations of the offerings

In general, the sacrifices detailed in the Israelite law were available only for unintentional sins. None of the five categories of sacrifice set out a procedure to deal with deliberate sin, even though that is the sin that most troubles the repentant sinner (Lev 4:2,13,22,27; 5:15,17; Num 15:30). The sacrificial system demonstrated that no system could solve the problem of sin or provide automatic cleansing. The sinner had no *right* to forgiveness. He could do nothing except turn to God and cast himself on God's mercy (2 Sam 24:14; Ps 51:1-2,16-17).

This does not mean that the sacrifices were useless or could be ignored. They still provided a means of communication by which the repentant sinner could approach God, express his repentance and ask God's forgiveness. The sacrifices pointed beyond themselves to something higher, the merciful love of God (Micah 7:18-20).

Cleansing and response

Animal sacrifices could not in themselves remove sin (Heb 10:1-4), but they at least showed that sacrificial death was necessary for the removal of sin (Heb 9:22). The one sacrificial death that has achieved what all the Old Testament sacrifices could not achieve is the sacrificial death of Jesus Christ (Heb 10:11-14,17-18). Unlike the animal sacrifices, Christ's sacrifice removes sin, cleanses the conscience, brings total forgiveness and secures eternal redemption (Heb 9:9-14,25-26; 10:14-18).

The book of Hebrews goes to some length to display the perfection of Christ's work, presenting him as both priest and sacrifice. In particular, it contrasts his sacrificial work with the sacrificial work of the Israelite high priest on the Day of Atonement (Heb 9:6-7,11-12,25-26; see DAY OF ATONEMENT; PRIEST).

Besides being man's only way of atonement, the sacrifice of Christ is an example to Christians of the sort of life they should live. Christ's sacrifice was a willing sacrifice, an act of obedience and love. God wants his people to show their obedience and love by willingly sacrificing themselves for the sake of others (Eph 5:2,25; cf. John 15:12-13; Rom 5:8; Heb 10:7,10).

The sacrifices of Christians, then, are spiritual sacrifices, which are offered in response to God's love and mercy (1 Peter 2:5). They are not atoning sacrifices, for Christ's one sacrifice has already brought complete release from sin's penalty (Heb 10:17-18). Christians offer to God the sacrifices of worship, praise and service (Rom 15:16; Phil 4:18; Heb 13:15). But they will be able to present such sacrifices properly only when they have first given themselves to God as living sacrifices (Rom 12:1; 2 Cor 8:5).

SADDUCEES

In New Testament times the two main parties within the Jewish religion were the Sadducees and the Pharisees. The beginnings of these two parties can be traced back to the second century BC, when Greek influence was having its effect on the Jewish people.

Origins

The influence of Greek ideas in Jewish affairs produced tension between those Jews who favoured it and those who resisted it. When conflict broke out between the two groups, the Greek ruler in Syria, Antiochus Epiphanes, used it as an excuse to invade Jerusalem and try to destroy the Jewish religion. (For details of this period of Jewish history see GREECE.) Under the leadership of a priestly family known as the Maccabees (or Hasmoneans) the Jews rebelled against Antiochus, and after three years of fighting regained religious freedom (165 BC).

When the Maccabees wanted to keep fighting and regain political freedom as well, the religiously strict Jews objected. They opposed the Maccabees' political ambitions just as they had opposed the

interference of Greek politics in Jewish affairs. These two factions were the forerunners of the Sadducees and the Pharisees. The former favoured political as well as religious freedom, whereas the latter were satisfied with religious freedom. The Maccabees carried on the war in spite of internal opposition, and after twenty years they won political independence (143 BC).

There was now a clear division among the Jews. The pro-political group consisted of powerful priests and wealthy leaders who were favoured by the Hasmonean rulers. The other group consisted largely of commoners who were politically powerless but favoured by most of the people. Later, a dispute concerning the Hasmonean ruler's right to be high priest led to the open formation of the Sadducee and Pharisee parties. (The name 'Sadducee' possibly comes from Zadok, the priest of Solomon's time whose descendants came to be regarded as the only legitimate priestly line; 1 Kings 1:38-39; Ezek 44:15-16; 48:11; see ZADOK.)

Religious power

Some of the Sadducees' religious beliefs further emphasized the differences between the two parties. The Pharisees followed strictly the traditions handed down from their forefathers, but the Sadducees had little interest in the traditions. They were concerned only with the commandments actually written in the law of Moses. Also, they did not believe in the continued existence of the soul after death, the bodily resurrection of the dead, the directing will of God in the events of life, or the existence of angelic beings. These were all important beliefs for the Pharisees (Matt 2:23; Acts 4:1-2; 23:7-8).

In spite of their dislike for the Pharisees, the Sadducees readily joined with them to oppose Jesus (Matt 16:1-4; 22:15,23,34). Jesus condemned them, along with the Pharisees, for their hypocrisy (Matt 16:6,12).

Most of the leading priests of New Testament times were Sadducees, and they enjoyed the support of the upper class Jews. The high priest, who was president of the Sanhedrin, was a Sadducee, and through him and his close associates the Sadducees exercised much power in the Sanhedrin (Acts 4:1-3; 5:17-21; see SANHEDRIN).

The Sadducees were particularly hostile to the early Christians. This was chiefly for two reasons. Firstly, the apostles' accusation of injustice on the part of the Sanhedrin was really an accusation against the ruling Sadducees (Acts 4:5-10; 5:27-28). Secondly, the church's rapid growth was based on the truth of the resurrection, which the Sadducees denied (Acts 4:1-2,10,17). The Sadducees had little following among the common people, and in fact were afraid of violence from them if they treated the Christians too harshly (Acts 4:2,17,21; 5:17,26). Only when the Pharisees turned against the Christians were the Sadducees able to use the full power of the Sanhedrin against the Christians (Acts 6:12-15; 7:58; 8:1; cf. Phil 3:5-6).

With the Romans' destruction of Jerusalem and the temple in AD 70, the Sadducees lost the priestly base that had maintained them. The party soon died out.

SALT

Apart from its obvious use in cooking, salt was widely used in the ancient world to keep perishable foods from decay (Lev 2:13; Job 6:6). Because of salt's uses and characteristics, the Bible refers to it to illustrate aspects of the lives of Christians. Just as salt gives food a good taste, so the gracious qualities of their new life in Christ should make the speech of Christians wholesome and pleasant (Col 4:6). If they are living as they should, Christians will be a good influence in a world corrupted by sin (Matt 5:13; Mark 9:50).

Because of its use in flavouring and preserving, salt symbolized a close and permanent relationship between people. It had a ceremonial use in making covenants, where it symbolized the unbroken loyalty that the two parties promised to the covenant (Lev 2:13; Num 18:19; 2 Chron 13:5; see COVENANT).

Sometimes, however, salt symbolized judgment and desolation. This was because salty land was useless for farming and became a barren waste. Therefore, a conqueror may have sprinkled salt over a destroyed city to symbolize that it was to be left in permanent desolation (Deut 29:23; Judg 9:45; Jer 17:6; Zeph 2:9).

The Israelites obtained their salt mainly from the region around the Dead Sea, which was itself so rich in salt that it was sometimes called the Salt Sea (Gen 14:3; Josh 3:16; 15:5; 18:19). Somewhere to the south-west of the Dead Sea, in the dry region of Israel known as the Negeb, was a place called the Valley of Salt (2 Sam 8:13; 2 Kings 14:7). (For further details of the Dead Sea and the Negeb see PALESTINE.)

SALVATION

God's salvation, as the Old Testament spoke of it, had a broad meaning. It referred to deliverance or preservation from disease, dangers, sufferings, death and the consequences of wrongdoing (Exod 14:30; Judg 2:11-16; Ps 34:6; 37:40; Jer 4:14; 17:14). The means of God's salvation may have been a warrior, a king, or some other national leader (Judg 3:9; 2 Kings 13:5), but in the highest sense the saviour was always God (1 Sam 14:23; Isa 33:22; 43:3,11,15; Hab 3:18).

In the New Testament, salvation may have the same broad meaning as in the Old Testament (Acts 27:20,43; 2 Cor 1:10; 2 Thess 3:2; 2 Peter 2:9), but its best known meaning is in relation to deliverance from sin and its consequences. This salvation comes from God through Jesus Christ (Matt 1:21; Luke 2:11; 19:10; John 3:17; 12:47; Acts 4:12; 1 Tim 1:15) and it is possible only because Jesus Christ atoned for sin in his death on the cross (1 Cor 1:18; Titus 2:14; see ATONEMENT; SIN).

This salvation is so great that no words can describe it fully. The Bible therefore uses many different pictures of salvation in an effort to help people understand what God has done.

One picture is that of the courtroom, where God the judge declares believers righteous and acquits them (Rom 3:26; 8:33; see JUSTIFICATION). Another picture is that of slavery, which shows that God has freed believers from the bondage of sin (1 Peter 1:18-19; see REDEMPTION). The picture of new birth shows that God gives life to those who are spiritually dead (1 Peter 1:23; see REGENERATION), and the picture of adoption shows how God places believers in his family and gives them the full status of sons (Rom 8:15; see ADOPTION).

A further picture is that of God's turning those who are his enemies into his friends (Rom 5:10-11; see RECONCILIATION). The picture of a sacrificial offering expresses further aspects of salvation; for example, the death of a sacrificial victim in the place of the sinner (Heb 9:26; see SACRIFICE), and the presentation of an offering to turn away God's anger against sin (Rom 3:25; see PROPITIATION). But regardless of whatever picture the Bible uses, it emphasizes constantly that salvation is solely by God's grace, and that people receive it through faith and repentance (Acts 5:31; 16:30-31; 20:21; 1 Cor 1:21; Eph 2:8-9; Titus 3:3-7; see FAITH; GRACE; REPENTANCE).

There are past, present and future aspects of salvation. The past aspect is that believers already have been saved because of Christ's death for them. Their sin has been dealt with, they are no longer under condemnation, and they have the assurance of eternal life (John 5:24; Rom 5:1-2; Eph 2:1,8; see ASSURANCE). The present aspect is that believers continue to experience the saving power of God in victory over sin in their daily lives (1 Cor 1:18; Phil 2:12; 2 Tim 1:8-9; see SANCTIFICATION). The future aspect is that believers will experience the fulfilment of their salvation at the return of Jesus Christ (Rom 8:24; 13:11; Phil 3:20; 1 Thess 5:9; Heb 9:28; 1 Peter 1:5; see RESURRECTION).

SAMARIA, SAMARITANS

A Samaritan was an inhabitant of Samaria, but there was a difference between the Samaria of the Old Testament and the Samaria of the New. In the time of Israel's Old Testament monarchy, Samaria was a city in central Israel and its inhabitants were Israelites. In New Testament times Samaria was the central region of Palestine and its inhabitants were non-Israelites.

Capital of the northern kingdom

Following the death of Solomon in 930 BC, the ancient kingdom of Israel was split into two. The breakaway northern section of ten tribes continued to call itself the kingdom of Israel; the southern section of two tribes became known as the kingdom

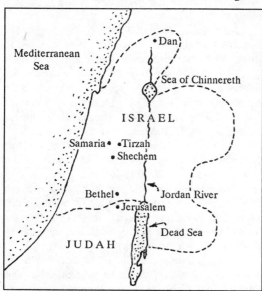

of Judah. The northerners established their capital first at Shechem, then at Tirzah, but when Omri came to the throne he built a new capital at Samaria. Samaria remained the capital till the end of the northern kingdom. The town, built on a hill, had a commanding position over the surrounding plain and nearby trade routes (1 Kings 16:23-24). It was well fortified and able to withstand enemy attacks (1 Kings 20:1-21; 2 Kings 6:24-7:20).

Just as Omri had made Samaria the political centre of his kingdom, so his son and successor Ahab made it the religious centre. The religion, however, was the corrupt religion of Baal imported by Ahab's heathen wife Jezebel. Ahab built a fully equipped Baal temple in Samaria (1 Kings 16:30-33), and although this was destroyed during Jehu's purge, false religion was never removed from Samaria (2 Kings 10:25-31; Jer 23:13). Israel's idolatry was the reason why God finally allowed the kingdom to be destroyed. In 722 BC the Assyrians captured Samaria, slaughtered the people, and carried off most of the survivors into foreign captivity (2 Kings 17:1-18).

Samaritans: a new people and a new religion

In keeping with their usual policy, the Assyrians resettled people from other parts of their empire into Samaria and other cities of the former northern kingdom (2 Kings 17:24). These people tried to avoid punishment from Israel's God by combining the worship of Yahweh with their own religious practices. They also intermarried with the Israelite people left in the land, producing a new racial group known as the Samaritans (2 Kings 17:25-33).

Because Samaritans were of mixed blood and mixed religion, tension developed between them and true Jews (cf. John 4:9). Succeeding Assyrian kings transported additional foreigners into Samaria (Ezra 4:2,9-10). Assyria itself was conquered by Babylon in 612 BC.

During the years 606-587 BC, the Babylonians conquered the southern kingdom Judah and took its people into captivity. In 539 BC Persia conquered Babylon and allowed the captive Jews to return to Jerusalem and rebuild their temple and city. By this time, as a result of Assyria's resettlement policy, the Samaritans were well established in the land. When they offered to help the Jews, the Jewish leaders rejected them, fearing they might introduce corrupt ideas into the Jewish religion (Ezra 4:1-3). The Samaritans reacted bitterly, and opposed the Jews throughout their building program (Ezra 4:4-24; Neh 4:1-23).

When, despite years of Samaritan opposition, the Jews completed their building program, the Samaritan leaders changed their tactics. By cunning and deceit some of them worked themselves into places of influence in Jerusalem. They corrupted the religion, defiled the temple and persuaded Jews and Samaritans to intermarry. Finally, in a sweeping reform, the Jerusalem governor Nehemiah drove those who were not true Jews out of the city (Neh 13:1-9,23-31).

The Samaritans then decided to show their opposition to the Jews and Jerusalem by establishing Mt Gerizim, beside the town of Shechem, as their national place of worship. Later they built a temple there. This only increased the hatred between Jews and Samaritans.

In using the five books of Moses to defend their beliefs and practices, the Samaritans became so extreme that they almost refused to accept the remaining books of the Old Testament as having any authority. Their chief beliefs were that there was one God, Moses was his only prophet, Moses' law was the only valid teaching, and the temple on Mt Gerizim was the only legitimate place of worship (Deut 27:12; John 4:9,20).

Today, near what used to be the town of Shechem, there is a small community that follows the ancient Samaritan religion.

Samaria in the New Testament

In New Testament times people commonly thought of Palestine as being divided into three regions: Judea in the south, Samaria in the centre and Galilee in the north. Under the Romans, Judea and Samaria were often grouped together. The centre of

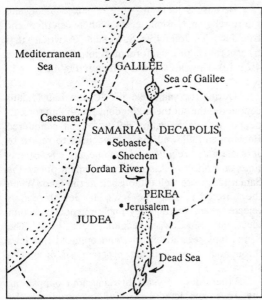

administration for the region was Caesarea, a city built on the coast by Herod the Great (Luke 3:1; Acts 1:8; 23:33). Herod also built a city on the site of ancient Samaria and named it Sebaste.

On one occasion when Jesus passed through Samaria, he spent two days preaching at Sychar (near Shechem) and many Samaritans believed (John 4:3-5,39-41). On another occasion people of a

Samaritan village showed the traditional Samaritan hatred for Jews by refusing to receive Jesus in their village (Luke 9:51-53).

But not all Samaritans were unfriendly. Jesus told stories about Samaritans who were kind and thankful, which was in contrast to the unloving and ungrateful attitude of many of the Jews (Luke 10:30-37; 17:11-18). After his resurrection Jesus commanded the Christians to take the gospel to Samaria, something that Philip and others did with great success (Acts 1:8; 8:1,4-6,25; 9:31; 15:3).

SAMSON

In the days between Israel's entrance into Canaan and the establishment of the kingdom, the Israelites were often oppressed by other peoples of the region. During one period, when the Philistines dominated them for forty years, the people had become so crushed that they had no more desire to fight. It was easier to accept the hardship of Philistine rule than to try to overthrow it (Judg 15:11-13). The man whom God raised up to stir the Israelites from this apathy was Samson. He began the revolt that would eventually lead to the overthrow of the Philistines (Judg 13:5b).

As a person dedicated to God according to the conditions of the Nazirite vow, Samson was not to drink wine, cut his hair or touch any dead body (Judg 13:5; cf. Num 6:2-8). Although he carried out mighty deeds through the special power of God's Spirit upon him (Judg 13:25; 14:6,19; 15:14), he was not careful to maintain his Nazirite dedication to God (Judg 14:8-9). When, towards the end of his life, he allowed the removal of the last symbol of this dedication (his uncut hair), God withdrew his divine power from him (Judg 16:19-20).

Samson had to fight his battles against the Philistines virtually unaided by his fellow Israelites. While they were complacent, he was looking for ways of unsettling the enemy. He lost no opportunity of doing as much damage as he could (Judg 14:4).

When, for example, the Philistines won a bet against him through cheating, Samson killed thirty of their citizens (Judg 14:18-19). When his wife was given to another man, Samson burnt the Philistines' fields (Judg 15:1-5). In retaliation for their murder of his wife and father-in-law, Samson killed more Philistines (Judg 15:6-8). When the Philistines made an attack on the town where he was staying in an attempt to capture him, he killed another thousand of them (Judg 15:15).

Samson became known as one of the judges of Israel. He was a judge not in the sense that he settled legal disputes, but in the sense that he executed judgments on the oppressors of God's people. His remarkable attacks, spread over twenty years, began the deliverance that David eventually achieved many years later (Judg 13:5b; 15:20; 2 Sam 8:1,11-12). His greatest triumph was on the day of his death when, through faith in the power of God, he killed all the Philistine rulers along with three thousand of their leading people (Judg 16:23,28,30; Heb 11:32-34). It was the turning point that gave Israel new hope.

SAMUEL

Samuel was born into a Levite family who lived at Ramah, in the tribal territory of Ephraim (1 Sam 1:19-20; 1 Chron 6:33-38). In accordance with a promise made before Samuel's birth, his mother took him as a young child to the tabernacle at Shiloh, where she dedicated him to God for life-long service. When his parents returned home, Samuel remained at Shiloh, to be brought up by the priest Eli (1 Sam 1:24,28; 2:11). He grew up to become Eli's helper in the duties of the tabernacle (1 Sam 2:18). By bringing God's message of judgment to Eli, he showed that God was preparing him to be a prophet (1 Sam 3:10-18).

When Eli died, Samuel succeeded him as chief administrator in Israel (1 Sam 4:18; 7:15). People everywhere acknowledged him as a prophet from God and the religious leader of the nation (1 Sam 3:20; 7:3-6; Acts 3:24; 13:20).

A national leader

There was an early indication of Samuel's leadership role after the capture and subsequent return of the ark by the Philistines. Samuel showed his authority among his people by demanding that they get rid of their foreign gods and by leading them in prayer and confession to God (1 Sam 7:3-6). The religious life of Israel now centred on Samuel, who set up an altar of sacrifice in Ramah (for the Philistines had destroyed the tabernacle; Ps 78:60-61; Jer 7:14). The priesthood had become so corrupt that God appointed Samuel to carry out priestly duties, even though he was not from a priestly family (1 Sam 2:27-36; 7:9; 10:8).

Israel's civil administration also centred on Samuel. He moved in an annual circuit around four major towns where he held district courts to settle disputes (1 Sam 7:15-17).

As Samuel grew old, his sons took over much of the administration. But instead of resisting the social corruption that had become widespread through the people's disobedience to God, they contributed to it (1 Sam 8:1-3). In search for improved conditions, the people asked Samuel to bring the old system to an end and give them a king after the pattern that existed in other nations. This was not so much a rejection of Samuel as a rejection of God. The people's troubles had come not from the system of government, but from their sins. The answer to their problems was to turn to God in a new attitude of faith and repentance, which they refused to do. Samuel warned that just as God had punished them for disobedience when they were under the judges, so he would punish them under the kings (1 Sam 8:4-22; 12:8-15).

Subsequently, the people got their king, and Samuel was no longer their civil leader. But he was still their spiritual leader, and he continued to teach them and pray for them (1 Sam 12:23-25).

With the corruption of the priesthood, God made increasing use of prophets, rather than priests, to speak to his people. The emotionalism of some of these prophets led to unusual behaviour at times (1 Sam 10:9-12; 19:20-24), but rather than silence the prophets, Samuel tried to redirect their spiritual zeal for the benefit of the nation. He established a school for prophets at Ramah, and others were established later at Bethel, Jericho and Gilgal (1 Sam 19:18-20; 2 Kings 2:3,5; 4:38).

Samuel and other national leaders

God revealed to Samuel that he would send to him the man whom God had chosen to be Israel's first king. That man was Saul, whom Samuel anointed in a brief private ceremony (1 Sam 9:15-16; 10:1). Some time later, Samuel called a meeting of the family and tribal leaders of Israel for a public selection of Israel's first king. Saul was chosen (1 Sam 10:17-25) and, after leading Israel to victory in his first battle, was crowned king in a national ceremony at Gilgal (1 Sam 11:12-15).

In time of approaching war, Saul was given one week during which Israel's leaders could gather the army together, and he himself could go to Gilgal to consult Samuel. There Samuel would offer sacrifices and pass on God's instructions (1 Sam 10:8). Saul was impatient and wanted complete power, religious as well as political. He therefore did not wait for Samuel but offered the sacrifices himself. Samuel announced that in judgment God would take the kingdom from Saul (1 Sam 13:8-14). He confirmed this judgment on a later occasion when Saul again disobeyed God (1 Sam 15:1-3,13-28).

God then sent Samuel to choose a person who would one day replace Saul as king. The person he chose was David (1 Sam 16:1-13). When, some years later, Saul became jealous of David and tried to kill him, David took refuge with Samuel. When Saul's messengers, and then Saul himself, tried to capture David, all of them were overcome by the power of God's Spirit, which still worked through Samuel and his followers (1 Sam 19:18-24).

To the day of his death and throughout the centuries that followed, Samuel was highly respected by the people of Israel (1 Sam 25:1; Jer 15:1). Saul so respected Samuel's power and wisdom that, after Samuel's death, he went to a woman who consulted the spirits of the dead in order to seek Samuel's help. But Samuel simply confirmed that God had rejected Saul and that the next day Saul would be dead (1 Sam 28:3-19).

SAMUEL, BOOKS OF

The two books of Samuel were originally one. They are part of the collection that the Hebrews referred to as the Former Prophets, that is, the books of Joshua, Judges, Samuel and Kings. (Concerning the significance of the name 'Former Prophets' see PROPHECY.)

Authorship

Though the author of 1 and 2 Samuel is not named, it seems that he took much of his material from the records kept by such people as Samuel, Nathan, Gad, David and the writer of the book of Jasher (1 Sam 10:25; 2 Sam 1:18; 1 Chron 27:24; 29:29). The books of Samuel are named after the man who is the chief character at the beginning of the story and who anointed the two kings whose reigns occupy the remainder of the story. Together the two books cover about one hundred years, from the end of the period of the judges to the end of the reign of David.

Religious purpose

The books of Samuel show how Israel's political life developed from the simple and often disorderly arrangement that existed in the time of the judges to an established hereditary monarchy. When Samuel succeeded Eli as judge over Israel, the nation's life was following the same pattern as illustrated in the book of Judges, with the people turning away from God and falling under foreign domination (1 Sam 3:11-13; 4:10-11). When, in response to Samuel's preaching, the people returned to God, God saved them (1 Sam 7:3-6,13,15-17).

When Samuel became old and was no longer able to exercise full control over the nation, troubles returned. In a desire for stability, the people asked

for a monarchy like that of other nations. But Israel's problems came from the people's sins, not from the system of government. Therefore, Samuel warned that although they would have their wish and

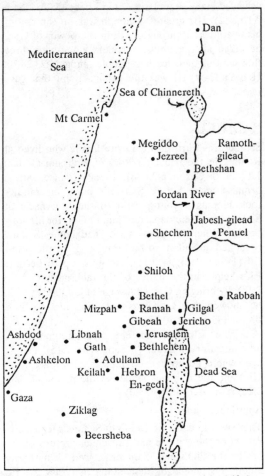

be given a king, they would still be punished if they disobeyed God. As it had been under the judges, so it would be under the kings (1 Sam 12:9-15).

Israel's first king, Saul, was similar to the judges in that the special power of God's Spirit came upon him in certain national crises (1 Sam 11:6-11). But because of his rebellion against God, God took this power from him and gave it to David (1 Sam 15:23; 16:13-14). David was the last of the Spirit-gifted leaders and the first of the hereditary kings. The people had wanted a system of government where the rule would pass from father to son without any need for God to act supernaturally through selected men. Now they had it.

With David a new era began, and the rest of the story deals with his reign. It demonstrates the truth of Samuel's earlier assertion that national stability would be achieved by devotion to God rather than by a change in the form of government.

Saul's reign was characterized by weakness and conflict, David's by strength and prosperity. The difference was not because of the monarchy as an institution, but because of David's submission to God and his desire to carry out God's will (Ps 89:19-37; Acts 13:22). The books of Samuel are not so much concerned with systems of government as with obedience to God. Their purpose is not simply to record historical events, but to show how God was working in the lives of his people.

Contents of 1 Samuel

The first seven chapters of 1 Samuel are concerned with Israel during the period when Eli, and then Samuel, were judges. By means of a lengthy story, the writer points out the significance of the birth of Samuel (1:1-2:11) in view of the judgment that was about to fall on Eli and his family (2:12-3:21). Israel, because of its sin, suffered God's judgment when the Philistines captured the ark (4:1-22), but the ark returned (5:1-7:1), Israel repented and the nation won a notable victory (7:2-17).

In their desire for greater national stability, the people of Israel asked for a king. Samuel told them that in acting like this they were rejecting God, but the people remained unmoved (8:1-22). God told Samuel to anoint Saul as king (9:1-10:16), and this private anointing was followed by Saul's public appointment to office (10:17-27). With a spectacular victory over the Ammonites, Saul soon became a popular hero (11:1-15), and Samuel retired from the national leadership (12:1-25). Saul had other notable victories, firstly over the Philistines (13:1-14:52), and then over the Amalekites (15:1-35), but in both cases his disobedience to God showed he was not fit to rule over God's people.

David was the man God chose to succeed Saul as king (16:1-23). He won fame through his victory over Goliath (17:1-58), and after further outstanding victories he was rapidly promoted in the Israelite army. His successes, however, stirred up Saul's jealousy, resulting in various attempts by Saul to kill him (18:1-19:24). David was forced to flee from Saul to save his life (20:1-21:15). Soon he was joined by hundreds of others who were discontented because of the injustices of Saul's rule (22:1-23). Yet in spite of Saul's unjust pursuit of him, David refused to attack his king (23:1-25:44).

At one stage David looked for refuge in enemy Philistia (26:1-27:12), and even set out with the Philistines when they were going to fight with Israel.

The Philistine leaders refused to accept him and sent him back (28:1-29:11). The result was that instead of fighting against Israel, David had a rewarding victory over some Amalekites who had been raiding in southern Israel (30:1-31). Meanwhile in the north the Philistines defeated Israel, and Saul was killed in battle (31:1-13).

Contents of 2 Samuel

David was made king in place of Saul, but some of Saul's followers refused to accept David. They made one of Saul's sons king, and fighting soon broke out between the two factions (1:1-3:1). After two years, Saul's faction was overthrown and David was the undisputed king (3:2-4:12).

In an effort to unite all Israel, David conquered Jerusalem (which had been under the control of non-Israelite people) and made it the new national capital (5:1-25). Determined to restore the true worship of God to its rightful place in the centre of the nation's life, he brought the ark to Jerusalem (6:1-23). In response to David's request to build God a permanent dwelling place, God promised David something more important, a lasting dynasty (7:1-29).

David won many battles (8:1-10:19), but he brought trouble upon himself through some foolish actions in which he was guilty of sexual immorality and murder (11:1-12:31). His own household was in turn torn apart by sexual immorality and murder (13:1-14:33), and his son Absalom overthrew him and seized the throne (15:1-16:23). War followed between Absalom and David, with the result that Absalom was killed (17:1-19:8). David then returned to Jerusalem to be re-established as king (19:9-43). Not long after, he had to deal with another revolt, but this time success came to him more swiftly (20:1-26).

The final four chapters form an appendix of miscellaneous matters. Various short stories indicate some of the difficult decisions that David at times faced (21:1-22). A lengthy psalm celebrates his victories over his enemies (22:1-51), and a shorter one speaks of the blessings that a God-fearing king brings to his people (23:1-7). After listing David's mighty men (23:8-39), the appendix closes with the story of a disastrous census that David once carried out (24:1-25).

SANCTIFICATION

The connection between sanctification and holiness is clearer in the original languages of the Bible than in the English of today. In Hebrew and Greek, the two words share the same root. To sanctify means to declare, acknowledge as, or make holy.

In the Old Testament

To Israelites of Old Testament times, the basic meaning of holiness was not a condition of moral purity, but a state of being different or separate from the common things of life. God was holy (Exod 15:11-12), and so were people and things set apart for him (Exod 19:6; 29:29,31; 30:25; Lev 27:30,33; Num 5:17). To sanctify a person or thing meant to separate it from the common affairs of life and consecrate it wholly to God (Exod 13:2; 19:10,23; 29:37,44; Lev 27:21).

Since sanctification meant separation from common use for God's use, sanctification soon included in it those ideas of moral purity that we today more commonly associate with the word. Both Old and New Testament writers emphasized that formal sanctification was of value only when it was accompanied by practical sanctification (2 Chron 29:15-16,34; 30:15,17; Rom 6:19,22). (For a fuller discussion on the biblical ideas of holiness see HOLINESS.)

In the New Testament

The New Testament speaks about the relationship aspect of sanctification (setting a person or thing apart for God) and the moral aspect (living an upright life). Jesus Christ was sanctified in both aspects. He was wholly consecrated to God (John 17:19; Acts 3:14) and he was morally perfect in his life (Heb 7:26; 1 Peter 2:22).

Although their experience differs from Christ's, Christians also may be spoken of as sanctified in the two senses we have been considering. In both cases it is through Christ that they are sanctified.

Firstly, through Christ's death believers are brought into a right relationship with God (1 Cor 1:30; Heb 10:10). God is the one who sanctifies them, as he cleanses them of their sin and declares them holy and righteous in his sight (2 Thess 2:13; Heb 2:12; 10:14-17; 1 Peter 1:2). In this sense, sanctification is another way of looking at the truth that is expressed in justification (1 Cor 6:11; see JUSTIFICATION). Believers are 'saints', meaning 'the sanctified ones'. They are 'God's holy people' (Rom 1:7; 1 Cor 1:2; Eph 1:1).

Secondly, sanctification means that Christians are to have a moral and spiritual change in their lives. God has declared them holy (because of what Christ has done on their behalf) and they must now make that true in practice. They *are* sanctified; now they must *be* sanctified (Rom 6:8-11,19-22; 1 Thess

4:3; 5:23; Heb 12:14). This will involve a battle with the old sinful nature (the flesh), but through the power of the living Christ within, they can have victory over the flesh and be progressively changed into the likeness of Christ (Rom 8:9-12; 12:1-2; Col 3:9-10,12; 1 Peter 1:14-15).

There are two other uses of the word 'sanctify' that should be noted. In the first, people are said to sanctify God when they acknowledge his holiness and reverence him as Lord (Num 20:12; Isa 8:13; 29:23; 1 Peter 3:15). In the second, God is said to sanctify the unbelieving husband whose wife has become a Christian. This does not mean that God makes the man into a Christian, but that he accepts the man as part of an equal marriage. God considers the marriage to be holy on account of the believing partner; it is a lawful union (1 Cor 7:14).

SANCTUARY

A sanctuary was a sanctified place, a place set apart for God and therefore considered to be holy (see SANCTIFICATION). Heaven, being God's dwelling place, could be called God's sanctuary (Ps 102:19; 150:1). Usually, however, the sanctuary referred to God's earthly dwelling place, the tabernacle, and later the temple (Exod 25:8; 1 Chron 28:10; Ps 68:24-26; see TABERNACLE; TEMPLE). The inner shrine, or Most Holy Place, was in particular known as the sanctuary; for it was there, over the ark of the covenant, that God symbolically dwelt (Lev 4:6; Ps 96:6; Heb 13:11).

Since Israel trusted in God and God dwelt in the sanctuary, to trust in God was to trust in the sanctuary. A sanctuary therefore came to have a secondary meaning as a place of refuge (Isa 8:14; Ezek 11:16; cf. Exod 21:12-14; 1 Kings 2:29; Num 35:6; see CITY OF REFUGE).

Other gods had their sanctuaries also. These were usually places where altars had been set up for the worship of false gods. The Baal sanctuaries, which Israelites often took over and used in their own form of false worship, were known as high places (Amos 7:9; see HIGH PLACES).

SANHEDRIN

With the re-establishment of the Jewish nation after the Jews' return from captivity in Babylon, there were significant developments in the Jewish religion. Many of these were connected with the establishment of synagogues (or meeting places) in the Jewish communities, and the rise of people known as scribes (or teachers of the law). The scribes usually had positions of power in the synagogues and used them as places from which to spread their teachings (see SCRIBES; SYNAGOGUE).

Under Ezra groups of elders and judges had been appointed to administer civil and religious law in Israel (Ezra 7:25-26; 10:14). It was probably on this basis that such people became leaders of the synagogues and rulers in the Jewish communities. As the scribes and other leaders on the synagogue committees grew in power, a system of local Jewish rule developed that eventually produced a council known as the Sanhedrin. Although any local Jewish council may have been called a Sanhedrin, the word was used most commonly for the supreme Jewish council in Jerusalem.

The Jerusalem Sanhedrin consisted of a maximum of seventy members, not counting the high priest. (The number was probably based on the ancient arrangement by which Moses and seventy elders administered Israel; see Num 11:24.) The composition of the Sanhedrin changed from time to time, depending on political developments within the nation. In New Testament times it consisted of scribes, elders, priests and other respected citizens, and included both Pharisees and Sadducees. The high priest acted as president (Matt 26:3,57-59; Luke 22:66; 23:50; Acts 4:5-7; 5:17-21,34; 22:30; 23:1-6). Any meeting of the Sanhedrin required at least twenty-three members to be present.

Rome gave the Sanhedrin authority to arrest, judge and punish Jewish people for offences relating to their religious law and for certain civil offences (Mark 14:43; Acts 5:17-21,40; 6:11-15; 9:2). The one exception concerned the death sentence. Although it could pass the death sentence, the Sanhedrin could not carry it out without permission from Rome (Matt 26:66; 27:1-2; John 18:30-31).

From details of Sanhedrin procedures recorded in ancient Jewish writings, it is clear that Jesus' trial, conviction and execution were illegal. The Jews' execution of Stephen was also illegal, but the Roman authorities probably considered it safer to ignore the incident and so avoid trouble with the Jews (Acts 7:57-58; cf. 18:14-17; Matt 27:24).

SARAH

At the time of her marriage to Abraham in Mesopotamia, Sarah's name was Sarai and Abraham's was Abram. God gave them their new names (Abraham meaning 'father of a multitude', Sarah meaning 'princess') to confirm to them that they would be the parents of a great people, the nation Israel (Gen 11:29; 17:5-6,15-16; Isa 51:2). From Mesopotamia

God directed Abraham and Sarah into Canaan, the land that he promised would be Israel's eventual homeland (Gen 12:1,5-8).

Abraham accepted God's promise by faith and, because of this, God accepted him as righteous (Gen 15:6). (For details of the New Testament teaching on faith in the lives of Abraham and Sarah see ABRAHAM.) However, Abraham's faith failed on occasions. Twice he deceived people by saying Sarah was his sister. This was partly true, as Sarah was a daughter of his father by a different wife; but it was wrong to tell only part of the truth in order to deceive (Gen 12:18-20; 20:11-12).

God had promised that Abraham and Sarah, in spite of their many years without children, would in due course produce a son through whom God's promises would be fulfilled. The older they grew, the less likely it seemed that Sarah would bear a child, so Sarah suggested that Abraham obtain the desired son through their slave-girl, Hagar. A son was born, but God said it was not the child he had promised (Gen 16:1-4,15; 17:18-19).

Sarah found it difficult to believe that a woman as old as she could bear a son, and therefore God sent special heavenly messengers to convince her. Sarah had to share Abraham's faith (Gen 18:10-14). The following year, when Abraham was about a hundred years old and Sarah about ninety, Sarah gave birth to Isaac, the son whom God had promised (Gen 17:17,19,21; 21:1-5). The faith of Abraham and Sarah had been tested constantly for twenty-five years (cf. Gen 12:4), and had shown itself to be genuine and enduring (Rom 4:17-21; Heb 11:11-12).

Earlier there had been friction between Sarah and Hagar (Gen 16:4-9). When it appeared again, Sarah said to Abraham that he should drive out Hagar and her son from the household (Gen 21:10). Although Sarah respected Abraham as head of the household, she also had a role in family decisions, and in this case God told Abraham to do as Sarah suggested (Gen 21:12; cf. 1 Peter 3:6). Isaac alone was to be heir to the promises God gave concerning his chosen land and people. Sarah lived to see her son grow into a mature and responsible leader. He was about thirty-seven years old when Sarah died (Gen 23:1,19).

SARDIS

The only biblical mention of the church in the town of Sardis is as the recipient of one of the letters that John sent to seven churches in the province of Asia (for map see ASIA). Nothing is known of the church apart from what is found in this letter.

So much had the church in Sardis followed the ways of the society around it, that it was Christian in name only. Spiritually it was dead. Unless the Christians woke up and changed their ways, God would act against them in swift judgment. There were some, however, who proved the genuineness of their faith by refusing to alter their behaviour to suit the majority. Such people were assured of God's reward (Rev 3:1-6).

SATAN

Among the angelic spirits of the unseen world there are those that are evil, though the Bible nowhere records how they fell into such a condition. The chief of these evil angelic spirits is one known as the adversary – the adversary of God, his people, and all that is good. The Hebrew word for 'adversary' is *satan*, which later became the name used in the Bible for this leader of evil (Job 1:6). He is also called the devil (Matt 4:1-12; 1 John 3:8; Rev 12:9), the prince of demons (Matt 9:34; 12:24; see also BEELZEBUL), the prince of this world (John 12:31; 14:30; 16:11), the god of this world (2 Cor 4:4), the prince of the power of the air (Eph 2:2), the evil one (Matt 13:19; Eph 6:16; 1 John 2:13; 3:12) and the accuser of the brethren (Rev 12:10; cf. Job 1:6-12; Zech 3:1).

God's rebellious servant

We should not think that Satan is in some way the equal of God, one being a good God and the other an evil God. God alone is God (Isa 44:6). Satan is no more than an angelic being created by God. There are good angels and evil angels, Satan being chief of the evil ones (Matt 25:31,41; Eph 6:12; Jude 9; Rev 12:7-9; see ANGELS; DEMONS). God, however, is above all and over all.

Also there are not, as it were, two kingdoms, a kingdom of good where God is absolute ruler and a kingdom of evil where Satan is absolute ruler. Satan is not a sovereign ruler but a rebel. Like all created beings, he is under the rule and authority of God and he can do his evil work only within the limits God allows (Job 1:12; 2:6; cf. Rev 20:2-3; 20:7-8). He is still the servant of God, even though a rebellious one (Job 1:6-7; 2:1-2; Zech 3:1-2). In spite of the evil he loves to do, he is still fulfilling God's purposes, even though unwillingly (Job 1:9-12; 1 Kings 22:19-23; cf. John 13:2,27; Acts 2:23; 1 Cor 5:5; 2 Cor 12:7; 1 Tim 1:20).

This does not mean that God tempts people to do evil. It is Satan, not God, who is the tempter (Gen 3:1-6; 1 Chron 21:1; Matt 4:1-11; 1 Cor 7:5;

James 1:13). God desires rather to save people from evil (Matt 6:13; 1 Cor 10:13). Yet God allows them to suffer the troubles and temptations that Satan brings in life, for through such things he tests and strengthens their faith (James 1:2-3,12; cf. Heb 2:18; 5:8-9; see TEMPTATION; TESTING).

Satan is hostile to God and fights against God's purposes (Matt 4:1-12; Mark 8:31-33). But in the long run Satan cannot be successful, because Jesus Christ, by his life, death and resurrection, has conquered him and delivered believers from his power (Matt 12:28-29; Luke 10:18; John 12:31; 16:11; Acts 26:18; Col 2:15; Heb 2:14-15; 1 John 3:8). (Concerning Jesus Christ's conquest of Satan see KINGDOM OF GOD.)

Man's enemy

Although Jesus has conquered Satan, the world at present sees neither Jesus' conquest nor Satan's defeat. God allows evil angels to continue to exist just as he allows evil people. He has condemned them but not yet destroyed them. The world will see Jesus' conquest and Satan's defeat in the great events at the end of the age, when Christ returns in power and glory (Rev 20:10).

In the meantime Satan continues to operate (Matt 13:24-26,37-39). He opposes all that is good and encourages all that is evil. At times he works with brutality and ferocity (1 Peter 5:8; Rev 2:10), at other times with cunning and deceit (2 Cor 2:11; 11:14; 1 Tim 3:7). He works not only through people who are obviously evil (Acts 13:8-10; Eph 2:1-3; 1 John 3:10,12; Rev 2:13), but also through those who appear to be good (Mark 8:33; John 8:44; Acts 5:3; Rev 2:9; 3:9).

Satan causes people physical suffering through disease (Luke 13:16; 2 Cor 12:7; see DISEASE), and evil spirits (Mark 3:20-27; 7:25; Acts 10:38; see MAGIC; UNCLEAN SPIRITS). He brings mental and spiritual suffering through the cunning of his deceit and temptations (1 Cor 7:5; 2 Thess 2:9-10: 2 Tim 2:24-26). Above all, he wants to prevent people from understanding and believing the gospel (Matt 13:19; 2 Cor 4:4).

Christians, because they have declared themselves on the side of God, may at times experience Satan's attacks more than others. They have a constant battle against Satan, but they do not fight entirely by their own strength. Certainly, they must make every effort to resist Satan and avoid doing those things that will give Satan an opportunity to tempt them (Eph 4:27; James 4:7), but God gives Christians the necessary armour to withstand Satan's attacks (Eph 6:11-13).

Just as Satan opposed Jesus in his ministry, so he will oppose Jesus' followers in their ministry (John 8:42-44; Acts 13:10; 1 Thess 2:18). But through the victory of Jesus, they too can have victory (Luke 10:17-18; 22:31-32; Rev 12:10-11).

SAUL, KING OF ISRAEL

Following Israel's demand to have a king as the other nations, God directed Samuel to Saul. At his first meeting with Saul, Samuel showed him privately that he was to be king (1 Sam 9:1-10:1). Later, at a gathering of representative family heads from all Israel, Saul was publicly chosen to be king (1 Sam 10:17-24). An official crowning ceremony followed in due course (1 Sam 11:14-15).

Victories and failures

Of the three signs that Samuel had announced to Saul as confirmation of the promised kingship, the most important was the coming of God's Spirit upon him (1 Sam 10:1-8). This changed Saul from an ordinary farmer into a national leader (1 Sam 10:9-13). Because certain people doubted Saul's suitability, he made no immediate change in the country's administration, but returned to his home in Gibeah (1 Sam 10:25-27). After leading Israel to victory in his first battle, he won the support of the whole nation (1 Sam 11:1-15).

Saul was to be under the spiritual direction of Samuel. But Saul wanted complete power, religious as well as political. Therefore, when a suitable occasion arose he rebelled against the limitation that God had placed on his authority. In punishment God announced that one day he would take the kingdom from Saul and give it to another (1 Sam 13:1-14). God confirmed this judgment on a later occasion when Saul again deliberately disobeyed his instructions through Samuel (1 Sam 15:1-34).

After this, Saul never saw Samuel again (1 Sam 15:35). Without Samuel's guidance, his rule from that time on was disastrous. When, at the end of his reign, he made a desperate attempt to consult the spirit of the dead Samuel, he merely received further confirmation of God's judgment upon him (1 Sam 28:3-19). (For details of events in this period of Saul's life see SAMUEL.)

Although Saul was at times calm and tolerant (1 Sam 10:27; 11:12-13), at other times he was rash and unpredictable (1 Sam 14:24-30,38-45; 18:10-11). Nevertheless, he brought stability and security to Israel through victories over all those nations that had previously attacked around Israel's borders (1 Sam 14:47-48; 15:7; 17:52-53).

Saul and David

God chose David as the man who would one day replace Saul as king. As David grew in experience and maturity, the special power of God's Spirit began to work through him rather than Saul (1 Sam 16:13-14). After David's victory over Goliath, Saul, unaware of God's purposes for David, made him his armour-bearer and full-time court musician (1 Sam 16:21-23; 18:2). Over the next few years Saul became more and more unstable, emotionally and mentally, while David became a popular hero through his military victories. Saul became suspicious that David might be the man to replace him, and in a fit of jealousy tried to kill him (1 Sam 18:5-11).

This began a long conflict between Saul and David. Saul tried by every possible means to get rid of David, but David steadfastly refused to do anything against Saul. Saul sent David on dangerous missions, hoping he might get killed, but his plans repeatedly failed (1 Sam 18:13-17,25). He sent his servants to kill David, and he himself tried to spear him, but all his efforts were without success (1 Sam 19:1,10-11). When David sought safety with Samuel, Saul and his servants pursued him, but the Spirit of God protected David by overpowering Saul and his men (1 Sam 19:18-24).

Year after year the chase went on. The mad Saul slaughtered any he thought had helped David (1 Sam 22:18-19), whereas David on two occasions spared Saul's life when he could easily have killed him (1 Sam 24:1-22; 26:6-25). (For details of events in this period of Saul's life see DAVID.)

Saul's tragic life came to an end during a battle with the Philistines on Mt Gilboa. When wounded in the fighting, he took his own life rather than allow himself to be captured and shamefully treated by his enemies (1 Sam 31:1-4). Loyal Israelites gave him an honourable burial (1 Sam 31:8-13), and David wrote a song in memory of him. The song also honoured Saul's son Jonathan, who died in the same battle (2 Sam 1:17-27).

SAUL OF TARSUS

See PAUL.

SCRIBES

In the days before mechanical printing, copies of documents, letters, government records and sacred writings were handwritten by skilled secretaries known as scribes (1 Kings 4:3; 2 Kings 18:18; 22:8; Jer 8:8; 38:18,26-27). The religious importance of scribes developed during the period that followed the Jews' return from captivity in 538 BC and the subsequent reconstruction of the Jewish nation. During the captivity there had been a renewal of interest in the law of Moses, and this increased following the return to Jerusalem. The result was a greater demand for copies of the law, and consequently greater prominence for the scribes (Neh 8:1-4,8; 9:3).

Because scribes had developed special skills in copying the details of the law exactly, people regarded them as experts on matters of the law (Ezra 7:6,10). Although the priests were supposed to be the teachers in Israel (Deut 33:10; Mal 2:7), people now went to the scribes, rather than the priests, when they had problems of the law that they wanted explained. During the centuries immediately before the Christian era, the scribes grew in power and prestige, and were chiefly responsible for the striking changes that came over the Jewish religion. They were also known as teachers of the law, lawyers and rabbis (Matt 22:35; 23:2-7).

Power of the scribes

The increased interest in the law produced not only the scribes as a class of teachers, but also the synagogues as places of worship (see SYNAGOGUE). The scribes developed the structure for synagogue

A scribe teaching his disciples

meetings, and controlled the synagogue teaching Matt 23:2,6; Luke 6:6-7; 20:46). They also developed and promoted the midrash as a form of teaching. (A midrash was an explanation of the 'deeper meaning' of a portion of Scripture, or in some cases a practical sermon based on a portion of Scripture.)

There was, however, a great difference between Ezra's explanations of the law and the expositions of the scribes of Jesus' time. Over the intervening centuries, the scribes had developed a system of their own, which consisted of countless laws to surround the central law of Moses. These new laws may have grown out of legal cases that the scribes had judged or traditions that had been handed down. The scribes then forced the Jewish people to obey these laws, till the whole lawkeeping system became a heavy burden (Matt 15:1-9; 23:2-4; see TRADITION).

As leaders in the synagogue and teachers of the people, the scribes enjoyed a respected status in the Jewish community (Matt 23:6-7). Some were members of the Sanhedrin, the supreme Jewish Council (Matt 26:57; see SANHEDRIN). In addition to controlling the synagogues, the scribes taught in the temple and established schools for the training of their disciples (Luke 2:46; Acts 22:3). They then sent these disciples to spread their teaching, till it became the chief force in the religious life of Israel (Matt 23:15).

Most of the scribes belonged to the party of the Pharisees (one of two major groups within Judaism; see PHARISEES; SADDUCEES), and are often linked with them in the biblical narratives (Matt 5:20; 12:38; 15:1; 23:2; Acts 5:34; 22:3). They opposed Jesus throughout his ministry, helped to crucify him, and later persecuted his followers (Matt 16:21; 21:15; 26:57; Acts 4:5-7; 6:12).

Later influences

With the destruction of Jerusalem in AD 70, the Jewish temple rituals ceased; but the influence of the scribes lived on. By AD 200, the scribes (now better known as rabbis) had put into writing the oral traditions that earlier scribes had built up around the law. This document was called the Mishnah.

After the completion of the Mishnah, the rabbis added to it their own commentary. This commentary was put into writing between AD 400 and 500, and was known as the Gemara. The Mishnah and the Gemara together made up the Talmud, which has remained the authoritative law for orthodox Jews ever since.

SCRIPTURES

Jews of New Testament times had a collection of sacred writings (now known as the Old Testament) which they referred to as the Scriptures. That is, they believed these writings originated with God and, although written by ordinary people, carried with them the absolute authority of God (Matt 21:42; 22:29; Luke 4:21; 24:27; John 5:39; 10:35; Acts 8:32; Rom 1:2; 4:3; 2 Tim 3:15-16; see INSPIRATION). During the time of the early church, Christians recognized the writings of Jesus' apostles and other leading Christians also as Scripture, and therefore as having equal authority with the Old Testament writings (1 Cor 14:37; 1 Tim 5:18; 2 Peter 3:16; see CANON).

Unity of the Scriptures

It is possible to become a Christian through only a very small portion of the Scriptures, but to grow as a Christian requires much more. If Christians want to know more about the character of God and the type of life that God requires of his people, they will need all God's Word, both Old Testament and New (see INTERPRETATION).

A better translation of the word 'testament' is 'covenant'. (For the biblical meaning of this word see COVENANT.) The Old and New Testaments are the books of the old and new covenants. The Old Testament shows how, under the old covenant, God chose the nation Israel as his people, and prepared it to be the channel through which he would provide a saviour for all mankind. The New Testament shows that this saviour, Jesus Christ, fulfilled the old covenant, then established a new covenant, by which people of all nations become God's people through faith.

There is, therefore, an underlying unity to the Scriptures. The Bible is one unbroken story that shows how mankind has rebelled against God, and how God in his grace has provided mankind with a way of salvation. Readers can understand the New Testament properly only if they understand the Old; and when they understand the New Testament, the Old will have more meaning. (Concerning the New Testament writers' use of Old Testament passages see QUOTATIONS.)

Sixty-six books make up the Bible. These were written over a period of perhaps 1400 years by a total of about forty writers. The writers were people of different nationalities, languages, occupations and temperaments, yet there is complete harmony within the Bible. Jesus considered the Bible of his time a unity and referred to it in the singular as 'the Scripture' (John 10:35). (Concerning the preparation of books and manuscripts in ancient times see MANUSCRIPTS; WRITING.)

Divisions of the Scriptures

Jews divided their Scriptures (our Old Testament) into three parts, which they called the Law, the Prophets and the Writings. Often they referred to the Writings as the Psalms, since Psalms was the largest, and possibly the first, book in the Writings (Luke 24:44). They often referred to the Scriptures in general simply as the Law (John 10:34; 1 Cor 14:21) or the Law and the Prophets (Matt 7:12; 22:40; Luke 16:16).

The Law consisted of the first five books of the Bible, commonly called the books of Moses (Mark 12:26; Acts 15:21; see PENTATEUCH). The Prophets consisted of the Former Prophets (Joshua, Judges, Samuel and Kings) and the Latter Prophets (Isaiah, Jeremiah, Ezekiel and the twelve so-called Minor Prophets) (see PROPHECY). The Writings consisted of Psalms, Job, Proverbs, Ruth, Song of Songs, Ecclesiastes, Lamentations, Esther, Daniel, Ezra, Nehemiah and Chronicles. This arrangement of books is indicated by Jesus' reference to the first and last martyrs mentioned in the Hebrew Bible (Matt 23:35; cf. Gen 4:8; 2 Chron 24:20-21). (For a book-by-book summary of the Bible's contents see BIBLE.)

Although there were no fixed divisions in the New Testament, the books may be conveniently grouped into three categories: the narrative books (the Four Gospels and the Acts of the Apostles), the letters (of Paul and of others), and the book of Revelation.

Names given to the books of the Bible are not part of the inspired writings, but have either established themselves by tradition or been given by translators. The names of some Old Testament books in the Christian Bible differ from those in the Hebrew Bible.

The order in which the books are arranged, whether in the Old Testament or the New, is simply the result of established practice and carries no divine authority. Also, the original writings were not divided into the chapters and verses that we are familiar with today. The chapter divisions were made in the thirteenth century AD, and the verse divisions in the sixteenth century.

SEA OF GALILEE

The Sea of Galilee is a freshwater lake in northern Palestine. It is approximately twenty kilometres long, twelve kilometres wide, and about two hundred metres below sea level. In Bible times it was known also as the Sea of Chinnereth (Num 34:11), the Lake of Gennesaret (Luke 5:1) and the Sea of Tiberias (John 6:1,16-25; 21:1). (For details see PALESTINE, sub-heading 'Upper Jordan and Sea of Galilee'.)

SECOND COMING

See JESUS CHRIST, sub-heading 'Christ's return and final triumph'. See also DAY OF THE LORD; ESCHATOLOGY; JUDGMENT; KINGDOM OF GOD; MILLENNIUM; RESURRECTION.

SEIR

Mount Seir was the chief mountain of the land of Edom. In common usage its name sometimes referred to the nation of Edom in general (Deut 2:1,4,12). (For details see EDOM.)

SELF-DISCIPLINE

Although Christians are not under the law, they are under grace (Rom 6:14). Although they are not slaves to sin, they are slaves to righteousness (Rom 6:17-18). Although they are free from the law, they are not free to do as they please; they must live rather to please God (Rom 7:4-6; Eph 5:10; Col 1:10). Therefore, they must exercise self-discipline, or self-control. This self-control is not opposed to control by the Holy Spirit. On the contrary it is one of the qualities that the Holy Spirit produces (Gal 5:22-23).

Christians must make every effort to develop self-discipline (1 Cor 9:25-27; 2 Peter 1:5-6), and this self-discipline applies to every area of their lives: thoughts (2 Cor 10:5), feelings (Lev 19:17-18; 1 Peter 2:11), speech (Ps 39:1; James 3:7-8), eating and drinking habits (Prov 23:2,20; Amos 6:4-6; Eph 5:18), sexual behaviour (1 Cor 7:9; 1 Thes 4:4-5) and in fact any situation in which they find themselves (1 Thes 5:22-23). Such personal discipline is essential in the lives of all Christians, regardless of status, sex or age (1 Tim 3:2,11; Titus 1:7-8; 2:2-6).

Self-discipline is necessary not only in avoiding what is wrong, but also in refraining from actions that in themselves may not be wrong at all. In certain circumstances Christians should deny themselves lawful freedoms out of consideration for others (Rom 14:15-16,20-22; 1 Cor 8:13; 10:23-24; see also DENY).

SEPTUAGINT

After the conquests of Alexander the Great in the fourth century BC, the Greek language spread throughout Alexander's empire and within a short time was the most commonly spoken language. In Alexandria in Egypt, the large Jewish population was almost entirely Greek-speaking, and for their sake the Hebrew Bible (our Old Testament) was translated into Greek. According to stories handed down by the Jews, the number of translators was about seventy. The translation was therefore called the Septuagint, meaning 'seventy' and abbreviated as LXX. The work was done some time during the third and second centuries BC. The quality of the translation varied, being good in some parts but poor in others.

Though the Septuagint was originally prepared for orthodox Jews of the pre-Christian era, the people who benefited most from it were the early Christians. In fact, the Septuagint's popularity with the Christians was one reason why it lost favour with the Jews. In New Testament times most of the Christians were Greek-speaking, even those of Jewish background, and the Septuagint provided them with a ready-made translation of the Old Testament in their own language. New Testament writers, in quoting from the Old Testament, usually used the Septuagint rather than translate from the Hebrew (see QUOTATIONS).

In matters concerning God and religion, the Septuagint was particularly helpful to preachers and writers of New Testament times. Greek religious words usually had meanings that related to pagan religious practices of the Greek world, and because of this the Septuagint translators chose their words carefully. Often they gave words new meaning or significance in the context of Hebrew Old Testament ideas.

This is important for present-day readers of the New Testament. In their consideration of teaching concerning God and Christian belief, they should understand Greek words in relation to the Hebrew words they represent, rather than in relation to the pagan ideas of the Greeks.

SERAPHIM

It seems that seraphim (plural of seraph) are angelic beings of one of the higher heavenly orders. They appear to be similar to cherubim and, like cherubim, are heavenly guardians who serve the Almighty. In the only biblical reference to them they have a special concern for holiness and morality (Isa 6:1-7; see CHERUBIM).

SERMON ON THE MOUNT

Matthew's Gospel is built around five main sermons or collections of teachings from Jesus. The first of these, Chapters 5-7, is known as the Sermon on the Mount, after the place where Jesus was teaching at the time (Matt 5:1). Although the section is a unified whole, many of the teachings within it occur in different settings in the other Gospels. It is likely, in view of Matthew's style of presentation, that the section contains more than the contents of a single sermon (see MATTHEW, GOSPEL OF). Jesus gave the teaching primarily to his disciples (Matt 5:1-2,13-14), though, as often happened, many others gathered to listen (Matt 7:28).

Ethics of the kingdom of God

Jesus' teaching set out for his followers the quality of life and behaviour that he required of those who entered his kingdom and came under his rule. Life in God's kingdom is characterized by humility, love, righteousness, mercy, sincerity, and dependence on God. Unlike life in human society in general, it has no place for pride, hatred, cruelty, aggression, hypocrisy and self-sufficiency (Matt 5:3-10,48; see KINGDOM OF GOD).

The Sermon on the Mount is not a new set of rules to replace the law of Moses. It does not lay down a legal code of ethics, but aims to work within people to produce a standard of behaviour that no law-code can produce, no matter how good it might be (Matt 5:17-18). The righteousness Jesus wants in his followers is more than outward conformity to certain laws (Matt 5:20). He wants a new attitude within – the principles of the law written on people's hearts. It is not enough, for instance, simply to refrain from murder; people must remove the spirit of hate and revenge from their hearts, for it is that spirit that produces murder (Matt 5:21-22; cf. Rom 8:4; Heb 8:10).

Teaching with authority

In the Sermon on the Mount, Jesus did not oppose or contradict the law of Moses. Rather he opposed the traditional interpretations and false applications taught by the Jewish teachers of the law (the scribes, or rabbis). Their concern for outward correctness failed to deal with inward attitudes (Matt 5:27-30).

Instead of being forgiving, the scribes used the law as an excuse for personal revenge. They took civil laws relating to penalties for crimes and applied them to personal relationships (Matt 5:38-42). They so twisted the meaning of the law that they could claim the law's authority for actions that were clearly contrary to the law (Matt 5:31-37). They even gave their own sayings equal authority with the law (Matt 5:43-47).

Jesus was opposed to this legalistic spirit. He was also opposed to the pride it produced through its concern for outward show (Matt 6:1-6,16-18). He wanted to change people in their hearts. He taught

his disciples how to pray (Matt 6:7-15; 7:7-12), how to have new attitudes of trust in God for all life's material needs (Matt 6:19-34), how to examine their attitudes (Matt 7:1-5) and how to be wise in deciding what is wholesome and what is not (Matt 7:6,15-23). Jesus' teaching, being from God, had an authority that was lacking in the traditional teaching of the scribes (Matt 7:28-29). But if people are to benefit from it, they must not only understand it but also act upon it (Matt 7:24-27).

SERVANT

Old and New Testaments alike use the one word 'servant' to translate a variety of words from the original languages. In many cases the word 'servant' is really 'slave'.

In English 'slave' and 'servant' suggest different classes of people, but this distinction is not so clear in the original languages. Often the words are used interchangeably. If there is a difference, it is usually one of suitability to context. 'Slave' may be used of a person in relation to his master, but 'servant' in relation to his work. The former may be in a context of submission to a superior (e.g. Matt 6:24; Rom 6:16-18; Eph 6:6-7; see SLAVE), the latter in the context of service for others (e.g. Matt 20:28: Luke 10:40; Rom 12:7; see MINISTER).

A special type of service

Christians are slaves of God and servants of God (1 Cor 4:1; 7:22-23). They are not to be ashamed of these titles, as if God has denied them ordinary human dignity or reduced them to some low and humiliating status. The Bible uses many pictures to describe the relationship between Christ and his people, and each picture illustrates only one aspect of a many-sided relationship.

Therefore, although Christians are sometimes called Christ's servants, other times they are called his friends and ambassadors. Service for him is a privilege (John 15:15,20; 2 Cor 5:20). Christ himself is an example of the type of servant a Christian should be (Luke 22:27; John 13:12-15; see SERVANT OF THE LORD).

Service for God can take many forms. It may consist of giving practical aid to those who are poor, hungry, or otherwise in need (Rom 15:25; 1 Tim 5:10; 2 Tim 1:18; Heb 6:10). Some people serve God through ministries of spreading the gospel and caring for churches (Acts 6:4; 20:24; 1 Cor 16:15; 2 Cor 3:6; Eph 3:7; 4:11-12; Col 4:17); others serve him by praying for those engaged in such works (Rom 15:30-31; 2 Cor 1:11; Phil 1:19). The title 'deacon', given to certain people who have various responsibilities in the church, means 'servant' (Phil 1:1; 1 Tim 3:8; see DEACON).

Motives and performance

Regardless of the special ministries entrusted to certain people, all Christians are in some sense God's servants. They have unlimited possibilities of service, and should consider that everything they do is a way of serving their Lord (Eph 6:5-8; Col 3:23). The service does not have to be in a religious setting. Christ sees everyday acts of kindness as service for him, even though the doers of those acts may not be aware of it (Matt 25:35-40). On the other hand, people may give an appearance of serving God, but if their chief concern is self-interest, they are not serving God at all (Matt 6:24).

To serve Christ means to serve others (Matt 25:35-40), and those who serve others receive God's rewards (Matt 20:25-28; 23:11-12). This does not mean that Christians serve God simply for what they can get in return. On the contrary they realize that whatever service they do is merely their duty (Luke 17:10). Yet God graciously promises to reward those who serve him faithfully (Matt 25:21; Luke 19:17; Heb 6:10; Rev 2:19,26; see REWARD).

SERVANT OF THE LORD

In a sense all God's people are servants of the Lord (Num 12:7; Ps 105:6; 1 Cor 4:1; Rev 22:3), but the Bible speaks of one particular figure who in a special sense is *the* servant of the Lord (Isa 42:1; 52:13). This particular 'servant of the Lord' is the subject of the present article. Concerning the more general usage of the expression see SERVANT.

Details about the servant of the Lord are found mainly in what are known as the four Servant Songs of Isaiah (Isa 42:1-4; 49:1-6; 50:4-9; 52:13-53:12). There is a threefold meaning to these songs.

Firstly, the nation Israel was chosen to be God's servant (Isa 41:8), but the nation as a whole was a failure (Isa 42:19). This leads to the second meaning, which is to the faithful minority within Israel. While the rest of the people rebelled against God, the believing remnant kept serving him loyally (Isa 49:4-6; see REMNANT). Even they, however, did not experience the full blessings that God intended for his people. The third and highest meaning of the servant applies to the Messiah, Jesus (Isa 53:12; Luke 22:37; Acts 3:13; 4:30; Phil 2:7).

Israel as a nation was Abraham's natural offspring (John 8:37; Rom 4:1; 11:1), the faithful remnant were his spiritual offspring (Rom 9:6-7; Gal 3:28-29), but the Messiah Jesus was the perfect offspring. In him the purposes of God for Israel reached their fulfilment (Gal 3:16).

Four Servant Songs

The first Servant Song outlines the ideal character of God's servant. Those ideals never became a reality for the nation Israel, and only to a limited extent did they characterize the faithful remnant. But they found their perfect expression in Jesus Christ (Isa 42:1-4; Matt 12:15-21).

God had a particular task for his servant, and the second Servant Song describes that task. God's servant was to take the light of his salvation to the Gentile nations. Again Israel as a whole failed, though some of the people were faithful (Isa 49:1-7; Acts 13:46-47). Jesus, by contrast, fulfilled the task perfectly, bringing salvation to Israel and to the Gentiles (Matt 1:21; Luke 2:32; Acts 26:23; Rom 15:8-12).

In the third Servant Song the emphasis is on the servant's patient endurance. This had some meaning in relation to Israel's experiences among hostile nations, and considerably more meaning in relation to the godly believers' experiences among their ungodly fellow Israelites. The full meaning is found only in the experiences of Jesus (Isa 50:4-9; Matt 26:67; 1 Peter 2:22-24).

The fourth Servant Song speaks of the servant's suffering and glory. God punished Israel for its sins by sending the nation into captivity in Babylon, but after the removal of sin he restored the nation to its land. Israel's sufferings at the hands of Babylon and its glory in the rebuilt Jerusalem were a picture of the sufferings of the Messiah and the glory that followed (Isa 52:13-15; Acts 2:23-24,36; Phil 2:8-11; 1 Peter 1:18-21).

Israel, God's unfaithful servant, suffered the judgment that its sin deserved; Jesus, the faithful servant, bore a judgment that he did not deserve. The godly remnant within Israel suffered because of the sins of others, and so did Jesus; but, more than that, Jesus suffered to *take away* the sins of others (Isa 53:4-6; Matt 8:17; 20:28; 1 Peter 2:22-25). He bore shame and injustice at the hands of wicked men (Isa 53:3,7-8; Matt 27:26-31; Acts 8:32-35), though he did at least receive a decent burial (Isa 53:9; Matt 27:57-60).

Yet, through all Jesus' experiences, God was bringing his purposes to fulfilment. Jesus' glorious resurrection showed God's complete satisfaction with his Son's atoning work. It also marked the beginning of a new age in which God's salvation goes to people throughout the world (Isa 53:10-12; Mark 10:45; Luke 24:46-47; Acts 2:23-24; 28:28; Rom 8:32-34; Rev 5:9-10).

SEVEN

One of the obvious features of the Bible is the frequent occurrence of the number 'seven'. The number seems to have been used to indicate one complete unit – fulness, completion, perfection (e.g. Gen 2:2).

This unit of seven features prominently in the organization of Israel's religious and community life. One day in seven was a holy day of rest, and this weekly unit provided the framework for various religious festivals (Exod 20:8-11; Lev 23:5-6,15,34; see SABBATH). The details of many of Israel's rituals were based on a unit of seven (Lev 4:6; 8:33; 13:4; 14:7-8,51; 23:18). Every seventh year was a year of rest for the land and release for debtors (Lev 25:1-4; Deut 15:1-2; see SABBATICAL YEAR). The symbolic 'seven' gave to ordinary events a special religious significance (Josh 6:4).

The expression 'seven times' seems to have been used as a figure of speech to indicate fulness or finality (Gen 4:15,24, Lev 26:18,21; 1 Kings 18:43-44; 2 Kings 5:10; Ps 12:6; 119:164; Isa 30:26; Dan 3:19; Matt 18:21-22; cf. Luke 8:2; 11:26; 20:29). A similar symbolic usage of the number 'seven' is common in the book of Revelation (Rev 1:20; 4:5; 5:1,6; 8:2; 10:3; 12:3; 13:1; 15:1).

SHALLUM

Two kings mentioned in the biblical record had the name Shallum, and each reigned for only a very short time. Shallum of Israel gained the throne through murdering the previous king, but one month later he himself was murdered (in 752 BC; 2 Kings 15:10,13-14). Shallum of Judah (who was also known as Jehoahaz) reigned only three months before Pharaoh Necho deposed him and took him captive to Egypt (in 609 BC; 2 Kings 23:30-34; Jer 22:11-12; see JEHOAHAZ). Several Old Testament characters of lesser importance also had the name Shallum.

SHARON

The thinly populated Plain of Sharon was part of Palestine's coastal plain south of Mt Carmel. Parts of it were marshland, though other parts contained good pastures and forests (1 Chron 5:16; 27:29; Isa 35:2; see PALESTINE). Its wildflowers were typical of the Palestinian plains (Song of Songs 2:1).

SHEBA

In south-western Arabia was the land known in Bible times as Sheba. It was located in the region of present-day Yemen and was occupied by a tribal group known as the Sabeans. Like people of other Arab tribal groups, those of Sheba were merchants and traders. They travelled widely throughout the East, dealing in gold, precious stones, cloth, spices and other merchandise (1 Kings 10:1-2; Ps 72:15; Isa 60:6; Jer 6:20; Ezek 27:22). They even engaged in slave trade (Joel 3:8) and, like other Arab nomads, they raided farms and villages (Job 1:15). When their queen on one occasion visited Israel's king Solomon, the two monarchs took the opportunity to have some useful trade exchanges (1 Kings 10:10,13). (Some African legends have connected this queen with Ethiopia.)

Sheba was also the name of a number of individuals mentioned in the Old Testament. The best known of these was the Benjaminite who tried unsuccessfully to lead the northern tribes to break away from the rule of David (2 Sam 20:1-22).

SHECHEM

The ancient town of Shechem lay in the valley between Mt Gerizim and Mt Ebal in central Canaan (Deut 27:12-13; Judg 9:7). It was the first recorded camping place of Abraham when he came to Canaan from Haran (Gen 12:4-6). (For maps of the region see PALESTINE.)

Abraham's grandson, Jacob, upon returning to Canaan from Paddan-aram, bought land in Shechem and settled there with his family and flocks (Gen 33:18-19). When a conflict developed with some of the local inhabitants, Jacob's sons massacred the men of Shechem and plundered the town (Gen 34:1-31). Jacob and his family then moved else-where, though at times they still pastured their flocks near Shechem (Gen 35:1-4; 37:12). Joseph's bones were later buried at Shechem in a field that Jacob had given to Joseph (Gen 48:22; Josh 24:32; John 4:5-6).

After the conquest of Canaan, the people of Israel gathered at Shechem to confirm the covenant. The blessings of the covenant were announced from Mt Gerizim on one side of the town, and the curses from Mt Ebal on the other. Just before Joshua's death, the leaders of Israel gathered at Shechem once more and declared their loyalty to the covenant (Deut 27:1-14; Josh 8:30-35; 24:1-28).

In the division of Canaan among the Israelites, Shechem fell within the tribal allotment of Ephraim, but was set apart for the Levites. It was one of the three cities of refuge west of Jordan (Josh 20:2,7; 21:20-21; see CITY OF REFUGE).

In the time of the judges, Abimelech tried to establish a kingdom in Shechem but his success was shortlived (Judg 9:1-6,16-57). In the time of the

Shechem, in the valley between Mt Gerizim and Mt Ebal

monarchy, after the death of Solomon, Rehoboam went to Shechem to be crowned king, no doubt hoping this would help him win the allegiance of the northern tribes. However, the northerners broke away and established their own kingdom, with its capital initially at Shechem (1 Kings 12:1,25). Within a few years they shifted the capital to Tirzah, and later again to Samaria (1 Kings 15:33; 16:8,24,29). Although Shechem lost its importance, it continued to exist, even after the Assyrians had destroyed the northern kingdom and taken most of the people into captivity (Jer 41:5).

When Assyria brought people from elsewhere to live in the deserted northern kingdom, these immigrants intermarried with the Israelites left in the land. In due course this produced a people of mixed blood and mixed religion who became known as the Samaritans. Shechem became the chief city of the Samaritans, and Mt Gerizim became to them a sacred mountain. There they built their temple, worshipped, and held religious festivals. The village of Sychar was nearby (John 4:5-6,20). (See SAMARIA, SAMARITANS.)

SHEEP

From earliest times people have kept sheep, whether for their meat or for their wool (Gen 4:2). In the dry semi-desert regions around Palestine, many of the Arabs and other tribal people moved with their flocks from place to place, looking for pastures and water (Gen 26:12-22; Exod 3:1; Isa 13:20). In other lands, where there was a better supply of grass and water, people who settled down permanently in one

area kept sheep as part of their farming activity. After settling down in Canaan, the Israelites, on the whole, belonged to this latter category (Deut 7:13; 1 Sam 17:15; 25:2).

Israelites kept sheep mainly for their wool, which they used to make clothing (Gen 38:13; Lev 13:47-48; Prov 27:26). Apart from those ceremonial sacrifices where worshippers ate the meat of the sheep in a ritual meal, Israelites killed sheep for meat only on special occasions (Lev 7:15; Deut 12:21; 1 Sam 25:18; Amos 6:4; see also LAMB).

A well known characteristic of sheep was that they were easily led astray and soon became lost. Because of this, people who were easily led astray were sometimes likened to sheep (Isa 53:6; Matt 10:6; 18:12). Sheep needed a shepherd to protect and lead them, and in the same way people need God to care for them and give them the right leadership in life (Num 27:17; Matt 10:16; John 10:11,27; 21:15-17; 1 Peter 5:1-4; see SHEPHERD).

SHEKEL

The shekel was the basic weight in use among Israelites of Bible times. It was equal to about sixteen grams, and was used to weigh all sorts of things (1 Sam 17:5,7; 2 Sam 14:26; Ezek 4:10). One of its most frequent uses was in weighing money. Since most money was weighed in silver, the shekel of silver became also a common monetary unit (Gen 23:16; Exod 21:32; 30:13; 2 Sam 24:24). (See also COINS; WEIGHTS.)

SHEKINAH

The Hebrew word transliterated 'Shekinah' refers to the glory of God that symbolizes his presence. The word is not found in the Old Testament, but was introduced into the Jewish religious vocabulary by rabbis of a later era.

These rabbis spoke of the Shekinah in order to encourage Israelites to have a higher idea of God. They wanted people to think of him as a dazzling light or a shining presence, rather than as a human-like figure with physical features such as hands, arms, eyes, mouth and the like. The Shekinah became particularly associated with God's symbolic presence in the tabernacle and later the temple (Exod 40:34-35; 1 Kings 8:11; Ezek 44:4). It also referred to other displays of God's glory or to the reality of his presence among his people (Num 14:10,22; Isa 60:1-2; see also GLORY).

SHEOL

When the Old Testament writers spoke about the afterlife, they referred to it by using the Hebrew word *sheol* (translated into the Greek as *hades*). Some early versions of the English Bible translated *sheol* and *hades* as 'hell', which is unfortunate, for that gives the wrong idea. Hell, as a place of fiery punishment, is the equivalent of the word *gehenna*. *Sheol* (or *hades*), by contrast, is simply the place or state of the dead. More recent English versions either transliterate the words as the proper nouns 'sheol' and 'hades', or translate them by such expressions as 'the world of the dead', 'the grave' and 'the pit'.

The Old Testament writers expressed their view of the afterlife in broad general terms. They saw that all people eventually die and go to sheol, whether they be rich or poor, good or bad (Job 3:13-19; Ps 88:1-5; Isa 38:18; Ezek 31:17; 32:18-32; cf. Luke 16:19-31). In fact, the writers often used 'sheol' simply as another word for 'death' (Gen 42:38; Ps 18:5; 86:13; 116:3; cf. Matt 16:18). But by speaking of sheol, they made it clear that death does not end human existence. They may have had very little knowledge concerning the state of the person in the afterlife, but they did not doubt that the person continued to exist.

People saw death as an enemy (Ps 6:5; 56:13; Eccles 8:8; cf. Rom 6:23; 1 Cor 15:26; Rev 6:8). The mysterious, silent, shadowy existence that lay beyond it was not something they looked forward to (Job 10:21-22; 17:13-16; Ps 94:17; 115:17; Isa 14:9-11; Ezek 26:19-20). The hope of the Old Testament believers was that God would not desert them in sheol, but would bring them into a new and joyful experience of life in the presence of God (Job 19:26; Ps 16:10-11; 49:15; 73:24; cf. Acts 2:27,31). For the wicked, however, sheol would bring nothing but terror (Deut 32:22; Job 31:11-12; Ps 55:15; Isa 14:19-20; Ezek 32:18-32).

During the latter part of the Old Testament era, believers became more firmly convinced that beyond death lay the resurrection (Dan 12:1-2). This confidence grew into bold assurance through the death and resurrection of Jesus Christ. Once Christ had conquered death and hades (sheol), man had no need to fear them any longer. God had now clearly shown immortal life to be a certainty (Matt 16:18; 2 Tim 1:10; Heb 2:14-15; Rev 1:18).

Since believers now shared Christ's conquest, they naturally looked upon those who were not believers as still under the power of death. They therefore associated the afterlife of the wicked dead with the unwelcome aspects of hades (Matt 11:23; 1 Pet 3:19-20; Rev 20:13). In relation to themselves, however, believers no longer thought of the afterlife as a gloomy existence in sheol or hades, but as a joyful experience of life with Christ in paradise (Luke 23:42; 2 Cor 5:8; Phil 1:23; see HEAVEN; PARADISE).

SHEPHELAH

'Shephelah' is a Hebrew word used to describe the low hill country between the coastal plain and the central mountains of Palestine. It was a fertile region, suitable for growing fruit trees and raising sheep and cattle (Josh 10:40; Judg 1:9; 2 Chron 9:27; 26:10; Jer 17:26; 32:44). For details see PALESTINE, sub-heading 'Shephelah'.

SHEPHERD

The occupation of shepherd was one of mankind's earliest occupations (Gen 4:2). In the dry semi-desert countries of the Bible story, shepherds lived a hard tough life, battling against heat, drought and wild animals (Gen 31:38-40; Amos 3:12). It is therefore not surprising that 'shepherd' became a word symbol for a leader of God's people. The emphasis is not only on care and leadership, but also on the ability to endure hardship. The shepherd must be prepared to battle against all opponents who threaten the welfare of those in his care (John 10:1,10-12; Acts 20:28-29).

Life of a shepherd

Shepherds were a common sight in Palestine and neighbouring countries. They lived in tents and moved around from place to place with their flocks in search of grass and water (Exod 3:1; Deut 8:15; Isa 13:20; see also SHEEP). Often the only water available was at wells that people had dug. These wells were frequently the cause of disputes (Gen 26:12-32).

After the Israelites took possession of Canaan, the shepherds among them settled down more or less permanently with their flocks. Yet they still faced the problem of finding good pastures and water, and still had to meet attacks by wild animals (1 Sam 17:34; Ps 23:2,4-5; Matt 10:16). Additional dangers came from thieves who stole sheep by night, and desert people who raided in groups (Gen 31:39; Job 1:14-15; 2 Chron 21:16-17; John 10:10). The shepherd's only weapons were a sling and a stick, though he may have used trained dogs to help him in his work (1 Sam 17:40,49; Job 30:1; Ps 23:4; Zech 11:7,10).

Sheep had to be protected and watched by shepherds constantly, otherwise they would wander away and be lost. If sheep became lost, the shepherd sometimes had to risk his life in searching for them and rescuing them (Ezek 34:8,12; Matt 18:12). The

Shepherd

shepherd was responsible to pay the owner the cost of any sheep lost while in his care, unless he could satisfy the owner that he was not to blame for the loss (Gen 31:39; Exod 22:10-13).

At night the shepherd usually kept his sheep in a walled enclosure called a fold, as an added protection against dangers (Num 32:36; Micah 2:12; Hab 3:17; Luke 2:8; John 10:1). He counted the sheep as they went in at night, to make sure that none was missing; then, in the morning, he led them out into the fields (Jer 33:13; Ezek 20:37; John 10:3,27; 17:12).

Leaders of God's people

The Old Testament often refers to the leaders of Israel as shepherds, and to the people as the flock (Num 27:17; Isa 63:11). Many of Israel's leaders were bad shepherds, and because of them the nation crumbled (Isa 56:11; Jer 50:6; Ezek 34:2-6; Zech 11:15-17).

In the New Testament also leaders of God's people are referred to as shepherds of the flock. As elders of a church they have the responsibility to lead it, feeding it with spiritual food and protecting it from spiritual harm (John 21:15-17; Acts 20:28-29; 1 Peter 5:1-3; see ELDER; PASTOR).

The true shepherd, however, is always God (Gen 49:24; Ps 23:1; Isa 40:11). This is seen clearly in the illustration Jesus used to picture himself as the good shepherd. He was so concerned for the sheep that he died for them (John 10:1-29; Heb 13:20; 1 Peter 2:25; 5:4; cf. Ezek 34:23-24).

SHILOH

One of the main routes from Egypt to northern Palestine was the road that passed along the top of the central hill country through the towns of Beersheba, Hebron, Jerusalem, Bethel, Shiloh and Shechem (Judg 21:19). (For map see PALESTINE.) Shiloh's convenient location on this road may have been one reason why it was Israel's central place of worship for most of the period of the judges. There that the nation's leaders set up the tabernacle and the people held religious festivals (Josh 18:1,8-10; 19:51; 22:9,12; Judg 18:31; 21:19-21; 1 Sam 1:3,9; 3:21; 4:3).

Some time later, because of the sins of the people, God allowed invaders to destroy Shiloh (Ps 78:60; Jer 7:12-14). This may have occurred during the period of Philistine oppression that led to the establishment of Israel's monarchy (1 Sam 4:2; 8:20). In the early days of the monarchy the tabernacle was set up at Nob, a town close to Jerusalem (1 Sam 21:1-6; 22:18-19). Later, Shiloh was partly rebuilt, but never again was the tabernacle set up there (1 Kings 14:4).

SHINAR

Shinar was an ancient name for the land of Babylon. Its chief towns were Babel, Erech and Accad, and its most famous warrior was Nimrod (Gen 10:9-10; 11:1-9; 14:1; Isa 11:11; Dan 1:2). (For details see BABEL; BABYLON.)

SHIP

Israelites were not seafaring people, partly because the Mediterranean coast south of Mt Carmel had shallow waters and sandy shores, with no good sites for harbours. North of Mt Carmel, however, there were good harbours at Tyre and Sidon. This was one reason why the Phoenicians became a great seafaring nation in Old Testament times (Ezek 27:2,25; 28:2; see PHOENICIA).

In the time of the Israelite monarchy, King Hiram of Phoenicia and King Solomon of Israel established a fleet of ships to operate between the Red Sea port of Ezion-geber and India. Because of the Israelites' lack of seafaring experience, Solomon had to rely on the Phoenician seamen to guide and teach his men. The ships used on this route were known as 'ships of Tarshish'. This was a technical name for a certain type of ocean-going cargo ship, not an indication of the port to which or from which a ship was sailing (1 Kings 9:26-28; 10:11,22; see TARSHISH).

'Ships of Tarshish', like other large ships, may have been driven by oars or by sails (Isa 33:21,23; Ezek 27:6-8,26,29). River boats, which were much smaller, may have been made of papyrus reeds (Isa 18:1-2).

God's judgment on the greedy commercial giant Phoenicia (Tyre) was pictured by the prophet Ezekiel as the sinking of a great ship. The ship had

Phoenician ship

been beautifully made of the best materials from all parts of the trading world. Its planks, masts, oars and decking were made of the best timbers, its sails of the finest linen, and its colours of the most expensive dyes. The oarsmen, sailors and craftsmen who made up its crew were highly skilled men from many countries. Tyre's trade, however, became so great that the ship became overloaded. When caught in a storm at sea, it sank. All its cargo was lost and all the crew drowned (Ezek 27:1-9,25-27; 28:2-8; cf. Rev 18:19).

In New Testament times huge grain ships sailed from Alexandria in Egypt to Greece and Rome (Acts 27:6; 28:11). They were capable of carrying large cargoes and several hundred people (Acts 27:18,37). Being sailing ships, they had to stay in port during winter months, when severe storms were likely to wreck them (Acts 27:9-20). During the stormy season the ship's crew wrapped strong ropes or metal bands around the hulls of the ships to hold their timbers together (Acts 27:17).

The smaller boats that sailed on the Lake of Galilee were used mainly for fishing or carrying passengers (Matt 4:21-22; 8:23-27; 9:1; Luke 5:2-7; John 6:22-23; 21:3). They were driven either by sails

or by oars, depending on the weather conditions (Mark 6:48; John 6:19).

SHUR

Shur was a desert region in the north of the Sinai Peninsular. It was bounded by Egypt on the west (the border being along the line of the present-day Suez Canal), and the Negeb on the east (the border being along the Brook of Egypt) (Gen 20:1; Exod 15:22; 1 Sam 15:7; 27:8). The main inland route from Egypt to Jerusalem passed through the Wilderness of Shur and the Judean towns of Beersheba and Hebron (Gen 13:1,18; 16:7; 21:14; 46:5). (For further details see PALESTINE, sub-heading 'Negeb'.)

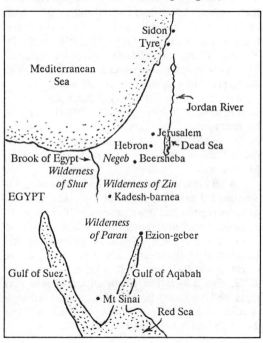

SIDON

The Mediterranean seaports of Tyre and Sidon were the two most important towns of Phoenicia. The Bible frequently mentions the two towns together as a way of referring to Phoenicia in general (Ezra 3:7; Isa 23:1,4; Zech 9:2; Mark 7:24). Sometimes mention of only one of the towns is sufficient. For example, Tyre, being the larger and more prosperous port, may have symbolized the greed and arrogance that Phoenicia as a whole developed because of its international shipping activity (Isa 23:1,8,17; Ezek 27:3,25; 28:5,9,16). In the same way Sidon, being a dominant religious centre, fittingly symbolized the corrupt Phoenician religion that at times troubled Israel (Judg 10:6; 1 Kings 16:31-33). (For details of Sidon's commerce, religion and history see PHOENICIA.)

SIGNS

In the Bible mighty works, miracles, wonders and signs are often linked together. This is because God's miracles are not merely extraordinary events, but extraordinary events with a meaning. They reveal something of the power and purposes of God (Exod 7:3; Deut 4:34; 7:19; Josh 24:17; John 2:11; Acts 2:22,43; Heb 2:4).

Jesus' miracles of raising the dead, healing the sick and casting out demons were clear evidence that the kingdom of God had come (Matt 11:2-6; 12:28; see KINGDOM OF GOD), and that Jesus was the Messiah, the Son of God (John 2:11; 4:54; 20:30-31). Yet many of the Jews refused to accept the evidence. They wanted Jesus to perform some special sign as added proof that he was the Messiah who had come from God. This was something Jesus consistently refused to do. The only sign to be given them would be the sign of Jesus' resurrection, by which the Father would show clearly that Jesus was his Son (Matt 12:38-40; 16:1-4; John 2:18-25; see MESSIAH; MIRACLES).

After Jesus' resurrection and ascension, his apostles did the same sorts of signs and miracles as Jesus himself had done previously. The power of Jesus now worked through them, enabling them to continue the work of Jesus by proclaiming the kingdom of God and establishing his church in the world (Acts 2:43; 3:6; 4:30; 5:12; 8:12-13; 2 Cor 12:12; Heb 2:3-4). The enemy of Christ also uses signs and wonders, but he does so in order to deceive people and lead them to destruction (Matt 24:24; 2 Thess 2:9-11; Rev 13:11-14).

SILAS

Among the more open-minded Jewish Christians in the Jerusalem church was Silas, sometimes called Silvanus. Besides being Jewish, he had the privileged status of Roman citizenship (Acts 15:22; 16:37). He was present at the conference in Jerusalem that discussed the problems created by Jewish legalists among the Gentile churches. When the Jerusalem leaders decided to send representatives to reassure the Gentile churches, Silas was one of the two they chose (Acts 15:22-27). He was a preacher whose messages strengthened the hearers (Acts 15:32).

Silas must have impressed Paul with his conduct at the conference in Jerusalem. As a result Paul chose him as his fellow worker for a missionary tour to the recently planted Gentile churches and beyond (Acts 15:40). He was with Paul through dangerous experiences in Philippi, Thessalonica, Berea and Corinth (Acts 16:19-17:15; 18:5-11), and Paul often spoke warmly of him as his fellow worker (2 Cor 1:19; 1 Thess 1:1; 2 Thess 1:1).

After his association with Paul, Silas worked closely with Peter. He visited Rome with Peter, and played a part in the writing of 1 Peter, a letter that Peter sent to the churches of northern Asia Minor (1 Peter 1:1; 5:12-13; see PETER, LETTERS OF).

SIMEON

Several people named Simeon feature in the biblical record. Historically, the most important was Simeon the son of Jacob, for he was father of the tribe of Simeon. Two New Testament men named Simeon are also significant.

In the Old Testament

Simeon was the second eldest of Jacob's twelve sons (Gen 35:22-23). He and the next son, Levi, were responsible for the ruthless massacre of the men of Shechem, an incident that Jacob deeply regretted (Gen 34:25,30). When Jacob blessed his sons before his death, he recalled the violence of Simeon and Levi, and prophesied that their descendants would be scattered in Israel (Gen 49:5-7).

When Canaan was divided among the twelve tribes, Simeon did not receive an independent tribal area of its own. It received part of the area of Judah (since Judah's area was too large for it) in the south of Canaan. The result was that Simeon soon lost its separate tribal identity and became part of the more powerful Judah (Josh 19:1,9; Judg 1:3,17). Towns belonging to Simeon were counted as belonging to Judah (Josh 19:1-5; cf. 15:21-31). Though absorbed by Judah, the Simeonites continued to maintain their own genealogical records (1 Chron 4:24,33; 12:24-25).

In the New Testament

At the time of Jesus' birth, only a few Jews had a true understanding of the sort of Saviour that the Messiah would be. One of these was an old man named Simeon. When he saw Mary presenting her baby to God in the temple, he praised God that the great Saviour had come (Luke 2:22-32). He saw that as people accepted or rejected Jesus, they would show the true condition of their hearts and so find either salvation or condemnation. He also warned Mary that sorrow lay ahead for her because of what people would do to her son (Luke 2:33-35).

The other Simeon mentioned in the New Testament was a prophet and teacher in the church at Antioch in Syria (Acts 13:1). His nickname 'Niger' (meaning 'black') suggests that he was dark skinned. Some have thought he might have been the man elsewhere called Simon of Cyrene, a place in North Africa (Mark 15:21). (See also SIMON.)

SIMON

The name 'Simon' in the New Testament is the equivalent of 'Simeon' in the Old Testament (see SIMEON). Two of Jesus' disciples were named Simon. The first was better known as Peter (Matt 10:2; see PETER). The other was known either by an Aramaic word transliterated 'Cananaean' or by the equivalent Greek word transliterated 'Zealot' (Matt 10:4; Luke 6:15; Acts 1:13). The name may have indicated his enthusiastic nature, or it may have referred to his association with the party of anti-Rome Jews known as the Zealots, or Patriots (see ZEALOT).

Five other people named Simon are mentioned in the Gospels. The first was a younger brother of Jesus (Matt 13:55). The second was a Pharisee who invited Jesus to his home but received Jesus' rebuke for his self-righteousness (Luke 7:36-50). The third was the owner of a house where a woman anointed Jesus just before his death (Matt 26:6). (For the suggestion that this man was the father or husband of Martha see MARTHA.) The fourth was a man from Cyrene in Africa who helped carry Jesus' cross to the crucifixion site (Mark 15:21). (He is possibly the person called Simeon in Acts 13:1.) The fifth was the father of Judas Iscariot (John 13:2,26).

Two more people named Simon feature in the book of Acts. One was a sorcerer in Samaria who believed Philip's preaching and was baptized. But he was still a sorcerer at heart, and thought that by paying the right amount of money, he could receive the Holy Spirit's power and so perform wonders. He was terrified when Peter announced a horrible judgment upon him, and asked Peter to pray on his behalf for God's mercy (Acts 8:9-24).

The other Simon was a tanner in Joppa, on the Mediterranean coast. Peter on one occasion stayed in Simon's house, and while there he had a vision that prepared him to visit Cornelius and other Gentiles in Caesarea (Acts 9:43; 10:1-23).

SIN

The Bible refers to sin by a variety of Hebrew and Greek words. This is partly because sin may appear in many forms, from deliberate wrongdoing and moral evil to accidental failure through weakness, laziness or ignorance (Exod 32:30; Prov 28:13; Matt 5:22,28; Rom 1:29-32; James 4:17). But the common characteristic of all sin is that it is against God (Ps 51:4; Rom 8:7). It is the breaking of God's law, that law being the expression of the perfection that God's absolute holiness demands (Isa 1:2; 1 John 3:4). It is the 'missing of the mark', that 'mark' being the perfect standard of the divine will (Deut 9:18; Rom 3:23). It is unbelief, for it rejects the truth God has revealed (Deut 9:23; Ps 78:21-22; John 3:18-19; 8:24; 16:9). It is ungodliness, and it makes a person guilty before God (Ps 1:5-6; Rom 1:18; James 2:10).

Origin of sin

From the activity of Satan in the Garden of Eden, it is clear that sin was present in the universe before Adam and Eve sinned. But the Bible does not record how evil originated. What it records is how evil entered the human race (see EVIL).

Because man was made in the image of God, the highest part of man's nature can be satisfied only by God. Man cannot be independent of God, just as the image of the moon on the water cannot exist independently of the moon (Gen 1:26-28; see MAN). Therefore, when God gave the created world to man, he placed a limit; for complete independence would not be consistent with man's status as being in God's image (Gen 2:15-17).

Man, however, went beyond the limit God set and fell into sin. Because of his ability to know God, he was tempted to put himself in the place of God. He wanted to rule his life independently of God and be the final judge of what was good and what was evil (Gen 3:1-6). Pride was at the centre of man's sin (Rom 1:21-23; 1 John 2:16; cf. Isa 10:15; 14:13-14; Obad 3a; see PRIDE).

Sin entered the life of man because man firstly doubted God, then ceased to trust him completely, and finally was drawn away by the desire to be his own master (James 1:14; cf. Ezek 28:2,6; John 16:9). Human sin originated in the heart of man; the act of disobedience was the natural outcome (Prov 4:23; Jer 17:9; Mark 7:21-23).

Above all, sin was against God — the rejection of his authority, wisdom and love. It was rebellion against God's revealed will (Gen 3:17; Rom 1:25; 1 John 3:4). And the more clearly God's will was revealed, the more clearly it showed man's sinfulness (Rom 3:20; 5:20; cf. John 15:22-24).

Results of sin

As a result of his sin, man fell under the judgment of God and came into a state of conflict with the natural world (Gen 3:17-19; Matt 24:39), with his fellow man (Gen 3:12-13; 1 John 3:12), with himself (Gen 3:7,11-13; Rom 7:15,19) and with God (Gen 3:8-10,22-24; Rom 3:10-18). The real penalty of sin, however, so far as man was concerned, was death (Gen 2:17; 3:19,22-24; Rom 6:23). This involves not only physical death but also spiritual death. It means separation from God, who is the source of spiritual life (John 3:3,7; Rom 6:16; 7:5,13; 1 Cor 15:56; Eph 2:1-5; see DEATH).

Ever since Adam's sin, the story of man is one of his running from God, loving himself instead of God, and doing his will instead of God's (Rom 1:19-23). The more man rejects God, the more he confirms his own stubbornness and hardness of heart (Matt 11:20-24; 13:12-13; Rom 1:28-32; Eph 4:18). Sin has placed man in the hopeless position of being separated from God and unable to bring himself back to God (Isa 59:2; Rom 3:19-20; Gal 3:10). God, however, has not left man in this helpless condition, but through the one obedient man, Jesus Christ, has reversed the effects of Adam's sin (Rom 5:6,8,15,18).

All sinned in Adam ('Original sin')

In Romans 5:12-21 the whole of mankind is viewed as having existed originally in Adam, and therefore as having sinned originally in Adam (Rom 5:12; cf. Acts 17:26). Adam *is* mankind; but because of his sin he is mankind separated from God and under his condemnation.

Because of Adam's sin (his 'one act of disobedience') the penalty of sin, death, passes on to all mankind; but because of Christ's death on the cross (his 'one act of obedience') the free gift of God, life, is available to all mankind. Adam, by his sin, brings condemnation; Christ, by his death, brings justification (Rom 5:17-20; 6:23; 1 Cor 6:9-11). If 'condemn' means 'declare guilty', 'justify' means 'declare righteous'; and this is what God, in his immeasurable grace, has done for the sinner who turns in faith to Jesus Christ (Rom 5:16; 8:33; see JUSTIFICATION).

Just as Adam is the representative head of man as sinful and separated from God, so Jesus Christ is the representative head of man as declared righteous and brought back to God. All who die, die because of their union with Adam; all who are made alive, are made alive because of their union with Christ (Rom 5:16; 1 Cor 15:22). Christ bears sin's penalty on behalf of sinful man, but more than that he brings repentant sinners into a right relationship with a just and holy God (Rom 4:24-25; 5:8; 2 Cor 5:21; Gal 3:10-13; Phil 3:9).

Human nature is corrupt ('Total depravity')

In addition to being sinners because of their union with Adam, people are sinners because of what they themselves do. They are born with a sinful nature inherited from Adam, and the fruits of this sinful nature are sinful thoughts and actions (Ps 51:5; John 3:6; Eph 4:17-18).

People do not need to be taught to do wrong; they do it naturally, from birth. Sinful words and deeds are only the outward signs of a much deeper evil — a sinful heart, mind and will (Prov 4:23; Jer 17:9; Mark 7:21-23; Gal 5:19-21; Eph 2:3). Every part of man is affected by this sinful nature. The corruption is total (Gen 6:5; 8:21; Isa 64:6; Rom 3:13-18; 7:18,21,23) and it affects all people (Rom 3:9-12,23; 1 John 1:8,10).

Total depravity means not that the whole of humanity is equally sinful, but that the whole of man's nature is affected by sin. All people are sinners, but not all show their sinful condition equally. The strong influences of conscience, will-power, civil laws and social customs may stop people from doing all that their hearts are capable of, and may even cause them to do good (Luke 6:33; 11:13; Rom 2:14-15; 13:3). But in spite of the good that people may do, human nature is still directed by sin. It has a natural tendency to rebel against God's law (Rom 7:11-13; 8:7-8; Gal 5:17-21; Col 2:23;). (See also FLESH.)

Man's hopeless position apart from God

Since human nature is in such a sinful condition, man is unable to make himself into something that is pleasing to God (Isa 64:6; Rom 8:7-8). The disease of sin has affected all that he is (his nature) and all that he does (his deeds). Every person is a sinner by nature and a sinner in practice (Ps 130:3; Rom 3:23; 1 John 1:8,10).

Man's position is hopeless. His sin has cut him off from God, and there is no way he can bring himself back to God (Isa 59:2; Hab 1:13; Col 1:21). He is a slave to sin and cannot free himself (John 8:34; Rom 7:21-23). He is under God's condemnation, and has no way of saving himself (Rom 3:19-20). He is the subject of the wrath of God and cannot avoid it (Rom 1:18). (See also JUDGMENT; PROPITIATION.)

This complete hopelessness may be summarized under the word 'dead'. Man is dead in his sin and unable to make himself alive. Yet God in his grace gives him new life, so that he can be spiritually 'born again' (John 3:3-8; Eph 2:1; see REGENERATION). This is entirely the work of God. It is made possible through the death of Jesus Christ, and is effectual in the lives of all those who in faith turn from their sin to God (John 1:13,29; 6:44-45; Acts 3:19; Rom 3:24-25; Eph 2:8-9). (See also ATONEMENT; RECONCILIATION; REDEMPTION.)

Having been forgiven their sin and freed from its power, believers then show it to be true by the way they live (Rom 6:1,14,18; Gal 5:1). Because of the continued presence of the old sinful nature (the flesh) they will not be sinless, but neither will they sin habitually (Rom 6:6-13). They can expect victory over sin, and even when they fail they can be assured that genuine confession brings God's gracious forgiveness (Matt 6:12-15; 1 John 1:6-10; 2:1-2; 3:10). (See also CONFESSION; FORGIVENESS; SANCTIFICATION.)

SINAI

The Sinai Peninsular is the dry region that lies south of Palestine between the two northern arms of the Red Sea. Within it are the semi-desert regions known as the Wilderness of Shur in the north and the Wilderness of Paran in the north-east. (For map see SHUR.)

In the biblical record the Sinai region's chief importance is as the location of the mountain in the south known as Horeb, or Mount Sinai. This was the place where God first met Moses and where he later established his covenant with the travelling Israelites (Exod 3:1,12; Acts 7:30). Through that covenant God formally made them his people and gave them this law (Exod 19:1-25; 24:16; 34:1-4,29; Lev 7:37-38; 27:34; Deut 1:6,19; 5:1-2; 1 Kings 8:9; Acts 7:38).

For about one year the people of Israel camped at Mt Sinai, organizing themselves for the new life that lay ahead in Canaan (Exod 19:1; Num 10:11). But because of their disobedience, they took about forty years to reach Canaan. They spent much of this time in the wilderness regions of the Sinai Peninsular, where the older generation passed away and a new generation grew up. It was this new generation that entered Canaan (Num 1:19; 10:12; 14:31-34; 26:63-65).

Several hundred years later, when the prophet Elijah felt that God's covenant people were a total failure, God brought him to Mt Sinai to reassure him. Though God would punish Israel, he would preserve the faithful minority and through them fulfil his covenant promises (1 Kings 19:8-18).

To Israelites, the covenant was inseparably linked with Sinai. But it was a covenant that was limited by time and restricted to one nation. The new covenant, by contrast, has no such limitations or restrictions. It comes into being through Jesus Christ and is identified not with Sinai but with heaven (Gal 4:24-27; Heb 12:18-29; see COVENANT).

SINGING

From ancient times to the present, singing has been used as a form of relaxation or amusement (2 Sam 19:35; Amos 6:4-5), an expression of joy (Prov 29:6; Isa 16:10; James 5:13), a form of celebration (Judg 5:1-2; 1 Sam 21:11), and a means of praising God (Exod 15:1; Ps 30:4; 66:4; 95:1-3; Acts 16:25; Rev 5:9; 15:3). Singing has often been associated with music and dancing (Gen 31:27; Exod 15:20-21; Isa 5:12; see DANCING; MUSIC).

In the temple worship that David organized, there were groups of singers who sang under a conductor to the accompaniment of music (1 Chron 15:16,22). This arrangement was followed by some of Israel's later leaders (2 Chron 29:30; Ezra 3:10-11). The psalms that these singers sang were sometimes divided into parts that individuals or sections of the choir sang in turn (Ezra 3:11; Ps 118; see PSALMS, BOOK OF).

Singing is an important part of the life of the church (1 Cor 14:26; cf. Mark 14:26). It should be an expression of praise to God that arises from a heart filled with joy and thanks. However, the songs must be based firmly on the Word of God, and people must sing them with understanding, not simply with a feeling of enjoyment. Only in this way will God be truly praised and the singers be truly built up in their Christian faith (1 Cor 14:15; Eph 5:19; Col 3:16).

In the early church, songs were an important means of summarizing Christian truth in a form that could be easily remembered and repeated. The New Testament contains what appear to be selections from early Christian songs (Phil 2:6-11; Col 1:15-20; 1 Tim 3:16; cf. also Luke 1:46-55,68-79; 2:14,29-32; Rev 4:11; 5:9-10; 11:17-18; 15:3-4.)

SLAVE

Slavery was well established throughout the ancient world long before Israel formally became a nation (Gen 15:2-3; 16:1-2; 17:12; 30:1-3). Israelite law recognized the evils of slavery, but it also recognized that slavery had for so long been part of society that it could not be removed quickly or easily.

The law given to Israel at Sinai was not a program for the ideal society, but a legal system designed to maintain order and administer justice among a people whose way of life was already well established. Nevertheless, it introduced values of human dignity that undermined the foundations on which slavery was built, and so started the process that led eventually to its removal.

Old Testament regulations

Unlike slaves in other countries, the Israelite slave had rights. He was given one full day's rest each week (Exod 20:10) and was protected against unjust treatment. If he suffered brutal punishment, he received compensation by being set free (Exod 21:26-27).

An Israelite slave could be held captive no more than six years (Exod 21:1-2; Deut 15:12). When he went out free, his master had to give him sufficient goods to enable him to begin his new life satisfactorily (Deut 15:13-14). If he had obtained a wife from among his fellow slaves, she was not automatically released with him. However, he could, if he wished, continue to work for the master and so keep his family together (Exod 21:3-6).

A female slave who had become a wife or concubine of the master (or his son) was not freed after six years; but neither could her master sell her to a foreigner if he no longer wanted her. If her family did not buy her back, her husband-master had to continue to look after her in accordance with her rights as his wife. If he failed to do this, he had to set her free (Exod 21:7-11).

Israelites were not to take fellow Israelites as slaves in payment for debts, and were to buy back any of their relatives who had sold themselves to foreigners in payment for debts (Lev 25:39-41; 25:47-49). Kidnapping for slavery was an offence that carried the death penalty (Deut 24:7), and the practice of returning runaway slaves to their masters was prohibited (Deut 23:15-16). International slave trading was condemned (Ezek 27:13; Joel 3:4-8; Amos 1:6,9; cf. Rev 18:13).

Most slaves in Israel were either descendants of the former inhabitants of the land or people taken captive in war (Lev 25:44-45; Num 31:9; Josh 9:21; 2 Sam 12:31; 1 Kings 9:20-21). Yet these slaves also had rights (Deut 21:10-14). They could even join in the full religious life of Israel, provided they had formally become part of the covenant people through the rite of circumcision (Exod 12:44; Deut 16:14).

All these restrictions helped to decrease the practice of slavery in Israel. But the process was much slower than it should have been, mainly because people of power and influence ignored the law. This was particularly so among corrupt officials and ruthless money-lenders (2 Kings 4:1; Neh 5:5; Amos 2:6; see LENDING).

Some New Testament examples

In the Roman Empire of New Testament times slavery was widespread. Even Jews had slaves among their people, though their treatment of slaves was usually better than that of non-Jewish peoples (Matt 13:27; 24:45; 25:14; 26:51; see also STEWARD).

As a result of the missionary expansion of the church, many slaves became Christians. In churches as well as households there were Christian slaves and Christian masters. Though Christian slaves were equal with their Christian masters in their standing before God (Acts 2:18; Gal 3:28; 1 Cor 7:22), they were not equal in their standing in society. Christian slaves and their Christian masters were not to take advantage of each other, but cooperate for their common good (Eph 6:5-9; Col 3:22; 1 Tim 6:1-2; see MASTER).

By encouraging Christian slaves to work with responsibility and dignity, Christianity helped to raise the status of slaves. They were not to think of themselves simply as tools of their masters (Col 3:22; Titus 2:9). They could use their positions as slaves to serve God, but if they got the opportunity to go free, they were advised to take it (1 Cor 7:20-21). Paul hoped that Christian masters would give Christian slaves their freedom, but he did not use his apostolic authority to force them to do so (Philem 8-10,14,21).

Man's relation to God

God's people of the Old Testament era sometimes likened their relation to God to that of a slave to his master. This applied to individuals (Exod 4:10; Num 12:7; Ps 19:13; Jer 7:25) and to the nation as a whole (Judg 2:7; Isa 41:8).

Although such a relationship indicated the submissive place of God's people (Deut 6:13-14; 10:12-13), it did not indicate shame or humiliation in their status. The word translated 'slave' often had the more general meaning of 'servant'. When referring to God's specially chosen ones, it indicated a position of honour (Ps 89:3; Isa 44:21). The same ideas are present in the New Testament, which speaks of Christians as God's slaves or servants (Matt 6:24; 10:24; Rom 1:1; Gal 1:10). (For further discussion concerning God's people as servants see SERVANT.)

Those who are true slaves of Jesus Christ will also be true slaves of one another (Matt 20:26-27; John 13:4-15; 1 Cor 9:19; 2 Cor 4:5). This is because of the new life they have through Jesus Christ (Gal 5:13; Phil 2:5-7). Formerly they were slaves to sin (John 8:34; Gal 4:8; Titus 3:3), but Christ has set them free from that bondage and now they are slaves of righteousness (Rom 6:16-19; Gal 5:1; see REDEMPTION). (Concerning freedom from bondage to the law see FREEDOM; LAW.)

SLEEP

Apart from having its common meaning of physical rest, 'sleep' is used in the Bible as another word for physical death (1 Kings 2:10; Job 14:12; Jer 51:39; Matt 27:52; John 11:11-14; 1 Cor 11:30; 15:20,51). This is because death is not permanent. One day all people will rise from death to meet the great judge of the universe and receive either his blessing or his punishment (Dan 12:2; John 5:28-29).

Sleep is used also as another word for spiritual laziness, whether of non-Christians (Eph 5:14) or Christians (Rom 13:11). Christians must not be ill-disciplined or careless, as those are who live in the 'night' of spiritual darkness. They must be spiritually alert and watchful, as they now belong to the 'day' of spiritual life and light (Rom 13:11-14; 1 Thess 5:4-8; cf. Matt 25:1-13).

SMYRNA

The port of Smyrna was in the Roman province of Asia, not far north of Ephesus. (For map see ASIA.) The church there was probably formed during Paul's three-year stay in Ephesus, when the Ephesian converts took the gospel to the surrounding area (Acts 19:8-10; Rev 2:8).

John's letter to the church in Smyrna shows that the Christians were very poor. Spiritually, however, they were rich (Rev 2:9). They were also persecuted, mainly by the Jews, who throughout Asia were bitterly anti-Christian (Rev 2:9; cf. Acts 21:27). God encouraged them with the promise that, no matter how much they might suffer in the present world, he would preserve the faithful for his heavenly kingdom (Rev 2:10-11).

SNAKE

Snakes were widespread throughout the Palestine region. Because of their poisonous bites and cunning habits, they were often spoken of as a picture of wicked people and wicked deeds (Gen 49:17; Deut 32:33; Ps 58:4; 140:3; Jer 46:22; Matt 3:7; 12:34; 2 Cor 11:3). The most striking use of the snake as a picture of one who is evil is in reference to the Devil, Satan, who is called 'that ancient snake' (Rev 12:9; cf. 3:1,14-15).

Some types of snakes were used by charmers and magicians in performing tricks (Eccles 10:11). It seems that Egyptian magicians hypnotized snakes to stiffen them, and in this way were able to imitate Aaron's miracle of turning a stick into a snake. But Aaron showed that his actions were miracles, not tricks, when his snake swallowed up those of the magicians (Exod 7:8-12; cf. 4:2-4).

On the journey from Egypt to Canaan, God punished his rebellious people with a plague of desert snakes whose bite produced burning pains and even death. When Moses prayed for the people, God replied by promising to heal those who stopped their complaining and demonstrated their trust in him by looking on a bronze snake that he had commanded Moses to make (Num 21:4-9; John 3:14-15; 1 Cor 10:9). This bronze snake later became an object of worship and had to be destroyed (2 Kings 18:4).

SODOM

It is believed that the cities of Sodom and Gomorrah were located near the southern end of the Dead Sea, but through earthquake activity the sea spread farther south and covered whatever remained of the ancient cities.

The area around Sodom was once suitable for raising flocks and herds, and for this reason Lot settled there (Gen 13:10-13). On one occasion when Sodom was invaded by plunderers, Lot was taken captive. But Abraham took some of his guards and workmen, defeated the invaders and recaptured Lot. Abraham acknowledged that God was the one who had given him victory, and he refused to accept any reward from the king of Sodom (Gen 14:1-24).

Sodom and Gomorrah were notoriously sinful, and homosexual practices were widespread (Gen 19:4-10). God determined to destroy the cities, but Abraham asked God to withhold his judgment if ten righteous men could be found. But ten righteous men could not be found and the two cities were destroyed. Lot and his family, however, escaped before the judgment fell (Gen 18:22-33; 19:12-14).

Petroleum, bitumen, salt and sulphur were abundant in this area (cf. Gen 14:10), and these became part of the means of judgment. The cities were destroyed probably through the lighting of natural gases by lightning, combined with earthquake disturbance. Yet the fiery destruction was also the work of God, for its timing and extent were exactly as God had previously announced (Gen 19:24-29).

In later generations people likened great moral sin to the sin of Sodom and Gomorrah, and likened a devastating judgment to the destruction of Sodom and Gomorrah (Deut 29:23; Isa 3:9; 13:19; Jer 23:14;

49:18; Ezek 16:46-56; Zeph 2:9; Matt 10:15; Luke 17:28-29; 2 Peter 2:6; Jude 7). Jesus warned that Jews of his day, who heard his teaching and saw his mighty works yet rejected him, would receive a more severe judgment than people of those wicked Gentile cities who had never heard of him. The people of Jesus' day had a greater privilege, and this placed upon them a greater responsibility (Matt 11:20-24).

SOLDIER

Christians are often likened to soldiers who have to clothe themselves with armour to fight against the evil forces of Satan (2 Cor 10:3-4; Eph 6:10-18; see ARMOUR; WEAPONS). They have to endure hardship and opposition, concentrating on the task God has given them, without losing heart (1 Tim 1:18; 2 Tim 2:3-4).

Israel's Old Testament history is full of stories of the heroic deeds of its soldiers. Not all these heroes were godly, though some were great men of God whose faith on occasions saved Israel (Heb 11:32). (For methods of warfare see WAR.)

Roman soldier

The soldiers mentioned in the New Testament are usually Romans. The Roman centurions, who feature in a number of New Testament stories, appear to have been men of quality. Some of them became Christians (Matt 8:5-13; 27:54; Acts 10:1-2; 23:17-18; 27:43).

SOLOMON

God's choice to succeed David as king over Israel was Solomon, the son born to David and Bathsheba after their first (and illegitimate) son had died

(2 Sam 12:24-25; 1 Chron 28:5). He was anointed as king before his father died, in order to overthrow the attempts of his brother Adonijah to seize the throne for himself (1 Kings 1:5-53).

Establishing his authority

Once David was dead, Solomon quickly dealt with Adonijah and the two leaders who had supported him. He interpreted a request from Adonijah as treason and executed him (1 Kings 2:13-25). He also executed the commander-in-chief of the army, Joab (1 Kings 2:28-34), and sent the priest Abiathar into exile (1 Kings 2:26-27). After this he executed Shimei, a relative of Saul who had always been hostile to the house of David (1 Kings 2:36-46; cf. 2 Sam 16:5-14).

By marrying the daughter of the king of Egypt, Solomon entered into a treaty with Egypt that guaranteed peace between the two nations (1 Kings 3:1). The formal treaty probably involved paying respect to foreign gods, a practice that was a repeated temptation to Solomon and brought him increasing trouble (1 Kings 11:1-8).

Solomon's love for lavish religious ceremony also led him into trouble (1 Kings 3:3-4), but his request for wisdom won God's approval (1 Kings 3:5-14). He soon proved his wisdom when he had to give a decision over which of two women was the mother of a disputed baby (1 Kings 3:16-28). His fame grew rapidly, and people came from countries far and near to hear his wisdom (1 Kings 4:29-34; 10:1-13; Matt 12:42). People made collections of his proverbs and songs, and some of these are preserved in the Bible (1 Kings 4:32; Ps 72, 127; Prov 1:1; 10:1; 25:1; Song of Songs 1:1). (For further details of Solomon's writings see PROVERBS.)

Under Solomon there was a large increase in the numbers of officials in the royal court, the national administration and the armed forces. To maintain all these people, Solomon revised the taxation system. He divided Israel into twelve zones, each of which had to maintain the government for one month of the year (1 Kings 4:7). Neighbouring nations within the Israelite empire also paid taxes (1 Kings 4:21).

Development, trade and wealth

David had prepared plans, finances and materials for Solomon to build God a temple in Jerusalem (1 Chron 22:2-16; 28:11; Acts 7:45-47). Solomon's plans, however, far exceeded David's. His temple would be more lavish than anything David had in mind, and his extensive building program would make Jerusalem a showpiece to the world.

Solomon bought costly building materials from Hiram, king of Tyre, and paid for them with produce taken from Israel's hard-working farmers (1 Kings 5:1-11). He also made all Israel's working men give three months work to the king each year, which provided a year-round workforce of 30,000 men. An additional 150,000, mainly Canaanites, were made full-time slaves (1 Kings 5:13-18). The temple was a richly ornamented building that took seven years to build (1 Kings 6:38; see TEMPLE).

This temple was only part of a much larger building program that Solomon had planned. He built a magnificent palace, which took a further thirteen years (1 Kings 7:1; 9:10), a military head-quarters called the House of the Forest of Lebanon (1 Kings 7:2; 10:17), an auditorium called the Hall of Pillars (1 Kings 7:6), a central law court called the Hall of Judgment (1 Kings 7:7) and a separate palace for his Egyptian queen (1 Kings 7:8). All these buildings, including the temple, were made of costly stone and best quality timber, and were enclosed in an area known as the Great Court (1 Kings 7:9-12).

Solomon also greatly strengthened Jerusalem's defences (1 Kings 9:15). In the country regions he rebuilt ruined cities, established army bases, and set up cities to store the farm produce that maintained his government (1 Kings 9:16-19).

To help finance his construction programs, Solomon borrowed huge amounts of gold from Hiram (1 Kings 9:14). Unable to repay his debts, Solomon decided to cut off twenty cities in northern Israel and give them to Hiram (1 Kings 9:10-11). This only increased the resentment that the people of northern Israel, and especially the farmers, felt towards Solomon and his showpiece city in the south. In spite of the hardship of the common people (1 Kings 12:4), Solomon spent extravagantly on himself (1 Kings 10:16-21,25,27; Song of Songs 3:7-10; cf. Matt 6:29).

David's power had come through military conquest, but Solomon's came through political and commercial treaties with neighbouring countries. One profitable operation was a sea-land trading partnership he established with Hiram of Phoenicia. Goods from the Mediterranean were collected at Hiram's port of Tyre, carried overland to Israel's Red Sea port of Ezion-geber, then shipped east (1 Kings 9:26-28; 10:22; for map see PHOENICIA).

Solomon gained additional income by taxing all goods that passed through Israel on the international trade routes (1 Kings 10:14-15). He further enriched himself by becoming the middleman in a profitable international horse and chariot trade (1 Kings 10:28-29).

A splendid kingdom lost

Although he taught wisdom to others, Solomon did not follow that wisdom himself. He ignored the instructions that God had given concerning the conduct of an Israelite king (Deut 17:15-17), and in particular earned God's wrath through worshipping the gods of the many foreign women whom he had taken as wives and concubines (1 Kings 11:1-10,33; Neh 13:26).

All the time that Solomon was developing his magnificent kingdom, he was preparing his own punishment. He had exploited the people in order to fulfil his ambitious plans, and now the people hated him. Soon they rebelled against him openly. The ten tribes to the north broke away from the Davidic rule, though for the sake of David, God withheld the inevitable judgment until after Solomon's death (1 Kings 11:11-13).

The rebellion against Solomon was led by a young man from the north, Jeroboam. Solomon had recognized Jeroboam's abilities earlier, and put him in charge of a large portion of the workforce from the northern tribes (1 Kings 11:28). When Solomon felt that Jeroboam was gaining support among the northerners, he tried to kill him, but Jeroboam escaped to the safety of Egypt (1 Kings 11:29-32,40). After Solomon's death, Jeroboam returned to Israel and successfully lead a breakaway rebellion (1 Kings 12:2-4,16-20).

SON

See ADOPTION; CHILD.

SON OF GOD

Like a number of biblical expressions, 'son of God' may have different meanings in different parts of the Bible. Adam is called the son of God, because he came into existence as a result of the creative activity of God (Luke 3:38; cf. Acts 17:28; Heb 12:9). Angels are sometimes called sons of God, probably in reference to the fact that they are spirit beings (Job 1:6; 38:7; Dan 3:25). The nation Israel was God's son, for God adopted it as his own (Exod 4:22-23; Rom 9:4). In a similar but higher sense, Christians are God's sons, again through God's gracious work of adoption (Rom 8:14-15; Gal 4:5-6; see ADOPTION).

In Old Testament Israel, the Davidic king was considered to be God's son, for through him God exercised his rule over his people (2 Sam 7:14; Ps

2:6-7). The promised Messiah would also be God's son, for he would belong to the Davidic line of kings. That Messiah was Jesus. But Jesus was more than God's son in the messianic sense. He was God's Son in the sense that he was God. He did not become the Son of God through being the Messiah; rather he became the Messiah because he was already the pre-existent Son of God (Matt 22:42-45; John 1:34,49; 20:31; see MESSIAH).

Eternally the Son

God is a trinity of Father, Son and Holy Spirit, all of whom are equally and eternally God (see TRINITY). Although Jesus is the Son, that does not mean that he was created by the Father or is inferior to the Father. On the contrary, he has the same godhead and character as the Father (Matt 11:27; John 1:1,14,18; 5:26; 8:18-19; 10:30,38; 14:9; Heb 1:1-3; 1 John 2:23; see WORD), has the powers, authority and responsibilities of the Father (John 3:35-36; 5:21-22,43; 13:3), and has the thought and purpose of the Father (John 5:17-20,30; 8:16,28-29; 14:10,24; see FATHER).

The relation between Jesus (the Son of God) and his Father is unique. It should not be confused with the relation between believers (sons of God) and their heavenly Father. In the case of Jesus, the sonship is eternal. The Father and the Son have always existed in a relation in which they are equally and unchangeably God. It is a relation that no created being can share (John 1:18; 5:37). In the case of believers, they become sons of God only through faith in Jesus. God *makes* them his sons by grace. Jesus was never *made* the Son of God. He always has been the Son (John 8:18-19; 17:1-5; 1 John 5:11-12).

Jesus was careful, when talking to believers, to make a distinction between 'my Father' and 'your Father' (Matt 5:16; Luke 2:49; 12:30; John 20:17). The believer is not a son of God in the same sense as Jesus is the Son of God. Nevertheless, believers become sons of God only through Jesus, the Son of God (Matt 11:27; John 1:12-13; Rom 8:16-17). Through Christ they come into a close personal relation with God the Father, and can even address him as 'Abba' as Jesus did (Mark 14:36; Rom 8:15; Gal 4:6; see ABBA).

The Son's mission

As the Son of God, Jesus shares in the deity and majesty of the Father; yet he is also humbly obedient to the Father. Although he existed with the Father from eternity, the Son willingly became man to fulfil his Father's purposes for the salvation of man and the conquest of evil (Rom 8:3; Gal 4:4-5; Heb 2:14-15).

When Jesus was born in Bethlehem, the Son of God added humanity to the deity that he already had. His entrance into human life involved the supernatural work of God in the womb of the virgin Mary, so that the baby born to her, though fully human, was also the unique Son of God (Luke 1:30-31,35; 2:42,49; see VIRGIN).

The earliest recorded words of Jesus indicate that even as a child he was conscious of his special relation with the Father (Luke 2:49). The Father reaffirmed this special relation at some of the great moments of Jesus' public ministry (Matt 3:17; 17:5; see BAPTISM; TRANSFIGURATION). Because the Son and the Father existed in this special relation, Satan tempted the Son to act independently of the Father. He tempted Jesus to use his divine powers contrary to the divine will (Matt 4:3,6).

There was often a difference between the way believers spoke of Jesus' sonship and the way Jesus himself spoke of it. Believers usually spoke of it in relation to Jesus' divine person and his unity with the Father (Matt 16:16; John 20:31; Col 1:13; 1 John 2:23; 4:15). Jesus also spoke of it in this way, but in addition he emphasized the meaning of his sonship in relation to his earthly ministry and complete submission to his Father (Mark 13:32; John 4:34; 5:19; 7:16; 8:28,42; cf. Heb 5:8).

The Father sent the Son to be the Saviour of the world, and the Son's obedience to this mission meant that he had to suffer and die (John 3:14-16; 12:27; Rom 5:10; 8:32; 1 John 4:9-10,14). The Son completed that work, being obedient even to death (John 17:4; Phil 2:8), and God declared his total satisfaction with the Son's work by raising him from death (Rom 1:4).

However, the mission that the Father entrusted to the Son involved more than saving those who believe. It involved overcoming all rebellion and restoring all things to a state of perfect submission to the sovereign God (John 5:20-29; 2 Cor 5:19; Eph 1:10; 1 John 3:8). That mission extends to the whole universe, and will reach its climax when the last enemy, death, has been banished for ever (1 Cor 15:25-26). The conquering power of the Son's victory at the cross will remove the last traces of sin. The Son will restore all things to the Father, and God's triumph will be complete. God will be everything to everyone (1 Cor 15:24,28).

Acknowledging the Son

One of the signs of the work of God in a person's life is his acknowledgment that Jesus Christ is the

Son of God (Matt 11:27; 16:16-17; 1 John 5:10). It seems that in the early church, a person's open confession of Jesus Christ as the Son of God was a formal declaration that he was a true believer (Acts 8:37; Heb 4:14; 1 John 2:23; 4:15).

Even Jesus' opponents recognized in his works and his teaching a claim to deity. For this they accused him of blasphemy and in the end crucified him (Matt 26:63-66; 27:42-43; John 5:18; 10:33,36; 19:7). God, however, demonstrated dramatically that Jesus was his Son by raising him from death and crowning him with glory in heaven (Rom 1:4; Eph 1:20; Heb 4:14; cf. John 6:62; 17:4-5). One day the Son will return to save his people and set in motion those events that will lead to God's final triumph (1 Thess 1:10; Titus 1:13). (See also JESUS CHRIST; SON OF MAN.)

SON OF MAN

Of all the titles commonly used of Jesus in the New Testament, 'Son of man' was the one most used by Jesus himself and least used by others. It hardly occurs at all outside the Gospels (Acts 7:56; Rev 1:13; 14:14), and inside the Gospels is used almost solely by Jesus. By using this unusual title for himself, Jesus made people think carefully about who he was and what his mission involved (John 12:34; 13:31-32).

A heavenly figure

The title 'son of man' comes from a vision recorded in the Old Testament book of Daniel. In this vision a person like a son of man came into the heavenly presence of God and received from him a universal and everlasting kingdom (Dan 7:13-14). The idea of the son of man was tied up with that of the kingdom of God, and this provided the background to Jesus' reference to himself as the Son of man.

With the coming of Jesus, the kingdom of God came visibly into the world of mankind. The world is under the power of Satan (2 Cor 4:4; 1 John 5:19), but Jesus delivered diseased and demonized people, showing that the rule and authority of God's kingdom can release people from Satan's power (Matt 4:23-24; 12:28; Luke 10:9,17-18; 17:20-21; see KINGDOM OF GOD). God's kingdom will reach its fullest expression when Jesus returns at the end of the age to punish evil, remove Satan and reign in righteousness (Dan 7:13-14; Matt 13:41-43; 24:30-31; Mark 8:38).

The vision in Daniel shows, however, that the Son of man shares the kingdom with his people (Dan 7:14,27). Jesus therefore promised those who followed him that they would share with him in the final triumph of his kingdom (Matt 19:28; 25:31-34; cf. 2 Tim 2:11-12; Rev 3:12,21; 20:4).

An earthly figure

In addition to this particular usage, the expression 'son of man' could be used in ordinary speech to apply to any man. It could be simply a poetic way of saying 'a person', and at times Jesus may have used it simply to mean 'I' or 'me' (Num 23:19; Ps 8:4; Ezek 2:1,3,8; Matt 11:19).

The twofold meaning of 'son of man' was especially appropriate as a title for Jesus. It pointed to his deity (he was the heavenly Son of God; John 3:13; 6:62) and to his humanity (he was a man, a member of the human race; Matt 8:20). The Son of man was the embodiment of God. In his unique person he carried the authority of God into the world of mankind (Mark 2:10,28; cf. John 5:27; see JESUS CHRIST; SON OF GOD).

Jesus' use of 'Son of man' in relation to the kingdom of God likewise combined heavenly and earthly aspects. The heavenly Son of man was in fact an earthly figure born in the royal line of David and having claim to the messianic throne. Because of the Jews' selfish nationalistic ideas of the Messiah and his kingdom, Jesus rarely spoke of himself specifically as the Messiah (see MESSIAH). By using the title 'Son of man', he was claiming to be the Messiah without actually using the title 'Messiah'. He knew the title 'Son of man' could be puzzling, but he wanted people to think about it. He wanted them to consider the evidence of his life and work, and discover for themselves the true identity of this one who called himself the Son of man (Matt 16:13-16; John 9:35-36; 12:34).

When the Jewish leaders finally understood Jesus' usage of the title (namely, that he claimed to be both the Davidic Messiah and the supernatural heavenly Messiah of Daniel 7:13-14), they accused him of blasphemy and had him crucified (Mark 14:61-64). This did not take Jesus by surprise, for he knew that the heavenly Son of man had also to become the suffering servant. He had to suffer and die before he could receive the kingdom (Mark 8:31; 9:12; 10:45; John 3:13-14; 8:28; see SERVANT OF THE LORD).

If, however, the crucified Son of man was to receive an eternal kingdom, his death had to be followed by resurrection (Mark 9:31; 10:33-34). Therefore God, in a triumphant declaration of the perfection of all that Jesus had done through his obedient life and sacrificial death, raised him up and gave him glory (1 Peter 1:21). The full revelation of that glory will take place when the Son of man returns in the triumph of his kingdom (Mark 8:38; 13:26; 14:62).

SONG OF SONGS

Solomon had the reputation of being one of Israel's greatest wisdom teachers and song writers (1 Kings 4:29-34). He was also one of its most famous lovers (1 Kings 11:1-4). It is therefore not surprising that he has been traditionally regarded as the author of the the biblical book that contains one of the world's best known collections of love songs, the Song of Songs. The book contains a number of references to the splendour of Solomon and his court, and is sometimes called the Song of Solomon (Song of Songs 1:1,5; 3:7-11; 8:11-12).

Interpretation

Although the book declares that it was written by Solomon, it is not necessarily about Solomon personally. A poet can write a poem about anybody. The reader has difficulty working out the identity of the people mentioned in the Song of Songs, because the poems can be understood in different ways. In some poems the words may all be from one speaker; in others, from several speakers. Some poems are the private reflections of individuals, others are dialogues; some describe actual circumstances or events, others recount dreams; some recall the past, others look to the future.

Since the reader has to work out for himself who is speaking in the various poems, a number of interpretations have been suggested. In some of the more recent versions of the Bible, the translators have tried to help the reader by inserting sub-headings. The variations in these subheadings reflect the variations in interpretation.

Among those who regard the book as a drama involving Solomon himself, there are two main interpretations. The first sees two main characters, Solomon and a Shulammite girl who fall in love and marry. The second sees three main characters — a young shepherd, his Shulammite lover, and King Solomon, who takes the girl from the shepherd and unsuccessfully tries to win her love.

Perhaps the book is best understood not as a drama, but as a collection of poems that recount the exchanges of love between an unnamed shepherd and an unnamed country girl. Yet there is a unity to the book. Certain features recur throughout, and there is a development in the love relationship.

The inclusion of such a book in the Bible is an indication of God's approval of sexual love. Always,

however, the love is in the context of a relationship where a man and a woman commit themselves to each other in marriage, to the exclusion of all others (Song of Songs 2:16; 6:3; 7:10).

Contents

In the opening poem the girl longs for her distant lover (1:1-7), after which each speaks in praise of the other (1:8-2:7). Then follows a group of three poems recounting memories and dreams. First the girl imagines her shepherd-lover coming to visit her at her home (2:8-17), then she recalls a dream she had about him (3:1-5), and finally she imagines her wedding day, when he comes and praises her beauty (3:6-5:1).

Another dream indicates the frustration the girl feels at being separated from her lover (5:2-6:3). Further poems express the intensely strong desires that the two have for each other (6:4-7:13), though they know how to restrain their physical expressions of love (8:1-4). The final poem, which pictures the homecoming of the two lovers, speaks of the power of love and the reward it brings (8:5-14).

SORCERY

See MAGIC.

SORROW

Sorrow is one of the consequences of sin in the world. This does not mean that each person's sorrow is because of his own sin; it means that sorrow occurs because of the damage sin has done in human society. Jesus was sorrowful because of what sin had done to the people of Jerusalem (Matt 23:37). He was sorrowful also because of what it had done to human relationships by bringing death and its consequent grief (John 11:33-36). But by his death and resurrection he conquered death and gave sorrowing believers hope (Rom 6:5-10,23; 8:31-37). The triumphant resurrection of Jesus guarantees the triumphant resurrection of all who believe in him (John 11:25-26; Rom 8:10-11; 1 Cor 15:20-23; see RESURRECTION).

Like Jesus, Christians sorrow because of the death of those they love; but they do not sorrow as unbelievers, who have nothing to look forward to beyond death (1 Thess 4:13-18; 5:9-11). Just as Jesus' resurrection changed the original disciples' sorrow to joy, so it gives joy to believers of all generations; and nothing, not even grief, can take that joy from them (John 16:20,22; Rom 8:38-39; Phil 3:21; 4:1,4-7; see JOY). The Christians' expressions of sorrow are therefore not the unrestrained demonstrations of grief that characterize those who have no hope in Christ (see FUNERAL).

Besides death, there are many troubles and sufferings in life that are likely to produce sorrow. Christians should not allow themselves to be overcome by such problems, but should turn them into experiences of learning and training that can help them become stronger Christians (James 1:2-4,12; 1 Peter 1:6-9; 4:12-14,19; see SUFFERING; TESTING). Christians are to be sympathetic to those who are downhearted because of their trials, and do all they can to help them triumph through them (Rom 12:15; see ENCOURAGEMENT).

The person who refuses to trust in God may find that sorrow can have a destructive effect on his life. Even sorrow for wrongdoing, if it is no more than shame or self-pity, can have deadly results (Matt 27:3-5). But if the person submits to God, sees his wrongdoing as God sees it and asks God to forgive him, his sorrow will soon be replaced by joy (Matt 5:4; Luke 7:38-39; 2 Cor 7:9-10; James 4:9-10; cf. Ezra 9:6,13,15). This will be a foretaste of the greater joy that will come in the new heavens and new earth, when sorrow will be banished for ever (Isa 65:17-19; Rev 7:17; 21:4).

SOUL

Like the word 'spirit', the word 'soul' has a variety of meanings in English. There is some variety also in the usages of the original words from which 'soul' has been translated. In the Hebrew of the Old Testament the word is *nephesh*. In the Greek of the New Testament the word is *psyche*.

Old Testament usage

The writers of the Old Testament did not speak of the soul as something that exists apart from the body. To them, soul (or *nephesh*) meant life. Both animals and people are *nephesh*, living creatures. Older English versions of the Bible have created misunderstanding by the translation 'man became a living soul' (Gen 2:7), for the words translated 'living soul' are the same words as earlier translated 'living creatures' (Gen 1:21,24). All animal life is *nephesh* (or *psyche*; Rev 8:9), though human *nephesh* is of a higher order than the *nephesh* of other animals (Gen 2:19-22).

From this it is easy to see how *nephesh* came to refer to the whole person. We should understand a person not as consisting of a combination of a lifeless body and a bodiless soul, but as a perfect unity, a living body. Thus *nephesh* may be translated 'person'; even if translated 'soul', it may mean no

more than 'person' or 'life' (Exod 1:5; Num 9:13; Ezek 18:4,27). Likewise when a person speaks of his (or another's) *nephesh*, he usually means simply himself (Ps 6:3-4; 35:9,13; Isa 1:14) or his life (Gen 36:18; 1 Kings 17:22; Ps 33:19).

New Testament usage

Similarly in the New Testament *psyche* can be used to mean no more than 'person' (Acts 2:41,43; 7:14; Rom 2:9; 13:1). Also, a person may speak of his (or another's) *psyche* as referring to the person himself (Matt 12:18; 26:38; Luke 1:46; 12:19; 1 Thess 2:8; Heb 10:38) or to his life (Matt 16:26; 1 Cor 15:45; Phil 2:30; 1 Peter 4:19). Sometimes 'soul' appears to be the same as 'heart', which in the Bible usually refers to the whole of a person's inner life (Prov 2:10; Acts 4:32; see HEART; MAN).

A person characterized by *psyche* is an ordinary person of the world, one who lives solely according to the principles and values of sinful human society. He is what Paul calls the 'natural person', in contrast to the 'spiritual person'. The latter is one who has new principles and values because of the Spirit of God within him (1 Cor 2:12-16; cf. Jude 19; see FLESH; SPIRIT).

Man's uniqueness

Both Old and New Testaments teach that when a person dies he does not cease to exist. His body returns to dust (Gen 3:19; Eccles 3:20), but he himself lives on in a place, or state, of the dead, which the Hebrew calls *sheol* and the Greek calls *hades* (Ps 6:5; 88:3-5; Luke 16:22-23; see HADES; SHEOL). The Old Testament does not say in what way man lives on after death. Certainly, he lives on as a conscious personal being, but that personal being is not complete, for it has no body (Ps 49:14; Ezek 26:20).

The New Testament also is unclear on the subject of a person's existence after death. It speaks of the bodiless person after death sometimes as a soul (Acts 2:27; Rev 6:9; 20:4), sometimes as a spirit (Heb 12:23; 1 Peter 3:18), but again the person, being bodiless, is not complete. Also, his existence as a bodiless person is only temporary, just as the decay of his body in the grave is only temporary. That is why the Bible encourages believers to look for their eternal destiny not in the endless existence of some bodiless 'soul' or 'spirit', but in the resurrection of the body to a new and glorious life (1 Cor 15:42-53; Phil 3:20-21).

Since there is far more to a person's life than what he experiences during his earthly existence, *psyche* naturally developed a meaning relating to more than normal earthly life. Eternal destiny also is involved (Matt 10:28; 16:26; Heb 10:38-39).

From this usage, *psyche* developed an even richer meaning. It became the word most commonly used among Christians to describe the higher or more spiritual aspect of human life that is popularly called the soul (Heb 6:19; 13:17; James 1:21; 1 Peter 1:9,22; 2:11,25; 3 John 2).

SPICES

From very early times spices were in great demand among the peoples of Palestine and surrounding countries. Some spices were grown locally, but many were imported from the East, bringing wealth to traders and to the governments who taxed them (Gen 37:25; 1 Kings 10:2; Song of Songs 3:6; Isa 60:6; Jer 6:20; Ezek 27:17; Rev 18:11-13). Among these spices were frankincense, myrrh, galbanum, stacte, onycha, cassia, aloes, cummin, dill, cinnamon, mint, rue, mustard, balm, sweet cane, henna, nard, saffron and calumus (Gen 37:25; Exod 30:23-24,34; Song of Songs 3:6; 4:13-14; Jer 6:20; Matt 23:23; Luke 11:42; 13:19).

Spices came from the gum of certain trees and from plants and herbs (Song of Songs 4:14). People used spices in preparing food and drinks (Song of Songs 8:2; Ezek 24:10; Matt 23:23), and in making a variety of oils, medicines, cosmetics, deodorants and disinfectants (Esther 2:12; Ps 45:8; Prov 7:17; Song of Songs 4:10,14; 5:13; Jer 8:22; 51:8; Luke 7:46; John 12:3; 19:39).

The preparation of these substances involved heating, drying, boiling, soaking and crushing. It was a specialized art in which some people became highly skilled (Exod 30:35; 1 Sam 8:13; 2 Chron 16:14). People placed great value on some of these substances, and preserved them in expensive boxes that they opened on special occasions (Isa 3:20; Mark 14:3; Luke 7:37-38).

Among Israelites the most sacred use of spices was in preparing oil and incense for use in religious rituals. Oil was used to anoint priests, and incense was burnt in the tabernacle (Exod 30:22-38; see OIL; INCENSE).

In relation to Jesus, people used spices, or substances made from them, to present in homage to him (Matt 2:11), to anoint and refresh him (Luke 7:46; John 12:3), and to offer him on the cross to deaden his pain (but he refused their offer) (Mark 15:23). Some used spices to prepare his body for burial (John 19:39) and others brought spices to anoint the body as it lay in the tomb (Mark 16:1).

SPIRIT

The Hebrew word that in the Old Testament is usually translated 'spirit' is *ruach*. The equivalent New Testament Greek word, also usually translated 'spirit', is *pneuma*. Both *ruach* and *pneuma* had very broad meanings. They could mean, among other things, wind (1 Kings 18:45; John 3:8), breath (Gen 7:15,22; Acts 9:1), human emotion (Gen 41:8; Num 5:14; John 13:21; Acts 18:25), human understanding (Isa 29:24; Mark 2:8), will-power (Jer 51:11; Acts 19:21), human life itself (Gen 45:27; Luke 8:55) and evil beings of the unseen world (1 Sam 16:23; Mark 1:23; see UNCLEAN SPIRITS). Both words were also used of God's Spirit, the living power of God at work (Judg 6:34; Acts 8:39; see HOLY SPIRIT).

Relationship with God

An examination of the usage of *ruach* in the Old Testament shows that its basic meaning has to do with something unseen and powerful that is full of life or life-giving. The word can be used of God who gives life to all human beings and animals (Job 33:4; Ps 104:30) and of the life that God gives to all human beings and animals (Gen 7:15,22).

According to this usage, *ruach* might be defined as the 'life-force' or 'breath of life' that God created. It belongs to him. He gives it to all people and animals for the time of their earthly existence and he takes it back at death (Num 16:22; Ps 104:29; Eccles 12:7). *Pneuma* can have a similar meaning in the New Testament (Heb 12:9; James 2:26).

However, both *ruach* and *pneuma* may be used specifically of the human spirit. That is, they may refer to the human spirit in a way that makes it different from the general life principle that humans share with animals (Prov 11:13; 15:13; 16:2,18-19,32; 1 Cor 2:11; 2 Cor 7:1; 1 Peter 3:4; see MAN). The New Testament goes further and uses *pneuma* to refer to that higher aspect of man's nature that enables him to communicate with God and have religious experiences (Rom 8:16; 1 Cor 5:5; 7:34; Gal 6:18; Phil 3:3).

'Spirit' may at times be simply another word for 'heart'. In such cases it speaks of a person's whole inner life (Ps 51:10,17; Prov 16:2; Matt 5:3; Rom 1:9; Philem 25; see HEART; MIND).

Through sin, man's spirit has been corrupted. It is not able to save him from disaster or bring him eternal life. It is, in a sense, dead, and needs to be born anew through the creative power of the Spirit of God (Ezek 36:26-27; John 3:6). This leads, then, to an even more restricted meaning of the word, particularly in the New Testament, where the reference is to the reborn spirit of the person whom God has created anew (Rom 8:10; 1 Cor 2:14-15; Eph 4:23; see REGENERATION; SOUL).

Life after death

Yet another usage of the word 'spirit' is in reference to life after death. When the life of the body comes to an end, a person does not cease to exist. Because he is no longer 'in the body', he is no longer in the physical world, but he continues to exist in the unseen world. He lives on in his spirit (Heb 12:23; 1 Peter 3:18; 4:6). This type of existence is only temporary, for man's destiny is not to live for ever in a bodiless spirit, but to experience eternal life in a renewed body (1 Cor 15:35-54; Phil 3:21; 1 John 3:2; see BODY).

SPORT

There are few references to sporting activity in the Old Testament, the main ones being to wrestling (Gen 32:24), archery (1 Sam 20:20,36) and sword-fighting (2 Samuel 2:14-16). The New Testament references to sport are mainly in those writings sent to people living in Greece and Asia Minor, where

Wrestling at the Greek Games

there was still much interest in sports that the Greeks had introduced in pre-Christian times. Many of these sports were associated with idolatrous practices, and therefore most Jewish people avoided them. Among the Greeks and other non-Jews they were very popular.

Chief among the sports mentioned in the New Testament are running and boxing. The winner received as his prize a circular crown made of leaves (1 Cor 9:24-25; 2 Tim 4:7-8). Self-discipline and perseverance were essential, and the person had to compete according to set rules, otherwise he was disqualified (1 Cor 9:25-27; Gal 5:7; 2 Tim 2:5; Heb 12:1-2).

Christians recognize that sport is a beneficial form of exercise (1 Tim 4:8) but, as in other areas of life, proper attitudes are more important than a successful result. Christians should not cheat, be

greedy, deliberately injure others, or allow sport to take the place of God in their lives (Matt 6:24; 22:39; Rom 12:1,9,17; Eph 4:22-27). The physical exercise that comes with sport is beneficial, but the benefits are only temporary. The benefits of spiritual exercise are eternal (1 Tim 4:8).

STARS

People in ancient times did not have the same knowledge of astronomy as people of today have. Nevertheless, they knew that the stars were beyond number and that they were an indication of the greatness of God who created them (Gen 1:16; 15:5; Job 9:7-10; Ps 8:3; 136:7-9; Amos 5:8). The Bible condemns the worship of stars and all forms of astrology (Deut 4:19; 2 Kings 21:3; 23:5; Isa 47:13; Acts 7:43).

The writers of the Bible repeatedly picture God's great interventions in judgment as being accompanied by spectacular irregularities among the sun, moon and stars (Isa 13:9-11; Ezek 32:7; Joel 2:31; 3:15; Matt 24:29-31; Rev 6:12-14).

STATE

See GOVERNMENT.

STEAL

There are many reasons why people steal, but the common feature of all stealing is that the thief unlawfully takes what belongs to someone else. For some people stealing is part of their way of life, and they may even have deliberately set out on a path of robbery and violence (Judg 9:25; Luke 10:30; John 10:10). For others stealing is contrary to their normal behaviour, but they may have been over-come by temptation in a moment of weakness (Josh 7:21; 1 Cor 10:12-13). Covetousness and greed are usually the cause of stealing (Micah 2:2; James 1:14-15; 4:1-2; see COVET), though some people steal because they are poor and in desperate need (Prov 30:8-9).

Regardless of the reason, stealing is wrong, though there may be degrees of seriousness. A hungry man who steals food is not as bad as a lustful man who steals another's wife (Prov 6:30-35). People who steal can easily have the appearance of respectability. Through deceit and cunning, they may be able to cheat the government, outclass their rivals and exploit the defenceless, but any dishonesty in such matters is still a form of stealing (1 Kings 21:1-15; Prov 21:6; Isa 1:23; Micah 6:10-13; John 12:4-6; Rom 13:6-7).

Those found guilty of stealing should make repayment to the lawful owner, as well as pay the legal penalty (Exod 20:15; 22:1-4). If a thief becomes a Christian, he must not be satisfied simply with correcting the past and deciding to earn an honest living in the future. He must have the added goal of giving generously to those in need (Eph 4:28).

STEPHEN

When some of the Greek-speaking Jews in the early Jerusalem church complained that their widows were being neglected, Stephen was one of seven men chosen to help sort out the problem. He was a man full of the Holy Spirit, strong in faith, gifted in the working of miracles and brilliant in debating with the opponents of Christianity (Acts 6:1-10).

Being a Greek-speaking Jew himself, Stephen went to the synagogue for Greek-speaking Jews in Jerusalem to try to turn his fellow Jews to Christ. But instead, they turned against him (Acts 6:11). Stephen saw that Christianity was not simply a remodelled Judaism. Through the life and work of Jesus, everything had changed. The Jewish laws, ceremonies, temple and priesthood had fulfilled their purpose and were no longer necessary. When Stephen preached these things, the Jews accused him of blasphemy and brought him before their Council, the Sanhedrin (Acts 6:12-15).

In defending his preaching, Stephen gave an outline of Israel's history, his aim being to demonstrate two main points. He showed firstly that God had never limited himself to one location (Acts 7:2,9,30,44,48), and secondly that the people of Israel had always rejected God's messengers (Acts 7:9,25,35,40). He applied these two points to the Jews of his time by saying that they were mistaken in thinking God dwelt in the Jerusalem temple, and that their rejection of Christ was in keeping with the stubbornness of their forefathers (Acts 7:48-53).

Furious at Stephen's words, the Jews rushed upon him, dragged him out of the city and stoned him to death (Acts 7:54-60). They then drove all the other Greek-speaking Jewish Christians out of Jerusalem (Acts 8:1-3). The result, however, was that Christianity spread throughout the region, as the expelled Christians preached the gospel wherever they went (Acts 8:4; 11:19).

STEWARD

In New Testament times the word 'steward' was usually used of the person appointed to look after his master's household or business. The steward's position meant that on the one hand he had control over those servants who were under him, but on the other he was answerable to his master for the way he carried out his responsibilities. It was essential, therefore, that a steward be trustworthy (Luke 12:42; 16:1-2; 1 Cor 4:2; cf. Gen 15:2; 24:1-67).

Christians are God's stewards, appointed by him to look after his interests in the world. This applies to their responsibilities in looking after the material things God has given them, and to their responsibilities in preaching the gospel and caring for God's people. They are answerable to God for the way they carry out these responsibilities (Gen 1:28-30; 1 Cor 4:1-5; 9:17; Col 1:25; 1 Thess 2:4; 2 Tim 1:14; 2:15; 1 Peter 4:10). (See also GIVING; SERVANT; WORK.)

STOICS

Athens was famous for the freedom it gave people to lecture publicly on such matters as religion, philosophy, politics and morals. There was, however, a council of philosophers, called the Areopagus, that exercised some control over public debate in the city. The council consisted of philosophers from two main schools, the Epicureans and the Stoics, and both were keen to hear the travelling preacher Paul give an account of his new religion (Acts 17:18-22; see AREOPAGUS).

Stoics took their name from the place in Athens where their founder, Zeno, taught his philosophy (about 300 BC). The Stoics believed that everything in life is determined by a universal Mind or Reason, which is the 'soul of the world'. Man must therefore accept whatever he meets in life without fear or complaint, and order his life to fit in with what nature has determined for him. In doing so he will find real contentment. Stoicism therefore had a number of distinctive features: rigid self-discipline, free of both pleasure and pain; moral earnestness, free of all feelings and desires; devotion to duty, free of all emotion; and reliance upon reason, free of all superstition and irrationality.

The Stoics would have agreed with Paul that there is a supreme God who is living, who is the source of all life, and who determines the times and places in which people live (Acts 17:24-26,28). But they dismissed Paul's belief in the resurrection as unworthy of serious consideration (Acts 17:32).

STONING

See EXECUTION.

STUMBLING BLOCK

In the figurative language of the Bible, a stumbling block is some sort of obstacle that either makes a person fall or hinders his doing what he should. (In some older English versions the word is sometimes translated 'offence'.)

The crucifixion of Jesus was a stumbling block to the Jews, because they would not believe that a person who died on a cross could be the Messiah sent by God. They expected the Messiah to be a mighty saviour who would rescue the nation Israel from its enemies and bring in an era of peace, joy and prosperity. A person who died on a cross, by contrast, was under the curse of God (Deut 21:23).

What the Jews did not understand was that when Jesus died on the cross, he bore God's curse in the place of those who had broken God's law. He did not die because of any wrong that he himself had committed (Gal 3:13).

The Jews refused to trust in Jesus' death on the cross for their forgiveness, but tried instead to win God's favour by their own good deeds. As a result the cross of Christ was to them a stumbling block (Rom 9:32-33; 1 Cor 1:23; Gal 5:11; 1 Peter 2:8). Jesus was always a stumbling block (offence) to those who had a wrong idea of his mission (Matt 11:6; 15:12; 16:23; Mark 6:3; John 6:61).

Something that causes a person to sin may also be called a stumbling block (Mark 9:42-43; Luke 17:1). Idolatry, for example, was a stumbling block to Jews of Old Testament times (Exod 23:33; Ezek 7:19-20; 14:3-4), and to some Christians of New Testament times. Through joining in idol feasts, these Christians were tempted to fall into idolatry and immorality (Rev 2:14).

Even if those who joined in idol feasts did not engage in idolatrous practices, others who followed them to the feasts may not have been able to resist the temptations to idolatry. Christians are therefore warned to be careful of their behaviour in everything they do. A bad example can be a stumbling block to those of weaker faith (Matt 17:27; 18:6-8; Rom 14:13; 1 Cor 8:7-12; 2 Cor 6:3).

SUFFERING

Before he sinned, man was in a state of harmony with God and with the natural world, and as a result was free of pain and suffering. But when he sinned, this state of harmony was ruined. God had given the natural world to man for his physical and spiritual well-being, but that world now became a cause of suffering. God had intended physical effort and bodily functions to bring pleasure, but now they brought pain and hardship (Gen 3:16-19).

Unanswered questions

It is therefore true to say that there is suffering in the world because there is sin in the world. It is not true to say, however, that the personal suffering of any one person is the direct result of that person's sin. The book of Job makes it plain that a person cannot know the moral reasons for another person's suffering. God alone knows (Job 42:2,7).

If suffering is not a measure of a person's sin, freedom from suffering is not a measure of a person's righteousness (Eccles 8:14; Luke 13:1-5; 1 Peter 2:19). In fact, very often the righteous suffer, while the wicked enjoy peace and prosperity (Ps 73:3-5,12-14). This is part of the mystery of human suffering. God does not satisfy people's curiosity concerning this mystery, but he does work in the lives of those who suffer, to bring them to a fuller knowledge of himself and therefore to glorify him (John 9:1-3; 2 Cor 1:3-7; see also DISEASE).

Satan takes pleasure in causing people to suffer (Luke 13:16; 2 Cor 12:7), but he can do his cruel work only to the extent God allows (Job 1:8-12; 2:1-8). The person who is in a right relationship with God may therefore see his suffering not as something essentially evil, but as something out of which good may come.

In some cases, for example, the believer may regard his suffering as a means of teaching him endurance, trust and other virtues. As a result he grows more towards the sort of person God wants him to be (Isa 38:17; Rom 5:3-5; 2 Cor 12:7-19). In other cases he may regard it as a fitting chastisement for some wrong he has done (Ps 38:1-8; 41:3-4; see CHASTISEMENT). Or he may regard it simply as one of the facts of life that he cannot explain but he must accept; though he must do so with faith and courage, not with resentment or bitterness (Ps 73:21-26; Rom 8:18; 2 Cor 4:17-18; 1 Peter 4:19; cf. Ps 13:1-2; Jer 20:14-18).

Although a person may in some circumstances exercise judgment against himself because of his suffering, he should not exercise similar judgment against another person who suffers. Instead he should look for ways of giving the sufferer the comfort and strength he requires (Mark 1:40-41; 14:34-41; 2 Cor 1:4).

Whether or not the believer understands why he suffers, he need have no doubt that God still loves him and will not leave him. He may have no explanation of God's purposes, but he can be confident that those purposes do exist and that they are perfect (Rom 8:28,37-39). Once it has passed, suffering may soon be forgotten. From the viewpoint of eternity it will appear brief indeed (John 16:21; 2 Cor 4:17).

God's provision

Jesus was fully man and lived in the world as other people. Therefore, he too experienced the suffering that is in the world through sin, even though he himself never sinned. Through his experiences he learnt the full meaning of obedience to God in a world of sin and suffering (Heb 2:10; 5:8).

Yet Jesus suffered not only because of the sins of others; he suffered to take away the sins of others. He was so identified with his fellow man that God's judgment on sinful people fell upon him. He died for them (Gal 2:20; 1 Peter 2:24).

Consequently, the expression 'the sufferings of Christ' developed the specific meaning of 'the death of Christ'. His death was not an accident, but the divinely ordered way of dealing with sin. In suffering for sin, Christ bore God's punishment on sin and so made it possible for people to be cleansed from sin and brought back to God (Isa 53:4-5,10; Matt 8:17; Mark 8:31; Heb 2:9; 13:12; 1 Peter 1:12; 2:21-24; 3:18). The sufferings of Christ, as well as bringing cleansing from sin, enable him to understand and help others who suffer (Heb 4:15-16).

When people by faith accept the benefits of Christ's death, they become united with Christ. To some extent they must suffer as he suffered. As the ungodly persecuted Jesus, so they will persecute his followers (John 15:18,20; Acts 14:22; 2 Cor 1:5; Phil 1:29; 3:10; 1 Peter 2:21; 4:13; see PERSECUTION). Such sufferings may test the genuineness of their faith, but may also produce in them greater strength and maturity of character (1 Peter 1:6-7; 5:10; cf. Heb 2:10; see TESTING). But Jesus' sufferings were followed by glory, and those who suffer for his sake can look forward to sharing in that glory (Rom 8:17-18; 1 Peter 5:10).

SUN

The Bible recognizes that the sun exercises control over certain processes of life in the world, and it sees this as a sign that God created the world and continues to care for it (Gen 1:14-18; Deut 33:13-14; Matt 5:45). The sun is a symbol of permanency and endurance (Ps 72:5,17; 89:36), but it is not eternal. It is something God has created, and therefore it must not become an object of worship (Deut 4:19; Ps 136:7-9; Ezek 8:16-18; Rom 1:18-23). The sun was darkened at the time of Jesus' crucifixion, and will be darkened again at the time of his return to judge the world (Matt 27:45; Mark 13:24-27).

SUSA (SHUSHAN)

The city of Susa was one of the oldest in the ancient world. It was capital of the ancient Mesopotamian kingdom of Elam. When Elam was absorbed by Persia, Susa became capital of Persia, and remained so throughout the era of the Persian Empire (Ezra 4:9; Neh 1:1; Esther 1:2,5; 4:8; 8:14; Dan 8:2; see PERSIA).

SWEAR

See OATH.

SYCHAR

The village of Sychar belonged to the Samaritans and was near the ancient town of Shechem (John 4:5-6). (For details see SHECHEM.)

SYNAGOGUE

During the time of the Jews' captivity in Babylon, they were unable to carry out sacrificial rituals. Not only were they in a foreign land, but their place of sacrifice, the Jerusalem temple, had been destroyed in 587 BC. The Jewish religious leaders therefore placed greater emphasis on teaching the moral commandments of the law than on teaching temple rituals. When the Jews returned to Jerusalem and rebuilt the temple (completed in 516 BC), they maintained this emphasis on teaching and explaining the law (Neh 8:1-4,7-8; 9:1-3). This teaching activity was partly responsible for the building of local meeting places known as synagogues (from a Greek word meaning 'to gather or bring together').

Community centre

A synagogue was a centre for prayer, worship, teaching and administration in any locality where there were enough Jews to make such a centre workable. It was a gathering point for the Jews in the locality, a place where they had fellowship and discussed community affairs. The gathering as well as the building could be called the synagogue (Luke 12:11). There was no altar in a synagogue and no sacrifices were offered there.

Wherever the Jews went they built synagogues, with the result that there were synagogues in many countries of the ancient world (Mark 1:21; Luke 4:16; Acts 9:1; 13:5,14; 17:1,10; 18:1,4; 19:8). These synagogues soon became more important in the development and operation of Judaism than the temple in Jerusalem. They helped give Judaism the particular features with which we are familiar in the New Testament.

The leaders of the synagogues were the recognized leaders in the Jewish community and were known as elders (Mark 15:1; Luke 7:3-5). They had power to punish wrongdoers, even to the extent of arresting them, whipping them, or expelling them from the synagogue community (Matt 10:17; 23:34; John 9:22; 16:2; Acts 22:19).

Religious services

In design a synagogue was a simple building. It consisted of a main meeting room entered through a porch, with an open court outside. During religious services, women and men sat on opposite sides of the room, with the leaders sitting in the chief seats, facing the audience (Matt 23:6). The chief leader was known as the ruler of the synagogue (Mark 5:22; Acts 18:8).

Synagogue services were conducted at least every Sabbath and were under the control of the leaders (Mark 1:21; Luke 13:14; Acts 13:14-15). The service opened with prayers, followed by readings from the Old Testament scrolls. These were kept in a special box and were handed to the reader by an attendant (Luke 4:16-17,20; Acts 15:21).

Since many Jews were not familiar with the Hebrew language, a paraphrase or interpretation of the Old Testament readings was usually given. (These paraphrases, known as targums, later became authorized interpretations and eventually were put into writing.) Then followed an address. This was usually based on the previously read portion of Scripture (Luke 4:20-21), and was given either by one of the leaders or by some other suitable person whom the leaders invited (Luke 4:16-17; 6:6; Acts 13:15; 17:10-11; 18:4). The service was closed with prayers.

By the time of Jesus, the people who most influenced the teaching given in the synagogues were the scribes, or teachers of the law. These people had risen to places of power during the centuries leading up to the New Testament era (see SCRIBES), but instead of teaching the law of Moses they taught Judaism, a system of religious regulations that they had developed (Matt 23:2-8; Mark 7:1-5; 12:38-39; Luke 6:6-7).

Because of the scribes, the synagogues became more of a hindrance than a help to God's people. Jesus often came into conflict with the synagogue authorities, and so did the early Christians (Matt 6:2,5; 10:17; 12:9-14; Luke 13:14-15; John 9:22; 12:42; Acts 14:1-2; 17:1-5; 18:4-7; Rev 2:9; 3:9).

SYRIA

The land of Syria bordered Israel to the north and stretched up into the mountains beyond the head-waters of the Euphrates River. The Old Testament mentions Syria chiefly in relation to its wars with Israel during the time of the divided kingdom. The New Testament mentions it chiefly in relation to the expansion of the early church.

Old Testament records

Originally Syria was known as Aram, and some versions of the Bible consistently use 'Aram' rather than 'Syria' in the Old Testament narratives (see ARAM). The land included parts of Mesopotamia, along with various smaller kingdoms such as Zobah, Geshur and Hamath (Deut 23:4; Judg 3:8; 1 Sam

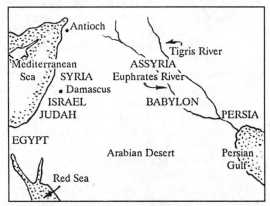

14:47; 2 Sam 3:3; 8:3,9). The capital of Syria during the time of its conflict with Israel was Damascus (1 Kings 11:24; Isa 7:8; see DAMASCUS).

The 'Israel' with whom Syria fought was the northern part of the divided Israelite nation, as distinct from Judah, the southern part. Syria's oppression of Israel began, it seems, during the reign of the Syrian king Ben-hadad I (1 Kings 15:16-22).

During the reign of the next king, Ben-hadad II, a combined army of Syria and neighbouring states attacked the Israelite capital, Samaria, but was defeated twice (1 Kings 20:1-31). The prophet Elisha on one occasion healed the commander-in-chief of the Syrian army, and on another was consulted when the Syrian king was ill (2 Kings 5:1-14; 8:7-8).

Ben-hadad II was assassinated by Hazael, who then seized the throne for himself. Hazael was a brutal enemy who repeatedly attacked Israel and butchered its people (2 Kings 8:12-15,28; 10:32; 12:17; 13:3,22; Amos 1:3-4). During the reign of the following king, Ben-hadad III, Israel regained much of the territory that it had lost to Hazael (2 Kings 13:25). Syria continued to decline in power, and

Israel at one stage took control of Damascus for a brief period (2 Kings 14:28).

With the rise of Assyria to power, both Syria and Israel were in danger of being conquered. The Syrian king Rezin and the Israelite king Pekah combined to attack Judah, with the aim of forcing Judah into a three-nation alliance that might be able to withstand Assyria. But Judah appealed to Assyria for help, and Assyria responded by conquering Syria and much of Israel (2 Kings 15:37; 16:5-9; Isa 7:1-9; 17:1-3). This marked the end of Syria as a separate and independent nation (732 BC).

Into the New Testament era

During the latter part of the fourth century BC, Alexander the Great established the Greek Empire throughout eastern Europe and western Asia. After Alexander's death in 323 BC, the empire split into sectors under the control of Alexander's Greek generals. One of these sectors was centred on Syria, and in 300 BC the city of Antioch was built as the administrative capital of the Syrian sector (see ANTIOCH IN SYRIA).

A dynasty of thirteen kings, most of them bearing the name Antiochus, reigned over Syria for about two and a half centuries. At first they commanded a large area stretching as far as Asia Minor in the west and Persia in the east. But over the years they consistently lost territory, till in the end they controlled only Syria itself. (For details of this era see GREECE.) Then, in 64 BC, they were conquered by Rome, and Syria became a province of the emerging Roman Empire (Luke 2:2).

Christianity first came to Syria through the efforts of Greek-speaking Jewish Christians who had been forced out of Jerusalem after the execution of Stephen (Acts 8:1; 9:1-2,10,19; 11:19-20). Paul was converted in Syria and carried out his first recorded evangelistic ministry there (Acts 19:1-22; Gal 1:21). He played an important part in the early growth of the church in Antioch (Acts 11:19-26), and when opportunities arose he visited churches throughout the province (Acts 15:41; 18:18-22).

TABERNACLE

When Israel left Egypt to begin a new life as an independent nation, God gave detailed arrangements for its organized religious life. According to these arrangements, Israel's place of worship was to be a tabernacle, or tent, set up in the centre of the camp. This tabernacle was the symbol of God's presence, a sign that God dwelt among his people. He was part of them, the centre of their national life.

It was known as the tent of meeting (Exod 39:32), for it was the place where God met with his people. It was also called the tent of the testimony (Exod 38:21), to remind the people that within it, in the ark, was the testimony of God, the law, which was to guide and control their lives.

The tabernacle was designed so that it could be easily put together, taken apart and transported. It was a prefabricated shrine that the people of Israel took with them on their journey to Canaan and set up at camps along the way. It consisted of a two-roomed timber structure inside a tent, which in turn was set in a large court surrounded by a fence. Within the rooms, and in the open court, were articles of sacred furniture.

Inside the tent

Probably the easiest way to picture the two-roomed structure under the tent is as a box-like frame with a cloth draped over it (as a tablecloth drapes over a table). The structure was 30 cubits long, 10 cubits wide and 10 cubits high (a cubit being about 44 centimetres or 18 inches). It was formed on the sides and rear by wooden frames that fitted vertically into metal bases and were joined horizontally with wooden bars. A row of timber columns formed the front, and another divided the structure into two rooms. All timber was overlaid with gold (Exod 26:15-37).

A multi-coloured embroidered linen covering was then draped over the entire structure, forming a ceiling overhead and walls on three sides. Curtains hung on columns formed the entrance and the internal partition (Exod 26:1-6,31-37). A covering of goats' hair was placed over the linen covering to give added protection (Exod 26:7-13).

This covered structure was shielded from the weather by a two-layer tent of animal skins pitched over the whole (Exod 26:14). Though brilliantly coloured inside, outwardly the shrine appeared as simply a tent; hence the name, tabernacle.

The front room of the structure was called the Holy Place and contained three articles of furniture. Against one wall was a table made of wood overlaid with gold. On it were twelve cakes of 'presence bread', in symbolic acknowledgment that Israel lived constantly in the presence of God, its provider. The cakes were renewed each Sabbath (Exod 25:23-30; Lev 24:5-9). Against the opposite wall was a seven-headed ornamented lampstand made entirely of gold (Exod 25:31-40; 26:35; see LAMP). Against the dividing curtain (or veil) was an altar used solely for burning incense. It was made of wood overlaid with gold. The daily offering of incense symbolized the

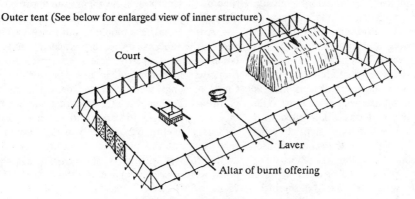

Outer tent (See below for enlarged view of inner structure)

Court

Laver

Altar of burnt offering

ABOVE: THE TABERNACLE AND ITS COURT

BELOW: ENLARGED CUTAWAY OF INNER STRUCTURE

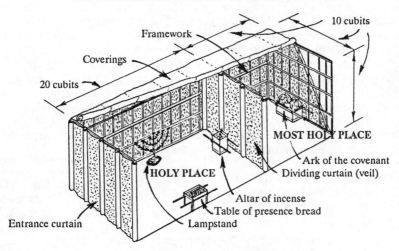

Framework

Coverings

20 cubits

10 cubits

MOST HOLY PLACE

Ark of the covenant

Dividing curtain (veil)

HOLY PLACE

Altar of incense

Table of presence bread

Entrance curtain

Lampstand

THE TABERNACLE

continual offering of the people's homage to God (Exod 30:1-10; see INCENSE).

The room behind the veil was called the Most Holy Place, or Holy of Holies, and was only half the size of the Holy Place. The only piece of furniture in this room was a wooden box, overlaid with gold, known as the ark of the covenant, or covenant box (Exod 25:10-16; 26:34). Its richly ornamented lid, called the mercy seat, was the symbolic throne of the invisible God. The symbolic guardians of this throne were two golden cherubim (Exod 25:17-21; 1 Sam 4:4; see CHERUBIM).

In giving this throne the name 'mercy', or 'grace', God reminded his people that in spite of all their religious exercises, they could be accepted into his presence and receive his forgiveness only by his

mercy (Exod 25:22; cf. Heb 4:16). Inside the ark were placed the stone tablets of the law (Deut 10:1-5), and later, Aaron's rod and the golden pot of manna (Heb 9:4).

Only priests could go into the Holy Place (Num 18:1-7; Heb 9:6). Only the high priest could go into the Most Holy Place, and then only once a year, on the Day of Atonement (Lev 16:11-15; Heb 9:7; see DAY OF ATONEMENT; PRIEST).

Courtyard and camp

This tabernacle-tent was set in a large court, 100 cubits long and 50 cubits wide, in which all the animal sacrifices were offered. Around the court was a fence of cloth attached to posts, with an entrance on the eastern side, opposite the entrance to the tent. The fence gave protection against desert winds and was high enough to prevent people outside from watching proceedings out of idle curiosity. It separated the tabernacle sufficiently from the camp to help create a feeling of reverence towards the tabernacle and its services (Exod 27:9-19).

All animal sacrifices were offered on a large altar that was made of wood overlaid with a metal variously described as bronze, copper or brass. The altar was a hollow box that was either filled with earth to form a mound on which the sacrifices were burnt, or had an internal grid for the same purpose. Halfway up the outside of the altar was a horizontal ledge supported by a grating. The priests may have stood on this ledge while offering the sacrifices (Exod 27:1-8).

Between the bronze altar and the entrance to the tent was a laver, or large basin, in which the priests washed before administering the sacrifices or entering the Holy Place. It also was made of bronze. The priests' washings had both a practical purpose and a symbolic significance, to demonstrate that cleansing from all uncleanness was necessary in the worship and service of God (Exod 30:17-21; 38:8; cf. 2 Chron 4:6).

The people of Israel camped in an orderly arrangement on the four sides of the tabernacle. Nearest the tabernacle, on the eastern side, were the priests. The three family divisions of the Levites were on the other three sides (Num 3:23,29,35,38). Further out were the common people according to their tribes, with three tribes on each of the four sides (Num 2:3,10,18,25).

Construction and maintenance

Building materials for the tabernacle came from the voluntary offerings of the people. They gave so generously that Moses had to restrain them (Exod 25:2; 36:5-7). In making the different parts of the tabernacle, the craftsmen had to conform to the overall pattern and dimensions that God gave (Exod 25:9,40), but they still had plenty of opportunity to use their skills in the structural and ornamental details (Exod 31:1-9). Moses inspected the separate parts of the tabernacle after they were finished (Exod 39:32-43), then supervised the erection of the whole (Exod 40:1-33).

Israelites no doubt saw symbolic significance in the differing values of materials outside and inside the tabernacle. As one moved from the outer court through the Holy Place into the Most Holy Place, the brilliance of the metals and the richness of the cloth hangings increased. It all helped to emphasize the majesty and holiness of Yahweh, the King of Israel who lived among his people, yet at the same time dwelt separately from them in unapproachable glory (Exod 40:34-35).

Apart from its symbolic significance to God's people, the tabernacle was very practically suited to Israel's circumstances. A tent over a prefabricated frame was most convenient for a travelling people. Cloth hangings were suitable for entrances and partitions. Timber was of a type that was plentiful in the region, light to carry, and did not warp or rot easily. Metals were of a type that would not rust. Some of the pieces of furniture were fitted at the corners with rings, through which carrying poles were placed to make transport easier (Exod 25:12-15,26-28; 27:6-7; 30:4-5).

Money for the maintenance of the tabernacle came from a special tax taken from the people whenever there was a national census. The tax was equal for all, but small enough for even the poorest to pay. The rich could gain no advantage. All God's people had an equal share in maintaining the tabernacle and its services (Exod 30:11-16).

Only Levites, however, could carry out the work of cleaning, repairing, erecting, dismantling and transporting the tabernacle. They were to do so according to the specific allocation of duties that God set out (Num 3:21-39; 4:1-33; see LEVITES). (Concerning the sacrifices offered at the tabernacle see SACRIFICE.)

Purpose fulfilled

Throughout their journey from Sinai to Canaan, the people of Israel set up the tabernacle at their camping places (Num 10:33-36; 33:1-49). When they entered Canaan, they set it up in their main camp at Gilgal (Josh 4:19; 10:6,15,43). After the conquest, they shifted the camp to a more central location at Shiloh, where again they set up the tabernacle (Josh 18:1; 19:51). It remained there for most of the next two hundred years (Judg 18:31; 1 Sam 1:3), though there was a period when it was in the neighbouring town of Bethel (Judg 20:26-27).

It seems that during Israel's time of conflict with the Philistines, the tabernacle was destroyed in an enemy attack upon Shiloh (Ps 78:60-61; Jer 7:12-14; 26:6,9). But the Israelites apparently rebuilt it, for later it was set up at Nob (1 Sam 21:1,6; Mark 2:26), and then at Gibeon (1 Chron 16:39; 21:29; 2 Chron 1:3,6).

For much of this time the ark of the covenant had become separated from the tabernacle (1 Sam 4:4,11; 7:2; 2 Sam 6:1-2,10-17; 2 Chron 1:3-4; see ARK). When Solomon built the temple in Jerusalem, he dismantled the tabernacle and stored it in the temple (1 Kings 8:1-11).

With the replacement of the movable tent by a permanent building, misunderstandings soon arose. Instead of realizing that God was among his people wherever they were, people thought that the temple in Jerusalem was the only place where he dwelt. When the early Christian preacher Stephen attacked this mistaken attitude, the Jews responded by killing him (Acts 7:44-50).

The New Testament book of Hebrews points out that the tabernacle had a purpose in demonstrating important truths concerning sinful man's approach to a holy God. The tabernacle system was a help to people in the era before Christ, but it also pointed to something far better. The truths that the tabernacle demonstrated reached their full expression in the new era that came with Jesus Christ (Heb 6:19-20; 8:1-5).

Although the tabernacle system was imperfect, it was not wrong in principle. It was imperfect only because it suffered those limitations of the pre-Christian era that Christ, and Christ alone, could overcome (Heb 9:1-14,24; 10:19-20).

TALENT

The talent was the heaviest weight used in Israel in Bible times. It weighed approximately 50 kilogram (110 pounds), was equal to 3,000 shekels, and was used mainly in weighing metals (Exod 38:27). Large quantities of money were usually weighed in talents, smaller quantities in shekels (1 Kings 10:10; 2 Kings 15:19; 18:14).

Silver was the metal most commonly used for money. Unless otherwise stated, a talent, when used as a monetary unit, meant a talent of silver (1 Kings 16:24; Ezra 8:25-27; Matt 18:23-24; 25:14-16). (See also COINS; WEIGHTS.)

TARSHISH

It is thought that Tarshish was a land in the western Mediterranean region, probably in Spain. It was rich in silver, iron, tin and lead (Jer 10:9; Ezek 27:12). Tarshish was one of the wealthy trading nations of the ancient world (Ps 72:10; Ezek 27:25) and built large ships to carry goods far and wide to many countries (Jonah 1:3; 4:2).

The ships of Tarshish were so successful that they became the model on which people throughout the region built their large merchant ships. As a result, 'ship of Tarshish' became the common name for any large ocean-going cargo ship, especially an ore-carrier. The name described a certain type of ship. It had nothing to do with the place where a

particular ship was made, or the place to which or from which it was sailing (1 Kings 10:22; 22:48; Isa 2:16; 23:1,14).

TARSUS

Chief city of the province of Cilicia, Tarsus was a large and important city in the days of the Roman Empire (Acts 21:39; for map see ACTS, BOOK OF). It was famous for its educational institutions, and was considered the centre of learning in Asia Minor (as Athens was in Greece and as Alexandria was in Egypt). Tarsus was Paul's home town (Acts 9:11,30; 11:25; 22:3) and this may have had some influence on his education. Paul's style of systematic thinking suggests a Greek educational background of the type available in Tarsus.

TAX COLLECTOR

The Roman taxation system operated on a plan where each state was divided into a number of regions, in each of which an appointed person was to provide Rome with an agreed amount of tax for

Collecting taxes on goods

that region. This person then had to arrange for others to help him collect the taxes. These taxes included both direct personal taxes and taxes on goods that people transported from one district to another (Matt 9:9). There were various grades of tax collectors (Luke 19:2).

All these tax collectors had to collect enough money to send to Rome the amount required, yet have enough left over as wages for themselves. The system gave much scope for corrupt practices (Luke 3:12-13; 19:8). As a result tax collectors had a bad reputation, and were usually associated with the most despised people in society (Matt 5:46; 9:10; 11:19; 18:17; Mark 2:15-17).

Jews hated both the Romans who ruled them and those who collected taxes for Rome, particularly if those tax collectors were Jews. It was almost as if they were traitors to their own people. Yet many tax collectors turned from their sin to believe in Jesus, and one even became a member of Jesus' chosen group of twelve apostles (Matt 9:9; 10:3; 21:31-32; Luke 18:13; 19:2,9; see MATTHEW).

TEACHER

God desires that his people learn about him and his Word, and therefore he has given teachers to instruct them (Deut 33:10; Eph 4:11). They may be people of different types and have different ways of teaching, but their teaching must have its origin in God himself. God is the only true teacher (Ps 25:4; 119:12; Matt 23:8-10; John 6:45; 1 Cor 2:12-13; 2 Tim 3:16).

A variety of teachers

Although God gives special teaching abilities to some, he does not expect these to be the only teachers. Parents are to teach their children the way of God (Deut 11:19; Eph 6:4; 2 Tim 3:14-15), and any godly person may teach others, though not necessarily in public meetings (2 Kings 12:2; Ps 34:11-14; Prov 10:21; Acts 18:26; Col 3:16; 2 Tim 2:24-25;).

In Old Testament times, Israel's religious and civil leaders had a wide-ranging responsibility to teach the law of God to the people (Exod 18:20; Deut 33:10; 2 Chron 17:7-9; Mal 2:7; see PRIEST). Prophets taught in the name of God, bringing his message to a people who were constantly turning from the path of devotion to him (Isa 30:20-21; Jer 23:22; 32:33; see PROPHET). Wisdom teachers gave instruction of a different kind, but it all helped to guide God's people in the way that was right (Prov 2:1-2; 4:10-11; 7:1-5; Eccles 12:9,13; see WISDOM LITERATURE).

Another group to gain prominence were the scribes, or teachers of the law. The early scribes were godly men who explained and applied God's law sensibly (Ezra 7:6,10; Neh 8:1-3,8), but by the time of Jesus the scribes had developed into a class of traditionalists whose teachings prevented people from entering the kingdom of God (Matt 15:9; 23:1-7,13; Luke 11:52; see SCRIBES).

The title 'teacher' (or, in the Hebrew, 'rabbi') was in common use in the time of Jesus. People used it when addressing teachers of the law, both good and bad (Matt 23:8; John 3:10), and likewise used it when addressing Jesus (Mark 9:5; John 1:38; 3:2; 6:25; 9:2). The teaching of Jesus, however, was in marked contrast to that of the scribes (Matt 7:28-29; 19:16-22).

Jesus the teacher

Jesus had not been trained in the schools of the rabbis, yet people were amazed at the authority of his teaching (Mark 11:18; Luke 4:22; John 7:15; cf. Acts 4:13). He taught in the synagogues, in the temple, in people's homes and in the open air (Matt 9:35; Mark 12:35; Luke 5:3; 10:38-39). He taught the masses publicly and his own disciples privately (Mark 6:34; 13:3), delivering his messages through discussions, arguments, parables and direct teaching (Matt 13:10; 22:41-46; John 3:1-14; 8:12-20; 16:29; see PARABLES).

A central theme of Jesus' teaching was that he had come from God (John 7:28-29; 8:28), that his teaching was from God (John 7:16) and that through him the kingdom of God had come among mankind (Matt 4:23; 5:1-3; Luke 17:21-22; see KINGDOM OF GOD). His teaching was so much a proclamation of the good news of the kingdom that any technical difference between teaching and preaching tended to disappear (Matt 9:35; Mark 6:6,12). (Elsewhere in the New Testament likewise there seems to be little difference between teaching and preaching; see PREACHING.)

Although Jesus enlightened people concerning the truth of the gospel, he also challenged them to make a response. His teaching was a call to a life of discipleship (Mark 8:34-38; Luke 9:57-62; 14:25-33; see DISCIPLE).

In training his disciples, Jesus taught them the truth that his Father had given him (John 17:8), so that after his return to the Father, they might carry on the work of the kingdom. They were to proclaim the good news, make disciples of Jesus, and teach them the truth that Jesus himself had taught (Matt 28:19-20). Jesus promised that in this task they would have his help, through the unseen teacher whom he would send to dwell within them, the Spirit of truth (John 14:18,25-26; 15:26; 16:13; see HOLY SPIRIT).

The work of apostles

Jesus' inner group of disciples, the apostles, were the teachers in the early church, and believers accepted their teaching as authoritative (Acts 2:42; 5:42). Even the teaching of additional apostles such as Paul was recognized by the church as being an authoritative interpretation of the life, work and teaching of Jesus (Acts 15:35; 1 Cor 14:37; 15:1-5; 1 Thess 2:13; see APOSTLE).

As the church grew, God provided for it further by giving to certain people the gift of teaching. These teachers did not have the unique position of apostles, but they had the God-given ability to understand and teach the Old Testament Scriptures and the apostolic doctrines (Rom 12:7; 1 Cor 12:28; Eph 4:11; 1 Tim 4:13-16). It seems that the office of apostle, having fulfilled the primary purpose for which Jesus appointed it, died out once the church was well established (Eph 2:20). The gift of teacher, however, has continued.

Teachers in the church

In the list of gifts that the risen Christ gave to the church (Eph 4:11), teachers are linked with pastors in a way that indicates that both words refer to the same people. Teachers must be pastors. Through their teaching they care for and feed the flock (Acts 20:28; see PASTOR). They aim to build up the church through producing greater ability among the church members to serve God and understand his Word (Eph 4:12).

The instruction that teachers give should cover the whole of God's Word (Acts 20:27; cf. Matt 28:20), so that Christians will increasingly develop the ability to discern between what is wholesome and what is not, and so grow towards spiritual maturity (Eph 4:13-14; Col 1:28; Heb 5:12-14). At the same time they will help bring healthy growth to the church as a whole (Eph 4:15-16). Teachers should not waste time arguing over senseless matters, but concentrate on the type of teaching that produces the knowledge of God, a sincere faith and a pure life (Col 1:28; 1 Tim 1:3-5; 4:6-8; 2 Tim 2:23-25; 4:1-2).

Those who are taught have a responsibility to support financially those who teach them (1 Cor 9:14; Gal 6:6; 1 Tim 5:17). At the same time they must beware of false teachers. They must therefore test what they hear, to make sure it is consistent with the Christian faith (1 Thess 5:20-21; 2 Thess 2:15; 1 Tim 6:3; cf. Acts 15:1; 1 Tim 1:7; 2 Tim 4:3-4; 1 John 4:1; 2 John 7-11; see HERESY).

Teachers, for their part, must make sure not only that what they teach is true, but that their lives are consistent with their teaching (1 Tim 4:15-16; James 3:1). They should also look for those who show signs of having the gift of teaching and help them develop it (2 Tim 2:2; cf. 1 Tim 4:13-14; Heb 5:12; see GIFTS OF THE SPIRIT).

TEMPLE

A temple was a house for a god, a place where the god dwelt and was worshipped. This was so in the case of the false gods that Israel's neighbours worshipped (1 Sam 5:2; 31:10; 1 Kings 16:32; 2 Kings 5:18), and in the case of the one and only true God whom Israel worshipped (Ps 5:7; 134:1; Hag 1:8-9; Matt 12:4; John 2:16; cf. 1 Cor 6:19; Rev 11:19).

However, the true God, who is the eternal one and the creator of all things, cannot be contained in a building. The Israelite temple, like the tabernacle before it, was only a symbol of God's presence. It symbolized that he dwelt among his people (Exod 25:8; 1 Kings 8:10-13; Acts 7:48-50). God's original plan for such a dwelling place was the tabernacle, which, being a tent, was a movable shrine that could be set up anywhere. This demonstrated to the people that God was not limited to one locality. The people were to remember this when they built their permanent temple in Jerusalem (2 Sam 7:5-7; Acts 7:44-46).

The site of the temple in Jerusalem was a piece of land that David had bought from a local farmer on the hill of Zion (Moriah) (2 Sam 24:18,22-25; 2 Chron 3:1; Ps 74:2; 78:68-69; cf. Gen 22:2). Each of the later temples was built on the same site, on top of the ruins of the previous temple. All three temples were based on the plan of the tabernacle, though they were larger and they included additional features.

Solomon's temple

Simply described, the temple built by Solomon was a rectangular stone building with a porch added to the front, and three storeys of storerooms added to the sides and rear (1 Kings 6:1-10). Two huge bronze pillars stood in front of the porch. They did not support the roof, but were purely ornamental (1 Kings 7:15-22). Entrance from the porch into the temple was through decorated folding doors (1 Kings 6:33-35). All stonework inside the building was covered with lavishly carved wood panelling, which in turn was overlaid with beaten gold (1 Kings 6:1-10,15,21-22,29).

An internal partition divided the main temple into two rooms. The larger front room was called the nave or Holy Place, the smaller rear room the inner

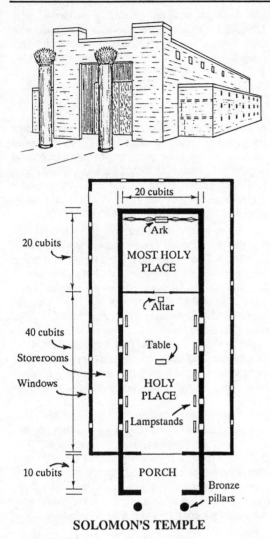

SOLOMON'S TEMPLE

(1 Kings 7:23-26). There were also ten mobile lavers, each consisting of a bronze basin set in a trolley, the four sides of which were enclosed with decorative panels (1 Kings 7:27-39).

The wealth of the temple's decorations and furnishings made it a target for enemy plunderers. At times the Judean kings themselves plundered it, usually to obtain funds to pay foreign overlords or invaders (1 Kings 14:25-26; 15:18; 2 Kings 16:8; 18:15). Some of Judah's more ungodly kings brought idols and other articles of foreign religion into the temple, and even introduced heathen practices (2 Kings 16:10-18; 21:4; 2 Chron 25:14).

As a result of Judah's unfaithfulness to God, the temple was frequently damaged or allowed to deteriorate. On a number of occasions godly kings repaired the temple and introduced reforms to restore it to its proper use (2 Kings 12:4-16; 2 Chron 29:3-11; 34:8-13). When the Babylonians destroyed Jerusalem in 587 BC, they stripped everything of value from the temple, then smashed or burnt what remained and took the people into captivity (2 Kings 25:8-17; cf. Ps 74:3-7).

Visions of Ezekiel

The captivity in Babylon would last no longer than seventy years, and the prophet Ezekiel wanted to prepare the people to return to their homeland. He therefore presented to them a plan for life in the rebuilt nation.

This plan, based on visions that Ezekiel saw, included a temple where God dwelt among his people in an ideal religious and political order. In this order the temple was not in the city, but in a large portion of land marked out for the priests (Ezek 45:1-4). The main building (the Holy Place and the Most Holy Place) was only one part of a huge complex of buildings, courtyards and various

sanctuary or Most Holy Place. The front room had windows, but not the rear room. This rear room contained the gold-covered ark of the covenant (covenant box), which symbolized the presence of God, and two winged creatures of gold (cherubim), which were symbolic guardians of the ark (1 Kings 6:31-32; 2 Chron 3:14; see ARK; CHERUBIM). The front room contained two pieces of gold-covered furniture, the altar of incense and the table of 'presence bread'. In addition there were ten golden lampstands, five on each of the two side walls (1 Kings 7:48-49; see LAMP).

In the open courtyard outside the building (1 Kings 6:36) stood a huge bronze altar of sacrifice (2 Chron 4:1). Also in the courtyard was a bronze laver, or tank, which held water for cleansing rites

Mobile laver used in the temple

facilities for priests and worshippers (Ezek 40:1-49; 41:1-42:14; 43:13-17; 46:19-24). Whatever symbolic value Ezekiel's visions may have had, his ideal temple was never built.

Zerubbabel's temple

When Persia conquered Babylon in 539 BC, the Persian king gave permission for the captive Jews to return to their land. Under the joint leadership of the governor Zerubbabel and the high priest Joshua, those who returned promptly began to rebuild the temple. They soon set up the altar, and in the second year they laid the foundation of the temple, but when local people opposed the builders, the work stopped (Ezra 3:1-3,8-10; 4:1-5,24). For sixteen years nobody worked on the temple. When the prophets Haggai and Zechariah roused the people to action, work restarted and within four years the temple was finished (Ezra 5:1-2; 6:15).

Little is known about this temple. It was not as large or as splendid as the former temple (Ezra 6:3-5; Hag 2:3; Zech 4:10), though like the former temple, it had storerooms for the people's offerings (Neh 13:4-9; Mal 3:10).

The best known events connected with this temple occurred in the second century BC. The leader of the Syrian sector of the former Greek Empire, Antiochus IV Epiphanes, being violently opposed to the Jews, found an excuse to invade and defile the temple. He set up an idolatrous altar, then took animals that the Jews considered unclean and offered them as sacrifices to the Greek gods. This led to a Jewish uprising under the leadership of a group known as the Maccabees. After three years of fighting, the Jews regained religious freedom and rededicated the temple (165 BC).

A century later, when the Romans invaded Palestine, the Jews converted the temple into a fortress that was strong enough to withstand the enemy for three months. Finally, in 63 BC, the Romans destroyed it.

Herod's temple

When Herod, who was not a genuine Jew, won Rome's appointment as 'king' of Judea, he tried to win the Jews' favour by building them a magnificent new temple. The main building took ten years to build and was finished about 9 BC, but builders were still working on the rest of the huge complex during the time of Jesus' public ministry (John 2:20). They finished the project in AD 64.

The main building consisted of two rooms, the Holy Place and the Most Holy Place, divided by a curtain (Matt 27:51). This building and its associated altar of burnt offering were set in a walled courtyard, which normally only the priests could enter (Luke 1:8-10).

Outside the Court of the Priests was another walled courtyard, known as the Court of Israel. Men could enter this courtyard, but not women. Beyond this was yet another walled courtyard, this one known as the Court of the Women, for it marked the limit beyond which women could not go. Entrance to this court was through the Beautiful gate (Acts 3:10), and inside the court were collection boxes for the temple offerings (Mark 12:41-44). No Gentiles were allowed into any of these courts, and any who attempted to do so risked death (Acts 21:28-31).

This fully enclosed area was set within a large open court called the Court of the Gentiles, for it was the only area open to Gentiles. Around the

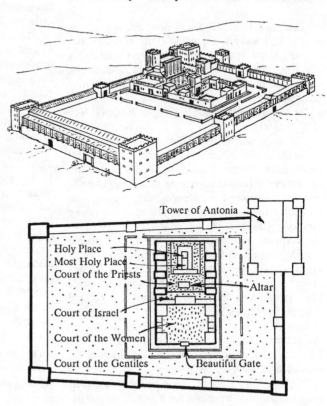

HEROD'S TEMPLE

Tower of Antonia

Holy Place
Most Holy Place
Court of the Priests

Altar

Court of Israel

Court of the Women

Court of the Gentiles

Beautiful Gate

perimeter of this court was a covered area where the teachers of the law taught (Luke 2:46; 19:47; John 10:23-24), where temple merchants carried out their business (John 2:14-16) and where the poor and the sick begged for help (Matt 21:14; Acts 3:11; 5:12,16).

In the north-eastern corner of the Court of the Gentiles was the Tower of Antonia. This was probably the praetorium, the palace where the Roman governor stayed when he came to Jerusalem to control the crowds at festival times (Matt 27:27; Mark 15:16; Acts 21:30-37). (Normally the governor lived at Caesarea; Acts 23:33.) The entire temple complex was surrounded by a wall made of huge stones (Mark 13:1).

The new temple

Jesus, being zealous for the true worship of God, condemned the Jews for their misuse of the temple. As a result the Jews became increasingly hostile towards him (John 2:13-22; Mark 11:15-19; cf. Mal 3:1). He condemned their religion as they practised it, and forecast that one of God's judgments on it would be the destruction of the temple (Mark 13:1-2).

Through Jesus, God was now building a new temple. This was not a building made of stones, but a community of people, the Christian church. This is a living temple, a community where God dwells, where his people worship him and where they maintain true holiness (John 4:21-24; 1 Cor 3:16-17; 2 Cor 6:16-18; Eph 2:21-22; 1 Peter 2:4-5; cf. Rev 21:22; 22:1-4).

It seems that many of the early Christians did not immediately understand that with the death and resurrection of Jesus, the temple had no further use in God's purposes for his people. They continued to go to the temple daily, worshipping, praying and witnessing to the resurrection life of Jesus (Luke 24:52-53; Acts 2:46-47; 3:1; 5:12,42).

Stephen, however, pointed out that if people thought Christianity was still part of the old temple-based religion, they were mistaken. The temple was in fact a hindrance to a proper understanding of Christianity (Acts 6:13; 7:44-50). The Jews reacted violently to Stephen's preaching and killed him; but at least there was now a clear distinction between the old temple-based religion and Christianity. The Christians' association with the temple was gone for ever (Acts 7:54-60; 8:1-3).

Within forty years the Jews also had lost their association with the temple; for in AD 70 the armies of Rome destroyed it (Mark 13:2; Luke 19:41-44). Since then, the Jews have had no temple.

TEMPTATION

In the original languages of the Bible, the words commonly translated 'temptation' had a range of meanings. These words were concerned basically with testing. In some cases the purpose of the testing may have been to prove the genuineness or quality of a person or thing. In other cases the purpose may have been to persuade a person to do wrong. In today's language, 'temptation' is usually used in the latter sense, and it is this sense that is the subject of the present article. (For other meanings of the word see TESTING.)

To be expected

God may allow people to meet temptations and trials in order to test their faith, but he will never tempt them to do evil. Rather he wants to deliver them from evil (Matt 6:13; 1 Cor 10:13; James 1:13; 2 Peter 2:9). Satan, not God, is the one who tempts people to do wrong (Gen 3:1-6; 1 Cor 7:5; 2 Cor 11:3; Eph 4:27; 6:11; 1 Peter 5:8-9). Some people blame God when they give in to temptation. The Scriptures point out that the source of their problem lies not with God, but with the sinful desires within their own hearts (James 1:13-14).

Sinful human nature creates within people a natural tendency towards sin. This increases the opportunities for temptation and makes them more likely to give in to it (Rom 7:11,14,21; Gal 5:17; Eph 4:22; 1 John 2:15-16; see FLESH).

But the temptation itself is not necessarily a sin. Jesus' nature was not corrupted by sin, and his behaviour was never spoiled by sin, yet he met temptation constantly (Luke 4:1,13; cf. Matt 16:23; 22:15; Mark 14:35; Luke 22:28; John 6:15; 12:27). In fact, the absence of sin in Jesus was the reason Satan attacked him all the more. Satan had tempted the sinless Adam, and now he tempted the sinless Jesus. But where Adam failed, Jesus triumphed (Matt 4:1-10; cf. Gen 3:1-6).

Israel failed temptation in the wilderness, but Jesus, the true fulfilment of Israel, triumphed over temptation in the wilderness (Matt 4:4,7,10; cf. Deut 6:13,16; 8:3). Jesus suffered the sorts of temptations that are common to mankind, but because he was victorious over them, he is able to help his people when they are tempted (Heb 2:18; 4:15).

No excuses

Temptation comes in many forms. Satan has many cunning methods, and people can easily get caught in his trap (2 Cor 2:11; 1 Thess 3:5; 1 Tim 6:9). But there can be no excuse for giving in to temptation, as there is always a way of escape (1 Cor 10:13).

Christians should not be over-confident in their own ability to overcome temptation (1 Cor 10:12). Instead they should be aware of the weakness of sinful human nature, and give it no opportunity to satisfy its desires (Rom 6:12; 13:14).

Although the sin lies in giving in to temptation rather than in the temptation itself, Christians must do all they can to avoid those situations likely to produce temptation (1 Cor 15:33; 2 Tim 2:22). This will require self-discipline as they develop better habits in their behaviour (Col 3:12-13; Gal 5:16), thinking (Rom 8:5; 2 Cor 10:5; Phil 4:8), talking (Eph 5:11-12; Titus 2:8) and praying (Matt 6:13; Mark 14:38). The guiding influence in helping God's people develop these better habits is the Word of God (Ps 119:11; 2 Tim 3:16-17).

The struggle against temptation is more than merely a struggle with the problems of everyday life. It is a battle against the evil powers of Satan (Eph 6:10-12). God has given his Word to his people to equip them for this battle (Matt 4:3-7; Eph 6:16-17), and he has given them the assurance of victory, provided they make the effort to resist the tempter. Each victory strengthens them and enables them to live more confidently and positively in a world still full of temptations (James 4:7; 1 Peter 5:9-10).

TEN COMMANDMENTS

See LAW.

TENT

Because tents could be easily put up and taken down, they were the normal dwelling places of ancient peoples who moved around from place to place with their flocks and herds. They were among

An eastern tent

the earliest dwelling places man invented (Gen 4:20; 9:21; 12:8; 18:1; 26:25; Song of Songs 1:8; Isa 38:12; Jer 49:28-29).

Tents were made of the skins of animals, the woven hair of animals, or heavy cloth. The material was stretched over poles and tied with cords to pegs in the ground. Tents were dark and drab externally, but internally they were usually colourful, because of the curtain hangings that divided them into rooms (Song of Songs 1:5; Isa 54:2).

Sometimes there were separate tents for men and women (Gen 18:6,9; 31:33). Armies camped in tents (2 Kings 7:7-8), and the Israelites camped in tents on their journey from Egypt to Canaan (Exod 16:16; 33:8; Num 16:26; 24:5; Deut 1:27).

Israel's place of worship, which they took with them on the journey, was in the form of a tent (Exod 26:14,36; see TABERNACLE). When David conquered Jerusalem he put the ark of the covenant in a tent he had erected for it in the city, in anticipation of the permanent temple he had planned for Jerusalem. This would replace the tabernacle-tent, which at that time was at Gibeon (1 Chron 16:1,39).

Bible writers use the tent as a picture of man's brief life. It comes to an inglorious end like a tent that collapses when its cords are cut (Job 4:21). But whereas the physical body is, like a tent, temporary, what God has prepared for the believer in the age to come is a permanent home (2 Cor 5:1).

TESTIMONY

See WITNESS.

TESTING

Some older versions of the Bible use the word 'temptation' in a variety of ways, some of them with the meaning rather of testing. Such testing is an action designed usually to prove the success or failure of a person or thing. This meaning of 'testing' is the subject of the present article. Concerning the better known meaning of temptation (that is, to tempt to do wrong) see TEMPTATION.

People may test the genuineness of metals by putting them into a fire. The purpose is to remove any impurities, so that the pure metal remains. In like manner God tests his people, allowing them to pass through trials in order to reveal whether their faith is genuine (Deut 8:2; Ps 66:10; Prov 17:3; Isa 48:10-11; Jer 20:12; 1 Peter 4:12). Those who pass the test find they are purified and strengthened by the experience (Gen 22:1; Deut

8:16; 13:3; Judg 2:22; Heb 11:17; James 1:2-3,12; 1 Peter 1:6-7; see REFINE).

The Bible tells Christians to test, or examine, themselves, to make sure they are really living by faith in Jesus Christ (2 Cor 13:5). This testing, in the sense of examination, must extend to all things, from matters of everyday living to matters concerning the church. As God's people choose what is worthwhile and reject what is worthless, they will grow towards maturity (Phil 1:10; 1 Thess 5:21; 1 Tim 3:10; Heb 5:14; 1 John 4:1).

Arrogant people sometimes try to test God by challenging him to do what they demand as a proof of his knowledge, power or love. Such a challenge is rebellion against God and may bring his punishment (Exod 17:7; Num 14:22; Deut 6:16; Ps 95:8-11; Matt 4:7; Acts 5:9; 15:10; 1 Cor 10:9). Jesus' opponents showed such an attitude when they challenged him to prove that he was the Son of God (Mark 8:11; 15:29-30; cf. Matt 4:5-7).

THADDAEUS

Little is known of Thaddaeus, apart from his appointment as one of Jesus' twelve apostles. From the comparison of the lists of names in the four Gospels, it seems that 'Thaddaeus' was another name for Judas the son of James (Matt 10:3; Mark 3:18; Luke 6:16; John 14:22; Acts 1:13). (In some versions he is called the brother of James and given an alternative name, Lebbaeus.)

THANKSGIVING

The lives of God's people are to be characterized by the offering of thanksgiving to God — always, for everything, and in all circumstances (Eph 5:19-20; Phil 4:6; 1 Thess 5:18). They are to give thanks for blessings, spiritual and physical (Col 1:12; 1 Tim 4:3-4), in their own lives and in the lives of others (Acts 28:15; 2 Thess 1:3; 2:13). Thanksgiving is part of praise, prayer and worship (Ps 95:1-7; 116:17; Col 4:2; Rev 7:12; 11:17). (See also PRAISE; PRAYER; WORSHIP.)

Believers should remind themselves constantly to thank God for all his blessings. They can do this by making sure that thanksgiving accompanies all their requests to God (Ps 30:12; 92:1-4; 103:1-5; Phil 4:6; Col 4:2; 1 Tim 2:1). They should be particularly thankful that God, in his love, has chosen them (2 Thess 2:13-14), made them sharers in his grace (1 Cor 1:4), equipped them with faith, hope and love (Col 1:3-5), and given them a part in the service of the gospel (2 Cor 1:11; Phil 1:4-5). By constantly

offering thanks to God, Christians help counter the influence of sin (Eph 5:4). By failing to offer thanks to God, they fail to give him the glory due to him (Luke 17:16-18).

THEBES

The city of Thebes was situated on the Nile River, over five hundred kilometres from its mouth. It was the most important city in Upper Egypt, and from 1570 to 1085 BC, the period of Egypt's greatest power and splendour, it was the country's capital. Its Hebrew name was No, and its god was Amon (Jer 46:25; Nahum 3:8). The wealth that poured into Thebes during those five hundred years helped to make the city the most magnificent in all Egypt.

One reason for Thebes' lengthy supremacy was the strong defence that the Nile River provided against enemy invasion. But these defences were not able to withstand the Assyrians, who in 663 BC plundered and destroyed the city (Ezek 30:14-16; Nahum 3:8-10). (For map and other details see EGYPT.)

THESSALONIANS, LETTERS TO

Thessalonica was a city in Macedonia in the north of Greece. Paul planted a church there during his second missionary journey, and soon after he wrote the church two letters that have been preserved in the New Testament.

Background to 1 Thessalonians

Paul's work in Thessalonica had been very fruitful, particularly among the non-Jewish population. This success stirred up the Jews' jealousy and opposition, and in the end Paul was forced to leave the city (Acts 17:1-9).

On arriving in Athens (in Achaia, the south of Greece), Paul sent his fellow worker Timothy back to Thessalonica to give additional help to the young church (1 Thess 3:1-2). Meanwhile, Paul went across to Corinth (also in Achaia), where Timothy met him after returning from Thessalonica (Acts 18:1-5; 1 Thess 3:6).

Timothy brought good news. The church in Thessalonica had grown much in only a short time, and had been so zealous in spreading the gospel into surrounding districts that Christians everywhere were praising God for it (1 Thess 1:6-9; 3:6). All this was in spite of the constant persecution that the church suffered (1 Thess 2:13-16).

In response to this good news, Paul wrote the letter known as 1 Thessalonians. He thanked God for the good news Timothy had brought concerning the Thessalonians, and encouraged them to maintain their enthusiasm and steadfastness. He also gave instruction in matters where the Christians' understanding was still uncertain. These included aspects of Christian behaviour and the nature of Christ's return.

Contents of 1 Thessalonians

In an opening expression of joyful praise, Paul thanks God for the Thessalonians' response to the gospel and their ongoing enthusiasm and growth (1:1-10). He reminds them of his own work in Thessalonica, and urges them to be honest and straightforward in all the work they do (2:1-12). He reminds them also that people who serve Christ can expect opposition (2:13-16).

Paul points out that he wanted to return to Thessalonica, but when he was unable to, he sent Timothy instead. He rejoices at the good news that Timothy has brought back (2:17-3:13). He goes on to give teaching about Christian behaviour in matters relating to marriage and work (4:1-12), and corrects some misunderstandings that people had concerning Christ's return (4:13-5:11). He closes his letter with a collection of brief statements on a variety of matters relevant both to individuals and to the church as a whole (5:12-28).

Background to 2 Thessalonians

Apparently the Thessalonians misunderstood some parts of the letter Paul had written to them, in particular those parts dealing with Christ's return. Some mistakenly thought that when Paul said Christ would return 'suddenly', he meant 'immediately'. If that was the case, they saw no purpose in working for a living and so became idle and lazy. Paul sent off his second letter to correct these, and related, misunderstandings.

Second Thessalonians was written only a short while after First Thessalonians. Paul was still in Corinth (he remained in Corinth for a year and a half; Acts 18:11) and he probably wrote the letter soon after hearing of the misunderstandings that had arisen over his previous letter.

Contents of 2 Thessalonians

As in his first letter, Paul begins by thanking God for the continued progress of the Thessalonian Christians. Although they are still suffering from persecution, they can be assured that the return of Jesus Christ will bring rest to them and punishment to their persecutors (1:1-12). Some thought that the Day of the Lord had begun, but Paul assures them it has not. There is yet to be a final great rebellion against God, but it will be overthrown by Christ

when he returns (2:1-12). By contrast, believers in Christ can face the future with confidence (2:13-17).

Paul asks prayer for himself, that his work for God in Corinth may be fruitful (3:1-5). He then deals with the problem of those who had become nuisances in the church through refusing to work (3:6-15). He concludes the letter in his usual manner by signing it personally (3:16-18).

THESSALONICA

After Alexander the Great established the Greek Empire (fourth century BC), the Greeks built many magnificent cities. One of these was Thessalonica in Alexander's home state of Macedonia. When the Greek Empire was later replaced by the Roman, Macedonia was made a Roman province, with Thessalonica as its political centre. The city was on the main route from Rome to Asia Minor, and is still an important city today.

There is only one recorded occasion on which Paul visited Thessalonica. This was on his second missionary journey, when he founded the church there, despite much opposition from the Jews. The church consisted mainly of Gentiles (Acts 17:1-7; 1 Thess 1:9). Although Paul worked to help support himself while in Thessalonica (1 Thess 2:9; 2 Thess 3:7-8), he received additional support from another Macedonian church, Philippi (Phil 4:16).

The church continued to grow after Paul left, and within a short time had spread the gospel throughout the surrounding countryside (1 Thess 1:6-8; 2:13-14). An important man in the church at Thessalonica was Aristarchus, who later went with Paul to Rome and remained there during Paul's imprisonment (Acts 20:4; 27:1-2; Col 4:10; Philem 24). (For details of the two letters Paul wrote to the church in Thessalonica see THESSALONIANS, LETTERS TO THE.)

THOMAS

It seems, from his name, that the apostle Thomas was a twin. The names Thomas and Didymus come from the words for 'twin' in the Aramaic and Greek languages respectively (Matt 10:3; John 11:16).

Three incidents show that Thomas was a straightforward person who expressed his feelings openly. The first occurred when Jesus, after leaving Judea to escape the Jews' attempt to kill him, decided to return. The disciples feared the dangers ahead and tried to dissuade him. When Jesus made it clear that he was determined to go, Thomas showed his courage and his pessimism by suggesting that they go with him so that they might die with him (John 10:39; 11:7-8,16).

The second incident occurred as the time drew near for Jesus to return to the Father. He reminded his disciples that they knew where he was going, but Thomas, with characteristic bluntness, replied that they did not (John 14:1-5).

The third incident occurred soon after the resurrection, when Thomas refused to believe the report that Jesus was alive. Upon meeting Jesus himself, he readily repented of his doubts and confessed Jesus to be his Lord and his God (John 20:24-29).

Thomas was one of the eleven apostles to hear Jesus' command to evangelize the world (Matt 28:16-20; Acts 1:6-13). According to tradition, his chief contribution to this task was to take the gospel to India.

THRESHING

See FARMING.

THRONE

People of the ancient world were familiar with the throne as a symbol of kingly power. A king usually sat on his throne when officiating at important ceremonies, when receiving homage or petitions

Throne of the King of Tyre

from his people, or when making legal judgments (1 Kings 2:19; 2 Kings 11:19; Esther 5:1; Prov 20:8). Often such thrones were lavishly adorned, befitting the majesty of the king in his exalted position (1 Kings 10:18-20).

God is repeatedly pictured in the Bible as the supreme Lord, the king and ruler of the universe who is high and lifted up, exalted on his throne. The angelic guardians of his throne are the cherubim, sometimes called 'living creatures' (Ps 80:1; 93:1-5; Isa 6:1-3; Ezek 1:22,26; 10:20-22; Matt 5:34; Rev 4:2,6; 5:11-14; see CHERUBIM).

The lid of the ark of the covenant in the tabernacle was a symbolic throne for the invisible God. Although sinful people have no right to enter God's presence, God in his mercy allows them to approach him in faith and so receive his forgiveness and help. His throne is therefore called a seat of mercy, a throne of grace (Exod 25:18; 1 Sam 4:4; Heb 4:16; 9:5; see TABERNACLE).

Jesus Christ, having become man and having been obedient to his Father's will even to death, has now been exalted to the highest place in heaven. This is signified by his being seated at the right hand of the throne of God (Phil 2:6-11; Heb 12:2). He, as the great high priest, is the believer's mediator before God in heaven, bringing the believer's real desires to the throne of God (Rom 8:34; Heb 7:24-25; 8:1).

The throne symbolizes rule and authority. Jesus Christ, therefore, in being pictured as seated on his throne, is King of kings and Lord of lords. He fulfils the promise given to David of a descendant who would sit on David's throne and rule for ever (2 Sam 7:12-16; Isa 11:1-9; Luke 1:32-33; Acts 2:30-33; Heb 1:8; Rev 19:16; see KING; MESSIAH). Believers in Jesus will share his reign with him (Matt 19:28; Rev 3:21). But the throne is also a place of judgment, where God will make the final separation between the righteous and the wicked (Matt 25:31-32; Rev 20:11-12; see JUDGMENT).

THYATIRA

Thyatira was an important manufacturing centre in the Roman province of Asia (present-day Turkey). It had factories for the manufacture of clothing, dyes, pottery and brasswork (Acts 16:14; Rev 2:18).

Towards the end of the first century, the church in Thyatira was troubled by a woman who was encouraging the Christians to join in idolatrous feasts and their accompanying immoral practices. The apostle John wrote to the church to warn the woman and her followers of the judgment for which they were heading, and to encourage the true Christians to remain faithful to God (Rev 2:19-29).

TIBERIAS

The town of Tiberias was on the western shore of Lake Galilee (also called the Sea of Galilee and the Sea of Tiberias) (John 6:1,23). Whereas towns on the northern shore were largely Jewish and were the scene of much of Jesus' ministry, Tiberias was almost entirely Gentile. There is no record that Jesus ever visited the town. (For map and other details see PALESTINE.)

TIGRIS

Two great rivers, the Tigris and the Euphrates, flowed through Mesopotamia, a fertile region that in biblical times was part of the lands of Aram, Assyria, Babylon and Persia (Gen 2:14-15; Dan

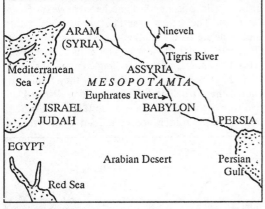

10:4). The Tigris is rarely mentioned in the Bible, though it features as the river on which Assyria's capital, Nineveh, was built (Nahum 2:6-8; cf. 3:8; see NINEVEH).

TIME

Life in the present world is inseparably bound up with time. Time is part of God's created order (Gen 1:14; Heb 1:2). By contrast God, being the eternal one and the creator of all things, is not limited in any way by time. This means that his view of time is different from man's (Isa 57:15; 1 Tim 1:17; 6:16; 2 Peter 3:8; see ETERNITY).

Nevertheless, God is able to use time to bring his purposes to fulfilment (Gal 4:4), and he gives it to man to use also (Eccles 5:18; 8:15). People are therefore responsible to God for the way they use their time (1 Peter 1:15-17). (Concerning systems for reckoning time see DAY; MONTH.)

As a wise, powerful and loving Creator, God sees that everything happens at the right time to maintain the world for the benefit of his creatures (Deut 11:14; 2 Kings 4:16; Eccles 3:11; Acts 14:17). He controls history, often announcing in advance the precise time for his actions (Exod 9:18; Isa 37:33-38; Acts 17:26). (Concerning the time element in the writings of the prophets see PROPHECY.) Jesus' birth, ministry, death and resurrection all took place at the time God had appointed (Gal 4:4; Mark 1:15; John 8:20; 12:23,27; 17:1). Christ's return will also occur when God's time has come (Mark 13:32; Acts 1:7; Rev 14:15; see DAY OF THE LORD).

Because history is moving constantly towards its great climax, Christians must use their time wisely (Ps 90:12; Col 4:5). They should see time not merely as a period measured by a clock or a calendar, but as an opportunity given them to use. This does not mean that they have to create unnecessary pressure by squeezing as much as they can into their time, but that they should live and behave as befits God's people (Eph 5:15-17; 1 Peter 4:1-3). The prospect of Christ's return is an incentive not to hectic activity but to more Christlike conduct (Rom 13:11-14; 1 John 2:18,28).

God wants people to use their time in worthwhile work, but his gift of the Sabbath shows that he also wants them to have time for rest (Exod 23:12; cf. Gen 2:2-3). People should not waste their time through laziness or worthless activities (Prov 10:4-5; 12:11; 18:9; 2 Thess 3:11-12; 1 Tim 5:13), but neither should they spend their time in constant activity that leaves no time for proper relaxation (Neh 13:15-21; Eccles 2:21-23; Amos 8:5; cf. Mark 6:30-31; Luke 10:40-42; see WORK).

In their concern for time, people should not try to calculate when present life will end. Rather they should use the opportunity of the present life to accept God's salvation and grow in Christian character (Acts 1:6-8; 2 Cor 6:1-2; Heb 3:13; 4:7; 5:12-14; 10:25; cf. Luke 12:16-20; James 4:13-16).

TIMOTHY

Most of the Bible's references to Timothy arise out of his close connection with Paul. The relationship between the two was such that Paul called Timothy his son, and spoke often of his love for Timothy and Timothy's devotion to him (1 Cor 4:17; Phil 2:19-20; 1 Tim 1:18).

Fitted for service

Timothy was born of a Greek father and a Jewish mother, and was brought up to know God. This was largely because his mother and grandmother taught him the Bible (Acts 16:1; 2 Tim 1:5; 3:14-15). He apparently first came in contact with Paul when Paul moved through the Galatian towns of Antioch, Iconium, Lystra and Derbe on his first missionary journey (2 Tim 3:10-11; cf. Acts 13:14-15:22). At that time Timothy was probably only a teenager.

By the time Paul passed through the Galatian towns again three years later, Timothy had so grown in his Christian life that Paul decided to take him as his assistant (Acts 16:1-3). In this he had the backing of Timothy's home churches, whose leaders publicly acknowledged Timothy's spiritual gifts (1 Tim 4:14). At this time Paul had Timothy circumcised, in the hope that this would gain acceptance for Timothy in the Jewish communities they wanted to reach with the gospel (Acts 16:3).

Timothy was not of naturally bold or forceful character. For this reason Paul repeatedly urged him to be more confident. Often Paul gave him tasks that would develop courage and win him greater respect throughout the churches (1 Cor 16:10-11; 1 Tim 1:3; 4:12-16; 2 Tim 1:6-8; 4:1-2).

Missionary travels

After travelling with Paul through Troas, Philippi, Thessalonica and Berea to Athens, Timothy was entrusted with his first individual mission. Paul sent him back to Thessalonica to help the young church.

The report that Timothy brought to Paul provided the basis for Paul's first letter to the Thessalonians (Acts 17:15; 1 Thess 3:1-2,6). By this time Paul was in Corinth, and Timothy helped in the preaching there (2 Cor 1:19).

During Paul's three-year stay in Ephesus (on his third missionary journey), Timothy was sent through Macedonia to Corinth, where he had to deal with serious disorders in the church (Acts 19:22; 1 Cor 4:17; 16:10). In due course he returned to Ephesus, and later accompanied Paul to Macedonia, from where Paul wrote the letter known as 2 Corinthians (2 Cor 1:1). He was still with Paul when Paul wrote to the Romans from Corinth (Rom 16:21). A short time later he was among the group of leading Christians who gathered in Troas to go with Paul to Jerusalem (Acts 20:4-6).

In Palestine Paul was imprisoned for two years (Acts 24:27). After that he was sent to Rome, where he was held prisoner for another two years (Acts 28:16,30). The letters that Paul wrote during this time indicate that Timothy was with him in Rome (Phil 1:1; Col 1:1; Philem 1). Upon his release, Paul set sail again, one of his travelling companions being Timothy. Upon coming to Ephesus, they found the church there troubled by false teaching. When Paul had to leave for Macedonia, he left Timothy behind in Ephesus. From Macedonia Paul then wrote a

letter to Timothy to encourage him in his difficult work (1 Tim 1:3).

Some time after this, the Roman authorities arrested Paul and took him to Rome again. He knew that this time he faced execution, and wrote once more to Timothy, asking him to come to Rome quickly (2 Tim 4:6-9). It is not known whether Timothy reached Rome before Paul was executed, but it is known that later Timothy himself was imprisoned for a time, then released (Heb 13:23). (See also TIMOTHY, LETTERS TO.)

TIMOTHY, LETTERS TO

Paul's letters to Timothy and Titus are commonly known as the Pastoral Letters. In them Paul shows a deep concern for the personal responsibilities that he had entrusted to Timothy and Titus in the places where he had left them. They show the warm personal relationship that Paul had with his fellow workers. They also show how church life had developed over the years since Paul first set out on his missionary travels.

Background to 1 Timothy

Towards the end of the book of Acts, Paul was taken prisoner to Rome and kept there for two years (Acts 28:16,30). In letters he wrote during that time, he expressed the hope that he would soon be released and so be able to visit churches in various places again (Phil 1:27; 2:24; Philem 22). Paul's hopes almost certainly came true, but since the book of Acts had by this time been completed, it contains no references to Paul's later travels. Paul's letters, however, provide information that enable us to work out at least some of his movements.

One place that Paul visited after leaving Rome was the island of Crete, where he found that the churches were badly in need of help. After staying a while, he sailed on, but he left Titus behind to help the churches of Crete further (Titus 1:5).

When Paul came to Ephesus he found similar problems. Many years earlier he had warned the elders of the Ephesian church that false teachers would create confusion among them (Acts 20:29-30), and now that had happened. The false teaching concerned some important matters, but contained much senseless talk on unimportant matters. People had tried to copy the Jewish teachers of the law by developing imaginative theories based on ancient myths, legends and genealogies (1 Tim 1:3-7; 6:3-5). Besides being unprofitable, the teaching created arguments and confusion. Some of it was dangerous to Christian faith, with the result that Paul had to

put the more serious offenders out of the church (1 Tim 1:19-20).

In due course Paul left Ephesus for Macedonia, but he left Timothy behind to help restore order and stability in the church. However, Paul was concerned for Timothy and the Ephesian church, so from Macedonia he wrote to give Timothy encouragement and direction in his difficult task. Paul felt at times that Timothy lacked boldness, and he hoped this letter would give Timothy the confidence he needed. At the same time Paul wrote a similar but shorter letter to Titus.

Contents of 1 Timothy

Paul begins his letter to Timothy with a warning about the false teachers. He contrasts the wrong type of teaching given at Ephesus with the gospel that he preaches (1:1-11), and then shows from his experiences that the truth of this gospel is sufficient for even the greatest of sinners (1:12-20).

In view of the disorder created by the false teachers, Paul gives Timothy instruction concerning the orderly arrangement that should characterize the church's life. He speaks of prayer and teaching, and of the conduct of both men and women in church meetings (2:1-15). After listing some basic requirements for elders and deacons (3:1-13), he contrasts the straightforward truth of the gospel with the deceptive nonsense taught by the false teachers (3:14-4:5). He advises Timothy how to deal with the false teachers and how to exercise his own gifts for the maximum benefit of all (4:6-16).

The final section of the letter deals with the various types of people within the church. It gives instruction concerning behaviour towards people in different age categories (5:1-2), care for widows (5:3-16), appointment and support of church leaders (5:17-25), attitudes of slaves and masters (6:1-2), treatment of false teachers (6:3-10), self-discipline and courage in God's servants (6:11-16) and the dangers of wealth (6:17-19). It concludes with an encouragement to Timothy to persist with the true Christian teaching and not to waste time arguing over senseless issues (6:20-21).

Background to 2 Timothy

Some time after writing 1 Timothy and Titus, Paul left northern Greece. It is not known exactly which route he followed, but among the places he visited was Corinth in southern Greece (2 Tim 4:20). He also visited Miletus, a town near Ephesus in western Asia Minor (2 Tim 4:20), and Troas, a town farther north (2 Tim 4:13). It seems that soon after this, Paul was arrested and taken to Rome once more.

From Rome he wrote his final letter, 2 Timothy (2 Tim 1:8; 2:9).

When the government authorities in Rome laid their charges against Paul, former friends deserted him. This was a great disappointment to Paul, but God protected him from violence and gave him the opportunity to make known the gospel to his captors (2 Tim 4:16-17). Paul knew he had little chance of being released; he expected rather to be executed (2 Tim 4:6-8). He therefore urged Timothy to come to Rome as quickly as possible (2 Tim 4:9), and to bring Mark with him (2 Tim 4:11). (Mark was probably working in Colossae, a town not far from Ephesus; cf. Col 4:10.)

Paul was lonely in prison. He had been visited by Onesiphorus of Ephesus (2 Tim 1:16-18) and by some of the local Roman Christians (2 Tim 4:21), but only Luke was able to stay with him (2 Tim 4:11). Various friends and fellow workers had gone to different places in the service of God, though Demas, who had been faithful to him during his previous imprisonment, had now left him for no good reason (2 Tim 4:10,12; cf. Col 4:14).

Apart from giving Timothy details concerning his circumstances in Rome, Paul wanted to give him added encouragement concerning the church in Ephesus. The Ephesian church was still troubled by false teaching, and Paul wanted Timothy to stand firm in his defence of the gospel.

Contents of 2 Timothy

The letter opens with Paul's encouraging Timothy to exercise his God-given gifts with boldness and to defend the gospel against all attacks (1:1-14). He mentions Onesiphorus as an example of whole-hearted faithfulness (1:15-18), and impresses upon Timothy the need for endurance (2:1-13).

Paul then deals specifically with the problem of the false teachers. He urges Timothy to concentrate on the main truths of the Christian faith and to avoid useless arguments (2:14-26). He warns that opposition to the truth of God will increase (3:1-9). In view of this, Timothy is to be an example to all, through enduring suffering patiently and preaching the Word constantly (3:10-4:5). Paul looks back on his own service for God with satisfaction (4:6-8), and concludes with details and advice in relation to his present circumstances in Rome (4:9-22).

TITHES

It seems to have been a custom from very early times for people to give a tithe (i.e. a tenth) of their goods to God as an act of worship and thanks. In this way they acknowledged God as the supreme controller of life's events and the sole giver of life's blessings. The custom existed as a voluntary act of devotion long before it became compulsory practice under the law of Moses.

The Bible records two pre-Mosaic examples of tithing. Abraham, on gaining a notable victory in the land God had promised him, offered to God a tithe of the goods he had seized in battle (Gen 14:17-24; Heb 7:4-10). Jacob, on fleeing for safety to a distant land, promised to give God a tithe of his possessions if God brought him back safely (Gen 28:20-22). In both cases the offering of the tithe was an acknowledgment that God was the sovereign controller in human affairs and the giver of all gifts.

The law of Moses

Under the law of Moses, Israelites had to give to God one tenth of all crops, fruit, flocks and herds. The tenth that a person offered had to be an honest sample of the whole, not an inferior portion that he had no use for himself. When tithing animals, for example, the owner counted the animals as they passed through the gate, setting aside every tenth one for God, regardless of whether it was good or bad (Lev 27:30,32-33).

If a person so desired, he could offer money instead of his produce or animals. The amount he paid was the value of the goods plus a fifth. This additional fifth was a type of fine, since the person was keeping for his own use something that rightly belonged to God (Lev 27:31).

The tithes were paid to the Levites, and so became the chief source of the Levites' income. Since the Levites spent their time in religious service for the people, they had no time to earn a normal living. This constant income from the tithes was payment for their work and compensation for their lack of a separate tribal area in Canaan (Num 18:21-24).

Having received tithes, the Levites then had to pay tithes. Their income was the produce of other people's farms, but when they offered a tenth of this produce to God, he accepted it as if it were their own. The Levites' tithes became the income of the priests (Num 18:25-32).

People presented their tithes by taking them to the central place of worship, where, with their households and the Levites, they joined in a joyous ceremonial meal (Deut 12:5-7,17-19). If the offerer lived so far from the tabernacle (or later the temple) that transporting his goods was a problem, he could sell his tithes locally and take the money instead (Deut 14:22-27).

Every third year the offerer had to distribute this tithe (or perhaps an additional tithe) in his own locality, so that the local poor could benefit from it as well as the Levites. In this case the offerer, after distributing his tithes, had to go to the central place of worship and declare before God that he had done according to the divine command (Deut 14:28-29; 26:12-15).

In addition to these compulsory tithes, there were sacrifices and offerings of various types. Some of these were required by law, but others were made voluntarily (2 Chron 31:5-6; Neh 10:37-38; 12:44; Mal 3:8-10). (For details see FEASTS; FIRSTBORN; FIRSTFRUITS; SACRIFICE; VOWS.)

New Testament times

In later years Jewish teachers of the law added their own laws to those given by Moses. The result was that by the time of Jesus, they had made the tithing system a heavy burden on the Jewish people. These teachers instructed Jews to keep the laws of tithing even to the smallest detail, assuring them that in doing so they would gain God's favour. But they neither taught nor practised the more important matters of faith, love, mercy and justice (Matt 23:4,23; Luke 11:42,46; 18:12).

The New Testament does not teach tithing as a binding law for Christians. Nevertheless, it upholds the principle of proportionate giving, the amount a person gives depending on the amount he earns (1 Cor 16:2; 2 Cor 8:12-14). God desires that people make their offerings willingly and joyfully, not under compulsion or grudgingly (2 Cor 8:3; 9:7). But he adds the promise that they need not fear poverty if they give much, because God is able to increase his supply so that the generous giver still has more than he needs (2 Cor 9:8-10). (See also GIVING.)

TITUS

It seems that Titus was originally from Antioch in Syria. When Paul and Barnabas took a gift from the Antioch church to the Jerusalem church, Titus went with them (Acts 11:27-30; Gal 2:1). By nationality he was a Greek (Gal 2:3).

Paul's representative to Corinth

Much of the Bible's information about Titus has to do with the church in Corinth. From Ephesus Paul had written at least one letter to the Corinthians, and had made a rushed visit to Corinth in an effort to deal with serious problems in the Corinthian church. When he heard that his efforts had only made people more rebellious, he wrote a severe letter and sent it to Corinth with Titus, his special representative (2 Cor 2:3-4,9; 7:8; 12:18). (For map see page 438.)

Paul's plan was for Titus to return from Corinth via Troas. Being eager to hear of the Corinthians' response to his letter, Paul went to Troas to meet Titus. Unable to wait patiently, he then went across to Macedonia in the hope of finding Titus there (2 Cor 2:12-13). Titus met Paul with the news that the severe letter had produced the desired results (2 Cor 7:5-6,13-15). Although this letter has not been preserved in the Bible, the letter that Paul wrote in response to Titus' good news has. It is called 2 Corinthians and it was taken to Corinth by Titus (2 Cor 8:16-18).

Titus was also Paul's appointed representative to encourage the Corinthian church to participate enthusiastically in an important project Paul was organizing. Paul was collecting money among the Gentile churches of Asia Minor and Greece to take to the needy Jewish Christians in Jerusalem (2 Cor 8:1-6,16-24).

Activities in other places

Many years later, after Paul had been released from his first imprisonment in Rome, Titus went with Paul to Crete to try to correct disorders in the churches there. When Paul left, Titus stayed behind to help the churches further (Titus 1:5). The book of Titus in our Bible is the letter Paul wrote to Titus at this time (see TITUS, LETTER TO).

Titus was such a valued worker that Paul could not leave him in Crete indefinitely. He therefore wrote to advise Titus that soon someone would come to take his place. Titus then apparently went to Nicopolis on the west coast of Greece to meet Paul as planned (Titus 3:12), and from there went north to Dalmatia (2 Tim 4:10). That is the last mention of him in the biblical record.

TITUS, LETTER TO

Paul's letter to Titus is in many ways similar to his first letter to Timothy, though it is much shorter. Paul apparently wrote the two letters about the same time.

Following his two-year imprisonment in Rome (Acts 28:16,30), Paul went on further travels. Among the places he visited was the Mediterranean island of Crete, where he found that the churches were in a state of confusion. He stayed a while to help the churches through their difficulties, but there were other cities and countries he wanted to visit. He therefore left Titus behind in Crete to help correct the problems (Titus 1:5), while he himself sailed on to Ephesus. There were problems in Ephesus also, but Paul could stay there for only a limited time. When he moved on to Macedonia, he left Timothy behind to carry on the work (1 Tim 1:3). (For map see page 438.)

From Macedonia Paul wrote two letters, one to Titus in Crete, the other to Timothy in Ephesus. Both letters were intended to encourage Paul's fellow workers in the tasks they faced, particularly in matters concerning leadership and teaching in the church. (For details of Paul's travels and writings of this time see TIMOTHY, LETTERS TO.)

Contents of the letter

After a lengthy introduction (1:1-4), Paul reminds Titus of the need to appoint elders in the Cretan churches and of the personal qualities that should characterize those elders. In particular they must be able to recognize and resist false teaching (1:5-16).

Paul gives Titus instructions concerning the behaviour that people of different ages and social backgrounds should exercise towards each other in the church (2:1-10). He reminds Titus that the grace of God changes lives (2:11-15), and that Christians must demonstrate this by the way they live (3:1-7). Titus must therefore teach the great truths of the Christian faith, and not waste time arguing over senseless topics (3:8-11). The letter closes with a few notes concerning Paul's plans for himself and Titus in the months ahead (3:12-15).

TOMB

See FUNERAL.

TONGUE

Speech is one of the most powerful forces man has available to him, for by his words he can bring great benefit or do great damage (Prov 12:18,25; 15:1,4; James 3:5,9). What a person says and the way he says it are therefore matters of the highest importance. Yet all people have difficulty with them. The person who can control his tongue can control his whole self (James 3:1-4,7-8; cf. Ps 141:3).

Control of the tongue

The root of man's problem with the tongue is man's evil heart. Sin has corrupted man's nature, and the wrong within him shows itself in an uncontrolled tongue (Mark 7:21-23; James 3:6). Christians, being indwelt by the Spirit, have divine help in resisting the pressures of the old nature. The Spirit teaches them to control the tongue and makes them realize the inconsistency of using the same tongue to bless

God and curse their fellows (Gal 5:17,22; Eph 4:30-31; Col 4:6; Titus 2:8; James 1:26; 3:9-12; see BLESSING; CURSE; MALICE; PRAISE).

Wrong use of the tongue does not have to be as obvious as cursing in order to be damaging. It may consist only of idle chatter, because even that can easily involve harmful gossip (Prov 11:9,13; 26:18-22; Eccles 5:3; see GOSSIP). Since the more a person speaks the more likely he is to sin, the wise person will limit his words and control the way he expresses them. A fool, by contrast, talks at length and so proclaims his folly (Prov 10:19; 12:23; 15:2; 17:27-28; 18:2,6-7; 2 Cor 11:16-19; Eph 5:4; see BOASTING; FOOLISHNESS).

Although a person may control his words, such control must be sincere. If he simply uses smooth words to hide evil feelings, he is a hypocrite (Ps 41:5-6; 55:21; Prov 10:18; 26:23-25; Matt 22:15-18; 23:28; see HYPOCRISY). A person must be truthful and straightforward with the words he uses. The cunning twisting of words can be merely a form of lying (Prov 12:19; 2 Cor 4:2; Eph 4:25; 1 Peter 3:10; see LIE). While a person should always speak the truth, he should do so in a spirit of love. His words give an indication of the quality of his character (Prov 10:11,20-21; 16:23; Eph 4:15; James 1:19; see TRUTH).

Christian witness

Words are an indication of a person's relationship with Christ. He may confess Christ as Lord, or deny all knowledge of him (Rom 10:9; Matt 26:70-74; see CONFESSION; DENIAL). But a confession of faith may be false (1 Tim 1:19), and a denial of Christ may be a temporary failure that a person soon corrects (John 21:15-17). Often a person's everyday speech, rather than his occasional public declaration, is a better indication of his spiritual condition. Such everyday speech will be used as evidence on the day of judgment (Matt 12:36-37).

Christian preachers in particular have to be careful with their words. They know that words are persuasive (Prov 16:21), and therefore they must be careful not to use their speaking abilities to gain control over people. They should want people to have their faith rooted in God and his Word, not in the preacher and his style (1 Cor 2:1-5; 3:5-7; 2 Cor 4:2; 11:6; 1 Thess 2:4; see PREACHING).

TONGUES

When the Bible says that people spoke in tongues ('other tongues' or 'strange tongues'), it means that their speech was in words that were not of their own language and that they did not understand, unless someone interpreted them. Beyond that simple definition, general statements about tongues become difficult, because of the different types and uses of tongues in the New Testament.

In the book of Acts

The birth of the New Testament church took place in Jerusalem on the Day of Pentecost, when about 120 disciples received the Holy Spirit as Jesus had promised (Acts 2:1-4; cf. 1:4-5). On that occasion the disciples spoke in tongues that people from other linguistic groups understood as their native languages (Acts 2:4-11).

There are only two other places in Acts where the writer records that people spoke in tongues, but in neither case is it clear whether the tongues were languages already in use or something completely different (Acts 10:44-46; 19:1-6). On each occasion there seems to have been a special reason for the people's speaking in tongues, as each case is a departure from what had been normal till that time. The speaking in tongues was a striking outward and visible demonstration that the people concerned had received the Holy Spirit and were introduced into the church the same as the original disciples were on the Day of Pentecost. (See also BAPTISM WITH THE SPIRIT.)

In Paul's letters

Tongues that were spoken in the normal meetings of the church seem to have had a different purpose. They were a gift that the Holy Spirit gave to certain people to exercise in their praise to God (1 Cor 12:10,30; 14:2). People were to use the gift publicly only if someone could interpret the words in the normal language of the worshippers, so that all present could benefit. This indicates that whereas the tongues referred to in Acts were irresistible, those referred to in Corinthians were under the control of the speaker (1 Cor 14:13,27-28). Also, those who spoke in tongues in the church were to do so one at a time, and no more than two or three in all (1 Cor 14:27).

It seems that the languages spoken in these cases (i.e. in the church) were different from any known languages. The Christians at Corinth, still influenced by attitudes from their former idolatrous days, were apparently impressed by these tongues, and considered that those who spoke them were spiritually superior. However, the situation got out of control, and people made some unusual, even blasphemous, statements. According to Paul, this was evidence that those who spoke in tongues were not necessarily speaking by the Holy Spirit (1 Cor 12:1-3; cf. 1 John 4:1-3).

Although Paul allowed the gift of tongues, he was cautious in encouraging people to seek it. He encouraged them rather to seek those gifts that proclaimed God's Word and consequently built up the hearers (1 Cor 12:28-31; 14:3-5). Any speaking that took place in the church had to have meaning to the audience (1 Cor 14:6-12,19). It had also to have meaning to the speaker, for he was not likely to be spiritually built up if he did not understand what he was saying (1 Cor 14:13-15).

The Corinthians' concern for the spectacular demonstrated their immaturity, and their misuse of tongues brought dishonour on the church (1 Cor 14:20-25). Like all the gifts of the Spirit, the gift of tongues was given to only some in the church, and it could be wrongly used or falsely copied (1 Cor 12:3,7,10,30; 13:1). Paul therefore emphasized that the evidence of the Spirit's work in a person's life was not whether he spoke in tongues, but whether his life displayed the fruit of the Spirit, which is Christlike character (Gal 5:22-23; see GIFTS OF THE SPIRIT).

TRACHONITIS

The region of Trachonitis lay to the north-east of Palestine, between Lake Galilee and Damascus. It was on the northern edge of the territory known in Old Testament times as Bashan (Num 32:33; Deut 32:14; see BASHAN). At the time Jesus began his public ministry, the governor of Trachonitis was Philip, a son of Herod the Great (Luke 3:1). (For map and other details see HEROD.)

TRADITION

In any society traditions develop as beliefs and practices are handed on from one generation to the next. The Jews of Jesus' day had many traditions. Some of these had been taught in the law of Moses (Luke 2:27,41-42), and others had grown up over the centuries (Luke 1:9). Many of the later traditions had been developed and taught by the scribes and Pharisees, and brought Jesus into conflict with the Jewish religious leaders (Matt 23:4-16; see SCRIBES; PHARISEES).

Jesus was not opposed to Jewish traditions. In fact, he kept some of them himself (Luke 4:16; John 10:22-23). But he was opposed to the teaching of traditions as binding on people. The Jewish leaders taught human traditions as if they were God's commandments; worse still, they rejected the genuine commandments of God in order to keep their traditions (Mark 7:7-13; cf. Col 2:8).

The tradition that Christians are to keep is twofold. First, they must keep the teaching passed down from Jesus through the apostles and recorded in the New Testament (Acts 2:42; 1 Cor 11:23; 15:3; 2 Tim 1:13-14; Jude 3; see GOSPEL). Second, they must maintain the standard of behaviour demanded by that teaching (1 Cor 11:1-2; Phil 4:9; 2 Thess 2:15; 3:6; see OBEDIENCE).

TRANSFIGURATION

Jesus' transfiguration took place on a high mountain, possibly Mt Hermon, not far from Caesarea Philippi in northern Palestine (Matt 16:13; 17:1). The event was a revelation of Christ's glory, witnessed by only three chosen disciples. Jesus had laid that glory aside in becoming man, but now it reappeared briefly, displayed through a human body. It was also a foretaste of the glory that Christ would receive after he had completed the work that he had come to do (Matt 17:2; John 17:4-5).

Moses and Elijah, the two people of the Old Testament era who appeared with Jesus, possibly symbolized the law and the prophets (Matt 17:3). Jesus was God's chosen one, to whom the Old Testament pointed. Their conversation with Jesus about his coming death confirmed what Jesus had told his disciples a few days earlier, namely, that though he was the Messiah, he was also the suffering servant. Though he was a glorious figure of heavenly origins, he had to die a shameful death (Luke 9:30-31; cf. Matt 16:16,21).

This was further confirmed in the words that the Father spoke from heaven. His statement of approval of his Son combined words from one of David's messianic psalms with words from one of the servant songs of Isaiah (Matt 17:5; cf. Ps 2:7; Isa 42:1).

The Father's final words, 'Hear him', indicated that this one, besides being the kingly Messiah and the suffering servant, was the great prophet who announced God's message to all mankind (Matt 17:5; cf. Deut 18:15; Acts 3:22-26). The entire transfiguration event showed God's satisfaction with all that Jesus had done and with all that he intended to do as the climax to his ministry approached. (See also MESSIAH; SERVANT OF THE LORD.)

TREATY

Treaties between people or nations were common in Bible times, as they are today. Such treaties were formal agreements that dealt with matters of mutual concern, such as peace, security and trade (Gen 21:25-33; 26:28-30; 1 Kings 9:26-28; 20:34; Isa 7:3; 30:1-5; 31:1).

God warned the Israelites of Moses' time that when they entered Canaan, they were not to make treaties with the former people of the land, but destroy them. In this way Israel would avoid the possibility of moral and religious corruption through adopting Canaanite practices (Exod 34:12-16).

Nevertheless, in the centuries that followed, a number of Israelite kings made treaties with neighbouring nations. One danger of this practice was that it led to the possibility of moral and religious corruption, because the two parties to the treaty usually paid respect to each other's gods. The treaty was sometimes strengthened by a marriage between members of the two royal families, which gave further opportunity for the introduction of foreign religious practices into Israel (1 Kings 3:1; 11:1-6; 16:30-33).

A treaty may also have been a sign of a lack of faith. This was particularly so when Israel (or Judah) trusted for military victory in an alliance with a foreign nation instead of trusting in God (1 Kings 15:18-20; Isa 30:1-3,15). Such a treaty would lead inevitably to political and religious domination by the foreign nation in whom Israel trusted (2 Kings 16:7-10; Isa 39:3-7; Hosea 7:8-10). By becoming a party to the treaty, Israel broke its covenant with God and so brought God's judgment upon itself (Hosea 7:11-13; 8:8-10; see COVENANT).

TREES

The two types of tree most often mentioned in the Bible are the fruit bearing trees, the fig and the olive (Deut 8:8; Mark 11:1,3; see FIG; OLIVE). The tree most valued for making buildings and furniture was the cedar. It grew in Lebanon and was the most beautiful, enduring and expensive timber available (Isa 2:12-13; 10:34; 35:2; 60:13; see LEBANON). The tabernacle, along with its furniture, was constructed of acacia wood, a timber that was readily available in the Sinai region. Acacia wood, being light, was very suitable for a portable structure such as the tabernacle (Exod 25:10; 26:15).

Among the other trees mentioned in the Bible are algum (2 Chron 2:8; 9:10), cypress (2 Chron 2:8), plane (Isa 60:13), myrtle (Isa 41:19; Neh 8:15), balsam (2 Sam 5:23), oak (Judg 6:11; 2 Sam 18:9), willow (Job 40:22; Ps 137:2), sycamine (Luke 17:6), broom (1 Kings 19:4), lotus (Job 40:22) and palm (Exod 15:27; Ps 92:12).

TRIBES

Israel was divided into twelve tribes according to the twelve sons of Jacob (Gen 35:22-26). In the division of Canaan, the tribe of Levi received no allotment of its own but was given cities within all the other tribes (Num 18:24; 35:1-8; see LEVITES). Joseph, by contrast, received two tribal allotments, one for each of his two sons, Ephraim and Manasseh. This double portion was the inheritance of the firstborn, an inheritance that Joseph received instead of the eldest son, Reuben (Gen 48:13-20; 49:22-26; 1 Chron 5:1-2).

The arrangement for dividing Canaan between the twelve tribes had two main features. First, the area of land for each tribe was in proportion to the

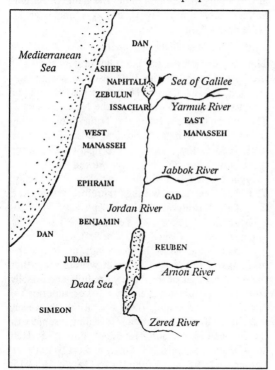

population of the tribe. Second, the location of each tribe within the land was decided by drawing lots (Num 26:52-56).

By their own choice, the tribes of Reuben, Gad and half of Manasseh did not settle in Canaan itself (i.e. the land between the Jordan River and the Mediterranean Sea). Instead they settled in the good pasture lands on the eastern side of the Jordan River. The remaining nine and a half tribes settled in Canaan (Josh 13:7-8). Judah and Simeon settled in the south. Benjamin, Dan, Ephraim and the other half of Manasseh settled in the centre. Issachar,

Zebulun, Naphtali and Asher settled in the north. (For details see separate entries for each tribe. For further history see ISRAEL.)

TRINITY

God is one, but he exists as a Trinity. Any attempt to define the Trinity is difficult and dangerous, as it is an attempt to do what the Bible does not do. However, by a study of the biblical teaching about God, we understand that although God is one, the form in which his godhead exists is that of three persons — Father, Son and Holy Spirit. Each of the three persons is fully God, yet there is only one God, not three.

One God, three persons

The Old Testament gives little clear teaching about the Trinity, for the emphasis there is on the oneness of God. Israel lived among nations that had many gods. The important truth impressed upon Israel was that there is only one God, and he is a unity (Deut 6:4).

Our understanding of the Trinity comes largely from the New Testament. This does not mean that the God of Old Testament times differed from the God of New Testament times, or that a God who was previously 'one' branched out into three. God has always existed in a Trinity. What is new in the New Testament is the revelation of the Trinity, not the Trinity itself.

The reason why the revelation of the Trinity is new in the New Testament is that it was related to the great acts of God in bringing his plan of salvation to completion in Christ. God did not reveal his truth to mankind in the form of abstract truths unrelated to the situation in which the people of the time lived. Rather he revealed his truth step by step as he brought man closer to the full salvation he had planned for him.

Nevertheless, with the fuller knowledge that Christians gain from the New Testament, they may see suggestions of the Trinity in the Old Testament. Such suggestions are there, even though believers of Old Testament times may not have seen them (cf. 1 Peter 1:10-12).

For example, in the Old Testament references to the creation there was an inseparable connection between God, the creative power of God's Word, and the life-giving power of God's Spirit (Gen 1:1-3; Job 33:4; Ps 33:6). But with the coming of Jesus, man gained a clearer understanding of the work of the Trinity in all the activity of God, including the creation (John 1:1-4). This understanding increased further as Jesus taught his followers and left with them the gift of the Holy Spirit, who would interpret his teaching and continue to enlighten them (John 16:13-15).

The revelation through Jesus Christ

When God became man in the person of Jesus Christ, much that was previously secret and hidden became open. Jesus revealed God to man (John 1:1,14,18).

God was now physically present in the world in the person of Jesus. Yet there was a sense in which he was not physically present in the world. Jesus made it plain that when people saw him they saw God (John 8:58-59), but he also made it plain that God existed elsewhere; for he himself came from God, and during his earthly life he spoke to God (John 6:38; 11:41-42).

Jesus explained this apparent contradiction by pointing out that he was God the Son, and that the one from whom he came and to whom he spoke was God the Father. Although these two persons were distinct, they were uniquely united (John 5:18,37; 8:42; 10:30; 11:41; 14:9; 16:26-28; see FATHER; SON OF GOD).

Having become man, God the Son now gave the additional revelation that there was a third person in the Godhead, the Holy Spirit. All three persons were involved in the miraculous coming of the Son into the world (Luke 1:35), and the life and ministry of Jesus that followed should have shown people that God existed as a Trinity — Father, Son and Holy Spirit (Matt 3:16-17; 12:28; Luke 4:18; John 3:34-35). Just before he completed his ministry, Jesus explained about the Holy Spirit more fully. He promised that after he returned to his Father, he and the Father would send the Holy Spirit to be with his disciples, as he himself had been previously (John 14:16-17,26; 15:26).

The Holy Spirit, though a separate person from the Father and the Son, is inseparably united with both (Acts 2:32-33). He comes from the Father as the bearer of the Father's power and presence (John 15:26; 16:7-11), and he comes from the Son as the bearer of the Son's power and presence (John 14:18; 16:7; Rom 8:9; see HOLY SPIRIT). Although there is a distinction between the three persons of the Godhead, there is no division. Each has his own personality and will, but he never acts independently of the others (John 14:26; Acts 16:6-7; Gal 4:6).

No change in God

This three-in-one and one-in-three unity of the Godhead is well illustrated in the command that

Jesus gave to his disciples to baptize their converts 'in the name of the Father and of the Son and of the Holy Spirit' (Matt 28:19). In Jewish thought the name represented the person (see NAME). Jesus here spoke of the name (singular), indicating one God, but at the same time he showed that this God existed in three persons. And these three persons were distinct from each other, yet uniquely and inseparably united.

As a God-fearing Jew, Jesus gave his complete allegiance to the one and only true God, and he taught others to do likewise (Deut 6:4; Matt 22:37). Jesus' statement therefore indicated that this God whom Israelites of former times worshipped under the name of Yahweh (Jehovah) was the same God as Christians worshipped under the name of Father, Son and Holy Spirit. The God who is 'one' is at the same time a Trinity.

Faith of the New Testament writers

The early disciples reached a fuller understanding of the Trinity through the life, teaching, death and triumph of Jesus Christ. They then passed on their insights through the writings of the New Testament. They never tried to define the Trinity, nor did they try to 'prove' it in a theoretical sense. Since they knew God as the one who gave his Son to die for them and gave his Spirit to indwell them, they thought of God in no other way than as a Trinity. The New Testament writings therefore assume the fact of the Trinity at all times (Eph 4:4-6; 5:18-20; 1 Thess 1:3-5; 1 Peter 1:2). Yet they also assume the oneness of God (Rom 3:30; 1 Cor 8:4).

In keeping with the teachings of Jesus, the teachings of the New Testament writers show that the three persons of the Trinity are fully and equally God. No one person is inferior to, or superior to, any other. Concerning their operations, however, there is a difference. The Son is willingly subject to the Father (John 5:30; 7:16; 12:49; Phil 2:5-8; Heb 10:5-7), and the Spirit is willingly subject to both the Father and the Son (John 14:26; 15:26; 16:13-15; Rom 8:26-27; Gal 4:6; Phil 1:19).

Because of the unity between the persons of the Trinity, all three are active in all the work of God. This work is not, as it were, divided among three persons. In a sense, what one does they all do. But the Bible story shows that there is also a sense in which their activities differ.

The name 'Father' speaks of one who has to do with the origin of things, and this is seen in the great works of creation, history and redemption (Mal 2:10; Eph 1:3-10; Heb 12:9; James 1:17). The Son is the one who reveals the Father, the one through whom the Father does these great works (John 10:25,38; 14:10; 2 Cor 5:19; Eph 1:3-10; Col 1:15-16). The Spirit is the one by whom God's power operates in the world, the one who applies the truth of God's great works to people's lives (John 14:17; 16:7-13; Acts 1:8; Rom 8:2-4; Gal 5:16-18; 1 Peter 1:2). God's salvation comes from the Father, through the Son, by the Spirit (Titus 3:4-6), and man's approach to God is by the Spirit, through the Son, to the Father (Eph 2:18).

Relationship with the triune God

In making statements about the Father, the Son and the Holy Spirit, the New Testament writers were not attempting a theoretical analysis of God. Their concern was not to set out in systematic form the character and activities of the persons of the Trinity, but to express the relationship that Christians have with God. Christians cannot fully understand the mysteries of the Godhead, but they should try to learn all they can about God; for the life they have in Christ depends on God being the sort of God he is – a Trinity.

Jesus Christ, for example, could not be man's Saviour if he were not the unique person that he is. The fact of the Trinity was essential to his birth (Luke 1:35), his life (John 3:34; 5:36-37; Heb 2:3-4; 1 John 5:6-9), his death (Rom 8:32; Gal 2:20; Heb 9:14), his resurrection (Acts 2:42; John 10:18; Rom 8:11) and his exaltation (Acts 5:30-32).

The fact of the Trinity is essential also for the life of believers: their indwelling by God (Eph 4:6; Col 1:27; 1 Cor 6:19); their sanctification (John 17:17; Heb 2:11; 1 Cor 6:11), their enjoyment of salvation (2 Cor 13:14), their exercise of prayer (Rom 8:26-27,34; Eph 2:18), their eternal security (John 10:28-29; Eph 4:30) and their ultimate victory over death (John 5:21; Rom 8:11).

Likewise the Trinity is involved in the life of the church (1 Cor 12:4-6) and in Christian service (2 Cor 3:5-6; 1 Tim 1:12; Acts 20:28). The Scriptures that Christians possess are a provision from the triune God (2 Tim 3:16-17; 1 Peter 1:10-11; 2 Peter 1:21). They are one of the means by which the same God wants to work in and through his people, as they build themselves up in their faith and prepare themselves for fellowship with him in the age to come (Jude 20-21).

TROAS

The city of Troas was situated alongside the site of ancient Troy in the region once known as Mysia. In New Testament times this region was part of the Roman province of Asia, and Troas was the main port in the province's north-west. (For map see ASIA.)

From Troas travellers sailed across the Aegean Sea to Macedonia, from where a major road led to Rome (Acts 16:8-11; 20:6-13). Troas therefore became an important town on the main route from Rome to Asia, and the Roman government gave it the status of a Roman colony. (Concerning Roman colonies see ROME, sub-heading 'Provinces of the Empire'.) Paul visited Troas several times on his journeys to and from Rome (Acts 16:8-11; 20:6-13; 2 Cor 2:12-13; 2 Tim 4:13).

TRUTH

There are various meanings of the word 'truth' in the Bible, some of which are similar to those we use today. A person or thing may be true, meaning the opposite of false (Deut 13:14; Prov 12:19; Rom 9:1; see LIE) or the opposite of insincere (Gen 42:16; Phil 1:18; 1 John 3:18; see HYPOCRISY). A thing may be called true in contrast to that which is only a shadow or picture (John 1:9; 15:1; Heb 9:24; see TYPE). The Bible often uses 'true' with the meaning of reliable, faithful or trustworthy (Gen 24:49; 47:29; Ps 57:10; Rev 22:6).

God is truth

All these meanings are in some way applied to God (Ps 19:9; Jer 10:9-10; 42:5; Micah 6:20; Rom 3:4; 1 Thess 1:9; Rev 16:7). Truth is God's very nature. He is the basic reality from which everything else springs (John 1:3-4,14; 8:26; Rom 1:25). God became man in Jesus, and therefore Jesus is truth in human form (John 14:6; Eph 4:21; Rev 3:7). As the Old Testament spoke of the God of truth or, to use the related word, the God of the Amen (Isa 65:16), so the New Testament speaks of Jesus as the Amen. He is the one in whom God's truth is perfectly expressed, and through whom God's promises are perfectly fulfilled (John 1:17; 2 Cor 1:20; Rev 3:14; see AMEN).

Jesus spoke repeatedly about the truth, and those who come to know him come to know the truth. Thereby they are freed from the bondage of sin, brought into a living relationship with the true God, and indwelt by him who is the Spirit of truth (John 8:32; 14:17; 16:13; 17:3; 2 John 1-2).

Truth, in the sense spoken of by Jesus, saves people, for it represents the full saving activity of God through Jesus Christ. Jesus' life and teaching were directed towards revealing and fulfilling God's truth (John 1:17; 8:32,45-46; 17:17,19; 18:37). A natural development from this was to speak of 'truth' as referring to the whole body of Christian teaching (2 Cor 4:2; Gal 2:5; 5:7; Eph 1:13; 1 Tim 2:4; 2 Tim 2:15). This is in keeping with the Old Testament usage of 'truth' as applying to the revealed Word of God (Ps 25:5; 86:11; 119:142; see REVELATION).

Christian character

Truth in all its aspects should characterize the lives of those who have come under the rule of him who is the truth (Exod 18:21; Ps 26:3; John 3:21; 2 Cor 13:8; Eph 4:15,25; 6:14; Titus 1:2; Heb 6:18; 3 John 4). Having become obedient to the truth, they must be loyal to the truth, without any trace of falsehood, insincerity or unfaithfulness (1 Cor 5:8; 2 Cor 4:2; Gal 4:16; 1 Peter 1:22).

Their possession of God's truth, however, is no reason for Christians to claim absolute authority for their own theories or opinions. The mind of man is limited and, like all man's capacities and abilities, is affected by sin (1 Cor 8:2). God alone is the possessor of absolute truth (Isa 55:8-9; Rom 11:33-34; see KNOWLEDGE).

TYCHICUS

Among the church representatives who went with Paul to present a gift to the Jerusalem church were two men from the province of Asia, Tychicus and Trophimus (Acts 20:4; 21:29). When Paul was later imprisoned for two years in Rome, Tychicus spent some time with him. Paul then sent him as his special representative to the churches of Ephesus and Colossae, to tell the Christians how he was faring in Rome. Tychicus probably also carried Paul's letters to the Ephesians and the Colossians (Eph 6:21-22; Col 4:7-8).

Tychicus continued to work with Paul after Paul's release from imprisonment. Paul considered sending him to relieve Titus in Crete (Titus 3:12), and later he sent him to relieve Timothy in Ephesus (2 Tim 4:12).

TYPE, TYPOLOGY

The New Testament teaches that certain things in the religious system of Israel were 'shadows', 'copies' or 'models' of the 'real' things that came through Jesus Christ (Col 2:17; Heb 8:5; 9:23-24; 10:1). The Old Testament provides examples, foreshadowings, illustrations and symbols of realities that we meet later in the New (Heb 9:8-9). All these examples, shadows, copies and symbols are commonly called 'types'. The particular kind of biblical interpretation that sees these 'types' fulfilled in the New Testament is called 'typology'.

Patterns in the Scriptures

New Testament writers point out repeatedly that the New Testament fulfils the Old. By this they mean that God brings to completion the plan he had been working out for mankind through the history of Israel. There is a pattern in God's activity, a repetition of his acts of judgment and salvation. This pattern reaches its completion and fulfilment in the life, death and resurrection of Jesus (Deut 4:25-31; Judg 2:13-16; 1 Kings 8:33-34; Ps 81:7-10; 89:29-37; Isa 1:16-20; Acts 2:36-39; Rom 3:21-26).

In reading the Old Testament we therefore see illustrations of man's failure and God's redemption. Judgment and salvation through the flood of Noah's day can picture the greater judgment and salvation through Christ's death. These truths are pictured also in Christian baptism (1 Peter 3:20-21).

Further examples are found in the Passover salvation and the events that followed. The Passover redemption foreshadows the greater redemption through Christ (1 Cor 5:7; see PASSOVER). The song sung by the Israelites who triumphed over the Egyptians becomes more meaningful when sung by Christians who triumph over their oppressors (Rev 15:3-4). Israel's experiences in the wilderness show what happens to unbelieving and rebellious people (1 Cor 10:1-11; Heb 3:7-4:10).

Lessons for a preparatory age

The Old Testament era was one of preparation. God was instructing his people by showing them their sin, his righteousness, and the outworking of his mercy in saving repentant sinners. This preparation was in expectation of the coming of Christ.

God is consistent in his character and in his dealings with man. The same great truths were present in Old and New Testament times, for the principles of God's salvation are unchanging. But until Christ came and revealed the means of that salvation, God taught the less enlightened Old Testament people in a form they could understand more easily. God intended the Old Testament 'types' (the illustrations, pictures and examples) to be simple, not complicated.

An example of this is the sacrifice offered for sin (Lev 4:1-12; 16:1-28). This was symbolic of the death of Christ (Heb 9:11-14), but apart from any connection with Christ's death it had a meaning of its own. The believer sacrificed an animal on the altar as a substitute for himself, in confession that because of his sin he deserved the death suffered by the animal. This was a very poor substitute for the complete forgiveness that comes only through the death of Christ (Heb 10:1-4,11-12), but as a simple God-given picture it had a purpose in its day (see SACRIFICE).

Fuller understanding through Christ

In general the New Testament writers emphasize the differences, rather than the similarities, between the Old Testament 'shadows' and the New Testament 'realities' (Heb 3:1-6; 7:11-12,23-28; 9:8-14,24-26; 10:11-14). Israel's rites and ceremonies illustrated God's truth to people who lived in an era before the coming of Jesus Christ, but they were imperfect representations of the reality, which is Christ. If Christians want to learn more of the excellencies of Christ, they will find them in the New Testament realities rather than in the Old Testament shadows (Col 2:17; Heb 7:19; 8:6-7).

The entire Old Testament revelation was a preparation for Christ, and this is the way the New Testament writers interpret it. For them typology was a Christian interpretation of history. (For the relevance of this to the New Testament writers' use of the Old Testament, see QUOTATIONS.)

This Christian view of the Bible does not give present-day readers the liberty to choose any Old Testament character or event and make it a 'type' of Christ and his work. They must not treat Old Testament passages as allegories; that is, they must not give words or things symbolic meanings that have no connection with the context. The first responsibility that readers have is to understand the straightforward meaning of each passage. As they understand its significance in God's progressive revelation, they will readily see its relevance for people today (Rom 15:4; 1 Cor 10:11; Heb 4:1-2; see INTERPRETATION).

TYRE

Along the Mediterranean coast north of Palestine lay the ancient land of Phoenicia, whose chief cities were the ports of Tyre and Sidon. The Bible rarely uses the name Phoenicia, preferring to refer to the country by the names of its chief cities, either separately or together (1 Kings 5:1; Ezra 3:7; Jer 47:4; Ezek 28:2,21; Zech 9:2; Mark 7:24; Luke 6:17; Acts 12:20). Other Phoenician towns along the Mediterranean coast were Zarephath and Byblos (1 Kings 17:9).

The Phoenicians were among the great sailors of the ancient world and had large shipping fleets working the trade routes of the Mediterranean Sea

(Isa 23:5,7). This brought much wealth to Phoenicia, particularly to Tyre, since it was the chief port (Ezek 27:3,25). But with wealth came arrogance, and this brought judgment from God (Ezek 28:5,9,16). The

Waterfront at Tyre

judgment on Phoenicia was usually pictured in the overthrow of Tyre or the downfall of its king (Ezek 27:2; 28:2,12). (For map and other details of Tyre, including its important rulers, commercial power and colourful history, see PHOENICIA.)

UNCLEAN SPIRITS

The most frequent mention of unclean spirits in the Bible is in relation to the ministry of Jesus. Elsewhere in the Bible evil spirits are called demons (see DEMONS). Satan is their leader, and he used them in an exceptional way to oppose Jesus' ministry (Mark 1:21-27; 3:11; 5:2,7; 6:7; 7:25). Jesus' victory over evil spirits was a sign that the kingdom of God had come and Satan was being conquered (Matt 4:23-24; 12:28; see KINGDOM OF GOD; SATAN).

When a person was possessed by a demon, his speech and behaviour changed. The demon may have enabled him to have supernatural knowledge or strength, which could be used in an orderly way, but could also produce behaviour similar to hysteria or epilepsy. This may have resulted in temporary blindness, deafness or dumbness (Matt 12:22; Mark 1:24-26; 5:2-5; 9:17-25; Acts 16:16-18).

Jesus and his disciples healed many who were possessed by evil spirits, but the Bible usually makes a distinction between such people and those who suffered from normal sicknesses and diseases (Matt 10:8; Mark 1:34; 6:13; Acts 5:16; 8:7; 16:16-18; see DISEASE). Those possessed by unclean spirits were not necessarily morally evil, and were not excluded from the synagogue. In fact, they were usually so tormented by the evil spirits that they showed great relief and gratitude when freed from them (Mark 1:21-26; 5:18-20; Luke 8:1-2).

Those whom Jesus cleansed from evil spirits had to beware of becoming self-satisfied. It was therefore important for them to be committed to Jesus as true followers, allowing God's Spirit to come into their lives and rule where previously Satan had ruled (Matt 12:43-45).

UNCLEANNESS

Since Israel's God was holy, Israel as a nation had to be holy (Lev 11:44-45). (For the biblical meaning of 'holy' see HOLINESS.) Laws of cleanliness applied this holiness to every part of the people's lives, including their daily food and bodily cleanliness. A person who broke one of these laws was considered defiled, or unclean, and had to be ceremonially cleansed before he could join again in the religious activities of God's covenant people (Exod 19:10-15; Num 19:20-22; John 11:55).

One duty of the priests was to teach the people to distinguish between the holy and the common, the clean and the unclean (Lev 10:10; Ezek 44:23). The system of ritual defilement reminded the people that the results of sin were widespread and could not be ignored (Lev 20:22-26). It also helped to keep the people physically healthy, by preventing them from eating harmful foods, encouraging personal hygiene and limiting the spread of disease.

Uncleanness of animals and things

Israel's laws concerning animals suitable for food were particularly useful in an age of little scientific knowledge. A few simple rules enabled people to recognize forbidden animals, even though they may not have known that meat from those animals could be harmful (Lev 11:1-23,46-47). The laws were not intended to govern the lives of people in other countries and eras (Acts 10:13-15; Rom 14:14,20; 1 Cor 10:31; 1 Tim 4:4).

Articles could become defiled through misuse or accidents. If washing could guarantee cleansing, as in the case of clothing, the articles were to be washed. If washing could not guarantee cleansing, as in the case of earthenware pots, the articles had to be destroyed (Lev 11:29-40; 15:8-11).

Uncleanness of persons

Contact with a dead body made a person unclean and required him to stay outside the community till he had bathed himself and washed his clothes. The isolation period was one day for handling the carcass of an animal, but a week for handling a human corpse. In the latter case, ritual sprinkling was also required (Lev 11:24-25; Num 19:11-19). There was a special cleansing ritual for restored lepers (Lev 14:1-57; see LEPROSY). If a person unknowingly ate meat from which the blood had not been properly drained, he had to carry out a cleansing ritual (Exod 22:31; Lev 17:14-16).

Ceremonial cleansing, including the offering of sacrifices, was necessary for a woman following childbirth. The ceremony was carried out forty days after the birth of a male child and eighty days after the birth of a female child (Lev 12:1-8; cf. Luke 2:21-24). There were strict laws concerning any infection or abnormality relating to sexual organs, whether male or female (Lev 15:1-15). Ceremonial uncleanness lasted one day after sexual intercourse, and seven days after normal menstruation. It was normally removed by bathing. Where a woman suffered lengthy or otherwise abnormal discharge, sacrifices also were required (Lev 15:16-33).

A serious defilement was that which resulted from the unlawful shedding of blood. Murder made the land unclean, and the uncleanness could be removed only by the death of the murderer; or, if the murderer could not be found, by the ritual slaughter of an animal in his place (Deut 21:1-9). Worship of idols also made the land unclean, and the uncleanness could be removed only by the removal of the people themselves from the land (Ezra 9:10-14; Jer 2:7; 16:18; Ezek 14:11; cf. 2 Kings 17:16-18; 21:11-15).

Practices of New Testament times

By the time of Jesus, the Jews had developed a far more detailed system of ritual cleansing. The hand-washing ritual of the Pharisees, for instance, required the pouring of water over their hands to cleanse them from the defilement of people and things they had touched in the Gentile world (Mark 7:1-4; John 2:6; 3:25; 18:28).

Jesus pointed out that such traditions caused misunderstandings of the law and prevented people from doing the more important things that the law required (Mark 7:5-9; see TRADITION). The laws of ceremonial cleansing pointed to a much deeper problem, the problem of sin, which affects every part of people's lives. Real defilement comes not from what people eat or how they eat it, but from sinful thoughts, words and actions. People are made unclean in God's sight by the evil that comes out of them, not by the food that goes into them (Mark 7:14-23; Titus 1:15; James 4:8).

This uncleanness can be removed only through the blood of Jesus Christ. His sacrificial death, by dealing with the root problem of sin, does what all the Israelite rituals were unable to do (Heb 9:13-14; 10:22; see BLOOD; SACRIFICE).

UR

The ancient city of Ur was in the land of Chaldea, which was part of a larger territory commonly known as Babylon. Though it is mentioned in the Bible only as the place from which Abraham originally came (Gen 11:27-31; 15:7; Neh 9:7), it was an important city in the ancient world. A powerful Sumerian dynasty had been centred there until overthrown by Amorites about 2000 BC. (For further details see AMORITES; BABYLON.)

URIM AND THUMMIM

It seems that the Urim and Thummim were small objects that the Israelite high priest kept in the flat pouch (or breastpiece) that he wore on the front of his clothing. They were used to find out God's will in matters requiring a clear-cut decision.

In seeking God's will through the Urim and Thummim, the priest put a question to God in a form that required an answer of either 'yes' or 'no'. He then took the Urim and Thummim out of the breastpiece to find out the answer. God may have said 'yes', 'no', or nothing at all (Exod 28:15-30; Num 27:21; 1 Sam 14:41; 23:9-12; 28:6; 30:7-8; Ezra 2:63; Neh 7:65). (Compare, for example, the drawing of two identical coins out of a pouch. Two 'heads' means 'yes'; two 'tails' means 'no'; a 'head' and a 'tail' means 'no answer'.)

UZZIAH

Much of the information about the period of Uzziah (or Azariah) comes from the prophets of the time, Amos and Hosea (Amos 1:1; Hosea 1:1). Uzziah was king of Judah for 52 years (791-739 BC; 2 Kings 15:1-2; 2 Chron 26:1), and for much of that time Judah was untroubled by foreign neighbours. Under Uzziah's leadership the nation prospered.

The favourable political conditions of the time enabled Uzziah to expand Judah's power in every direction. To the south and west he overran Arab and Philistine territory (2 Chron 26:6-7), spreading his influence to the borders of Egypt and taking control of Edom's Red Sea port of Ezion-geber (or Elath) (2 Chron 26:2,8). To the east he overpowered Ammon (2 Chron 26:8), and to the north he enjoyed peace with the similarly prosperous Israelite kingdom of Jeroboam II (2 Kings 14:23-25; see JEROBOAM). He fortified Jerusalem, built up the armed forces, and equipped his troops with the most modern weapons (2 Chron 26:9,11-15).

Uzziah's conquests gave him control over land and sea trade routes, and his concern for agricultural development increased farm productivity (2 Chron 26:10). Unfortunately, the prosperity brought with it greed and corruption. Those who profited most from the economic growth were the powerful city people, such as government officials, merchants and judges. Ordinary people, the majority of whom were poor farmers, suffered much from the corruption and oppression of the rich. This injustice was fiercely condemned by the prophets of the time, Amos and Hosea (Amos 5:10-12; 6:1; 8:4-6; Hosea 12:7-9; see also AMOS; HOSEA).

Early in his reign Uzziah ruled well, because he followed the godly instruction of his chief adviser (2 Chron 26:5). Later in his reign his power led to pride, which in turn led to his downfall. Despite opposition from the priests, he insisted on taking over the high priest's position, so that he could become the religious head of the nation as well as the political head. God punished him with leprosy, and his son Jotham had to act as joint ruler till Uzziah's death (2 Chron 26:16-23). In the year of Uzziah's death the prophet Isaiah, following Amos and Hosea, began to bring his messages of judgment to the corrupt nation (Isa 1:1; 6:1).

VICTORY

Songs celebrating victory in war were common among ancient people. Israel's victory songs were marked by great praise to God, because Israelites acknowledged that God was the one who gave them victory (Exod 15:1-18; Judg 5:1-31; Ps 18:1-50; see also WAR).

The New Testament uses the illustration of warfare in giving teaching about the Christian's conflict with evil, a conflict in which God again is the one who brings victory (2 Cor 10:3-4; Eph 6:10-18; see also ARMOUR; WEAPONS). Satan is the enemy of God's people, but Christians can be assured of victory over him because of Christ's victory over him (Luke 4:1-13; 10:18; Rev 12:7-11; see SATAN; TEMPTATION). Because of Satan's power in the world, Christians have a conflict with the world and its evil ways, but again through faith in Christ they are guaranteed victory (Rom 8:35-37; James 4:4; 1 John 2:15; 5:19; see WORLD).

Within themselves likewise Christians have a conflict. Their old human nature, the flesh, still tries to rule them, but Christ has conquered the flesh so that they may no longer be under its power. By faith Christ's victory becomes theirs (Rom 8:1-4; see FLESH).

The final victory will be the conquest of death at Christ's return. All God's people will be raised to new life in glorified spiritual bodies, and will be free for ever from the effects of sin. Having established complete authority over all things, Christ will then deliver his victorious kingdom to the Father (1 Cor 15:24-28,54; see RESURRECTION).

VINE

See GRAPES.

VIRGIN

One of the unique features concerning the birth of Jesus was his conception in the womb of his mother while she was still a virgin. Yet the Bible gives no detailed reasons for this. The Gospel writers clearly taught it, but, without attempting to explain its mysteries, they pointed to the goal God had in view. God had become man for the purpose of saving man (Matt 1:21-23; Luke 2:11,29-32; cf. Heb 2:14-15).

Words translated 'virgin'

In the Old Testament there are two Hebrew words translated 'virgin'. In the New Testament only one Greek word is translated 'virgin', though that Greek word is used as the equivalent of either of the Hebrew words.

Of the two Hebrew words, the more commonly used is the one that refers to a young woman who had never had sexual intercourse (Gen 24:16; Lev 21:14; Judg 21:12; 2 Sam 13:2,18; cf. 2 Cor 11:2). Israelites considered it important that a woman be a virgin at the time of her marriage, and their law set out penalties for the loss of virginity before marriage (Exod 22:16-17; Deut 22:13-19; see ADULTERY; FORNICATION). Prophets sometimes used the word poetically, particularly in relation to nations and cities. The word indicated a variety of qualities such as purity, honour, privilege and safety against attack (Isa 37:22; 47:1; Jer 14:17; 31:4; 46:11).

The other Hebrew word is less specific and has been translated by such words as virgin, maiden, girl and young woman. It refers to any young woman of marriageable age. In some contexts the word may imply virginity, but in other contexts the question of virginity is irrelevant (Gen 24:43; Exod 2:8; Ps 68:25; Prov 30:19; Song of Songs 1:3; cf. Matt 25:1; Acts 21:9; 1 Cor 7:25-38).

Isaiah used this latter word when giving the Judean king Ahaz a sign of promise at the time of a combined Israelite-Syrian attack on Judah. He promised Ahaz that God would be with Judah. This divine protection would become so evident over the following months, that in thanks to God one of the Judean young women would name her new-born child Immanuel, meaning 'God with us'. Not only would this be a sign to reassure the royal household, but before the child was three years old Israel and Syria would be powerless to trouble Judah further (Isa 7:10-16).

When the virgin Mary gave birth to Jesus, Matthew saw this as a greater fulfilment of the words that Isaiah spoke to Ahaz. But the word translated 'young woman' in the promise to Ahaz was ambiguous. Isaiah used the word with its broader meaning of 'young woman', but Matthew used it with its narrower meaning of 'virgin'. In the time of Ahaz, God promised to be with his people and protect them; but with the birth of Jesus, God came physically to live with man in man's world (Matt 1:23; John 1:14).

Miraculous conception of Jesus

God is the source of all life. Usually he begins the process of human life in the womb of a woman through using a human father, but when he himself became man he began the process miraculously, by the work of his Spirit in the womb of the virgin Mary (Matt 1:18,20; Luke 1:26-35; see MIRACLE). However, the development of the child in Mary's womb and the birth of the child at the appointed time seem to have been normal. The child, though without a human father, was fully human (Luke 1:42; 2:6-7; Gal 4:4).

The virgin conception of Jesus shows that Jesus was not some ordinary person to whom God added deity, but a unique person whose existence came about through God's direct activity. God did not make a human being into God; he became a human being. Jesus was not someone whom God adopted as his Son; he was actually God's Son. He had existed eternally as the Son of God, and his coming into the world without the function of an earthly father was a clear demonstration of his divine origin (Luke 1:35; John 1:14; see SON OF GOD).

Moreover, the direct activity of God in the conception of Jesus ensured that the child would be holy. There could be no chance that sin, which affects everything man does, could affect him (Luke 1:35; 1 John 3:5). Jesus was the beginning of a new creation, separate from and unspoiled by sin. He was not under the curse of sin, but in the end he bore the sin of others, so that they through him might be part of God's new creation (2 Cor 5:17,21; Col 3:9-10; Titus 3:4-7).

VISION

Many of the visions mentioned in the Bible seem to be little different from dreams (Gen 46:2; Job 33:15; Dan 7:1-2; Acts 16:9). The main difference seems to be that a dream occurred while a person was asleep, but a vision may have occurred while a person was either asleep or awake (1 Sam 3:3-15; Ps 89:19; Dan 2:19; 8:1-26; 9:20-23; Luke 1:22; Acts 9:10-17; 10:3,9-17). Also, dreams were a common experience among people in general, whereas visions were usually given by God to selected people for specific purposes (Gen 15:1; 2 Sam 7:17; Nahum 1:1; Dan 7:1; 8:1; Acts 11:4-18; 18:9). In such cases people were not to boast about their visions, but give glory to God (2 Cor 12:1-10). (Concerning the interpretation of visions see DREAM.)

Visions were often associated with prophets. Prophets were God's messengers to the people, and God may have given them his messages through visions (Num 12:6; 2 Sam 7:17; Isa 1:1; Amos 3:7). To say there was 'no vision in the land' usually meant there were no prophets in the land; or, if there were prophets, they had no message from God. The people were going through a spiritual drought (1 Sam 3:1; Prov 29:18; Lam 2:9; Ezek 7:26; Amos 8:11-12; see PROPHET).

False prophets usually claimed to have seen visions. In this way they hoped to gain acceptance among the people, and consequently receive a good income (Jer 14:14; 23:16-17; Micah 3:5-7).

After the destruction of Jerusalem and the taking of the Jewish people into captivity in Babylon, visions had a more prominent place in the prophetic ministry (Ezek 1:4,15; 8:1-4; 37:1-6; Dan 7:1-4; 8:1). This developed further after the people returned to Jerusalem (Zech 1:8,18; 2:1), and continued to develop right through into New Testament times (Rev 1:12; 4:1).

These visions were largely concerned with the persecution that God's people suffered because of the ungodly nations who ruled them. The message of the visions was that all nations and all events were under the control of God. When his pre-determined time had come, he would intervene in the affairs of the world, overthrow evil, set up his kingdom and bring in the era of the new heavens and the new earth (Dan 9:24-27; Zech 5:5-11; 6:1-8; Rev 18:1-24; 20:1-15; 21:1-8; 22:1-5). (For details see APOCALYPTIC LITERATURE.)

VOW

A vow was a promise that a person made to God to do something (or not to do something), usually in return for God's favour (Num 21:1-3; 1 Sam 1:11; Ps 56:12-13; 132:1-5). In some cases, however, a vow was not concerned with some specific blessing from God, but was purely an act of devotion by which a person offered to God worship and service (Num 6:1-8; Ps 61:8; 65:1; 76:11; cf. Acts 18:18; see also NAZIRITE).

Israelite regulations

All vows were voluntary, but once a person made a vow he had to keep it. A vow was as binding as an oath, and a broken vow brought God's judgment (Num 30:2; Deut 23:21-23; Eccles 5:4-6; see OATH). Therefore, a person was not to make a vow in haste, but was to consider carefully what it involved (Prov 20:25; cf. Judg 10:30-40; see JEPHTHAH).

To protect people from the consequences of rash vows, Israelite law placed a special responsibility upon the head of the household. If he heard his wife or daughter make a rash vow, he could cancel it, provided he acted immediately he heard the vow. If he at first allowed the vow then later changed his mind and forced the person to break it, God held him responsible for the broken vow (Num 30:1-16). Normally, when a person had fulfilled a vow, he was released from it by a ceremony that involved offering a sacrifice of dedication (Deut 12:6,26; Ps 50:14; 66:13).

The Levitical law set out details concerning the types of things a person could vow to God and the way he could offer them. If the offering he vowed was a person, he could not offer the person as a sacrifice, but had to buy back (redeem) the person by a payment of money to the sanctuary. The priests estimated the amount of money according to the usefulness of the person offered (Lev 27:1-8).

Animals, houses and land that were vowed to God usually became the property of the sanctuary. The priests were free to decide whether to use the vowed articles or sell them. If a person vowed an article then later wanted to keep it for himself, he could buy it back from the sanctuary at a price estimated by the priests. However, he had to add a fine of one fifth of its value, since he was keeping for himself something he had vowed to God (Lev 27:9-27).

If the priests caught a person being dishonest, such as trying to offer an inferior animal instead of the one he had vowed, he lost both (Lev 27:10). No one could vow to God anything that belonged to

God already, such as the firstborn of animals (Lev 27:26,28-29).

Misuse of the system

The Israelite regulations for vows should have made people aware of the need for complete honesty, sincerity and devotion to God. Yet some people soon found ways of using the system deceitfully and for their own benefit. They used the making of vows to hide treachery (2 Sam 15:7-10), immorality (Prov 7:14) and selfishness (Mal 1:14).

A well known example of the misuse of vows concerned the Jews of Jesus' time. A person would vow his possessions or money to the temple in such a way that they became the property of the temple upon his death. They were 'corban', meaning 'given to God'. Having promised the things to God, the person said he was no longer free to give them to anyone else, not even to his needy parents. Yet he himself continued to enjoy the use of those things as long as he lived. As usual, Jesus condemned such people, for they cunningly used the details of legal regulations to excuse them from more important responsibilities (Mark 7:9-13).

WALK

The Bible sometimes speaks of people's conduct or manner of life as their 'way' or 'walk'. The two expressions are closely connected: people move along a way by walking (Lev 26:23-24; 1 Kings 6:12; 2 Kings 20:3; Prov 8:20; 20:7; Acts 9:31; Eph 2:10; 5:2; 1 John 2:11).

Frequently, the Bible uses the word 'walk' when contrasting people's way of life before they were Christians with their new life in Christ (Rom 6:4; Eph 2:1-2; 5:8; Col 3:7-8). Their new way of life is controlled by the Spirit rather than by the flesh (Rom 8:4; Gal 5:16,25). It is characterized by love rather than by selfishness (Rom 14:15,19), and is influenced by the person in whom they believe rather than by the things they see in the world around them (John 12:35; 2 Cor 5:7). It is lived in fellowship with God rather than in obedience to sin (1 John 1:6-7), and is patterned on the life of Christ rather than on the life of their fellows (1 John 2:6,11; 2 John 6). (See also WAY.)

WAR

Conflicts between nations occur for a variety of reasons, but always they are evidence of sin in the world. Some nations go to war because they are aggressive, others because they have to defend themselves against aggression. But in neither case do nations have unlimited right to do as they like. This applies even when nations are God's instrument to carry out his judgment on the wicked (Isa 10:5-14; Hab 2:12-13,16-17).

Instructions for Israel

According to God's plan for Israel, the conquest of Canaan was not merely for political or material gain, but had a moral and religious purpose. God had given the Canaanites time to repent but they had consistently refused. Finally, their sin reached the extent where God could postpone judgment no longer (Gen 15:16; Deut 9:5). The destruction of the Canaanites along with their idols, and at times their animals and possessions, was also of significance in God's purposes for Israel. It helped to protect Israel from the corrupt religion, moral filth and physical disease that characterized life throughout Canaan (Deut 7:1-2,16,25-26; 20:16-18).

This policy of total destruction applied only to Israel's conquest of Canaan. The Israelites were not to destroy non-Canaanite cities unless the people refused Israel's terms of peace. They attacked only when all else failed. Even then they were to attack only the soldiers, not the women and children (Deut 20:10-15; cf. Judg 11:12-28), and they were not to destroy the natural environment (Deut 20:19-20). They were to treat prisoners of war well, and if they took any of the captive women as wives, they had to treat them with consideration and respect (Deut 21:10-14; cf. 2 Kings 6:21-22).

Not all Israelite men were required to fight for their country. Those excused from military service included any who had recently committed themselves to some undertaking that could be ruined if they suddenly abandoned it (Deut 20:1-7). If any went out to battle but then became afraid, they were to be sent home (Deut 20:8; cf. Judg 7:3).

Israel's leaders usually consulted priests or prophets before going to war, to ensure they were acting with God's approval (1 Sam 30:7-8; 2 Kings 3:11). They could be confident of victory if God was on their side (Josh 23:10; 2 Chron 20:15; Ps 68:1). They could celebrate their triumphs with victory songs (Exod 15:1-3; Judg 5:1-5; Ps 18:1-6), but they were not to delight in war, and neither were their enemies (Ps 68:30). God gained no pleasure from bloodshed, even when it resulted in victory (1 Chron 22:8; Ps 11:5). He preferred to work for peace (Isa 9:6-7; Micah 4:3-4; Zech 9:9-10).

The Old Testament record

In the early days of their settlement in Canaan, the Israelites enjoyed a fairly peaceful existence and saw no need for a regular army. Later, when hostile neighbours began to invade Israel's territory, a local leader would arise to assemble a fighting force and drive out the enemy (Judg 3:1-3; 5:14-15; 6:33-35; 7:24; 10:18; see JUDGES, BOOK OF).

With the appointment of Saul as Israel's first king, a regular army was established (1 Sam 11:6-8; 13:2; 17:2). At that time most of Israel's fighting was done by foot soldiers who used swords, spears, and bows and arrows (1 Sam 31:1-4; 2 Sam 2:23; see ARMOUR; WEAPONS). Armies set up their bases in well protected camps (1 Sam 17:20; 25:13), and usually went to war in spring or summer, when weather conditions were favourable (2 Sam 11:1; 2 Kings 13:20).

David improved Israel's army till it was the strongest among the nations of the region (2 Sam 8:1-18). As he seized the chariot forces of conquered enemies, Israel's army began to use chariots. The following king, Solomon, enlarged Israel's chariot force considerably (2 Sam 8:4; 15:1; 1 Kings 4:26; 9:22; 10:26; cf. 22:35; see CHARIOT). A later king, Uzziah, further modernized the army by providing it with better armour and weapons, including special equipment for use against besieging armies (2 Chron 26:14-15).

Siege was a common part of warfare, and was often considered essential if an aggressor failed to take a city in a surprise attack or head-on assault. The more powerful armies had huge pieces of siege equipment, some of which were designed to shoot

Siege warfare

over the city walls, others to break down the walls. The attackers usually heaped earth against the walls to enable them to get closer to the top, where the walls were thinner and easier to break through (2 Kings 6:24; 25:1; Ezek 4:2). Meanwhile, people inside the city slowly starved to death or died of disease (2 Kings 25:2-3; Jer 32:24; Lam 2:10-12; 2:19-21; 4:4-9). The victorious siege often ended with senseless butchery, rape, plunder and destruction

(2 Kings 25:4-17; Ps 74:4-8; 79:1-3; Lam 5:11-12; Nahum 2:5-9; 3:1-3).

Christians and war

As long as there is sin in the world there will be war (Matt 24:6; James 4:1), and governments will be forced to protect their people from aggression. The Old Testament record seems to support the view that this use of force by a government is within the authority given it by God. That authority allows it to punish wrongdoers and preserve the well-being of its citizens (Rom 13:4; 1 Tim 2:1-2; 1 Peter 2:13-14; see GOVERNMENT).

Christians, however, should never try to expand or defend the kingdom of God through war (Matt 26:52-54; John 18:36). God alone has the right to impose his kingdom by force, and he will exercise that right when Jesus Christ returns and finally destroys all enemies (Rev 16:1-21; 17:14; 19:11-21; see KINGDOM OF GOD).

In the meantime, Christians live in a world where they are members of God's kingdom and at the same time members of earthly nations (see NATION). God's kingdom is of a different type from the 'kingdoms' of the world, and Christians must not apply the legal procedures of civil government to their personal behaviour. Civil law requires legal retaliation for wrongdoing, and therefore imposes a punishment to suit the offence. Christian morality requires believers to forgive those who do them wrong (Matt 5:38-42; cf. Rom 12:17-21 with Rom 13:1-6).

War is one of those cases where Christians at times see tension between these two responsibilities. In the New Testament, as in the Old, believers seem to have had no objection to engaging in military service themselves or accepting the protection that those in military service provided for them (Luke 3:14; 7:2-9; Acts 10:1-4; 23:17-35; Heb 11:33-34). But in the century immediately following the apostolic era, most Christians were strongly pacifist. They believed all war to be wrong and they refused to participate in military service.

Throughout the history of the church, sincere Christians have held a variety of views ranging from total pacifism to total commitment to military service. Some Christians, while not believing all involvement in war to be wrong, believe it to be wrong for *Christians* to take part in war. Others, still condemning war, consider that when the state of affairs becomes so bad that the ideal is no longer possible, they may be forced to accept the lesser of two wrongs (cf. Matt 19:8). While refusing to initiate aggression themselves, they consider that to resist an evil attacker is not as bad as allowing the evil to triumph unhindered. They do not enjoy such action, but at the same time they do not believe they should leave the protection of the defenceless entirely to non-Christians (cf. Isa. 1:17).

Even if Christians believe it is right for them to take part in war, they must not accept the decisions of their government without question. Governments can make decisions that are so unjust or immoral that a Christian may feel he must disobey them if he is to remain obedient to God. God alone can demand absolute obedience (cf. Dan 3:17-18; Acts 4:19; 5:29). Whatever the circumstances, Christians must, like their God, work to achieve justice and peace (cf. Isa 2:4; 9:2-7; 11:1-9; Matt 5:6,9; see JUSTICE; PEACE).

WATER

In a hot and dry country such as Palestine, water was extremely important. God promised his people that if they were obedient to him, he would always send them enough rain to ensure a constant supply for all their needs. But if they were disobedient, he would send them droughts and famine (Deut 28:12-24; Joel 2:23; Amos 4:7-8). (For further details concerning the problems of water in Palestine see PALESTINE; WEATHER.)

The refreshing and life-giving benefits of water made it a popular biblical symbol to picture the spiritual refreshment and eternal life that God gives to those who trust in him (Ps 1:3; 23:1-3; Isa 44:3; 55:1; Jer 17:13; John 4:14; 7:37-39; Rev 21:6; 22:1-2). Water could, however, be a means of judgment (Gen 6:17; Exod 14:23,26-27; Ps 32:6; Matt 7:24-27; 2 Peter 2:5).

Water was also used in the cleansing rituals of the Israelite religion. Ceremonial washings for the priests spoke of the purity required of those in official religious positions (Exod 29:4-5). At times the washing had additional practical benefits (Exod 30:18-21). If people became ceremonially unclean, they had to be ceremonially cleansed with water. Again there were cases where the washing had additional practical benefits (Lev 14:1-9; 15:16-18; Num 19:11-13; see UNCLEANNESS).

Ritual cleansings may have involved bathing the whole body (Num 19:7), bathing only parts of the body (Exod 30:19), or merely sprinkling (Num 8:7). The water used in the rituals in some cases was pure water, in others a specially prepared mixture (Lev 15:13; Num 19:17).

In figurative speech, water was a picture of cleansing from sin (Ps 51:1-2; Ezek 36:25-26; John 13:5-10; Acts 22:16; Eph 5:26; Heb 10:22; see also BAPTISM). Such cleansing can occur only through the activity of God, who in his mercy removes sin and creates new life within the cleansed sinner (John 3:5-7; 1 Cor 6:9-11; Titus 3:5-7; Rev 7:14,17; see REGENERATION).

WAY

During the time of the early church, Christianity was known as 'the way' (Acts 9:2; 19:9,23; 22:4; 24:14,22). Possibly this was because Christians spoke of their newfound life as the way of the Lord, the way of life, or the way of salvation (cf. Matt 7:13-14; Luke 20:21; John 1:23; 14:6; Acts 16:17). This usage was common also among believers in Old Testament times (Ps 16:11; 18:21,30,32; 27:11).

Since the way of God led to true life and true enjoyment, that 'way' may have meant God's will and God's commandments (Job 21:14; Ps 37:23-24; 119:27,37; Jer 5:4; Matt 22:16; Rom 11:33; Rev 15:3). The word could also refer to a person's manner of life in general. In that sense the way of the righteous was often contrasted with the way of the wicked (Ps 1:1,6; 37:5; Prov 4:18-19; 14:12; Jer 7:3; Rom 3:16; 1 Cor 12:31; James 5:20). (See also WALK.)

WEALTH

God created the material world and gave it to man for his enjoyment (Gen 1:26; 2:16; 1 Tim 4:4). But there is always the danger that man will misuse God's gifts. Although both Old and New Testaments state that wealth may be a gift from God that a person should enjoy (Eccles 5:19; 1 Tim 6:17), the statement in each case is preceded by a warning of the danger of misuse (Eccles 5:10; 1 Tim 6:10).

Wealth is not necessarily a sign of divine reward for godliness. In some cases it may be (Deut 28:1-6; Ps 112:1-3; 2 Cor 9:10-11), but in others it may have resulted from greed or injustice (Isa 3:14-15; James 5:1-6; Rev 3:17).

One of the dangers of wealth is that it gives such a feeling of independence that people may not trust God as they should (Deut 8:17-18; Ps 10:3; 52:7; Prov 18:11; 28:11; Mark 10:23; 1 Tim 6:17). Some people become so concerned with making themselves rich that their wealth becomes a god. Only by getting rid of it can they find eternal life (Matt 6:24; 13:22; 19:16,21-22). Although Jesus did not tell all his followers to get rid of their wealth, he warned of the consequences of putting the desire for wealth before devotion to God or concern for others (Matt 6:19-21; Luke 12:16-21; 16:19-25).

Christians have to be alert constantly to the dangers associated with money, as the desire for it can lead to spiritual ruin (Prov 11:28; 1 Tim 6:9-10). They should be satisfied with what they have and trust in God's care for them through life's varied circumstances (Matt 6:33; Luke 12:15; Phil 4:11-12; Heb 13:5).

The Bible does not always condemn wealth, for the wealthy can help others by their generous giving (Deut 15:1-11; Matt 27:57-60; Luke 12:33; 16:9-13; Acts 4:36-37; 20:35; 2 Cor 8:14; 9:6-7; 1 Tim 6:17-19; see GIVING). But the Bible consistently condemns luxury, for it combines self-centred extravagance with indifference for others (Isa 5:8-12; Amos 6:4-6; Luke 6:24-25; 16:19; James 5:1-5).

People who use their wealth to gain power are also condemned, particularly when they oppress people who have no way of resisting them (Jer 22:13-17; Amos 4:1; 5:11-12; Micah 2:1-2; James 2:6; 5:1-6; see POOR). Christians, by contrast, should follow the example of Jesus and put other people's interests before their own (2 Cor 8:9; Phil 2:4-8).

WEAPONS

In ancient warfare the chief weapon was the sword. Swords were of many types and could be either single-edged or double-edged (Judg 3:16,21; 7:22; 20:37; 1 Sam 25:13; 31:4; Matt 26:47; Acts 12:2). The Bible often speaks of the sword figuratively, some-

Syrian soldier with sword, spear and shield

times as a symbol of judgment (Ezek 30:24; 32:10; Rev 19:15,21), other times as a symbol of the Word of God (Eph 6:17; Heb 4:12).

Spears and lances may have been made entirely of metal, or of wood with a metal head (Num 25:7;

1 Sam 13:19; 17:7; 18:11; 26:12; Jer 46:4; John 19:34; Acts 23:23). Bows and arrows were widely used in warfare and were usually made of wood (2 Kings 9:24; 13:15; 2 Chron 14:8; Ps 7:12; 11:2; 44:6; Zech 9:10). Slings of leather were used to throw stones. Though originally used by shepherds to fight wild animals, they were later used in warfare (1 Sam 17:40; 1 Chron 12:2).

The Bible often likens the Christian life to warfare with unseen spiritual forces. Christians must therefore clothe themselves with the armour of God and go to battle using the weapons of righteousness (2 Cor 6:6-7; 10:3-4; Eph 6:11-13; 1 Tim 1:18; see ARMOUR; WAR).

WEATHER

The climate of Palestine was, on the whole, hot and dry. The hot season, from April to September, was almost without rain. During this season farmers depended for water mainly on heavy dews, wells, or reservoirs that had been filled with water during the dry season (Gen 26:18,21-22; 2 Chron 26:10; Isa 18:4). The rain came in the cooler season, beginning with early rains about October and concluding with later rains about March (Deut 11:14; Jer 3:3; 5:24; Joel 2:23; see FARMING).

Over the whole year the amount of rain that fell in Palestine varied from about 350 mm (14 inches) on the coastal plain to about 700 mm (28 inches) in the central mountains. The Negeb, the dry region to the south, received less than 200 mm (8 inches) a year, and the lower Jordan Valley only about 100 mm (4 inches). (For map of the regions see PALESTINE.)

The temperature in Palestine for most of the year was between 23 and 30 degrees Celsius, often reaching 40 degrees in the lower Jordan Valley. In the central mountains the temperature dropped to about 10 degrees in the middle of winter, but only at Mt Hermon in the far north was there usually any snow (Jer 18:14; cf. Deut 3:9).

Israelites had to bear in mind constantly that their God was in control of the weather. He was the God of nature (Ps 68:9-10; 104:1-30; Jer 10:13). If they obeyed him, he would bless them with good weather and agricultural prosperity; if they turned away from him and followed other gods, he would send them droughts and other disasters (Deut 28:1-24; see NATURE).

When they settled in Canaan, the Israelites found that the Canaanite gods were also regarded as gods of nature. Before long the Israelites fell to the temptation to combine the worship of these gods

457

with the worship of their own God, Yahweh (Judg 2:11-13; Hosea 2:5-13; see BAAL).

WEIGHTS

It is not possible today to give exact equivalents of the weights and measures referred to in the Bible. It seems that there was no official system in operation throughout Palestine, and weights and measures may have varied from place to place and from era to era.

The important requirement of the Israelite law was that weights and measures be honest (Lev 19:5-36; Deut 25:13-16). This was a requirement that

Weighing goods

greedy and dishonest merchants ignored. When selling grain they used undersized measures, and when weighing the buyer's money they used extra heavy weights (Amos 8:4-5). But God saw their dishonesty and announced his judgment upon them (Prov 11:1; Micah 6:11).

The heaviest weight in use in Israel was the talent, which probably weighed about 50 kilograms (1 Chron 29:7; Rev 16:21; see TALENT). A talent was divided into sixty minas (1 Kings 10:17), and a mina into fifty shekels. Thus a shekel, which was the basic weight, weighed between sixteen and seventeen grams (Ezek 4:10; see SHEKEL). Half a shekel was called a beka (Exod 38:26), and a twentieth of a shekel a gerah (Exod 30:13).

WIDOW

In Bible times widows usually found life difficult, partly because they were defenceless against people able to take advantage of them. Without anyone to support and protect them, many widows became lonely and poor. The law of Moses recognized that widows needed special protection against social

injustice (Exod 2:22; Deut 24:17; Jer 7:5-7; Mark 12:40-44; Luke 18:1-5).

Throughout the Bible God shows a special concern for widows and he expects people in general to have similar concern (Deut 10:18; 14:29; 24:19; Ps 68:5; 146:9; Prov 15:25; Isa 1:17; James 1:27). Christians in the Jerusalem church showed such concern when they organized a daily distribution of food to the widows among them (Acts 6:1-3). Later, other churches followed their example, though some families abused the system by using the church's welfare program as a way of avoiding their responsibilities. Paul therefore suggested that the church support only those widows who were over sixty years of age and who had no other means of support. Widows in Christian families were to be supported by those families (1 Tim 5:3-16).

Paul reminded Christians that a widow in the church was free to remarry, provided she married another Christian and provided the circumstances were favourable (Rom 7:2-3; 1 Cor 7:26-27,39-40). In the case of younger widows, he advised in favour of remarriage (1 Tim 5:11-15).

A custom in Old Testament times was that when a man died having no children, his brother had the duty of producing a son through the widow. Legally this child was considered to be the son of the dead man and so carried on his family name and inheritance. If the living brother refused to do his duty, he was publicly disgraced for allowing his brother's family name to die out (Gen 38:8-10; Deut 25:5-10; Ruth 1:1-14; 3:1-4:12; Matt 22:24).

WIFE

When God created mankind, he created it male and female, with an equality between the sexes. Men and women are equal in worth and status, having been created jointly in the image of God (Gen 1:27; 2:21-23; cf. Gal 3:28). But physically and emotionally they are different, for God has made them to fulfil different roles. Although there may be cases where God's will is that a person remain single (1 Cor 7:7-8,32-35), in general his will is that people marry. In marriage two equal human beings, a man and a woman, have two different functions, those of husband and wife (Gen 2:24-25).

The marriage partnership

The husband's exclusively male characteristics mean that he starts the process that produces children in the family, and perhaps this is why he carries the ultimate responsibility for the family. The wife's exclusively female characteristics enable her to bear children, and perhaps this is why she has a special responsibility for the children's care (1 Cor 11:3; 1 Tim 2:15). Both the husband and the wife have a responsibility to 'rule' or 'manage' the family (1 Tim 3:4; 5:14), and in their different ways they contribute to its stability and well-being. As in other areas of life, each is dependent on the other (1 Cor 11:11-12; see also HUSBAND).

The wife should submit to her husband in his role as head of the family (Eph 5:22-24; Titus 2:4-5; 1 Peter 3:1,5-6), but this is balanced by the requirement that the husband should submit to his wife (Eph 5:21; 1 Peter 3:7). The husband should exercise self-sacrificing love for his wife (Eph 5:25-29; Col 3:19), but this is balanced by the requirement that the wife should exercise self-sacrificing love for her husband (Eph 5:1-2). Each gives for the sake of the other. The relationship between them is patterned on the relationship between Christ and the church (Eph 5:24-25,32; see also MARRIAGE).

Ideals and reality

In an Old Testament picture of the ideal wife, there is an equality of trust and understanding between her and her husband (Prov 31:10-12). She is both discerning and diligent, whether in helping the family income or in carrying out household tasks (Prov 31:13-19). Her generous service for others extends beyond her family to those who are less fortunate, with the result that all in the community respect both her and her household (Prov 31:20-26). In particular, she is loved and honoured by her husband and children (Prov 31:27-31).

There will be marital harmony where husband and wife recognize each other's strengths and learn to depend on each other and support each other. A wife may find, for instance, that her husband is especially dependent on her in cases where he acknowledges her superior insight, judgment or decisiveness (Gen 21:12; Judg 4:4; 13:22-23; 1 Sam 1:23; Prov 19:14; Acts 18:26; cf. 1 Sam 25:1-42). In other circumstances a wife may gladly accept the judgment of her husband and realize that in the chosen course of action what he needs most is her support (Gen 31:3-5,14-17; Exod 18:5-8; 1 Cor 9:5; cf. Job 2:9-10; Prov 19:13).

A wife must not allow loyalty to her husband to lead her into wrongdoing (cf. Acts 5:1-2,9). The husband's headship in marriage does not mean he can command absolute obedience. The only person to whom a wife must give absolute obedience is God (cf. Acts 4:19; 5:29).

Special difficulties may arise in the case where the wife becomes a Christian after marriage, but her husband remains a non-Christian. The wife should not try to divorce her husband, but neither should she be aggressive in trying to make him a Christian. She should rather live with him in such a way that he may see the worth of the Christian life and perhaps become a believer himself (1 Cor 7:12-16; 1 Peter 3:1-6; see also DIVORCE).

WINE
See GRAPES.

WISDOM
One of God's desires for mankind is that people learn and develop practical wisdom, so that they might live intelligently and honestly. In this way their lives will be useful, bringing pleasure to God and benefits to themselves and others (Prov 1:2-7; 2:7-11; Eph 5:15-16).

Practical and God-centred

The wisdom that the Bible encourages is concerned with the practical affairs of everyday living rather than with philosophical theories. People live in a real world and have to deal with real people (Deut 1:13-15; 34:9; 1 Kings 3:9; Acts 6:3; 7:10). The basis of that wisdom, however, is not human cleverness but obedient reverence for God. God is the source of true wisdom and he gives it to those who seek it (Prov 1:7; 2:6; 9:10; Dan 2:20; Rom 16:27; 1 Cor 1:30; James 1:5-8).

Without such reverence, wisdom may be selfish and worldly, characterized by ungodly attitudes such as jealousy and deceit. Godly wisdom, by contrast, is characterized by humility, uprightness and a concern for others (Prov 8:12-16; 10:8; 11:2; Isa 5:21; James 3:13-18).

This godly wisdom is available to all who are prepared to leave the folly of their self-centred ways and accept it from God (Prov 1:20-23; 8:1-6; 9:1-6). It will enable them to overcome the temptations of life (Prov 6:23-27). But if they refuse it, they will inevitably bring upon themselves disappointment, shame and despair (Prov 1:20,24-26; 5:11-13; 7:1-23; Eccles 10:1-3).

In Old Testament times the chief teachers of this practical wisdom were people known as 'the wise' (Jer 18:18). Though different from priests and prophets, these teachers of wisdom were godly men who sought to persuade people by giving practical advice based on experience (1 Kings 4:30-31; Prov 25:1; 31:1; Eccles 12:9-10).

The wisdom teachers knew that the average person had enough common sense to recognize the wisdom of the instruction. Sometimes they taught by means of short, easily remembered statements such as those collected in the biblical book of Proverbs. Other times they taught by arguments and debates, such as those recorded in the books of Job and Ecclesiastes and in certain psalms. (For details see WISDOM LITERATURE.)

However, the wisdom teachers never forgot that true wisdom was not something they themselves invented. Wisdom existed long before man was created. In fact, it was through wisdom that God created man, and it is through wisdom that man can now live a meaningful life (Prov 8:12-31).

God's wisdom and man's

Although God is the source of any wisdom that man possesses, man's wisdom is still limited. God's wisdom is not. It is infinite and therefore is beyond man's understanding (Isa 40:28; Rom 11:33-34). In his wisdom God created the universe, and by his wisdom he governs it (Ps 104:24; Prov 3:19; Rev 7:12). His plan of salvation for his sinful creatures demonstrates to people and angels his unsearchable wisdom (Rom 11:33; Eph 3:10).

The wisdom of God in salvation was expressed in Jesus Christ, both in his life and in his death (Matt 12:42; 13:54; 1 Cor 1:23-24,30; Col 2:3). Again the wisdom was concerned not with philosophical notions but with practical action. Jesus died for sinful people so that they might be saved. To those who refuse to believe, salvation through Jesus' death on the cross seems foolish. Actually, they are the ones who are foolish, for they reject what God in his wisdom has done, and try by their own misguided wisdom to save themselves (1 Cor 1:18-25). People may think they are wise, but they must humble themselves and trust in God's wisdom if they are to be saved (1 Cor 3:18-20).

Because salvation depends on humble trust in God and not on human wisdom, the true preacher of the gospel will not try to impress people with his wisdom. Rather he will command them to repent of their sins and trust in the death of Jesus Christ for their salvation (1 Cor 2:1-5).

Once people have repented and believed, they must make every effort to learn more of God. Then they will begin to grow in true wisdom. This wisdom is not the proud and worldly type that prevents people from trusting in God, but is a new wisdom based on the character of God who gives it (1 Cor 2:6-7; Eph 5:15; Col 1:28). Only as believers increase in the knowledge of God and his Word can their wisdom develop and be of use to God, to themselves

and to others (Ps 90:12; Dan 12:3; Eph 1:9,17-19; Col 1:9-10; 3:16).

WISDOM LITERATURE

Among the different types of writings found in the Bible are those known as the wisdom writings. The best known of these are the books of Proverbs, Job and Ecclesiastes. A number of psalms also belong to this class of literature (e.g. Ps 10, 14, 19, 37, 49, 73, 112).

Teachers of wisdom

God used many different types of people to instruct and guide ancient Israelites in the sort of life he desired for them. He used priests to teach and supervise his law (Deut 33:10; Mal 2:7). He used prophets to bring direct messages from himself that would stir the people to change their ways and develop right attitudes (Amos 3:1,7; 4:1-3; 5:14-15). He also used teachers known as 'the wise' (Jer 18:18). These were men who received no special revelations from God, but who simply examined the everyday affairs of life and, on the basis of their findings, offered advice to their hearers (Eccles 12:9-10).

The biblical literature that comes from these wisdom teachers is of two main types. The first, represented by the book of Proverbs, gives the principles of right and wrong as they apply to life in general; for example, the righteous will prosper but the wicked will perish (Prov 11:5-8). The second, represented by the books of Job and Ecclesiastes, looks at the exceptions; for example, the righteous often have all sorts of troubles, while the wicked enjoy peace and prosperity (Job 12:4; 21:7-13; Eccles 7:15; 8:14).

These two types of wisdom are not in conflict, but simply show different aspects of life. The same teacher could look at life's problems from several viewpoints. The book of Proverbs recognizes that the same principle may not apply equally in all cases (Prov 26:4-5), while the books of Job and Ecclesiastes recognize that the general principles are still the basis for wise teaching (Job 28:20-28; Eccles 7:1-13).

The wisdom teachers of the Bible were godly men who made an honest effort to examine life, with all its inconsistencies, so that they might help people live more meaningful lives. Though they were aware of an afterlife (Job 19:26), their main concern was to deal with problems in the present life.

Wisdom teachers taught in public places where they could reach the common people (Prov 1:20-21;

8:1-3; Eccles 12:9-10), and in their own schools where they instructed their disciples (Prov 2:1; 3:1; Eccles 12:12). They taught in a variety of ways. At times they taught by giving direct instruction and asking questions (Prov 1:2,5; 5:1; Eccles 1:3,10; 2:22; 3:9,21-22); other times they used proverbs, picture language and riddles (Prov 1:6; 8:1; 10:1). They recounted stories and experiences from real life (Prov 24:30-34; Eccles 4:13-16; 9:13-18) and they told parables (2 Sam 12:1-6). Some of the wisdom teachers became official advisers to the nation's rulers (2 Sam 15:12,34; 16:23; 20:18).

Source of true wisdom

Wise men were active not only in Israel but also in countries throughout the region of the Bible's story (1 Kings 4:30; Jer 49:7; 50:35; Acts 7:22). Some of Israel's wisdom sayings had parallels in other countries, and wisdom teachers from various nations visited each other to test each other's knowledge and increase their own (1 Kings 4:30-34; 10:1). The Israelites readily borrowed wisdom teaching from their neighbours when it displayed sound common sense (Prov 30:1; 31:1; cf. John 1:9).

At the same time, the Israelite wisdom teachers did not allow their teaching to be corrupted by the idolatry, immorality and self-seeking that were often a feature of the teaching of their neighbours. The characteristic that marked Israelite wisdom as being different from that of all others was the Israelites' view of God. For them, the fear of God was the basis of true wisdom (Job 28:28; Prov 1:7; Eccles 12:13). The wisdom taught by the wise men of Israel came from those who reverenced God's law and wanted to apply it to the details of everyday living. Their insight came from their knowledge of God.

WITNESS

The word 'witness' had many usages and meanings in the Bible. It was commonly used to refer to a person who saw, knew or experienced something (Deut 17:6; Acts 5:30-32), or to that person's open declaration of what he saw, knew or experienced. His witness was his testimony (Exod 20:16; John 3:11).

'Witness' was used also to denote a person who guaranteed, or swore to, the truth of something (Ruth 4:9; 1 Sam 12:5; 2 Cor 1:23); or it may have denoted that person's oath or guarantee of the truth (Acts 10:43; Rom 3:21). Even a lifeless object could be a witness, in the sense of being a guarantee or confirmation of something, such as a verbal agreement (Gen 31:44-50; Josh 24:27). Actions likewise

could be a witness, in the sense of being evidence (John 5:36).

The law of Israel

When God established his covenant with Israel at Mt Sinai, he gave the Ten Commandments as the basis of the covenant requirements laid upon his people. The two tablets of stone containing the Ten Commandments were a witness, or testimony, to God's demands and to Israel's acceptance of them (Exod 24:3,12). They were therefore called the testimony (Exod 25:21), the ark of the covenant in which they were placed was called the ark of the testimony (Exod 25:16), and the tabernacle (or tent) in which the ark was kept was called the tabernacle of the testimony (Exod 38:21).

Other uses of 'witness' in relation to Israel's laws were concerned with evidence in lawsuits. The main requirement was that there be at least two witnesses if the judges were to accept or act upon any accusation (Deut 19:15; cf. Matt 18:15-16). To discourage people from making accusations secretly or lightly, the law required them, in certain cases, to participate publicly in the punishment if the accused was found guilty (Deut 17:6-7).

It was wrong, however, for a witness to remain silent when he had evidence to present (Lev 5:1). If the judges found that a witness had given false evidence, they inflicted upon him the punishment that he had tried to bring upon the accused (Deut 19:16-21; cf. Mark 14:55-56).

The witness of Jesus

'Witness' had a specific meaning in relation to the life of Jesus Christ. John the Baptist was a witness to Jesus in the sense that he pointed people to Jesus as the Saviour who had come from God. John was a witness to the truth (John 1:7,15; 5:33). The works Jesus did were also a witness, for they showed clearly that he was the Messiah who had come from God. The Old Testament Scriptures were another witness (John 5:36-39).

With all these witnesses, there was no basis for the Pharisees' objection that Jesus had no witnesses to support his claim to be the God-sent Saviour (John 8:12-13). Jesus came from God as the one who revealed God to the world, and therefore he was a witness to the truth of God (John 3:11; 18:37). His witness was supported by the witness of the Father, and therefore the Pharisees should have accepted it (John 8:14-18).

Those who lived with Jesus were witnesses to the truth that he was God-become-man, the Saviour of the world (1 John 1:1-3; 4:14). Other believers, whether in the first century or the present day, bear the same witness to him, because of the Spirit who bears witness within them (John 15:26; 1 John 5:7,10-11).

Witness in the early church

After Jesus' resurrection and ascension, the disciples boldly bore witness to him as Lord and Messiah. They emphasized the facts of his life, death, and particularly his resurrection, for they were personal eye-witnesses of those events (Acts 2:22-24,32-33; 5:30-32; 10:36-43; 13:27-31).

These personal eye-witnesses were the first to spread the gospel (Luke 24:46-49; Acts 1:8), but other believers also bore witness to Jesus when they preached the gospel (Acts 20:24; 23:11). The gospel was sometimes called the witness, or testimony, of Christ (1 Cor 1:6; 2:1; 2 Thess 1:10).

Often Christians, as well as the gospel they preached, came under attack. In these circumstances they had to bear the same testimony to the truth as Jesus had borne (Acts 22:20; 1 Tim 6:13-14; Rev 1:9). Some were killed because of their witness to Jesus (Rev 2:13; 11:7; 12:11). In fact, bearing witness to Jesus became so closely associated with being killed for Jesus' sake that the word for 'witness' (Greek: *martyria*) produced the word 'martyr' (Rev 6:9; 17:6; 20:4).

WOE

See CURSE.

WOMEN

The biblical account of the origins of the human race makes it clear that humankind, as existing in God's image, consists of people of two sexes who are equal in status and worth in God's sight (Gen 1:27). The male and the female, though of opposite sexes, are complementary to each other. As partners they form a unit (Gen 2:18,23). (For details relating to the role of women in marriage and the family see MARRIAGE; WIFE; FAMILY.)

Wrong attitudes corrected

Through the different physical, psychological and emotional characteristics he placed within the sexes, God equipped men and women for different roles in human society. He gave the ultimate responsibility for leadership to the man, but when sin entered the human race, the man misused his position to dominate the woman (Gen 3:16). As societies developed, men increasingly denied women their rights and exploited them.

Israelite law helped restore the status of women by giving them rights in matters such as marriage (Deut 22:13-21; cf. Gen 24:57-58), divorce (Deut 24:1-4), work (Deut 15:12) and inheritance (Num 27:8). Some women were prophets (Exod 15:20; Judg 4:4; Luke 2:36) and some rose to prominent positions in the nation's leadership (Num 12:4; Judg 4:4-6; 5:7; 2 Kings 22:14-16).

Both the words and the works of Jesus show that he treated women no differently from men. His openness with women was a surprise and a rebuke to those men who considered women inferior (Matt 15:21-28; Mark 5:25-34; Luke 7:36-50; 10:38-42; John 4:7-27; 8:1-11; 11:5,20-33). A number of women, having become believers in Jesus, travelled with him and the apostles to help look after their everyday needs. During the events surrounding his trial and crucifixion, some of these women were more faithful to him than were the apostles (Luke 8:1-3; Mark 15:40-41; 16:1-2).

Women in the church

Life in the early church demonstrated that there is no difference between men and women in their status as believers (Gal 3:28), their reception of the Holy Spirit (Acts 2:17-18), or their possession of spiritual gifts (1 Cor 12:7,12-14).

Women prayed and prophesied publicly (Acts 1:14; 21:9), though the custom was that when they did so they covered their heads (1 Cor 11:5,13,16). This practice was apparently to maintain harmony with what local people considered to be culturally acceptable (1 Cor 11:6,13). Paul saw in it a reflection of the woman's role in God's order for church and society (1 Cor 11:3,7-9), though he did not see it as meaning that she was inferior to the man (1 Cor 11:11-12).

Paul was always concerned that public meetings of the church be orderly (1 Cor 14:40). Just as he expected the speaker in tongues to be silent when there was no interpreter present (1 Cor 14:28), and the speaker of prophecy to be silent when another person received a revelation (1 Cor 14:29-30), so he expected the women to be silent when they were tempted to question the speaker (1 Cor 14:34-35).

Although Paul permitted women to prophesy (1 Cor 11:4; cf. Acts 2:17; 21:9), he would not permit them to be the authoritative teachers or leaders of the church. He believed that, in general, they were more likely than men to be misled by false teaching (1 Tim 2:12-14; cf. 2 Tim 3:6-7). He considered that women should regard their first responsibility as bringing up their children to know and follow God (1 Tim 2:15; 5:14).

However, not all women have children. This indicates that Paul was not laying down a fixed law to be applied in all cases (cf. 1 Cor 7:34). Rather he was expressing what he considered to be a general principle. He himself acknowledged that at times a woman may have a more prominent teaching role than her husband (Acts 18:2,26; Rom 16:3-4; 2 Tim 4:19). Many women worked with him and used their spiritual gifts in a variety of ministries (Acts 16:13-15; Rom 16:7,12-15; Phil 4:2-3). Women were recognized for their work in the churches (Rom 16:1-2; 1 Tim 5:10) and served alongside men as deacons (1 Tim 3:8,11). But there were times when women were just as guilty as men in leading people astray through false teaching (Rev 2:20).

WONDERS

See MIRACLES; SIGNS.

WORD

To the Israelites of Old Testament times, God's word was not simply something written down or spoken out, but something active. It had within it the power of God, so that when God expressed his will, that will was carried out. When God said, 'Let there be light', there was light (Gen 1:3). Through the active word of God, the universe was created (Gen 1:3,6,9,14,20,24,26; Heb 11:3; 2 Peter 3:5). God's word could not fail. Whatever it said would happen had to happen (Isa 55:10-11). God's word had such life and power that people often thought of it almost as if it was a person — the living agent or messenger of God (Ps 33:6; 107:20; 147:15,18).

Jesus the Word

In the New Testament Jesus is called the Word (Greek: *logos*) (1 John 1:1-3). Greek philosophers of the first century used *logos* in reference to what they believed to be the principle of reason in the universe, but this is not necessarily the way the Bible uses the word. The word *logos* as used in the New Testament may contain some reference to the Greek ideas, but it is better understood in relation to the Old Testament meaning of 'word'.

The Word of God is the living and active agent of God. It existed before creation and was the means by which God created. The New Testament shows that this Word is more than merely likened to a person, it *is* a person; no longer 'it', but 'he'. He is not only with God, he is God. This Word is Jesus Christ, who became man. He is the living Word, the living expression of God. His words and deeds are the words and deeds of God (John 1:1-4,14; cf. Gen

1:1,3; Col 1:15-17; Heb 1:1-3; Rev 19:13,16). (For details see JESUS CHRIST; SON OF GOD.)

The written and spoken Word

Because God has spoken to mankind through Jesus Christ, Jesus Christ is the Word. Similarly, because he has spoken through the Scriptures, the Scriptures are the Word (Ps 119:105; Matt 15:6; John 10:35). When, however, the Bible writers speak of the written or spoken Word of God, they are usually referring not to a one-volume book such as our Bible, but to the Word of God as announced or preached by God's representatives. (For details of the Bible as the Word of God see INSPIRATION; SCRIPTURES.)

Prophets, for example, were God's spokesmen, and their announcements were the authoritative Word of God for his people (Isa 1:2-4,18; Jer 23:22; Ezek 1:3; Hosea 4:1; Joel 1:1; Amos 1:3; Heb 1:1-2; see PROPHECY). Likewise the preaching of the gospel by the New Testament apostles was the proclamation of the Word of God (Acts 4:31; 13:44; Eph 1:13; Col 1:5-6; 1 Peter 1:23,25; see GOSPEL; PREACHING). The instruction in Christian doctrine that followed was the teaching of the Word of God (Acts 18:11; Col 3:16; 1 Thess 2:13; Heb 13:7; see TEACHER).

This spoken Word became also the written Word and, like the personal Word Jesus, was living and active. It is still living and active today, and does God's work in the hearts and lives of those who hear it or read it (Heb 4:12).

WORK

In the original languages of the Bible, the word 'work' had a broad meaning. It was often used of action or behaviour in general (Ps 9:16; Amos 8:7; Eph 2:8-9; 2 Tim 1:9; see GOOD WORKS). Its specific usages may be grouped into three main categories, namely, ordinary physical work, particular service for God, and the works of God himself

Physical work

From the beginning God intended man to work. In so doing, man would develop his physical and mental abilities and at the same time learn how to benefit from the created world that God had given him (Gen 1:28; 2:15). It is not work that is the result of sin, but the pain and suffering that result from work in a world dominated by sin. As a result of his sin, man no longer had the spiritual power that God originally gave him. Consequently, the physical creation, which was intended for his enjoyment, became the means of his torment. Work, instead of bringing physical pleasure, brought pain and hardship (Gen 3:16-19; Eccles 2:22-23).

Work is part of God's plan for the proper functioning of human life. God desires that people find dignity and enjoyment in the work they do. This

Brickmakers at work in ancient Egypt

applies not just to work that earns money, but to unpaid work such as household and community tasks (Eccles 2:24; 9:10; cf. Ps 104:19-24).

Christians have additional reasons for taking interest in whatever they do, as their aim is to please Christ, their unseen master. They will work honestly whether or not someone is watching, and will find satisfaction in doing all tasks well, whether or not those tasks are enjoyable (Col 3:23; Eph 6:6-8; 1 Peter 2:18). The Christian who works solely for the purpose of getting income is not serving Christ (Matt 6:24).

Although diligence in work is necessary if a person is to earn a living honestly (1 Thess 2:9; 2 Thess 3:8), it should not be used as an excuse for selfish ambition. Work becomes a god when a person's chief concern is to make himself rich (Matt 19:21-22; Luke 12:16-21; James 3:16; 4:13-5:6; see WEALTH). It also becomes a god when a person does not know how to cease from it. Rest and recreation, both physical and mental, are part of the weekly work cycle that the Creator intended for his creatures (Gen 2:3; Exod 20:8-11; cf. Mark 6:31; Luke 10:38-41; see SABBATH).

God is not pleased with those who are lazy or who refuse to work (Prov 13:4; 18:9; 21:25; Eccles 10:18; 2 Thess 3:6,10-12). But he is sympathetic to people who, for various reasons, are not able to work, and he expects others to help them (Deut 15:7-11; Prov 17:5; Isa 58:7; Luke 14:12-14; 16:19-26; Rom 12:13; Eph 4:28).

All workers, whether employers or employees, are entitled to a just reward for their work. This includes the right to honest profits and fair wages

(Lev 19:13; Prov 14:23; 31:16-24; Eccles 5:18-19; 11:1,4,6; Luke 10:7; 19:13-17; Col 4:1). The Bible consistently condemns an over-concern with income, especially when it produces dishonesty, violence and exploitation (Deut 24:14-15; Prov 20:17; 21:6; Jer 22:13,17; Amos 8:4-6; Luke 3:10-14; 1 Tim 6:9; James 5:4). All Christians, employers and employees alike, are answerable to a heavenly master who favours no one on the basis of social class (Eph 6:5,9). He expects all his people to trust in him and to put the interests of his kingdom before their own (Matt 6:25-33).

Particular service for God

Though God's people must carry out all work as if it is his work, they recognize that certain activities are in a special sense God's work. Such activities are those that concern the preaching of the gospel, the planting of churches and the building up of God's people. All Christians are, to some extent, involved in this work, for all have been given tasks according to their God-given abilities (1 Cor 12:4-7; see GIFTS OF THE SPIRIT). Therefore, all Christians will one day have their work assessed, as a result of which they will either receive a reward or suffer loss (1 Cor 3:10-15; see REWARD).

God may set apart certain people for specific types of work (Acts 13:2; 14:26; Eph 4:11-13; 1 Tim 1:18; 3:1). Such people should do their work with perseverance, honesty and joy, even though the work may at times bring them suffering and distress (Rom 15:17-20; 1 Cor 15:58; 2 Cor 11:24-29; Phil 2:30). Christians respect their fellow believers who endure faithfully for the sake of Christ (1 Cor 16:10; 1 Thess 5:13; 1 Tim 4:15-16).

Nevertheless, true workers for God do not seek praise for themselves. They are not like hawkers trying to sell goods for their own gain. They work from pure motives, avoid any suggestion of deceit or dishonesty, and are concerned only for the glory of God and the well-being of others (2 Cor 2:17; 4:1-2,5,15; Gal 1:10; 1 Thess 2:3-8; see SERVANT; STEWARD).

If people spend their whole time in the service of the church, they have the right to be supported financially by those who benefit from their work. They might also receive support from those who receive no direct benefit from their work (1 Cor 9:4-7; 2 Cor 11:8-9; Gal 6:6,10; Phil 4:15-16; 1 Tim 5:17-18). Some, however, may choose at times to earn their living by doing secular work, to avoid creating misunderstanding or financial hardship in a particular church (Acts 18:3; 1 Cor 9:12-15; 1 Thess 2:9; 2 Thess 3:8-9).

The works of God

The Bible speaks of the works of God as evidence of his power, love, faithfulness, righteousness, majesty and almost all other aspects of the divine character (Ps 111:2-8). Always God's works are a cause for people everywhere to worship and praise him (Ps 92:5; 103:22).

Frequently the Bible refers to God's works in relation to creation (Gen 2:2; Ps 8:3; 19:1; 104:24; Heb 1:10) and the control of history (Ps 46:8-9; 66:3; 107:24; 111:6; Isa 26:11-13; 28:21; Rev 15:2-4). In particular, it speaks of God's works with reference to his miracles (Deut 11:3-7; Judg 2:7; John 9:1-7; see MIRACLES). But no matter in what context it speaks of the works of God, those works are usually concerned with two main themes, judgment and salvation (Ps 77:11-15; 111:6-9; Isa 28:21; Acts 13:41; Phil 1:6; see GOD).

With the coming of Jesus, God's works were in a special sense done through him. Those works were clear evidence, particularly to the Jews, that Jesus had been sent by the Father (John 5:36) and that through Jesus people could come to the Father (John 14:6,10-11). But most of the Jews rejected the evidence (John 5:37-38; 10:25-26,37-38). They were stubbornly resistant to Jesus' claims (John 10:32-33), and his miraculous works only roused them to greater opposition (John 10:20,31,39).

Jesus, however, did not turn back from his task. He continued to do his Father's work till that work was finished (John 4:34; 5:17; 9:4; 15:24; 17:4; 19:30). Through faith in him and his finished work, people can have forgiveness of sins and eternal life (John 6:28-29; 20:30-31; see JESUS CHRIST).

WORLD

In the Bible, as in ordinary speech, 'the world' may refer to the physical world of God's creation or to the people who inhabit that world (Ps 90:2; 98:7,9; Matt 25:34; John 3:16; Rom 10:18). Because of sin, the world has become a place where Satan rules in people's lives (John 12:31; Rom 5:12; 2 Cor 4:4; 1 John 5:19). Therefore, the Bible frequently speaks of the present world, or present age, as something that is evil and that is opposed to God (John 7:7; 17:25; James 4:4; 1 John 2:15). The world in this sense is the subject of the present article – the world of sinful mankind along with all the wrong attitudes that characterize sinful mankind.

Living in the world

Chief among the characteristics of the ordinary (unbelieving) people of the world are covetousness and pride. Their lives are governed according to what they want to get or want to do, without any regard for God (1 John 2:16). This is worldliness, and it is an evil that the Bible warns Christians against. The lives of Christians are to be governed by an attitude that trusts in God, not in personal possessions or ambitions. To be constantly worried about such things is the attitude of unbelievers, not of Christians (Matt 6:31-32).

The temptation to worldliness may not lie in the more obviously sinful things of life. It may lie in those everyday things that are not sinful in themselves at all, such as food, work, possessions and concern for the future. These things can become wrong when people have wrong attitudes towards them (cf. Rom 1:25).

If Christians cannot see the relation that these things have to the life of faith in God, their attitude to them can readily become worldly. Ambition can very easily become selfish ambition, wisdom become worldly wisdom, and thoughts for the future become faithless anxiety (Matt 6:33-34; 1 Cor 1:20; 2:7-8,12; 3:19; James 3:13-17; 4:13-17).

Worldly people are those whose values in life are determined by what they understand of the world they see around them. Godly people are those whose values are determined by what they understand of God (2 Cor 4:18; 5:7; 1 John 2:17). This does not mean that the godly must rid themselves of all possessions, power and status. But it does mean that they will not pursue those things at all costs, and will even sacrifice them when they conflict with their commitment to Jesus Christ (Matt 19:29; Gal 2:20; 6:14; Phil 3:7-8).

Overcoming the world

Some Christians build a set of laws for themselves to live by, hoping that the laws will prevent them from doing what they believe to be worldly. Yet the very act of making laws to live by is worldly. Such people refuse to trust in the indwelling Spirit to direct their enjoyment of the freedom God has given them. Instead they trust in the methods of those who still 'belong to the world', who still live 'in the flesh' (Gal 3:3; 4:9-11; 5:1; Col 2:20-23; see FLESH). The Christians' liberty does not mean they are free to commit sin (Rom 6:1-2,12; Gal 5:13; 1 John 3:4-6), but neither do man-made laws help them overcome sin (Col 2:23; see FREEDOM).

Christians cannot overcome the temptations of the world by using the methods of the world. They can overcome them only by trusting in the power of Christ, who has conquered Satan, the prince of the world (John 12:31; 14:30; 16:11,33; 1 John 5:4-5; see TEMPTATION). One day this same Christ will return, to free the world completely from Satan's power (Rev 19:16; 20:2-3,10).

Meanwhile Christians have to live in an evil world, while not joining in the sins of the world. They may find that, as a result, the people of the world will hate them (John 15:18; 17:14-17). But they must remain faithful to Christ and keep themselves from being corrupted by the world's evil. Only in this way can they properly carry out their function of delivering people from the corruption of sin (Matt 5:13-16; John 17:18; James 1:27).

WORSHIP

Both the Hebrew (Old Testament) and the Greek (New Testament) words usually translated 'worship' indicate a type of humble submission; for example, the submission of a servant to a master. The inferior kneels or bows down, showing an attitude of deep respect for the superior (Gen 18:2; 33:3; 42:6; 49:8; 2 Sam 24:20; Matt 8:2; 9:18; 18:26).

This is the underlying idea in man's worship of God. Man humbles himself before his Creator as one who serves, honours, fears and adores him. He worships as one who appreciates God's infinite worth (Gen 24:26-27; Exod 4:31; 12:27; Ps 95:6; Matt 2:2; 28:9; Rev 4:10; 5:14; 11:16). Yet worship is not something grim, dull or cheerless. It is something joyful, for it is the enjoyment of God himself (Ps 89:15-16; 98:4-6; Luke 1:46-47; 1 Peter 1:8).

Forms of worship

Worship is both an attitude in which a person lives and a spiritual exercise that he carries out (Exod 33:10; Rom 12:1). It is an activity not only of the spirit, but also of the mind (1 Cor 14:15). It is something that is done individually and collectively (Gen 22:5; 24:52; 1 Chron 29:20; Acts 20:7 1 Cor 14:26). 'Worship' is a term so broad in meaning that it may be used in some places to denote the highest exercises of the soul, in others to denote the formal exercises of insincere religion (1 Sam 15:30; 2 Sam 12:20; Jer 7:2-3).

In Old Testament times the Israelites expressed their worship in ceremonial forms such as sacrifices and festivals (1 Sam 1:3; Ps 132:7). But true worship always required right behaviour, humility of spirit and confession of known sin. The rituals themselves were of no use if the person did not worship God in his heart and life (Ps 15:1; 50:7-15; Isa 29:13; Micah

6:6-8). Organized forms of worship were established firstly for the tabernacle (see FEASTS; SACRIFICE; TABERNACLE), then for the temple (see MUSIC; SINGING; TEMPLE), and later for the synagogue (see SYNAGOGUE).

The early Christians continued to attend the temple for prayer and worship (Acts 2:46; 3:1), but before long they made a clear break with Judaism and gradually developed their own form of public worship. It consisted mainly of praying, singing, reading the Scriptures, teaching Christian truth and celebrating the Lord's Supper (Acts 2:42; 20:7; 1 Cor 14:15-16; 1 Tim 4:13; see CHURCH; GIFTS OF THE SPIRIT).

Because the Christians' worship was collective, the participants had to maintain a degree of order in the procedures they followed. The worship of the church was a united act, not a disjointed collection of individual expressions of devotion (1 Cor 12:25; 14:16-17,33,40). As in Old Testament times, the spiritual condition of the worshippers was more important than their formal expressions of worship (Mark 7:6-7; John 4:23-24; Phil 3:3).

Worship, besides being 'in the spirit', must be 'in truth' (John 4:24). People must worship out of an understanding of the truth of God, and that truth has been revealed through the Scriptures (John 16:14). If a clearer understanding of the Scriptures leads to a more worthy worship, the Bible should have a place in worship, whether individual or collective. As God reveals more of his person and work through the Scriptures, believers will be filled with love and awe, and will respond with humble yet adoring worship (Rev 1:12-17).

In true worship there is therefore a two-way movement. There is a movement from God to man and from man to God; in other words, communion (1 John 1:1-13). This is well expressed in the Lord's Supper (1 Cor 10:16-17; 11:24-26; see COMMUNION; FELLOWSHIP; LORD'S SUPPER).

True and false worship

Any giving of honour to God is, in a sense, worship (Ps 22:27-29; Acts 8:27; 16:14), but the higher forms of worship arise out of an exercise of the soul that words cannot express. The greater the appreciation that believers have of God's holy character and gracious works, the more they adore him and praise him. They worship him as their Creator and their Redeemer. They bring him homage, adoration and praise because of who he is and what he has done (Ps 103:1-5; 104:1-4,31-35; Rev 4:8-11; 5:9-14). God's deeds, whether in creation, history or redemption, are a cause for unceasing worship and praise from mankind (Ps 33:1-19; 99:1-5; Rom 11:33-36; Eph 3:14-21; Jude 24-25).

God alone is to be worshipped (Acts 10:25-26; 14:11-15; Rev 22:8-9). The person who worships any other god, person or thing is guilty of idolatry (Exod 20:4-5; 32:8; Deut 4:19; 8:19; Rom 1:25; see IDOLATRY). Just as the worship of God means submission to his sovereign rule, so the worship of idols means submission to the evil power of false gods (Exod 20:5; Deut 11:16; 29:26; Josh 24:15; Matt 4:10; 1 Cor 10:20; Heb 1:6-7). If anyone other than God claims for himself divine worship, he is guilty of blasphemy (Matt 4:9-10; Mark 2:7; 14:61-64; Rev 13:4-8; 19:20; see BLASPHEMY).

There is a sense in which all creation worships God (Ps 96:1; 97:1; 148:3-4). In particular, the spirit beings who live in God's heavenly presence worship him unceasingly, as if that were the purpose for which they were created (Ps 148:1-2; Isa 6:2-3; Heb 1:6; Rev 4:8-11).

The people of God's earth also worship him. In the case of those who have responded to the grace of God and accepted the gift of his Son, their worship is enriched by their unspeakable gratitude (2 Cor 8:9; 9:15). They worship Jesus Christ, and they worship the Father through Christ, whose Spirit now indwells them (John 16:13-14; Eph 2:18; Col 1:15-23; Jude 24-25). Yet their worship at present is very far short of perfection. Only in the age to come, when they see and know God clearly, will they worship as they ought (1 Cor 13:12; Rev 22:3-4).

WRATH

God's attitude of opposition to all that is evil is usually called his wrath, or anger. Man's wrath is inconsistent and, because of the effects of sin in human nature, may express itself in outbursts of bad temper (James 1:20; see ANGER). God's wrath is consistent and pure. It is his holy, righteous and just reaction to sin — the only proper reaction for one who is himself holy, righteous and just (Exod 32:9-10; Jer 21:12; Nahum 1:2,6; Mark 3:5; John 2:14-17; Rom 1:18; Heb 12:29). God, as the supreme judge, can neither take pleasure in sin nor ignore it. Therefore, all people, being sinners, are the objects of his wrath (Ps 7:11; Eph 2:3; Col 3:5-6).

However, God takes no pleasure in punishing sin. He is longsuffering towards sinners, and gives them the opportunity to repent of their sin and ask his forgiveness (Ezek 33:11,14-16; 2 Peter 3:9; see PATIENCE). Many mistakenly think that because God does not immediately act against them in judgment, they have escaped his judgment. They may even think that God is as carefree about sin as they are, and so they sin all the more. But they only guarantee for themselves a more severe judgment when God's wrath finally falls upon them (2 Chron 36:16; Ps 50:19-21; 78:37-40; Eccles 8:11; Rom 2:4-6).

The final great outpouring of God's wrath will take place at the close of the age, when Jesus Christ returns in power and glory to execute judgment on the ungodly (Rom 2:5; 2 Thess 1:7-10; Rev 6:17; 14:10,19; 19:11-16). God's people will not experience this wrath, for they have been saved from it through Jesus Christ (1 Thess 1:10; 5:9). Jesus, in bearing their sin, has borne God's wrath on their behalf (Rom 5:9; 2 Cor 5:21; 1 Peter 2:24). But those who refuse to trust in Jesus as their substitute must bear God's wrath themselves (John 3:36). (For a fuller discussion on the relationship between God's love and God's wrath see PROPITIATION.)

WRITING

As ancient nations and communities developed, people became increasingly aware of the benefits that writing brought. Over the centuries they used a variety of materials and methods in their efforts to develop the art and improve their skills.

One of the early practices was to engrave letters on a smooth surface of bare stone, clay, or stone covered with plaster. The writing was done with a sharp-pointed instrument, usually on rectangular tablets of a size that people could easily handle (Exod 32:15-16; Deut 27:2-3; Job 19:24; Isa 8:1). A more common practice for writings and records of lesser importance was to write in ink on pieces of pottery (technically known as ostraca).

Engraved tablets of stone or clay effectively preserved the writing, but their size and weight limited their usefulness. A more convenient material was developed from a reed known as papyrus (from which we get the English word 'paper') or byblos. Dried flat strips of papyrus were stuck together to form a flat sheet, which a person wrote upon using a pen and ink. The pen also was made from a papyrus reed (2 John 12; 3 John 13).

Papyrus writing sheets were often joined to form a long strip, which was then rolled into a scroll (Jer 36:2; Rev 5:1). The Greeks called a scroll a *biblion* (after the byblos, or papyrus, plant). From this word we get the word 'Bible' as a name for that collection of scrolls, or books, that Christians acknowledge as the Scriptures. Since papyrus did not last well, writers sometimes used specially dried animal skin (parchment) instead. Parchment was much more expensive than papyrus, and usually people used it only for those writings that were more important or in more constant use (Luke 4:17,20; 2 Tim 4:13).

Papyrus plants

Although the word 'book' sometimes appears in English translations of the Old and New Testaments, the article referred to was not a book in the sense that we understand today (i.e. a collection of sheets bound together). It was most likely a scroll. The book form developed early in the second century AD. Christians found this form particularly useful, not simply because books were easier to read than scrolls, but because the sacred writings could be kept together more conveniently. A few books could contain the writings of many scrolls. This kind of book has become known as a codex. (See also MANUSCRIPTS.)

YAHWEH

Yahweh, or Jehovah, was the personal name of God by which the Israelites knew him as *their* God – and their God was the one and only true God (Exod 4:22; 32:27; Deut 6:4; 1 Sam 17:45). When they wanted to name a place after some special event where they had seen God at work, they often formed the name by combining God's name with a suitable Hebrew word (Gen 22:8,14; Exod 17:15; Judg 6:24; Ezek 48:35). They also combined shortened forms of Yahweh (Jehovah) with other words to form names for people (2 Kings 11:1-2,4,21).

Usage in Hebrew

The word 'Jehovah' probably never existed in the Hebrew language. Originally Hebrew was written with consonants only, the readers supplying the vowels as they read. The word from which 'Jehovah' comes consists of the consonants YHWH, and was probably pronounced 'Yahweh'. Transliterations of the word in other languages support this as the likely pronunciation.

Absolute certainty, however, is not possible, as there are no Hebrew records old enough to preserve the original pronunciation. By the time written Hebrew had established the practice of adding vowels to the consonants, the Jews no longer spoke the name YHWH. They claimed this was because of their reverence for God's name, but for many it was more because of superstition. Whatever the reason, the practice became universal that when Jews read the Scriptures, instead of speaking the word YHWH, they substituted the word *adonai*, meaning 'lord' or 'master'.

When, about 300 BC, a new version of the Hebrew Bible added vowels to the consonants for the first time, it put the vowels of *adonai* to the consonants YHWH. This resulted in the word 'Jehovah', though the Jews continued to substitute the word *adonai* for YHWH when speaking. Many English versions of the Bible have avoided the pronunciation problem by using the expression 'the LORD' (in capital letters) for YHWH. (See also JESUS CHRIST, sub-heading 'Jesus as Lord'.)

Meaning of the name

Both the origin and the meaning of the name Yahweh are uncertain. Abraham, Isaac and Jacob knew God by his name Yahweh (Gen 15:7; 26:24-25; 28:20-21), though they did not understand its full significance. They knew that God was the creator of the universe, the one who controlled all things and was able to fulfil the promises he had made to them, but they did not live to see those promises fulfilled (Gen 15:5-6,13-15).

Several hundred years later, when God was about to bring the descendants of these men out of slavery in Egypt, God's people were given a fuller understand of the significance of the name Yahweh. Yahweh was their God according to the covenant he had made with Abraham, and now he would save them according to that covenant (Gen 15:18; Exod 2:24; 3:16). In other words, Yahweh was more than just a covenant God; he was a covenant redeemer. In making himself known to the Israelite slaves as a redeemer, Yahweh was showing a characteristic of himself that Abraham, Isaac and Jacob had never seen (Exod 6:2-8).

Although the events of Israel's salvation from Egypt displayed Yahweh's character, the meaning of the name was still mysterious. The name YHWH was connected with the Hebrew words 'I am'. God gave no simple explanation of what his name meant, but he reassured his people by stating his name in words that may be translated 'I am who I am' or 'I will be what I will be'. Yahweh revealed himself as the one who is eternal, absolute, unchangeable, always active, always present, and answerable to no one. He would be to his people whatever he chose to be, and they were to trust that he would never fail them (Exod 3:13-14; see also GOD).

Other names of God

Besides referring to God by his personal name Yahweh, the Bible refers to him by the ordinary Hebrew words for 'God' such as *El, Elohim* and related words (Gen 1:1; Josh 3:10). These words were used even for false gods (Gen 31:30; Exod 15:11). Sometimes *El* was joined to other words to form more descriptive titles, such as *El Elyon*, the Most High God (Gen 14:18) and *El Shaddai*, God Almighty (Gen 17:1; 28:3; 35:11). Anyone, Hebrew or otherwise, might acknowledge the great creator and all-powerful ruler of the universe as God (*El*), but the Hebrews added to this that *El* was Yahweh (Gen 14:19,22; Deut 4:24; 6:4,20).

As with Yahweh, *El* and *Elohim* were sometimes used when naming places after memorable experiences (Gen 21:33; 28:19; 32:30; 33:20). They were used also in names given to people (Gen 28:2; Exod 31:2; 1 Sam 1:20).

YOKE

A yoke was a piece of curved wood placed over the neck of an animal to enable it to pull a plough or a cart (Num 19:2). According to a commonly used

Yoked oxen at work

metaphor, the yoke was a symbol of hardship and bondage (Gen 27:40; 1 Kings 12:4; Isa 9:4; Jer 27:8; 28:1-16; 1 Tim 6:1). In this sense Jewish law-keeping was a harsh yoke. It was a burden that the Jewish

religious leaders forced upon the people (Acts 15:10; Gal 5:1; cf. Matt 23:4).

When people submit to Jesus Christ as their master, they take upon themselves his yoke. Christ's yoke, however, is not harsh or heavy, but easy and light. Obedience to him does not create weariness, but brings refreshment, joy and meaning to life (Matt 11:28-30; 1 John 5:3).

Farmers sometimes yoked animals together to form a pair or a team (1 Kings 19:19; Luke 14:19; Phil 4:3); but Israelite law did not allow them to yoke together two animals of a different kind, such as an ox and an ass (Deut 22:10). Paul used this to illustrate that a Christian should not enter into a binding relationship (such as marriage) with a non-Christian (2 Cor 6:14).

ZADOK

Zadok and Abiathar were the two Levitical priests who became members of David's royal court (2 Sam 8:17). At the time of Absalom's rebellion, they helped David by remaining in Jerusalem to become spies on David's behalf (2 Sam 15:24-37; 19:11). Later, however, in the palace conflict over David's successor, Zadok supported Solomon, and Abiathar supported Adonijah. As a result Solomon promoted Zadok to chief priest and sent Abiathar into exile (1 Kings 1:5-8,43-45; 2:26,35).

Since Zadok belonged to the line of chief priests that went back through Phinehas and Eleazar to Aaron (Ezra 7:2-5), his appointment to the high priesthood was in keeping with the plan and promise of God (Num 25:10-13). His descendants followed him as chief priests till the destruction of Jerusalem in 587 BC (2 Chron 31:10). Because they remained faithful to God throughout that period, they were designated the chief priests in the religious system that Ezekiel looked for in the rebuilt nation (Ezek 40:46; 44:15).

History shows that following the reconstruction of Israel, descendants of Zadok continued to be the chief priests for several centuries. The Sadducees, who formed the priestly party that later became powerful in Israel, possibly took their name from Zadok (see SADDUCEES).

ZEALOT

In the opening years of the New Testament era, the Romans exercised their rule over Judea firstly through Herod the Great and then through Herod's son, Archelaus. But in AD 6 the Romans replaced Archelaus with a governor sent out from Rome, and

Judea for the first time came under direct Roman rule (cf. Matt 2:22).

Since Rome could no longer collect Judea's taxes through the Herods, it conducted a census of the province in preparation for collecting the taxes direct. A group of Jews, led by a man called Judas the Galilean, rebelled against this direct taxation, claiming that God's people should not pay taxes to a pagan emperor. Because of their zeal in trying to keep Israel free from pagan influence, they became known as Zealots (or Patriots). They formed one of the minor political parties in Israel (Acts 5:37). One of the twelve apostles was possibly at some time a member of the Zealots (Luke 6:15; Acts 1:13).

The Zealots maintained their opposition to Rome in spite of persecution and even the execution of some of their members. From time to time other anti-Roman extremists joined them. Among these was a group known as the Assassins, who hid daggers in their clothing and murdered any whom they suspected of being on the side of the Romans (Acts 21:38).

In AD 66, bitter at the mismanagement of Jewish affairs by the corrupt governors of Judea, the Zealots led an open rebellion against Rome. The Jews were divided among themselves, with various extremists competing for leadership. Nevertheless, they held Jerusalem against the Romans for four years. During this time Rome had systematically conquered Galilee, Perea and Judea. Finally, in AD 70, they conquered Jerusalem, destroying the temple and most of the city. This marked the end of the national life of Israel.

ZEBULUN

The tribe of Zebulun was descended from the sixth son of Jacob and Leah (Gen 30:19-20). Jacob's blessing of this tribe indicated it would inherit part of Canaan's coastal region, but the territory it actually occupied was a few kilometres inland, in the hill country that rose from the coastal plain. Trade routes that passed through the region brought the tribe prosperity (Gen 49:13; Deut 33:18-19; Josh 19:10-16; for map see TRIBES). On occasions the men of Zebulun, along with those of neighbouring Naphtali, fought heroically for Israel (Judg 5:18; 6:35; 1 Chron 12:33-34,40).

In New Testament times the territory that formerly belonged to Zebulun was part of Galilee and included within it the town of Nazareth. The glory of Zebulun was that from its territory came the Messiah, who brought God's light into a dark world (Isa 9:1; Matt 4:12-16; see NAZARETH).

ZECHARIAH

The Bible mentions about thirty people who had the name Zechariah. Many of these were priests, prophets or rulers.

Of the rulers named Zechariah, one was a king of Israel. He was the fifth king of the dynasty of Jehu, and with his murder in 752 BC, Jehu's dynasty ended as bloodily as it had begun (2 Kings 15:8-12).

The most important of the prophets named Zechariah was the man whose book is part of the Old Testament. He lived in Jerusalem during the period that followed the Jews' return from captivity and, with Haggai, he roused the people to get on with the job of rebuilding the temple (Ezra 5:1-2; 6:14-15; Zech 1:1; see ZECHARIAH, BOOK OF).

Of the priests named Zechariah, the best known in Old Testament times was the man who rebuked King Joash and the people of Jerusalem for their idolatry. By command of the king, the leaders of Jerusalem murdered him. In a divine judgment on the murderers, the leaders of Jerusalem were killed in an enemy invasion and the king was assassinated by two of his palace officials (in 796 BC; 2 Chron 24:17-26; Luke 11:49-51).

Another priest named Zechariah lived in New Testament times. This man was the father of John the Baptist. For many years he and his wife had not been able to have children, even though they had prayed earnestly and lived righteously before God. One day, while Zechariah was on duty in the temple, an angel from God told him that in answer to their prayers, God was about to give them a son. This son, whom they were to name John, was to be the forerunner of the Messiah (Luke 1:5-17).

Zechariah could hardly believe the good news and wanted a sign to confirm it. The sign he received was also a penalty for his unbelief: he was made dumb till the baby was born (Luke 1:18-23,57-66). Upon regaining his speech, Zechariah immediately began to praise God. His first words of praise were for the promised Messiah (Luke 1:67-75). He then offered praise for his son John, who would prepare the people for the Messiah's arrival by calling them to repentance (Luke 1:76-79).

ZECHARIAH, BOOK OF

After the decree of Cyrus in 539 BC that released the Jews from captivity, a number returned to their homeland. They settled in Jerusalem under the leadership of the governor Zerubbabel and the high priest Joshua, and set about rebuilding the city and the temple (Ezra 1:1-4; 2:1-2). Soon they had set up the altar and laid the foundation of the temple, but when local people began persecuting them, they became discouraged and stopped work (Ezra 4:1-5,24). For sixteen years no work was done on the temple. Then, in 520 BC, God raised up two prophets, Haggai and Zechariah, to stir up the people to get to work again and finish the temple (Ezra 5:1-2; Hag 1:1; Zech 1:1).

Characteristics of the book

The prophets' preaching for the first six months was largely concerned with encouraging the people through the early difficulties. Haggai began the preaching with two stirring messages (Hag 1:1-15 and 2:1-9), after which Zechariah delivered his first message (Zech 1:1-6). Haggai followed this with two more messages (Hag 2:10-19 and 2:20-23), after which Zechariah delivered his second message (Zech 1:7-6:15). Zechariah's next recorded message was preached when the construction had reached the half-way point (Zech 7:1-8:23). The temple was finished in 516 BC, after four and a half years work (Ezra 6:14-15).

Haggai and Zechariah were both concerned with rousing the people from their spiritual laziness and getting them to work on the temple, but the preaching of Zechariah went further. Through him God was preparing his people for the task for which he had chosen them, namely, the coming of the Messiah, the establishment of his kingdom and the salvation of people worldwide. Zechariah was therefore concerned to bring about a lasting spiritual change in the lives of the people.

The latter half of Zechariah's book, which consists of two messages delivered probably late in his life, shows that the task the people faced was not an easy one. There would be bitter conflicts with the forces of evil, but in the end God's kingdom would triumph.

In contrast to the straightforward preaching of Haggai, Zechariah's preaching was often mysterious and colourful. His book shows characteristics of the apocalyptic literature that developed in Israel over the next few centuries. Apocalyptic writers presented their messages in the form of visions in which symbolic figures and numbers usually featured (see APOCALYPTIC LITERATURE).

Contents of the book

After an initial call to repentance (1:1-6), Zechariah recounts eight visions, all of which concern the rebuilding of the temple and God's purposes for his people. The first three visions give encouragement to the workmen (1:7-2:13), the central pair give encouragement to the leaders, Joshua and Zerubbabel (3:1-4:14), and the last three give assurance of final victory (5:1-6:8). A short narrative recounts the crowning of the high priest (6:9-15).

At the half-way point in the building program, some representatives of the people asked Zechariah if they should still keep certain fasts to mourn the destruction of the former temple. In response Zechariah warns not to mourn over the past, but to have confidence for the future (7:1-8:23).

In the first of the two longer messages given later in life, Zechariah speaks of the punishment of enemies and the restoration of freedom. He draws a striking contrast between the worthless leadership of unspiritual people and the type of leadership God wants (9:1-11:17). In the second message he warns that the victory Israel looked for will be achieved only at great cost and with much sorrow. He again notes the difference between the false shepherds and the true shepherd, and looks forward to the final triumph of the Messiah's kingdom (12:1-14:21).

ZEDEKIAH

The most important of several biblical characters named Zedekiah was the man who became the last king of Judah. Others who bore the name Zedekiah were a prophet in the court of Ahab (1 Kings 2:11,24), an administrator in the government of Jehoiakim (Jer 36:12), a son of Jehoiakim (1 Chron 3:16) and a false prophet among the Jewish captives in Babylon (Jer 29:21-23).

King of Judah

Zedekiah the king was the third son of Josiah to sit upon the throne of Judah. He was known also as Mattaniah (2 Kings 23:30,34; 24:17). The king of Babylonian appointed him king after the former king and all Judah's best people had been taken captive to Babylon (in 597 BC; 2 Kings 24:10-17). Little is known of the early part of Zedekiah's reign, except that in his fourth year he paid a visit to Babylon (Jer 51:59).

With all Jerusalem's best administrators now captive in Babylon, Zedekiah's government was immature and weak. His officials encouraged him to seek help from Egypt and rebel against Babylon. Jeremiah, who had been bringing God's message to Judah for more than thirty years, opposed this policy. He warned that it would lead only to the horrors of siege and destruction. He advised the people to submit to Babylon, and so at least soften the judgment that was to fall upon them (2 Kings 24:18-20; 2 Chron 36:11-14; Jer 27:1,12-15).

Zedekiah, however, followed the advice of the pro-Egypt party and rebelled against Babylon. As a result he brought upon Jerusalem the besieging armies of Babylon (2 Kings 24:20b; 25:1; Jer 32:1-2). When he asked Jeremiah to pray that God would remove the Babylonians, Jeremiah replied that God would not remove them. The time of Jerusalem's judgment had come. Jeremiah advised that it would be better to surrender and be taken captive to Babylon than to resist and die in the siege (Jer 21:1-10). He also warned Zedekiah of the judgment to fall on him personally (Jer 34:1-7).

When Egypt came to Jerusalem's aid, Babylon lifted the siege temporarily, but Jeremiah warned Zedekiah that Babylon would return and crush both Egypt and Judah (Jer 37:1-10). Meanwhile in Babylon, Ezekiel likewise warned of the increased suffering that Zedekiah's rebellion against Babylon would bring upon Jerusalem (Ezek 17:12-21).

Back in Jerusalem, the pro-Egypt party accused Jeremiah of being a traitor and had him imprisoned. The weak Zedekiah easily gave in to Jeremiah's opponents (Jer 37:15; 38:5-6), but then was just as easily persuaded by a friend of Jeremiah to change his mind (Jer 38:7-10). Zedekiah had secret meetings with Jeremiah in the hope of receiving better news, but Jeremiah merely repeated his former announcements (Jer 37:16-21; 38:14-28).

After eighteen months of siege, the Babylonian army broke through the walls of Jerusalem (2 Kings 25:1-4; Jer 39:1-3). Zedekiah tried to escape by night, but enemy soldiers quickly captured him. They then executed his sons in front of him, blinded him and took him in chains to Babylon, where later he died (2 Kings 25:4-7; Ezek 12:10-13; 21:25-27). Jerusalem was destroyed, its remaining people and treasures taken to Babylon, and the kingdom of Judah brought to an end (2 Kings 25:8-21; 587 BC).

ZEPHANIAH

So far as we know, Zephaniah was the first prophet to appear in Judah since Isaiah and Micah, whose work had come to an end seventy years earlier. His preaching marked the beginning of a new era of prophetic activity in Judah, but it was an era that was to end in the destruction of Jerusalem. Among the prophets who followed him were Jeremiah, Nahum and Habakkuk.

Background to the book

For much of the seventy years before Zephaniah, the wicked Manasseh had reigned. After his reign the spiritual condition of Judah was worse than that for which God had destroyed the Canaanites in the time of Joshua. The destruction of Judah appeared to be inevitable (2 Kings 21:1-16).

The new era was marked not only by the preaching of Zephaniah, but also by the religious reforms of the new king, Josiah (who had come to the throne in 640 BC). It seems that Zephaniah and Josiah were related (Zeph 1:1). Josiah's reforms, which lasted many years, were aimed at removing idolatry and restoring the true worship of God in Jerusalem. (For details of the reforms see 2 Kings 22:3-23:25; 2 Chron 34:1-35:27.)

Zephaniah saw that the improvements in the external forms of religion, though commendable, were no substitute for true reform in heart and life. The wrong attitudes promoted by Manasseh were so deeply rooted that Josiah's reforms could not remove them (2 Kings 23:26-27). As Zephaniah announced God's judgment on the nation, he urged people to repent of their wrongdoing and come to a true knowledge of God.

Contents of the book

The preaching of Zephaniah was concerned largely with the certainty of God's judgment on sinners. The violence, cheating and false religion of Manasseh's time were still widespread in Jerusalem (1:1-18). But there was hope for those who humbly turned from their sin to the Lord (2:1-3). Examples from the surrounding nations impressed upon the people that evildoers could not escape God's judgment (2:4-15). Jerusalem's sin guaranteed a terrible judgment for the city (3:1-8), though when all the sinners had been destroyed, those who had truly repented would enjoy God's blessing (3:9-20).

ZERUBBABEL

When Persia conquered Babylon in 539 BC, the Persian king Cyrus released the captive Jews to return to their homeland and rebuild Jerusalem. The original leader of the Jews was Sheshbazzar (Ezra 1:8; 5:14), but his leadership was soon replaced by the joint leadership of the governor Zerubbabel and the high priest Joshua (Ezra 2:2; Hag 1:1). (An alternative view is that Sheshbazzar was another name for Zerubbabel.)

Rebuilding the temple

The year after they arrived in Jerusalem, the Jews began rebuilding the temple. Within a short time they met opposition from the local non-Jewish people, with the result that they became discouraged and the work stopped (Ezra 4:24). For about sixteen years no work was done, though the people still had time and money to build costly houses for themselves. It seems that Zerubbabel was as much at fault as the common people in this. Only when Haggai and Zechariah began their stirring preaching in 520 BC did Zerubbabel, Joshua and the rest of the people get to work again (Ezra 5:1-2; Hag 1:1-6,14-15).

Much of Haggai and Zechariah's preaching was designed to challenge and encourage Zerubbabel and Joshua (Hag 2:4). Zerubbabel, having control of the work, was told that through God's power he would overcome the mountain of obstacles he faced. As his hands had begun the work on the temple, so his hands would finish it (Zech 4:6-10). The promise was fulfilled four and a half years after the prophets began their preaching (Ezra 6:15).

Ancestor of the Messiah

Zerubbabel was a direct descendant of David in the line of kings that had reigned in Jerusalem before its destruction by Babylon (Matt 1:6-12). He was entitled to the throne of Israel, but since Israel was still under Persian rule, he could be no more than governor. When the Israelites held a symbolic coronation ceremony during the rebuilding of the temple, they were careful to avoid any suggestion of treason. They therefore placed the crown on Joshua instead of on Zerubbabel; but the words used in the ceremony referred to Zerubbabel. As a descendant of David, Zerubbabel was like a new 'branch' springing from the 'tree' of David's dynasty, a 'tree' that Babylon had earlier 'cut down' (Zech 6:11-13; cf. Isa 11:1).

'The Branch' was a name that Israelites used of the great descendant of David who would come as their Messiah (Isa 4:2; 11:1; Jer 23:5; 33:15). The name was freely applied to Zerubbabel because, as leader of the rebuilt nation, he was part of the fulfilment of the promise given to David. Through him the Messiah would come (Hag 2:21-23; Zech 3:8-10; Matt 1:6,12,16; cf. 2 Sam 7:16).

ZIN

Much of southern Palestine was a dry region known as the Negeb. Within this region lay the barren Wilderness of Zin. It lay south-west of the Dead Sea, between the Dead Sea and Kadesh-barnea (Num 20:1-2; 27:14; 33:36; 34:3-5). (For map and other details see PALESTINE, sub-heading 'Negeb'.)

ZION

Mount Zion was the name given to that hill section of Jerusalem that lay inside the city wall along the eastern side. A Canaanite fortress on the southern part of this hill had enabled the inhabitants of Jerusalem to withstand enemy attacks for centuries. When David conquered the city he determined to build a temple for God on Zion, though the site chosen was to the north rather than the south (2 Sam 5:6-9; 24:18-25; 2 Chron 3:1; Ps 78:68-69; Isa 8:18; for map see JERUSALEM). The temple was built during the reign of David's son, Solomon (1 Chron 22:8-10).

Since the temple was God's symbolic dwelling place, Israelites regarded Zion as a holy hill and Jerusalem as a holy city (Ps 2:6; 9:11; Isa 52:1). They often used the name Zion figuratively to refer to both the temple and the city (2 Kings 19:31; Ps 9:14; 51:18; 87:1-3; Matt 21:5; see JERUSALEM; TEMPLE). Because of the people's wickedness and idolatry, Jerusalem, far from being a holy city, was a sinful city (Isa 1:21; 10:11; Micah 3:10).

Nevertheless, Zion was the location of God's symbolic dwelling place, and psalmists and prophets mentioned it repeatedly. To them it spoke of God and his salvation of Israel (Ps 20:1-2; 53:6; Isa 28:16; Micah 4:2,7; cf. Rom 11:26).

New Testament writers used Zion as a symbol of a far greater salvation, a salvation that is not limited to one city, one nation, one people or one era. To them it spoke of the heavenly Jerusalem, whose citizens are those 'born from above' (Heb 12:22-24; Gal 3:26-29; 4:26-28; Rev 3:12; 21:1-4).

ZOAN

The city of Zoan was one of Egypt's great cities (Ezek 30:14). It was located in the Nile Delta (Ps 78:12), was very old (Num 13:22), and for several hundred years was Egypt's capital (Isa 19:11). It was probably the city earlier known as Rameses (see EGYPT; RAMESES).